Oxford
Colour French
Dictionary Plus

Revised second edition

FRENCH—ENGLISH
ENGLISH—FRENCH

FRANÇAIS—ANGLAIS
ANGLAIS—FRANÇAIS

OXFORD
UNIVERSITY PRESS

OXFORD
UNIVERSITY PRESS

Great Clarendon Street, Oxford OX2 6DP

Oxford University Press is a department of the University of Oxford.
It furthers the University's objective of excellence in research, scholarship,
and education by publishing worldwide in

Oxford New York

Auckland Bangkok Buenos Aires Cape Town Chennai
Dar es Salaam Delhi Hong Kong Istanbul Karachi Kolkata
Kuala Lumpur Madrid Melbourne Mexico City Mumbai Nairobi
São Paulo Shanghai Taipei Tokyo Toronto

Oxford is a registered trade mark of Oxford University Press
in the UK and in certain other countries

Published in the United States
by Oxford University Press Inc., New York

© Oxford University Press 1995, 1998, 2001, 2004

Database right Oxford University Press (maker)

The moral rights of the author have been asserted

First published 1995 as the Oxford Colour French Dictionary
Revised edition published 1998
Second edition published 2001
Revised second edition published 2004

British Library Cataloguing in Publication Data

Data available

Library of Congress Cataloging in Publication Data

Data available

ISBN 0-19-860900-0
ISBN 0-19-860898-5 (US edition)

10 9 8 7 6 5 4 3 2

Typeset by Tradespools Ltd
Printed in Great Britian
by the Bath Press

Contents

Preface

The *Oxford Colour French Dictionary Plus* is a dictionary
designed primarily for students of French. The clear
presentation and colour headwords make it easily accessible.
It contains completely new sections, not found in the *Oxford
Colour French Dictionary*, on French life and culture,
letter-writing, and French grammar, making it even more
useful for students up to intermediate level.

List of contributors

Revised Second Edition

Marianne Chalmers

Second Edition

Editors:

Marianne Chalmers
Rosalind Combley
Catherine Roux
Laura Wedgeworth

Supplementary Material:

Marianne Chalmers
Martine Pierquin
Glynnis Chantrell
Valerie Grundy
Natalie Pomier

Proof-reading:

Andrew Hodgson

First Edition

Editors:

Michael Janes
Dora Latiri-Carpenter
Edwin Carpenter

Introduction

This dictionary is designed as an effective and practical reference tool for the student, adult learner, traveller, and business professional. It provides user-friendly treatment of core vocabulary across a broad spectrum of written and spoken language.

Enhanced coverage

The wordlist of the previous edition has been comprehensively revised to reflect recent additions to both languages and to cover such topics as **computing** and the **Internet**.

A further new feature of the dictionary is the special status given to more complex grammatical words which provide the basic structure of both languages. These *function words* are given a special layout to make them instantly accessible and offer clearly presented translation options and examples, with **short usage notes** to warn of possible pitfalls.

Coverage of verbs has been significantly extended so that all **French verbs** in the text are cross-referenced to the appropriate section of the expanded verb tables. Examples of the three main French verb groups, as well as *avoir* and *être*, are conjugated in the most commonly used tenses. A quick reference guide giving the English translation of an example verb in the principal tenses has been included, followed by exemplified guidance on **how to conjugate a reflexive verb**.

Easy reference

The dictionary layout has been designed to be **clear**, streamlined, and easy to consult. The wordlist has been fully **alphabetized**, with all English compounds and French hyphenated compounds in their correct alphabetical positions. **Bullet points** separate each new part of speech within an entry, making it easy to scan. Nuances of sense or usage are pinpointed by semantic indicators (in condensed type in round brackets) or by typical collocates (*in italics in round brackets*) with which the word frequently occurs, quickly guiding the user to the appropriate translation. Extra help is given in the form of **symbols** to mark the register of language unambiguously. An exclamation mark Ⓘ indicates colloquial language and a cross Ⓧ indicates slang.

Each headword is followed by its **phonetic transcription** between slashes, except in the case of English compound headwords where the pronunciation can be derived from that of each of the component parts. The symbols used for the pronunciation are those of the International Phonetic Alphabet. Any unpredictable plural forms or irregular English conjugations, comparative and superlative forms are also given in brackets.

This dictionary is designed to present essential information in an accessible format, providing the user with a fast track to **clear and effective communication**.

Proprietary terms

This dictionary includes some words which are, or are asserted to be, proprietary terms or trademarks. The presence or absence of such assertions should not be regarded as affecting the legal status of any proprietary name or trademark.

The pronunciation of French

Vowels

a	*as in*	patte	/pat/		ɑ	*as in*	pâte	/pɑt/
ɑ̃		clan	/klɑ̃/		e		dé	/de/
ɛ		belle	/bɛl/		ɛ̃		lin	/lɛ̃/
ə		demain	/dəmɛ̃/		i		gris	/gʀi/
o		gros	/gʀo/		ɔ		corps	/kɔʀ/
ɔ̃		long	/lɔ̃/		œ		leur	/lœʀ/
œ̃		brun	/bʀœ̃/		ø		deux	/dø/
u		fou	/fu/		y		pur	/pyʀ/

Semi-Vowels

j	*as in*	fille	/fij/
ɥ		huit	/ɥit/
w		oui	/wi/

Consonants

Aspiration of 'h'

Where it is impossible to make a liason this is indicated by /'/ immediately after the slash e.g. *haine* /'ɛn/.

b	*as in*	bal	/bal/		ŋ	*as in*	camping	/kɑ̃piŋ/
d		dent	/dɑ̃/		p		porte	/pɔʀt/
f		foire	/fwaʀ/		ʀ		rire	/ʀiʀ/
g		gomme	/gɔm/		s		sang	/sɑ̃/
k		clé	/kle/		ʃ		chien	/ʃjɛ̃/
l		lien	/ljɛ̃/		t		train	/tʀɛ̃/
m		mer	/mɛʀ/		v		voile	/vwal/
n		nage	/naʒ/		z		zèbre	/zɛbʀ/
ɲ		gnon	/ɲɔ̃/		ʒ		jeune	/ʒœn/

Glossary of grammatical terms

Abbreviation A shortened form of a word or phrase made by leaving out some letters or by using only the initial letter of each word: etc., DNA

Active In the active form the subject of the verb performs the action: **she whistled = elle a sifflé**

Adjective A word describing a noun: **a** *red* **pencil = un crayon** *rouge*

Adverb A word that describes or changes the meaning of a verb, an adjective, or another adverb: **he drives** *fast* **= il conduit** *vite*; *fairly* **often =** *assez* **souvent**

Article The definite article, **the = le, la, l', les**, and indefinite article, **a/an = un, une**, are used in front of a noun

Attributive An adjective or noun is attributive when it is used directly before a noun: **the** *big* **dog = le** *grand* **chien;** *birthday* **card = carte d'anniversaire**

Auxiliary verb One of the verbs used to form the perfect, pluperfect, and future perfect tenses. In French the auxiliary verbs are **avoir** and **être: I have read the letter = j'***ai* **lu la lettre; he had already gone = il** *était* **déjà parti**

Cardinal number A whole number representing a quantity: **one, two, three = un/une, deux, trois**

Clause A self-contained section of a sentence that contains a subject and a verb

Collective noun A noun that is singular in form but refers to a group of persons or things, e.g. **royalty, grain**

Collocate A word that regularly occurs with another; in French **livre** is a typical collocate of the verb **lire**

Comparative The form of an adjective or adverb for comparing two or more nouns or pronouns, often using **more, less** or **as (plus, moins, aussi): smaller = plus petit; more frequently = plus fréquemment; as intelligent = aussi intelligent**

Compound adjective An adjective formed from two separate words : **tout-puissant = all-powerful; nord-américain = North American**

Compound noun A noun formed from two or more separate words: **porte-clés = keyring**

Conditional tense A tense of a verb that expresses what would happen if something else occurred: **I would invite them = je les inviterais**

Conjugation Variation of the form of a verb to show tense, person, mood, etc.

Conjunction A word used to link clauses: **and = et, because = parce que**

Definite article: **the = le, la, l', les**

Demonstrative pronoun A pronoun indicating the person or thing referred to: *this one* **is cheaper =** *celui-ci* **est moins cher**

Determiner A word that comes before a noun to show how it is being used: **the = le, la, l', les; some = du/de l'/de la/des; my = mon/ma/mes**

Direct object the noun or pronoun directly affected by the verb: **she ate *the apple* = elle a mangé *la pomme***

Direct speech A speaker's actual words or the use of these in writing

Ending Letters added to the stem of verbs, as well as to nouns and adjectives, according to tense, number, gender

Exclamation A sound, word, or remark expressing a strong feeling such as anger, fear, or joy: **ouch! = aïe!**

Feminine One of the two noun genders in French: **la femme = the woman; la carte = the card**

Future tense The tense of a verb that refers to something that will happen in the future: **I will go = j'irai**

Gender One of the two groups of nouns in French: masculine and feminine

Imperative A form of a verb that expresses a command: **hurry up! – dépêche-toi!**

Imperfect tense The tense of a verb that refers to an uncompleted or a habitual action in the past: **I went there every day = j'y allais tous les jours**

Impersonal verb A verb used in English only with 'it' and in French only with 'il': **it is raining = il pleut**

Indefinite article: a/an = un, une

Indefinite pronoun A pronoun that does not identify a specific person or object: **one = on; something = quelque chose**

Indicative form The form of a verb used when making a statement of fact or asking questions of fact: **we like animals = nous aimons les animaux**

Indirect object The noun or pronoun indirectly affected by the verb, at which the direct object is aimed: **she gave *him* the key = elle *lui* a donné la clé**

Indirect speech A report of what someone has said which does not reproduce the exact words

Infinitive The basic part of a verb: **to play = jouer**

Inflect To change the ending or form of a word to show its tense or its grammatical relation to other words: **donne** and **donnez** are inflected forms of the verb **donner**

Interrogative pronoun A pronoun that asks a question: **who? = qui?**

Intransitive verb A verb that does not have a direct object: **he died yesterday = il est mort hier**

Invariable adjective An adjective that has the same form in the feminine as the masculine, as French **ivoire, transmanche**

Invariable noun A noun that has the same form in the plural as the singular as English **sheep, species**, French **précis, rabais**

Irregular verb A verb that does not follow one of the set patterns and has its own individual forms, e.g. English **to be**, French **être**

Masculine One of the two noun genders in French: **le garçon = the boy; le livre = the book**

Modal verb A verb that is used with another verb to express permission, obligation, possibility, such as **might**, **should**. The French modal verbs are **devoir**, **pouvoir**, **savoir**, **vouloir**, **falloir**

Negative Expressing refusal or denial: **there aren't any = il n'y en a pas**; **he won't go = il ne veut pas partir**

Noun A word that names a person or thing

Number The state of being either singular or plural

Object The word or group of words which is immediately affected by the action indicated by the verb, as **livre** in **il a lu le livre**, or **voiture** in **elle lave la voiture**

Ordinal number A number that shows the position of a person or thing in a series: **the *third* time = la *troisième* fois**, **the *fourth* door on the left = la *quatrième* porte à gauche**

Part of speech A grammatical term for the function of a word; noun, verb, adjective, etc., are parts of speech

Passive In the passive form the subject of the verb experiences the action rather than performs it: **he was punished = il a été puni**

Past participle The part of a verb used to form past tenses: **she had *gone* = elle était *partie***

Perfect tense The tense of a verb that refers to an action that has taken place in a period of time that includes the present: **I have already eaten = j'ai déjà mangé**; **my bike has been stolen = on m'a volé mon vélo**

Person Any of the three groups of personal pronouns and forms taken by verbs. In the singular the **first person** (e.g. **I/je**) refers to the person speaking; **the second**

person (e.g. **you/tu**) refers to the person spoken to; the **third person** (e.g. **he**, **she**, **it/il**, **elle**) refers to the person spoken about. The corresponding plural forms are **we/nous**, **you/vous**, **they/ils**, **elles**

Personal pronoun A pronoun that refers to a person or thing

Phrasal verb A verb in English combined with a preposition or an adverb to have a particular meaning: **run away = se sauver**

Phrase A self-contained section of a sentence that does not contain a full verb

Pluperfect tense The tense of a verb that refers to something that happened before a particular point in the past: **when I arrived, he *had* already *left* = quand je suis arrivé, il *était* déjà *parti***

Plural Of nouns, etc., referring to more than one: **the children = les enfants**

Possessive adjective An adjective that shows possession, belonging to someone or something: **my = mon/ma/mes**

Possessive pronoun a pronoun that shows possession, belonging to someone or something: **mine = le mien/la mienne/les miens/les miennes**

Predicative An adjective is predicative when it comes after a verb such as **be** or **become** in English, or after **être** or **devenir** in French: **she is beautiful = elle est belle**

Prefix A group of letters added to the beginning of a word to change its meaning, e.g. **anti-**, **ultra-**, **non-**

Preposition A word that stands in front of a noun or pronoun, usually indicating movement, position or time: *on the chair* = *sur la chaise*; *towards the car* = *vers la voiture*

Present participle The part of a verb in English that ends in –ing; the corresponding ending in French is **-ant**

Present tense The tense of a verb that refers to something happening now: **I make = je fais**

Pronoun A word that stands instead of a noun: **he = il, she = elle, mine = le mien/la mienne/ les miens/les miennes**

Proper noun A name of a person, place, institution etc. written with a capital letter at the start; **France, the Alps, Madeleine, l'Europe** are all proper nouns

Reflexive pronoun A pronoun that goes with a reflexive verb: in French **me, te, se, nous, vous, se**

Reflexive verb a verb whose object is the same as its subject. In French it is used with a reflexive pronoun and conjugated with **être**: **you should wash yourself = tu devrais te laver**

Regular verb A verb that follows a set pattern in its different forms

Relative pronoun A pronoun that introduces a subordinate clause, relating to a person or thing mentioned in the main clause: **the book *which* I chose = le livre *que* j'ai choisi**

Reported speech Another name for **Indirect speech**

Sentence A sequence of words, with a subject and a verb, that can stand on their own to make a statement, ask a question, or give a command

Singular Of nouns, etc., referring to just one: **the tree = l'arbre**

Stem The part of a verb to which endings are added; **donn-** is the stem of **donner**

Subject In a clause or sentence, the noun or pronoun that causes the action of the verb: **he caught the ball = il a attrapé le ballon**

Subjunctive A verb form that is used to express doubt or uncertainty in English. It is more widely used in French, particularly after certain conjunctions and with verbs of wishing, fearing, ordering, forbidding followed by **que**: **I want you to be good = je veux que tu sois sage**; **you may be right = il est possible que tu aies raison**

Subordinate clause A clause which adds information to the main clause of a sentence, but cannot function as a sentence by itself, e.g. **when it rang** in **she answered the phone when it rang**

Suffix A group of letters joined to the end of a word to form another word, as **–eur** in **grandeur** or **–able** in **véritable**

Superlative The form of an adjective or adverb that makes it the 'most' or 'least': **the *biggest* house = *la plus grande* maison; the *cheapest* CD = le CD *le moins cher***

Tense The form of a verb that tells when the action takes place: present, future, imperfect, perfect, pluperfect are all tenses

Transitive verb A verb that is used with a direct object: **I wrote the letter = j'ai écrit la lettre**

Verb A word or group of words that describes an action: **the children are playing = les enfants jouent**

Abbreviations/Abréviations

adjective	*a*	adjectif
abbreviation	*abbr, abrév*	abréviation
adverb	*adv*	adverbe
anatomy	*Anat*	anatomie
archeology	*Archeol, Archéol*	archéologie
architecture	*Archit*	architecture
motoring	*Auto*	automobile
auxiliary	*aux*	auxiliaire
aviation	*Aviat*	aviation
botany	*Bot*	botanique
commerce	*Comm*	commerce
computing	*Comput*	informatique
conjunction	*conj*	conjonction
cookery	*Culin*	culinaire
determiner	*det, dét*	déterminant
electricity	*Electr; Électr*	électricité
figurative	*fig*	sens figuré
geography	*Geog, Géog*	géographie
geology	*Geol, Géol*	géologie
grammar	*Gram*	grammaire
humorous	*hum*	humoristique
interjection	*interj*	interjection
invariable	*inv*	invariable
law	*Jur*	droit
linguistics	*Ling*	linguistique
literal	*lit*	littéral
phrase	*loc*	locution
medicine	*Med, Méd*	médecine
military	*Mil*	armée
music	*Mus*	musique
noun	*n*	nom
nautical	*Naut*	nautisme
feminine noun	*nf*	nom féminin
masculine noun	*nm*	nom masculin
masculine and feminine noun	*nm,f or nmf or nm/f*	nom masculin et féminin
computing	*Ordinat*	informatique

pejorative	*pej, péj*	péjoratif
philosophy	*Phil*	philosophie
photography	*Photo*	photographie
plural	*pl*	pluriel
politics	*Pol*	politique
possessive	*poss*	possessif
past participle	*pp*	participe passé
prefix	*pref, préf*	préfixe
preposition	*prep, prép*	préposition
present participle	*pres p*	participe présent
pronoun	*pron*	pronom
psychology	*Psych*	psychologie
past	*pt*	prétérit
something	*qch*	quelque chose
somebody	*qn*	quelqu'un
railway	*Rail*	chemin de fer
relative pronoun	*rel pron, pron rel*	pronom relatif
religion	*Relig*	religion
somebody	*sb*	quelqu'un
school	*School, Scol*	scolaire
sport	*Sport*	sport
something	*sth*	quelque chose
technology	*Tech*	technologie
theatre	*Theat, Théât*	théâtre
television	*TV*	télévision
university	*Univ*	université
American English	*US*	anglais américain
auxiliary verb	*v aux*	verbe auxiliaire
intransitive verb	*vi*	verbe intransitif
reflexive verb	*vpr*	verbe pronominal
transitive verb	*vt*	verbe transitif
transitive and intransitive verb	*vt/i*	verbe transitif et intransitif
translation equivalent	≈	équivalent approximatif
trademark	®	marque déposée
colloquial	🄸	familier
slang	🆇	argot

a /a/ ⇒AVOIR [5].

....

à /a/ *préposition*

à+le = au
à+les = aux

····▸ (avec verbe de mouvement) to.

····▸ (pour indiquer où l'on se trouve) ∼ **la maison** at home; ∼ **Nice** in Nice.

····▸ (âge, date, heure) ∼ **l'âge de...** at the age of...; **au XIXe siècle** in the 19th century; ∼ **deux heures** at two o'clock.

····▸ (description) with; **aux yeux verts** with green eyes.

····▸ (appartenance) ∼ **qui est ce stylo?** whose pen is this?; **c'est vous?** is this yours?

····▸ (avec nombre) ∼ **90 km/h** at 90 km per hour; ∼ **10 minutes d'ici** 10 minutes from here; **des tomates** ∼ **2 euros le kilo** tomatoes at 2 euros a kilo; **un timbre** ∼ **2 euros** a 2-euro stamp; **nous avons fait le travail** ∼ **deux** two of us did the work; **mener 5** ∼ **4** to lead 5 (to) 4.

····▸ (avec être) **c'est** ∼ **moi** it's my turn; **je suis** ∼ **vous tout de suite** I'll be with you in a minute; **c'est** ∼ **toi de décider** it's up to you to decide.

····▸ (hypothèse) ∼ **ce qu'il paraît** apparently; ∼ **t'entendre** to hear you talk.

····▸ (exclamatif) ∼ **ta santé!** cheers!; ∼ **demain/bientôt!** see you tomorrow/soon!

····▸ (moyen) ∼ **la main** by hand; ∼ **vélo** by bike; ∼ **pied** on foot; **chauffage au gaz** gas heating.

....

abaissement /abɛsmɑ̃/ *nm* (de taux, de prix) cut; (de seuil) lowering.

abaisser /abese/ [1] *vt* lower; (*levier*) pull *ou* push down; (fig) humiliate. □ **s'**∼ *vpr* go down, drop; (fig) demean oneself; **s'**∼ **à** stoop to.

abandon /abɑ̃dɔ̃/ *nm* abandonment; (de personne) desertion; (de course) withdrawal; (naturel) abandon; **à l'**∼ in a state of neglect.

abandonner /abɑ̃dɔne/ [1] *vt* abandon; (*épouse, cause*) desert; (renoncer à) give up, abandon; (céder) give (à to); (*course*) withdraw from; (Ordinat) abort. □ **s'**∼ **à** *vpr* give oneself up to.

abasourdir /abazurdir/ [2] *vt* stun.

abat-jour /abaʒur/ *nm inv* lampshade.

abats /aba/ *nmpl* offal.

abattement /abatmɑ̃/ *nm* dejection; (faiblesse) exhaustion; (Comm) reduction; ∼ **fiscal** tax allowance.

abattre /abatr/ [11] *vt* knock down; (*arbre*) cut down; (*animal*) slaughter; (*avion*) shoot down; (affaiblir) weaken; (démoraliser) demoralize; **ne pas se laisser** ∼ not let things get one down. □ **s'**∼ *vpr* come down, fall (down).

abbaye /abei/ *nf* abbey.

abbé /abe/ *nm* priest; (supérieur d'une abbaye) abbot.

abcès /apsɛ/ *nm* abscess.

abdiquer /abdike/ [1] *vt/i* abdicate.

abdomen /abdɔmɛn/ *nm* abdomen.

abdominal (*pl* -aux) /abdɔminal/ *a* abdominal. **abdominaux** *nmpl* (Sport) stomach exercises.

abeille /abɛj/ *nf* bee.

aberrant, ~e /abɛRɑ̃, -t/ *a* absurd.

abêtir /abetiR/ [2] *vt* turn into a moron.

abîme /abim/ *nm* abyss.

abimer /abime/ [1] *vt* damage, spoil. □ **s'**~ *vpr* get damaged *ou* spoilt.

ablation /ablasjɔ̃/ *nf* removal.

aboiement /abwamɑ̃/ *nm* bark, barking; ~s barking.

abolir /abɔliR/ [2] *vt* abolish.

abondance /abɔ̃dɑ̃s/ *nf* abundance; (prospérité) affluence. **abondant**, ~e *a* abundant, plentiful.

abonder /abɔ̃de/ [1] *vi* abound (en in); ~ **dans le sens de qn** agree wholeheartedly with sb.

abonné, ~e /abɔne/ *nm, f* (lecteur) subscriber; (voyageur, spectateur) season-ticket holder.

abonnement /abɔnmɑ̃/ *nm* (à un journal) subscription; (de bus, Théât) season-ticket; (au gaz) standing charge.

abonner (**s'**) /(s)abɔne/ [1] *vpr* subscribe (à to).

abord /abɔR/ *nm* access; ~s surroundings; **d'**~ first.

abordable /abɔRdabl/ *a* (prix) affordable; (personne) approachable; (texte) accessible.

aborder /abɔRde/ [1] *vt* approach; (lieu) reach; (problème) tackle. ● *vi* reach land.

aborigène /abɔRiʒɛn/ *nm* aborigine.

aboutir /abutiR/ [2] *vi* succeed, achieve a result; ~ **à** end (up) in, lead to; **n'**~ **à rien** come to nothing.

aboutissement /abutismɑ̃/ *nm* outcome; (de carrière, d'évolution) culmination.

aboyer /abwaje/ [31] *vi* bark.

abrégé /abReʒe/ *nm* summary.

abréger /abReʒe/ [14] [40] *vt* (texte) shorten, abridge; (mot) abbreviate, shorten; (visite) cut short.

abreuver /abRœve/ [1] *vt* water; (fig) overwhelm (de with). □ **s'**~ *vpr* drink.

abréviation /abRevjasjɔ̃/ *nf* abbreviation.

abri /abRi/ *nm* shelter; **à l'**~ under cover; (en lieu sûr) safe; **à l'**~ **de** sheltered from; **se mettre à l'**~ take shelter.

abricot /abRiko/ *nm* apricot.

abriter /abRite/ [1] *vt* shelter; (recevoir) house. □ **s'**~ *vpr* (take) shelter.

abrupt, ~e /abRypt/ *a* steep, sheer; (fig) abrupt.

abruti, ~e /abRyti/ *nm, f* 🔲 idiot.

absence /apsɑ̃s/ *nf* absence; **il a des** ~s sometimes his mind goes blank.

absent, ~e /apsɑ̃, -t/ *a* (personne) absent, away; (chose) missing; **il est toujours** ~ he's still away; **d'un air** ~ absently. ● *nm, f* absentee.

absenter (**s'**) /(s)apsɑ̃te/ [1] *vpr* go *ou* be away; (sortir) go out, leave.

absolu, ~e /apsɔly/ *a* absolute.

absorbant, ~e /apsɔRbɑ̃, -t/ *a* (travail) absorbing; (matière) absorbent.

absorber /apsɔRbe/ [1] *vt* absorb;

être absorbé par qch be engrossed in sth.

abstenir (s') /(s)apstənir/ [58] *vpr* abstain; **s'~ de** refrain from.

abstrait, **~e** /apstrɛ, -t/ *a & nm* abstract.

absurde /apsyrd/ *a* absurd.

abus /aby/ *nm* abuse, misuse; (injustice) abuse; **~ de confiance** breach of trust.

abuser /abyze/ [1] *vt* deceive. ●*vi* go too far; **~ de** abuse, misuse; (profiter de) take advantage of; (alcool) overindulge in. □**s'~** *vpr* be mistaken.

abusif, **-ive** /abyzif, -v/ *a* excessive; (impropre) wrong; (injuste) unfair.

académie /akademi/ *nf* academy; (circonscription) local education authority.

acajou /akaʒu/ *nm* mahogany.

accablant, **~e** /akablɑ̃, -t/ *a* (chaleur) oppressive; (fait, témoignage) damning.

accabler /akable/ [1] *vt* overwhelm; **~ d'impôts** burden with taxes; **~ d'injures** heap insults upon.

accéder /aksede/ [14] *vi* **~ à** (lieu) reach; (pouvoir, trône) accede to; (requête) grant; (Ordinat) access; **~ à la propriété** become a homeowner.

accélérateur /akseleratœr/ *nm* accelerator.

accélérer /akselere/ [14] *vt/i* accelerate. □**s'~** *vpr* speed up.

accent /aksɑ̃/ *nm* accent; (sur une syllabe) stress, accent; **mettre l'~ sur** stress; **~ aigu/grave/ circonflexe** acute/grave/circumflex accent.

accentuer /aksɑ̃tɥe/ [1] *vt* (lettre, syllabe) accent; (fig) emphasize, accentuate. □**s'~** *vpr* become more pronounced, increase.

accepter /aksɛpte/ [1] *vt* accept; **~ de faire** agree to do.

accès /aksɛ/ *nm* access; (porte) entrance; (de fièvre) bout; (de colère) fit; (d'enthousiasme) burst; (Ordinat) access; **les ~ de** (voies) the approaches to; **facile d'~** easy to get to.

accessoire /akseswar/ *a* secondary, incidental. ●*nm* accessory; (Théât) prop.

accident /aksidɑ̃/ *nm* accident; **~ de train/d'avion** train/plane crash; **par ~** by accident.

accidenté, **~e** *a* (personne) injured (in an accident); (voiture) damaged; (terrain) uneven, hilly.

accidentel, **~le** *a* accidental.

acclamer /aklame/ [1] *vt* cheer, acclaim.

accommoder /akɔmɔde/ [1] *vt* adapt (à to); (cuisiner) prepare; (assaisonner) flavour. □**s'~ de** *vpr* make the best of.

accompagnateur, **-trice** /akɔ̃paɲatœr, -tris/ *nm, f* (Mus) accompanist; (guide) guide; **~ d'enfants** accompanying adult.

accompagner /akɔ̃paɲe/ [1] *vt* accompany. □**s'~ de** *vpr* be accompanied by.

accomplir /akɔ̃plir/ [2] *vt* carry out, fulfil. □**s'~** *vpr* take place, happen; (vœu) be fulfilled.

accord /akɔr/ *nm* agreement; (harmonie) harmony; (Mus) chord; **être d'~** agree (pour to); **se mettre d'~** come to an agreement, agree; **d'~!** all right!, OK!

accorder /akɔrde/ [1] *vt* grant; (couleurs) match; (Mus) tune; (attribuer) (valeur, importance) assign. □**s'~** *vpr* (se mettre d'accord) agree; (s'octroyer) allow oneself; **s'~ avec** (s'entendre avec) get on with.

accotement /akɔtmɑ̃/ *nm* verge; **~ non stabilisé** soft verge.

accouchement /akuʃmɑ̃/ *nm* childbirth; (*travail*) labour.

accoucher /akuʃe/ [1] *vi* give birth (**de** to); (être en travail) be in labour. ● *vt* deliver. **accoucheur** *nm* **médecin** ~ obstetrician.

accoudoir /akudwaʀ/ *nm* armrest.

accoupler /akuple/ [1] *vt* (Tech) couple. □ **s'**~ *vpr* mate.

accourir /akuʀiʀ/ [20] *vi* run up.

accoutumance /akutymɑ̃s/ *nf* familiarization; (Méd) addiction.

accoutumer /akutyme/ [1] *vt* accustom. □ **s'**~ *vpr* get accustomed.

accro /akʀo/ *nmf* 🗆 (drogué) addict; (amateur) fan.

accroc /akʀo/ *nm* tear, rip; (fig) hitch.

accrochage /akʀoʃaʒ/ *nm* hanging; hooking; (Auto) collision; (dispute) clash; (Mil) encounter.

accrocher /akʀoʃe/ [1] *vt* (suspendre) hang up; (attacher) hook, hitch; (déchirer) catch; (heurter) hit; (attirer) attract. □ **s'**~ *vpr* cling, hang on (à to); (se disputer) clash.

accroissement /akʀwasmɑ̃/ *nm* increase (**de** in).

accroître /akʀwɑtʀ/ [24] *vt* increase. □ **s'**~ *vpr* increase.

accroupir (s') /(s)akʀupiʀ/ [2] *vpr* squat.

accru, ~**e** /akʀy/ *a* increased, greater.

accueil /akœj/ *nm* reception, welcome.

accueillant, ~**e** /akœjɑ̃, -t/ *a* friendly, welcoming.

accueillir /akœjiʀ/ [25] *vt* receive, welcome; (*film, livre*) receive; (prendre en charge) (*réfugiés, patients*) take care of, cater for.

accumuler /akymyle/ [1] *vt* (*énergie*) store up; (*capital*) accumulate. □ **s'**~ *vpr* (*neige, ordures*) pile up; (*dettes*) accrue.

accusation /akyzasjɔ̃/ *nf* accusation; (Jur) charge; **l'**~ (magistrat) the prosecution.

accusé, ~**e** /akyze/ *a* marked. ● *nm, f* defendant, accused.

accuser /akyze/ [1] *vt* accuse (**de** of); (blâmer) blame (**de** for); (Jur) charge (**de** with); (fig) emphasize; ~ **réception de** acknowledge receipt of.

acharné, ~**e** /aʃaʀne/ *a* relentless, ferocious.

acharnement *nm* (énergie) furious energy; (ténacité) determination.

acharner (s') /(s)aʃaʀne/ [1] *vpr* persevere; **s'**~ **sur** set upon; (poursuivre) hound; **s'**~ **à faire** (s'évertuer) try desperately; (s'obstiner) keep on doing.

achat /aʃa/ *nm* purchase; ~**s** shopping; **faire l'**~ **de** buy; **faire des** ~**s** do some shopping.

acheminer /aʃ(ə)mine/ [1] *vt* dispatch, convey; (*courrier*) handle. □ **s'**~ **vers** head for.

acheter /aʃ(ə)te/ [6] *vt* buy; ~ **qch à qn** (pour lui) buy sth for sb; (chez lui) buy sth from sb.
acheteur, -**euse** *nm, f* buyer; (client de magasin) shopper.

achèvement /aʃɛvmɑ̃/ *nm* completion.

achever /aʃ(ə)ve/ [6] *vt* finish (off). □ **s'**~ *vpr* end.

acide /asid/ *a* acid, sharp. ● *nm* acid.

acier /asje/ *nm* steel.

acné /akne/ *nf* acne.

acompte /akɔ̃t/ *nm* deposit, part-payment.

à-côté (*pl* ~**s**) /akote/ *nm* side issue; ~**s** (argent) extras.

acoustique /akustik/ *nf* acoustics (+ *sg*). ● *a* acoustic.

acquéreur /akeʀœʀ/ *nm* purchaser, buyer.

A

acquérir /akeʀiʀ/ [7] *vt* acquire, gain; (*biens*) purchase, acquire.

acquis, ~e /aki, -z/ *a* acquired; (*fait*) established; **tenir qch pour ~** take sth for granted. ● *nm* experience. **acquisition** *nf* acquisition; purchase.

acquitter /akite/ [1] *vt* acquit; (*dette*) settle. □ **s'~ de** *vpr* (*promesse*) fulfil; (*devoir*) discharge.

âcre /ɑkʀ/ *a* acrid.

acrobatie /akʀɔbasi/ *nf* acrobatics (+ *pl*); **~ aérienne** aerobatics (+ *pl*).

acte /akt/ *nm* act, action, deed; (Théât) act; (Jur) deed; **~ de naissance/mariage** birth/marriage certificate; **~s** (compte rendu) proceedings; **prendre ~ de** note.

acteur /aktœʀ/ *nm* actor.

actif, -ive /aktif, -v/ *a* active; (*population*) working. ● *nm* (Comm) assets; **avoir à son ~** have to one's credit *ou* name.

action /aksjɔ̃/ *nf* action; (Comm) share; (Jur) action; (effet) effect; (initiative) initiative. **actionnaire** *nmf* shareholder.

activer /aktive/ [1] *vt* speed up; (*feu*) boost. □ **s'~** *vpr* hurry up; (s'affairer) be very busy.

activité /aktivite/ *nf* activity; **en ~** (*volcan*) active; (*fonctionnaire*) working; (*usine*) in operation.

actrice /aktʀis/ *nf* actress.

actualité /aktɥalite/ *nf* topicality; **l'~** current affairs; **les ~s** news; **d'~** topical.

actuel, ~le /aktɥɛl/ *a* current, present; (d'actualité) topical. **actuellement** *adv* currently, at the present time.

acupuncture /akypɔ̃ktyʀ/ *nf* acupuncture.

adaptateur /adaptatœʀ/ *nm* (Électr) adapter.

adapter /adapte/ [1] *vt* adapt;

(fixer) fit. □ **s'~** *vpr* adapt (oneself); (Tech) fit.

additif /aditif/ *nm* (note) rider; (substance) additive.

addition /adisjɔ̃/ *nf* addition; (au café) bill; (US) check. **additionner** [1] *vt* add; (totaliser) add (up).

adepte /adɛpt/ *nmf* follower; (d'activité) enthusiast.

adéquat, ~e /adekwa, -t/ *a* suitable; (suffisant) adequate.

adhérent, ~e /aderɑ̃, -t/ *nm, f* member.

adhérer /adere/ [14] *vi* adhere, stick (à to); **~ à** (*club*) be a member of; (s'inscrire à) join.

adhésif, -ive /adezif, -v/ *a* adhesive; **ruban ~** sticky tape.

adhésion /adezjɔ̃/ *nf* membership; (soutien) support.

adieu (*pl* ~x) /adjø/ *interj & nm* goodbye, farewell.

adjectif /adʒɛktif/ *nm* adjective.

adjoint, ~e /adʒwɛ̃, -t/ *nm, f* assistant; **~ au maire** deputy mayor. ● *a* assistant.

adjuger /adʒyʒe/ [40] *vt* award; (aux enchères) auction. □ **s'~** *vpr* take (for oneself).

admettre /admɛtʀ/ [42] *vt* let in, admit; (tolérer) allow; (reconnaître) admit, acknowledge; (*candidat*) pass.

administrateur, -trice /administʀatœʀ, -tʀis/ *nm, f* administrator, director; (Jur) trustee; **~ de site Internet** Webmaster.

administratif, -ive /administʀatif, -v/ *a* administrative; (*document*) official. **administration** *nf* administration; (gestion) management; **l'A~** Civil Service.

administrer /administʀe/ [1] *vt* run, manage; (*justice, biens, antidote*) administer.

admirateur, -trice /admiʀatœʀ, -tʀis/ *nm, f* admirer.

admiration /admiʀasjɔ̃/ *nf* admiration.

admirer /admiʀe/ [1] *vt* admire.

admission /admisjɔ̃/ *nf* admission.

ADN *abrév m* (**acide désoxyribonucléique**) DNA.

adolescence /adɔlesɑ̃s/ *nf* adolescence. **adolescent, ~e** *nm, f* adolescent, teenager.

adopter /adɔpte/ [1] *vt* adopt. **adoptif, -ive** *a* (*enfant*) adopted; (*parents*) adoptive.

adorer /adɔʀe/ [1] *vt* love; (plus fort) adore; (Relig) worship, adore.

adosser /adɔse/ [1] *vt* lean (**à, contre** against). □ **s'~** *vpr* lean back (**à, contre** against).

adoucir /adusiʀ/ [2] *vt* soften; (*boisson*) sweeten; (*chagrin*) ease. □ **s'~** *vpr* soften; (*chagrin*) ease; (*temps*) become milder.
adoucissant *nm* (fabric) softener.

adresse /adʀɛs/ *nf* address; (habileté) skill; **~ électronique** e-mail address.

adresser /adʀese/ [1] *vt* send; (écrire l'adresse sur) address; (*remarque*) address; **~ la parole à** speak to. □ **s'~ à** *vpr* address; (aller voir) (*personne*) go and ask ou see; (*bureau*) enquire at; (viser, intéresser) be directed at.

adroit, ~e /adʀwa, -t/ *a* skilful, clever.

adulte /adylt/ *nmf* adult. ● *a* adult; (*plante, animal*) fully-grown.

adultère /adyltɛʀ/ *a* adulterous. ● *nm* adultery.

adverbe /advɛʀb/ *nm* adverb.

adversaire /advɛʀsɛʀ/ *nmf* opponent, adversary.

aérer /aeʀe/ [1] *vt* air; (*texte*) space out. □ **s'~** *vpr* get some air.

aérien, ~ne /aeʀjɛ̃, -jɛn/ *a* air; (*photo*) aerial; (*câble*) overhead.

aérobic /aeʀɔbik/ *nm* aerobics (+ *sg*).

aérogare /aeʀɔgaʀ/ *nf* air terminal.

aéroglisseur /aeʀɔglisœʀ/ *nm* hovercraft.

aérogramme /aeʀɔgʀam/ *nm* airmail letter; (US) aerogram.

aéronautique /aeʀɔnotik/ *a* aeronautical. ● *nf* aeronautics (+ *sg*).

aéroport /aeʀɔpɔʀ/ *nm* airport.

aérospatial, ~e (*mpl* **-iaux**) /aeʀɔspasjal, -jo/ *a* aerospace.

affaiblir /afebliʀ/ [2] *vt* weaken. □ **s'~** *vpr* get weaker.

affaire /afɛʀ/ *nf* affair, matter; (Jur) case; (histoire, aventure) affair; (occasion) bargain; (entreprise) business; (transaction) deal; (question, problème) matter; **~s** (Comm) business; (Pol) affairs; (problèmes personnels) business; (effets personnels) things; **c'est mon ~** that's my business; **avoir ~ à** a deal with; **ça fera l'~** that will do the job; **ça fera leur ~** that's just what they need; **tirer qn d'~** help sb out of a tight spot; **se tirer d'~** get out of trouble.

affairé, ~e /afeʀe/ *a* busy.

affaisser (s') /(s)afese/ [1] *vpr* (*terrain, route*) sink, subside; (*poutre*) sag; (*personne*) collapse.

affamé, ~e /afame/ *a* starving.

affectation /afɛktasjɔ̃/ *nf* (nomination) (à une fonction) appointment; (dans un lieu) posting; (de matériel, d'argent) allocation; (comportement) affectation.

affecter /afɛkte/ [1] *vt* (feindre) affect; (toucher, affliger) affect; (destiner) assign; (nommer) appoint, post.

affectif, -ive /afɛktif, -v/ *a* emotional.

A

affection /afɛksjɔ̃/ *nf* affection; (maladie) complaint.

affectueux, -euse /afɛktɥø, -z/ *a* affectionate.

affichage /afiʃaʒ/ *nm* billposting; (électronique) display.

affiche /afiʃ/ *nf* (public) notice; (publicité) poster; (Théât) bill; **être à l'~** (*film*) be showing; (*pièce*) be on.

afficher /afiʃe/ [1] *vt* (annonce) put up; (événement) announce; (sentiment) display; (Ordinat) display.

affirmatif, -ive /afiʀmatif, -v/ *a* affirmative. **affirmation** *nf* assertion.

affirmer /afiʀme/ [1] *vt* assert; (soutenir) maintain.

affligé, ~e /afliʒe/ *a* distressed. **~ de** afflicted with.

affluer /aflye/ [1] *vi* flood in; (*sang*) rush.

affolant, ~e /afɔlɑ̃, -t/ *a* alarming.

affoler /afɔle/ [1] *vt* throw into a panic. □ **s'~** *vpr* panic.

affranchir /afʀɑ̃ʃiʀ/ [2] *vt* stamp; (à la machine) frank; (esclave) emancipate; (fig) free. **affranchissement** *nm* (tarif) postage.

affreux, -euse /afʀø, -z/ *a* (laid) hideous; (mauvais) awful.

affrontement /afʀɔ̃tmɑ̃/ *nm* confrontation.

affronter /afʀɔ̃te/ [1] *vt* confront. □ **s'~** *vpr* confront each other.

affûter /afyte/ [1] *vt* sharpen.

afin /afɛ̃/ *prép & conj* **~ de faire** in order to do; **~ que** so that.

africain, ~e /afʀikɛ̃, -ɛn/ *a* African. **A~, ~e** *nm, f* African.

Afrique /afʀik/ *nf* Africa; **~ du Sud** South Africa.

agacer /agase/ [10] *vt* irritate, annoy.

âge /aʒ/ *nm* age; (vieillesse) (old)

age; **quel ~ avez-vous?** how old are you?; **~ adulte** adulthood; **~ mûr** maturity; **d'un certain ~** middle-aged.

âgé, ~e /aʒe/ *a* elderly; **~ de cinq ans** five years old.

agence /aʒɑ̃s/ *nf* agency, bureau, office; (succursale) branch; **~ d'interim** employment agency; **~ de voyages** travel agency; **~ publicitaire** advertising agency.

agenda /aʒɛ̃da/ *nm* diary; **~ électronique** electronic organizer.

agent /aʒɑ̃/ *nm* agent; (fonctionnaire) official; **~ (de police)** policeman; **~ de change** stockbroker; **~ commercial** sales representative.

agglomération /aglɔmeʀasjɔ̃/ *nf* town, built-up area.

aggraver /agʀave/ [1] *vt* aggravate, make worse. □ **s'~** *vpr* get worse.

agile /aʒil/ *a* agile, nimble.

agir /aʒiʀ/ [2] *vi* act; (se comporter) behave; (avoir un effet) work, have effect. □ **s'~ de** *vpr* (être nécessaire) **il s'agit de faire** we/you etc. must do; (être question de) **il s'agit de faire** it is a matter of doing; **dans ce livre il s'agit de** this book is about; **dont il s'agit** in question; **il s'agit de ton fils** it's about your son; **de quoi s'agit-il?** what is it about?

agitation /aʒitasjɔ̃/ *nf* bustle; (trouble) agitation; (malaise social) unrest.

agité, ~e /aʒite/ *a* restless, fidgety; (troublé) agitated; (mer) rough.

agiter /aʒite/ [1] *vt* (bras, mouchoir) wave; (liquide, boîte) shake; (troubler) agitate; (discuter) debate. □ **s'~** *vpr* bustle about; (enfant) fidget; (foule, pensées) stir.

agneau (*pl* **~x**) /aɲo/ *nm* lamb.

agrafe /agʀaf/ *nf* hook; (pour

papiers) staple. **agrafeuse** *nf* stapler.

agrandir /agʀɑ̃diʀ/ [2] *vt* enlarge; (*maison*) extend. □ **s'~** *vpr* expand, grow. **agrandissement** *nm* extension; (de photo) enlargement.

agréable /agʀeabl/ *a* pleasant.

agréé, ~e /agʀee/ *a* (*agence*) authorized; (*nourrice, médecin*) registered; (*matériel*) approved.

agréer /agʀee/ [15] *vt* accept; **~ à** please; **veuillez ~, Monsieur, mes salutations distinguées** (personne non nommée) yours faithfully; (personne nommée) yours sincerely.

agrégation /agʀegasjɔ̃/ *nf* highest examination for recruitment of teachers. **agrégé, ~e** *nm, f* teacher (who has passed the agrégation).

agrément /agʀemɑ̃/ *nm* charm; (plaisir) pleasure; (accord) assent.

agresser /agʀese/ [1] *vt* attack; (pour voler) mug.

agressif, -ive /agʀesif, -v/ *a* aggressive. **agression** *nf* attack; (pour voler) mugging; (Mil) aggression.

agricole /agʀikɔl/ *a* agricultural; (ouvrier, produit) farm.
agriculteur *nm* farmer.
agriculture *nf* agriculture, farming.

agripper /agʀipe/ [1] *vt* grab. □ **s'~** *vpr* cling (**à** to).

agroalimentaire /agʀɔalimɑ̃tɛʀ/ *nm* food industry.

agrumes /agʀym/ *nmpl* citrus fruit(s).

ai /e/ ⇒**avoir** [5].

aide /ɛd/ *nf* help, assistance; (en argent) aid; **à l'~ de** with the help of; **venir en ~ à** help; **~ à domicile** home help; **~ familiale** mother's help; **~ sociale** social security; (US) welfare. ● *nmf* assistant.

aide-mémoire *nm inv* handbook of key facts.

aider /ede/ [1] *vt/i* help, assist; (subventionner) aid, give aid to; **~ à faire** help to do. □ **s'~ de** *vpr* use.

aïeul, ~e /ajœl/ *nm, f* grandparent.

aigle /ɛgl/ *nm* eagle.

aigre /ɛgʀ/ *a* sour, sharp; (fig) sharp.

aigrir /egʀiʀ/ [2] *vt* embitter. □ **s'~** *vpr* turn sour; (personne) become embittered.

aigu, ~ë /egy/ *a* (douleur, problème) acute; (objet) sharp; (voix) shrill; (Mus) high(-pitched); (accent) acute.

aiguille /eguij/ *nf* needle; (de montre) hand; (de balance) pointer; **~ à tricoter** knitting needle.

aiguilleur /eguijœʀ/ *nm* pointsman; **~ du ciel** air traffic controller.

aiguiser /eg(ɥ)ize/ [1] *vt* sharpen; (fig) stimulate.

ail (pl **~s** ou **aulx**) /aj, o/ *nm* garlic.

aile /ɛl/ *nf* wing.

ailier /elje/ *nm* winger; (US) end.

aille /aj/ ⇒**ALLER** [8].

ailleurs /ajœʀ/ *adv* elsewhere, somewhere else; **d'~** besides, moreover; **nulle part ~** nowhere else; **par ~** moreover, furthermore; **partout ~** everywhere else.

aimable /ɛmabl/ *a* kind.

aimant /ɛmɑ̃/ *nm* magnet.

aimer /eme/ [1] *vt* like; (d'amour) love; **j'aimerais faire** I'd like to do; **~ bien** quite like; **~ mieux** ou **autant** prefer.

aîné, ~e /ene/ *a* eldest; (de deux) elder. ● *nm, f* eldest (child); (premier de deux) elder; **~s** elders; **il est mon ~** he is older than me ou my senior.

ainsi /ɛ̃si/ *adv* like this, thus; (donc) so; **et ~ de suite** and so on; **pour ~ dire** so to speak, as it were; **~ que** as well as; (comme) as.

air /ɛʀ/ *nm* air; (mine) look, air; (mélodie) tune; **~ conditionné** air-conditioning; **avoir l'~** look, appear; **avoir l'~ de** look like; **avoir l'~ de faire** appear to be doing; **en l'~** (up) in the air; (*promesses*) empty; **prendre l'~** get some fresh air.

aire /ɛʀ/ *nf* area; **~ d'atterrissage** landing-strip; **~ de pique-nique** picnic area; **~ de repos** rest area; **~ de services** (motorway) services.

aisance /ɛzɑ̃s/ *nf* ease; (richesse) affluence.

aise /ɛz/ *nf* joy; **à l'~** (sur un siège) comfortable; (pas gêné) at ease; (fortuné) comfortably off; **mal à l'~** uncomfortable; ill at ease; **aimer ses ~s** like one's creature comforts; **mettre qn à l'~** put sb at ease; **se mettre à l'~** make oneself comfortable.

aisé, ~e /eze/ *a* easy; (fortuné) well-off.

aisselle /ɛsɛl/ *nf* armpit.

ait /ɛ/ ⇒AVOIR [5].

ajourner /aʒuʀne/ [1] *vt* postpone; (*début, procès*) adjourn.

ajout /aʒu/ *nm* addition.

ajouter /aʒute/ [1] *vt* add (**à** to); **~ foi à** lend credence to. □ **s'~** *vpr* be added.

ajuster /aʒyste/ [1] *vt* adjust; (*cible*) aim at; (adapter) fit; **~ son coup** adjust one's aim.

alarme /alaʀm/ *nf* alarm; **donner l'~** raise the alarm.

alarmer /alaʀme/ [1] *vt* alarm. □ **s'~** *vpr* become alarmed (**de** at).

Albanie /albani/ *nf* Albania.

alcool /alkɔl/ *nm* alcohol; (eau de vie) brandy; **~ à brûler** methylated spirit. **alcoolique** *a & nmf* alcoholic. **alcoolisé, ~e** *a* (*boisson*) alcoholic. **alcoolisme** *nm* alcoholism.

alcootest /alkɔtɛst/ *nm* breath test; (appareil) Breathalyser®.

aléa /alea/ *nm* hazard. **aléatoire** *a* unpredictable, uncertain; (Ordinat) random.

alentours /alɑ̃tuʀ/ *nmpl* surroundings; **aux ~ de** (de lieu) around; (de chiffre, date) about, around.

alerte /alɛʀt/ *a* (personne) alert; (vif) lively. ● *nf* alert; **~ à la bombe** bomb scare. **alerter** [1] *vt* alert.

algèbre /alʒɛbʀ/ *nf* algebra.

Algérie /alʒeʀi/ *nf* Algeria.

algue /alg/ *nf* seaweed; **les ~s** (Bot) algae.

aliéné, ~e /aljene/ *nm, f* insane person.

aliéner /aljene/ [14] *vt* alienate; (céder) give up. □ **s'~** *vpr* alienate.

aligner /aliɲe/ [1] *vt* (objets) line up, make lines of; (chiffres) string together; **~ sur** bring into line with. □ **s'~** *vpr* line up, **s'~ sur** align oneself on.

aliment /alimɑ̃/ *nm* food.

alimentaire /alimɑ̃tɛʀ/ *a* (industrie) food; (habitudes) dietary; **produits ~s** foodstuffs.

alimentation /alimɑ̃tasjɔ̃/ *nf* feeding, supply(ing); (régime) diet; (aliments) food; **magasin d'~** grocery shop *ou* store.

alimenter /alimɑ̃te/ [1] *vt* feed; (fournir) supply; (fig) sustain. □ **s'~** *vpr* eat.

allaiter /alete/ [1] *vt* (bébé) breast-feed; (US) nurse; (animal) suckle.

allée /ale/ *nf* path, lane; (menant à une maison) drive(way); (dans un

cinéma, magasin) aisle; (rue) road; ~s
et venues comings and goings.

allégé, ~e /aleʒe/ a diet; (beurre,
yaourt) low-fat.

alléger /aleʒe/ [14] [40] vt make
lighter; (fardeau, chargement)
lighten; (fig) (souffrance) alleviate.

allégresse /alegʀɛs/ nf gaiety,
joy.

alléguer /alege/ [14] vt (exemple)
invoke; (prétexter) allege.

Allemagne /almaɲ/ nf Germany.

allemand, ~e /almɑ̃, -d/ a
German. ● nm (Ling) German.
A~, ~e nm, f German.

aller /ale/ [8]

●verbe auxiliaire

····▸ je vais l'appeler I'm going to
call him; j'allais partir I was
about to leave; va savoir! who
knows?; ~ en s'améliorant be
improving.

●verbe intransitif

····▸ (se déplacer) go; allons-y! let's
go!; allez! come on!

····▸ (se porter) comment allez-vous?,
comment ça va? how are you?; ça
va (bien) I'm fine; qu'est-ce qui ne
va pas? what's the matter?; ça ne
va pas la tête? ⚆ are you mad?
⚆.

····▸ (mettre en valeur) ~ à qn suit sb;
ça te va bien it really suits you.

····▸ (convenir) ça va ma coiffure? is
my hair OK?; ça ne va pas du
tout that's no good at all.

◻ s'en aller verbe pronominal

····▸ go; va-t'en go away!; ça ne
s'en va pas (tache) it won't come
out.

●nom masculin

····▸ outward journey; ~ (simple)
single (ticket); (US) one-way
(ticket); ~ retour return (ticket);

(US) round trip (ticket); à l'~ on
the way out.

allergie /alɛʀʒi/ nf allergy.

allergique a allergic (à to).

alliance /aljɑ̃s/ nf alliance;
(bague) wedding-ring; (mariage)
marriage.

allier /alje/ [45] vt combine; (Pol)
ally. ◻ s'~ vpr combine; (Pol)
form an alliance; (famille)
become related (à to).

allô /alo/ interj hallo, hello.

allocation /alɔkasjɔ̃/ nf
allowance; ~ chômage
unemployment benefit; ~s
familiales family allowance.

allonger /alɔ̃ʒe/ [40] vt lengthen;
(bras, jambe) stretch (out);
(coucher) lay down. ◻ s'~ vpr get
longer; (s'étendre) lie down; (s'étirer)
stretch (oneself) out.

allouer /alwe/ [1] vt allocate;
(prêt) grant.

allumer /alyme/ [1] vt (bougie,
gaz) light; (lampe, appareil) turn
on; (pièce) switch the light(s) on
in; (fig) arouse. ◻ s'~ vpr
(lumière, appareil) come on.

allumette /alymɛt/ nf match.

allure /alyʀ/ nf speed, pace;
(démarche) walk; (apparence)
appearance; à toute ~ at full
speed; avoir de l'~ have style;
avoir des ~s de look like; avoir
une drôle d'~ be funny-looking.

allusion /alyzjɔ̃/ nf allusion (à
to); (implicite) hint (à at); faire ~ à
allude to; hint at.

alors /alɔʀ/ adv (à ce moment-là)
then; (de ce fait) so; (dans ce cas-là)
then; ça ~! well!; et ~? so what?
● conj ~ que (pendant que) while;
(tandis que) when, whereas.

alouette /alwɛt/ nf lark.

alourdir /aluʀdiʀ/ [2] vt weigh
down; (rendre plus important)
increase.

aloyau (*pl* ~x) /alwajo/ *nm* sirloin.

Alpes /alp/ *nfpl* **les** ~ the Alps.

alphabet /alfabɛ/ *nm* alphabet. **alphabétique** *a* alphabetical.

alphabétiser /alfabetize/ [1] *vt* teach to read and write.

alpiniste /alpinist/ *nmf* mountaineer.

altérer /altere/ [14] *vt* (*fait, texte*) distort; (*abîmer*) spoil; (*donner soif à*) make thirsty. □ **s'**~ *vpr* deteriorate.

alternance /altɛrnɑ̃s/ *nf* alternation; **en** ~ alternately.

altitude /altityd/ *nf* altitude, height.

amabilité /amabilite/ *nf* kindness.

amaigrir /amegrir/ [?] *vt* make thin(ner).

amande /amɑ̃d/ *nf* almond; (*d'un fruit à noyau*) kernel.

amant /amɑ̃/ *nm* lover.

amarre /amar/ *nf* (mooring) rope; ~**s** moorings.

amas /ama/ *nm* heap, pile.

amasser /amase/ [1] *vt* amass, gather; (*empiler*) pile up. □ **s'**~ *vpr* pile up; (*gens*) gather.

amateur /amatœr/ *nm* amateur; ~ **de** lover of; **d'**~ amateur; (*péj*) amateurish.

ambassade /ɑ̃basad/ *nf* embassy. **ambassadeur, -drice** *nm, f* ambassador.

ambiance /ɑ̃bjɑ̃s/ *nf* atmosphere. **ambiant, ~e** *a* surrounding.

ambigu, ~ë /ɑ̃bigy/ *a* ambiguous.

ambitieux, -ieuse /ɑ̃bisjø, -z/ *a* ambitious. **ambition** *nf* ambition.

ambulance /ɑ̃bylɑ̃s/ *nf* ambulance.

ambulant, ~e /ɑ̃bylɑ̃, -t/ *a* itinerant, travelling.

âme /ɑm/ *nf* soul; ~ **sœur** soul mate.

amélioration /ameljɔrasjɔ̃/ *nf* improvement.

améliorer /ameljɔre/ [1] *vt* improve. □ **s'**~ *vpr* improve.

aménagement /amenaʒmɑ̃/ *nm* (de magasin) fitting out; (de grenier) conversion; (de territoire) development; (de cuisine) equipping.

aménager /amenaʒe/ [40] *vt* (*magasin*) fit out; (*transformer*) convert; (*territoire*) develop; (*cuisine*) equip.

amende /amɑ̃d/ *nf* fine; **faire** ~ **honorable** make amends.

amener /am(ə)ne/ [6] *vt* bring; (*causer*) bring about; ~ **qn à faire** cause sb to do. □ **s'**~ *vpr* 🔟 turn up.

amer, -ère /amɛr/ *a* bitter.

américain, ~e /amerikɛ̃, -ɛn/ *a* American. **A~, ~e** *nm, f* American.

Amérique /amerik/ *nf* America; ~ **centrale/latine** Central/Latin America; ~ **du Nord/Sud** North/South America.

amertume /amɛrtym/ *nf* bitterness.

ami, ~e /ami/ *nm, f* friend; (amateur) lover; **un** ~ **des bêtes** an animal lover. ● *a* friendly.

amiable /amjabl/ *a* amicable; **à l'**~ (*divorcer*) by mutual consent; (*se séparer*) on friendly terms; (*séparation*) amicable.

amical, ~e (*mpl* -**aux**) /amikal, -o/ *a* friendly.

amiral (*pl* -**aux**) /amiral, -o/ *nm* admiral.

amitié /amitje/ *nf* friendship; ~**s** (en fin de lettre) kind regards; **prendre qn en** ~ take a liking to sb.

amnistie /amnisti/ *nf* amnesty.

amoindrir /amwɛ̃dRiR/ [2] vt reduce.

amont: en ~ /ɑ̃namɔ̃/ loc upstream.

amorcer /amɔRse/ [10] vt start; (hameçon) bait; (pompe) prime; (arme à feu) arm.

amortir /amɔRtiR/ [2] vt (choc) cushion; (bruit) deaden; (dette) pay off; **~ un achat** make a purchase pay for itself.

amortisseur /amɔRtisœR/ nm shock absorber.

amour /amuR/ nm love; **pour l'~ de** for the sake of.

amoureux, -euse /amuRø, -z/ a (personne) in love; (relation, regard) loving; (vie) love; **~ de qn** in love with sb. ● nm, f lover.

amour-propre /amuRpRɔpR/ nm self-esteem.

amphithéâtre /ɑ̃fiteatR/ nm amphitheatre; (d'université) lecture hall.

ampleur /ɑ̃plœR/ nf extent, size; (de vêtement) fullness; **prendre de l'~** spread, grow.

amplifier /ɑ̃plifje/ [45] vt amplify; (fig) expand, develop. □ **s'~** vpr (son) grow; (scandale) intensify.

ampoule /ɑ̃pul/ nf (électrique) bulb; (sur la peau) blister; (Méd) phial, ampoule.

amusant, ~e /amyzɑ̃, -t/ a (blague) funny; (soirée) enjoyable, entertaining.

amuse-gueule /amyzgœl/ nm inv cocktail snack.

amusement /amyzmɑ̃/ nm amusement; (passe-temps) entertainment.

amuser /amyze/ [1] vt amuse; (détourner l'attention de) distract. □ **s'~** vpr enjoy oneself; (jouer) play.

amygdale /amidal/ nf tonsil.

an /ɑ̃/ nm year; **avoir dix ~s** be ten years old; **un garçon de deux ~s** a two-year-old boy; **à soixante ~s** at the age of sixty; **les moins de dix-huit ~s** under eighteens.

analogie /analɔʒi/ nf analogy.

analogue /analɔg/ a similar, analogous (à to).

analphabète /analfabɛt/ a & nmf illiterate.

analyse /analiz/ nf analysis; (Méd) test. **analyser** [1] vt analyse; (Méd) test.

ananas /anana(s)/ nm pineapple.

anarchie /anaRʃi/ nf anarchy.

anatomie /anatɔmi/ nf anatomy.

ancêtre /ɑ̃sɛtR/ nm ancestor.

anchois /ɑ̃ʃwa/ nm anchovy.

ancien, ~ne /ɑ̃sjɛ̃, -jɛn/ a old; (de jadis) ancient; (meuble) antique; (précédent) former, ex-, old; (dans une fonction) senior; **~ combattant** veteran. ● nm, f senior; (par l'âge) elder. **anciennement** adv formerly. **ancienneté** nf age, seniority.

ancre /ɑ̃kR/ nf anchor; **jeter/lever l'~** cast/weigh anchor.

andouille /ɑ̃duj/ nf sausage (filled with chitterlings); (idiot 🄳) fool; **faire l'~** fool around.

âne /ɑn/ nm donkey, ass; (imbécile 🄳) dimwit 🄳.

anéantir /aneɑ̃tiR/ [2] vt destroy; (exterminer) annihilate; (accabler) overwhelm.

anémie /anemi/ nf anaemia.

ânerie /ɑnRi/ nf stupid remark.

anesthésie /anɛstezi/ nf (opération) anaesthetic.

ange /ɑ̃ʒ/ nm angel; **aux ~s** in seventh heaven.

angine /ɑ̃ʒin/ nf throat infection.

anglais, ~e /ɑ̃glɛ, -z/ a English. ● nm (Ling) English. **A~, ~e** nm, f Englishman, Englishwoman.

angle /ɑ̃gl/ nm angle; (coin) corner.

Angleterre /ɑ̃glətɛR/ nf England.

anglophone /ãglɔfɔn/ a English-speaking. ● nmf English speaker.

angoissant, ~e /ãgwasã, -t/ a alarming; (effrayant) harrowing.

angoisse /ãgwas/ nf anxiety. **angoissé**, ~e a anxious. **angoisser** [1] vi worry.

animal (pl -aux) /animal, -o/ nm animal; ~ **familier**, ~ **de compagnie** pet. ● a (mpl -aux) animal.

animateur, -trice /animatœʀ, -tʀis/ nm, f organizer, leader; (TV) host, hostess.

animation /animasjɔ̃/ nf liveliness; (affairement) activity; (au cinéma) animation; (activité dirigée) organized activity.

animé, ~e /anime/ a lively; (affairé) busy; (être) animate.

animer /anime/ [1] vt liven up; (débat, atelier) lead; (spectacle) host; (pousser) drive; (encourager) spur on. □ s'~ vpr liven up.

anis /ani(s)/ nm (Culin) aniseed; (Bot) anise.

anneau (pl ~x) /ano/ nm ring; (de chaîne) link.

année /ane/ nf year; ~ **bissextile** leap year; ~ **civile** calendar year.

annexe /anɛks/ a (document) attached; (question) related; (bâtiment) adjoining. ● nf (bâtiment) annexe; (US) annex; (document) appendix; (électronique) attachment. **annexer** [1] vt annex; (document) attach.

anniversaire /anivɛʀsɛʀ/ nm birthday; (d'un événement) anniversary. ● a anniversary.

annonce /anɔ̃s/ nf announcement; (publicitaire) advertisement; (indice) sign.

annoncer /anɔ̃se/ [10] vt announce; (prédire) forecast; (être l'indice de) herald. □ s'~ vpr (crise, tempête) be brewing; s'~ **bien/mal**

look good/bad. **annonceur** nm advertiser.

annuaire /anɥɛʀ/ nm year-book; ~ **(téléphonique)** (telephone) directory.

annuel, ~**le** /anɥɛl/ a annual, yearly.

annulation /anylasjɔ̃/ nf cancellation; (de sanction, loi) repeal; (de mesure) abolition.

annuler /anyle/ [1] vt cancel; (contrat) nullify; (jugement) quash; (loi) repeal. □ s'~ vpr cancel each other out.

anodin, ~e /anɔdɛ̃, -in/ a insignificant; (sans risques) harmless, safe.

anonymat /anɔnima/ nm anonymity; **garder l'**~ remain anonymous. **anonyme** a anonymous.

anorexie /anɔʀɛksi/ nf anorexia.

anormal, ~e (mpl -aux) /anɔʀmal, -o/ a abnormal.

anse /ãs/ nf handle; (baie) cove.

Antarctique /ãtaʀktik/ nm Antarctic.

antenne /ãtɛn/ nf aerial; (US) antenna; (d'insecte) antenna; (succursale) agency; (Mil) outpost; **à l'**~ on the air; ~ **chirurgicale** mobile emergency unit; ~ **parabolique** satellite dish.

antérieur, ~e /ãteʀjœʀ/ a previous, earlier; (placé devant) front; ~ **à** prior to.

antiaérien, ~**ne** /ãtiaeʀjɛ̃, -ɛn/ a anti-aircraft; **abri** ~ air-raid shelter.

antiatomique /ãtiatɔmik/ a **abri** ~ nuclear fall-out shelter.

antibiotique /ãtibjɔtik/ nm antibiotic.

anticipation /ãtisipasjɔ̃/ nf d'~ (livre, film) science fiction; **par** ~ in advance.

anticiper /ãtisipe/ [1] vt ~ **(sur)**

anticipate; (effectuer à l'avance) bring forward.

anticorps /ɑ̃tikɔʀ/ *nm* antibody.

antidater /ɑ̃tidate/ [1] *vt* backdate, antedate.

antigel /ɑ̃tiʒɛl/ *nm* antifreeze.

Antilles /ɑ̃tij/ *nfpl* **les** ~ the West Indies.

antipathique /ɑ̃tipatik/ *a* unpleasant.

antiquaire /ɑ̃tikɛʀ/ *nmf* antique dealer.

antiquité /ɑ̃tikite/ *nf* (objet) antique; **l'A**~ antiquity.

antisémite /ɑ̃tisemit/ *a* anti-Semitic.

antiseptique /ɑ̃tisɛptik/ *a & nm* antiseptic.

antivol /ɑ̃tivɔl/ *nm* anti-theft device; (Auto) steering lock.

anxiété /ɑ̃ksjete/ *nf* anxiety.

anxieux, -ieuse /ɑ̃ksjø, -z/ *a* anxious. ● *nm, f* worrier.

août /u(t)/ *nm* August.

apaiser /apeze/ [1] *vt* calm down; (colère, militant) appease; (douleur) soothe; (faim) satisfy. □ **s'**~ *vpr* (tempête) die down.

apathie /apati/ *nf* apathy.

apathique *a* apathetic.

apercevoir /apɛʀsəvwaʀ/ [52] *vt* see. □ **s'**~ **de** *vpr* notice; **s'**~ **que** notice *ou* realize that.

aperçu /apɛʀsy/ *nm* (échantillon) glimpse, taste; (intuition) insight.

apéritif /apeʀitif/ *nm* aperitif, drink.

aphte /aft/ *nm* mouth ulcer.

apitoyer /apitwaje/ [31] *vt* move (to pity). □ **s'**~ *vpr* **s'**~ **sur** (**le sort de**) **qn** feel sorry for sb.

aplanir /aplaniʀ/ [2] *vt* level; (fig) iron out.

aplatir /aplatiʀ/ [2] *vt* flatten (out). □ **s'**~ *vpr* (s'immobiliser) flatten oneself.

aplomb /aplɔ̃/ *nm* balance; (fig) self-confidence; **d'**~ (en équilibre)

steady; **je ne suis pas bien d'**~ 🔲 I don't feel very well.

apogée /apɔʒe/ *nm* peak.

apologie /apɔlɔʒi/ *nf* panegyric.

apostrophe /apɔstʀɔf/ *nf* apostrophe; (remarque) remark.

apothéose /apɔteoz/ *nf* high point; (d'événement) grand finale.

apparaître /apaʀɛtʀ/ [18] *vi* appear; **il apparaît que** it appears that.

appareil /apaʀɛj/ *nm* device; (électrique) appliance; (Anat) system; (téléphone) phone; (avion) plane; (Culin) mixture; (système administratif) apparatus; ~ (**dentaire**) brace; (dentier) dentures; ~ (**photo**) camera; **c'est Gabriel à l'**~ it's Gabriel on the phone; ~ **auditif** hearing aid; ~ **électroménager** household electrical appliance.

appareiller /apaʀeje/ [1] *vi* (navire) cast off, put to sea.

apparemment /apaʀamɑ̃/ *adv* apparently.

apparence /apaʀɑ̃s/ *nf* appearance; **en** ~ outwardly; (apparemment) apparently.

apparent, ~e /apaʀɑ̃, -t/ *a* apparent; (visible) conspicuous.

apparenté, ~e /apaʀɑ̃te/ *a* related; (semblable) similar.

apparition /apaʀisjɔ̃/ *nf* appearance; (spectre) apparition.

appartement /apaʀtəmɑ̃/ *nm* flat; (US) apartment.

appartenir /apaʀtəniʀ/ [58] *vi* belong (**à** to); **il lui appartient de** it is up to him to.

appât /apɑ/ *nm* bait; (fig) lure.

appauvrir /apovʀiʀ/ [2] *vt* impoverish. □ **s'**~ *vpr* become impoverished.

appel /apɛl/ *nm* call; (Jur) appeal; (supplique) appeal, plea; (Mil) call-up; (US) draft; **faire** ~ appeal; **faire** ~ **à** (recourir à) call on; (invoquer) appeal to; (évoquer) call up; (exiger) call for; **faire l'~** (Scol) call the register; (Mil) take a roll-call; **~ d'offres** (Comm) invitation to tender; **faire un ~ de phares** flash one's headlights.

appeler /aple/ [38] vt call; (téléphoner) phone, call; (nécessiter) call for; **en ~ à** appeal to; **appelé à** (destiné) destined for. □ **s'~** vpr be called; **il s'appelle Tim** his name is Tim ou he is called Tim.

appellation /apelasjɔ̃/ nf name, designation.

appendice /apɛ̃dis/ nm appendix. **appendicite** nf appendicitis.

appesantir /apəzɑ̃tiʀ/ [2] vt weigh down. □ **s'~** vpr grow heavier; **s'~ sur** dwell upon.

appétissant, ~e /apetisɑ̃, -t/ a appetizing.

appétit /apeti/ nm appetite; **bon ~!** enjoy your meal!

applaudir /aplodiʀ/ [2] vt/i applaud. **applaudissements** nmpl applause.

application /aplikasjɔ̃/ nf (soin) care, (de loi) (respect) application; (mise en œuvre) implementation; (Ordinat) application program.

appliqué, ~e /aplike/ a (travail) painstaking; (sciences) applied; (élève) hard-working.

appliquer /aplike/ [1] vt apply; (loi) enforce. □ **s'~** vpr apply oneself, (à to), take great care (à faire to do); **s'~ à** (concerner) apply to.

appoint /apwɛ̃/ nm support; **d'~** extra; **faire l'~** give the correct money.

apport /apɔʀ/ nm contribution.

apporter /apɔʀte/ [1] vt bring; (aide, précision) give; (causer) bring about.

appréciation /apʀesjasjɔ̃/ nf estimate, evaluation; (de monnaie)

appreciation; (jugement) assessment.

apprécier /apʀesje/ [45] vt appreciate; (évaluer) assess; (objet) value, appraise.

appréhender /apʀeɑ̃de/ [1] vt dread, fear; (arrêter) apprehend.

apprendre /apʀɑ̃dʀ/ [50] vt learn; (être informé de) hear, learn; (de façon indirecte) hear of; **~ qch à qn** teach sb sth; (informer) tell sb sth; **~ à faire** learn to do; **~ à qn à faire** teach sb to do; **~ que** learn that; (être informé) hear that.

apprenti, ~e /apʀɑ̃ti/ nm, f apprentice. **apprentissage** nm apprenticeship; (d'un sujet) learning.

apprêter /apʀete/ [1] vt prepare; (bois) prime; (mur) size. □ **s'~ à** vpr prepare to.

apprivoiser /apʀivwaze/ [1] vt tame.

approbation /apʀɔbasjɔ̃/ nf approval.

approchant, ~e /apʀɔʃɑ̃, -t/ a close, similar.

approcher /apʀɔʃe/ [1] vt (objet) move near(er) (de to); (personne) approach; **~ de** get nearer ou closer to. ● vi approach □ **s'~ de** vpr approach, move near(er) to.

approfondir /apʀɔfɔ̃diʀ/ [2] vt deepen; (fig) go into sth in depth; (connaissances) improve.

approprié, ~e /apʀɔpʀije/ a appropriate.

approprier (s') /(s)apʀɔpʀije/ [45] vpr appropriate.

approuver /apʀuve/ [1] vt approve; (trouver louable) approve of; (soutenir) agree with.

approvisionner /apʀɔvizjɔne/ [1] vt supply (en with); (compte en banque) pay money into. □ **s'~** vpr stock up.

approximatif, -ive /apʀɔksimatif, -v/ a approximate.

appul /apɥi/ *nm* support; (de fenêtre) sill; (pour objet) rest; **à l'~ de** in support of; **prendre ~ sur** lean on.

appui-tête (*pl* appuis-tête) /apɥitɛt/ *nm* headrest.

appuyer /apɥije/ [31] *vt* lean, rest; (presser) press; (soutenir) support, back. ● *vi* **~ sur** press (on); (fig) stress. □ **s'~ sur** *vpr* lean on; (compter sur) rely on.

après /apʀɛ/ *prép* after; (au-delà de) after, beyond; **~ avoir fait** after doing; **~ tout** after all; **~ coup** after the event; **d'~** (selon) according to; (en imitant) from; (adapté de) based on. ● *adv* after (wards); (plus tard) later; **le bus d'~** the next bus. ● *conj* **~ qu'il est parti** after he left. **après-demain** *adv* the day after tomorrow. **après-guerre** (*pl* ~s) *nm ou f* postwar period. **après-midi** *nm ou f inv* afternoon. **après-rasage** (*pl* ~s) *nm* aftershave. **après-ski** *nm inv* moonboot. **après-vente** *a inv* after-sales.

a priori /apʀijɔʀi/ *adv* (à première vue) offhand, on the face of it; (sans réfléchir) out of hand. ● *nm* preconception.

à-propos /apʀopo/ *nm* timing, timeliness; (fig) presence of mind.

apte /apt/ *a* capable (à of); (ayant les qualités requises) suitable (à for); (en état) fit (à for).

aptitude /aptityd/ *nf* aptitude, ability.

aquarelle /akwaʀɛl/ *nf* watercolour.

aquatique /akwatik/ *a* aquatic; (Sport) water.

arabe /aʀab/ *a* Arab; (Ling) Arabic; (désert) Arabian. ● *nm* (Ling) Arabic. **A~** *nmf* Arab.

Arabie /aʀabi/ *nf* **~ Saoudite** Saudi Arabia.

arachide /aʀaʃid/ *nf* groundnut; **huile d'~** groundnut oil.

araignée /aʀeɲe/ *nf* spider.

arbitraire /aʀbitʀɛʀ/ *a* arbitrary.

arbitre /aʀbitʀ/ *nm* referee; (au cricket, tennis) umpire; (expert) arbiter; (Jur) arbitrator. **arbitrer** [1] *vt* (match) referee, umpire; (Jur) arbitrate in.

arbre /aʀbʀ/ *nm* tree; (Tech) shaft.

arbuste /aʀbyst/ *nm* shrub.

arc /aʀk/ *nm* (arme) bow; (courbe) curve; (voûte) arch; **~ de cercle** arc of a circle.

arc-en-ciel (*pl* arcs-en-ciel) /aʀkɑ̃sjɛl/ *nm* rainbow.

arche /aʀʃ/ *nf* arch; **~ de Noé** Noah's ark.

archéologie /aʀkeɔlɔʒi/ *nf* archaeology.

archevêque /aʀʃəvɛk/ *nm* archbishop.

architecte /aʀʃitɛkt/ *nmf* architect. **architecture** *nf* architecture.

Arctique /aʀktik/ *nm* Arctic.

ardent, ~e /aʀdɑ̃, -t/ *a* burning; (passionné) ardent; (foi) fervent. **ardeur** *nf* ardour; (chaleur) heat.

ardoise /aʀdwaz/ *nf* slate; **~ électronique** notepad computer.

arène /aʀɛn/ *nf* arena; **~s** amphitheatre; (pour corridas) bullring.

arête /aʀɛt/ *nf* (de poisson) bone; (bord) ridge.

argent /aʀʒɑ̃/ *nm* money; (métal) silver; **~ comptant** cash; **prendre pour ~ comptant** take at face value; **~ de poche** pocket money. **argenté, ~e** /aʀʒɑ̃te/ *a* silver(y); (métal) (silver-)plated.

argenterie /aʀʒɑ̃tʀi/ *nf* silverware.

Argentine /aʀʒɑ̃tin/ *nf* Argentina.

argile /aʀʒil/ *nf* clay.

argot /aʀgo/ *nm* slang.

argument /aʀgymɑ̃/ *nm*
argument; ∼ **de vente** selling
point. **argumenter** [1] *vi* argue.

aristocratie /aʀistɔkʀasi/ *nf*
aristocracy.

arithmétique /aʀitmetik/ *nf*
arithmetic. ● *a* arithmetical.

armature /aʀmatyʀ/ *nf*
framework; (de tente) frame.

arme /aʀm/ *nf* arm, weapon; ∼ **à
feu** firearm; ∼**s** (blason) coat of
arms.

armée /aʀme/ *nf* army; ∼ **de l'air**
Air Force; ∼ **de terre** Army.

armer /aʀme/ [1] *vt* arm; (fusil)
cock; (navire) equip; (renforcer)
reinforce; (Photo) wind on; □ **s'**∼
de *vpr* arm oneself with.

armoire /aʀmwaʀ/ *nf* cupboard;
(penderie) wardrobe; (US) closet; ∼
à pharmacie medicine cabinet.

armure /aʀmyʀ/ *nf* armour.

arnaque /aʀnak/ *nf* 🄲 swindling;
c'est de l'∼ it's a swindle.

arobas(e) /aʀɔbas, aʀɔbaz/ *nm* at
sign.

aromate /aʀɔmat/ *nm* herb,
spice.

aromatisé, ∼**e** /aʀɔmatize/ *a*
flavoured.

arôme /aʀom/ *nm* aroma; (additif)
flavouring.

arpenter /aʀpɑ̃te/ [1] *vt* pace up
and down; (terrain) survey.

arqué, ∼**e** /aʀke/ *a* arched;
(jambes) bandy.

arrache-pied: d'∼ /daʀaʃpje/ *loc*
relentlessly.

arracher /aʀaʃe/ [1] *vt* pull out
ou off; (plante) pull *ou* dig up;
(cheveux, page) tear *ou* pull out;
(par une explosion) blow off; ∼ **à**
(enlever à) snatch from; (fig) force
ou wrest from. □ **s'**∼ **qch** *vpr*
fight over sth.

arranger /aʀɑ̃ʒe/ [40] *vt* arrange,
fix up; (réparer) put right; (régler)
sort out; (convenir à) suit. □ **s'**∼ *vpr*

(se mettre d'accord) come to an
arrangement; (se débrouiller)
manage (**pour** to).

arrestation /aʀɛstasjɔ̃/ *nf* arrest.

arrêt /aʀɛ/ *nm* stopping; (de
combats) cessation; (de production)
halt; (lieu) stop; (pause) pause; (Jur)
ruling; **aux** ∼**s** (Mil) under arrest;
à l'∼ (véhicule) stationary;
(machine) idle; **faire un** ∼ (make
a) stop; **sans** ∼ (sans escale)
nonstop; (sans interruption)
constantly; ∼ **maladie** sick leave;
∼ **de travail** (grève) stoppage; (Méd)
sick leave.

arrêté /aʀete/ *nm* order; ∼
municipal bylaw.

arrêter /aʀete/ [1] *vt* stop; (date)
fix; (appareil) turn off; (renoncer à)
give up; (appréhender) arrest. ● *vi*
stop. □ **s'**∼ *vpr* stop; **s'**∼ **de faire**
stop doing.

arrhes /aʀ/ *nfpl* deposit; **verser
des** ∼ pay a deposit.

arrière /aʀjɛʀ/ *a inv* back, rear.
● *nm* back, rear; (football) back; **à
l'**∼ in *ou* at the back; **en** ∼
behind; (marcher, tomber)
backwards; **en** ∼ **de** behind.

arrière-boutique (pl ∼**s**) *nf* back
room (of the shop). **arrière-
garde** (pl ∼**s**) *nf* rearguard.
arrière-goût (pl ∼**s**) *nm* after-
taste. **arrière-grand-mère** (pl
arrière-grands-mères) *nf* great-
grandmother. **arrière-grand-
père** (pl **arrière-grands-pères**)
nm great-grandfather. **arrière-
pays** *nm inv* backcountry.
arrière-pensée (pl ∼**s**) *nf*
ulterior motive. **arrière-plan** *nm*
(pl ∼**s**) background.

arrimer /aʀime/ [1] *vt* secure;
(cargaison) stow.

arrivage /aʀivaʒ/ *nm*
consignment.

arrivée /aʀive/ *nf* arrival; (Sport)
finish.

arriver /aʀive/ [1] *vi* (aux être)

arrive, come; (*réussir*) succeed; (se
produire) happen; ~ **à** (atteindre)
reach; ~ **à faire** manage to do; **je
n'arrive pas à faire** I can't do; **en ~
à faire** get to the stage of doing; **il
arrive que** it happens that; **il lui
arrive de faire** he (sometimes)
does.

arriviste /aʀivist/ *nmf* go-getter,
self-seeker.

arrondir /aʀɔ̃diʀ/ [2] *vt* (make)
round; (*somme*) round off. □ **s'~**
vpr become round(ed).

arrondissement /aʀɔ̃dismɑ̃/ *nm*
district.

arroser /aʀoze/ [1] *vt* water;
(*repas*) wash down (with a
drink); (*rôti*) baste; (*victoire*)
drink to. **arrosoir** *nm* watering-
can.

art /aʀ/ *nm* art; (*don*) knack (**de
faire** of doing); ~**s et métiers** arts
and crafts; ~**s ménagers** home
economics (+ *sg*).

artère /aʀtɛʀ/ *nf* artery; (**grande**)
~ main road.

arthrite /aʀtʀit/ *nf* arthritis.

arthrose /aʀtʀoz/ *nf*
osteoarthritis.

artichaut /aʀtiʃo/ *nm* artichoke.

article /aʀtikl/ *nm* article; (Comm)
item, article; **à l'~ de la mort** at
death's door; ~ **de fond** feature
(article); ~**s de voyage** travel
goods.

articulation /aʀtikylasjɔ̃/ *nf*
articulation; (Anat) joint.

articuler /aʀtikyle/ [1] *vt*
articulate; (*structurer*) structure;
(*assembler*) connect (**sur** to).

artificiel, ~**le** /aʀtifisjɛl/ *a*
artificial.

artisan /aʀtizɑ̃/ *nm* artisan,
craftsman; **l'~ de** (fig) the
architect of.

artisanal, ~**e** (*mpl* ~**aux**)
/aʀtizanal/ *a* craft; (*méthode*)
traditional; (*amateur*) home-made;

de fabrication ~**e** hand-made,
hand-crafted.

artiste /aʀtist/ *nmf* artist.

artistique *a* artistic.

as[1] /a/ ⇒AVOIR [5].

as[2] /ɑs/ *nm* ace.

ascenseur /asɑ̃sœʀ/ *nm* lift; (US)
elevator.

ascension /asɑ̃sjɔ̃/ *nf* ascent;
l'A~ Ascension.

aseptiser /asɛptize/ [1] *vt*
disinfect; (*stériliser*) sterilize;
aseptisé (péj) sanitized.

asiatique /azjatik/ *a* Asian. **A~**
nmf Asian.

Asie /azi/ *nf* Asia.

asile /azil/ *nm* refuge; (Pol)
asylum; (*pour malades, vieillards*)
home; ~ **de nuit** night shelter.

aspect /aspɛ/ *nm* appearance;
(*facettes*) aspect; (*perspective*) side; **à
l'~ de** at the sight of.

asperge /aspɛʀʒ/ *nf* asparagus.

asperger /aspɛʀʒe/ [40] *vt* spray.

asphyxier /asfiksje/ [45] *vt*
(*personne*) asphyxiate;
(*entreprise, réseau*) paralyse.
□ **s'~** *vpr* suffocate; gas oneself;
(*entreprise, réseau*) become
paralysed.

aspirateur /aspiʀatœʀ/ *nm*
vacuum cleaner.

aspirer /aspiʀe/ [1] *vt* inhale;
(*liquide*) suck up. ● *vi* ~ **à** aspire
to.

aspirine® /aspiʀin/ *nf* aspirin.

assainir /aseniʀ/ [2] *vt* clean up.

assaisonnement /asɛzɔnmɑ̃/
nm seasoning.

assassin /asasɛ̃/ *nm* murderer;
(Pol) assassin. **assassiner** [1] *vt*
murder; (Pol) assassinate.

assaut /aso/ *nm* assault,
onslaught; **donner l'~ à**, **prendre
d'~** storm.

assemblage /asɑ̃blaʒ/ *nm*
assembly; (*combinaison*) collection;
(Tech) joint.

assemblée /asɑ̃ble/ *nf* meeting; (gens réunis) gathering; (Pol) assembly.

assembler /asɑ̃ble/ [1] *vt* assemble, put together; (réunir) gather. □ **s'~** *vpr* gather, assemble.

asseoir /aswaʀ/ [9] *vt* sit (down), seat; (bébé, malade) sit up; (affermir) establish; (baser) base. □ **s'~** *vpr* sit (down).

assez /ase/ *adv* (suffisamment) enough; (plutôt) quite, fairly; ~ **grand/rapide** big/fast enough (**pour** to); ~ **de** enough; **j'en ai ~ (de)** I've had enough (of).

assidu, ~**e** /asidy/ *a* (zélé) assiduous; (régulier) regular; ~ **auprès de** attentive to. **assiduité** *nf* assiduousness, regularity.

assiéger /asjeʒe/ [14] [40] *vt* besiege.

assiette /asjɛt/ *nf* plate; (équilibre) seat; ~ **anglaise** assorted cold meats; ~ **creuse/plate** soup-/ dinner-plate; **ne pas être dans son ~** feel out of sorts.

assigner /asiɲe/ [1] *vt* assign; (limite) fix.

assimilation /asimilasjɔ̃/ *nf* assimilation; (comparaison) likening, comparison.

assimiler /asimile/ [1] *vt* ~ **à** liken to; (classer) class as. □ **s'~** *vpr* assimilate; (être comparable) be comparable (**à** to).

assis, ~**e** /asi, -z/ *a* sitting (down), seated. ●⇒ASSEOIR [9].

assise /asiz/ *nf* (base) foundation; ~**s** (tribunal) assizes; (congrès) conference, congress.

assistance /asistɑ̃s/ *nf* audience; (aide) assistance; **l'A~ (publique)** welfare services.

assistant, ~**e** /asistɑ̃, -t/ *nm,f* assistant; (Scol) foreign language assistant; ~**s** (spectateurs) members of the audience; ~**e sociale** social worker; ~ **personnel numérique** personal digital assistant, PDA.

assister /asiste/ [1] *vt* assist; ~ **à** attend, be (present) at; (accident) witness; **assisté par ordinateur** computer-assisted.

association /asɔsjasjɔ̃/ *nf* association.

associé, ~**e** /asɔsje/ *nm, f* partner, associate. ●*a* associate.

associer /asɔsje/ [45] *vt* associate; (mêler) combine (**à** with); ~ **qn à** (projet) involve sb in; (bénéfices) give sb a share of. □ **s'~** *vpr* (sociétés, personnes) become associated, join forces (**à** with); (s'harmoniser) combine (**à** with); **s'~ à** (joie, opinion de qn) share; (projet) take part in.

assommer /asɔme/ [1] *vt* knock out; (animal) stun; (fig) overwhelm; (ennuyer 🔲) bore.

Assomption /asɔ̃psjɔ̃/ *nf* Assumption.

assortiment /asɔrtimɑ̃/ *nm* assortment.

assortir /asɔrtiʀ/ [2] *vt* match (**à** with, to); ~ **de** accompany with. □ **s'~** *vpr* match; **s'~ à qch** match sth.

assoupir (s') /(s)asupiʀ/ [2] *vpr* doze off; (s'apaiser) subside.

assouplir /asupliʀ/ [2] *vt* make supple; (fig) make flexible.

assourdir /asurdiʀ/ [2] *vt* (personne) deafen; (bruit) muffle.

assouvir /asuviʀ/ [2] *vt* satisfy.

assujettir /asyʒetiʀ/ [2] *vt* subjugate, subdue; ~ **à** subject to.

assumer /asyme/ [1] *vt* assume; (coût) meet; (accepter) come to terms with, accept.

assurance /asyʀɑ̃s/ *nf* (self-) assurance; (garantie) assurance; (contrat) insurance; ~**s sociales**

social insurance; ~ **automobile/ maladie** car/health insurance.

assuré, ~e /asyʀe/ a certain, assured; (*sûr de soi*) confident, assured. ● *nm, f* insured party.

assurer /asyʀe/ [1] vt ensure; (*fournir*) provide; (*exécuter*) carry out; (Comm) insure; (*stabiliser*) steady; (*frontières*) make secure; ~ **à qn que** assure sb that; ~ **qn de** assure sb of; ~ **la gestion/ défense de** manage/defend. □ **s'~** vpr take out insurance; **s'~ de/ que** make sure of/that; **s'~ qch** (*se procurer*) secure sth. **assureur** *nm* insurer.

astérisque /asteʀisk/ *nm* asterisk.

asthmatique /asmatik/ a & *nmf* asthmatic.

asthme /asm/ *nm* asthma.

asticot /astiko/ *nm* maggot.

astreindre /astʀɛ̃dʀ/ [22] vt ~ **qn à qch** force sth on sb; ~ **qn à faire** force sb to do.

astrologie /astʀɔlɔʒi/ *nf* astrology. **astrologue** *nmf* astrologer.

astronaute /astʀonot/ *nmf* astronaut.

astronomie /astʀonɔmi/ *nf* astronomy.

astuce /astys/ *nf* smartness; (*truc*) trick; (*plaisanterie*) wisecrack.

astucieux, -ieuse /astysjø, -z/ a smart, clever.

atelier /atəlje/ *nm* (*local*) workshop; (*de peintre*) studio; (*séance de travail*) workshop.

athée /ate/ *nmf* atheist. ● a atheistic.

athlète /atlɛt/ *nmf* athlete. **athlétisme** *nm* athletics.

Atlantique /atlɑ̃tik/ *nm* Atlantic (Ocean).

atmosphère /atmɔsfɛʀ/ *nf* atmosphere.

atomique /atɔmik/ a atomic; (*énergie, centrale*) nuclear.

atomiseur /atɔmizœʀ/ *nm* spray.

atout /atu/ *nm* trump (card); (*avantage*) asset.

atroce /atʀɔs/ a atrocious.

attabler (s') /(s)atable/ [1] vpr sit down at table.

attachant, ~e /ataʃɑ̃, -t/ a charming.

attache /ataʃ/ *nf* (*agrafe*) fastener; (*lien*) tie.

attaché, ~e /ataʃe/ a **être ~ à** (*aimer*) be attached to. ● *nm, f* (Pol) attaché.

attacher /ataʃe/ [1] vt tie (up); (*ceinture, robe*) fasten; (*bicyclette*) lock; ~ **à** (*attribuer à*) attach to. ● vi (Culin) stick. □ **s'~** vpr fasten, do up; **s'~ à** (*se lier à*) become attached to; (*se consacrer à*) apply oneself to.

attaquant, ~e /atakɑ̃, -t/ *nm, f* attacker; (*au football*) striker; (*au football américain*) forward.

attaque /atak/ *nf* attack; ~ (*cérébrale*) stroke; **il va en faire une ~** he'll have a fit; ~ **à main armée** armed attack.

attaquer /atake/ [1] vt attack; (*banque*) raid. ● vi attack. □ **s'~ à** vpr attack; (*problème, sujet*) tackle.

attardé, ~e /ataʀde/ a backward; (*idées*) outdated; (*en retard*) late.

attarder (s') /(s)ataʀde/ [1] vpr linger.

atteindre /atɛ̃dʀ/ [22] vt reach; (*blesser*) hit; (*affecter*) affect.

atteint, ~e /atɛ̃, -t/ a ~ **de** suffering from.

atteinte /atɛ̃t/ *nf* attack (à on); **porter ~ à** attack; (*droit*) infringe.

atteler /atle/ [38] vt (*cheval*) harness; (*remorque*) couple. □ **s'~ à** vpr get down to.

attelle /atɛl/ *nf* splint.

attenant, ∼e /atnã, -t/ *a* ∼ (à) adjoining.

attendant: en ∼ /ãnatãdã/ *loc* meanwhile.

attendre /atãdʀ/ [3] *vt* wait for; (*bébé*) expect; (être le sort de ∼) await; (escompter) expect; ∼ que qn fasse wait for sb to do. ● *vi* wait; (au téléphone) hold. □ s'∼ à *vpr* expect.

attendrir /atãdʀiʀ/ [2] *vt* move (to pity). □ s'∼ *vpr* be moved to pity.

attendu[1] /atãdy/ *prép* given, considering; ∼ que considering that.

attendu[2], ∼e /atãdy/ *a* (escompté) expected; (espéré) long-awaited.

attentat /atãta/ *nm* assassination attempt; ∼ (à la bombe) (bomb) attack.

attente /atãt/ *nf* wait(ing); (espoir) expectations (∼ *pl*).

attenter /atãte/ [1] *vi* ∼ à make an attempt on; (fig) violate.

attentif, -ive /atãtif, -v/ *a* attentive; (scrupuleux) careful; ∼ à mindful of; (soucieux) careful of.

attention /atãsjõ/ *nf* attention; (soin) care; ∼ (à)! watch out (for)!; faire ∼ à (écouter) pay attention to; (prendre garde à) watch out for; (prendre soin de) take care of; faire ∼ à faire be careful to do.

attentionné, ∼e *a* considerate.

attentisme /atãtism/ *nm* wait-and-see policy.

atténuer /atenɥe/ [1] *vt* (*violence*) reduce; (*critique*) tone down; (*douleur*) ease; (*faute*) mitigate. □ s'∼ *vpr* subside.

atterrir /ateʀiʀ/ [2] *vi* land.

atterrissage *nm* landing.

attestation /atɛstasjõ/ *nf* certificate.

attester /atɛste/ [1] *vt* testify to; ∼ que testify that.

attirant, ∼e /atiʀã, -t/ *a* attractive.

attirer /atiʀe/ [1] *vt* draw, attract; (causer) bring. □ s'∼ *vpr* bring upon oneself; (*amis*) win.

attiser /atize/ [1] *vt* (*feu*) poke; (*sentiment*) stir up.

attitré, ∼e /atitʀe/ *a* accredited; (habituel) usual, regular.

attitude /atityd/ *nf* attitude; (maintien) bearing.

attraction /atʀaksjõ/ *nf* attraction.

attrait /atʀɛ/ *nm* attraction.

attraper /atʀape/ [1] *vt* catch; (*corde, main*) catch hold of; (*habitude, accent*) pick up; (*maladie*) catch; se faire ∼ 🄳 get told off.

attrayant, ∼e /atʀɛjã, -t/ *a* attractive.

attribuer /atʀibɥe/ [1] *vt* allocate; (*prix*) award; (imputer) attribute. □ s'∼ *vpr* claim (for oneself). **attribution** *nf* awarding, allocation.

attrouper (s') /(s)atʀupe/ [1] *vpr* gather.

au /o/ →à.

aubaine /obɛn/ *nf* godsend, opportunity.

aube /ob/ *nf* dawn, daybreak.

auberge /obɛʀʒ/ *nf* inn; ∼ de jeunesse youth hostel.

aubergine /obɛʀʒin/ *nf* aubergine; (US) eggplant.

aucun, ∼e /okœ̃, okyn/ *a* (dans une phrase négative) no, not any; (positif) any. ● *pron* (dans une phrase négative) none, not any; (positif) any; ∼ des deux neither of the two; d'∼s some. **aucunement** *adv* not at all, in no way.

audace /odas/ *nf* daring; (impudence) audacity.

audacieux, -ieuse /odasjø, -z/ *a* daring.

au-delà /od(ə)la/ *adv* beyond. ● *prép* ∼ de beyond.

au-dessous /od(ə)su/ *adv* below.

● *prép* ～ **de** below; (couvert par) under.

au-dessus /od(ə)sy/ *adv* above.
● *prép* ～ **de** above.

au-devant /od(ə)vã/ *prép* **aller** ～ **de qn** go to meet sb; **aller** ～ **des désirs de qn** anticipate sb's wishes.

audience /odjãs/ *nf* audience; (d'un tribunal) hearing; (succès, attention) success.

audimat® /odimat/ *nm* **l'**～ the TV ratings.

audiovisuel, ～**le** /odjɔvizɥεl/ *a* audio-visual.

auditeur, **-trice** /oditœʀ, -tʀis/ *nm,f* listener.

audition /odisjɔ̃/ *nf* hearing; (Théât, Mus) audition.

auditoire /oditwaʀ/ *nm* audience.

augmentation /ogmãtasjɔ̃/ *nf* increase; ～ **(de salaire)** (pay) rise; (US) raise.

augmenter /ogmãte/ [1] *vt/i* increase; (*employé*) give a pay rise *ou* raise to.

augure /ogyʀ/ *nm* (devin) oracle; **être de bon/mauvais** ～ be a good/ bad sign.

aujourd'hui /oʒuʀdɥi/ *adv* today.

auparavant /opaʀavã/ *adv* (avant) before; (précédemment) previously; (en premier lieu) beforehand.

auprès /opʀε/ *prép* ～ **de** (à côté de) beside, next to; (comparé à) compared with; **s'excuser/se plaindre** ～ **de** apologize/complain to.

auquel /okεl/ ⇒LEQUEL.

aura, **aurait** /oʀa, oʀε/ ⇒AVOIR [5].

aurore /oʀɔʀ/ *nf* dawn.

aussi /osi/ *adv* (également) too, also, as well; (dans une comparaison) as; (si, tellement) so; ～ **bien que** as well as. ● *conj* (donc) so, consequently.

aussitôt /osito/ *adv* immediately; ～ **que** as soon as, the moment; ～ **arrivé** as soon as he arrived.

austère /ostεʀ/ *a* austere.

Australie /ɔstʀali/ *nf* Australia.

australien, ～**ne** /ɔstʀaljε̃, -εn/ *a* Australian. **A**～, ～**ne** *nm,f* Australian.

autant /otã/ *adv* (travailler, manger) as much (**que** as); ～ **(de)** (quantité) as much (**que** as); (nombre) as many (**que** as); (tant) so much, so many; ～ **faire** one had better do; **d'**～ **plus que** all the more than; **en faire** ～ do the same; **pour** ～ for all that.

autel /otεl/ *nm* altar.

auteur /otœʀ/ *nm* author; **l'**～ **du crime** the perpetrator of the crime.

authentifier /otãtifje/ [45] *vt* authenticate.

authentique /otãtik/ *a* authentic.

auto /oto/ *nf* car; ～ **tamponneuse** dodgem, bumper car.

autobus /otɔbys/ *nm* bus.

autocar /otɔkaʀ/ *nm* coach.

autochtone /otɔktɔn/ *nmf* native.

autocollant, ～**e** /otɔkɔlã, -t/ *a* self-adhesive. ● *nm* sticker.

autodidacte /otɔdidakt/ *nmf* self-taught person.

auto-école (*pl* ～**s**) /otɔekɔl/ *nf* driving school.

automate /otɔmat/ *nm* automaton, robot.

automatique /otɔmatik/ *a* automatic.

automatisation /otɔmatizasjɔ̃/ *nf* automation.

automne /otɔn/ *nm* autumn; (US) fall.

automobile /otɔmɔbil/ *a* motor, car; (US) automobile. ● *nf* (motor) car; **l'**～ the motor industry; (Sport) motoring. **automobiliste** *nmf* motorist.

autonome /otɔnɔm/ *a* autonomous; (Ordinat) stand-alone.

autoradio /otɔʀadjo/ *nm* car radio.

autorisation /otɔʀizasjõ/ *nf* permission, authorization; (permis) permit.

autorisé, **~e** /otɔʀize/ *a* (opinions) authoritative; (approuvé) authorized.

autoriser /otɔʀize/ [1] *vt* authorize, permit; (rendre possible) allow (of); (donner un droit) **~ qn à faire** entitle sb to do.

autoritaire /otɔʀitɛʀ/ *a* authoritarian.

autorité /otɔʀite/ *nf* authority; **faire ~** be authoritative.

autoroute /otɔʀut/ *nf* motorway; (US) highway; **~ de l'information** (Ordinat) information superhighway.

auto-stop /otostɔp/ *nm* hitch-hiking; **faire de l'~** hitch hike; **prendre qn en ~** give a lift to sb.

autour /otuʀ/ *adv* around; **tout ~** all around. ● *prép* **~ de** around.

autre /otʀ/ *a* other; **un ~ jour/livre** another day/book; **~ chose/part** something/somewhere else; **quelqu'un/rien d'~** somebody/nothing else; **quoi d'~?** what else?; **d'~ part** on the other hand; (de plus) moreover, besides; **vous ~s Anglais** you English. ● *pron* **un ~, une ~** another (one); **l'~** the other (one); **les ~s** the others; (autrui) others; **d'~s** (some) others; **l'un l'~** each other; **l'un et l'~** both of them; **d'un jour à l'~** (bientôt) any day now; **entre ~s** among other things.

autrefois /otʀəfwa/ *adv* in the past; (précédemment) formerly.

autrement /otʀəmɑ̃/ *adv*

differently; (sinon) otherwise; (plus 𝕞) far more; **~ dit** in other words.

Autriche /otʀiʃ/ *nf* Austria.

autrichien, ~ne /otʀiʃjɛ̃, -jɛn/ *a* Austrian. **A~, ~ne** *nm, f* Austrian.

autruche /otʀyʃ/ *nf* ostrich.

autrui /otʀɥi/ *pron* others, other people.

aux /o/ ⇒À.

auxiliaire /oksiljɛʀ/ *a* auxiliary. ● *nmf* (assistant) auxiliary. ● *nm* (Gram) auxiliary.

auxquels, -quelles /okɛl/ ⇒LEQUEL.

aval: en ~ /ɑ̃naval/ *loc* downstream.

avaler /avale/ [1] *vt* swallow.

avance /avɑ̃s/ *nf* advance; (sur un concurrent) lead; **~ (de fonds)** advance; **à l'~** in advance; **d'~** already; **en ~** early; (montre) fast; **en ~ (sur)** (menant) ahead (of).

avancement /avɑ̃smɑ̃/ *nm* promotion.

avancé, ~e /avɑ̃se/ *a* advanced.

avancer /avɑ̃se/ [10] *vi* move forward, advance; (travail) make progress; (montre) be fast; (faire saillie) jut out. ● *vt* move forward; (dans le temps) bring forward; (argent) advance; (montre) put forward. □ **s'~** *vpr* move forward, advance; (se hasarder) commit oneself.

avant /avɑ̃/ *nm* front; (Sport) forward. ● *a inv* front. ● *prép* before; **~ de faire** before doing; **en ~ de** in front of; **~ peu** shortly; **~ tout** above all. ● *adv* (dans le temps) before, beforehand; (d'abord) first; **en ~** (dans l'espace) forward(s); (dans le temps) ahead; **le bus d'~** the previous bus. ● *conj* **~ que** before; **~ qu'il (ne) fasse** before he does.

avantage /avãtaʒ/ *nm*
advantage; (Comm) benefit.

avantager /avãtaʒe/ [40] *vt*
favour; (embellir) show off to
advantage.

avantageux, -euse /avãtaʒø, -z/
a advantageous, favourable;
(*prix*) attractive.

avant-bras /avãbRa/ *nm inv*
forearm.

avant-centre (*pl* **avants-
centres**) /avãsãtR/ *nm* centre
forward.

avant-coureur (*pl* ~s)
/avãkuRœR/ *a* precursory,
foreshadowing.

avant-dernier, -ière (*pl* ~s)
/avãdɛRnje, -jɛR/ *a & nm,f* last
but one.

avant-goût (*pl* ~s) /avãgu/ *nm*
foretaste.

avant-hier /avãtjɛR/ *adv* the day
before yesterday.

avant-poste (*pl* ~s) /avãpɔst/
nm outpost.

avant-première (*pl* ~s)
/avãpRəmjɛR/ *nf* preview.

avant-propos /avãpRɔpo/ *nm inv*
foreword.

avare /avaR/ *a* miserly; ~ **de**
sparing with. ● *nmf* miser.

avarié, ~e /avaRje/ *a* (*aliment*)
spoiled.

avatar /avataR/ *nm* misfortune.

avec /avɛk/ *prép* with. ● *adv* 🔟
with it *ou* them.

avènement /avɛnmã/ *nm*
advent; (d'un roi) accession.

avenir /avniR/ *nm* future; **à l'**~ in
future; **d'**~ with (future)
prospects.

aventure /avãtyR/ *nf* adventure;
(sentimentale) affair. **aventureux,
-euse** *a* adventurous; (hasardeux)
risky.

avérer (**s'**) /(s)aveRe/ [14] *vpr*
prove (to be).

averse /avɛRs/ *nf* shower.

avertir /avɛRtiR/ [2] *vt* inform;
(mettre en garde, menacer) warn.
avertissement *nm* warning.

avertisseur /avɛRtisœR/ *nm*
alarm; (Auto) horn; ~ **d'incendie**
fire-alarm; ~ **lumineux** warning
light.

aveu (*pl* ~**x**) /avø/ *nm*
confession; **de l'**~ **de** by the
admission of.

aveugle /avœgl/ *a* blind. ● *nmf*
blind man, blind woman.

aviateur, -trice /avjatœR, -tRis/
nm, f aviator.

aviation /avjasjõ/ *nf* flying;
(industrie) aviation; (Mil) air force.

avide /avid/ *a* greedy (de for);
(anxieux) eager (de for); ~ **de faire**
eager to do.

avion /avjõ/ *nm* plane, aeroplane,
aircraft; (US) airplane; ~ **à
réaction** jet.

aviron /aviRõ/ *nm* oar; **l'**~ (Sport)
rowing.

avis /avi/ *nm* opinion; (conseil)
advice; (renseignement) notification;
(Comm) advice; **à mon** ~ in my
opinion; **changer d'**~ change
one's mind; **être d'**~ **que** be of the
opinion that; ~ **au lecteur**
foreword.

avisé, ~e /avize/ *a* sensible; **être
bien/mal** ~ **de** be well-/ill-advised
to.

aviser /avize/ [1] *vt* advise,
notify. ● *vi* decide what to do.
□ **s'**~ **de** *vpr* suddenly realize;
s'~ **de faire** take it into one's
head to do.

avocat, ~e /avɔka, -t/ *nm, f*
barrister; (US) attorney; (fig)
advocate; ~ **de la défense** counsel
for the defence. ● *nm* (fruit)
avocado (pear).

avoine /avwan/ *nf* oats (+ *pl*).

avoir /avwaʀ/ [5]

● *verbe auxiliaire*

····➤ have; **il nous a appelés hier** he called us yesterday.

● *verbe transitif*

····➤ (possession) have (got).

····➤ (obtenir) get; (au téléphone) get through to.

····➤ (duper) ⚅ have; **on m'a eu!** I've been had!

····➤ ~ **chaud/faim** be hot/hungry.

····➤ ~ **dix ans** be ten years old.

● **avoir à** *verbe + préposition*

····➤ to have to; **j'ai beaucoup à faire** I have a lot to do; **tu n'as qu'à leur écrire** all you have to do is write to them.

● **en avoir pour** *verbe + préposition*

····➤ **j'en ai pour une minute** I will only be a minute; **j'en ai eu pour 100 euros** it cost me 100 euros.

● **il y a** *verbe impersonnel*

····➤ there is; there are; **qu'est-ce qu'il y a?** what's the matter?; **il est venu il y a cinq ans** he came here five years ago; **il y a au moins 5 km jusqu'à la gare** it's at least 5 km to the station.

● *nom masculin*

····➤ (dans un magasin) credit note.

····➤ (biens) asset (+ *pl*).

avortement /avɔʀtəmɑ̃/ *nm* (Méd) abortion.

avorter /avɔʀte/ [1] *vi* (*projet*) abort; (*se faire*) ~ have an abortion.

avoué, ~**e** /avwe/ *a* avowed. ● *nm* solicitor; (US) attorney.

avouer /avwe/ [1] *vt* (*amour, ignorance*) confess; (*crime*) confess to, admit. ● *vi* confess.

avril /avʀil/ *nm* April.

axe /aks/ *nm* axis; (essieu) axle; (d'une politique) main line(s), basis; ~ **(routier)** main road.

ayant /ɛjɑ̃/ ⇒AVOIR [5].

azote /azɔt/ *nm* nitrogen.

azur /azyʀ/ *nm* sky-blue.

baba /baba/ *nm* ~ **(au rhum)** (rum) baba; **en rester** ~ ⚅ be flabbergasted.

babillard /babijaʀ/ *nm* ~ **électronique** (Internet) bulletin board system, BBS.

babines /babin/ *nfpl* **se lécher les** ~ lick one's chops.

babiole /babjɔl/ *nf* trinket.

bâbord /bɑbɔʀ/ *nm* port (side).

baby-foot /babifut/ *nm inv* table football.

bac /bak/ *nm* (Scol) ⇒BACCALAURÉAT; (bateau) ferry; (récipient) tub; (plus petit) tray.

baccalauréat /bakalɔʀea/ *nm* school leaving certificate.

bâche /bɑʃ/ *nf* tarpaulin.

bachelier, -ière /baʃəlje, -jɛʀ/ *nm, f* holder of the *baccalauréat*.

bachoter /baʃɔte/ [1] *vi* cram (for an exam).

bâcler /bɑkle/ [1] *vt* botch (up).

bactérie /bakteʀi/ *nf* bacterium; ~**s** bacteria.

badaud, ~**e** /bado, -d/ *nm, f* onlooker.

badigeonner /badiʒɔne/ [1] *vt* whitewash; (barbouiller) daub.

badiner /badine/ [1] *vi* banter.

baffe /baf/ *nf* ⚅ slap.

baffle /bafl/ *nm* speaker.

bafouiller /bafuje/ [1] *vt/i* stammer.

bagage /bagaʒ/ *nm* bag; (connaissances) knowledge; ~s luggage; ~ à main hand luggage.

bagarre /bagaʀ/ *nf* fight.

bagatelle /bagatɛl/ *nf* trifle; (somme) trifling amount.

bagnard /baɲaʀ/ *nm* convict.

bagnole /baɲɔl/ *nf* 🗉 car.

bague /bag/ *nf* (bijou) ring.

baguette /bagɛt/ *nf* stick; (de chef d'orchestre) baton; (chinoise) chopstick; (pain) baguette; ~ magique magic wand; ~ de tambour drumstick.

baie /bɛ/ *nf* (Géog) bay; (fruit) berry; ~ (vitrée) picture window; (Ordinat) bay.

baignade /bɛɲad/ *nf* swimming.

baigner /beɲe/ [1] *vt* bathe; (enfant) bath. ●*vi* ~ dans l'huile swim in grease. □ se ~ *vpr* have a swim. **baigneur, -euse** *nm, f* swimmer.

baignoire /bɛɲwaʀ/ *nf* bath(tub).

bail (*pl* **baux**) /baj, bo/ *nm* lease.

bâiller /baje/ [1] *vi* yawn; (être ouvert) gape.

bailleur /bajœʀ/ *nm* ~ de fonds (Comm) sleeping partner.

bain /bɛ̃/ *nm* bath; (baignade) swim; prendre un ~ de soleil sunbathe; ~ de bouche mouthwash; être dans le ~ (fig) be in the swing of things; se remettre dans le ~ get back into the swing of things; prendre un ~ de foule mingle with the crowd.

bain-marie (*pl* **bains-marie**) /bɛ̃maʀi/ *nm* double boiler.

baiser /beze/ [1] *vt* (main) kiss; 🗷 screw 🗷. ●*nm* kiss.

baisse /bɛs/ *nf* fall, drop; être en ~ be going down.

baisser /bese/ [1] *vt* lower; (radio, lampe) turn down. ●*vi* (niveau) go down, fall; (santé,

forces) fail. □ se ~ *vpr* bend down.

bal (*pl* ~**s**) /bal/ *nm* dance; (habillé) ball; (lieu) dance-hall; ~ costumé fancy-dress ball.

balade /balad/ *nf* stroll; (en auto) drive.

balader /balade/ [1] *vt* take for a stroll. □ se ~ *vpr* (à pied) (go for a) stroll; (en voiture) go for a drive; (voyager) travel.

baladeur /baladœʀ/ *nm* personal stereo.

balafre /balafʀ/ *nf* gash; (cicatrice) scar.

balai /balɛ/ *nm* broom.

balance /balɑ̃s/ *nf* scales (+ *pl*); la B~ Libra.

balancer /balɑ̃se/ [10] *vt* swing; (doucement) sway; (lancer 🗉) chuck 🗉; (se débarrasser de 🗉) chuck out 🗉. ●*vi* sway. □ se ~ *vpr* swing; sway; s'en ~ 🗉 not to give a damn 🗉.

balancier /balɑ̃sje/ *nm* (d'horloge) pendulum; (d'équilibriste) pole.

balançoire /balɑ̃swaʀ/ *nf* swing.

balayage /balejaʒ/ *nm* sweeping; (cheveux) highlights.

balayer /baleje/ [31] *vt* sweep (up); (vent) sweep away; (se débarrasser de) sweep aside.

balbutiement /balbysimɑ̃/ *nm* stammering; les ~s (fig) the first steps.

balcon /balkɔ̃/ *nm* balcony; (Théât) dress circle.

baleine /balɛn/ *nf* whale.

balise /baliz/ *nf* beacon; (bouée) buoy; (Auto) (road) sign. **baliser** [1] *vt* mark out (with beacons); (route) signpost; (sentier) mark out.

balivernes /balivɛʀn/ *nfpl* nonsense.

ballant, ~e /balɑ̃, -t/ *a* dangling.

balle /bal/ *nf* (projectile) bullet; (Sport) ball; (paquet) bale.

ballerine /balʀin/ nf (danseuse) ballerina; (chaussure) ballet pump.

ballet /balɛ/ nm ballet.

ballon /balɔ̃/ nm (Sport) ball; ∼ (de baudruche) balloon; ∼ de football football.

ballonné, ∼e /balɔne/ a bloated.

balnéaire /balneɛʀ/ a seaside.

balourd, ∼e /baluʀ, -d/ nm, f oaf. ●a uncouth.

balustrade /balystʀad/ nf railing.

ban /bɑ̃/ nm round of applause; ∼s (de mariage) banns; **mettre au ∼ de** cast out from.

banal, ∼e (mpl ∼s) /banal/ a commonplace, banal.

banane /banan/ nf banana.

banc /bɑ̃/ nm bench; (de poissons) shoal; ∼ des accusés dock; ∼ d'essai (test) testing ground.

bancaire /bɑ̃kɛʀ/ a (secteur) banking; (chèque) bank.

bancal, ∼e (mpl ∼s) /bɑ̃kal/ a wobbly; (solution) shaky.

bande /bɑ̃d/ nf (groupe) gang; (de papier) strip; (rayure) stripe; (de film) reel; (pansement) bandage; ∼ dessinée comic strip; ∼ (magnétique) tape; ∼ sonore sound-track.

bande-annonce (pl bandes-annonces) /bɑ̃dnɔ̃s/ nf trailer.

bandeau (pl ∼x) /bɑ̃do/ nm headband; (sur les yeux) blindfold; ∼ publicitaire (Ordinat) banner.

bander /bɑ̃de/ [1] vt bandage; (arc) bend; (muscle) tense; ∼ les yeux à blindfold.

banderole /bɑ̃dʀɔl/ nf banner.

bandit /bɑ̃di/ nm bandit. **banditisme** nm crime.

bandoulière: **en ∼** /ɑ̃bɑ̃duljɛʀ/ loc across one's shoulder.

banlieue /bɑ̃ljø/ nf suburbs; **de ∼** suburban. **banlieusard, ∼e** nm, f (suburban) commuter.

bannir /baniʀ/ [2] vt banish.

banque /bɑ̃k/ nf bank; (activité) banking; ∼ de données databank.

banqueroute /bɑ̃kʀut/ nf bankruptcy.

banquet /bɑ̃kɛ/ nm banquet.

banquette /bɑ̃kɛt/ nf seat.

banquier, -ière /bɑ̃kje, -jɛʀ/ nm, f banker.

baptême /batɛm/ nm baptism, christening. **baptiser** [1] vt baptize, christen; (nommer) call.

bar /baʀ/ nm (lieu) bar.

baragouiner /baʀagwine/ [1] vt/i gabble; (langue) speak a few words of.

baraque /baʀak/ nf hut, shed; (maison []) house.

baratin /baʀatɛ̃/ nm [] sweet ou smooth talk.

barbare /baʀbaʀ/ a barbaric. ●nmf barbarian.

barbe /baʀb/ nf beard; ∼ à papa candy-floss; (US) cotton candy; **quelle ∼!** [] what a drag! [].

barbelé /baʀbəle/ a **fil ∼** barbed wire.

barber /baʀbe/ [1] vt [] bore.

barboter /baʀbɔte/ [1] vi (dans l'eau) paddle, splash. ●vt (voler []) pinch.

barbouiller /baʀbuje/ [1] vt (souiller) smear (de with); **tu es tout barbouillé** your face is all dirty; **être barbouillé** feel queasy.

barbu, ∼e /baʀby/ a bearded.

barème /baʀɛm/ nm list, table; (échelle) scale.

baril /baʀil/ nm barrel.

bariolé, ∼e /baʀjɔle/ a multicoloured.

baromètre /baʀɔmɛtʀ/ nm barometer.

baron, ∼ne /baʀɔ̃, -ɔn/ nm, f baron, baroness.

barque /baʀk/ nf (small) boat.

barrage /baʀaʒ/ nm dam; (sur route) roadblock.

barre /baʀ/ nf bar; (trait) line, stroke; (Naut) helm; ~ **de boutons** (Ordinat) toolbar.

barreau (pl ~x) /baʀo/ nm bar; (d'échelle) rung; **le** ~ (Jur) the bar.

barrer /baʀe/ [1] vt block; (porte) bar; (rayer) cross out; (Naut) steer. □ **se** ~ vpr ᵃ leave.

barrette /baʀɛt/ nf (hair) slide.

barrière /baʀjɛʀ/ nf (porte) gate; (clôture) fence; (obstacle) barrier.

bar-tabac (pl **bars-tabac**) /baʀtaba/ nm café (selling stamps and cigarettes).

bas, basse /ba, bas/ a (niveau, table) low; (action) base; **au** ~ **mot** at the lowest estimate; **en** ~ **âge** young; ~ **morceaux** (viande) cheap cuts. ● nm bottom; (chaussette) stocking; ~ **de laine** (fig) nest-egg. ● adv low; **en** ~ down below; (dans une maison) downstairs; **en** ~ **de la page** at the bottom of the page; **plus** ~ further down ou lower down; **mettre** ~ give birth (to). **bas de casse** nm inv lower case. **bas-côté** (pl ~s) nm (de route) verge; (US) shoulder.

bascule /baskyl/ nf (balance) scales (+ pl); **cheval/fauteuil à** ~ rocking-horse/-chair.

basculer /baskyle/ [1] vi topple over; (benne) tip up.

base /baz/ nf base; (fondement) basis; (Pol) rank and file; **de** ~ basic. **base de données** nf database.

baser /baze/ [1] vt base. □ **se** ~ **sur** vpr go by.

bas-fonds /bafɔ̃/ nmpl (eau) shallows; (fig) dregs.

basilic /bazilik/ nm basil.

basilique /bazilik/ nf basilica.

basque /bask/ a Basque. **B**~ nmf Basque.

basse /bas/ ⇒**BAS**.

basse-cour (pl **basses-cours**) /baskuʀ/ nf farmyard.

bassesse /bases/ nf baseness; (action) base act.

bassin /basɛ̃/ nm (pièce d'eau) pond; (de piscine) pool; (Géog) basin; (Anat) pelvis; (plat) bowl; ~ **houiller** coalfield.

bassine /basin/ nf bowl.

basson /basɔ̃/ nm bassoon.

bas-ventre (pl ~s) /bavɑ̃tʀ/ nm lower abdomen.

bat /ba/ ⇒**BATTRE** [11].

bataille /bataj/ nf battle; (fig) fight.

bâtard, ~e /batar, -d/ a (solution) hybrid. ● nm, f bastard.

bateau (pl ~x) /bato/ nm boat; ~ **pneumatique** rubber dinghy. **bateau-mouche** (pl **bateaux-mouches**) nm sightseeing boat.

bâti,~e /bati/ a **bien** ~ well-built.

bâtiment /batimɑ̃/ nm building; (industrie) building trade; (navire) vessel.

bâtir /batiʀ/ [2] vt build.

bâton /batɔ̃/ nm stick; **conversation à** ~**s rompus** rambling conversation; ~ **de rouge** lipstick.

battant /batɑ̃/ nm (vantail) flap; **porte à deux** ~**s** double door.

battement /batmɑ̃/ nm (de cœur) beat(ing); (temps) interval; (Mus) beat.

batterie /batʀi/ nf (Mil, Électr) battery; (Mus) drums; ~ **de cuisine** pots and pans.

batteur /batœʀ/ nm (Mus) drummer; (Culin) whisk.

battre /batʀ/ [11] vt/i beat; (cartes) shuffle; (Culin) whisk; (l'emporter sur) beat; ~ **des ailes** flap its wings; ~ **des mains** clap; ~ **des paupières** blink; ~ **en retraite** beat a retreat; ~ **la semelle** stamp one's feet; ~ **son plein** be in full swing. □ **se** ~ vpr fight.

baume /bom/ nm balm.

bavard, ∼e /bavaʀ, -d/ a talkative. ● nm, f chatterbox.

bavardage /bavaʀdaʒ/ nm chatter, gossip. **bavarder** [1] vi chat; (jacasser) chatter, gossip.

bave /bav/ nf dribble, slobber; (de limace) slime. **baver** [1] vi dribble, slobber. **baveux**, -euse a dribbling; (omelette) runny.

bavoir /bavwaʀ/ nm bib.

bavure /bavyʀ/ nf smudge; (erreur) blunder. ∼ policière police blunder.

bazar /bazaʀ/ nm bazaar; (objets 🔲) clutter.

BCBG abrév mf (**bon chic bon genre**) posh.

BD abrév f (**bande dessinée**) comic strip.

béant, ∼e /beɑ̃, -t/ a gaping.

béat, ∼e /bea, -t/ a (hum) blissful; ∼ d'admiration wide-eyed with admiration.

beau (**bel** before vowel or mute h), **belle** (mpl ∼x) /bo, bɛl/ a beautiful; (femme) beautiful; (homme) handsome; (temps) fine, nice. ● nm beauty. ● adv il fait ∼ the weather is nice; au ∼ milieu right in the middle; bel et bien well and truly; de plus belle more than ever; faire le ∼ sit up and beg; on a ∼ essayer/insister however much one tries/insists.

beaucoup /boku/ adv a lot, very much; ∼ de (nombre) many; (quantité) a lot of; pas ∼ (de) not many; (quantité) not much; ∼ plus/mieux much more/better; ∼ trop far too much; de ∼ by far.

beau-fils (pl **beaux-fils**) /bofis/ nm (remariage) stepson.

beau-frère (pl **beaux-frères**) /bofʀɛʀ/ nm brother-in-law.

beau-père (pl **beaux-pères**) /bopɛʀ/ nm father-in-law; (remariage) stepfather.

beauté /bote/ nf beauty; finir en ∼ end magnificently.

beaux-arts /bozaʀ/ nmpl fine arts.

beaux-parents /bopaʀɑ̃/ nmpl parents-in-law.

bébé /bebe/ nm baby. **bébé-éprouvette** (pl **bébés-éprouvette**) nm test-tube baby.

bec /bɛk/ nm beak; (de théière) spout; (de casserole) lip; (bouche 🔲) mouth; ∼ de gaz gas street-lamp.

bécane /bekan/ nf 🔲 bike.

bêche /bɛʃ/ nf spade.

bégayer /begeje/ [31] vt/i stammer.

bègue /bɛg/ nmf stammerer. ● a être ∼ stammer.

bégueule /begœl/ a prudish.

beige /bɛʒ/ a & nm beige.

beignet /bɛɲɛ/ nm fritter.

bel /bɛl/ ⇒BEAU.

bêler /bele/ [1] vi bleat.

belette /bəlɛt/ nf weasel.

belge /bɛlʒ/ a Belgian. **B**∼ nmf Belgian.

Belgique /bɛlʒik/ nf Belgium.

bélier /belje/ nm ram; le **B**∼ Aries.

belle /bɛl/ ⇒BEAU.

belle-fille (pl **belles-filles**) /bɛlfij/ nf daughter-in-law; (remariage) stepdaughter.

belle-mère (pl **belles-mères**) /bɛlmɛʀ/ nf mother-in-law; (remariage) stepmother.

belle-sœur (pl **belles-sœurs**) /bɛlsœʀ/ nf sister-in-law.

belliqueux, -euse /belikø, -z/ a warlike.

bémol /bemɔl/ nm (Mus) flat.

bénédiction /benediksjɔ̃/ nf blessing.

bénéfice /benefis/ nm (gain) profit; (avantage) benefit.

bénéficiaire /benefisjɛʀ/ nmf beneficiary.

bénéficier /benefisje/ [45] vi ~ de benefit from; (jouir de) enjoy, have.

bénéfique /benefik/ a beneficial.

Bénélux /benelyks/ nm Benelux.

bénévole /benevɔl/ a voluntary.

bénin, -igne /benɛ̃, -iɲ/ a minor; (tumeur) benign.

bénir /benir/ [2] vt bless. **bénit, ~e** a (eau) holy; (pain) consecrated.

benjamin, ~e /bɛ̃ʒamɛ̃, -in/ nm, f youngest child.

benne /bɛn/ nf (de grue) scoop; ~ à ordures (camion) waste disposal truck; (conteneur) skip; ~ (basculante) dump truck.

béquille /bekij/ nf crutch; (de moto) stand.

berceau (pl ~x) /bɛrso/ nm (de bébé, civilisation) cradle.

bercer /bɛrse/ [10] vt (balancer) rock; (apaiser) lull; (leurrer) delude.

béret /berɛ/ nm beret.

berge /bɛrʒ/ nf (bord) bank.

berger, -ère /bɛrʒe, -ɛr/ nm, f shepherd, shepherdess.

berne: en ~ /ɑ̃bɛrn/ loc at half-mast.

berner /bɛrne/ [1] vt fool.

besogne /bəzɔɲ/ nf task, job.

besoin /bəzwɛ̃/ nm need; avoir ~ de need; au ~ if need be; dans le ~ in need.

bestiole /bɛstjɔl/ nf ▣ bug.

bétail /betaj/ nm livestock.

bête /bɛt/ a stupid. ● nf animal; ~ noire pet hate; ~ sauvage wild beast; chercher la petite ~ be overfussy.

bêtise /betiz/ nf stupidity; (action) stupid thing.

béton /betɔ̃/ nm concrete; ~ armé reinforced concrete; en ~ (mur) concrete; (argument ▣) watertight. **bétonnière** nf concrete mixer.

betterave /bɛtrav/ nf beet; ~ rouge beetroot.

beugler /bøgle/ [1] vi bellow; (radio) blare out.

beur /bœr/ nmf & a ▣ second-generation North African living in France.

beurre /bœr/ nm butter. **beurré, ~e** a buttered; ▣ drunk. **beurrier** nm butter-dish.

bévue /bevy/ nf blunder.

biais /bjɛ/ nm (moyen) way; par le ~ de by means of; de ~, en ~ at an angle.

bibelot /biblo/ nm ornament.

biberon /bibrɔ̃/ nm (feeding) bottle; nourrir au ~ bottle-feed.

bible /bibl/ nf bible; la B~ the Bible.

bibliographie /biblijɔgrafi/ nf bibliography.

bibliothécaire /biblijɔtekɛr/ nmf librarian.

bibliothèque /biblijɔtɛk/ nf library; (meuble) bookcase.

bic® /bik/ nm biro®.

bicarbonate /bikarbɔnat/ nm ~ (de soude) bicarbonate (of soda).

biceps /bisɛps/ nm biceps.

biche /biʃ/ nf doe; ma ~ darling.

bichonner /biʃɔne/ [1] vt pamper.

bicyclette /bisiklɛt/ nf bicycle.

bide /bid/ nm (ventre ▣) paunch; (échec ▣) flop.

bidet /bidɛ/ nm bidet.

bidon /bidɔ̃/ nm can; (plus grand) drum; (ventre ▣) belly; c'est du ~ ▣ it's a load of hogwash ▣. ● a inv ▣ phoney.

bidonville /bidɔ̃vil/ nf shanty town.

bidule /bidyl/ nm ▣ thing.

Biélorussie /bjelɔrysi/ nf Byelorussia.

bien /bjɛ̃/ adv well; (très) quite, very; ~ des (nombre) many; tu as

~ **de la chance** you are very
lucky; **j'aimerais** ~ I would like to;
ce n'est pas ~ **de** it is not nice to;
~ **sûr** of course. ● *nm* good;
(patrimoine) possession; ~**s de
consommation** consumer goods. ●
a inv good; (passable) all right; (en
forme) well; (à l'aise) comfortable;
(beau) attractive; (respectable) nice,
respectable. ● *conj* ~ **que** (al-)
though; ~ **que ce soit** although it
is. **bien-aimé,** ~**e** *a & nm,f*
beloved. **bien-être** *nm* well-
being.

bienfaisance /bjɛ̃fəzɑ̃s/ *nf*
charity; **fête de** ~ charity event.
bienfaisant, ~**e** *a* beneficial.

bienfait /bjɛ̃fɛ/ *nm* (kind) favour;
(avantage) beneficial effect.
bienfaiteur, -trice *nm, f*
benefactor.

bien-pensant, ~**e** /bjɛ̃pɑ̃sɑ̃, -t/ *a*
right-thinking.

bienséance /bjɛ̃seɑ̃s/ *nf*
propriety.

bientôt /bjɛ̃to/ *adv* soon; **à** ~ see
you soon.

bienveillance /bjɛ̃vɛjɑ̃s/ *nf*
kind-(li)ness.

bienvenu, ~**e** /bjɛ̃vny/ *a*
welcome. ● *nm, f* **être le** ~, **être la**
~ **e be welcome.**

bienvenue /bjɛ̃vny/ *nf* welcome;
souhaiter la ~ **à** welcome.

bière /bjɛʀ/ *nf* beer; (cercueil)
coffin; ~ **blonde** lager; ~ **brune** ≈
stout; ~ **pression** draught beer.

bifteck /biftɛk/ *nm* steak.

bifurquer /bifyʀke/ [1] *vi* branch
off, fork.

bigarré, ~**e** /bigaʀe/ *a* motley.

bigoudi /bigudi/ *nm* curler.

bijou (*pl* ~**x**) /biʒu/ *nm* jewel; ~**x
en** or gold jewellery. **bijouterie** *nf*
(boutique) jewellery shop; (Comm)
jewellery. **bijoutier, -ière** *nm, f*
jeweller.

bilan /bilɑ̃/ *nm* outcome; (d'une
catastrophe) (casualty) toll; (Comm)
balance sheet; **faire le** ~ **de**
assess; ~ **de santé** check-up.

bile /bil/ *nf* bile; **se faire de la** ~ 🄸
worry.

bilingue /bilɛ̃g/ *a* bilingual.

billard /bijaʀ/ *nm* billiards (+ *pl*);
(table) billiard-table.

bille /bij/ *nf* (d'enfant) marble; (de
billard) billiard-ball.

billet /bijɛ/ *nm* ticket; (lettre) note;
(article) column; ~ **(de banque)**
(bank) note; ~ **de 50 euros**
50-euro note.

billetterie /bijɛtʀi/ *nf* cash
dispenser.

billion /biljɔ̃/ *nm* billion; (US)
trillion.

bimensuel, ~**e** /bimɑ̃sɥɛl/ *a*
fortnightly, bimonthly.

binette /binɛt/ *nf* hoe; (visage)
face; (Internet) smiley.

biochimie /bjoʃimi/ *nf*
biochemistry.

biodégradable /bjodegʀadabl/ *a*
biodegradable.

biographie /bjɔgʀafi/ *nf*
biography.

biologie /bjɔlɔʒi/ *nf* biology.
biologique *a* biological; (produit)
organic.

bioterrorisme /bjoteʀɔʀism/ *nm*
bioterrorism.

bis /bis/ *nm & interj* encore.

biscornu, ~**e** /biskɔʀny/ *a*
crooked; (bizarre) cranky 🄸.

biscotte /biskɔt/ *nf* continental
toast.

biscuit /biskɥi/ *nm* biscuit; (US)
cookie; ~ **salé** cracker; ~ **de
Savoie** sponge-cake.

bise /biz/ *nf* 🄸 kiss; (vent) north
wind.

bison /bizɔ̃/ *nm* buffalo.

bisou /bizu/ *nm* 🄸 kiss.

bistro(t) /bistʀo/ *nm* 🄸 café, bar.

bit /bit/ *nm* (Ordinat) bit.

bitume /bitym/ *nm* asphalt.

bizarre /bizaʀ/ a odd, strange.
bizarrerie nf peculiarity.

blafard, ~e /blafaʀ, -d/ a pale.

blague /blag/ nf ▯ joke; **sans ~!** no kidding! ▯.

blaguer /blage/ [1] ▯ vi joke.

blaireau (pl ~x) /blɛʀo/ nm shaving-brush; (animal) badger.

blâmer /blame/ [1] vt criticize.

blanc, **blanche** /blɑ̃, blɑ̃ʃ/ a white; (papier, page) blank. ● nm white; (espace) blank; **~ d'œuf** egg white; **~ de poireau** white part of the leek; **~ de poulet** chicken breast; **le ~** (linge) whites; **laisser en ~** leave blank. **B~, Blanche** nm, f white man, white woman.
blanche nf (Mus) minim.

blanchiment /blɑ̃ʃimɑ̃/ nm (d'argent) laundering.

blanchir /blɑ̃ʃiʀ/ [2] vt whiten; (personne: fig) clear; (argent) launder; (Culin) blanch; **~ (à la chaux)** whitewash. ● vi turn white.

blanchisserie /blɑ̃ʃisʀi/ nf laundry.

blason /blazɔ̃/ nm coat of arms.

blasphème /blasfɛm/ nm blasphemy.

blé /ble/ nm wheat.

blême /blɛm/ a pallid.

blessant, ~e /blesɑ̃, -t/ a hurtful.

blessé, ~e /blese/ nm, f casualty, injured person.

blesser /blese/ [1] vt injure, hurt; (par balle) wound; (offenser) hurt. □ **se ~** vpr injure ou hurt oneself. **blessure** nf wound.

bleu, ~e /blø/ a blue; (Culin) very rare; **~ marine/turquoise** navy blue/turquoise; **avoir une peur ~e** be scared stiff. ● nm blue; (contusion) bruise; **~ (de travail)** overalls (+ pl).

bleuet /blø/ nm cornflower.

blindé, ~e /blɛ̃de/ a armoured; (fig) immune (**contre** to); **porte ~e** security car. ● nm armoured car, tank.

blinder /blɛ̃de/ [1] vt armour; (fig) harden.

bloc /blɔk/ nm block; (de papier) pad; **serrer à ~** tighten hard; **en ~** (matériau) in a block; (nier) outright.

blocage /blɔkaʒ/ nm (des prix) freeze, freezing; (des roues) locking; (Psych) block.

bloc-notes (pl **blocs-notes**) /blɔknɔt/ nm note-pad.

blocus /blɔkys/ nm blockade.

blond, ~e /blɔ̃, -d/ a fair, blond. ● nm, f fair-haired man, fair-haired woman.

bloquer /blɔke/ [1] vt block; (porte, machine) jam; (roues) lock; (prix, crédits) freeze. □ **se ~** vpr jam; (roues) lock; (freins) jam; (ordinateur) crash; **bloqué par la neige** snowbound.

blottir (se) /(sə)blɔtiʀ/ [2] vpr snuggle, huddle (**contre** against).

blouse /bluz/ nf overall. **blouse blanche** nf white coat.

blouson /bluzɔ̃/ nm jacket, blouson.

bluffer /blœfe/ [1] vt/i bluff.

bobine /bɔbin/ nf (de fil, film) reel; (Électr) coil.

bobo /bobo/ nm ▯ sore, cut; **avoir ~** have a pain.

bocal (pl **-aux**) /bɔkal, -o/ nm jar.

bœuf (pl ~s) /bœf, bø/ nm bullock; (US) steer; (viande) beef; **~s** oxen.

bogue /bɔg/ nm (Ordinat) bug.

bohème /bɔɛm/ a & nmf bohemian.

boire /bwaʀ/ [12] vt/i (personne, plante) drink; (argile) soak up; **~ un coup** ▯ have a drink.

bois /bwa/ ⇒BOIRE [12]. ● nm

(matériau, forêt) wood; **de ~, en ~** wooden. ● *nmpl* (de cerf) antlers.

boiseries /bwazʀi/ *nfpl* panelling.

boisson /bwasõ/ *nf* drink.

boit /bwa/ ⇒BOIRE [12].

boîte /bwat/ *nf* box; (de conserves) tin, can; (entreprise Ⅱ) firm; **en ~** tinned, canned; **~ à gants** glove compartment; **~ aux lettres** letter-box; **~ aux lettres électronique** mailbox; **~ de nuit** night-club; **~ postale** post-office box; **~ de vitesses** gear box.

boiter /bwate/ [1] *vi* limp.

boiteux, -euse *a* lame; (*raisonnement*) shaky.

boîtier /bwatje/ *nm* case.

bol /bɔl/ *nm* bowl; **~ d'air** a breath of fresh air; **avoir du ~** Ⅱ be lucky.

bolide /bɔlid/ *nm* racing car.

Bolivie /bɔlivi/ *nf* Bolivia.

bombardement /bõbaʀdəmã/ *nm* bombing; shelling.

bombarder /bõbaʀde/ [1] *vt* bomb; (par obus) shell; **~ qn de** (fig) bombard sb with. **bombardier** *nm* (Aviat) bomber.

bombe /bõb/ *nf* bomb; (atomiseur) spray, aerosol.

bombé, ~e /bõbe/ *a* rounded; (*route*) cambered.

bon, bonne /bõ, bon/ *a* good; (qui convient) right; **~ à/pour** (approprié) fit to/for; **bonne année** happy New Year; **~ anniversaire** happy birthday; **~ appétit/voyage** enjoy your meal/trip; **bonne chance/nuit** good luck/night; **~ sens** common sense; **bonne femme** (péj) woman; **de bonne heure** early; **à quoi ~?** what's the point? ● *adv* sentir **~** smell nice; **tenir ~** stand firm; **il fait ~** the weather is mild. ● *interj* right, well. ● *nm* (billet) voucher, coupon; **~ de commande**

order form; **pour de ~** for good. **bonne** *nf* (domestique) maid.

bonbon /bõbõ/ *nm* sweet; (US) candy.

bonbonne /bõbon/ *nf* demijohn; (de gaz) cylinder.

bond /bõ/ *nm* leap; **faire un ~** (de surprise) jump.

bonde /bõd/ *nf* plug; (trou) plughole.

bondé, ~e /bõde/ *a* packed.

bondir /bõdiʀ/ [2] *vi* leap; (de surprise) jump.

bonheur /bɔnœʀ/ *nm* happiness; (chance) (good) luck; **au petit ~** haphazardly; **par ~** luckily.

bonhomme (*pl* **bonshommes**) /bonom, bõzom/ *nm* fellow; **~ de neige** snowman. ● *a inv* good-hearted.

bonifier (se) /(sə)bonifje/ [45] *vpr* improve.

bonjour /bõʒuʀ/ *nm* & *interj* hallo, hello, good morning *ou* afternoon.

bon marché /bõmaʀʃe/ *a inv* cheap. ● *adv* cheap(ly).

bonne /bon/ ⇒BON.

bonne-maman (*pl* **bonnes-mamans**) /bonmamã/ *nf* Ⅱ granny.

bonnement /bonmã/ *adv* **tout ~** quite simply.

bonnet /bonɛ/ *nm* hat; (de soutien-gorge) cup; **~ de bain** swimming cap. **bonneterie** *nf* hosiery.

bonsoir /bõswaʀ/ *nm* good evening; (en se couchant) good night.

bonté /bõte/ *nf* kindness.

bonus /bonys/ *nm* (Auto) no-claims bonus.

boots /buts/ *nmpl* ankle boots.

bord /bɔʀ/ *nm* edge; (rive) bank; **à ~ (de)** on board; **au ~ de la mer** at the seaside; **au ~ des larmes** on the verge of tears; **~ de la route** roadside.

B

bordeaux /bɔʀdo/ a inv maroon.
●nm inv Bordeaux.

bordel /bɔʀdɛl/ nm brothel;
(désordre 🆃) shambles.

border /bɔʀde/ [1] vt line, border;
(tissu) edge; (personne, lit) tuck
in.

bordereau (pl ~x) /bɔʀdəʀo/ nm
(document) slip.

bordure /bɔʀdyʀ/ nf border; **en ~
de** on the edge of.

borgne /bɔʀɲ/ a one-eyed.

borne /bɔʀn/ nf boundary
marker; (pour barrer le passage)
bollard; **~ (kilométrique)** ≈
milestone; **~s** limits.

borné, **~e** /bɔʀne/ a (esprit)
narrow; (personne) narrow-
minded.

borner (se) /(sə)bɔʀne/ [1] vpr
confine oneself (**à** to).

bosniaque /bɔsnjak/ a Bosnian.
B~ nmf Bosnian.

Bosnie /bɔsni/ nf Bosnia.

bosse /bɔs/ nf bump; (de chameau)
hump; **avoir la ~ de** 🆃 have a gift
for; **avoir roulé sa ~** have been
around. **bosselé**, **~e** a dented;
(terrain) bumpy.

bosser /bɔse/ [1] vi 🆃 work
(hard).

bossu, **~e** /bɔsy/ a
hunchbacked. ●nm, f hunchback.

botanique /bɔtanik/ nf botany.
●a botanical.

botte /bɔt/ nf boot; (de fleurs,
légumes) bunch; (de paille) bundle,
bale; **~s de caoutchouc**
wellingtons.

botter /bɔte/ [1] vt 🆃 **ça me botte**
I like the idea.

bottin® /bɔtɛ̃/ nm phone book.

bouc /buk/ nm (billy-)goat; (barbe)
goatee; **~ émissaire** scapegoat.

boucan /bukã/ nm 🆃 din.

bouche /buʃ/ nf mouth; (lèvres)
lips; **~ bée** open-mouthed; **~
d'égout** manhole; **~ d'incendie**

(fire) hydrant; **~ de métro**
entrance to the underground ou
subway (US). **bouche-à-bouche**
nm inv mouth-to-mouth
resuscitation. **bouche-à-oreille**
nm inv word of mouth.

bouché, **~e** /buʃe/ a (profession,
avenir) oversubscribed; (stupide:
péj) stupid.

bouchée /buʃe/ nf mouthful.

boucher¹ /buʃe/ [1] vt block;
(bouteille) cork. □ **se ~** vpr get
blocked; **se ~ le nez** hold one's
nose.

boucher², **-ère** /buʃe, -ɛʀ/ nm, f
butcher. **boucherie** nf butcher's
(shop); (carnage) butchery.

bouchon /buʃɔ̃/ nm stopper; (en
liège) cork; (de stylo, tube) cap; (de
pêcheur) float; (embouteillage) traffic
jam; **~ de cérumen** plug of
earwax.

boucle /bukl/ nf (de ceinture)
buckle; (de cheveux) curl; (forme)
loop; **~ d'oreille** earring. **bouclé**,
~e a (cheveux) curly.

boucler /bukle/ [1] vt fasten;
(enfermer 🆃) shut up; (encercler) seal
off; (budget) balance; (terminer)
finish off. ●vi curl.

bouclier /buklije/ nm shield.

bouddhiste /budist/ a & nmf
Buddhist.

bouder /bude/ [1] vi sulk. ●vt
stay away from.

boudin /budɛ̃/ nm black pudding.

boue /bu/ nf mud.

bouée /bwe/ nf buoy; **~ de sauvetage** lifebuoy.

boueux, **-euse** /buø, -z/ a muddy.

bouffe /buf/ nf 🆃 food, grub.

bouffée /bufe/ nf puff, whiff;
(d'orgueil) fit; **~ de chaleur** (Méd) hot
flush.

bouffi, **~e** /bufi/ a bloated.

bouffon, **~ne** /bufɔ̃, -ɔn/ a
farcical. ●nm buffoon.

bougeoir /buʒwaʀ/ *nm* candlestick.

bougeotte /buʒɔt/ *nf* **avoir la ~** 🔲 have the fidgets.

bouger /buʒe/ [40] *vt/i* move. □ **se ~** *vpr* 🔲 move.

bougie /buʒi/ *nf* candle; (Auto) spark(ing)-plug.

bouillant, ~e /bujɑ̃, -t/ *a* boiling; (très chaud) boiling hot.

bouillie /buji/ *nf* (pour bébé) baby cereal; (péj) mush; **en ~** crushed, mushy.

bouillir /bujiʀ/ [13] *vi* boil; (fig) seethe; **faire ~** boil.

bouilloire /bujwaʀ/ *nf* kettle.

bouillon /bujɔ̃/ *nm* (de cuisson) stock; (potage) broth.

bouillonner /bujɔne/ [1] *vi* bubble.

bouillotte /bujɔt/ *nf* hot-water bottle.

boulanger, -ère /bulɑ̃ʒe, -ɛʀ/ *nm, f* baker. **boulangerie** *nf* bakery. **boulangerie-pâtisserie** *nf* bakery (selling cakes and pastries).

boule /bul/ *nf* ball; **~s** (jeu) boules; **jouer aux ~s** play boules; **une ~ dans la gorge** a lump in one's throat; **~ de neige** snowball.

bouleau (*pl* **~x**) /bulo/ *nm* (silver) birch.

boulet /bulɛ/ *nm* (de forçat) ball and chain; **~ (de canon)** cannonball; **~ de charbon** coal nut.

boulette /bulɛt/ *nf* (de pain, papier) pellet; (bévue) blunder; **~ de viande** meat ball.

boulevard /bulvaʀ/ *nm* boulevard.

bouleversant, ~e /bulvɛʀsɑ̃, -t/ *a* deeply moving. **bouleversement** *nm* upheaval. **bouleverser** [1] *vt* turn upside down; (pays, plans) disrupt; (émouvoir) upset.

boulimie /bulimi/ *nf* bulimia.

boulon /bulɔ̃/ *nm* bolt.

boulot, ~te /bulo, -ɔt/ *a* (rond 🔲) dumpy. ●*nm* (travail 🔲) work.

boum /bum/ *nm & interj* bang. ●*nf* (fête 🔲) party.

bouquet /bukɛ/ *nm* (de fleurs) bunch, bouquet; (d'arbres) clump; **c'est le ~!** 🔲 that's the last straw!

bouquin /bukɛ̃/ *nm* 🔲 book. **bouquiner** [1] *vt/i* 🔲 read. **bouquiniste** *nmf* second-hand bookseller.

bourbier /buʀbje/ *nm* mire; (fig) tangle.

bourde /buʀd/ *nf* blunder.

bourdon /buʀdɔ̃/ *nm* bumble-bee. **bourdonnement** *nm* buzzing.

bourg /buʀ/ *nm* (market) town (centre), village centre.

bourgeois, ~e /buʀʒwa, -z/ *a & nm,f* middle-class (person); (péj) bourgeois. **bourgeoisie** *nf* middle class(es).

bourgeon /buʀʒɔ̃/ *nm* bud.

bourgogne /buʀgɔɲ/ *nm* Burgundy.

bourlinguer /buʀlɛ̃ge/ [1] *vi* 🔲 travel about.

bourrage /buʀaʒ/ *nm* **~ de crâne** brainwashing.

bourratif, -ive /buʀatif, -v/ *a* stodgy.

bourreau (*pl* **~x**) /buʀo/ *nm* executioner; **~ de travail** (fig) workaholic.

bourrelet /buʀlɛ/ *nm* weather-strip, draught excluder; (de chair) roll of fat.

bourrer /buʀe/ [1] *vt* cram (de with); (pipe) fill; **~ de** (nourriture) stuff with; **~ de coups** thrash; **~ le crâne à qn** brainwash sb.

bourrique /buʀik/ *nf* donkey; 🔲 pig-headed person.

bourru, ~e /buʀy/ *a* gruff.

bourse /buʀs/ *nf* purse;

(subvention) grant; **la B~** the Stock Exchange.

boursier, -ière /buʀsje, -jɛʀ/ a (valeurs) Stock Exchange. ●nm, f grant holder.

boursoufler /buʀsufle/ [1] vt (visage) cause to swell; (peinture) blister.

bousculade /buskylad/ nf crush; (précipitation) rush. **bousculer** [1] vt (pousser) jostle; (presser) rush; (renverser) knock over.

bousiller /buzije/ [1] vt ▣ wreck.

boussole /busɔl/ nf compass.

bout /bu/ nm end; (de langue, bâton) piece; (morceau) bit; **à ~** exhausted; **à ~ de souffle** out of breath; **à ~ portant** point-blank; **au ~ de** (après) after; **venir à ~ de** (finir) manage to finish; **d'un ~ à l'autre** throughout; **au ~ du compte** in the end; **~ filtre** filter-tip.

bouteille /butɛj/ nf bottle; **~ d'oxygène** oxygen cylinder.

boutique /butik/ nf shop; (de mode) boutique.

bouton /butɔ̃/ nm button; (sur la peau) spot, pimple; (pousse) bud; (de porte, radio) knob; **~ de manchette** cuff-link. **boutonner** [1] vt button (up). **boutonnière** nf buttonhole. **bouton-pression** (pl **boutons-pression**) nm press-stud; (US) snap.

bouture /butyʀ/ nf cutting.

bovin, ~e /bɔvɛ̃, -in/ a bovine. **bovins** nmpl cattle (pl).

box (pl ~ ou **boxes**) /bɔks/ nm lock-up garage; (de dortoir) cubicle; (d'écurie) (loose) box; (Jur) dock.

boxe /bɔks/ nf boxing.

boyau (pl ~x) /bwajo/ nm gut; (corde) catgut; (galerie) gallery; (de bicyclette) tyre; (US) tire.

boycotter /bɔjkɔte/ [1] vt boycott.

BP abrév f (**boîte postale**) PO Box.

bracelet /bʀaslɛ/ nm bracelet; (de montre) watchstrap.

braconnier /bʀakɔnje/ nm poacher.

brader /bʀade/ [1] vt sell off. **braderie** nf clearance sale.

braguette /bʀagɛt/ nf fly.

braille /bʀaj/ nm & a Braille.

brailler /bʀaje/ [1] vt/i bawl.

braise /bʀɛz/ nf embers (+ pl).

braiser /bʀeze/ [1] vt (Culin) braise.

brancard /bʀɑ̃kaʀ/ nm stretcher; (de charrette) shaft.

branche /bʀɑ̃ʃ/ nf branch.

branché, ~e /bʀɑ̃ʃe/ a ▣ trendy.

branchement /bʀɑ̃ʃmɑ̃/ nm connection. **brancher** [1] vt (prise) plug in; (à un réseau) connect.

brandir /bʀɑ̃diʀ/ [2] vt brandish.

branler /bʀɑ̃le/ [1] vi be shaky.

braquer /bʀake/ [1] vt (arme) aim; (regard) fix; (roue) turn; (banque: ▣) hold up; **~ qn contre** turn sb against. ●vi (Auto) turn (the wheel). ▢ **se ~** vpr dig one's heels in.

bras /bʀa/ nm arm; (de rivière) branch; (Tech) arm; **~ dessus ~ dessous** arm in arm; **~ droit** (fig) right hand man; **~ de mer** sound; **en ~ de chemise** in one's shirtsleeves. ●nmpl (fig) labour, hands.

brasier /bʀazje/ nm blaze.

brassard /bʀasaʀ/ nm armband.

brasse /bʀas/ nf breast-stroke; **~ papillon** butterfly (stroke).

brasser /bʀase/ [1] vt mix; (bière) brew; (affaires) handle a lot of. **brasserie** nf brewery; (café) brasserie.

brave /bʀav/ a (bon) good; (valeureux) brave. **braver** [1] vt defy.

B

bravo /bʀavo/ *interj* bravo. ● *nm* cheer.

bravoure /bʀavuʀ/ *nf* bravery.

break /bʀɛk/ *nm* estate car; (US) station-wagon.

brebis /bʀəbi/ *nf* ewe.

brèche /bʀɛʃ/ *nf* gap, breach; **être sur la ~** be on the go.

bredouille /bʀəduj/ *a* empty-handed.

bredouiller /bʀəduje/ [1] *vt/i* mumble.

bref, brève /bʀɛf, -v/ *a* short, brief. ● *adv* in short; **en ~** in short.

Brésil /bʀezil/ *nm* Brazil.

Bretagne /bʀətaɲ/ *nf* Brittany.

bretelle /bʀətɛl/ *nf* (de sac, maillot) strap; (d'autoroute) access road; **~s** (pour pantalon) braces; (US) suspenders.

breton, ~ne /bʀətɔ̃, -ɔn/ *a & nm* (Ling) Breton. **B~, ~ne** *nm, f* Breton.

breuvage /bʀœvaʒ/ *nm* beverage.

brève /bʀɛv/ ⇒BREF.

brevet /bʀəvɛ/ *nm* (d'invention) patent; (diplôme) diploma.

breveté, ~e /bʀəvte/ *a* patented.

bribes /bʀib/ *nfpl* scraps.

bricolage /bʀikɔlaʒ/ *nm* do-it-yourself (jobs).

bricole /bʀikɔl/ *nf* trifle.

bricoler /bʀikɔle/ [1] *vi* do DIY; (US) fix things, tinker with.

bricoleur, -euse /bʀikɔlœʀ, -øz/ *nm, f* handyman, handywoman.

bride /bʀid/ *nf* bridle.

bridé, ~e /bʀide/ *a* **yeux ~s** slanting eyes.

brider /bʀide/ [1] *vt* (cheval) bridle; (fig) keep in check.

brièvement /bʀijɛvmɑ̃/ *adv* briefly.

brigade /bʀigad/ *nf* (de police) squad; (Mil) brigade; (fig) team.

brigadier *nm* (de gendarmerie) sergeant.

brigand /bʀigɑ̃/ *nm* robber.

brillant, ~e /bʀijɑ̃, -t/ *a* (couleur) bright; (luisant) shiny; (remarquable) brilliant. ● *nm* (éclat) shine; (diamant) diamond.

briller /bʀije/ [1] *vi* shine.

brimade /bʀimad/ *nf* vexation.

brimer [1] *vt* bully, harass; **se sentir brimé** feel put down.

brin /bʀɛ̃/ *nm* (de muguet) sprig; (d'herbe) blade; (de paille) wisp; **un ~ de** (un peu) a bit of.

brindille /bʀɛ̃dij/ *nf* twig.

brioche /bʀijɔʃ/ *nf* brioche, sweet bun; (ventre 🔟) paunch.

brique /bʀik/ *nf* brick.

briquet /bʀikɛ/ *nm* (cigarette-) lighter.

brise /bʀiz/ *nf* breeze.

briser /bʀize/ [1] *vt* break. □ **se ~** *vpr* break.

britannique /bʀitanik/ *a* British. **B~** *nmf* Briton; **les B~s** the British

brocante /bʀɔkɑ̃t/ *nf* bric à brac trade; (marché) flea market.

broche /bʀɔʃ/ *nf* brooch; (Culin) spit; **à la ~** spit-roasted.

broché, ~e /bʀɔʃe/ *a* paperback.

brochet /bʀɔʃɛ/ *nm* pike.

brochette /bʀɔʃɛt/ *nf* skewer.

brochure /bʀɔʃyʀ/ *nf* brochure, booklet.

broder /bʀɔde/ [1] *vt/i* embroider.

broderie *nf* embroidery.

broncher /bʀɔ̃ʃe/ [1] *vi* **sans ~** without turning a hair.

bronchite /bʀɔ̃ʃit/ *nf* bronchitis.

bronze /bʀɔ̃z/ *nm* bronze.

bronzé, ~e /bʀɔ̃ze/ *a* (sun-)tanned.

bronzer /bʀɔ̃ze/ [1] *vi* (personne) get a (sun-)tan.

brosse /bʀɔs/ *nf* brush; **~ à dents** toothbrush; **~ à habits** clothes brush; **en ~** (*coiffure*) in a crew cut.

brosser /bʀɔse/ [1] *vt* brush; (fig) paint. □ **se ~** *vpr* **se ~ les dents/ les cheveux** brush one's teeth/ hair.

brouette /bʀuɛt/ *nf* wheelbarrow.

brouhaha /bʀuaa/ *nm* hubbub.

brouillard /bʀujaʀ/ *nm* fog.

brouille /bʀuj/ *nf* quarrel.

brouiller /bʀuje/ [1] *vt* (*vue*) blur; (*œufs*) scramble; (*amis*) set at odds; **~ les pistes** cloud the issue. □ **se ~** *vpr* (*ciel*) cloud over; (*amis*) fall out.

brouillon, ~ne /bʀujɔ̃, -ɔn/ *a* untidy. ● *nm* (rough) draft.

brousse /bʀus/ *nf* **la ~** the bush.

brouter /bʀute/ [1] *vt/i* graze.

broyer /bʀwaje/ [31] *vt* crush; (*moudre*) grind.

bru /bʀy/ *nf* daughter-in-law.

bruine /bʀɥin/ *nf* drizzle.

bruissement /bʀɥismɑ̃/ *nm* rustling.

bruit /bʀɥi/ *nm* noise; **~ de couloir** (fig) rumour.

bruitage /bʀɥitaʒ/ *nm* sound effects.

brûlant, ~e /bʀylɑ̃, -t/ *a* burning (hot); (*sujet*) red-hot; (*passion*) fiery.

brûlé /bʀyle/ *nm* burning; **ça sent le ~** I can smell something burning. ● ⇒BRÛLER [1].

brûler /bʀyle/ [1] *vt/i* burn; (*essence*) use (up); (*cierge*) light (à to); **~ un feu (rouge)** jump the lights; **~ d'envie de faire** be longing to do. □ **se ~** *vpr* burn oneself.

brûlure /bʀylyʀ/ *nf* burn; **~s d'estomac** heartburn.

brume /bʀym/ *nf* mist. **brumeux, -euse** *a* misty; (*esprit*) hazy.

brun, ~e /bʀœ̃, -yn/ *a* brown, dark. ● *nm* brown. ● *nm, f* dark-

haired person. **brunir** [2] *vi* turn brown; (*bronzer*) get a tan.

brushing /bʀœʃiŋ/ *nm* blow-dry.

brusque /bʀysk/ *a* (*personne*) abrupt; (*geste*) violent; (*soudain*) sudden.

brusquer /bʀyske/ [1] *vt* be abrupt with; (*précipiter*) rush.

brut, ~e /bʀyt/ *a* (*diamant*) rough; (*champagne*) dry; (*pétrole*) crude; (Comm) gross.

brutal, ~e (*mpl* **-aux**) /bʀytal, -o/ *a* brutal. **brutalité** *nf* brutality. **brute** /bʀyt/ *nf* brute.

Bruxelles /bʀysɛl/ *npr* Brussels.

bruyant, ~e /bʀɥijɑ̃, -t/ *a* noisy.

bruyère /bʀyjɛʀ/ *nf* heather.

bu /by/ ⇒BOIRE [12].

bûche /byʃ/ *nf* log; **~ de Noël** Christmas log; **ramasser une ~** 🅱 fall.

bûcher /byʃe/ [1] *vt/i* 🅱 slog away (at) 🅱. ● *nm* (*supplice*) stake.

bûcheron /byʃʀɔ̃/ *nm* lumberjack.

budget /bydʒɛ/ *nm* budget. **budgétaire** *a* budgetary.

buée /bɥe/ *nf* condensation.

buffet /byfɛ/ *nm* sideboard; (*table garnie*) buffet.

buffle /byfl/ *nm* buffalo.

buisson /bɥisɔ̃/ *nm* bush.

buissonnière /bɥisɔnjɛʀ/ *af* **faire l'école ~** play truant.

bulbe /bylb/ *nm* bulb.

bulgare /bylgaʀ/ *a & nm* Bulgarian. **B~** *nmf* Bulgarian.

Bulgarie /bylgaʀi/ *nf* Bulgaria.

bulldozer /byldozɛʀ/ *nm* bulldozer.

bulle /byl/ *nf* bubble.

bulletin /byltɛ̃/ *nm* bulletin, report; (Scol) report; **~ d'information** news bulletin; **~ météorologique** weather report; **~ (de vote)** ballot-paper; **~ de salaire** pay-slip.

buraliste /byʀalist/ *nmf*
tobacconist.

bureau (*pl* ~x) /byʀo/ *nm* office;
(meuble) desk; (comité) board; ~
d'études design office; ~ **de poste**
post office; ~ **de tabac**
tobacconist's (shop); ~ **de vote**
polling station.

bureaucrate /byʀokʀat/ *nmf*
bureaucrat. **bureaucratie** *nf*
bureaucracy. **bureaucratique** *a*
bureaucratic.

bureautique /byʀotik/ *nf* office
automation.

burlesque /byʀlɛsk/ *a* (histoire)
ludicrous; (film) farcical.

bus /bys/ *nm* bus.

buste /byst/ *nm* bust.

but /by(t)/ *nm* target; (dessein)
aim, goal; (football) goal; **avoir pour**
~ **de** aim to; **de** ~ **en blanc** point-
blank; **dans le** ~ **de** with the
intention of; **aller droit au** ~ go
straight to the point.

butane /bytan/ *nm* butane, Calor
gas®.

buté, ~**e** /byte/ *a* obstinate.

buter /byte/ [1] *vi* ~ **contre** knock
against; (problème) come up
against. ● *vt* antagonize. □ **se** ~
vpr (s'entêter) become obstinate.

buteur /bytœʀ/ *nm* (au football)
striker.

butin /bytɛ̃/ *nm* booty, loot.

butte /byt/ *nf* mound; **en** ~ **à**
exposed to.

buvard /byvaʀ/ *nm* blotting-
paper.

buvette /byvɛt/ *nf* (refreshment)
bar.

buveur, -euse /byvœʀ, -øz/ *nm, f*
drinker.

c' /s/ ⇒CE.

....

ça /sa/

● *pronom démonstratif*

····▸ (sujet) it; that; ~ **flotte** it floats;
~ **suffit!** that's enough!; ~ **y est!**
that's it!; ~ **sent le brûlé** there's a
smell of burning; ~ **va?** how are
things?

····▸ (objet) (proche) this; (plus éloigné)
that; **c'est** ~ that's right.

····▸ (dans expressions) **où** ~?
where?; **quand** ~? when?; **et
avec** ~? anything else?

....

çà /sa/ *adv* ~ **et là** here and
there.

cabane /kaban/ *nf* hut; (à outils)
shed.

cabaret /kabaʀɛ/ *nm* cabaret.

cabillaud /kabijo/ *nm* cod.

cabine /kabin/ *nf* (à la piscine)
cubicle; (de bateau) cabin; (de
camion) cab; (d'ascenseur) cage; ~
d'essayage fitting room; ~ **de
pilotage** cockpit; ~ **de plage** beach
hut; ~ (**téléphonique**) phone
booth, phone box.

cabinet /kabinɛ/ *nm* (de médecin)
surgery; (US) office; (d'avocat)
office; (clientèle) practice; (cabinet
collectif) firm; (Pol) Cabinet; (pièce)
room; ~**s** (toilettes) toilet; (US)
bathroom; ~ **de toilette** bathroom.

câble /kɑbl/ *nm* cable; (corde)
rope; (TV) cable TV. **câbler** *vt* [1]
cable; (TV) install cable television
in.

cabosser /kabɔse/ [1] *vt* dent.

cabotage /kabɔtaʒ/ *nm* coastal navigation.

cabrer (se) /(sə)kabʀe/ [1] *vpr* (*cheval*) rear; **se ~ contre** rebel against.

cabriole /kabʀijɔl/ *nf* **faire des ~s** caper about.

cacahuète /kakawɛt/ *nf* peanut.

cacao /kakao/ *nm* cocoa.

cachalot /kaʃalo/ *nm* sperm whale.

cache /kaʃ/ *nm* mask. ● *nf* hiding place; **~ d'armes** arms cache.

cache-cache /kaʃkaʃ/ *nm inv* hide-and-seek.

cache-nez /kaʃne/ *nm inv* scarf.

cacher /kaʃe/ [1] *vt* hide, conceal (à from). □ **se ~** *vpr* hide; (se trouver caché) be hidden.

cachet /kaʃɛ/ *nm* (de cire) seal; (à l'encre) stamp; (de la poste) postmark; (comprimé) tablet; (d'artiste) fee; (chic) style, cachet.

cachette /kaʃɛt/ *nf* hiding-place; **en ~** in secret.

cachot /kaʃo/ *nm* dungeon.

cachottier, -ière /kaʃɔtje, -jɛʀ/ *a* secretive.

cacophonie /kakɔfɔni/ *nf* cacophony.

cactus /kaktys/ *nm* cactus.

cadavérique /kadaveʀik/ *a* (*teint*) deathly pale.

cadavre /kadavʀ/ *nm* corpse; (de victime) body.

caddie /kadi/ *nm* (de supermarché)® trolley; (au golf) caddie.

cadeau (*pl* **~x**) /kado/ *nm* present, gift; **faire un ~ à qn** give sb a present.

cadenas /kadna/ *nm* padlock.

cadence /kadɑ̃s/ *nf* rhythm, cadence; (de travail) rate; **en ~** in time; (*marcher*) in step.

cadet, ~te /kadɛ, -t/ *a* youngest; (entre deux) younger. ● *nm, f* youngest (child); younger (child).

cadran /kadʀɑ̃/ *nm* dial; **~ solaire** sundial.

cadre /kadʀ/ *nm* frame; (lieu) setting; (milieu) surroundings; (limites) scope; (contexte) framework; **dans le ~ de** (à l'occasion de) on the occasion of; (dans le contexte de) in the framework of. ● *nm* (personne) executive; **les ~s** the managerial staff.

cadrer /kadʀe/ [1] *vi* **~ avec** tally with. ● *vt* (*photo*) centre.

cafard /kafaʀ/ *nm* (insecte) cockroach; **avoir le ~** 🄳 be down in the dumps.

café /kafe/ *nm* coffee; (bar) café; **~ crème** espresso with milk; **~ en grains** coffee beans; **~ au lait** white coffee.

cafetière /kaftjɛʀ/ *nf* coffee-pot; **~ électrique** coffee machine.

cage /kaʒ/ *nf* cage; **~ d'ascenseur** lift shaft; **~ d'escalier** stairwell; **~ thoracique** rib cage.

cageot /kaʒo/ *nm* crate.

cagibi /kaʒibi/ *nm* storage room.

cagneux, -euse /kaɲø, -z/ *a* **avoir les genoux ~** be knock-kneed.

cagnotte /kaɲɔt/ *nf* kitty.

cagoule /kagul/ *nf* hood; (passe-montagne) balaclava.

cahier /kaje/ *nm* notebook; (Scol) exercise book; **~ de textes** homework notebook; **~ des charges** (Tech) specifications (+ *pl*).

cahot /kao/ *nm* bump, jolt. **cahoteux, -euse** *a* bumpy.

caïd /kaid/ *nm* 🄳 big shot.

caille /kɑj/ *nf* quail.

cailler /kaje/ [1] *vi* curdle; **ça caille** 🄳 it's freezing. □ **se ~** *vpr* (*sang*) clot; (*lait*) curdle. **caillot** *nm* (blood) clot.

caillou (*pl* ~**x**) /kaju/ *nm* stone; (*galet*) pebble.

caisse /kɛs/ *nf* crate, case; (*tiroir, machine*) till; (*guichet*) cash desk; (*au supermarché*) check-out; (*bureau*) office; (Mus) drum; ~ **enregistreuse** cash register; ~ **d'épargne** savings bank; ~ **de retraite** pension fund. **caissier, -ière** *nm, f* cashier.

cajoler /kaʒɔle/ [1] *vt* coax.

calcaire /kalkɛʀ/ *a* (*sol*) chalky; (*eau*) hard.

calciné, ~e /kalsine/ *a* charred.

calcul /kalkyl/ *nm* calculation; (Scol) arithmetic; (*différentiel*) calculus; ~ **biliaire** gallstone.

calculatrice /kalkylatʀis/ *nf* calculator. **calculer** [1] *vt* calculate. **calculette** *nf* (pocket) calculator.

cale /kal/ *nf* wedge; (*pour roue*) chock; (*de navire*) hold; ~ **sèche** dry dock.

calé, ~e /kale/ *a* 🄵 clever.

caleçon /kalsɔ̃/ *nm* boxer shorts (+ *pl*); underpants (+ *pl*); (*de femme*) leggings.

calembour /kalɑ̃buʀ/ *nm* pun.

calendrier /kalɑ̃dʀije/ *nm* calendar; (fig) schedule, timetable.

calepin /kalpɛ̃/ *nm* notebook.

caler /kale/ [1] *vt* wedge. ● *vi* stall; (*abandonner* 🄵) give up.

calfeutrer /kalføtʀe/ [1] *vt* (*fissure*) stop up; (*porte*) draught proof.

calibre /kalibʀ/ *nm* calibre; (d'un œuf, fruit) grade.

calice /kalis/ *nm* (Relig) chalice; (Bot) calyx.

califourchon: **à ~** /akalifuʀʃɔ̃/ *loc* astride.

câlin, ~e /kɑlɛ̃, -in/ *a* (*regard, ton*) affectionate; (*personne*) cuddly.

calmant /kalmɑ̃/ *nm* sedative.

calme /kalm/ *a* calm. ● *nm* peace; calm; (*maîtrise de soi*) composure; **du ~**! calm down!

calmer /kalme/ [1] *vt* (*personne*) calm down; (*situation*) defuse; (*douleur*) ease; (*soif*) quench. □ **se ~** *vpr* (*personne, situation*) calm down; (*agitation, tempête*) die down; (*douleur*) ease.

calomnie /kalɔmni/ *nf* (*orale*) slander; (*écrite*) libel. **calomnier** [45] *vt* slander; libel. **calomnieux, -ieuse** *a* slanderous; libellous.

calorie /kalɔʀi/ *nf* calorie.

calque /kalk/ *nm* tracing; (**papier**) ~ tracing paper; (fig) exact copy.

calquer /kalke/ [1] *vt* trace; (fig) copy; ~ **qch sur** model sth on.

calvaire /kalvɛʀ/ *nm* (*croix*) Calvary; (fig) suffering.

calvitie /kalvisi/ *nf* baldness.

camarade /kamaʀad/ *nmf* friend; (Pol) comrade; ~ **de jeu** playmate. **camaraderie** *nf* friendship.

cambouis /kɑ̃bwi/ *nm* dirty oil.

cambrer /kɑ̃bʀe/ [1] *vt* arch. □ **se ~** *vpr* arch one's back.

cambriolage /kɑ̃bʀijɔlaʒ/ *nm* burglary. **cambrioler** [1] *vt* burgle. **cambrioleur, -euse** *nm, f* burglar.

camelot /kamlo/ *nm* 🄵 street vendor.

camelote /kamlɔt/ *nf* 🄵 junk.

caméra /kameʀa/ *nf* (cinéma, télévision) camera.

caméscope® /kameskɔp/ *nm* camcorder.

camion /kamjɔ̃/ *nm* lorry, truck. **camion-citerne** (*pl* **camions-citernes**) *nm* tanker. **camionnage** *nm* haulage. **camionnette** *nf* van. **camionneur** *nm* lorry *ou* truck driver; (*entrepreneur*) haulage contractor.

camisole /kamizɔl/ nf ~ (de force) straitjacket.

camoufler /kamufle/ [1] vt camouflage.

camp /kɑ̃/ nm camp; (Sport, Pol) side.

campagnard, ~e /kɑ̃paɲaʀ, -d/ a country. ●nm, f countryman, countrywoman.

campagne /kɑ̃paɲ/ nf country; countryside; (Mil, Pol) campaign.

campement /kɑ̃pmɑ̃/ nm camp, encampment.

camper /kɑ̃pe/ [1] vi camp. ●vt (esquisser) sketch. □ se ~ vpr plant oneself. **campeur, -euse** nm, f camper.

camping /kɑ̃piŋ/ nm camping; faire du ~ go camping; (terrain de) ~ campsite. **camping-car** (pl ~s) nm camper-van; (US) motorhome. **camping-gaz®** nm inv (réchaud) camping stove.

Canada /kanada/ nm Canada.

canadien, ~ne /kanadjɛ̃, -ɛn/ a Canadian. **C~, ~ne** nm, f Canadian. **canadienne** nf (veste) fur-lined jacket; (tente) ridge tent.

canaille /kanɑj/ nf rogue.

canal (pl -aux) /kanal, -o/ nm (artificiel) canal; (bras de mer) channel; (Tech, TV) channel; (moyen) channel; par le ~ de through. **canalisation** nf (tuyaux) mains (+ pl). **canaliser** [1] vt (eau) canalize; (fig) channel.

canapé /kanape/ nm sofa.

canard /kanaʀ/ nm duck; (journal 🄸) rag.

canari /kanaʀi/ nm canary.

cancans /kɑ̃kɑ̃/ nmpl 🄸 gossip.

cancer /kɑ̃sɛʀ/ nm cancer; le C~ Cancer. **cancéreux, -euse** a cancerous. **cancérigène** a carcinogenic.

cancre /kɑ̃kʀ/ nm dunce.

candeur /kɑ̃dœʀ/ nf ingenuousness.

candidat, ~e /kɑ̃dida, -t/ nm, f (à un examen, Pol) candidate; (à un poste) applicant, candidate (à for).

candidature /kɑ̃didatyʀ/ nf application; (Pol) candidacy; **poser sa ~ à un poste** apply for a job.

candide /kɑ̃did/ a ingenuous.

cane /kan/ nf (female) duck. **caneton** nm duckling.

canette /kanɛt/ nf (bouteille) bottle; (boîte) can.

canevas /kanva/ nm canvas; (ouvrage) tapestry; (plan) framework, outline.

caniche /kaniʃ/ nm poodle.

canicule /kanikyl/ nf scorching heat; (vague de chaleur) heatwave.

canif /kanif/ nm penknife.

canine /kanin/ nf canine (tooth).

caniveau (pl ~x) /kanivo/ nm gutter.

cannabis /kanabis/ nm cannabis.

canne /kan/ nf (walking) stick; ~ à pêche fishing rod; ~ à sucre sugar cane.

cannelle /kanɛl/ nf cinnamon.

cannibale /kanibal/ a & nmf cannibal.

canoë /kanɔe/ nm canoe; (Sport) canoeing.

canon /kanɔ̃/ nm (big) gun; (ancien) cannon; (d'une arme) barrel; (principe, règle) canon.

canot /kano/ nm dinghy, (small) boat; ~ de sauvetage lifeboat; ~ pneumatique rubber dinghy. **canotier** nm boater.

cantatrice /kɑ̃tatʀis/ nf opera singer.

cantine /kɑ̃tin/ nf canteen.

cantique /kɑ̃tik/ nm hymn.

cantonner /kɑ̃tɔne/ [1] vt (Mil) billet. □ se ~ dans vpr confine oneself to.

canular /kanylaʀ/ nm hoax.

caoutchouc /kautʃu/ nm

rubber; (élastique) rubber band; ~ **mousse** foam rubber.

cap /kap/ *nm* cape, headland; (direction) course; (obstacle) hurdle; **franchir le ~ de la cinquantaine** pass the fifty mark; **mettre le ~ sur** steer a course for.

capable /kapabl/ *a* capable (**de** of); ~ **de faire** able to do, capable of doing.

capacité /kapasite/ *nf* ability; (contenance, potentiel) capacity.

cape /kap/ *nf* cape; **rire sous ~** laugh up one's sleeve.

capillaire /kapilɛʀ/ *a* (lotion, soins) hair; (vaisseau) ~ capillary.

capitaine /kapitɛn/ *nm* captain.

capital, ~e (*mpl* -**aux**) /kapital, -o/ *a* key, crucial, fundamental; (peine, lettre) capital. ● *nm* (*pl* -**aux**) (Comm) capital; (fig) stock; **capitaux** (Comm) capital; ~-**risque** venture capital; ~-**risqueur** venture capitalist. **capitale** *nf* (ville, lettre) capital.

capitalisme /kapitalism/ *nm* capitalism.

capitonné, ~e /kapitone/ *a* padded.

capituler /kapityle/ [1] *vi* capitulate.

caporal (*pl* -**aux**) /kapɔʀal, -o/ *nm* corporal.

capot /kapo/ *nm* (Auto) bonnet; (US) hood.

capote /kapɔt/ *nf* (Auto) hood; (US) top; (préservatif 🔲) condom.

capoter /kapɔte/ [1] *vi* overturn; (fig) collapse.

câpre /kɑpʀ/ *nf* (Culin) caper.

caprice /kapʀis/ *nm* whim; (colère) tantrum; **faire un ~** throw a tantrum. **capricieux, -ieuse** *a* capricious; (appareil) temperamental.

Capricorne /kapʀikɔʀn/ *nm* **le ~** Capricorn.

capsule /kapsyl/ *nf* capsule; (de bouteille) cap.

capter /kapte/ [1] *vt* (eau) collect; (émission) get; (signal) pick up; (fig) win, capture.

captif, -ive /kaptif, -v/ *a & nm,f* captive.

captiver /kaptive/ [1] *vt* captivate.

capturer /kaptyʀe/ [1] *vt* capture.

capuche /kapyʃ/ *nf* hood. **capuchon** *nm* hood; (de stylo) cap.

car /kaʀ/ *conj* because, for. ● *nm* coach; (US) bus.

carabine /kaʀabin/ *nf* rifle.

caractère /kaʀaktɛʀ/ *nm* (lettre) character; (nature) nature; ~**s d'imprimerie** block letters; **avoir bon/mauvais ~** be good-natured/ bad-tempered; **avoir du ~** have character.

caractériel, ~le /kaʀakteʀjɛl/ *a* (trait) character; (enfant) disturbed.

caractériser /kaʀakteʀize/ [1] *vt* characterize. □ **se ~ par** *vpr* be characterized by.

caractéristique *a & nf* characteristic.

carafe /kaʀaf/ *nf* carafe.

Caraïbes /kaʀaib/ *nfpl* **les ~** the Caribbean.

carambolage /kaʀɑ̃bɔlaʒ/ *nm* pile-up.

caramel /kaʀamɛl/ *nm* caramel; (bonbon) toffee.

carapace /kaʀapas/ *nf* shell.

caravane /kaʀavan/ *nf* (Auto) caravan; (US) trailer; (convoi) caravan.

carbone /kaʀbɔn/ *nm* carbon; (papier) ~ carbon (paper).

carboniser [1] *vt* burn (to ashes).

carburant /kaʀbyʀɑ̃/ *nm* (motor) fuel.

carburateur /kaʀbyʀatœʀ/ *nm* carburettor; (US) carburetor.

carcan /kaʀkɑ̃/ *nm* constraints (+ *pl*).

C

carcasse /kaʀkas/ nf (squelette) carcass; (armature) frame; (de voiture) shell.

cardiaque /kaʀdjak/ a heart. ● nmf heart patient.

cardinal, ~e (mpl -aux) /kaʀdinal, -o/ a & nm cardinal.

Carême /kaʀɛm/ nm le ~ Lent.

carence /kaʀɑ̃s/ nf shortcomings (+ pl); inadequacy; (Méd) deficiency; (absence) lack.

caresse /kaʀɛs/ nf caress; (à un animal) stroke. **caresser** [1] vt caress, stroke; (espoir) cherish.

cargaison /kaʀgɛzɔ̃/ nf cargo.

cargo /kaʀgo/ nm cargo boat.

caricature /kaʀikatyʀ/ nf caricature.

carie /kaʀi/ nf (trou) cavity; la ~ (dentaire) tooth decay.

carillon /kaʀijɔ̃/ nm chimes (+ pl); (horloge) chiming clock.

caritatif, -ive /kaʀitatif, -v/ a **association caritative** charity.

carnage /kaʀnaʒ/ nm carnage.

carnassier, -ière /kaʀnasje, -jɛʀ/ a carnivorous.

carnaval (pl ~s) /kaʀnaval/ nm carnival.

carnet /kaʀnɛ/ nm notebook; (de tickets, timbres) book; ~ **d'adresses** address book; ~ **de chèques** chequebook.

carotte /kaʀɔt/ nf carrot.

carpe /kaʀp/ nf carp.

carré, ~e /kaʀe/ a (forme, mesure) square; (fig) straightforward; **un mètre** ~ one square metre. ● nm square; (de terrain) patch.

carreau (pl ~x) /kaʀo/ nm (window) pane; (par terre, au mur) tile; (dessin) check; (aux cartes) diamonds (+ pl); à ~x (tissu) check(ed); (papier) squared.

carrefour /kaʀfuʀ/ nm crossroads (+ sg).

carrelage /kaʀlaʒ/ nm tiling; (sol) tiles.

carrément /kaʀemɑ̃/ adv (complètement) completely; (stupide, dangereux) downright; (dire) straight out; **elle a** ~ **démissionné** she went straight ahead and resigned.

carrière /kaʀjɛʀ/ nf career; (terrain) quarry.

carrossable /kaʀɔsabl/ a suitable for vehicles.

carrosse /kaʀɔs/ nm (horse-drawn) coach.

carrosserie /kaʀɔsʀi/ nf (Auto) body(work).

carrure /kaʀyʀ/ nf shoulders; (fig) necessary qualities, calibre.

cartable /kaʀtabl/ nm satchel.

carte /kaʀt/ nf card; (Géog) map; (Naut) chart; (au restaurant) menu; ~s (jeu) cards; **à la** ~ (manger) à la carte; (horaire) personalized; **donner** ~ **blanche à** give a free hand to; ~ **de crédit** credit card; ~ **de fidélité** loyalty card; ~ **grise** (car) registration document; ~ **d'identité** identity card; ~ **magnétique** swipe card; ~ **de paiement** debit card; ~ **postale** postcard; ~ **à puce** smart card; ~ **de séjour** resident's permit; ~ **des vins** wine list; ~ **de visite** (business) card.

cartilage /kaʀtilaʒ/ nm cartilage.

carton /kaʀtɔ̃/ nm cardboard; (boîte) (cardboard) box; ~ **à dessin** portfolio; **faire un** ~ 🔲 do well.

cartonné, ~e /kaʀtone/ a **livre** ~ hardback.

cartouche /kaʀtuʃ/ nf cartridge; (de cigarettes) carton. **cartouchière** nf cartridge-belt.

cas /kɑ/ nm case; **au** ~ **où** in case; ~ **urgent** emergency; **en aucun** ~ on no account; **en** ~ **de** in the event of, in case of; **en tout** ~ in any case; (du moins) at least; **faire** ~ **de** set great store by; ~ **de conscience** moral dilemma.

casanier, -ière /kazanje, -jɛʀ/ *a* home-loving.

cascade /kaskad/ *nf* waterfall; (au cinéma) stunt; (fig) spate, series (+ *sg*).

cascadeur, -euse /kaskadœʀ, -øz/ *nm, f* stuntman, stuntwoman.

case /kɑz/ *nf* hut; (de damier) square; (compartiment) pigeon-hole; (sur un formulaire) box.

caser /kaze/ [1] *vt* Ⓘ (mettre) put; (loger) put up; (dans un travail) find a job for; (marier: péj) marry off.

caserne /kazɛʀn/ *nf* barracks; ~ **de sapeurs-pompiers** fire station.

casier /kazje/ *nm* pigeon-hole, compartment; (à bouteilles, chaussures) rack; ~ **judiciaire** criminal record.

casque /kask/ *nm* (de motard) crash helmet; (de cycliste) cycle helmet; (chez le coiffeur) (hair-)drier; ~ (à écouteurs) headphones; ~ **anti-bruit** ear defenders; ~ **de protection** safety helmet.

casquette /kaskɛt/ *nf* cap.

cassant, ~e /kasɑ̃, -t/ *a* brittle; (brusque) curt.

cassation /kasasjɔ̃/ *nf* **cour de** ~ appeal court.

casse /kɑs/ *nf* (objets) breakages; (lieu) breaker's yard; **mettre à la** ~ scrap.

casse-cou /kasku/ *nmf inv* daredevil.

casse-croûte /kaskrut/ *nm inv* snack.

casse-noix /kasnwa/ *nm inv* nutcrackers (+ *pl*).

casse-pieds /kaspje/ *nmf inv* Ⓘ pain (in the neck) Ⓘ.

casser /kase/ [1] *vt* break; (annuler) annul; ~ **les pieds à qn** Ⓘ annoy sb. ● *vi* break. □ **se** ~ *vpr* break; (partir Ⓘ) be off Ⓘ.

casserole /kasʀɔl/ *nf* saucepan.

casse-tête /kastɛt/ *nm inv*

(problème) headache; (jeu) brain teaser.

cassette /kasɛt/ *nf* casket; (de magnétophone) cassette, tape; (de vidéo) video tape; ~ **audionumérique** digital audio tape.

cassis /kasi(s)/ *nm inv* blackcurrant.

cassure /kasyʀ/ *nf* break.

castor /kastɔʀ/ *nm* beaver.

castration /kastʀasjɔ̃/ *nf* castration.

catalogue /katalɔg/ *nm* catalogue.

catalyseur /katalizœʀ/ *nm* catalyst; (Auto) catalytic convertor.

catastrophe /katastʀɔf/ *nf* disaster, catastrophe.

catastrophique *a* catastrophic.

catch /katʃ/ *nm* (all-in) wrestling.

catéchisme /kateʃism/ *nm* catechism.

catégorie /kategɔʀi/ *nf* category.

catégorique *a* categorical.

cathédrale /katedʀal/ *nf* cathedral.

catholique /katɔlik/ *a* Catholic. **pas très** ~ a bit fishy.

catimini: en ~ /katimini/ *loc* on the sly.

cauchemar /koʃmaʀ/ *nm* nightmare.

cause /koz/ *nf* cause; (raison) reason; (Jur) case; **à** ~ **de** because of; **en** ~ (en jeu, concerné) involved; **pour** ~ **de** on account of; **mettre en** ~ implicate; **remettre en** ~ call into question.

causer /koze/ [1] *vt* cause; (discuter de Ⓘ) ~ **travail** talk shop; ~ **de** talk about. ● *vi* chat.

causerie *nf* talk.

causette /kozɛt/ *nf* (Internet) chat; **faire la** ~ chat.

caution /kosjɔ̃/ *nf* surety; (Jur) bail; (appui) backing; (garantie) deposit; **libéré sous ~** released on bail. **cautionner** [1] *vt* guarantee; (soutenir) back.

cavalcade /kavalkad/ *nf* stampede, rush.

cavalier, -ière /kavalje, -jɛʀ/ *a* offhand; **allée cavalière** bridle path. ● *nm, f* rider; (pour danser) partner. ● *nm* (aux échecs) knight.

cave /kav/ *nf* cellar. ● *a* sunken.

caveau (*pl* ~**x**) /kavo/ *nm* vault.

caverne /kavɛʀn/ *nf* cave.

CCP *abrév m* (**compte chèque postal**) post office account.

CD *abrév m* (**compact disc**) CD.

CD-ROM *abrév m inv* (**compact disc read only memory**) CD-ROM.

....

ce, c', cet, cette (*pl* **ces**) /sə, s, sɛt, se/

c' before e. **cet** before vowel or mute h.

●**ce, cet, cette** (*pl* **ces**) *adjectif démonstratif*

····▸ this; (plus éloigné) that; **ces** these; (plus éloigné) those; **cette nuit** (passée) last night; (à venir) tonight.

●**ce, c'** *pronom démonstratif*

····▸ **c'est** it's *ou* it is; **c'est un policier** he's a policeman; ~ **sont eux qui l'ont fait** THEY did it; **qui est-~?** who is it?

····▸ **ce que/qui** what; ~ **que je ne comprends pas** what I don't understand; **elle est venue, ~ qui est étonnant** she came, which is surprising; ~ **que tu as de la chance!** how lucky you are!; **tout ~ que je sais** all I know; **tout ~ qu'elle trouve/peut** everything she finds/can.

....

CE *abrév f* (**Communauté européenne**) EC.

ceci /səsi/ *pron* this.

cécité /sesite/ *nf* blindness.

céder /sede/ [14] *vt* give up; ~ **le passage** give way; (vendre) sell. ● *vi* (se rompre) give way; (se soumettre) give in.

cédérom /sederɔm/ *nm* CD-ROM.

cédille /sedij/ *nf* cedilla.

cèdre /sɛdʀ/ *nm* cedar.

CEI *abrév f* (**Communauté des États indépendants**) CIS.

ceinture /sɛ̃tyʀ/ *nf* belt; (taille) waist; ~ **de sauvetage** lifebelt; ~ **de sécurité** seatbelt.

cela /səla/ *pron* it, that; (pour désigner) that; ~ **va de soi** it is obvious; ~ **dit/fait** having said/done that.

célèbre /selɛbʀ/ *a* famous.

célébrer [14] *vt* celebrate.

célébrité *nf* fame; (personne) celebrity.

céleri /sɛlʀi/ *nm* (en branches) celery. **céleri-rave** (*pl* **céleris-raves**) *nm* celeriac.

célibat /seliba/ *nm* celibacy; (état) single status.

célibataire /selibatɛʀ/ *a* single. ● *nm* bachelor. ● *nf* single woman.

celle, celles /sɛl/ ⇒CELUI.

cellulaire /selylɛʀ/ *a* cell; **emprisonnement** ~ solitary confinement; **fourgon** *ou* **voiture** ~ prison van; **téléphone** ~ cellular phone.

cellule /selyl/ *nf* cell; ~ **souche** stem cell.

celui, celle (*pl* **ceux, celles**) /səlɥi, sɛl, sø/ *pron* the one; ~ **de mon ami** my friend's; ~**-ci** this (one); ~**-là** that (one); **ceux-ci** these (ones); **ceux-là** those (ones).

cendre /sɑ̃dʀ/ *nf* ash.

cendrier /sɑ̃dʀije/ *nm* ashtray.

censé, ~e /sɑ̃se/ *a* **être ~ faire** be supposed to do.

censeur /sɑ̃sœʀ/ nm censor; (Scol) administrator in charge of discipline.

censure /sɑ̃syʀ/ nf censorship. **censurer** [1] vt censor; (critiquer) censure.

cent /sɑ̃/ a (a) hundred; **20 pour ~** 20 per cent. ● n (quantité) hundred; **~ un** a hundred and one; (centième d'euro) cent.

centaine /sɑ̃tɛn/ nf hundred; **une ~ (de)** (about) a hundred.

centenaire /sɑ̃tnɛʀ/ nm (anniversaire) centenary.

centième /sɑ̃tjɛm/ a & nmf hundredth.

centimètre /sɑ̃timɛtʀ/ nm centimetre; (ruban) tape-measure.

central, ~e (mpl -aux) /sɑ̃tʀal, -o/ a central. ● nm (pl -aux) ~ **(téléphonique)** (telephone) exchange. **centrale** nf power station.

centre /sɑ̃tʀ/ nm centre; ~ **d'appel** call centre; ~ **commercial** shopping centre; (US) mall; ~ **de formation** training centre; ~ **hospitalier** hospital. **centrer** [1] vt centre. **centre-ville** (pl centres-villes) nm town centre.

centuple /sɑ̃typl/ nm le ~ **de** a hundred times; **au ~** a hundredfold.

cep /sɛp/ nm vine stock.

cépage /sepaʒ/ nm grape variety.

cèpe /sɛp/ nm cep.

cependant /səpɑ̃dɑ̃/ adv however.

céramique /seʀamik/ nf ceramic; (art) ceramics (+ sg).

cercle /sɛʀkl/ nm circle; (cerceau) hoop; (association) society, club; ~ **vicieux** vicious circle.

cercueil /sɛʀkœj/ nm coffin.

céréale /seʀeal/ nf cereal; ~**s** (Culin) (breakfast) cereal.

cérébral, ~e (mpl -aux) /seʀebʀal, -o/ a cerebral.

cérémonie /seʀemɔni/ nf ceremony; **sans ~s** (repas) informal; (recevoir) informally.

cerf /sɛʀ/ nm stag.

cerfeuil /sɛʀfœj/ nm chervil.

cerf-volant (pl cerfs-volants) /sɛʀvolɑ̃/ nm kite.

cerise /s(ə)ʀiz/ nf cherry. **cerisier** nm cherry tree.

cerner /sɛʀne/ [1] vt surround; (question) define; **avoir les yeux cernés** have rings under one's eyes.

certain, ~e /sɛʀtɛ̃, -ɛn/ a certain; (sûr) certain, sure (**de** of; **que** that); **d'un ~ âge** no longer young; **un ~ temps** some time. **certainement** adv (probablement) most probably; (avec certitude) certainly. **certains, -es** pron some people.

certes /sɛʀt/ adv (sans doute) admittedly; (bien sûr) of course.

certificat /sɛʀtifika/ nm certificate.

certifier /sɛʀtifje/ [45] vt certify; ~ **qch à qn** assure sb of sth; **copie certifiée conforme** certified true copy.

certitude /sɛʀtityd/ nf certainty.

cerveau (pl ~x) /sɛʀvo/ nm brain.

cervelle /sɛʀvɛl/ nf (Anat) brain; (Culin) brains.

ces /se/ ⇒CE.

césarienne /sezaʀjɛn/ nf Caesarean (section).

cesse /sɛs/ nf **n'avoir de ~ que** have no rest until; **sans ~** constantly, incessantly.

cesser /sese/ [1] vt stop; ~ **de faire** stop doing. ● vi cease; **faire ~** put an end to.

cessez-le-feu /seselfø/ nm inv ceasefire.

cession /sɛsjɔ̃/ nf transfer.

c'est-à-dire /setadiʀ/ *conj* that is (to say).

cet, cette /sɛt/ ⇒CE.

ceux /sø/ ⇒CELUI.

chacun, ~e /ʃakœ̃, -yn/ *pron* each (one), every one; (tout le monde) everyone; **~ d'entre nous** each (one) of us.

chagrin /ʃagʀɛ̃/ *nm* sorrow; **avoir du ~** be sad.

chahut /ʃay/ *nm* row, din.

chahuter /ʃayte/ [1] *vi* make a row. ● *vt* (*enseignant*) be rowdy with; (*orateur*) heckle.

chaîne /ʃɛn/ *nf* chain; (de télévision) channel; **~ (d'assemblage)** assembly line; **~s** (Auto) snow chains; **~ de montagnes** mountain range; **~ de montage/fabrication** assembly/ production line; **~ hi-fi** hi-fi system; **~ laser** CD player; **en ~** (*accidents*) multiple; (*réaction*) chain. **chaînette** *nf* (small) chain. **chaînon** *nm* link.

chair /ʃɛʀ/ *nf* flesh; **bien en ~** plump; **en ~ et en os** in the flesh; **~ à saucisses** sausage meat; **la ~ de poule** gooseflesh, goose pimples. ● *a inv* (*couleur*) **~** flesh-coloured.

chaire /ʃɛʀ/ *nf* (d'église) pulpit; (Univ) chair.

chaise /ʃɛz/ *nf* chair; **~ longue** deckchair.

châle /ʃal/ *nm* shawl.

chaleur /ʃalœʀ/ *nf* heat; (moins intense) warmth; (d'un accueil, d'une couleur) warmth. **chaleureux, -euse** *a* warm.

chalumeau (*pl* **~x**) /ʃalymo/ *nm* blowtorch.

chalutier /ʃalytje/ *nm* trawler.

chamailler (se) /(sə)ʃamaje/ [1] *vpr* squabble.

chambre /ʃɑ̃bʀ/ *nf* (bed)room; (Pol, Jur) chamber; **faire ~ à part** sleep in separate rooms; **~ à air** inner tube; **~ d'amis** spare *ou* guest room; **~ de commerce (et d'industrie)** Chamber of Commerce; **~ à coucher** bedroom; **~ à un lit/deux lits** single/twin room; **~ pour deux personnes** double room; **~ forte** strong-room; **~ d'hôte** bed and breakfast, B and B. **chambrer** [1] *vt* (vin) bring to room temperature.

chameau (*pl* **~x**) /ʃamo/ *nm* camel.

chamois /ʃamwa/ *nm* chamois.

champ /ʃɑ̃/ *nm* field; **~ de bataille** battlefield; **~ de courses** racecourse; **~ de tir** firing range.

champêtre /ʃɑ̃pɛtʀ/ *a* rural.

champignon /ʃɑ̃piɲɔ̃/ *nm* mushroom; (moisissure) fungus; **~ de Paris** button mushroom.

champion, ~ne /ʃɑ̃pjɔ̃, -ɔn/ *nm, f* champion. **championnat** *nm* championship.

chance /ʃɑ̃s/ *nf* (good) luck; (possibilité) chance; **avoir de la ~** be lucky; **quelle ~!** what luck!

chanceler /ʃɑ̃sle/ [38] *vi* stagger; (fig) falter, waver.

chancelier /ʃɑ̃səlje/ *nm* chancellor.

chanceux, -euse /ʃɑ̃sø, -z/ *a* lucky.

chandail /ʃɑ̃daj/ *nm* sweater.

chandelier /ʃɑ̃dəlje/ *nm* candlestick.

chandelle /ʃɑ̃dɛl/ *nf* candle; **dîner aux ~s** candlelight dinner.

change /ʃɑ̃ʒ/ *nm* (foreign) exchange; (taux) exchange rate.

changement /ʃɑ̃ʒmɑ̃/ *nm* change; **~ de vitesse** (dispositif) gears.

changer /ʃɑ̃ʒe/ [40] *vt* change; **~ qch de place** move sth; (échanger) change (**pour, contre** for); **~ de nom/voiture** change one's name/ car; **~ de place/train** change places/trains; **~ de direction**

change direction; ~ **d'avis** *ou*
d'idée change one's mind; ~ **de
vitesse** change gear. □ **se** ~ *vpr*
change, get changed.

chanson /ʃɑ̃sɔ̃/ *nf* song.

chant /ʃɑ̃/ *nm* singing; (*chanson*)
song; (*Relig*) hymn.

chantage /ʃɑ̃taʒ/ *nm* blackmail.

chanter /ʃɑ̃te/ [1] *vt* sing; **si cela
vous chante** 🔲 if you feel like it.
● *vi* sing; **faire** ~ (*délit*) blackmail.

chanteur, -euse *nm, f* singer.

chantier /ʃɑ̃tje/ *nm* building site;
~ **naval** shipyard; **mettre en** ~ get
under way, start.

chaos /kao/ *nm* chaos.

chaparder /ʃaparde/ [1] *vt* 🔲
pinch 🔲, filch.

chapeau (*pl* ~**x**) /ʃapo/ *nm* hat;
~**!** well done!

chapelet /ʃaplɛ/ *nm* rosary; (*fig*)
string.

chapelle /ʃapɛl/ *nf* chapel.

chapelure /ʃaplyʀ/ *nf* (*Culin*)
breadcrumbs.

chaperonner /ʃapʀɔne/ [1] *vt*
chaperone.

chapiteau (*pl* ~**x**) /ʃapito/ *nm*
marquee; (*de cirque*) big top; (*de
colonne*) capital.

chapitre /ʃapitʀ/ *nm* chapter;
(*fig*) subject.

chaque /ʃak/ *a* every, each.

char /ʃaʀ/ *nm* (*Mil*) tank; (*de
carnaval*) float; (*charrette*) cart; (*dans
l'antiquité*) chariot.

charabia /ʃaʀabja/ *nm* 🔲
gibberish.

charade /ʃaʀad/ *nf* riddle.

charbon /ʃaʀbɔ̃/ *nm* coal; (*Méd*)
anthrax; ~ **de bois** charcoal.

charcuterie /ʃaʀkytʀi/ *nf* pork
butcher's shop; (*aliments*) (*cooked*)
pork meats. **charcutier, -ière**
nm, f pork butcher.

chardon /ʃaʀdɔ̃/ *nm* thistle.

charge /ʃaʀʒ/ *nf* load, burden;
(Mil, Électr, Jur) charge; (*responsabilité*)
responsibility; **avoir qn à** ~ be
responsible for; ~**s** expenses; (*de
locataire*) service charges; **être à la**
~ **de** (*personne*) be the
responsibility of; (*frais*) be
payable by; ~**s sociales** social
security contributions; **prendre en**
~ take charge of.

chargé, ~e /ʃaʀʒe/ *a* (*véhicule*)
loaded; (*journée, emploi du
temps*) busy; (*langue*) coated.
● *nm, f* ~
de mission head of mission; ~
d'affaires chargé d'affaires, ~ **de
cours** lecturer.

chargement /ʃaʀʒəmɑ̃/ *nm*
loading; (*objets*) load.

charger /ʃaʀʒe/ [40] *vt* load;
(Ordinat, Photo) load; (*attaquer*)
charge; (*batterie*) charge; ~ **qn de**
(*fardeau*) weigh sb down with;
(*tâche*) entrust sb with; ~ **qn de
faire** make sb responsible for
doing. ● *vi* (*attaquer*) charge. □ **se**
~ **de** *vpr* take charge *ou* care of.

charlot /ʃaʀjo/ *nm* (*à roulettes*)
trolley; (US) cart; (*charrette*) cart.

charitable /ʃaʀitabl/ *a*
charitable.

charité /ʃaʀite/ *nf* charity; **faire la**
~ **à** give (*money*) to.

charlatan /ʃaʀlatɑ̃/ *nm*
charlatan.

charmant, ~e /ʃaʀmɑ̃, -t/ *a*
charming.

charme /ʃaʀm/ *nm* charm; (*qui
envoûte*) spell. **charmer** [1] *vt*
charm. **charmeur, -euse** *nm, f*
charmer.

charnel, ~le /ʃaʀnɛl/ *a* carnal.

charnière /ʃaʀnjɛʀ/ *nf* hinge; **à la**
~ **de** at the meeting point
between.

charnu, ~e /ʃaʀny/ *a* plump,
fleshy.

charpente /ʃaʀpɑ̃t/ *nf*
framework; (*carrure*) build.

charpentier /ʃaʀpɑ̃tje/ nm carpenter.

charrette /ʃaʀɛt/ nf cart.

charrue /ʃaʀy/ nf plough.

chasse /ʃas/ nf hunting; (au fusil) shooting; (poursuite) chase; (recherche) hunt(ing); ~ **d'eau** (toilet) flush; ~ **sous-marine** harpoon fishing.

chasse-neige /ʃasnɛʒ/ nm inv snowplough.

chasser /ʃase/ [1] vt hunt; (au fusil) shoot; (faire partir) chase away; (odeur, employé) get rid of. ●vi go hunting; (au fusil) go shooting.

chasseur, -euse /ʃasœʀ, -øz/ nm, f hunter. ●nm bellboy; (US) bellhop; (avion) fighter plane.

châssis /ʃasi/ nm frame; (Auto) chassis.

chasteté /ʃastəte/ nf chastity.

chat¹ /ʃa/ nm cat; (mâle) tomcat.

chat² /tʃæt/ nm (Internet) chat.

châtaigne /ʃatɛɲ/ nf chestnut. **châtaignier** nm chestnut tree. **châtain** a inv chestnut (brown).

château (pl ~x) /ʃato/ nm castle; (manoir) manor; ~ **d'eau** water tower; ~ **fort** fortified castle.

châtiment /ʃatimɑ̃/ nm punishment.

chaton /ʃatɔ̃/ nm (chat) kitten.

chatouillement /ʃatujmɑ̃/ nm tickling. **chatouiller** [1] vt tickle. **chatouilleux, -euse** a ticklish; (susceptible) touchy.

châtrer /ʃatʀe/ [1] vt castrate; (chat) neuter.

chatte /ʃat/ nf female cat.

chaud, ~e /ʃo, -d/ a warm; (brûlant) hot; (vif: fig) warm. ●nm heat; **au** ~ in the warm(th); **avoir** ~ be warm; be hot; **il fait** ~ it is warm; it is hot; **pour te tenir** ~ to keep you warm. **chaudement** adv warmly; (disputé) hotly.

chaudière /ʃodjɛʀ/ nf boiler.

chaudron /ʃodʀɔ̃/ nm cauldron.

chauffage /ʃofaʒ/ nm heating; ~ **central** central heating.

chauffard /ʃofaʀ/ nm (péj) reckless driver.

chauffer /ʃofe/ [1] vt/i heat (up); (moteur, appareil) overheat. □ **se** ~ vpr warm oneself (up).

chauffeur /ʃofœʀ/ nm driver; (aux gages de qn) chauffeur.

chaume /ʃom/ nm (de toit) thatch.

chaussée /ʃose/ nf road(way).

chausse-pied (pl ~s) /ʃospje/ nm shoehorn.

chausser /ʃose/ [1] vt (chaussures) put on; (enfant) put shoes on (to). ●vi ~ **bien** (aller) fit well; ~ **du 35** take a size 35 shoe. □ **se** ~ vpr put one's shoes on.

chaussette /ʃosɛt/ nf sock.

chausson /ʃosɔ̃/ nm slipper; (de bébé) bootee; ~ **de danse** ballet shoe; ~ **aux pommes** apple turnover.

chaussure /ʃosyʀ/ nf shoe; ~ **de ski** ski boot; ~ **de marche** hiking boot.

chauve /ʃov/ a bald.

chauve-souris (pl **chauves-souris**) /ʃovsuʀi/ nf bat.

chauvin, ~e /ʃovɛ̃, -in/ a chauvinistic. ●nm, f chauvinist.

chavirer /ʃaviʀe/ [1] vt (bateau) capsize; (objets) tip over.

chef /ʃɛf/ nm leader, head; (supérieur) boss, superior; (Culin) chef; (de tribu) chief; **architecte en** ~ chief ou head architect; ~ **d'accusation** (Jur) charge; ~ **d'équipe** foreman; (Sport) captain; ~ **d'État** head of State; ~ **de famille** head of the family; ~ **de file** (Pol) leader; ~ **de gare** stationmaster; ~ **d'orchestre** conductor; ~ **de service**

department head; ~ **de train** guard; (US) conductor.

chef-d'œuvre (pl **chefs-d'œuvre**) /ʃedœvʀ/ nm masterpiece.

chef-lieu (pl **chefs-lieux**) /ʃɛfljø/ nm county town, administrative centre.

chemin /ʃəmɛ̃/ nm road; (étroit) lane; (de terre) track; (pour piétons) path; (passage) way; (direction, trajet) way; **avoir du ~ à faire** have a long way to go; ~ **de fer** railway; **par ~ de fer** by rail; ~ **de halage** towpath; ~ **vicinal** country lane.

cheminée /ʃəmine/ nf chimney; (intérieure) fireplace; (encadrement) mantelpiece; (de bateau) funnel.

cheminot /ʃəmino/ nm railwayman; (US) railroad man.

chemise /ʃəmiz/ nf shirt; (dossier) folder; (de livre) jacket; ~ **de nuit** nightdress. **chemisette** nf short-sleeved shirt. **chemisier** nm blouse.

chêne /ʃɛn/ nm oak.

chenil /ʃəni(l)/ nm (pension) kennels (+ sg).

chenille /ʃənij/ nf caterpillar; **véhicule à ~s** tracked vehicle.

cheptel /ʃɛptɛl/ nm livestock.

chèque /ʃɛk/ nm cheque; ~ **sans provision** bad cheque; ~ **de voyage** traveller's cheque. **chéquier** nm chequebook.

cher, chère /ʃɛʀ/ a (coûteux) dear, expensive; (aimé) dear; (dans la correspondance) dear. ● adv (coûter, payer) a lot (of money); (en importance) dearly. ● nm, f **mon ~, ma chère** my dear.

chercher /ʃɛʀʃe/ [1] vt look for; (aide, paix, gloire) seek; **aller ~** go and get ou fetch, go for; ~ **à faire** attempt to do; ~ **la petite bête** be finicky.

chercheur, -euse /ʃɛʀʃœʀ, -øz/ nm, f research worker.

chèrement /ʃɛʀmɑ̃/ adv dearly.

chéri, ~e /ʃeʀi/ a beloved. ● nm, f darling.

chérir /ʃeʀiʀ/ [2] vt cherish.

chétif, -ive /ʃetif, -v/ a puny.

cheval (pl **-aux**) /ʃəval, -o/ nm horse; **à ~** on horseback; **à ~ sur** astride, straddling; **faire du ~** ride, go horse-riding.

chevalerie /ʃəvalʀi/ nf chivalry.

chevalet /ʃəvalɛ/ nm easel; (de menuisier) trestle.

chevalier /ʃəvalje/ nm knight.

chevalière /ʃəvaljɛʀ/ nf signet ring.

cheval-vapeur (pl **chevaux-vapeur**) /ʃəvalvapœʀ/ nm horsepower.

chevaucher /ʃəvoʃe/ [1] vt sit astride. □ **se** ~ vpr overlap.

chevelu, ~e /ʃəvly/ a (péj) long-haired; (Bot) hairy.

chevelure /ʃəvlyʀ/ nf hair.

chevet /ʃəvɛ/ nm **au ~ de** at the bedside of; **livre de ~** bedside book.

cheveu (pl ~**x**) /ʃəvø/ nm (poil) hair; ~**x** (chevelure) hair; **avoir les** ~**x longs** have long hair.

cheville /ʃəvij/ nf ankle; (fiche) peg, pin; (pour mur) (wall) plug.

chèvre /ʃɛvʀ/ nf goat.

chevreuil /ʃəvʀœj/ nm roe (deer); (Culin) venison.

chevron /ʃəvʀɔ̃/ nm (poutre) rafter; **à ~s** herringbone.

chez /ʃe/ prép (au domicile de) at the house of; (parmi) among; (dans le caractère ou l'œuvre de) in; **aller ~ qn** go to sb's house; ~ **le boucher** at ou to the butcher's; ~ **soi** at home; **rentrer ~ soi** go home. **chez-soi** nm inv home.

chic /ʃik/ a inv smart; (gentil) kind. ● nm style; **avoir le ~ pour** have a knack for; ~ **(alors)!** great!

chicane /ʃikan/ nf double bend;

chercher ~ **à qn** pick a quarrel with sb.

chiche /ʃiʃ/ a mean (**de** with); ~ **que je le fais!** 🔲 I bet you I can do it.

chichis /ʃiʃi/ nmpl 🔲 fuss.

chicorée /ʃikɔʀe/ nf (frisée) endive; (à café) chicory.

chien /ʃjɛ̃/ nm dog; ~ **d'aveugle** guide dog; ~ **de garde** watch-dog. **chienne** nf dog, bitch.

chiffon /ʃifɔ̃/ nm rag; (pour nettoyer) duster; ~ **humide** damp cloth. **chiffonner** [1] vt crumple; (préoccuper 🔲) bother.

chiffre /ʃifʀ/ nm figure; (numéro) number; (code) code; ~**s arabes/ romains** Arabic/Roman numerals; ~**s** (**statistiques**) statistics; ~ **d'affaires** turnover.

chiffrer /ʃifʀe/ [1] vt put a figure on, assess; (texte) encode. □ **se** ~ **à** vpr come to.

chignon /ʃiɲɔ̃/ nm bun, chignon.

Chili /ʃili/ nm Chile.

chimère /ʃimɛʀ/ nf fantasy.

chimie /ʃimi/ nf chemistry. **chimique** a chemical. **chimiste** nmf chemist.

chimpanzé /ʃɛ̃pɑ̃ze/ nm chimpanzee.

Chine /ʃin/ nf China.

chinois, ~**e** /ʃinwa, -z/ a Chinese. ● nm (Ling) Chinese. **C**~, ~**e** nm, f Chinese.

chiot /ʃjo/ nm pup(py).

chips /ʃips/ nf inv crisp; (US) chip.

chirurgie /ʃiʀyʀʒi/ nf surgery; ~ **esthétique** plastic surgery. **chirurgien** nm surgeon.

chlore /klɔʀ/ nm chlorine.

choc /ʃɔk/ nm (heurt) impact, shock; (émotion) shock; (collision) crash; (affrontement) clash; (Méd) shock; **sous le** ~ in shock.

chocolat /ʃɔkɔla/ nm chocolate; (à boire) drinking chocolate; ~ **au lait** milk chocolate; ~ **chaud** hot chocolate; ~ **noir** plain ou dark chocolate.

chœur /kœʀ/ nm (antique) chorus; (chanteurs, nef) choir; **en** ~ in chorus.

choisir /ʃwaziʀ/ [2] vt choose, select.

choix /ʃwa/ nm choice, selection; **fromage ou dessert au** ~ a choice of cheese or dessert; **de** ~ choice; **de premier** ~ top quality.

chômage /ʃomaʒ/ nm unemployment; **au** ~, **en** ~ unemployed; **mettre en** ~ **technique** lay off.

chômeur, -euse /ʃomœʀ, -øz/ nm, f unemployed person; **les** ~**s** the unemployed.

choquer /ʃɔke/ [1] vt shock; (commotionner) shake.

choral, ~**e** (mpl ~**s**) /kɔʀal/ a choral. **chorale** nf choir, choral society.

chorégraphie /kɔʀegʀafi/ nf choreography.

choriste /kɔʀist/ nmf (à l'église) chorister; (à l'opéra) member of the chorus ou choir.

chose /ʃoz/ nf thing; (très) **peu de** ~ nothing much; **pas grand** ~ not much.

chou (pl ~**x**) /ʃu/ nm cabbage; ~ (**à la crème**) cream puff; ~ **de Bruxelles** Brussels sprout; **mon petit** ~ 🔲 my dear.

chouchou, ~**te** /ʃuʃu, -t/ nm, f (de professeur) pet; (du public) darling.

choucroute /ʃukʀut/ nf sauerkraut.

chouette /ʃwɛt/ nf owl. ● a 🔲 super.

chou-fleur (*pl* **choux-fleurs**) /ʃuflœʀ/ *nm* cauliflower.

choyer /ʃwaje/ [31] *vt* pamper.

chrétien, **∼ne** /kʀetjɛ̃, -jɛn/ *a & nm,f* Christian.

Christ /kʀist/ *nm* le ∼ Christ.

chrome /kʀom/ *nm* chromium, chrome.

chromosome /kʀomozom/ *nm* chromosome.

chronique /kʀonik/ *a* chronic. ● *nf* (rubrique) column; (nouvelles) news; (annales) chronicle.

chronologique /kʀonoloʒik/ *a* chronological.

chronomètre /kʀonomɛtʀ/ *nm* stopwatch. **chronométrer** [14] *vt* time.

chrysanthème /kʀizɑ̃tɛm/ *nm* chrysanthemum.

chuchoter /ʃyʃote/ [1] *vt/i* whisper.

chut /ʃyt/ *interj* shh, hush.

chute /ʃyt/ *nf* fall; (déchet) offcut; ∼ (d'eau) waterfall; ∼ **de pluie** rainfall; ∼ **des cheveux** hair loss; ∼ **des ventes** drop in sales; ∼ **5%** 5% drop. **chuter** [1] *vi* fall.

Chypre /ʃipʀ/ *nf* Cyprus.

ci /si/ *adv* here; **∼-gît** here lies; **cet homme-∼** this man; **ces maisons-∼** these houses.

ci-après /siapʀe/ *adv* below.

cible /sibl/ *nf* target.

ciboulette /sibulɛt/ *nf* (Culin) chives (+ *pl*).

cicatrice /sikatʀis/ *nf* scar.

cicatriser /sikatʀize/ [1] *vt* heal. □ **se ∼** *vpr* heal.

ci-dessous /sidəsu/ *adv* below.

ci-dessus /sidəsy/ *adv* above.

cidre /sidʀ/ *nm* cider.

ciel (*pl* **cieux**, **ciels**) /sjɛl, sjø/ *nm* sky; (Relig) heaven; **cieux** (Relig) heaven.

cierge /sjɛʀʒ/ *nm* (church) candle.

cigale /sigal/ *nf* cicada.

cigare /sigaʀ/ *nm* cigar.

cigarette /sigaʀɛt/ *nf* cigarette.

cigogne /sigoɲ/ *nf* stork.

ci-joint /siʒwɛ̃/ *adv* enclosed.

cil /sil/ *nm* eyelash.

cime /sim/ *nf* peak, tip.

ciment /simɑ̃/ *nm* cement.

cimetière /simtjɛʀ/ *nm* cemetery, graveyard; ∼ **de voitures** breaker's yard.

cinéaste /sineast/ *nmf* film-maker.

cinéma /sinema/ *nm* cinema; (US) movie theater.

cinémathèque *nf* film archive; (salle) film theatre.

cinématographique *a* cinema.

cinéphile /sinefil/ *nmf* film lover.

cinglant, **∼e** /sɛ̃glɑ̃, -t/ *a* (vent) biting; (remarque) scathing.

cinglé, **∼e** /sɛ̃gle/ *a* 🔲 crazy.

cinq /sɛ̃k/ *a & nm* five.

cinquante /sɛ̃kɑ̃t/ *a & nm* fifty.

cinquième /sɛ̃kjɛm/ *a & nmf* fifth.

cintre /sɛ̃tʀ/ *nm* coat-hanger; (Archit) curve.

cirage /siʀaʒ/ *nm* polish.

circoncision /siʀkɔ̃sizjɔ̃/ *nf* circumcision.

circonflexe /siʀkɔ̃flɛks/ *a* circumflex.

circonscription /siʀkɔ̃skʀipsjɔ̃/ *nf* district; ∼ **électorale** constituency; (US) district; (de conseiller, maire) ward.

circonscrire /siʀkɔ̃skʀiʀ/ [30] *vt* (incendie, épidémie) contain; (sujet) define.

circonspect, **∼e** /siʀkɔ̃spɛkt/ *a* circumspect.

circonstance /siʀkɔ̃stɑ̃s/ *nf* circumstance; (situation) situation; (occasion) occasion; ∼**s atténuantes** mitigating circumstances.

circuit /siʀkɥi/ nm circuit; (trajet) tour, trip.

circulaire /siʀkylɛʀ/ a & nf circular.

circulation /siʀkylasjɔ̃/ nf circulation; (de véhicules) traffic.

circuler /siʀkyle/ [1] vi (se répandre, être distribué) circulate; (aller d'un lieu à un autre) get around; (en voiture) travel; (piéton) walk; (être en service) (bus, train) run; **faire ~** (badauds) move on; (rumeur) spread.

cire /siʀ/ nf wax.

ciré /siʀe/ nm oilskin.

cirer /siʀe/ [1] vt polish.

cirque /siʀk/ nm circus; (arène) amphitheatre; (désordre: fig) chaos; **faire le ~** 🄴 make a racket 🄴.

ciseau (pl ~x) /sizo/ nm chisel; **~x** scissors.

ciseler /sizle/ [6] vt chisel.

citadelle /sitadɛl/ nf citadel.

citadin, ~e /sitadɛ̃, -in/ nm,f city-dweller. ● a city.

citation /sitasjɔ̃/ nf quotation; (Jur) summons.

cité /site/ nf city; (logements) housing estate; **~ universitaire** (university) halls of residence.

citer /site/ [1] vt quote, cite; (Jur) summon.

citerne /sitɛʀn/ nf tank.

citoyen, ~ne /sitwajɛ̃, -ɛn/ nm,f citizen.

citron /sitʀɔ̃/ nm lemon; **~ vert** lime. **citronnade** nf lemon squash, (still) lemonade.

citrouille /sitʀuj/ nf pumpkin.

civet /sivɛ/ nm stew; **~ de lièvre** jugged hare.

civière /sivjɛʀ/ nf stretcher.

civil, ~e /sivil/ a civil; (non militaire) civilian; (poli) civil. ● nm civilian; **dans le ~** in civilian life; **en ~** in plain clothes.

civilisation /sivilizasjɔ̃/ nf civilization.

civiliser /sivilize/ [1] vt civilize. □ **se ~** vpr become civilized.

civique /sivik/ a civic.

clair, ~e /klɛʀ/ a clear; (éclairé) light, bright; (couleur) light; **le plus ~ de** most of. ● adv clearly; **il faisait ~** it was already light. ● nm **~ de lune** moonlight; **tirer une histoire au ~** get to the bottom of things. **clairement** adv clearly.

clairière /klɛʀjɛʀ/ nf clearing.

clairsemé, ~e /klɛʀsəme/ a sparse.

clamer /klame/ [1] vt proclaim.

clameur /klamœʀ/ nf clamour.

clan /klɑ̃/ nm clan.

clandestin, ~e /klɑ̃dɛstɛ̃, -in/ a secret; (journal) underground; (immigration, travail) illegal; **passager ~** stowaway.

clapier /klapje/ nm (rabbit) hutch.

clapoter /klapɔte/ [1] vi lap.

claquage /klakaʒ/ nm strained muscle; **se faire un ~** pull a muscle.

claque /klak/ nf slap.

claquer /klake/ [1] vi bang; (porte) slam, bang; (fouet) crack; (se casser 🄴) conk out; (mourir 🄴) snuff it 🄴; **~ des doigts** snap one's fingers; **~ des mains** clap one's hands; **il claque des dents** his teeth are chattering. ● vt (porte) slam, bang; (dépenser 🄴) blow; (fatiguer 🄴) tire out.

claquettes /klakɛt/ nfpl tap dancing.

clarifier /klaʀifje/ [45] vt clarify.

clarinette /klaʀinɛt/ nf clarinet.

clarté /klaʀte/ nf light, brightness; (netteté) clarity.

classe /klas/ nf class; (salle: Scol) classroom; (cours) class, lesson; **aller en ~** go to school; **faire la ~**

teach; ~ **ouvrière/moyenne** working/middle class.

classement /klasmɑ̃/ *nm* classification; (d'élèves) grading; (de documents) filing; (rang) place, grade; (de coureur) placing.

classer /klase/ [1] *vt* classify; (par mérite) grade; (*papiers*) file; (Jur) (*affaire*) close. □ **se ~** *vpr* rank.

classeur /klasœʀ/ *nm* (meuble) filing cabinet; (chemise) file; (à anneaux) ring binder.

classification /klasifikasjɔ̃/ *nf* classification.

classique /klasik/ *a* classical; (de qualité) classic; (habituel) classic, standard. ● *nm* classic; (auteur) classical author.

clavecin /klavsɛ̃/ *nm* harpsichord.

clavicule /klavikyl/ *nf* collarbone.

clavier /klavje/ *nm* keyboard; ~ **numérique** keypad.

clé, clef /kle/ *nf* key; (outil) spanner; (Mus) clef; ~ **anglaise** (monkey-)wrench; ~ **de contact** ignition key; ~ **à molette** adjustable spanner; ~ **de voûte** keystone. ● *a inv* key.

clémence /klemɑ̃s/ *nf* (de climat) mildness; (indulgence) leniency.

clergé /klɛʀʒe/ *nm* clergy.

clérical, ~e (*mpl* **-aux**) /kleʀikal, -o/ *a* clerical.

clic /klik/ *nm* (Ordinat) click.

cliché /klife/ *nm* cliché; (Photo) negative.

client, ~e /klijɑ̃, -t/ *nm, f* customer; (d'un avocat) client; (d'un médecin) patient; (d'hôtel) guest; (de taxi) passenger.

clientèle /klijɑ̃tɛl/ *nf* customers, clientele; (d'un avocat) clients, practice; (d'un médecin) patients, practice; (soutien) custom.

cligner /kliɲe/ [1] *vi* ~ **des yeux** blink; ~ **de l'œil** wink.

clignotant /kliɲɔtɑ̃/ *nm* (Auto) indicator, turn.

clignoter /kliɲɔte/ [1] *vi* blink; (lumière) flicker; (comme signal) flash.

climat /klima/ *nm* climate.

climatisation /klimatizasjɔ̃/ *nf* air-conditioning.

clin d'œil /klɛ̃dœj/ *nm* wink; **en un ~** in a flash.

clinique /klinik/ *a* clinical. ● *nf* (private) clinic.

clinquant, ~e /klɛ̃kɑ̃, -t/ *a* showy.

clip /klip/ *nm* video.

cliquer /klike/ [1] *vi* (Ordinat) click (**sur** on).

cliqueter /klikte/ [38] *vi* (couverts) clink; (clés, monnaie) jingle; (ferraille) rattle. **cliquetis** *nm* clink(ing), jingle, rattle.

clivage /klivaʒ/ *nm* divide.

clochard, ~e /klɔʃaʀ, -d/ *nm, f* tramp.

cloche /klɔʃ/ *nf* bell; (imbécile ▪) idiot; ~ **à fromage** cheese-cover.

cloche-pied: à ~ /aklɔʃpje/ *loc* **sauter à ~** hop on one leg.

clocher /klɔʃe/ *nm* bell-tower; (pointu) steeple; **de ~** parochial.

cloison /klwazɔ̃/ *nf* partition; (fig) barrier.

cloître /klwatʀ/ *nm* cloister.

cloîtrer (se) [1] *vpr* shut oneself away.

clonage /klonaʒ/ *nm* cloning.

cloner /klone/ [1] *vt* clone.

cloque /klɔk/ *nf* blister.

clos, ~e /klo, -z/ *a* closed.

clôture /klotyʀ/ *nf* fence; (fermeture) closure; (de magasin, bureau) closing; (de débat, liste) close; (en Bourse) close of trading.

clôturer [1] *vt* enclose, fence in; (festival, séance) close.

clou /klu/ *nm* nail; (furoncle) boil; (de spectacle) star attraction; **les ~s**

(passage) pedestrian crossing; (US) crosswalk.

clouer /klue/ [1] vt nail down; (fig) pin down; **être cloué au lit** be confined to one's bed; **~ le bec à qn** shut sb up.

clouté, **~e** /klute/ a studded; **passage ~** pedestrian crossing; (US) crosswalk.

coaliser (se) /(sə)koalize/ [1] vpr join forces.

coalition /koalisjɔ̃/ nf coalition.

cobaye /kobaj/ nm guinea-pig.

cocaïne /kokain/ nf cocaine.

cocasse /kokas/ a comical.

coccinelle /koksinɛl/ nf ladybird; (US) ladybug.

cocher /koʃe/ [1] vt tick (off), check. ● nm coachman.

cochon, **~ne** /koʃɔ̃, -ɔn/ nm, f (personne ▣) pig. ● a ▣ filthy. ● nm pig. **cochonnerie** nf (saleté ▣) filth; (marchandise ▣) rubbish, junk.

cocon /kokɔ̃/ nm cocoon.

cocorico /kokoriko/ nm cock-a-doodle-doo.

cocotier /kokotje/ nm coconut palm.

cocotte /kokot/ nf (marmite) casserole; **~ minute®** pressure-cooker; **ma ~** ▣ my dear.

cocu, **~e** /koky/ nm, f ▣ deceived husband, deceived wife.

code /kod/ nm code; **~s** dipped headlights; **se mettre en ~s** dip one's headlights; **~ (à) barres** bar code; **~ confidentiel (d'identification)** PIN number; **~ postal** post code; (US) zip code; **~ de la route** Highway Code. **coder** [1] vt code, encode.

coéquipier, **-ière** /koekipje, -jɛʀ/ nm, f team mate.

cœur /kœʀ/ nm heart; (aux cartes) hearts (+ pl); **~ d'artichaut** artichoke heart; **~ de palmier** palm heart; **à ~ ouvert**

(opération) open-heart; (parler) freely; **avoir bon ~** be kind-hearted; **de bon ~** willingly; (rire) heartily; **par ~** by heart; **avoir mal au ~** feel sick ou nauseous; **je veux en avoir le ~ net** I want to be clear in my own mind (about it).

coffre /kofʀ/ nm chest; (pour argent) safe; (Auto) boot; (US) trunk. **coffre-fort** (pl **coffres-forts**) nm safe.

coffret /kofʀɛ/ nm casket, box; (de livres, cassettes) boxed set.

cogner /kone/ [1] vt/i knock. □ **se ~** vpr knock oneself; **se ~ la tête** bump one's head.

cohabiter /koabite/ [1] vi live together.

cohérent, **~e** /koeʀɑ̃, -t/ a coherent; (homogène) consistent.

cohue /koy/ nf crowd.

coi, **~te** /kwa, -t/ a silent.

coiffe /kwaf/ nf headgear.

coiffer /kwafe/ [1] vt do the hair of; (chapeau) put on; (surmonter) cap; **~ qn d'un chapeau** put a hat on sb; **coiffé de** wearing; **être bien/mal coiffé** have tidy/untidy hair. □ **se ~** vpr do one's hair.

coiffeur, **-euse** /kwafœʀ, -øz/ nm, f hairdresser. **coiffeuse** nf dressing-table.

coiffure /kwafyʀ/ nf hairstyle; (métier) hairdressing; (chapeau) hat.

coin /kwɛ̃/ nm corner; (endroit) spot; (cale) wedge; **au ~ du feu** by the fireside; **dans le ~** locally; **du ~** local.

coincer /kwɛ̃se/ [10] vt jam; (caler) wedge; (attraper ▣) catch. □ **se ~** vpr get jammed.

coïncidence /koɛ̃sidɑ̃s/ nf coincidence.

coing /kwɛ̃/ nm quince.

coït /koit/ nm intercourse.

col /kol/ nm collar; (de bouteille) neck; (de montagne) pass; **~ blanc** white-collar worker; **~ roulé**

polo-neck; (US) turtle-neck; ~ de l'utérus cervix; **se casser le ~ du fémur** break one's hip.

colère /kɔlɛʀ/ *nf* anger; (accès) fit of anger; **en ~** angry; **se mettre en ~** lose one's temper; **faire une ~** throw a tantrum.

coléreux, -euse /kɔleʀø, -z/ *a* quick-tempered.

colin /kɔlɛ̃/ *nm* (merlu) hake; (lieu noir) coley.

colique /kɔlik/ *nf* diarrhoea; (Méd) colic.

colis /kɔli/ *nm* parcel.

collaborateur, -trice /kɔlabɔʀatœʀ, -tʀis/ *nm, f* collaborator; (journaliste) contributor; (collègue) colleague.

collaboration /kɔlabɔʀasjɔ̃/ *nf* collaboration (à on); (à ouvrage, projet) contribution (à to).

collaborer /kɔlabɔʀe/ [1] *vi* collaborate (à on); **~ à** (journal) contribute to.

collant, ~e /kɔlã, -t/ *a* (moulant) skin-tight; (poisseux) sticky. ● *nm* (bas) tights, (US) panty hose.

colle /kɔl/ *nf* glue; (en pâte) paste; (problème Ⅲ) poser; (Scol Ⅲ) detention.

collecter /kɔlɛkte/ [1] *vt* collect.

collectif, -ive /kɔlɛktif, -v/ *a* collective; (billet, voyage) group.

collection /kɔlɛksjɔ̃/ *nf* collection; (ouvrages) series (+ sg); (du même auteur) set. **collectionner** [1] *vt* collect. **collectionneur, -euse** *nm, f* collector.

collectivité /kɔlɛktivite/ *nf* community; **~ locale** local authority.

collège /kɔlɛʒ/ *nm* secondary school (up to age 15); (US) junior high school; (assemblée) college. **collégien, ~ne** *nm, f* schoolboy, schoolgirl.

collègue /kɔlɛg/ *nmf* colleague.

coller /kɔle/ [1] *vt* stick; (avec colle liquide) glue; (affiche) stick up; (mettre Ⅲ) stick; (par une question Ⅲ) stump; (Scol Ⅲ) **se faire ~** get a detention; **je me suis fait ~ en maths** I failed *ou* flunked maths. ● *vi* stick (à to); (être collant) be sticky; **~ à** (convenir à) fit, correspond to.

collet /kɔlɛ/ *nm* (piège) snare; **~ monté** prim and proper; **mettre la main au ~ de qn** collar sb.

collier /kɔlje/ *nm* necklace; (de chien) collar.

colline /kɔlin/ *nf* hill.

collision /kɔlizjɔ̃/ *nf* (choc) collision; (lutte) clash; **entrer en ~ (avec)** collide (with).

collyre /kɔliʀ/ *nm* eye drops (+ pl).

colmater /kɔlmate/ [1] *vt* plug, seal.

colombe /kɔlɔ̃b/ *nf* dove.

Colombie /kɔlɔ̃bi/ *nf* Colombia.

colon /kɔlɔ̃/ *nm* settler.

colonel /kɔlɔnɛl/ *nm* colonel.

colonie /kɔlɔni/ *nf* colony; **~ de vacances** children's holiday camp.

colonne /kɔlɔn/ *nf* column; **~ vertébrale** spine; **en ~ par deux** in double file.

colorant /kɔlɔʀã/ *nm* colouring.

colorier /kɔlɔʀje/ [45] *vt* colour (in).

colosse /kɔlɔs/ *nm* giant.

colza /kɔlza/ *nm* rape(-seed).

coma /kɔma/ *nm* coma; **dans le ~** in a coma.

combat /kɔ̃ba/ *nm* fight; (Sport) match; **~s** fighting. **combatif, -ive** *a* eager to fight; (esprit) fighting.

combattre /kɔ̃batʀ/ [11] *vt/i* fight.

combien /kɔ̃bjɛ̃/ *adv* **~ (de)** (quantité) how much; (nombre) how many; (temps) how long; **~ il a changé!** (comme) how he has changed!; **~ y a-t-il d'ici à …?** how far is it to …?; **on est le ∼ aujourd'hui?** what's the date today?

combinaison /kɔ̃binɛzɔ̃/ *nf* combination; (*de femme*) slip; (*bleu de travail*) boiler suit; (*US*) overalls; **∼ d'aviateur** flying-suit; **∼ de plongée** wetsuit.

combine /kɔ̃bin/ *nf* trick; (*fraude*) fiddle; (*intrigue*) scheme.

combiné /kɔ̃bine/ *nm* (*de téléphone*) receiver, handset.

combiner /kɔ̃bine/ [1] *vt* (*réunir*) combine; (*calculer*) devise; **∼ de faire** plan to do.

comble /kɔ̃bl/ *a* packed. ● *nm* height; **∼s** (*mansarde*) attic, loft; **c'est le ∼!** that's the (absolute) limit!

combler /kɔ̃ble/ [1] *vt* fill; (*perte, déficit*) make good; (*désir*) fulfil; **∼ qn de cadeaux** lavish gifts on sb.

combustible /kɔ̃bystibl/ *nm* fuel.

comédie /kɔmedi/ *nf* comedy; (*histoire* 🔟) fuss; **∼ musicale** musical; **jouer la ∼** put on an act. **comédien, ∼ne** *nm, f* actor, actress.

comestible /kɔmɛstibl/ *a* edible.

comète /kɔmɛt/ *nf* comet.

comique /kɔmik/ *a* comical, funny; (*genre*) comic. ● *nm* (*acteur*) comic; (*comédie*) comedy; (*côté drôle*) comical aspect.

commandant /kɔmɑ̃dɑ̃/ *nm* commander; (*dans l'armée de terre*) major; **∼ (de bord)** captain; **∼ en chef** Commander-in-Chief.

commande /kɔmɑ̃d/ *nf* (Comm) order; (Tech) control; **∼s** (*d'avion*) controls.

commandement /kɔmɑ̃dmɑ̃/ *nm* command; (Relig) commandment.

commander /kɔmɑ̃de/ [1] *vt* command; (*acheter*) order; (*étude,*

œuvre d'art) commission; **∼ à** (*maîtriser*) control; **∼ à qn de** command sb to. ● *vi* be in command.

comme /kɔm/ *adv* **∼ c'est bon!** it's so good!; **∼ il est mignon!** isn't he sweet! ● *conj* (*dans une comparaison*) as; (*dans une équivalence, illustration*) like; (*en tant que*) as; (*puisque*) as, since; (*au moment où*) as; **vif ∼ l'éclair** as quick as a flash; **travailler ∼ sage-femme** work as a midwife; **∼ ci ∼ ça** so-so; **∼ il faut** properly; **∼ pour faire** as if to do; **jolie ∼ tout** as pretty as anything; **qu'est-ce qu'il y a ∼ légumes?** what is there in the way of vegetables?

commencer /kɔmɑ̃se/ [10] *vt/i* begin, start; **∼ à faire** begin *ou* start to do.

comment /kɔmɑ̃/ *adv* how; **∼?** (*répétition*) pardon?; (*surprise*) what?; **∼ est-il?** what is he like?; **le ∼ et le pourquoi** the whys and wherefores.

commentaire /kɔmɑ̃tɛʀ/ *nm* comment; (*d'un texte, événement*) commentary. **commentateur, -trice** *nm, f* commentator.

commenter /kɔmɑ̃te/ [1] *vt* comment on; (*film, visite*) provide a commentary for; (*radio, TV*) commentate.

commérages /kɔmeʀaʒ/ *nmpl* gossip.

commerçant, ∼e /kɔmɛʀsɑ̃, -t/ *a* (*rue*) shopping; (*personne*) business-minded. ● *nm, f* shopkeeper.

commerce /kɔmɛʀs/ *nm* trade, commerce; (*magasin*) business; **faire du ∼** be in business; **∼ électronique** e-commerce.

commercial, ∼e (*mpl* **-iaux**) /kɔmɛʀsjal, -jo/ *a* commercial. **commercialiser** [1] *vt* market.

commettre /kɔmɛtʀ/ [42] *vt* commit.

commis /kɔmi/ *nm* (de magasin) assistant; (de bureau) clerk.

commissaire /kɔmisɛR/ *nm* commissioner; (Sport) steward; ~ **(de police)** (police) superintendent. **commissaire-priseur** (*pl* **commissaires-priseurs**) *nm* auctioneer.

commissariat /kɔmisaRja/ *nm* ~ **(de police)** police station.

commission /kɔmisjɔ̃/ *nf* commission; (course) errand; (message) message; ~**s** shopping.

commode /kɔmɔd/ *a* handy, convenient; (facile) easy; **il n'est pas** ~ he's a difficult customer. ● *nf* chest (of drawers).
commodité *nf* convenience.

commotion /kɔmosjɔ̃/ *nf* ~ **(cérébrale)** concussion.

commun, ~**e** /kɔmœ̃, yn/ *a* common; (*effort, action*) joint; (*frais, pièce*) shared; **en** ~ jointly; **avoir** *ou* **mettre en** ~ share; **le** ~ **des mortels** ordinary mortals.
communal, ~**e** (*mpl* -**aux**) *a* of the commune, local.

communauté /kɔmynote/ *nf* community.

commune /kɔmyn/ *nf* (circonscription, collectivité) commune.

communicatif, -**ive** /kɔmynikatif, -v/ *a* (*personne*) talkative; (*gaieté*) infectious.

communication /kɔmynikasjɔ̃/ *nf* communication; (téléphonique) call; ~**s** (relations) communications (+ *pl*); **voies** *ou* **moyens de** ~ communications (+ *pl*).

communier /kɔmynje/ [45] *vi* (Relig) receive communion; (fig) commune.

communiqué /kɔmynike/ *nm* statement; (de presse) communiqué.

communiquer /kɔmynike/ [1] *vt* pass on, communicate; (*date, décision*) announce. ● *vi* communicate. □ **se** ~ **à** *vpr* spread to.

communiste /kɔmynist/ *a & nmf* communist.

commutateur /kɔmytatœR/ *nm* (Électr) switch.

compagne /kɔ̃paɲ/ *nf* companion.

compagnie /kɔ̃paɲi/ *nf* company; **tenir** ~ **à** keep company; **en** ~ **de** together with; ~ **aérienne** airline.

compagnon /kɔ̃paɲɔ̃/ *nm* companion.

comparable /kɔ̃paRabl/ *a* comparable (à to). **comparaison** *nf* comparison; (littéraire) simile.

comparaître /kɔ̃paRɛtR/ [18] *vi* (Jur) appear (**devant** before).

comparatif, -**ive** /kɔ̃paRatif, v/ *a & nm* comparative.

comparer /kɔ̃paRe/ [1] *vt* compare (**a** with). □ **se** ~ *vpr* compare oneself; (être comparable) be comparable.

compartiment /kɔ̃paRtimɑ̃/ *nm* compartment.

comparution /kɔ̃paRysjɔ̃/ *nf* (Jur) appearance.

compas /kɔ̃pa/ *nm* (pair of) compasses; (boussole) compass.

compassion /kɔ̃pasjɔ̃/ *nf* compassion.

compatible /kɔ̃patibl/ *a* compatible.

compatir /kɔ̃patir/ [2] *vi* sympathize; ~ **à** share in.

compatriote /kɔ̃patRijɔt/ *nmf* compatriot.

compensation /kɔ̃pɑ̃sasjɔ̃/ *nf* compensation. **compenser** [1] *vt* compensate for, make up for.

compère /kɔ̃pɛR/ *nm* accomplice.

compétence /kɔpetɑ̃s/ *nf* competence; (fonction) domain, sphere; **entrer dans les ∼s de qn** be in sb's domain. **compétent, ∼e** *a* competent.

compétition /kɔ̃petisjɔ̃/ *nf* competition; (sportive) event; **de ∼** competitive.

complaire (se) /(sə)kɔ̃plɛR/ [47] *vpr* **se ∼ dans** delight in.

complaisance /kɔ̃plɛzɑ̃s/ *nf* kindness; (indulgence) indulgence.

complément /kɔ̃plemɑ̃/ *nm* supplement; (Gram) complement; **∼ (d'objet)** (Gram) object; **∼ d'information** further information. **complémentaire** *a* complementary; (renseignements) supplementary.

complet, -ète /kɔ̃plɛ, -t/ *a* complete; (train, hôtel) full. ● *nm* suit.

compléter /kɔ̃plete/ [14] *vt* complete; (agrémenter) complement. □ **se ∼** *vpr* complement each other.

complexe /kɔ̃plɛks/ *a* complex. ● *nm* (sentiment, bâtiments) complex.

complexé, ∼e /kɔ̃plekse/ *a* **être ∼** have a lot of hang-ups.

complice /kɔ̃plis/ *nm* accomplice.

compliment /kɔ̃plimɑ̃/ *nm* compliment; **∼s** (félicitations) compliments, congratulations.

compliquer /kɔ̃plike/ [1] *vt* complicate. □ **se ∼** *vpr* become complicated.

complot /kɔ̃plo/ *nm* plot.

comportement /kɔ̃pɔRtəmɑ̃/ *nm* behaviour; (de joueur, voiture) performance.

comporter /kɔ̃pɔRte/ [1] *vt* (être composé de) comprise; (inclure) include; (risque) entail. □ **se ∼** *vpr* behave; (joueur, voiture) perform.

composant /kɔ̃pozɑ̃/ *nm* component.

composé, ∼e /kɔ̃poze/ *a*

composite; (salade) mixed; (guindé) affected. ● *nm* compound.

composer /kɔ̃poze/ [1] *vt* make up, compose; (chanson, visage) compose; (numéro) dial; (page) typeset. ● *vi* (transiger) compromise. □ **se ∼ de** *vpr* be made up *ou* composed of.

compositeur, -trice *nm, f* (Mus) composer.

composter /kɔ̃pɔste/ [1] *vt* (billet) punch.

compote /kɔ̃pɔt/ *nf* stewed fruit; **∼ de pommes** stewed apples.

compréhensible /kɔ̃pReɑ̃sibl/ *a* understandable; (intelligible) comprehensible.

compréhensif, -ive /kɔ̃pReɑ̃sif, -v/ *a* understanding.

compréhension /kɔ̃pReɑ̃sjɔ̃/ *nf* understanding, comprehension.

comprendre /kɔ̃pRɑ̃dR/ [50] *vt* understand; (comporter) comprise, be made up of. □ **se ∼** *vpr* (personnes) understand each other; **ça se comprend** that is understandable.

compresse /kɔ̃pRɛs/ *nf* compress.

comprimé /kɔ̃pRime/ *nm* tablet.

comprimer /kɔ̃pRime/ [1] *vt* compress; (réduire) reduce.

compris, ∼e /kɔ̃pRi, -z/ *a* included; (d'accord) agreed; **∼ entre** (contained) between; **service (non) ∼** service (not) included; **tout ∼** (all) inclusive; **y ∼** including.

compromettre /kɔ̃pRɔmɛtR/ [42] *vt* compromise. **compromis** *nm* compromise.

comptabilité /kɔ̃patibilite/ *nf* accountancy; (comptes) accounts; (service) accounts department.

comptable /kɔ̃tabl/ *a* accounting. ● *nmf* accountant.

comptant /kɔ̃tɑ̃/ *adv* (payer) (in) cash; (acheter) for cash.

compte /kɔ̃t/ *nm* count; (facture,

comptabilité) account; (nombre exact) right number; ~ **bancaire,** ~ **en banque** bank account; **prendre qch en** ~, **tenir** ~ **de qch** take sth into account; **se rendre** ~ **de** realize; **demander/rendre des** ~**s** ask for/ give an explanation; **à bon** ~ cheaply; **s'en tirer à bon** ~ get off lightly; **travailler à son** ~ be self-employed; **faire le** ~ **de** count; **pour le** ~ **de** on behalf of; **sur le** ~ **de** about; **au bout du** ~ all things considered; ~ **à rebours** countdown.

compte-gouttes /kɔ̃tgut/ *nm inv* (Méd) dropper; **au** ~ (fig) in dribs and drabs.

compter /kɔ̃te/ [1] *vt* count; (prévoir) allow, reckon on; (facturer) charge for; (avoir) have; (classer) consider; ~ **faire** intend to do. • *vi* (calculer, importer) count; ~ **avec** reckon with; ~ **parmi** (figurer) be considered among; ~ **sur** rely on, count on.

compte(-)rendu /kɔ̃trãdy/ *nm* report; (de film, livre) review.

compteur /kɔ̃tœʀ/ *nm* meter; ~ **de vitesse** speedometer.

comptine /kɔ̃tin/ *nf* nursery rhyme.

comptoir /kɔ̃twaʀ/ *nm* counter; (de café) bar.

comte /kɔ̃t/ *nm* count.

comté /kɔ̃te/ *nm* county.

comtesse /kɔ̃tɛs/ *nf* countess.

con, ~**ne** /kɔ̃, kɔn/ *a* ⊠ bloody stupid ⊠. • *nm, f* ⊠ bloody fool ⊠.

concentrer /kɔ̃sɑ̃tʀe/ [1] *vt* concentrate. □ **se** ~ *vpr* be concentrated.

concept /kɔ̃sɛpt/ *nm* concept.

concerner /kɔ̃sɛʀne/ [1] *vt* concern; **en ce qui me concerne** as far as I am concerned.

concert /kɔ̃sɛʀ/ *nm* concert; **de** ~ in unison.

concerter /kɔ̃sɛʀte/ [1] *vt* organize, prepare. □ **se** ~ *vpr* confer.

concession /kɔ̃sesjɔ̃/ *nf* concession; (terrain) plot.

concevoir /kɔ̃svwaʀ/ [52] *vt* (imaginer, engendrer) conceive; (comprendre) understand; (élaborer) design.

concierge /kɔ̃sjɛʀʒ/ *nmf* caretaker.

concilier /kɔ̃silje/ [45] *vt* reconcile. □ **se** ~ *vpr* (s'attirer) win (over).

concis, ~**e** /kɔ̃si, -z/ *a* concise.

conclure /kɔ̃klyʀ/ [16] *vt* conclude; ~ **à** conclude in favour of. • *vi* ~ **en faveur de/contre** find in favour of/against. **conclusion** *nf* conclusion.

concombre /kɔ̃kɔ̃bʀ/ *nm* cucumber.

concordance /kɔ̃kɔʀdɑ̃s/ *nf* agreement.

concourir /kɔ̃kuʀiʀ/ [20] *vi* compete. • *vt* ~ **à** contribute towards.

concours /kɔ̃kuʀ/ *nm* competition; (examen) competitive examination; (aide) help; (de circonstances) combination.

concret, -ète /kɔ̃kʀɛ, -t/ *a* concrete.

concrétiser /kɔ̃kʀetize/ [1] *vt* give concrete form to. □ **se** ~ *vpr* materialize.

conçu, ~**e** /kɔ̃sy/ *a* **bien/mal** ~ well/badly designed.

concubinage /kɔ̃kybinaʒ/ *nm* cohabitation; **vivre en** ~ live together, cohabit.

concurrence /kɔ̃kyʀɑ̃s/ *nf* competition; **faire** ~ **à** compete with; **jusqu'à** ~ **de** up to a limit of.

concurrencer /kɔ̃kyʀɑ̃se/ [10] *vt* compete with.

concurrent, ~**e** /kɔ̃kyʀɑ̃, -t/

nm, f competitor; (Scol) candidate.
● *a* rival.

condamnation /kɔ̃danasjɔ̃/ *nf*
condemnation; (peine) sentence;
~ **centralisée des portières** central
locking. **condamné**, ~**e** *nm, f*
condemned man, condemned
woman. **condamner** [1] *vt*
(censurer, obliger) condemn; (Jur)
sentence; (*porte*) block up.

condition /kɔ̃disjɔ̃/ *nf* condition;
~**s** (prix) terms; **à** ~ **de** *ou* **que**
provided (that); **sans** ~
unconditional(ly); **sous** ~
conditionally.

conditionnel, ~**le** /kɔ̃disjɔnɛl/
a conditional. ● *nm* conditional
(tense).

conditionnement /kɔ̃disjɔnmɑ̃/
nm conditioning; (emballage)
packaging.

condoléances /kɔ̃dɔleɑ̃s/ *nfpl*
condolences.

conducteur, **-trice** /kɔ̃dyktœr,
-tris/ *nm, f* driver.

conduire /kɔ̃dyir/ [17] *vt* take (à
to); (guider) lead; (Auto) drive;
(*affaire*) conduct; ~ **à** (faire aboutir)
lead to. ● *vi* drive. ◻ **se** ~ *vpr*
behave.

conduit /kɔ̃dyi/ *nm* duct.

conduite /kɔ̃dyit/ *nf* conduct,
behaviour; (Auto) driving; (tuyau)
pipe; **voiture avec** ~ **à droite** right-
hand drive car.

confection /kɔ̃fɛksjɔ̃/ *nf* making;
de ~ ready-made; **la** ~ the
clothing industry.

conférence /kɔ̃ferɑ̃s/ *nf*
conference; (exposé) lecture; ~ **au**
sommet summit meeting.
conférencier, **-ière** *nm, f*
lecturer.

confesser /kɔ̃fese/ [1] *vt* confess.
◻ **se** ~ *vpr* go to confession.

confiance /kɔ̃fjɑ̃s/ *nf* trust; **avoir**
~ **en** trust.

confiant, ~**e** /kɔ̃fjɑ̃, -t/ *a* (assuré)
confident; (sans défiance) trusting.

confidence /kɔ̃fidɑ̃s/ *nf*
confidence.

confidentiel, ~**le** /kɔ̃fidɑ̃sjɛl/ *a*
confidential.

confier /kɔ̃fje/ [45] *vt* ~ **à qn**
entrust sb with; ~ **un secret à qn**
tell sb a secret. ◻ **se** ~ **à** *vpr*
confide in.

confiner /kɔ̃fine/ [1] *vt* confine;
~ **à** border on. ◻ **se** ~ *vpr*
confine oneself (à, dans to).

confirmation /kɔ̃firmasjɔ̃/ *nf*
confirmation. **confirmer** [1] *vt*
confirm.

confiserie /kɔ̃fizri/ *nf* sweet
shop; ~**s** confectionery.

confisquer /kɔ̃fiske/ [1] *vt*
confiscate.

confit, ~**e** /kɔ̃fi, -t/ *a* candied;
(*fruits*) crystallized. ● *nm* ~ **de**
canard confit of duck.

confiture /kɔ̃fityr/ *nf* jam.

conflit /kɔ̃fli/ *nm* conflict.

confondre /kɔ̃fɔ̃dr/ [3] *vt*
confuse, mix up; (étonner)
confound. ◻ **se** ~ *vpr* merge; **se**
~ **en excuses** apologize profusely.

conforme /kɔ̃fɔrm/ *a* **être** ~ **à**
comply with; (être en accord) be in
keeping with.

conformer /kɔ̃fɔrme/ [1] *vt*
adapt. ◻ **se** ~ **à** *vpr* conform to.

conformité /kɔ̃fɔrmite/ *nf*
compliance, conformity; **agir en** ~
avec act in accordance with.

confort /kɔ̃fɔr/ *nm* comfort; **tout**
~ with all mod cons.
confortable *a* comfortable.

confrère /kɔ̃frɛr/ *nm* colleague.

confronter /kɔ̃frɔ̃te/ [1] *vt*
confront; (*textes*) compare. ◻ **se**
~ **à** *vpr* be confronted with.

confus, ~**e** /kɔ̃fy, -z/ *a* confused;
(gêné) embarrassed.

congé /kɔ̃ʒe/ *nm* holiday; (arrêt
momentané) time off, leave; (avis de

départ) notice; **en** ~ on holiday *ou* leave; ~ **de maladie/maternité** sick/maternity leave; **jour de** ~ day off; **prendre** ~ **de** take one's leave of.

congédier /kɔ̃ʒedje/ [45] *vt* dismiss.

congélateur /kɔ̃ʒelatœʀ/ *nm* freezer.

congeler /kɔ̃ʒle/ [6] *vt* freeze.

congère /kɔ̃ʒɛʀ/ *nf* snowdrift.

congrès /kɔ̃gʀɛ/ *nm* conference; (Pol) congress.

conjoint, ~**e** /kɔ̃ʒwɛ̃, -t/ *nm, f* spouse. ● *a* joint.

conjonctivite /kɔ̃ʒɔ̃ktivit/ *nf* conjunctivitis.

conjoncture /kɔ̃ʒɔ̃ktyʀ/ *nf* situation; (économique) economic climate.

conjugaison /kɔ̃ʒygɛzɔ̃/ *nf* conjugation.

conjugal, ~**e** (*mpl* -**aux**) /kɔ̃ʒy-gal, -o/ *a* conjugal, married.

conjuguer /kɔ̃ʒyge/ [1] *vt* (Gram) conjugate; (*efforts*) combine. □ **se** ~ *vpr* (Gram) be conjugated; (*facteurs*) be combined.

conjurer /kɔ̃ʒyʀe/ [1] *vt* (éviter) avert, (implorer) beg.

connaissance /kɔnɛsɑ̃s/ *nf* knowledge; (personne) acquaintance; ~**s** (science) knowledge; **faire la** ~ **de** meet; (apprécier une personne) get to know; **perdre/reprendre** ~ lose/regain consciousness; **sans** ~ unconscious.

connaisseur /kɔnɛsœʀ/ *nm* expert, connoisseur.

connaître /kɔnɛtʀ/ [18] *vt* know; (*difficultés, faim, succès*) experience; **faire** ~ make known. □ **se** ~ *vpr* (se rencontrer) meet; **s'y** ~ **en** know (all) about.

connecter /kɔnɛkte/ [1] *vt* connect; **être/ne pas être connecté**

be on-/off-line. □ **se** ~ **à** *vpr* (Ordinat) log on to.

connerie /kɔnʀi/ *nf* ▣ **faire une** ~ do something stupid; **dire des** ~**s** talk rubbish.

connu, ~**e** /kɔny/ *a* well-known.

conquérant, ~**e** /kɔ̃keʀɑ̃, -t/ *nm, f* conqueror.

conquête /kɔ̃kɛt/ *nf* conquest.

consacrer /kɔ̃sakʀe/ [1] *vt* devote; (Relig) consecrate; (sanctionner) sanction. □ **se** ~ **à** *vpr* devote oneself to.

conscience /kɔ̃sjɑ̃s/ *nf* conscience; (perception) awareness; (de collectivité) consciousness; **avoir/prendre** ~ **de** be/become aware of; **perdre/reprendre** ~ lose/regain consciousness; **avoir bonne/mauvaise** ~ have a clear/guilty conscience.

conscient, ~**e** /kɔ̃sjɑ̃, -t/ *a* conscious; ~ **de** aware *ou* conscious of.

conseil /kɔ̃sɛj/ *nm* (pièce of) advice; (assemblée) council, committee; (séance) meeting; (personne) consultant; ~ **d'administration** board of directors; ~ **en gestion** management consultant; ~ **des ministres** Cabinet. ~ **municipal** town council.

conseiller[1] /kɔ̃seje/ [1] *vt* advise; ~ **à qn** advise sb to; ~ **qch à qn** recommend sth to sb.

conseiller[2], -**ère** /kɔ̃seje, -jɛʀ/ *nm, f* adviser, counsellor; ~ **municipal** town councillor; ~ **d'orientation** careers adviser.

consentement /kɔ̃sɑ̃tmɑ̃/ *nm* consent.

conséquence /kɔ̃sekɑ̃s/ *nf* consequence; **en** ~ (comme il convient) accordingly; **en** ~ (de quoi) as a result of which.

conséquent, ~**e** /kɔ̃sekɑ̃, -t/ *a* consistent, logical; (important)

conservateur, -trice /kɔ̃sɛʀvatœʀ, -tʀis/ *a* conservative. ● *nm, f* (Pol) conservative; (de musée) curator. ● *nm* preservative.

conservation /kɔ̃sɛʀvasjɔ̃/ *nf* preservation; (d'espèce, patrimoine) conservation.

conservatoire /kɔ̃sɛʀvatwaʀ/ *nm* academy.

conserve /kɔ̃sɛʀv/ *nf* tinned *ou* canned food; **en ~** tinned, canned; **boîte de ~** tin, can.

conserver /kɔ̃sɛʀve/ [1] *vt* keep; (en bon état) preserve; (Culin) preserve. □ **se ~** *vpr* (Culin) keep.

considérer /kɔ̃sideʀe/ [14] *vt* consider; (respecter) esteem; **~ comme** consider to be.

consigne /kɔ̃siɲ/ *nf* (de gare) left-luggage office; (US) baggage checkroom; (somme) deposit; (ordres) orders; **~ automatique** left-luggage lockers; (US) baggage lockers.

consistance /kɔ̃sistɑ̃s/ *nf* consistency; (fig) substance, weight. **consistant, ~e** *a* solid; (épais) thick.

consister /kɔ̃siste/ [1] *vi* **~ en/ dans** consist of/in; **~ à faire** consist in doing.

consoler /kɔ̃sɔle/ [1] *vt* console. □ **se ~** *vpr* find consolation; **se ~ de qch** get over sth.

consolider /kɔ̃sɔlide/ [1] *vt* strengthen; (fig) consolidate.

consommateur, -trice /kɔ̃sɔmatœʀ, -tʀis/ *nm, f* (Comm) consumer; (dans un café) customer.

consommation /kɔ̃sɔmasjɔ̃/ *nf* consumption; (accomplissement) consummation; (boisson) drink; **de ~** (Comm) consumer.

consommer /kɔ̃sɔme/ [1] *vt* consume, use; (manger) eat; (boire) drink; (mariage) consummate.

□ **se ~** *vpr* (être mangé) be eaten; (être utilisé) be used.

consonne /kɔ̃sɔn/ *nf* consonant.

constat /kɔ̃sta/ *nm* (official) report; **~ (à l')amiable** accident report drawn up by those involved.

constatation /kɔ̃statasjɔ̃/ *nf* observation, statement of fact.

constater [1] *vt* note, notice; (certifier) certify.

consternation /kɔ̃stɛʀnasjɔ̃/ *nf* dismay.

constipé, ~e /kɔ̃stipe/ *a* constipated; (fig) uptight.

constituer /kɔ̃stitɥe/ [1] *vt* (composer) make up, constitute; (organiser) form; (être) constitute; **constitué de** made up of. □ **se ~ prisonnier** *vpr* **se ~** give oneself up.

constitution /kɔ̃stitysjɔ̃/ *nf* formation, setting up; (Pol, Méd) constitution.

constructeur /kɔ̃stʀyktœʀ/ *nm* manufacturer, builder.

construction /kɔ̃stʀyksjɔ̃/ *nf* building; (structure, secteur) construction; (fabrication) manufacture.

construire /kɔ̃stʀɥiʀ/ [17] *vt* build; (système, phrase) construct.

consulat /kɔ̃syla/ *nm* consulate.

consultation /kɔ̃syltasjɔ̃/ *nf* consultation; (réception: Méd) surgery; (US) office; **heures de ~** surgery *ou* office (US) hours.

consulter /kɔ̃sylte/ [1] *vt* consult. ● *vi* (médecin) hold surgery, see patients. □ **se ~** *vpr* consult together.

contact /kɔ̃takt/ *nm* contact; (toucher) touch; **au ~ de** on contact with; (personne) by contact with, by seeing; **mettre/couper le ~** (Auto) switch on/off the ignition;

substantial; **par ~** consequently, therefore.

prendre ~ **avec** get in touch with. **contacter** [1] vt contact.

contagieux, -ieuse /kɔ̃taʒjø, -z/ a contagious.

conte /kɔ̃t/ nm tale; ~ **de fées** fairy tale.

contempler /kɔ̃tɑ̃ple/ [1] vt contemplate.

contemporain, ~e /kɔ̃tɑ̃pɔʀɛ̃, -ɛn/ a & nm,f contemporary.

contenance /kɔ̃t(ə)nɑ̃s/ nf (volume) capacity; (allure) bearing; **perdre** ~ lose one's composure.

contenir /kɔ̃t(ə)niʀ/ [58] vt contain; (avoir une capacité de) hold. □ **se** ~ vpr contain oneself.

content, ~e /kɔ̃tɑ̃, -t/ a pleased, happy (**de** with); ~ **de faire** pleased ou happy to do.

contenter /kɔ̃tɑ̃te/ [1] vt satisfy. □ **se** ~ **de** vpr content oneself with.

contenu /kɔ̃t(ə)ny/ nm (de récipient) contents (+ pl); (de texte) content.

conter /kɔ̃te/ [1] vt tell, relate.

contestation /kɔ̃tɛstasjɔ̃/ nf dispute; (opposition) protest.

contester /kɔ̃tɛste/ [1] vt question, dispute; (s'opposer) protest against. ● vi protest.

contour, -euse /kɔ̃tœʀ, -øz/ nm,f storyteller.

contigu, ~ë /kɔ̃tigy/ a adjacent (**à** to).

continent /kɔ̃tinɑ̃/ nm continent.

continu, ~e /kɔ̃tiny/ a continuous.

continuer /kɔ̃tinɥe/ [1] vt continue. ● vi continue, go on; ~ **à** ou **de faire** carry on ou go on ou continue doing.

contorsionner (se) /(sə)kɔ̃tɔʀsjɔne/ [1] vpr wriggle.

contour /kɔ̃tuʀ/ nm outline, contour; ~**s** (d'une route) twists and turns, bends.

contourner /kɔ̃tuʀne/ [1] vt go

round, by-pass; (difficulté) get round.

contraceptif, -ive /kɔ̃tʀasɛptif, -v/ a contraceptive. ● nm contraceptive. **contraception** nf contraception.

contracter /kɔ̃tʀakte/ [1] vt (maladie) contract; (dette) incur; (muscle) tense; (assurance) take out. □ **se** ~ vpr contract.

contractuel, ~le /kɔ̃tʀaktɥɛl/ nm,f (agent) traffic warden.

contradictoire /kɔ̃tʀadiktwaʀ/ a contradictory; (débat) open.

contraignant, ~e /kɔ̃tʀɛɲɑ̃, -t/ a restricting.

contraindre /kɔ̃tʀɛ̃dʀ/ [22] vt force, compel (**à faire** to do).

contrainte /kɔ̃tʀɛ̃t/ nf constraint.

contraire /kɔ̃tʀɛʀ/ a opposite; ~ **à** contrary to. ● nm opposite; **au** ~ on the contrary; **au** ~ **de** unlike.

contrarier /kɔ̃tʀaʀje/ [45] vt annoy; (projet, volonté) frustrate; (chagriner) upset.

contraste /kɔ̃tʀast/ nm contrast.

contrat /kɔ̃tʀa/ nm contract.

contravention /kɔ̃tʀavɑ̃sjɔ̃/ nf (parking) ticket; **en** ~ in breach (**à** of).

contre /kɔ̃tʀ(ə)/ prép against; (en échange de) for; **par** ~ on the other hand; **tout** ~ close by. **contre-attaque** (pl ~**s**) nf counter-attack. **contre-attaquer** [1] vt counter-attack. **contre-balancer** [10] vt counterbalance.

contrebande /kɔ̃tʀəbɑ̃d/ nf contraband; **faire la** ~ **de** smuggle.

contrebas: en ~ /ɑ̃kɔ̃tʀəba/ loc below.

contrebasse /kɔ̃tʀəbas/ nf double bass.

contrecœur: à ~ /akɔ̃tʀəkœʀ/ loc reluctantly.

contrecoup /kɔ̃tʀəku/ nm effects, repercussions.

contredire /kɔ̃trədiʀ/ [37] vt contradict. □ se ~ vpr contradict oneself.

contrée /kɔ̃tre/ nf region; (pays) land.

contrefaçon /kɔ̃trəfasɔ̃/ nf (objet imité, action) forgery.

contre-indiqué, -e /kɔ̃trɛ̃dike/ a (Méd) contra-indicated; (déconseillé) not recommended.

contre-jour: à ~ /akɔ̃trəʒuʀ/ loc against the light.

contrepartie /kɔ̃trəparti/ nf compensation; en ~ in exchange, in return.

contreplaqué /kɔ̃trəplake/ nm plywood.

contresens /kɔ̃trəsɑ̃s/ nm misinterpretation; (absurdité) nonsense; à ~ the wrong way.

contretemps /kɔ̃trətɑ̃/ nm hitch; à ~ (fig) at the wrong time.

contribuable /kɔ̃tribɥabl/ nmf taxpayer.

contribuer /kɔ̃tribɥe/ [1] vt contribute (à to, towards).

contrôle /kɔ̃trol/ nm (maîtrise) control; (vérification) check; (des prix) control; (poinçon) hallmark; (Scol) test; ~ **continu** continuous assessment; ~ **des changes** exchange control; ~ **des naissances** birth control; ~ **de soi-même** self-control; ~ **technique** (des véhicules) MOT (test).

contrôler /kɔ̃trole/ [1] vt (vérifier) check; (surveiller, maîtriser) control. □ se ~ vpr control oneself.

contrôleur, -euse /kɔ̃trolœr, -øz/ nm, f inspector.

convaincre /kɔ̃vɛ̃kʀ/ [59] vt convince; ~ **qn de faire** persuade sb to do.

convalescence /kɔ̃valesɑ̃s/ nf convalescence; **être en** ~ be convalescing.

convenable /kɔ̃vnabl/ a (correct) decent, proper; (approprié) suitable; (acceptable) reasonable, acceptable.

convenance /kɔ̃vnɑ̃s/ nf **à ma** ~ to my satisfaction; **les** ~**s** convention.

convenir /kɔ̃vniʀ/ [58] vt/i be suitable; ~ **à** suit; ~ **que** admit that; ~ **de qch** (avouer) admit sth; (s'accorder sur) agree on sth; ~ **de faire** agree to do; **il convient de** it is advisable to; (selon les bienséances) it would be right to.

convention /kɔ̃vɑ̃sjɔ̃/ nf agreement, convention; (clause) article, clause; ~**s** (convenances) convention; **de** ~ conventional; ~ **collective** industrial agreement.

convenu, -e /kɔ̃vny/ a agreed.

conversation /kɔ̃vɛʀsasjɔ̃/ nf conversation.

convertir /kɔ̃vɛʀtiʀ/ [2] vt convert (à to; en into). □ se ~ vpr be converted, convert.

conviction /kɔ̃viksjɔ̃/ nf conviction; **avoir la** ~ **que** be convinced that.

convivial, -e (mpl **-iaux**) /kɔ̃vivjal, -jo/ a convivial; (Ordinat) user-friendly.

convocation /kɔ̃vɔkasjɔ̃/ nf (Jur) summons; (d'une assemblée) convening; (document) notification to attend.

convoi /kɔ̃vwa/ nm convoy; (train) train; ~ **(funèbre)** funeral procession.

convoquer /kɔ̃vɔke/ [1] vt (assemblée) convene; (personne) summon; **être convoqué pour un entretien** be called for interview.

coopération /kɔɔperasjɔ̃/ nf cooperation; (Mil) civilian national service abroad.

coordination /kɔɔʀdinasjɔ̃/ nf coordination. **coordonnées** nfpl coordinates; (adresse) address and telephone number.

copain /kɔpɛ̃/ *nm* friend; (*petit ami*) boyfriend.

copie /kɔpi/ *nf* copy; (Scol) paper; ~ **d'examen** exam paper *ou* script; ~ **de sauvegarde** back-up copy.

copier /kɔpje/ [45] *vt/i* copy; ~ **sur** (Scol) copy *ou* crib from.

copieux, -ieuse /kɔpjø, -z/ *a* copious.

copine /kɔpin/ *nf* friend; (*petite amie*) girlfriend.

coq /kɔk/ *nm* cockerel.

coque /kɔk/ *nf* shell; (*de bateau*) hull.

coquelicot /kɔkliko/ *nm* poppy.

coqueluche /kɔklyʃ/ *nf* whooping cough.

coquet, ~te /kɔkɛ, -t/ *a* flirtatious; (*élégant*) pretty; (*somme* 🎯) tidy.

coquetier /kɔktje/ *nm* eggcup.

coquillage /kɔkijaʒ/ *nm* shellfish; (*coquille*) shell.

coquille /kɔkij/ *nf* shell; (*faute*) misprint; ~ **Saint-Jacques** scallop.

coquin, ~e /kɔkɛ̃, -in/ *a* mischievous. ●*nm, f* rascal.

cor /kɔr/ *nm* (Mus) horn; (*au pied*) corn.

corail (*pl* **-aux**) /kɔraj, -o/ *nm* coral.

corbeau (*pl* **~x**) /kɔrbo/ *nm* (*oiseau*) crow.

corbeille /kɔrbɛj/ *nf* basket; ~ **à papier** waste-paper basket.

corbillard /kɔrbijar/ *nm* hearse.

cordage /kɔrdaʒ/ *nm* rope; ~**s** (Naut) rigging.

corde /kɔrd/ *nf* rope; (*d'arc, de violon*) string; ~ **à linge** washing line; ~ **à sauter** skipping-rope; ~ **raide** tightrope; ~**s vocales** vocal cords.

cordon /kɔrdɔ̃/ *nm* string, cord; ~ **de police** police cordon.

cordonnier /kɔrdɔnje/ *nm* cobbler.

Corée /kɔre/ *nf* Korea.

coriace /kɔrjas/ *a* tough.

corne /kɔrn/ *nf* horn.

corneille /kɔrnɛj/ *nf* crow.

cornemuse /kɔrnəmyz/ *nf* bagpipes (+ *pl*).

corner /kɔrne/ [1] *vt* (*page*) turn down the corner of; **page cornée** dog-eared page. ●*vi* (Auto) hoot, honk.

cornet /kɔrnɛ/ *nm* (*paper*) cone; (*crème glacée*) cornet, cone.

corniche /kɔrniʃ/ *nf* cornice; (*route*) cliff road.

cornichon /kɔrniʃɔ̃/ *nm* gherkin.

corporel, ~le /kɔrpɔrɛl/ *a* bodily; (*châtiment*) corporal.

corps /kɔr/ *nm* body; (Mil) corps; **combat ~ à ~** hand-to-hand combat; ~ **électoral** electorate; ~ **enseignant** teaching profession.

correct, ~e /kɔrɛkt/ *a* proper, correct; (*exact*) correct.

correcteur, -trice /kɔrɛktœr, -tris/ *nm, f* (*d'épreuves*) proofreader; (Scol) examiner; ~ **liquide** correction fluid; ~ **d'orthographe** spell-checker.

correction /kɔrɛksjɔ̃/ *nf* correction; (*d'examen*) marking, grading; (*punition*) beating.

correspondance /kɔrɛspɔ̃dɑ̃s/ *nf* correspondence; (*de train, d'autobus*) connection; **vente par** ~ mail order; **faire des études par** ~ do a correspondence course.

correspondant, ~e /kɔrɛspɔ̃dɑ̃, -t/ *a* corresponding. ●*nm, f* correspondent; penfriend; (*au téléphone*) **votre** ~ the person you are calling.

correspondre /kɔrɛspɔ̃dr/ [3] *vi* (*s'accorder, écrire*) correspond; (*chambres*) communicate. ●*v +prép* ~ **à** (*être approprié à*) match, suit; (*équivaloir à*) correspond to. □ **se** ~ *vpr* correspond.

corrida /kɔrida/ *nf* bullfight.

corriger /kɔʀiʒe/ [40] vt correct; (devoir) mark, grade, correct; (punir) beat; (guérir) cure.

corsage /kɔʀsaʒ/ nm bodice; (chemisier) blouse.

corsaire /kɔʀsɛʀ/ nm pirate.

Corse /kɔʀs/ nf Corsica. ● nmf Corsican. **corse** a Corsican.

corsé, **~e** /kɔʀse/ a (vin) full-bodied; (café) strong; (scabreux) racy; (problème) tough.

cortège /kɔʀtɛʒ/ nm procession; ~ **funèbre** funeral procession.

corvée /kɔʀve/ nf chore.

cosmonaute /kɔsmɔnot/ nmf cosmonaut.

cosmopolite /kɔsmɔpɔlit/ a cosmopolitan.

cosse /kɔs/ nf (de pois) pod.

cossu, **~e** /kɔsy/ a (gens) well-to-do; (demeure) opulent.

costaud, **~e** /kɔsto, -d/ 🄸 a strong. ● nm strong man.

costume /kɔstym/ nm suit; (Théât) costume.

cote /kɔt/ nf (classification) mark; (en Bourse) quotation; (de cheval) odds (de on); (de candidat, acteur) rating; ~ **d'alerte** danger level; **avoir la** ~ be popular.

côte /kot/ nf (littoral) coast; (pente) hill; (Anat) rib; (Culin) chop; ~ **à ~** side by side; **la C~ d'Azur** the (French) Riviera.

côté /kote/ nm side; (direction) way; **à ~** nearby; **voisin d'à ~** next-door neighbour; **à ~ de** next to; (comparé à) compared to; **à ~ de la cible** wide of the target; **aux ~s de** by the side of; **de ~** (regarder) sideways; (sauter) to one side; **mettre de ~** put aside; **de ce ~** this way; **de chaque ~** on each side; **de tous les ~s** on every side; (partout) everywhere; **du ~ de** (vers) towards; (dans les environs de) near.

côtelette /kotlɛt/ nf chop.

coter /kote/ [1] vt (Comm) quote;

coté en Bourse listed on the Stock Exchange; **très coté** highly rated.

cotiser /kɔtize/ [1] vi pay one's contributions (**à** to); (à un club) pay one's subscription. □ **se ~** vpr club together.

coton /kɔtɔ̃/ nm cotton; ~ **hydrophile** cotton wool.

cou /ku/ nm neck.

couchant /kuʃɑ̃/ nm sunset.

couche /kuʃ/ nf layer; (de peinture) coat; (de bébé) nappy; (US) diaper; **~s** (Méd) childbirth; **~s sociales** social strata.

coucher /kuʃe/ [1] vt put to bed; (loger) put up; (étendre) lay down; ~ (**par écrit**) set down. ● vi sleep. □ **se ~** vpr go to bed; (s'étendre) lie down; (soleil) set. ● nm ~ (**de soleil**) sunset; **au ~ du soleil** at sunset.

couchette /kuʃɛt/ nf (de train) couchette; (Naut) berth.

coude /kud/ nm elbow; (de rivière, chemin) bend; ~ **à ~** side by side.

cou-de-pied (pl **cous-de-pied**) /kudpje/ nm instep.

coudre /kudʀ/ [19] vt/i sew.

couette /kwɛt/ nf duvet, continental quilt.

couler /kule/ [1] vi flow, run; (fromage, nez) run; (fuir) leak; (bateau) sink; (entreprise) go under; **faire ~ un bain** run a bath. ● vt (bateau) sink; (sculpture, métal) cast. □ **se ~** vpr slip (**dans** into).

couleur /kulœʀ/ nf colour; (peinture) paint; (aux cartes) suit; **~s** (teint) colour; **de ~** (homme, femme) coloured; **en ~s** (télévision, film) colour.

couleuvre /kulœvʀ/ nf grass snake.

coulisse /kulis/ nf (de tiroir) runner; **à ~** (porte, fenêtre) sliding;

~s (Théât) wings; **dans les** ~s (fig) behind the scenes.

couloir /kulwaʀ/ *nm* corridor; (Sport) lane; ~ **de bus** bus lane.

coup /ku/ *nm* blow; (choc) knock; (Sport) stroke; (de crayon, chance, cloche) stroke; (de fusil, pistolet) shot; (fois) time; (aux échecs) move; **donner un** ~ **de pied/poing à** kick/ punch; **à** ~ **sûr** definitely; **après** ~ after the event; **boire un** ~ 🖪 have a drink; ~ **sur** in rapid succession; **du** ~ as a result; **d'un seul** ~ in one go; **du premier** ~ first go; **sale** ~ dirty trick; **sous le** ~ **de la fatigue/colère** out of tiredness/anger; **sur le** ~ instantly; **tenir le** ~ hold out; **manquer son** ~ 🖪 blow it 🖪; ~ **de chiffon** wipe (with a rag); ~ **de coude** nudge; ~ **de couteau** stab; ~ **d'envoi** kick-off; ~ **d'État** (Pol) coup; ~ **de fou** shot; ~ **de fil** 🖪 phone call; ~ **de filet** haul, (fig) police raid; ~ **de foudre** love at first sight; ~ **franc** free kick; ~ **de frein** sudden braking; ~ **de grâce** coup de grâce; ~ **de main** helping hand; ~ **d'œil** glance; ~ **de pied** kick; ~ **de poing** punch; ~ **de soleil** sunburn; ~ **de sonnette** ring (on a bell); ~ **de téléphone** (tele-) phone call; ~ **de tête** wild impulse; ~ **de théâtre** dramatic event; ~ **de tonnerre** thunderclap; ~ **de vent** gust of wind.

coupable /kupabl/ *a* guilty. ● *nmf* culprit.

coupe /kup/ *nf* cup; (de champagne) goblet; (à fruits) dish; (de vêtement) cut; (dessin) section; ~ **de cheveux** haircut.

couper /kupe/ [1] *vt* cut; (arbre) cut down; (arrêter) cut off; (voyage) break up; (appétit) take away; (vin) water down; ~ **par** take a short cut via; ~ **la parole à qn** cut sb short. ● *vi* cut. □ **se** ~ *vpr* cut oneself; **se** ~ **le doigt** cut one's

finger; (routes) intersect; **se** ~ **de** cut oneself off from.

couple /kupl/ *nm* couple; (d'animaux) pair.

coupure /kupyʀ/ *nf* cut; (billet de banque) note; (de presse) cutting; (pause, rupture) break; ~ (**de courant**) power cut.

cour /kuʀ/ *nf* (court)yard; (du roi) court; (tribunal) court; ~ (**de récréation**) playground; ~ **martiale** court-martial; **faire la** ~ **à** court.

courageux, -euse /kuʀaʒø, -z/ *a* courageous.

couramment /kuʀamɑ̃/ *adv* frequently; (parler) fluently.

courant, ~e /kuʀɑ̃, -t/ *a* standard, ordinary; (en cours) current. ● *nm* current; (de mode, d'idées) trend; ~ **d'air** draught; **dans le** ~ **de** in the course of; **être/mettre au** ~ do know/tell about; (à jour) be/bring up to date on.

courbature /kuʀbatyʀ/ *nf* ache; **avoir des** ~s be stiff, ache.

courber /kuʀbe/ [1] *vt* bend.

coureur, -euse /kuʀœʀ, -øz/ *nm,f* (Sport) runner; ~ **automobile** racing driver; ~ **cycliste** racing cyclist. ● *nm* womanizer.

courgette /kuʀʒɛt/ *nf* courgette; (US) zucchini.

courir /kuʀiʀ/ [20] *vi* run; (se hâter) rush; (nouvelles) go round; ~ **après qn/qch** chase after sb/ sth. ● *vt* (risque) run; (danger) face; (épreuve sportive) run *ou* compete in; (fréquenter) do the rounds of; (filles) chase (after).

couronne /kuʀɔn/ *nf* crown; (de fleurs) wreath.

couronnement /kuʀɔnmɑ̃/ *nm* coronation, crowning; (fig) crowning achievement.

courrier /kuʀje/ *nm* post, mail; (à écrire) letters; ~ **du cœur** problem page; ~ **électronique** e-mail.

cours /kuʀ/ nm (leçon) class; (série de leçons) course; (prix) price; (cote) (de valeur, denrée) price; (de devises) exchange rate; (déroulement, d'une rivière) course; (allée) avenue; **au ∼ de** in the course of; **avoir ∼** (monnaie) be legal tender; (fig) current; (Scol) have a lesson; **∼ d'eau** river, stream; **∼ du soir** evening class; **∼ particulier** private lesson; **∼ magistral** (Univ) lecture; **en ∼** current; (travail) in progress; **en ∼ de route** along the way.

course /kuʀs/ nf running; (épreuve de vitesse) race; (activité) racing; (entre rivaux: fig) race; (de projectile) flight; (voyage) journey; (commission) errand; **∼s** (achats) shopping; (de chevaux) races; **faire la ∼ avec qn** race sb.

coursier, -ière /kuʀsje, -jɛʀ/ nm, f messenger.

court, ∼e /kuʀ, -t/ a short. ● adv short; **à ∼ de** short of; **pris de ∼** caught unawares. ● nm **∼ (de tennis)** (tennis) court.

courtier, -ière /kuʀtje, -jɛʀ/ nm, f broker.

courtiser /kuʀtize/ [1] vt woo, court.

courtois, ∼e /kuʀtwa, -z/ a courteous. **courtoisie** nf courtesy.

cousin, ∼e /kuzɛ̃, -in/ nm, f cousin; **∼ germain** first cousin.

coussin /kusɛ̃/ nm cushion.

coût /ku/ nm cost; **le ∼ de la vie** the cost of living.

couteau (pl ∼x) /kuto/ nm knife; **∼ à cran d'arrêt** flick knife.

coûter /kute/ [1] vt/i cost; **coûte que coûte** at all costs; **au prix coûtant** at cost (price).

coutume /kutym/ nf custom.

couture /kutyʀ/ nf sewing; (métier) dressmaking; (points) seam.

couturier nm fashion designer.
couturière nf dressmaker.

couvée /kuve/ nf brood.

couvent /kuvɑ̃/ nm convent.

couver /kuve/ [1] vt (œufs) hatch; (personne) overprotect, pamper; (maladie) be coming down with, be sickening for. ● vi (feu) smoulder; (mal) be brewing.

couvercle /kuvɛʀkl/ nm (de marmite, boîte) lid; (qui se visse) screwtop.

couvert, ∼e /kuvɛʀ, -t/ a covered (de with); (habillé) covered up; (ciel) overcast. ● nm (à table) place setting; (prix) cover charge; **∼s** (couteaux etc.) cutlery; **mettre le ∼** lay the table; (abri) cover; **à ∼** (Mil) under cover; **à ∼ de** (fig) safe from.

couverture /kuvɛʀtyʀ/ nf cover; (de lit) blanket; (toit) roofing; (dans la presse) coverage; **∼ chauffante** electric blanket.

couvre-feu (pl ∼x) /kuvʀəfø/ nm curfew.

couvre-lit (pl ∼s) /kuvʀəli/ nm bedspread.

couvrir /kuvʀiʀ/ [21] vt cover. □ **se ∼** vpr (s'habiller) wrap up; (se coiffer) put one's hat on; (ciel) become overcast.

covoiturage /kɔvwatyʀaʒ/ nm car sharing.

cracher /kʀaʃe/ [1] vi spit; (radio) crackle. ● vt spit (out); (fumée) belch out.

crachin /kʀaʃɛ̃/ nm drizzle.

craie /kʀɛ/ nf chalk.

craindre /kʀɛ̃dʀ/ [22] vt be afraid of, fear; (être sensible à) be easily damaged by.

crainte /kʀɛ̃t/ nf fear (pour for); **de ∼ de/que** for fear of/that. **craintif, -ive** a timid.

crampon /kʀɑ̃põ/ nm (de chaussure) stud.

cramponner (se) /(sə)kʀɑ̃pɔne/ [1] *vpr* se ~ à cling to.

cran /kʀɑ̃/ *nm* (entaille) notch; (trou) hole; (courage 🔲) guts 🔲, courage; ~ **de sûreté** safety catch.

crâne /kʀɑn/ *nm* skull.

crapaud /kʀapo/ *nm* toad.

craquer /kʀake/ [1] *vi* crack, snap; (*plancher*) creak; (*couture*) split; (fig) (*personne*) break down; (céder) give in. ● *vt* (*allumette*) strike; (*vêtement*) split.

crasse /kʀas/ *nf* grime.

cravache /kʀavaʃ/ *nf* (horse) whip.

cravate /kʀavat/ *nf* tie.

crayon /kʀejɔ̃/ *nm* pencil; ~ **de couleur** coloured pencil; ~ **à bille** ballpoint pen; ~ **optique** light pen.

créateur, -trice /kʀeatœʀ, -tʀis/ *a* creative. ● *nm, f* creator, designer.

crèche /kʀɛʃ/ *nf* day nursery, crèche; (Relig) crib.

crédit /kʀedi/ *nm* credit; (somme allouée) funds; **à** ~ on credit; **faire** ~ give credit (**à** to).

créer /kʀee/ [15] *vt* create, (*produit*) design; (*société*) set up.

crémaillère /kʀemajɛʀ/ *nf* **pendre la** ~ have a house-warming party.

crème /kʀɛm/ *a inv* cream. ● *nm* (café) ~ espresso with milk. ● *nf* cream; (dessert) cream dessert; ~ **anglaise** egg custard; ~ **fouettée** whipped cream; ~ **pâtissière** confectioner's custard. **crémerie** *nf* dairy. **crémeux, -euse** *a* creamy. **crémier, -ière** *nm, f* dairyman, dairywoman.

créneau (*pl* ~**x**) /kʀeno/ *nm* (trou, moment) slot, window; (dans le marché) gap; **faire un** ~ parallel-park.

crêpe /kʀɛp/ *nf* (galette) pancake.

● *nm* (tissu) crêpe; (matière) crêpe (rubber).

crépitement /kʀepitmɑ̃/ *nm* crackling; (d'huile) sizzling.

crépuscule /kʀepyskyl/ *nm* twilight, dusk.

cresson /kʀəsɔ̃/ *nm* (water)cress.

crête /kʀɛt/ *nf* crest; (de coq) comb.

crétin, ~e /kʀetɛ̃, -in/ *nm, f* 🔲 moron 🔲.

creuser /kʀøze/ [1] *vt* dig; (évider) hollow out; (fig) go into in depth. □ **se** ~ *vpr* (écart) widen; **se** ~ (**la cervelle**) 🔲 rack one's brains.

creux, -euse /kʀø, -z/ *a* hollow; (heures) off-peak. ● *nm* hollow; (de l'estomac) pit; **dans le** ~ **de la main** in the palm of the hand.

crevaison /kʀəvɛzɔ̃/ *nf* puncture.

crevasse /kʀavas/ *nf* crack; (de glacier) crevasse; (de la peau) chap.

crevé, ~e /kʀave/ *a* 🔲 worn out.

crever /kʀave/ [1] *vt* burst; (*pneu*) puncture, burst; (*exténuer* 🔲) exhaust; (*œil*) put out. ● *vi* (*pneu, sac*) burst; (*mourir* 🔲) die.

crevette /kʀavɛt/ *nf* ~ **grise** shrimp; ~ **rose** prawn.

cri /kʀi/ *nm* cry; (de douleur) scream, cry; **pousser un** ~ cry out, scream.

criard, ~e /kʀijaʀ, -d/ *a* (couleur) garish; (voix) shrill.

crier /kʀije/ [45] *vi* (fort) shout, cry (out); (de douleur) scream; (grincer) creak. ● *vt* (ordre) shout (out).

crime /kʀim/ *nm* crime; (meurtre) murder.

criminel, ~le /kʀiminɛl/ *a* criminal. ● *nm, f* criminal; (assassin) murderer.

crinière /kʀinjɛʀ/ *nf* mane.

crise /kʀiz/ *nf* crisis; (Méd) attack; (de colère) fit; ~ **cardiaque** heart attack; ~ **de foie** bilious attack; ~ **de nerfs** hysterics (+ *pl*).

crisper /kʀispe/ [1] *vt* tense; (*énerver* ▣) irritate. □ **se ~** *vpr* tense; (*mains*) clench.

critère /kʀitɛʀ/ *nm* criterion.

critique /kʀitik/ *a* critical. ● *nf* criticism; (*article*) review; (*commentateur*) critic; **la ~** (*personnes*) the critics. **critiquer** [1] *vt* criticize.

Croate /kʀɔat/ *a* Croatian. **C~** *nmf* Croatian.

Croatie /kʀɔasi/ *nf* Croatia.

croche /kʀɔʃ/ *nf* quaver.

croche-pied (*pl* **~s**) /kʀɔʃpje/ *nm* ▣ **faire un ~ à** trip up.

crochet /kʀɔʃɛ/ *nm* hook; (*détour*) detour; (*signe*) (square) bracket; (*tricot*) crochet; **faire au ~** crochet.

crochu, ~e /kʀɔʃy/ *a* hooked.

crocodile /kʀɔkɔdil/ *nm* crocodile.

croire /kʀwaʀ/ [23] *vt* believe (à, en in); (*estimer*) think, believe (que that). ● *vi* believe.

croisade /kʀwazad/ *nf* crusade.

croisement /kʀwazmã/ *nm* crossing; (*fait de passer à côté de*) passing; (*carrefour*) crossroads.

croiser /kʀwaze/ [1] *vi* (*bateau*) cruise. ● *vt* cross; (*passant, véhicule*) pass; **~ les bras** fold one's arms; **~ les jambes** cross one's legs; (*animaux*) crossbreed. □ **se ~** *vpr* (*véhicules, piétons*) pass each other; (*lignes*) cross.

croisière /kʀwazjɛʀ/ *nf* cruise.

croissance /kʀwasãs/ *nf* growth.

croissant, ~e /kʀwasã, -t/ *a* growing. ● *nm* crescent; (*pâtisserie*) croissant.

croix /kʀwa/ *nf* cross; **~ gammée** swastika; **C~-Rouge** Red Cross.

croquant, ~e /kʀɔkã, -t/ *a* crunchy.

croque-monsieur /kʀɔkməsjø/ *nm inv* toasted ham and cheese sandwich.

croque-mort (*pl* **~s**) /kʀɔkmɔʀ/ *nm* ▣ undertaker.

croquer /kʀɔke/ [1] *vt* crunch; (*dessiner*) sketch; **chocolat à ~** plain chocolate. ● *vi* be crunchy.

croquis /kʀɔki/ *nm* sketch.

crotte /kʀɔt/ *nf* dropping.

crotté, ~e /kʀɔte/ *a* muddy.

crottin /kʀɔtɛ̃/ *nm* (horse) dropping.

croupir /kʀupiʀ/ [2] *vi* stagnate.

croustillant, ~e /kʀustijã, -t/ *a* crispy; (*pain*) crusty; (fig) spicy.

croûte /kʀut/ *nf* crust; (*de fromage*) rind; (*de plaie*) scab; **en ~** (Culin) in pastry.

croûton /kʀutɔ̃/ *nm* (bout de pain) crust; (avec potage) croûton.

CRS *abrév m* (**Compagnie républicaine de sécurité**) French riot police; **un ~** *a* member of the French riot police.

cru¹ /kʀy/ ⇒CROIRE [23].

cru², ~e /kʀy/ *a* raw; (*lumière*) harsh; (*propos*) crude. ● *nm* vineyard; (vin) vintage wine.

crû /kʀy/ ⇒CROÎTRE [24].

cruauté /kʀyote/ *nf* cruelty.

cruche /kʀyʃ/ *nf* jug, pitcher.

crucial, ~e (*mpl* **-iaux**) /kʀysjal, -jo/ *a* crucial.

crudité /kʀydite/ *nf* (de langage) crudeness; **~s** (Culin) raw vegetables.

crue /kʀy/ *nf* rise in water level; **en ~** in spate.

crustacé /kʀystase/ *nm* shellfish.

cube /kyb/ *nm* cube. ● *a* (*mètre*) cubic.

cueillir /kœjiʀ/ [25] *vt* pick, gather; (*personne* ▣) pick up.

cuiller, cuillère /kɥijɛʀ/ *nf* spoon; **~ à soupe** soup spoon; (*mesure*) tablespoonful.

cuir /kɥiʀ/ *nm* leather; **~ chevelu** scalp.

cuire /kɥiʀ/ [17] *vt* cook; **~ (au**

four) bake. ● *vi* cook; **faire ~** cook.

cuisine /kɥizin/ *nf* kitchen; (art) cookery, cooking; (aliments) food; **faire la ~** cook.

cuisiner /kɥizine/ [1] *vt* cook; (interroger Ⅱ) grill. ● *vi* cook.

cuisinier, -ière /kɥizinje, -jɛʀ/ *nm, f* cook. **cuisinière** *nf* (appareil) cooker, stove.

cuisse /kɥis/ *nf* thigh; (de poulet) thigh; (de grenouille) leg.

cuisson /kɥisɔ̃/ *nf* cooking.

cuit, ~e /kɥi, -t/ *a* cooked; **bien ~** well done *ou* cooked; **trop ~** overdone.

cuivre /kɥivʀ/ *nm* copper; **~ (jaune)** brass; **~s** (Mus) brass.

cul /ky/ *nm* (derrière 图) backside, bottom, arse 图

culbuter /kylbyte/ [1] *vi* (personne) tumble; (objet) topple (over). ● *vt* knock over.

culminer /kylmine/ [1] *vi* reach its highest point *ou* peak.

culot /kylo/ *nm* (audace Ⅱ) nerve, cheek; (Tech) base.

culotte /kylɔt/ *nf* (de femme) pants (+ *pl*), knickers (+ *pl*); (US) panties (+ *pl*); **~ de cheval** riding breeches; **en ~ courte** in short trousers.

culpabilité /kylpabilite/ *nf* guilt.

culte /kylt/ *nm* cult, worship; (religion) religion; (office protestant) service.

cultivateur, -trice /kyltivatœʀ, -tʀis/ *nm, f* farmer.

cultiver /kyltive/ [1] *vt* cultivate; (plantes) grow.

culture /kyltyʀ/ *nf* cultivation; (de plantes) growing; (agriculture) farming; (éducation) culture; (connaissances) knowledge; **~s** (terrains) lands under cultivation; **~ physique** physical training.

culturel, ~le /kyltyʀɛl/ *a* cultural.

cumuler /kymyle/ [1] *vt* accumulate; (fonctions) hold concurrently.

cure /kyʀ/ *nf* (course of) treatment.

curé /kyʀe/ *nm* (parish) priest.

cure-dent (*pl* ~s) /kyʀdɑ̃/ *nm* toothpick.

curer /kyʀe/ [1] *vt* clean. □ **se ~** *vpr* **se ~ les dents/ongles** clean one's teeth/nails.

curieux, -ieuse /kyʀjø, -z/ *a* curious. ● *nm, f* (badaud) onlooker.

curiosité /kyʀjozite/ *nf* curiosity; (objet) curio; (spectacle) unusual sight.

curriculum vitae /kyʀikylɔm vite/ *nm inv* curriculum vitae; (US) résumé.

curseur /kyʀsœʀ/ *nm* cursor.

cutané, ~e /kytane/ *a* skin.

cuve /kyv/ *nf* vat; (à mazout, eau) tank.

cuvée /kyve/ *nf* (de vin) vintage.

cuvette /kyvɛt/ *nf* bowl; (de lavabo) (wash)basin; (des cabinets) pan, bowl.

CV *abrév m* (**curriculum vitae**) CV.

cyberbranché, ~e /sibɛʀbʀɑ̃ʃe/ *a* cyberwired.

cybercafé /sibɛʀkafe/ *nm* cybercafe.

cyberespace /sibɛʀsɛpas/ *nm* cyberspace.

cybernaute /sibɛʀnot/ *nmf* Netsurfer.

cybernétique /sibɛʀnetik/ *nf* cybernetics (+ *pl*).

cyclisme /siklism/ *nm* cycling.

cycliste /siklist/ *nmf* cyclist. ● *nm* cycling shorts. ● *a* cycle.

cyclone /siklon/ *nm* cyclone.

cygne /siɲ/ *nm* swan.

cynique /sinik/ *a* cynical. ● *nm* cynic.

d' /d/ ⇒DE.

d'abord /dabɔR/ *adv* first; (au début) at first.

dactylo /daktilo/ *nf* typist. **dactylographier** [45] *vt* type.

dada /dada/ *nm* hobby-horse.

daim /dɛ̃/ *nm* (fallow) deer; (cuir) suede.

dallage /dalaʒ/ *nm* paving. **dalle** *nf* slab.

daltonien, ~ne /daltɔnjɛ̃, -ɛn/ *a* colour-blind.

dame /dam/ *nf* lady; (cartes, échecs) queen; **~s** (jeu) draughts; (US) checkers.

damier /damje/ *nm* draught-board; (US) checker-board; **à ~** chequered.

damner /dane/ [1] *vt* damn.

dandiner (se) /(sə)dãdine/ [1] *vpr* waddle.

Danemark /danmaRk/ *nm* Denmark.

danger /dãʒe/ *nm* danger; **en ~** in danger; **mettre en ~** endanger.

dangereux, -euse /dãʒ(ə)Rø, -z/ *a* dangerous.

danois, ~e /danwa, -z/ *a* Danish. ●*nm* (Ling) Danish. **D~, ~e** *nm, f* Dane.

dans /dã/ *prép* in; (mouvement) into; (à l'intérieur de) inside, in; **être ~ un avion** be on a plane; **~ dix jours** in ten days' time; **boire ~ un verre** drink out of a glass; **~ les 10 francs** about 10 francs.

danse /dãs/ *nf* dance; (art) dancing.

danser /dãse/ [1] *vt/i* dance. **danseur, -euse** *nm, f* dancer.

darne /daRn/ *nf* steak (of fish).

date /dat/ *nf* date; **~ limite** deadline; **~ limite de vente** sell-by date; **~ de péremption** use-by date.

dater /date/ [1] *vt/i* date; **à ~ de** as from.

datte /dat/ *nf* (fruit) date.

daube /dob/ *nf* casserole.

dauphin /dofɛ̃/ *nm* (animal) dolphin.

davantage /davãtaʒ/ *adv* more; (plus longtemps) longer; **~ de** more; **je n'en sais pas ~** that's as much as I know.

....

de, d' /də, d/

d' before vowel or mute h.

●*préposition*

····▸ of; **le livre ~ mon ami** my friend's book; **un pont ~ fer** an iron bridge.

····▸ (provenance) from.

····▸ (temporel) from; **~ 8 heures à 10 heures** from 8 till 10.

····▸ (mesure, manière) **dix mètres ~ haut** ten metres high; **pleurer ~ rage** cry with rage.

····▸ (agent) by; **un livre ~ Marcel Aymé** a book by Marcel Aymé.

●**de, de l', de la, du,** (*pl* **des**) *déterminant*

····▸ some; **du pain** (some) bread; **des fleurs** (some) flowers; **je ne bois jamais ~ vin** I never drink wine.

de + le = du
de + les = des

....

dé /de/ *nm* (à jouer) dice; (à coudre) thimble; **~s** (jeu) dice.

débâcle /debɑkl/ *nf* (Géog) breaking up; (Mil) rout.

déballer /debale/ [1] vt unpack;
(révéler) spill out.

débarbouiller /debaʀbuje/ vt
wash the face of. □ **se ~** vpr
wash one's face.

débarcadère /debaʀkadɛʀ/ nm
landing-stage.

débardeur /debaʀdœʀ/ nm
(vêtement) tank top.

débarquement /debaʀkəmɑ̃/ nm
disembarkation. **débarquer** [1]
vt/i disembark, land; (arriver 🗊)
turn up.

débarras /debaʀa/ nm junk
room; **bon ~!** good riddance!

débarrasser /debaʀase/ [1] vt
clear (**de** of); **~ qn de** relieve sb
of; (défaut, ennemi) rid sb of. □ **se
~ de** vpr get rid of.

débat /deba/ nm debate.

débattre /debatʀ/ [11] vt debate.
● vi **~ de** discuss. □ **se ~** vpr
struggle (to get free).

débauche /deboʃ/ nf
debauchery; (fig) profusion.

débaucher /deboʃe/ [1] vt
(licencier) lay off; (distraire) tempt
away.

débile /debil/ a weak; 🗊 stupid.
● nmf moron 🗊.

débit /debi/ nm (rate of) flow;
(élocution) delivery; (de compte)
debit; **~ de tabac** tobacconist's
shop; **~ de boissons** bar.

débiter /debite/ [1] vt (compte)
debit; (fournir) produce; (vendre)
sell; (dire: péj) spout; (couper) cut
up.

débiteur, -trice /debitœʀ, -tʀis/
nm, f debtor. ● a (compte) in
debit.

déblayer /debleje/ [31] vt clear.

déblocage /deblɔkaʒ/ nm (de prix)
deregulating. **débloquer** [1] vt
(prix, salaires) unfreeze.

déboiser /debwaze/ [1] vt clear
(of trees).

déboîter /debwate/ [1] vi

(véhicule) pull out. ● vt (membre)
dislocate.

débordement /debɔʀdəmɑ̃/ nm
(de joie) excess.

déborder /debɔʀde/ [1] vi
overflow. ● vt (dépasser) extend
beyond; **~ de** (joie etc.) be
brimming over with.

débouché /debuʃe/ nm opening;
(carrière) prospect; (Comm) outlet;
(sortie) end, exit.

déboucher /debuʃe/ [1] vt
(bouteille) uncork; (évier)
unblock. ● vi come out (**de** from);
~ sur (rue) lead into.

débourser /debuʀse/ [1] vt pay
out.

debout /dəbu/ adv standing; (levé,
éveillé) up; **être ~, se tenir ~** be
standing, stand; **se mettre ~**
stand up.

déboutonner /debutɔne/ [1] vt
unbutton. □ **se ~** vpr unbutton
oneself; (vêtement) come undone.

débrancher /debʀɑ̃ʃe/ [1] vt
(prise) unplug; (système)
disconnect.

débrayer /debʀeje/ [31] vi (Auto)
declutch; (faire grève) stop work.

débris /debʀi/ nmpl fragments;
(détritus) rubbish (+ sg); debris.

débrouillard, -e /debʀujaʀ, -d/
a 🗊 resourceful.

débrouiller /debʀuje/ [1] vt
disentangle; (problème) solve.
□ **se ~** vpr manage.

début /deby/ nm beginning; **faire
ses ~s** (en public) make one's
début; **à mes ~s** when I started
out. **débutant, ~e** nm, f
beginner. **débuter** [1] vi begin;
(dans un métier etc.) start out.

déca /deka/ nm 🗊 decaf.

deçà: en ~ /ɑ̃dəsa/ loc this side.
● prép **en ~ de** this side of.

décacheter /dekaʃte/ [6] vt
open.

décade /dekad/ *nf* ten days; (décennie) decade.

décadent, ~e /dekadã, -t/ *a* decadent.

décalage /dekalaʒ/ *nm* (écart) gap; ~ **horaire** time difference. **décaler** [1] *vt* shift.

décalquer /dekalke/ [1] *vt* trace.

décamper /dekãpe/ [1] *vi* clear off.

décanter /dekãte/ *vt* allow to settle. □ **se ~** *vpr* settle.

décapant /dekapã/ *nm* chemical agent; (pour peinture) paint stripper. ● *a* (humour) caustic.

décapotable /dekapɔtabl/ *a* convertible.

décapsuleur /dekapsylœʀ/ *nm* bottle-opener.

décédé, ~e /desede/ *a* deceased. **décéder** [14] *vi* die.

déceler /desle/ [6] *vt* detect; (démontrer) reveal.

décembre /desãbʀ/ *nm* December.

décemment /desamã/ *adv* decently. **décence** *nf* decency. **décent, ~e** *a* decent.

décennie /deseni/ *nf* decade.

décentralisation /desãtralizasjɔ̃/ *nf* decentralization. **décentraliser** [1] *vt* decentralize.

déception /desɛpsjɔ̃/ *nf* disappointment.

décerner /desɛʀne/ [1] *vt* award.

décès /desɛ/ *nm* death.

décevant, ~e /des(ə)vã, -t/ *a* disappointing. **décevoir** [52] *vt* disappoint.

déchaîner /deʃene/ [1] *vt* (enthousiasme) rouse. □ **se ~** *vpr* go wild.

décharge /deʃaʀʒ/ *nf* (de fusil) discharge; ~ **électrique** electric shock; ~ **publique** municipal dump.

décharger /deʃaʀʒe/ [40] *vt*

unload; ~ **qn de** relieve sb from. □ **se ~** *vpr* (batterie, pile) go flat.

déchausser (se) /(sə)deʃose/ [1] *vpr* take off one's shoes; (dent) work loose.

dèche /dɛʃ/ *nf* 🔲 **dans la ~** broke.

déchéance /deʃeãs/ *nf* decay.

déchet /deʃɛ/ *nm* (reste) scrap; (perte) waste; ~**s** (ordures) refuse.

déchiffrer /deʃifʀe/ [1] *vt* decipher.

déchiqueter /deʃikte/ [38] *vt* tear to shreds.

déchirement /deʃiʀmã/ *nm* heartbreak; (conflit) split.

déchirer /deʃiʀe/ [1] *vt* (par accident) tear; (lacérer) tear up; (arracher) tear off *ou* out; (diviser) tear apart. □ **se ~** *vpr* tear.

déchirure *nf* tear.

décibel /desibɛl/ *nm* decibel.

décidément /desidemã/ *adv* really.

décider /deside/ [1] *vt* decide on; (persuader) persuade; ~ **que**/**de** decide that/to; ~ **de qch** decide on sth. □ **se ~** *vpr* make up one's mind (**à** to).

décimal, ~e (*mpl* ~**aux**) /desimal, -o/ *a & nf* decimal.

décisif, -ive /desizif, -v/ *a* decisive.

décision /desizjɔ̃/ *nf* decision.

déclaration /deklaʀasjɔ̃/ *nf* declaration; (commentaire politique) statement; ~ **d'impôts** tax return.

déclarer /deklaʀe/ [1] *vt* declare; (naissance) register; **déclaré coupable** found guilty; ~ **forfait** (Sport) withdraw. □ **se ~** *vpr* (feu) break out.

déclencher /deklãʃe/ [1] *vt* (Tech) set off; (conflit) spark off; (avalanche) start; (rire) provoke. □ **se ~** *vpr* (Tech) go off.

déclencheur *nm* (Photo) shutter release.

déclic /deklik/ *nm* click.

déclin /deklɛ̃/ nm decline.

déclinaison /deklinɛzõ/ nf (Ling) declension.

décliner /dekline/ [1] vt (refuser) decline; (dire) state; (Ling) decline.

décocher /dekɔʃe/ [1] vt (coup) fling; (regard) shoot.

décollage /dekɔlaʒ/ nm take-off.

décoller /dekɔle/ [1] vt unstick. ● vi (avion) take off. □ se ~ vpr come off.

décolleté, ~e /dekɔlte/ a low-cut. ● nm low neckline.

décolorer /dekɔlɔre/ [1] vt fade; (cheveux) bleach. □ se ~ vpr fade.

décombres /dekõbʀ/ nmpl rubble.

décommander /dekɔmɑ̃de/ [1] vt cancel.

décomposer /dekõpoze/ [1] vt break up; (substance) decompose. □ se ~ vpr decompose.

décompte /dekõt/ nm deduction; (détail) breakdown

décongeler /dekõʒle/ [6] vt thaw.

déconseillé, ~e /dekõsɛje/ a not recommended, inadvisable.

déconseiller /dekõsɛje/ [1] vt ~ qch à qn advise sb against sth.

décontracté, ~e /dekõtrakte/ a relaxed.

déconvenue /dekõvny/ nf disappointment.

décor /dekɔʀ/ nm (paysage) scenery; (de cinéma, théâtre) set; (cadre) setting; (de maison) décor.

décoratif, -ive /dekɔʀatif, -v/ a decorative.

décorateur, -trice /dekɔʀatœʀ, -tʀis/ nm, f (de cinéma) set designer. **décoration** nf decoration. **décorer** [1] vt decorate.

décortiquer /dekɔʀtike/ [1] vt shell; (fig) dissect.

découdre (se) /(sə)dekudʀ/ [19] vpr come unstitched.

découler /dekule/ [1] vi ~ de follow from.

découper /dekupe/ [1] vt cut up; (viande) carve; (détacher) cut out.

découragement /dekuʀaʒmɑ̃/ nm discouragement.

décourager /dekuʀaʒe/ [40] vt discourage. □ se ~ vpr become discouraged.

décousu, ~e /dekuzy/ a (vêtement) which has come unstitched; (idées) disjointed.

découvert, ~e /dekuvɛʀ, -t/ a (tête) bare; (terrain) open. ● nm (de compte) overdraft; à ~ exposed; (fig) openly.

découverte /dekuvɛʀt/ nf discovery; à la ~ de in search of.

découvrir /dekuvʀiʀ/ [21] vt discover; (voir) see; (montrer) reveal. □ se ~ vpr (se décoiffer) take one's hat off; (ciel) clear.

décrasser /dekʀase/ [1] vt clean.

décrépit, ~e /dekʀepi, -t/ a decrepit. **décrépitude** nf decay.

décret /dekʀɛ/ nm decree.

décréter [14] vt order; (dire) declare.

décrié, ~e /dekʀije/ a criticized.

décrire /dekʀiʀ/ [30] vt describe.

décroché, ~e /dekʀɔʃe/ a (téléphone) off the hook.

décrocher /dekʀɔʃe/ [1] vt unhook; (obtenir 🗓) get. ● vi (abandonner 🗓) give up; ~ (le téléphone) pick up the phone.

décroître /dekʀwatʀ/ [24] vi decrease.

déçu, ~e /desy/ a disappointed.

décupler /dekyple/ [1] vt/i increase tenfold.

dédaigner /dedɛɲe/ [1] vt scorn.

dédain /dedɛ̃/ nm scorn.

dédale /dedal/ nm maze.

dedans /dədɑ̃/ adv & nm inside; en ~ on the inside.

dédicacer /dedikase/ [10] *vt* dedicate; (signer) sign.

dédier /dedje/ [45] *vt* dedicate.

dédommagement /dedɔmaʒmɑ̃/ *nm* compensation. **dédommager** [40] *vt* compensate (**de** for).

déduction /dedyksjɔ̃/ *nf* deduction; ~ **d'impôts** tax deduction.

déduire /dedɥiʀ/ [17] *vt* deduct; (conclure) deduce.

déesse /dees/ *nf* goddess.

défaillance /defajɑ̃s/ *nf* (panne) failure; (évanouissement) blackout. **défaillant**, ~**e** *a* (système) faulty; (personne) faint.

défaire /defɛʀ/ [33] *vt* undo; (valise) unpack; (démonter) take down. □ **se** ~ *vpr* come undone; **se** ~ **de** rid oneself of.

défait, ~**e** /defɛ, -t/ *a* (cheveux) ruffled; (visage) haggard; (nœud) undone. **défaite** *nf* defeat.

défaitiste /defetist/ *a & nmf* defeatist.

défalquer /defalke/ [1] *vt* (somme) deduct.

défaut /defo/ *nm* fault, defect; (d'un verre, diamant, etc.) flaw; (pénurie) shortage; **à** ~ **de** for lack of; **pris en** ~ caught out; **faire** ~ (argent etc.) be lacking; **par** ~ (Jur) in one's absence; ~ **de paiement** non-payment.

défavorable /defavɔʀabl/ *a* unfavourable.

défavoriser /defavɔʀize/ [1] *vt* discriminate against.

défectueux, -**euse** /defɛktɥø, -z/ *a* faulty, defective.

défendre /defɑ̃dʀ/ [3] *vt* defend; (interdire) forbid; ~ **à qn de** forbid sb to. □ **se** ~ *vpr* defend oneself; (se protéger) protect oneself; (se débrouiller) manage; **se** ~ **de** (refuser) refrain from.

défense /defɑ̃s/ *nf* defence; ~ **de fumer** no smoking; (d'éléphant) tusk.

défenseur *nm* defender.

défensif, -**ive** *a* defensive.

déferler /defɛʀle/ [1] *vi* (vagues) break; (violence) erupt.

défi /defi/ *nm* challenge; (provocation) defiance; **mettre au** ~ challenge.

déficience /defisjɑ̃s/ *nf* deficiency. **déficient**, ~**e** *a* deficient.

déficit /defisit/ *nm* deficit. **déficitaire** *a* in deficit.

défier /defje/ [45] *vt* challenge; (braver) defy.

défilé /defile/ *nm* procession; (Mil) parade; (fig) (continual) stream; (Géog) gorge; ~ **de mode** fashion parade.

défiler /defile/ [1] *vi* march; (visiteurs) stream; (images) flash by; (chiffres, minutes) add up. □ **se** ~ *vpr* 🄳 sneak off.

défini, ~**e** /defini/ *a* (Ling) definite.

définir /definiʀ/ [2] *vt* define.

définitif, -**ive** /definitif, -v/ *a* final, definitive; **en définitive** in the end.

définition /definisjɔ̃/ *nf* definition; (de mots croisés) clue.

définitivement /definitivmɑ̃/ *adv* definitively, permanently.

déflagration /deflagʀasjɔ̃/ *nf* explosion.

déflation /deflasjɔ̃/ *nf* deflation. **déflationniste** *a* deflationary.

défoncé, ~**e** /defɔ̃se/ *a* (terrain) full of potholes; (siège) broken; (drogué: 🄳) high.

défoncer /defɔ̃se/ [10] *vt* (porte) break down; (mâchoire) break. □ **se** ~ *vpr* 🄳 to give one's all.

déformation /defɔʀmasjɔ̃/ *nf* distortion. **déformer** [1] *vt* put out of shape; (faits, pensée) distort.

défouler (**se**) /(sə)defule/ [1] *vpr* let off steam.

défrayer /defʀeje/ [31] *vt* (payer) pay the expenses of; ~ **la chronique** be the talk of the town.

défricher /defʀiʃe/ [1] *vt* clear.

défroisser /defʀwase/ [1] *vt* smooth out.

défunt, ~**e** /defœ̃, -t/ *a* (mort) late. ● *nm,f* deceased.

dégagé, ~**e** /degaʒe/ *a* (ciel) clear; (*front*) bare; **d'un ton ~** casually.

dégagement /degaʒmɑ̃/ *nm* clearing; (football) clearance.

dégager /degaʒe/ [40] *vt* (exhaler) give off; (désencombrer) clear; (faire ressortir) bring out; (*ballon*) clear. □ **se ~** *vpr* free oneself; (ciel, rue) clear; (*odeur*) emanate.

dégarnir (se) /(sə)degaʀniʀ/ [2] *vpr* clear, empty; (*personne*) be going bald.

dégâts /dega/ *nmpl* damage (+ *sg*).

dégel /deʒɛl/ *nm* thaw. **dégeler** [6] *vi* thaw (out).

dégénéré, ~**e** /deʒeneʀe/ *a* & *nm,f* degenerate.

dégivrer /deʒivʀe/ [1] *vt* (Auto) de-ice; (*réfrigérateur*) defrost.

déglinguer /deglɛ̃ge/ 🄳 [1] *vt* bust. □ **se ~** *vpr* break down.

dégonflé, ~**e** /degɔ̃fle/ *a* (pneu) flat; (lâche 🄳) yellow 🄳.

dégonfler /degɔ̃fle/ [1] *vt* deflate. ● *vi* (blessure) go down. □ **se ~** *vpr* 🄳 chicken out.

dégouliner /deguline/ [1] *vi* trickle.

dégourdi, ~**e** /deguʀdi/ *a* smart.

dégourdir /deguʀdiʀ/ [2] *vt* (membre, liquide) warm up. □ **se ~** *vpr* **se ~ les jambes** stretch one's legs.

dégoût /degu/ *nm* disgust.

dégoûtant, ~**e** /degutɑ̃, -t/ *a* disgusting.

dégoûter /degute/ [1] *vt* disgust; ~ **qn de qch** put sb off sth.

dégradant, ~**e** /degʀadɑ̃, -t/ *a* degrading.

dégradation /degʀadasjɔ̃/ *nf* damage; **commettre des ~s** cause damage.

dégrader /degʀade/ [1] *vt* (abîmer) damage. □ **se ~** *vpr* (se détériorer) deteriorate.

dégrafer /degʀafe/ [1] *vt* unhook.

degré /dəgʀe/ *nm* degree; (d'escalier) step.

dégressif, -ive /degʀesif, -v/ *a* graded; **tarif ~** tapering charge.

dégrèvement /degʀɛvmɑ̃/ *nm* ~ **fiscal** *ou* **d'impôts** tax reduction.

dégringolade /degʀɛ̃gɔlad/ *nf* tumble.

dégrossir /degʀosiʀ/ [2] *vt* (bois) trim; (*projet*) rough out.

déguerpir /degɛʀpiʀ/ [2] *vi* clear off.

dégueulasse /degœlas/ *a* 🄳 disgusting, lousy.

dégueuler /degœle/ [1] *vt* 🄳 throw up.

déguisement /degizmɑ̃/ *nm* (de carnaval) fancy dress; (pour duper) disguise.

déguiser /degize/ [1] *vt* dress up; (pour duper) disguise. □ **se ~** *vpr* (au carnaval etc.) dress up; (pour duper) disguise oneself.

déguster /degyste/ [1] *vt* taste, sample; (savourer) enjoy.

dehors /dəɔʀ/ *adv* **en ~ de** outside; (hormis) apart from; **jeter/ mettre ~** throw/put out. ● *nm* outside.

● *nmpl* (aspect de qn) exterior.

déjà /deʒa/ *adv* already; (avant) before, already.

déjeuner /deʒœne/ [1] *vi* have lunch; (le matin) have breakfast. ● *nm* lunch; **petit ~** breakfast.

delà /dəla/ *adv & prép* **au ~ (de)**, **par ~** beyond.

délai /delɛ/ *nm* time-limit; (attente) wait; (sursis) extension (of time);

sans ~ immediately; **dans un** ~ **de 2 jours** within 2 days; **finir dans les** ~s finish within the deadline; **dans les plus brefs** ~s as soon as possible.

délaisser /delese/ [1] vt (négliger) neglect.

délassement /delasmɑ̃/ nm relaxation.

délation /delasjɔ̃/ nf informing.

délavé, ~e /delave/ a faded.

délayer /deleje/ [31] vt mix (with liquid); (idée) drag out.

délecter (se) /(sə)delɛkte/ [1] vpr se ~ de delight in.

délégué, ~e /delege/ nm, f delegate.

délibéré, ~e /delibeʀe/ a deliberate; (résolu) determined.

délicat, ~e /delika, -t/ a delicate; (plein de tact) tactful. **délicatesse** nf delicacy; (tact) tact. **délicatesses** nfpl (kind) attentions.

délice /delis/ nm delight. **délicieux, -ieuse** a (au goût) delicious; (charmant) delightful.

délier /delje/ [45] vt untie; (délivrer) free. □ se ~ vpr come untied.

délimiter /delimite/ [1] vt determine, demarcate.

délinquance /delɛ̃kɑ̃s/ nf delinquency. **délinquant, ~e** a & nm, f delinquent.

délirant, ~e /deliʀɑ̃, -t/ a delirious; (frénétique) frenzied; Ⓘ wild.

délire /deliʀ/ nm delirium; (fig) frenzy. **délirer** [1] vi be delirious (de with); Ⓘ be off one's rocker Ⓘ.

délit /deli/ nm offence.

délivrance /delivʀɑ̃s/ nf release; (soulagement) relief; (remise) issue. **délivrer** [1] vt free, release; (pays) liberate; (remettre) issue.

déloyal, ~e (mpl -aux) /delwajal, -jo/ a disloyal; (procédé) unfair.

deltaplane /dɛltaplan/ nm hang-glider.

déluge /delyʒ/ nm downpour; **le D~** the Flood.

démagogie /demagɔʒi/ nm demagogy. **démagogue** nmf demagogue.

demain /dəmɛ̃/ adv tomorrow.

demande /dəmɑ̃d/ nf request; ~ **d'emploi** job application; ~ **en mariage** marriage proposal.

demander /dəmɑ̃de/ [1] vt ask for; (chemin, heure) ask; (nécessiter) require; ~ **que/si** ask that/if; ~ **qch à qn** ask sb sth; ~ **à qn de** ask sb to; ~ **en mariage** propose to. □ se ~ vpr se ~ si/où wonder if/where.

demandeur, -euse /dəmɑ̃dœʀ, -øz/ nm, f ~ **d'emploi** job seeker; ~ **d'asile** asylum-seeker.

démangeaison /demɑ̃ʒezɔ̃/ nf itch(ing).

démanteler /demɑ̃tle/ [6] vt break up.

démaquillant /demakijɑ̃/ nm make-up remover. **démaquiller (se)** [1] vpr remove one's make-up.

démarchage /demaʀʃaʒ/ nm door-to-door selling.

démarche /demaʀʃ/ nf walk, gait; (procédé) step.

démarcheur, -euse /demaʀʃœʀ, -øz/ nm, f (door-to-door) canvasser.

démarrage /demaʀaʒ/ nm start.

démarrer /demaʀe/ [1] vi (moteur) start (up); (partir) move off; (fig) get moving. ● vt Ⓘ get moving.

démarreur /demaʀœʀ/ nm starter.

démêlant /demelɑ̃/ nm

conditioner. **démêler** [1] vt
disentangle.

déménagement /demenaʒmɑ̃/
nm move; (transport) removal.

déménager /demenaʒe/ [40] vi
move (house). ● vt (meubles)
remove.

déménageur /demenaʒœR/ nm
removal man.

démence /demɑ̃s/ nf insanity.

démener (se) /(sə)demne/ [6]
vpr move about wildly; (fig) put
oneself out.

dément, ~e /demɑ̃, -t/ a insane.
● nm, f lunatic.

démenti /demɑ̃ti/ nm denial.

démentir /demɑ̃tiR/ [46] vt deny;
(contredire) refute; ~ que deny that.

démerder (se) /(sə)domɛRde/ [1]
vpr 🖼 manage.

démettre /demɛtR/ [42] vt
(poignet etc.) dislocate; ~ qn de
relieve sb of. □ se ~ vpr resign
(de from).

demeure /dəmœR/ nf residence;
mettre en ~ de order to.

demeurer /dəmœRe/ [1] vi live;
(rester) remain.

demi, ~e /dəmi/ a half(-). ● nm, f
half. ● nm (bière) (half-pint) glass
of beer; (football) half-back. ● adv
à ~ half; (ouvrir, fermer) half-
way; à la ~e at half past; une
heure et ~e an hour and a half; (à
l'horloge) half past one; une
~-journée/-livre half a day/pound.
demi-cercle (pl ~s) nm
semicircle. **demi-finale** (pl ~s)
nf semifinal. **demi-frère** (pl ~s)
nm half-brother, stepbrother.
demi-heure (pl ~s) nf half-hour,
half an hour. **demi-litre** (pl ~s)
nm half a litre. **demi-mesure** (pl
~s) nf half-measure. à demi-
mot adv without having to
express every word. **demi-
pension** nf half-board. **demi-
queue** nm boudoir grand piano.

demi-sel a inv slightly salted.

demi-sœur (pl ~s) nf half-sister,
stepsister.

démission /demisjɔ̃/ nf
resignation.

demi-tarif (pl ~s) /dəmitaRif/
nm half-fare.

demi-tour (pl ~s) /dəmituR/ nm
about turn; (Auto) U-turn; faire ~
turn back.

démocrate /demɔkRat/ nmf
democrat. ● a democratic.

démocratie nf democracy.

démodé, ~e /demode/ a old-
fashioned.

demoiselle /dəmwazɛl/ nf young
lady; (célibataire) single lady; ~
d'honneur bridesmaid.

démolir /demɔliR/ [2] vt
demolish.

démon /demɔ̃/ nm demon; le D~
the Devil. **démoniaque** a
fiendish.

démonstration /demɔ̃stRasjɔ̃/ nf
demonstration; (de force) show.

démonter /demɔ̃te/ [1] vt take
apart, dismantle; (installation)
take down; (fig) disconcert. □ se
~ vpr come apart.

démontrer /demɔ̃tRe/ [1] vt
demonstrate; (indiquer) show.

démoraliser /demɔRalize/ [1] vt
demoralize.

démuni, ~e /demyni/ a
impoverished; ~ de without.

démunir /demyniR/ [2] vt ~ de
deprive of. □ se ~ de vpr part
with.

dénaturer /denatyRe/ [1] vt
(faits) distort.

dénigrement /denigRəmɑ̃/ nm
denigration.

dénivellation /denivɛlasjɔ̃/ nf
(pente) slope.

dénombrer /denɔ̃bRe/ [1] vt
count.

dénomination /denɔminasjɔ̃/ nf
designation.

D

dénommé, ~e /denɔme/ nm, f le
~ X the said X.

dénoncer /denɔ̃se/ [10] vt
denounce. □ se ~ vpr give
oneself up. **dénonciateur, -trice**
nm, f informer.

dénouement /denumɑ̃/ nm
outcome; (Théât) dénouement.

dénouer /denwe/ [1] vt undo.
□ se ~ vpr (nœud) come undone.

dénoyauter /denwajote/ [1] vt
stone.

denrée /dɑ̃ʀe/ nf ~ alimentaire
foodstuff.

dense /dɑ̃s/ a dense. **densité** nf
density.

dent /dɑ̃/ nf tooth; **faire ses** ~s
teethe; ~ **de lait** milk tooth; ~ **de
sagesse** wisdom tooth; (de roue)
cog. **dentaire** a dental.

denté, ~e /dɑ̃te/ a (roue) toothed

dentelé, ~e /dɑ̃tle/ a jagged.

dentelle /dɑ̃tɛl/ nf lace.

dentier /dɑ̃tje/ nm dentures (+
pl), false teeth (+ pl).

dentifrice /dɑ̃tifʀis/ nm
toothpaste.

dentiste /dɑ̃tist/ nmf dentist.

dentition /dɑ̃tisjɔ̃/ nf teeth,
dentition.

dénudé, ~e /denyde/ a bare.

dénué, ~e /denye/ a ~ **de**
devoid of.

dénuement /denymɑ̃/ nm
destitution.

déodorant /deɔdɔʀɑ̃/ nm
deodorant.

dépannage /depanaʒ/ nm repair;
(Ordinat) troubleshooting.
dépanner [1] vt repair; (fig) help
out. **dépanneuse** nf breakdown
lorry.

dépareillé, ~e /depaʀeje/ a odd,
not matching.

départ /depaʀ/ nm departure;
(Sport) start; **au** ~ **de Nice** from
Nice; **au** ~ (d'abord) at first.

département /depaʀtəmɑ̃/ nm
department.

dépassé, ~e /depase/ a
outdated.

dépasser /depase/ [1] vt go past,
pass; (véhicule) overtake; (excéder)
exceed; (rival) surpass; **ça me
dépasse** 🔲 it's beyond me. ● vi
stick out.

dépaysement /depeizmɑ̃/ nm
change of scenery; (désagréable)
disorientation.

dépêche /depɛʃ/ nf dispatch.

dépêcher /depeʃe/ [1] vt
dispatch. □ se ~ vpr hurry (up).

dépendance /depɑ̃dɑ̃s/ nf
dependence; (à une drogue)
dependency; (bâtiment)
outbuilding.

dépendre /depɑ̃dʀ/ [3] vt take
down. ● vi depend (de on); ~ **de**
(appartenir à) belong to.

dépens /depɑ̃/ nmpl aux ~ **de** at
the expense of.

dépense /depɑ̃s/ nf expense;
expenditure.

dépenser /depɑ̃se/ [1] vt/i spend;
(énergie etc.) use up. □ se ~ vpr
get some exercise.

dépérir /depeʀiʀ/ [2] vi wither.

dépêtrer (se) /(sə)depetʀe/ [1]
vpr get oneself out (de of).

dépeupler /depœple/ [1] vt
depopulate. □ se ~ vpr become
depopulated.

déphasé, ~e /defaze/ a 🔲 out of
step.

dépilatoire /depilatwaʀ/ a & nm
depilatory.

dépistage /depistaʒ/ nm
screening. **dépister** [1] vt detect;
(criminel) track down.

dépit /depi/ nm resentment; **par**
~ out of pique; **en** ~ **de** despite;
en ~ **du bon sens** in a very
illogical way. **dépité**, ~e a
vexed.

déplacé, ~e /deplase/ a (remarque) uncalled for.

déplacement /deplasmã/ nm (voyage) trip.

déplacer /deplase/ [10] vt move. □ se ~ vpr move; (voyager) travel.

déplaire /deplɛʀ/ [47] vi ~ à (irriter) displease; ça me déplaît I don't like it.

déplaisant, ~e /deplɛzã, -t/ a unpleasant, disagreeable.

dépliant /deplijã/ nm leaflet.

déplier /deplije/ [45] vt unfold.

déploiement /deplwamã/ nm (démonstration) display; (militaire) deployment.

déplorable /deplɔʀabl/ a deplorable. **déplorer** [1] vt (trouver regrettable) deplore; (mort) lament

déployer /deplwaje/ [31] vt (ailes, carte) spread; (courage) display; (armée) deploy.

déportation /depɔʀtasjɔ̃/ nf (en 1940) internment in a concentration camp.

déposer /depoze/ [1] vt put down; (laisser) leave; (passager) drop; (argent) deposit; (plainte) lodge; (armes) lay down. ●vi (Jur) testify. □ se ~ vpr settle.

dépositaire /depozitɛʀ/ nmf (Comm) agent.

déposition /depozisjɔ̃/ nf (Jur) statement.

dépôt /depo/ nm (entrepôt) warehouse; (d'autobus) depot; (particules) deposit; (garantie) deposit; **laisser en** ~ give for safe keeping; ~ **légal** formal deposit of a publication with an institution.

dépouille /depuj/ nf skin, hide; ~ (mortelle) mortal remains.

dépouiller /depuje/ [1] vt (courrier) open; (scrutin) count; (écorcher) skin; ~ **qn de** strip sb of.

dépourvu, ~e /depuʀvy/ a ~ de

devoid of; **prendre au** ~ catch unawares.

déprécier /depʀesje/ [45] vt depreciate. □ se ~ vpr depreciate.

déprédations /depʀedasjɔ̃/ nfpl damage (+ sg).

dépression /depʀesjɔ̃/ nf depression; ~ **nerveuse** nervous breakdown.

déprimer /depʀime/ [1] vt depress.

....

depuis /dəpɥi/

●**préposition**

····▸ (point de départ) since; ~ **quand attendez-vous?** how long have you been waiting?

····▸ (durée) for; ~ **toujours** always; ~ **peu** recently.

●**adverbe**

····▸ since; **il a eu une attaque le mois dernier,** ~ **nous sommes inquiets** he had a stroke last month and we've been worried ever since.

●**depuis que** conjonction

····▸ since, ever since; **Sophie a beaucoup changé depuis que Camille est née** Sophie has changed a lot since Camille was born.

....

député /depyte/ nm ≈ Member of Parliament.

déraciné, -e /deʀasine/ nm, f rootless person.

déraillement /deʀajmã/ nm derailment.

dérailler /deʀaje/ [1] vi be derailed; (fig 🔲) be talking nonsense; **faire** ~ derail. **dérailleur** nm (de vélo) derailleur.

déraisonnable /deʀɛzɔnabl/ a unreasonable.

dérangement /deʀãʒmã/ nm

bother; (désordre) disorder, upset;
en ~ out of order; les ~s the
fault reporting service.

déranger /deʀɑ̃ʒe/ [40] vt (gêner)
bother, disturb; (dérégler) upset,
disrupt. □ se ~ vpr (aller) go; (fig)
put oneself out; **ça te dérangerait
de…?** would you mind…?

dérapage /deʀapaʒ/ nm skid.
déraper [1] vi skid; (fig) (prix) get
out of control.

déréglé, ~e /deʀegle/ a (vie)
dissolute; (estomac) upset; (mécanisme) (that is) not running
properly.

dérégler /deʀegle/ [14] vt make
go wrong. □ se ~ vpr go wrong.

dérision /deʀizjɔ̃/ nf mockery;
tourner en ~ ridicule.

dérive /deʀiv/ nf aller à la ~ drift.
dérivé /deʀive/ nm by-product.
dériver /deʀive/ [1] vi (bateau)
drift; ~ de stem from.

dermatologie /dɛʀmatɔlɔʒi/ nf
dermatology.

dernier, -ière /dɛʀnje, -jɛʀ/ a
last; (nouvelles, mode) latest;
(étage) top. ● nm, f last (one); **ce
~ the latter; le ~ de mes soucis**
the least of my worries.

dernièrement /dɛʀnjɛʀmɑ̃/ adv
recently.

dérober /deʀɔbe/ [1] vt steal.
□ se ~ vpr slip away; **se ~ à**
(obligation) shy away from.

dérogation /deʀɔgasjɔ̃/ nf
special authorization.

déroger /deʀɔʒe/ [40] vi ~ à
depart from.

déroulement /deʀulmɑ̃/ nm
(d'une action) development.

dérouler /deʀule/ [1] vt (fil etc.)
unwind. □ se ~ vpr unwind; (avoir
lieu) take place; (récit, paysage)
unfold.

déroute /deʀut/ nf (Mil) rout.
dérouter /deʀute/ [1] vt
disconcert.

derrière /dɛʀjɛʀ/ prép & adv
behind. ● nm back, rear; (postérieur
▯) behind ▯; **de ~** (fenêtre)
back, rear; (pattes) hind.

des /de/ ⇒DE.

dès /dɛ/ prép (right) from; ~ **lors**
from then on; ~ **que** as soon as.

désabusé, ~e /dezabyze/ a
disillusioned.

désaccord /dezakɔʀ/ nm
disagreement.

désaffecté, ~e /dezafɛkte/ a
disused.

désagréable /dezagʀeabl/ a
unpleasant.

désagrément /dezagʀemɑ̃/ nm
annoyance, inconvenience.

désaltérer (se) /(sə)dezaltere/
[14] vpr quench one's thirst.

désamorcer /dezamɔʀse/ [10] vt
(situation, obus) defuse.

désapprobation /dezapʀɔbasjɔ̃/
nf disapproval. **désapprouver** [1]
vt disapprove of.

désarçonner /dezaʀsɔne/ [1] vt
throw.

désarmement /dezaʀməmɑ̃/ nm
(Pol) disarmament.

désarroi /dezaʀwa/ nm distress.
désastre /dezastʀ/ nm disaster.
désastreux, -euse a disastrous.

désavantage /dezavɑ̃taʒ/ nm
disadvantage. **désavantager** [40]
vt put at a disadvantage.

désaveu (pl ~x) /dezavø/ nm
denial. **désavouer** [1] vt deny.

descendance /desɑ̃dɑ̃s/ nf
descent; (enfants) descendants (+
pl). **descendant, ~e** nm, f
descendant.

descendre /desɑ̃dʀ/ [3] vi (aux
être) go down; (venir) come down;
(passager) get off ou out; (nuit)
fall; ~ **à pied** walk down; ~ **par
l'ascenseur** take the lift down; ~
de (être issu de) be descended
from; ~ **à l'hôtel** go to a hotel; ~
dans la rue (Pol) take to the

streets. ● vt (aux avoir) (escalier etc.) go ou come down; (objet) take down; (abattre ▯) shoot down.

descente /desɑ̃t/ nf descent; (à ski) downhill; (raid) raid; **dans la ~** going downhill; **~ de lit** bedside rug.

descriptif, -ive /deskriptif, -v/ a descriptive. **description** nf description.

désemparé, ~e /dezɑ̃pare/ a distraught.

désendettement /dezɑ̃dɛtmɑ̃/ nm reduction of the debt.

déséquilibré, ~e /dezekilibre/ a unbalanced; ▯ crazy. ● nm,f lunatic. **déséquilibrer** [1] vt throw off balance.

désert, ~e /dezɛʀ, -t/ a deserted. ● nm desert.

déserter /dezɛʀte/ [1] vt/i desert. **déserteur** nm deserter.

désertique /dezɛʀtik/ a desert.

désespérant, ~e /dezɛspeʀɑ̃, -t/ a utterly disheartening.

désespéré, ~e /dezɛspere/ a in despair; (état, cas) hopeless; (effort) desperate.

désespérer /dezɛspere/ [14] vt drive to despair. ● vi despair, lose hope; **~ de** despair of. ▫ se **~** vpr despair.

désespoir /dezɛspwaʀ/ nm despair; **en ~ de cause** as a last resort.

déshabillé, ~e /dezabije/ a undressed. ● nm négligee.

déshabiller /dezabije/ [1] vt undress. ▫ se **~** vpr get undressed.

désherbant /dezɛʀbɑ̃/ nm weed-killer.

déshérité, ~e /dezerite/ a (région) deprived; (personne) the underprivileged.

déshériter /dezerite/ [1] vt disinherit.

déshonneur /dezɔnœʀ/ nm disgrace.

déshonorer /dezɔnɔʀe/ [1] vt dishonour.

déshydrater /dezidʀate/ [1] vt dehydrate. ▫ se **~** vpr get dehydrated.

désigner /deziɲe/ [1] vt (montrer) point to ou out; (élire) appoint; (signifier) designate.

désillusion /dezilyzjɔ̃/ nf disillusionment.

désinence /dezinɑ̃s/ nf (Gram) ending.

désinfectant /dezɛ̃fɛktɑ̃/ nm disinfectant. **désinfecter** [1] vt disinfect.

désintéressé, ~e /dezɛ̃terese/ a (personne, acte) selfless.

désintéresser (se) /(sə)dezɛ̃terese/ [1] vpr se **~ de** lose interest in.

désintoxiquer /dezɛ̃tɔksike/ [1] vt detoxify; **se faire ~** to undergo detoxification.

désinvolte /dezɛ̃vɔlt/ a casual. **désinvolture** nf casualness.

désir /deziʀ/ nm wish, desire; (convoitise) desire.

désirer /dezire/ [1] vt want; (sexuellement) desire; **vous désirez?** what would you like?

désireux, -euse /deziʀø, -z/ a **~ de faire** anxious to do.

désistement /dezistəmɑ̃/ nm withdrawal.

désobéir /dezɔbeiʀ/ [2] vi **~ (à)** disobey. **désobéissant, ~e** a disobedient.

désobligeant, ~e /dezɔbliʒɑ̃, -t/ a disagreeable, unkind.

désodorisant /dezɔdɔʀizɑ̃/ nm air freshener.

désodoriser /dezɔdɔʀize/ [1] vt freshen up.

désœuvré, ~e /dezœvʀe/ a at a loose end. **désœuvrément** nm lack of anything to do.

D

désolation /dezɔlasjõ/ *nf*
distress.

désolé, **~e** /dezɔle/ *a* (au regret)
sorry; (*région*) desolate.

désoler /dezɔle/ [1] *vt* distress.
□ **se** ~ *vpr* be upset (**de qch**
about sth).

désopilant, **~e** /dezɔpilã, -t/ *a*
hilarious.

désordonné, **~e** /dezɔrdɔne/ *a*
untidy; (*mouvements*)
uncoordinated.

désordre /dezɔrdr/ *nm*
untidiness; (Pol) disorder; **en** ~
untidy.

désorganiser /dezɔrganize/ [1]
vt disorganize.

désorienter /dezɔrjɑ̃te/ [1] *vt*
disorient.

désormais /dezɔrmɛ/ *adv* from
now on.

desquels, desquelles /dekɛl/
⇒LEQUEL.

dessécher /deseʃe/ [1] *vt* dry
out. □ **se** ~ *vpr* dry out, become
dry; (*plante*) wither.

dessein /desɛ̃/ *nm* intention; **à** ~
intentionally.

desserrer /desere/ [1] *vt* loosen;
il n'a pas desserré les dents he
never once opened his mouth.
□ **se** ~ *vpr* come loose.

dessert /desɛr/ *nm* dessert; **en** ~
for dessert.

desservir /desɛrvir/ [46] *vt/i*
(*débarrasser*) clear away; (*autobus*)
serve.

dessin /desɛ̃/ *nm* drawing; (*motif*)
design; (*discipline*) art; (*contour*)
outline; **professeur de** ~ art
teacher; ~ **animé** (*cinéma*) cartoon;
~ **humoristique** cartoon.

dessinateur, -trice /desinatœr,
-tris/ *nm, f* artist; (*industriel*)
draughtsman.

dessiner /desine/ [1] *vt/i* draw;
(fig) outline. □ **se** ~ *vpr* appear,
take shape.

dessoûler /desule/ [1] *vt/i* sober
up.

dessous /dəsu/ *adv* underneath.
● *nm* underside, underneath.
● *nmpl* underwear; **les** ~ **d'une
histoire** what is behind a story; **du**
~ bottom; (*voisins*) downstairs;
en ~, **par-**~ underneath.
dessous-de-plat *nm inv* (heat-
resistant) table-mat. **dessous-
de-table** *nm inv* backhander.
dessous-de-verre *nm inv*
coaster.

dessus /dəsy/ *adv* on top (of it),
on it. ● *nm* top; **du** ~ top;
(*voisins*) upstairs; **avoir le** ~ get
the upper hand. **dessus-de-lit**
nm inv bedspread.

destabiliser /destabilize/ [1] *vt*
destabilize, unsettle.

destin /destɛ̃/ *nm* (sort) fate;
(*avenir*) destiny.

destinataire /destinatɛr/ *nmf*
addressee.

destination /destinasjõ/ *nf*
destination; (*fonction*) purpose; **vol
à** ~ **de** flight to.

destinée /destine/ *nf* destiny.

destiner /destine/ [1] *vt* ~ **à**
intend for; (*vouer*) destine for; **le
commentaire m'est destiné** this
comment is aimed at me; **être
destiné à faire** be intended to do;
(*obligé*) be destined to do. □ **se** ~
à *vpr* (*carrière*) intend to take up.

destituer /destitɥe/ [1] *vt*
discharge.

destructeur, -trice /destryktœr,
-tris/ *a* destructive. **destruction**
nf destruction.

désuet, -ète /dezɥɛ, -t/ *a*
outdated.

détachant /detaʃã/ *nm* stain
remover.

détacher /detaʃe/ [1] *vt* untie;
(*ôter*) remove, detach; (*déléguer*)
second. □ **se** ~ *vpr* come off,

break away; (*nœud etc.*) come undone; (*ressortir*) stand out.

détail /detaj/ *nm* detail; (de compte) breakdown; (Comm) retail; **au ~** (*vendre etc.*) retail; **de ~** (*prix etc.*) retail; **en ~** in detail; **entrer dans les ~s** go into detail.

détaillant, ~e /detajã, -t/ *nm, f* retailer.

détaillé, ~e /detaje/ *a* detailed.

détailler /detaje/ [1] *vt* (*rapport*) detail; **~ ce que qn fait** scrutinize what sb does.

détaler /detale/ [1] *vi* ▣ bolt.

détartrant /detaRtRã/ *nm* descaler.

détecter /detɛkte/ [1] *vt* detect. **détecteur** *nm* detector.

détective /detɛktiv/ *nm* detective.

déteindre /detɛdR/ [22] *vi* (dans l'eau) run (**sur** on to); (au soleil) fade; **~ sur** (fig) rub off on.

détendre /detãdR/ [3] *vt* slacken; (*ressort*) release; (*personne*) relax. □ **se ~** *vpr* (*ressort*) slacken; (*personne*) relax.

détendu, ~e *a* (calme) relaxed.

détenir /det(ə)niR/ [58] *vt* hold; (*secret, fortune*) possess.

détente /detãt/ *nf* relaxation; (Pol) détente; (saut) spring; (gâchette) trigger; **être lent à la ~** ▣ be slow on the uptake.

détenteur, -trice /detãtœr, -tris/ *nm, f* holder.

détention /detãsjõ/ *nf* detention; **~ provisoire** custody.

détenu, ~e /detny/ *nm, f* prisoner.

détergent /detɛRʒã/ *nm* detergent.

détérioration /deterjɔRasjõ/ *nf* deterioration; (dégât) damage.

détériorer /deterjɔRe/ [1] *vt* damage. □ **se ~** *vpr* deteriorate.

détermination /detɛRminasjõ/ *nf* determination. **déterminé, ~e**

a (résolu) determined; (précis) definite. **déterminer** [1] *vt* determine.

déterrer /detere/ [1] *vt* dig up.

détestable /detɛstabl/ *a* (caractère, temps) foul.

détester /detɛste/ [1] *vt* hate. □ **se ~** *vpr* hate each other.

détonation /detɔnasjõ/ *nf* explosion, detonation.

détour /detuR/ *nm* (crochet) detour; (fig) roundabout means; (virage) bend.

détournement /detuRnəmã/ *nm* hijack(ing); (de fonds) embezzlement.

détourner /detuRne/ [1] *vt* (*attention*) divert; (*tête, yeux*) turn away; (*avion*) hijack; (*argent*) embezzle. □ **se ~ de** *vpr* stray from.

détraquer /detRake/ [1] *vt* make go wrong; (*estomac*) upset. □ **se ~** *vpr* (*machine*) go wrong.

détresse /detRɛs/ *nf* distress; **dans la ~, en ~** in distress.

détritus /detRitys/ *nmpl* rubbish (+ *sg*).

détroit /detRwa/ *nm* strait.

détromper /detRõpe/ [1] *vt* set straight. □ **se ~** *vpr* **détrompe-toi!** you'd better think again!

détruire /detRųiR/ [17] *vt* destroy.

dette /dɛt/ *nf* debt.

deuil /dœj/ *nm* (période) mourning; (décès) bereavement; **porter le ~** be in mourning; **faire son ~ de qch** give sth up as lost.

deux /dø/ *a & nm* two; **~ fois** twice; **tous (les) ~** both.

deuxième *a & nmf* second.

deux-pièces *nm inv* (maillot de bain) two-piece; (logement) two-room flat. **deux-points** *nm inv* (Gram) colon. **deux-roues** *nm inv* two-wheeled vehicle.

dévaliser /devalize/ [1] vt rob, clean out.

dévalorisant, ~e /devalɔRizɑ̃, -t/ a demeaning.

dévaloriser /devalɔRize/ [1] vt (monnaie) devalue. □ **se** ~ vpr (personne) put oneself down.

dévaluation /devalɥasjɔ̃/ nf devaluation.

dévaluer /devalɥe/ [1] vt devalue. □ **se** ~ vpr devalue.

devancer /dəvɑ̃se/ [10] vt be ou go ahead of; (arriver) arrive ahead of; (prévenir) anticipate.

devant /d(ə)vɑ̃/ prép in front of; (distance) ahead of; (avec mouvement) past; (en présence de) in front of; (face à) in the face of; **avoir du temps** ~ **soi** have plenty of time. ● adv in front; (à distance) ahead; **de** ~ front. ● nm front; **prendre les** ~**s** take the initiative.

devanture /dəvɑ̃tyR/ nf shop front; (vitrine) shop window.

développement /devlɔpmɑ̃/ nm development; (de photos) developing.

développer /devlɔpe/ [1] vt develop. □ **se** ~ vpr (corps, talent) develop; (entreprise) grow, expand.

devenir /dəvniR/ [58] vi (aux être) become; **qu'est-il devenu?** what has become of him?

dévergondé, ~e /devɛRgɔ̃de/ a & nm,f shameless (person).

déverser /devɛRse/ [1] vt (liquide) pour; (ordures, pétrole) dump. □ **se** ~ vpr (rivière) flow; (égout, foule) pour.

dévêtir /devetiR/ [61] vt undress. □ **se** ~ vpr get undressed.

déviation /devjasjɔ̃/ nf diversion.

dévier /devje/ [45] vt divert; (coup) deflect. ● vi (ballon, balle) veer; (personne) deviate.

devin /dəvɛ̃/ nm soothsayer.

deviner /dəvine/ [1] vt guess; (apercevoir) distinguish.

devinette /dəvinɛt/ nf riddle.

devis /dəvi/ nm estimate, quote.

dévisager /devizaʒe/ [40] vt stare at.

devise /dəviz/ nf motto; ~**s** (monnaie) (foreign) currency.

dévisser /devise/ [1] vt unscrew.

dévitaliser /devitalize/ [1] vt (dent) carry out root canal treatment on.

dévoiler /devwale/ [1] vt reveal.

devoir /dəvwaR/ [26]

● verbe auxiliaire

····~ **faire** (obligation, hypothèse) must do; (nécessité) have got to do; **je dois dire que...** I have to say that...; **il a dû partir** (nécessité) he had to leave; (hypothèse) he must have left.

····▸ (prévision) **je devais lui dire** I was to tell her; **elle doit rentrer bientôt** she's due back soon.

····▸ (conseil) **tu devrais** you should.

● verbe transitif

····▸ (argent, excuses) owe; **combien je vous dois?** (en achetant) how much is it?

□ **se devoir** verbe pronominal

····▸ **je me dois de le faire** it's my duty to do it.

● nom masculin

····▸ duty; **faire son** ~ do one's duty.

····▸ (Scol) ~ (surveillé) test; **les** ~**s** homework (+ sg); **faire ses** ~**s** do one's homework.

dévorer /devɔRe/ [1] vt devour.

dévot, ~e /devo, -ɔt/ a devout.

dévoué, ~e /devwe/ a devoted. **dévouement** nm devotion.

dévouer (se) /(sə)devwe/ [1] vpr

devote oneself (**à** to); (**se sacrifier**) sacrifice oneself.

dextérité /dɛksteʀite/ *nf* skill.

diabète /djabɛt/ *nm* diabetes. **diabétique** *a* & *nmf* diabetic.

diable /djabl/ *nm* devil.

diagnostic /djagnɔstik/ *nm* diagnosis. **diagnostiquer** [1] *vt* diagnose.

diagonal, ~e (*mpl* **-aux**) /djagɔnal, -o/ *a* diagonal. **diagonale** *nf* diagonal; **en ~e** diagonally.

diagramme /djagʀam/ *nm* diagram; (graphique) graph.

dialecte /djalɛkt/ *nm* dialect.

dialogue /djalɔg/ *nm* dialogue. **dialoguer** [1] *vi* have talks, enter into a dialogue.

diamant /djamɑ̃/ *nm* diamond.

diamètre /djamɛtʀ/ *nm* diameter.

diapositive /djapozitiv/ *nf* slide.

diarrhée /djaʀe/ *nf* diarrhoea.

dictateur /diktatœʀ/ *nm* dictator.

dicter /dikte/ [1] *vt* dictate. **dictée** *nf* dictation.

dictionnaire /diksjɔnɛʀ/ *nm* dictionary.

dicton /diktɔ̃/ *nm* saying.

dièse /djɛz/ *nm* (Mus) sharp.

diesel /djezɛl/ *nm* & *a inv* diesel.

diète /djɛt/ *nf* restricted diet.

diététicien, ~ne /djetetisjɛ̃, -ɛn/ *nm, f* dietician.

diététique /djetetik/ *nf* dietetics. ● *a* **produit** *ou* **aliment ~** dietary product; **magasin ~** health food shop *ou* store.

dieu (*pl* **~x**) /djø/ *nm* god; **D~** God.

diffamation /difamasjɔ̃/ *nf* slander; (par écrit) libel. **diffamer** [1] *vt* slander; (par écrit) libel.

différé: en ~ /ɑ̃difeʀe/ *loc* (émission) pre-recorded.

différemment /difeʀamɑ̃/ *adv* differently.

différence /difeʀɑ̃s/ *nf* difference; **à la ~ de** unlike.

différencier /difeʀɑ̃sje/ [45] *vt* differentiate. □ **se ~** *vpr* differentiate oneself; **se ~ de** (différer de) differ from.

différend /difeʀɑ̃/ *nm* difference (of opinion).

différent, ~e /difeʀɑ̃, -t/ *a* different (**de** from).

différer /difeʀe/ [14] *vt* postpone. ● *vi* differ (**de** from).

difficile /difisil/ *a* difficult; (exigeant) fussy. **difficilement** *adv* with difficulty.

difficulté /difikylte/ *nf* difficulty; **faire des ~s** raise objections.

diffus, ~e /dify, -z/ *a* diffuse.

diffuser /difyze/ [1] *vt* (émission) broadcast; (nouvelle) spread; (lumière, chaleur) diffuse; (Comm) distribute. **diffusion** *nf* broadcasting; diffusion; distribution.

digérer /diʒeʀe/ [14] *vt* digest; (endurer ▯) stomach. **digeste** *a* digestible.

digestif, -ive /diʒɛstif, -v/ *a* digestive. ● *nm* after-dinner liqueur.

digital, ~e (*mpl* **-aux**) /diʒital, -o/ *a* digital.

digne /diɲ/ *a* (noble) dignified; (approprié) worthy; **~ de** worthy of; **~ de foi** trustworthy.

digue /dig/ *nf* dyke; (US) dike.

dilater /dilate/ [1] *vt* dilate. □ **se ~** *vpr* dilate; (estomac) distend.

dilemme /dilɛm/ *nm* dilemma.

dilettante /diletɑ̃t/ *nmf* amateur.

diluant /dilɥɑ̃/ *nm* thinner.

diluer /dilɥe/ [1] *vt* dilute.

dimanche /dimɑ̃ʃ/ *nm* Sunday.

dimension /dimɑ̃sjɔ̃/ *nf* (taille) size; (mesure) dimension; (aspect) dimension.

diminuer /diminɥe/ [1] *vt* reduce, decrease; (plaisir,

courage) dampen; (*dénigrer*)
diminish. ● *vi* (se réduire) decrease;
(*faiblir*) (*bruit, flamme*) die down;
(*ardeur*) cool. **diminutif** *nm*
diminutive; (*surnom*) pet name.
diminution *nf* decrease (**de** in);
(*réduction*) reduction; (*affaiblissement*)
diminishing.

dinde /dɛ̃d/ *nf* turkey.

dîner /dine/ [1] *vi* have dinner.
● *nm* dinner.

dingue /dɛ̃g/ *a* ⊞ crazy.

dinosaure /dinozɔR/ *nm*
dinosaur.

diphtongue /diftɔ̃g/ *nf*
diphthong.

diplomate /diplɔmat/ *nmf*
diplomat. ● *a* diplomatic.
diplomatique *a* diplomatic.

diplôme /diplom/ *nm* certificate,
diploma; (Univ) degree. **diplômé,**
∼e *a* qualified.

dire /diR/ [27] *vt* say; (*secret,
vérité, heure*) tell; (*penser*) think;
∼ que say that; **∼ à qn que** tell sb
that; **∼ à qn de** tell sb to; **ça me dit
de faire** I feel like doing; **on dirait
que** it would seem that, it seems
that; **dis/dites donc!** hey! ◻ **se ∼**
vpr (*mot*) be said; (*penser*) tell
oneself; (se prétendre) claim to be.
● *nm* **au ∼ de, selon les ∼s de**
according to.

direct, ∼e /diRɛkt/ *a* direct. ● *nm*
(*train*) express train; **en ∼**
(*émission*) live.

directeur, -trice /diRɛktœR,
-tRis/ *nm, f* director; (chef de service)
manager, manageress; (de journal)
editor; (d'école) headteacher; (US)
principal; **∼ de banque** bank
manager; **∼ commercial** sales
manager; **∼ des ressources
humaines** human resources
manager.

direction /diRɛksjɔ̃/ *nf* (sens)
direction; (de société) management;
(Auto) steering; **en ∼ de** (going to).

dirigeant, ∼e /diRiʒɑ̃, -t/ *nm, f*
(Pol) leader; (Comm) manager. ● *a*
(*classe*) ruling.

diriger /diRiʒe/ [40] *vt* (*service,
école, parti, pays*) run;
(*entreprise, usine*) manage;
(*travaux*) supervise; (*véhicule*)
steer; (*orchestre*) conduct;
(braquer) aim; (tourner) turn. ◻ **se ∼**
vpr (s'orienter) find one's way; **se ∼
vers** head for, make for.

dis /di/ ⇒DIRE [27].

discernement /disɛRnəmɑ̃/ *nm*
discernment.

disciplinaire *a* disciplinary.
discipline *nf* discipline.

discontinu, ∼e /diskɔ̃tiny/ *a*
intermittent.

discordant, ∼e /diskɔRdɑ̃, -t/ *a*
discordant.

discothèque /diskɔtɛk/ *nf*
record library; (boîte de nuit) disco
(thèque).

discours /diskuR/ *nm* speech;
(propos) views.

discret, -ète /diskRɛ, -t/ *a*
discreet.

discrétion /diskResjɔ̃/ *nf*
discretion; **à ∼** (*vin*) unlimited;
(*manger, boire*) as much as one
desires.

discrimination /diskRiminasjɔ̃/
nf discrimination.
discriminatoire *a*
discriminatory.

disculper /diskylpe/ [1] *vt*
exonerate. ◻ **se ∼** *vpr* vindicate
oneself.

discussion /diskysjɔ̃/ *nf*
discussion; (querelle) argument.

discutable /diskytabl/ *a*
debatable; (critiquable)
questionable.

discuter /diskyte/ [1] *vt* discuss;
(contester) question. ● *vi* (parler)
talk; (répliquer) argue; **∼ de**
discuss.

disette /dizɛt/ *nf* food shortage.

disgrâce /disgʀɑs/ *nf* disgrace.

disgracieux, -ieuse /disgʀasjø, -z/ *a* ugly, unsightly.

disjoindre /disʒwɛ̃dʀ/ [22] *vt* take apart. □ **se** ~ *vpr* come apart.

disloquer /dislɔke/ [1] *vt* (*membre*) dislocate; (*machine*) break (apart). □ **se** ~ *vpr* (*parti, cortège*) break up; (*meuble*) come apart.

disparaître /dispaʀɛtʀ/ [18] *vi* disappear; (*mourir*) die; **faire** ~ get rid of. **disparition** *nf* disappearance; (*mort*) death.

disparate /dispaʀat/ *a* ill-assorted.

disparu, ~e /dispaʀy/ *a* missing. ● *nm, f* missing person; (*mort*) dead person.

dispensaire /dispãsɛʀ/ *nm* clinic.

dispense /dispãs/ *nf* exemption.

dispenser /dispãse/ [1] *vt* exempt (**de** from). □ **se** ~ **de** *vpr* avoid.

disperser /dispɛʀse/ [1] *vt* (*éparpiller*) scatter; (*répartir*) disperse. □ **se** ~ *vpr* disperse.

disponibilité /dispɔnibilite/ *nf* availability. **disponible** *a* available.

dispos, ~e /dispo, -z/ *a* **frais et** ~ fresh and alert.

disposé, ~e /dispoze/ *a* **bien/mal** ~ in a good/bad mood; ~ **à** prepared to; ~ **envers** disposed towards.

disposer /dispoze/ [1] *vt* arrange; ~ **à** (*engager à*) incline to. ● *vi* ~ **de** have at one's disposal. □ **se** ~ **à** *vpr* prepare to.

dispositif /dispozitif/ *nm* device; (*ensemble de mesures*) operation.

disposition /dispozisjɔ̃/ *nf* arrangement, layout; (*tendance*) tendency; ~**s** (*humeur*) mood; (*préparatifs*) arrangements; (*mesures*)

measures; (*aptitude*) aptitude; **mettre à la** ~ **de** place *ou* put at the disposal of.

disproportionné, ~e /dispʀɔpɔʀsjɔne/ *a* disproportionate; ~ **à** out of proportion with.

dispute /dispyt/ *nf* quarrel.

disputer /dispyte/ [1] *vt* (*match*) play; (*course*) run in; (*prix*) fight for; (*gronder* 🔲) tell off. □ **se** ~ *vpr* quarrel; (*se battre pour*) fight over; (*match*) be played.

disquaire /diskɛʀ/ *nmf* record dealer.

disque /disk/ *nm* (Mus) record; (Sport) discus; (*cercle*) disc, disk; (Ordinat) disk; ~ **compact** compact disc; ~ **dur** hard disk; ~ **optique compact** CD ROM; ~ **souple** floppy disk.

disquette /diskɛt/ *nf* floppy disk, diskette; ~ **de sauvegarde** back-up disk.

disséminer /disemine/ [1] *vt* spread, scatter.

dissertation /disɛʀtasjɔ̃/ *nf* essay, paper.

disserter /disɛʀte/ [1] *vi* ~ **sur** speak about; (*par écrit*) write about.

dissident, ~e /disidã, -t/ *a* & *nm, f* dissident.

dissimulation /disimylasjɔ̃/ *nf* concealment; (*fig*) deceit.

dissimuler /disimyle/ [1] *vt* conceal (**à** from). □ **se** ~ *vpr* conceal oneself.

dissipé, ~e /disipe/ *a* (*élève*) unruly.

dissiper /disipe/ [1] *vt* (*fumée, crainte*) dispel; (*fortune*) squander; (*personne*) distract. □ **se** ~ *vpr* disappear; (*élève*) grow restless.

dissolvant /disɔlvã/ *nm* solvent; (*pour ongles*) nail polish remover.

dissoudre /disudʀ/ [53] *vt* dissolve. □ **se** ~ *vpr* dissolve.

D

dissuader /disɥade/ [1] vt
dissuade (**de** from).

dissuasion /disɥazjɔ̃/ nf
dissuasion; **force de** ~ deterrent
force.

distance /distɑ̃s/ nf distance;
(écart) gap; **à** ~ at ou from a
distance.

distancer /distɑ̃se/ [10] vt
outdistance.

distendre /distɑ̃dʀ/ [3] vt
(estomac) distend; (corde) stretch.

distinct, ~**e** /distɛ̃(kt), -ɛ̃kt/ a
distinct.

distinctif, -ive /distɛ̃ktif, -v/ a
(trait) distinctive; (signe,
caractère) distinguishing.

distinction /distɛ̃ksjɔ̃/ nf
distinction; (récompense) honour.

distinguer /distɛ̃ge/ [1] vt
distinguish.

distraction /distʀaksjɔ̃/ nf
absent-mindedness; (passe-temps)
entertainment, leisure; (détente)
recreation.

distraire /distʀɛʀ/ [29] vt amuse;
(rendre inattentif) distract; ~ **qn de**
qch take sb's mind off sth. □ se
~ vpr amuse oneself.

distrait, ~**e** /distʀɛ, -t/ a absent-
minded; (élève) inattentive.

distrayant, ~**e** /distʀɛjɑ̃, -t/ a
entertaining.

distribuer /distʀibɥe/ [1] vt hand
out, distribute; (répartir) distribute;
(tâches, rôles) allocate; (cartes)
deal; (courrier) deliver.

distributeur /distʀibytœʀ/ nm
(Auto, Comm) distributor; ~
(automatique) vending-machine;
~ **de billets** (**de banque**) cash
dispenser. **distribution** nf
distribution; (du courrier) delivery;
(acteurs) cast; (secteur) retailing.

district /distʀikt/ nm district.

dit[1], **dites** /di, dit/ ⇒DIRE [27].

dit[2], ~**e** /di, dit/ a (décidé) agreed;
(surnommé) known as.

diurne /djyʀn/ a diurnal;
(activité) daytime.

divagations /divagasjɔ̃/ nfpl
ravings.

divergence /divɛʀʒɑ̃s/ nf
divergence. **divergent**, ~**e** a
divergent. **diverger** [40] vi
diverge.

divers, ~**e** /divɛʀ, -s/ a (varié)
diverse; (différent) various; (frais)
miscellaneous; **dépenses** ~**es**
sundries. **diversifier** [45] vt
diversify.

diversité /divɛʀsite/ nf diversity,
variety.

divertir /divɛʀtiʀ/ [2] vt amuse,
entertain. □ se ~ vpr amuse
oneself; (passer du bon temps) enjoy
oneself. **divertissement** nm
amusement, entertainment.

dividende /dividɑ̃d/ nm
dividend.

divin, ~**e** /divɛ̃, -in/ a divine.
divinité nf divinity.

diviser /divize/ [1] vt divide. □ se
~ vpr become divided; **se** ~ **par**
sept be divisible by seven. **division** nf division.

divorce /divɔʀs/ nm divorce.

divorcé, ~**e** /divɔʀse/ a
divorced. ● nm, f divorcee.

divorcer /divɔʀse/ [10] vi ~
(d'avec) divorce.

dix /dis/ (/di/ before consonant,
/diz/ before vowel) a & nm ten.

dix-huit /dizɥit/ a & nm eighteen.

dixième /dizjɛm/ a & nmf tenth.

dix-neuf /diznœf/ a & nm
nineteen.

dix-sept /disɛt/ a & nm
seventeen.

docile /dɔsil/ a docile.

docteur /dɔktœʀ/ nm doctor.

doctorat /dɔktɔʀa/ nm doctorate,
PhD.

document /dɔkymɑ̃/ nm
document. **documentaire** a &
nm documentary.

documentaliste /dɔkymɑ̃talist/ *nmf* information officer; (Scol) librarian.

documentation /dɔkymɑ̃tasjɔ̃/ *nf* information, literature; **centre de ~** resource centre.

documenté, ~e /dɔkymɑ̃te/ *a* well-documented.

documenter /dɔkymɑ̃te/ [1] *vt* provide with information. □ **se ~** *vpr* collect information.

dodo /dodo/ *nm* faire **~** (langage enfantin) sleep.

dodu, ~e /dody/ *a* plump.

dogmatique /dɔgmatik/ *a* dogmatic. **dogme** *nm* dogma.

doigt /dwa/ *nm* finger; **un ~ de a** drop of; **montrer qch du ~** point at sth; **à deux ~s de** a hair's breadth away from; **~ de pied** toe. **doigté** *nm* (Mus) fingering, touch; (diplomatie) tact.

dois, doit /dwa/ ⇒DEVOIR [26].

doléances /dɔleɑ̃s/ *nfpl* grievances.

dollar /dɔlar/ *nm* dollar.

domaine /dɔmɛn/ *nm* estate, domain; (fig) domain, field.

domestique /dɔmɛstik/ *a* domestic. ● *nmf* servant.

domestiquer [1] *vt* domesticate.

domicile /dɔmisil/ *nm* home, **à ~** at home; (*livrer*) to the home.

domicilié, ~e /dɔmisilje/ *a* resident; **être ~ à Paris** live *ou* be resident in Paris.

dominant, ~e /dɔminɑ̃, -t/ *a* dominant. **dominante** *nf* dominant feature.

dominer /dɔmine/ [1] *vt* dominate; (*surplomber*) tower over, dominate; (*sujet*) master; (*peur*) overcome. ● *vi* dominate; (*équipe*) be in the lead; (*prévaloir*) stand out.

domino /dɔmino/ *nm* domino.

dommage /dɔmaʒ/ *nm* (tort) harm; **~(s)** (dégâts) damage; **c'est ~** it's a pity *ou* shame; **quel ~** what a pity *ou* shame.

dommages-intérêts *nmpl* (Jur) damages.

dompter /dɔ̃te/ [1] *vt* tame.

dompteur, -euse *nm, f* tamer.

DOM-TOM /dɔmtɔm/ *abrév mpl* **(départements et territoires d'outre-mer)** French overseas departments and territories.

don /dɔ̃/ *nm* (cadeau, aptitude) gift.

donateur, -trice *nm, f* donor.

donation *nf* donation.

donc /dɔ̃k/ *conj* so, then; (par conséquent) so, therefore; **quoi ~?** what did you say?; **tiens ~!** fancy that!

donjon /dɔ̃ʒɔ̃/ *nm* (tour) keep.

donné, ~e /dɔne/ *a* (fixé) given; (pas cher 🅸) dirt cheap; **étant ~ que** given that.

donnée /dɔne/ *nf* (élément d'information) fact; **~s** data.

donner /dɔne/ [1] *vt* give; (*vieilles affaires*) give away; (distribuer) give out; (*fruits, résultats*) produce; (*film*) show; (*pièce*) put on; **ça donne soif/faim** it makes one thirsty/hungry; **~ qch à réparer** take sth to be repaired; **~ lieu à** give rise to. ● *vi* **~ sur** look out on to; **~ dans** tend towards. □ **se ~ à** *vpr* devote oneself to; **se ~ du mal** go to a lot of trouble (**pour faire** to do).

dont /dɔ̃/

● *pronom*

····▸ (personne) **la fille ~ je te parlais** the girl I was telling you about; **l'homme ~ la fille a dit...** the man whose daughter said...

····▸ (chose) which, **l'affaire ~ il parle** the matter which he is referring to; **la manière ~ elle parle** the way she speaks; **ce ~ il parle** what he's talking about.

····➤ (provenance) from which.

····➤ (parmi lesquels) **deux personnes ~ toi** two people, one of whom is you; **plusieurs thèmes ~ l'identité et le racisme** several topics including identity and racism.

dopage /dɔpaʒ/ *nm* (de cheval) doping; (d'athlète) illegal drug-use.

doper /dɔpe/ [1] *vt* dope. □ **se ~** *vpr* take drugs.

doré, ~e /dɔʀe/ *a* (couleur d'or) golden; (qui rappelle l'or) gold; (avec de l'or) gilt; **la jeunesse ~e** gilded youth.

dorénavant /dɔʀenavɑ̃/ *adv* henceforth.

dorer /dɔʀe/ [1] *vt* gild; (Culin) brown.

dormir /dɔʀmiʀ/ [46] *vi* sleep; (être endormi) be asleep; **~ debout** be asleep on one's feet; **une histoire à ~ debout** a cock-and-bull story.

dortoir /dɔʀtwaʀ/ *nm* dormitory.

dorure /dɔʀyʀ/ *nf* gilding.

dos /do/ *nm* back; (de livre) spine; **à ~ de** riding on; **au ~ de** (chèque) on the back of; **de ~** from behind; **~ crawlé** backstroke.

dosage /dozaʒ/ *nm* (mélange) mixture; (quantité) amount, proportions. **dose** *nf* dose. **doser** [1] *vt* measure out; (contrôler) use in a controlled way.

dossier /dɔsje/ *nm* (documents) file; (Jur) case; (de chaise) back; (TV, presse) special feature.

dot /dɔt/ *nf* dowry.

douane /dwan/ *nf* customs.

douanier, -ière /dwanje, -jɛʀ/ *a* customs. ● *nm* customs officer.

double /dubl/ *a & adv* double. ● *nm* (copie) duplicate; (sosie) double; **le ~ (de)** twice as much

ou as many (as); **le ~ messieurs** the men's doubles.

double-cliquer /dublklike/ [1] *vt* double-click.

doubler /duble/ [1] *vt* double; (dépasser) overtake; (vêtement) line; (film) dub; (classe) repeat; (cap) round. ● *vi* double.

doublure /dublyʀ/ *nf* (étoffe) lining; (acteur) understudy.

douce /dus/ ⇒DOUX.

doucement /dusmɑ̃/ *adv* gently; (sans bruit) quietly; (lentement) slowly.

douceur /dusœʀ/ *nf* (mollesse) softness; (de climat) mildness; (de personne) gentleness; (friandise) sweet; (US) candy; **en ~** smoothly.

douche /duʃ/ *nf* shower.

doucher (se) /duʃe/ [1] **~** *vpr* have *ou* take a shower.

doudoune /dudun/ *nf* Ⓘ down jacket.

doué, ~e /dwe/ *a* gifted; **~ de** endowed with.

douille /duj/ *nf* (Électr) socket.

douillet, ~te /dujɛ, -t/ *a* cosy, comfortable; (personne: péj) soft.

douleur /dulœʀ/ *nf* pain; (chagrin) sorrow, grief. **douloureux, -euse** *a* painful.

doute /dut/ *nm* doubt; **sans ~** no doubt; **sans aucun ~** without doubt.

douter /dute/ [1] *vt* **~ de** doubt; **~ que** doubt that. ● *vi* doubt. □ **se ~ de** *vpr* suspect; **je m'en doutais** I thought so.

douteux, -euse /dutø, -z/ *a* dubious, doubtful.

Douvres /duvʀ/ *npr* Dover.

doux, douce /du, dus/ *a* (moelleux) soft; (sucré) sweet; (clément, pas fort) mild; (pas brusque, bienveillant) gentle.

douzaine /duzɛn/ *nf* about twelve; (douze) dozen; **une ~ d'œufs** a dozen eggs.

D

douze /duz/ a & nm twelve.
douzième a & nmf twelfth.

doyen, ∼ne /dwajɛ̃, -ɛn/ nm, f
dean; (en âge) most senior person.

dragée /dRaʒe/ nf sugared
almond.

draguer /dRage/ [1] vt (rivière)
dredge; (filles Ⅱ) chat up.

drainer /dRene/ [1] vt drain.

dramatique /dRamatik/ a
dramatic; (tragique) tragic. ● nf
(television) drama.

dramatiser /dRamatize/ [1] vt
dramatize.

dramaturge /dRamatyRʒ/ nmf
dramatist.

drame /dRam/ nm (genre) drama;
(pièce) play; (événement tragique)
tragedy.

drap /dRa/ nm sheet; (tissu)
(woollen) cloth.

drapeau (pl ∼x) /dRapo/ nm
flag.

drap-housse (pl draps-
housses) /dRaus/ nm fitted
sheet.

dressage /dREsaʒ/ nm training;
(compétition équestre) dressage.

dresser /dREse/ [1] vt put up,
erect; (tête) raise; (animal) train;
(liste, plan) draw up; ∼ l'oreille
prick up one's ears. □ se ∼ vpr
(bâtiment) stand; (personne) draw
oneself up. **dresseur, -euse** nm, f
trainer.

dribbler /dRible/ [1] vi (Sport)
dribble.

drive /dRajv/ nm (Ordinat) drive.

drogue /dRɔg/ nf drug; la ∼
drugs.

drogué, ∼e /dRɔge/ nm, f drug
addict.

droguer /dRɔge/ [1] vt (malade)
drug heavily; (victime) drug. □ se
∼ vpr take drugs.

droguerie /dRɔgRi/ nf hardware

shop. **droguiste** nmf owner of a
hardware shop.

droit, ∼e /dRwa, -t/ a (contraire de
gauche) right; (non courbe) straight;
(loyal) upright; **angle** ∼ right
angle. ● adv straight. ● nm right;
∼(s) (taxe) duty; **le ∼** (Jur) law;
avoir ∼ à be entitled to; **avoir le ∼
de** be allowed to; **être dans son ∼**
be in the right; ∼ **d'auteur**
copyright; ∼ **d'inscription**
registration fee; ∼s **d'auteur**
royalties.

droite /dRwat/ nf (contraire de
gauche) right; **à** ∼ on the right;
(direction) (to the) right; **la** ∼ the
right (side); (Pol) the right (wing);
(ligne) straight line. **droitier,
-ière** a right-handed.

drôle /dRol/ a (amusant) funny;
(bizarre) funny, odd. **drôlement**
adv funnily; (très Ⅱ) really.

dru, ∼e /dRy/ a thick; **tomber** ∼
fall thick and fast.

drugstore /dRœgstɔR/ nm
drugstore.

du /dy/ ⇒DE.

dû, due /dy/ a due. ● nm due;
(argent) dues; ∼ **à** due to.
● ⇒DEVOIR [26].

duc, duchesse /dyk, dyʃɛs/ nm, f
duke, duchess.

duo /dɥo/ nm (Mus) duet; (fig) duo.

dupe /dyp/ nf dupe.

duplex /dyplɛks/ nm split-level
apartment; (US) duplex; (émission)
link-up.

duplicata /dyplikata/ nm inv
duplicate.

duquel /dykɛl/ ⇒LEQUEL.

dur, ∼e /dyR/ a hard; (sévère)
harsh, hard; (viande) tough; (col,
brosse) stiff; ∼ **d'oreille** hard of
hearing. ● adv hard. ● nm, f
tough nut Ⅱ; (Pol) hardliner.

durable /dyRabl/ a lasting.

durant /dyRɑ̃/ prép (au cours de)
during; (avec mesure de temps) for;

~ **des heures** for hours; **des heures** ~ for hours and hours.

durcir /dyʀsiʀ/ [2] *vt* harden. ● *vi* (*terre*) harden; (*ciment*) set; (*pain*) go hard. □ **se** ~ *vpr* harden.

durée /dyʀe/ *nf* length; (*période*) duration; **de courte** ~ short-lived; **pile longue** ~ long-life battery.

durer /dyʀe/ [1] *vi* last.

dureté /dyʀte/ *nf* hardness; (*sévérité*) harshness.

duvet /dyvɛ/ *nm* down; (*sac*) sleeping-bag.

dynamique /dinamik/ *a* dynamic.

dynamite /dinamit/ *nf* dynamite.

dynamo /dinamo/ *nf* dynamo.

eau (*pl* ~**x**) /o/ *nf* water; ~ **courante** running water; ~ **de mer** seawater; ~ **de source** spring water; ~ **douce/salée** fresh/salt water; ~ **de pluie** rainwater; ~ **potable** drinking water; ~ **de Javel** bleach; ~ **minérale** mineral water; ~ **gazeuse** sparkling water; ~ **plate** still water; ~ **de toilette** eau de toilette; ~**x usées** dirty water; ~**x et forêts** forestry commission (+ *sg*); **tomber à l'**~ (*fig*) fall through; **prendre l'**~ take in water. **eau-de-vie** (*pl* **eaux-de-vie**) *nf* brandy.

ébahi, ~**e** /ebai/ *a* dumbfounded.

ébauche /eboʃ/ *nf* (*dessin*) sketch; (*fig*) attempt.

ébéniste /ebenist/ *nm* cabinet-maker.

éblouir /ebluiʀ/ [2] *vt* dazzle.

éboueur /ebwœʀ/ *nm* dustman.

ébouillanter /ebujɑ̃te/ [1] *vt* scald.

éboulement /ebulmɑ̃/ *nm* landslide.

ébouriffé, ~**e** /eburife/ *a* dishevelled.

ébrécher /ebreʃe/ [14] *vt* chip.

ébruiter /ebruite/ [1] *vt* spread about. □ **s'**~ *vpr* get out.

ébullition /ebylisjɔ̃/ *nf* boiling; **en** ~ boiling.

écaille /ekaj/ *nf* (*de poisson*) scale; (*de peinture, roc*) flake; (*matière*) tortoiseshell.

écarlate /ekaʀlat/ *a* scarlet.

écarquiller /ekaʀkije/ [1] *vt* ~ **les yeux** open one's eyes wide.

écart /ekaʀ/ *nm* gap; (*de prix*) difference; (*embardée*) swerve; ~ **de conduite** lapse in behaviour; **être à l'**~ be isolated; **se tenir à l'**~ **de** stand apart from; (*fig*) keep out of the way of.

écarté, ~**e** /ekaʀte/ *a* (*lieu*) remote; **les jambes** ~**es** (with) legs apart; **les bras** ~**s** with one's arms out.

écarter /ekaʀte/ [1] *vt* (*séparer*) move apart; (*membres*) spread; (*branches*) part; (*éliminer*) dismiss; ~ **qch de** move sth away from; ~ **qn de** keep sb away from. □ **s'**~ *vpr* (*s'éloigner*) move away; (*quitter son chemin*) move aside; **s'**~ **de** stray from.

ecchymose /ekimoz/ *nf* bruise.

écervelé, ~**e** /esɛʀvəle/ *a* scatterbrained. ● *nm, f* scatterbrain.

échafaudage /eʃafodaʒ/ *nm* scaffolding; (*amas*) heap.

échalote /eʃalɔt/ *nf* shallot.

échancré, ~**e** /eʃɑ̃kʀe/ *a* low-cut.

échange /eʃɑ̃ʒ/ *nm* exchange; **en** ~ (**de**) in exchange (for).

échanger [40] *vt* exchange (**contre** for).

échangeur /eʃɑ̃ʒœʀ/ *nm* (Auto) interchange.

échantillon /eʃɑ̃tijɔ̃/ *nm* sample.

échappatoire /eʃapatwaʀ/ *nf* way out.

échappement /eʃapmɑ̃/ *nm* exhaust.

échapper /eʃape/ [1] *vi* ~ **à** escape; (**en fuyant**) escape (from); ~ **des mains de** slip out of the hands of; **ça m'a échappé** (fig) it just slipped out; **l'~ belle** have a narrow *ou* lucky escape. □ **s'~** *vpr* escape.

écharde /eʃaʀd/ *nf* splinter.

écharpe /eʃaʀp/ *nf* scarf; (**de** maire) sash; **en ~** (*bras*) in a sling.

échasse /eʃas/ *nf* stilt.

échauffement /eʃofmɑ̃/ *nm* (Sport) warm up.

échauffer /eʃofe/ [1] *vt* heat; (fig) excite. □ **s'~** *vpr* warm up.

échéance /eʃeɑ̃s/ *nf* due date (for payment); (**délai**) deadline; (**obligation**) (financial) commitment.

échéant: le cas ~ /ləkazeʃeɑ̃/ *loc* if need be.

échec /eʃɛk/ *nm* failure; ~**s** (jeu) chess; ~ **et mat** checkmate.

échelle /eʃɛl/ *nf* ladder; (**dimension**) scale.

échelon /eʃlɔ̃/ *nm* rung; (**hiérarchique**) grade; (**niveau**) level.

échevelé, ~**e** /eʃəvle/ *a* dishevelled.

écho /eko/ *nm* echo; ~**s** (**dans la** presse) gossip.

échographie /ekɔgʀafi/ *nf* (ultrasound) scan.

échouer /eʃwe/ [1] *vi* (*bateau*) run aground; (**ne pas réussir**) fail; ~ **à un examen** fail an exam. ● *vt* (*bateau*) ground. □ **s'~** *vpr* run aground.

échu, ~**e** /eʃy/ *a* (*délai*) expired.

éclabousser /eklabuse/ [1] *vt* splash.

éclair /eklɛʀ/ *nm* (flash of) lightning; (fig) flash; (**gâteau**) éclair. ● *a inv* (*visite*) brief.

éclairage /eklɛʀaʒ/ *nm* lighting.

éclaircie /eklɛʀsi/ *nf* sunny interval.

éclaircir /eklɛʀsiʀ/ [2] *vt* lighten; (*mystère*) clear up. □ **s'~** *vpr* (*ciel*) clear; (*mystère*) become clearer. **éclaircissement** *nm* clarification.

éclairer /eklɛʀe/ [1] *vt* light (up); (*personne*) (fig) enlighten; (*situation*) throw light on. ● *vi* give light. □ **s'~** *vpr* become clearer.

éclaireur, -euse /eklɛʀœʀ, -øz/ *nm,f* (boy) scout, (girl) guide.

éclat /ekla/ *nm* fragment; (**de** lumière) brightness; (**splendeur**) brilliance; ~ **de rire** burst of laughter.

éclatant, ~**e** /eklatɑ̃, -t/ *a* brilliant; (*soleil*) dazzling.

éclater /eklate/ [1] *vi* burst; (**exploser**) go off; (*verre*) shatter; (*guerre*) break out; (*groupe*) split up; ~ **de rire** burst out laughing.

éclipse /eklips/ *nf* eclipse.

éclosion /eklozjɔ̃/ *nf* hatching, opening.

écluse /eklyz/ *nf* (de canal) lock.

écœurant, ~**e** /ekœʀɑ̃, -t/ *a* (*gâteau*) sickly; (fig) disgusting. **écœurer** [1] *vt* sicken.

éco-guerrier, -lère (*pl* **éco-guerriers, ières**) /ekogɛʀie, ɛʀ/ *nmf* eco-warrior.

école /ekɔl/ *nf* school; ~ **maternelle/primaire/secondaire** nursery/primary/secondary school; ~ **normale** teachers' training college. **écolier, -ière** *nm,f* schoolboy, schoolgirl.

écologie /ekɔlɔʒi/ *nf* ecology.

écologique *a* ecological, green.

écologiste *nmf* (chercheur)

ecologist; (dans l'âme)
environmentalist; (Pol) Green.
économie /ekɔnɔmi/ *nf*
economy; (discipline) economics;
~s (argent) savings; **une ~ de** (gain)
a saving of. **économique** *a* (Pol)
economic; (bon marché)
economical.
économiser /ekɔnɔmize/ [1] *vt/i*
save.
écorce /ekɔRs/ *nf* bark; (de fruit)
peel.
écorcher /ekɔRʃe/ [1] *vt* (genou)
graze; (animal) skin. □ **s'~** *vpr*
graze oneself. **écorchure** *nf*
graze.
écossais, ~e /ekɔsɛ, -z/ *a*
Scottish. **É~, ~e** *nm, f* Scot.
Écosse /ekɔs/ *nf* Scotland.
écoulement /ekulmã/ *nm* flow.
écouler /ekule/ [1] *vt* dispose of,
sell. □ **s'~** *vpr* (liquide) flow;
(temps) pass.
écourter /ekuRte/ [1] *vt* shorten.
écoute /ekut/ *nf* listening; **à l'~**
(de) listening in (to); **heures de
grande ~** prime time; **~s
téléphoniques** phone tapping.
écouter /ekute/ [1] *vt* listen to.
● *vi* listen; **~ aux portes**
eavesdrop. **écouteur** *nm*
earphones (+ *pl*); (de téléphone)
receiver.
écran /ekRã/ *nm* screen; **~ total**
sun-block.
écraser /ekRaze/ [1] *vt* crush;
(piéton) run over; (cigarette) stub
out. □ **s'~** *vpr* crash (**contre** into).
écrémé, ~e /ekReme/ *a*
skimmed; **demi-~** semi-skimmed.
écrevisse /ekRəvis/ *nf* crayfish.
écrier (s') /(s)ekRije/ [45] *vpr*
exclaim.
écrin /ekRɛ̃/ *nm* case.
écrire /ekRiR/ [30] *vt/i* write;
(orthographier) spell. □ **s'~** *vpr* (mot)
be spelt.
écrit /ekRi/ *nm* document;

(examen) written paper; **par ~** in
writing.
écriteau (*pl* **~x**) /ekRito/ *nm*
notice.
écriture /ekRityR/ *nf* writing; **~s**
(Comm) accounts.
écrivain /ekRivɛ̃/ *nm* writer.
écrou /ekRu/ *nm* (Tech) nut.
écrouler (s') /(s)ekRule/ [1] *vpr*
collapse.
écru, ~e /ekRy/ *a* (couleur)
natural; (tissu) raw.
écueil /ekœj/ *nm* reef; (fig)
danger.
éculé, ~e /ekyle/ *a* (soulier)
worn at the heel; (fig) well-worn.
écume /ekym/ *nf* foam; (Culin)
scum.
écumer /ekyme/ [1] *vt* skim. ● *vi*
foam.
écureuil /ekyRœj/ *nm* squirrel.
écurie /ekyRi/ *nf* stable.
écuyer, -ère /ekɥije, -jɛR/ *nm, f*
(horse) rider.
eczéma /ɛgzema/ *nm* eczema.
EDF *abrév f* (**Électricité de
France**) French electricity board.
édifice /edifis/ *nm* building.
édifier /edifje/ [45] *vt* construct;
(porter à la vertu) edify.
Édimbourg /edɛ̃buR/ *npr*
Edinburgh.
édit /edi/ *nm* edict.
éditer /edite/ [1] *vt* publish;
(annoter) edit. **éditeur, -trice** *nm, f*
publisher; (réviseur) editor.
édition /edisjɔ̃/ *nf* (activité)
publishing; (livre, disque) edition.
éditique /editik/ *nf* electronic
publishing.
éditorial, ~e (*pl* **-iaux**) /editɔ-
Rjal, -jo/ *a & nm* editorial.
édredon /edRədɔ̃/ *nm* eiderdown.
éducateur, -trice /edykatœR,
-tRis/ *nm, f* youth worker.

éducatif, -ive /edykatif, -v/ *a* educational.

éducation /edykasjɔ̃/ *nf* (façon d'élever) upbringing; (enseignement) education; (manières) manners; ~ **physique** physical education.

éduquer /edyke/ [1] *vt* (élever) bring up; (former) educate.

effacé, ~e /efase/ *a* (modeste) unassuming.

effacer /efase/ [10] *vt* (gommer) rub out; (à l'écran) delete; (*souvenir*) erase. □ **s'~** *vpr* fade; (s'écarter) step aside.

effarer /efaʀe/ [1] *vt* alarm; **être effaré** be astounded.

effaroucher /efaʀuʃe/ [1] *vt* scare away.

effectif, -ive /efɛktif, -v/ *a* effective. ●*nm* (d'école) number of pupils; **~s** numbers. **effectivement** *adv* effectively; (en effet) indeed.

effectuer /efɛktɥe/ [1] *vt* carry out, make.

efféminé, ~e /efemine/ *a* effeminate.

effervescent, ~e /efɛʀvesɑ̃, -t/ *a* **comprimé ~** effervescent tablet.

effet /efɛ/ *nm* effect; (impression) impression; **~s** (habits) clothes, things; **sous l'~ d'une drogue** under the influence of drugs; **en ~** indeed; **faire de l'~** have an effect, be effective; **faire bon/ mauvais ~** make a good/bad impression; **ça fait un drôle d'~** it feels strange.

efficace /efikas/ *a* effective; (*personne*) efficient. **efficacité** *nf* effectiveness; (de personne) efficiency.

effleurer /eflœʀe/ [1] *vt* touch lightly; (*sujet*) touch on; **ça ne m'a pas effleuré** it did not cross my mind.

effondrement /efɔ̃dʀəmɑ̃/ *nm* collapse. **effondrer (s')** [1] *vpr* collapse.

efforcer (s') /(s)efɔʀse/ [10] *vpr* try (hard) (**de** to).

effort /efɔʀ/ *nm* effort.

effraction /efʀaksjɔ̃/ *nf* **entrer par ~** break in.

effrayant, ~e /efʀejɑ̃, -t/ *a* frightening; (fig) frightful.

effrayer /efʀeje/ [31] *vt* frighten; (décourager) put off. □ **s'~** *vpr* be frightened.

effréné, ~e /efʀene/ *a* wild.

effriter (s') /(s)efʀite/ [1] *vpr* crumble.

effroi /efʀwa/ *nm* dread.

effronté, ~o /cfʀɔ̃te/ *a* cheeky. ●*nm, f* cheeky boy, cheeky girl.

effroyable /efʀwajabl/ *a* dreadful.

égal, ~e (*mpl* **-aux**) /egal, -o/ *a* equal; (*surface, vitesse*) even. ●*nm, f* equal; **ça m'est/lui est ~** it is all the same to me/him; **sans ~** matchless; **d'~ à ~** between equals. **également** *adv* equally; (aussi) as well. **égaler** [1] *vt* equal.

égaliser /egalize/ [1] *vt/i* (Sport) equalize; (niveler) level out; (*cheveux*) trim.

égalitaire /egaliteʀ/ *a* egalitarian.

égalité /egalite/ *nf* equality; (de surface) evenness; **être à ~** be level.

égard /egaʀ/ *nm* consideration; **~s** respect (+ *sg*); **par ~ pour** out of consideration for; **à cet ~** in this respect; **à l'~ de** with regard to; (envers) towards.

égarer /egaʀe/ [1] *vt* mislay; (tromper) lead astray. □ **s'~** *vpr* get lost; (se tromper) go astray.

égayer /egeje/ [31] *vt* (*personne*) cheer up; (*pièce*) brighten up.

église /egliz/ *nf* church.

égoïsme /egɔism/ *nm* selfishness, egoism.

égoïste /egɔist/ *a* selfish. ● *nmf* egoist.

égorger /egɔʀʒe/ [40] *vt* slit the throat of.

égout /egu/ *nm* sewer.

égoutter /egute/ [1] *vt* drain. □ s'~ *vpr* (*vaisselle*) drain; (*lessive*) drip dry. **égouttoir** *nm* draining-board.

égratigner /egʀatiɲe/ [1] *vt* scratch. **égratignure** *nf* scratch.

Égypte /eʒipt/ *nf* Egypt.

éjecter /eʒɛkte/ [1] *vt* eject.

élaboration /elabɔʀasjɔ̃/ *nf* elaboration. **élaborer** [1] *vt* elaborate.

élan /elɑ̃/ *nm* (*animal*) moose; (Sport) run-up; (*vitesse*) momentum; (fig) surge.

élancé, ~e /elɑ̃se/ *a* slender.

élancement /elɑ̃smɑ̃/ *nm* twinge.

élancer (s') /(s)elɑ̃se/ [10] *vpr* leap forward, dash; (*arbre, édifice*) soar.

élargir /elaʀʒiʀ/ [2] *vt* (*route*) widen; (*connaissances*) broaden. □ s'~ *vpr* (*famille*) expand; (*route*) widen; (*écart*) increase; (*vêtement*) stretch.

élastique /elastik/ *a* elastic. ● *nm* elastic band; (*tissu*) elastic.

électeur, -trice /elɛktœʀ, -tʀis/ *nm, f* voter. **élection** *nf* election. **électoral, ~e** (*mpl* -aux) *a* (*réunion*) election. **électorat** *nm* electorate, voters (+ *pl*).

électricien, ~ne /elɛktʀisjɛ̃, ɛn/ *nm, f* electrician. **électricité** *nf* electricity.

électrifier /elɛktʀifje/ [45] *vt* electrify.

électrique /elɛktʀik/ *a* electric; (*installation*) electrical.

électrocuter /elɛktʀɔkyte/ [1] *vt* electrocute.

électroménager /elɛktʀɔmenaʒe/ *nm* l'~ household appliances (+ *pl*).

électron /elɛktʀɔ̃/ *nm* electron.

électronicien, ~ne *nm, f* electronics engineer.

électronique /elɛktʀɔnik/ *a* electronic. ● *nf* electronics.

élégance /elegɑ̃s/ *nf* elegance. **élégant, ~e** *a* elegant.

élément /elemɑ̃/ *nm* element; (*meuble*) unit. **élémentaire** *a* elementary.

éléphant /elefɑ̃/ *nm* elephant.

élevage /ɛlvaʒ/ *nm* (stock-) breeding.

élévation /elevasjɔ̃/ *nf* rise; (*hausse*) rise; (*plan*) elevation; ~ de terrain rise in the ground.

élève /elɛv/ *nmf* pupil.

élevé, ~e /ɛlve/ *a* high; (*noble*) elevated; **bien ~** well-mannered.

élever /ɛlve/ [6] *vt* (*lever*) raise; (*enfants*) bring up, raise; (*animal*) breed. □ s'~ *vpr* rise; (*dans le ciel*) soar up; **s'~ à** amount to. **éleveur, -euse** *nm, f* (stock-) breeder.

éligible /eliʒibl/ *a* eligible.

élimination /eliminasjɔ̃/ *nf* elimination.

éliminatoire /eliminatwaʀ/ *a* qualifying. ● *nf* (Sport) heat.

éliminer /elimine/ [1] *vt* eliminate.

élire /eliʀ/ [39] *vt* elect.

elle /ɛl/ *pron* she; (*complément*) her; (*chose*) it. **elle-même** *pron* herself; itself. **elles** *pron* they; (*complément*) them. **elles-mêmes** *pron* themselves.

élocution /elɔkysjɔ̃/ *nf* diction.

éloge /elɔʒ/ *nm* praise; **faire l'~ de** praise; **~s** praise (+ *sg*).

éloigné, ~e /elwaɲe/ *a* distant; **~ de** far away from; **parent ~** distant relative.

éloigner /elwaɲe/ [1] *vt* take

away *ou* remove (**de** from); (*danger*) ward off; (*visite*) put off. □ **s'~** *vpr* go *ou* move away (**de** from); (*affectivement*) become estranged (**de** from).

élongation /elɔ̃gasjɔ̃/ *nf* strained muscle.

éloquent, **~e** /elɔkɑ̃, -t/ *a* eloquent.

élu, **~e** /ely/ *a* elected. ● *nm,f* (Pol) elected representative.

élucider /elyside/ [1] *vt* elucidate.

éluder /elyde/ [1] *vt* evade.

émacié, **~e** /emasje/ *a* emaciated.

e-mail /imɛl/ *nm* e-mail; **envoyer un ~ à qn** e-mail sb.

émail (*pl* -**aux**) /emaj, -o/ *nm* enamel.

émanciper /emɑ̃sipe/ [1] *vt* emancipate. □ **s'~** *vpr* become emancipated.

émaner /emane/ [1] *vi* emanate.

emballage /ɑ̃balaʒ/ *nm* (dur) packaging; (souple) wrapping.

emballer /ɑ̃bale/ [1] *vt* pack; (en papier) wrap; **ça ne m'emballe pas** Ⓘ I'm not really taken by it. □ **s'~** *vpr* (*moteur*) race; (*cheval*) bolt; (*personne*) get carried away; (*prices*) shoot up.

embarcadère /ɑ̃baʀkadɛʀ/ *nm* landing-stage.

embarcation /ɑ̃baʀkasjɔ̃/ *nf* boat.

embardée /ɑ̃baʀde/ *nf* swerve.

embarquement /ɑ̃baʀkəmɑ̃/ *nm* (de passagers) boarding; (de fret) loading.

embarquer /ɑ̃baʀke/ [1] *vt* take on board; (*frêt*) load; (emporter Ⓘ) cart off. ● *vi* board. □ **s'~** *vpr* board; **s'~ dans** embark upon.

embarras /ɑ̃baʀa/ *nm* (gêne) embarrassment; (difficulté) difficulty.

embarrasser /ɑ̃baʀase/ [1] *vt* (encombrer) clutter (up); (fig) embarrass. □ **s'~ de** *vpr* burden oneself with.

embauche /ɑ̃boʃ/ *nf* hiring.

embaucher /ɑ̃boʃe/ [1] *vt* hire, take on.

embaumer /ɑ̃bome/ [1] *vt* (*pièce*) fill; (*cadavre*) embalm. ● *vi* be fragrant.

embellir /ɑ̃beliʀ/ [2] *vt* make more attractive; (*récit*) embellish.

embêtant, **~e** /ɑ̃bətɑ̃, -t/ *a* Ⓘ annoying.

embêter /ɑ̃bete/ [1] *vt* bother. □ **s'~** *vpr* be bored.

emblée: d'~ /dɑ̃ble/ *loc* right away.

emblème /ɑ̃blɛm/ *nm* emblem.

emboîter /ɑ̃bwate/ [1] *vt* fit together; **~ le pas à qn** (imiter) follow suit. □ **s'~** *vpr* fit together; (**s'**)**~ dans** fit into.

embonpoint /ɑ̃bɔ̃pwɛ̃/ *nm* stoutness.

embourber (s') /(s)ɑ̃buʀbe/ [1] *vpr* get stuck in the mud; (fig) get bogged down.

embouteillage /ɑ̃butɛjaʒ/ *nm* traffic jam.

emboutir /ɑ̃butiʀ/ [2] *vt* (Auto) crash into.

embraser (s') /(s)ɑ̃bʀaze/ [1] *vpr* catch fire.

embrasser /ɑ̃bʀase/ [1] *vt* kiss; (adopter, contenir) embrace. □ **s'~** *vpr* kiss.

embrayage /ɑ̃bʀɛjaʒ/ *nm* clutch.

embrayer [31] *vi* engage the clutch.

embrouiller /ɑ̃bʀuje/ [1] *vt* confuse; (*fils*) tangle. □ **s'~** *vpr* become confused.

embryon /ɑ̃bʀijɔ̃/ *nm* embryo.

embûches /ɑ̃byʃ/ *nfpl* traps.

embuer (s') /(s)ɑ̃bɥe/ [1] *vpr* mist up.

embuscade /ɑ̃byskad/ *nf* ambush.

émeraude /ɛmʀod/ *nf* emerald.

émerger /emɛʀʒe/ [40] *vi* emerge; (fig) stand out.

émeri /ɛmʀi/ *nm* emery.

émerveillement /emɛʀvɛjmɑ̃/ *nm* amazement, wonder.

émerveiller /emɛʀveje/ [1] *vt* fill with wonder. □ s'∼ *vpr* marvel at.

émetteur /emɛtœʀ/ *nm* transmitter.

émettre /emɛtʀ/ [42] *vt* (*son*) produce; (*message*) send out; (*timbre, billet*) issue; (*opinion*) express.

émeute /emøt/ *nf* riot.

émietter /emjete/ [1] *vt* crumble. □ s'∼ *vpr* crumble.

émigrant, ∼e /emigʀɑ̃, -t/ *nm, f* emigrant. **émigration** *nf* emigration. **émigrer** [1] *vi* emigrate.

émincer /emɛ̃se/ [10] *vt* cut into thin slices.

éminent, ∼e /eminɑ̃, -t/ *a* eminent.

émissaire /emisɛʀ/ *nm* emissary.

émission /emisjɔ̃/ *nf* (*programme*) programme; (*de chaleur, gaz*) emission; (*de timbre*) issue.

emmagasiner /ɑ̃magazine/ [1] *vt* store.

emmanchure /ɑ̃mɑ̃ʃyʀ/ *nf* armhole.

emmêler /ɑ̃mele/ [1] *vt* tangle. □ s'∼ *vpr* get mixed up.

emménager /ɑ̃menaʒe/ [40] *vi* move in; ∼ **dans** move into.

emmener /ɑ̃mne/ [6] *vt* take; (*comme prisonnier*) take away.

emmerder /ɑ̃mɛʀde/ [1] 🔲 *vt* ∼ **qn** get on sb's nerves. □ s'∼ *vpr* be bored.

emmitoufler /ɑ̃mitufle/ [1] *vt* wrap up warmly. □ s'∼ *vpr* wrap oneself up warmly.

émoi /emwa/ *nm* turmoil; (plaisir) excitement.

émotif, **-ive** /emɔtif, -v/ *a* emotional. **émotion** *nf* emotion; (peur) fright. **émotionnel**, ∼le *a* emotional.

émousser /emuse/ [1] *vt* blunt.

émouvant, ∼e /emuvɑ̃, -t/ *a* moving.

empailler /ɑ̃paje/ [1] *vt* stuff.

empaqueter /ɑ̃pakte/ [38] *vt* package.

emparer (s') /(s)ɑ̃paʀe/ [1] *vpr* s'∼ **de** get hold of.

empêchement /ɑ̃pɛʃmɑ̃/ *nm* . **avoir un** ∼ to be held up.

empêcher /ɑ̃peʃe/ [1] *vt* prevent; ∼ **de faire** prevent *ou* stop (from) doing; (il) **n'empêche que** still. □ s'∼ *vpr* **il ne peut pas s'en** ∼ he cannot help it.

empereur /ɑ̃pʀœʀ/ *nm* emperor.

empester /ɑ̃peste/ [1] *vt* stink out; (*essence*) stink of. ● *vi* stink.

empêtrer (s') /(s)ɑ̃petʀe/ [1] *vpr* become entangled.

empiéter /ɑ̃pjete/ [14] *vi* ∼ **sur** encroach upon.

empiffrer (s') /(s)ɑ̃pifʀe/ [1] *vpr* 🔲 stuff oneself.

empiler /ɑ̃pile/ [1] *vt* pile up. □ s'∼ *vpr* pile up.

empire /ɑ̃piʀ/ *nm* empire.

emplacement /ɑ̃plasmɑ̃/ *nm* site.

emplâtre /ɑ̃plɑtʀ/ *nm* (Méd) plaster.

emploi /ɑ̃plwa/ *nm* (travail) job; (embauche) employment; (utilisation) use; **un** ∼ **de chauffeur** a job as a driver; ∼ **du temps** timetable. **employé**, ∼e *nm, f* employee.

employer /ɑ̃plwaje/ [31] *vt* (*personne*) employ; (utiliser) use. □ s'∼ *vpr* be used; **s'**∼ **à** devote oneself to. **employeur**, **-euse** *nm, f* employer.

empoigner /ɑ̃pwaɲe/ [1] *vt* grab. □ s'∼ *vpr* come to blows.

empoisonnement /ɑ̃pwazɔnmɑ̃/ *nm* poisoning.

empoisonner /ɑ̃pwazɔne/ [1] *vt* poison; (embêter 🔲) annoy. □ **s'~** *vpr* to poison oneself.

emporter /ɑ̃pɔʀte/ [1] *vt* take (away); (entraîner) sweep away; (arracher) tear off. □ **s'~** *vpr* lose one's temper; **l'~** get the upper hand (**sur** of); **plat à ~** take-away.

empoté, **~e** /ɑ̃pɔte/ *a* clumsy.

empreinte /ɑ̃pʀɛ̃t/ *nf* mark; **~** (digitale) fingerprint; **~ de pas** footprint.

empressé, **~e** /ɑ̃pʀese/ *a* eager, attentive.

empresser (**s'**) /(s)ɑ̃pʀese/ [1] *vpr* hasten to; **s'~ auprès de** be attentive to.

emprise /ɑ̃pʀiz/ *nf* influence.

emprisonnement /ɑ̃pʀizɔnmɑ̃/ *nm* imprisonment. **emprisonner** [1] *vt* imprison.

emprunt /ɑ̃pʀœ̃/ *nm* loan; **faire un ~** take out a loan.

emprunté, **~e** /ɑ̃pʀœ̃te/ *a* awkward.

emprunter /ɑ̃pʀœ̃te/ [1] *vt* borrow (**à** from); (route) take; (fig) assume. **emprunteur**, **-euse** *nm, f* borrower.

ému, **~e** /emy/ *a* moved; (intimidé) nervous.

émule /emyl/ *nmf* imitator.

....

en /ɑ̃/

➡ Pour les expressions comme **en principe, en train de, s'en aller**, etc. ⇒**principe, train, aller**, etc.

● *préposition*

····▸ (lieu) in.

····▸ (avec mouvement) to.

····▸ (temps) in.

····▸ (manière, état) in; **~ faisant** by *ou* while doing; **je t'appelle ~**

rentrant I will call you when I get back.

····▸ (en qualité de) as.

····▸ (transport) by.

····▸ (composition) made of; **table ~ bois** wooden table.

● *pronom*

····▸ **~ avoir/vouloir** have/want some; **ne pas ~ avoir/vouloir** not have/want any; **j'~ ai deux** I've got two; **prends-~ plusieurs** take several; **il m'~ reste un** I have one left; **j'~ suis content** I am pleased with him/her/it/them; **je m'~ souviens** I remember them.

····▸ **~ êtes-vous sûr?** are you sure?

....

encadrement /ɑ̃kadʀəmɑ̃/ *nm* framing; (de porte) frame. **encadrer** [1] *vt* frame; (entourer d'un trait) circle; (superviser) supervise.

encaisser /ɑ̃kese/ [1] *vt* (argent) collect; (chèque) cash; (coups 🔲) take.

encart /ɑ̃kaʀ/ *nm* **~ publicitaire** (advertising) insert.

en-cas /ɑ̃kɑ/ *nm* (stand-by) snack.

encastré, **~e** /ɑ̃kastʀe/ *a* built-in.

encaustique /ɑ̃kɔstik/ *nf* wax polish.

enceinte /ɑ̃sɛ̃t/ *af* pregnant; **~ de 3 mois** 3 months pregnant. ● *nf* enclosure; **~** (acoustique) speaker.

encens /ɑ̃sɑ̃/ *nm* incense.

encercler /ɑ̃seʀkle/ [1] *vt* surround.

enchaînement /ɑ̃ʃɛnmɑ̃/ *nm* (suite) chain; (d'idées) sequence.

enchaîner /ɑ̃ʃene/ [1] *vt* chain (up); (phrases) link (up). ● *vi* continue. □ **s'~** *vpr* follow on.

enchanté, **~e** /ɑ̃ʃɑ̃te/ *a* (ravi) delighted. **enchanter** [1] *vt* delight; (ensorceler) enchant.

enchère /ɑ̃ʃɛʀ/ *nf* bid; **mettre** *ou* **vendre aux** ~**s** sell by auction.

enchevêtrer /ɑ̃ʃəvetʀe/ [1] *vt* tangle. □ **s'**~ *vpr* become tangled.

enclave /ɑ̃klav/ *nf* enclave.

enclencher /ɑ̃klɑ̃ʃe/ [1] *vt* engage.

enclin, ~**e** /ɑ̃klɛ̃, -in/ *a* ~ **à** inclined to.

enclos /ɑ̃klo/ *nm* enclosure.

enclume /ɑ̃klym/ *nf* anvil.

encoche /ɑ̃kɔʃ/ *nf* notch.

encolure /ɑ̃kɔlyʀ/ *nf* neck.

encombrant, ~**e** /ɑ̃kɔ̃bʀɑ̃, -t/ *a* cumbersome.

encombre /ɑ̃kɔ̃bʀ/ *nm* **sans** ~ without any problems.

encombrement /ɑ̃kɔ̃bʀəmɑ̃/ *nm* (Auto) traffic congestion; (volume) bulk.

encombrer /ɑ̃kɔ̃bʀe/ [1] *vt* clutter (up); (obstruer) obstruct. □ **s'**~ **de** *vpr* burden oneself with.

encontre: à l'~ **de** /alɑ̃kɔ̃tʀədə/ *loc* against.

encore /ɑ̃kɔʀ/ *adv* (toujours) still; (de nouveau) again; (de plus) more; (aussi) also; ~ **plus grand** even larger; ~ **un café** another coffee; **pas** ~ not yet; **si** ~ if only; **et puis quoi** ~? 🔲 what next?

encouragement /ɑ̃kuʀaʒmɑ̃/ *nm* encouragement. **encourager** [40] *vt* encourage.

encourir /ɑ̃kuʀiʀ/ [20] *vt* incur.

encrasser /ɑ̃kʀase/ [1] *vt* clog up (with dirt).

encre /ɑ̃kʀ/ *nf* ink. **encrier** *nm* ink-well.

encyclopédie /ɑ̃siklɔpedi/ *nf* encyclopaedia.

endettement /ɑ̃dɛtmɑ̃/ *nm* debt.

endetter /ɑ̃dɛte/ [1] *vt* put into debt. □ **s'**~ *vpr* get into debt.

endiguer /ɑ̃dige/ [1] *vt* dam; (fig) curb.

endimanché, ~**e** /ɑ̃dimɑ̃ʃe/ *a* in one's Sunday best.

endive /ɑ̃div/ *nf* chicory.

endoctriner /ɑ̃dɔktʀine/ [1] *vt* indoctrinate.

endommager /ɑ̃dɔmaʒe/ [40] *vt* damage.

endormi, ~**e** /ɑ̃dɔʀmi/ *a* asleep; (apathique) sleepy.

endormir /ɑ̃dɔʀmiʀ/ [46] *vt* send to sleep; (médicalement) put to sleep; (duper) dupe (**avec** with). □ **s'**~ *vpr* fall asleep.

endosser /ɑ̃dose/ [1] *vt* (vêtement) put on; (assumer) take on; (Comm) endorse.

endroit /ɑ̃dʀwa/ *nm* place; (de tissu) right side; **à l'**~ the right way round; **par** ~**s** in places.

enduire /ɑ̃dɥiʀ/ [17] *vt* coat. **enduit** *nm* coating.

endurance /ɑ̃dyʀɑ̃s/ *nf* endurance. **endurant**, ~**e** *a* tough.

endurcir /ɑ̃dyʀsiʀ/ [2] *vt* strengthen. □ **s'**~ *vpr* become hard(ened).

endurer /ɑ̃dyʀe/ [1] *vt* endure.

énergétique /enɛʀʒetik/ *a* energy; (food) high-calorie.

énergie *nf* energy; (Tech) power. **énergique** *a* energetic.

énervant, ~**e** /enɛʀvɑ̃, -t/ *a* irritating, annoying.

énerver /enɛʀve/ [1] *vt* irritate. □ **s'**~ *vpr* get worked up.

enfance /ɑ̃fɑ̃s/ *nf* childhood; **la petite** ~ infancy.

enfant /ɑ̃fɑ̃/ *nmf* child. **enfantillage** *nm* childishness. **enfantin**, ~**e** *a* simple, easy; (puéril) childish; (jeu, langage) children's.

enfer /ɑ̃fɛʀ/ *nm* (Relig) Hell; (fig) hell.

enfermer /ɑ̃fɛʀme/ [1] *vt* shut up. □ **s'**~ *vpr* shut oneself up.

enfiler /ɑ̃file/ [1] *vt* (aiguille)

thread; (*vêtement*) slip on; (*rue*) take.

enfin /ɑ̃fɛ̃/ *adv* (de soulagement) at last; (en dernier lieu) finally; (résignation, conclusion) well; ∼ **presque** well nearly.

enflammé, ∼e /ɑ̃flame/ *a* (Méd) inflamed; (*discours*) fiery; (*lettre*) passionate.

enflammer /ɑ̃flame/ [1] *vt* set fire to. □ **s'**∼ *vpr* catch fire.

enfler /ɑ̃fle/ [1] *vt* (*histoire*) exaggerate. ● *vi* (*partie du corps*) swell (up); (*mer*) swell; (*rumeur, colère*) spread. □ **s'**∼ *vpr* (*colère*) mount; (*rumeur*) grow.

enfoncer /ɑ̃fɔ̃se/ [10] *vt* (*épingle*) push *ou* drive in; (*chapeau*) push down; (*porte*) break down. ● *vi* sink. □ **s'**∼ *vpr* sink (**dans** into).

enfouir /ɑ̃fwiʀ/ [2] *vt* bury.

enfourcher /ɑ̃fuʀʃe/ [1] *vt* mount.

enfreindre /ɑ̃fʀɛ̃dʀ/ [22] *vt* infringe, break.

enfuir (s') /(s)ɑ̃fɥiʀ/ [35] *vpr* run away.

enfumé, ∼e /ɑ̃fyme/ *a* filled with smoke.

engagé, ∼e /ɑ̃ɡaʒe/ *a* committed.

engagement /ɑ̃ɡaʒmɑ̃/ *nm* (promesse) promise; (Pol, Comm) commitment.

engager /ɑ̃ɡaʒe/ [40] *vt* (lier) bind, commit, (embaucher) take on; (commencer) start; (introduire) insert; (investir) invest. □ **s'**∼ *vpr* (promettre) commit oneself; (commencer) start; (soldat) enlist; (concurrent) enter; **s'**∼ **à faire** undertake to do; **s'**∼ **dans** (voie) enter.

engelure /ɑ̃ʒlyʀ/ *nf* chilblain.

engendrer /ɑ̃ʒɑ̃dʀe/ [1] *vt* (causer) generate.

engin /ɑ̃ʒɛ̃/ *nm* device; (véhicule) vehicle; (missile) missile.

engloutir /ɑ̃ɡlutiʀ/ [2] *vt* swallow (up).

engouement /ɑ̃ɡumɑ̃/ *nm* passion.

engouffrer /ɑ̃ɡufʀe/ [1] *vt* ▯ gobble up. □ **s'**∼ **dans** *vpr* rush in.

engourdir /ɑ̃ɡuʀdiʀ/ [2] *vt* numb. □ **s'**∼ *vpr* go numb.

engrais /ɑ̃ɡʀɛ/ *nm* manure; (chimique) fertilizer.

engrenage /ɑ̃ɡʀənaʒ/ *nm* gears (+ *pl*); (fig) spiral.

engueuler /ɑ̃ɡœle/ [1] ▯ *vt* shout at. □ **s'**∼ *vpr* have a row.

enhardir (s') /(s)ɑ̃aʀdiʀ/ [2] *vpr* become bolder.

énième /ɛnjɛm/ *a* umpteenth.

énigmatique /enigmatik/ *a* enigmatic. **énigme** *nf* enigma; (devinette) riddle.

enivrer /ɑ̃nivʀe/ [1] *vt* intoxicate. □ **s'**∼ *vpr* get intoxicated.

enjambée /ɑ̃ʒɑ̃be/ *nf* stride.

enjamber [1] *vt* step over; (*pont*) span.

enjeu (*pl* ∼**x**) /ɑ̃ʒø/ *nm* stake.

enjoué, ∼e /ɑ̃ʒwe/ *a* cheerful.

enlacer /ɑ̃lase/ [10] *vt* entwine.

enlèvement /ɑ̃lɛvmɑ̃/ *nm* (de colis) removal; (d'ordures) collection; (rapt) kidnapping.

enlever /ɑ̃lve/ [6] *vt* remove (**à** from); (*vêtement*) take off; (*tache, organe*) take out, remove; (kidnapper) kidnap; (gagner) win.

enliser (s') /(s)ɑ̃lize/ [1] *vpr* get bogged down.

enneigé, ∼e /ɑ̃neʒe/ *a* snow-covered.

ennemi, ∼e /ɛnmi/ *a* & *nm* enemy; ∼ **de** (fig) hostile to.

ennui /ɑ̃nɥi/ *nm* problem; (tracas) boredom; **s'attirer des** ∼**s** run into trouble.

ennuyer /ɑ̃nɥije/ [31] *vt* bore; (irriter) annoy; (préoccuper) worry; **si**

cela ne t'ennuie pas if you don't mind. □ s'~ *vpr* get bored.

ennuyeux, -euse /ănɥijø, -z/ *a* boring; (fâcheux) annoying.

énoncé /enɔse/ *nm* wording, text; (Gram) utterance.

énoncer /enɔse/ [10] *vt* express, state.

enorgueillir (s') /(s)ănɔrgœjir/ [2] *vpr* s'~ de pride oneself on.

énorme /enɔrm/ *a* enormous.

enquête /ăkɛt/ *nf* (Jur) investigation, inquiry; (sondage) survey; **mener l'~** lead the inquiry. **enquêter** [1] *vi* ~ **(sur)** investigate. **enquêteur, -euse** *nm, f* investigator.

enquiquinant, ~e /ăkikină, -t/ *a* 🄸 irritating.

enraciné, ~e /ărasine/ *a* deep-rooted.

enragé, ~e /ăraʒe/ *a* furious; (chien) rabid; (fig) fanatical.

enrager /ăraʒe/ [40] *vi* be furious; **faire ~ qn** annoy sb.

enregistrement /ăr(ə)ʒistrəmă/ *nm* recording; (des bagages) check-in. **enregistrer** [1] *vt* (Mus, TV) record; (mémoriser) take in; (bagages) check in.

enrhumer (s') /(s)ărɥme/ [1] *vpr* catch a cold.

enrichir /ăriʃir/ [2] *vt* enrich. □ s'~ *vpr* grow rich(er). **enrichissant, ~e** *a* (expérience) rewarding.

enrober /ărɔbe/ [1] *vt* coat (de with).

enrôler /ărole/ [1] *vt* recruit. □ s'~ *vpr* enlist, enrol.

enroué, ~e /ărwe/ *a* hoarse.

enrouler /ărule/ [1] *vt* wind, wrap. □ s'~ *vpr* wind; **s'~ dans une couverture** roll oneself up in a blanket.

ensanglanté, ~e /ăsăglăte/ *a* bloodstained.

enseignant, ~e /ăsɛɲă, -t/ *nm, f* teacher. ●*a* teaching.

enseigne /ăsɛɲ/ *nf* sign.

enseignement /ăsɛɲəmă/ *nm* (profession) teaching; (instruction) education.

enseigner /ăsɛɲe/ [1] *vt/i* teach; ~ **qch à qn** teach sb sth.

ensemble /ăsăbl/ *adv* together. ●*nm* group; (Mus) ensemble; (vêtements) outfit; (cohésion) unity; (maths) set; **dans l'~** on the whole; **d'~** (idée) general; **l'~ de** (totalité) all of, the whole of.

ensevelir /ăsəvlir/ [2] *vt* bury.

ensoleillé, ~e /ăsɔleje/ *a* sunny.

ensorceler /ăsɔrsəle/ [38] *vt* bewitch.

ensuite /ăsɥit/ *adv* next, then; (plus tard) later.

ensuivre (s') /(s)ăsɥivr/ [57] *vpr* follow; **et tout ce qui s'ensuit** and all the rest of it.

entaille /ătaj/ *nf* cut; (profonde) gash; (encoche) notch.

entamer /ătame/ [1] *vt* start; (inciser) cut into; (ébranler) shake.

entasser /ătase/ [1] *vt* (livres) pile; (argent) hoard; (personnes) cram (dans into). □ s'~ *vpr* (objets) pile up (dans into); (personnes) squeeze (dans into).

entendement /ătădmă/ *nm* understanding; **ça dépasse l'~** it's beyond belief.

entendre /ătădr/ [3] *vt* hear; (comprendre) understand; (vouloir dire) mean; ~ **parler de** hear of; ~ **dire que** hear that. □ s'~ *vpr* (être d'accord) agree; **s'~ (bien)** get on (avec with); **cela s'entend** of course.

entendu, ~e /ătădy/ *a* (convenu) agreed; (sourire, air) knowing; **bien ~** of course; **(c'est) ~!** all right!

entente /ătăt/ *nf* understanding; **bonne ~** good relationship.

enterrement /ɑ̃tɛrmɑ̃/ *nm* funeral.

enterrer /ɑ̃tere/ [1] *vt* bury.

en-tête /ɑ̃tɛt/ *nm* heading; **à ~** headed.

entêté, ~e /ɑ̃tete/ *a* stubborn. **entêtement** *nm* stubbornness. **entêter (s')** [1] *vpr* persist (**à, dans** in).

enthousiasme /ɑ̃tuzjasm/ *nm* enthusiasm. **enthousiasmer** [1] *vt* fill with enthusiasm. **enthousiaste** *a* enthusiastic.

enticher (s') /(s)ɑ̃tiʃe/ [1] *vpr* **s'~ de** become infatuated with.

entier, -ière /ɑ̃tje, -jɛr/ *a* whole; (absolu) absolute; (entêté) unyielding. ● *nm* whole; **en ~** entirely.

entonnoir /ɑ̃tɔnwar/ *nm* funnel; (trou) crater.

entorse /ɑ̃tɔrs/ *nf* sprain; (fig) **~ à** (loi) infringement of.

entortiller /ɑ̃tɔrtije/ [1] *vt* wind, wrap (**autour** around); (duper [I]) get round.

entourage /ɑ̃turaʒ/ *nm* circle of family and friends; (bordure) surround.

entouré, ~e /ɑ̃ture/ *a* (personne) supported.

entourer /ɑ̃ture/ [1] *vt* surround (**de** with); (réconforter) rally round; **~ qch de mystère** shroud sth in mystery.

entracte /ɑ̃trakt/ *nm* interval.

entraide /ɑ̃trɛd/ *nf* mutual aid. **entraider (s')** [1] *vpr* help each other.

entrain /ɑ̃trɛ̃/ *nm* zest, spirit.

entraînement /ɑ̃trɛnmɑ̃/ *nm* (Sport) training.

entraîner /ɑ̃trene/ [1] *vt* (emporter) carry away; (provoquer) lead to; (Sport) train; (actionner) drive. □ **s'~** *vpr* train. **entraîneur** *nm* trainer.

entrave /ɑ̃trav/ *nf* hindrance. **entraver** [1] *vt* hinder.

entre /ɑ̃tr(ə)/ *prép* between; (parmi) among(st); **~ autres** among other things; **l'un d'~ nous/eux** one of us/them.

entrebâillé, ~e /ɑ̃trəbaje/ *a* ajar, half-open.

entrechoquer (s') /(s)ɑ̃trəʃɔke/ [1] *vpr* knock against each other.

entrecôte /ɑ̃trəkot/ *nf* rib steak.

entrecouper /ɑ̃trəkupe/ [1] *vt* **~ de** intersperse with.

entrecroiser (s') /(s)ɑ̃trəkrwaze/ [1] *vpr* (routes) intertwine.

entrée /ɑ̃tre/ *nf* entrance; (vestibule) hall; (accès) admission, entry; (billet) ticket; (Culin) starter; (Ordinat) **tapez sur E~** press Enter; **'~ interdite'** 'no entry'.

entrejambes /ɑ̃trəʒɑ̃b/ *nm* crotch.

entremets /ɑ̃trəmɛ/ *nm* dessert.

entremise /ɑ̃trəmiz/ *nf* intervention; **par l'~ de** through.

entreposer /ɑ̃trəpoze/ [1] *vt* store.

entrepôt /ɑ̃trəpo/ *nm* warehouse.

entreprenant, ~e /ɑ̃trəprənɑ̃, -t/ *a* (actif) enterprising; (séducteur) forward.

entreprendre /ɑ̃trəprɑ̃dr/ [50] *vt* start on, undertake; (personne) buttonhole; **~ de faire** undertake to do.

entrepreneur /ɑ̃trəprənœr/ *nm* (de bâtiment) contractor; (chef d'entreprise) firm manager.

entreprise /ɑ̃trəpriz/ *nf* (projet) undertaking; (société) firm, business, company.

entrer /ɑ̃tre/ [1] *vi* (aux être) go in, enter; (venir) come in, enter; **~ dans** go *ou* come into, enter; (club) join; **~ en collision** collide (**avec** with); **faire ~** (personne) show in; **laisser ~** let in; **~ en guerre** go to war. ● *vt* (données) enter.

entre-temps /ɑ̃tʀətɑ̃/ *adv* meanwhile.

entretenir /ɑ̃tʀət(ə)niʀ/ [58] *vt* (*appareil*) maintain; (*vêtement*) look after; (*alimenter*) keep going; (*feu*) keep going; (*amitié*) keep alive; ~ **qn de** converse with sb about. □ **s'**~ *vpr* speak (**de** about; **avec** to).

entretien *nm* maintenance; (*discussion*) talk; (*pour un emploi*) interview.

entrevoir /ɑ̃tʀəvwaʀ/ [63] *vt* make out; (*brièvement*) glimpse.

entrevue /ɑ̃tʀəvy/ *nf* meeting.

entrouvert, ~**e** /ɑ̃tʀuvɛʀ, -t/ *a* ajar, half-open.

énumération /enymeʀasjɔ̃/ *nf* enumeration. **énumérer** [14] *vt* enumerate.

envahir /ɑ̃vaiʀ/ [2] *vt* invade, overrun; (*douleur, peur*) overcome.

enveloppe /ɑ̃vlɔp/ *nf* envelope; (*emballage*) wrapping; ~ **budgétaire** budget. **envelopper** [1] *vt* wrap (up); (*fig*) envelop.

envergure /ɑ̃vɛʀgyʀ/ *nf* wingspan; (*importance*) scope; (*qualité*) calibre.

envers /ɑ̃vɛʀ/ *prép* toward(s), to. ● *nm* (*de tissu*) wrong side; **à l'**~ (*tableau*) upside down; (*devant derrière*) back to front; (*chaussette*) inside out.

envie /ɑ̃vi/ *nf* urge; (*jalousie*) envy; **avoir** ~ **de qch** feel like sth; **avoir** ~ **de faire** want to do; (*moins urgent*) feel like doing; **faire** ~ **à qn** make sb envious.

envier /ɑ̃vje/ [45] *vt* envy. **envieux, -ieuse** *a* envious.

environ /ɑ̃viʀɔ̃/ *adv* about.

environnant, ~**e** /ɑ̃viʀɔnɑ̃, -t/ *a* surrounding.

environnement /ɑ̃viʀɔnmɑ̃/ *nm* environment.

environs /ɑ̃viʀɔ̃/ *nmpl* vicinity;

aux ~ **de** (*lieu*) in the vicinity of; (*heure*) round about.

envisager /ɑ̃vizaʒe/ [40] *vt* consider; (*imaginer*) envisage; ~ **de faire** consider doing.

envoi /ɑ̃vwa/ *nm* dispatch; (*paquet*) consignment; **faire un** ~ send; **coup d'**~ (*Sport*) kick-off.

envoler (s') /(s)ɑ̃vɔle/ [1] *vpr* fly away; (*avion*) take off; (*papiers*) blow away.

envoyé, ~**e** /ɑ̃vwaje/ *nm, f* envoy; ~ **spécial** special correspondent.

envoyer /ɑ̃vwaje/ [32] *vt* send; (*lancer*) throw.

éolienne /eɔljɛn/ *nf* windmill; **ferme d'**~**s** wind farm.

épais, ~**se** /epɛ, -s/ *a* thick.

épaisseur *nf* thickness.

épaissir /epesiʀ/ [2] *vt/i* thicken. □ **s'**~ *vpr* thicken; (*mystère*) deepen.

épanoui, ~**e** /epanwi/ *a* (*personne*) beaming, radiant.

épanouir (s') /(s)epanwiʀ/ [2] *vpr* (*fleur*) open out; (*visage*) beam; (*personne*) blossom. **épanouissement** *nm* (*éclat*) blossoming, full bloom.

épargne /epaʀɲ/ *nf* savings.

épargner /epaʀɲe/ [1] *vt/i* save; (*ne pas tuer*) spare; ~ **qch à qn** spare sb sth.

éparpiller /epaʀpije/ [1] *vt* scatter. □ **s'**~ *vpr* scatter.

épars, ~**e** /epaʀ, -s/ *a* scattered.

épatant, ~**e** /epatɑ̃, -t/ *a* Ⓘ amazing.

épaule /epol/ *nf* shoulder.

épave /epav/ *nf* wreck.

épée /epe/ *nf* sword.

épeler /ɛple/ [6] *vt* spell.

éperdu, ~**e** /epɛʀdy/ *a* wild, frantic.

éperon /epʀɔ̃/ *nm* spur.

éphémère /efemɛʀ/ *a* ephemeral.

épi /epi/ *nm* (de blé) ear; (mèche) tuft of hair; ~ **de maïs** corn cob.

épice /epis/ *nf* spice. **épicé,** ~**e** *a* spicy.

épicerie /episʀi/ *nf* grocery shop; (produits) groceries. **épicier, -ière** *nm, f* grocer.

épidémie /epidemi/ *nf* epidemic.

épiderme /epidɛʀm/ *nm* skin.

épier /epje/ [45] *vt* spy on.

épilepsie /epilɛpsi/ *nf* epilepsy. **épileptique** *a & nmf* epileptic.

épiler /epile/ [1] *vt* remove unwanted hair from; (sourcils) pluck.

épilogue /epilɔg/ *nm* epilogue; (fig) outcome.

épinard /epinaʀ/ *nm* ~**s** spinach (+ sg).

épine /epin/ *nf* thorn, prickle; (d'animal) prickle, spine; ~ **dorsale** backbone. **épineux, -euse** *a* thorny.

épingle /epɛ̃gl/ *nf* pin; ~ **de nourrice,** ~ **de sûreté** safety-pin.

épisode /epizɔd/ *nm* episode; à ~**s** serialized.

épitaphe /epitaf/ *nf* epitaph.

épluche-légumes /eplyʃlegym/ *nm inv* (potato) peeler.

éplucher /eplyʃe/ [1] *vt* peel; (examiner: fig) scrutinize.

épluchure /eplyʃyʀ/ *nf* ~**s** peelings.

éponge /epɔ̃ʒ/ *nf* sponge.

éponger /epɔ̃ʒe/ [40] *vt* (liquide) mop up; (surface, front) mop; (fig) (dettes) wipe out.

épopée /epɔpe/ *nf* epic.

époque /epɔk/ *nf* time, period; à l'~ at the time; **d'**~ period.

épouse /epuz/ *nf* wife.

épouser /epuze/ [1] *vt* marry; (forme, idée) adopt.

épousseter /epuste/ [38] *vt* dust.

épouvantable /epuvɑ̃tabl/ *a* appalling.

épouvantail /epuvɑ̃taj/ *nm* scarecrow.

épouvante /epuvɑ̃t/ *nf* terror. **épouvanter** [1] *vt* terrify.

époux /epu/ *nm* husband; **les** ~ the married couple.

éprendre (s') /(s)epʀɑ̃dʀ/ [50] *vpr* **s'**~ **de** fall in love with.

épreuve /epʀœv/ *nf* test; (Sport) event; (malheur) ordeal; (Photo, d'imprimerie) proof; **mettre à l'**~ put to the test.

éprouver /epʀuve/ [1] *vt* (ressentir) experience; (affliger) distress; (tester) test.

éprouvette /epʀuvɛt/ *nf* test-tube.

EPS *abrév f* (**éducation physique et sportive**) PE.

épuisé, ~**e** /epɥize/ *a* exhausted; (livre) out of print. **épuisement** *nm* exhaustion.

épuiser /epɥize/ [1] *vt* (fatiguer, user) exhaust. □ **s'**~ *vpr* become exhausted.

épuration /epyʀasjɔ̃/ *nf* purification; (Pol) purge. **épurer** [1] *vt* purify; (Pol) purge.

équateur /ekwatœʀ/ *nm* equator.

équilibre /ekilibʀ/ *nm* balance; **être** *ou* **se tenir en** ~ (personne) balance; (objet) be balanced. **équilibré,** ~**e** *a* well-balanced.

équilibrer /ekilibʀe/ [1] *vt* balance. □ **s'**~ *vpr* balance each other.

équilibriste /ekilibʀist/ *nmf* acrobat.

équipage /ekipaʒ/ *nm* crew.

équipe /ekip/ *nf* team; ~ **de nuit/jour** night/day shift.

équipé, ~**e** /ekipe/ *a* equipped; **cuisine** ~**e** fitted kitchen.

équipement /ekipmɑ̃/ *nm* equipment; ~**s** (installations) amenities, facilities.

équiper /ekipe/ [1] *vt* equip (de with). □ **s'**~ *vpr* equip oneself.

équipier, -ière /ekipje, -jɛʀ/ *nm, f* team member.

équitable /ekitabl/ *a* fair.

équitation /ekitasjɔ̃/ *nf* (horse-) riding.

équivalence /ekivalɑ̃s/ *nf* equivalence. **équivalent, ~e** *a* equivalent.

équivaloir /ekivalwaʀ/ [60] *vi* ~ **à** be equivalent to.

équivoque /ekivɔk/ *a* equivocal; (louche) questionable. ● *nf* ambiguity.

érable /eʀabl/ *nm* maple.

érafler /eʀafle/ [1] *vt* scratch. **éraflure** *nf* scratch.

éraillé, ~e /eʀaje/ *a* (voix) raucous.

ère /ɛʀ/ *nf* era.

éreintant, ~e /eʀɛ̃tɑ̃, -t/ *a* exhausting. **éreinter** (s') [1] *vpr* wear oneself out.

ériger /eʀiʒe/ [40] *vt* erect. □ **s'~ en** *vpr* set (oneself) up as.

éroder /eʀɔde/ [1] *vt* erode. **érosion** *nf* erosion.

errer /eʀe/ [1] *vi* wander.

erreur /eʀœʀ/ *nf* mistake, error; **dans l'~** mistaken; **par ~** by mistake; **~ judiciaire** miscarriage of justice.

erroné, ~e /eʀɔne/ *a* erroneous.

érudit, ~e /eʀydi, -t/ *a* scholarly. ● *nm, f* scholar.

éruption /eʀypsjɔ̃/ *nf* eruption; (Méd) rash.

es /ɛ/ ⇒ÊTRE [4].

escabeau (pl ~x) /ɛskabo/ *nm* step-ladder.

escadron /ɛskadʀɔ̃/ *nm* (Mil) company.

escalade /ɛskalad/ *nf* climbing; (Pol, Comm) escalation. **escalader** [1] *vt* climb.

escale /ɛskal/ *nf* (d'avion) stopover; (port) port of call; **faire ~ à** (avion, passager) stop over at; (navire, passager) put in at.

escalier /ɛskalje/ *nm* stairs (+ pl); **~ mécanique** *ou* **roulant** escalator.

escalope /ɛskalɔp/ *nf* escalope.

escargot /ɛskaʀgo/ *nm* snail.

escarpé, ~e /ɛskaʀpe/ *a* steep.

escarpin /ɛskaʀpɛ̃/ *nm* court shoe; (US) pump.

escient: **à bon ~** /abɔ̃nesjɑ̃/ *loc* wisely.

esclandre /ɛsklɑ̃dʀ/ *nm* scene.

esclavage /ɛsklavaʒ/ *nm* slavery. **esclave** *nmf* slave.

escompte /ɛskɔ̃t/ *nm* discount. **escompter** [1] *vt* expect; (Comm) discount.

escorte /ɛskɔʀt/ *nf* escort.

escrime /ɛskʀim/ *nf* fencing.

escroc /ɛskʀo/ *nm* swindler.

escroquer /ɛskʀɔke/ [1] *vt* swindle; **~ qch à qn** swindle sb out of sth. **escroquerie** *nf* swindle.

espace /ɛspas/ *nm* space; **~s verts** gardens and parks.

espacer /ɛspase/ [10] *vt* space out. □ **s'~** *vpr* become less frequent.

espadrille /ɛspadʀij/ *nf* rope sandal.

Espagne /ɛspaɲ/ *nf* Spain.

espagnol, ~e /ɛspaɲɔl/ *a* Spanish. ● *nm* (Ling) Spanish. **E~, ~e** *nm, f* Spaniard.

espèce /ɛspɛs/ *nf* kind, sort; (race) species; **en ~s** (argent) in cash; **~ d'idiot!** ⚆ you idiot! ⚆.

espérance /ɛspeʀɑ̃s/ *nf* hope.

espérer /ɛspeʀe/ [14] *vt* hope for; **~ faire/que** hope to do/that. ● *vi* hope.

espiègle /ɛspjɛgl/ *a* mischievous.

espion, ~ne /ɛspjɔ̃, -ɔn/ *nm, f* spy. **espionnage** *nm* espionage, spying. **espionner** [1] *vt* spy (on).

espoir /ɛspwaʀ/ *nm* hope; **reprendre ~** feel hopeful again.

esprit /ɛspʀi/ nm (intellect) mind; (humour) wit; (fantôme) spirit; (ambiance) atmosphere; **perdre l'~** lose one's mind; **reprendre ses ~s** come to; **faire de l'~** try to be witty.

esquimau, ~de (mpl ~x) /ɛskimo, -d/ nm,f Eskimo.

esquinter /ɛskɛ̃te/ [1] vt 🔲 ruin.

esquisse /ɛskis/ nf sketch; (fig) outline.

esquiver /ɛskive/ [1] vt dodge. □ **s'~** vpr slip away.

essai /esɛ/ nm (épreuve) test, trial; (tentative) try; (article) essay; (au rugby) try; **~s** (Auto) qualifying round (+ sg); **à l'~** on trial.

essaim /esɛ̃/ nm swarm.

essayage /esɛjaʒ/ nm fitting; **salon d'~** fitting room.

essayer /eseje/ [31] vt/i try; (vêtement) try (on); (voiture) try (out); **~ de faire** try to do.

essence /esɑ̃s/ nf (carburant) petrol; (nature, extrait) essence; **~ sans plomb** unleaded petrol.

essentiel, ~le /esɑ̃sjɛl/ a essential. ● nm **l'~** the main thing; (quantité) the main part.

essieu (pl ~x) /esjø/ nm axle.

essor /esɔʀ/ nm expansion; **prendre son ~** expand.

essorage /esɔʀaʒ/ nm spin-drying. **essorer** [1] vt (linge) spin-dry; (en tordant) wring.

essoreuse /esɔʀøz/ nf spin-drier; **~ à salade** salad spinner.

essoufflé, ~e /esufle/ a out of breath.

essuie-glace /esɥiglas/ nm inv windscreen wiper.

essuie-mains /esɥimɛ̃/ nm inv hand-towel.

essuie-tout /esɥitu/ nm inv kitchen paper.

essuyer /esɥije/ [31] vt wipe; (subir) suffer. □ **s'~** vpr dry ou wipe oneself.

est¹ /ɛ/ ⇒ÊTRE [4].

est² /ɛst/ nm east. ● a inv east; (partie) eastern; (direction) easterly.

estampe /ɛstɑ̃p/ nf print.

esthète /ɛstɛt/ nmf aesthete.

esthéticienne /ɛstetisjɛn/ nf beautician.

esthétique /ɛstetik/ a aesthetic.

estimation /ɛstimasjɔ̃/ nf (de coûts) estimate; (valeur) valuation.

estime /ɛstim/ nf esteem.

estimer /ɛstime/ [1] vt (tableau) value; (calculer) estimate; (respecter) esteem; (considérer) consider (que that).

estival, ~e (mpl -aux) /ɛstival, -o/ a summer. **estivant, ~e** nm,f summer visitor.

estomac /ɛstɔma/ nm stomach.

estomaqué, ~e /ɛstɔmake/ a 🔲 stunned.

Estonie /ɛstɔni/ nf Estonia.

estrade /ɛstʀad/ nf platform.

estragon /ɛstʀagɔ̃/ nm tarragon.

estropié, ~e /ɛstʀɔpje/ nm,f cripple. ● a crippled.

estuaire /ɛstɥɛʀ/ nm estuary.

et /e/ conj and; **~ moi?** what about me?; **~ alors?** so what?

étable /etabl/ nf cow-shed.

établi, ~e /etabli/ a established; **un fait bien ~** a well-established fact. ● nm work-bench.

établir /etabliʀ/ [2] vt establish; (liste, facture) draw up; (personne, camp, record) set up. □ **s'~** vpr (personne) settle; **s'~ à son compte** set up on one's own.

établissement /etablismɑ̃/ nm (entreprise) organization; (institution) establishment; **~ scolaire** school.

étage /etaʒ/ nm floor, storey; (de fusée) stage; **à l'~** upstairs; **au premier ~** on the first floor.

étagère /etaʒɛʀ/ nf shelf; (meuble) shelving unit.

étain /etɛ̃/ nm pewter.

E

étais, était /etɛ/ ⇒ÊTRE [4].

étalage /etalaʒ/ nm display; (vitrine) shop-window; **faire ~ de** flaunt. **étalagiste** nmf window-dresser.

étaler /etale/ [1] vt spread; (journal) spread (out); (pâte) roll out; (exposer) display; (richesse) flaunt. □ **s'~** vpr (prendre de la place) spread out; (tomber 🗉) fall flat; **s'~ sur** (paiement) be spread over.

étalon /etalɔ̃/ nm (cheval) stallion; (modèle) standard.

étanche /etɑ̃ʃ/ a watertight; (montre) waterproof.

étancher /etɑ̃ʃe/ [1] vt (soif) quench.

étang /etɑ̃/ nm pond.

étant /etɑ̃/ ⇒ÊTRE [4].

étape /etap/ nf stage; (lieu d'arrêt) stopover; (fig) stage.

état /eta/ nm state; (liste) statement; (métier) profession; **en bon/mauvais ~** in good/bad condition; **en ~ de** in a position to; **en ~ de marche** in working order; **faire ~ de** (citer) mention; **être dans tous ses ~s** be in a state; **~ civil** civil status; **~ des lieux** inventory of fixtures. **État** nm State.

état-major (pl **états-majors**) /etamaʒɔR/ nm (officiers) staff (+ pl).

États-Unis /etazyni/ nmpl **~ (d'Amérique)** United States (of America).

étau (pl **~x**) /eto/ nm vice.

étayer /eteje/ [31] vt prop up.

été¹ /ete/ ⇒ÊTRE [4].

été² /ete/ nm summer.

éteindre /etɛ̃dR/ [22] vt (feu) put out; (lumière, radio) turn off. □ **s'~** vpr (feu, lumière) go out; (appareil) go off; (mourir) die. **éteint, ~e** a (feu) out; (volcan) extinct.

étendard /etɑ̃daR/ nm standard.

étendre /etɑ̃dR/ [3] vt (nappe) spread (out); (bras, jambes) stretch (out); (linge) hang out; (agrandir) extend. □ **s'~** vpr (s'allonger) lie down; (se propager) spread; (plaine) stretch; **s'~ sur** (sujet) dwell on.

étendu, ~e /etɑ̃dy/ a extensive. **étendue** nf area; (d'eau) stretch; (importance) extent.

éternel, ~le /etɛRnɛl/ a (vie) eternal; (fig) endless.

éterniser (s') /(s)etɛRnize/ [1] vpr (durer) drag on.

éternité /etɛRnite/ nf eternity.

éternuement /etɛRnymɑ̃/ nm sneeze. **éternuer** [1] vi sneeze.

êtes /ɛt/ ⇒ÊTRE [4].

éthique /etik/ a ethical. ● nf ethics (+ sg).

ethnie /ɛtni/ nf ethnic group. **ethnique** a ethnic.

étincelant, ~e /etɛ̃slɑ̃, -t/ a sparkling. **étinceler** [38] vi sparkle. **étincelle** nf spark.

étiqueter /etikte/ [38] vt label. **étiquette** nf label; (protocole) etiquette.

étirer /etiRe/ [1] vt stretch. □ **s'~** vpr stretch.

étoffe /etɔf/ nf fabric.

étoffer /etɔfe/ [1] vt expand. □ **s'~** vpr fill out.

étoile /etwal/ nf star; **à la belle ~** in the open; **~ filante** shooting star; **~ de mer** starfish.

étonnant, ~e /etɔnɑ̃, -t/ a (curieux) surprising; (formidable) amazing. **étonnement** nm surprise; (plus fort) amazement.

étonner /etɔne/ [1] vt amaze. □ **s'~** vpr be amazed (de at).

étouffant, ~e /etufɑ̃, -t/ a stifling.

étouffer /etufe/ [1] vt/i suffocate; (sentiment, révolte) stifle; (feu) smother; (bruit) muffle; **on étouffe**

it is stifling. □ **s'~** *vpr* suffocate; (en mangeant) choke.

étourderie /eturdəri/ *nf* thoughtlessness; (acte) careless mistake.

étourdi, ~e /eturdi/ *a* absent-minded. ● *nm, f* scatterbrain.

étourdir /eturdir/ [2] *vt* stun; (fatiguer) make sb's head spin. **étourdissant, ~e** *a* stunning.

étourneau (*pl ~x*) /eturno/ *nm* starling.

étrange /etrɑ̃ʒ/ *a* strange.

étranger, ~ère /etrɑ̃ʒe, -ɛr/ *a* (inconnu) strange, unfamiliar; (d'un autre pays) foreign. ● *nm, f* foreigner; (inconnu) stranger; **à l'~** abroad; **de l'~** from abroad.

étrangler /etrɑ̃gle/ [1] *vt* strangle; (col) throttle. □ **s'~** *vpr* choke.

....

être /ɛtr/ [4]

● *verbe auxiliaire*

····➤ (du passé) have; **elle est partie/ venue hier** she left/came yesterday.

····➤ (de la voix passive) be.

● *verbe intransitif* (*aux avoir*)

····➤ be; **~ médecin** be a doctor; **je suis à vous** I'm all yours; **j'en suis à me demander si…** I'm beginning to wonder whether…, **qu'en est-il de…?** what's the news about…?

····➤ (appartenance) be, belong to.

····➤ (heure, date) be; **nous sommes le 3 mars** it's March 3.

····➤ (aller) be; **je n'y ai jamais été** I've never been; **il a été le voir** he went to see him.

····➤ **c'est** it is *or* it's; **c'est moi qui l'ai fait** I did it; **est-ce que tu veux du thé?** do you want some tea?

● *nom masculin*

····➤ being; **~ humain** human being.

····➤ (personne) person; **un ~ cher** a loved one.

....

étreindre /etrɛ̃dr/ [22] *vt* embrace. **étreinte** *nf* embrace.

étrennes /etrɛn/ *nfpl* (New Year's) gift (+ *sg*); (argent) money.

étrier /etrije/ *nm* stirrup.

étriqué, ~e /etrike/ *a* tight.

étroit, ~e /etrwa, -t/ *a* narrow; (vêtement) tight; (liens, surveillance) close; **à l'~** cramped. **étroitement** *adv* closely. **étroitesse** *nf* narrowness.

étude /etyd/ *nf* study; (enquête) survey; (bureau) office; (salle d')~ (Scol) prep room; **à l'~** under consideration; **faire des ~s (de)** study; **il n'a pas fait d'~s** he didn't go to university; **~ de marché** market research.

étudiant, ~e /etydjɑ̃, -t/ *nm, f* student.

étudier /etydje/ [45] *vt/i* study.

étui /etyi/ *nm* case.

étuve /etyv/ *nf* steam room.

eu, ~e /y/ ⇒AVOIR [5].

euro /øro/ *nm* euro.

Europe /ørɔp/ *nf* Europe.

européen, ~ne /ørɔpeɛ̃, -ɛɛn/ *a* European. **E~, ~ne** *nm, f* European.

euthanasie /øtanazi/ *nf* euthanasia.

eux /ø/ *pron* they; (complément) them. **eux-mêmes** *pron* themselves.

évacuation /evakɥasjɔ̃/ *nf* evacuation; (d'eaux usées) discharge. **évacuer** [1] *vt* evacuate.

évadé, ~e /evade/ *a* escaped. ● *nm, f* escaped prisoner. **évader (s')** [1] *vpr* escape.

évaluation /evalɥasjɔ̃/ *nf*

assessment. **évaluer** [1] vt assess.

évangile /evãʒil/ nm gospel; l'É~ the Gospel.

évanouir (s') /(s)evanwiʀ/ [2] vpr faint; (disparaître) vanish.

évaporation /evapɔʀasjɔ̃/ nf evaporation. **évaporer** (s') [1] vpr evaporate.

évasif, -ive /evazif, -v/ a evasive.

évasion /evazjɔ̃/ nf escape.

éveil /evɛj/ nm awakening; en ~ alert.

éveillé, ~e /eveje/ a awake; (intelligent) alert.

éveiller /eveje/ [1] vt awake(n); (susciter) arouse. □ s'~ vpr awake.

événement /evɛnmã/ nm event.

éventail /evãtaj/ nm fan; (gamme) range.

éventrer /evãtʀe/ [1] vt (sac) rip open.

éventualité /evãtɥalite/ nf possibility; dans cette ~ in that event.

éventuel, ~le /evãtɥɛl/ a possible. **éventuellement** adv possibly.

évêque /evɛk/ nm bishop.

évertuer (s') /(s)evɛʀtɥe/ [1] vpr s'~ à struggle hard to.

éviction /eviksjɔ̃/ nf eviction.

évidemment /evidamã/ adv obviously; (bien sûr) of course.

évidence /evidãs/ nf obviousness; (fait) obvious fact; être en ~ be conspicuous; mettre en ~ (fait) highlight. **évident, ~e** a obvious, evident.

évier /evje/ nm sink.

évincer /evɛ̃se/ [10] vt oust.

éviter /evite/ [1] vt avoid (de faire doing); ~ qch à qn (dérangement) save sb sth.

évocateur, -trice /evɔkatœʀ, -tʀis/ a evocative. **évocation** nf evocation.

évolué, ~e /evɔlɥe/ a highly developed.

évoluer /evɔlɥe/ [1] vi evolve; (situation) develop; (se déplacer) glide. **évolution** nf evolution; (d'une situation) development.

évoquer /evɔke/ [1] vt call to mind, evoke.

exacerber /ɛgzasɛʀbe/ [1] vt exacerbate.

exact, ~e /ɛgza(kt), -akt/ a (précis) exact, accurate; (juste) correct; (personne) punctual. **exactement** adv exactly. **exactitude** nf exactness; punctuality.

ex æquo /ɛgzeko/ adv être ~ tie (avec qn with sb).

exagération /ɛgzaʒeʀasjɔ̃/ nf exaggeration. **exagéré, ~e** a excessive.

exagérer /ɛgzaʒeʀe/ [14] vt/i exaggerate; (abuser) go too far.

exalté, ~e /ɛgzalte/ nm, f fanatic. **exalter** [1] vt excite; (glorifier) exalt.

examen /ɛgzamɛ̃/ nm examination; (Scol) exam.

examinateur, -trice nm, f examiner. **examiner** [1] vt examine.

exaspération /ɛgzaspeʀasjɔ̃/ nf exasperation. **exaspérer** [14] vt exasperate.

exaucer /ɛgzose/ [10] vt grant; (personne) grant the wish(es) of.

excédent /ɛksedã/ nm surplus; ~ de bagages excess luggage; ~ de la balance commerciale trade surplus. **excédentaire** a excess, surplus.

excéder /ɛksede/ [14] vt (dépasser) exceed; (agacer) irritate.

excellence /ɛksɛlãs/ nf excellence. **excellent, ~e** a excellent. **exceller** [1] vi excel (dans in).

excentricité /ɛksãtʀisite/ nf

eccentricity. **excentrique** a & nmf eccentric.

excepté, ~e /ɛksɛpte/ a & prép except.

excepter /ɛksɛpte/ [1] vt except.

exception /ɛksɛpsjɔ̃/ nf exception; **à l'~ de** except for; **d'~** exceptional; **faire ~** be an exception. **exceptionnel**, ~le a exceptional.

exceptionnellement adv exceptionally.

excès /ɛksɛ/ nm excess; **~ de vitesse** speeding.

excessif, -ive /ɛksesif, -v/ a excessive.

excitant, ~e /ɛksitɑ̃, -t/ a stimulating; (palpitant) exciting. ● nm stimulant.

exciter /ɛksite/ vt excite; (irriter) get excited. □ s'~ vpr get excited.

exclamer (s') /(s)ɛksklɑme/ [1] vpr exclaim.

exclure /ɛksklyʀ/ [16] vt exclude, (expulser) expel; (empêcher) preclude.

exclusif, -ive /ɛksklyzif, -v/ a exclusive.

exclusion /ɛksklyzjɔ̃/ nf exclusion.

exclusivité /ɛksklyzivite/ nf (Comm) exclusive rights (+ pl); **projeter en ~** show exclusively.

excursion /ɛkskyʀsjɔ̃/ nf excursion; (à pied) hike.

excuse /ɛkskyz/ nf excuse; ~s apology (+ sg); **faire des ~s** apologize.

excuser /ɛkskyze/ [1] vt excuse; **excusez-moi** excuse me. □ s'~ vpr apologize (**de** for).

exécrable /ɛgzekʀabl/ a dreadful. **exécrer** [14] vt loathe.

exécuter /ɛgzekyte/ [1] vt carry out, execute; (Mus) perform; (tuer) execute.

exécutif, -ive /ɛgzekytif, -v/ a & nm (Pol) executive.

exécution /ɛgzekysjɔ̃/ nf execution; (Mus) performance.

exemplaire /ɛgzɑ̃plɛʀ/ a exemplary. ● nm copy.

exemple /ɛgzɑ̃pl/ nm example; **par ~** for example; **donner l'~** set an example.

exempt, ~e /ɛgzɑ̃, -t/ a ~ **de** exempt (**de** from).

exempter /ɛgzɑ̃te/ [1] vt exempt (**de** from). **exemption** nf exemption.

exercer /ɛgzɛʀse/ [10] vt exercise; (influence, contrôle) exert; (former) train, exercise; ~ **un métier** have a job; ~ **le métier de...** work as a... □ s'~ vpr practise.

exercice /ɛgzɛʀsis/ nm exercise; (de métier) practice; **en ~** in office; (médecin) in practice.

exhaler /ɛgzale/ [1] vt emit.

exhaustif, -ive /ɛgzostif, -v/ a exhaustive.

exhiber /ɛgzibe/ [1] vt exhibit.

exhorter /ɛgzɔʀte/ [1] vt exhort (**à** to).

exigeant, ~e /ɛgziʒɑ̃, -t/ a demanding; **être ~ avec qn** demand a lot of sb. **exigence** nf demand. **exiger** [40] vt demand.

exigu, ~ë /ɛgzigy/ a tiny.

exil /ɛgzil/ nm exile. **exilé**, ~e nm, f exile.

exiler /ɛgzile/ [1] vt exile. □ s'~ vpr go into exile.

existence /ɛgzistɑ̃s/ nf existence. **exister** [1] vi exist.

exode /ɛgzɔd/ nm exodus.

exonérer /ɛgzɔneʀe/ [14] vt exempt (**de** from).

exorbitant, ~e /ɛgzɔʀbitɑ̃, -t/ a exorbitant.

exorciser /ɛgzɔʀsize/ [1] vt exorcize.

exotique /ɛgzɔtik/ a exotic.

E

expansé, ~**e** /ɛkspɑ̃se/ *a* (Tech) expanded.

expansif, -ive /ɛkspɑ̃sif, -v/ *a* expansive. **expansion** *nf* expansion.

expatrié, ~**e** /ɛkspatʀije/ *nm, f* expatriate.

expectative /ɛkspɛktativ/ *nf* **être dans l'**~ wait and see.

expédient /ɛkspedjɑ̃/ *nm* expedient; **vivre d'**~**s** live by one's wits; **user d'**~**s** resort to expedients.

expédier /ɛkspedje/ [45] *vt* send, dispatch; (*tâche* ⑩) polish off. **expéditeur, -trice** *nm, f* sender.

expéditif, -ive /ɛkspeditif, -v/ *a* quick.

expédition /ɛkspedisjɔ̃/ *nf* (envoi) dispatching; (voyage) expedition.

expérience /ɛkspeʀjɑ̃s/ *nf* experience; (scientifique) experiment.

expérimental, ~**e** (*mpl* **-aux**) /ɛksperimɑ̃tal, o/ *a* experimental. **expérimentation** *nf* experimentation.

expérimenté, ~**e** *a* experienced. **expérimenter** [1] *vt* test, experiment with.

expert, ~**e** /ɛkspɛʀ, -t/ *a* expert. ● *nm* expert; (d'assurances) adjuster. **expert-comptable** (*pl* **experts-comptables**) *nm* accountant.

expertise /ɛkspɛʀtiz/ *nf* valuation; (de dégâts) assessment. **expertiser** [1] *vt* value; (dégâts) assess.

expier /ɛkspje/ [45] *vt* atone for.

expiration /ɛkspiʀasjɔ̃/ *nf* expiry.

expirer /ɛkspiʀe/ [1] *vi* breathe out; (finir, mourir) expire.

explicatif, -ive /ɛksplikatif, -v/ *a* explanatory.

explication /ɛksplikasjɔ̃/ *nf*

explanation; (fig) discussion; ~ **de texte** (Scol) literary commentary.

explicite /ɛksplisit/ *a* explicit.

expliquer /ɛksplike/ [1] *vt* explain. □ **s'**~ *vpr* explain oneself; (discuter) discuss things; (être explicable) be understandable.

exploit /ɛksplwa/ *nm* exploit.

exploitant, ~**e** /ɛksplwatɑ̃, -t/ *nm, f* ~ (**agricole**) farmer.

exploitation /ɛksplwatasjɔ̃/ *nf* exploitation; (d'entreprise) running; (ferme) farm.

exploiter /ɛksplwate/ [1] *vt* exploit; (ferme) run; (mine) work.

explorateur, -trice /ɛksplɔʀatœʀ, -tʀis/ *nm, f* explorer. **exploration** *nf* exploration. **explorer** [1] *vt* explore.

exploser /ɛksploze/ [1] *vi* explode; **faire** ~ explode; (bâtiment) blow up.

explosif, -ive /ɛksplozif, -v/ *a* & *nm* explosive. **explosion** *nf* explosion.

exportateur, -trice /ɛkspɔʀtatœʀ, -tʀis/ *nm, f* exporter. ● *a* exporting. **exportation** *nf* export. **exporter** [1] *vt* export.

exposant, ~**e** /ɛkspozɑ̃, -t/ *nm, f* exhibitor.

exposé, ~**e** /ɛkspoze/ *nm* talk (**sur** on); (d'une action) account; **faire l'**~ **de la situation** give an account of the situation. ● *a* ~ **au nord** facing north.

exposer /ɛkspoze/ [1] *vt* display, show; (expliquer) explain; (soumettre, mettre en danger) expose (**à** to); (vie) endanger. □ **s'**~ **à** *vpr* expose oneself to.

exposition /ɛkspozisjɔ̃/ *nf* (d'art) exhibition; (de faits) exposition; (géographique) aspect.

exprès[1] /ɛkspʀɛ/ *adv* specially; (délibérément) on purpose.

exprès², **-esse** /ɛkspRɛs/ a express.

express /ɛkspRɛs/ a & nm inv (**café**) ∼ espresso; (**train**) ∼ fast train.

expressif, **-ive** /ɛkspResif, -v/ a expressive. **expression** nf expression.

exprimer /ɛkspRime/ [1] vt express. □ **s'**∼ vpr express oneself.

expulser /ɛkspylse/ [1] vt expel; (*locataire*) evict; (*joueur*) send off. **expulsion** nf (d'élève) expulsion; (de locataire) eviction; (d'immigré) deportation.

exquis, **-e** /ɛkski, -z/ a exquisite.

extase /ɛkstɑz/ nf ecstasy.

extasier (**s'**) /(s)ɛkstazje/ [45] vpr **s'**∼ **sur** be ecstatic about.

extensible /ɛkstɑ̃sibl/ a (*tissu*) stretch.

extension /ɛkstɑ̃sjɔ̃/ nf extension; (*expansion*) expansion.

exténuer /ɛkstenɥe/ [1] vt exhaust.

extérieur, **∼e** /ɛksteRjœR/ a outside; (*signe, gaieté*) outward; (*politique*) foreign. ● nm outside, exterior; (de personne) exterior; **à l'**∼ (**de**) outside. **extérioriser** [1] vt show, externalize.

extermination /ɛkstɛRminasjɔ̃/ nf extermination. **exterminer** [1] vt exterminate.

externe /ɛkstɛRn/ a external. ● nmf (Scol) day pupil.

extincteur /ɛkstɛ̃ktœR/ nm fire extinguisher.

extinction /ɛkstɛ̃ksjɔ̃/ nf extinction; **avoir une** ∼ **de voix** have lost one's voice.

extorquer /ɛkstɔRke/ [1] vt extort.

extra /ɛkstRa/ a inv first-rate. ● nm inv (*repas*) (special) treat.

extraction /ɛkstRaksjɔ̃/ nf extraction.

extrader /ɛkstRade/ [1] vt extradite.

extraire /ɛkstRɛR/ [29] vt extract. **extrait** nm extract.

extraordinaire /ɛkstRaɔRdinɛR/ a extraordinary.

extravagance /ɛkstRavagɑ̃s/ nf extravagance. **extravagant**, ∼**e** a extravagant.

extraverti, ∼**e** /ɛkstRavɛRti/ nm, f extrovert.

extrême /ɛkstRɛm/ a & nm extreme. **extrêmement** adv extremely.

Extrême-Orient /ɛkstRɛmɔRjɑ̃/ nm Far East.

extrémiste /ɛkstRemist/ nmf extremist.

extrémité /ɛkstRemite/ nf end; (mains, pieds) extremity.

exubérance /ɛgzybeRɑ̃s/ nf exuberance. **exubérant**, ∼**e** a exuberant.

F abrév f (**franc, francs**) franc, francs.

fabricant, ∼**e** /fabRikɑ̃, -t/ nm, f manufacturer. **fabrication** nf making; manufacture.

fabrique /fabRik/ nf factory. **fabriquer** [1] vt make; (industriellement) manufacture; (fig) make up.

fabuler /fabyle/ [1] vi fantasize.

fabuleux, **-euse** /fabylø, -z/ a fabulous.

fac /fak/ nf ① university.

façade /fasad/ *nf* front; (fig)
façade.

face /fas/ *nf* face; (d'un objet) side;
en ∼ (de), d'en ∼ opposite; **en ∼
de** (fig) faced with; **∼ à** facing; (fig)
faced with; **faire ∼ à** face. **face-à-
face** *nm inv* (débat) one-to-one
debate.

fâcher /faʃe/ [1] *vt* anger; **fâché**
angry; (désolé) sorry. **□ se ∼** *vpr*
get angry; (se brouiller) fall out.

facile /fasil/ *a* easy; (caractère)
easygoing.

facilité /fasilite/ *nf* easiness;
(aisance) ease; (aptitude) ability; **∼s**
(possibilités) facilities,
opportunities; **∼s d'importation**
import opportunities; **∼s de
paiement** easy terms.

faciliter /fasilite/ [1] *vt* facilitate,
make easier.

façon /fasɔ̃/ *nf* way; (de vêtement)
cut; **de cette ∼** in this way; **de ∼ à**
so as to; **de toute ∼** anyway; **∼s**
(chichis) fuss; **faire des ∼s** stand on
ceremony; **sans ∼s** (repas)
informal; (personne)
unpretentious. **façonner** [1] *vt*
shape; (faire) make.

fac-similé (*pl* **∼s**) /faksimile/
nm facsimile.

facteur, -trice /faktœr, -tris/
nm, f postman, postwoman. ● *nm*
(élément) factor.

facture /faktyr/ *nf* bill; (Comm)
invoice; **∼ détaillée** itemized bill.
facturer [1] *vt* invoice.
facturette *nf* credit card slip.

facultatif, -ive /fakyltatif, -v/ *a*
optional.

faculté /fakylte/ *nf* faculty;
(possibilité) power; (Univ) faculty.

fade /fad/ *a* insipid.

faible /fɛbl/ *a* weak; (espoir,
quantité, écart) slight; (revenu,
intensité) low; **∼ d'esprit** feeble-
minded. ● *nm* (personne) weakling;

(penchant) weakness. **faiblesse** *nf*
weakness. **faiblir** [2] *vi* weaken.

faïence /fajɑ̃s/ *nf* earthenware.

faillir /fajir/ [2] *vi* **j'ai failli acheter**
I almost bought.

faillite /fajit/ *nf* bankruptcy; (fig)
collapse.

faim /fɛ̃/ *nf* hunger; **avoir ∼** be
hungry; **rester sur sa ∼** (fig) be left
wanting more.

fainéant, ∼e /feneɑ̃, -t/ *a* idle.
● *nm, f* idler.

∙∙

faire /fɛr/ [33]
➡ Pour les expressions comme
  **faire attention, faire la
  cuisine,** etc. ⇒**attention,
  cuisine,** etc.

● *verbe transitif*

∙∙∙▶ (préparer, créer) make; **∼ une
tarte/une erreur** make a tart/a
mistake.

∙∙∙▶ (se livrer à une activité) do; **∼ du
droit** do law; **∼ du foot/du violon**
play football/the violin; **qu'est-ce
qu'elle fait?** (dans la vie) what does
she do?; (en ce moment précis) what
is she doing?

∙∙∙▶ (dans les calculs, mesures, etc.) **10
et 10 font 20** 10 and 10 make 20;
ça fait 25 euros that's 25 euros; **∼
60 kilos** weigh 60 kilos; **il fait 1,75
m** he's 1.75 m tall.

∙∙∙▶ (dans les expressions de temps) **ça
fait une heure que j'attends** I have
been waiting for an hour.

∙∙∙▶ (imiter) **∼ le clown** act the
clown; **faire le malade** pretend to
be ill.

∙∙∙▶ (parcourir) **∼ 10 km** do *ou* cover
10 km; **∼ les musées** go round
the museums.

∙∙∙▶ (entraîner, causer) **ça ne fait rien** it
doesn't matter; **l'accident a fait 8
morts** 8 people died in the
accident.

····➤ (dire) say; **'excusez-moi', fit-elle** 'excuse me', she said.

● *verbe auxiliaire*

····➤ (**faire** + infinitif + qn) make; **~ pleurer qn** make sb cry.

····➤ (**faire** + infinitif + qch) have, get; **~ réparer sa voiture** have *ou* get one's car mended.

····➤ (**ne faire que** + infinitif) (continuellement) **ne ~ que pleurer** do nothing but cry; (seulement) **je ne fais qu'obéir** I'm only following orders.

● *verbe intransitif*

····➤ (agir) do, act; **~ vite** act quickly; **fais comme tu veux** do as you please; **fais comme chez toi** make yourself at home.

····➤ (paraître) look; **~ joli** look pretty; **ça fait cher** it's expensive.

····➤ (en parlant du temps) **il fait chaud/ gris** it's hot/overcast.

□ **se faire** *verbe pronominal*

····➤ (obtenir, confectionner) make; **se ~ des amis** make friends; **se ~ un thé** make (oneself) a cup of tea.

····➤ (**se faire** + infinitif) **se ~ gronder** be scolded; **se ~ couper les cheveux** have one's hair cut.

····➤ (devenir) **il se fait tard** it's getting late.

····➤ (être d'usage) **ça ne se fait pas** it's not the done thing.

····➤ (emploi impersonnel) **comment se fait-il que tu sois ici?** how come you're here?

····➤ □ **se faire à** get used to; **je ne m'y fais pas** I can't get used to it.

····➤ □ **s'en faire** worry; **ne t'en fais pas** don't worry.

! Lorsque **faire** remplace un verbe plus précis, on traduira quelquefois par ce dernier: **faire une visite** *pay a visit*, **faire un nid** *build a nest*.

faire-part /fɛʀpaʀ/ *nm inv* announcement.

fais /fɛ/ ⇒FAIRE [33].

faisan /fəzɑ̃/ *nm* pheasant.

faisceau (*pl* ~x) /fɛso/ *nm* (rayon) beam; (fagot) bundle.

fait, ~e /fɛ, fɛt/ *a* done; (*fromage*) ripe; **pour ~** made for; **tout ~** ready made; **c'est bien ~ pour toi** it serves you right. ● *nm* fact; (événement) event; **au ~ (de)** informed (of); **de ce ~** therefore; **du ~ de** on account of; **~ divers** (trivial) news item; **~ nouveau** new development; **prendre qn sur le ~** catch sb in the act.
● ⇒FAIRE [33].

faîte /fɛt/ *nm* top; (fig) peak.

faîtes /fɛt/ ⇒FAIRE [33].

falaise /falɛz/ *nf* cliff.

falloir /falwaʀ/ [34] *vi* **il faut qch/ qn** we/you *etc.* need sth/so; **il lui faut du pain** he needs bread, **il faut rester** we/you *etc.* have to *ou* must stay; **il faut que j'y aille** I have to *ou* must go; **il faudrait que tu partes** you should leave; **il aurait fallu le faire** we/you *etc.* should have done it; **comme il faut** (*manger, se tenir*) properly; (*personne*) respectable, proper.
□ **s'en ~** *vpr* **il s'en est fallu de peu qu'il gagne** he nearly won; **il s'en faut de beaucoup que je sois** I am far from being.

falsifier /falsifje/ [45] *vt* falsify; (*signature, monnaie*) forge.

famé, ~e /fame/ *a* **mal ~** disreputable, seedy.

fameux, -euse /famø, -z/ *a* famous; (excellent Ⅱ) first-rate.

familial, ~e (*mpl* **-iaux**) /familjal, -jo/ *a* family.

familiale /familjal/ *nf* estate car; (US) station wagon.

familiariser /familjaʀize/ [1] vt familiarize (avec with). □ **se ~** vpr familiarize oneself.

familier, -ière /familje, -jɛʀ/ a familiar; (amical) informal.

famille /famij/ nf family; **en ~** with one's family.

famine /famin/ nf famine.

fanatique /fanatik/ a fanatical. ● nmf fanatic.

fanfare /fɑ̃faʀ/ nf brass band; (musique) fanfare.

fantaisie /fɑ̃tezi/ nf imagination, fantasy; (caprice) whim; (de) **~** (boutons etc.) fancy. **fantaisiste** a unorthodox; (personne) eccentric.

fantasme /fɑ̃tasm/ nm fantasy.

fantastique /fɑ̃tastik/ a fantastic.

fantôme /fɑ̃tom/ nm ghost; **cabinet(-)~** (Pol) shadow cabinet.

faon /fɑ̃/ nm fawn.

FAQ abrév f (**Foire aux questions**) (Internet) FAQ, Frequently Asked Questions.

farce /faʀs/ nf (practical) joke; (Théât) farce; (hachis) stuffing.

farcir /faʀsiʀ/ [2] vt stuff.

fard /faʀ/ nm make-up; **~ à paupières** eye-shadow; **piquer un ~** blush.

fardeau (pl **~x**) /faʀdo/ nm burden.

farfelu, ~e /faʀfəly/ a & nm,f eccentric.

farine /faʀin/ nf flour. **farineux, -euse** a floury. **farineux** nmpl starchy food.

farouche /faʀuʃ/ a shy; (peu sociable) unsociable; (violent) fierce.

fascicule /fasikyl/ nm (brochure) booklet; (partie d'un ouvrage) fascicule.

fasciner /fasine/ [1] vt fascinate.

fascisme /faʃism/ nm fascism.

fasse /fas/ ⇒FAIRE [33].

fast-food /fastfud/ nm fast-food place.

fastidieux, -ieuse /fastidjø, -z/ a tedious.

fatal, ~e (mpl **~s**) /fatal/ a inevitable; (mortel) fatal. **fatalité** nf (destin) fate.

fatigant, ~e /fatigɑ̃, -t/ a tiring; (ennuyeux) tiresome.

fatigue /fatig/ nf fatigue, tiredness.

fatigué, ~e /fatige/ a tired.

fatiguer /fatige/ [1] vt tire; (yeux, moteur) strain. ● vi (moteur) labour. □ **se ~** vpr get tired, tire (de of).

faubourg /fobuʀ/ nm suburb.

faucher /foʃe/ [1] vt (herbe) mow; (voler 🖪) pinch; **~ qn** (véhicule, tir) mow sb down.

faucon /fokɔ̃/ nm falcon, hawk.

faudra, faudrait /fodʀa, fodʀɛ/ ⇒FALLOIR [34].

faufiler (se) /(sə)fofile/ [1] vpr edge one's way, squeeze.

faune /fon/ nf wildlife, fauna.

faussaire /fosɛʀ/ nmf forger.

fausse /fos/ ⇒FAUX².

fausser /fose/ [1] vt buckle; (fig) distort; **~ compagnie à qn** give sb the slip.

faut /fo/ ⇒FALLOIR [34].

faute /fot/ nf mistake; (responsabilité) fault; (délit) offence; (péché) sin; **en ~** at fault; **~ de** for want of; **~ de quoi** failing which; **sans ~** without fail; **~ de frappe** typing error; **~ de goût** bad taste; **~ professionnelle** professional misconduct.

fauteuil /fotœj/ nm armchair; (de président) chair; (Théât) seat; **~ roulant** wheelchair.

fautif, -ive /fotif, -v/ a guilty; (faux) faulty. ● nm,f guilty party.

fauve /fov/ a (couleur) fawn, tawny. ● nm wild cat.

faux¹ /fo/ nf scythe.

faux², **fausse** /fo, fos/ a false; (falsifié) fake, forged; (numéro, calcul) wrong; (voix) out of tune; c'est ~! that is wrong!; ~ témoignage perjury; faire ~ bond à qn stand sb up; fausse couche miscarriage; ~ frais incidental expenses. ● adv (chanter) out of tune. ● nm forgery. **faux-filet** (pl ~s) nm sirloin.

faveur /favœʀ/ nf favour; de ~ (régime) preferential; en ~ de in favour of.

favorable /favɔʀabl/ a favourable.

favori, ~**te** /favɔʀi, -t/ a & nm,f favourite. **favoriser** [1] vt favour.

fax /faks/ nm fax. **faxer** [1] vt fax.

fébrile /febʀil/ a feverish.

fécond, ~**e** /fekɔ̃, -d/ a fertile. **féconder** [1] vt fertilize. **fécondité** nf fertility.

fédéral, ~**e** (mpl -**aux**) /federal, -o/ a federal. **fédération** nf federation.

fée /fe/ nf fairy. **féerie** nf magical spectacle. **féerique** a magical.

feindre /fɛ̃dʀ/ [22] vt feign; ~ de pretend to.

fêler /fele/ [1] vt crack. □ se ~ vpr crack.

félicitations /felisitasjɔ̃/ nfpl congratulations (pour on). **féliciter** [1] vt congratulate (de on).

félin, ~**e** /felɛ̃, -in/ a & nm feline.

femelle /fəmɛl/ a & nf female.

féminin, ~**e** /feminɛ̃, -in/ a feminine; (sexe) female; (mode, équipe) women's. ● nm feminine. **féministe** nmf feminist.

femme /fam/ nf woman; (épouse) wife; ~ au foyer housewife; ~ de chambre chambermaid; ~ de ménage cleaning lady.

fémur /femyʀ/ nm thigh-bone.

fendre /fɑ̃dʀ/ [3] vt (couper) split; (fissurer) crack. □ se ~ vpr crack.

fenêtre /fənɛtʀ/ nf window.

fenouil /fənuj/ nm fennel.

fente /fɑ̃t/ nf (ouverture) slit, slot; (fissure) crack.

féodal, ~**e** (mpl -**aux**) /feodal, -o/ a feudal.

fer /fɛʀ/ nm iron; ~ (à repasser) iron; ~ à cheval horseshoe; ~ de lance spearhead; ~ forgé wrought iron.

fera, **ferait** /fəʀa, fəʀɛ/ ⇒FAIRE [33].

férié, ~**e** /feʀje/ a jour ~ public holiday.

ferme /fɛʀm/ nf farm; (maison) farm(house). ● a firm. ● adv (travailler) hard.

fermé, ~**e** /fɛʀme/ a closed; (gaz, radio) off.

fermenter /fɛʀmɑ̃te/ [1] vi ferment.

fermer /fɛʀme/ [1] vt/i close, shut; (cesser d'exploiter) close ou shut down; (gaz, robinet) turn off. □ se ~ vpr close, shut.

fermeté /fɛʀməte/ nf firmness.

fermeture /fɛʀmətyʀ/ nf closing; (dispositif) catch; ~ annuelle annual closure; ~ éclair® zip(-fastener); (US) zipper.

fermier, -**ière** /fɛʀmje, -jɛʀ/ a farm. ● nm farmer. **fermière** nf farmer's wife.

féroce /feʀɔs/ a ferocious.

ferraille /feʀaj/ nf scrap-iron.

ferrer /feʀe/ [1] vt (cheval) shoe.

ferroviaire /feʀɔvjɛʀ/ a rail(way).

ferry /feʀi/ nm ferry.

fertile /fɛʀtil/ a fertile; ~ en (fig) rich in. **fertiliser** [1] vt fertilize. **fertilité** nf fertility.

fervent, ~**e** /fɛʀvɑ̃, -t/ a fervent. ● nm,f enthusiast (de of).

fesse /fɛs/ nf buttock. **fessée** nf spanking, smack.

festin /fɛstɛ̃/ nm feast.

festival (pl ~**s**) /fɛstival/ nm festival.

fêtard, ~e /fɛtaʀ, -d/ *nm, f* ▣ party animal.

fête /fɛt/ *nf* holiday; (religieuse) feast; (du nom) name-day; (réception) party; (en famille) celebration; (foire) fair; (folklorique) festival; **~ des Mères** Mother's Day; **~ foraine** fun-fair; **faire la ~** live it up; **les ~s (de fin d'année)** the Christmas season. **fêter** [1] *vt* celebrate; (*personne*) give a celebration for.

fétiche /fetiʃ/ *nm* fetish; (fig) mascot.

feu¹ (*pl* ~**x**) /fø/ *nm* fire; (lumière) light; (de réchaud) burner; **à ~ doux/vif** on a low/high heat; **~ rouge/vert/orange** red/green/ amber light; **aux ~x, tournez à droite** turn right at the traffic lights; **avez-vous du ~?** (pour cigarette) have you got a light?; **au ~!** fire!; **mettre le ~ à** set fire to; **prendre ~** catch fire; **jouer avec le ~** play with fire; **ne pas faire long ~** not last; **~ d'artifice** firework display; **~ de joie** bonfire; **~ de position** sidelight.

feu² /fø/ *a inv* (mort) late.

feuillage /fœjaʒ/ *nm* foliage.

feuille /fœj/ *nf* leaf; (de papier) sheet; (formulaire) form; **~ d'impôts** tax return; **~ de paie** payslip.

feuilleté, ~e /fœjte/ *a* **pâte ~e** puff pastry. ● *nm* savoury pasty.

feuilleter /fœjte/ [1] *vt* leaf through.

feuilleton /fœjtɔ̃/ *nm* (à suivre) serial; (histoire complète) series.

feutre /føtʀ/ *nm* felt; (chapeau) felt hat; (crayon) felt-tip (pen).

fève /fɛv/ *nf* broad bean.

février /fevʀije/ *nm* February.

fiable /fjabl/ *a* reliable.

fiançailles /fjɑ̃saj/ *nfpl* engagement.

fiancé, ~e /fjɑ̃se/ *a* engaged. ● *nm* fiancé. **fiancée** *nf* fiancée.

fiancer (se) [10] *vpr* become engaged (**avec** to).

fibre /fibʀ/ *nf* fibre; **~ de verre** fibreglass.

ficeler /fisle/ [38] *vt* tie up.

ficelle /fisɛl/ *nf* string.

fiche /fiʃ/ *nf* (index) card; (formulaire) form, slip; (Électr) plug.

ficher¹ /fiʃe/ [1] *vt* (enfoncer) drive (**dans** into).

ficher² /fiʃe/ [1] ▣ *vt* (faire) do; (donner) give; (mettre) put; **~ le camp** clear off. □ **se ~ de** *vpr* make fun of; **il s'en fiche** he couldn't care less.

fichier /fiʃje/ *nm* file.

fichu, ~e /fiʃy/ *a* ▣ (mauvais) rotten; (raté) done for; **mal ~** terrible.

fictif, -ive /fiktif, -v/ *a* fictitious.

fiction *nf* fiction.

fidèle /fidɛl/ *a* faithful. ● *nmf* (client) regular; (Relig) believer; **~s** (à l'église) congregation. **fidélité** *nf* fidelity.

fier¹, fière /fjɛʀ/ *a* proud (**de** of).

fier² (se) /(sə)fje/ [45] *vpr* **se ~ à** trust.

fierté /fjɛʀte/ *nf* pride.

fièvre /fjɛvʀ/ *nf* fever; **avoir de la ~** have a temperature; **~ aphteuse** foot-and-mouth disease. **fiévreux, -euse** *a* feverish.

figer /fiʒe/ [40] *vi* (graisse) congeal; (sang) clot; **figé sur place** frozen to the spot. □ **se ~** *vpr* (*personne, sourire*) freeze; (*graisse*) congeal; (*sang*) clot.

figue /fig/ *nf* fig.

figurant, ~e /figyʀɑ̃, -t/ *nm, f* (au cinéma) extra.

figure /figyʀ/ *nf* face; (forme, personnage) figure; (illustration) picture.

figuré, ~e /figyʀe/ *a* (sens) figurative.

figurer /figyʀe/ [1] *vi* appear. ● *vt* represent. □ **se ~** *vpr* imagine.

fil /fil/ *nm* thread; (métallique,

électrique) wire; (de couteau) edge; (à coudre) cotton; **au ~ de** with the passing of; **~ de l'eau** with the current; **~ de fer** wire; **au bout du ~** 🕾 on the phone.

file /fil/ *nf* line; (voie: Auto) lane; **~ (d'attente)** queue; (US) (*liquide*) **indienne** in single file.

filer /file/ [1] *vt* spin; (suivre) shadow; **~ qch à qn** 🕾 slip sb sth. ● *vi* ladder, run; (*bas*) (*liquide*) run; (aller vite 🕾) speed along, fly by; (partir 🕾) dash off; (disparaître 🕾) **~ entre les mains** slip through one's fingers; **~ doux** do as one's told.

filet /file/ *nm* net; (d'eau) trickle; (de viande) fillet; **~ (à bagages)** (luggage) rack; **~ à provisions** string bag (*for shopping*).

filiale /filjal/ *nf* subsidiary (company).

filière /filjɛʀ/ *nf* (official) channels; (de trafiquants) network; **passer par** *ou* **suivre la ~** (*employé*) work one's way up.

fille /fij/ *nf* girl; (opposé à fils) daughter. **fillette** *nf* little girl.

filleul /fijœl/ *nm* godson.

filleule /fijœl/ *nf* god-daughter.

film /film/ *nm* film; **~ d'épouvante/muet/parlant** horror/ silent/talking film; **~ dramatique** drama. **filmer** [1] *vt* film.

filon /filɔ̃/ *nm* (Géol) seam; (travail lucratif 🕾) money spinner; **avoir trouvé le bon ~** be onto a good thing.

fils /fis/ *nm* son.

filtre /filtʀ/ *nm* filter. **filtrer** [1] *vt/i* filter; (*personne*) screen.

fin¹ /fɛ̃/ *nf* end; **à la ~** finally; **en ~ de compte** all things considered; **~ de semaine** weekend; **mettre ~ à** put an end to; **prendre ~** come to an end.

fin², **~e** /fɛ̃, in/ *a* fine; (tranche,

couche) thin; (taille) slim; (plat) exquisite; (esprit, vue) sharp; **~es herbes** mixed herbs. ● *adv* (couper) finely.

final, **~e** (*mpl* **-aux**) /final, -o/ *a* final.

finale /final/ *nm* (Mus) finale. ● *nf* (Sport) final; (Gram) final syllable. **finalement** *adv* finally; (somme toute) after all. **finaliste** *nmf* finalist.

finance /finɑ̃s/ *nf* finance. **financer** [10] *vt* finance. **financier**, **-ière** /finɑ̃sje, -jɛʀ/ *a* financial. ● *nm* financier.

finesse /fines/ *nf* fineness; (de taille) slimness; (acuité) sharpness; **~s** (de langue) niceties.

finir /finiʀ/ [2] *vt/i* finish, end; (arrêter) stop; (manger) finish (up); **en ~ avec** have done with; **~ par faire** end up doing; **ça va mal ~** it will turn out badly.

finlandais, **~e** /fɛ̃lɑ̃dɛ, -z/ *a* Finnish. **F~**, **~e** *nm*, *f* Finn. **Finlande** /fɛ̃lɑ̃d/ *nf* Finland.

finnois, **~e** /finwa/ *a* Finnish. ● *nm* (Ling) Finnish.

firme /firm/ *nf* firm.

fisc /fisk/ *nm* tax authorities. **fiscal**, **~e** (*mpl* **-aux**) *a* tax, fiscal. **fiscalité** *nf* tax system.

fissure /fisyʀ/ *nf* crack.

fixe /fiks/ *a* fixed; (stable) steady; **à heure ~** at a set time, **menu à prix ~** set menu. ● *nm* basic pay.

fixer /fikse/ [1] *vt* fix; **~ (du regard)** stare at; **être fixé** (*personne*) have made up one's mind. □ **se ~** *vpr* (s'attacher) be attached; (s'installer) settle down.

flacon /flakɔ̃/ *nm* bottle.

flagrant, **~e** /flagʀɑ̃, -t/ *a* flagrant, blatant; **en ~ délit** in the act.

flair /flɛʀ/ *nm* (sense of) smell; (fig) intuition.

flamand, **~e** /flamɑ̃, -d/ *a*

Flemish. ● *nm* (Ling) Flemish. F∼,
∼e *nm, f* Fleming.
flamant /flamɑ̃/ *nm* flamingo.
flambeau (*pl* ∼x) /flɑ̃bo/ *nm*
torch.
flambée /flɑ̃be/ *nf* blaze; (fig)
explosion.
flamber /flɑ̃be/ [1] *vi* blaze;
(*prix*) shoot up. ● *vt* (*aiguille*)
sterilize; (*volaille*) singe.
flamme /flam/ *nf* flame; (fig)
ardour; **en** ∼**s** ablaze.
flan /flɑ̃/ *nm* custard tart.
flanc /flɑ̃/ *nm* side; (d'animal,
d'armée) flank.
flâner /flɑne/ [1] *vi* stroll.
flânerie *nf* stroll.
flanquer /flɑ̃ke/ [1] *vt* flank; (jeter
🔲) chuck; (donner 🔲) give; ∼ **à la
porte** kick out.
flaque /flak/ *nf* (d'eau) puddle; (de
sang) pool.
flash (*pl* ∼**es**) /flaʃ/ *nm* (Photo)
flash; (information) news flash; ∼
publicitaire commercial.
flatter /flate/ [1] *vt* flatter. □ **se** ∼
de *vpr* pride oneself on.
flatteur, -euse /flatœr, -øz/ *a*
flattering. ● *nm, f* flatterer.
fléau (*pl* ∼x) /fleo/ *nm* (désastre)
scourge; (personne) pest.
flèche /flɛʃ/ *nf* arrow; (de clocher)
spire; **monter en** ∼ spiral; **partir en**
∼ shoot off.
flécher /fleʃe/ [14] *vt* mark *ou*
signpost (with arrows). **fléchette**
nf dart.
fléchir /fleʃir/ [2] *vt* bend;
(*personne*) move, sway. ● *vi*
(faiblir) weaken; (*prix*) fall;
(*poutre*) sag, bend.
flemme /flɛm/ *nf* 🔲 laziness; **j'ai
la** ∼ **de faire** I can't be bothered
doing.
flétrir (**se**) /(sə)fletrir/ [2] *vpr*
(*plante*) wither; (*fruit*) shrivel;
(*beauté*) fade.
fleur /flœr/ *nf* flower; **à** ∼ **de**

terre/d'eau just above the ground/
water; **à** ∼**s** flowery; ∼ **de l'âge**
prime of life; **en** ∼**s** in flower.
fleurir /flœrir/ [2] *vi* flower;
(*arbre*) blossom; (fig) flourish.
● *vt* decorate with flowers.
fleuriste *nmf* florist.
fleuve /flœv/ *nm* river.
flic /flik/ *nm* 🔲 cop.
flipper /flipœr/ *nm* pinball
(machine).
flirter /flœrte/ [1] *vi* flirt.
flocon /flɔkɔ̃/ *nm* flake.
flore /flɔr/ *nf* flora.
florissant, ∼e /flɔrisɑ̃, -t/ *a*
flourishing.
flot /flo/ *nm* flood, stream; **être à**
∼ be afloat; **les** ∼**s** the waves.
flottant, ∼e /flɔtɑ̃, -t/ *a*
(*vêtement*) loose; (indécis)
indecisive.
flotte /flɔt/ *nf* fleet; (pluie 🔲) rain;
(eau 🔲) water.
flottement /flɔtmɑ̃/ *nm* (incertitude)
indecision.
flotter /flɔte/ [1] *vi* float;
(*drapeau*) flutter; (*nuage, parfum,
pensées*) drift; (pleuvoir 🔲) rain.
flotteur *nm* float.
flou, ∼e /flu/ *a* out of focus; (fig)
vague.
fluctuer /flyktɥe/ [1] *vi* fluctuate.
fluet, ∼te /flyɛ, -t/ *a* thin.
fluide /flɥid/ *a & nm* fluid.
fluor /flyɔr/ *nm* (pour les dents)
fluoride.
fluorescent, ∼e /flyɔresɑ̃, -t/ *a*
fluorescent.
flûte /flyt/ *nf* flute; (verre)
champagne glass.
fluvial, ∼e (*mpl* **-iaux**) /flyvjal,
-jo/ *a* river.
flux /fly/ *nm* flow; ∼ **et reflux** ebb
and flow.
FM *abrév f* (**frequency
modulation**) FM.
fœtus /fetys/ *nm* foetus.

foi /fwa/ *nf* faith; **être de bonne/ mauvaise ∼** be acting in good/bad faith; **ma ∼!** well (indeed)!

foie /fwa/ *nm* liver.

foin /fwɛ̃/ *nm* hay.

foire /fwaʀ/ *nf* fair; **faire la ∼** 🗊 live it up.

fois /fwa/ *nf* time; **une ∼** once; **deux ∼** twice; **à la ∼** at the same time; **des ∼** (parfois) sometimes; **une ∼ pour toutes** once and for all.

fol /fɔl/ ⇒FOU.

folie /fɔli/ *nf* madness; (bêtise) foolish thing, folly; **faire une ∼, faire des ∼s** be extravagant.

folklore /fɔlklɔʀ/ *nm* folklore. **folklorique** *a* folk; 🗊 eccentric.

folle /fɔl/ ⇒FOU.

foncé, ∼e /fɔ̃se/ *a* dark.

foncer /fɔ̃se/ [10] *vt* darken. ● *vi* (s'assombrir) darken; (aller vite 🗊) dash along; **∼ sur** 🗊 charge at.

foncier, -ière /fɔ̃sje, -jɛʀ/ *a* fundamental; (Comm) real estate.

fonction /fɔ̃ksjɔ̃/ *nf* function; (emploi) position; **∼s** (obligations) duties; **en ∼ de** according to; **∼ publique** civil service; **voiture de ∼** company car. **fonctionnaire** *nmf* civil servant. **fonctionnement** *nm* working.

fonctionner /fɔ̃ksjɔne/ [1] *vi* work; **faire ∼** work.

fond /fɔ̃/ *nm* bottom; (de salle, magasin, etc.) back; (essentiel) basis; (contenu) content; (plan) background; (Sport) long-distance running; **à ∼** thoroughly; **au ∼** basically; **de ∼** (bruit) background; **de ∼ en comble** from top to bottom; **au** *ou* **dans le ∼** really; **∼ de teint** foundation, make-up base.

fondamental, ∼e (*mpl* **-aux**) /fɔ̃damɑ̃tal, -o/ *a* fundamental.

fondateur, -trice /fɔ̃datœʀ, -tʀis/ *nm, f* founder. **fondation** *nf* foundation.

fonder /fɔ̃de/ [1] *vt* found; (baser) base (**sur** on); (**bien**) **fondé** well-founded. □ **se ∼ sur** *vpr* be guided by, be based on.

fonderie /fɔ̃dʀi/ *nf* foundry.

fondre /fɔ̃dʀ/ [3] *vt/i* melt; (dans l'eau) dissolve; (mélanger) merge; **faire ∼** melt; dissolve; **∼ en larmes** burst into tears; **∼ sur** swoop on. □ **se ∼** *vpr* merge.

fonds /fɔ̃/ *nm* fund; **∼ de commerce** business. ● *nmpl* (capitaux) funds.

fondu, ∼e /fɔ̃dy/ *a* melted; (métal) molten.

font /fɔ̃/ ⇒FAIRE [33].

fontaine /fɔ̃tɛn/ *nf* fountain; (source) spring.

fonte /fɔ̃t/ *nf* melting; (fer) cast iron; **∼ des neiges** thaw.

foot /fut/ *nm* 🗊 football.

football /futbol/ *nm* football.

footing /futiŋ/ *nm* jogging.

forain /fɔʀɛ̃/ *nm* fairground entertainer; **marchand ∼** stall-holder.

forçat /fɔʀsa/ *nm* convict.

force /fɔʀs/ *nf* force; (physique) strength; (hydraulique etc.) power; **∼s** (physiques) strength; **à ∼ de** by sheer force of; **de ∼, par la ∼** by force; **∼ de dissuasion** deterrent; **∼ de frappe** strike force, deterrent; **∼ de l'âge** prime of life; **∼s de l'ordre** police (force); **∼s de marché** market forces.

forcé, ∼e /fɔʀse/ *a* forced; (inévitable) inevitable; **c'est ∼ qu'il fasse** 🗊 he's bound to do. **forcément** *adv* necessarily; (évidemment) obviously.

forcené, ∼e /fɔʀsəne/ *a* frenzied. ● *nm, f* maniac.

forcer /fɔʀse/ [10] *vt* force (**à faire** to do); (voix) strain; **∼ la dose** 🗊 overdo it. ● *vi* force; (exagérer)

F

overdo it. □ se ~ vpr force oneself.

forer /fɔʀe/ [1] vt drill.

forestier, -ière /fɔʀɛstje, -jɛʀ/ a forest. ● nm, f forestry worker.

forêt /fɔʀɛ/ nf forest.

forfait /fɔʀfɛ/ nm (Comm) (prix fixe) fixed price; (offre promotionnelle) package. **forfaitaire** a (prix) fixed.

forger /fɔʀʒe/ [40] vt forge; (inventer) make up.

forgeron /fɔʀʒəʀɔ̃/ nm blacksmith.

formaliser (se) /(sə)fɔʀmalize/ [1] vpr take offence (de at).

formalité /fɔʀmalite/ nf formality.

format /fɔʀma/ nm format. **formater** [1] vt (Ordinat) format.

formation /fɔʀmasjɔ̃/ nf formation; (professionnelle) training; (culture) education; ~ permanente ou continue continuing education.

forme /fɔʀm/ nf form; (contour) shape, form; ~s (de femme) figure; être en ~ be in good shape, be on form; en ~ de in the shape of; en bonne et due ~ in due form.

formel, ~le /fɔʀmɛl/ a formal; (catégorique) positive.

former /fɔʀme/ [1] vt form; (instruire) train. □ se ~ vpr form.

formidable /fɔʀmidabl/ a fantastic.

formulaire /fɔʀmylɛʀ/ nm form.

formule /fɔʀmyl/ nf formula; (expression) expression; (feuille) form; ~ de politesse polite phrase, letter ending. **formuler** [1] vt formulate.

fort, ~e /fɔʀ, -t/ a strong; (grand) big; (pluie) heavy; (bruit) loud; (pente) steep; (élève) clever; au plus ~ de at the height of; c'est une ~e tête she/he's headstrong. ● adv (frapper) hard; (parler) loud; (très) very; (beaucoup) very

much. ● nm (atout) strong point; (Mil) fort.

fortifiant /fɔʀtifjɑ̃/ nm tonic.

fortifier /45/ vt fortify.

fortune /fɔʀtyn/ nf fortune; de ~ (improvisé) makeshift; faire ~ make one's fortune.

forum /fɔʀɔm/ nm forum; ~ de discussion (Internet) newsgroup.

fosse /fos/ nf pit; (tombe) grave; ~ d'orchestre orchestra pit; ~ septique septic tank.

fossé /fose/ nm ditch; (fig) gulf; ~ numérique digital divide.

fossette /fosɛt/ nf dimple.

fossile /fɔsil/ nm fossil.

fou (fol before vowel or mute h), **folle** /fu, fɔl/ a mad; (course, regard) wild; (énorme ▣) tremendous; ~ de crazy about; le ~ rire the giggles. ● nm madman; (bouffon) jester. **folle** nf madwoman.

foudre /fudʀ/ nf lightning.

foudroyant, ~e /fudʀwajɑ̃, -t/ a (mort, maladie) violent.

foudroyer /fudʀwaje/ [31] vt (orage) strike; (maladie etc.) strike down; ~ qn du regard look daggers at sb.

fouet /fwɛ/ nm whip; (Culin) whisk.

fougère /fuʒɛʀ/ nf fern.

fougue /fug/ nf ardour. **fougueux, -euse** a ardent.

fouille /fuj/ nf search; (Archéol) excavation.

fouiller /fuje/ [1] vt/i search; (creuser) dig; ~ dans (tiroir) rummage through.

fouillis /fuji/ nm jumble.

foulard /fulaʀ/ nm scarf.

foule /ful/ nf crowd; une ~ de (fig) a mass of.

foulée /fule/ nf stride; il l'a fait dans la ~ he did it while he was at ou about it.

fouler /fule/ [1] vt (raisin) press; (sol) set foot on; ~ qch aux pieds

trample sth underfoot; (fig) ride
roughshod over sth. □ **se ~** *vpr*
se ~ le poignet/le pied sprain
one's wrist/foot; **ne pas se ~** ▣
not strain oneself.

four /fuʀ/ *nm* oven; (de potier) kiln;
(Théât) flop; **~ à micro-ondes**
microwave oven; **~ crématoire**
crematorium.

fourbe /fuʀb/ *a* deceitful.

fourche /fuʀʃ/ *nf* fork; (à foin)
pitchfork. **fourchette** *nf* fork;
(Comm) bracket, range.

fourgon /fuʀgɔ̃/ *nm* van.

fourmi /fuʀmi/ *nf* ant; **avoir des
~s** have pins and needles.

fourmiller /fuʀmije/ [1] *vi* swarm
(de with).

fourneau (*pl* **~x**) /fuʀno/ *nm*
stove.

fourni, **~e** /fuʀni/ *a* (épais) thick.

fournir /fuʀniʀ/ [2] *vt* supply,
provide; (client) supply; (effort)
put in; **~ à qn** supply sb with.
□ **se ~ chez** *vpr* shop at.

fournisseur /fuʀnisœʀ/ *nm*
supplier; **~ d'accès à l'Internet**
Internet service provider.

fourniture /fuʀnityʀ/ *nf* supply.

fourrage /fuʀaʒ/ *nm* fodder.

fourré, **~e** /fuʀe/ *a* (vêtement)
fur-lined; (gâteau etc.) filled (with
jam, cream, etc.). ● *nm* thicket.

fourre-tout /fuʀtu/ *nm inv* (sac)
holdall.

fourreur /fuʀœʀ/ *nm* furrier.

fourrière /fuʀjɛʀ/ *nf* (lieu) pound.

fourrure /fuʀyʀ/ *nf* fur.

foutre /futʀ/ [3] *vt* ▣ = **ficher²** [1].

foutu, **~e** /futy/ *a* ▣ = **fichu**.

foyer /fwaje/ *nm* home; (âtre)
hearth; (club) club; (d'étudiants)
hostel; (Théât) foyer; (Photo) focus;
(centre) centre.

fracas /fʀaka/ *nm* din; (de train)
roar; (d'objet qui tombe) crash.

fracassant, **~e** *a* (bruyant)
deafening; (violent) shattering.

fraction /fʀaksjɔ̃/ *nf* fraction.

fracture /fʀaktyʀ/ *nf* fracture; **~
du poignet** fractured wrist.

fragile /fʀaʒil/ *a* fragile; (peau)
sensitive; (cœur) weak. **fragilité**
nf fragility.

fragment /fʀagmɑ̃/ *nm* bit,
fragment. **fragmenter** [1] *vt* split,
fragment.

F

fraîchement /fʀɛʃmɑ̃/ *adv*
(récemment) freshly; (avec froideur)
coolly. **fraîcheur** *nf* coolness;
(nouveauté) freshness. **fraîchir** [2]
vi freshen, become colder.

frais¹, **fraîche** /fʀɛ, ʃ/ *a* fresh,
(temps, accueil) cool; (peinture)
wet; **~ et dispos** fresh; **il fait ~** it
is cool. ● *adv* (récemment) newly,
freshly. ● *nm* **mettre au ~** put in a
cool place; **prendre le ~** get some
fresh air.

frais² /fʀɛ/ *nmpl* expenses; (droits)
fees; **aux ~ de** at the expense of;
faire des ~ spend a lot of money;
~ généraux (Comm) overheads,
running expenses; **~ de scolarité**
school fees.

fraise /fʀɛz/ *nf* strawberry.

fraisier *nm* strawberry plant;
(gâteau) strawberry gateau.

framboise /fʀɑ̃bwaz/ *nf*
raspberry. **framboisier** *nm*
raspberry bush.

franc, **franche** /fʀɑ̃, ʃ/ *a* frank;
(regard) frank, candid; (cassure)
clean; (net) clear; (libre) free; (véritable) downright.

français, **~e** /fʀɑ̃sɛ, -z/ *a* French.
● *nm* (Ling) French. **F~**, **~e** *nm, f*
Frenchman, Frenchwoman.

France /fʀɑ̃s/ *nf* France.

franchement /fʀɑ̃ʃmɑ̃/ *adv*
frankly; (nettement) clearly; (tout à
fait) really.

franchir /fʀɑ̃ʃiʀ/ [2] *vt* (obstacle)

get over; (*distance*) cover; (*limite*) exceed; (*traverser*) cross.

franchise /fʀɑ̃ʃiz/ *nf* (qualité) frankness; (Comm) franchise; (exemption) exemption; ~ **douanière** exemption from duties.

franc-maçon (*pl* **francs-maçons**) /fʀɑ̃masɔ̃/ *nm* Freemason. **franc-maçonnerie** *nf* Freemasonry.

franco /fʀɑ̃ko/ *adv* postage paid.

francophone /fʀɑ̃kɔfɔn/ *a* French-speaking. ● *nmf* French speaker.

franc-parler /fʀɑ̃paʀle/ *nm inv* outspokenness.

frange /fʀɑ̃ʒ/ *nf* fringe.

frappe /fʀap/ *nf* (de texte) typing.

frappé, ~**e** /fʀape/ *a* chilled.

frapper /fʀape/ [1] *vt/i* strike; (battre) hit, strike; (*monnaie*) mint; (à la porte) knock, bang; **frappé de panique** panic-stricken.

fraternel, ~**le** /fʀatɛʀnɛl/ *a* brotherly. **fraternité** *nf* brotherhood.

fraude /fʀod/ *nf* fraud; (à un examen) cheating; **passer qch en** ~ smuggle sth in. **frauder** [1] *vt/i* cheat. **frauduleux, -euse** *a* fraudulent.

frayer /fʀeje/ [31] *vt* open up. □ **se** ~ *vpr* **se** ~ **un passage** force one's way (**à travers, dans** through).

frayeur /fʀejœʀ/ *nf* fright.

fredonner /fʀədɔne/ [1] *vt* hum.

free-lance /fʀilɑ̃s/ *a & nmf* freelance.

freezer /fʀizœʀ/ *nm* freezer.

frein /fʀɛ̃/ *nm* brake; **mettre un** ~ **à** curb; ~ **à main** hand brake.

freiner /fʀene/ [1] *vt* slow down; (modérer, enrayer) curb. ● *vi* (Auto) brake.

frêle /fʀɛl/ *a* frail.

frelon /fʀəlɔ̃/ *nm* hornet.

frémir /fʀemiʀ/ [2] *vi* shudder, shake; (*feuille, eau*) quiver.

frêne /fʀɛn/ *nm* ash.

frénésie /fʀenezi/ *nf* frenzy. **frénétique** *a* frenzied.

fréquemment /fʀekamɑ̃/ *adv* frequently. **fréquence** *nf* frequency. **fréquent**, ~**e** *a* frequent. **fréquentation** *nf* frequenting.

fréquentations /fʀekɑ̃tasjɔ̃/ *nfpl* acquaintances; **avoir de mauvaises** ~ keep bad company.

fréquenter /fʀekɑ̃te/ [1] *vt* frequent; (*école*) attend; (*personne*) see.

frère /fʀɛʀ/ *nm* brother.

fret /fʀɛt/ *nm* freight.

friand, ~**e** /fʀijɑ̃, -d/ *a* ~ **de** very fond of.

friandise /fʀijɑ̃diz/ *nf* sweet; (US) candy; (gâteau) cake.

fric /fʀik/ *nm* 🔲 money.

friction /fʀiksjɔ̃/ *nf* friction; (massage) rub-down.

frigidaire® /fʀiʒidɛʀ/ *nm* refrigerator.

frigo /fʀigo/ *nm* 🔲 fridge. **frigorifique** *a* (*vitrine etc.*) refrigerated.

frileux, -euse /fʀilø, -z/ *a* sensitive to cold.

frime /fʀim/ *nf* 🔲 **c'est de la** ~ it's all pretence; **pour la** ~ for show.

frimousse /fʀimus/ *nf* face.

fringale /fʀɛ̃gal/ *nf* 🔲 ravenous appetite.

fringant, ~**e** /fʀɛ̃gɑ̃, -t/ *a* dashing.

fringues /fʀɛ̃g/ *nfpl* 🔲 gear.

friper /fʀipe/ [1] *vt* crumple, crease. □ **se** ~ *vpr* crumple, crease.

fripon, ~**ne** /fʀipɔ̃, -ɔn/ *nm, f* rascal. ● *a* mischievous.

fripouille /fʀipuj/ *nf* rogue.

frire /fʀiʀ/ [56] *vt/i* fry; **faire** ~ fry.

frise /fʁiz/ *nf* frieze.

friser /fʁize/ [1] *vt/i* (*cheveux*) curl; (*personne*) curl the hair of; **frisé** curly.

frisson /fʁisɔ̃/ *nm* (de froid) shiver; (de peur) shudder. **frissonner** [1] *vi* shiver; shudder.

frit, **~e** /fʁi, -t/ *a* fried.

frite /fʁit/ *nf* chip; avoir la **~** ▯ feel good.

friteuse /fʁitøz/ *nf* chip pan; (électrique) (deep) fryer.

friture /fʁityʁ/ *nf* fried fish; (huile) (frying) oil *ou* fat.

frivole /fʁivɔl/ *a* frivolous.

froid, **~e** /fʁwa, -d/ *a & nm* cold; avoir/prendre **~** be/catch cold; il fait **~** it is cold. **froidement** *adv* coldly; (*calculer*) coolly. **froideur** *nf* coldness.

froisser /fʁwase/ [1] *vt* crumple; (fig) offend. □ se **~** *vpr* crumple; (fig) take offence; se **~** un muscle strain a muscle.

frôler /fʁole/ [1] *vt* brush against, skim; (fig) come close to.

fromage /fʁɔmaʒ/ *nm* cheese.

fromager, **-ère** /fʁɔmaʒe, ɛʁ/ *a* cheese. ● *nm, f* (fabricant) cheese-maker; (marchand) cheesemonger.

froment /fʁɔmɑ̃/ *nm* wheat.

froncer /fʁɔ̃se/ [10] *vt* gather; **~ les sourcils** frown.

front /fʁɔ̃/ *nm* forehead; (Mil, Pol) front; **de ~** at the same time; (de face) head-on; (côte à côte) abreast; **faire ~ à** face up to. **frontal**, **~e** (*mpl* **-aux**) *a* frontal; (Ordinat) front-end.

frontalier, **-ière** /fʁɔ̃talje, -jɛʁ/ *a* border; **travailleur ~** commuter from across the border.

frontière /fʁɔ̃tjɛʁ/ *nf* border, frontier.

frottement /fʁɔtmɑ̃/ *nm* rubbing; (Tech) friction. **frotter** [1] *vt/i* rub; (*allumette*) strike.

frottis /fʁɔti/ *nm* **~ vaginal** cervical smear.

frousse /fʁus/ *nf* ▯ fear; avoir la **~** ▯ be scared.

fructifier /fʁyktifje/ [45] *vi* faire **~** put to work.

fructueux, **-euse** /fʁyktɥø, -z/ *a* fruitful.

frugal, **~e** (*mpl* **-aux**) /fʁygal, -o/ *a* frugal.

fruit /fʁɥi/ *nm* fruit; **des ~s** (some) fruit; **~s de mer** seafood. **fruité**, **~e** *a* fruity.

frustrant, **~e** /fʁystʁɑ̃, -t /* *a* frustrating. **frustrer** [1] *vt* frustrate.

fuel /fjul/ *nm* fuel oil.

fugitif, **-ive** /fyʒitif, -v/ *a* (*passager*) fleeting. ● *nm, f* fugitive.

fugue /fyg/ *nf* (Mus) fugue; faire une **~** run away.

fuir /fɥiʁ/ [35] *vi* flee, run away; (*eau, robinet, etc.*) leak. ● *vt* (quitter) flee; (éviter) shun.

fuite /fɥit/ *nf* flight; (de liquide, d'une nouvelle) leak; **en ~** on the run; **mettre en ~** put to flight; **prendre la ~** take flight.

fulgurant, **~e** /fylgyʁɑ̃, -t/ *a* (*vitesse*) lightning.

fumé, **~e** /fyme/ *a* (*poisson, verre*) smoked.

fumée /fyme/ *nf* smoke; (vapeur) steam.

fumer /fyme/ [1] *vt/i* smoke.

fumeur, **-euse** /fymœʁ, -øz/ *nm, f* smoker; **zone non-~s** no smoking area.

fumier /fymje/ *nm* manure.

funambule /fynɑ̃byl/ *nmf* tightrope walker.

funèbre /fynɛbʁ/ *a* funeral; (fig) gloomy.

funérailles /fyneʁaj/ *nfpl* funeral.

funéraire /fyneʁɛʁ/ *a* funeral.

funeste /fynɛst/ *a* fatal.

F

fur: au ∼ et à mesure /ofyʀeaməzyʀ/ *loc* as one goes along, progressively; **au ∼ et à mesure que** as.

furet /fyʀɛ/ *nm* ferret.

fureur /fyʀœʀ/ *nf* fury; (*passion*) passion; **avec ∼** furiously; passionately; **mettre en ∼** infuriate; **faire ∼** be all the rage.

furieux, -ieuse /fyʀjø, -z/ *a* furious.

furoncle /fyʀɔ̃kl/ *nm* boil.

furtif, -ive /fyʀtif, -v/ *a* furtive.

fuseau (*pl* ∼**x**) /fyzo/ *nm* ski trousers; (*pour filer*) spindle; ∼ **horaire** time zone.

fusée /fyze/ *nf* rocket.

fusible /fyzibl/ *nm* fuse.

fusil /fyzi/ *nm* rifle, gun; (*de chasse*) shotgun; ∼ **mitrailleur** machine-gun.

fusion /fyzjɔ̃/ *nf* fusion; (Comm) merger. **fusionner** [1] *vt/i* merge.

fut /fy/ ⇒ÊTRE [5].

fût /fy/ *nm* (*tonneau*) barrel; (*d'arbre*) trunk.

futé, ∼e /fyte/ *a* cunning.

futile /fytil/ *a* futile.

futur, ∼e /fytyʀ/ *a* future; **∼e femme/maman** wife-/mother-to-be. ● *nm* future.

fuyant, ∼e /fɥijɑ̃, -t/ *a* (*front, ligne*) receding; (*personne*) evasive.

fuyard, ∼e /fɥijaʀ, -d/ *nm, f* runaway.

gabardine /gabaʀdin/ *nf* raincoat.

gabarit /gabaʀi/ *nm* size; (*patron*) template; (fig) calibre.

gâcher /gɑʃe/ [1] *vt* (*gâter*) spoil; (*gaspiller*) waste.

gâchette /gɑʃɛt/ *nf* trigger.

gâchis /gɑʃi/ *nm* waste.

gaffe /gaf/ *nf* 🆔 blunder; **faire ∼** be careful (à of).

gage /gaʒ/ *nm* security; (*de bonne foi*) pledge; (*de jeu*) forfeit; ∼**s** (*salaire*) wages; **en ∼ de** as a token of; **mettre en ∼** pawn; **tueur à ∼s** hired killer.

gageure /gaʒyʀ/ *nf* challenge.

gagnant, ∼e /gaɲɑ̃, -t/ *a* winning. ● *nm, f* winner.

gagne-pain /gaɲpɛ̃/ *nm inv* job.

gagner /gaɲe/ [1] *vt* (*match, prix*) win; (*argent, pain*) earn; (*terrain*) gain; (*temps*) save; (*atteindre*) reach; (*convaincre*) win over; ∼ **sa vie** earn one's living. ● *vi* win; (fig) gain.

gai, ∼e /ge/ *a* cheerful; (*ivre*) merry. **gaiement** *adv* cheerfully. **gaieté** *nf* cheerfulness.

gain /gɛ̃/ *nm* (*salaire*) earnings; (*avantage*) gain; (*économie*) saving; ∼**s** (Comm) profits; (*au jeu*) winnings.

gaine /gɛn/ *nf* (*corset*) girdle; (*étui*) sheath.

galant, ∼e /galɑ̃, -t/ *a* courteous; (*amoureux*) romantic.

galaxie /galaksi/ *nf* galaxy.

gale /gal/ *nf* (*de chat etc.*) mange.

galère /galɛʀ/ *nf* (navire) galley;
c'est la ∼! ⊡ what an ordeal!

galérer /galeʀe/ [14] *vi* ⊡ (peiner)
have a hard time.

galerie /galʀi/ *nf* gallery; (Théât)
circle; (de voiture) roof-rack; ∼
marchande shopping arcade.

galet /galɛ/ *nm* pebble.

galette /galɛt/ *nf* flat cake; ∼ **des
Rois** Twelfth Night cake.

Galles /gal/ *nfpl* **le pays de ∼**
Wales.

gallois, ∼e /galwa, -z/ *a* Welsh.
●*nm* (Ling) Welsh. **G∼, ∼e** *nm, f*
Welshman, Welshwoman.

galon /galɔ̃/ *nm* braid; (Mil) stripe;
prendre du ∼ be promoted.

galop /galo/ *nm* canter; **aller au ∼**
canter; **grand ∼** gallop; ∼ **d'essai**
trial run. **galoper** [1] *vi* (cheval)
canter; (au grand galop) gallop;
(personne) run.

galopin /galopɛ̃/ *nm* ⊡ rascal.

gambader /gɑ̃bade/ [1] *vi* leap
about.

gamelle /gamɛl/ *nf* (de soldat)
mess kit; (d'ouvrier) lunch-box.

gamin, ∼e /gamɛ̃, -in/ *a* childish;
(air) youthful. ●*nm, f* ⊡ kid.

gamme /gam/ *nf* (Mus) scale;
(série) range; **haut de ∼**
up-market, top of the range; **bas
de ∼** down-market, bottom of the
range.

gang /gɑ̃g/ *nm* ⊡ gang.

ganglion /gɑ̃glijɔ̃/ *nm* ganglion.

gangster /gɑ̃gstɛʀ/ *nm* gangster;
(escroc) crook.

gant /gɑ̃/ *nm* glove; ∼ **de ménage**
rubber glove; ∼ **de toilette** face-
flannel, face-cloth.

garage /gaʀaʒ/ *nm* garage.
garagiste *nmf* garage owner;
(employé) car mechanic.

garant, ∼e /gaʀɑ̃, -t/ *nm, f*
guarantor. ●*a* **se porter ∼ de**
vouch for.

garanti, ∼e /gaʀɑ̃ti/ *a*
guaranteed.

garantie /gaʀɑ̃ti/ *nf* guarantee.
∼**s** (de police d'assurance) cover.

garantir [2] *vt* guarantee;
(protéger) protect (**de** from).

garçon /gaʀsɔ̃/ *nm* boy; (jeune
homme) young man; (célibataire)
bachelor; ∼ (**de café**) waiter; ∼
d'honneur best man. **garçonnière**
nf bachelor flat.

garde[1] /gaʀd/ *nf* guard; (d'enfants,
de bagages) care; (service) guard
(duty); (infirmière) nurse; **de ∼** on
duty; ∼ **à vue** (police) custody;
mettre en ∼ warn; **prendre ∼** be
careful (**à** of); (**droit de**) ∼ custody
(**de** of).

garde[2] /gaʀd/ *nm* guard; (de
propriété, parc) warden; ∼ **champêtre**
village policeman; ∼ **du corps**
bodyguard.

garde-à-vous /gaʀdavu/ *nm inv*
(Mil) **se mettre au ∼** stand to
attention.

garde-chasse (*pl* ∼**s**) /gaʀdə-
ʃas/ *nm* gamekeeper.

garde-manger /gaʀdmɑ̃ʒe/ *nm
inv* meat safe; (placard) larder.

garder /gaʀde/ [1] *vt* (conserver,
maintenir) keep; (vêtement) keep
on; (surveiller) look after; (défendre)
guard; ∼ **le lit** stay in bed. □ **se ∼**
vpr (denrée) keep; **se ∼ de faire**
be careful not to do.

garderie /gaʀdəʀi/ *nf* day
nursery.

garde-robe (*pl* ∼**s**) /gaʀdəʀɔb/
nf wardrobe.

gardien, ∼ne /gaʀdjɛ̃, -ɛn/ *nm, f*
(de locaux) security guard; (de prison,
réserve) warden; (d'immeuble)
caretaker; (de musée) attendant;
(de zoo) keeper; (de traditions)
guardian; ∼ **de but** goalkeeper; ∼
de la paix policeman; ∼ **de nuit**
night watchman; **gardienne
d'enfants** childminder.

G

gare /gaʀ/ nf (Rail) station; ~ **routière** coach station; (US) bus station. ● interj ~ (à toi) watch out!

garer /gaʀe/ [1] vt park. □ se ~ vpr park; (s'écarter) move out of the way.

gargouille /gaʀguj/ nf waterspout; (sculptée) gargoyle. **gargouiller** [1] vi gurgle; (stomach) rumble.

garni, ~e /gaʀni/ a (plat) served with vegetables; **bien ~** (rempli) well-filled.

garnir /gaʀniʀ/ [2] vt (remplir) fill; (décorer) decorate; (couvrir) cover; (doubler) line; (Culin) garnish. **garniture** nf (légumes) vegetables; (ornement) trimming; (de voiture) trim.

gars /ga/ nm 🔲 lad; (adulte) guy, bloke.

gas-oil /gazwal/ nm diesel (oil).

gaspillage /gaspijaʒ/ nm waste. **gaspiller** [1] vt waste.

gastrique /gastʀik/ a gastric.

gastronome /gastʀɔnɔm/ nmf gourmet.

gâteau (pl ~x) /gɑto/ nm cake; ~ **sec** biscuit; (US) cookie; **un papa ~** a doting dad.

gâter /gɑte/ [1] vt spoil. □ se ~ vpr (viande) go bad; (dent) rot; (temps) get worse.

gâterie /gɑtʀi/ nf little treat.

gâteux, -euse /gɑtø, -z/ a senile.

gauche /goʃ/ a left; (maladroit) awkward. ● nf left; **à ~** on the left; (direction) (to the) left; **la ~** the left (side); (Pol) the left (wing).

gaucher, -ère /goʃe, -ɛʀ/ a left-handed.

gaufre /gofʀ/ nf waffle. **gaufrette** nf wafer.

gaulois, ~e /golwa, -z/ a Gallic; (fig) bawdy. **G~, ~e** nm, f Gaul.

gaver /gave/ [1] vt force-feed;

(fig) cram. □ se ~ **de** vpr gorge oneself with; (fig) devour.

gaz /gaz/ nm inv gas; ~ **d'échappement** exhaust fumes; ~ **lacrymogène** tear-gas.

gaze /gaz/ nf gauze.

gazer /gaze/ [1] vi 🔲 **ça gaze?** how's things?

gazette /gazɛt/ nf newspaper.

gazeux, -euse /gazø, -z/ a (boisson) fizzy; (eau) sparkling.

gazoduc /gazɔdyk/ nm gas pipeline.

gazon /gazɔ̃/ nm lawn, grass.

gazouiller /gazuje/ [1] vi (oiseau) chirp; (bébé) babble.

GDF abrév m (Gaz de France) French gas board.

géant, ~e /ʒeɑ̃, -t/ a giant. ● nm giant. **géante** nf giantess.

geindre /ʒɛ̃dʀ/ [22] vi groan, moan.

gel /ʒɛl/ nm frost; (produit) gel; (Comm) freeze; ~ **coiffant** hair gel.

gelée /ʒ(ə)le/ nf frost; (Culin) jelly; ~ **blanche** hoarfrost.

geler /ʒəle/ [6] vt/i freeze; **on gèle** (on a froid) it's freezing; **il** ou **ça gèle** (il fait froid) it's freezing.

gélule /ʒelyl/ nf (Méd) capsule.

Gémeaux /ʒemo/ nmpl Gemini.

gémir /ʒemiʀ/ [2] vi groan.

gênant, ~e /ʒenɑ̃, -t/ a embarrassing; (irritant) annoying; (incommode) cumbersome.

gencive /ʒɑ̃siv/ nf gum.

gendarme /ʒɑ̃daʀm/ nm policeman, gendarme. **gendarmerie** nf police force; (local) police station.

gendre /ʒɑ̃dʀ/ nm son-in-law.

gène /ʒɛn/ nm gene.

gêne /ʒɛn/ nf discomfort; (confusion) embarrassment; (dérangement) trouble, inconvenience; (pauvreté) poverty.

gêné, ~e /ʒene/ a embarrassed; (désargenté) short of money.

généalogie /ʒenealɔʒi/ *nf*
genealogy.

gêner /ʒene/ [1] *vt* bother,
disturb; (troubler) embarrass;
(entraver) block; (faire mal) hurt.

général, ~e (*mpl* **-aux**) /ʒeneral,
-o/ *a* general; **en ~** in general.
● *nm* (*pl* **-aux**) general.

généralement /ʒeneralmɑ̃/ *adv*
generally.

généraliser /ʒeneralize/ [1] *vt*
make general. ● *vi* generalize.
□ **se ~** *vpr* become widespread
ou general.

généraliste /ʒeneralist/ *nmf*
general practitioner, GP.

généralité /ʒeneralite/ *nf*
general point.

génération /ʒenerasjɔ̃/ *nf*
generation.

généreux, ~euse /ʒenerø, -z/ *a*
generous.

générique /ʒenerik/ *nm* (au
cinéma) credits. ● *a* generic.

générosité /ʒenerozite/ *nf*
generosity.

génétique /ʒenetik/ *a* genetic.
● *nf* genetics.

Genève /ʒənɛv/ *npr* Geneva.

génial, ~e (*mpl* **-iaux**) /ʒenjal,
-jo/ *a* brilliant; (fantastique 🅸)
fantastic.

génie /ʒeni/ *nm* genius; **~ civil**
civil engineering.

génital, ~e (*mpl* **-aux**) /ʒenital,
-o/ *a* genital.

génocide /ʒenɔsid/ *nm* genocide.

génoise /ʒenwaz/ *nf* sponge
(cake).

génome /ʒenom/ *nm* genome.

génothèque /ʒenɔtɛk/ *nf* gene
bank.

genou (*pl* **~x**) /ʒənu/ *nm* knee;
être à ~x be kneeling.

genre /ʒɑ̃r/ *nm* sort, kind; (Gram)
gender; (allure) **avoir bon/mauvais
~** to look nice/disreputable;
(comportement) **c'est bien son ~** it's

just like him/her.

gens /ʒɑ̃/ *nmpl* people.

gentil, ~le /ʒɑ̃ti, -j/ *a* kind, nice;
(sage) good. **gentillesse** *nf*
kindness. **gentiment** *adv* kindly.

géographie /ʒeɔgrafi/ *nf*
geography.

geôlier, -ière /ʒolje, -jɛr/ *nm, f*
gaoler, jailer.

géologie /ʒeolɔʒi/ *nf* geology.

géomètre /ʒeomɛtr/ *nm*
surveyor.

géométrie /ʒeometri/ *nf*
geometry. **géométrique** *a*
geometric.

gérance /ʒerɑ̃s/ *nf* management.

gérant, ~e /ʒerɑ̃, -t/ *nm, f*
manager, manageress; **~
d'immeuble** landlord's agent.

gerbe /ʒɛrb/ *nf* (de fleurs) bunch,
bouquet; (d'eau) spray; (de blé)
sheaf.

gercer /ʒɛrse/ [10] *vt* chap, **avoir
les lèvres gercées** have chapped
lips. ● *vi* become chapped.
gerçure *nf* crack, chap.

gérer /ʒere/ [14] *vt* manage, run;
(traiter: fig) (crise, situation) handle.

germe /ʒɛrm/ *nm* germ; **~s de
soja** bean sprouts.

germer /ʒɛrme/ [1] *vi* germinate.

gestation /ʒɛstasjɔ̃/ *nf* gestation.

geste /ʒɛst/ *nm* gesture.

gesticuler /ʒɛstikyle/ [1] *vi*
gesticulate.

gestion /ʒɛstjɔ̃/ *nf* management.
gestionnaire *nmf* administrator.

ghetto /gɛto/ *nm* ghetto.

gibier /ʒibje/ *nm* (animaux) game.

giboulée /ʒibule/ *nf* shower.

gicler /ʒikle/ [1] *vi* squirt; **faire ~**
squirt.

gifle /ʒifl/ *nf* slap in the face.
gifler [1] *vt* slap.

gigantesque /ʒigɑ̃tɛsk/ *a*
gigantic.

G

gigot /ʒigo/ nm leg (of lamb).

gigoter /ʒigɔte/ [1] vi wriggle; (nerveusement) fidget.

gilet /ʒilɛ/ nm waistcoat; (cardigan) cardigan; ~ **de sauvetage** life-jacket.

gingembre /ʒɛ̃ʒɑ̃bʀ/ nm ginger.

girafe /ʒiʀaf/ nf giraffe.

giratoire /ʒiʀatwaʀ/ a **sens ~** roundabout.

girofle /ʒiʀɔfl/ nm **clou de ~** clove.

girouette /ʒiʀwɛt/ nf weathercock, weathervane.

gisement /ʒizmɑ̃/ nm deposit.

gitan, ~e /ʒitɑ̃, -an/ nm, f gypsy.

gîte /ʒit/ nm (maison) home; (abri) shelter; ~ **rural** holiday cottage.

givre /ʒivʀ/ nm frost; (sur pare-brise) ice.

givré, ~e /ʒivʀe/ a 🔢 crazy.

glace /glas/ nf ice; (crème) ice-cream; (vitre) window; (miroir) mirror; (verre) glass.

glacé, ~e /glase/ a (vent, accueil) icy; (hands) frozen; (gâteau) iced.

glacer /glase/ [10] vt freeze; (gâteau, boisson) chill; (pétrifier) chill. □ **se ~** vpr freeze.

glacier /glasje/ nm (Géog) glacier; (vendeur) ice-cream seller. **glacière** nf coolbox. **glaçon** nm ice-cube.

glaïeul /glajœl/ nm gladiolus.

glaise /glɛz/ nf clay.

gland /glɑ̃/ nm acorn; (ornement) tassel.

glande /glɑ̃d/ nf gland.

glander /glɑ̃de/ [1] vi 🔢 laze around.

glaner /glane/ [1] vt glean.

glauque /glok/ a (fig) murky; (street) squalid.

glissade /glisad/ nf (jeu) slide; (dérapage) skid.

glissant, ~e /glisɑ̃, -t/ a slippery.

glissement /glismɑ̃/ nm sliding; gliding; (fig) shift; ~ **de terrain** landslide.

glisser /glise/ [1] vi slide; (être glissant) be slippery; (sur l'eau) glide; (déraper) slip; (véhicule) skid. ● vt (objet) slip (**dans** into); (remarque) slip in. □ **se ~** vpr slip (**dans** into).

glissière /glisjɛʀ/ nf slide; **porte à ~** sliding door; ~ **de sécurité** (Auto) crash-barrier; **fermeture à ~** zip.

global, ~e (mpl -**aux**) /glɔbal, -o/ a (entier, général) overall.

globalement adv as a whole.

globe /glɔb/ nm globe; ~ **oculaire** eyeball; ~ **terrestre** globe.

globule /glɔbyl/ nm (du sang) corpuscle.

gloire /glwaʀ/ nf glory, fame. **glorieux, -ieuse** a glorious. **glorifier** [45] vt glorify.

glose /gloz/ nf gloss.

glossaire /glɔsɛʀ/ nm glossary.

gloussement /glusmɑ̃/ nm chuckle; (de poule) cluck.

glouton, ~ne /glutɔ̃, -ɔn/ a gluttonous. ● nm, f glutton.

gluant, ~e /glyɑ̃, -t/ a sticky.

glucose /glykoz/ nm glucose.

glycérine /gliseʀin/ nf glycerin(e).

GO abrév fpl (**grandes ondes**) long wave.

goal /gol/ nm 🔢 goalkeeper.

gobelet /gɔblɛ/ nm cup; (en verre) tumbler.

gober /gɔbe/ [1] vt swallow (whole); **je ne peux pas le ~** 🔢 I can't stand him.

goéland /gɔelɑ̃/ nm (sea)gull.

gogo: à ~ /agogo/ loc 🔢 galore, in abundance.

goinfre /gwɛ̃fʀ/ nm (glouton 🔢) pig. **goinfrer (se)** [1] vpr 🔢 stuff oneself (**de** with).

golf /gɔlf/ *nm* golf; (terrain) golf course.

golfe /gɔlf/ *nm* gulf.

gomme /gɔm/ *nf* rubber; (US) eraser; (résine) gum. **gommer** [1] *vt* rub out.

gond /gɔ̃/ *nm* hinge; **sortir de ses ∼s** 🔲 go mad.

gondoler (se) /(sə)gɔ̃dɔle/ [1] *vpr* (bois) warp; (métal) buckle.

gonflé, ∼e /gɔ̃fle/ *a* swollen; **il est ∼** 🔲 he's got a nerve.

gonflement /gɔ̃fləmɑ̃/ *nm* swelling.

gonfler /gɔ̃fle/ [1] *vt* (ballon, pneu) pump up, blow up; (augmenter) increase; (exagérer) inflate. ● *vi* swell.

gorge /gɔʀʒ/ *nf* throat; (poitrine) breast; (vallée) gorge.

gorgée /gɔʀʒe/ *nf* sip, gulp.

gorger /gɔʀʒe/ [40] *vt* fill (**de** with); **gorgé de** full of. □ **se ∼** *vpr* gorge oneself (**de** with).

gorille /gɔʀij/ *nm* gorilla; (garde 🔲) bodyguard.

gosier /gozje/ *nm* throat.

gosse /gɔs/ *nmf* 🔲 kid.

gothique /gɔtik/ *a* Gothic.

goudron /gudʀɔ̃/ *nm* tar. **goudronner** [1] *vt* tarmac.

gouffre /gufʀ/ *nm* abyss, gulf.

goujat /guʒa/ *nm* lout, boor.

goulot /gulo/ *nm* neck, **boire au ∼** drink from the bottle.

goulu, ∼e /guly/ *a* gluttonous. ● *nm, f* glutton.

gourde /guʀd/ *nf* (à eau) flask; (idiot 🔲) fool.

gourer (se) /(sə)guʀe/ [1] *vpr* 🔲 make a mistake.

gourmand, ∼e /guʀmɑ̃, -d/ *a* greedy. ● *nm, f* glutton.

gourmandise /guʀmɑ̃diz/ *nf* greed; **∼s** sweets.

gourmet /guʀmɛ/ *nm* gourmet.

gourmette /guʀmɛt/ *nf* chain bracelet.

gousse /gus/ *nf* **∼ d'ail** clove of garlic.

goût /gu/ *nm* taste; (gré) liking; **prendre ∼ à** develop a taste for; **avoir bon ∼** (aliment) taste nice; (personne) have good taste; **donner du ∼ à** give flavour.

goûter /gute/ [1] *vt* taste; (apprécier) enjoy; **∼ à** ou **de** taste. ● *vi* have tea. ● *nm* tea, snack.

goutte /gut/ *nf* drop; (Méd) gout. **goutte-à-goutte** *nm inv* drip. **goutter** [1] *vi* drip.

gouttière /gutjɛʀ/ *nf* gutter.

gouvernail /guvɛʀnaj/ *nm* rudder; (barre) helm.

gouvernement /guvɛʀnəmɑ̃/ *nm* government.

gouverner /guvɛʀne/ [1] *vt/i* govern; (dominer) control.

gouverneur *nm* governor.

grâce /gʀɑs/ *nf* (charme) grace; (faveur) favour; (volonté) grace; (Jur) pardon; (Relig) grace; **∼ à** thanks to; **rendre ∼(s) à** give thanks to.

gracier /gʀasje/ [45] *vt* pardon.

gracieusement /gʀasjøzmɑ̃/ *adv* gracefully; (gratuitement) free (of charge).

gracieux, -ieuse /gʀasjø, -z/ *a* graceful.

grade /gʀad/ *nm* rank; **monter en ∼** be promoted.

gradin /gʀadɛ̃/ *nm* tier, step; **en ∼s** terraced; **les ∼s** terraces.

gradué, ∼e /gʀadɥe/ *a* graded, graduated; **verre ∼** measuring jug.

graffiti /gʀafiti/ *nmpl* graffiti.

grain /gʀɛ̃/ *nm* grain; (Naut) squall; **∼ de beauté** beauty spot; **∼ de café** coffee bean; **∼ de poivre** pepper corn; **∼ de raisin** grape.

graine /gʀɛn/ *nf* seed.

graisse /gʀɛs/ *nf* fat; (lubrifiant)

grease. **graisser** [1] *vt* grease.
graisseux, -euse *a* greasy.
grammaire /gʀam(m)ɛʀ/ *nf*
grammar.
gramme /gʀam/ *nm* gram.
grand, ∼e /gʀɑ̃, -d/ *a* big, large;
(haut) tall; (intense, fort) great;
(brillant) great; (principal) main; (plus
âgé) big, elder; (adulte) grown-up;
au ∼ air in the open air; **au ∼ jour**
in broad daylight; (fig) in the
open; **en ∼e partie** largely; **∼e
banlieue** outer suburbs; **∼
ensemble** housing estate; **∼es
lignes** (Rail) main lines; **∼ magasin**
department store; **∼e personne**
grown-up; **∼ public** general
public; **∼e surface** hypermarket;
∼es vacances summer holidays.
● *adv* (ouvrir) wide; **∼ ouvert**
wide open; **voir ∼** think big.
● *nm, f* (adulte) grown-up; (enfant)
big boy, big girl; (Scol) senior.
Grande-Bretagne /gʀɑ̃dbʀətaɲ/
nf Great Britain.
grand-chose /gʀɑ̃ʃoz/ *pron* **pas
∼** not much, not a lot.
grandeur /gʀɑ̃dœʀ/ *nf* greatness;
(dimension) size; **folie des ∼s**
delusions of grandeur.
grandir /gʀɑ̃diʀ/ [2] *vi* grow;
(bruit) grow louder. ● *vt* (talons)
make taller; (loupe) magnify.
grand-mère (pl **grands-mères**)
/gʀɑ̃mɛʀ/ *nf* grandmother.
grand-père (pl **grands-pères**)
/gʀɑ̃pɛʀ/ *nm* grandfather.
grands-parents /gʀɑ̃paʀɑ̃/ *nmpl*
grandparents.
grange /gʀɑ̃ʒ/ *nf* barn.
granulé /gʀanyle/ *nm* granule.
graphique /gʀafik/ *a* graphic;
(Ordinat) graphics; **informatique ∼**
computer graphics. ● *nm* graph.
graphologie /gʀafɔlɔʒi/ *nf*
graphology.
grappe /gʀap/ *nf* cluster; **∼ de
raisin** bunch of grapes.

gras, ∼se /gʀɑ, -s/ *a* (gros) fat;
(aliment) fatty; (surface, peau,
cheveux) greasy; (épais) thick;
(caractères) bold; **faire la ∼se
matinée** sleep late. ● *nm* (Culin) fat.
gratifiant, ∼e /gʀatifjɑ̃, -t/ *a*
gratifying; (travail) rewarding.
gratifier /gʀatifje/ [45] *vt* favour,
reward (**de** with).
gratin /gʀatɛ̃/ *nm* gratin (baked
dish with cheese topping); (élite 🆃)
upper crust.
gratis /gʀatis/ *adv* free.
gratitude /gʀatityd/ *nf* gratitude.
gratte-ciel /gʀatsjɛl/ *nm inv*
skyscraper.
gratter /gʀate/ [1] *vt/i* scratch;
(avec un outil) scrape; **ça me gratte** 🆃
it itches. □ **se ∼** *vpr* scratch
oneself; **se ∼ la tête** scratch one's
head.
gratuiciel /gʀatɥisjɛl/ *nm*
(Internet) freeware.
gratuit, ∼e /gʀatɥi, -t/ *a* free;
(acte) gratuitous. **gratuitement**
adv free (of charge).
grave /gʀav/ *a* (maladie, accident,
problème) serious; (solennel) grave;
(voix) deep; (accent) grave.
gravement *adv* seriously,
gravely.
graver /gʀave/ [1] *vt* engrave; (sur
bois) carve.
gravier /gʀavje/ *nm* **du ∼** gravel.
gravité /gʀavite/ *nf* gravity.
graviter /gʀavite/ [1] *vi* revolve.
gravure /gʀavyʀ/ *nf* engraving;
(de tableau, photo) print, plate.
gré /gʀe/ *nm* (volonté) will; (goût)
taste; **à son ∼** (agir) as one likes;
de bon ∼ willingly; **bon ∼ mal ∼**
like it or not; **je vous en saurais ∼**
I'd be grateful for that.
grec, ∼que /gʀɛk/ *a* Greek. ● *nm*
(Ling) Greek. **G∼, ∼que** *nm, f*
Greek.
Grèce *nf* /gʀɛs/ Greece.
greffe /gʀɛf/ *nf* graft; (d'organe)

transplant. **greffer** /gʀefe/ [1] vt graft; transplant.

greffier, -ière /gʀefje, -jɛʀ/ nm, f clerk of the court.

grêle /gʀɛl/ a (maigre) spindly; (voix) shrill. ● nf hail.

grêler /gʀele/ [1] vi hail; **il grêle** it's hailing. **grêlon** nm hailstone.

grelot /gʀəlo/ nm (little) bell.

grelotter /gʀəlɔte/ [1] vi shiver.

grenade /gʀənad/ nf (fruit) pomegranate; (explosif) grenade.

grenat /gʀəna/ a inv dark red.

grenier /gʀənje/ nm attic; (pour grain) loft.

grenouille /gʀənuj/ nf frog.

grès /gʀɛ/ nm sandstone; (poterie) stoneware.

grésiller /gʀezije/ [1] vi sizzle; (radio) crackle.

grève /gʀɛv/ nf (rivage) shore; (cessation de travail) strike; **faire ~, être en ~** be on strike; **se mettre en ~** go on strike. **gréviste** nmf striker.

gribouiller /gʀibuje/ [1] vt/i scribble.

grief /gʀijɛf/ nm grievance.

grièvement /gʀijɛvmɑ̃/ adv seriously.

griffe /gʀif/ nf claw; (de couturier) label; **coup de ~** scratch.

griffé, ~e /gʀife/ a (vêtement, article) designer.

griffer /gʀife/ [1] vt scratch, claw.

grignoter /gʀiɲɔte/ [1] vt/i nibble.

gril /gʀil/ nm (de cuisinière) grill; (plaque) grill pan.

grillade /gʀijad/ nf (viande) grill.

grillage /gʀijaʒ/ nm wire netting.

grille /gʀij/ nf railings; (portail) (metal) gate; (de fenêtre) bars; (de cheminée) grate; (fig) grid. **grille-pain** nm inv toaster.

griller /gʀije/ [1] vt (pain) toast;

(viande) grill; (ampoule) blow; (feu rouge) go through; (appareil) burn out. ● vi (ampoule) blow; (Culin) **faire ~** (viande) grill; (pain) toast.

grillon /gʀijɔ̃/ nm cricket.

grimace /gʀimas/ nf (funny) face; (de douleur, dégoût) grimace; **faire des ~s** make faces; **faire la ~** pull a face, grimace.

grimper /gʀɛ̃pe/ [1] vt climb. ● vi climb; **~ sur ou dans un arbre** climb a tree.

grincement /gʀɛ̃smɑ̃/ nm creak(ing).

grincer /gʀɛ̃se/ [10] vi creak; **~ des dents** grind one's teeth.

grincheux, -euse /gʀɛ̃ʃø, -z/ a grumpy.

grippe /gʀip/ nf influenza, flu.

grippé, ~e /gʀipe/ a **être ~** have (the) flu; (mécanisme) be seized up ou jammed.

gris, ~e /gʀi, -z/ a grey; (saoul) tipsy.

grivois, ~e /gʀivwa, -z/ a bawdy.

grog /gʀɔg/ nm hot toddy.

grogner /gʀɔɲe/ [1] vi (animal) growl; (personne) grumble.

grognon /gʀɔɲɔ̃/ am grumpy.

groin /gʀwɛ̃/ nm snout.

gronder /gʀɔ̃de/ [1] vi (tonnerre, volcan) rumble; (chien) growl; (conflit) be brewing. ● vt scold.

groom /gʀum/ nm bellboy.

gros, ~se /gʀo, -s/ a big, large; (gras) fat; (important) big; (épais) thick; (lourd) heavy; (buveur, fumeur) heavy; **~ bonnet** Ⓘ bigwig; **~ lot** jackpot; **~ mot** swear word; **~ plan** close-up; **~se caisse** bass drum; **~ titre** headline. ● nm, f fat man, fat woman. ● adv (écrire) big; (risquer, gagner) a lot. ● nm **le ~ de** the bulk of; **de ~** (Comm) wholesale; **en ~** roughly; (Comm) wholesale.

groseille /gʀozɛj/ *nf* redcurrant; **~ à maquereau** gooseberry.

grossesse /gʀosɛs/ *nf* pregnancy.

grosseur /gʀosœʀ/ *nf* (volume) size; (enflure) lump.

grossier, -ière /gʀosje, -jɛʀ/ *a* (sans finesse) coarse, rough; (rudimentaire) crude; (vulgaire) coarse; (impoli) rude; (erreur) gross. **grossièrement** *adv* (sommairement) roughly; (vulgairement) coarsely. **grossièreté** *nf* coarseness; crudeness; rudeness; (mot) rude word.

grossir /gʀosiʀ/ [2] *vt* (faire augmenter) increase, boost; (agrandir) enlarge; (exagérer) exaggerate; **~ les rangs** *ou* **la foule** swell the ranks. ●*vi* (personne) put on weight; (augmenter) grow.

grossiste /gʀosist/ *nmf* wholesaler.

grosso modo /gʀosomodo/ *adv* roughly.

grotesque /gʀotɛsk/ *a* grotesque; (ridicule) ludicrous.

grotte /gʀot/ *nf* cave; grotto.

grouiller /gʀuje/ [1] *vi* swarm; **~ de** be swarming with.

groupe /gʀup/ *nm* group; (Mus) group, band; **~ électrogène** generating set; **~ scolaire** school; **~ de travail** working party.

groupement /gʀupmɑ̃/ *nm* grouping.

grouper /gʀupe/ [1] *vt* put together; □ **se ~** *vpr* group (together).

grue /gʀy/ *nf* (machine, oiseau) crane.

gruyère /gʀyjɛʀ/ *nm* gruyère (cheese).

gué /ge/ *nm* ford; **passer** *ou* **traverser à ~** ford.

guenon /gənɔ̃/ *nf* female monkey.

guépard /gepaʀ/ *nm* cheetah.

guêpe /gɛp/ *nf* wasp.

guère /gɛʀ/ *adv* **ne ~** hardly; **il n'y a ~ d'espoir** there is no hope; **elle n'a ~ dormi** she didn't sleep much, she hardly slept.

guérilla /geʀija/ *nf* guerrilla warfare; (groupe) guerillas.

guérir /geʀiʀ/ [2] *vt* (personne, maladie, mal) cure (de of); (plaie, membre, mal) heal. ●*vi* get better; (blessure) heal; **~ de** recover from. **guérison** *nf* curing; healing; (de personne) recovery.

guerre /gɛʀ/ *nf* war; **en ~** at war; **faire la ~** wage war (à against); **~ civile** civil war; **~ mondiale** world war.

guerrier, -ière /geʀje, -jɛʀ/ *a* warlike. ●*nm, f* warrior.

guet /gɛ/ *nm* watch; **faire le ~** be on the watch. **guet-apens** (*pl* **guets-apens**) *nm* ambush.

guetter /gete/ [1] *vt* watch; (attendre) watch out for.

gueule /gœl/ *nf* mouth; (figure ▯) face; **ta ~!** ▯ shut up!; **~ de bois** ▯ hangover.

gueuleton /gœltɔ̃/ *nm* ▯ blow-out, slap-up meal.

gui /gi/ *nm* mistletoe.

guichet /giʃɛ/ *nm* window, counter; (de gare) ticket-office; (Théât) box-office; **jouer à ~s fermés** (pièce) be sold out; **~ automatique** cash dispenser.

guide /gid/ *nm* guide. ●*nf* (fille scout) girl guide.

guider /gide/ [1] *vt* guide.

guidon /gidɔ̃/ *nm* handlebars.

guignol /giɲɔl/ *nm* puppet; (personne) clown; (spectacle) puppet-show.

guillemets /gijmɛ/ *nmpl* quotation marks, inverted

commas; **entre ~** in inverted commas.

guillotine /gijɔtin/ *nf* guillotine.

guimauve /gimov/ *nf* marshmallow; **c'est de la ~** 🔲 it's slushy *ou* schmaltzy 🔲.

guindé, **~e** /gɛ̃de/ *a* stiff, formal; *(style)* stilted.

guirlande /giʀlɑ̃d/ *nf* garland; tinsel.

guitare /gitaʀ/ *nf* guitar.

gym /ʒim/ *nf* gymnastics; (Scol) physical education, PE.

gymnase /ʒimnɑz/ *nm* gym-(nasium). **gymnastique** *nf* gymnastics.

gynécologie /ʒinekɔlɔʒi/ *nf* gynaecology.

habile /abil/ *a* skilful, clever.

habillé, **~e** /abije/ *a* *(vêtement)* smart; *(soirée)* formal.

habillement /abijmɑ̃/ *nm* clothing.

habiller /abije/ [1] *vt* dress **(de** in); *(équiper)* clothe; *(recouvrir)* cover **(de** with). □ **s'~** *vpr* get dressed; *(élégamment)* dress up.

habit /abi/ *nm* *(de personnage)* outfit; *(de cérémonie)* tails; **~s** clothes.

habitant, **~e** /abitɑ̃, -t/ *nm, f* *(de maison, quartier)* resident; *(de pays)* inhabitant.

habitat /abita/ *nm* *(mode de peuplement)* settlement; *(conditions)* housing.

habitation /abitasjɔ̃/ *nf* *(logement)* house.

habité, **~e** /abite/ *a* *(terre)* inhabited.

habiter /abite/ [1] *vi* live. ● *vt* live in.

habitude /abityd/ *nf* habit; **avoir l'~ de** be used to; **d'~** usually; **comme d'~** as usual.

habitué, **~e** /abitɥe/ *nm, f* *(client)* regular.

habituel, **~le** /abitɥɛl/ *a* usual. **habituellement** *adv* usually.

habituer /abitɥe/ [1] *vt* **~ qn à** get sb used to. □ **s'~ à** *vpr* get used to.

hache /'aʃ/ *nf* axe.

haché, **~e** /'aʃe/ *a* *(viande)* minced; *(phrases)* jerky.

hacher /'aʃe/ [1] *vt* mince; *(au couteau)* chop.

hachis /'aʃi/ *nm* minced meat; (US) ground meat; **~ Parmentier** ≈ shepherd's pie.

hachisch /'aʃiʃ/ *nm* hashish.

hachoir /'aʃwaʀ/ *nm* *(appareil)* mincer; *(couteau)* chopper; *(planche)* chopping board.

haie /'ɛ/ *nf* hedge; *(de personnes)* line; **course de ~s** hurdle race.

haillon /'ajɔ̃/ *nm* rag.

haine /'ɛn/ *nf* hatred.

haïr /'aiʀ/ [36] *vt* hate.

hâlé /'ɑle/ *a* (sun-)tanned.

haleine /alɛn/ *nf* breath; **travail de longue ~** long job.

haleter /'alte/ [6] *vi* pant.

hall /'ol/ *nm* hall; *(de gare)* concourse.

halle /'al/ *nf* market hall; **~s** covered market.

halte /'alt/ *nf* stop; **faire ~** stop. ● *interj* stop; (Mil) halt.

haltère /altɛʀ/ *nm* dumbbell; **faire des ~s** to do weightlifting.

hameau (*pl* **~x**) /'amo/ *nm* hamlet.

hameçon /amsɔ̃/ *nm* hook.

hanche /'ɑ̃ʃ/ *nf* hip.

handicap /'ɑ̃dikap/ *nm* handicap. **handicapé**, ~e *a & nm,f* disabled (person).

hangar /'ɑ̃gaʀ/ *nm* shed; (pour avions) hangar.

hanter /'ɑ̃te/ [1] *vt* haunt.

hantise /'ɑ̃tiz/ *nf* dread; **avoir la ~ de** dread.

haras /'aʀɑ/ *nm* stud-farm.

harasser /'aʀase/ [1] *vt* exhaust.

harcèlement /'aʀsɛlmɑ̃/ *nm* ~ **sexuel** sexual harassment.

harceler /'aʀsəle/ [6] *vt* harass.

hardi, ~e /'aʀdi/ *a* bold.

hareng /'aʀɑ̃/ *nm* herring.

hargne /'aʀɲ/ *nf* (aggressive) bad temper.

haricot /'aʀiko/ *nm* bean; ~ **vert** French bean; (US) green bean.

harmonie /aʀmɔni/ *nf* harmony. **harmonieux**, **-ieuse** *a* harmonious.

harmoniser /aʀmɔnize/ [1] *vt* harmonize. □ **s'~** *vpr* harmonize.

harnacher /'aʀnaʃe/ [1] *vt* harness.

harnais /'aʀnɛ/ *nm* harness.

harpe /'aʀp/ *nf* harp.

harpon /'aʀpɔ̃/ *nm* harpoon.

hasard /'azaʀ/ *nm* chance; (coïncidence) coincidence; **les ~s de** the fortunes of; **au ~** (choisir etc.) at random; (flâner) aimlessly. **hasardeux**, **-euse** *a* risky.

hasarder /'azaʀde/ [1] *vt* risk; (remarque) venture.

hâte /'ɑt/ *nf* haste; **à la ~**, **en ~** hurriedly; **avoir ~ de** look forward to.

hâter /'ɑte/ [1] *vt* hasten. □ **se ~** *vpr* hurry (**de** to).

hâtif, **-ive** /'ɑtif, -v/ *a* hasty; (précoce) early.

hausse /'os/ *nf* rise (**de** in); ~ **des prix** price rise; **en ~** rising.

hausser /'ose/ [1] *vt* raise; (épaules) shrug.

haut, ~e /'o, 'ot/ *a* high; (de taille) tall; **à voix ~e** aloud; ~ **en couleur** colourful; **plus ~** higher up; (dans un texte) above; **en ~ lieu** in high places. ● *adv* high; **tout ~** out loud. ● *nm* top; **des ~s et des bas** ups and downs; **en ~** (regarder) up; (à l'étage) upstairs; **en ~ (de)** at the top (of).

hautbois /'obwa/ *nm* oboe.

haut-de-forme /'odfɔʀm/ (*pl* **hauts-de-forme**) *nm* top hat.

hauteur /'otœʀ/ *nf* height; (colline) hill; (arrogance) haughtiness; **être à la ~** be up to it; **à la ~ de** (ville) near; **être à la ~ de la situation** be equal to the situation.

haut-le-cœur /'olkœʀ/ *nm inv* nausea.

haut-parleur (*pl* ~**s**) /'opaʀlœʀ/ *nm* loudspeaker.

havre /'ɑvʀ/ *nm* haven (**de** of).

hayon /'ajɔ̃/ *nm* (Auto) hatchback.

hebdomadaire /ɛbdɔmadɛʀ/ *a & nm* weekly.

hébergement /ebɛʀʒəmɑ̃/ *nm* accommodation.

héberger /ebɛʀʒe/ [40] *vt* (ami) put up; (réfugiés) take in.

hébreu (*pl* ~x) /ebʀø/ *am* Hebrew. ● *nm* (Ling) Hebrew; **c'est de l'~!** it's all Greek to me!

Hébreu (*pl* ~x) /ebʀø/ *nm* Hebrew; **les ~x** the Hebrews.

hécatombe /ekatɔ̃b/ *nf* slaughter.

hectare /ɛktaʀ/ *nm* hectare (= 10,000 square metres).

hélas /'elɑs/ *interj* alas. ● *adv* sadly.

hélice /elis/ *nf* propeller.

hélicoptère /elikɔptɛʀ/ *nm* helicopter.

helvétique /ɛlvetik/ *a* Swiss.

hématome /ematom/ *nm* bruise.

hémorragie /emɔʀaʒi/ *nf* haemorrhage.

hémorroïdes /emɔʀɔid/ *nfpl*
piles, haemorrhoids.

hennir /'eniʀ/ [2] *vi* neigh.

hépatite /epatit/ *nf* hepatitis.

herbe /ɛʀb/ *nf* grass; (Méd, Culin)
herb; **en ~** in the blade; (fig)
budding.

héréditaire /eʀeditɛʀ/ *a*
hereditary.

hérédité /eʀedite/ *nf* heredity.

hérisser /'eʀise/ [1] *vt* bristle; **~
qn** (fig) ruffle sb. □ **se ~** *vpr*
bristle.

hérisson /'eʀisɔ̃/ *nm* hedgehog.

héritage /eʀitaʒ/ *nm* inheritance;
(spirituel) heritage.

hériter /eʀite/ [1] *vt/i* inherit (**de**
from); **~ de qch** inherit sth.

héritier, -ière *nm, f* heir, heiress.

hermétique /ɛʀmetik/ *a* airtight;
(fig) unfathomable.

hernie /'ɛʀni/ *nf* hernia.

héroïne /eʀɔin/ *nf* (femme)
heroine; (drogue) heroin.

héroïque /eʀɔik/ *a* heroic.

héros /'eʀo/ *nm* hero.

hésiter /ezite/ [1] *vi* hesitate (**à**
to); **j'hésite** I'm not sure.

hétérogène /eteʀɔʒɛn/ *a*
heterogeneous.

hétérosexuel, ~le /eteʀɔsek-
sɥɛl/ *nm/f & a* heterosexual.

hêtre /'ɛtʀ/ *nm* beech.

heure /œʀ/ *nf* time; (soixante
minutes) hour; **quelle ~ est-il?** what
time is it?; **il est dix ~s** it is ten
o'clock; **à l'~** (venir, être) on
time; **d'~ en ~** by the hour;
toutes les deux ~s every two
hours; **~ de pointe** rush-hour; **~
de cours** (Scol) period; **~ indue**
ungodly hour; **~s creuses** off-
peak periods; **~s supplémentaires**
overtime.

heureusement /œʀøzmɑ̃/ *adv*
fortunately, luckily.

heureux, -euse /œʀø, -z/ *a*
happy; (chanceux) lucky, fortunate.

heurt /'œʀ/ *nm* collision; (conflit)
clash; **sans ~** smoothly.

heurter /'œʀte/ [1] *vt* (cogner) hit;
(mur) bump into, hit; (choquer)
offend. □ **se ~ à** *vpr* bump into,
hit; (fig) come up against.

hexagone /ɛgzagɔn/ *nm*
hexagon; **l'~** France.

hiberner /ibɛʀne/ [1] *vi*
hibernate.

hibou (*pl* **~x**) /'ibu/ *nm* owl.

hier /jɛʀ/ *adv* yesterday; **~ soir**
last night, yesterday evening.

hiérarchie /'jeʀaʀʃi/ *nf*
hierarchy.

hilare /ilaʀ/ *a* (visage) merry; **être
~** be laughing.

hindou, ~e /ɛ̃du/ *a & nm, f*
Hindu. **H~, ~e** *nm, f* Hindu.

hippique /ipik/ *a* equestrian; **le
concours ~** showjumping.

hippodrome /ipodʀom/ *nm*
racecourse.

hippopotame /ipɔpɔtam/ *nm*
hippopotamus.

hirondelle /iʀɔ̃dɛl/ *nf* swallow.

hisser /'ise/ [1] *vt* hoist, haul.
□ **se ~** *vpr* heave oneself up.

histoire /istwaʀ/ *nf* (récit) story;
(étude) history; (affaire) business;
~(s) (chichis) fuss; (ennuis) trouble.

historique *a* historical.

hiver /ivɛʀ/ *nm* winter. **hivernal,
~e** (*mpl* **-aux**) *a* winter; (glacial)
wintry.

H.L.M. *abbrév m ou f* (**habitation
à loyer modéré**) block of council
flats; (US) low-rent apartment
building.

hocher /'ɔʃe/ [1] *vt* **~ la tête** (pour
dire oui) nod; (pour dire non) shake
one's head.

hochet /'ɔʃɛ/ *nm* rattle.

hockey /'ɔkɛ/ *nm* hockey; **~ sur
glace** ice hockey.

hollandais, ~e /'ɔlɑ̃dɛ, -z/ *a*
Dutch. ● *nm* (Ling) Dutch. **H~,**

~e *nm, f* Dutchman, Dutchwoman.

Hollande /'ɔlɑ̃d/ *nf* Holland.

homard /'ɔmaʀ/ *nm* lobster.

homéopathie /ɔmeɔpati/ *nf* homoeopathy.

homicide /ɔmisid/ *nm* homicide; ~ **involontaire** manslaughter.

hommage /ɔmaʒ/ *nm* tribute; ~s (salutations) respects; **rendre ~ à** pay tribute to.

homme /ɔm/ *nm* man; (espèce) man(kind); ~ **d'affaires** businessman; ~ **de la rue** man in the street; ~ **d'État** statesman; ~ **politique** politician.

homogène /ɔmɔʒɛn/ *a* homogeneous.

homonyme /ɔmɔnim/ *nm* (personne) namesake.

homosexualité /ɔmɔsɛksɥalite/ *nf* homosexuality.

homosexuel, ~le /ɔmɔsɛksɥɛl/ *a & nm,f* homosexual.

Hongrie /'ɔ̃gʀi/ *nf* Hungary.

hongrois, ~e /'ɔ̃gʀwa, -z/ *a* Hungarian. ● *nm* (Ling) Hungarian. **H~, ~e** *nm, f* Hungarian.

honnête /ɔnɛt/ *a* honest; (juste) fair. **honnêteté** *nf* honesty.

honneur /ɔnœʀ/ *nm* honour; (mérite) credit; **d'~** (invité, place) of honour; **en l'~ de** in honour of; **en quel ~?** ▣ why?; **faire ~ à** (équipe, famille) bring credit to.

honorable /ɔnɔʀabl/ *a* honourable; (convenable) respectable.

honoraire /ɔnɔʀɛʀ/ *a* honorary. **honoraires** *nmpl* fees.

honorer /ɔnɔʀe/ [1] *vt* honour; (faire honneur à) do credit to.

honte /'ɔ̃t/ *nf* shame; **avoir ~** be ashamed (de of); **faire ~ à** make ashamed. **honteux, -euse** *a* (personne) ashamed (de of); (action) shameful.

hôpital (*pl* -aux) /ɔpital, -o/ *nm* hospital.

hoquet /'ɔkɛ/ *nm* **le ~** (the) hiccups.

horaire /ɔʀɛʀ/ *a* hourly. ● *nm* timetable; ~s **libres** flexitime.

horizon /ɔʀizɔ̃/ *nm* horizon; (Fig) outlook.

horizontal, ~e (*mpl* -aux) /ɔʀizɔ̃tal, -o/ *a* horizontal.

horloge /ɔʀlɔʒ/ *nf* clock.

hormis /'ɔʀmi/ *prép* save.

hormonal, ~e (*mpl* -aux) /ɔʀmɔnal, -o/ *a* hormonal, hormone.

hormone /ɔʀmon/ *nf* hormone.

horreur /ɔʀœʀ/ *nf* horror; **avoir ~ de** hate.

horrible /ɔʀibl/ *a* horrible.

horrifier /ɔʀifje/ [45] *vt* horrify.

hors /'ɔʀ/ *prép* ~ **de** outside, (avec mouvement) out of; ~ **d'atteinte** out of reach; ~ **d'haleine** out of breath; ~ **de prix** extremely expensive; ~ **pair** outstanding; ~ **de soi** beside oneself. **hors-bord** *nm inv* speedboat. **hors-d'œuvre** *nm inv* hors-d'œuvre. **hors-jeu** *a inv* offside. **hors-la-loi** *nm inv* outlaw. **hors-piste** *nm* off-piste skiing. **hors-taxe** *a inv* duty-free.

horticulteur, -trice /ɔʀtikyltœʀ, -tʀis/ *nm, f* horticulturist.

hospice /ɔspis/ *nm* home.

hospitalier, -ière /ɔspitalje, -jɛʀ/ *a* hospitable; (Méd) hospital. **hospitaliser** [1] *vt* take to hospital. **hospitalité** *nf* hospitality.

hostile /ɔstil/ *a* hostile. **hostilité** *nf* hostility.

hôte /ot/ *nm* (maître) host; (invité) guest.

hôtel /otɛl/ *nm* hotel; ~ (particulier) (private) mansion; ~ **de ville** town hall.

hôtelier, -ière /otəlje, -jɛʀ/ *a*

hotel. ● *nm, f* hotel keeper.
hôtellerie *nf* hotel business.
hôtesse /otɛs/ *nf* hostess; ~ **de l'air** stewardess.
hotte /'ɔt/ *nf* basket; ~ **aspirante** extractor (hood), (US) ventilator.
houblon /'ublɔ̃/ *nm* **le** ~ hops.
houille /'uj/ *nf* coal; ~ **blanche** hydroelectric power.
houle /'ul/ *nf* swell. **houleux, -euse** *a* (*mer*) rough; (*débat*) stormy.
housse /'us/ *nf* cover; ~ **de siège** seat cover.
houx /'u/ *nm* holly.
huées /'ɥe/ *nfpl* boos. **huer** [1] *vt* boo.
huile /ɥil/ *nf* oil; (personne ⚇) bigwig. **huiler** [1] *vt* oil. **huileux, -euse** *a* oily.
huis /'ɥi/ *nm* **à** ~ **clos** in camera.
huissier /ɥisje/ *nm* (Jur) bailiff, (portier) usher.
huit /'ɥi(t)/ *a* eight; ~ **jours** a week; **lundi en** ~ a week on Monday. ● *nm* eight. **huitième** *a* & *nmf* eighth.
huître /ɥitʀ/ *nf* oyster.
humain, ~e /ymɛ̃, -ɛn/ *a* human; (compatissant) humane.
humanitaire *a* humanitarian.
humanité *nf* humanity.
humble /œbl/ *a* humble.
humeur /ymœʀ/ *nf* mood; (tempérament) temper; **de bonne/ mauvaise** ~ in a good/bad mood.
humide /ymid/ *a* damp; (chaleur, climat) humid; (lèvres, yeux) moist. **humidité** *nf* humidity.
humilier /ymilje/ [45] *vt* humiliate.
humoristique /ymɔʀistik/ *a* humorous.
humour /ymuʀ/ *nm* humour; **avoir de l'**~ have a sense of humour.
hurlement /'yʀləmɑ̃/ *nm* howl (ing). **hurler** [1] *vt/i* howl.

hutte /'yt/ *nf* hut.
hydratant, ~e /idʀatɑ̃, -t/ *a* (lotion) moisturizing.
hydravion /idʀavjɔ̃/ *nm* seaplane.
hydroélectrique /idʀɔelɛktʀik/ *a* hydroelectric.
hydrogène /idʀɔʒɛn/ *nm* hydrogen.
hygiène /iʒjɛn/ *nf* hygiene. **hygiénique** *a* hygienic.
hymne /imn/ *nm* hymn; ~ **national** national anthem.
hyperlien /ipɛʀljɛ̃/ *nm* (Internet) hyperlink.
hypermarché /ipɛʀmaʀʃe/ *nm* (supermarché) hypermarket.
hypertension /ipɛʀtɑ̃sjɔ̃/ *nf* high blood-pressure.
hypertexte /ipɛʀtɛkst/ *nm* (Internet) hypertext.
hypnotiser /ipnotize/ [1] *vt* hypnotize.
hypocrisie /ipɔkʀizi/ *nf* hypocrisy.
hypocrite /ipɔkʀit/ *a* hypocritical. ● *nmf* hypocrite.
hypothèque /ipotɛk/ *nf* mortgage.
hypothèse /ipotɛz/ *nf* hypothesis.
hystérie /isteʀi/ *nf* hysteria.

ici /isi/ *adv* (dans l'espace) here; (dans le temps) now; **d'**~ **demain** by tomorrow; **d'**~ **là** in the meantime; **d'**~ **peu** shortly; ~ **même** in this very place; **jusqu'**~

until now; (dans le passé) until then.

idéal, ~e (*mpl* -aux) /ideal, -o/ *a* & *nm* ideal. **idéaliser** [1] *vt* idealize.

idée /ide/ *nf* idea; (esprit) mind; **avoir dans l'~ de faire** plan to do; **il ne me viendrait jamais à l'~ de faire** it would never occur to me to do; **~ fixe** obsession; **~ reçue** conventional opinion.

identification /idɑ̃tifikasjɔ̃/ *nf* identification. **identifier** [45] *vt*, **s'identifier** *vpr* identify (à with).

identique /idɑ̃tik/ *a* identical.

identité /idɑ̃tite/ *nf* identity.

idéologie /ideɔlɔʒi/ *nf* ideology.

idiome /idjom/ *nm* idiom.

idiot, ~e /idjo, -ɔt/ *a* idiotic. ● *nm, f* idiot. **idiotie** *nf* idiocy; (acte, parole) idiotic thing.

idole /idɔl/ *nf* idol.

if /if/ *nm* yew.

ignare /iɲaʀ/ *a* ignorant. ● *nmf* ignoramus.

ignoble /iɲɔbl/ *a* vile.

ignorance /iɲɔʀɑ̃s/ *nf* ignorance.

ignorant, ~e /iɲɔʀɑ̃, -t/ *a* ignorant. ● *nm, f* ignoramus.

ignorer /iɲɔʀe/ [1] *vt* not know; **je l'ignore** I don't know; (personne) ignore.

il /il/ *pron* (personne, animal familier) he; (chose, animal) it; (impersonnel) it; **~ est vrai que** it is true that; **~ neige/pleut** it is snowing/raining; **~ y a** there is; (pluriel) there are; (temps) ago; (durée) for; **~ y a 2 ans** 2 years ago; **~ y a plus d'une heure que j'attends** I've been waiting for over an hour.

île /il/ *nf* island; **~ déserte** desert island; **~s anglo-normandes** Channel Islands; **~s Britanniques** British Isles.

illégal, ~e (*mpl* ~aux) /ilegal, -o/ *a* illegal.

illégitime /ileʒitim/ *a* illegitimate.

illettré, ~e /iletʀe/ *a* & *nm,f* illiterate.

illicite /ilisit/ *a* illicit; (Jur) unlawful.

illimité, ~e /ilimite/ *a* unlimited.

illisible /ilizibl/ *a* illegible; (livre) unreadable.

illogique /ilɔʒik/ *a* illogical.

illuminé, ~e /ilymine/ *a* lit up; (monument) floodlit.

illusion /ilyzjɔ̃/ *nf* illusion; **se faire des ~s** delude oneself. **illusoire** *a* illusory.

illustre /ilystʀ/ *a* illustrious.

illustré, ~e /ilystʀe/ *a* illustrated. ● *nm* comic.

illustrer /ilystʀe/ [1] *vt* illustrate. □ **s'~** *vpr* become famous.

îlot /ilo/ *nm* islet; (de maisons) block.

ils /il/ *pron* they.

image /imaʒ/ *nf* picture; (métaphore) image; (reflet) reflection. **imagé, ~e** *a* full of imagery.

imaginaire /imaʒinɛʀ/ *a* imaginary. **imaginatif, -ive** *a* imaginative. **imagination** *nf* imagination.

imaginer /imaʒine/ [1] *vt* imagine; (inventer) think up. □ **s'~** *vpr* (se représenter) imagine (que that); (croire) think (que that).

imbécile /ɛ̃besil/ *a* idiotic. ● *nmf* idiot.

imbiber /ɛ̃bibe/ [1] *vt* soak (de with). □ **s'~** *vpr* become soaked (de with).

imbriqué, ~e /ɛ̃bʀike/ *a* (lié) interlinked, interlocking; (tuiles) overlapping.

imbu, ~e /ɛ̃by/ *a* **~ de** full of.

imitateur, -trice /imitatœʀ, -tʀis/ *nm, f* imitator; (comédien) impersonator. **imiter** [1] *vt* imitate; (personnage) impersonate; (*signature*) forge; (faire comme) do the same as.

immatriculation /imatʀikylasjɔ̃/ *nf* registration.

immatriculer /imatʀikyle/ [1] *vt* register; **se faire ~** register; **faire ~ une voiture** have a car registered.

immédiat, ~e /imedja, -t/ *a* immediate. ● *nm* **dans l'~** for the time being.

immense /imɑ̃s/ *a* huge, immense.

immerger /imɛʀʒe/ [40] *vt* immerse. □ **s'~** *vpr* immerse oneself (**dans** in).

immeuble /imœbl/ *nm* block of flats, building; **~ de bureaux** office building *ou* block.

immigrant, ~e /imigʀɑ̃, -t/ *a* & *nm,f* immigrant. **immigration** *nf* immigration. **immigré, ~e** *a* & *nm,f* immigrant. **immigrer** [1] *vi* immigrate.

imminent, ~e /iminɑ̃, -t/ *a* imminent.

immobile /imɔbil/ *a* still, motionless.

immobilier, -ière /imɔbilje, -jɛʀ/ *a* property; **agence immobilière** estate agent's office; (US) real estate office; **agent ~** estate agent; (US) real estate agent. ● *nm* **l'~** property; (US) real estate.

immobiliser /imɔbilize/ [1] *vt* immobilize; (*stopper*) stop. □ **s'~** *vpr* stop.

immonde /imɔ̃d/ *a* filthy.

immoral, ~e (*mpl* **-aux**) /imɔʀal, -o/ *a* immoral.

immortel, ~le /imɔʀtɛl/ *a* immortal.

immuable /imɥabl/ *a* unchanging.

immuniser /imynize/ [1] *vt* immunize; **immunisé contre** (à l'abri de) immune to. **immunité** *nf* immunity.

impact /ɛ̃pakt/ *nm* impact.

impair, ~e /ɛ̃pɛʀ/ *a* (*numéro*) odd. ● *nm* blunder, faux pas.

imparfait, ~e /ɛ̃paʀfɛ, -t/ *a* & *nm* imperfect.

impasse /ɛ̃pɑs/ *nf* (*rue*) dead end; (*situation*) deadlock.

impatient, ~e /ɛ̃pasjɑ̃, -t/ *a* impatient.

impatienter /ɛ̃pasjɑ̃te/ [1] *vt* annoy. □ **s'~** *vpr* get impatient (**contre qn** with sb).

impayé, ~e /ɛ̃peje/ *a* unpaid.

impeccable /ɛ̃pekabl/ *a* (*propre*) impeccable, spotless; (*soigné*) perfect.

impensable /ɛ̃pɑ̃sabl/ *a* unthinkable.

impératif, -ive /ɛ̃peʀatif, -v/ *a* imperative. ● *nm* (Gram) imperative; (*contrainte*) imperative; **~s** (*exigences*) requirements, demands (**de** of).

impératrice /ɛ̃peʀatʀis/ *nf* empress.

impérial, ~e (*mpl* **-iaux**) /ɛ̃peʀjal, -jo/ *a* imperial.

impérieux, -ieuse /ɛ̃peʀjø, -z/ *a* imperious; (*pressant*) pressing.

imperméable /ɛ̃pɛʀmeabl/ *a* impervious (à to); (*manteau, tissu*) waterproof. ● *nm* raincoat.

impersonnel, ~le /ɛ̃pɛʀsɔnɛl/ *a* impersonal.

impertinent, ~e /ɛ̃pɛʀtinɑ̃, -t/ *a* impertinent.

imperturbable /ɛ̃pɛʀtyʀbabl/ *a* unshakeable, unruffled.

impétueux, -euse /ɛ̃petɥø, -z/ *a* impetuous.

impitoyable /ɛ̃pitwajabl/ *a* merciless.

implant /ɛ̃plɑ̃/ *nm* implant.

implanter /ɛ̃plɑ̃te/ [1] *vt* establish, set up. □ **s'~** *vpr* become established.

implication /ɛ̃plikasjɔ̃/ *nf*
(conséquence) implication;
(participation) involvement.

impliquer /ɛ̃plike/ [1] *vt* (mêler)
implicate (**dans** in); (signifier)
imply, mean (**que** that); (nécessiter)
involve (**de faire** doing).

implorer /ɛ̃plɔʀe/ [1] *vt* implore,
beg for.

impoli, **~e** /ɛ̃pɔli/ *a* impolite,
rude.

importance /ɛ̃pɔʀtɑ̃s/ *nf*
importance; (taille) size; (ampleur)
extent; **sans ~** unimportant.

important, **~e** /ɛ̃pɔʀtɑ̃, -t/ *a*
important; (en quantité)
considerable, sizeable, big; (*air*)
self-important. ● *nm* **l'~** the
important thing.

importateur, **-trice** /ɛ̃pɔʀtatœʀ,
-tʀis/ *nm, f* importer. ● *a*
importing. **importation** *nf*
import.

importer /ɛ̃pɔʀte/ [1] *vt* (Comm)
import. ● *vi* matter, be important
(**à** to); **il importe que** it is
important that; **n'importe, peu
importe** it does not matter;
n'importe comment anyhow;
n'importe où anywhere; **n'importe
qui** anybody; **n'importe quoi**
anything.

importun, **~e** /ɛ̃pɔʀtœ̃, -yn/ *a*
troublesome. ● *nm, f* nuisance.

imposer /ɛ̃poze/ [1] *vt* impose (**à**
on); (taxer) tax; **en ~ à qn** impress
sb. □ **s'~** *vpr* (*action*) be
essential; (se faire reconnaître) stand
out; (s'astreindre à) **s'~ de faire**
force oneself to do.

imposition /ɛ̃pozisjɔ̃/ *nf* taxation;
~ des mains laying-on of hands.

impossible /ɛ̃posibl/ *a*
impossible. ● *nm* **faire l'~** do
one's utmost.

impôt /ɛ̃po/ *nm* tax; **~s**
(contributions) tax(ation), taxes; **~
sur le revenu** income tax.

impotent, **~e** /ɛ̃pɔtɑ̃, -t/ *a*
disabled.

imprécis, **~e** /ɛ̃pʀesi, -z/ *a*
imprecise.

imprégner /ɛ̃pʀeɲe/ [14] *vt* fill
(**de** with); (imbiber) impregnate (**de**
with). □ **s'~ de** *vpr* (fig) immerse
oneself in.

impression /ɛ̃pʀesjɔ̃/ *nf*
impression; (de livre) printing.
impressionnant *a* impressive;
(choquant) disturbing.
impressionner [1] *vt* impress;
(choquer) disturb.

imprévisible /ɛ̃pʀevizibl/ *a*
unpredictable.

imprévu, **~e** /ɛ̃pʀevy/ *a*
unexpected. ● *nm* unexpected
incident; **sauf ~** unless anything
unexpected happens.

imprimante /ɛ̃pʀimɑ̃t/ *nf* (Ordinat)
printer; **~ à jet d'encre** ink-jet
printer; **~ (à) laser** laser printer.

imprimé, **~e** /ɛ̃pʀime/ *a* printed.
● *nm* printed form.

imprimer /ɛ̃pʀime/ [1] *vt* print;
(marquer) imprint. **imprimerie** *nf*
(art) printing; (lieu) printing works.
imprimeur *nm* printer.

improbable /ɛ̃pʀɔbabl/ *a*
unlikely, improbable.

impropre /ɛ̃pʀɔpʀ/ *a* incorrect; **~
à** unfit for.

improviste: à l'~ /alɛ̃pʀɔvist/ *loc*
unexpectedly.

imprudence /ɛ̃pʀydɑ̃s/ *nf*
carelessness; (acte) careless
action.

imprudent, **~e** /ɛ̃pʀydɑ̃, -t/ *a*
careless; **il est ~ de** it is unwise
to.

impudent, **~e** /ɛ̃pydɑ̃, -t/ *a*
impudent.

impuissant, **~e** /ɛ̃pɥisɑ̃, -t/ *a*
helpless; (Méd) impotent; **~ à faire**
powerless to do.

impulsif, **-ive** /ɛ̃pylsif, -v/ *a*
impulsive. **impulsion** *nf* (poussée,

influence) impetus; (instinct, mouvement) impulse.

impur, ~e /ɛ̃pyʀ/ a impure.

imputer /ɛ̃pyte/ [1] vt ~ **à** attribute to, impute to.

inabordable /inabɔʀdabl/ a (prix) prohibitive.

inacceptable /inaksɛptabl/ a unacceptable.

inactif, -ive /inaktif, -v/ a inactive.

inadapté, ~e /inadapte/ a maladjusted. ● nm, f (Psych) maladjusted person.

inadmissible /inadmisibl/ a unacceptable.

inadvertance /inadvɛʀtɑ̃s/ nf par ~ by mistake.

inanimé, ~e /inanime/ a (évanoui) unconscious; (mort) lifeless; (matière) inanimate.

inaperçu, ~e /inapɛʀsy/ a unnoticed.

inapte /inapt/ a unsuited (à to); ~ **à faire** incapable of doing; ~ **au service militaire** unfit for military service.

inattendu, ~e /inatɑ̃dy/ a unexpected.

inaugurer /inogyʀe/ [1] vt inaugurate.

incapable /ɛ̃kapabl/ a incapable (de qch of sth); ~ **de faire** unable to do, incapable of doing. ● nmf incompetent.

incapacité /ɛ̃kapasite/ nf inability, incapacity; **être dans l'~ de faire** be unable to do.

incarcérer /ɛ̃kaʀseʀe/ [14] vt imprison, incarcerate.

incarnation /ɛ̃kaʀnasjɔ̃/ nf embodiment, incarnation.

incarné, ~e a (ongle) ingrowing.

incassable /ɛ̃kɑsabl/ a unbreakable.

incendiaire /ɛ̃sɑ̃djɛʀ/ a incendiary; (propos) inflammatory. ● nmf arsonist.

incendie /ɛ̃sɑ̃di/ nm fire; ~ **criminel** arson. **incendier** [45] vt set fire to.

incertain, ~e /ɛ̃sɛʀtɛ̃, -ɛn/ a uncertain; (contour) vague; (temps) unsettled. **incertitude** nf uncertainty.

inceste /ɛ̃sɛst/ nm incest.

incidence /ɛ̃sidɑ̃s/ nf effect.

incident /ɛ̃sidɑ̃/ nm incident; ~ **technique** technical hitch.

incinérer /ɛ̃sineʀe/ [14] vt incinerate; (mort) cremate.

inciser /ɛ̃size/ [1] vt make an incision in; (abcès) lance. **incisif, -ive** a incisive. **incision** nf incision; (d'abcès) lancing.

incitation /ɛ̃sitasjɔ̃/ nf (Jur) incitement (à to); (encouragement) incentive. **inciter** [1] vt incite (à to); (encourager) encourage.

inclinaison /ɛ̃klinɛzɔ̃/ nf incline; (de la tête) tilt.

inclination /ɛ̃klinasjɔ̃/ nf (penchant) inclination; (geste) (du buste) bow; (de la tête) nod.

incliner /ɛ̃kline/ [1] vt tilt, lean; (courber) bend; (inciter) encourage (à to); ~ **la tête** (approuver) nod; (révérence) bow. ● vi ~ **à** be inclined to. □ **s'~** vpr lean forward; (se courber) bow down (devant before); (céder) give in, yield (devant to); (chemin) slope.

inclure /ɛ̃klyʀ/ [16] vt include; (enfermer) enclose; **jusqu'au lundi inclus** up to and including Monday.

incohérence /ɛ̃kɔeʀɑ̃s/ nf incoherence; (contradiction) discrepancy. **incohérent, ~e** a incoherent, inconsistent.

incolore /ɛ̃kɔlɔʀ/ a colourless; (verre) clear.

incommoder /ɛ̃kɔmɔde/ [1] vt inconvenience, bother.

incompatible /ɛ̃kɔ̃patibl/ a incompatible.

incompétent, ~e /ɛ̃kɔ̃petɑ̃, -t/ *a* incompetent.

incomplet, **-ète** /ɛ̃kɔ̃plɛ, -t/ *a* incomplete.

incompréhension /ɛ̃kɔ̃preɑ̃sjɔ̃/ *nf* lack of understanding.

incompris, ~e /ɛ̃kɔ̃pri, -z/ *a* misunderstood.

inconcevable /ɛ̃kɔ̃svabl/ *a* inconceivable.

incongru, ~e /ɛ̃kɔ̃gry/ *a* unseemly.

inconnu, ~e /ɛ̃kɔny/ *a* unknown (à to). ● *nm, f* stranger. ● *nm* l'~ the unknown.

inconscience /ɛ̃kɔ̃sjɑ̃s/ *nf* unconsciousness; (folie) madness.

inconscient, ~e /ɛ̃kɔ̃sjɑ̃, -t/ *a* unconscious (de of); (fou) mad. ● *nm* (Psych) subconscious.

incontestable /ɛ̃kɔ̃tɛstabl/ *a* indisputable.

incontrôlable /ɛ̃kɔ̃trolabl/ *a* unverifiable; (non maîtrisé) uncontrollable.

inconvenant, ~e /ɛ̃kɔ̃vnɑ̃, -t/ *a* improper.

inconvénient /ɛ̃kɔ̃venjɑ̃/ *nm* disadvantage, drawback; (objection) objection.

incorporer /ɛ̃kɔrpɔre/ [1] *vt* incorporate; (Culin) blend (à into); (Mil) enlist.

incorrect, ~e /ɛ̃kɔrɛkt/ *a* (faux) incorrect; (malséant) improper; (impoli) impolite; (déloyal) unfair.

incrédule /ɛ̃kredyl/ *a* incredulous.

incriminer /ɛ̃krimine/ [1] *vt* (*personne*) incriminate; (*conduite, action*) attack.

incroyable /ɛ̃krwajabl/ *a* incredible.

incruster /ɛ̃kryste/ [1] *vt* inlay (de with).

incubateur /ɛ̃kybatœr/ *nm* incubator.

inculpation /ɛ̃kylpasjɔ̃/ *nf* charge (de, pour of). **inculpé**, ~e *nm, f* accused. **inculper** [1] *vt* charge (de with).

inculquer /ɛ̃kylke/ [1] *vt* instil (à into).

inculte /ɛ̃kylt/ *a* uncultivated; (*personne*) uneducated.

incurver /ɛ̃kyrve/ [1] *vt* curve, bend. □ s'~ *vpr* curve, bend.

Inde /ɛ̃d/ *nf* India.

indécent, ~e /ɛ̃desɑ̃, -t/ *a* indecent.

indécis, ~e /ɛ̃desi, -z/ *a* (de nature) indecisive; (temporairement) undecided.

indéfini, ~e /ɛ̃defini/ *a* (Gram) indefinite; (vague) undefined; (sans limites) indeterminate.

indemne /ɛ̃dɛmn/ *a* unharmed.

indemniser /ɛ̃dɛmnize/ [1] *vt* compensate (de for).

indemnité /ɛ̃dɛmnite/ *nf* indemnity, compensation; (allocation) allowance; ~s de licenciement redundancy payment.

indépendance /ɛ̃depɑ̃dɑ̃s/ *nf* independence. **indépendant**, ~e *a* independent.

indéterminé, ~e /ɛ̃detɛrmine/ *a* unspecified.

index /ɛ̃dɛks/ *nm* forefinger; (liste) index.

indicateur, **-trice** /ɛ̃dikatœr, -tris/ *nm, f* (police) informer. ● *nm* (livre) guide; (Tech) indicator.

indicatif, **-ve** /ɛ̃dikatif, -v/ *a* indicative (de of). ● *nm* (à la radio) signature tune; (téléphonique) dialling code; (Gram) indicative.

indication /ɛ̃dikasjɔ̃/ *nf* indication; (renseignement) information; (directive) instruction.

indice /ɛ̃dis/ *nm* sign; (dans une enquête) clue; (des prix) index; (évaluation) rating; ~ d'écoute audience ratings.

indifférence /ɛ̃difeRɑ̃s/ *nf* indifference.

indifférent, ~e /ɛ̃difeRɑ̃, -t/ *a* indifferent (à to); **ça m'est ~** it makes no difference to me.

indigène /ɛ̃diʒɛn/ *a & nmf* native, indigenous; (du pays) local. ● *nmf* native.

indigent, ~e /ɛ̃diʒɑ̃, -t/ *a* destitute.

indigeste /ɛ̃diʒɛst/ *a* indigestible. **indigestion** *nf* indigestion.

indigne /ɛ̃diɲ/ *a* unworthy (de of); (acte) vile. **indigner (s')** [1] *vpr* become indignant (de at).

indiqué, ~e /ɛ̃dike/ *a* (heure) appointed; (opportun) appropriate; (conseillé) recommended.

indiquer /ɛ̃dike/ [1] *vt* (montrer) show, indicate; (renseigner sur) point out, tell; (déterminer) give, state, appoint; **~ du doigt** point to *ou* out *ou* at.

indirect, ~e /ɛ̃diRɛkt/ *a* indirect. **indiscipliné, ~e** /ɛ̃disipline/ *a* unruly.

indiscret, -ète /ɛ̃diskRɛ, -t/ *a* (personne) inquisitive; (question) indiscreet.

indiscutable /ɛ̃diskytabl/ *a* unquestionable.

indispensable /ɛ̃dispɑ̃sabl/ *a* indispensable; **il est ~ qu'il vienne** it is essential that he comes.

individu /ɛ̃dividy/ *nm* individual. **individuel, ~le** /ɛ̃dividɥɛl/ *a* (pour une personne) individual; (qui concerne l'individu) personal; **chambre ~le** single room; **maison ~le** detached house.

indolore /ɛ̃dɔlɔR/ *a* painless.

Indonésie /ɛ̃dɔnezi/ *nf* Indonesia.

indu, ~e /ɛ̃dy/ *a* **à une heure ~e** at some ungodly hour.

induire /ɛ̃dɥiR/ [17] *vt* infer (de from); (inciter) induce (à faire to do); **~ en erreur** mislead.

indulgence /ɛ̃dylʒɑ̃s/ *nf* indulgence; (de jury) leniency.

indulgent, ~e *a* indulgent; (clément) lenient.

industrialisé, ~e /ɛ̃dystRijalize/ *a* industrialized.

industrie /ɛ̃dystRi/ *nf* industry.

industriel, ~le /ɛ̃dystRijɛl/ *a* industrial. ● *nm* industrialist.

inédit, ~e /inedi, -t/ *a* unpublished; (fig) original.

inefficace /inefikas/ *a* (remède, mesure) ineffective; (appareil, système) inefficient.

inégal, ~e (mpl -aux) /inegal, -o/ *a* unequal; (irrégulier) uneven. **inégalable** *a* matchless. **inégalité** *nf* (injustice) inequality; (irrégularité) unevenness; (disproportion) disparity.

inéluctable /inelyktabl/ *a* inescapable.

inepte /inɛpt/ *a* inept, absurd. **inerte** /inɛRt/ *a* inert; (immobile) lifeless; (sans énergie) apathetic. **inertie** *nf* inertia; (fig) apathy.

inespéré, ~e /inɛspere/ *a* unhoped for.

inestimable /inɛstimabl/ *a* priceless; (aide) invaluable.

inexact, ~e /inɛgza(kt), -kt/ *a* (imprécis) inaccurate; (incorrect) incorrect.

in extremis /inɛkstremis/ *adv* (par nécessité) as a last resort; (au dernier moment) at the last minute. ● *a* last-minute.

infaillible /ɛ̃fajibl/ *a* infallible.

infâme /ɛ̃fɑm/ *a* vile.

infantile /ɛ̃fɑ̃til/ *a* (puéril) infantile; (maladie) childhood; (mortalité) infant.

infarctus /ɛ̃faRktys/ *nm* coronary, heart attack.

infatigable /ɛ̃fatigabl/ *a* tireless.

infect, ~e /ɛ̃fɛkt/ *a* revolting.

infecter /ɛ̃fɛkte/ [1] *vt* infect. □ **s'~** *vpr* become infected.

infectieux, -ieuse *a* infectious.
infection *nf* infection.
inférieur, ~e /ɛ̃ferjœr/ *a* (plus bas) lower; (moins bon) inferior (à to); **~ à** (plus petit que) smaller than; (plus bas que) lower than. ● *nm, f* inferior. **infériorité** *nf* inferiority.
infernal, ~e (*mpl* **-aux**) /ɛ̃fɛrnal, -o/ *a* infernal.
infester /ɛ̃fɛste/ [1] *vt* infest.
infidèle /ɛ̃fidɛl/ *a* unfaithful (à to). **infidélité** *nf* unfaithfulness; (acte) infidelity.
infiltrer (s') /sɛ̃filtre/ [1] *vpr* s'~ (dans) (personnes, idées) infiltrate; (liquide) seep through.
infime /ɛ̃fim/ *a* tiny, minute.
infini, ~e /ɛ̃fini/ *a* infinite. ● *nm* infinity; **à l'~** endlessly.
infinité /ɛ̃finite/ *nf* **l'~** infinity; **une ~ de** an endless number of.
infinitif /ɛ̃finitif/ *nm* infinitive.
infirme /ɛ̃firm/ *a* disabled. ● *nmf* disabled person. **infirmerie** *nf* sickbay, infirmary. **infirmier** *nm* (male) nurse. **infirmière** *nf* nurse. **infirmité** *nf* disability.
inflammable /ɛ̃flamabl/ *a* in-flammable.
inflation /ɛ̃flasjɔ̃/ *nf* inflation.
infliger /ɛ̃fliʒe/ [40] *vt* inflict; (sanction) impose.
influence /ɛ̃flyɑ̃s/ *nf* influence. **influencer** [10] *vt* influence. **influent, ~e** *a* influential.
influer /ɛ̃flye/ *vi* **~ sur** influence.
informateur, -trice /ɛ̃fɔrmatœr, -tris/ *nm, f* informant; (pour la police) informer.
informaticien, ~ne /ɛ̃fɔrmatisjɛ̃, -ɛn/ *nm, f* computer scientist.
information /ɛ̃fɔrmasjɔ̃/ *nf* information; (Jur) inquiry; **une ~** (some) information; (nouvelle) (some) news; **les ~s** the news.

informatique /ɛ̃fɔrmatik/ *nf* computer science; (techniques) information technology.
informatiser [1] *vt* computerize.
informer /ɛ̃fɔrme/ [1] *vt* inform (de about, of). □ s'~ *vpr* enquire (de about).
inforoute /ɛ̃fɔrut/ *nf* (Ordinat) information highway.
infortune /ɛ̃fɔrtyn/ *nf* misfortune.
infraction /ɛ̃fraksjɔ̃/ *nf* offence; **~ à** (loi, règlement) breach of.
infrastructure /ɛ̃frastryktyr/ *nf* infrastructure; (équipements) facilities.
infructueux, -euse /ɛ̃fryktɥø, -z/ *a* fruitless.
infuser /ɛ̃fyze/ [1] *vt/i* infuse, brew. **infusion** *nf* herbal tea, infusion.
ingénier (s') /(s)ɛ̃ʒenje/ [45] *vpr* **s'~ à** strive to.
ingénieur /ɛ̃ʒenjœr/ *nm* engineer.
ingénieux, -ieuse /ɛ̃ʒenjø, -z/ *a* ingenious. **ingéniosité** *nf* ingenuity.
ingénu, ~e /ɛ̃ʒeny/ *a* naïve.
ingérence /ɛ̃ʒerɑ̃s/ *nf* interference.
ingérer (s') /sɛ̃ʒere/ [14] *vpr* **s'~ dans** interfere in.
ingrat, ~e /ɛ̃gra, -t/ *a* (personne) ungrateful; (travail) unrewarding, thankless; (visage) unattractive.
ingrédient /ɛ̃gredjɑ̃/ *nm* ingredient.
ingurgiter /ɛ̃gyrʒite/ [1] *vt* swallow.
inhabité, ~e /inabite/ *a* uninhabited.
inhabituel, ~le /inabitɥɛl/ *a* unusual.
inhumain, ~e /inymɛ̃, -ɛn/ *a* inhuman.
inhumation /inymasjɔ̃/ *nf* burial.

initial, ~e (*mpl* **-iaux**) /inisjal, -jo/ *a* initial. **initiale** *nf* initial.

initialisation /inisjalizasjɔ̃/ *nf* (Ordinat) formatting. **initialiser** [1] *vt* format.

initiation /inisjasjɔ̃/ *nf* initiation; (formation) introduction (**à** to); **cours d'~** introductory course.

initiative /inisjativ/ *nf* initiative.

initier /inisje/ [45] *vt* initiate (**à** into); (faire découvrir) introduce (**à** to). □ **s'~** *vpr* **s'~ à qch** learn sth.

injecter /ɛ̃ʒɛkte/ [1] *vt* inject; **injecté de sang** bloodshot.

injection *nf* injection.

injure /ɛ̃ʒyʀ/ *nf* insult. **injurier** [45] *vt* insult. **injurieux, -ieuse** *a* insulting.

injuste /ɛ̃ʒyst/ *a* unjust, unfair. **injustice** *nf* injustice.

inné, ~e /inne/ *a* innate, inborn.

innocence /inosɑ̃s/ *nf* innocence. **innocent, ~e** *a* & *nm,f* innocent. **innocenter** [1] *vt* clear, prove innocent.

innombrable /inɔ̃bʀabl/ *a* countless.

innovateur, -trice /inovatœʀ, -tʀis/ *nm,f* innovator. **innovation** *nf* innovation. **innover** [1] *vi* innovate.

inodore /inodɔʀ/ *a* odourless.

inoffensif, -ive /inofɑ̃sif, -v/ *a* harmless.

inondation /inɔ̃dasjɔ̃/ *nf* flood; (action) flooding.

inonder /inɔ̃de/ [1] *vt* flood; (mouiller) soak; (envahir) inundate (**de** with); **inondé de soleil** bathed in sunlight.

inopiné, ~e /inopine/ *a* unexpected; (mort) sudden.

inopportun, ~e /inopɔʀtœ̃, -yn/ *a* inopportune, ill-timed.

inoubliable /inublijabl/ *a* unforgettable.

inouï, ~e /inwi/ *a* incredible; (événement) unprecedented.

inox® /inɔks/ *nm* stainless steel.

inoxydable /inɔksidabl/ *a* **acier ~** stainless steel.

inqualifiable /ɛ̃kalifjabl/ *a* unspeakable.

inquiet, -iète /ɛ̃kjɛ, -t/ *a* worried. **inquiétant, ~e** *a* worrying.

inquiéter /ɛ̃kjete/ [14] *vt* worry. □ **s'~** *vpr* worry (**de** about).

inquiétude *nf* anxiety, worry.

insaisissable /ɛ̃sezisabl/ *a* (personne) elusive; (nuance) indefinable.

insalubre /ɛ̃salybʀ/ *a* unhealthy.

insatisfaisant, ~e /ɛ̃satisfəzɑ̃, -t/ *a* unsatisfactory. **insatisfait, ~e** *a* (mécontent) dissatisfied; (frustré) unfulfilled.

inscription /ɛ̃skʀipsjɔ̃/ *nf* inscription; (immatriculation) enrolment.

inscrire /ɛ̃skʀiʀ/ [30] *vt* write (down); (graver, tracer) inscribe; (personne) enrol; (sur une liste) put down. □ **s'~** *vpr* put one's name down; **s'~ à** (école) enrol at; (club, parti) join; (examen) enter for.

insecte /ɛ̃sɛkt/ *nm* insect.

insécurité /ɛ̃sekyʀite/ *nf* insecurity.

insensé, ~e /ɛ̃sɑ̃se/ *a* mad.

insensibilité /ɛ̃sɑ̃sibilite/ *nf* insensitivity. **insensible** *a* insensitive (**à** to); (graduel) imperceptible.

insérer /ɛ̃seʀe/ [14] *vt* insert. □ **s'~** *vpr* be inserted; **s'~ dans** be part of.

insigne /ɛ̃siɲ/ *nm* badge; **~s** (d'une fonction) insignia.

insignifiant, ~e /ɛ̃siɲifjɑ̃, -t/ *a* insignificant.

insinuation /ɛ̃sinɥasjɔ̃/ *nf* insinuation.

insinuer /ɛ̃sinɥe/ [1] *vt* insinuate. □ **s'~** *vpr* (socialement) ingratiate oneself (**auprès de qn** with sb);

s'~ dans (se glisser) slip into; (*idée, nuance*) creep into.
insipide /ɛ̃sipid/ *a* insipid.
insistance /ɛ̃sistɑ̃s/ *nf* insistence. **insistant, ~e** *a* insistent.
insister /ɛ̃siste/ [1] *vi* insist (**pour faire** on doing); **~ sur** stress.
insolation /ɛ̃sɔlasjɔ̃/ *nf* (Méd) sunstroke.
insolent, ~e /ɛ̃sɔlɑ̃, -t/ *a* insolent.
insolite /ɛ̃sɔlit/ *a* unusual.
insolvable /ɛ̃sɔlvabl/ *a* insolvent.
insomnie /ɛ̃sɔmni/ *nf* insomnia.
insonoriser /ɛ̃sɔnɔrize/ [1] *vt* soundproof.
insouciance /ɛ̃susjɑ̃s/ *nf* lack of concern. **insouciant, ~e** *a* carefree.
insoutenable /ɛ̃sutnabl/ *a* unbearable; (*argument*) untenable.
inspecter /ɛ̃spɛkte/ [1] *vt* inspect. **inspecteur, -trice** *nm, f* inspector. **inspection** *nf* inspection.
inspiration /ɛ̃spirasjɔ̃/ *nf* inspiration; (*respiration*) breath.
inspirer /ɛ̃spire/ [1] *vt* inspire; **~ la méfiance à qn** inspire distrust in sb. ● *vi* breathe in. □ **s'~ de** *vpr* be inspired by.
instabilité /ɛ̃stabilite/ *nf* instability; unsteadiness. **instable** *a* unstable; (*temps*) unsettled.
installation /ɛ̃stalasjɔ̃/ *nf* installation; (de local) fitting out; (de locataire) settling in. **installations** *nfpl* facilities.
installer /ɛ̃stale/ [1] *vt* install; (*meuble*) put in; (*étagère*) put up; (*gaz, téléphone*) connect; (équiper) fit out. □ **s'~** *vpr* settle (down); (*emménager*) settle in; **s'~ comme** set oneself up as.
instance /ɛ̃stɑ̃s/ *nf* authority;

(*prière*) entreaty; **avec ~** with insistence; **en ~** pending; **en ~ de** in the course of, on the point of.
instant /ɛ̃stɑ̃/ *nm* moment, instant; **à l'~** this instant.
instantané, ~e /ɛ̃stɑ̃tane/ *a* instantaneous; (*café*) instant.
instar: à l'~ de /alɛstardə/ *loc* like.
instaurer /ɛ̃store/ [1] *vt* institute.
instigateur, -trice /ɛ̃stigatœr, -tris/ *nm, f* instigator.
instinct /ɛ̃stɛ̃/ *nm* instinct; **d'~** instinctively. **instinctif, -ive** *a* instinctive.
instituer /ɛ̃stitɥe/ [1] *vt* establish.
institut /ɛ̃stity/ *nm* institute; **~ de beauté** beauty parlour.
instituteur, -trice /ɛ̃stitytœr, -tris/ *nm, f* primary-school teacher.
institution /ɛ̃stitysjɔ̃/ *nf* institution; (*école*) private school.
instructif, -ive /ɛ̃stryktif, -v/ *a* instructive.
instruction /ɛ̃stryksjɔ̃/ *nf* (formation) education; (Mil) training; (*document*) directive; **~s** (ordres, mode d'emploi) instructions; (Ordinat) (énoncé) instruction; (pas de séquence) statement.
instruire /ɛ̃strɥir/ [17] *vt* teach, educate; **~ de** inform of. □ **s'~** *vpr* learn, educate oneself; **s'~ de** enquire about. **instruit, ~e** *a* educated.
instrument /ɛ̃strymɑ̃/ *nm* instrument; (outil) tool; (moyen: fig) instrument; **~ de gestion** management tool; **~s de bord** (Aviat) controls.
insu: à l'~ de /alɛsydə/ *loc* without the knowledge of.
insuffisance /ɛ̃syfizɑ̃s/ *nf* (pénurie) shortage; (médiocrité) inadequacy. **insuffisant, ~e** *a*

inadequate; (en nombre) insufficient.

insulaire /ɛ̃sylɛʀ/ a island. ● nmf islander.

insuline /ɛ̃sylin/ nf insulin.

insulte /ɛ̃sylt/ nf insult. **insulter** [1] vt insult.

insupportable /ɛ̃sypɔʀtabl/ a unbearable.

insurger (s') /(s)ɛ̃syʀʒe/ [40] vpr rebel.

intact, ~e /ɛ̃takt/ a intact.

intangible /ɛ̃tɑ̃ʒibl/ a intangible; (principe) inviolable.

intarissable /ɛ̃taʀisabl/ a inexhaustible.

intégral, ~e (mpl -aux) /ɛ̃tegʀal, -o/ a complete; (texte, édition) unabridged; (paiement) full, in full. **intégralement** adv in full. **intégralité** nf whole.

intègre /ɛ̃tɛgʀ/ a upright.

intégrer /ɛ̃tegʀe/ [14] vt integrate. □ s'~ vpr (personne) integrate; (maison) fit in.

intégriste /ɛ̃tegʀist/ nmf fundamentalist.

intégrité /ɛ̃tegʀite/ nf integrity.

intellect /ɛ̃telɛkt/ nm intellect. **intellectuel**, ~le a & nm,f intellectual.

intelligence /ɛ̃teliʒɑ̃s/ nf intelligence; (compréhension) understanding; (complicité) agreement; agir d'~ avec qn act in agreement with sb. **intelligent**, ~e a intelligent.

intempéries /ɛ̃tɑ̃peʀi/ nfpl severe weather.

intempestif, -ive /ɛ̃tɑ̃pɛstif, -v/ a untimely.

intenable /ɛ̃tnabl/ a unbearable; (enfant) impossible.

intendance /ɛ̃tɑ̃dɑ̃s/ nf (Scol) bursar's office.

intendant, ~e /ɛ̃tɑ̃dɑ̃, -t/ nm (Mil) quartermaster. ● nm,f (Scol) bursar.

intense /ɛ̃tɑ̃s/ a intense; (circulation) heavy. **intensif**, -ive a intensive. **intensité** nf intensity.

intenter /ɛ̃tɑ̃te/ [1] vt ~ un procès ou une action institute proceedings (à, contre against).

intention /ɛ̃tɑ̃sjɔ̃/ nf intention (de faire of doing); à l'~ de qn for sb. **intentionnel**, ~le a intentional.

interactif, -ive /ɛ̃teʀaktif, -v/ a (TV, vidéo) interactive.

interaction /ɛ̃teʀaksjɔ̃/ nf interaction.

intercaler /ɛ̃teʀkale/ [1] vt insert.

intercéder /ɛ̃teʀsede/ [14] vi intercede (en faveur de on behalf of).

intercepter /ɛ̃teʀsɛpte/ [1] vt intercept.

interdiction /ɛ̃teʀdiksjɔ̃/ nf ban; ~ de fumer no smoking.

interdire /ɛ̃teʀdiʀ/ [37] vt forbid; (officiellement) ban, prohibit; ~ à qn de faire forbid sb to do.

interdit, ~e /ɛ̃teʀdi, -t/ a prohibited, forbidden; (étonné) dumbfounded.

intéressant, ~e /ɛ̃teʀesɑ̃, -t/ a interesting; (avantageux) attractive.

intéressé, ~e /ɛ̃teʀese/ a (en cause) concerned; (pour profiter) self-interested. ● nm, f person concerned.

intéresser /ɛ̃teʀese/ [1] vt interest; (concerner) concern. □ s'~ à vpr be interested in.

intérêt /ɛ̃teʀɛ/ nm interest; (égoïsme) self-interest; ~(s) (Comm) interest; vous avez ~ à it is in your interest to.

interface /ɛ̃teʀfas/ nf (Ordinat) interface.

intérieur, ~e /ɛ̃teʀjœʀ/ a inner, inside; (mur, escalier) internal; (vol, politique) domestic; (vie, calme) inner. ● nm interior; (de boîte, tiroir) inside; **à l'~ (de)** inside; (fig) within. **intérieurement** adv inwardly.

intérim /ɛ̃teʀim/ nm interim; **assurer l'~** deputize (**de** for); **par ~** on an interim basis; **président par ~** acting president; **faire de l'~** temp.

intérimaire /ɛ̃teʀimɛʀ/ a temporary, interim. ● nmf (secrétaire) temp; (médecin) locum.

interjection /ɛ̃teʀʒɛksjɔ̃/ nf interjection.

interlocuteur, -trice /ɛ̃teʀlɔkytœʀ, -tʀis/ nm, f **son ~** the person one is speaking to.

interloqué, ~e /ɛ̃teʀlɔke/ a **être ~** be taken aback.

intermède /ɛ̃teʀmɛd/ nm interlude.

intermédiaire /ɛ̃teʀmedjɛʀ/ a intermediate. ● nmf intermediary. ● nm **sans ~** without an intermediary, direct; **par l'~ de** through.

interminable /ɛ̃teʀminabl/ a endless.

intermittence /ɛ̃teʀmitɑ̃s/ nf **par ~** intermittently.

internat /ɛ̃teʀna/ nm boarding-school.

international, ~e (mpl **-aux**) /ɛ̃teʀnasjɔnal, -o/ a international.

internaute /ɛ̃teʀnot/ nmf (Ordinat) Netsurfer, Internet user.

interne /ɛ̃teʀn/ a internal; (cours, formation) in-house. ● nmf (Scol) boarder; (Méd) house officer; (US) intern.

internement /ɛ̃teʀnəmɑ̃/ nm (Pol) internment. **interner** [1] vt (Pol) intern; (Méd) commit.

Internet /ɛ̃teʀnet/ nm Internet; **sur ~** on the Internet.

interpellation /ɛ̃teʀpelasjɔ̃/ nf (Pol) questioning. **interpeller** [1] vt shout to; (apostropher) shout at; (interroger) question.

interphone /ɛ̃teʀfɔn/ nm intercom; (d'immeuble) entry phone.

interposer (s') /(s)ɛ̃teʀpoze/ [1] vpr intervene.

interprétariat /ɛ̃teʀpretaʀja/ nm interpreting. **interprétation** nf interpretation; (d'artiste) performance. **interprète** nmf interpreter; (artiste) performer. **interpréter** [14] vt interpret; (jouer) play; (chanter) sing.

interrogateur, -trice /ɛ̃teʀɔgatœʀ, -tʀis/ a questioning. **interrogatif, -ive** a interrogative. **interrogation** nf question; (action) questioning; (épreuve) test. **interrogatoire** nm interrogation. **interroger** [40] vt question; (élève) test.

interrompre /ɛ̃teʀɔ̃pʀ/ [3] vt break off, interrupt; (personne) interrupt. □ **s'~** vpr break off. **interrupteur** nm switch. **interruption** nf interruption; (arrêt) break.

interurbain, ~e /ɛ̃teʀyʀbɛ̃, -ɛn/ a long-distance, trunk.

intervalle /ɛ̃teʀval/ nm space; (temps) interval; **dans l'~** in the meantime.

intervenir /ɛ̃teʀvəniʀ/ [58] vi (agir) intervene (**auprès de qn** with sb); (survenir) occur, take place; (Méd) operate. **intervention** nf intervention; (Méd) operation.

intervertir /ɛ̃teʀvɛʀtiʀ/ [2] vt invert; (rôles) reverse.

interview /ɛ̃teʀvju/ nf interview. **interviewer** [1] vt interview.

intestin /ɛ̃tɛstɛ̃/ nm intestine.

intime /ɛ̃tim/ a intimate; (fête, vie) private; (dîner) quiet. ● nmf intimate friend.

intimider /ɛ̃timide/ [1] vt intimidate.

intimité /ɛ̃timite/ nf intimacy; (vie privée) privacy.

intituler /ɛ̃tityle/ [1] vt call,

entitle. □ s'∼ *vpr* be called *ou* entitled.

intolérable /ɛtɔlɛrabl/ *a* intolerable. **intolérance** *nf* intolerance. **intolérant**, ∼e *a* intolerant.

intonation /ɛtɔnasjɔ̃/ *nf* intonation.

intox /ɛtɔks/ *nf* 🄳 brainwashing.

intoxication /ɛtɔksikasjɔ̃/ *nf* poisoning; (fig) brainwashing; ∼ **alimentaire** food poisoning. **intoxiquer** [1] *vt* poison; (fig) brainwash.

intraitable /ɛtrɛtabl/ *a* inflexible.

Intranet /ɛtranɛt/ *nm* Intranet.

intransigeant, ∼e /ɛtrɑ̃ziʒɑ̃, -t/ *a* intransigent.

intransitif, -ive /ɛtrɑ̃zitif, -v/ *a* intransitive.

intraveineux, -euse /ɛtravɛnø, -z/ *a* intravenous.

intrépide /ɛtrepid/ *a* fearless.

intrigue /ɛtrig/ *nf* intrigue; (scénario) plot.

intrinsèque /ɛtrɛ̃sɛk/ *a* intrinsic.

Introduction /ɛtrɔdyksjɔ̃/ *nf* introduction; (insertion) insertion.

introduire /ɛtrɔdɥir/ [17] *vt* introduce, bring in; (insérer) put in, insert; ∼ **qn** show sb in. □ s'∼ *vpr* get in; s'∼ **dans** get into, enter.

introuvable /ɛtruvabl/ *a* that cannot be found.

introverti, ∼e /ɛtrɔvɛrti/ *nm, f* introvert. ●*a* introverted.

intrus, ∼e /ɛtry, -z/ *nm, f* intruder. **intrusion** *nf* intrusion.

intuitif, -ive /ɛtɥitif, -iv/ *a* intuitive. **intuition** *nf* intuition.

inusable /inyzabl/ *a* hard-wearing.

inusité, ∼e /inyzite/ *a* little used.

inutile /inytil/ *a* useless; (vain) needless. **inutilement** *adv* needlessly. **inutilisable** *a* unusable.

invalide /ɛ̃valid/ *a* & *nmf* disabled (person).

invariable /ɛ̃varjabl/ *a* invariable.

invasion /ɛ̃vazjɔ̃/ *nf* invasion.

invectiver /ɛ̃vɛktive/ [1] *vt* abuse.

inventaire /ɛ̃vɑ̃tɛr/ *nm* inventory; (Comm) stocklist; **faire l'∼** draw up an inventory; (Comm) do a stocktake.

inventer /ɛ̃vɑ̃te/ [1] *vt* invent. **inventeur, -trice** *nm, f* inventor. **inventif, -ive** *a* inventive. **invention** *nf* invention.

inverse /ɛ̃vɛrs/ *a* opposite; (ordre) reverse; **en sens ∼** in *ou* from the opposite direction. ●*nm* reverse; **c'est l'∼** it's the other way round. **inversement** *adv* conversely. **inverser** [1] *vt* reverse, invert.

Investir /ɛvɛstir/ [2] *vt* invest. **investissement** *nm* investment.

investiture /ɛ̃vɛstityr/ *nf* (de candidat) nomination; (de président) investiture.

invétéré, ∼e /ɛ̃vetere/ *a* inveterate; (menteur) compulsive; (enraciné) deep-rooted.

invisible /ɛ̃vizibl/ *a* invisible.

invitation /ɛ̃vitasjɔ̃/ *nf* invitation. **invité**, ∼e *nm, f* guest. **inviter** [1] *vt* invite (à to).

involontaire /ɛ̃vɔlɔ̃tɛr/ *a* involuntary; (témoin, héros) unwitting.

invoquer /ɛ̃vɔke/ [1] *vt* call upon, invoke.

invraisemblable /ɛ̃vrɛsɑ̃blabl/ *a* improbable, unlikely; (incroyable) incredible. **invraisemblance** *nf* improbability.

iode /jɔd/ *nm* iodine.

ira, irait /ira, irɛ/ ⇒ALLER [8].

Irak /iʀak/ nm Iraq.

Iran /iʀɑ̃/ nm Iran.

iris /iʀis/ nm iris.

irlandais, ~e /iʀlɑ̃dɛ, -z/ a Irish. **I~, ~e** nm, f Irishman, Irishwoman.

Irlande /iʀlɑ̃d/ nf Ireland.

ironie /iʀɔni/ nf irony. **ironique** a ironic.

irrationnel, ~le /iʀasjɔnɛl/ a irrational.

irréalisable /iʀealizabl/ a (idée, rêve) unachievable; (projet) unworkable.

irrécupérable /iʀekypeʀabl/ a irretrievable; (capital) irrecoverable.

irréel, ~le /iʀeɛl/ a unreal.

irréfléchi, ~e /iʀefleʃi/ a thoughtless.

irrégulier, -ière /iʀegylje, -jɛʀ/ a irregular.

irrémédiable /iʀemedjabl/ a irreparable.

irremplaçable /iʀɑ̃plasabl/ a irreplaceable.

irréparable /iʀepaʀabl/ a (objet) beyond repair; (tort, dégâts) irreparable.

irréprochable /iʀepʀɔʃabl/ a flawless.

irrésistible /iʀezistibl/ a irresistible; (drôle) hilarious.

irrésolu, ~e /iʀezɔly/ a indecisive; (problème) unsolved.

irrespirable /iʀɛspiʀabl/ a stifling.

irresponsable /iʀɛspɔ̃sabl/ a irresponsible.

irrigation /iʀigasjɔ̃/ nf irrigation. **irriguer** [1] vt irrigate.

irritable /iʀitabl/ a irritable.

irriter /iʀite/ [1] vt irritate. □ **s'~** vpr get annoyed (**de** at).

irruption /iʀypsjɔ̃/ nf faire ~ dans burst into.

Islam /islam/ nm Islam. **islamique** a Islamic.

islandais, ~e /islɑ̃dɛ, -z/ a Icelandic. ● nm (Ling) Icelandic. **I~, ~e** nm, f Icelander.

Islande /islɑ̃d/ nf Iceland.

isolant /izɔlɑ̃/ nm insulating material. **isolation** nf insulation.

isolé, ~e /izɔle/ a isolated. **isolement** nm isolation.

isoler /izɔle/ [1] vt isolate; (Électr) insulate. □ **s'~** vpr isolate oneself.

isoloir /izɔlwaʀ/ nm polling booth.

Isorel® /izɔʀɛl/ nm hardboard.

Israël /isʀaɛl/ nm Israel. **israélien, ~ne** a Israeli.

israélite /isʀaelit/ a Jewish. ● nmf Jew.

issu, ~e /isy/ a être ~ **de** (personne) come from; (résulter de) result ou stem from.

issue /isy/ nf (sortie) exit; (résultat) outcome; (fig) solution; **à l'~ de** at the conclusion of; ~ **de secours** emergency exit; **rue** ou **voie sans** ~ dead end.

Italie /itali/ nf Italy.

italien, ~ne /italjɛ̃, -ɛn/ a Italian. ● nm (Ling) Italian. **I~, ~ne** nm, f Italian.

italique /italik/ nm italics.

itinéraire /itineʀɛʀ/ nm itinerary, route.

I.U.T. abrév m (**Institut universitaire de technologie**) university institute of technology.

I.V.G. abrév f (**interruption volontaire de grossesse**) abortion.

ivoire /ivwaʀ/ nm ivory.

ivre /ivʀ/ a drunk. **ivresse** nf drunkenness; (fig) exhilaration. **ivrogne** nmf drunk(ard).

j' /ʒ/ ⇒JE.

jacinthe /ʒasɛ̃t/ nf hyacinth.

jadis /ʒadis/ adv long ago.

jaillir /ʒajir/ [2] vi (liquide) spurt (out); (lumière) stream out; (apparaître) burst forth, spring out.

jalonner /ʒalɔne/ [1] vt mark (out).

jalousie /ʒaluzi/ nf jealousy; (store) (venetian) blind. **jaloux, -ouse** a jealous.

jamais /ʒamɛ/ adv ever; ne ~ never; il ne boit ~ he never drinks; à ~ for ever; si ~ if ever.

jambe /ʒɑ̃b/ nf leg.

jambon /ʒɑ̃bɔ̃/ nm ham. **jambonneau** (pl ~x) nm knuckle of ham.

janvier /ʒɑ̃vje/ nm January.

Japon /ʒapɔ̃/ nm Japan.

japonais, ~e /ʒapɔnɛ, -z/ a Japanese. ● nm (Ling) Japanese. **J~, ~e** nm, f Japanese.

japper /ʒape/ [1] vi yap.

jaquette /ʒakɛt/ nf (de livre, femme) jacket; (d'homme) morning coat.

jardin /ʒardɛ̃/ nm garden; ~ d'enfants nursery (school); ~ public public park. **jardinage** nm gardening. **jardiner** [1] vi do some gardening, garden. **jardinier, -ière** nm, f gardener.

jardinière /ʒardinjɛr/ nf (meuble) plant-stand; ~ de légumes mixed vegetables.

jarretelle /ʒartɛl/ nf suspender; (US) garter.

jarretière /ʒartjɛr/ nf garter.

jatte /ʒat/ nf bowl.

jauge /ʒoʒ/ nf capacity; (de navire) tonnage; (compteur) gauge; ~ d'huile dipstick.

jaune /ʒon/ a & nm yellow; (péj) scab; ~ d'œuf (egg) yolk; rire ~ give a forced laugh. **jaunir** [2] vt/ i turn yellow. **jaunisse** nf jaundice.

javelot /ʒavlo/ nm javelin.

jazz /dʒaz/ nm jazz.

J.C. abrév m (**Jésus-Christ**) 500 avant/après ~ 500 B.C./A.D.

je, j' /ʒə, ʒ/ pron I.

jean /dʒin/ nm jeans; un ~ a pair of jeans.

jet¹ /ʒɛ/ nm throw; (de liquide, vapeur) jet; ~ d'eau fountain.

jet² /dʒɛt/ nm (avion) jet.

jetable /ʒətabl/ a disposable.

jetée /ʒəte/ nf pier.

jeter /ʒəte/ [38] vt throw; (au rebut) throw away; (regard, ancre, lumière) cast; (cri) utter; (bases) lay; ~ un coup d'œil have ou take a look (à at). □ se ~ vpr se ~ contre crash ou bash into; se ~ dans (fleuve) flow into; se ~ sur (se ruer sur) rush at.

jeton /ʒətɔ̃/ nm token; (pour compter) counter; (au casino) chip.

jeu (pl ~x) /ʒø/ nm game; (amusement) play; (au casino) gambling; (Théât) acting; (série) set; (de lumière, ressort) play; en ~ (honneur) at stake; (forces) at work; ~ de cartes (paquet) pack of cards; ~ d'échecs (boîte) chess set; ~ de mots pun; ~ télévisé television quiz; ~ vidéo video game; ~x de grattage scratch cards.

jeudi /ʒødi/ nm Thursday.

jeun: à ~ /aʒœ̃/ loc on an empty stomach.

jeune /ʒœn/ a young; ~ fille girl; ~ pousse (Comm) start-up; ~s mariés newlyweds. ● nmf young person; les ~s young people.

jeûne /ʒøn/ nm fast.

jeunesse /ʒœnɛs/ *nf* youth; (apparence) youthfulness; **la ~** (jeunes) the young.

joaillerie /ʒɔajRi/ *nf* jewellery; (magasin) jeweller's shop.

joie /ʒwa/ *nf* joy.

joindre /ʒwɛ̃dR/ [22] *vt* join (à to); (mains, pieds) put together; (efforts) combine; (contacter) contact; (dans une enveloppe) enclose. □ **se ~ à** *vpr* join.

joint, **~e** /ʒwɛ̃, -t/ *a* (efforts) joint; (pieds) together. ● *nm* joint; (de robinet) washer.

joli, **~e** /ʒɔli/ *a* pretty, nice; (somme, profit) nice; **c'est du ~!** (ironique) charming! **c'est bien ~ mais** it is all very well but.

joncher /ʒɔ̃ʃe/ [1] *vt* litter, be strewn over; **jonché de** littered with.

jonction /ʒɔ̃ksjɔ̃/ *nf* junction.

jongleur, **-euse** /ʒɔ̃glœR, øz/ *nm, f* juggler.

jonquille /ʒɔ̃kij/ *nf* daffodil.

joue /ʒu/ *nf* cheek.

jouer /ʒwe/ [1] *vt/i* play; (Théât) act; (au casino) gamble; (fonctionner) work; (film, pièce) put on; (cheval) back; (être important) count; **~ à** (jeu, Sport) play; **~ de** (Mus) play; **~ la comédie** put on an act; **bien joué!** well done!

jouet /ʒwɛ/ *nm* toy; (personne: fig) plaything; (victime) victim.

joueur, **-euse** /ʒwœR, -øz/ *nm, f* player; (parieur) gambler.

joufflu, **~e** /ʒufly/ *a* chubby-cheeked; (visage) chubby.

jouir /ʒwiR/ [2] *vi* (sexe) come; **~ de** (droit, avantage) enjoy; (bien, concession) enjoy the use of.

jouissance *nf* pleasure; (usage) use (**de qch** of sth).

joujou (pl **~x**) /ʒuʒu/ *nm* ▣ toy.

jour /ʒuR/ *nm* day; (opposé à nuit) day(time); (lumière) daylight; (aspect) light; (ouverture) gap; **de nos**

~s nowadays; **du ~ au lendemain** overnight; **il fait ~** it is (day)light; **~ chômé** *ou* **férié** public holiday; **~ de fête** holiday; **~ ouvrable**, **~ de travail** working day; **mettre à ~** update; **mettre au ~** uncover; **au grand ~** in the open; **donner le ~** give birth; **voir le ~** be born; **vivre au ~ le jour** live from day to day.

journal (pl **-aux**) /ʒuRnal, -o/ *nm* (news)paper; (spécialisé) journal; (intime) diary; (à la radio) news; **~ de bord** log-book.

journalier, **-ière** /ʒuRnalje, -jɛR/ *a* daily.

journalisme /ʒuRnalism/ *nm* journalism. **journaliste** *nmf* journalist.

journée /ʒuRne/ *nf* day.

jovial, **~e** (mpl **-iaux**) /ʒɔvjal, -jo/ *a* jovial.

joyau (pl **~x**) /ʒwajo/ *nm* gem.

joyeux, **-euse** /ʒwajø, -z/ *a* merry, joyful; **~ anniversaire** happy birthday.

jubiler /ʒybile/ [1] *vi* be jubilant.

jucher /ʒyʃe/ [1] *vt* perch. □ **se ~** *vpr* perch.

judaïsme /ʒydaism/ *nm* Judaism.

judiciaire /ʒydisjɛR/ *a* judicial.

judicieux, **-ieuse** /ʒydisjø, -z/ *a* judicious.

judo /ʒydo/ *nm* judo.

juge /ʒyʒ/ *nm* judge; (arbitre) referee; **~ de paix** Justice of the Peace; **~ de touche** linesman.

jugé: au ~ /oʒyʒe/ *loc* by guesswork.

jugement /ʒyʒmɑ̃/ *nm* judgement; (criminel) sentence.

juger /ʒyʒe/ [40] *vt/i* judge; (estimer) consider (**que** that); **~ de** judge.

juguler /ʒygyle/ [1] *vt* stamp out; curb.

juif, **-ive** /ʒɥif, -v/ *a* Jewish. ● *nm, f* Jew.

juillet /ʒɥijɛ/ *nm* July.

juin /ʒɥɛ̃/ nm June.

jumeau, -elle (mpl ~x) /ʒymo, -ɛl/ a & nm, f twin. **jumeler** [38] vt (villes) twin.

jumelles /ʒymɛl/ nfpl binoculars.

jument /ʒymɑ̃/ nf mare.

junior /ʒynjɔʀ/ a & nmf junior.

jupe /ʒyp/ nf skirt.

jupon /ʒypɔ̃/ nm slip, petticoat.

juré, ~e /ʒyʀe/ nm, f juror. ● a sworn.

jurer /ʒyʀe/ [1] vt swear (que that). ● vi (pester) swear; (contraster) clash (avec with).

juridiction /ʒyʀidiksjɔ̃/ nf jurisdiction; (tribunal) court of law.

juridique /ʒyʀidik/ a legal.

juriste /ʒyʀist/ nmf legal expert.

juron /ʒyʀɔ̃/ nm swear-word.

jury /ʒyʀi/ nm (Jur) jury; (examinateurs) panel of judges.

jus /ʒy/ nm juice; (de viande) gravy; ~ **de fruit** fruit juice.

jusque /ʒysk(ə)/ prep **jusqu'à** (up) to, as far as; (temps) until, till; (limite) up to; (y compris) even, **jusqu'à ce que** until; **jusqu'à présent** until now; **jusqu'en** until; **jusqu'où?** how far?; ~ **dans, ~ sur** as far as.

juste /ʒyst/ a fair, just; (légitime) just; (correct, exact) right; (vrai) true; (vêtement) tight; (quantité) on the short side; **le ~ milieu** the happy medium. ● adv rightly, correctly; (chanter) in tune, (seulement, exactement) just; (un peu) ~ (calculer, mesurer) a bit fine ou close; **au** ~ exactly; **c'était** ~ (presque raté) it was a close thing.

justement adv (précisément) precisely; (à l'instant) just; (avec justesse) correctly; (légitimement) justifiably.

justesse /ʒystɛs/ nf accuracy; **de** ~ just, narrowly.

justice /ʒystis/ nf justice; (autorités) law; (tribunal) court.

justifier /ʒystifje/ [45] vt justify.

● vi ~ **de** prove. □ **se** ~ vpr justify oneself.

juteux, -euse /ʒytø, -z/ a juicy.

juvénile /ʒyvenil/ a youthful; (délinquance, mortalité) juvenile.

kaki /kaki/ a inv & nm khaki.

kangourou /kɑ̃guʀu/ nm kangaroo.

karaté /kaʀate/ nm karate.

kart /kaʀt/ nm go-cart.

kascher /kaʃɛʀ/ a inv kosher.

kayak /kajak/ nm kayak.

képi /kepi/ nm kepi.

kermesse /kɛʀmɛs/ nf fête.

kidnapper /kidnape/ [1] vt kidnap.

kilo /kilo/ nm kilo.

kilogramme /kilogʀam/ nm kilogram.

kilométrage /kilometʀaʒ/ nm ≈ mileage. **kilomètre** nm kilometre.

kinésithérapeute /kineziteʀapøt/ nmf physiotherapist. **kinésithérapie** nf physiotherapy.

kiosque /kjɔsk/ nm kiosk; ~ **à musique** bandstand.

kit /kit/ nm kit. ~ **mains libres conducteur** hands-free kit.

klaxon® /klaksɔn/ nm (Auto) horn. **klaxonner** [1] vi sound one's horn.

Ko abrév m (**kilo-octet**) (Ordinat) KB.

KO abrév m (**knock-out**) KO Ⅱ.

K-way® /kawɛ/ nm inv windcheater.

kyste /kist/ nm cyst.

l', la /l, la/ ⇒LE.

là /la/

● *adverbe*

····▸ (dans ce lieu) there; (ici) here; (chez soi) in; **c'est ~ que** this is where; **~ où** where; **par ~** (dans cette direction) this way; (dans cette zone) around there; **de ~** hence.

····▸ (à ce moment) then; **c'est ~ que** that's when.

····▸ **cet homme-~** that man; **ces maisons-~** those houses.

● *interjection*

····▸ **~! c'est fini** there (now), it's all over!

là-bas /laba/ *adv* there; (à l'endroit que l'on indique) over there.

label /labɛl/ *nm* seal, label.

laboratoire /labɔʀatwaʀ/ *nm* laboratory.

laborieux, -ieuse /labɔʀjø, -z/ *a* laborious; (*personne*) industrious; **classes laborieuses** working classes.

labour /labuʀ/ *nm* ploughing; (US) plowing. **labourer** [1] *vt* plough; (US) plow; (*déchirer*) rip at.

labyrinthe /labiʀɛ̃t/ *nm* maze, labyrinth.

lac /lak/ *nm* lake.

lacer /lase/ [10] *vt* lace up.

lacet /lasɛ/ *nm* (de chaussure) (shoe-)lace; (de route) sharp bend.

lâche /lɑʃ/ *a* cowardly; (détendu) loose; (sans rigueur) lax. ● *nmf* coward.

lâcher /lɑʃe/ [1] *vt* let go of; (laisser tomber) drop; (abandonner) give up; (laisser) leave; (libérer) release; (*flèche, balle*) fire; (*juron, phrase*) come out with; (desserrer) loosen; **~ prise** let go. ● *vi* give way.

lâcheté /lɑʃte/ *nf* cowardice.

lacrymogène /lakʀimɔʒɛn/ *a* **gaz ~** tear gas.

lacune /lakyn/ *nf* gap.

là-dedans /lad(ə)dɑ̃/ *adv* (près) in here; (plus loin) in there.

là-dessous /lad(ə)su/ *adv* (près) under here; (plus loin) under there.

là-dessus /lad(ə)sy/ *adv* (sur une surface) on here; (plus loin) on there; (sur ce) with that; (quelque temps après) after that; **qu'avez-vous à dire ~?** what have you got to say about it?

ladite /ladit/ ⇒LEDIT.

lagune /lagyn/ *nf* lagoon.

là-haut /lao/ *adv* (en hauteur) up here; (plus loin) up there; (à l'étage) upstairs.

laïc /laik/ *nm* layman.

laid, ~e /lɛ, lɛd/ *a* ugly; (*action*) vile. **laideur** *nf* ugliness.

lainage /lɛnaʒ/ *nm* woollen garment.

laine /lɛn/ *nf* wool; **de ~** woollen.

laïque /laik/ *a* (état, loi) secular; (habit, personne) lay; (école) nondenominational. ● *nmf* layman, laywoman.

laisse /lɛs/ *nf* lead, leash; **tenir en ~** keep on a lead.

laisser /lese/ [1] *vt* (déposer) leave, drop off; (confier) leave (à qn with sb); (abandonner) leave; (rendre) **~ qn perplexe/froid** leave sb puzzled/cold; **~ qch à qn** (céder, prêter) let sb have sth; (donner) (*choix, temps*) give sb sth. □ **se ~**

vpr se ~ **persuader/insulter** let oneself be persuaded/insulted; **elle ne se laisse pas faire** she won't be pushed around; **laisse-toi faire** leave it to me/him/her *etc.*; **se ~ aller** let oneself go. ● *v aux* ~ **qn/qch faire** let sb/sth do; **laisse-moi faire** (ne m'aide pas) let me do it; (je m'en occupe) leave it to me; **laisse faire!** so what! **laisser-aller** *nm inv* carelessness; (dans la tenue) scruffiness. **laissez-passer** *nm inv* pass.

lait /lɛ/ *nm* milk; ~ **longue conservation** long-life *ou* UHT milk; **frère/sœur de** ~ foster-brother/-sister. **laitage** *nm* milk product. **laiterie** *nf* dairy. **laiteux, -euse** *a* milky.

laitier, -ière /letje, -jɛʀ/ *a* dairy. ● *nm, f* (livreur) milkman, milkwoman.

laiton /lɛtɔ̃/ *nm* brass.

laitue /lety/ *nf* lettuce.

lama /lama/ *nm* llama.

lambeau (*pl* ~**x**) /lɑ̃bo/ *nm* shred; **en** ~**x** in shreds.

lame /lam/ *nf* blade; (lamelle) strip; (vague) wave; ~ **de fond** ground swell; ~ **de rasoir** razor blade.

lamentable /lamɑ̃tabl/ *a* deplorable. **lamenter (se)** [1] *vpr* moan (**sur** about, over).

lampadaire /lɑ̃padɛʀ/ *nm* standard lamp; (de rue) street lamp.

lampe /lɑ̃p/ *nf* lamp; (ampoule) bulb; (de radio) valve; ~ **(de poche)** torch; (US) flashlight; ~ **à souder** blowlamp; ~ **de chevet** bedside lamp; ~ **solaire**, ~ **à bronzer** sunlamp.

lance /lɑ̃s/ *nf* spear; (de tournoi) lance; (tuyau) hose; ~ **d'incendie** fire hose.

lancement /lɑ̃smɑ̃/ *nm* throwing; (de navire, de missile, mise sur le marché) launch.

lance-missiles /lɑ̃smisil/ *nm inv* missile launcher.

lance-pierres /lɑ̃spjɛʀ/ *nm inv* catapult.

lancer /lɑ̃se/ [10] *vt* throw; (avec force) hurl; (navire, idée, artiste) launch; (émettre) give out; (regard) cast; (moteur) start. □ **se** ~ *vpr* (Sport) gain momentum; (se précipiter) rush; **se** ~ **dans** (explication) launch into; (passe-temps) take up. ● *nm* throw; (action) throwing.

lancinant, -e /lɑ̃sinɑ̃, -t/ *a* (douleur) shooting; (problème) nagging.

landau /lɑ̃do/ *nm* pram; (US) baby carriage.

lande /lɑ̃d/ *nf* heath, moor.

langage /lɑ̃gaʒ/ *nm* language; ~ **machine/de programmation** machine/programming language.

langouste /lɑ̃gust/ *nf* spiny lobster. **langoustine** *nf* Dublin Bay prawn.

langue /lɑ̃g/ *nf* (Anat) tongue; (Ling) language; **il m'a tiré la** ~ he stuck his tongue out at me; **de** ~ **anglaise** (personne) English-speaking; (journal) English-language; ~ **maternelle** mother tongue; ~ **vivante** modern language.

lanière /lanjɛʀ/ *nf* strap.

lanterne /lɑ̃tɛʀn/ *nf* lantern; (électrique) lamp; (de voiture) sidelight.

lapin /lapɛ̃/ *nm* rabbit; **poser un** ~ **à qn** 🔟 stand sb up; **le coup du** ~ rabbit punch; (en voiture) whiplash injury.

lapsus /lapsys/ *nm* slip (of the tongue).

laque /lak/ *nf* lacquer; (pour cheveux) hairspray; (peinture) gloss paint.

laquelle /lakɛl/ ⇒LEQUEL.

lard /laʀ/ *nm* streaky bacon.

large /larʒ/ *a* wide, broad; (grand) large; (généreux) generous; **avoir les idées ~s** be broad-minded; **~ d'esprit** broad-minded. ●*adv* (calculer, mesurer) on the generous side; **voir ~** think big. ●*nm* **faire 10 cm de ~** be 10 cm wide; **le ~** (mer) the open sea; **au ~ de** (Naut) off. **largement** *adv* widely; (ouvrir) wide; (amplement) amply; (généreusement) generously; (au moins) easily.

largesse /larʒɛs/ *nf* generous gift.

largeur /larʒœr/ *nf* width, breadth; **~ d'esprit** broad-mindedness.

larguer /large/ [1] *vt* drop; **~ les amarres** cast off.

larme /larm/ *nf* tear; (goutte □) drop; **en ~s** in tears.

larmoyant, **~e** /larmwajã, -t/ *a* full of tears. **larmoyer** [31] *vi* (yeux) water; (pleurnicher) whine.

larynx /larɛ̃ks/ *nm* larynx.

las, **~se** /lɑ, lɑs/ *a* weary.

lasagnes /lazaɲ/ *nfpl* lasagna.

laser /lazɛr/ *nm* laser.

lasser /lɑse/ [1] *vt* weary. □ **se ~** *vpr* grow tired, get weary (**de** of).

latéral, **~e** (*mpl* **-aux**) /lateral, -o/ *a* lateral.

latin, **~e** /latɛ̃, -in/ *a* Latin. ●*nm* (Ling) Latin.

latte /lat/ *nf* lath; (de plancher) board; (de siège) slat; (de mur, plafond) lath.

lauréat, **~e** /lɔrea, -t/ *a* prize-winning. ●*nm, f* prize-winner.

laurier /lɔrje/ *nm* (Bot) laurel; (Culin) bay-leaves.

lavable /lavabl/ *a* washable.

lavabo /lavabo/ *nm* wash-basin; **~s** toilet(s).

lavage /lavaʒ/ *nm* washing; **~ de cerveau** brainwashing.

lavande /lavãd/ *nf* lavender.

lave /lav/ *nf* lava.

lave-glace (*pl* **~s**) /lavglas/ *nm* windscreen washer.

lave-linge /lavlɛ̃ʒ/ *nm inv* washing machine.

laver /lave/ [1] *vt* wash; **~ qn de** (fig) clear sb of. □ **se ~** *vpr* wash (oneself); **se ~ les mains** wash one's hands.

laverie /lavri/ *nf* **~ (automatique)** launderette; (US) laundromat.

lave-vaisselle /lavvɛsɛl/ *nm inv* dishwasher.

laxatif, **-ive** /laksatif, -v/ *a & nm* laxative.

layette /lɛjɛt/ *nf* baby clothes.

le, **la**, **l'** (*pl* **les**) /lə, la, l, le/ **l'** before vowel or mute h.

●*déterminant*

····▸ the.

····▸ (notion générale) **aimer la musique** like music; **l'amour** love.

····▸ (possession) **avoir les yeux verts** have green eyes; **il s'est cassé la jambe** he broke his leg.

····▸ (prix) **3 euros ~ kilo** 3 euros a kilo.

····▸ (temps) **~ lundi** on Mondays; **tous les mardis** every Tuesday.

····▸ (avec nom propre) **les Dury** the Durys; **la reine Margot** Queen Margot; **la Belgique** Belgium.

····▸ (avec adjectif) the; **je veux la rouge** I want the red one; **les riches** the rich.

●*pronom*

····▸ (homme) him; (femme) her; (chose, animal) it; (au pluriel) them.

····▸ (remplaçant une phrase) **je te l'avais bien dit** I told you so; **je ~ croyais aussi** I thought so too.

lécher /leʃe/ [14] *vt* lick; (flamme) lick; (mer) lap.

lèche-vitrines /lɛʃvitʀin/ *nm inv* faire du ~ go window-shopping.

leçon /ləsɔ̃/ *nf* lesson; **faire la ~ à** lecture; ~ **particulière** private lesson; ~s **de conduite** driving lessons.

lecteur, -trice /lɛktœʀ, -tʀis/ *nm, f* reader; (Univ) foreign language assistant; ~ **de cassettes** cassette player; ~ **de disquettes** (disk) drive; ~ **laser** CD player; ~ **optique** optical scanner.

lecture /lɛktyʀ/ *nf* reading.

ledit, ladite (*pl* **lesdit(e)s**) /lədi, ladit, ledi(t)/ *a* the aforementioned.

légal, ~e (*mpl* **-aux**) /legal, -o/ *a* legal. **légaliser** [1] *vt* legalize. **légalité** *nf* legality; (loi) law.

légendaire /leʒɑ̃dɛʀ/ *a* legendary. **légende** *nf* (histoire, inscription) legend; (de carte) key; (d'illustration) caption.

léger, -ère /leʒe, -ɛʀ/ *a* light; (bruit, faute, maladie) slight; (café, argument) weak; (imprudent) thoughtless; (frivole) fickle; **à la légère** thoughtlessly. **légèrement** *adv* lightly; (agir) thoughtlessly; (un peu) slightly. **légèreté** *nf* lightness; thoughtlessness.

légion /leʒjɔ̃/ *nf* legion.

législatif, -ive /leʒislatif, -v/ *a* legislative; **élections législatives** general election.

législature /leʒislatyʀ/ *nf* term of office.

légitime /leʒitim/ *a* (Jur) legitimate; (fig) rightful; **agir en état de ~ défense** act in self-defence. **légitimité** *nf* legitimacy.

legs /lɛg/ *nm* legacy; (d'effets personnels) bequest.

léguer /lege/ [14] *vt* bequeath.

légume /legym/ *nm* vegetable.

lendemain /lɑ̃dmɛ̃/ *nm* **le ~** the next day; (fig) the future; **le ~ de** the day after; **le ~ matin/soir** the

next morning/evening; **du jour au ~** from one day to the next.

lent, ~e /lɑ̃, -t/ *a* slow. **lentement** *adv* slowly. **lenteur** *nf* slowness.

lentille /lɑ̃tij/ *nf* (Culin) lentil; (verre) lens; ~s **de contact** contact lenses.

léopard /leopaʀ/ *nm* leopard.

lèpre /lɛpʀ/ *nf* leprosy.

....

lequel, laquelle (*pl* **lesquel-(le)s**), **auquel** (*pl* **auxquel(le)s**), **duquel** (*pl* **desquel(le)s**) /ləkɛl, lakɛl, lekɛl, okɛl, dykɛl, dekɛl/

à + lequel	= auquel
à + lesquel(le)s	= auxquel(le)s;
de + lequel	= duquel,
de + lesquel(le)s	= desquel(le)s

●*pronom*

····▸ (relatif) (personne) who; (complément indirect) whom; (autres cas) which; **l'ami auquel tu as écrit** the friend to whom you wrote; **les voisins chez lesquels Sophie est allée** the neighbours whose house Sophie went to.

····▸ (interrogatif) which; ~ **tu veux?** which one do you want?

●*adjectif*

····▸ **auquel cas** in which case.

....

les /le/ ⇒LE.

lesbienne /lɛsbjɛn/ *nf* lesbian.

léser /leze/ [14] *vt* wrong.

lésiner /lezine/ [1] *vi* **ne pas ~ sur** not stint on.

lesquels, lesquelles /lekɛl/ ⇒LEQUEL.

lessive /lesiv/ *nf* (poudre) washing-powder; (liquide) washing liquid; (linge, action) washing.

leste /lɛst/ *a* agile, nimble; (grivois) coarse.

Lettonie /letɔni/ *nf* Latvia.

lettre /lɛtʀ/ *nf* letter; **à la ~, au pied de la ~** literally; **en toutes ~s** in full; **les ~s** (Univ) (the) arts.
leucémie /løsemi/ *nf* leukaemia.

leur (*pl* ~s) /lœʀ/
●*pronom personnel invariable*
····▸them; **donne-le ~** give it to them; **je ~ fais confiance** I trust them.
●*adjectif possessif*
····▸their; **~s enfants** their children; **à ~ arrivée** when they arrived.
●**le leur, la leur**, (*pl* **les leurs**) *pronom possessif*
····▸theirs; **chacun le ~** one each; **je suis des ~s** I am one of them.

levain /ləvɛ̃/ *nm* leaven.
levé, ~e /ləve/ *a* (debout) up.
levée /ləve/ *nf* (de peine, de sanctions) lifting; (de courrier) collection; (de troupes, d'impôts) levying.
lever /ləve/ [6] *vt* lift (up), raise; (interdiction) lift; (séance) close; (armée, impôts) levy. ●*vi* (pâte) rise. □ **se ~** *vpr* get up; (soleil, rideau) rise; (jour) break. ●*nm* **au ~** on getting up; **~ du jour** daybreak; **~ de rideau** (Théât) curtain (up); **~ du soleil** sunrise.
levier /ləvje/ *nm* lever; **~ de changement de vitesse** gear lever.
lèvre /lɛvʀ/ *nf* lip.
lévrier /levʀije/ *nm* greyhound.
levure /ləvyʀ/ *nf* yeast; **~ chimique** baking powder.
lexique /lɛksik/ *nm* vocabulary; (glossaire) lexicon.
lézard /lezaʀ/ *nm* lizard.
lézarde /lezaʀd/ *nf* crack.
liaison /ljɛzɔ̃/ *nf* connection; (transport, Ordinat) link; (contact) contact; (Gram, Mil) liaison;

(amoureuse) affair; **être en ~ avec** be in contact with; **assurer la ~ entre** liaise between.
liane /ljan/ *nf* creeper.
Liban /libɑ̃/ *nm* Lebanon.
libeller /libele/ [1] *vt* (chèque) write; (contrat) draw up; **libellé à l'ordre de** made out to.
libellule /libelyl/ *nf* dragonfly.
libéral, ~e (*mpl* **-aux**) /libeʀal, -o/ *a* liberal; **les professions ~es** the professions.
libérateur, -trice /libeʀatœʀ, -tʀis/ *a* liberating. ●*nm, f* liberator. **libération** *nf* release; (de pays) liberation.
libérer /libeʀe/ [14] *vt* (personne) free, release; (pays) liberate, free; (bureau, lieux) vacate; (gaz) release. □ **se ~** *vpr* free oneself.
liberté /libɛʀte/ *nf* freedom, liberty; (loisir) free time; **être/ mettre en ~** be/set free; **~ conditionnelle** parole; **~ provisoire** provisional release (pending trial); **~ surveillée** probation; **~s publiques** civil liberties.
Libertel /libɛʀtɛl/ *nm* (Internet) Freenet.
libraire /libʀɛʀ/ *nmf* bookseller. **librairie** *nf* bookshop.
libre /libʀ/ *a* free; (place, pièce) vacant, free; (passage) clear; (école) private (usually religious); **~ de qch/de faire** free from sth/to do. **libre-échange** *nm* free trade. **libre-service** (*pl* **libres-services**) *nm* (magasin) self-service shop; (restaurant) self-service restaurant.
licence /lisɑ̃s/ *nf* licence; (Univ) degree.
licencié, ~e /lisɑ̃sje/ *nm, f* graduate; **~ ès lettres/sciences** Bachelor of Arts/Science.
licenciements /lisɑ̃simɑ̃/ *nm* redundancy; (pour faute) dismissal.

licencier [45] *vt* make redundant; (pour faute) dismiss.

licorne /likɔʀn/ *nf* unicorn.

liège /ljɛʒ/ *nm* cork.

lien /ljɛ̃/ *nm* (rapport) link; (attache) bond, tie; (corde) rope; **~s affectifs/de parenté** emotional/family ties.

lier /lje/ [45] *vt* tie (up), bind; (relier) link; (engager, unir) bind; **~ conversation** strike up a conversation; **ils sont très liés** they are very close. □ **se ~ avec** *vpr* make friends with.

lierre /ljɛʀ/ *nm* ivy.

lieu (*pl* **~x**) /ljø/ *nm* place; **~x** (locaux) premises; (d'un accident) scene; **sur les ~x** at the scene; **au ~ de** instead of; **avoir ~** take place; **donner ~ à** give rise to; **tenir ~ de** serve as; **s'il y a ~** if necessary; **en premier ~** firstly; **en dernier ~** lastly; **~ commun** commonplace; **~ de rencontre** meeting place.

lièvre /ljɛvʀ/ *nm* hare.

lifting /liftiŋ/ *nm* face-lift.

ligne /liɲ/ *nf* line; (trajet) route; (de métro, train) line; (formes) lines; (de femme) figure; **en ~** (joueurs) lined up; (au téléphone) on the phone; (Ordinat) on line; **~ spécialisée** (Internet) dedicated line.

ligoter /ligɔte/ [1] *vt* tie up.

ligue /lig/ *nf* league. **liguer (se)** [1] *vpr* join forces (**contre** against).

lilas /lila/ *nm & a inv* lilac.

limace /limas/ *nf* slug.

limande /limɑ̃d/ *nf* (poisson) dab.

lime /lim/ *nf* file; **~ à ongles** nail file.

limitation /limitasjɔ̃/ *nf* limitation; **~ de vitesse** speed limit.

limite /limit/ *nf* limit; (de jardin, champ) boundary; **à la ~ de** (fig) verging on, bordering on; **à la ~**
if it comes to it, at a pinch; **dans une certaine ~** up to a point; **dans la ~ du possible** as far as possible. ● *a* (vitesse, âge) maximum; **cas ~** borderline case; **date ~** deadline; **date ~ de vente** sell-by date.

limiter /limite/ [1] *vt* limit; (délimiter) form the border of. □ **se ~** *vpr* limit oneself (**à** to).

limonade /limɔnad/ *nf* lemonade.

limpide /lɛ̃pid/ *a* limpid, clear.

lin /lɛ̃/ *nm* (tissu) linen.

linge /lɛ̃ʒ/ *nm* linen; (lessive) washing; (torchon) cloth; **~ (de corps)** underwear. **lingerie** *nf* underwear. **lingette** *nf* wipe.

lingot /lɛ̃go/ *nm* ingot.

linguistique /lɛ̃gɥistik/ *a* linguistic. ● *nf* linguistics.

lion /ljɔ̃/ *nm* lion; **le L~** Leo. **lionceau** (*pl* **~x**) *nm* lion cub. **lionne** *nf* lioness.

liquidation /likidasjɔ̃/ *nf* liquidation; (vente) (clearance) sale; **entrer en ~** go into liquidation.

liquide /likid/ *a* liquid. ● *nm* (argent) **~** ready money; **payer en ~** pay cash; **~ de frein** brake fluid.

liquider /likide/ [1] *vt* liquidate; (vendre) sell.

lire /liʀ/ [39] *vt/i* read. ● *nf* lira.

lis¹ /li/ ⇒LIRE[39].

lis² /lis/ *nm* (fleur) lily.

lisible /lizibl/ *a* legible; (roman) readable.

lisière /lizjɛʀ/ *nf* edge.

lisse /lis/ *a* smooth.

liste /list/ *nf* list; **~ d'attente** waiting list; **~ électorale** register of voters; **être sur (la) ~ rouge** be ex-directory.

listing /listiŋ/ *nm* printout.

lit /li/ *nm* bed; **se mettre au ~** get into bed; **~ de camp** camp-bed;

$\sim$ **d'enfant** cot; $\sim$ **d'une personne** single bed; $\sim$ **de deux personnes, grand** $\sim$ double bed.

literie /litʀi/ *nf* bedding.

litière /litjɛʀ/ *nf* litter.

litige /litiʒ/ *nm* dispute.

litre /litʀ/ *nm* litre.

littéraire /liteʀɛʀ/ *a* literary; (*études, formation*) arts.

littéral, ~e (*mpl* **-aux**) /liteʀal, -o/ *a* literal.

littérature /liteʀatyʀ/ *nf* literature.

littoral (*pl* **-aux**) /litoʀal, -o/ *nm* coast.

Lituanie /lityani/ *nf* Lithuania.

livide /livid/ *a* deathly pale.

livraison /livʀɛzɔ̃/ *nf* delivery.

livre /livʀ/ *nf* (monnaie, poids) pound. ● *nm* book; $\sim$ **de bord** log-book; $\sim$ **de compte** books; $\sim$ **de poche** paperback.

livrer /livʀe/ [1] *vt* (Comm) deliver; (*abandonner*) give over (à to); (*remettre*) (*coupable, document*) hand over (à to); **livré à soi-même** left to oneself. □ **se** $\sim$ *vpr* (se rendre) give oneself up (à to); **se** $\sim$ **à** (*boisson, actes*) indulge in; (*ami*) confide in.

livret /livʀɛ/ *nm* book; (Mus) libretto; $\sim$ **de caisse d'épargne** savings book; $\sim$ **scolaire** school report (book).

livreur, -euse /livʀœʀ, -øz/ *nm, f* delivery man, delivery woman.

local¹, ~e (*mpl* **-aux**) /lɔkal, -o/ *a* local.

local² (*pl* **-aux**) /lɔkal, -o/ *nm* premises; **locaux** premises.

localement /lɔkalmɑ̃/ *adv* locally.

localiser /lɔkalize/ [1] *vt* (*repérer*) locate; (*circonscrire*) localize.

locataire /lɔkatɛʀ/ *nmf* tenant; (de chambre) lodger.

location /lɔkasjɔ̃/ *nf* (de maison) renting; (de voiture, de matériel) hire,

rental; (de place) booking, reservation; (par propriétaire) renting out; hiring out; **en** $\sim$ (*voiture*) on hire, rented; (*habiter*) in rented accommodation.

locomotive /lɔkɔmɔtiv/ *nf* engine, locomotive.

locution /lɔkysjɔ̃/ *nf* phrase.

loft /lɔft/ *nm* loft (apartment).

loge /lɔʒ/ *nf* (de concierge, de franc-maçons) lodge; (d'acteur) dressing-room; (de spectateur) box.

logement /lɔʒmɑ̃/ *nm* accommodation; (appartement) flat; (habitat) housing.

loger /lɔʒe/ [40] *vt* (*réfugié, famille*) house; (*ami*) put up; (*client*) accommodate. ● *vi* live. □ **se** $\sim$ *vpr* live; **trouver à se** $\sim$ find accommodation; **se** $\sim$ **dans** (*balle*) lodge itself in.

logiciel /lɔʒisjɛl/ *nm* software; $\sim$ **contributif** shareware; $\sim$ **d'application** application software; $\sim$ **de groupe** groupware; $\sim$ **de jeux** games software; $\sim$ **de navigation** browser; $\sim$ **public** freeware.

logique /lɔʒik/ *a* logical. ● *nf* logic.

logis /lɔʒi/ *nm* dwelling.

logistique /lɔʒistik/ *nf* logistics.

loi /lwa/ *nf* law.

loin /lwɛ̃/ *adv* far (away); **au** $\sim$ far away; **de** $\sim$ from far away; (de beaucoup) by far; $\sim$ **de là** far from it; **plus** $\sim$ further; **il revient de** $\sim$ (fig) he had a close shave.

lointain, ~e /lwɛ̃tɛ̃, -ɛn/ *a* distant. ● *nm* distance; **dans le** $\sim$ in the distance.

loisir /lwaziʀ/ *nm* (spare) time; $\sim$**s** (temps libre) leisure, spare time; (distractions) leisure activities; **à** $\sim$ at one's leisure; **avoir le** $\sim$ **de faire** have time to do.

londonien, ~ne /lɔ̃dɔnjɛ̃, -ɛn/ *a* London. **L~, ~e** *nm, f* Londoner.

Londres /lɔ̃dʀ/ npr London.

long, longue /lɔ̃, lɔ̃g/ a long; à ~ **terme** long-term; **être ~ à faire** be a long time doing. ● nm **de ~** (mesure) long; **de ~ en large** back and forth; **(tout) le ~ de** (all) along. ● adv **en dire ~ sur qn/qch** say a lot about sb/sth; **en savoir plus ~ sur** know more about.

longer /lɔ̃ʒe/ [40] vt go along; (limiter) border.

longitude /lɔ̃ʒityd/ nf longitude.

longtemps /lɔ̃tɑ̃/ adv a long time; **avant ~** before long; **trop ~** too long; **ça prendra ~** it will take a long time; **prendre plus ~ que prévu** take longer than anticipated.

longuement /lɔ̃gmɑ̃/ adv (longtemps) for a long time; (en détail) at length.

longueur /lɔ̃gœʀ/ nf length; **~s** (de texte) over-long parts; **à ~ de journée** all day long; **en ~** lengthwise; **~ d'onde** wavelength.

lopin /lɔpɛ̃/ nm **~ de terre** patch of land.

loque /lɔk/ nf **~s** rags; **~ (humaine)** (human) wreck.

loquet /lɔkɛ/ nm latch.

lors de /lɔʀdə/ prép (au moment de) at the time of; (pendant) during.

lorsque /lɔʀsk(ə)/ conj when.

losange /lɔzɑ̃ʒ/ nm diamond.

lot /lo/ nm (portion) share; (aux enchères) lot; (Ordinat) batch; (destin) lot; **gagner le gros ~** hit the jackpot.

loterie /lɔtʀi/ nf lottery.

lotion /losjɔ̃/ nf lotion.

lotissement /lɔtismɑ̃/ nm (à construire) building plot; (construit) (housing) development.

louable /luabl/ a praiseworthy.

louange /luɑ̃ʒ/ nf praise.

louche /luʃ/ a shady, dubious. ● nf ladle.

loucher /luʃe/ [1] vi squint.

louer /lwe/ [1] vt (approuver) praise (de for); (prendre en location) (maison) rent; (voiture, matériel) hire; (place) book, reserve; (donner en location) (maison) rent out; (matériel) rent out, hire out; **à ~** to let, for rent (US).

loufoque /lufɔk/ a 🔲 crazy.

loup /lu/ nm wolf.

loupe /lup/ nf magnifying glass.

louper /lupe/ [1] vt 🔲 miss; (examen) flunk 🔲.

lourd, ~e /luʀ, -d/ a heavy; (faute) serious; **~ de dangers** fraught with danger; **il fait ~** it's close ou muggy.

loutre /lutʀ/ nf otter.

louveteau (pl ~x) /luvto/ nm wolf cub; (scout) Cub (Scout).

loyal, ~e (mpl -aux) /lwajal, -o/ a loyal, faithful; (honnête) fair.

loyauté nf loyalty; fairness.

loyer /lwaje/ nm rent.

lu /ly/ →LIRE [39].

lubrifiant /lybʀifjɑ̃/ nm lubricant.

lucide /lysid/ a lucid **lucidité** nf lucidity.

lucratif, -ive /lykʀatif, -v/ a lucrative; **à but non ~** non-profit-making.

ludiciel /lydisjɛl/ nm (Ordinat) games software.

lueur /lɥœʀ/ nf (faint) light, glimmer; (fig) glimmer, gleam.

luge /lyʒ/ nf toboggan.

lugubre /lygybʀ/ a gloomy.

L

lui /lɥi/

● pronom

⋯▸ (masculin) (sujet) he; **~, il est à l'étranger** he's abroad; **c'est ~!** it's him!; (objet) him; (animal) it; **c'est à ~** it's his; **elle conduit mieux que ~** she's a better driver than he is.

⋯▸ (féminin) her; **je ~ ai annoncé** I told her.

····▸ (masculin/féminin) **donne-le-~**
: give it to him/her.

lui-même /lɥimɛm/ *pron* himself;
(animal) itself.

luire /lɥiʀ/ [17] *vi* shine; (reflet
humide) glisten; (reflet chaud, faible)
glow.

lumière /lymjɛʀ/ *nf* light; **~s**
(connaissances) knowledge; **faire
(toute) la ~ sur une affaire** clear a
matter up.

luminaire /lyminɛʀ/ *nm* lamp.

lumineux, -euse /lyminø, -z/ *a*
luminous; (éclairé) illuminated;
(*rayon*) of light; (radieux) radiant;
source lumineuse light source.

lunaire /lynɛʀ/ *a* lunar.

lunatique /lynatik/ *a*
temperamental.

lunch /lœnʃ/ *nm* buffet lunch.

lundi /lœdi/ *nm* Monday.

lune /lyn/ *nf* moon; **~ de miel**
honeymoon.

lunettes /lynɛt/ *nfpl* glasses; (de
protection) goggles; **~ de ski/
natation** ski/swimming goggles; **~
noires** dark glasses; **~ de soleil**
sun-glasses.

lustre /lystʀ/ *nm* (éclat) lustre;
(objet) chandelier.

lutin /lytɛ̃/ *nm* goblin.

lutte /lyt/ *nf* fight, struggle; (Sport)
wrestling. **lutter** [1] *vi* fight,
struggle; (Sport) wrestle. **lutteur,
-euse** *nm, f* fighter; (Sport)
wrestler.

luxe /lyks/ *nm* luxury; **de ~**
luxury; (*produit*) de luxe.

Luxembourg /lyksɑ̃buʀ/ *nm*
Luxemburg.

luxer (se) /(sə)lykse/ [1] *vpr* **se
~ le genou** dislocate one's knee.

luxueux, -euse /lyksɥø, -z/ *a*
luxurious.

lycée /lise/ *nm* (secondary)
school. **lycéen, ~ne** *nm, f* pupil
(at secondary school).

lyophilisé, ~e /ljɔfilize/ *a*
freeze-dried.

lyrique /liʀik/ *a* (*poésie*) lyric;
(passionné) lyrical; **artiste/théâtre ~**
opera singer/house.

lys /lis/ *nm* lily.

m' /m/ ⇒ME.

ma /ma/ ⇒MON.

macabre /makabʀ/ *a* macabre.

macadam /makadam/ *nm*
Tarmac®.

macaron /makaʀɔ̃/ *nm* (gâteau)
macaroon; (insigne) badge.

macédoine /masedwan/ *nf*
mixed diced vegetables; **~ de
fruits** fruit salad.

macérer /maseʀe/ [14] *vt/i* soak;
(dans du vinaigre) pickle.

mâcher /mɑʃe/ [1] *vt* chew; **ne
pas ~ ses mots** not mince one's
words.

machin /maʃɛ̃/ *nm* ▯ (chose)
thing; (dont on ne trouve pas le nom)
whatsit ▯.

machinal, ~e (*mpl* -aux)
/maʃinal, -o/ *a* automatic.
machinalement *adv*
mechanically, automatically.

machination /maʃinasjɔ̃/ *nf*
plot; **des ~s** machinations.

machine /maʃin/ *nf* machine;
(d'un train, navire) engine; **~ à écrire**
typewriter; **~ à laver/coudre**
washing-/sewing-machine; **~ à
sous** fruit machine; (US) slot-
machine. **machine-outil** (*pl*
machines-outils) *nf* machine
tool. **machinerie** *nf* machinery.

machiniste /maʃinist/ *nm* (Théât)
stage-hand; (conducteur) driver.

mâchoire /maʃwaʀ/ *nf* jaw.

mâchonner /maʃɔne/ [1] *vt*
chew.

maçon /masɔ̃/ *nm* (entrepreneur)
builder; (poseur de briques)
bricklayer; (qui construit en pierre)
mason. **maçonnerie** *nf* (briques)
brickwork; (pierres) stonework,
masonry; (travaux) building.

madame (*pl* **mesdames**)
/madam, medam/ *nf* (à une
inconnue) (dans une lettre) **M∼** Dear
Madam; **bonjour, ∼** good
morning; **mesdames et messieurs**
ladies and gentlemen; (à une femme
dont on connaît le nom) (dans une lettre)
Chère M∼ Dear Mrs *ou* Ms X;
bonjour, ∼ good morning Mrs *ou*
Ms X; **oui M∼ le Ministre** yes
Minister; (formule de respect) **oui M∼**
yes madam.

mademoiselle (*pl*
mesdemoiselles) /madmwazɛl,
medmwazɛl/ *nf* (à une inconnue)
(dans une lettre) **M∼** Dear Madam;
bonjour, ∼ good morning; **entrez
mesdemoiselles** come in (ladies);
(à une jeune fille dont on connaît le nom)
(dans une lettre) **Chère M∼** Dear Ms
ou Miss X; **bonjour, ∼** good
morning Miss *ou* Ms X.

magasin /magazɛ̃/ *nm* shop,
store; (entrepôt) warehouse; (d'une
arme) magazine; **en ∼** in stock.

magazine /magazin/ *nm*
magazine; (émission) programme.

Maghreb /magrɛb/ *nm* North
Africa.

magicien, ∼ne /maʒisjɛ̃, -ɛn/
nm, f magician.

magie /maʒi/ *nf* magic. **magique**
a magic; (mystérieux) magical.

magistral, ∼e (*mpl* **-aux**)
/maʒistral, -o/ *a* masterly; (grand:
hum) tremendous; **cours ∼**
lecture.

magistrat /maʒistra/ *nm*
magistrate.

magistrature /maʒistratyr/ *nf*
judiciary; (fonction) public office.

magner (se) /(sə)maɲe/ [1] *vpr*
🆇 get a move on.

magnétique /maɲetik/ *a*
magnetic. **magnétiser** [1] *vt*
magnetize. **magnétisme** *nm*
magnetism.

magnétophone /maɲetɔfɔn/ *nm*
tape recorder; (à cassettes) cassette
recorder.

magnétoscope /maɲetɔskɔp/
nm video recorder.

magnificence /maɲifisɑ̃s/ *nf*
magnificence. **magnifique** *a*
magnificent.

magot /mago/ *nm* 🆇 hoard (of
money)

magouille /maguj/ *nf* 🆇
scheming, skulduggery.

magret /magrɛ/ *nm* **∼ de canard**
duck breast.

mai /mɛ/ *nm* May.

maigre /mɛgr/ *a* thin; (viande)
lean; (yaourt) low-fat; (fig) poor,
meagre; **faire ∼** abstain from
meat. **maigreur** *nf* thinness;
leanness; (fig) meagreness.

maigrir /megrir/ [2] *vi* get thin-
(ner); (en suivant un régime) slim.
● *vt* make thin(ner).

maille /maj/ *nf* stitch; (de filet)
mesh; **∼ qui file** ladder, run; **avoir
∼ à partir avec qn** have a brush
with sb.

maillet /majɛ/ *nm* mallet.

maillon /majɔ̃/ *nm* link.

maillot /majo/ *nm* (Sport) shirt,
jersey; **∼ (de corps)** vest; (US)
undershirt; **∼ (de bain)**
(swimming) costume.

main /mɛ̃/ *nf* hand; **donner la ∼ à
qn** hold sb's hand; **se donner la ∼**
hold hands; **en ∼s propres** in
person; **en bonnes ∼s** in good
hands; **∼ courante** handrail; **se**

M

faire la ∼ get the hang of it; **perdre la** ∼ lose one's touch; **sous la** ∼ to hand; **vol à** ∼ **armée** armed robbery; **fait (à la)** ∼ handmade; **haut les** ∼**s!** hands up! **main-d'œuvre** (pl **mains-d'œuvre**) nf labour; (ouvriers) labour force.

main-forte /mɛ̃fɔʀt/ nf inv **prêter** ∼ **à qn** come to sb's aid.

maint, ∼**e** /mɛ̃, mɛ̃t/ a many a (+ sg); ∼**s** many; **à** ∼**es reprises** many times.

maintenant /mɛ̃t(ə)nɑ̃/ adv now; (de nos jours) nowadays; (l'époque actuelle) today.

maintenir /mɛ̃t(ə)niʀ/ [58] vt keep, maintain; (soutenir) support, hold up; (affirmer) maintain; (decision) stand by. □ **se** ∼ vpr (tendance) persist; (prix, malade) remain stable.

maintien /mɛ̃tjɛ̃/ nm (attitude) bearing; (conservation) maintenance.

maire /mɛʀ/ nm mayor.

mairie /meʀi/ nf town hall; (administration) town council.

mais /mɛ/ conj but; ∼ **oui** of course; ∼ **non** of course not.

maïs /mais/ nm maize, corn; (Culin) sweetcorn.

maison /mɛzɔ̃/ nf house; (foyer) home; (immeuble) building; ∼ **(de commerce)** firm; **à la** ∼ at home; **rentrer** ou **aller à la** ∼ go home; ∼ **des jeunes (et de la culture)** youth club; ∼ **de repos** rest home; ∼ **de convalescence** convalescent home; ∼ **de retraite** old people's home; ∼ **mère** parent company. ●a inv (Culin) home-made.

maître, -esse /mɛtʀ, -ɛs/ a (qui contrôle) **être** ∼ **de soi** be one's own master; ∼ **de la situation** in control of the situation; (principal) (idée, qualité) key, main. ●nm, f (Scol) teacher; (d'animal) owner,

master. ●nm (expert, guide) master; (dirigeant) leader; ∼ **e** (pl **maîtres de conférences** senior lecturer; ∼ **d'hôtel** head waiter; (domestique) butler. **maître-assistant**, ∼ **e** (pl **maîtres-assistants**) nm, f lecturer.

maître-chanteur (pl **maîtres-chanteurs**) nm blackmailer.

maître-nageur (pl **maîtres-nageurs**) nm swimming instructor. **maîtresse** nf (amante) mistress.

maîtrise /metʀiz/ nf mastery; (contrôle) control; (Mil) supremacy; (Univ) master's degree; ∼ **(de soi)** self-control.

maîtriser /metʀize/ [1] vt (sujet, technique) master; (incendie, sentiment, personne) control. □ **se** ∼ vpr have self-control.

maïzena® /maizena/ nf cornflour.

majesté /maʒɛste/ nf majesty.

majestueux, -euse /maʒɛstɥø, z/ a majestic.

majeur, ∼**e** /maʒœʀ/ a major, main; (Jur) of age; **en** ∼**e partie** mostly; **la** ∼**e partie de** most of. ●nm middle finger.

majoration /maʒɔʀasjɔ̃/ nf increase (**de** in). **majorer** [1] vt increase.

majoritaire /maʒɔʀitɛʀ/ a majority; **être** ∼ be in the majority. **majorité** nf majority; **en** ∼ chiefly.

Majorque /maʒɔʀk/ nf Majorca.

majuscule /maʒyskyl/ a capital. ●nf capital letter.

mal[1] /mal/ adv badly; (incorrectement) wrong(ly); **aller** ∼ (personne) be unwell; (affaires) go badly; ∼ **entendre/comprendre** not hear/understand properly; ∼ **en point** in a bad state; **pas** ∼ quite a lot. ●a inv bad, wrong; **c'est** ∼ **de** it is wrong ou bad to; **ce n'est pas** ∼ 🄸 it's not bad; **Nick**

n'est pas ∼ ⬚ Nick is not bad-looking.

mal² (*pl* **maux**) /mal, mo/ *nm* evil; (*douleur*) pain, ache; (*maladie*) disease; (*effort*) trouble; (*dommage*) harm; (*malheur*) misfortune; **avoir ∼ à la tête/à la gorge** have a headache/a sore throat; **avoir le ∼ de mer/du pays** be seasick/homesick; **faire ∼** hurt; **se faire ∼** hurt oneself; **j'ai ∼** it hurts; **faire du ∼ à** hurt, harm; **se donner du ∼ pour faire qch** go to a lot of trouble to do sth.

malade /malad/ *a* sick, ill; (*bras, œil*) bad; (*plante, poumons, côlon*) diseased; **tomber ∼** fall ill; (*fou* ⬚) mad. ●*nmf* sick person; (*d'un médecin*) patient; **∼ mental** mentally ill person.

maladie /maladi/ *nf* illness, disease; (*manie* ⬚) mania.

maladif, -ive /maladif, -v/ *a* sickly; (*jalousie, peur*) pathological.

maladresse /maladʀɛs/ *nf* clumsiness; (*erreur*) blunder.

maladroit, ∼e /maladʀwa, -t/ *a* clumsy; (*sans tact*) tactless.

malaise /malɛz/ *nm* feeling of faintness; (*gêne*) uneasiness; (*état de crise*) unrest.

malaisé, ∼e /maleze/ *a* difficult.

Malaisie /malɛzi/ *nf* Malaysia.

malaria /malaʀja/ *nf* malaria.

malaxer /malakse/ [1] *vt* (*pétrir*) knead; (*mêler*) mix.

malchance /malʃɑ̃s/ *nf* misfortune. **malchanceux, -euse** *a* unlucky.

mâle /mɑl/ *a* male; (*viril*) manly. ●*nm* male.

malédiction /malediksjɔ̃/ *nf* curse.

maléfice /malefis/ *nm* evil spell. **maléfique** *a* evil.

malentendant, ∼e /malɑ̃tɑ̃dɑ̃, -t/ *a* hard of hearing.

malentendu /malɑ̃tɑ̃dy/ *nm* misunderstanding.

malfaçon /malfasɔ̃/ *nf* defect.

malfaisant, ∼e /malfəzɑ̃, -t/ *a* harmful; (*personne*) evil.

malfaiteur /malfɛtœʀ/ *nm* criminal.

malformation /malfɔʀmasjɔ̃/ *nf* malformation.

malgré /malgʀe/ *prép* in spite of, despite; **∼ tout** nevertheless.

malheur /malœʀ/ *nm* misfortune; (*accident*) accident; **par ∼** unfortunately; **faire un ∼** ⬚ be a big hit; **porter ∼** be *ou* bring bad luck.

malheureusement /malœʀøzmɑ̃/ *adv* unfortunately.

malheureux, -euse /malœʀø, -z/ *a* unhappy; (*regrettable*) unfortunate; (*sans succès*) unlucky; (*insignifiant*) paltry, pathetic. ●*nm, f* (poor) wretch.

malhonnête /malɔnɛt/ *a* dishonest. **malhonnêteté** *nf* dishonesty.

malice /malis/ *nf* mischief; **sans ∼** harmless; **avec ∼** mischievously. **malicieux, -ieuse** *a* mischievous.

malignité /malinite/ *nf* malignancy. **malin, -igne** *a* clever, smart; (*méchant*) malicious; (*tumeur*) malignant; (*difficile* ⬚) difficult.

malingre /malɛ̃gʀ/ *a* puny.

malle /mal/ *nf* (*valise*) trunk; (Auto) boot; (US) trunk.

mallette /malɛt/ *nf* (small) suitcase; (*pour le bureau*) briefcase.

malmener /malmǝne/ [6] *vt* manhandle; (fig) give a rough ride to.

malnutrition /malnytʀisjɔ̃/ *nf* malnutrition.

malodorant, ∼e /malɔdɔʀɑ̃, -t/ *a* smelly, foul-smelling.

M

malpoli, ~e /malpɔli/ a rude, impolite.

malpropre /malprɔpr/ a dirty.

malsain, ~e /malsɛ̃, -ɛn/ a unhealthy.

malt /malt/ nm malt.

Malte /malt/ nf Malta.

maltraiter /maltrete/ [1] vt ill-treat.

malveillance /malvɛjɑ̃s/ nf malice. **malveillant**, ~e a malicious.

maman /mamɑ̃/ nf mum(my), mother; (US) mom(my).

mamelle /mamɛl/ nf teat.

mamelon /mamlɔ̃/ nm (Anat) nipple; (colline) hillock.

mamie /mami/ nf ▣ granny.

mammifère /mamifɛr/ nm mammal.

manche /mɑ̃ʃ/ nf sleeve; (Sport, Pol) round. ● nm (d'un instrument) handle; ~ **à balai** broomstick; (Aviat) joystick. **M**~ nf **la M**~ the Channel; **le tunnel sous la M**~ the Channel tunnel.

manchette /mɑ̃ʃɛt/ nf cuff; (de journal) headline.

manchot, ~te /mɑ̃ʃo, -ɔt/ nm, f one-armed person; (sans bras) armless person. ● nm (oiseau) penguin.

mandarine /mɑ̃darin/ nf tangerine, mandarin (orange).

mandat /mɑ̃da/ nm (postal) money order; (Pol) mandate; (procuration) proxy; (de police) warrant; ~ **d'arrêt** arrest warrant.

mandataire /mɑ̃datɛr/ nm representative; (Jur) proxy.

manège /manɛʒ/ nm riding school; (à la foire) merry-go-round; (manœuvre) trick, ploy.

manette /manɛt/ nf lever; (de jeu) joystick.

mangeable /mɑ̃ʒabl/ a edible.

mangeoire /mɑ̃ʒwar/ nf trough; (pour oiseaux) feeder.

manger /mɑ̃ʒe/ [40] vt eat; (fortune) go through; (profits) eat away at; (économies) use up; (ronger) eat into. ● vi eat; **donner à** ~ **à** feed. ● nm food.

mangue /mɑ̃g/ nf mango.

maniable /manjabl/ a easy to handle.

maniaque /manjak/ a fussy. ● nmf fusspot; (fou) maniac; (fanatique) fanatic; **un** ~ **de l'ordre** a stickler for tidiness.

manie /mani/ nf habit; (marotte) obsession.

maniement /manimɑ̃/ nm handling. **manier** [45] vt handle.

manière /manjɛr/ nf way, manner; ~**s** (politesse) manners; (chichis) fuss; **à la** ~ **de** in the style of; **de** ~ **à** so as to; **de toute** ~ anyway, in any case.

maniéré, ~e /manjere/ a affected.

manif /manif/ nf ▣ demo.

manifestant, ~e /manifɛstɑ̃, -t/ nm, f demonstrator.

manifestation /manifɛstasjɔ̃/ nf expression, manifestation; (de maladie, phénomène) appearance; (Pol) demonstration; (événement) event; ~ **culturelle** cultural event.

manifeste /manifɛst/ a obvious. ● nm manifesto.

manifester /manifɛste/ [1] vt show, manifest; (désir, crainte) express. ● vi (Pol) demonstrate. □ **se** ~ vpr (sentiment) show itself; (apparaître) appear; (répondre à un appel) come forward.

manigance /manigɑ̃s/ nf little plot. **manigancer** [10] vt plot.

manipulation /manipylasjɔ̃/ nf handling; (péj) manipulation.

manivelle /manivɛl/ nf handle, crank.

mannequin /mankɛ̃/ nm (personne) model; (statue) dummy.

manœuvrer /manœvre/ [1] vt

manoeuvre; (*machine*) operate.
● *vi* manoeuvre.

manoir /manwaʀ/ *nm* manor.

manque /mɑ̃k/ *nm* lack (**de** of);
(lacune) gap; ~ **à gagner** loss of
earnings; **en (état de)** ~ having
withdrawal symptoms.

manqué, ~**e** /mɑ̃ke/ *a* (*écrivain*)
failed; **garçon** ~ tomboy.

manquement /mɑ̃kmɑ̃/ *nm* ~ **à**
breach of.

manquer /mɑ̃ke/ [1] *vt* miss;
(gâcher) spoil; ~ **à** (*devoir*) fail in;
~ **de** be short of, lack; **il/ça lui
manque** he misses him/it; ~ (**de**)
faire (faillir) nearly do; **ne manquez
pas de** be sure to; ~ **à sa parole**
break one's word. ● *vi* be short
ou lacking; (être absent) be absent;
(en moins, disparu) be missing; **il me
manque 20 francs** I'm 20 francs
short.

mansarde /mɑ̃saʀd/ *nf* attic
(room).

manteau (*pl* ~**x**) /mɑ̃to/ *nm*
coat.

manucure /manykyʀ/ *nmf*
manicurist. ● *nf* (soins) manicure.

manuel, ~**le** /manɥɛl/ *a* manual.
● *nm* (livre) manual; (Scol)
textbook.

manufacture /manyfaktyʀ/ *nf*
factory; (fabrication) manufacture.

manufacturer [1] *vt*
manufacture.

manuscrit, ~**e** /manyskʀi, -t/ *a*
handwritten. ● *nm* manuscript.

mappemonde /mapmɔ̃d/ *nf*
world map; (sphère) globe.

maquereau (*pl* ~**x**) /makʀo/ *nm*
(poisson) mackerel. ⊡ pimp.

maquette /makɛt/ *nf* (scale)
model; ~ (**de mise en page**)
paste-up.

maquillage /makijaʒ/ *nm*
make-up.

maquiller /makije/ [1] *vt* make

up; (truquer) doctor, fake. □ **se** ~
vpr make (oneself) up.

maquis /maki/ *nm* (paysage)
scrub; (Mil) Maquis, underground.

maraîcher, -**ère** /maʀeʃe, -ɛʀ/
nm, f market gardener; (US) truck
farmer.

marais /maʀɛ/ *nm* marsh.

marasme /maʀasm/ *nm* slump,
stagnation; **dans le** ~ in the
doldrums.

marbre /maʀbʀ/ *nm* marble.

marc /maʀ/ *nm* (eau-de-vie) marc;
~ **de café** coffee grounds.

marchand, ~**e** /maʀʃɑ̃, -d/ *a*
(valeur) market. ● *nm, f* trader;
(de charbon, vins) merchant; ~ **de
couleurs** ironmonger; (US)
hardware merchant; ~ **de
journaux** newsagent; ~ **de légumes**
greengrocer; ~ **de poissons**
fishmonger.

marchander /maʀʃɑ̃de/ [1] *vt*
haggle over. ● *vi* haggle.

marchandise /maʀʃɑ̃diz/ *nf*
goods.

marche /maʀʃ/ *nf* (démarche, trajet)
walk; (rythme) pace; (Mil, Mus, Pol)
march; (d'escalier) step; (Sport)
walking; (de machine) operation,
working; (de véhicule) running; **en**
~ (*train*) moving; (*moteur,
machine*) running; **faire** ~ **arrière**
(véhicule) reverse; **mettre en** ~
start (up); **se mettre en** ~ start
moving.

marché /maʀʃe/ *nm* market;
(contrat) deal; **faire son** ~ do one's
shopping; ~ **aux puces** flea
market; ~ **noir** black market.

marchepied /maʀʃəpje/ *nm* (de
train, camion) step.

marcher /maʀʃe/ [1] *vi* walk;
(poser le pied) tread (**sur** on); (aller)
go; (fonctionner) work, run;
(prospérer) go well; (*film, livre*) do
well; (consentir ⊡) agree; **faire** ~ **qn**
⊡ pull sb's leg.

M

mardi /maʀdi/ nm Tuesday; **M~ gras** Shrove Tuesday.

mare /maʀ/ nf (étang) pond; (flaque) pool.

marécage /maʀekaʒ/ nm marsh; (sous les tropiques) swamp.

maréchal (pl -aux) /maʀeʃal, -o/ nm field marshal.

maréchal-ferrant (pl -aux-ferrants /maʀeʃalfeʀɑ̃/ nm blacksmith.

marée /maʀe/ nf tide; (poissons) fresh fish; ~ **haute/basse** high/low tide; ~ **noire** oil slick.

marelle /maʀɛl/ nf hopscotch.

margarine /maʀgaʀin/ nf margarine.

marge /maʀʒ/ nf margin; **en ~ de** (à l'écart de) on the fringe(s) of; ~ **bénéficiaire** profit margin.

marginal, ~e (mpl -aux) /maʀʒinal, -o/ a marginal. ● nm, f drop-out.

marguerite /maʀgəʀit/ nf daisy; (qui imprime) daisy-wheel.

mari /maʀi/ nm husband.

mariage /maʀjaʒ/ nm marriage; (cérémonie) wedding.

marié, ~e /maʀje/ a married. ● nm, f (bride)groom, bride; **les ~s** the bride and groom.

marier /maʀje/ [45] vt marry. □ **se ~** vpr get married, marry; **se ~ avec** marry, get married to.

marin, ~e /maʀɛ̃, -in/ a sea. ● nm sailor.

marine /maʀin/ nf navy; ~ **marchande** merchant navy. ● a inv navy (blue).

marionnette /maʀjɔnɛt/ nf puppet; (à fils) marionette.

maritalement /maʀitalmɑ̃/ adv (vivre) as husband and wife.

maritime /maʀitim/ a maritime, coastal; (agent, compagnie) shipping.

marmaille /maʀmaj/ nf ▣ brats.

marmelade /maʀməlad/ nf

stewed fruit; ~ **d'oranges** (orange) marmalade.

marmite /maʀmit/ nf (cooking-) pot.

marmonner /maʀmɔne/ [1] vt mumble.

marmot /maʀmo/ nm ▣ kid.

Maroc /maʀɔk/ nm Morocco.

maroquinerie /maʀɔkinʀi/ nf (magasin) leather goods shop.

marquant, ~e /maʀkɑ̃, -t/ a (remarquable) outstanding; (qu'on n'oublie pas) memorable.

marque /maʀk/ nf mark; (de produits) brand, make; (décompte) score; **à vos ~s!** (Sport) on your marks!; **de ~** (Comm) brand name; (fig) important; ~ **de fabrique** trademark; ~ **déposée** registered trademark.

marquer /maʀke/ [1] vt mark; (indiquer) show, say; (écrire) note down; (point, but) score; (joueur) mark; (influencer) leave its mark on; (exprimer) (volonté, sentiment) show. ● vi (laisser une trace) leave a mark; (événement) stand out; (Sport) score.

marquis, ~e /maʀki, -z/ nm, f marquis, marchioness.

marraine /maʀɛn/ nf godmother.

marrant, ~e /maʀɑ̃, -t/ a ▣ funny.

marre /maʀ/ adv **en avoir ~** ▣ be fed up (**de** with).

marrer (se) /(sə)maʀe/ [1] vpr ▣ laugh, have a (good) laugh.

marron /maʀɔ̃/ nm chestnut; (couleur) brown; (coup ▣) thump; ~ **d'Inde** horse chestnut. ● a inv brown.

mars /maʀs/ nm March.

marteau (pl ~x) /maʀto/ nm hammer; ~ (**de porte**) (door) knocker; ~ **piqueur** ou **pneumatique** pneumatic drill; **être ~** ▣ be mad.

marteler /maʀtəle/ [6] vt

hammer; (*poings, talons*) pound; (*scander*) rap out.
martial, ~e (*mpl* -**iaux**) /maʀsjal, -jo/ *a* military; (*art*) martial.
martien, ~**ne** /maʀsjɛ̃, -ɛn/ *a & nm, f* Martian.
martyr, ~**e** /maʀtiʀ/ *nm, f* martyr. ● *a* martyred; (*enfant*) battered.
martyre /maʀtiʀ/ *nm* (Relig) martyrdom; (fig) agony, suffering.
martyriser /maʀtiʀize/ [1] *vt* (Relig) martyr; (*torturer*) torture; (*enfant*) batter.
marxisme /maʀksism/ *nm* Marxism. **marxiste** *a & nmf* Marxist.
masculin, ~**e** /maskylɛ̃, -in/ *a* masculine; (*sexe*) male; (*mode, équipe*) men's. ● *nm* masculine.
masochisme /mazɔʃism/ *nm* masochism.
masochiste /mazɔʃist/ *nmf* masochist. ● *a* masochistic.
masque /mask/ *nm* mask; ~ **de beauté** face pack. **masquer** [1] *vt* (*cacher*) hide, conceal (à from); (*lumière*) block (off).
massacre /masakʀ/ *nm* massacre. **massacrer** [1] *vt* massacre; (*abîmer* ⊞) ruin.
massage /masaʒ/ *nm* massage.
masse /mas/ *nf* (volume) mass; (*gros morceau*) lump, mass; (*outil*) sledge-hammer; **en** ~ (*vendre*) in bulk; (*venir*) in force; **produire en** ~ mass-produce; **la** ~ (*foule*) the masses; **une** ~ **de** ⊞ masses of; **la** ~ **de** the majority of.
masser /mase/ [1] *vt* (*assembler*) assemble; (*pétrir*) massage. □ **se** ~ *vpr* (*gens, foule*) mass.
massif, -**ive** /masif, -v/ *a* massive; (*or, argent*) solid. ● *nm* (de fleurs) clump; (*parterre*) bed; (Géog) massif. **massivement** *adv* (*en masse*) in large numbers.

massue /masy/ *nf* club, bludgeon.
mastic /mastik/ *nm* putty; (pour trous) filler.
mastiquer /mastike/ [1] *vt* (*mâcher*) chew.
mat /mat/ *a* (*couleur*) matt; (*bruit*) dull; (*teint*) olive; **être** ~ (aux échecs) be in checkmate.
mât /mɑ/ *nm* mast; (pylône) pole; ~ **de drapeau** flagpole.
match /matʃ/ *nm* match; (US) game; **faire** ~ **nul** tie, draw; ~ **aller** first leg; ~ **retour** return match.
matelas /matla/ *nm* mattress; ~ **pneumatique** air bed.
matelassé, ~**e** /matlase/ *a* padded; (*tissu*) quilted.
matelot /matlo/ *nm* sailor.
mater /mate/ [1] *vt* (*révolte*) put down; (*personne*) bring into line.
matérialiser (se) /(sə)mateʀjalize/ [1] *vpr* materialize.
matérialiste /mateʀjalist/ *a* materialistic. ● *nmf* materialist.
matériau (pl ~**x**) /mateʀjo/ *nm* material.
matériel, ~**le** /mateʀjɛl/ *a* material. ● *nm* equipment, materials; ~ **informatique** hardware.
maternel, ~**le** /matɛʀnɛl/ *a* maternal; (comme d'une mère) motherly. **maternelle** *nf* nursery school.
maternité /matɛʀnite/ *nf* maternity hospital; (état de mère) motherhood; **de** ~ maternity.
mathématicien, ~**ne** /matematisjɛ̃, -ɛn/ *nm, f* mathematician.
mathématique /matematik/ *a* mathematical. **mathématiques** *nfpl* mathematics (+ *sg*).
maths /mat/ *nfpl* ⊞ maths (+ *sg*).
matière /matjɛʀ/ *nf* matter; (produit) material; (sujet) subject; **en**

~ **de** as regards; ~ **plastique** plastic; ~**s grasses** fat content; ~**s premières** raw materials.

matin /matɛ̃/ nm morning; **de bon** ~ early in the morning.

matinal, ~**e** (mpl **-aux**) /matinal, -o/ a morning; (de bonne heure) early; **être** ~ be up early; (d'habitude) be an early riser.

matinée /matine/ nf morning; (spectacle) matinée.

matou /matu/ nm tomcat.

matraque /matʀak/ nf (de police) truncheon; (US) billy (club).
matraquer [1] vt club, beat; (produit, chanson) plug.

matrimonial, ~**e** (mpl **-iaux**) /matʀimɔnjal, -jo/ a matrimonial; **agence** ~**e** marriage bureau.

maturité /matyʀite/ nf maturity.

maudire /modiʀ/ [41] vt curse.

maudit, ~**e** /modi, -t/ a 🞂 blasted, damned.

maugréer /mogʀee/ [15] vi grumble.

mausolée /mozɔle/ nm mausoleum.

maussade /mosad/ a gloomy.

mauvais, ~**e** /mɔvɛ, -z/ a bad; (erroné) wrong; (malveillant) evil; (désagréable) nasty, bad; (mer) rough; **le** ~ **moment** the wrong time; ~**e herbe** weed; ~**e langue** gossip; ~**e passe** tight spot; ~ **traitements** ill-treatment. ● adv (sentir) bad; **il fait** ~ the weather is bad. ● nm **le bon et le** ~ the good and the bad.

mauve /mov/ a & nm mauve.

mauviette /movjɛt/ nf weakling, wimp.

maux /mo/ ⇒ MAL².

maximal, ~**e** (mpl **-aux**) /maksimal, -o/ a maximum.

maxime /maksim/ nf maxim.

maximum /maksimɔm/ a maximum. ● nm maximum; **au** ~ as much as possible; (tout au plus)

at most; **faire le** ~ do one's utmost.

mazout /mazut/ nm (fuel) oil.

me, m' /mə, m/ pron me; (indirect) (to) me; (réfléchi) myself.

méandre /meɑ̃dʀ/ nm meander.

mec /mek/ nm 🞂 bloke, guy.

mécanicien, ~**ne** /mekanisjɛ̃, -jɛn/ nm, f mechanic. ● nm train driver.

mécanique /mekanik/ a mechanical; (jouet) clockwork; **problème** ~ engine trouble. ● nf mechanics (+ sg); (mécanisme) mechanism. **mécaniser** [1] vt mechanize.

mécanisme /mekanism/ nm mechanism.

méchamment /meʃamɑ̃/ adv spitefully. **méchanceté** nf nastiness; (action) wicked action.

méchant, ~**e** /meʃɑ̃, -t/ a (cruel) wicked; (désagréable, grave) nasty; (enfant) naughty; (chien) vicious; (sensationnel 🞂) terrific. ● nm, f (enfant) naughty child.

mèche /mɛʃ/ nf (de cheveux) lock; (de bougie) wick; (d'explosif) fuse; (outil) drill bit; **de** ~ **avec** in league with.

méconnaissable /mekɔnɛsabl/ a unrecognizable.

méconnaître /mekɔnɛtʀ/ [18] vt misunderstand, misread; (mésestimer) underestimate.

méconnu, ~**e** /mekɔny/ a unrecognized; (artiste) neglected.

mécontent, ~**e** /mekɔ̃tɑ̃, -t/ a dissatisfied (de with); (irrité) annoyed (de at, with). **mécontentement** nm dissatisfaction; annoyance. **mécontenter** [1] vt dissatisfy; (irriter) annoy.

médaille /medaj/ nf medal; (insigne) badge; (bijou) medallion. **médaillé**, ~**e** nm, f medallist.

médaillon /medajɔ̃/ *nm* medallion; (bijou) locket.

médecin /medsɛ̃/ *nm* doctor.

médecine /medsin/ *nf* medicine.

média /medja/ *nm* medium; **les** ∼**s** the media.

médiateur, -trice /medjatœr, -tris/ *nm, f* mediator.

médiatique /medjatik/ *a* (événement, personnalité) media.

médical, ∼e (*mpl* **-aux**) /medikal, -o/ *a* medical.

médicament /medikamɑ̃/ *nm* medicine, drug.

médico-légal, ∼e (*mpl* **-aux**) /medikɔlegal, -o/ *a* forensic.

médiéval, ∼e (*mpl* **-aux**) /medjeval, -o/ *a* medieval.

médiocre /medjɔkr/ *a* mediocre, poor. **médiocrité** *nf* mediocrity.

médire /medir/ [37] *vi* ∼ **de** speak ill of, malign.

médisance /medizɑ̃s/ *nf* ∼(**s**) malicious gossip.

méditer /medite/ [1] *vi* meditate (**sur** on). ● *vt* contemplate; (paroles, conseils) mull over; ∼ **de** plan to.

Méditerranée /mediterane/ *nf* **la** ∼ the Mediterranean.

méditerranéen, ∼ne /mediteraneɛ̃, -ɛn/ *a* Mediterranean.

médium /medjɔm/ *nm* (personne) medium.

méduse /medyz/ *nf* jellyfish.

meeting /mitiŋ/ *nm* meeting.

méfait /mefɛ/ *nm* misdeed; **les** ∼**s de** (conséquences) the ravages of.

méfiance /mefjɑ̃s/ *nf* suspicion, distrust. **méfiant, ∼e** *a* suspicious, distrustful.

méfier (se) /(sə)mefje/ [45] *vpr* be wary *ou* careful; **se** ∼ **de** distrust, be wary of.

mégaoctet /megaɔkte/ *nm* (Ordinat) megabyte.

mégère /meʒɛr/ *nf* (femme) shrew.

mégot /mego/ *nm* cigarette end.

meilleur, ∼e /mɛjœr/ *a* (comparatif) better (**que** than); (superlatif) best; **le** ∼ **livre** the best book; **mon** ∼ **ami** my best friend; ∼ **marché** cheaper. ● *nm, f* **le** ∼, **la** ∼**e** the best (one). ● *adv* (sentir) better; **il fait** ∼ the weather is better.

mél /mel/ *nm* e-mail; **envoyer un** ∼ send an e-mail.

mélancolie /melɑ̃kɔli/ *nf* melancholy.

mélange /melɑ̃ʒ/ *nm* mixture, blend.

mélanger /melɑ̃ʒe/ [40] *vt* mix; (thés, parfums) blend. □ **se** ∼ *vpr* mix; (thés, parfums) blend; (idées) get mixed up.

mélasse /melas/ *nf* black treacle; (US) molasses.

mêlée /mele/ *nf* free for all; (au rugby) scrum.

mêler /mele/ [1] *vt* mix (**à** with); (qualités) combine; (embrouiller) mix up; ∼ **qn à** (impliquer dans) involve sb in. □ **se** ∼ *vpr* mix; combine; **se** ∼ **à** (se joindre à) mingle with; (participer à) join in; **se** ∼ **de** meddle in; **mêle-toi de ce qui te regarde** mind your own business.

méli-mélo (*pl* **mélis-mélos**) /melimelo/ *nm* jumble.

mélo /melo/ 🔲 *nm* melodrama. ● *a inv* slushy, schmaltzy 🔲.

mélodie /melɔdi/ *nf* melody. **mélodieux, -ieuse** *a* melodious. **mélodique** *a* melodic.

mélodramatique /melodramatik/ *a* melodramatic. **mélodrame** *nm* melodrama.

mélomane /meloman/ *nmf* music lover.

melon /məlɔ̃/ *nm* melon; (chapeau) ∼ bowler (hat).

M

membrane /mãbʀan/ *nf* membrane.

membre /mãbʀ/ *nm* (Anat) limb; (adhérent) member.

même /mɛm/ *a* same; **ce livre ∼** this very book; **la bonté ∼** kindness itself; **en ∼ temps** at the same time. ●*pron* **le ∼, la ∼** the same (one). ●*adv* even; **à ∼ (sur)** directly on; **à ∼ de** in a position to; **de ∼ (aussi)** too; (de la même façon) likewise; **de ∼ que** just as; **∼si** even if.

mémé /meme/ *nf* 🄸 granny.

mémo /memo/ *nm* note, memo.

mémoire /memwaʀ/ *nm* (rapport) memorandum; (Univ) dissertation; **∼s** (souvenirs écrits) memoirs. ●*nf* memory; **à la ∼ de** to the memory of; **de ∼** from memory; **∼ morte/ vive** (Ordinat) ROM/RAM.

mémorable /memoʀabl/ *a* memorable.

menace /mønas/ *nf* threat. **menacer** [10] *vt* threaten (**de faire** to do).

ménage /menaʒ/ *nm* (couple) couple; (travail) housework; (famille) household; **se mettre en ∼** set up house.

ménagement /menaʒmã/ *nm* **avec ∼s** gently; **sans ∼s** (dire) bluntly; (jeter, pousser) roughly.

ménager¹, **-ère** /menaʒe, -ɛʀ/ *a* household, domestic; **travaux ∼s** housework.

ménager² /menaʒe/ [40] *vt* be gentle with, handle carefully; (utiliser) be careful with; (organiser) prepare (carefully); **ne pas ∼ ses efforts** spare no effort.

ménagère /menaʒɛʀ/ *nf* housewife.

ménagerie /menaʒʀi/ *nf* menagerie.

mendiant, **∼e** /mãdjã, -t/ *nm, f* beggar.

mendier /mãdje/ [45] *vt* beg for. ●*vi* beg.

mener /møne/ [6] *vt* lead; (entreprise, pays) run; (étude, enquête) carry out; (politique) pursue; **∼ à** (accompagner à) take to; (faire aboutir) lead to; **∼ à bien** see through. ●*vi* lead.

méningite /menɛ̃ʒit/ *nf* meningitis.

menotte /mønɔt/ *nf* 🄸 hand; **∼s** handcuffs.

mensonge /mãsɔ̃ʒ/ *nm* lie; (action) lying. **mensonger**, **-ère** *a* untrue, false.

mensualité /mãsɥalite/ *nf* monthly payment.

mensuel, **∼le** /mãsɥɛl/ *a* monthly. ●*nm* monthly (magazine). **mensuellement** *adv* monthly.

mensurations /mãsyʀasjɔ̃/ *nfpl* measurements.

mental, **∼e** (*mpl* **-aux**) /mãtal, -o/ *a* mental; **malade ∼** mentally ill person; **handicapé ∼** mentally handicapped person.

mentalité /mãtalite/ *nf* mentality.

menteur, **-euse** /mãtœʀ, -øz/ *nm, f* liar. ●*a* untruthful.

menthe /mãt/ *nf* mint.

mention /mãsjɔ̃/ *nf* mention; (annotation) note; (Scol) grade; **rayer la ∼ inutile** delete as appropriate. **mentionner** [1] *vt* mention.

mentir /mãtiʀ/ [46] *vi* lie.

menton /mãtɔ̃/ *nm* chin.

menu, **∼e** /møny/ *a* (petit) tiny; (fin) fine; (insignifiant) minor. ●*adv* (couper) fine. ●*nm* (carte) menu; (repas) meal; (Ordinat) menu; **∼ déroulant** pull-down menu.

menuiserie /mønɥizʀi/ *nf* carpentry, joinery. **menuisier** *nm* carpenter, joiner.

méprendre (se) /(sə)mepʀãdʀ/

[50] *vpr* **se ~ sur** be mistaken about.

mépris /mepʀi/ *nm* contempt, scorn (de for); **au ~ de** regardless of.

méprisable /mepʀizabl/ *a* contemptible, despicable.

méprise /mepʀiz/ *nf* mistake.

méprisant, ~e /mepʀizɑ̃, -t/ *a* scornful. **mépriser** [1] *vt* scorn, despise.

mer /mɛʀ/ *nf* sea; (marée) tide; **en pleine ~** out at sea.

mercenaire /mɛʀsənɛʀ/ *nm & a* mercenary.

mercerie /mɛʀs(ə)ʀi/ *nf* haberdashery; (US) notions store. **mercier, -ière** *nm, f* haberdasher; (US) notions seller.

merci /mɛʀsi/ *interj* thank you, thanks (de, pour for); **~ beaucoup, ~ bien** thank you very much. ● *nm* thank you. ● *nf* mercy.

mercredi /mɛʀkʀədi/ *nm* Wednesday; **~ des Cendres** Ash Wednesday.

merde /mɛʀd/ *nf* 🖪 shit 🖪.

mère /mɛʀ/ *nf* mother; **~ de famille** mother.

méridional, ~e (*mpl* **-aux**) /meʀidjɔnal, -o/ *a* southern. ● *nm, f* Southerner.

mérite /meʀit/ *nm* merit; **avoir du ~ à faire** deserve credit for doing.

mériter /meʀite/ [1] *vt* deserve; **~ d'être lu** be worth reading.

méritoire /meʀitwaʀ/ *a* commendable.

merlan /mɛʀlɑ̃/ *nm* whiting.

merle /mɛʀl/ *nm* blackbird.

merveille /mɛʀvɛj/ *nf* wonder, marvel; **à ~** wonderfully; **faire des ~s** work wonders.

merveilleux, -euse /mɛʀvɛjø, -z/ *a* wonderful, marvellous.

mes /me/ ⇒MON.

mésange /mezɑ̃ʒ/ *nf* tit(mouse).

mésaventure /mezavɑ̃tyʀ/ *nf*

misadventure; **par ~** by some misfortune.

mesdames /medam/ ⇒MADAME.

mesdemoiselles /medmwazɛl/ ⇒MADEMOISELLE.

mésentente /mezɑ̃tɑ̃t/ *nf* disagreement.

mesquin, ~e /mɛskɛ̃, -in/ *a* mean-minded, petty; (chiche) mean. **mesquinerie** *nf* meanness.

message /mesaʒ/ *nm* message; **un ~ électronique** an e-mail; **~ texte** text message.

messager, -ère /mesaʒe, -ɛʀ/ *nm, f* messenger. ● *nm* **~ de poche** pager.

messagerie /mesaʒʀi/ *nf* (transports) freight forwarding; (télécommunications) messaging; **~ électronique** electronic mail; **~ vocale** voice mail.

messe /mɛs/ *nf* (Relig) mass.

messieurs /mesjø/ ⇒MONSIEUR.

mesure /məzyʀ/ *nf* measurement; (quantité, unité) measure; (disposition) measure, step; (cadence) time; **en ~ in** time; (modération) moderation; **à ~ que** as; **dans la ~ où** in so far as; **dans une certaine ~** to some extent; **en ~ de** in a position to; **sans ~** to excess; (fait) **sur ~** made-to-measure.

mesuré, ~e /məzyʀe/ *a* measured; (attitude) moderate.

mesurer /məzyʀe/ [1] *vt* measure; (juger) assess; (argent, temps) ration. ● *vi* **~ 15 mètres de long** be 15 metres long. □ **se ~ avec** *vpr* pit oneself against.

met /mɛ/ ⇒METTRE [42].

métal (*pl* **-aux**) /metal, -o/ *nm* metal. **métallique** *a* (objet) metal; (éclat) metallic.

métallurgie /metalyʀʒi/ *nf* (industrie) metalworking industry.

métamorphoser /metamɔʀfoze/

M

[1] *vt* transform. □ **se ~** *vpr* be transformed; **se ~ en** metamorphose into.

métaphore /metafɔʀ/ *nf* metaphor.

météo /meteo/ *nf* (bulletin) weather forecast.

météore /meteɔʀ/ *nm* meteor.

météorologie /meteɔʀɔlɔʒi/ *nf* meteorology.

météorologique /meteɔʀɔlɔʒik/ *a* meteorological; **conditions ~s** weather conditions.

méthode /metɔd/ *nf* method; (ouvrage) course, manual.

méthodique *a* methodical.

méticuleux, -euse /metikylø, -z/ *a* meticulous.

métier /metje/ *nm* job; (manuel) trade; (intellectuel) profession; (expérience) experience, skill; **~ (à tisser)** loom; **remettre qch sur le ~** rework sth.

métis, ~se /metis/ *a* mixed race. ● *nm, f* person of mixed race.

métrage /metʀaʒ/ *nm* length; **court ~** short (film); **long ~** feature-length film.

mètre /mɛtʀ/ *nm* metre; (règle) rule; **~ ruban** tape-measure.

métreur, -euse /metʀœʀ, -øz/ *nm, f* quantity surveyor.

métrique /metʀik/ *a* metric.

métro /metʀo/ *nm* underground; (US) subway.

métropole /metʀɔpɔl/ *nf* metropolis; (pays) mother country.

métropolitain, ~e *a* metropolitan.

mets /mɛ/ *nm* dish. ● ⇒METTRE [42].

mettable /mɛtabl/ *a* wearable.

metteur /mɛtœʀ/ *nm* **~ en scène** director.

mettre /mɛtʀ/ [42] *vt* put; (radio, chauffage) put *ou* switch on; (réveil) set; (installer) put in; (revêtir) put on; (porter habituellement)

(vêtement, lunettes) wear; (prendre) take; (investir, dépenser) put; (écrire) write, say; **elle a mis deux heures** it took her two hours; **~ la table** lay the table; **~ en question** question; **~ en valeur** highlight; (terrain) develop; **mettons que** let's suppose that. ● *vi* **~ bas** (animal) give birth. □ **se ~** *vpr* (vêtement, maquillage) put on; (se placer) (objet) go; (personne) (debout) stand; (assis) sit; (couché) lie; **se ~ en short** put shorts on; **se ~ debout** stand up; **se ~ au lit** go to bed; **se ~ à table** sit down at table; **se ~ en ligne** line up; **se ~ du sable dans les yeux** get sand in one's eyes; **se ~ au chinois/tennis** take up Chinese/tennis; **se ~ au travail** set to work; **se ~ à faire** start to do.

meuble /mœbl/ *nm* piece of furniture; **~s** furniture.

meublé /møble/ *nm* furnished flat.

meubler /møble/ [1] *vt* furnish; (fig) fill. □ **se ~** *vpr* buy furniture.

meugler /møgle/ [1] *vi* moo.

meule /møl/ *nf* millstone; **~ de foin** haystack.

meunier, -ière /mønje, -jɛʀ/ *nm, f* miller.

meurs, meurt /mœʀ/ ⇒MOURIR [43].

meurtre /mœʀtʀ/ *nm* murder.

meurtrier, -ière /mœʀtʀije, -jɛʀ/ *a* deadly. ● *nm, f* murderer, murderess.

meurtrir /mœʀtʀiʀ/ [2] *vt* bruise.

meute /møt/ *nf* pack of hounds.

Mexique /mɛksik/ *nm* Mexico.

mi- /mi/ *préf* mid-, half-; **à mi-chemin** half-way; **à mi-pente** half-way up the hill; **à la mi-juin** in mid-June.

miauler /mjole/ [1] *vi* miaow.

micro /mikʀo/ *nm* microphone, mike; (Ordinat) micro.

microbe /mikʀɔb/ *nm* germ.

microfilm /mikʀɔfilm/ *nm* microfilm.

micro-onde /mikʀɔõd/ *nf* microwave; **un four à ~s** microwave (oven). **micro-ondes** *nm inv* microwave (oven).

micro-ordinateur (*pl* ~s) /mikʀɔɔʀdinatœʀ/ *nm* personal computer.

microphone /mikʀɔfɔn/ *nm* microphone.

microprocesseur /mikʀɔpʀɔsɛsœʀ/ *nm* microprocessor.

microscope /mikʀɔskɔp/ *nm* microscope.

midi /midi/ *nm* twelve o'clock, midday, noon; (déjeuner) lunchtime; (sud) south. **Midi** *nm* **le M~** the South of France.

mie /mi/ *nf* soft part (of the loaf); **un pain de ~** a sandwich loaf.

miel /mjɛl/ *nm* honey.

mielleux, -euse /mjɛlø, -z/ *a* unctuous.

mien, ~ne /mjɛ̃, -ɛn/ *pron* **le ~, la ~ne, les ~(ne)s** mine.

miette /mjɛt/ *nf* crumb; (fig) scrap; **en ~s** in pieces.

mieux /mjø/ *a inv* better (**que** than); **le** *ou* **la** *ou* **les ~** (the) best. ● *nm* best; (progrès) improvement; **faire de son ~** do one's best; **le ~ serait de** the best thing would be to. ● *adv* better; **le** *ou* **la** *ou* **les ~** (de deux) the better; (de plusieurs) the best; **elle va ~** she is better; **j'aime ~ rester** I'd rather stay; **il vaudrait ~ partir** it would be best to leave; **tu ferais ~ de faire** you would be best to do.

mièvre /mjɛvʀ/ *a* insipid.

mignon, ~ne /miɲɔ̃, -ɔn/ *a* cute; (gentil) kind.

migraine /migʀɛn/ *nf* headache; (plus fort) migraine.

migration /migʀasjõ/ *nf* migration.

mijoter /miʒɔte/ [1] *vt/i* simmer; (tramer 🔲) cook up.

mil /mil/ *nm* a thousand.

milice /milis/ *nf* militia.

milieu (*pl* ~x) /miljø/ *nm* middle; (environnement) environment; (appartenance sociale) background; (groupe) circle; (voie) middle way; (criminel) underworld; **au ~ de** in the middle of; **en plein** *ou* **au beau ~ de** right in the middle (of).

militaire /militɛʀ/ *a* military. ● *nm* soldier, serviceman.

militant, ~e /militɑ̃, -t/ *nm,f* militant.

militer /milite/ [1] *vi* be a militant; **~ pour** militate in favour of.

mille¹ /mil/ *a & nm inv* a thousand; **deux ~** two thousand; **mettre dans le ~** (fig) hit the nail on the head.

mille² /mil/ *nm* **~ (marin)** (nautical) mile.

millénaire /milenɛʀ/ *nm* millennium. ● *a* a thousand years old.

mille-pattes /milpat/ *nm inv* centipede.

millésime /milezim/ *nm* date; (de vin) vintage.

millet /mijɛ/ *nm* millet.

milliard /miljaʀ/ *nm* thousand million, billion. **milliardaire** *nmf* multimillionaire.

millième /miljɛm/ *a & nmf* thousandth.

millier /milje/ *nm* thousand; **un ~ (de)** about a thousand.

millimètre /milimɛtʀ/ *nm* millimetre.

million /miljõ/ *nm* million; **deux ~s (de)** two million. **millionnaire** *nmf* millionaire.

mime /mim/ *nmf* mime-artist.

M

● *nm* (art) mime. **mimer** [1] *vt* mime; (imiter) mimic.

mimique /mimik/ *nf* expressions and gestures.

minable /minabl/ *a* ▣ (logement) shabby; (médiocre) pathetic, crummy.

minauder /minode/ [1] *vi* simper.

mince /mɛ̃s/ *a* thin; (svelte) slim; (faible) (espoir, majorité) slim.
● *interj* ▣ blast ▣, darn it ▣.

minceur /mɛ̃sœʀ/ *nf* thinness; slimness.

mincir /mɛ̃siʀ/ [2] *vi* get slimmer; **ça te mincit** it makes you look slimmer.

mine /min/ *nf* expression; (allure) appearance; **avoir bonne** ~ look well; **faire** ~ **de** make as if to; (exploitation, explosif) mine; (de crayon) lead; ~ **de charbon** coal-mine.

miner /mine/ [1] *vt* (saper) undermine; (garnir d'explosifs) mine.

minerai /minʀɛ/ *nm* ore.

minéral, ~e (*mpl* **-aux**) /mineʀal, -o/ *a* mineral. ● *nm* (*pl* **-aux**) mineral.

minéralogique /mineʀalɔʒik/ *a* **plaque** ~ numberplate; (US) license plate.

minet, ~te /minɛ, -t/ *nm, f* (chat ▣) pussy(cat).

mineur, ~e /minœʀ/ *a* minor; (Jur) under age. ● *nm, f* (Jur) minor. ● *nm* (ouvrier) miner.

miniature /minjatyʀ/ *nf & a* miniature.

minier, -ière /minje, -jɛʀ/ *a* mining.

minimal, ~e (*mpl* **-aux**) /minimal, o/ *a* minimal, minimum.

minime /minim/ *a* minimal, minor. ● *nmf* (Sport) junior.

minimum /minimɔm/ *a* minimum. ● *nm* minimum; **au** ~ (pour le moins) at the very least; **en faire un** ~ do as little as possible.

ministère /ministɛʀ/ *nm* ministry; (gouvernement) government; ~ **public** public prosecutor's office. **ministériel, ~le** *a* ministerial, government.

ministre /ministʀ/ *nm* minister; (au Royaume-Uni) Secretary of State; (US) Secretary.

Minitel® /minitɛl/ *nm* Minitel (telephone videotext system).

minorer /minɔʀe/ [1] *vt* reduce.

minoritaire /minɔʀitɛʀ/ *a* minority; **être** ~ be in the minority. **minorité** *nf* minority.

minuit /minɥi/ *nm* midnight.

minuscule /minyskyl/ *a* minute. ● *nf* (lettre) ~ lower case.

minute /minyt/ *nf* minute; **'talons** ~' 'heels repaired while you wait'.

minuterie /minytʀi/ *nf* time-switch.

minutie /minysi/ *nf* meticulousness.

minutieux, -ieuse /minysjø, -z/ *a* meticulous.

mioche /mjɔʃ/ *nm, f* ▣ kid.

mirabelle /miʀabɛl/ *nf* (mirabelle) plum.

miracle /miʀakl/ *nm* miracle; **par** ~ miraculously.

miraculeux, -euse /miʀakylø, -z/ *a* miraculous.

mirage /miʀaʒ/ *nm* mirage.

mire /miʀ/ *nf* (fig) centre of attraction; (TV) test card.

mirobolant, ~e /miʀɔbɔlɑ̃, -t/ *a* ▣ marvellous.

miroir /miʀwaʀ/ *nm* mirror.

miroiter /miʀwate/ [1] *vi* shimmer, sparkle.

mis, ~e /mi, miz/ *a* **bien** ~ well-dressed. ● ⇒METTRE [42].

mise /miz/ *nf* (argent) stake; (tenue) attire; ~ **à feu** blast-off; ~ **au point** adjustment; (fig) clarification; ~ **de fonds** capital

outlay; ~ **en garde** warning; ~ **en plis set**; ~ **en scène** direction.
miser /mize/ [1] vt (*argent*) bet, stake (**sur** on). ● vi ~ **sur** (parier) place a bet on; (compter sur) bank on.
misérable /mizeʀabl/ a miserable, wretched; (indigent) destitute; (minable) seedy, squalid.
misère /mizeʀ/ nf destitution; (malheur) trouble, woe. **miséreux, -euse** nm, f destitute person.
miséricorde /mizeʀikɔʀd/ nf mercy.
missel /misɛl/ nm missal.
missile /misil/ nm missile.
mission /misjɔ̃/ nm mission. **missionnaire** nmf missionary.
missive /misiv/ nf missive.
mistral /mistʀal/ nm (vent) mistral.
mitaine /mitɛn/ nf fingerless mitt.
mite /mit/ nf (clothes-)moth.
mi-temps /mitɑ̃/ nf inv (arrêt) half-time, (période) half. ● nm inv part-time work; **à** ~ part-time.
miteux, -euse /mitø, -z/ a shabby.
mitigé, ~e /mitiʒe/ a (modéré) lukewarm; (succès) qualified.
mitonner /mitɔne/ [1] vt cook slowly with care; (fig) cook up.
mitoyen, ~ne /mitwajɛ̃, -ɛn/ a **mur** ~ party wall.
mitrailler /mitʀaje/ [1] vt machine-gun; (fig) bombard.
mitraillette /mitʀajɛt/ nf submachine gun. **mitrailleuse** nf machine gun.
mi-voix: à ~ /amivwa/ loc in a low voice.
mixeur /miksœʀ/ nm liquidizer, blender; (batteur) mixer.
mixte /mikst/ a mixed; (commission) joint; (école) coeducational; (peau) combination.

mobile /mɔbil/ a mobile; (pièce) moving; (feuillet) loose. ● nm (art) mobile; (raison) motive.
mobilier /mɔbilje/ nm furniture.
mobilisation /mɔbilizasjɔ̃/ nf mobilization. **mobiliser** [1] vt mobilize.
mobilité /mɔbilite/ nf mobility.
mobylette® /mɔbilɛt/ nf moped.
moche /mɔʃ/ a ⊞ (laid) ugly; (mauvais) lousy.
modalités /mɔdalite/ nfpl (conditions) terms; (façon de fonctionner) practical details.
mode /mɔd/ nf fashion; (coutume) custom; **à la** ~ fashionable. ● nm method, mode; (genre) way; ~ **d'emploi** directions (for use).
modèle /mɔdɛl/ a model. ● nm model; (exemple) example; (Comm) (type) model; (taille) size; (style) style; ~ **familial** family size; ~ **réduit** (small-scale) model.
modeler /mɔdle/ [6] vt model (**sur** on). □ **se** ~ **sur** vpr model oneself on.
modem /mɔdɛm/ nm modem.
modérateur, -trice /mɔdeʀatœʀ, -tʀis/ a moderating. **modération** nf moderation.
modéré, ~e /mɔdeʀe/ a & nm, f moderate.
modérer /mɔdeʀe/ [14] vt (propos) moderate; (désirs, sentiments) curb. □ **se** ~ vpr restrain oneself.
moderne /mɔdɛʀn/ a modern.
moderniser [1] vt modernize.
modeste /mɔdɛst/ a modest. **modestie** nf modesty.
modification /mɔdifikasjɔ̃/ nf modification.
modifier /mɔdifje/ [45] vt change, modify. □ **se** ~ vpr change, alter.
modique /mɔdik/ a modest.
modiste /mɔdist/ nf milliner.

M

moduler /mɔdyle/ [1] vt
modulate; (adapter) adjust.

moelle /mwal/ nf marrow; ~
épinière spinal cord; ~ **osseuse**
bone marrow.

moelleux, -euse /mwalø, -z/ a
soft; (onctueux) smooth.

mœurs /mœR(s)/ nfpl (morale)
morals; (usages) customs; (manières)
habits, ways.

moi /mwa/ pron me; (indirect) (to)
me; (sujet) I. ● nm self.

moignon /mwaɲɔ̃/ nm stump.

moi-même /mwamɛm/ pron
myself.

moindre /mwɛ̃dR/ a (moins grand)
lesser; le ou la ~, les ~s the
slightest, the least.

moine /mwan/ nm monk.

moineau (pl ~x) /mwano/ nm
sparrow.

moins /mwɛ̃/ prép minus; (pour
dire l'heure) to; **une heure ~ dix** ten
to one. ● adv less (que than); le
ou la ou les ~ the least; le ~
grand/haut the smallest/lowest; ~
de (avec un nom non dénombrable) less
(que than); ~ **de dix francs** less
than ten francs; ~ **de livres** fewer
books; **au** ~, **du** ~ at least; **à** ~
que unless; **de** ~ less; **de** ~ **en** ~
less and less; **en** ~ less; (manquant)
missing.

mois /mwa/ nm month.

moisi, ~e /mwazi/ a mouldy.
● nm mould; **de** ~ (odeur) musty.
moisir [2] vi go mouldy.
moisissure nf mould.

moisson /mwasɔ̃/ nf harvest.

moissonner /mwasɔne/ [1] vt
harvest, reap. **moissonneur,
-euse** nm, f harvester.

moite /mwat/ a sticky, clammy.

moitié /mwatje/ nf half; (milieu)
halfway mark; **s'arrêter à la** ~
stop halfway through; **à** ~ **vide**
half empty; **à** ~ **prix** (at) half-
price; **la** ~ **de** half (of). **moitié-
moitié** adv half-and-half.

mol /mɔl/ ⇒MOU.

molaire /mɔlɛR/ nf molar.

molécule /mɔlekyl/ nf molecule.

molester /mɔlɛste/ [1] vt
manhandle, rough up.

molle /mɔl/ ⇒MOU.

mollement /mɔlmɑ̃/ adv softly;
(faiblement) feebly. **mollesse** nf
softness; (faiblesse) feebleness;
(apathie) listlessness.

mollet /mɔlɛ/ nm (de jambe) calf.

mollir /mɔliR/ [2] vi soften; (céder)
yield.

môme /mom/ nmf Ⓕ kid.

moment /mɔmɑ̃/ nm moment;
(période) time; (petit) ~ short
while; **au** ~ **où** when; **par** ~s now
and then; **du** ~ **où** ou **que** (pourvu
que) as long as, provided that;
(puisque) since; **en ce** ~ at the
moment.

momentané, ~e /mɔmɑ̃tane/ a
momentary. **momentanément**
adv momentarily; (en ce moment) at
present.

momie /mɔmi/ nf mummy.

mon, ma (mon before vowel or
mute h) (pl **mes**) /mɔ̃, ma, mɔ̃,
me/ a my.

Monaco /mɔnako/ npr Monaco.

monarchie /mɔnaRʃi/ nf
monarchy.

monarque /mɔnaRk/ nm
monarch.

monastère /mɔnastɛR/ nm
monastery.

monceau (pl ~x) /mɔ̃so/ nm
heap, pile.

mondain, ~e /mɔ̃dɛ̃, -ɛn/ a
society, social.

monde /mɔ̃d/ nm world; **du** ~ (a
lot of); (quelqu'un) somebody; **le (grand)** ~ (high)
society; **se faire (tout) un** ~ **de qch**
make a great deal of fuss about

sth; **pas le moins du ~** not in the least.

mondial, ~e (*mpl* **-iaux**) /mɔ̃djal, -jo/ *a* world; (*influence*) worldwide. **mondialement** *adv* the world over. **mondialisation** /mɔ̃djalizasjɔ̃/ *nf* globalization.

monétaire /mɔnetɛʀ/ *a* monetary.

moniteur, -trice /mɔnitœʀ, -tʀis/ *nm, f* instructor; (de colonie de vacances) group leader; (US) (camp) counselor.

monnaie /mɔnɛ/ *nf* currency; (pièce) coin; (appoint) change; **faire la ~ de** get change for; **faire de la ~ à qn** give sb change; **menue** *ou* **petite ~** small change.

monnayer /mɔneje/ [31] *vt* convert into cash.

monologue /mɔnɔlɔg/ *nm* monologue.

monopole /mɔnɔpɔl/ *nm* monopoly. **monopoliser** [1] *vt* monopolize.

monospace /mɔnɔspas/ *nm* (Auto) people carrier.

monotone /mɔnɔtɔn/ *a* monotonous. **monotonie** *nf* monotony.

Monseigneur (*pl* **Messeigneurs**) /mɔ̃sɛɲœʀ/ *nm* (à un duc, archevêque) Your Grace; (à un prince) Your Highness.

monsieur (*pl* **messieurs**) /məsjø, mesjø/ *nm* (à un inconnu) (dans une lettre) **M~** Dear Sir; **bonjour, ~** good morning; **mesdames et messieurs** ladies and gentlemen; (à un homme dont on connaît le nom) (dans une lettre) **Cher M~** Dear Mr X; **bonjour, ~** good morning Mr X; **M~ le curé** Father X; **oui M~ le ministre** yes Minister; (homme) man; (formule de respect) sir.

monstre /mɔ̃stʀ/ *nm* monster. ● *a* Ⅲ colossal.

monstrueux, -euse /mɔ̃stʀyø, -z/ *a* monstrous. **monstruosité** *nf* monstrosity.

mont /mɔ̃/ *nm* mountain; **le ~ Everest** Mount Everest; **être toujours par ~s et par vaux** be always on the move.

montage /mɔ̃taʒ/ *nm* (assemblage) assembly; (au cinéma) editing.

montagne /mɔ̃taɲ/ *nf* mountain; (région) mountains; **~s russes** roller-coaster. **montagneux, -euse** *a* mountainous.

montant, ~e /mɔ̃tɑ̃, -t/ *a* rising; (col) high; (chemin) uphill. ● *nm* amount; (pièce de bois) upright.

mont-de-piété (*pl* **monts-de-piété**) /mɔ̃dpjete/ *nm* pawnshop.

monte-charge /mɔ̃tʃaʀʒ/ *nm inv* goods lift.

montée /mɔ̃te/ *nf* ascent, climb; (de prix) rise; (de coûts, risques) increase; (côte) hill.

monter /mɔ̃te/ [1] *vt* (*aux.* avoir) take up; (à l'étage) take upstairs; (escalier, rue, pente) go up; (assembler) assemble; (tente, échafaudage) put up; (col, manche) set in; (organiser) (pièce) stage; (société) set up; (attaque, garde) mount. ● *vi* (*aux.* être) go *ou* come up; (à l'étage) go *ou* come upstairs; (avion) climb; (route) go uphill, climb; (augmenter) rise; (marée) come up; **~ sur** (trottoir, toit) get up on; (cheval, bicyclette) get on; **~ à l'échelle/l'arbre** climb the ladder/tree; **~ dans** (voiture) get in; (train, bus, avion) get on; **~ à bord** climb on board; **~ à** (cheval) ride; **~ à bicyclette/moto** ride a bike/motorbike.

monteur, -euse /mɔ̃tœʀ, -øz/ *nm, f* (Tech) fitter; (au cinéma) editor.

montre /mɔ̃tʀ/ *nf* watch; **faire ~ de** show.

montrer /mɔ̃tʀe/ [1] *vt* show (à to); **~ du doigt** point to. □ **se ~**

vpr show oneself; (être) be; (s'avérer) prove to be.

monture /mɔ̃tyʀ/ *nf* (cheval) mount; (de lunettes) frames (+ *pl*); (de bijou) setting.

monument /mɔnymɑ̃/ *nm* monument; ~ **aux morts** war memorial. **monumental** (*mpl* **-aux**) *a* monumental.

moquer (se) /(sə)mɔke/ [1] *vpr* **se ~ de** make fun of; **je m'en moque** Ⅰ I couldn't care less. **moquerie** *nf* mockery. **moqueur, -euse** *a* mocking.

moquette /mɔkɛt/ *nf* fitted carpet; (US) wall-to-wall carpeting.

moral, ~e (*mpl* **-aux**) /mɔʀal, -o/ *a* moral. ● *nm* (*pl* **-aux**) morale; **ne pas avoir le ~** feel down; **avoir le ~** be in good spirits; **ça m'a remonté le ~** it gave me a boost.

morale /mɔʀal/ *nf* moral code; (mœurs) morals; (de fable) moral; **faire la ~ à** lecture. **moralité** *nf* (de personne) morals (+ *pl*); (d'action, œuvre) morality; (de fable) moral.

moralisateur, -trice /mɔʀalizatœʀ, -tʀis/ *a* moralizing.

morbide /mɔʀbid/ *a* morbid.

morceau (*pl* ~**x**) /mɔʀso/ *nm* piece, bit; (de sucre) lump; (de viande) cut; (passage) passage; **manger un ~** Ⅰ have a bite to eat; **mettre en ~x** smash *ou* tear to bits.

morceler /mɔʀsəle/ [6] *vt* divide up.

mordant, ~e /mɔʀdɑ̃, -t/ *a* scathing; (froid) biting. ● *nm* vigour, energy.

mordiller /mɔʀdije/ [1] *vt* nibble at.

mordre /mɔʀdʀ/ [3] *vi* bite (dans into); ~ **sur** (ligne) go over; (territoire) encroach on; ~ **à l'hameçon** bite. ● *vt* bite.

mordu, ~e /mɔʀdy/ Ⅰ *nm, f* fan. ● *a* smitten; ~ **de** crazy about.

morfondre (se) /(sə)mɔʀfɔ̃dʀ/ [3] *vpr* wait anxiously; (languir) mope.

morgue /mɔʀg/ *nf* morgue, mortuary; (attitude) arrogance.

moribond, ~e /mɔʀibɔ̃, -d/ *a* dying.

morne /mɔʀn/ *a* dull.

morphine /mɔʀfin/ *nf* morphine.

mors /mɔʀ/ *nm* (de cheval) bit.

morse /mɔʀs/ *nm* (animal) walrus; (code) Morse code.

morsure /mɔʀsyʀ/ *nf* bite.

mort¹ /mɔʀ/ *nf* death.

mort², ~e /mɔʀ, -t/ *a* dead; ~ **de fatigue** dead tired. ● *nm, f* dead man, dead woman; **les ~s** the dead.

mortalité /mɔʀtalite/ *nf* mortality; (**taux de) ~** death rate.

mortel, ~le /mɔʀtɛl/ *a* mortal; (accident) fatal; (poison, silence) deadly. ● *nm, f* mortal. **mortellement** *adv* mortally.

mortifié, ~e /mɔʀtifje/ *a* mortified.

mort-né, ~e /mɔʀne/ *a* stillborn.

mortuaire /mɔʀtɥɛʀ/ *a* (cérémonie) funeral.

morue /mɔʀy/ *nf* cod.

mosaïque /mɔzaik/ *nf* mosaic.

mosquée /mɔske/ *nf* mosque.

mot /mo/ *nm* word; (lettre, message) note; ~ **d'ordre** watchword; ~ **de passe** password; ~**s croisés** crossword (puzzle).

motard /mɔtaʀ/ *nm* biker; (policier) police motorcyclist.

moteur, -trice /mɔtœʀ, -tʀis/ *a* (Méd) motor; (force) driving; **à 4 roues motrices** 4-wheel drive. ● *nm* engine, motor; **barque à ~** motor launch; ~ **de recherche** (Internet) search engine.

motif /mɔtif/ *nm* (raisons) grounds

(+ *pl*); (cause) reason; (Jur) motive; (dessin) pattern.

motion /mosjɔ̃/ *nf* motion.

motivation /motivasjɔ̃/ *nf* motivation. **motiver** [1] *vt* motivate.

moto /moto/ *nf* motor cycle. **motocycliste** *nmf* motorcyclist.

motorisé, **~e** /motorize/ *a* motorized.

motrice /motris/ ⇒MOTEUR.

motte /mot/ *nf* lump; (de beurre) slab; (de terre) clod; **~ de gazon** turf.

mou (**mol** *before vowel or mute h*), **molle** /mu, mol/ *a* soft; (*ventre*) flabby; (*sans conviction*) feeble; (*apathique*) sluggish, listless. ● *nm* slack; **avoir du ~** be slack.

mouchard, **~e** /muʃar, -d/ *nm, f* informer; (Scol) sneak.

mouche /muʃ/ *nf* fly; (de cible) bull's eye.

moucher (**se**) /(sə)muʃe/ [1] *vpr* blow one's nose.

moucheron /muʃrɔ̃/ *nm* midge.

moucheté, **~e** /muʃte/ *a* speckled.

mouchoir /muʃwar/ *nm* handkerchief, hanky; **~ en papier** tissue.

moue /mu/ *nf* pout; **faire la ~** pout.

mouette /mwɛt/ *nf* (sea)gull.

moufle /mufl/ *nf* (gant) mitten.

mouillé, **~e** /muje/ *a* wet.

mouiller /muje/ [1] *vt* wet, make wet; **~ l'ancre** drop anchor. □ **se ~** *vpr* get (oneself) wet.

moulage /mulaʒ/ *nm* cast.

moule /mul/ *nf* (coquillage) mussel. ● *nm* mould; **~ à gâteau** cake tin; **~ à tarte** flan dish. **mouler** [1] *vt* mould; (*statue*) cast.

moulin /mulɛ̃/ *nm* mill; **~ à café** coffee grinder; **~ à poivre** pepper mill; **~ à vent** windmill.

moulinet /mulinɛ/ *nm* (de canne à pêche) reel; **faire des ~s avec qch** twirl sth around.

moulinette® /mulinɛt/ *nf* vegetable mill.

moulu, **~e** /muly/ *a* ground; (fatigué 🔲) worn out.

moulure /mulyr/ *nf* moulding.

mourant, **~e** /murɑ̃, -t/ *a* dying. ● *nm, f* dying person.

mourir /murir/ [43] *vi* (*aux. être*) die; **~ d'envie de** be dying to; **~ de faim** be starving; **~ d'ennui** be dead bored.

mousquetaire /muskətɛr/ *nm* musketeer.

mousse /mus/ *nf* moss; (écume) froth, foam; (de savon) lather; (dessert) mousse; **~ à raser** shaving foam. ● *nm* ship's boy

mousseline /muslin/ *nf* muslin; (de soie) chiffon.

mousser /muse/ [1] *vi* froth, foam, (savon) lather.

mousseux, **-euse** /musø, -z/ *a* frothy. ● *nm* sparkling wine.

mousson /musɔ̃/ *nf* monsoon.

moustache /mustaʃ/ *nf* moustache; **~s** (d'animal) whiskers.

moustique /mustik/ *nm* mosquito.

moutarde /mutard/ *nf* mustard.

mouton /mutɔ̃/ *nm* sheep; (peau) sheepskin; (viande) mutton.

mouvant, **~e** /muvɑ̃, -t/ *a* changing; (*terrain*) shifting, unstable.

mouvement /muvmɑ̃/ *nm* movement; (agitation) bustle; (en gymnastique) exercise; (impulsion) impulse; (tendance) tend, tendency; **en ~** in motion.

mouvementé, **~e** /muvmɑ̃te/ *a* eventful.

moyen, **~ne** /mwajɛ̃, -ɛn/ *a* average; (médiocre) poor; **de taille moyenne** medium-sized. ● *nm* means, way; **~s** means; (dons)

M

ability; **au ~ de** by means of; **il n'y a pas ~ de** it is not possible to. **Moyen Âge** *nm* Middle Ages (+ *pl*).

moyennant /mwajɛnɑ̃/ *prép* (pour) for; (grâce à) with.

moyenne /mwajɛn/ *nf* average; (Scol) pass-mark; **en ~** on average; **~ d'âge** average age.

moyennement *adv* moderately.

Moyen-Orient /mwajɛnɔrjɑ̃/ *nm* Middle East.

moyeu (*pl* **~x**) /mwajø/ *nm* hub.

mû, mue /my/ *a* driven (**par** by).

mucoviscidose /mykɔvisidoz/ *nf* cystic fibrosis.

mue /my/ *nf* moulting; (de voix) breaking of the voice.

muer /mɥe/ [1] *vi* moult; (voix) break. □ **se ~ en** *vpr* change into.

muet, ~te /mɥɛ, -t/ *a* (Méd) dumb; (fig) speechless (**de** with); (silencieux) silent. ● *nm, f* mute.

mufle /myfl/ *nm* nose, muzzle; (personne 🖭) boor, lout.

mugir /myʒir/ [2] *vi* (vache) moo; (bœuf) bellow; (fig) howl.

muguet /mygɛ/ *nm* lily of the valley.

mule /myl/ *nf* (female) mule; (pantoufle) mule.

mulet /mylɛ/ *nm* (male) mule.

multicolore /myltikɔlɔr/ *a* multicoloured.

multimédia /myltimedja/ *a* & *nm* multimedia.

multinational, ~e (*mpl* **-aux**) /myltinasjɔnal, -o/ *a* multinational. **multinationale** *nf* multinational (company).

multiple /myltipl/ *nm* multiple. ● *a* numerous, many; (naissances) multiple.

multiplication /myltiplikasjɔ̃/ *nf* multiplication.

multiplicité /myltiplisite/ *nf* multiplicity.

multiplier /myltiplije/ [45] *vt* multiply; (risques) increase. □ **se ~** *vpr* multiply; (accidents) be on the increase; (difficultés) increase.

multitude /myltityd/ *nf* multitude, mass.

municipal, ~e (*mpl* **-aux**) /mynisipal, -o/ *a* municipal; **conseil ~** town council.

municipalité *nf* (ville) municipality; (conseil) town council.

munir /mynir/ [2] *vt* **~ de** provide with. □ **se ~ de** *vpr* (apporter) bring; (emporter) take.

munitions /mynisjɔ̃/ *nfpl* ammunition.

mur /myr/ *nm* wall; **~ du son** sound barrier.

mûr, ~e /myr/ *a* ripe; (personne) mature.

muraille /myrɑj/ *nf* (high) wall.

mural, ~e (*mpl* **-aux**) /myral, -o/ *a* wall; **peinture ~e** mural.

mûre /myr/ *nf* blackberry.

mûrir /myrir/ [2] *vi* ripen; (abcès) come to a head; (personne, projet) mature. ● *vt* (fruit) ripen; (personne) mature.

murmure /myrmyr/ *nm* murmur.

muscade /myskad/ *nf* **noix ~** nutmeg.

muscle /myskl/ *nm* muscle. **musclé, ~e** *a* muscular.

musculaire *a* muscular.

musculation /myskylasjɔ̃/ *nf* bodybuilding.

musculature /myskylatyr/ *nf* muscles (+ *pl*).

museau (*pl* **~x**) /myzo/ *nm* muzzle; (de porc) snout.

musée /myze/ *nm* museum; (de peinture) art gallery.

muselière /myzəljɛr/ *nf* muzzle.

musette /myzɛt/ *nf* haversack.

muséum /myzeɔm/ *nm* natural
history museum.

musical, ∼e (*mpl* **-aux**)
/myzikal, -o/ *a* musical.

musicien, ∼ne /myzisjɛ̃, -ɛn/ *a*
musical. ● *nm, f* musician.

musique /myzik/ *nf* music;
(orchestre) band.

must /mœst/ *nm* Ⓔ must.

musulman, ∼e /myzylmɑ̃, -an/ *a*
& *nm,f* Muslim.

mutation /mytasjɔ̃/ *nf* change;
(biologique) mutation; (d'un employé)
transfer.

muter /myte/ [1] *vt* transfer. ● *vi*
mutate.

mutilation /mytilasjɔ̃/ *nf*
mutilation. **mutiler** [1] *vt*
mutilate. **mutilé**, ∼e *nm, f*
disabled person.

mutin, ∼e /mytɛ̃, -in/ *a*
mischievous. ● *nm* mutineer;
(prisonnier) rioter.

mutinerie /mytinʀi/ *nf* mutiny;
(de prisonniers) riot.

mutisme /mytism/ *nm* silence.

mutuel, ∼le /mytɥɛl/ *a* mutual.

mutuelle *nf* mutual insurance
company. **mutuellement** *adv*
mutually; (l'un l'autre) each other.

myope /mjɔp/ *a* short-sighted.
myopie *nf* short sightedness.

myosotis /mjozɔtis/ *nm* forget-
me-not.

myrtille /miʀtij/ *nf* bilberry,
blueberry.

mystère /mistɛʀ/ *nm* mystery.

mystérieux, **-ieuse** /misteʀjø, -z/
a mysterious.

mystification /mistifikasjɔ̃/ *nf*
hoax.

mysticisme /mistisism/ *nm*
mysticism.

mystique /mistik/ *a* mystic(al).
● *nmf* mystic. ● *nf* mystique.

mythe /mit/ *nm* myth. **mythique**
a mythical.

mythologie /mitɔlɔʒi/ *nf*
mythology.

n' /n/ ⇒NE.

nacre /nakʀ/ *nf* mother-of-pearl.

nage /naʒ/ *nf* swimming; (manière)
stroke; **traverser à la** ∼ swim
across; **en** ∼ sweating.

nageoire /naʒwaʀ/ *nf* fin; (de
mammifère) flipper.

nager /naʒe/ [40] *vt/i* swim.
nageur, **-euse** *nm,f* swimmer.

naguère /nagɛʀ/ *adv* (autrefois)
formerly.

naïf, **-ive** /naif, -v/ *a* naïve.

nain, ∼e /nɛ̃, nɛn/ *nm,f* & *a*
dwarf.

naissance /nesɑ̃s/ *nf* birth;
donner ∼ **à** give birth to; (fig) give
rise to.

naître /nɛtʀ/ [44] *vi* be born;
(résulter) arise (de from); **faire** ∼
(susciter) give rise to.

naïveté /naivte/ *nf* naïvety.

nappe /nap/ *nf* tablecloth; (de
pétrole, gaz) layer; ∼ **phréatique**
ground water.

napperon /napʀɔ̃/ *nm* (cloth)
tablemat.

narco-dollars /naʀkodɔlaʀ/
nmpl drug money.

narcotique /naʀkɔtik/ *a* & *nm*
narcotic. **narco(-)trafiquant**, ∼e
(*pl* ∼s) *nm, f* drug trafficker.

narguer /naʀge/ [1] *vt* taunt;
(autorité) flout.

narine /naʀin/ *nf* nostril.

nasal, ∼e (*mpl* **-aux**) /nazal, -o/
a nasal.

naseau (*pl* ∼x) /nazo/ *nm*
nostril.

natal, ~e (*mpl* ~s) /natal/ *a* native.

natalité /natalite/ *nf* birth rate.

natation /natasjɔ̃/ *nf* swimming.

natif, **-ive** /natif, -v/ *a* native.

nation /nasjɔ̃/ *nf* nation.

national, ~e (*mpl* **-aux**) /nasjɔnal, -o/ *a* national. **nationale** *nf* A road; (US) highway. **nationaliser** [1] *vt* nationalize.

nationalité /nasjɔnalite/ *nf* nationality.

natte /nat/ *nf* (de cheveux) plait; (US) braid; (tapis de paille) mat.

nature /natyʀ/ *nf* nature; ~ **morte** still life; **de** ~ **à** likely to; **payer en** ~ pay in kind. ● *a inv* plain; (*yaourt*) natural; (*thé*) black.

naturel, ~**le** /natyʀɛl/ *a* natural. ● *nm* nature; (simplicité) naturalness; (Culin) au ~ plain; (*thon*) in brine. **naturellement** *adv* naturally; (bien sûr) of course.

naufrage /nofʀaʒ/ *nm* shipwreck; **faire** ~ be shipwrecked; (*bateau*) be wrecked.

nauséabond, ~e /nozeabɔ̃, -d/ *a* nauseating.

nausée /noze/ *nf* nausea.

nautique /notik/ *a* nautical; **sports** ~**s** water sports.

naval, ~e (*mpl* ~s) /naval/ *a* naval; **chantier** ~ shipyard.

navet /navɛ/ *nm* turnip; (film: péj) flop; (US) turkey.

navette /navɛt/ *nf* shuttle (service); **faire la** ~ shuttle back and forth.

navigateur, **-trice** /navigatœʀ, -tʀis/ *nm,f* sailor; (qui guide) navigator; (Internet) browser.

navigation *nf* navigation; (trafic) shipping; (Internet) browsing.

naviguer /navige/ [1] *vi* sail; (piloter) navigate; (Internet) browse; ~ **dans l'Internet** surf the Internet.

navire /naviʀ/ *nm* ship.

navré, ~e /navʀe/ *a* sorry (de to).

------

ne, **n'** /nə, n/

n' before vowel or mute h.

● *adverbe*

····▸ **je n'ai que 10 euros** I've only got 10 euros.

····▸ **tu n'avais qu'à le dire!** you only had to say so!

····▸ **je crains qu'il** ~ **parte** I am afraid he will leave.

❗ Pour les expressions comme ne... guère, ne... jamais, ne... pas, ne... plus, etc. ⇒**guère, jamais, pas, plus**, etc.

------

né, ~e /ne/ *a* born; ~e **Martin** née Martin; (dans composés) **dernier-**~ last-born. ● ⇒**NAÎTRE** [44].

néanmoins /neɑ̃mwɛ̃/ *adv* nevertheless.

néant /neɑ̃/ *nm* nothingness; **réduire à** ~ (effet, efforts) negate, nullify; (espoir) dash; '**revenus:** ~' 'income: nil'.

nécessaire /neseseʀ/ *a* necessary. ● *nm* (sac) bag; (trousse) kit; **le** ~ (l'indispensable) the necessities *ou* essentials; **faire le** ~ do what is necessary.

nécessité /nesesite/ *nf* necessity; **de première** ~ vital.

nécessiter /nesesite/ [1] *vt* necessitate.

néerlandais, ~e /neɛʀlɑ̃dɛ, -z/ *a* Dutch. ● *nm* (Ling) Dutch. **N**~, ~e *nm, f* Dutchman, Dutchwoman.

néfaste /nefast/ *a* harmful (à to).

négatif, **-ive** /negatif, -v/ *a & nm* negative.

négligé, ~e /negliʒe/ *a* (travail)

careless; (*tenue*) scruffy. ● *nm*
(*tenue*) negligee.

négligent, **~e** /negliʒɑ̃, -t/ *a*
careless, negligent.

négliger /negliʒe/ [40] *vt* neglect;
(*ne pas tenir compte de*) ignore,
disregard; **~ de faire** fail to do.
□ **se ~** *vpr* neglect oneself.

négoce /negɔs/ *nm* business,
trade. **négociant**, **~e** *nm*, *f*
merchant.

négociation /negɔsjasjɔ̃/ *nf*
negotiation. **négocier** [45] *vt/i*
negotiate.

nègre /nɛgʀ/ *a* (*musique, art*)
Negro. ● *nm* (*écrivain*) ghost
writer.

neige /nɛʒ/ *nf* snow. **neiger** [40]
vi snow.

nénuphar /nenyfaʀ/ *nm* waterlily.

nerf /nɛʀ/ *nm* nerve; (*vigueur*)
stamina; **être sur les ~s** be on
edge.

nerveux, **-euse** /nɛʀvø, -z/ *a*
nervous; (*irritable*) nervy; (*centre,
cellule*) nerve; (*voiture*)
responsive. **nervosité** *nf*
nervousness; (*irritabilité*)
touchiness.

net, **~te** /nɛt/ *a* (*clair, distinct*) clear;
(*propre*) clean; (*notable*) marked;
(*soigné*) neat; (*prix, poids*) net. ●
N~ *nm* (Ordinat) net. ● *adv*
(*s'arrêter*) dead; (*refuser*) flatly;
(*parler*) plainly; (*se casser*)
cleanly; (*tuer*) outright.
nettement *adv* (*expliquer*)
clearly; (*augmenter, se détériorer*)
markedly; (*indiscutablement*)
distinctly, decidedly. **netteté** *nf*
clearness.

netéconomie /nɛtekɔnɔmi/ *nf*
e-economy.

nétiquette /netikɛt/ *nf*
netiquette.

nettoyage /nɛtwajaʒ/ *nm*
cleaning; **~ à sec** dry-cleaning;
produit de ~ cleaner; **~ ethnique**
ethnic cleansing.

nettoyer /nɛtwaje/ [31] *vt* clean.

neuf¹ /nœf/ (/nœv/ *before vowels
and mute h*) *a inv* & *nm* nine.

neuf², **-euve** /nœf, -v/ *a* new; **tout
~** brand new. ● *nm* new; **remettre
à ~** brighten up; **du ~** a new
development; **quoi de ~?** what's
new?

neutre /nøtʀ/ *a* neutral; (Gram)
neuter. ● *nm* (Gram) neuter.

neuve /nœv/ ⇒NEUF².

neuvième /nœvjɛm/ *a* & *nm*, *f*
ninth.

neveu (*pl* **~x**) /nəvø/ *nm*
nephew.

névrose /nevʀoz/ *nf* neurosis.
névrosé, **~e** *a* & *nm*, *f* neurotic.

nez /ne/ *nm* nose; **~ à ~** face to
face; **~ retroussé** turned-up nose.

ni /ni/ *conj* neither, nor; **~ grand
~ petit** neither big nor small; **~
l'un ~ l'autre ne fument** neither
(one nor the other) smokes; **sortir
sans manteau ~ chapeau** go
without a coat or hat; **elle n'a dit
~ oui ~ non** she didn't say either
yes or no.

niais, **~e** /njɛ, -z/ *a* silly.

niche /niʃ/ *nf* (de chien) kennel;
(*cavité*) niche.

nicher /niʃe/ [1] *vi* nest. □ **se ~**
vpr nest; (se cacher) hide.

nicotine /nikɔtin/ *nf* nicotine.

nid /ni/ *nm* nest; **faire un ~** build
a nest. **nid-de-poule** (*pl* **nids-de-
poule**) *nm* pot-hole.

nièce /njɛs/ *nf* niece.

nier /nje/ [45] *vt* deny.

nigaud, **~e** /nigo, -d/ *nm*, *f* fool.

nippon, **~ne** /nipɔ̃, -ɔn/ *a*
Japanese. **N~**, **~ne** *nm*, *f*
Japanese.

niveau (*pl* **~x**) /nivo/ *nm* level;
(*compétence*) standard; (*étage*)
storey; (US) story; **au ~** up to
standard; **mettre à ~** (Ordinat)
upgrade; **~ à bulle** (d'air) spirit-
level; **~ de vie** standard of living.

niveler /nivle/ [6] *vt* level.

N

noble /nɔbl/ *a* noble. ● *nm, f* nobleman, noblewoman.
noblesse *nf* nobility.

noce /nɔs/ *nf* (fête 🔲) party; (invités) wedding guests; **~s** wedding; **faire la ~** 🔲 live it up.

nocif, -ive /nɔsif, -v/ *a* harmful.

nocturne /nɔktyʀn/ *a* nocturnal. ● *nm* (Mus) nocturne. ● *nf* (Sport) evening fixture; (de magasin) late-night opening.

Noël /nɔɛl/ *nm* Christmas.

nœud /nø/ *nm* (Naut) knot; (pour lier) knot; (pour orner) bow; **~s** (fig) ties; **~ coulant** slipknot, noose; **~ papillon** bow-tie.

noir, ~e /nwaʀ/ *a* black; (obscur, sombre) dark; (triste) gloomy. ● *nm* black; (obscurité) dark; **travail au ~** moonlighting. ● *nm, f* (personne) Black.

noircir /nwaʀsiʀ/ [2] *vt* blacken; **~ la situation** paint a black picture of the situation. ● *vi* (banane) go black; (mur) get dirty; (métal) tarnish. □ **se ~** *vpr* (ciel) darken.

noire /nwaʀ/ *nf* (Mus) crotchet.

noisette /nwazɛt/ *nf* hazelnut; (de beurre) knob.

noix /nwa/ *nf* nut; (du noyer) walnut; (de beurre) knob; **~ de cajou** cashew nut; **~ de coco** coconut; **à la ~** 🔲 useless.

nom /nɔ̃/ *nm* name; (Gram) noun; **au ~ de** on behalf of; **~ et prénom** full name; **~ déposé** registered trademark; **~ de famille** surname; **~ de jeune fille** maiden name; **~ de plume** pen name; **~ propre** proper noun.

nomade /nɔmad/ *a* nomadic; (Internet) mobile. ● *nmf* nomad.

nombre /nɔ̃bʀ/ *nm* number; **au ~ de** (parmi) among; (l'un de) one of;

en (grand) **~** in large numbers; **sans ~** countless.

nombreux, -euse /nɔ̃bʀø, -z/ *a* (en grand nombre) many, numerous; (important) large; **de ~ enfants** many children; **nous étions très ~** there were a great many of us.

nombril /nɔ̃bʀil/ *nm* navel.

nomination /nɔminasjɔ̃/ *nf* appointment.

nommer /nɔme/ [1] *vt* name; (élire) (à un poste) appoint; (à un lieu) post. □ **se ~** *vpr* (s'appeler) be called.

non /nɔ̃/ *adv* no; (pas) not; **~ (pas) que** not that; **il vient, ~?** he is coming, isn't he?; **moi ~ plus** neither am/do/can/*etc.* I. ● *nm inv* no.

non- /nɔ̃/ *préf* non-; **~-fumeur** non-smoker.

nonante /nɔnɑ̃t/ *a & nm* ninety.

non-sens /nɔ̃sɑ̃s/ *nm inv* absurdity.

nord /nɔʀ/ *a inv* (façade, côte) north; (frontière, zone) northern. ● *nm* north; **le ~ de l'Europe** northern Europe; **vent de ~** northerly (wind); **aller vers le ~** go north; **le Nord** the North; **du Nord** northern. **nord-est** *nm* north-east.

nordique /nɔʀdik/ *a* Scandinavian.

nord-ouest /nɔʀwɛst/ *nm* north-west.

normal, ~e (*mpl* **-aux**) /nɔʀmal, -o/ *a* normal. **normale** *nf* normality; (norme) norm; (moyenne) average.

normand, ~e /nɔʀmɑ̃, -d/ *a* Norman. **N~, ~e** *nm, f* Norman.

Normandie /nɔʀmɑ̃di/ *nf* Normandy.

norme /nɔʀm/ *nf* norm; (de production) standard; **~s de sécurité** safety standards.

Norvège /nɔʀvɛʒ/ *nf* Norway.

norvégien, ~ne /nɔʀveʒjɛ̃, -ɛn/ a Norwegian. **N~**, **~ne** nm, f Norwegian.

nos /no/ ⇒NOTRE.

nostalgie /nɔstalʒi/ nf nostalgia; **avoir la ~ de son pays** be homesick. **nostalgique** a nostalgic.

notaire /nɔtɛʀ/ nm notary public.

notamment /nɔtamɑ̃/ adv notably.

note /nɔt/ nf (remarque) note; (chiffrée) mark, grade; (facture) bill; (Mus) note; **~ (de service)** memorandum.

noter /nɔte/ [1] vt note, notice; (écrire) note (down); (devoir) mark; (US) grade; **bien/mal noté** (employé) highly/poorly rated.

notice /nɔtis/ nf note; (mode d'emploi) instructions, directions.

notifier /nɔtifje/ [45] vt notify (à to).

notion /nɔsjɔ̃/ nf notion; **avoir des ~s de** have a basic knowledge of.

notoire /nɔtwaʀ/ a well-known; (criminel) notorious.

notre (pl nos) /nɔtʀ, no/ a our.

nôtre /notʀ/ pron le ou la ~, les ~s ours.

nouer /nwe/ [1] vt tie, knot; (relations) strike up.

nouille /nuj/ nf (Culin) noodle; **des ~s** noodles, pasta; (idiot 🄻) idiot.

nounours /nunuʀs/ nm 🄻 teddy bear.

nourri, **~e** /nuʀi/ a être logé ~ have bed and board; **~ au sein** breastfed.

nourrice /nuʀis/ nf childminder.

nourrir /nuʀiʀ/ [2] vt feed; (espoir, crainte) harbour; (projet) nurture; (passion) fuel. ● vi be nourishing. □ se ~ vpr eat; se ~ **de** feed on. **nourrissant**, **~e** a nourishing.

nourrisson /nuʀisɔ̃/ nm infant.

nourriture /nuʀityʀ/ nf food.

nous /nu/ pron (sujet) we; (complément) us; (indirect) (to) us; (réfléchi) ourselves; (l'un l'autre) each other; **la voiture est à ~** the car is ours. **nous-mêmes** pron ourselves.

nouveau (**nouvel** before vowel or mute h), **nouvelle** (mpl ~x) /nuvo, nuvɛl/ a new; **nouvel an** new year; **~x mariés** newly-weds; **~ venu**, **nouvelle venue** newcomer. ● nm, f (élève) new boy, new girl. ● nm du ~ (fait nouveau) a new development; **de ~**, **à ~** again. **nouveau-né** (pl ~s) nm newborn baby.

nouveauté /nuvote/ nf novelty; (chose) new thing; (livre) new publication; (disque) new release.

nouvelle /nuvɛl/ nf (pièce of news; (récit) short story; **~s** news.

Nouvelle-Zélande /nuvɛlzelɑ̃d/ nf New Zealand.

novembre /nɔvɑ̃bʀ/ nm November.

noyade /nwajad/ nf drowning.

noyau (pl ~x) /nwajo/ nm (de fruit) stone; (US) pit; (de cellule) nucleus; (groupe) group; (centre: fig) core.

noyer /nwaje/ [31] vt drown; (inonder) flood. □ se ~ vpr drown; (volontairement) drown oneself; **se ~ dans un verre d'eau** make a mountain out of a molehill. ● nm walnut-tree.

nu, **~e** /ny/ a (corps, personne) naked; (mains, mur, fil) bare; **à l'œil ~** to the naked eye. ● nm nude; **mettre à ~** expose.

nuage /nɥaʒ/ nm cloud.

nuance /nɥɑ̃s/ nf shade; (de sens) nuance; (différence) difference. **nuancer** [10] vt (opinion) qualify.

nucléaire /nykleɛʀ/ a nuclear. ● nm le ~ nuclear energy.

nudisme /nydism/ nm nudism.

N

nudité /nydite/ *nf* nudity; (de lieu) bareness.

nuée /nɥe/ *nf* swarm, host.

nues /ny/ *nfpl* **tomber des** ~ be amazed; **porter qn aux** ~ praise sb to the skies.

nuire /nɥiʀ/ [17] *vi* ~ **à** harm.

nuisible /nɥizibl/ *a* harmful (**à** to).

nuit /nɥi/ *nf* night; **cette** ~ tonight; (hier) last night; **il fait** ~ it is dark; ~ **blanche** sleepless night; **la** ~, **de** ~ at night; ~ **de noces** wedding night.

nul, ~**le** /nyl/ *a* (aucun) no; (zéro) nil; (qui ne vaut rien) useless; (non valable) null; (contrat) void; (testament) invalid; **match** ~ draw; ~ **en sciences** no good at science; **nulle part** nowhere; ~ **autre** no one else. ● *pron* no one. **nullement** *adv* not at all. **nullité** *nf* uselessness; (personne) nonentity.

numérique /nymeʀik/ *a* numerical; (montre, horloge) digital.

numéro /nymeʀo/ *nm* number; (de journal) issue; (spectacle) act; ~ **de téléphone** telephone number; ~ **vert** freephone number. **numéroter** [1] *vt* number.

nuque /nyk/ *nf* nape (of the neck).

nurse /nœʀs/ *nf* nanny.

nutritif, -ive /nytʀitif, -v/ *a* nutritious; (valeur) nutritional.

oasis /ɔazis/ *nf* oasis.

obéir /ɔbeiʀ/ [2] *vt* ~ **à** obey. ● *vi* obey. **obéissance** *nf* obedience. **obéissant**, ~**e** *a* obedient.

obèse /ɔbɛz/ *a* obese.

objecter /ɔbʒɛkte/ [1] *vt* object.

objectif, -ive /ɔbʒɛktif, -v/ *a* objective. ● *nm* objective; (Photo) lens.

objection /ɔbʒɛksjɔ̃/ *nf* objection; **soulever des** ~s raise objections.

objet /ɔbʒɛ/ *nm* (chose) object; (sujet) subject; (but) purpose, object; **être** *ou* **faire l'**~ **de** be the subject of; ~ **d'art** objet d'art; ~s **trouvés** lost property; (US) lost and found.

obligation /ɔbligasjɔ̃/ *nf* obligation; (Comm) bond; **être dans l'**~ **de** be under obligation to.

obligatoire /ɔbligatwaʀ/ *a* compulsory. **obligatoirement** *adv* (par règlement) of necessity; (inévitablement) inevitably.

obligeance /ɔbliʒɑ̃s/ *nf* **avoir l'**~ **de faire** be kind enough to do.

obliger /ɔbliʒe/ [40] *vt* compel, force (**à faire** to do); (aider) oblige; **être obligé de** have to (**de** for).

oblique /ɔblik/ *a* oblique; **regard** ~ sidelong glance; **en** ~ at an angle.

oblitérer /ɔbliteʀe/ [14] *vt* (timbre) cancel.

obnubilé, ~**e** /ɔbnybile/ *a* obsessed.

obscène /ɔpsɛn/ *a* obscene.

obscur, ~**e** /ɔpskyʀ/ *a* dark;

(confus, humble) obscure; (vague) vague.

obscurcir /ɔpskyʀsiʀ/ [2] vt make dark; (fig) obscure. □ s'∼ vpr (ciel) darken.

obscurité /ɔpskyʀite/ nf darkness; (de passage, situation) obscurity.

obsédant, ∼e /ɔpsedã, -t/ a nagging; (problème) nagging; (musique, souvenir) haunting.

obsédé, ∼e /ɔpsede/ nm, f ∼ (sexuel) sex maniac; ∼ du ski/jazz ski/jazz freak.

obséder /ɔpsede/ [14] vt obsess.

obsèques /ɔpsɛk/ nfpl funeral.

observateur, -trice /ɔpsɛʀvatœʀ, -tʀis/ a observant. ●nm, f observer.

observation /ɔpsɛʀvasjɔ̃/ nf observation; (remarque) remark, comment; (reproche) criticism; (obéissance) observance; en ∼ under observation.

observer /ɔpsɛʀve/ [1] vt (regarder) observe; (surveiller) watch, observe; (remarquer) notice, observe; faire ∼ qch point sth out (à to).

obsession /ɔpsesjɔ̃/ nf obsession.

obstacle /ɔpstakl/ nm obstacle; (pour cheval) fence, jump; (pour athlète) hurdle; faire ∼ à stand in the way of, obstruct.

obstétrique /ɔpstetʀik/ nf obstetrics (+ sg).

obstiné, ∼e /ɔpstine/ a stubborn, obstinate.

obstiner (s') /(s)ɔpstine/ [1] vpr persist (à in).

obstruction /ɔpstʀyksjɔ̃/ nf obstruction; (de conduit) blockage.

obstruer /ɔpstʀye/ [1] vt obstruct, block.

obtenir /ɔptəniʀ/ [58] vt get, obtain. **obtention** nf obtaining.

obus /ɔby/ nm shell.

occasion /ɔkazjɔ̃/ nf opportunity (de faire of doing); (circonstance) occasion; (achat) bargain; (article non neuf) second-hand buy; à l'∼ sometimes; d'∼ second-hand.

occasionnel, ∼le a occasional.

occasionner /ɔkazjɔne/ [1] vt cause.

occident /ɔksidã/ nm (direction) west; l'O∼ the West.

occidental, ∼e (mpl -aux) /ɔksidãtal, -o/ a western. **O∼, ∼e** (mpl -aux) nm, f westerner.

occulte /ɔkylt/ a occult.

occupant, ∼e /ɔkypã, -t/ nm, f occupant. ●nm (Mil) forces of occupation.

occupation /ɔkypasjɔ̃/ nf occupation.

occupé, ∼e /ɔkype/ a busy; (place, pays) occupied; (téléphone) engaged, busy; (toilettes) engaged.

occuper /ɔkype/ [1] vt occupy; (poste) hold; (espace, temps) take up. □ s'∼ vpr (s'affairer) keep busy (à faire doing); s'∼ de (personne, problème) take care of; (bureau, firme) be in charge of; (se mêler) occupe-toi de tes affaires mind your own business.

occurrence: en l'∼ /ãlɔkyʀãs/ loc in this case.

océan /ɔseã/ nm ocean.

Océanie /ɔseani/ nf Oceania.

ocre /ɔkʀ/ a inv ochre.

octante /ɔktãt/ a eighty.

octet /ɔktɛ/ nm byte.

octobre /ɔktɔbʀ/ nm October.

octogone /ɔktɔgɔn/ nm octagon.

octroyer /ɔktʀwaje/ [31] vt grant.

oculaire /ɔkylɛʀ/ a témoin ∼ eye-witness; troubles ∼s eye trouble.

oculiste /ɔkylist/ nmf ophthalmologist.

odeur /ɔdœʀ/ nf smell.

odieux, -ieuse /ɔdjø, -z/ a odious.

odorant, ~**e** /ɔdɔRɑ̃, -t/ a sweet-smelling.

odorat /ɔdɔRa/ nm sense of smell.

œil (pl **yeux**) /œj, jø/ nm eye; **à l'**~ ▯ for free; **à mes yeux** in my view; **faire de l'**~ **à** make eyes at; **faire les gros yeux à** glare at; **ouvrir l'**~ keep one's eyes open; ~ **poché** black eye; **fermer les yeux** shut one's eyes; (fig) turn a blind eye.

œillères /œjɛR/ nfpl blinkers.

œillet /œjɛ/ nm (plante) carnation; (trou) eyelet.

œuf (pl ~**s**) /œf, ø/ nm egg; ~ **à la coque/dur/sur le plat** boiled/hard-boiled/fried egg.

œuvre /œvR/ nf (ouvrage, travail) work; ~ **d'art** work of art; ~ **(de bienfaisance)** charity; **être à l'**~ be at work; **mettre en** ~ (réforme, moyens) implement; **mise en** ~ implementation. ●nm (ensemble spécifié) **l'**~ **entier de Beethoven** the complete works of Beethoven.

œuvrer /œvRe/ [1] vi work.

offense /ɔfɑ̃s/ nf insult.

offenser /ɔfɑ̃se/ [1] vt offend. □ **s'**~ vpr take offence (de at).

offensive /ɔfɑ̃siv/ nf offensive.

offert, ~**e** /ɔfɛR, -t/ ⇒OFFRIR [21].

office /ɔfis/ nm office; (Relig) service; (de cuisine) pantry; **faire** ~ **de** act as; **d'**~ without consultation, automatically; ~ **du tourisme** tourist information office.

officiel, -le /ɔfisjɛl/ a official. ●nm official.

officier /ɔfisje/ [45] vi (Relig) officiate. ●nm officer.

officieux, -ieuse /ɔfisjø, -z/ a unofficial.

offre /ɔfR/ nf offer; (aux enchères) bid; **l'**~ **et la demande** supply and demand; '~**s d'emploi**' 'situations vacant'.

offrir /ɔfRiR/ [21] vt offer (de faire to do); (cadeau) give; (acheter) buy; ~ **à boire à** (chez soi) give a drink to; (au café) buy a drink for. □ **s'**~ vpr (se proposer) offer oneself (comme as); (solution) present itself; (s'acheter) treat oneself to.

ogive /ɔʒiv/ nf ~ **nucléaire** nuclear warhead.

OGM abrév m (**organisme génétiquement modifié**) GMO, genetically modified organism.

oie /wa/ nf goose.

oignon /ɔɲɔ̃/ nm (légume) onion; (de fleur) bulb.

oiseau (pl ~**x**) /wazo/ nm bird.

oisif, -ive /wazif, -v/ a idle.

olive /ɔliv/ nf & a inv olive. **olivier** nm olive tree.

olympique /ɔlɛ̃pik/ a Olympic.

ombrage /ɔ̃bRaʒ/ nm shade; **prendre** ~ **de** take offence at. **ombragé,** ~**e** a shady.

ombre /ɔ̃bR/ nf (pénombre) shade; (contour) shadow; (soupçon: fig) hint, shadow; **dans l'**~ (agir, rester) behind the scenes; **faire de l'**~ **à qn** be in sb's light.

ombrelle /ɔ̃bRɛl/ nf parasol.

omelette /ɔmlɛt/ nf omelette.

omettre /ɔmɛtR/ [42] vt omit, leave out.

omnibus /ɔmnibys/ nm stopping ou local train.

omoplate /ɔmɔplat/ nf shoulder blade.

on /ɔ̃/ pron (tu, vous) you; (nous) we; (ils, elles) they; (les gens) people, they; (quelqu'un) someone; (indéterminé) one, you; ~ **dit** people say, they say, it is said; ~ **m'a demandé mon avis** I was asked for my opinion.

oncle /ɔ̃kl/ nm uncle.

onctueux, -euse /ɔktɥø, -z/ a smooth.

onde /ɔd/ nf wave; ~s courtes/ longues short/long wave; sur les ~s on the air.

on-dit /ɔdi/ nm inv les ~ hearsay.

onduler /ɔdyle/ [1] vi undulate; (cheveux) be wavy.

onéreux, -euse /ɔnerø, -z/ a costly.

ongle /ɔgl/ nm (finger)nail; ~ de pied toenail; se faire les ~s do one's nails.

ont /ɔ̃/ ⇒AVOIR [5].

ONU abrév f (**Organisation des Nations unies**) UN.

onze /ɔz/ a & nm eleven.

onzième a & nmf eleventh.

OPA abrév f (**offre publique d'achat**) takeover bid.

opéra /ɔpera/ nm opera; (édifice) opera house. **opéra-comique** (pl **opéras-comiques**) nm light opera.

opérateur, -trice /ɔperatœr, -tris/ nm, f operator.

opération /ɔperasjɔ̃/ nf operation; (Comm) deal; (calcul) calculation; ~ escargot slow-moving protest convoy.

opératoire /ɔperatwar/ a (Méd) surgical; bloc ~ operating suite.

opérer /ɔpere/ [14] vt (personne) operate on; (exécuter) carry out, make; ~ qn d'une tumeur operate on sb to remove a tumour; se faire ~ have surgery ou an operation. ● vi (Méd) operate; (faire effet) work. □ s'~ vpr (se produire) occur.

opiniâtre /ɔpinjɑtr/ a tenacious.

opinion /ɔpinjɔ̃/ nf opinion.

opportuniste /ɔpɔrtynist/ nmf opportunist.

opposant, ~e /ɔpozɑ̃, -t/ nm, f opponent.

opposé, ~e /ɔpoze/ a (sens, angle, avis) opposite; (factions) opposing; (intérêts) conflicting; être ~ à be opposed to. ● nm opposite; à l'~ de (contrairement à) contrary to, unlike.

opposer /ɔpoze/ [1] vt (objets) place opposite each other; (personnes) match, oppose; (contraster) contrast; (résistance, argument) put up. □ s'~ vpr (personnes) confront each other; (styles) contrast; s'~ à oppose.

opposition /ɔpozisjɔ̃/ nf opposition; par ~ à in contrast with; entrer en ~ avec come into conflict with; faire ~ à un chèque stop a cheque.

oppressant, ~e /ɔpresɑ̃, -t/ a oppressive.

opprimer /ɔprime/ [1] vt oppress.

opter /ɔpte/ [1] vi ~ pour opt for.

opticien, ~ne /ɔptisjɛ̃, -ɛn/ nm, f optician.

optimisme /ɔptimism/ nm optimism.

optimiste /ɔptimist/ nmf optimist. ● a optimistic.

option /ɔpsjɔ̃/ nf option.

optique /ɔptik/ a (verre) optical. ● nf (science) optics (+ sg); (perspective) perspective.

or¹ /ɔr/ nm gold; d'~ golden; en ~ gold; (occasion) golden.

or² /ɔr/ conj now, well; (indiquant une opposition) and yet.

orage /ɔraʒ/ nm (thunder)storm. **orageux, -euse** a stormy.

oral, ~e (mpl -aux) /ɔral, -o/ a oral. ● nm (pl -aux) oral.

orange /ɔrɑ̃ʒ/ a inv orange; (Aut) (feu) amber; (US) yellow. ● nf orange. **orangeade** nf orangeade. **oranger** nm orange tree.

orateur, -trice /ɔratœr, -tris/ nm, f speaker.

orbite /ɔrbit/ nf orbit; (d'œil) socket.

orchestre /ɔRkɛstR/ *nm*
orchestra; (de jazz) band; (parterre)
stalls.

ordinaire /ɔRdinɛR/ *a* ordinary;
(habituel) usual; (*qualité*) standard;
(médiocre) very average. ● *nm* l'~
the ordinary; (nourriture) the
standard fare; **d'~, à l'~** usually.
ordinairement *adv* usually.

ordinateur /ɔRdinatœR/ *nm*
computer; ~ **personnel/de bureau**
personal/desktop computer; ~
portable laptop (computer); ~
hôte (Internet) host.

ordonnance /ɔRdonɑ̃s/ *nf* (ordre,
décret) order; (de médecin)
prescription.

ordonné, ~e /ɔRdone/ *a* tidy.

ordonner /ɔRdone/ [1] *vt* order (à
qn de sb to); (agencer) arrange;
(Méd) prescribe; (*prêtre*) ordain.

ordre /ɔRdR/ *nm* order; (propreté)
tidiness; **aux ~s de qn** at sb's
disposal; **avoir de l'~** be tidy; **en**
~ tidy, in order; **de premier** ~
first-rate; **d'~ officiel** of an
official nature; **l'~ du jour**
(programme) agenda; **mettre de l'** ~
dans tidy up; **jusqu'à nouvel** ~
until further notice; **un** ~ **de**
grandeur an approximate idea.

ordure /ɔRdyR/ *nf* filth; ~**s**
(détritus) rubbish; (US) garbage; ~**s**
ménagères household refuse.

oreille /ɔRɛj/ *nf* ear.

oreiller /ɔReje/ *nm* pillow.

oreillons /ɔRɛjɔ̃/ *nmpl* mumps.

orfèvre /ɔRfɛvR/ *nm* goldsmith.

organe /ɔRgan/ *nm* organ.

organigramme /ɔRganigRam/
nm organization chart; (Ordinat)
flowchart.

organique /ɔRganik/ *a* organic.

organisateur, -trice
/ɔRganizatœR, -tRis/ *nm, f*
organizer.

organisation /ɔRganizasjɔ̃/ *nf*
organization.

organiser /ɔRganize/ [1] *vt*
organize. □ **s'~** *vpr* organize
oneself, get organized.

organisme /ɔRganism/ *nm* body,
organism.

orge /ɔRʒ/ *nf* barley.

orgelet /ɔRʒəlɛ/ *nm* sty.

orgue /ɔRg/ *nm* organ; ~ **de**
Barbarie barrel-organ. **orgues**
nfpl organ.

orgueil /ɔRgœj/ *nm* pride. **or-**
gueilleux, -euse *a* proud.

orient /ɔRjɑ̃/ *nm* (direction) east;
l'O~ the Orient.

oriental, ~e (*mpl* **-aux**) /ɔRjɑ̃tal,
-o/ *a* eastern; (de l'Orient) oriental.
O~, ~e (*mpl* **-aux**) *nm, f* Asian.

orientation /ɔRjɑ̃tasjɔ̃/ *nf*
direction; (tendance politique)
leanings (+ *pl*); (de maison) aspect;
(Sport) orienteering; ~
professionnelle careers advice; ~
scolaire curriculum counselling.

orienter /ɔRjɑ̃te/ [1] *vt* position;
(*personne*) direct. □ **s'~** *vpr* (se
repérer) find one's bearings; **s'~**
vers turn towards.

origan /ɔRigɑ̃/ *nm* oregano.

originaire /ɔRiʒinɛR/ *a* **être** ~ **de**
be a native of.

original, ~e (*mpl* **-aux**) /ɔRiʒinal,
-o/ *a* original; (curieux) eccentric.
● *nm* (œuvre) original. ● *nm, f*
eccentric. **originalité** *nf*
originality; eccentricity.

origine /ɔRiʒin/ *nf* origin; **à l'~**
originally; **d'~** (*pièce, pneu*)
original; **être d'~ noble** come
from a noble background.

originel, ~le /ɔRiʒinɛl/ *a*
original.

orme /ɔRm/ *nm* elm.

ornement /ɔRnəmɑ̃/ *nm*
ornament.

orner /ɔRne/ [1] *vt* decorate.

orphelin, ~e /ɔRfəlɛ̃, -in/ *nm, f*
orphan. ● *a* orphaned.
orphelinat *nm* orphanage.

orteil /ɔʀtɛj/ nm toe.

orthodoxe /ɔʀtɔdɔks/ a orthodox.

orthographe /ɔʀtɔgʀaf/ nf spelling.

ortie /ɔʀti/ nf nettle.

os /ɔs, o/ nm bone.

OS abrév m ⇒OUVRIER SPÉCIALISÉ.

osciller /ɔsile/ [1] vi sway; (Tech) oscillate; (hésiter) waver; (fluctuer) fluctuate.

osé, ~e /oze/ a daring.

oseille /ozɛj/ nf (plante) sorrel.

oser /oze/ [1] vi dare.

osier /ozje/ nm wicker.

ossature /ɔsatyʀ/ nf skeleton, frame.

ossements /ɔsmã/ nmpl bones, remains.

osseux, -euse /ɔsø, -z/ a bony; (Méd) bone.

otage /ɔtaʒ/ nm hostage.

OTAN /ɔtã/ abrév f (Organisation du traité de l'Atlantique Nord) NATO.

otarie /ɔtaʀi/ nf eared seal.

ôter /ote/ [1] vt remove (à qn from sb); (déduire) take away.

otite /ɔtit/ nf ear infection.

ou /u/ conj or; ~ bien or else; ~ (bien)... ~ (bien)... either... or...; vous ~ moi either you or me.

où /u/ pron where; (dans lequel) in which; (sur lequel) on which; (auquel) at which; d'~ from which; (pour cette raison) hence; par ~ through which; ~ qu'il soit wherever he may be; juste au moment ~ just as; le jour ~ the day when. ● adv where; d'~? where from?

ouate /wat/ nf cotton wool; (US) absorbent cotton.

oubli /ubli/ nm forgetfulness; (trou de mémoire) lapse of memory; (négligence) oversight; tomber dans l'~ sink into oblivion.

oublier /ublije/ [45] vt forget;

(omettre) leave out, forget. □ s'~ vpr (chose) be forgotten.

ouest /wɛst/ a inv (façade, côte) west; (frontière, zone) western. ● nm west; l'~ de l'Europe western Europe; vent d'~ westerly (wind); aller vers l'~ go west; l'O~ the West; de l'O~ western.

oui /wi/ adv & nm inv yes.

ouï-dire, par ~ /paʀwidiʀ/ loc by hearsay.

ouïe /wi/ nf hearing; (de poisson) gill.

ouragan /uʀagã/ nm hurricane.

ourlet /uʀlɛ/ nm hem.

ours /uʀs/ nm bear; ~ blanc polar bear; ~ en peluche teddy bear.

outil /uti/ nm tool. **outillage** nm tools (+ pl). **outiller** [1] vt equip.

outrage /utʀaʒ/ nm (grave) insult.

outrance /utʀãs/ nf à ~ excessively. **outrancier, -ière** a extreme.

outre /utʀ/ prép besides. ● adv passer ~ pay no heed; ~ mesure unduly; en ~ in addition. **outre-mer** adv overseas.

outrepasser /utʀəpase/ [1] vt exceed.

outrer /utʀe/ [1] vt exaggerate; (indigner) incense.

ouvert, ~e /uvɛʀ, -t/ a open; (gaz, radio) on. ● ⇒OUVRIR [21].

ouverture /uvɛʀtyʀ/ nf opening; (Mus) overture; (Photo) aperture; ~s (offres) overtures; ~ d'esprit open-mindedness.

ouvrable /uvʀabl/ a jour ~ working day; aux heures ~s during business hours.

ouvrage /uvʀaʒ/ nm (travail, livre) work; (couture) (piece of) needlework.

ouvre-boîtes /uvʀəbwat/ nm inv tin-opener.

O

ouvre-bouteilles /uvrəbutɛj/ *nm inv* bottle-opener.

ouvreur, -euse /uvrœr, -øz/ *nm, f* usherette.

ouvrier, -ière /uvrije, -jɛr/ *nm, f* worker; ∼ **qualifié/spécialisé** skilled/unskilled worker. ● *a* working-class; (*conflit*) industrial; **syndicat** ∼ trade union.

ouvrir /uvrir/ [21] *vt* open (up); (*gaz, robinet*) turn on. ● *vi* open (up). □ **s'**∼ *vpr* open (up); **s'**∼ **à qn** open one's heart to sb.

ovaire /ɔvɛr/ *nm* ovary.

ovale /ɔval/ *a & nm* oval.

ovni /ɔvni/ *abrév m* (**objet volant non-identifié**) UFO.

ovule /ɔvyl/ *nm* (à féconder) ovum; (gynécologique) pessary.

oxygène /ɔksiʒɛn/ *nm* oxygen.

oxygéner (s') /(s)ɔksiʒene/ [14] *vpr* get some fresh air.

ozone /ozon/ *nf* ozone; **la couche d'**∼ the ozone layer.

pacifique /pasifik/ *a* peaceful; (*personne*) peaceable; (Géog) Pacific. **P**∼ *nm* **le P**∼ the Pacific.

pacotille /pakɔtij/ *nf* junk, rubbish.

PACS /paks/ *abrév nm* (**pacte civil de solidarité**) contract of civil union.

pacser (se) /pakse/ [1] *vpr* sign a contract of civil union (PACS).

pagaie /pagɛ/ *nf* paddle.

pagaille /pagaj/ *nf* 🛙 mess.

page /paʒ/ *nf* page; **mise en** ∼ layout; **tourner la** ∼ turn over a new leaf; **être à la** ∼ be up to

date; ∼ **d'accueil** (Internet) home page.

paie /pɛ/ *nf* pay.

paiement /pɛmɑ̃/ *nm* payment.

païen, ∼ne /pajɛ̃, -ɛn/ *a & nm, f* pagan.

paillasson /pajasɔ̃/ *nm* doormat.

paille /paj/ *nf* straw. ● *a* (*cheveux*) straw-coloured.

paillette /pajɛt/ *nf* (sur robe) sequin; (de savon) flake.

pain /pɛ̃/ *nm* bread; (miche) loaf (of bread); (de savon, cire) bar; ∼ **d'épices** gingerbread; ∼ **grillé** toast.

pair, ∼e /pɛr/ *a* (nombre) even. ● *nm* (personne) peer; **aller de** ∼ go together (**avec** with); **au** ∼ (jeune fille) au pair. **paire** *nf* pair.

paisible /pezibl/ *a* peaceful.

paître /pɛtr/ [44] *vi* graze.

paix /pɛ/ *nf* peace; **fiche-moi la** ∼! 🛙 leave me alone!

Pakistan /pakistɑ̃/ *nm* Pakistan.

palace /palas/ *nm* luxury hotel.

palais /palɛ/ *nm* palace; (Anat) palate; ∼ **de Justice** law courts; ∼ **des sports** sports stadium.

pâle /pɑl/ *a* pale.

Palestine /palɛstin/ *nf* Palestine.

palier /palje/ *nm* (d'escalier) landing; (étape) stage.

pâlir /pɑlir/ [2] *vt/i* (turn) pale.

palissade /palisad/ *nf* fence.

pallier /palje/ [45] *vt* compensate for.

palmarès /palmarɛs/ *nm* list of prize-winners.

palme /palm/ *nf* palm leaf; (de nageur) flipper. **palmé, ∼e** *a* (patte) webbed.

palmier /palmje/ *nm* palm (tree).

palper /palpe/ [1] *vt* feel.

palpiter /palpite/ [1] *vi* (battre) pound; (frémir) quiver.

paludisme /palydism/ *nm* malaria.

pamplemousse /pɑ̃pləmus/ *nm* grapefruit.

panaché, ~e /panaʃe/ *a* (bariolé, mélangé) motley; **glace ~e** mixed-flavour ice cream. ● *nm* shandy.

pancarte /pɑ̃kaʀt/ *nf* sign; (de manifestant) placard.

pané, ~e /pane/ *a* breaded.

panier /panje/ *nm* basket; (de basket-ball) basket; **mettre au ~** 🅘 throw out; **~ à salade** salad shaker; (fourgon 🅘) police van.

panique /panik/ *nf* panic.

paniquer [1] *vi* panic.

panne /pan/ *nf* breakdown; **être en ~** have broken down; **être en ~ sèche** have run out of petrol; **~ d'électricité** *ou* **de courant** power failure.

panneau (*pl* **~x**) /pano/ *nm* sign; (publicitaire) hoarding; (de porte) panel; **~ (d'affichage)** notice board; **~ (de signalisation)** road sign.

panoplie /panɔpli/ *nf* (jouet) outfit; (gamme) range.

pansement /pɑ̃smɑ̃/ *nm* dressing; **~ adhésif** plaster.

panser [1] *vt* (*plaie*) dress; (*personne*) dress the wound(s) of; (*cheval*) groom.

pantalon /pɑ̃talɔ̃/ *nm* trousers (+ *pl*).

panthère /pɑ̃tɛʀ/ *nf* panther.

pantin /pɑ̃tɛ̃/ *nm* puppet.

pantomime /pɑ̃tɔmim/ *nf* mime; (spectacle) mime show.

pantoufle /pɑ̃tufl/ *nf* slipper.

paon /pɑ̃/ *nm* peacock.

papa /papa/ *nm* dad(dy).

pape /pap/ *nm* pope.

paperasse /papʀas/ *nf* (péj) bumf.

papeterie /papetʀi/ *nf* (magasin) stationer's shop.

papier /papje/ *nm* paper; (formulaire) form; **~s (d'identité)** (identity) papers; **~ absorbant** kitchen paper; **~ aluminium** tin foil; **~ buvard** blotting paper; **~ cadeau** wrapping paper; **~ calque** tracing paper; **~ carbone** carbon paper; **~ collant** adhesive tape; **~ hygiénique** toilet paper; **~ journal** newspaper; **~ à lettres** writing paper; **~ mâché** papier mâché; **~ peint** wallpaper; **~ de verre** sandpaper.

papillon /papijɔ̃/ *nm* butterfly; (contravention 🅘) parking-ticket; **~ de nuit** moth.

papoter /papɔte/ [1] *vi* 🅘 chatter.

paquebot /pakbo/ *nm* liner.

pâquerette /pɑkʀɛt/ *nf* daisy.

Pâques /pɑk/ *nfpl & nm* Easter.

paquet /pakɛ/ *nm* packet; (de cartes) pack; (colis) parcel; **un ~ de** (beaucoup 🅘) a mass of.

par /paʀ/ *prép* by; (à travers) through; (motif) out of, from; (provenance) from; **commencer/finir ~ qch** begin/end with sth; **commencer/finir ~ faire** begin by/end up by doing; **~ an/mois** a *ou* per year/month; **~ jour** a day; **~ personne** each, per person; **~ avion** (lettre) (by) airmail; **~-ci, ~-là** here and there; **~ contre** on the other hand; **~ ici/là** this/that way.

parachute /paʀaʃyt/ *nm* parachute. **parachutiste** *nmf* parachutist; (Mil) paratrooper.

parader /paʀade/ [1] *vi* show off.

paradis /paʀadi/ *nm* (Relig) heaven; (lieu idéal) paradise; **~ fiscal** tax haven.

paradoxal, ~e (*mpl* **-aux**) /paʀadɔksal, -o/ *a* paradoxical.

paraffine /paʀafin/ *nf* paraffin wax.

parages /paʀaʒ/ *nmpl* **dans les ~** around.

P

paragraphe /paʀagʀaf/ *nm* paragraph.

paraître /paʀɛtʀ/ [18] *vi* (se montrer) appear; (sembler) seem, appear; (*ouvrage*) be published, come out; **il paraît qu'ils...** apparently they...; **oui, il paraît** so I hear.

parallèle /paʀalɛl/ *a* parallel; (*illégal*) unofficial. ● *nm* parallel; **faire le ∼** make a connection. ● *nf* parallel (line).

paralyser /paʀalize/ [1] *vt* paralyse. **paralysie** *nf* paralysis.

parapente /paʀapɑ̃t/ *nm* paraglider; (*activité*) paragliding.

parapher /paʀafe/ [1] *vi* initial; (*signer*) sign.

parapluie /paʀaplɥi/ *nm* umbrella.

parasite /paʀazit/ *nm* parasite; **∼s** (radio) interference (+ *sg*).

parasol /paʀasɔl/ *nm* sunshade.

paratonnerre /paʀatɔnɛʀ/ *nm* lightning conductor *ou* rod.

paravent /paʀavɑ̃/ *nm* screen.

parc /paʀk/ *nm* park; (de bétail) pen; (de bébé) play-pen; (entrepôt) depot; **∼ relais** park and ride; **∼ de stationnement** car park.

parce que /paʀsk(ə)/ *conj* because.

parchemin /paʀʃəmɛ̃/ *nm* parchment.

parcmètre /paʀkmɛtʀ/ *nm* parking meter.

parcourir /paʀkuʀiʀ/ [20] *vt* travel *ou* go through; (distance) travel; (des yeux) glance at *ou* over.

parcours /paʀkuʀ/ *nm* route; (voyage) journey.

par-delà /paʀdəla/ *prép* beyond.

par-derrière /paʀdɛʀjɛʀ/ *adv* (*attaquer*) from behind; (*critiquer*) behind sb's back.

par-dessous /paʀdəsu/ *prép & adv* under(neath).

pardessus /paʀdəsy/ *nm* overcoat.

par-dessus /paʀdəsy/ *prép & adv* over; **∼ bord** overboard; **∼ le marché** 🄸 into the bargain; **∼ tout** above all.

par-devant /paʀdəvɑ̃/ *adv* (*passer*) by the front.

pardon /paʀdɔ̃/ *nm* forgiveness; (**je vous demande**) **∼!** (I am) sorry!; (pour demander qch) excuse me.

pardonner /paʀdɔne/ [1] *vt* forgive; **∼ qch à qn** forgive sb for sth.

pare-brise /paʀbʀiz/ *nm inv* windscreen.

pare-chocs /paʀʃɔk/ *nm inv* bumper.

pareil, ∼le /paʀɛj/ *a* similar (à to); (tel) such (a); **c'est ∼** it's the same; **ce n'est pas ∼** it's not the same thing. ● *nm, f* equal. ● *adv* 🄸 the same.

parent, ∼e /paʀɑ̃, -t/ *a* related (de to). ● *nm, f* relative, relation; **∼s** (père et mère) parents; **∼ isolé** single parent; **réunion de ∼s d'élèves** parents' evening.

parenté /paʀɑ̃te/ *nf* relationship.

parenthèse /paʀɑ̃tɛz/ *nf* bracket, parenthesis; (fig) digression.

parer /paʀe/ [1] *vt* (esquiver) parry; (orner) adorn. ● *vi* **∼ à** deal with; **∼ au plus pressé** tackle the most urgent things first.

paresse /paʀɛs/ *nf* laziness.

paresseux, -euse /paʀɛsø, -z/ *a* lazy. ● *nm, f* lazy person.

parfait, ∼e /paʀfɛ, -t/ *a* perfect. **parfaitement** *adv* perfectly; (bien sûr) absolutely.

parfois /paʀfwa/ *adv* sometimes.

parfum /paʀfœ̃/ *nm* (senteur) scent; (substance) perfume, scent; (goût) flavour. **parfumé, ∼e** *a* fragrant; (savon) scented; (thé) flavoured.

parfumer /paʁfyme/ [1] *vt*
(embaumer) scent; (*gâteau*) flavour.
□ se ~ *vpr* put on one's perfume.
parfumerie *nf* (produits) perfumes;
(boutique) perfume shop.

pari /paʁi/ *nm* bet.

Paris /paʁi/ *npr* Paris.

parisien, ~ne /paʁizjɛ̃, -ɛn/ *a*
Parisian; (*banlieue*) Paris. **P**~,
~ne *nm, f* Parisian.

parking /paʁkiŋ/ *nm* car park.

parlement /paʁləmɑ̃/ *nm*
parliament.

parlementaire /paʁləmɑ̃tɛʁ/ *a*
parliamentary. ● *nmf* Member of
Parliament.

parlementer /paʁləmɑ̃te/ [1] *vi*
negotiate.

parler /paʁle/ [1] *vi* talk (à to); ~
de talk about; **tu parles d'un
avantage!** call that a benefit!; **de
quoi ça parle?** what is it about?
● *vt* (*langue*) speak; (*politique,
affaires*) talk. □ se ~ *vpr*
(*personnes*) talk (to each other);
(*langue*) be spoken. ● *nm* speech;
(dialecte) dialect.

parmi /paʁmi/ *prép* among(st).

paroi /paʁwa/ *nf* wall; ~ rocheuse
rock face.

paroisse /paʁwas/ *nf* parish.

parole /paʁɔl/ *nf* (mot, promesse)
word; (langage) speech; **demander
la** ~ ask to speak; **prendre la** ~
(begin to) speak, **tenir** ~ keep
one's word; **croire qn sur** ~ take
sb's word for it.

parquet /paʁkɛ/ *nm* (parquet)
floor; **lame de** ~ floorboard; **le** ~
(Jur) prosecution.

parrain /paʁɛ̃/ *nm* godfather; (fig)
sponsor.

parsemer /paʁsəme/ [6] *vt* strew
(de with).

part /paʁ/ *nf* share, part; **à** ~ (de
côté) aside; (séparément) separate;
(excepté) apart from; **d'une** ~ on
the one hand; **d'autre** ~ on the

other hand; (de plus) moreover; **de
la** ~ **de** from; **de toutes** ~s from
all sides; **de** ~ **et d'autre** on both
sides; **faire** ~ **à qn** inform sb (de
of); **faire la** ~ **des choses** make
allowances; **prendre** ~ **à** take part
in; (*joie, douleur*) share; **pour ma**
~ as for me.

partage /paʁtaʒ/ *nm* (division)
dividing; (répartition) sharing out;
recevoir qch en ~ be left sth in a
will.

partager /paʁtaʒe/ [40] *vt* divide;
(distribuer) share out; (avoir en
commun) share. □ se ~ **qch** *vpr*
share sth.

partenaire /paʁtənɛʁ/ *nmf*
partner.

parterre /paʁtɛʁ/ *nm* flower-bed;
(Théât) stalls.

parti /paʁti/ *nm* (Pol) party;
(décision) decision; (un mariage)
match; ~ **pris** bias; **prendre** ~ get
involved; **prendre** ~ **pour qn** side
with sb; **j'en ai pris mon** ~ I've
come to terms with that.

partial, ~e (*mpl* -**iaux**) /paʁsjal,
-jo/ *a* biased.

participe /paʁtisip/ *nm* (Gram)
participle.

participant, ~e /paʁtisipɑ̃, -t/
nm, f participant (à in).

participation /paʁtisipasjɔ̃/ *nf*
participation; (financière)
contribution; (d'un artiste)
appearance.

participer /paʁtisipe/ [1] *vi* ~ **à**
take part in, participate in;
(*profits, frais*) share.

particule /paʁtikyl/ *nf* particle.

particulier, -ière /paʁtikylje,
-jɛʁ/ *a* (spécifique) particular;
(bizarre) unusual; (privé) private;
rien de ~ nothing special. ● *nm*
private individual; **en** ~ in particular, particularly. **particulièrement** *adv* particularly.

partie /paʁti/ *nf* part; (cartes, Sport)

P

game; (Jur) party; **une ~ de pêche** a fishing trip; **en ~** partly, in part; **en grande ~** largely; **faire ~ de** be part of; (adhérer à) be a member of; **faire ~ intégrante de** be an integral part of.

partiel, ~le /parsjɛl/ a partial. ● nm (Univ) exam based on a module.

partir /partir/ [46] vi (aux être) go; (quitter un lieu) leave, go; (tache) come out; (bouton) come off; (coup de feu) go off; (commencer) start; **~ pour le Brésil** leave for Brazil; **~ du principe que** work on the assumption that; **à ~ de** from; **à ~ de maintenant** from now on.

partisan, ~e /partizã, -an/ nm, f supporter. ● nm (Mil) partisan; **être ~ de** be in favour of.

partition /partisjɔ̃/ nf (Mus) score.

partout /partu/ adv everywhere; **~ où** wherever.

paru /pary/ ⇒PARAÎTRE [18].

parure /paryr/ nf finery; (bijoux) set of jewels; (de draps) set.

parution /parysjɔ̃/ nf publication.

parvenir /parvənir/ [58] vi (aux être) **~ à** reach; **~ à faire** manage to do; **faire ~** send.

parvenu, ~e /parvəny/ nm, f upstart.

pas¹ /pa/

Pour les expressions comme **pas encore, pas mal**, etc. ⇒**encore, mal**, etc.

● adverbe

····▸ not; **ne ~** not; **je ne sais ~** I don't know; **je ne pense ~** I don't think so; **il a aimé, moi ~** he liked it, I didn't; **~ cher/poli** cheap/impolite.

····▸ **~ du tout** not at all; **~ de chance!** tough luck!

····▸ **on a bien ri, ~ vrai?** 🄸 we had a good laugh, didn't we?

> ❗ In spoken colloquial French **ne… pas** is often shortened to **pas**. You will often hear **j'ai pas compris** instead of **je n'ai pas compris** (I didn't understand). Note that this would not be correct in written French.

pas² /pa/ nm step; (bruit) footstep; (trace) footprint; (vitesse) pace; **à deux ~ (de)** a step away (from); **marcher au ~** march; **rouler au ~** move very slowly; **à ~ de loup** stealthily; **faire les cent ~** walk up and down; **faire le premier ~** make the first move; **~ de porte** doorstep; **~ de vis** (Tech) thread.

passage /pasaʒ/ nm (traversée) crossing; (visite) visit; (chemin) way, passage; (d'une œuvre) passage; **de ~** (voyageur) visiting; (amant) casual; **la tempête a tout emporté sur son ~** the storm swept everything away; **~ clouté** pedestrian crossing; **~ interdit** (panneau) no thoroughfare; **~ à niveau** level crossing; **~ souterrain** subway.

passager, -ère /pasaʒe, -ɛr/ a temporary. ● nm, f passenger; **~ clandestin** stowaway.

passant, ~e /pasã, -t/ a (rue) busy. ● nm, f passer-by. ● nm (anneau) loop.

passe /pas/ nf pass; **bonne/ mauvaise ~** good/bad patch; **en ~ de** on the road to.

passé, ~e /pase/ a (révolu) past; (dernier) last; (fané) faded; **~ de mode** out of fashion. ● nm past. ● prép after.

passe-partout /paspartu/ nm

inv master-key. ● *a inv* for all occasions.

passeport /paspɔʀ/ *nm* passport.

passer /pase/ [1] *vi (aux être ou avoir)* go past, pass; *(aller)* go; *(venir)* come; *(temps, douleur)* pass; *(film)* be on; *(couleur)* fade; **laisser ~** let through; *(occasion)* miss; **~ devant** (à pied) walk past; (en voiture) drive past; **~ par** go through; **où est-il passé?** where did he get to?; **~ outre** take no notice; **passons!** let's forget about it!; **passons aux choses sérieuses** let's turn to serious matters; **~ dans la classe supérieure** go up a year; **~ pour un idiot** look a fool. ● *vt (aux avoir)* (franchir) pass, cross; (donner) pass, hand; *(temps)* spend; *(enfiler)* slip on; *(vidéo, disque)* put on; *(examen)* take, sit; *(commande)* place; (faire) **~ le temps** while away the time; **~ l'aspirateur** hoover; **~ un coup de fil à qn** give sb a ring; **je vous passe Mme X** (par le standard) I'll put you through to Mrs X; (en donnant l'appareil) I'll pass you over to Mrs X; **~ qch en fraude** smuggle sth. □ **se ~** *vpr* happen, take place; (s'écouler) go by; **se ~ de** go *ou* do without.

passerelle /pasʀɛl/ *nf* footbridge; (de navire) gangway; (d'avion) (passenger) footbridge; (Internet) gateway.

passe-temps /pastã/ *nm inv* pastime.

passif, -ive /pasif, -v/ *a* passive. ● *nm* (Comm) liabilities.

passion /pasjõ/ *nf* passion. **passionnant, ~e** *a* fascinating.

passionné, ~e /pasjone/ *a* passionate; **être ~ de** have a passion for.

passionner /pasjone/ [1] *vt* fascinate. □ **se ~ pour** *vpr* have a passion for.

passoire /paswaʀ/ *nf* (à thé) strainer; (à légumes) colander.

pastèque /pastɛk/ *nf* watermelon.

pasteur /pastœʀ/ *nm* (Relig) minister.

pastille /pastij/ *nf* (médicament) pastille, lozenge.

patate /patat/ *nf* 🔲 spud; **~ (douce)** sweet potato.

patauger /patoʒe/ [40] *vi* splash about.

pâte /pat/ *nf* paste; (à gâteau) dough; (à tarte) pastry; (à frire) batter; **~s (alimentaires)** pasta (+ *sg*); **~ à modeler** Plasticine®; **~ d'amandes** marzipan.

pâté /pate/ *nm* (Culin) pâté; (d'encre) blot; (de sable) sandpie; **~ en croûte** ≈ pie; **~ de maisons** block (of houses).

pâtée /pate/ *nf* feed, mash.

patente /patãt/ *nf* trade licence.

paternel, ~le /patɛʀnɛl/ *a* paternal. **paternité** *nf* paternity.

pathétique /patetik/ *a* moving.

patience /pasjãs/ *nf* patience. **patient, ~e** *a & nm,f* patient. **patienter** [1] *vi* wait.

patin /patɛ̃/ *nm* skate; **~ à roulettes** roller-skate.

patinage /patinaʒ/ *nm* skating. **patiner** [1] *vi* skate; (roue) spin. **patinoire** *nf* ice rink.

pâtisserie /patisʀi/ *nf* cake shop; (gâteau) pastry; (secteur) cake making. **pâtissier, -ière** *nm, f* confectioner, pastry-cook.

patrie /patʀi/ *nf* homeland.

patrimoine /patʀimwan/ *nm* heritage.

patriote /patʀijɔt/ *a* patriotic. ● *nmf* patriot.

patron, ~ne /patʀõ, -ɔn/ *nm, f* employer, boss; (propriétaire) owner, boss; (saint) patron saint. ● *nm* (couture) pattern. **patronal,**

∼**e** (*mpl* **-aux**) *a* employers'.
patronat /patʁɔna/ *nm* employers (+ *pl*).
patrouille /patʁuj/ *nf* patrol.
patte /pat/ *nf* leg; (pied) foot; (de chat) paw; ∼**s** (favoris) sideburns; **marcher à quatre** ∼**s** walk on all fours; (bébé) crawl; ∼**s de derrière** hind legs.
paume /pom/ *nf* (de main) palm.
paumé, ∼**e** /pome/ *nm, f* ⊞ misfit.
paupière /popjɛʁ/ *nf* eyelid.
pause /poz/ *nf* pause; (halte) break.
pauvre /povʁ/ *a* poor. ● *nmf* poor man, poor woman. **pauvreté** *nf* poverty.
pavé /pave/ *nm* cobblestone.
pavillon /pavijɔ̃/ *nm* (maison) house; (drapeau) flag.
payant, ∼**e** /pɛjɑ̃, -t/ *a* (hôte) paying; **c'est** ∼ you have to pay to get in.
payer /peje/ [31] *vt/i* pay; (service, travail) pay for; ∼ **qch à qn** buy sb sth; **faire** ∼ **qn** charge sb; **il me le paiera!** he'll pay for this. □ **se** ∼ *vpr* **se** ∼ **qch** buy oneself sth; **se** ∼ **la tête de** make fun of.
pays /pei/ *nm* country; (région) region; **du** ∼ local.
paysage /peizaʒ/ *nm* landscape.
paysan, ∼**ne** /peizɑ̃, -an/ *nm, f* farmer, country person; (péj) peasant. ● *a* (agricole) farming; (rural) country.
Pays-Bas /peiba/ *nmpl* **les** ∼ the Netherlands.
PCV *abrév m* (**paiement contre vérification**) **téléphoner en** ∼ reverse the charges.
PDG *abrév m* (**président-directeur général**) chairman and managing director.
péage /peaʒ/ *nm* toll; (lieu) tollgate.
peau (*pl* ∼**x**) /po/ *nf* skin; (cuir)

hide; ∼ **de chamois** shammy (leather); ∼ **de mouton** sheepskin; **être bien/mal dans sa** ∼ be/not be at ease with oneself.
pêche /pɛʃ/ *nf* (fruit) peach; (activité) fishing; (poissons) catch; ∼ **à la ligne** angling.
péché /peʃe/ *nm* sin.
pêcher /peʃe/ *vt* (poisson) catch; (dénicher ⊞) dig up. ● *vi* fish.
pêcheur *nm* fisherman; (à la ligne) angler.
pécuniaire /pekynjɛʁ/ *a* financial.
pédagogie /pedagɔʒi/ *nf* education.
pédale /pedal/ *nf* pedal.
pédalo® /pedalo/ *nm* pedal boat.
pédant, ∼**e** /pedɑ̃, -t/ *a* pedantic.
pédestre /pedɛstʁ/ *a* **faire de la randonnée** ∼ go walking *ou* hiking.
pédiatre /pedjatʁ/ *nmf* paediatrician.
pédicure /pedikyʁ/ *nmf* chiropodist.
peigne /pɛɲ/ *nm* comb.
peigner /peɲe/ [1] *vt* comb; (personne) comb the hair of. □ **se** ∼ *vpr* comb one's hair.
peignoir /pɛɲwaʁ/ *nm* dressing-gown.
peindre /pɛ̃dʁ/ [22] *vt* paint.
peine /pɛn/ *nf* sadness, sorrow; (effort, difficulté) trouble; (Jur) sentence; **avoir de la** ∼ feel sad; **faire de la** ∼ **à** hurt; **ce n'est pas la** ∼ **de sonner** you don't need to ring the bell; **j'ai de la** ∼ **à le croire** I find it hard to believe; **se donner** *ou* **prendre la** ∼ **de faire** go to the trouble of doing; ∼ **de mort** death penalty. ● *adv* **à** ∼ hardly.
peiner /pene/ [1] *vi* struggle. ● *vt* sadden.
peintre /pɛ̃tʁ/ *nm* painter; ∼ **en bâtiment** house painter.
peinture /pɛ̃tyʁ/ *nf* painting;

(matière) paint; ~ à l'huile oil painting.

péjoratif, -ive /peʒɔRatif, -v/ a pejorative.

pelage /pəlaʒ/ nm coat, fur.

pêle-mêle /pɛlmɛl/ adv in a jumble.

peler /pəle/ [6] vt/i peel.

pèlerinage /pɛlRinaʒ/ nm pilgrimage.

pelle /pɛl/ nf shovel; (d'enfant) spade.

pellicule /pelikyl/ nf film; ~s (cheveux) dandruff.

pelote /pɔlɔt/ nf (of wool) ball.

peloton /p(ə)lɔtɔ̃/ nm platoon; (Sport) pack; ~ d'exécution firing squad.

pelotonner (se) /(sə)plɔtɔne/ [1] vpr curl up.

pelouse /p(ə)luz/ nf lawn.

peluche /p(ə)lyʃ/ nf (matière) plush; (jouet) cuddly toy; en ~ (lapin, chien) fluffy.

pénal, ~e (mpl -aux) /penal, -o/ a penal. **pénaliser** |1| vt penalize. **pénalité** nf penalty.

penchant /pɑ̃ʃɑ̃/ nm inclination; (goût) liking (pour for).

pencher /pɑ̃ʃe/ [1] vt tilt; ~ pour favour. ● vi lean (over), tilt. □ se ~ vpr lean (forward). se ~ sur (problème) examine.

pendaison /pɑ̃dɛzɔ̃/ nf hanging.

pendant¹ /pɑ̃dɑ̃/ prép (au cours de) during; (durée) for; ~ que while.

pendant², ~e /pɑ̃dɑ̃, -t/ a hanging; **jambes ~es** with one's legs dangling. ● nm (contrepartie) matching piece (de to); ~ d'oreille drop ear-ring.

pendentif /pɑ̃dɑ̃tif/ nm pendant.

penderie /pɑ̃dRi/ nf wardrobe.

pendre /pɑ̃dR/ [3] vt/i hang. □ se ~ vpr hang (à from); (se tuer) hang oneself.

pendule /pɑ̃dyl/ nf clock. ● nm pendulum.

pénétrer /penetRe/ [14] vi ~ (dans) enter; faire ~ une crème rub a cream in. ● vt penetrate.

pénible /penibl/ a (travail) hard; (nouvelle) painful; (enfant) tiresome.

péniche /peniʃ/ nf barge.

pénitence /penitɑ̃s/ nf (Relig) penance; (punition) punishment; faire ~ repent.

pénitentiaire /penitɑ̃sjɛR/ a (établissement) penal.

pénombre /penɔ̃bR/ nf half-light.

pensée /pɑ̃se/ nf (idée) thought; (fleur) pansy.

penser /pɑ̃se/ [1] vt/i think; ~ à (réfléchir à) think about; (se souvenir de, prévoir) think of; ~ faire think of doing; faire ~ à remind one of.

pensif, -ive /pɑ̃sif, -v/ a pensive.

pension /pɑ̃sjɔ̃/ nf (Scol) boarding school; (repas, somme) board; (allocation) pension; ~ (de famille) guest house; ~ alimentaire (Jur) alimony. **pensionnaire** nmf (Scol) boarder; (d'hôtel) guest.

pensionnat nm boarding school.

pente /pɑ̃t/ nf slope; en ~ sloping.

Pentecôte /pɑ̃tkot/ nf la ~ Whitsun.

pénurie /penyRi/ nf shortage.

pépin /pepɛ̃/ nm (graine) pip; (ennui 🗊) hitch.

pépinière /pepinjɛR/ nf (tree) nursery.

perçant, ~e /pɛRsɑ̃, -t/ a (cri) shrill; (regard) piercing.

perce-neige /pɛRsənɛʒ/ nm or f inv snowdrop.

percepteur /pɛRsɛptœR/ nm tax inspector.

percer /pɛRse/ [10] vt pierce; (avec perceuse) drill; (mystère) penetrate. ● vi break through; (dent) come through. **perceuse** nf drill.

P

percevoir /pɛRsəvwaR/ [52] vt
perceive; (impôt) collect.

perche /pɛRʃ/ nf (bâton) pole.

percher (se) /(sə)pɛRʃe/ [1] vpr
perch.

percolateur /pɛRkɔlatœR/ nm
coffee machine.

percuter /pɛRkyte/ [1] vt
(véhicule) crash into.

perdant, ~e /pɛRdɑ̃, -t/ a losing.
● nm, f loser.

perdre /pɛRdR/ [3] vt/i lose;
(gaspiller) waste; ~ ses poils (chat)
moult. □ se ~ vpr get lost; (rester
inutilisé) go to waste.

perdrix /pɛRdRi/ nf partridge.

perdu, ~e /pɛRdy/ a lost;
(endroit) isolated; (balle) stray;
c'est du temps ~ it's a waste of
time.

père /pɛR/ nm father; ~ de famille
father, family man; ~ spirituel
father figure; le ~ Noël Santa
Claus.

perfection /pɛRfɛksjɔ̃/ nf
perfection.

perfectionner /pɛRfɛksjɔne/ [1]
vt (technique) perfect; (art) refine.
□ se ~ vpr improve; se ~ en
anglais improve one's English.

perforer /pɛRfɔRe/ [1] vt
perforate; (billet, bande) punch.

performance /pɛRfɔRmɑ̃s/ nf
performance.

perfusion /pɛRfyzjɔ̃/ nf drip; sous
~ on a drip.

péridurale /peRidyRal/ nf
epidural.

péril /peRil/ nm peril; à tes risques
et ~s at your own risk.

périlleux, -euse /peRijø, -z/ a
perilous.

périmé, ~e /peRime/ a (produit)
past its use-by date; (désuet)
outdated.

période /peRjɔd/ nf period.

périodique /peRjɔdik/ a period-
ic(al). ● nm (journal) periodical.

péripétie /peRipesi/ nf
(unexpected) event, adventure.

périphérique /peRifeRik/ a
peripheral. ● nm (boulevard) ~
ring road.

périple /peRipl/ nm journey.

périr /peRiR/ [2] vi perish, die.

perle /pɛRl/ nf (d'huître) pearl; (de
verre) bead.

permanence /pɛRmanɑ̃s/ nf
permanence; (Scol) study room;
de ~ on duty; en ~ permanently;
assurer une ~ keep the office
open.

permanent, ~e /pɛRmanɑ̃, -t/ a
permanent; (constant) constant;
formation ~e continuous
education. **permanente** nf
(coiffure) perm.

permettre /pɛRmɛtR/ [42] vt
allow; ~ à qn de allow sb to. □ se
~ vpr (achat) afford; se ~ de faire
take the liberty of doing.

permis, ~e /pɛRmi, -z/ a
allowed. ● nm licence, permit; ~
(de conduire) driving licence.

permission /pɛRmisjɔ̃/ nf
permission; en ~ (Mil) on leave.

Pérou /peRu/ nm Peru.

perpendiculaire /pɛRpɑ̃dikylɛR/
a & nf perpendicular.

perpétuité /pɛRpetɥite/ nf à ~
for life.

perplexe /pɛRplɛks/ a perplexed.

perquisition /pɛRkizisjɔ̃/ nf
(police) search.

perron /peRɔ̃/ nm (front) steps.

perroquet /peRɔkɛ/ nm parrot.

perruche /peRyʃ/ nf budgerigar.

perruque /peRyk/ nf wig.

persécuter /pɛRsekyte/ [1] vt
persecute.

persévérance /pɛRseveRɑ̃s/ nf
perseverance. **persévérer** [14] vi
persevere.

persienne /pɛRsjɛn/ nf (outside)
shutter.

persil /pɛRsi/ nm parsley.

persistance /pɛʀsistɑ̃s/ nf
persistence. **persistant, ~e** a
persistent; (feuillage) evergreen.

persister /pɛʀsiste/ [1] vi persist
(à faire in doing).

personnage /pɛʀsɔnaʒ/ nm
character; (personne célèbre)
personality.

personnalité /pɛʀsɔnalite/ nf
personality.

personne /pɛʀsɔn/ nf person, ~s
people. ● pron nobody, no-one;
je n'ai vu ~ I didn't see anybody.

personnel, ~le /pɛʀsɔnɛl/ a
personal; (égoïste) selfish. ● nm
staff.

perspective /pɛʀspɛktiv/ nf (art,
point de vue) perspective; (vue)
view; (éventualité) prospect.

perspicace /pɛʀspikas/ a
shrewd. **perspicacité** nf
shrewdness.

persuader /pɛʀsɥade/ [1] vt
persuade (de faire to do).
persuasif, -ive /pɛʀsɥazif, -v/ a
persuasive.

perte /pɛʀt/ nf loss, (ruine) ruin; à
~ **de vue** as far as the eye can
see; ~ **de** (temps, argent) waste
of; ~ **sèche** total loss; **~s** (Méd)
discharge.

pertinent, ~e /pɛʀtinɑ̃, -t/ a
pertinent.

perturbateur, -trice /pɛʀtyʀ-
batœʀ, -tʀis/ nm, f disruptive
element. **perturbation** nf
disruption. **perturber** [1] vt
disrupt; (personne) perturb.

pervers, ~e /pɛʀvɛʀ, -s/ a
(dépravé) perverted; (méchant)
wicked.

pervertir /pɛʀvɛʀtiʀ/ [2] vt
pervert.

pesant, ~e /pəzɑ̃, -t/ a heavy.
pesanteur /pəzɑ̃tœʀ/ nf
heaviness; **la ~** (force) gravity.

pesée /pəze/ nf weighing; (effort)
pressure.

pèse-personne (pl ~s) /pɛzpɛʀ-
sɔn/ nm (bathroom) scales.

peser /pəze/ [6] vt/i weigh; ~ **sur**
bear upon.

pessimiste /pesimist/ a
pessimistic. ● nmf pessimist.

peste /pɛst/ nf plague; (personne
🅵) pest.

pet /pɛ/ nm 🅵 fart 🅵.

pétale /petal/ nm petal.

petard /petaʀ/ nm banger.

péter /pete/ [14] vi 🅵 fart 🅵, go
bang; (casser) snap.

pétillant, ~e /petijɑ̃, -t/ a
(boisson) sparkling; (personne)
bubbly.

pétiller /petije/ [1] vi (feu)
crackle; (champagne, yeux)
sparkle; ~ **d'intelligence** sparkle
with intelligence.

petit, ~e /p(ə)ti/ a small; (avec
nuance affective) little; (jeune) young,
small; (défaut) minor; (mesquin)
petty; **en ~** in miniature; ~ **à ~**
little by little; **un ~ peu** a little
bit; ~ **ami** boyfriend, **~e amie**
girlfriend; **~es annonces** small
ads; **~e cuillère** teaspoon; ~
déjeuner breakfast; ~ **pois** garden
pea. ● nm, f little child; (Scol)
junior; **~s** (de chat) kittens; (de
chien) pups. **petite-fille** (pl
petites-filles) nf granddaughter.

petit-fils (pl **petits-fils**) nm
grandson.

pétition /petisjɔ̃/ nf petition.

petits-enfants /pətizɑ̃fɑ̃/ nmpl
grandchildren.

pétrin /petʀɛ̃/ nm **dans le ~** 🅵 in
a fix 🅵.

pétrir /petʀiʀ/ [2] vt knead.

pétrole /petʀɔl/ nm oil; ~ **brut**
crude oil.

pétrolier, -ière /petʀɔlje, -jɛʀ/ a
oil. ● nm (navire) oil-tanker.

peu /pø/ adv ~ **(de)** (quantité) little,
not much; (nombre) few, not many;
~ **intéressant** not very interesting;

P

il mange ∼ he doesn't eat very much. ● *pron* few. ● *nm* little; **un** ∼ **(de)** a little; **à** ∼ **près** more or less; **de** ∼ only just; ∼ **à** ∼ gradually; ∼ **après/avant** shortly after/before; ∼ **de chose** not much; ∼ **nombreux** few; ∼ **souvent** seldom; **pour** ∼ **que** if.

peuple /pœpl/ *nm* people. **peupler** [1] *vt* populate.

peuplier /pøplije/ *nm* poplar.

peur /pœʀ/ *nf* fear; **avoir** ∼ be afraid (**de** of); **de** ∼ for fear of; **faire** ∼ **à** frighten. **peureux, -euse** *a* fearful.

peut /pø/ ⇒POUVOIR [49].

peut-être /pøtɛtʀ/ *adv* perhaps, maybe; ∼ **qu'il viendra** he might come.

peux /pø/ ⇒POUVOIR [49].

phare /faʀ/ *nm* (tour) lighthouse; (de véhicule) headlight; ∼ **antibrouillard** fog lamp.

pharmacie /faʀmasi/ *nf* (magasin) chemist's (shop), pharmacy; (science) pharmacy; (armoire) medicine cabinet. **pharmacien, ∼ne** *nm, f* chemist, pharmacist.

phénomène /fenɔmɛn/ *nm* phenomenon; (personne 🆘) eccentric.

philosophe /filɔzɔf/ *nmf* philosopher. ● *a* philosophical. **philosophie** *nf* philosophy. **philosophique** *a* philosophical.

phobie /fɔbi/ *nf* phobia.

phonétique /fɔnetik/ *a* phonetic. ● *nf* phonetics.

phoque /fɔk/ *nm* (animal) seal.

photo /fɔto/ *nf* photo; (art) photography; **prendre en** ∼ take a photo of; ∼ **d'identité** passport photograph.

photocopie /fɔtɔkɔpi/ *nf* photocopy. **photocopier** [45] *vt* photocopy.

photographe /fɔtɔgʀaf/ *nmf* photographer. **photographie** *nf*

photograph; (art) photography. **photographier** [45] *vt* take a photo of.

phrase /fʀɑz/ *nf* sentence.

physicien, ∼ne /fizisjɛ̃, -ɛn/ *nm, f* physicist.

physique /fizik/ *a* physical. ● *nm* physique; **au** ∼ physically. ● *nf* physics (+ *sg*).

piano /pjano/ *nm* piano.

pianoter /pjanɔte/ [1] *vi* tinkle; ∼ **sur** (*ordinateur*) tap at.

PIB *abrév m* (**produit intérieur brut**) GDP.

pic /pik/ *nm* (outil) pickaxe; (sommet) peak; (oiseau) woodpecker; **à** ∼ (*falaise*) sheer; (*couler*) straight to the bottom; **tomber à** ∼ 🆘 come just at the right time.

pichet /piʃɛ/ *nm* jug.

picorer /pikɔʀe/ [1] *vt/i* peck.

picotement /pikɔtmɑ̃/ *nm* tingling. **picoter** [1] *vt* sting; (*yeux*) sting.

pie /pi/ *nf* magpie.

pièce /pjɛs/ *nf* (d'habitation) room; (de monnaie) coin; (Théât) play; (pour raccommoder) patch; (écrit) document; (morceau) piece; ∼ (de théâtre) play; **dix francs (la)** ∼ ten francs each; ∼ **détachée** part; ∼ **d'identité** identity paper; ∼**s jointes** enclosures; (courrier électronique) attachments; ∼**s justificatives** written proof; ∼ **montée** tiered cake; ∼ **de rechange** spare part; **un deux-**∼**s** a two-room flat.

pied /pje/ *nm* foot; (de meuble) leg; (de lampe) base; (de verre) stem; (d'appareil photo) stand; **être** ∼**s nus** be bare-foot; **à** ∼ on foot; **au** ∼ **de la lettre** literally; **avoir** ∼ be able to touch the bottom; **jouer au tennis comme un** ∼ 🆘 be hopeless at tennis; **mettre sur** ∼ set up; **sur un** ∼ **d'égalité** on an equal footing; **mettre les ~s dans le plat** Ⓕ put one's foot in it; **c'est le ~** Ⓕ it's great. **pied-bot** (*pl* **pieds-bots**) *nm* club-foot.

piédestal /pjedɛstal/ *nm* pedestal.

piège /pjɛʒ/ *nm* trap.

piéger /pjeʒe/ [14] [40] *vt* trap; **lettre/voiture piégée** letter/car bomb.

piercing /piʀsiŋ/ *nm* body piercing.

pierre /pjɛʀ/ *nf* stone; **~ précieuse** precious stone; **~ tombale** tombstone.

piétiner /pjetine/ [1] *vi* (avancer lentement) shuffle along; (fig) make no headway; **~ d'impatience** hop up and down with impatience. ●*vt* trample (on).

piéton /pjetõ/ *nm* pedestrian.

pieu (*pl* **~x**) /pjø/ *nm* post, stake.

pieuvre /pjœvʀ/ *nf* octopus.

pieux, -ieuse /pjø, -z/ *a* pious.

pigeon /piʒõ/ *nm* pigeon.

piger /piʒe/ [40] *vt/i* Ⓕ understand, get (it).

pile /pil/ *nf* (tas) pile; (Électr) battery; **~ ou face?** heads or tails? ●*adv* (s'arrêter Ⓕ) dead; **à dix heures ~** Ⓕ at ten on the dot.

pilier /pilje/ *nm* pillar.

pillage /pijaʒ/ *nm* looting. **pillard, ~e** *nm, f* looter. **piller** [1] *vt* loot.

pilote /pilɔt/ *nm* (Aviat, Naut) pilot; (Auto) driver. ●*a* pilot. **piloter** [1] *vt* (Aviat, Naut) pilot; (Auto) drive.

pilule /pilyl/ *nf* pill; **la ~** the pill.

piment /pimã/ *nm* hot pepper; (fig) spice. **pimenté, ~e** *a* spicy.

pin /pɛ̃/ *nm* pine.

pinard /pinaʀ/ *nm* Ⓕ plonk Ⓕ, cheap wine.

pince /pɛ̃s/ *nf* (outil) pliers (+ *pl*); (levier) crowbar; (de crabe) pincer; (à sucre) tongs (+ *pl*); **~ à épiler** tweezers (+ *pl*); **~ à linge** clothes peg.

pinceau (*pl* **~x**) /pɛ̃so/ *nm* paintbrush.

pincée /pɛ̃se/ *nf* pinch (**de** of).

pincer /pɛ̃se/ [10] *vt* pinch; (attraper Ⓕ) catch. □ **se ~** *vpr* catch oneself; **se ~ le doigt** catch one's finger.

pince-sans-rire /pɛ̃ssãʀiʀ/ *nmf inv* **c'est un ~** he has a deadpan sense of humour.

pingouin /pɛ̃gwɛ̃/ *nm* penguin.

pingre /pɛ̃gʀ/ *a* stingy.

pintade /pɛ̃tad/ *nf* guinea fowl.

piocher /pjɔʃe/ [1] *vt/i* dig; (étudier Ⓕ) study hard, slog away (at).

pion /pjõ/ *nm* (de jeu) counter; (aux échecs) pawn; (Scol Ⓕ) supervisor.

pipe /pip/ *nf* pipe; **fumer la ~** smoke a pipe.

piquant, ~e /pikã, -t/ *a* (barbe) prickly; (goût) pungent; (remarque) cutting. ●*nm* prickle.

pique /pik/ *nm* (aux cartes) spades.

pique-nique (*pl* **~s**) /piknik/ *nm* picnic.

piquer /pike/ [1] *vt* (épine) prick; (épice) burn, sting; (abeille, ortie) sting; (serpent, moustique) bite; (enfoncer) stick; (coudre) (machine-) stitch; (curiosité) excite; (voler Ⓕ) pinch. ●*vi* (avion) dive; (goût) be hot. □ **se ~** *vpr* prick oneself.

piquet /pikɛ/ *nm* stake; (de tente) peg; (de parasol) pole; **~ de grève** (strike) picket.

piqûre /pikyʀ/ *nf* prick; (d'abeille) sting; (de serpent) bite; (point) stitch; (Méd) injection, jab; **faire une ~ à qn** give sb an injection.

pirate /piʀat/ *nm* pirate; **~ informatique** computer hacker; **~ de l'air** hijacker.

pire /piʀ/ *a* worse (**que** than); **les ~s mensonges** the most wicked lies. ●*nm* **le ~** the worst; **au ~** at worst.

pis /pi/ *nm* (de vache) udder. ●*a*

P

inv & adv worse; **aller de mal en ~** go from bad to worse.

piscine /pisin/ *nf* swimming-pool; **~ couverte** indoor swimming-pool.

pissenlit /pisɑ̃li/ *nm* dandelion.

pistache /pistaʃ/ *nf* pistachio.

piste /pist/ *nf* track; (de personne, d'animal) track, trail; (Aviat) runway; (de cirque) ring; (de ski) slope; (de danse) floor; (Sport) racetrack; **~ cyclable** cycle lane.

pistolet /pistɔlɛ/ *nm* gun, pistol; (de peintre) spray-gun.

piteux, -euse /pitø, -z/ *a* pitiful.

pitié /pitje/ *nf* pity; **il me fait ~** I feel sorry for him.

piton /pitɔ̃/ *nm* (à crochet) hook; (sommet pointu) peak.

pitoyable /pitwajabl/ *a* pitiful.

pitre /pitʀ/ *nm* clown; **faire le ~** clown around.

pittoresque /pitɔʀɛsk/ *a* picturesque.

pivot /pivo/ *nm* pivot. **pivoter** [1] *vi* revolve; (*personne*) swing round.

placard /plakaʀ/ *nm* cupboard; (affiche) poster. **placarder** [1] *vt* (*affiche*) post up; (*mur*) cover with posters.

place /plas/ *nf* place; (espace libre) room, space; (siège) seat, place; (prix d'un trajet) fare; (esplanade) square; (emploi) position; (de parking) space; **à la ~ de** instead of; **en ~, à sa ~** in its place; **faire ~ à** give way to; **sur ~** on the spot; **remettre qn à sa ~** put sb in his place; **ça prend de la ~** it takes up a lot of room; **se mettre à la ~ de qn** put oneself in sb's shoes *ou* place.

placement /plasmɑ̃/ *nm* (d'argent) investment.

placer /plase/ [10] *vt* place; (*invité, spectateur*) seat; (*argent*) invest. □ **se ~** *vpr* (*personne*) take up a position.

plafond /plafɔ̃/ *nm* ceiling.

plage /plaʒ/ *nf* beach; **~ horaire** time slot.

plagiat /plaʒja/ *nm* plagiarism.

plaider /plede/ [1] *vt/i* plead. **plaidoirie** *nf* (defence) speech. **plaidoyer** *nm* plea.

plaie /plɛ/ *nf* wound; (personne Ⅲ) nuisance.

plaignant, ~e /plɛɲɑ̃, -t/ *nm, f* plaintiff.

plaindre /plɛ̃dʀ/ [22] *vt* pity. □ **se ~** *vpr* complain (de about); **se ~ de** (souffrir de) complain of.

plaine /plɛn/ *nf* plain.

plainte /plɛ̃t/ *nf* complaint; (gémissement) groan. **plaintif, -ive** *a* plaintive.

plaire /plɛʀ/ [47] *vi* **~ à** please; **ça lui plaît** he likes it; **elle lui plaît** he likes her; **ça me plaît de faire** I like *ou* enjoy doing; **s'il vous plaît** please. □ **se ~** *vpr* **il se plaît ici** he likes it here.

plaisance /plɛzɑ̃s/ *nf* **la (navigation de) ~** boating.

plaisant, ~e /plɛzɑ̃, -t/ *a* pleasant; (drôle) amusing.

plaisanter /plɛzɑ̃te/ [1] *vi* joke. **plaisanterie** *nf* joke. **plaisantin** *nm* joker.

plaisir /plɛziʀ/ *nm* pleasure; **faire ~ à** please; **pour le ~** for fun *ou* pleasure.

plan /plɑ̃/ *nm* plan; (de ville) map; (de livre) outline; **~ d'eau** artificial lake; **~ social** planned redundancy programme; **premier ~** foreground.

planche /plɑ̃ʃ/ *nf* board, plank; (gravure) plate; **~ à repasser** ironing-board; **~ à voile** windsurfing board; (Sport) windsurfing.

plancher /plɑ̃ʃe/ *nm* floor.

planer /plane/ [1] *vi* glide; **~ sur** (*mystère, danger*) hang over.

planète /planɛt/ *nf* planet.

planeur /plancer/ *nm* glider.

planifier /planifje/ [45] *vt* plan.

plant /plɑ̃/ *nm* seedling; (de légumes) patch.

plante /plɑ̃t/ *nf* plant; ~ d'appartement houseplant; ~ des pieds sole (of the foot).

planter /plɑ̃te/ [1] *vt* (*plante*) plant; (enfoncer) drive in; (*tente*) put up; **rester planté** ▣ stand still.

plaque /plak/ *nf* plate; (de marbre) slab; (insigne) badge; ~ **chauffante** hotplate; ~ **commémorative** plaque; ~ **minéralogique** numberplate; ~ **de verglas** patch of ice.

plaquer /plake/ [1] *vt* (*bois*) veneer; (aplatir) flatten; (rugby) tackle; (abandonner ▣) ditch ▣; **tout** ~ chuck it all.

plastique /plastik/ *a & nm* plastic; **en** ~ plastic.

plastiquer /plastike/ [1] *vt* blow up.

plat, ~**e** /pla, -t/ *a* flat. ● *nm* (Culin) dish; (partie de repas) course; (de la main) flat ● **à plat** *adv* (*poser*) flat; (*batterie, pneu*) flat; **à** ~ **ventre** flat on one's face.

platane /platan/ *nm* plane tree.

plateau (*pl* ~**x**) /plato/ *nm* tray; (de cinéma) set; (de balance) pan; (Géog) plateau; ~ **de fromages** cheeseboard; ~ **de fruits de mer** seafood platter. **plate-bande** (*pl* **plates-bandes**) *nf* flower-bed.

platine /platin/ *nm* platinum. ● *nf* (tourne-disque) turntable; ~ **laser** compact disc player.

plâtre /plɑtʀ/ *nm* plaster; (Méd) (plaster) cast.

plein, ~**e** /plɛ̃, -ɛn/ *a* full (**de** of); (total) complete. ● *nm* **faire le** ~ (d'essence) fill up (the tank); **à** ~ fully; **à** ~ **temps** full-time; **en** ~ **air** in the open air; **en** ~ **milieu**/

visage right in the middle/the face; **en** ~**e nuit** in the middle of the night. ● *adv* **avoir des idées** ~ **la tête** be full of ideas. **pleinement** *adv* fully.

pleurer /plœʀe/ [1] *vi* cry, weep (**sur** over); (*yeux*) water. ● *vt* mourn.

pleurnicher /plœʀniʃe/ [1] *vi* ▣ snivel.

pleurs /plœʀ/ *nmpl* tears; **en** ~ in tears.

pleuvoir /pløvwaʀ/ [48] *vi* rain; (fig) rain *ou* shower down; **il pleut** it is raining; **il pleut à verse** *ou* **des cordes** it is pouring.

pli /pli/ *nm* fold; (de jupe) pleat; (de pantalon) crease; (lettre) letter; (habitude) habit; (faux) ~ crease.

pliant, ~**e** /plijɑ̃, -t/ *a* folding. ● *nm* folding stool, camp-stool.

plier /plije/ [45] *vt* fold; (courber) bend; (soumettre) submit (**à** to). ● *vi* bend. □ **se** ~ *vpr* fold; **se** ~ **à** submit to.

plinthe /plɛ̃t/ *nf* skirting-board.

plissé, ~**e** /plise/ *a* (*jupe*) pleated.

plisser /plise/ [1] *vt* crease; (*yeux*) screw up.

plomb /plɔ̃/ *nm* lead; (fusible) fuse; ~**s** (de chasse) lead shot; **de** *ou* **en** ~ lead. **plombage** *nm* filling.

plomberie /plɔ̃bʀi/ *nf* plumbing. **plombier** *nm* plumber.

plongée /plɔ̃ʒe/ *nf* diving; **en** ~ (*sous-marin*) submerged.

plongeoir /plɔ̃ʒwaʀ/ *nm* diving-board.

plonger /plɔ̃ʒe/ [40] *vi* dive; (*route*) plunge. ● *vt* plunge. □ **se** ~ *vpr* plunge into; **se** ~ **dans** (fig) (*lecture*) bury oneself in.

plongeur, **-euse** *nm, f* diver; (de restaurant) dishwasher.

plu /ply/ ⇒PLAIRE [47], PLEUVOIR [48].

pluie /plɥi/ *nf* rain; (averse)

P

shower; ~ **battante/diluvienne** driving/torrential rain.

plume /plym/ *nf* feather; (pointe) nib.

plumeau (*pl* ~x) /plymo/ *nm* feather duster.

plumier /plymje/ *nm* pencil box.

plupart: **la** ~ /laplypar/ *loc* **la** ~ **des** (*gens, cas*) most; **la** ~ **du temps** most of the time; **pour la** ~ for the most part.

pluriel, ~**le** /plyrjɛl/ *a & nm* plural.

....

plus /ply, plys, plyz/

● *adverbe de comparaison*

⋯▶ more (**que** than); ~ **âgé/tard** older/later; ~ **beau** more beautiful; ~ **j'y pense...** the more I think about it...; **deux fois** ~ twice as much; **deux fois** ~ **cher** twice as expensive.

⋯▶ **le** ~ the most; **le** ~ **grand** the biggest; (de deux) the bigger.

⋯▶ ~ **de** (*pain*) more; (*dix jours*) more than; **il est** ~ **de 8 heures** it is after 8 o'clock.

⋯▶ **de** ~ more (**que** than); (en outre) moreover; **les enfants de** ~ **de 10 ans** children over 10 years old; **de** ~ **en** ~ more and more.

⋯▶ **en** ~ on top of that; **c'est en** ~ it's extra; **en** ~ **de** in addition to.

⋯▶ ~ **ou moins** more or less.

⋯▶ **au** ~ **tard** at the latest.

● *adverbe de négation*

⋯▶ **ne** ~ (*temps*) no longer, not any more; **je n'y vais** ~ I don't go there any longer *ou* any more.

⋯▶ **ne** ~ **de** (quantité) no more; **il n'y a** ~ **de pain** there is no more bread.

⋯▶ ~ **que deux jours!** only two days left!

● *préposition & nom masculin*

⋯▶ (maths) plus.

....

plusieurs /plyzjœr/ *a & pron* several.

plus-value (*pl* ~s) /plyvaly/ *nf* (bénéfice) profit.

plutôt /plyto/ *adv* rather (**que** than).

pluvieux, -**ieuse** /plyvjø, -z/ *a* rainy.

PME *abrév f* (**petites et moyennes entreprises**) SME.

PNB *abrév m* (**produit national brut**) GNP.

pneu (*pl* ~s) /pnø/ *nm* tyre. **pneumatique** *a* inflatable.

poche /pɔʃ/ *nf* pocket; (sac) bag; ~s (sous les yeux) bags.

pocher /pɔʃe/ [1] *vt* (œuf) poach.

pochette /pɔʃɛt/ *nf* (de documents) folder; (sac) bag, pouch; (d'allumettes) book; (de disque) sleeve; (mouchoir) pocket handkerchief.

poêle /pwal/ *nf* ~ (à frire) frying-pan. ● *nm* stove.

poème /pɔɛm/ *nm* poem. **poésie** *nf* poetry; (poème) poem. **poète** *nm* poet. **poétique** *a* poetic.

poids /pwa/ *nm* weight; ~ **coq/ lourd/plume** bantam weight/ heavyweight/featherweight; ~ **lourd** (camion) lorry, juggernaut; (US) truck.

poignard /pwaɲar/ *nm* dagger. **poignarder** [1] *vt* stab.

poigne /pwaɲ/ *nf* **avoir de la** ~ have a strong grip.

poignée /pwaɲe/ *nf* (de porte) handle; (quantité) handful; ~ **de main** handshake.

poignet /pwaɲɛ/ *nm* wrist; (de chemise) cuff.

poil /pwal/ *nm* hair; (pelage) fur; (de brosse) bristle; ~s (de tapis) pile; **à** ~ ⊞ naked; ~ **à gratter**

itching powder. **poilu, ~e** a hairy.

poinçon /pwɛ̃sɔ̃/ nm awl; (marque) hallmark. **poinçonner** [1] vt (billet) punch.

poing /pwɛ̃/ nm fist.

point /pwɛ̃/ nm (endroit, Sport) point; (marque visible) spot, dot; (de couture) stitch; (pour évaluer) mark; **enlever un ~ par faute** take a mark off for each mistake; **à ~** (Culin) medium; (arriver) at the right time; **faire le ~** take stock; **mettre au ~** (photo) focus; (technique) develop; **mettre les choses au ~** get things clear; **Camille n'est pas encore au ~ pour ses examens** Camille is not ready for her exams; **sur le ~ de** about to; **au ~ que** to the extent that; **~** (final) full stop, period; **deux ~s** colon; **~ d'interrogation/d'exclamation** question/exclamation mark; **~s de suspension** suspension points; **~ virgule** semicolon; **~ culminant** peak; **~ du jour** daybreak; **~ mort** (Auto) neutral; **~ de repère** landmark; **~ de suture** (Méd) stitch; **~ de vente** point of sale; **~ de vue** point of view. ● adv (ne) **~** not.

pointe /pwɛ̃t/ nf point, tip; (clou) tack; (de grille) spike; (fig) touch (de of); **de ~** (industrie) high-tech; **en ~** pointed; **heure de ~** peak hour; **sur la ~ des pieds** on tiptoe.

pointer /pwɛ̃te/ [1] vt (cocher) tick off; (diriger) point, aim. ● vi (employé) (en arrivant) clock in; (en sortant) clock out. □ **se ~** vpr 🆒 turn up.

pointillé /pwɛ̃tije/ nm dotted line.

pointilleux, -euse /pwɛ̃tijø, -z/ a fastidious, particular.

pointu, ~e /pwɛ̃ty/ a pointed; (aiguisé) sharp.

pointure /pwɛ̃tyʀ/ nf size.

poire /pwaʀ/ nf pear.

poireau (pl ~x) /pwaʀo/ nm leek.

poirier /pwaʀje/ nm pear tree.

pois /pwa/ nm pea; (motif) dot; **robe à ~** polka dot dress.

poison /pwazɔ̃/ nm poison.

poisseux, -euse /pwasø, -z/ a sticky.

poisson /pwasɔ̃/ nm fish; **~ rouge** goldfish; **~ d'avril** April fool; **les P~s** Pisces.

poissonnerie nf fish shop.

poissonnier, -ière nm, f fishmonger.

poitrine /pwatʀin/ nf chest; (seins) bosom.

poivre /pwavʀ/ nm pepper. **poivré, ~e** a peppery. **poivrière** nf pepper-pot.

poivron /pwavʀɔ̃/ nm sweet pepper.

polaire /pɔlɛʀ/ a polar. ● nf (veste) fleece.

pôle /pol/ nm pole.

polémique /pɔlemik/ nf debate. ● a controversial.

poli, ~e /pɔli/ a (personne) polite.

police /pɔlis/ nf (force) police (+ pl); (discipline) (law and) order; (d'assurance) policy.

policier, -ière /pɔlisje, -jɛʀ/ a police; (roman) detective. ● nm policeman.

polir /pɔliʀ/ [2] vt polish.

politesse /pɔlitɛs/ nf politeness; (parole) polite remark.

politicien, ~ne /pɔlitisjɛ̃, -ɛn/ nm, f (péj) politician.

politique /pɔlitik/ a political; **homme ~** politician. ● nf politics; (ligne de conduite) policy.

pollen /pɔlɛn/ nm pollen.

polluant, ~e /pɔlɥɑ̃, -t/ a polluting. ● nm pollutant.

polluer /pɔlɥe/ [1] vt pollute.

pollution nf pollution.

P

polo /pɔlo/ *nm* (Sport) polo; (vêtement) polo shirt.

Pologne /pɔlɔɲ/ *nf* Poland.

polonais, **~e** /pɔlɔnɛ, -z/ *a* Polish. ● *nm* (Ling) Polish. **P~**, **~e** *nm, f* Pole.

poltron, **~ne** /pɔltRɔ̃, -ɔn/ *a* cowardly. ● *nm, f* coward.

polygame /pɔligam/ *nmf* polygamist.

polyvalent, **~e** /pɔlivalɑ̃, -t/ *a* varied; (*personne*) versatile.

pommade /pɔmad/ *nf* ointment.

pomme /pɔm/ *nf* apple; (d'arrosoir) rose; **~ d'Adam** Adam's apple; **~ de pin** pine cone; **~ de terre** potato; **~s frites** chips; (US) French fries; **tomber dans les ~s** 🔟 pass out.

pommette /pɔmɛt/ *nf* cheekbone.

pommier /pɔmje/ *nm* apple tree.

pompe /pɔ̃p/ *nf* pump; (splendeur) pomp; **~ à incendie** fire-engine; **~s funèbres** undertaker's (+ *sg*).

pomper /pɔ̃pe/ [1] *vt* pump; (copier 🔟) copy, crib; **~ l'air à qn** 🔟 get on sb's nerves.

pompier /pɔ̃pje/ *nm* fireman.

pomponner (se) /(sə)pɔ̃pɔne/ [1] *vpr* get dolled up.

poncer /pɔ̃se/ [10] *vt* sand.

ponctuation /pɔ̃ktɥasjɔ̃/ *nf* punctuation.

ponctuel, **~le** /pɔ̃ktɥɛl/ *a* punctual.

pondre /pɔ̃dR/ [3] *vt/i* lay.

poney /pɔnɛ/ *nm* pony.

pont /pɔ̃/ *nm* bridge; (de navire) deck; (de graissage) ramp; **faire le ~** get an extended weekend; **~ aérien** airlift. **pont-levis** (*pl* **ponts-levis**) *nm* drawbridge.

populaire /pɔpylɛR/ *a* popular; (*expression*) colloquial; (*quartier, origine*) working-class.

popularité *nf* popularity.

population /pɔpylasjɔ̃/ *nf* population.

porc /pɔR/ *nm* pig; (viande) pork.

porcelaine /pɔRsəlɛn/ *nf* china, porcelain.

porc-épic (*pl* **porcs-épics**) /pɔRkepik/ *nm* porcupine.

porcherie /pɔRʃəRi/ *nf* pigsty.

pornographie /pɔRnɔgRafi/ *nf* pornography.

port /pɔR/ *nm* port, harbour; **à bon ~** safely; **~ maritime** seaport; (transport) carriage; (d'armes) carrying; (de barbe) wearing.

portable /pɔRtabl/ *nm* (Ordinat) laptop (computer); (telephone) mobile (phone).

portail /pɔRtaj/ *nm* gate.

portatif, **-ive** /pɔRtatif, -v/ *a* portable.

porte /pɔRt/ *nf* door; (passage) doorway; (de jardin, d'embarquement) gate; **mettre à la ~** throw out; **~ d'entrée** front door.

porté, **~e** /pɔRte/ *a* **~ à** inclined to; **~ sur** keen on.

porte-avions /pɔRtavjɔ̃/ *nm inv* aircraft carrier.

porte-bagages /pɔRtbagaʒ/ *nm inv* (de vélo) carrier.

porte-bonheur /pɔRtbɔnœR/ *nm inv* lucky charm.

porte-clefs /pɔRtəkle/ *nm inv* key ring.

porte-documents /pɔRtdɔkymɑ̃/ *nm inv* briefcase.

portée /pɔRte/ *nf* (d'une arme) range; (de voûte) span; (d'animaux) litter; (impact) significance; (Mus) stave; **à ~ de (la) main** within (arm's) reach; **hors de ~ (de)** out of reach (of); **à la ~ de qn** at sb's level.

porte-fenêtre (*pl* **portes-fenêtres**) /pɔRtfənɛtR/ *nf* French window.

portefeuille /pɔRtəfœj/ *nm* wallet; (de ministre) portfolio.

porte-jarretelles /pɔrtʒartɛl/ *nm inv* suspender belt.

portemanteau (*pl* ~**x**) /pɔrtmɑ̃to/ *nm* coat *ou* hat stand.

porte-monnaie /pɔrtmɔnɛ/ *nm inv* purse.

porte-parole /pɔrtparɔl/ *nm inv* spokesperson.

porter /pɔrte/ [1] *vt* carry; (*vêtement, bague*) wear; (*fruits, responsabilité, nom*) bear; (*coup*) strike; (*amener*) bring; (*inscrire*) enter. ● *vi* (*bruit*) carry; (*coup*) hit home; ~ **sur** rest on; (*concerner*) be about. □ **se** ~ *vpr* **bien se** ~ be *ou* feel well; **se** ~ **candidat** stand as a candidate.

porteur, -euse /pɔrtœr, -øz/ *nm,f* (de nouvelles) bearer; (Méd) carrier. ● *nm* (Rail) porter.

portier /pɔrtje/ *nm* doorman.

portière /pɔrtjɛr/ *nf* door.

porto /pɔrto/ *nm* port (wine).

portrait /pɔrtrɛ/ *nm* portrait. **portrait-robot** (*pl* **portraits-robots**) *nm* identikit®, photofit®.

portuaire /pɔrtɥɛr/ *a* port.

portugais, ~e /pɔrtygɛ, -z/ *a* Portuguese. ● *nm* (Ling) Portuguese. **P~, ~e** *nm,f* Portuguese.

Portugal /pɔrtygal/ *nm* Portugal.

pose /poz/ *nf* installation; (attitude) pose; (Photo) exposure.

posé, ~e /poze/ *a* calm, serious.

poser /poze/ [1] *vt* put (down); (*installer*) install, put in; (*fondations*) lay; (*question*) ask; (*problème*) pose; ~ **sa candidature** apply (**à** for). ● *vi* (*modèle*) pose. □ **se** ~ *vpr* (avion, oiseau) land; (regard) fall; (se présenter) arise.

positif, -ive /pozitif, -v/ *a* positive.

position /pozisjɔ̃/ *nf* position; **prendre** ~ take a stand.

posologie /pozɔlɔʒi/ *nf* dosage.

posséder /pɔsede/ [14] *vt* (*propriété*) own, possess; (*diplôme*) have.

possessif, -ive /pɔsesif, -v/ *a* possessive.

possession /pɔsesjɔ̃/ *nf* possession; **prendre** ~ **de** take possession of.

possibilité /pɔsibilite/ *nf* possibility.

possible /pɔsibl/ *a* possible; **dès que** ~ as soon as possible; **le plus tard** ~ as late as possible. ● *nm* **le** ~ what is possible; **faire son** ~ do one's utmost.

postal, ~e (*mpl* **-aux**) /pɔstal, -o/ *a* postal.

poste /pɔst/ *nf* (service) post; (bureau) post office; ~ **aérienne** airmail; **mettre à la** ~ post; ~ **restante** poste restante. ● *nm* (lieu, emploi) post; (de radio, télévision) set; (téléphone) extension (number); ~ **d'essence** petrol station; ~ **d'incendie** fire point; ~ **de pilotage** cockpit; ~ **de police** police station; ~ **de secours** first-aid post.

poster¹ /pɔste/ [1] *vt* (*lettre, personne*) post.

poster² /pɔstɛr/ *nm* poster.

postérieur, ~e /pɔsterjœr/ *a* later; (*partie*) back; ~ **à** after. ● *nm* 🔲 posterior.

posthume /pɔstym/ *a* posthumous.

postiche /pɔstiʃ/ *a* false.

postier, -ière /pɔstje, -jɛr/ *nm,f* postal worker.

post-scriptum /pɔstskriptɔm/ *nm inv* postscript.

postuler /pɔstyle/ [1] *vt/i* apply (**à** for); (*principe*) postulate.

pot /po/ *nm* pot; (en plastique) carton; (en verre) jar; (chance 🔲) luck; (boisson 🔲) drink; ~ **catalytique** catalytic converter; ~ **d'échappement** exhaust pipe.

P

potable /pɔtabl/ *a* eau ∼ drinking water.

potage /pɔtaʒ/ *nm* soup.

potager, -ère /pɔtaʒe, -ɛʀ/ *a* vegetable. ● *nm* vegetable garden.

pot-au-feu /pɔtofø/ *nm inv* (plat) stew.

pot-de-vin (*pl* **pots-de-vin**) /podvɛ̃/ *nm* bribe.

poteau (*pl* ∼x) /pɔto/ *nm* post; (télégraphique) pole; ∼ **indicateur** signpost.

potelé, ∼e /pɔtle/ *a* plump.

potentiel, ∼le /pɔtɑ̃sjɛl/ *a & nm* potential.

poterie /pɔtʀi/ *nf* pottery; (objet) piece of pottery. **potier** *nm* potter.

potins /pɔtɛ̃/ *nmpl* gossip (+ *sg*).

potiron /pɔtiʀɔ̃/ *nm* pumpkin.

pou (*pl* ∼x) /pu/ *nm* louse.

poubelle /pubɛl/ *nf* dustbin.

pouce /pus/ *nm* thumb; (de pied) big toe; (mesure) inch.

poudre /pudʀ/ *nf* powder; ∼ (à canon) gunpowder; en ∼ (lait) powdered; (chocolat) drinking.

poudrier /pudʀije/ *nm* (powder) compact.

pouf /puf/ *nm* pouffe.

poulailler /pulaje/ *nm* hen house.

poulain /pulɛ̃/ *nm* foal; (protégé) protégé.

poule /pul/ *nf* hen; (Culin) fowl; (femme 🅇) tart.

poulet /pulɛ/ *nm* chicken.

pouliche /puliʃ/ *nf* filly.

poulie /puli/ *nf* pulley.

pouls /pu/ *nm* pulse.

poumon /pumɔ̃/ *nm* lung.

poupe /pup/ *nf* stern.

poupée /pupe/ *nf* doll.

pour /puʀ/ *prép* for; (envers) to; (à la place de) on behalf of; (comme) as; ∼ **cela** for that reason; ∼ **cent**

per cent; ∼ **de bon** for good; ∼ **faire** (in order) to do; ∼ **que** so that; ∼ **moi** (à mon avis) as for me; **trop poli** ∼ too polite to; ∼ **ce qui est de** as for; **être** ∼ be in favour. ● *nm inv* **le** ∼ **et le contre** the pros and cons.

pourboire /puʀbwaʀ/ *nm* tip.

pourcentage /puʀsɑ̃taʒ/ *nm* percentage.

pourparlers /puʀpaʀle/ *nmpl* talks.

pourpre /puʀpʀ/ *a & nm* crimson; (violet) purple.

pourquoi /puʀkwa/ *conj & adv* why. ● *nm inv* **le** ∼ **et le comment** the why and the wherefore.

pourra, pourrait /puʀa, puʀɛ/ ⇒POUVOIR [49].

pourri, ∼e /puʀi/ *a* rotten.

pourrir [2] *vt/i* rot. **pourriture** *nf* rot.

poursuite /puʀsɥit/ *nf* pursuit (de of); ∼s (Jur) legal action (+ *sg*).

poursuivre /puʀsɥivʀ/ [57] *vt* pursue; (continuer) continue (with); ∼ **(en justice)** take to court; (droit civil) sue. ● *vi* continue. □ **se** ∼ *vpr* continue.

pourtant /puʀtɑ̃/ *adv* yet.

pourvoir /puʀvwaʀ/ [63] *vi* ∼ **à** provide for; **pourvu de** supplied with.

pourvu que /puʀvyk(ə)/ *conj* (condition) provided (that); (souhait) let us hope (that).

pousse /pus/ *nf* growth; (bourgeon) shoot.

poussé, ∼e /puse/ *a* (études) advanced; (enquête) thorough.

poussée /puse/ *nf* pressure; (coup) push; (de prix) upsurge; (Méd) attack.

pousser /puse/ [1] *vt* push; (cri) let out; (soupir) heave; (continuer) continue; (exhorter) urge (à to); (forcer) drive (à to). ● *vi* push;

(grandir) grow; **faire** ~ (*cheveux*) let grow; (*plante*) grow. □ **se** ~ *vpr* move over *ou* up; **pousse-toi!** move over!

poussette /pusɛt/ *nf* pushchair.

poussière /pusjɛʀ/ *nf* dust. **poussiéreux, -euse** *a* dusty.

poussin /pusɛ̃/ *nm* chick.

poutre /putʀ/ *nf* beam; (en métal) girder.

pouvoir /puvwaʀ/ [49] *v aux* (possibilité) can, be able; (permission, éventualité) may, can; **il peut/pouvait/pourrait venir** he can/could/might come; **je n'ai pas pu** I couldn't; **j'ai pu faire** (réussi à) I managed to do; **je n'en peux plus** I am exhausted; **il se peut que** it may be that. ● *nm* power; (gouvernement) government; **au** ~ **in** power; ~**s publics** authorities.

prairie /pʀeʀi/ *nf* meadow.

praticien, ~ne /pʀatisjɛ̃, -ɛn/ *nm, f* practitioner.

pratiquant, ~e /pʀatikɑ̃, -t/ *a* practising. ● *nm, f* churchgoer.

pratique /pʀatik/ *a* practical. ● *nf* practice; (expérience) experience; **la** ~ **du golf/du cheval** golfing/riding. **pratiquement** *adv* (en pratique) in practice; (presque) practically.

pratiquer /pʀatike/ [1] *vt/i* practise; (Sport) play; (faire) make.

pré /pʀe/ *nm* meadow.

préalable /pʀealabl/ *a* preliminary, prior. ● *nm* precondition; **au** ~ first.

préambule /pʀeɑ̃byl/ *nm* preamble.

préavis /pʀeavi/ *nm* notice.

précaire /pʀekɛʀ/ *a* precarious. **précarité** *nf* (d'emploi) insecurity.

précaution /pʀekosjɔ̃/ *nf* (mesure) precaution; (prudence) caution.

précédent, ~e /pʀesedɑ̃, -t/ *a* previous. ● *nm* precedent.

précéder /pʀesede/ [14] *vt/i* precede.

précepteur, -trice /pʀesɛptœʀ, -tʀis/ *nm, f* (private) tutor.

prêcher /pʀeʃe/ [1] *vt/i* preach.

précieux, -ieuse /pʀesjø, -z/ *a* precious.

précipitamment /pʀesipitamɑ̃/ *adv* hastily. **précipitation** *nf* haste.

précipiter /pʀesipite/ [1] *vt* throw, precipitate; (hâter) hasten. □ **se** ~ *vpr* (se dépêcher) rush (**sur** at, on to); (se jeter) throw oneself; (s'accélérer) speed up.

précis, ~e /pʀesi, -z/ *a* precise, specific; (mécanisme) accurate; **dix heures** ~**es** ten o'clock sharp. ● *nm* summary.

préciser /pʀesize/ [1] *vt* specify; **précisez votre pensée** could you be more specific. □ **se** ~ *vpr* become clear(er). **précision** *nf* precision; (détail) detail.

précoce /pʀekɔs/ *a* (enfant) precocious.

préconiser /pʀekɔnize/ [1] *vt* advocate.

précurseur /pʀekyʀsœʀ/ *nm* forerunner.

prédicateur /pʀedikatœʀ/ *nm* preacher.

prédilection /pʀedilɛksjɔ̃/ *nf* preference.

prédire /pʀediʀ/ [37] *vt* predict.

prédominer /pʀedɔmine/ [1] *vi* predominate.

préface /pʀefas/ *nf* preface.

préfecture /pʀefɛktyʀ/ *nf* prefecture; ~ **de police** police headquarters.

préféré, ~e /pʀefeʀe/ *a & nm, f* favourite.

préférence /pʀefeʀɑ̃s/ *nf* preference; **de** ~ preferably.

préférentiel, ~le /pʀefeʀɑ̃sjɛl/ *a* preferential.

préférer /pʀefeʀe/ [14] *vt* prefer

(à to); ~ **faire** prefer to do; **je ne préfère pas** I'd rather not; **j'aurais préféré ne pas savoir** I wish I hadn't found out.

préfet /pʀefɛ/ *nm* prefect; ~ **de police** prefect *ou* chief of police.

préfixe /pʀefiks/ *nm* prefix.

préhistorique /pʀeistɔʀik/ *a* prehistoric.

préjudice /pʀeʒydis/ *nm* harm, prejudice; **porter** ~ **à** harm.

préjugé /pʀeʒyʒe/ *nm* prejudice; **être plein de** ~**s** be very prejudiced.

prélasser (se) /(sə)pʀelase/ [1] *vpr* loll (about).

prélèvement /pʀelɛvmɑ̃/ *nm* deduction; (de sang) sample. **prélever** [6] *vt* deduct (**sur** from); (*sang*) take.

préliminaire /pʀeliminɛʀ/ *a* & *nm* preliminary; ~**s** (*sexuels*) foreplay.

prématuré, ~**e** /pʀematyʀe/ *a* premature. ● *nm* premature baby.

premier, -ière /pʀəmje, -jɛʀ/ *a* first; (*rang*) front, first; (*enfance*) early; (*nécessité, souci*) prime; (*qualité*) top, prime; **de** ~ **ordre** first-rate; ~ **ministre** Prime Minister. ● *nm,f* first (one). ● *nm* (date) first; (*étage*) first floor; **en** ~ first. **première** *nf* (Rail) first class; (*exploit jamais vu*) first; (*cinéma, Théât*) première; (*Aut*) (*vitesse*) first (gear). **premièrement** *adv* firstly.

prémunir /pʀemyniʀ/ [2] *vt* protect (**contre** against).

prenant, ~**e** /pʀənɑ̃, -t/ *a* (*activité*) engrossing; (*enfant*) demanding.

prénatal, ~**e** (*mpl* ~**s**) /pʀenatal/ *a* antenatal.

prendre /pʀɑ̃dʀ/ [50] *vt* take; (*attraper*) catch, get; (*acheter*) get; (*repas*) have; (engager, adopter) take on; (*poids*) put on; (chercher) pick

up; **qu'est-ce qui te prend?** what's the matter with you? ● *vi* (*liquide*) set; (*feu*) catch; (*vaccin*) take. □ **se** ~ *vpr* **se** ~ **pour** think one is; **s'en** ~ **à** attack; (rendre responsable) blame; **s'y** ~ set about (it).

preneur, -euse /pʀənœʀ, -øz/ *nm,f* buyer; **être** ~ be willing to buy; **trouver** ~ find a buyer.

prénom /pʀenɔ̃/ *nm* first name.

prénommer /pʀenɔme/ [1] *vt* call. □ **se** ~ *vpr* be called.

préoccupation /pʀeɔkypasjɔ̃/ *nf* (souci) worry; (idée fixe) preoccupation.

préoccuper /pʀeɔkype/ [1] *vt* worry; (absorber) preoccupy. □ **se** ~ **de** *vpr* think about.

préparation /pʀepaʀasjɔ̃/ *nf* preparation. **préparatoire** *a* preparatory.

préparer /pʀepaʀe/ [1] *vt* prepare; (*repas, café*) make; **plats préparés** ready-cooked meals. □ **se** ~ *vpr* prepare oneself (à for); (s'apprêter) get ready; (être proche) be brewing.

préposé, ~**e** /pʀepoze/ *nm,f* employee; (des postes) postman, postwoman.

préposition /pʀepozisjɔ̃/ *nf* preposition.

préretraite /pʀeʀətʀɛt/ *nf* early retirement.

près /pʀɛ/ *adv* near, close; ~ **de** near (to), close to; (presque) nearly; **à cela** ~ except that; **de** ~ closely.

présage /pʀezaʒ/ *nm* omen.

presbyte /pʀɛsbit/ *a* long-sighted, far-sighted.

prescrire /pʀɛskʀiʀ/ [30] *vt* prescribe.

préséance /pʀeseɑ̃s/ *nf* precedence.

présence /pʀezɑ̃s/ *nf* presence; (Scol) attendance.

présent, ~e /pʀezã, -t/ a
present. ● nm (temps, cadeau)
present; à ~ now.

présentateur, **-trice** /pʀesãta-
tœʀ, -tʀis/ nm, f presenter.

présentation /pʀezãtasjõ/ nf (de
personne) introduction; (exposé)
presentation.

présenter /pʀezãte/ [1] vt
present; (personne) introduce (à
to); (montrer) show. ● vi ~ **bien**
have a pleasing appearance. □ se
~ vpr introduce oneself (à to);
(aller) go; (apparaître) appear;
(candidat) come forward;
(occasion) arise; se ~ à (examen)
sit for; (élection) stand for; se ~
bien look good.

préservatif /pʀezɛʀvatif/ nm
condom.

préserver /pʀezɛʀve/ [1] vt
protect.

présidence /pʀezidãs/ nf (d'État)
presidency; (de société)
chairmanship.

président, ~e /pʀezidã, -t/ nm, f
president; (de société, comité)
chairman, chairwoman;
~**-directeur général** managing
director.

présidentiel, ~**le** /pʀezidãsjɛl/ a
presidential.

présider /pʀezide/ [1] vt preside.

présomptueux, **-euse** /pʀezõp-
tɥø, -z/ a presumptuous.

presque /pʀɛsk(ə)/ adv almost,
nearly; ~ **jamais** hardly ever; ~
rien hardly anything; ~ **pas** (de)
hardly any.

presqu'île /pʀɛskil/ nf peninsula.

pressant, ~e /pʀesã, -t/ a
pressing, urgent.

presse /pʀɛs/ nf (journaux, appareil)
press.

pressentiment /pʀesãtimã/ nm
premonition. **pressentir** [46] vt
have a premonition of.

pressé, ~e /pʀese/ a in a hurry;
(orange, citron) freshly squeezed.

presser /pʀese/ [1] vt squeeze,
press; (appuyer sur, harceler) press;
(hâter) hasten; (inciter) urge (de to).
● vi (temps) press; (affaire) be
pressing. □ se ~ vpr (se hâter)
hurry; (se grouper) crowd.

pressing /pʀesiŋ/ nm (teinturerie)
dry-cleaner's.

pression /pʀesjõ/ nf pressure;
(bouton) press-stud.

prestance /pʀestãs/ nf
(imposing) presence.

prestation /pʀestasjõ/ nf
allowance; (d'artiste) performance.

prestidigitation /pʀestidiʒita-
sjõ/ nf conjuring.

prestige /pʀestiʒ/ nm prestige.

prestigieux, **-ieuse** a
prestigious.

présumer /pʀezyme/ [1] vt
presume; ~ **que** assume that; ~
de overrate.

prêt, ~e /pʀɛ, -t/ a ready (à qch
for sth, à faire to do). ● nm loan.

prêt-à-porter nm inv ready-to-
wear clothes.

prétendre /pʀetãdʀ/ [3] vt claim
(que that), (vouloir) intend; **on le
prétend riche** he is said to be very
rich. **prétendu**, ~e a so-called.
prétendument adv supposedly,
allegedly.

prétentieux, **-ieuse** /pʀetãsjø,
-z/ a pretentious.

prêter /pʀete/ [1] vt lend (à to);
(attribuer) attribute; ~ **son aide à
qn** give sb some help; ~ **attention**
pay attention; ~ **serment** take an
oath. ● vi ~ **à** lead to.

prêteur, **-euse** /pʀetœʀ, -øz/ nm, f
(money-)lender; ~ **sur gages**
pawnbroker.

prétexte /pʀetɛkst/ nm pretext,
excuse.

prêtre /pʀɛtʀ/ nm priest.

preuve /pʀœv/ nf proof; **des** ~s

evidence (+ *sg*); **faire ~ de** show; **faire ses ~s** prove oneself.

prévaloir /pʀevalwaʀ/ [60] *vi* prevail.

prévenant, **~e** /pʀevnɑ̃, -t/ *a* thoughtful.

prévenir /pʀevniʀ/ [58] *vt* (*menacer*) warn; (*informer*) tell; (*médecin*) call; (*éviter, anticiper*) prevent.

préventif, -ive /pʀevɑ̃tif, -v/ *a* preventive.

prévention /pʀevɑ̃sjɔ̃/ *nf* prevention; **faire de la ~** take preventive action; **~ routière** road safety.

prévenu, **~e** /pʀevny/ *nm, f* defendant.

prévisible /pʀevizibl/ *a* predictable. **prévision** *nf* prediction; (*météorologique*) forecast.

prévoir /pʀevwaʀ/ [63] *vt* foresee; (*temps*) forecast; (*organiser*) plan (for), provide for; (*envisager*) allow (for); **prévu pour** (*jouet*) designed for; **comme prévu** as planned.

prévoyance /pʀevwajɑ̃s/ *nf* foresight. **prévoyant**, **~e** *a* far-sighted.

prier /pʀije/ [45] *vi* pray. ● *vt* pray to; (*demander à*) ask (**de** to); **je vous en prie** please; (*il n'y a pas de quoi*) don't mention it.

prière /pʀijɛʀ/ *nf* prayer; (*demande*) request; **~ de** (*vous êtes prié de*) will you please.

primaire /pʀimɛʀ/ *a* primary.

prime /pʀim/ *nf* free gift; (*d'employé*) bonus; (*subvention*) subsidy; (*d'assurance*) premium.

primé, **~e** /pʀime/ *a* prize-winning.

primeurs /pʀimœʀ/ *nfpl* early fruit and vegetables.

primevère /pʀimvɛʀ/ *nf* primrose.

primitif, -ive /pʀimitif, -v/ *a* primitive; (*d'origine*) original. ● *nm, f* primitive.

primordial, **~e** (*mpl* **-iaux**) /pʀimɔʀdjal, -jo/ *a* essential.

prince /pʀɛ̃s/ *nm* prince. **princesse** *nf* princess.

principal, **~e** (*mpl* **-aux**) /pʀɛ̃sipal, -o/ *a* main, principal. ● *nm* headmaster; (*chose*) main thing.

principe /pʀɛ̃sip/ *nm* principle; **en ~** in theory; (*d'habitude*) as a rule.

printanier, -ière /pʀɛ̃tanje, -jɛʀ/ *a* spring(-like).

printemps /pʀɛ̃tɑ̃/ *nm* spring.

prioritaire /pʀijɔʀitɛʀ/ *a* priority; **être ~** have priority. **priorité** *nf* priority; (Auto) right of way.

pris, **~e** /pʀi, -z/ *a* (*place*) taken; (*personne, journée*) busy; (*nez*) stuffed up; **~ de** (*peur, fièvre*) stricken with; **~ de panique** panic-stricken. ● ⇒PRENDRE [50].

prise /pʀiz/ *nf* hold, grip; (*animal attrapé*) catch; (Mil) capture; **~ (de courant)** (*mâle*) plug; (*femelle*) socket; **~ multiple** multiplug adapter; **avoir ~ sur qn** have a hold over sb; **aux ~s avec** to grips with; **~ de conscience** awareness; **~ de contact** first contact, initial meeting; **~ de position** stand; **~ de sang** blood test.

prisé, **~e** /pʀize/ *a* popular.

prison /pʀizɔ̃/ *nf* prison, jail; (*réclusion*) imprisonment. **prisonnier, -ière** *nm, f* prisoner.

privation /pʀivasjɔ̃/ *nf* deprivation; (*sacrifice*) hardship.

privatiser /pʀivatize/ [1] *vt* privatize.

privé /pʀive/ *a* private. ● *nm* (Comm) private sector; (Scol) private schools (+ *pl*); **en ~** in private.

priver /pʀive/ [1] vt ~ de deprive of. □ se ~ (de) vpr go without.

privilège /pʀivilɛʒ/ nm privilege. **privilégié**, ~e nm, f privileged person.

prix /pʀi/ nm price; (récompense) prize; **à tout** ~ at all costs; **au** ~ **de** (fig) at the expense of; ~ **coûtant**, ~ **de revient** cost price; **à** ~ **fixe** set price.

probabilité /pʀɔbabilite/ nf probability. **probable** a probable, likely. **probablement** adv probably.

probant, ~e /pʀɔbã, -t/ a convincing, conclusive.

problème /pʀɔblɛm/ nm problem.

procédé /pʀɔsede/ nm process; (manière d'agir) practice.

procéder /pʀɔsede/ [14] vi proceed; ~ **à** carry out.

procès /pʀɔsɛ/ nm (criminel) trial; (civil) lawsuit, proceedings (+ pl).

processus /pʀɔsesys/ nm process; ~ **de paix** peace process.

procès-verbal (pl **procès-verbaux**) /pʀɔsɛvɛʀbal, -o/ nm minutes (+ pl); (contravention) ticket.

prochain, ~e /pʀɔʃɛ̃, -ɛn/ a (suivant) next; (proche) imminent; (avenir) near. ● nm fellow man. **prochainement** adv soon.

proche /pʀɔʃ/ a near, close; (avoisinant) neighbouring; (parent, ami) close; ~ **de** close ou near to; **de** ~ **en** gradually; **dans un** ~ **avenir** in the near future; **être** ~ (imminent) be approaching. ● nm close relative; (ami) close friend.

Proche-Orient /pʀɔʃɔʀjɑ̃/ nm Near East.

proclamation /pʀɔklamasjɔ̃/ nf declaration, proclamation. **proclamer** [1] vt declare, proclaim.

procuration /pʀɔkyʀasjɔ̃/ nf proxy.

procurer /pʀɔkyʀe/ [1] vt bring (à to). □ se ~ vpr obtain.

procureur /pʀɔkyʀœʀ/ nm public prosecutor.

prodige /pʀɔdiʒ/ nm (fait) marvel; (personne) prodigy; **enfant/musicien** ~ child/musical prodigy. **prodigieux**, -ieuse a tremendous, prodigious.

prodigue /pʀɔdig/ a wasteful; **fils** ~ prodigal son.

producteur, -trice /pʀɔdyktœʀ, -tʀis/ a producing. ● nm, f producer. **productif**, -ive a productive. **production** nf production; (produit) product. **productivité** nf productivity.

produire /pʀɔdɥiʀ/ [17] vt produce. □ se ~ vpr (survenir) happen; (acteur) perform.

produit /pʀɔdɥi/ nm product; ~s (de la terre) produce (+ sg); ~ **chimique** chemical; ~s **alimentaires** foodstuffs; ~ **de consommation** consumer goods; ~ **intérieur brut** gross domestic product, ~ **national brut** gross national product.

proéminent, ~e /pʀɔeminã, -t/ a prominent.

profane /pʀɔfan/ a secular. ● nmf lay person.

proférer /pʀɔfeʀe/ [14] vt utter.

professeur /pʀɔfesœʀ/ nm teacher; (Univ) lecturer; (avec chaire) professor.

profession /pʀɔfesjɔ̃/ nf occupation; ~ **libérale** profession. **professionnel**, ~le /pʀɔfesjɔnɛl/ a professional; (école) vocational. ● nm, f professional.

profil /pʀɔfil/ nm profile.

profit /pʀɔfi/ nm profit; **au** ~ **de** in aid of. **profitable** a profitable.

profiter /pʀɔfite/ [1] vi ~ **à** benefit; ~ **de** take advantage of.

profond, ~e /pʀɔfɔ̃, -d/ a deep; (sentiment, intérêt) profound;

P

(*causes*) underlying; **au plus ~ de** in the depths of. **profondément** *adv* deeply; (*différent, triste*) profoundly; (*dormir*) soundly. **profondeur** *nf* depth.

progéniture /prɔʒenityr/ *nf* offspring.

progiciel /prɔʒisjɛl/ *nm* (Ordinat) package.

programmation /prɔgramasjɔ̃/ *nf* programming.

programme /prɔgram/ *nm* programme; (Scol) (*d'une matière*) syllabus; (*général*) curriculum; (Ordinat) program. **programmer** [1] *vt* (*ordinateur, appareil*) program; (*émission*) schedule. **programmeur, -euse** *nm, f* computer programmer.

progrès /prɔgrɛ/ *nm & nmpl* progress; **faire des ~** make progress. **progresser** [1] *vi* progress. **progressif, -ive** *a* progressive. **progression** *nf* progression.

prohibitif, -ive /prɔibitif, -v/ *a* prohibitive.

proie /prwa/ *nf* prey; **en ~ à** tormented by.

projecteur /prɔʒɛktœr/ *nm* floodlight; (Mil) searchlight; (cinéma) projector.

projectile /prɔʒɛktil/ *nm* missile.

projection /prɔʒɛksjɔ̃/ *nf* projection; (*séance*) show.

projet /prɔʒɛ/ *nm* plan; (*ébauche*) draft; **~ de loi** bill.

projeter /prɔʒte/ [38] *vt* (*prévoir*) plan (**de** to); (*film*) project, show; (*jeter*) hurl, project.

prolétaire /prɔletɛr/ *nmf* proletarian.

prologue /prɔlɔg/ *nm* prologue.

prolongation /prɔlɔ̃gasjɔ̃/ *nf* extension; **~s** (football) extra time.

prolonger /prɔlɔ̃ʒe/ [40] *vt* extend. □ **se ~** *vpr* go on.

promenade /prɔmnad/ *nf* walk;

(à bicyclette, à cheval) ride; (en auto) drive, ride; **faire une ~** go for a walk.

promener /prɔmne/ [6] *vt* take for a walk; **~ son regard sur** cast an eye over. □ **se ~** *vpr* walk; (**aller**) **se ~** go for a walk.

promeneur, -euse *nm, f* walker.

promesse /prɔmɛs/ *nf* promise.

prometteur, -euse /prɔmɛtœr, -øz/ *a* promising.

promettre /prɔmɛtr/ [42] *vt/i* promise. ● *vi* be promising. □ **se ~ de** *vpr* resolve to.

promoteur /prɔmotœr/ *nm* (immobilier) property developer.

promotion /prɔmosjɔ̃/ *nf* promotion; (Univ) year; (Comm) special offer.

prompt, ~e /prɔ̃, -t/ *a* swift.

promu, ~e /prɔmy/ *a* **être ~** be promoted.

prôner /prone/ [1] *vt* extol.

pronom /prɔnɔ̃/ *nm* pronoun. **pronominal, ~e** (*mpl* **-aux**) *a* pronominal.

prononcé, ~e /prɔnɔ̃se/ *a* strong.

prononcer /prɔnɔ̃se/ [10] *vt* pronounce; (*discours*) make. □ **se ~** *vpr* (*mot*) be pronounced; (*personne*) make a decision (**pour** in favour of). **prononciation** *nf* pronunciation.

pronostic /prɔnɔstik/ *nm* forecast; (Méd) prognosis.

propagande /prɔpagɑ̃d/ *nf* propaganda.

propager /prɔpaʒe/ [40] *vt* spread. □ **se ~** *vpr* spread.

prophète /prɔfɛt/ *nm* prophet. **prophétie** *nf* prophecy.

propice /prɔpis/ *a* favourable.

proportion /prɔpɔrsjɔ̃/ *nf* proportion; (en mathématiques) ratio; **toutes ~s gardées** relatively speaking. **proportionné, ~e** *a* proportionate (**à** to).

proportionnel, **∼le** *a* proportional.

proportionnellement *adv* proportionately.

propos /pʀopo/ *nm* intention; (sujet) subject; **à ∼** at the right time; (dans un dialogue) by the way; **à ∼ de** about; **à tout ∼** at every possible occasion. ● *nmpl* (paroles) remarks.

proposer /pʀopoze/ [1] *vt* suggest, propose; (offrir) offer. □ **se ∼** *vpr* volunteer (**pour** to).

proposition *nf* proposal; (affirmation) proposition; (Gram) clause.

propre /pʀopʀ/ *a* (non sali) clean; (soigné) neat; (honnête) decent; (à soi) own; (sens) literal; **∼ à** (qui convient) suited to; (spécifique) particular to. ● *nm* **mettre au ∼** write out again neatly; **c'est du ∼!** (ironique) well done!

proprement /pʀopʀəmɑ̃/ *adv* (avec soin) neatly; (au sens strict) strictly; **le bureau ∼ dit** the office itself.

propreté /pʀopʀəte/ *nf* cleanliness.

propriétaire /pʀopʀijetɛʀ/ *nmf* owner; (Comm) proprietor; (qui loue) landlord, landlady.

propriété /pʀopʀijete/ *nf* property; (droit) ownership.

propulser /pʀopylse/ [1] *vt* propel.

proroger /pʀoʀoʒe/ [40] *vt* (contrat) defer; (passeport) extend.

proscrire /pʀoskʀiʀ/ [30] *vt* proscribe.

proscrit, **∼e** /pʀoskʀi, -t/ *a* proscribed. ● *nm, f* (exilé) exile.

prose /pʀoz/ *nf* prose.

prospectus /pʀospɛktys/ *nm* leaflet.

prospère /pʀospɛʀ/ *a* flourishing, thriving. **prospérer** [14] *vi* thrive,

prosper. **prospérité** *nf* prosperity.

prosterner (**se**) /(sə)pʀostɛʀne/ [1] *vpr* prostrate oneself; **prosterné devant** prostrate before.

prostituée /pʀostitɥe/ *nf* prostitute. **prostitution** *nf* prostitution.

protecteur, **-trice** /pʀotɛktœʀ, -tʀis/ *nm, f* protector. ● *a* protective.

protection /pʀotɛksjɔ̃/ *nf* protection.

protégé, **∼e** /pʀoteʒe/ *nm, f* protégé.

protéger /pʀoteʒe/ [40] *vt* protect. □ **se ∼** *vpr* protect oneself.

protéine /pʀotein/ *nf* protein.

protestant, **∼e** /pʀotɛstɑ̃, -t/ *a & nm, f* Protestant.

protestation /pʀotɛstasjɔ̃/ *nf* protest. **protester** [1] *vt/i* protest.

protocole /pʀotokol/ *nm* protocol.

protubérant, **∼e** /pʀotybeʀɑ̃/ *a* protruding.

proue /pʀu/ *nf* bow, prow.

prouesse /pʀuɛs/ *nf* feat, exploit.

prouver /pʀuve/ [1] *vt* prove.

provenance /pʀovnɑ̃s/ *nf* origin; **en ∼ de** from.

provençal, **∼e** (*mpl* **-aux**) /pʀo-vɑ̃sal, -o/ *a & nm, f* Provençal.

provenir /pʀovniʀ/ [58] *vi* **∼ de** come from.

proverbe /pʀovɛʀb/ *nm* proverb.

province /pʀovɛ̃s/ *nf* province; **de ∼** provincial; **la ∼** the provinces (+ *pl*). **provincial**, **∼e** (*mpl* **-iaux**) *a & nm, f* provincial.

proviseur /pʀovizœʀ/ *nm* headmaster, principal.

provision /pʀovizjɔ̃/ *nf* supply, store; (sur un compte) credit (balance); (acompte) deposit; **∼s** (vivres) food shopping.

P

provisoire /pʀɔvizwaʀ/ a provisional.

provocant, ∼e /pʀɔvɔkɑ̃, -t/ a provocative. **provocation** nf provocation. **provoquer** [1] vt cause; (sexuellement) arouse; (défier) provoke.

proxénète /pʀɔksenɛt/ nm pimp, procurer.

proximité /pʀɔksimite/ nf proximity; **à ∼ de** close to.

prude /pʀyd/ a prudish.

prudemment /pʀydamɑ̃/ adv (conduire) carefully; (attendre) cautiously. **prudence** nf caution. **prudent**, ∼e a (au volant) careful; (à agir) cautious; (sage) wise.

prune /pʀyn/ nf plum.

pruneau (pl ∼x) /pʀyno/ nm prune.

prunelle /pʀynɛl/ nf (pupille) pupil; (fruit) sloe.

prunier /pʀynje/ nm plum tree.

psaume /psom/ nm psalm.

pseudonyme /psødɔnim/ nm pseudonym.

psychanalyse /psikanaliz/ nf psychoanalysis. **psychanalyste** nmf psychoanalyst.

psychiatre /psikjatʀ/ nmf psychiatrist. **psychiatrie** nf psychiatry. **psychiatrique** a psychiatric.

psychique /psiʃik/ a mental, psychological.

psychologie /psikɔlɔʒi/ nf psychology. **psychologique** a psychological. **psychologue** nmf psychologist.

pu /py/ ⇒POUVOIR [49].

puant, ∼e /pɥɑ̃, -t/ a stinking.

pub /pyb/ nf ▯ **la ∼** advertising; **une ∼** an advert.

puberté /pybɛʀte/ nf puberty.

public, -que /pyblik/ a public. ●nm public; (assistance) audience; (Scol) state schools (+ pl); **en ∼** in public.

publication /pyblikasjɔ̃/ nf publication.

publicitaire /pyblisitɛʀ/ a publicity. **publicité** nf publicity, advertising; (annonce) advertisement.

publier /pyblije/ [45] vt publish.

publiquement /pyblikmɑ̃/ adv publicly.

puce /pys/ nf flea; (électronique) chip; **marché aux ∼s** flea market.

pudeur /pydœʀ/ nf modesty.

pudibond, ∼e /pydibɔ̃, -d/ a prudish.

pudique /pydik/ a modest.

puer /pɥe/ [1] vi stink. ●vt stink of.

puéricultrice /pɥeʀikyltʀis/ nf pediatric nurse.

puéril, ∼e /pɥeʀil/ a puerile.

puis /pɥi/ adv then.

puiser /pɥize/ [1] vt draw (dans from). ●vi ∼ **dans qch** dip into sth.

puisque /pɥisk(ə)/ conj since, as.

puissance /pɥisɑ̃s/ nf power; **en ∼** potential.

puissant, ∼e /pɥisɑ̃, -t/ a powerful.

puits /pɥi/ nm well; (de mine) shaft.

pull(-over) /pyl(ɔvɛʀ)/ nm pullover, jumper.

pulpe /pylp/ nf pulp.

pulsation /pylsasjɔ̃/ nf (heart-) beat.

pulvériser /pylveʀize/ [1] vt pulverize; (liquide) spray.

punaise /pynɛz/ nf (insecte) bug; (clou) drawing-pin.

punch[1] /pɔ̃ʃ/ nm (boisson) punch.

punch[2] /pœnʃ/ nm **avoir du ∼** have drive.

punir /pyniʀ/ [2] vt punish. **punition** nf punishment.

pupille /pypij/ nf (de l'œil) pupil. ●nmf (enfant) ward.

pupitre /pypitʀ/ nm (Scol) desk; ~ **à musique** music stand.

pur /pyʀ/ a pure; (*whisky*) neat.

purée /pyʀe/ nf purée; (de pommes de terre) mashed potatoes (+ *pl*).

pureté /pyʀte/ nf purity.

purgatoire /pyʀgatwaʀ/ nm purgatory.

purge /pyʀʒ/ nf purge. **purger** [40] vt (Pol, Méd) purge; (*peine*: Jur) serve.

purifier /pyʀifje/ [45] vt purify.

puritain, ~e /pyʀitɛ̃, -ɛn/ nm, f puritan. ● a puritanical.

pur-sang /pyʀsɑ̃/ nm inv (cheval) thoroughbred.

pus /py/ nm pus.

putain /pytɛ̃/ nf whore.

puzzle /pœzl/ nm jigsaw (puzzle).

P-V abrév m (**procès-verbal**) ticket, traffic fine.

pyjama /piʒama/ nm pyjamas (+ *pl*); **un** ~ a pair of pyjamas.

pylône /pilon/ nm pylon.

Pyrénées /piʀene/ nfpl **les** ~ the Pyrenees.

pyromane /piʀɔman/ nmf arsonist.

QG abrév m (**quartier général**) HQ.

QI abrév m (**quotient intellectuel**) IQ.

qu' /k/ ⇒QUE.

quadriller /kadʀije/ [1] vt (*armée*) take control of; (*police*) spread one's net over; **papier quadrillé** squared paper.

quadrupède /kadʀypɛd/ nm quadruped.

quadruple /kadʀypl/ a quadruple. ● nm **le** ~ **de** four times. **quadrupler** [1] vt/i quadruple.

quai /ke/ nm (de gare) platform; (de port) quay; (de rivière) bank.

qualification /kalifikasjɔ̃/ nf qualification; (compétence pratique) skills (+ *pl*).

qualifié, ~e /kalifje/ a (diplômé) qualified; (*main-d'œuvre*) skilled.

qualifier /kalifje/ [45] vt qualify; (décrire) describe (**de** as). □ **se** ~ vpr qualify (**pour** for).

qualité /kalite/ nf quality; (titre) occupation; (fonction) position; **en sa** ~ **de** in his ou her capacity as.

quand /kɑ̃/ adv when; ~ **même** all the same. ● conj when; (toutes les fois que) whenever; ~ **bien même** even if.

quant à /kɑ̃ta/ prép as for.

quantité /kɑ̃tite/ nf quantity; **une** ~ **de** a lot of; **des** ~**s** (**de**) masses ou lots (of).

quarantaine /kaʀɑ̃tɛn/ nf (Méd) quarantine; **une** ~ (**de**) about forty; **avoir la** ~ be in one's forties.

quarante /kaʀɑ̃t/ a & nm forty.

quart /kaʀ/ nm quarter; (Naut) watch; **onze heures moins le** ~ quarter to eleven; ~ (**de litre**) quarter litre; ~ **de finale** quarter-final; ~ **d'heure** quarter of an hour; ~ **de tour** ninety-degree turn.

quartier /kaʀtje/ nm area, district; (zone ethnique) quarter; (de lune, pomme, bœuf) quarter; (d'une orange) segment; ~**s** (Mil) quarters; **de** ~, **du** ~ local; ~ **général** headquarters; **avoir** ~ **libre** be free.

quasiment /kazimɑ̃/ adv almost, practically.

Q

quatorze /katɔʀz/ *a & nm*
fourteen.

quatre /katʀ(ə)/ *a & nm* four.
quatre-vingt(s) *a & nm* eighty.
quatre-vingt-dix *a & nm* ninety.

quatrième /katʀijɛm/ *a & nmf*
fourth. ● *nf* (Auto) fourth gear.

quatuor /kwatɥɔʀ/ *nm* quartet.

que, qu' /kə, k/
qu' before vowel or mute h.

● *conjonction*
••••➤ that; **je crains ~...** I'm worried
that...
••••➤ (souhait, volonté) **je veux ~ tu
viennes** I want you to come; **~ tu
viennes ou non** whether you
come or not; **qu'il entre** let him
come in.
••••➤ (comparaison) than; **plus grand
~ toi** taller than you.

● *pronom interrogatif*
••••➤ what; **~ voulez-vous manger?**
what would you like to eat?

● *pronom relatif*
••••➤ (personne) whom, that; **l'homme
~ j'ai rencontré** the man (whom)
I met.
••••➤ (chose) that, which; **le cheval ~
Nick m'a offert** the horse (which)
Nick gave me.

● *adverbe*
••••➤ **~ c'est joli!** it's so pretty!; **~
de monde!** what a lot of people!

Québec /kebɛk/ *nm* Quebec.

quel, quelle (*pl* **quel(le)s**) /kɛl/
● *adjectif interrogatif*
••••➤ which, what; **~ auteur a
écrit...?** which writer wrote...?;
~ jour sommes-nous? what day
is it today?

● *adjectif exclamatif*
••••➤ what; **~ idiot!** what an idiot!;
quelle horreur! that's horrible!

● *adjectif relatif*
••••➤ **~ que soit son âge** whatever
his age; **quelles que soient tes
raisons** whatever your reasons;
~ que soit le gagnant whoever
the winner is.

quelconque /kɛlkɔ̃k/ *a* any,
some; (banal) ordinary; (médiocre)
poor, second rate.

quelque /kɛlkə/ *a* some; **~s** a
few, some. ● *adv* (environ) about,
some; **et ~** Ⓘ and a bit; **~ chose**
something; (dans les phrases
interrogatives) anything; **~ part**
somewhere; **~ peu** somewhat.

quelquefois /kɛlkəfwa/ *adv*
sometimes.

quelques-uns, -unes /kɛlkəzœ̃,
-yn/ *pron* some, a few.

quelqu'un /kɛlkœ̃/ *pron*
someone, somebody; (dans les
phrases interrogatives) anyone,
anybody.

querelle /kəʀɛl/ *nf* quarrel.
quereller (se) [1] *vpr* quarrel.
querelleur, -euse *a* quarrelsome.

question /kɛstjɔ̃/ *nf* question;
(affaire) matter, question; **poser une
~** ask a question; **en ~** in
question; **il est ~ de** (cela concerne)
it is about; (on parle de) there is
talk of; **il n'en est pas ~** it is out
of the question; **pas ~!** no way!

questionnaire /kɛstjɔnɛʀ/ *nm*
questionnaire.

questionner /kɛstjɔne/ [1] *vt*
question.

quête /kɛt/ *nf* (Relig) collection;
(recherche) search; **en ~ de** in
search of.

queue /kø/ *nf* tail; (de poêle)
handle; (de fruit) stalk; (de fleur)
stem; (file) queue; (US) line; (de
train) rear; **faire la ~** queue (up);

(US) line up; ~ **de cheval** ponytail; **faire une** ~ **de poisson à qn** (Auto) cut in front of sb.

qui /ki/

● *pronom interrogatif*

····➤ (sujet) who; ~ **a fait ça?** who did that?

····➤ (complément) whom; **à** ~ **est ce livre?** whose book is this?

● *pronom relatif*

····➤ (personne sujet) who; **c'est Isabelle qui vient d'appeler** it's Isabelle who's just called.

····➤ (autres cas) that, which; **qu'est-ce** ~ **te prend?** what is the matter with you?; **invite** ~ **tu veux** invite whoever you want; ~ **que ce soit** whoever it is, anybody.

quiche /kiʃ/ *nf* quiche.

quiconque /kikɔ̃k/ *pron* whoever; (n'importe qui) anyone.

quille /kij/ *nf* (de bateau) keel; (jouet) skittle.

quincaillerie /kɛ̃kajʀi/ *nf* hardware; (magasin) hardware shop. **quincaillier, -ière** *nm, f* hardware dealer.

quintal (*pl* -**aux**) /kɛ̃tal, -o/ *nm* quintal, one hundred kilos.

quinte /kɛ̃t/ *nf* ~ **de toux** coughing fit.

quintuple /kɛ̃typl/ *a* quintuple. ● *nm* **le** ~ **de** five times. **quintupler** [1] *vt/i* quintuple, increase fivefold.

quinzaine /kɛ̃zɛn/ *nf* **une** ~ **(de)** about fifteen.

quinze /kɛ̃z/ *a & nm inv* fifteen; ~ **jours** two weeks.

quiproquo /kipʀɔko/ *nm* misunderstanding.

quittance /kitɑ̃s/ *nf* receipt.

quitte /kit/ *a* quits (**envers** with); ~ **à faire** even if it means doing.

quitter /kite/ [1] *vt* leave; (vêtement) take off; **ne quittez pas!** hold the line, please! □ **se** ~ *vpr* part.

qui-vive /kiviv/ *nm inv* **être sur le** ~ be alert.

quoi /kwa/ *pron* what; (après une préposition) which; **de** ~ **vivre** (assez) enough to live on; **de** ~ **écrire** something to write with; ~ **qu'il dise** whatever he says; ~ **que ce soit** anything; **il n'y a pas de** ~ my pleasure; **il n'y a pas de** ~ **s'inquiéter** there's nothing to worry about.

quoique /kwak(ə)/ *conj* although, though.

quota /kɔta/ *nm* quota.

quote-part (*pl* **quotes-parts**) /kɔtpaʀ/ *nf* share.

quotidien, ~ne /kɔtidjɛ̃, -ɛn/ *a* daily; (banal) everyday. ● *nm* daily (paper); (vie quotidienne) everyday life. **quotidiennement** *adv* daily.

rabâcher /ʀabɑʃe/ [1] *vt* keep repeating.

rabais /ʀabɛ/ *nm* reduction, discount. **rabaisser** [1] *vt* (déprécier) belittle; (réduire) reduce.

rabat-joie /ʀabaʒwa/ *nm inv* killjoy.

rabattre /ʀabatʀ/ [11] *vt* (chapeau, visière) pull down; (refermer) shut; (diminuer) reduce; (déduire) take off; (col, drap) turn down. □ **se** ~ *vpr* (se refermer) close; (*véhicule*) cut back in; se ~ sur make do with.

rabot /Rabo/ *nm* plane.

rabougri, ~**e** /Rabugri/ *a* stunted.

racaille /Rakaj/ *nf* rabble.

raccommoder /Rakɔmɔde/ [1] *vt* mend; (*personnes* 🔲) reconcile.

raccompagner /Rakɔ̃paɲe/ [1] *vt* see *ou* take back (*home*).

raccord /RakɔR/ *nm* link; (*de papier peint*) join; (*retouche*) touch-up. **raccorder** [1] *vt* connect, join.

raccourci /Rakursi/ *nm* short cut; en ~ in short.

raccourcir /RakursiR/ [2] *vt* shorten. ● *vi* get shorter.

raccrocher /RakRɔʃe/ [1] *vt* hang back up; (*passant*) grab hold of; (*relier*) connect; ~ le combiné *ou* le téléphone hang up. ● *vi* hang up. □ se ~ à *vpr* cling to; (*se relier à*) be connected to *ou* with.

race /Ras/ *nf* race; (*animale*) breed; de ~ (*chien*) pedigree; (*cheval*) thoroughbred.

racheter /Raʃte/ [6] *vt* buy (back); (*acheter encore*) buy more; (*nouvel objet*) buy another; (*société*) buy out; ~ des chaussettes buy new socks. □ se ~ *vpr* make amends.

racial, ~**e** (*mpl* -**iaux**) /Rasjal, -o/ *a* racial.

racine /Rasin/ *nf* root; ~ carrée/ cubique square/cube root.

racisme /Rasism/ *nm* racism. **raciste** *a & nmf* racist.

racket /Raket/ *nm* racketeering.

raclée /Rakle/ *nf* 🔲 thrashing.

racler /Rakle/ [1] *vt* scrape. □ se ~ *vpr* se ~ la gorge clear one's throat.

racolage /Rakɔlaʒ/ *nm* soliciting.

raconter /Rakɔ̃te/ [1] *vt* (*histoire*) tell; (*vacances*) tell about; (*vie, épisode*) describe; ~ à qn que tell

sb that, say to sb that; qu'est-ce que tu racontes? what are you talking about?

radar /RadaR/ *nm* radar.

radeau (*pl* ~**x**) /Rado/ *nm* raft.

radiateur /RadjatœR/ *nm* radiator; (*électrique*) heater.

radiation /Radjasjɔ̃/ *nf* radiation.

radical, ~**e** (*mpl* -**aux**) /Radikal, -o/ *a* radical. ● *nm* (*pl* -**aux**) radical.

radieux, -**ieuse** /Radjø, -z/ *a* radiant.

radin, ~**e** /Radɛ̃, -in/ *a* 🔲 stingy 🔲.

radio /Radjo/ *nf* radio; à la ~ on the radio; (*radiographie*) X-ray.

radioactif, -**ive** /Radjɔaktif, -v/ *a* radioactive. **radioactivité** *nf* radioactivity.

radiocassette /Radjɔkasɛt/ *nf* radio cassette player.

radiodiffuser /Radjɔdifyze/ [1] *vt* broadcast.

radiographie /RadjɔgRafi/ *nf* (*photographie*) X-ray.

radiomessageur /Radjɔmesa-ʒœR/ *nm* pager.

radis /Radi/ *nm* radish; ne pas avoir un ~ 🔲 be broke.

radoter /Radɔte/ [1] *vi* 🔲 talk drivel.

radoucir (se) /(sə)RadusiR/ [2] *vpr* (*humeur*) improve; (*temps*) become milder.

rafale /Rafal/ *nf* (*de vent*) gust; (*de mitraillette*) burst.

raffermir /RafɛRmiR/ [2] *vt* strengthen. □ se ~ *vpr* become stronger.

raffiné, ~**e** /Rafine/ *a* refined. **raffinement** *nm* refinement.

raffiner /Rafine/ [1] *vt* refine. **raffinerie** *nf* refinery.

raffoler /Rafɔle/ [1] *vt* 🔲 ~ de be crazy about 🔲.

raffut /Rafy/ *nm* 🔲 din.

rafle /Rɑfl/ *nf* (*police*) raid.

rafraîchir /RafreʃiR/ [2] *vt* cool (down); (*mur*) give a fresh coat of paint to; (*personne, mémoire*) refresh. □ se ~ *vpr* (boire) refresh oneself; (*temps*) get cooler.
rafraîchissant, ~e *a* refreshing.

rafraîchissement /Rafreʃismɑ̃/ *nm* (boisson) cold drink; ~s refreshments.

ragaillardir /RagajaRdiR/ [2] *vt* Ⓘ cheer up.

rage /Raʒ/ *nf* rage; (maladie) rabies; **faire ~** (*bataille, incendie*) rage; (*maladie*) be rife; **~ de dents** raging toothache. **rageant**, ~e *a* infuriating.

ragots /Rago/ *nmpl* Ⓘ gossip.

ragoût /Ragu/ *nm* stew.

raid /Rɛd/ *nm* (Mil) raid; (Sport) trek.

raide /Rɛd/ *a* stiff; (*côte*) steep; (*corde*) tight; (*cheveux*) straight. ● *adv* (monter, descendre) steeply. **raideur** *nf* stiffness; steepness.

raidir /RediR/ [2] *vt* (*corps*) tense. □ se ~ *vpr* tense up; (*position*) harden; (*corde*) tighten.

raie /Rɛ/ *nf* (ligne) line; (bande) strip; (de cheveux) parting; (poisson) skate.

raifort /RefɔR/ *nm* horseradish.

rail /Raj/ *nm* rail, track; **le ~** (transport) rail.

raisin /Rɛzɛ̃/ *nm* **le ~** grapes; **~ sec** raisin; **un grain de ~** a grape.

raison /Rɛzɔ̃/ *nf* reason; **à ~ de** at the rate of; **avec ~** rightly; **avoir ~** be right (**de faire** to do); **avoir ~ de qn** get the better of sb; **donner ~ à** prove right; **en ~ de** because of; **~ de plus** all the more reason; **perdre la ~** lose one's mind.

raisonnable /Rɛzɔnabl/ *a* reasonable, sensible.

raisonnement /Rɛzɔnmɑ̃/ *nm* reasoning; (propositions) argument.

raisonner /Rɛzɔne/ [1] *vi* think. ● *vt* (personne) reason with.

rajeunir /RaʒœniR/ [2] *vt* ~ **qn** make sb (look) younger; (moderniser) modernize; (Méd) rejuvenate. ● *vi* (personne) look younger.

rajuster /Raʒyste/ [1] *vt* straighten; (salaires) (re)adjust.

ralenti, ~e /Ralɑ̃ti/ *a* slow. ● *nm* (au cinéma) slow motion; **tourner au ~** tick over, idle.

ralentir /Ralɑ̃tiR/ [2] *vt/i* slow down. □ se ~ *vpr* slow down.

ralentisseur /Ralɑ̃tisœR/ *nm* speed ramp.

râler /Rale/ [1] *vi* groan; (protester Ⓘ) moan.

rallier /Ralje/ [45] *vt* rally; (rejoindre) rejoin. □ se ~ *vpr* rally; **se ~ à** (avis) come round to; (parti) join.

rallonge /Ralɔ̃ʒ/ *nf* (de table) leaf; (de fil électrique) extension lead.

rallonger [40] *vt* lengthen; (séjour, fil, table) extend.

rallumer /Ralyme/ [1] *vt* (feu) relight; (lampe) switch on again; (ranimer: fig) revive.

rallye /Rali/ *nm* rally.

ramassage /Ramasaʒ/ *nm* (cueillette) gathering; (d'ordures) collection; **~ scolaire** school bus service.

ramasser /Ramase/ [1] *vt* pick up; (récolter) gather; (recueillir, rassembler) collect. □ se ~ *vpr* huddle up, curl up.

rame /Ram/ *nf* (aviron) oar; (train) train.

ramener /Ramne/ [1] *vt* (rapporter, faire revenir) bring back; (reconduire) take back; **~ à** (réduire à) reduce to. □ se ~ *vpr* Ⓘ turn up; **se ~ à** (problème) come down to.

ramer /Rame/ [1] *vi* row.

ramollir /RamɔliR/ [2] *vt* soften. □ se ~ *vpr* become soft.

R

ramoneur /ʀamɔnœʀ/ *nm* (chimney) sweep.

rampe /ʀɑ̃p/ *nf* banisters; (pente) ramp; ∼ **d'accès** (Auto) slip road; ∼ **de lancement** launching pad.

ramper /ʀɑ̃pe/ [1] *vi* crawl.

rancard /ʀɑ̃kaʀ/ *nm* 🔲 date.

rancart /ʀɑ̃kaʀ/ *nm* **mettre** *ou* **jeter au** ∼ 🔲 scrap.

rance /ʀɑ̃s/ *a* rancid.

rancœur /ʀɑ̃kœʀ/ *nf* resentment.

rançon /ʀɑ̃sɔ̃/ *nf* ransom. **rançonner** [1] *vt* rob, extort money from.

rancune /ʀɑ̃kyn/ *nf* grudge; **sans** ∼! no hard feelings! **rancunier, -ière** *a* vindictive.

randonnée /ʀɑ̃dɔne/ *nf* walk, ramble; **la** ∼ **à cheval** pony trekking; **faire une** ∼ go walking *ou* rambling.

rang /ʀɑ̃/ *nm* row; (hiérarchie, condition) rank; **se mettre en** ∼ line up; **au premier** ∼ in the first row; (fig) at the forefront; **de second** ∼ (péj) second-rate.

rangée /ʀɑ̃ʒe/ *nf* row.

rangement /ʀɑ̃ʒmɑ̃/ *nm* (de pièce) tidying (up); (espace) storage space.

ranger /ʀɑ̃ʒe/ [40] *vt* put away; (chambre) tidy (up); (disposer) place. □ **se** ∼ *vpr* (véhicule) park; (s'écarter) stand aside; (conducteur) pull over; (s'assagir) settle down; **se** ∼ **à** (avis) accept.

ranimer /ʀanime/ [1] *vt* revive; (Méd) resuscitate. □ **se** ∼ *vpr* come round.

rap /ʀap/ *nm* rap (music).

rapace /ʀapas/ *nm* bird of prey. ● *a* grasping.

rapatriement /ʀapatʀimɑ̃/ *nm* repatriation. **rapatrier** [45] *vt* repatriate.

râpe /ʀɑp/ *nf* (Culin) grater; (lime) rasp.

râpé, ∼e /ʀɑpe/ *a* (vêtement) threadbare; (fromage) grated.

râper /ʀɑpe/ [1] *vt* grate; (bois) rasp.

rapide /ʀapid/ *a* fast, rapid. ● *nm* (train) express (train); (cours d'eau) rapids (+ *pl*). **rapidement** *adv* fast, rapidly. **rapidité** *nf* speed.

rappel /ʀapɛl/ *nm* recall; (deuxième avis) reminder; (de salaire) back pay; (Méd) booster; (de diplomate) recall; (de réservistes) call-up; (Théât) curtain call.

rappeler /ʀaple/ [38] *vt* (par téléphone) call back; (réserviste) call up; (diplomate) recall; (évoquer) recall; ∼ **qch à qn** remind sb of sth. □ **se** ∼ *vpr* remember, recall.

rappeur, -euse /ʀapœʀ, øz/ *nmf* rapper.

rapport /ʀapɔʀ/ *nm* connection; (compte-rendu) report; (profit) yield; ∼**s** (relations) relations; **en** ∼ **avec** (accord) in keeping with; **mettre/se mettre en** ∼ **avec** put/get in touch with; **par** ∼ **à** (comparé à) compared with; (vis-à-vis de) with regard to; ∼**s** (sexuels) intercourse.

rapporter /ʀapɔʀte/ [1] *vt* (ici) bring back; (là-bas) take back, return; (profit) bring in; (dire, répéter) report. ● *vi* (Comm) bring in a good return; (moucharder 🔲) tell tales. □ **se** ∼ **à** *vpr* relate to.

rapporteur, -euse /ʀapɔʀtœʀ, -øz/ *nm, f* (mouchard) tell-tale. ● *nm* protractor.

rapprochement /ʀapʀɔʃmɑ̃/ *nm* reconciliation; (Pol) rapprochement; (rapport) connection; (comparaison) parallel.

rapprocher /ʀapʀɔʃe/ *vt* move closer (**de** to); (réconcilier) bring together; (comparer) compare; (date, rendez-vous) bring forward. □ **se** ∼ *vpr* get *ou* come closer (**de** to); (personnes, pays) come together; (s'apparenter) be close (**de** to).

rapt /ʀapt/ *nm* abduction.

raquette /ʀakɛt/ nf (de tennis) racket; (de ping-pong) bat.

rare /ʀɑʀ/ a rare; (insuffisant) scarce. **rarement** adv rarely, seldom. **rareté** nf rarity; scarcity.

ras, ∼e /ʀɑ, ʀɑz/ adv coupé ∼ cut short. ● a (herbe, poil) short; à ∼ de terre very close to the ground; en avoir ∼ le bol Ⓤ be really fed up; ∼e campagne open country; à ∼ bord to the brim.

raser /ʀɑze/ [1] vt shave; (cheveux, barbe) shave off; (frôler) skim; (abattre) raze. □ se ∼ vpr shave.

rasoir /ʀɑzwaʀ/ nm razor. ● a inv Ⓤ boring.

rassasier /ʀasazje/ [45] vt satisfy, fill up, être rassasié de have had enough of.

rassemblement /ʀasɑ̃bləmɑ̃/ nm gathering; (manifestation) rally.

rassembler /ʀasɑ̃ble/ [1] vt gather; (forces, courage) summon up; (idées) collect. □ se ∼ vpr gather.

rassis, ∼e /ʀasi, -z/ a (pain) stale.

rassurer /ʀasyʀe/ [1] vt reassure. □ se ∼ vpr reassure oneself; **rassure-toi** don't worry.

rat /ʀa/ nm rat.

rate /ʀat/ nf spleen.

raté, ∼e /ʀate/ nm, f (personne) failure. ● nm avoir des ∼s (voiture) backfire.

râteau (pl ∼x) /ʀɑto/ nm rake.

râtelier /ʀɑtəlje/ nm hayrack; (dentier Ⓤ) dentures.

rater /ʀate/ [1] vt (train, rendez-vous, cible) miss; (gâcher) make a mess of, spoil; (examen) fail. ● vi fail.

ratio /ʀasjo/ nm ratio.

rationaliser /ʀasjɔnalize/ [1] vt rationalize.

rationnel, ∼le /ʀasjɔnɛl/ a rational.

rationnement /ʀasjɔnmɑ̃/ nm rationing.

ratisser /ʀatise/ [1] vt rake; (fouiller) comb.

rattacher /ʀataʃe/ [1] vt (lacets) tie up again; (ceinture de sécurité, collier) refasten; (relier) link; (incorporer) join.

rattrapage /ʀatʀapaʒ/ nm (Comm) adjustment; **cours de** ∼ remedial lesson.

rattraper /ʀatʀape/ [1] vt catch; (rejoindre) catch up with; (retard, erreur) make up for. □ se ∼ vpr catch up; (se dédommager) make up for it; **se** ∼ **à** catch hold of.

rature /ʀatyʀ/ nf deletion.

rauque /ʀok/ a raucous, harsh.

ravager /ʀavaʒe/ [40] vt devastate, ravage.

ravages /ʀavaʒ/ nmpl **faire des** ∼ wreak havoc.

ravaler /ʀavale/ [1] vt (façade) clean; (colère) swallow.

ravi, ∼e /ʀavi/ a delighted (que that).

ravin /ʀavɛ̃/ nm ravine.

ravir /ʀaviʀ/ [2] vt delight; ∼ qch à qn rob sb of sth.

ravissant, ∼e /ʀavisɑ̃, -t/ a beautiful.

ravisseur, **-euse** /ʀavisœʀ, -øz/ nm, f kidnapper.

ravitaillement /ʀavitajmɑ̃/ nm provision of supplies (de to); (denrées) supplies; ∼ **en essence** refuelling.

ravitailler /ʀavitaje/ [1] vt provide with supplies; (avion) refuel. □ se ∼ vpr stock up.

raviver /ʀavive/ [1] vt revive; (feu, colère) rekindle.

rayé, ∼e /ʀeje/ a striped.

rayer /ʀeje/ [31] vt scratch; (biffer) cross out; '∼ **la mention inutile**' 'delete as appropriate'.

rayon /ʀɛjɔ̃/ *nm* ray; (étagère) shelf; (de magasin) department; (de roue) spoke; (de cercle) radius; ∼ **d'action** range; ∼ **de miel** honeycomb; ∼ **X** X-ray; **en connaître un** ∼ 🔲 know one's stuff 🔲.

rayonnement /ʀɛjɔnmɑ̃/ *nm* (éclat) radiance; (influence) influence; (radiations) radiation.

rayonner [1] *vi* radiate; (de joie) beam; (se déplacer) tour around (*from a central point*).

rayure /ʀɛjyʀ/ *nf* scratch; (dessin) stripe; **à** ∼**s** striped.

raz-de-marée /ʀɑdmaʀe/ *nm inv* tidal wave; ∼ **électoral** electoral landslide.

réacteur /ʀeaktœʀ/ *nm* jet engine; (nucléaire) reactor.

réaction /ʀeaksjɔ̃/ *nf* reaction; ∼ **en chaîne** chain reaction; **moteur à** ∼ jet engine.

réagir /ʀeaʒiʀ/ [2] *vi* react; ∼ **sur** have an effect on.

réalisateur, -trice /ʀealizatœʀ, -tʀis/ *nm, f* (au cinéma) director; (TV) producer.

réalisation /ʀealizasjɔ̃/ *nf* (de rêve) fulfilment; (œuvre) achievement; (TV, cinéma) production; **projet en** ∼ project in progress.

réaliser /ʀealize/ [1] *vt* carry out; (*effort, bénéfice, achat*) make; (*rêve*) fulfil; (*film*) direct; (*capital*) realize; (se rendre compte de) realize. □ **se** ∼ *vpr* be fulfilled.

réalisme /ʀealism/ *nm* realism.

réaliste /ʀealist/ *a* realistic. ● *nmf* realist.

réalité /ʀealite/ *nf* reality.

réanimation /ʀeanimasjɔ̃/ *nf* resuscitation; **service de** ∼ intensive care. **réanimer** [1] *vt* resuscitate.

réarmement /ʀeaʀməmɑ̃/ *nm* rearmament.

rébarbatif, -ive /ʀebaʀbatif, -v/ *a* forbidding, off-putting.

rebelle /ʀəbɛl/ *a* rebellious; (*soldat*) rebel; ∼ **à** resistant to. ● *nmf* rebel.

rébellion /ʀebeljɔ̃/ *nf* rebellion.

rebondir /ʀəbɔ̃diʀ/ [2] *vi* bounce; rebound; (fig) get moving again.

rebondissement /ʀəbɔ̃dismɑ̃/ *nm* (new) development.

rebord /ʀəbɔʀ/ *nm* edge; ∼ **de la fenêtre** window ledge *ou* sill.

rebours: **à** ∼ /aʀəbuʀ/ *loc* (*compter, marcher*) backwards.

rebrousse-poil: **à** ∼ /aʀəbʀuspwal/ *loc* the wrong way; (fig) **prendre qn à** ∼ rub sb up the wrong way.

rebrousser /ʀəbʀuse/ [1] *vt* ∼ **chemin** turn back.

rebut /ʀəby/ *nm* **mettre** *ou* **jeter au** ∼ scrap.

rebutant, ∼**e** /ʀəbytɑ̃, -t/ *a* off-putting.

recaler /ʀəkale/ [1] *vt* 🔲 fail; **se faire** ∼, **être recalé** fail.

recel /ʀəsɛl/ *nm* receiving.

receler [6] *vt* (*objet volé*) receive; (cacher) conceal.

récemment /ʀesamɑ̃/ *adv* recently.

recensement /ʀəsɑ̃smɑ̃/ *nm* census; (inventaire) inventory.

recenser [1] *vt* (*population*) take a census of; (*objets*) list.

récent, ∼**e** /ʀesɑ̃, -t/ *a* recent.

récépissé /ʀesepise/ *nm* receipt.

récepteur /ʀeseptœʀ/ *nm* receiver.

réception /ʀesɛpsjɔ̃/ *nf* reception; (de courrier) receipt.

réceptionniste *nmf* receptionist.

récession /ʀesesjɔ̃/ *nf* recession.

recette /ʀəsɛt/ *nf* (Culin) recipe; (argent) takings; ∼**s** (Comm) receipts.

receveur, -euse /ʀəs(ə)vœʀ, -øz/ nm, f (de bus) conductor; **∼ des contributions** tax collector.

recevoir /ʀəs(ə)vwaʀ/ [52] vt receive, get; (client, malade) see; (invités) welcome, receive; **être reçu à un examen** pass an exam.

rechange: **de ∼** /dəʀəʃɑ̃ʒ/ loc (roue, vêtements) spare; (solution) alternative.

réchapper /ʀeʃape/ [1] vt/i **∼ de** come through, survive.

recharge /ʀəʃaʀʒ/ nf (de stylo) refill.

réchaud /ʀeʃo/ nm stove.

réchauffement /ʀeʃofmɑ̃/ nm (de température) rise (**de** in); **le ∼ de la planète** global warming.

réchauffer /ʀeʃofe/ [1] vt warm up. □ **se ∼** vpr warm oneself up; (temps) get warmer.

rêche /ʀɛʃ/ a rough.

recherche /ʀəʃɛʀʃ/ nf search (**de** for); (raffinement) meticulousness; **∼(s)** (Univ) research; **∼s** (enquête) investigations; **∼ d'emploi** job-hunting.

recherché, ∼e /ʀəʃɛʀʃe/ a in great demand; (style) original, recherché (péj); **∼ pour meurtre** wanted for murder.

rechercher /ʀəʃɛʀʃe/ [1] vt search for.

rechute /ʀəʃyt/ nf (Méd) relapse; **faire une ∼** have a relapse.

récidiver /ʀesidive/ [1] vi commit a second offence.

récif /ʀesif/ nm reef.

récipient /ʀesipjɑ̃/ nm container.

réciproque /ʀesipʀɔk/ a mutual, reciprocal.

réciproquement /ʀesipʀɔkmɑ̃/ adv each other; **et ∼** and vice versa.

récit /ʀesi/ nm (compte-rendu) account, story; (histoire) story.

réciter /ʀesite/ [1] vt recite.

réclamation /ʀeklamasjɔ̃/ nf complaint; (demande) claim.

réclame /ʀeklam/ nf advertisement; **faire de la ∼** advertise; **en ∼** on offer.

réclamer /ʀeklame/ [1] vt call for, demand. ● vi complain.

reclus, ∼e /ʀəkly, -z/ nm, f recluse. ● a reclusive.

réclusion /ʀeklyzjɔ̃/ nf imprisonment.

récolte /ʀekɔlt/ nf (action) harvest; (produits) crop, harvest; (fig) crop. **récolter** [1] vt harvest, gather; (fig) collect, get.

recommandation /ʀəkɔmɑ̃dasjɔ̃/ nf recommendation.

recommandé /ʀəkɔmɑ̃de/ nm registered letter; **envoyer en ∼** send by registered post.

recommander /ʀəkɔmɑ̃de/ [1] vt recommend.

recommencer /ʀəkɔmɑ̃se/ [10] vt (reprendre) begin ou start again; (refaire) repeat. ● vi start ou begin again; **ne recommence pas** don't do it again.

récompense /ʀekɔ̃pɑ̃s/ nf reward; (prix) award. **récompenser** [1] vt reward (**de** for).

réconcilier /ʀekɔ̃silje/ [45] vt reconcile. □ **se ∼** vpr become reconciled (**avec** with).

reconduire /ʀəkɔ̃dɥiʀ/ [17] vt see home; (à la porte) show out; (renouveler) renew.

réconfort /ʀekɔ̃fɔʀ/ nm comfort.

reconnaissance /ʀəkɔnɛsɑ̃s/ nf gratitude; (fait de reconnaître) recognition; (Mil) reconnaissance. **reconnaissant, ∼e** a grateful (**de** for).

reconnaître /ʀəkɔnɛtʀ/ [18] vt recognize; (admettre) admit (**que** that); (Mil) reconnoitre; (enfant, tort) acknowledge. □ **se ∼** vpr

R

(s'orienter) know where one is; (l'un l'autre) recognize each other.

reconstituer /Rəkɔ̃stitɥe/ [1] vt reconstitute; (crime) reconstruct; (époque) recreate.

reconversion /Rəkɔ̃vɛRsjɔ̃/ nf (de main-d'œuvre) redeployment.

recopier /Rəkɔpje/ [45] vt copy out.

record /RəkɔR/ nm & a inv record.

recouper /Rəkupe/ [1] vt confirm. □ se ~ vpr check, tally, match up.

recourbé, ~e /RəkuRbe/ a curved; (nez) hooked.

recourir /RəkuRiR/ [20] vi ~ à (expédient, violence) resort to; (remède, méthode) have recourse to.

recours /RəkuR/ nm resort; **avoir ~ à** have recourse to, resort to; **avoir ~ à qn** turn to sb.

recouvrer /RəkuvRe/ [1] vt recover.

recouvrir /RəkuvRiR/ [21] vt cover.

récréation /RekReasjɔ̃/ nf recreation; (Scol) break; (US) recess.

recroqueviller (se) /(sə)RəkRɔkvije/ [1] vpr curl up.

recrudescence /RəkRydesɑ̃s/ nf new outbreak.

recrue /RəkRy/ nf recruit.

recrutement /RəkRytmɑ̃/ nm recruitment. **recruter** [1] vt recruit.

rectangle /Rɛktɑ̃gl/ nm rectangle. **rectangulaire** a rectangular.

rectifier /Rɛktifje/ [45] vt correct, rectify.

recto /Rɛkto/ nm au ~ on the front of the page.

reçu, ~e /Rəsy/ a accepted; (candidat) successful. ●nm receipt. ●⇒RECEVOIR [52].

recueil /Rəkœj/ nm collection.

recueillement /Rəkœjmɑ̃/ nm meditation.

recueillir /RəkœjiR/ [25] vt collect; (prendre chez soi) take in. □ se ~ vpr meditate.

recul /Rəkyl/ nm retreat; (éloignement) distance; (déclin) decline; **avoir un mouvement de ~** recoil; **être en ~** be on the decline; **avec le ~** with hindsight.

reculé, ~e /Rəkyle/ a (région) remote.

reculer /Rəkyle/ [1] vt move back; (véhicule) reverse; (différer) postpone. ●vi move back; (voiture) reverse; (armée) retreat; (régresser) fall; (céder) back down; **~ devant** (fig) shrink from. □ se ~ vpr move back.

récupération /RekypeRasjɔ̃/ nf (de l'organisme, de dette) recovery; (d'objets) salvage.

récupérer /RekypeRe/ [14] vt recover; (vieux objets) salvage. ●vi recover.

récurer /RekyRe/ [1] vt scour; **poudre à ~** scouring powder.

récuser /Rekyze/ [1] vt challenge. □ se ~ vpr state that one is not qualified to judge.

recyclage /Rəsiklaʒ/ nm (de personnel) retraining; (de matériau) recycling.

recycler /Rəsikle/ [1] vt (personne) retrain; (chose) recycle. □ se ~ vpr retrain.

rédacteur, -trice /RedaktœR, -tRis/ nm, f author, writer; (de journal, magazine) editor.

rédaction /Redaksjɔ̃/ nf writing; (Scol) essay, composition; (personnel) editorial staff.

redevable /Rədvabl/ a **être ~ à qn de** (argent) owe sb; (fig) be indebted to sb for.

redevance /Rədvɑ̃s/ nf (de

télévision) licence fee; (de téléphone) rental charge.

rédiger /Rediʒe/ [40] *vt* write; (*contrat*) draw up.

redire /RədiR/ [27] *vt* repeat; **avoir ou trouver à ~ à** find fault with.

redondant, ~e /Rədõdã, -t/ *a* superfluous.

redonner /Rədɔne/ [1] *vt* (*rendre*) give back; (*donner davantage*) give more; (*donner de nouveau*) give again.

redoubler /Rəduble/ [1] *vt* increase; (*classe*) repeat; **~ de prudence** be even more careful. ● *vi* (Scol) repeat a year; (*s'intensifier*) intensify.

redoutable /Rədutabl/ *a* formidable.

redouter /Rədute/ [1] *vt* dread.

redressement /RədREsmã/ *nm* (*reprise*) recovery; **~ judiciaire** receivership

redresser /RədRese/ [1] *vt* straighten (out *ou* up); (*situation*) right, redress; (*économie, entreprise*) turn around. □ **se ~** *vpr* (*personne*) straighten (oneself) up; (*se remettre debout*) stand up; (*pays, économie*) recover.

réduction /Redyksjõ/ *nf* reduction.

réduire /RedqiR/ [17] *vt* reduce (à to). □ **se ~** *vpr* be reduced *ou* cut; **se ~ à** (*revenir à*) come down to.

réduit, ~e /Redqi, -t/ *a* (*objet*) small-scale; (*limité*) limited. ● *nm* cubbyhole.

rééducation /Reedykasjõ/ *nf* (de handicapé) rehabilitation; (Méd) physiotherapy. **rééduquer** [1] *vt* (*personne*) rehabilitate; (*membre*) restore normal movement to.

réel, ~le /Reel/ *a* real. ● *nm* reality. **réellement** *adv* really.

réexpédier /ReɛkspedJe/ [45] *vt* forward; (*retourner*) send back.

refaire /RəfɛR/ [33] *vt* do again; (*erreur, voyage*) make again; (*réparer*) do up, redo.

réfectoire /RefɛktwaR/ *nm* refectory.

référence /Referãs/ *nf* reference.

référendum /Referɛ̃dɔm/ *nm* referendum.

référer /Refere/ [14] *vi* **en ~ à** consult. □ **se ~ à** *vpr* refer to, consult.

refermer /RəfɛRme/ [1] *vt* close (again). □ **se ~** *vpr* close (again).

réfléchi, ~e /RefleʃJ/ *a* (*personne*) thoughtful; (*verbe*) reflexive.

réfléchir /RefleʃiR/ [2] *vi* think (à, sur about). ● *vt* reflect. □ **se ~** *vpr* be reflected.

reflet /Rəflɛ/ *nm* reflection; (*nuance*) sheen.

refléter /Rəflete/ [14] *vt* reflect. □ **se ~** *vpr* be reflected.

réflexe /Reflɛks/ *a* reflex. ● *nm* reflex; (*réaction*) reaction.

réflexion /Reflɛksjõ/ *nf* (*pensée*) thought, reflection; (*remarque*) remark, comment; **à la ~** on second thoughts.

refluer /Rəflye/ [1] *vi* flow back; (*foule*) retreat; (*inflation*) go down.

reflux /Rəfly/ *nm* (*marée*) ebb, tide.

réforme /RefɔRm/ *nf* reform. **réformer** [1] *vt* reform; (*soldat*) invalid out.

refouler /Rəfule/ [1] *vt* (*larmes*) hold back; (*désir*) repress; (*souvenir*) suppress.

refrain /Rəfrɛ̃/ *nm* chorus; **le même ~** the same old story.

refréner /Rəfrene/ [14] *vt* curb, check.

réfrigérateur /RefRiʒeRatœR/ *nm* refrigerator.

refroidir /RəfRwadiR/ [2] *vt/i* cool

R

(down). □ **se ~** *vpr* (*personne, temps*) get cold. **refroidissement** *nm* cooling; (rhume) chill.

refuge /Rəfyʒ/ *nm* refuge; (chalet) mountain hut.

réfugié, ~e /Refyʒje/ *nm, f* refugee. **réfugier (se)** [45] *vpr* take refuge.

refus /Rəfy/ *nm* refusal; **ce n'est pas de ~** Ⅱ I wouldn't say no. **refuser** /Rəfyze/ [1] *vt* refuse (**de** to); (*client, spectateur*) turn away; (*recaler*) fail; (à un poste) turn down. □ **se ~ à** *vpr* (*évidence*) reject; **se ~ à faire** refuse to do.

regain /Rəgɛ̃/ *nm* **~ de** renewal *ou* revival of; (Comm) rise.

régal (*pl* ~s) /Regal/ *nm* treat, delight.

régaler /Regale/ [1] *vt* **~ qn de** treat sb to. □ **se ~** *vpr* (de nourriture) **je me régale** it's delicious.

regard /Rəgar/ *nm* (expression, coup d'œil) look; (vue) eye; (yeux) eyes; **~ fixe** stare; **au ~ de** with regard to; **en ~ de** compared with.

regardant, ~e /Rəgardɑ̃, -t/ *a* **~ avec son argent** careful with money; **peu ~** (**sur**) not fussy (about).

regarder /Rəgarde/ [1] *vt* look at; (observer) watch; (considérer) consider; (concerner) concern; **~ fixement** stare at; **~ à** think about, pay attention to. ● *vi* look. □ **se ~** *vpr* (soi-même) look at oneself; (*personnes*) look at each other.

régate /Regat/ *nf* regatta.

régie /Reʒi/ *nf* **~ d'État** public corporation; (radio, TV) control room; (au cinéma) production; (Théât) stage management.

régime /Reʒim/ *nm* (organisation) system; (Pol) regime; (Méd) diet; (de moteur) speed; (de bananes) bunch; **se mettre au ~** go on a diet; **à ce ~** at this rate.

régiment /Reʒimɑ̃/ *nm* regiment.

région /Reʒjɔ̃/ *nf* region.

régional, ~e (*mpl* **-aux**) *a* regional.

régir /Reʒir/ [2] *vt* govern.

régisseur /Reʒisœr/ *nm* (Théât) stage manager; **~ de plateau** (TV) floor manager; (au cinéma) studio manager.

registre /Rəgistr/ *nm* register.

réglage /Reglaʒ/ *nm* adjustment; (de moteur) tuning.

règle /Rɛgl/ *nf* rule; (instrument) ruler; **~s** (de femme) period; **en ~** in order.

réglé, ~e /Regle/ *a* (vie) ordered; (arrangé) settled; (papier) ruled.

règlement /Rɛgləmɑ̃/ *nm* (règles) regulations; (solution) settlement; (paiement) payment. **réglementaire** *a* (uniforme) regulation. **réglementation** *nf* regulation, rules. **réglementer** [1] *vt* regulate, control.

régler /Regle/ [14] *vt* settle; (*machine*) adjust; (programmer) set; (*facture*) settle; (*personne*) settle up with; **~ son compte à** Ⅱ settle a score with.

réglisse /Reglis/ *nf* liquorice.

règne /Rɛɲ/ *nm* reign; (végétal, animal, minéral) kingdom.

regret /Rəgrɛ/ *nm* regret; **à ~** with regret.

regretter /Rəgrete/ [1] *vt* regret; (*personne*) miss; (pour s'excuser) be sorry.

regrouper /Rəgrupe/ [1] *vt* group *ou* bring together. □ **se ~** *vpr* gather *ou* group together.

régularité /Regylarite/ *nf* regularity; (de rythme, progrès) steadiness; (de surface, écriture) evenness.

régulier, -ière /Regylje, -jɛr/ *a* regular; (qualité, vitesse) steady, even; (ligne, paysage) even; (légal) legal; (honnête) honest.

rehausser /Rəose/ [1] vt raise; (faire valoir) enhance.

rein /Rɛ̃/ nm kidney; ~s (dos) small of the back.

reine /Rɛn/ nf queen.

réinsertion /Reɛ̃sɛRsjɔ̃/ nf reintegration.

réintégrer /Reɛ̃tegRe/ [14] vt (lieu) return to; (Jur) reinstate; (personne) reintegrate.

réitérer /Reitere/ [14] vt repeat.

rejaillir /RəʒajiR/ [2] vi ~ sur splash back onto; ~ sur qn (succès) reflect on sb.

rejet /Rəʒɛ/ nm rejection; ~s (déchets) waste.

rejeter /Rəʒte/ [38] vt throw back; (refuser) reject; (déverser) discharge; ~ une faute sur qn shift the blame for a mistake onto sb.

rejeton /Rəʒtɔ̃/ nm (enfant 🗊) offspring (inv).

rejoindre /Rəʒwɛ̃dR/ [22] vt go back to, rejoin; (rattraper) catch up with; (rencontrer) join, meet up with. □ se ~ vpr (personnes) meet up; (routes) join, meet.

réjoui, ~e /Reʒwi/ a joyful.

réjouir /ReʒwiR/ [2] vt delight. □ se ~ vpr be delighted (de at).

réjouissances nfpl festivities.

réjouissant, ~e a cheering.

relâche /Rəlɑʃ/ nm (repos) break, rest; faire ~ (Théât) be closed.

relâcher /Rəlɑʃe/ [1] vt slacken; (personne) release; (discipline) relax. □ se ~ vpr slacken.

relais /Rəlɛ/ nm (Sport) relay; (hôtel) hotel; (intermédiaire) intermediary; prendre le ~ de take over from.

relancer /Rəlɑ̃se/ [10] vt boost, revive; (renvoyer) throw back.

relatif, -ive /Rəlatif, -v/ a relative; ~ à relating to.

relation /Rəlasjɔ̃/ nf relationship; (ami) acquaintance; (personne puissante) connection; ~s

relations; ~s extérieures foreign affairs; en ~ avec qn in touch with sb.

relativement /Rəlativmɑ̃/ adv relatively; ~ à in relation to.

relativité /Rəlativite/ nf relativity.

relax /Rəlaks/ a inv 🗊 laid-back.

relaxer (se) /(sə)Rəlakse/ [1] vpr relax.

relayer /Rəleje/ [31] vt relieve; (émission) relay. □ se ~ vpr take over from one another.

reléguer /Rələge/ [14] vt relegate.

relent /Rəlɑ̃/ nm stink; (fig) whiff.

relève /Rəlɛv/ nf relief; prendre ou assurer la ~ take over (de from).

relevé, ~e /Rəlve/ a spicy. ● nm (de compteur) reading; (facture) bill; ~ bancaire, ~ de compte bank statement; faire le ~ de list.

relever /Rəlve/ [6] vt pick up; (personne tombée) help up; (remonter) raise; (col) turn up; (compteur) read; (défi) accept; (relayer) relieve; (remarquer, noter) note; (plat) spice up; (rebâtir) rebuild; ~ de come within the competence of; (Méd) recover from. □ se ~ vpr (personne) get up (again); (pays, économie) recover.

relief /Rəljɛf/ nm relief; mettre en ~ highlight.

relier /Rəlje/ [45] vt link (up) (à to); (livre) bind.

religieux, -ieuse /Rəliʒjø, -z/ a religious. ● nm, f monk, nun.

religion /Rəliʒjɔ̃/ nf religion.

reliure /RəljyR/ nf binding.

reluire /RəlɥiR/ [17] vi shine.

remaniement /Rəmanimɑ̃/ nm revision; ~ ministériel cabinet reshuffle.

remarquable /RəmaRkabl/ a remarkable.

R

remarque /Rəmark/ *nf* remark; (par écrit) comment.

remarquer /Rəmarke/ [1] *vt* notice; (dire) say; **faire ~** point out (à to); **se faire ~** draw attention to oneself; **remarque(z)** mind you.

remblai /Rãblɛ/ *nm* embankment.

remboursement /Rãbursəmã/ *nm* (d'emprunt, dette) repayment; (Comm) refund.

rembourser /Rãburse/ [1] *vt* (dette, emprunt) repay; (billet, frais) refund; (client) give a refund to; (ami) pay back.

remède /Rəmɛd/ *nm* remedy; (médicament) medicine.

remédier /Rəmedje/ [45] *vi* ~ à remedy.

remerciements /RəmɛRsimã/ *nmpl* thanks. **remercier** [45] *vt* thank (de for); (licencier) dismiss.

remettre /RəmɛtR/ [42] *vt* put back; (vêtement) put back on; (donner) hand over; (devoir, démission) hand in; (faire fonctionner) switch back on; (restituer) give back; (différer) put off; (ajouter) add; (se rappeler) remember; **~ en cause** *ou* **en question** call into question. □ **se ~** *vpr* (guérir) recover; **se ~ au tennis** take up tennis again; **se ~ au travail** get back to work; **se ~ à faire** start doing again; **s'en ~ à** leave it to it.

remise /Rəmiz/ *nf* (abri) shed; (rabais) discount; (transmission) handing over; (ajournement) postponement; **~ en cause** *ou* **en question** calling into question; **~ des prix** prizegiving; **~ des médailles** medals ceremony; **~ de peine** remission.

remontant /Rəmõtã/ *nm* tonic.

remontée /Rəmõte/ *nf* ascent; (d'eau, de prix) rise; **~ mécanique** ski lift.

remonte-pente (*pl* ~s) /Rəmõt-pãt/ *nm* ski tow.

remonter /Rəmõte/ [1] *vi* go *ou* come (back) up; (prix, niveau) rise (again); (revenir) go back (à to); **~ dans le temps** go back in time. ● *vt* (rue, escalier) go *ou* come (back) up; (relever) raise; (montre) wind up; (objet démonté) put together again; (personne) buck up.

remontoir /RəmõtwaR/ *nm* winder.

remords /RəmɔR/ *nm* remorse; **avoir du** *or* **des ~** feel remorse.

remorque /RəmɔRk/ *nf* trailer; **en ~** on tow. **remorquer** [1] *vt* tow.

remous /Rəmu/ *nm* eddy; (de bateau) backwash; (fig) turmoil.

rempart /RãpaR/ *nm* rampart.

remplaçant, ~e /Rãplasã, -t/ *nm, f* replacement; (joueur) reserve, substitute.

remplacement /Rãplasmã/ *nm* replacement; **faire des ~s** do supply teaching. **remplacer** [10] *vt* replace.

rempli, ~e /Rãpli/ *a* full (de of); (journée) busy.

remplir /RãpliR/ [2] *vt* fill (up); (formulaire) fill in *ou* out; (condition) fulfil; (devoir, tâche, rôle) carry out. □ **se ~** *vpr* fill (up). **remplissage** *nm* filling; (de texte) padding.

remporter /RãpɔRte/ [1] *vt* take back; (victoire) win.

remuant, ~e /Rəmɥã, -t/ *a* boisterous.

remue-ménage /Rəmymenaʒ/ *nm inv* commotion, bustle.

remuer /Rəmɥe/ [1] *vt* move; (thé, café) stir; (passé) rake up. ● *vi* move; (gigoter) fidget. □ **se ~** *vpr* move.

rémunération /RemyneRasjõ/ *nf* payment.

renaissance /Rənɛsãs/ *nf* rebirth.

renard /RənaR/ *nm* fox.

renchérir /ʀɑ̃ʃeʀiʀ/ [2] *vi* (dans une vente) raise the bidding; ~ **sur** go one better than. ● *vt* increase, put up.

rencontre /ʀɑ̃kɔ̃tʀ/ *nf* meeting; (de routes) junction; (Mil) encounter; (match) match; (US) game.

rencontrer /ʀɑ̃kɔ̃tʀe/ [1] *vt* meet; (heurter) hit; (trouver) find. □ **se** ~ *vpr* meet.

rendement /ʀɑ̃dmɑ̃/ *nm* yield; (travail) output.

rendez-vous /ʀɑ̃devu/ *nm* appointment; (d'amoureux) date; (lieu) meeting-place; **prendre** ~ (**avec**) make an appointment (with).

rendormir (se) /(sə)ʀɑ̃dɔʀmiʀ/ [46] *vpr* go back to sleep.

rendre /ʀɑ̃dʀ/ [3] *vt* give back, return; (donner en retour) return; (monnaie) give; (justice) dispense; (jugement) pronounce; ~ **heureux/possible** make happy/possible; (vomir 🄼) vomit: ~ **compte de** report on; ~ **service (à)** help; ~ **visite à** visit. ● *vi* (terres) yield; (activité) be profitable. □ **se** ~ *vpr* (capituler) surrender; (aller) go (à to); **se** ~ **utile** make oneself useful.

rêne /ʀɛn/ *nf* rein.

renfermé, ~e /ʀɑ̃fɛʀme/ *a* withdrawn. ● *nm* **sentir le** ~ smell musty.

renflé, ~e /ʀɑ̃fle/ *a* bulging.

renforcer /ʀɑ̃fɔʀse/ [10] *vt* reinforce.

renfort /ʀɑ̃fɔʀ/ *nm* reinforcement; **à grand** ~ **de** with a great deal of.

renier /ʀənje/ [45] *vt* (personne, œuvre) disown; (foi) renounce.

renifler /ʀənifle/ [1] *vt/i* sniff.

renne /ʀɛn/ *nm* reindeer.

renom /ʀənɔ̃/ *nm* renown; (réputation) reputation. **renommé,**

~**e** *a* famous. **renommée** *nf* (célébrité) fame; (réputation) reputation.

renoncement /ʀənɔ̃smɑ̃/ *nm* renunciation.

renoncer /ʀənɔ̃se/ [10] *vi* ~ **à** (habitude, ami) give up, renounce; (projet) abandon; ~ **à faire** abandon the idea of doing.

renouer /ʀənwe/ [1] *vt* tie up (again); (amitié) renew; ~ **avec qn** get back in touch with sb; (après une dispute) make up with sb.

renouveau (*pl* ~**x**) /ʀənuvo/ *nm* revival.

renouveler /ʀənuvle/ [38] *vt* renew; (réitérer) repeat; (remplacer) replace. □ **se** ~ *vpr* be renewed; (incident) recur, happen again.

renouvellement /ʀənuvɛlmɑ̃/ *nm* renewal.

rénovation /ʀenɔvasjɔ̃/ *nf* (d'édifice) renovation; (d'institution) reform.

renseignement /ʀɑ̃sɛɲ(ə)mɑ̃/ *nm* ~(**s**) information, (bureau des) ~**s** information desk; (service des) ~**s téléphoniques** directory enquiries.

renseigner /ʀɑ̃seɲe/ [1] *vt* inform, give information to. □ **se** ~ *vpr* enquire, make enquiries, find out.

rentabilité /ʀɑ̃tabilite/ *nf* profitability. **rentable** *a* profitable.

rente /ʀɑ̃t/ *nf* (private) income; (pension) annuity. **rentier, -ière** *nm, f* person of private means.

rentrée /ʀɑ̃tʀe/ *nf* return; (revenu) income; **la** ~ **parlementaire** the reopening of Parliament; **la** ~ (**des classes**) the start of the new school year; **faire sa** ~ make a comeback.

rentrer /ʀɑ̃tʀe/ [1] *vi* (aux être) go *ou* come back home, return home; (entrer) go *ou* come in;

R

(entrer à nouveau) go *ou* come back in; (*revenu*) come in; (*élèves*) go back (to school); ~ **dans** (heurter) smash into; **tout est rentré dans l'ordre** everything is back to normal; ~ **dans ses frais** break even. ●*vt* (*aux avoir*) bring in; (*griffes*) draw in; (*vêtement*) tuck in.

renverser /Rɑ̃vɛRSe/ [1] *vt* knock over *ou* down; (*piéton*) knock down; (*liquide*) upset, spill; (*mettre à l'envers*) turn upside down; (*gouvernement*) overthrow; (*inverser*) reverse. □ **se** ~ *vpr* (*véhicule*) overturn; (*verre, vase*) fall over.

renvoi /Rɑ̃vwa/ *nm* return; (*d'employé*) dismissal; (*d'élève*) expulsion; (*report*) postponement; (*dans un livre, fichier*) cross-reference; (*rot*) burp.

renvoyer /Rɑ̃vwaje/ [32] *vt* send back, return; (*employé*) dismiss; (*élève*) expel; (*ajourner*) postpone; (*référer*) refer; (*réfléchir*) reflect.

repaire /RəpɛR/ *nm* den.

répandre /Repɑ̃dR/ [3] *vt* (*liquide*) spill; (*étendre, diffuser*) spread; (*odeur*) give off. □ **se** ~ *vpr* spread; (*liquide*) spill; **se** ~ **en injures** let out a stream of abuse.

répandu, ~**e** /Repɑ̃dy/ *a* widespread.

réparateur, **-trice** /RepaRatœR, -tRis/ *nm* engineer. **réparation** *nf* repair; (*compensation*) compensation. **réparer** [1] *vt* repair, mend; (*faute*) make amends for; (*remédier à*) put right.

repartie /Rəparti/ *nf* retort; **avoir de la** ~ always have a ready reply.

repartir /RəpartiR/ [46] *vi* start again; (*voyageur*) set off again; (*s'en retourner*) go back; (*secteur économique*) pick up again.

répartir /RepartiR/ [2] *vt* distribute; (*partager*) share out;

(*étaler*) spread. **répartition** *nf* distribution.

repas /Rəpa/ *nm* meal.

repassage /Rəpasaʒ/ *nm* ironing.

repasser /Rəpase/ [1] *vi* come *ou* go back; ~ **devant qch** go past sth again. ●*vt* (*linge*) iron; (*examen*) retake, resist; (*film*) show again.

repêcher /Rəpeʃe/ [1] *vt* recover, fish out; (*candidat*) allow to pass.

repentir[1] /Rəpɑ̃tiR/ *nm* repentance.

repentir[2] (**se**) /(sə)Rəpɑ̃tiR/ [2] *vpr* repent (**de** of); **se** ~ **de** (regretter) regret.

répercuter /RepɛRkyte/ [1] *vt* (*bruit*) send back. □ **se** ~ *vpr* echo; **se** ~ **sur** have repercussions on.

repère /RəpɛR/ *nm* mark; (*jalon*) marker; (*événement*) landmark; (*référence*) reference point.

repérer /Rəpere/ [14] *vt* locate, spot. □ **se** ~ *vpr* get one's bearings.

répertoire /RepɛRtwaR/ *nm* (artistique) repertoire; (*liste*) directory; ~ **téléphonique** telephone directory; (*personnel*) telephone book. **répertorier** [45] *vt* index.

répéter /Repete/ [14] *vt* repeat; (*Théât*) rehearse. ●*vi* rehearse. □ **se** ~ *vpr* be repeated; (*personne*) repeat oneself.

répétition /Repetisjɔ̃/ *nf* repetition; (*Théât*) rehearsal.

répit /Repi/ *nm* respite, break.

replier /Rəplije/ [45] *vt* fold (up); (*ailes, jambes*) tuck in. □ **se** ~ *vpr* withdraw (**sur soi-même** into oneself).

réplique /Replik/ *nf* reply; (*riposte*) retort; (*objection*) objection; (*Théât*) line; (*copie*) replica. **répliquer** [1] *vt/i* reply; (*riposter*) retort; (*objecter*) answer back.

répondeur /Repɔ̃dœR/ *nm* answering machine.

répondre /Repɔ̃dR/ [3] *vt* (*injure, bêtise*) reply with; ~ **que** answer *ou* reply that; ~ **à** (être conforme à) answer; (*affection, sourire*) return; (*avances, appel, critique*) respond to; ~ **de** answer for. ● *vi* answer, reply; (être insolent) answer back; (réagir) respond (**à** to).

réponse /Repɔ̃s/ *nf* answer, reply; (fig) response.

report /RəpɔR/ *nm* (transcription) transfer; (renvoi) postponement.

reportage /RəpɔRtaʒ/ *nm* report; (par écrit) article.

reporter¹ /RəpɔRte/ [1] *vt* take back; (ajourner) put off; (transcrire) transfer. □ **se ~ à** *vpr* refer to.

reporter² /RəpɔRtɛR/ *nm* reporter.

repos /Rəpo/ *nm* rest; (paix) peace. **reposant, ~e** *a* restful.

reposer /Rəpoze/ [1] *vt* put down again; (délasser) rest. ● *vi* rest (**sur** on); **laisser ~** (*pâte*) leave to stand. □ **se ~** *vpr* rest; **se ~ sur** rely on.

repousser /Rəpuse/ [1] *vt* push back; (écarter) push away; (dégoûter) repel; (décliner) reject; (ajourner) postpone, put back. ● *vi* grow again.

reprendre /RəpRɑ̃dR/ [50] *vt* take back; (*confiance, conscience*) regain; (*souffle*) get back; (*évadé*) recapture; (recommencer) resume; (redire) repeat; (modifier) alter; (blâmer) reprimand; ~ **du pain** take some more bread; **on ne m'y reprendra pas** I won't be caught out again. ● *vi* (recommencer) resume; (*affaires*) pick up. □ **se ~** *vpr* (se ressaisir) pull oneself together; (se corriger) correct oneself.

représailles /RəpRezaj/ *nfpl* reprisals.

représentant, ~e /RəpRezɑ̃tɑ̃, -t/ *nm, f* representative.

représentation /RəpRezɑ̃tasjɔ̃/ *nf* representation; (Théât) performance.

représenter /RəpRezɑ̃te/ [1] *vt* represent; (figures) depict, show; (*pièce de théâtre*) perform. □ **se ~** *vpr* (s'imaginer) imagine.

répression /RepResjɔ̃/ *nf* repression; (d'élan) suppression.

réprimande /RepRimɑ̃d/ *nf* reprimand.

réprimer /RepRime/ [1] *vt* (*peuple*) repress; (*sentiment*) suppress; (*fraude*) crack down on.

reprise /RəpRiz/ *nf* resumption; (Théât) revival; (TV) repeat; (de tissu) darn, mend; (essor) recovery; (Comm) part-exchange, trade-in; **à plusieurs ~s** on several occasions.

repriser /RəpRize/ [1] *vt* darn, mend.

reproche /RəpRɔʃ/ *nm* reproach; **faire des ~s à** find fault with.

reprocher /RəpRɔʃe/ [1] *vt* ~ **qch à qn** reproach *ou* criticize sb for sth.

reproducteur, -trice /RəpRɔdyktœR, -tRis/ *a* reproductive.

reproduire /RəpRɔdɥiR/ [17] *vt* reproduce; (répéter) repeat. □ **se ~** *vpr* reproduce; (se répéter) recur.

reptile /Reptil/ *nm* reptile.

repu, ~e /Rəpy/ *a* satiated, replete.

républicain, ~e /Repyblikɛ̃, -ɛn/ *a & nm, f* republican.

république /Repyblik/ *nf* republic; ~ **populaire** people's republic.

répudier /Repydje/ [45] *vt* repudiate; (*droit*) renounce.

répugnance /Repyɲɑ̃s/ *nf* repugnance; (hésitation) reluctance; **avoir de la ~ pour** loathe.

répugnant, ~e *a* repulsive.

R

répugner /ʀepyɲe/ [1] vt be repugnant to, disgust; ~ à (effort, violence) be averse to; ~ à faire be reluctant to do.

répulsion /ʀepylsjɔ̃/ nf repulsion.

réputation /ʀepytasjɔ̃/ nf reputation.

réputé, ~e /ʀepyte/ a renowned (pour for); (école, compagnie) reputable; ~ pour être reputed to be.

requérir /ʀəkeʀiʀ/ [7] vt require, demand.

requête /ʀəkɛt/ nf request; (Jur) petition.

requin /ʀəkɛ̃/ nm shark.

requis, ~e /ʀəki, -z/ a (exigé) required; (nécessaire) necessary.

RER abrév m (réseau express régional) Parisian rapid transit rail system.

rescapé, ~e /ʀɛskape/ nm, f survivor. ● a surviving.

rescousse /ʀɛskus/ nf à la ~ to the rescue.

réseau (pl ~x) /ʀezo/ nm network; ~ local local area network, LAN; le ~ des ~x (Ordinat) Internet.

réservation /ʀezɛʀvasjɔ̃/ nf reservation, booking.

réserve /ʀezɛʀv/ nf reserve; (restriction) reservation, reserve; (indienne) reservation; (entrepôt) store-room; en ~ in reserve; les ~s (Mil) the reserves.

réserver /ʀezɛʀve/ [1] vt reserve; (place) book, reserve. □ se ~ vpr se ~ qch save sth for oneself; se ~ pour save oneself for; se ~ le droit de reserve the right to.

réservoir /ʀezɛʀvwaʀ/ nm tank; (lac) reservoir.

résidence /ʀezidɑ̃s/ nf residence; ~ secondaire second home; ~ universitaire hall of residence.

résident, ~e /ʀezidɑ̃, -t/ nm, f resident; (étranger) foreign resident.

résider /ʀezide/ [1] vi reside; ~ dans qch (difficulté) lie in.

résigner (se) /(sə)ʀeziɲe/ [1] vpr se ~ à faire resign oneself to doing.

résilier /ʀezilje/ [45] vt terminate.

résine /ʀezin/ nf resin.

résistance /ʀezistɑ̃s/ nf resistance; (fil électrique) element.

résistant, ~e a tough.

résister /ʀeziste/ [1] vi resist; ~ à (agresseur, assaut, influence, tentation) resist; (corrosion, chaleur) withstand.

résolu, ~e /ʀezɔly/ a resolute; ~ à faire determined to do.
● ⇒RÉSOUDRE [53].

résolution /ʀezɔlysjɔ̃/ nf (fermeté) resolution; (d'un problème) solving.

résonner /ʀezɔne/ [1] vi resound.

résorber /ʀezɔʀbe/ [1] vt reduce. □ se ~ vpr be reduced.

résoudre /ʀezudʀ/ [53] vt solve; (crise, conflit) resolve. □ se ~ à vpr (se décider) resolve to; (se résigner) resign oneself to.

respect /ʀɛspɛ/ nm respect.

respectabilité nf respectability.

respecter /ʀɛspɛkte/ [1] vt respect; faire ~ (loi, décision) enforce.

respectueux, -euse /ʀɛspɛktɥø, -z/ a respectful; ~ de l'environnement environmentally friendly.

respiration /ʀɛspiʀasjɔ̃/ nf breathing; (haleine) breath.

respiratoire a respiratory, breathing.

respirer /ʀɛspiʀe/ [1] vi breathe; (se reposer) catch one's breath.
● vt breathe (in); (exprimer) radiate.

resplendir /ʀɛsplɑ̃diʀ/ [2] vi

shine (de with). **resplendissant**, ~e a brilliant, radiant.

responsabilité /rɛspɔ̃sabilite/ nf responsibility; (légale) liability.

responsable /rɛspɔ̃sabl/ a responsible (de for); ~ de (chargé de) in charge of. ● nmf person in charge; (coupable) person responsible.

resquiller /rɛskije/ [1] vi ▣ (dans le train) fare-dodge; (au spectacle) get in without paying; (dans la queue) jump the queue.

ressaisir (se) /(sə)rəsezir/ [2] vpr pull oneself together; (équipe sportive, valeurs boursières) make a recovery.

ressemblance /rəsɑ̃blɑ̃s/ nf resemblance.

ressemblant, ~e /rəsɑ̃blɑ̃, -t/ a être ~ (portrait) be a good likeness.

ressembler /rəsɑ̃ble/ [1] vi à ~ resemble, look like. □ se ~ vpr be alike; (physiquement) look alike.

ressentiment /rəsɑ̃timɑ̃/ nm resentment.

ressentir /rəsɑ̃tir/ [46] vt feel. □ se ~ de vpr feel the effects of.

resserrer /rəsere/ [1] vt tighten; (contracter) compress; (vêtement) take in. □ se ~ vpr tighten; (route) narrow; (se regrouper) move closer together.

ressort /rəsɔr/ nm (objet) spring; (fig) energy; être du ~ de be the province of; (Jur) be within the jurisdiction of; en dernier ~ as a last resort.

ressortir /rəsɔrtir/ [46] vi go ou come back out; (se voir) stand out; (film, disque) be re-released; faire ~ bring out; il ressort que it emerges that. ● vt take out again; (redire) come out with again; (disque, film) re-release.

ressortissant, ~e /rəsɔrtisɑ̃, -t/ nm, f national.

ressource /rəsurs/ nf resource; ~s resources; à bout de ~ at one's wits' end.

ressusciter /resysite/ [1] vi come back to life. ● vt bring back to life; (fig) revive.

restant, ~e /rɛstɑ̃, -t/ a remaining. ● nm remainder.

restaurant /rɛstɔrɑ̃/ nm restaurant.

restauration /rɛstɔrasjɔ̃/ nf restoration; (hôtellerie) catering.

restaurer /rɛstɔre/ [1] vt restore. □ se ~ vpr eat.

reste /rɛst/ nm rest; (d'une soustraction) remainder; ~s remains (de of); (nourriture) leftovers; un ~ de poulet some left-over chicken; au ~, du ~ moreover, besides.

rester /rɛste/ [1] vi (aux être) stay, remain; (subsister) be left, remain; il reste du pain there is some bread left (over); il me reste du pain I have some bread left (over); il me reste à it remains for me to; en ~ à go no further than; en ~ là stop there.

restituer /rɛstitɥe/ [1] vt (rendre) return; (recréer) reproduce; (rétablir) reconstruct.

restreindre /rɛstrɛ̃dr/ [22] vt restrict. □ se ~ vpr (dans les dépenses) cut back.

résultat /rezylta/ nm result.

résulter /rezylte/ [1] vi ~ de result from, be the result of.

résumé /rezyme/ nm summary; en ~ in short; (pour finir) to sum up. **résumer** [1] vt summarize.

résurrection /rezyrɛksjɔ̃/ nf resurrection; (renouveau) revival.

rétablir /retablir/ [2] vt restore; (personne) restore to health. □ se ~ vpr (ordre, silence) be restored; (guérir) recover.

rétablissement nm restoration; (de malade, monnaie) recovery.

R

retard /ʀətaʀ/ *nm* lateness; (sur un programme) delay; (infériorité) backwardness; **avoir du ~** be late; (montre) be slow; **en ~** late; (retardé) behind; **en ~ sur l'emploi du temps** behind schedule; **rattraper** *ou* **combler son ~** catch up; **prendre du ~** fall behind.

retardataire /ʀətaʀdatɛʀ/ *nmf* latecomer. ● *a* late.

retarder /ʀətaʀde/ [1] *vt* **~ qn/ qch** delay sb/sth, hold sb/sth up; (par rapport à une heure convenue) make sb/sth late; (montre) put back. ● *vi* (montre) be slow; (personne) be out of touch.

retenir /ʀətniʀ/ [58] *vt* hold back; (souffle, attention, prisonnier) hold; (eau, chaleur) retain, hold; (larmes) hold back; (garder) keep; (retarder) detain, hold up; (réserver) book; (se rappeler) remember; (déduire) deduct; (accepter) accept. □ **se ~** *vpr* (se contenir) restrain oneself; **se ~ à** hold on to; **se ~ de faire** stop oneself from doing.

rétention /ʀetɑ̃sjɔ̃/ *nf* retention.

retentir /ʀətɑ̃tiʀ/ [2] *vi* ring out, resound; **~ sur** have an impact on. **retentissant**, **~e** *a* resounding. **retentissement** *nm* (effet) effect.

retenue /ʀətny/ *nf* restraint; (somme) deduction; (Scol) detention.

réticent, **~e** /ʀetisɑ̃, -t/ *a* (hésitant) hesitant; (qui rechigne) reluctant; (réservé) reticent.

rétine /ʀetin/ *nf* retina.

retiré, **~e** /ʀətiʀe/ *a* (vie) secluded; (lieu) remote.

retirer /ʀətiʀe/ [1] *vt* (sortir) take out; (ôter) take off; (argent, offre, candidature) withdraw; (écarter) (main, pied) withdraw; (billet, bagages) collect, pick up; (avantage) derive; **~ à qn** take away from sb. □ **se ~** *vpr* withdraw, retire.

retombées /ʀətɔ̃be/ *nfpl* (conséquences) effects; **~ radioactives** nuclear fall-out.

retomber /ʀətɔ̃be/ [1] *vi* (faire une chute) fall again; (retourner au sol) land, come down; **~ dans** (erreur) fall back into.

retouche /ʀətuʃ/ *nf* alteration; (de photo, tableau) retouch.

retour /ʀətuʀ/ *nm* return; **être de ~** be back (de from); **~ en arrière** flashback; **par ~ du courrier** by return of post; **en ~** in return.

retourner /ʀətuʀne/ [1] *vt* (aux avoir) turn over; (vêtement) turn inside out; (maison) turn upside down; (lettre, compliment) return; (émouvoir 🔟) shake, upset. ● *vi* (aux être) go back, return. □ **se ~** *vpr* turn round; (dans son lit) twist and turn; **s'en ~** go back; **se ~ contre** turn against.

retrait /ʀətʀɛ/ *nm* withdrawal; (des eaux) receding; **être (situé) en ~ (de)** be set back (from).

retraite /ʀətʀɛt/ *nf* retirement; (pension) retirement pension; (fuite, refuge) retreat; **mettre à la ~** pension off; **prendre sa ~** retire.

retraité, **~e** /ʀətʀete/ *a* retired. ● *nm, f* (old-age) pensioner.

retrancher /ʀətʀɑ̃ʃe/ [1] *vt* remove; (soustraire) deduct, subtract. □ **se ~** *vpr* (Mil) entrench oneself; **se ~ derrière** take refuge behind.

retransmettre /ʀətʀɑ̃smɛtʀ/ [42] *vt* broadcast.

rétrécir /ʀetʀesiʀ/ [2] *vt* make narrower; (vêtement) take in. ● *vi* (tissu) shrink. □ **se ~** *vpr* (rue) narrow.

rétribution /ʀetʀibysjɔ̃/ *nf* payment.

rétroactif, **-ive** /ʀetʀoaktif, -v/ *a* retrospective; **augmentation à effet ~** backdated pay rise.

retrousser /RətRuse/ [1] *vt* pull up; (*manche*) roll up.

retrouvailles /RətRuvɑj/ *nfpl* reunion.

retrouver /RətRuve/ [1] *vt* find (again); (rejoindre) meet (again); (*forces, calme*) regain; (*lieu*) be back in; (se rappeler) remember. □ **se** ~ *vpr* find oneself (back); (se réunir) meet (again); (être présent) be found; **s'y** ~ (s'orienter, comprendre) find one's way; (rentrer dans ses frais 🗊) break even.

rétroviseur /RetRɔvizœR/ *nm* (Auto) (rear-view) mirror.

réunion /Reynjɔ̃/ *nf* meeting; (rencontre) gathering; (après une séparation) réunion; (d'objets) collection.

réunir /ReyniR/ [2] *vt* gather, collect; (rapprocher) bring together; (convoquer) call together; (raccorder) join; (*qualités*) combine. □ **se** ~ *vpr* meet.

réussi, ~e /Reysi/ *a* successful.

réussir /ReysiR/ [2] *vi* succeed, be successful; ~ **à faire** succeed in doing, manage to do; ~ **à un examen** pass an exam; ~ **à qn** (*méthode*) work well for sb; (*climat, mode de vie*) agree with sb. ● *vt* (*vie*) make a success of.

réussite /Reysit/ *nf* success; (jeu) patience.

revaloir /RəvalwaR/ [60] *vt* **je vous revaudrai cela** (en mal) I'll pay you back for this; (en bien) I'll repay you some day.

revanche /Rəvɑ̃ʃ/ *nf* revenge; (Sport) return *ou* revenge match; **en** ~ on the other hand.

rêvasser /Revase/ [1] *vi* daydream.

rêve /Rɛv/ *nm* dream; **faire un** ~ have a dream.

réveil /Revɛj/ *nm* waking up, (fig) awakening; (pendule) alarm clock.

réveillé, ~e /Reveje/ *a* awake.

réveille-matin /Revɛjmatɛ̃/ *nm inv* alarm clock.

réveiller /Reveje/ [1] *vt* wake (up); (*sentiment, souvenir*) awaken; (*curiosité*) arouse. □ **se** ~ *vpr* wake up.

réveillon /Revɛjɔ̃/ *nm* (Noël) Christmas Eve; (nouvel an) New Year's Eve. **réveillonner** [1] *vi* see Christmas *ou* the New Year in.

révéler /Revele/ [14] *vt* reveal. □ **se** ~ *vpr* be revealed; **se** ~ **facile** turn out to be easy, prove easy.

revendeur, -euse /RəvɑdœR, -øz/ *nm, f* dealer, stockist; ~ **de drogue** drug dealer.

revendication /Rəvɑdikasjɔ̃/ *nf* claim. **revendiquer** [1] *vt* claim.

revendre /RəvɑdR/ [3] *vt* sell (again); **avoir de l'énergie à** ~ have energy to spare.

revenir /RəvniR/ [58] *vi* (aux être) come back, return (à to); ~ **à** (*activité*) go back to; (se résumer à) come down to; (échoir à) fall to; ~ **à 100 francs** cost 100 francs; ~ **de** (*maladie, surprise*) get over; ~ **sur ses pas** retrace one's steps; **faire** ~ (Culin) brown; **ça me revient!** now I remember!; **je n'en reviens pas!** 🗊 I can't get over it!

revenu /Rəvny/ *nm* income; (de l'État) revenue.

rêver /Reve/ [1] *vt/i* dream (à of; de faire of doing).

réverbère /RevɛRbɛR/ *nm* street lamp.

révérence /ReveRɑ̃s/ *nf* reverence; (salut d'homme) bow; (salut de femme) curtsy.

rêverie /RɛvRi/ *nf* daydream; (activité) daydreaming.

revers /RəvɛR/ *nm* reverse; (de main) back; (d'étoffe) wrong side; (de veste) lapel; (de pantalon) turn-up;

R

(de manche) cuff; (tennis) backhand; (fig) set-back.

revêtement /Rəvɛtmã/ nm covering; (de route) surface; ~ **de sol** floor covering. **revêtir** [61] vt cover; (habit) put on; (prendre, avoir) assume.

rêveur, -euse /Rɛvœr, -øz/ a dreamy. ● nm, f dreamer.

réviser /Revize/ [1] vt revise; (machine, véhicule) service. **révision** nf revision; service.

revivre /Rəvivr/ [62] vi come alive again. ● vt relive.

révocation /Revɔkasjɔ̃/ nf repeal; (d'un fonctionnaire) dismissal.

revoir¹ /Rəvwar/ [63] vt see (again); (réviser) revise.

revoir² /Rəvwar/ nm au ~ goodbye.

révolte /Revɔlt/ nf revolt. **révolté, ~e** nm, f rebel.

révolter /Revɔlte/ [1] vt appal, revolt. □ **se ~** vpr revolt.

révolu, ~e /Revɔly/ a past; **avoir 21 ans ~s** be over 21 years of age.

révolution /Revɔlysjɔ̃/ nf revolution. **révolutionnaire** a & nmf revolutionary. **révolutionner** [1] vt revolutionize.

revolver /Revɔlvɛr/ nm revolver, gun.

révoquer /Revɔke/ [1] vt repeal; (fonctionnaire) dismiss.

revue /Rəvy/ nf (examen, défilé) review; (magazine) magazine; (spectacle) variety show.

rez-de-chaussée /Redʃose/ nm inv ground floor; (US) first floor.

RF abrév f (**République Française**) French Republic.

rhinocéros /Rinɔserɔs/ nm rhinoceros.

rhubarbe /Rybarb/ nf rhubarb.

rhum /Rɔm/ nm rum.

rhumatisme /Rymatism/ nm rheumatism.

rhume /Rym/ nm cold; ~ **des foins** hay fever.

ri /Ri/ ⇒RIRE [54].

ricaner /Rikane/ [1] vi snigger.

riche /Riʃ/ a rich (en in). ● nmf rich man, rich woman.

richesse /Riʃɛs/ nf wealth; (de sol, décor) richness; ~**s** wealth; (ressources) resources.

ride /Rid/ nf wrinkle; (sur l'eau) ripple.

rideau (pl ~**x**) /Rido/ nm curtain; (métallique) shutter; (fig) screen.

ridicule /Ridikyl/ a ridiculous. ● nm (d'une situation) absurdity; (le grotesque) **le ~** ridicule. **ridiculiser** [1] vt ridicule.

rien /Rjɛ̃/ pron nothing; (quoi que ce soit) anything; **de ~!** don't mention it!; ~ **de bon** nothing good; **elle n'a ~ dit** she didn't say anything; ~ **d'autre/de plus** nothing else/more; ~ **du tout** nothing at all; ~ **que** (seulement) just, only; **trois fois ~** next to nothing; **il n'y est pour ~** he has nothing to do with it; ~ **à faire!** (c'est impossible) it's no good!; (refus) no way! ①. ● nm un ~ **de** a touch of; **être puni pour un ~** be punished for the slightest thing; **se disputer pour un ~** fight over nothing; **en un ~ de temps** in next to no time.

rieur, -euse /Rijœr, -øz/ a cheerful; (yeux) laughing.

rigide /Riʒid/ a rigid.

rigolade /Rigɔlad/ nf fun.

rigoler /Rigɔle/ [1] vi laugh; (s'amuser) have some fun; (plaisanter) joke.

rigolo, ~te /Rigɔlo, -ɔt/ a ① funny. ● nm, f ① joker.

rigoureux, -euse /Rigurø, -z/ a rigorous; (hiver) harsh; (sévère) strict; (travail, recherches) meticulous.

rigueur /Rigœr/ nf rigour; **à la ~**

at a pinch; **être de ~** be
obligatory; **tenir ~ à qn de qch**
bear sb a grudge for sth.

rime /Rim/ *nf* rhyme.

rimer /Rime/ [1] *vi* rhyme (**avec**
with); **cela ne rime à rien** it makes
no sense.

rinçage /Rɛ̃saʒ/ *nm* rinse; (action)
rinsing.

rincer /Rɛ̃se/ [10] *vt* rinse.

riposte /Ripɔst/ *nf* retort.

riposter /Ripɔste/ [1] *vi* retaliate;
~ à (*attaque*) counter; (*insulte*)
reply to. ● *vt* retort (**que** that).

rire /RiR/ [54] *vi* laugh (**de** at);
(plaisanter) joke; (s'amuser) have fun;
c'était pour ~ it was a joke. ● *nm*
laugh; **des ~s** laughter.

risée /Rize/ *nf* **la ~ de** the
laughing-stock of.

risque /Risk/ *nm* risk. **risqué, ~e**
a risky; (osé) daring.

risquer /Riske/ [1] *vt* risk (**de faire**
of doing); (être passible de) face; **il
risque de pleuvoir** it might rain; **tu
risques de te faire mal** you might
hurt yourself. □ **se ~ à/dans** *vpr*
venture to/into.

ristourne /Risturn/ *nf* discount.

rite /Rit/ *nm* rite; (habitude) ritual.
rituel, ~le *a & nm* ritual.

rivage /Rivaʒ/ *nm* shore.

rival, ~e (*mpl* **-aux**) /Rival, -o/ *a
& nm, f* rival. **rivaliser** [1] *vi*
compete (**avec** with). **rivalité** *nf*
rivalry.

rive /Riv/ *nf* (de fleuve) bank; (de
lac) shore.

riverain, ~e /RivRɛ̃, -ɛn/ *a*
riverside. ● *nm, f* riverside
resident; (d'une rue) resident.

rivière /RivjɛR/ *nf* river.

riz /Ri/ *nm* rice. **rizière** *nf* paddy
field.

robe /Rɔb/ *nf* (de femme) dress; (de
juge) robe; (de cheval) coat; **~ de
chambre** dressing-gown.

robinet /Rɔbinɛ/ *nm* tap; (US)
faucet.

robot /Rɔbo/ *nm* robot; **~ ménager**
food processor.

robuste /Rɔbyst/ *a* robust.

roche /Rɔʃ/ *nf* rock.

rocher /Rɔʃe/ *nm* rock.

rock /Rɔk/ *nm* (Mus) rock.

rodage /Rɔdaʒ/ *nm* **en ~** (Auto)
running in.

roder /Rɔde/ [1] *vt* (Auto) run in;
être rodé (personne) have got the
hang of things.

rôder /Rode/ [1] *vi* roam;
(suspect) prowl.

rogne /Rɔɲ/ *nf* Ⅱ anger; **en ~** in a
temper.

rogner /Rɔɲe/ [1] *vt* trim; **~ sur**
cut down on.

rognon /Rɔɲɔ̃/ *nm* (Culin) kidney.

roi /Rwa/ *nm* king; **les R~ mages**
the Magi; **la fête des R~** Twelfth
Night.

rôle /Rol/ *nm* role, part.

romain, ~e /Rɔmɛ̃, -ɛn/ *a* Roman.
R~, ~e *nm, f* Roman. **romaine**
nf (laitue) cos.

roman /Rɔmɑ̃/ *nm* novel; (genre)
fiction.

romance /Rɔmɑ̃s/ *nf* ballad.

romancier, -ière /Rɔmɑ̃sje, -jɛR/
nm, f novelist.

romanesque /Rɔmanɛsk/ *a*
romantic; (fantastique) fantastic;
(récit) fictional; **œuvres ~s**
novels, fiction.

romantique /Rɔmɑ̃tik/ *a & nmf*
romantic. **romantisme** *nm*
romanticism.

rompre /Rɔ̃pR/ [3] *vt* break;
(relations) break off. ● *vi* (se
séparer) break up; **~ avec** (fiancé)
break up with; (parti) break
away from; (tradition) break with.
□ **se ~** *vpr* break.

ronce /Rɔ̃s/ *nf* bramble.

rond, ~e /Rɔ̃, -d/ *a* round; (gras)
plump; (ivre Ⅱ) drunk. ● *nm*

R

(cercle) ring; (tranche) slice; **en ~** in a circle; **il n'a pas un ~** 🔲 he hasn't got a penny.

ronde /Rɔ̃d/ nf (de policier) beat; (de soldat, gardien) watch; (Mus) semibreve.

rondelle /Rɔ̃dɛl/ nf (Tech) washer; (tranche) slice.

rondement /Rɔ̃dmɑ̃/ adv promptly; (franchement) frankly.

rondeur /Rɔ̃dœR/ nf roundness; (franchise) frankness; (embonpoint) plumpness.

rondin /Rɔ̃dɛ̃/ nm log.

rond-point (pl **ronds-points**) /Rɔ̃pwɛ̃/ nm roundabout; (US) traffic circle.

ronfler /Rɔ̃fle/ [1] vi snore; (moteur) purr.

ronger /Rɔ̃ʒe/ [40] vt gnaw (at); (vers, acide) eat into. □ **se ~** vpr **se ~ les ongles** bite one's nails.

rongeur /Rɔ̃ʒœR/ nm rodent.

ronronner /Rɔ̃Rɔne/ [1] vi purr.

rosbif /Rɔsbif/ nm roast beef.

rose /Roz/ nf rose. ● a & nm pink.

rosé, **~e** /Roze/ a pinkish. ● nm rosé.

roseau (pl **~x**) /Rozo/ nm reed.

rosée /Roze/ nf dew.

rosier /Rozje/ nm rose bush.

rossignol /Rɔsiɲɔl/ nm nightingale.

rotatif, **-ive** /Rɔtatif, -v/ a rotary.

roter /Rɔte/ [1] vi 🔲 burp.

rôti /Roti/ nm joint; (cuit) roast; **~ de porc** roast pork.

rotin /Rɔtɛ̃/ nm (rattan) cane.

rôtir /RotiR/ [2] vt roast.

rôtissoire /RotiswaR/ nf roasting spit.

rotule /Rɔtyl/ nf kneecap.

rouage /Rwaʒ/ nm (Tech) wheel; **les ~s** the works; (d'une organisation: fig) wheels.

roucouler /Rukule/ [1] vi coo.

roue /Ru/ nf wheel; **~ dentée** cog(wheel); **~ de secours** spare wheel.

rouer /Rwe/ [1] vt **~ de coups** thrash.

rouge /Ruʒ/ a red; (fer) red-hot. ● nm red; (vin) red wine; (fard) blusher; **~ à lèvres** lipstick. ● nmf (Pol) red. **rouge-gorge** (pl **rouges-gorges**) nm robin.

rougeole /Ruʒɔl/ nf measles (+ sg).

rouget /Ruʒɛ/ nm red mullet.

rougeur /RuʒœR/ nf redness; (tache) red blotch.

rougir /RuʒiR/ [2] vi turn red; (de honte) blush.

rouille /Ruj/ nf rust. **rouillé**, **~e** a rusty.

rouiller /Ruje/ [1] vi rust. □ **se ~** vpr get rusty.

rouleau (pl **~x**) /Rulo/ nm roll; (outil, vague) roller; **~ à pâtisserie** rolling pin; **~ compresseur** steamroller.

roulement /Rulmɑ̃/ nm rotation; (bruit) rumble; (alternance) rotation; (de tambour) roll; **~ à billes** ball-bearing; **travailler par ~** work in shifts.

rouler /Rule/ [1] vt roll; (ficelle, manches) roll up; (pâte) roll out; (duper 🔲) cheat. ● vi (véhicule, train) go, travel; (conducteur) drive. □ **se ~ dans** vpr roll in; (couverture) roll oneself up in.

roulette /Rulɛt/ nf (de meuble) castor; (de dentiste) drill; (jeu) roulette; **comme sur des ~s** very smoothly.

roulotte /Rulɔt/ nf caravan.

roumain, **~e** /Rumɛ̃, -ɛn/ a Romanian. **R~**, **~e** nm, f Romanian.

Roumanie /Rumani/ nf Romania.

rouquin, **~e** /Rukɛ̃, -in/ 🔲 a red-haired. ● nm, f redhead.

rouspéter /ʀuspete/ [14] vi 🔲 grumble, moan.

rousse /ʀus/ ⇒ROUX.

roussir /ʀusiʀ/ [2] vt scorch. ● vi turn brown.

route /ʀut/ nf road; (Naut, Aviat) route; (direction) way; (voyage) journey; (chemin: fig) path; **en ∼** on the way; **en ∼!** let's go!; **mettre en ∼** start; **∼ nationale** trunk road, main road; **se mettre en ∼** set out.

routier, -ière /ʀutje, -jɛʀ/ a road. ● nm long-distance lorry ou truck driver; (restaurant) transport café; (US) truck stop.

routine /ʀutin/ nf routine.

roux, rousse /ʀu, ʀus/ a red, russet; (personne) red-haired; (chat) ginger. ● nm, f redhead.

royal, ∼e (mpl -aux) /ʀwajal, -jo/ a royal; (cadeau) fit for a king.

royaume /ʀwajom/ nm kingdom.

Royaume-Uni /ʀwajomyni/ nm United Kingdom.

royauté /ʀwajote/ nf royalty.

RTT abrév f (**réduction du temps de travail**) reduction in working hours.

ruban /ʀybɑ̃/ nm ribbon; (de chapeau) band; **∼ adhésif** sticky tape; **∼ magnétique** magnetic tape.

rubéole /ʀybeɔl/ nf German measles (+ sg).

rubis /ʀybi/ nm ruby.

rubrique /ʀybʀik/ nf heading; (article) column.

ruche /ʀyʃ/ nf beehive.

rude /ʀyd/ a (au toucher) rough; (pénible) tough; (grossier) coarse; (fameux 🔲) tremendous.

rudement /ʀydmɑ̃/ adv (frapper) hard; (traiter) harshly; (très 🔲) really.

rudimentaire /ʀydimɑ̃tɛʀ/ a rudimentary.

rue /ʀy/ nf street.

ruée /ʀɥe/ nf rush.

ruer /ʀɥe/ [1] vi (cheval) buck. □ **se ∼** vpr rush (**dans** into; **vers** towards); **se ∼ sur** pounce on.

rugby /ʀygbi/ nm rugby.

rugir /ʀyʒiʀ/ [2] vi roar.

rugueux, -euse /ʀygø, -z/ a rough.

ruine /ʀɥin/ nf ruin; **en ∼(s)** in ruins. **∼ ruiner** vt ruin.

ruisseau (pl ∼x) /ʀɥiso/ nm stream; (rigole) gutter.

rumeur /ʀymœʀ/ nf (nouvelle) rumour; (son) murmur, hum.

ruminer /ʀymine/ [1] vi (animal) ruminate; (méditer) meditate.

rupture /ʀyptyʀ/ nf break; (action) breaking; (de contrat) breach; (de pourparlers) breakdown; (de relations) breaking off; (de couple, coalition) break-up.

rural, ∼e (mpl -aux) /ʀyʀal, -o/ a rural.

ruse /ʀyz/ nf cunning; **une ∼** a trick, a ruse. **rusé, ∼e** a cunning.

russe /ʀys/ a Russian. ● nm (Ling) Russian. **R∼** nmf Russian.

Russie /ʀysi/ nf Russia.

rustique /ʀystik/ a rustic.

rythme /ʀitm/ nm rhythm; (vitesse) rate; (de la vie) pace.

rythmique a rhythmical.

s' /s/ ⇒SE.

sa /sa/ ⇒SON¹.

SA abrév f (**société anonyme**) PLC.

sabbatique /sabatik/ a (année) sabbatical year.

sable /sɑbl/ nm sand; **∼s**

mouvants quicksands. **sabler** *vt* [1] grit.

sablier /sablije/ *nm* (Culin) eggtimer.

sablonneux, -euse /sablɔnø, -z/ *a* sandy.

sabot /sabo/ *nm* (de cheval) hoof; (chaussure) clog; (de frein) shoe; ∼ **de Denver®** (wheel) clamp.

saboter /sabɔte/ [1] *vt* sabotage; (bâcler) botch.

sac /sak/ *nm* bag; (grand, en toile) sack; **mettre à** ∼ (*maison*) ransack; (*ville*) sack; ∼ **à dos** rucksack; ∼ **à main** handbag; ∼ **de couchage** sleeping-bag; **mettre dans le même** ∼ lump together.

saccadé, ∼**e** /sakade/ *a* jerky.

saccager /sakaʒe/ [40] *vt* (abîmer) wreck; (*maison*) ransack; (*ville, pays*) sack.

saccharine /sakaʀin/ *nf* saccharin.

sachet /saʃɛ/ *nm* (small) bag; (d'aromates) sachet; ∼ **de thé** tea-bag.

sacoche /sakɔʃ/ *nf* bag; (de vélo) saddlebag.

sacre /sakʀ/ *nm* (de roi) coronation; (d'évêque) consecration. **sacré,** ∼**e** *a* sacred; (maudit 🄸) damned.

sacrement *nm* sacrament. **sacrer** [1] *vt* crown; consecrate.

sacrifice /sakʀifis/ *nm* sacrifice.

sacrifier /sakʀifje/ [45] *vt* sacrifice; ∼ **à** conform to. □ **se** ∼ *vpr* sacrifice oneself.

sacrilège /sakʀilɛʒ/ *nm* sacrilege. ● *a* sacrilegious.

sadique /sadik/ *a* sadistic. ● *nmf* sadist.

sage /saʒ/ *a* wise; (docile) good, well behaved. ● *nm* wise man.

sage-femme (*pl* **sages-femmes**) /saʒfam/ *nf* midwife.

sagesse /saʒɛs/ *nf* wisdom.

Sagittaire /saʒitɛʀ/ *nm* **le** ∼ Sagittarius.

saignant, ∼**e** /sɛɲã, -t/ *a* (Culin) rare.

saigner /seɲe/ [1] *vt/i* bleed; ∼ **du nez** have a nosebleed.

saillant, ∼**e** /sajã, -t/ *a* prominent.

sain, ∼**e** /sɛ̃, sɛn/ *a* healthy; (*moralement*) sane; ∼ **et sauf** safe and sound.

saindoux /sɛ̃du/ *nm* lard.

saint, ∼**e** /sɛ̃, -t/ *a* holy; (bon, juste) saintly. ● *nm, f* saint. **Saint-Esprit** *nm* Holy Spirit. **sainteté** *nf* holiness; (d'un lieu) sanctity. **Sainte Vierge** *nf* Blessed Virgin. **Saint-Sylvestre** *nf* New Year's Eve.

sais /sɛ/ ⇒SAVOIR [55].

saisie /sezi/ *nf* (Jur) seizure; (Comput) keyboarding; ∼ **de données** data capture.

saisir /seziʀ/ [2] *vt* grab (hold of); (*proie*) seize; (*occasion, biens*) seize; (comprendre) grasp; (frapper) strike; (Ordinat) keyboard, capture; **saisi de** (*peur*) stricken by, overcome by. □ **se** ∼ **de** *vpr* seize. **saisissant,** ∼**e** *a* (*spectacle*) gripping.

saison /sɛzɔ̃/ *nf* season; **la morte** ∼ the off season. **saisonnier, -ière** *a* seasonal.

sait /sɛ/ ⇒SAVOIR [55].

salade /salad/ *nf* (plat) salad; (plante) lettuce. **saladier** *nm* salad bowl.

salaire /salɛʀ/ *nm* wages (+ *pl*), salary.

salarié, ∼**e** /salaʀje/ *a* wage-earning. ● *nm, f* wage earner.

sale /sal/ *a* dirty; (mauvais) nasty.

salé, ∼**e** /sale/ *a* (*goût*) salty; (plat) salted; (opposé à sucré) savoury; (grivois 🄸) spicy; (excessif 🄸) steep. **saler** [1] *vt* salt.

saleté /salte/ *nf* dirtiness; (crasse)

dirt; (obscénité) obscenity; ~(s) (camelote) rubbish; (détritus) mess.

salir /saliʀ/ [2] vt (make) dirty; (réputation) tarnish. □ se ~ vpr get dirty. **salissant**, ~e a dirty; (étoffe) easily dirtied.

salive /saliv/ nf saliva.

salle /sal/ nf room; (grande, publique) hall; (de restaurant) dining room; (Théât, cinéma) auditorium; **cinéma à trois ~s** three-screen cinema; ~ **à manger** dining room; ~ **d'attente** waiting room; ~ **de bains** bathroom; ~ **de bavardage**, ~ **de causette** chatroom; ~ **de séjour** living room; ~ **de classe** classroom; ~ **d'embarquement** departure lounge; ~ **d'opération** operating theatre; ~ **des ventes** saleroom.

salon /salɔ̃/ nm lounge; (de coiffure, beauté) salon; (exposition) show; ~ **de thé** tea-room; ~ **virtuel** chatroom.

salopette /salɔpɛt/ nf dungarees (+ pl); (d'ouvrier) overalls (+ pl).

saltimbanque /saltɛ̃bɑ̃k/ nmf (street) acrobat.

salubre /salybʀ/ a healthy.

saluer /salɥe/ [1] vt greet; (en partant) take one's leave of; (de la tête) nod to; (de la main) wave to; (Mil) salute; (accueillir favorablement) welcome.

salut /saly/ nm greeting; (de la tête) nod; (de la main) wave; (Mil) salute; (rachat) salvation. ● interj (bonjour ▯) hello; (au revoir ▯) bye.

salutation /salytasjɔ̃/ nf greeting.

samedi /samdi/ nm Saturday.

SAMU /samy/ abrév m (**Service d'assistance médicale d'urgence**) ≈ mobile accident unit.

sanction /sɑ̃ksjɔ̃/ nf sanction. **sanctionner** [1] vt sanction; (punir) punish.

sandale /sɑ̃dal/ nf sandal.

sang /sɑ̃/ nm blood; **se faire du mauvais** ~ ou **un** ~ **d'encre** be worried stiff. **sang-froid** nm inv self-control. **sanglant**, ~e a bloody.

sangle /sɑ̃gl/ nf strap.

sanglier /sɑ̃glije/ nm wild boar.

sanglot /sɑ̃glo/ nm sob. **sangloter** [1] vi sob.

sanguin, ~e /sɑ̃gɛ̃, -in/ a (groupe) blood.

sanguinaire /sɑ̃ginɛʀ/ a bloodthirsty.

sanitaire /sanitɛʀ/ a (directives) health; (conditions) sanitary; (appareils, installations) bathroom, sanitary. **sanitaires** nmpl bathroom.

sans /sɑ̃/ prép without; ~ **ça**, ~ **quoi** otherwise; ~ **arrêt** nonstop; ~ **encombre/faute/tarder** without incident/fail/delay; ~ **fin/goût/limite** endless/tasteless/limitless; ~ **importance/pareil/précédent/travail** unimportant/unparalleled/unprecedented/unemployed; **j'ai aimé mais** ~ **plus** it was good, it wasn't great.

sans-abri /sɑ̃zabʀi/ nmf inv homeless person.

sans-gêne /sɑ̃ʒɛn/ a inv inconsiderate, thoughtless. ● nm inv thoughtlessness.

sans-papiers /sɑ̃papje/ nm inv illegal immigrant.

santé /sɑ̃te/ nf health; **à ta** ou **votre** ~! cheers!

saoul, ~e /su, sul/ ⇒SOÛL.

sapin /sapɛ̃/ nm fir(tree); ~ **de Noël** Christmas tree.

sarcasme /saʀkasm/ nm sarcasm. **sarcastique** a sarcastic.

sardine /saʀdin/ nf sardine.

sas /sɑs/ nm (Naut, Aviat) airlock.

satané, ~e /satane/ a ▯ damned.

satellite /satelit/ nm satellite.

S

satin /satɛ̃/ nm satin.

satire /satiʀ/ nf satire.

satisfaction /satisfaksjɔ̃/ nf satisfaction.

satisfaire /satisfɛʀ/ [33] vt satisfy. ● vi ~ à fulfil. **satisfaisant**, ~e a (acceptable) satisfactory. **satisfait**, ~e a satisfied (**de** with).

saturer /satyʀe/ [1] vt saturate.

sauce /sos/ nf sauce; ~ **tartare** tartar sauce. **saucière** nf sauceboat.

saucisse /sosis/ nf sausage.

saucisson /sosisɔ̃/ nm (slicing) sausage.

sauf[1] /sof/ prép except; ~ **erreur** if I'm not mistaken; ~ **imprévu** unless anything unforeseen happens; ~ **avis contraire** unless otherwise stated.

sauf[2], **-ve** /sof, sov/ a safe, unharmed.

sauge /soʒ/ nf (Culin) sage.

saule /sol/ nm willow; ~ **pleureur** weeping willow.

saumon /somɔ̃/ nm salmon. ● a inv salmon-(pink).

sauna /sona/ nm sauna.

saupoudrer /supudʀe/ [1] vt sprinkle (**de** with).

saut /so/ nm jump; **faire un** ~ **chez qn** pop round to sb's (place); **le** ~ (Sport) jumping; ~ **en hauteur/longueur** high/long jump; ~ **périlleux** somersault; **au** ~ **du lit** on getting up.

sauté, ~e /sote/ a & nm (Culin) sauté.

saute-mouton /sotmutɔ̃/ nm inv leap-frog.

sauter /sote/ [1] vi jump; (exploser) blow up; (fusible) blow; (se détacher) come off; **faire** ~ (détruire) blow up; (fusible) blow; (casser) break; ~ **à la corde** skip; ~ **aux yeux** be obvious; ~ **au cou de qn** fling one's arms round sb; ~ **sur**

une occasion jump at an opportunity. ● vt jump (over); (page, classe) skip.

sauterelle /sotʀɛl/ nf grasshopper.

sautiller /sotije/ [1] vi hop.

sauvage /sovaʒ/ a wild; (primitif, cruel) savage; (farouche) unsociable; (illégal) unauthorized. ● nmf unsociable person; (brute) savage.

sauve /sov/ ⇒SAUF[2].

sauvegarde /sovgaʀd/ [1] vt safeguard; (Ordinat) back up.

sauver /sove/ [1] vt save; (d'un danger) rescue, save; (matériel) salvage. □ **se** ~ vpr (fuir) run away; (partir 🄸) be off. **sauvetage** nm rescue. **sauveteur** nm rescuer. **sauveur** nm saviour.

savant, ~e /savã, -t/ a learned; (habile) skilful. ● nm scientist.

saveur /savœʀ/ nf flavour; (fig) savour.

savoir /savwaʀ/ [55] vt know; **elle sait conduire/nager** she can drive/ swim; **faire** ~ **à qn que** inform sb that; (**pas**) **que je sache** (not) as far as I know; **à** ~ namely. ● nm learning.

savon /savɔ̃/ nm soap; **passer un** ~ **à qn** 🄸 give sb a telling-off. **savonnette** nf bar of soap.

savourer /savuʀe/ [1] vt savour. **savoureux**, **-euse** a tasty; (fig) spicy.

scandale /skãdal/ nm scandal; (tapage) uproar; (en public) noisy scene; **faire** ~ shock people; **faire un** ~ make a scene. **scandaleux**, **-euse** a scandalous. **scandaliser** [1] vt scandalize, shock.

scander /skãde/ [1] vt (vers) scan; (slogan) chant.

scandinave /skãdinav/ a Scandinavian. **S**~ nmf Scandinavian.

Scandinavie /skɑ̃dinavi/ nf
Scandinavia.

scarabée /skaʀabe/ nm beetle.

sceau (pl ∼x) /so/ nm seal.

scélérat /selera/ nm scoundrel.

sceller /sele/ [1] vt seal.

scène /sɛn/ nf scene; (estrade, art
dramatique) stage; **mettre en** ∼
(pièce) stage; (film) direct; **mise
en** ∼ direction; ∼ **de ménage**
domestic dispute.

scepticisme /sɛptisism/ nm
scepticism.

sceptique /sɛptik/ a sceptical.
● nmf sceptic.

schéma /ʃema/ nm diagram.
schématique a schematic;
(sommaire) sketchy. **schématiser**
[1] vt simplify.

schizophrène /skizɔfʀɛn/ a &
nmf schizophrenic.

sciatique /sjatik/ a (nerf)
sciatic. ● nf sciatica.

scie /si/ nf saw.

sciemment /sjamɑ̃/ adv
knowingly.

science /sjɑ̃s/ nf science; (savoir)
knowledge.

science-fiction /sjɑ̃sfiksjɔ̃/ nf
science fiction.

scientifique /sjɑ̃tifik/ a
scientific. ● nmf scientist.

scier /sje/ [45] vt saw.

scintiller /sɛ̃tije/ [1] vi glitter;
(étoile) twinkle.

scission /sisjɔ̃/ nf split.

sclérose /skleʀoz/ nf sclerosis;
∼ **en plaques** multiple sclerosis.

scolaire /skɔlɛʀ/ a school.
scolarisé, ∼**e** a going to school.
scolarité nf schooling.

score /skɔʀ/ nm score.

scorpion /skɔʀpjɔ̃/ nm scorpion;
le S∼ Scorpio.

scotch /skɔtʃ/ nm (boisson) Scotch
(whisky); (ruban adhésif)®
Sellotape®.

scout, ∼**e** /skut/ nm & a scout.

scrupule /skʀypyl/ nm scruple.
scrupuleux, -**euse** a scrupulous.

scruter /skʀyte/ [1] vt examine,
scrutinize.

scrutin /skʀytɛ̃/ nm (vote) ballot;
(élections) polls (+ pl).

sculpter /skylte/ [1] vt sculpt,
carve. **sculpteur** nm sculptor.
sculpture nf sculpture.

SDF abrév mf (**sans domicile
fixe**) homeless person.

∙∙∙∙∙∙∙∙∙∙∙∙∙∙∙∙∙∙∙∙∙∙∙∙∙∙∙∙∙∙∙∙∙∙∙

se, s' /sə, s/

s' before vowel or mute h.

● pronom
∙∙∙➤ himself, (féminin) herself;
(indéfini) oneself; (non humain) itself;
(au pluriel) themselves; ∼ **laver les
mains** wash one's hands;
(réciproque) each other, one
another; **ils se détestent** they
hate each other.

❗ The translation of se will
vary according to which
verb it is associated with.
You should therefore refer
to the verb to find it. For
example, **se promener, se
taire** will be treated
respectively under **promener**
and **taire**.

∙∙∙∙∙∙∙∙∙∙∙∙∙∙∙∙∙∙∙∙∙∙∙∙∙∙∙∙∙∙∙∙∙∙∙

séance /seɑ̃s/ nf session; (Théât,
cinéma) show; ∼ **de pose** sitting; ∼
tenante forthwith.

seau (pl ∼x) /so/ nm bucket,
pail.

sec, sèche /sɛk, sɛʃ/ a dry;
(fruits) dried; (coup, bruit) sharp;
(cœur) hard; (whisky) neat. ● nm
à ∼ (sans eau) dry; (sans argent)
broke; **au** ∼ in a dry place.

sèche-cheveux /sɛʃʃəvø/ nm
inv hairdrier.

sèchement /sɛʃmɑ̃/ adv drily.

sécher /seʃe/ [14] vt/i dry;
(cours: 🄸) skip; (ne pas savoir 🄸) be

S

stumped. □ **se ~** *vpr* dry oneself.
sécheresse /seʃʀɛs/ *nf* (de climat) dryness;
(temps sec) drought. **séchoir** *nm*
drier.

second, ~e /səɡɔ̃, -d/ *a & nm,f*
second. ● *nm* (adjoint) second in
command; (étage) second floor.
secondaire *a* secondary.
seconde *nf* (instant) second;
(vitesse) second gear.

seconder /səɡɔ̃de/ [1] *vt* assist.

secouer /səkwe/ [1] *vt* shake;
(*poussière, torpeur*) shake off.
□ **se ~** *vpr* ▣ (se dépêcher) get a
move on; (réagir) shake oneself
up.

secourir /səkuʀiʀ/ [20] *vt* assist,
help. **secouriste** *nmf* first-aid
worker.

secours /səkuʀ/ *nm* assistance,
help; **au ~!** help!; **de ~** (*sortie*)
emergency; (*équipe, opération*)
rescue. ● *nmpl* (Méd) first aid.

secousse /səkus/ *nf* jolt, jerk;
(séisme) tremor.

secret, -ète /səkʀɛ, -t/ *a* secret.
● *nm* secret; (discrétion) secrecy; **le
~ professionnel** professional
confidentiality; **~ de Polichinelle**
open secret; **en ~** in secret,
secretly.

secrétaire /səkʀetɛʀ/ *nmf*
secretary; **~ de direction** personal
assistant. ● *nm* (meuble) writing-
desk; **~ d'État** junior minister.

secrétariat /səkʀetaʀja/ *nm*
secretarial work; (bureau)
secretariat.

sectaire /sɛktɛʀ/ *a* sectarian.

secte /sɛkt/ *nf* sect.

secteur /sɛktœʀ/ *nm* area;
(Comm) sector; (circuit: Électr) mains
(+ *pl*).

section /sɛksjɔ̃/ *nf* section; (Scol)
stream; (Mil) platoon. **sectionner**
[1] *vt* sever.

sécuriser /sekyʀize/ [1] *vt*
reassure.

sécurité /sekyʀite/ *nf* security;
(absence de danger) safety; **en ~**
safe, secure. **Sécurité sociale** *nf*
social services, social security
services.

sédatif /sedatif/ *nm* sedative.

sédentaire /sedɑ̃tɛʀ/ *a*
sedentary.

séducteur, -trice /sedyktœʀ,
-tʀis/ *a* seductive. ● *nm, f*
seducer. **séduction** *nf* seduction;
(charme) charm.

séduire /seduiʀ/ [17] *vt* charm;
(plaire à) appeal to; (sexuellement)
seduce. **séduisant, ~e** *a*
attractive.

ségrégation /seɡʀeɡasjɔ̃/ *nf*
segregation.

seigle /sɛɡl/ *nm* rye.

seigneur /sɛɲœʀ/ *nm* lord; **le S~**
the Lord.

sein /sɛ̃/ *nm* breast; **au ~ de**
within.

séisme /seism/ *nm* earthquake.

seize /sɛz/ *a & nm* sixteen.

séjour /seʒuʀ/ *nm* stay; (pièce)
living room. **séjourner** [1] *vi*
stay.

sel /sɛl/ *nm* salt; (piquant) spice.

sélectif, -ive /selɛktif, -v/ *a*
selective.

sélection /selɛksjɔ̃/ *nf* selection.
sélectionner [1] *vt* select.

selle /sɛl/ *nf* saddle; **~s** (Méd)
stools.

sellette /sɛlɛt/ *nf* **sur la ~**
(*personne*) in the hot seat.

selon /səlɔ̃/ *prép* according to; **~
que** depending on whether.

semaine /səmɛn/ *nf* week; **en ~**
during the week.

sémantique /semɑ̃tik/ *a*
semantic. ● *nf* semantics.

semblable /sɑ̃blabl/ *a* similar (à
to). ● *nm* fellow (creature).

semblant /sɑ̃blɑ̃/ *nm* **faire ~ de**

pretend to; **un ~ de** a semblance of.

sembler /sɑ̃ble/ [1] *vi* seem (à to; que that); **il me semble que** it seems to me that.

semelle /səmɛl/ *nf* sole; **~ compensée** wedge heel.

semence /s(ə)mɑ̃s/ *nf* seed.

semer /s(ə)me/ [6] *vt* (*graine, doute*) sow; (*jeter, parsemer*) strew; (*personne* 🄸) lose; **~ la panique** spread panic.

semestre /səmɛstʁ/ *nm* half-year; (Univ) semester. **semestriel, ~le** *a* (*revue*) biannual; (*examen*) end-of-semester.

séminaire /seminɛʁ/ *nm* (Relig) seminary; (Univ) seminar.

semi-remorque /s(ə)miʁ(ə) mɔʁk/ *nm* articulated lorry.

semis /s(ə)mi/ *nm* (plant) seedling.

semoule /s(ə)mul/ *nf* semolina.

sénat /sena/ *nm* senate. **sénateur** *nm* senator.

sénile /senil/ *a* senile.

senior /senjɔʁ/ *a* (âgé) senior; (*mode, publication*) for senior citizens. ● *nmf* senior citizen.

sens /sɑ̃s/ *nm* (Méd) sense, (signification) meaning, sense; (direction) direction. **à mon ~** to my mind; **à ~ unique** (*rue*) one-way; **ça n'a pas de ~** it doesn't make sense; **~ commun** common sense; **~ giratoire** roundabout; **~ interdit** no-entry sign; (rue) one-way street; **dans le ~ des aiguilles d'une montre** clockwise; **dans le ~ inverse des aiguilles d'une montre** anticlockwise; **~ dessus dessous** upside down; **~ devant derrière** back to front.

sensation /sɑ̃sasjɔ̃/ *nf* feeling, sensation; **faire ~** create a sensation. **sensationnel, ~le** *a* sensational.

sensé, ~e /sɑ̃se/ *a* sensible.

sensibiliser /sɑ̃sibilize/ [1] *vt* **~ l'opinion** increase people's awareness (**à qch** to sth).

sensibilité /sɑ̃sibilite/ *nf* sensitivity. **sensible** *a* sensitive (à to); (appréciable) noticeable. **sensiblement** *adv* noticeably.

sensoriel, ~le /sɑ̃sɔʁjɛl/ *a* sensory.

sensualité /sɑ̃sɥalite/ *nf* sensuousness; sensuality. **sensuel, ~le** *a* sensual.

sentence /sɑ̃tɑ̃s/ *nf* sentence.

senteur /sɑ̃tœʁ/ *nf* scent.

sentier /sɑ̃tje/ *nm* path.

sentiment /sɑ̃timɑ̃/ *nm* feeling; **faire du ~** sentimentalize; **j'ai le ~ que...** I get the feeling that... **sentimental, ~e** (*mpl* -aux) *a* sentimental.

sentir /sɑ̃tiʁ/ [46] *vt* feel; (*odeur*) smell; (pressentir) sense; **~ la lavande** smell of lavender; **je ne peux pas le ~** 🄸 I can't stand him. ● *vi* smell. □ **se ~** *vpr* **se ~ fier/mieux** feel proud/better.

séparation /sepaʁasjɔ̃/ *nf* separation.

séparatiste /sepaʁatist/ *a & nmf* separatist.

séparé, ~e /sepaʁe/ *a* separate; (*conjoints*) separated.

séparer /sepaʁe/ [1] *vt* separate; (en deux) split. □ **se ~** *vpr* separate, part (**de** from); (se détacher) split; **se ~ de** (se défaire de) part with.

sept /sɛt/ *a & nm* seven.

septante /sɛptɑ̃t/ *a & nm* seventy.

septembre /sɛptɑ̃bʁ/ *nm* September.

septentrional, ~e (*mpl* -aux) /sɛptɑ̃tʁijɔnal, -o/ *a* northern.

septième /sɛtjɛm/ *a & nmf* seventh.

sépulture /sepyltyʁ/ *nf* burial; (lieu) burial place.

séquelles /sekɛl/ *nfpl* (maladie) aftereffects; (fig) aftermath (+ *sg*).

S

séquence /sekɑ̃s/ *nf* sequence.

séquestrer /sekɛstʀe/ [1] *vt* confine (illegally).

sera, serait /səʀa, səʀɛ/ ⇒ÊTRE [4].

serbe /sɛʀb/ *a* Serbian. **S~** *nmf* Serbian.

Serbie /sɛʀbi/ *nf* Serbia.

serein, ~e /səʀɛ̃, -ɛn/ *a* serene.

sérénité /seʀenite/ *nf* serenity.

sergent /sɛʀʒɑ̃/ *nm* sergeant.

série /seʀi/ *nf* series (+ *sg*); (d'objets) set; **de ~** (*véhicule etc.*) standard; **fabrication** *ou* **production en ~** mass production.

sérieusement /seʀjøzmɑ̃/ *adv* seriously.

sérieux, -ieuse /seʀjø, -z/ *a* serious; (*digne de confiance*) reliable; (*chances, raison*) good. ●*nm* seriousness; **garder son ~** keep a straight face; **prendre au ~** take seriously.

serin /səʀɛ̃/ *nm* canary.

seringue /səʀɛ̃g/ *nf* syringe.

serment /sɛʀmɑ̃/ *nm* oath; (promesse) vow.

sermon /sɛʀmɔ̃/ *nm* sermon. **sermonner** [1] *vt* lecture.

séropositif, -ive /seʀopozitif, -v/ *a* HIV positive.

serpent /sɛʀpɑ̃/ *nm* snake; **~ à sonnettes** rattlesnake.

serpillière /sɛʀpijɛʀ/ *nf* floorcloth.

serre /sɛʀ/ *nf* (de jardin) greenhouse; (griffe) claw.

serré, ~e /seʀe/ *a* (habit, nœud, écrou) tight; (personnes) packed, crowded; (lutte, mailles) close; (écriture) cramped; (cœur) heavy.

serrer /seʀe/ [1] *vt* (saisir) grip; (presser) squeeze; (vis, corde, ceinture) tighten; (poing, dents) clench; **~ qn dans ses bras** hug sb; **~ les rangs** close ranks; **~ qn** (vêtement) be tight on sb; **~ qn de près** follow sb closely; **~ la main à**

shake hands with. ●*vi* **~ à droite** keep over to the right. □ **se ~** *vpr* (se rapprocher) squeeze (up).

serrure /seʀyʀ/ *nf* lock. **serrurier** *nm* locksmith.

servante /sɛʀvɑ̃t/ *nf* (maid) servant.

serveur, -euse /sɛʀvœʀ, -øz/ *nm, f* (homme) waiter; (femme) waitress. ●*nm* (Ordinat) server.

serviable /sɛʀvjabl/ *a* helpful.

service /sɛʀvis/ *nm* service; (fonction, temps de travail) duty; (pourboire) service (charge); (dans une société) department; **~ (non) compris** service (not) included; **être de ~** be on duty; **pendant le ~** (when) on duty; **rendre ~ à qn** be a help to sb; **~ à thé** tea set; **~ d'ordre** stewards (+ *pl*); **~ après-vente** after-sales service; **~ militaire** military service; **les ~s secrets** the secret service (+ *sg*).

serviette /sɛʀvjɛt/ *nf* (de toilette) towel; (cartable) briefcase; **~ (de table)** serviette, napkin; **~ hygiénique** sanitary towel.

servir /sɛʀviʀ/ [46] *vt/i* serve; (être utile) be of use, serve; **~ qn (à table)** wait on sb; **ça sert à** (outil, récipient) it is used for; **ça me sert à/de** I use it to/as; **ça ne sert à rien** (action) it's pointless; **~ de** serve as, be used as; **~ à qn de guide** act as a guide for sb. □ **se ~** *vpr* (à table) help oneself (de to); **se ~ de** use. **serviteur** *nm* servant.

ses /se/ ⇒SON¹.

session /sesjɔ̃/ *nf* session.

seuil /sœj/ *nm* doorstep; (entrée) doorway; (fig) threshold.

seul, ~e /sœl/ *a* alone, on one's own; (unique) only; **un ~ exemple** only one example; **pas un ~ ami** not a single friend; **lui ~ le sait** only he knows; **dans le ~ but de** with the sole aim of; **parler tout ~**

talk to oneself; **faire qch tout ~** do sth on one's own. ●*nm, f* **le ~, la ~e** the only one. **seulement** *adv* only.

sève /sɛv/ *nf* sap.

sévère /sevɛʁ/ *a* severe. **sévérité** *nf* severity.

sévices /sevis/ *nmpl* physical abuse (+ *sg*).

sévir /seviʁ/ [2] *vi* (*fléau*) rage; **~ contre** punish.

sevrer /səvʁe/ [6] *vt* wean.

sexe /sɛks/ *nm* sex; (*organes*) genitals (+ *pl*). **sexiste** *a* sexist. **sexualité** *nf* sexuality. **sexuel, ~le** *a* sexual.

shampooing /ʃɑ̃pwɛ̃/ *nm* shampoo.

shérif /ʃeʁif/ *nm* sheriff.

short /ʃɔʁt/ *nm* shorts (+ *pl*).

si (**s'** before **il, ils**) /si, s/ *conj* if; (*interrogation indirecte*) if, whether; **~ on allait se promener?** what about a walk?, s'il vous **ou** te plaît please; **~ oui** if so; **~ seulement** if only. ●*adv* (*tellement*) so; (*oui*) yes; **un ~ bon repas** such a good meal; **~ habile qu'il soit** however skilful he may be, **~ bien que** with the result that.

sida /sida/ *nm* (Méd) Aids.

sidérurgie /sideʁyʁʒi/ *nf* steel industry.

siècle /sjɛkl/ *nm* century; (*époque*) age.

siège /sjɛʒ/ *nm* seat; (Mil) siege; **~ éjectable** ejector seat; **~ social** head office, headquarters (+ *pl*). **siéger** [14] [40] *vi* (*assemblée*) sit.

sien, ~ne /sjɛ̃, -ɛn/ *pron* **le ~, la ~ne, les ~(ne)s** (homme) his; (femme) hers; (chose) its; **les ~s** (famille) one's family.

sieste /sjɛst/ *nf* nap, siesta.

sifflement /sifləmɑ̃/ *nm* whistling; **un ~** a whistle.

siffler /sifle/ [1] *vi* whistle; (avec un sifflet) blow one's whistle;

(*serpent, gaz*) hiss. ●*vt* (*air*) whistle; (*chien*) whistle to **ou** for; (*acteur*) hiss.

sifflet /siflɛ/ *nm* whistle; **~s** (huées) boos.

sigle /sigl/ *nm* acronym.

signal (*pl* **-aux**) /siɲal, -o/ *nm* signal; **~ sonore** (de répondeur) tone.

signalement /siɲalmɑ̃/ *nm* description.

signaler /siɲale/ [1] *vt* indicate; (par une sonnerie, un écriteau) signal; (dénoncer, mentionner) report; (faire remarquer) point out.

signalisation /siɲalizasjɔ̃/ *nf* signalling, signposting; (signaux) signals (+ *pl*).

signataire /siɲatɛʁ/ *nmf* signatory.

signature /siɲatyʁ/ *nf* signature; (action) signing; **~ électronique** digital signature.

signe /siɲ/ *nm* sign; (de ponctuation) mark; **faire ~ à qn** wave at sb; (contacter) contact; **faire ~ à qn de** beckon sb to; **faire ~ que non** shake one's head; **faire ~ que oui** nod.

signer /siɲe/ [1] *vt* sign. □ **se ~** *vpr* (Relig) cross oneself.

signet /siɲɛ/ *nm* (pour livre, Internet) bookmark; **~s favoris** (Internet) hotlist.

significatif, -ive /siɲifikatif, -v/ *a* significant.

signification /siɲifikasjɔ̃/ *nf* meaning. **signifier** [45] *vt* mean, signify; (faire connaître) make known (à to).

silence /silɑ̃s/ *nm* silence; (Mus) rest; **garder le ~** keep silent.

silencieux, -ieuse /silɑ̃sjø, -z/ *a* silent. ●*nm* silencer.

silex /silɛks/ *nm inv* flint.

silhouette /silwɛt/ *nf* outline, silhouette.

sillon /sijɔ̃/ *nm* furrow; (de disque) groove.

S

sillonner /sijɔne/ [1] vt crisscross.

similaire /similɛʀ/ a similar. **similitude** nf similarity.

simple /sɛ̃pl/ a simple; (non double) single. ● nm ~ **dames/messieurs** ladies'/men's singles (+ pl). **simple d'esprit** nmf simpleton. **simplement** adv simply. **simplicité** nf simplicity; (naïveté) simpleness.

simplification /sɛ̃plifikasjɔ̃/ nf simplification. **simplifier** [45] vt simplify.

simpliste /sɛ̃plist/ a simplistic.

simulacre /simylakʀ/ nm pretence, sham.

simulation /simylasjɔ̃/ nf simulation. **simuler** [1] vt simulate.

simultané, ~e /simyltane/ a simultaneous.

sincère /sɛ̃sɛʀ/ a sincere. **sincérité** nf sincerity.

singe /sɛ̃ʒ/ nm monkey; (grand) ape. **singer** [40] vt mimic, ape.

singulier, -ière /sɛ̃gylje, -jɛʀ/ a peculiar, remarkable; (Gram) singular. ● nm (Gram) singular.

sinistre /sinistʀ/ a sinister. ● nm disaster; (incendie) blaze; (dommages) damage.

sinistré, ~e /sinistʀe/ a stricken. ● nm, f disaster victim.

sinon /sinɔ̃/ conj (autrement) otherwise; (sauf) except (**que** that); **difficile** ~ **impossible** difficult if not impossible.

sinueux, -euse /sinɥø, -z/ a winding; (fig) tortuous.

sirène /siʀɛn/ nf (appareil) siren; (femme) mermaid.

sirop /siʀo/ nm (de fruits, Méd) syrup; (boisson) cordial.

sismique /sismik/ a seismic.

site /sit/ nm site; ~ **touristique** place of interest; ~ **Internet** or **Web** Web site.

sitôt /sito/ adv ~ **entré** immediately after coming in; ~ **que** as soon as; **pas de** ~ not for a while.

situation /sitɥasjɔ̃/ nf situation; (emploi) job, position; ~ **de famille** marital status.

situé, ~e /sitɥe/ a situated.

situer /sitɥe/ [1] vt situate, locate. □ **se** ~ vpr (se trouver) be situated.

six /sis/ (/si/ before consonant, /siz/ before vowel) a & nm six. **sixième** a & nmf sixth.

sketch (pl ~es) /skɛtʃ/ nm (Théât) sketch.

ski /ski/ nm (matériel) ski; (Sport) skiing; **faire du** ~ ski; ~ **de fond** cross-country skiing; ~ **nautique** water skiing. **skier** [45] vi ski.

slave /slav/ a Slav; (Ling) Slavonic.

slip /slip/ nm (d'homme) underpants (+ pl); (de femme) knickers (+ pl); ~ **de bain** (swimming) trunks (+ pl); (du bikini) bikini bottom.

slogan /slɔgã/ nm slogan.

Slovaquie /slɔvaki/ nf Slovakia.

Slovénie /slɔveni/ nf Slovenia.

smoking /smɔkiŋ/ nm dinner jacket.

SNCF abrév f (**Société nationale des Chemins de fer français**) *French national railway company.*

snob /snɔb/ nmf snob. ● a snobbish. **snobisme** nm snobbery.

sobre /sɔbʀ/ a sober.

social, ~e (mpl **-iaux**) /sɔsjal, -jo/ a social.

socialisme /sɔsjalism/ nm socialism. **socialiste** nmf & a socialist.

société /sɔsjete/ nf society; (entreprise) company; ~ **point com** dot-com.

socle /sɔkl/ nm (de colonne, statue) plinth; (de lampe) base.

socquette /sɔkɛt/ nf ankle sock.

soda /sɔda/ nm fizzy drink.

sœur /sœr/ nf sister.

soi /swa/ pron oneself; **derrière ~** behind one; **en ~** in itself; **aller de ~** be obvious.

soi-disant /swadizɑ̃/ a inv so-called. ● adv supposedly.

soie /swa/ nf silk.

soif /swaf/ nf thirst; **avoir ~** be thirsty; **donner ~** make one thirsty.

soigné, **~e** /swaɲe/ a (apparence) tidy, neat; (travail) carefully done.

soigner /swaɲe/ [1] vt (s'occuper de) look after, take care of; (tenue, style) take care over; (maladie) treat. □ **se ~** vpr look after oneself.

soigneusement /swaɲøzmɑ̃/ adv carefully. **soigneux**, **-euse** a careful (de about); (ordonné) tidy.

soi-même /swamɛm/ pron oneself.

soin /swɛ̃/ nm care; (ordre) tidiness; **~s** care; (Méd) treatment; **avec ~** carefully; **avoir ou prendre ~ de qn/de faire** take care of sb/to do; **premiers ~s** first aid (+ sg).

soir /swar/ nm evening; **à ce ~** see you tonight.

soirée /sware/ nf evening; (réception) party.

soit /swa/ conj (à savoir) that is to say; **~ ... ~** either … or. ● ⇒ÊTRE [4].

soixante /swasɑ̃t/ a & nm sixty. **soixante-dix** a & nm seventy.

soja /sɔʒa/ nm (graines) soya beans (+ pl); (plante) soya.

sol /sɔl/ nm ground; (de maison) floor; (terrain agricole) soil.

solaire /sɔlɛr/ a solar; (huile, filtre) sun.

soldat /sɔlda/ nm soldier.

solde¹ /sɔld/ nf (salaire) pay.

solde² /sɔld/ nm (Comm) balance; **les ~s** the sales; **~s** (écrit en vitrine) sale; **en ~** (acheter) at sale price.

solder /sɔlde/ [1] vt sell off at sale price; (compte) settle. □ **se ~ par** vpr (aboutir à) end in.

sole /sɔl/ nf (poisson) sole.

soleil /sɔlɛj/ nm sun; (fleur) sunflower; **il y a du ~** it's sunny.

solennel, **~le** /sɔlanɛl/ a solemn.

solfège /sɔlfɛʒ/ nm musical theory.

solidaire /sɔlidɛr/ a (mécanismes) interdependent; (collègues) (mutually) supportive; **être ~ de qn** support sb. **solidarité** nf solidarity.

solide /sɔlid/ a solid; (personne) strong. ● nm solid.

solidifier /sɔlidifje/ [45] vt solidify. □ **se ~** vpr solidify.

solitaire /sɔlitɛr/ a solitary. ● nmf (personne) loner. **solitude** nf solitude.

solliciter /sɔlisite/ [1] vt seek; (faire appel à) call upon; **être très sollicité** be very much in demand.

sollicitude /sɔlisityd/ nf concern.

solo /sɔlo/ nm & a inv (Mus) solo.

solution /sɔlysjɔ̃/ nf solution.

solvable /sɔlvabl/ a solvent.

solvant /sɔlvɑ̃/ nm solvent.

sombre /sɔ̃br/ a dark, (triste) sombre.

sombrer /sɔ̃bre/ [1] vi sink (dans into).

sommaire /sɔmɛr/ a (exécution) summary; (description) rough. ● nm contents (+ pl); **au ~** on the programme.

sommation /sɔmasjɔ̃/ nf (Mil) warning; (Jur) notice.

somme /sɔm/ nf sum; **en ~, ~ toute** in short; **faire la ~ de** add (up), total (up). ● nm nap.

sommeil /sɔmɛj/ nm sleep; **avoir**

S

~ be *ou* feel sleepy; **en** ~ (*projet*) put on ice. **sommeiller** [1] *vi* doze; (*fig*) lie dormant.

sommelier /sɔməlje/ *nm* wine steward.

sommer /sɔme/ [1] *vt* summon.

sommes /sɔm/ ⇒ÊTRE [4].

sommet /sɔmɛ/ *nm* top; (*de montagne*) summit; (*de triangle*) apex; (*gloire*) height.

sommier /sɔmje/ *nm* bed base.

somnambule /sɔmnãbyl/ *nm* sleepwalker.

somnifère /sɔmnifɛʀ/ *nm* sleeping pill.

somnolent, ~**e** /sɔmnɔlã, -t/ *a* drowsy. **somnoler** [1] *vi* doze.

somptueux, -euse /sɔ̃ptɥø, -z/ *a* sumptuous.

son¹, sa (**son** *before vowel or mute h*) (*pl* **ses**) /sɔ̃, sa, sɔ̃, se/ *a* (*homme*) his; (*femme*) her; (*chose*) its; (*indéfini*) one's.

son² /sɔ̃/ *nm* (*bruit*) sound; (*de blé*) bran; **baisser le** ~ turn the volume down.

sondage /sɔ̃daʒ/ *nm* ~ (**d'opinion**) (opinion) poll.

sonde /sɔ̃d/ *nf* (*de forage*) drill; (*Méd*) (*d'évacuation*) catheter; (*d'examen*) probe.

sonder /sɔ̃de/ [1] *vt* (*population*) poll; (*explorer*) sound; (*terrain*) drill; (*intentions*) sound out.

songe /sɔ̃ʒ/ *nm* dream.

songer /sɔ̃ʒe/ [40] *vt* ~ **que** think that; ~ **à** think about. **songeur, -euse** *a* pensive.

sonné, ~**e** /sɔne/ *a* (*étourdi*) groggy; 🄸 crazy.

sonner /sɔne/ [1] *vt/i* ring; (*clairon, glas*) sound; (*heure*) strike; (*domestique*) ring for; **midi sonné** well past noon; ~ **de** (*clairon*) sound, blow.

sonnerie /sɔnʀi/ *nf* ringing; (*de clairon*) sounding; (*sonnette*) bell.

sonnet /sɔnɛ/ *nm* sonnet.

sonnette /sɔnɛt/ *nf* bell.

sonore /sɔnɔʀ/ *a* resonant; (*onde, effets*) sound; (*rire*) resounding.

sonorisation /sɔnɔʀizasjɔ̃/ *nf* (*matériel*) public address system.

sonorité /sɔnɔʀite/ *nf* resonance; (*d'un instrument*) tone.

sont /sɔ̃/ ⇒ÊTRE [4].

sophistiqué, ~**e** /sɔfistike/ *a* sophisticated.

sorcellerie /sɔʀsɛlʀi/ *nf* witchcraft. **sorcier** *nm* (*guérisseur*) witch doctor; (*maléfique*) sorcerer. **sorcière** *nf* witch.

sordide /sɔʀdid/ *a* sordid; (*lieu*) squalid.

sort /sɔʀ/ *nm* (*destin, hasard*) fate; (*condition*) lot; (*maléfice*) spell; **tirer** (**qch**) **au** ~ draw lots (for sth).

sortant, ~**e** /sɔʀtã, -t/ *a* (*président etc.*) outgoing.

sorte /sɔʀt/ *nf* sort, kind; **de** ~ **que** so that; **en quelque** ~ in a way; **de la** ~ in this way; **faire en** ~ **que** make sure that.

sortie /sɔʀti/ *nf* exit; (*promenade, dîner*) outing; (*déclaration* 🄸) remark; (*parution*) publication; (*de disque, film*) release; (*d'un ordinateur*) output; ~**s** (*argent*) outgoings.

sortilège /sɔʀtilɛʒ/ *nm* (magic) spell.

sortir /sɔʀtiʀ/ [46] *vi* (*aux être*) go out, leave; (*venir*) come out; (*aller au spectacle*) go out; (*livre, film*) come out; (*plante*) come up; ~ **de** (*pièce*) leave; (*milieu social*) come from; (*limites*) go beyond; ~ **du commun** *ou* **de l'ordinaire** be out of the ordinary. ● *vt* (*aux avoir*) take out; (*livre, modèle*) bring out; (*dire* 🄸) come out with; ~ **qn de** get sb out of; **être sorti d'affaire** be in the clear. □ **s'en** ~ *vpr* cope, manage.

sosie /sozi/ *nm* double.

sot, ~**te** /so, sɔt/ *a* silly.

sottise /sɔtiz/ *nf* silliness; (action,

remarque) foolish thing; **faire des** ~s be naughty.

sou /su/ *nm* ① ~s money; **sans le** ~ without a penny; **près de ses** ~s tight-fisted.

soubresaut /subʀəso/ *nm* (sudden) start.

souche /suʃ/ *nf* (d'arbre) stump; (de famille) stock; (de carnet) counterfoil.

souci /susi/ *nm* (inquiétude) worry; (préoccupation) concern; (plante) marigold; **se faire du** ~ worry.

soucier (se) /(sə)susje/ [45] *vpr* **se** ~ **de** care about. **soucieux, -ieuse** *a* concerned (**de** about).

soucoupe /sukup/ *nf* saucer; ~ **volante** flying saucer.

soudain, ~e /sudɛ̃, -ɛn/ *a* sudden. ● *adv* suddenly.

soude /sud/ *nf* soda.

souder /sude/ [1] *vt* weld, solder; **famille très soudée** close-knit family. □ **se** ~ *vpr* (os) knit (together).

soudoyer /sudwaje/ [31] *vt* bribe.

souffle /sufl/ *nm* (haleine) breath; (respiration) breathing; (explosion) blast; (vent) breath of air; **le** ~ **coupé** out of breath; **à couper le** ~ breathtaking.

souffler /sufle/ [1] *vi* blow; (haleter) puff. ● *vt* (bougie) blow out; (poussière, fumée) blow; (verre) blow; (par explosion) destroy; (chuchoter) whisper; ~ **la réplique à** prompt. **souffleur, -euse** *nm, f* (Théât) prompter.

souffrance /sufʀɑ̃s/ *nf* suffering; **en** ~ (affaire) pending. **souffrant, ~e** *a* unwell.

souffrir /sufʀiʀ/ [21] *vi* suffer (**de** from). ● *vt* (endurer) suffer; **il ne peut pas le** ~ he cannot stand *ou* bear him.

soufre /sufʀ/ *nm* sulphur.

souhait /swɛ/ *nm* wish; **à tes** ~s!

bless you!; **paisible à** ~ incredibly peaceful. **souhaitable** *a* desirable.

souhaiter /swete/ [1] *vt* ~ **qch à qn** wish sb sth; ~ **que/faire** hope that/to do; ~ **la bienvenue à qn** welcome sb.

soûl, ~e /su, sul/ *a* drunk. ● *nm* **tout son** ~ as much as one can.

soulagement /sulaʒmɑ̃/ *nm* relief. **soulager** [40] *vt* relieve.

soûler /sule/ [1] *vt* make drunk. □ **se** ~ *vpr* get drunk.

soulèvement /sulɛvmɑ̃/ *nm* uprising.

soulever /sulve/ [6] *vt* lift, raise; (question, poussière) raise; (enthousiasme) arouse; (foule) stir up. □ **se** ~ *vpr* lift *ou* raise oneself up; (se révolter) rise up.

soulier /sulje/ *nm* shoe.

souligner /suliɲe/ [1] *vt* underline; (yeux) outline; (taille) emphasize.

soumettre /sumɛtʀ/ [42] *vt* (assujettir) subject (**à** to); (présenter) submit (**à** to). □ **se** ~ *vpr* submit (**à** to). **soumis, ~e** *a* submissive. **soumission** *nf* submission.

soupape /supap/ *nf* valve.

soupçon /supsɔ̃/ *nm* suspicion; **un** ~ **de** (un peu de) a touch of. **soupçonner** [1] *vt* suspect. **soupçonneux, -euse** *a* suspicious.

soupe /sup/ *nf* soup.

souper /supe/ [6] *vi* have supper. ● *nm* supper.

soupeser /supəze/ [1] *vt* judge the weight of; (fig) weigh up.

soupière /supjɛʀ/ *nf* (soup) tureen.

soupir /supiʀ/ *nm* sigh; **pousser un** ~ heave a sigh.

soupirer /supire/ [1] *vi* sigh.

souple /supl/ *a* supple; (règlement, caractère) flexible.

S

souplesse *nf* suppleness; (de règlement) flexibility.

source /suRs/ *nf* (de rivière, origine) source; (eau) spring; **prendre sa ~ à** rise in; **de ~ sûre** from a reliable source; **~ thermale** hot spring.

sourcil /suRsi/ *nm* eyebrow.

sourciller /suRsije/ [1] *vi* **sans ~** without batting an eyelid.

sourd, **~e** /suR, -d/ *a* deaf; (bruit, douleur) dull; **faire la ~e oreille** turn a deaf ear. ● *nm, f* deaf person.

sourd-muet (*pl* **sourds-muets**), **sourde-muette** (*pl* **sourdes-muettes**) /suRmɥe, suRdmɥet/ *a* deaf and dumb. ● *nm, f* deaf-mute.

souricière /suRisjɛR/ *nf* mousetrap; (fig) trap.

sourire /suRiR/ [54] *vi* smile (à at); **~ à** (fortune) smile on. ● *nm* smile; **garder le ~** keep smiling.

souris /suRi/ *nf* mouse; **des ~** mice.

sournois, **~e** /suRnwa, -z/ *a* sly, underhand.

sous /su/ *prép* under, beneath; **~ la main** handy; **~ la pluie** in the rain; **~ peu** shortly; **~ terre** underground.

sous-alimenté, **~e** /suzalimɑ̃te/ *a* undernourished.

souscription /suskRipsjɔ̃/ *nf* subscription. **souscrire** [30] *vi* **~ à** subscribe to.

sous-entendre /suzɑ̃tɑ̃dR/ [3] *vt* imply. **sous-entendu** *nm* innuendo, insinuation.

sous-estimer /suzɛstime/ [1] *vt* underestimate.

sous-jacent, **~e** /suʒasɑ̃, -t/ *a* underlying.

sous-marin, **~e** /sumaRɛ̃, -in/ *a* underwater; (plongée) deep-sea. ● *nm* submarine.

soussigné, **~e** /susiɲe/ *a & nm, f* undersigned.

sous-sol /susɔl/ *nm* (cave) basement.

sous-titre /sutitR/ *nm* subtitle.

soustraction /sustRaksjɔ̃/ *nf* (déduction) subtraction.

soustraire /sustRɛR/ [29] *vt* (déduire) subtract; (retirer) take away (à from). □ **se ~ à** *vpr* escape from.

sous-traitant /sutRɛtɑ̃/ *nm* subcontractor.

sous-verre /suvɛR/ *nm inv* glass mount.

sous-vêtement /suvɛtmɑ̃/ *nm* underwear.

soute /sut/ *nf* (de bateau) hold; **~ à charbon** coal-bunker.

soutenir /sutniR/ [59] *vt* support; (effort, rythme) sustain; (résister à) withstand; **~ que** maintain that.

soutenu, **~e** /sutny/ *a* (constant) sustained; (style) formal.

souterrain, **~e** /sutɛRɛ̃, -ɛn/ *a* underground. ● *nm* underground passage.

soutien /sutjɛ̃/ *nm* support.

soutien-gorge (*pl* **soutiens-gorge**) /sutjɛ̃gɔRʒ/ *nm* bra.

soutirer /sutiRe/ [1] *vt* **~ à qn** extract from sb.

souvenir¹ /suvniR/ *nm* memory, recollection; (objet) memento; (cadeau) souvenir; **en ~ de** in memory of.

souvenir² (**se**) /(sə)suvniR/ [59] *vpr* **se ~ de** remember; **se ~ que** remember that.

souvent /suvɑ̃/ *adv* often.

souverain, **~e** /suvRɛ̃, -ɛn/ *a* sovereign. ● *nm, f* sovereign.

soviétique /sɔvjetik/ *a* Soviet.

soyeux, **-euse** /swajø, -z/ *a* silky.

spacieux, **-ieuse** /spasjø, -z/ *a* spacious.

sparadrap /spaRadRa/ *nm* (sticking) plaster.

spatial, ~e (*mpl* -**iaux**) /spasjal, -jo/ *a* space.

speaker, ~**ine** /spikœR, -kRin/ *nm, f* announcer.

spécial, ~e (*mpl* -**iaux**) /spesjal, -jo/ *a* special; (*bizarre*) odd. **spécialement** *adv* (*exprès*) specially; (*très*) especially.

spécialiser (**se**) /səspesjalize/ [1] *vpr* specialize (**dans** in). **spécialiste** *nmf* specialist. **spécialité** *nf* speciality; (US) specialty.

spécifier /spesifje/ [45] *vt* specify.

spécifique /spesifik/ *a* specific.

spécimen /spesimɛn/ *nm* specimen.

spectacle /spɛktakl/ *nm* show; (*vue*) sight, spectacle.

spectaculaire /spɛktakylɛR/ *a* spectacular.

spectateur, -**trice** /spɛktatœR, -tRis/ *nm, f* (*Sport*) spectator; (*témoin oculaire*) onlooker; **les** ~**s** (*Théât*) the audience (+ *sg*).

spectre /spɛktR/ *nm* (*revenant*) spectre; (*images*) spectrum.

spéculateur, -**trice** /spekylatœR, -tRis/ *nm, f* speculator. **spéculation** *nf* speculation. **spéculer** [1] *vi* speculate.

spéléologie /speleɔlɔʒi/ *nf* cave exploration, pot-holing.

spermatozoïde /spɛRmatozoid/ *nm* spermatozoon. **sperme** *nm* sperm.

sphère /sfɛR/ *nf* sphere.

spirale /spiral/ *nf* spiral.

spirituel, ~**le** /spiRityɛl/ *a* spiritual; (*amusant*) witty.

spiritueux /spiRityø/ *nm* (*alcool*) spirit.

splendeur /splɑ̃dœR/ *nf* splendour. **splendide** *a* splendid.

sponsoriser /spɔ̃sɔRize/ [1] *vt* sponsor.

spontané, ~e /spɔ̃tane/ *a* spontaneous. **spontanéité** *nf* spontaneity.

sport /spɔR/ *a inv* (*vêtements*) casual. ● *nm* sport; **veste/voiture de** ~ sports jacket/car.

sportif, -**ive** /spɔRtif, -v/ *a* (*personne*) sporty; (*physique*) athletic; (*résultats*) sports. ● *nm, f* sportsman, sportswoman.

spot /spɔt/ *nm* spotlight; ~ (**publicitaire**) ad.

square /skwaR/ *nm* small public garden.

squatter /skwate/ [1] *vt* squat in.

squelette /skəlɛt/ *nm* skeleton. **squelettique** *a* skeletal.

SSII *abrév f* (**société de services et d'ingénierie informatiques**) computer services company.

stabiliser /stabilize/ [1] *vt* stabilize. **stable** *a* stable.

stade /stad/ *nm* (Sport) stadium; (*phase*) stage.

stage /staʒ/ *nm* (*cours*) course; (*professionnel*) placement. **stagiaire** *nmf* course member; (*apprenti*) trainee.

stagner /stagne/ [1] *vi* stagnate.

stand /stɑ̃d/ *nm* stand; (*de fête foraine*) stall.

standard /stɑ̃daR/ *nm* switchboard. ● *a inv* standard. **standardiser** [1] *vt* standardize. **standardiste** /stɑ̃daRdist/ *nmf* switchboard operator.

standing /stɑ̃diŋ/ *nm* status, standing; **de** ~ (*hôtel*) luxury.

starter /staRtɛR/ *nm* (Auto) choke.

station /stasjɔ̃/ *nf* station; (*halte*) stop; ~ **debout** standing position; ~ **de taxis** taxi rank; ~ **balnéaire/ de ski** seaside/ski resort; ~ **thermale** spa.

stationnaire /stasjɔnɛR/ *a* stationary.

stationnement /stasjɔnmɑ̃/ *nm* parking. **stationner** [1] *vi* park.

station-service (*pl* **stations-**

S

service) /stasjɔ̃sɛRvis/ *nf* service station.

statique /statik/ *a* static.

statistique /statistik/ *nf* statistic; (science) statistics (+ *sg*). ● *a* statistical.

statue /staty/ *nf* statue.

statuer /statɥe/ [1] *vi* ~ **sur** give a ruling on.

statut /staty/ *nm* status. **statutaire** *a* statutory.

sténo /steno/ *nf* (sténographie) shorthand. **sténodactylo** *nf* shorthand typist. **sténographie** *nf* shorthand.

stéréo /steReo/ *nf & a inv* stereo.

stéréotype /steReɔtip/ *nm* stereotype.

stérile /steRil/ *a* sterile.

stérilet /steRilɛ/ *nm* coil, IUD.

stérilisation /steRilizasjɔ̃/ *nf* sterilization. **stériliser** [1] *vt* sterilize.

stéroïde /steRɔid/ *a & nm* steroid.

stimulant /stimylɑ̃/ *nm* stimulus; (médicament) stimulant.

stimulateur /stimylatœR/ *nm* ~ **cardiaque** (Méd) pacemaker.

stimuler /stimyle/ [1] *vt* stimulate.

stipuler /stipyle/ [1] *vt* stipulate.

stock /stɔk/ *nm* stock. **stocker** [1] *vt* stock.

stoïque /stɔik/ *a* stoical. ● *nmf* stoic.

stop /stɔp/ *interj* stop. ● *nm* stop sign; (feu arrière) brake light; **faire du** ~ 🔲 hitch-hike. **stopper** [1] *vt/i* stop.

store /stɔR/ *nm* blind; (de magasin) awning.

strapontin /stRapɔ̃tɛ̃/ *nm* folding seat, jump seat.

stratégie /stRateʒi/ *nf* strategy. **stratégique** *a* strategic.

stress /stRɛs/ *nm* stress. **stressant**, ~**e** *a* stressful.

stressé, ~**e** *a* stressed. **stresser** [1] *vt* put under stress.

strict /stRikt/ *a* strict; (tenue, vérité) plain; **le** ~ **minimum** the bare minimum. **strictement** *adv* strictly.

strident, ~**e** /stRidɑ̃, -t/ *a* shrill.

strophe /stRɔf/ *nf* stanza, verse.

structure /stRyktyR/ *nf* structure.

studieux, -ieuse /stydjø, -z/ *a* studious.

studio /stydjo/ *nm* (d'artiste, de télévision) studio; (logement) studio flat.

stupéfaction /stypefaksjɔ̃/ *nf* amazement. **stupéfait**, ~**e** *a* amazed.

stupéfiant, ~**e** /stypefjɑ̃, -t/ *a* astounding. ● *nm* drug, narcotic.

stupéfier /stypefje/ [45] *vt* amaze.

stupeur /stypœR/ *nf* amazement; (Méd) stupor.

stupide /stypid/ *a* stupid.

stupidité *nf* stupidity.

style /stil/ *nm* style.

styliste /stilist/ *nmf* fashion designer.

stylo /stilo/ *nm* pen; ~ **(à) bille** ball-point pen; ~ **(à) encre** fountain pen.

su /sy/ ⇒SAVOIR [55].

suave /sɥav/ *a* sweet.

subalterne /sybaltɛRn/ *a & nmf* subordinate.

subconscient /sypkɔ̃sjɑ̃/ *nm* subconscious.

subir /sybiR/ [2] *vt* be subjected to; (traitement, expériences) undergo.

subit, ~**e** /sybi, -t/ *a* sudden.

subjectif, -ive /sybʒɛktif, -v/ *a* subjective.

subjonctif /sybʒɔ̃ktif/ *nm* subjunctive.

subjuguer /sybʒyge/ [1] *vt* (charmer) captivate.

sublime /syblim/ *a* sublime.

submerger /sybmɛrʒe/ [40] *vt* submerge; (fig) overwhelm.

subordonné, ~e /sybɔrdɔne/ *a & nm, f* subordinate.

subside /sybzid/ *nm* grant.

subsidiaire /sybzidjɛr/ *a* subsidiary; **question** ~ tiebreaker.

subsistance /sybzistãs/ *nf* subsistence. **subsister** [1] *vi* subsist; (durer, persister) exist.

substance /sypstãs/ *nf* substance.

substantiel, ~le /sypstãsjɛl/ *a* substantial.

substantif /sypstãtif/ *nm* noun.

substituer /sypstitɥe/ [1] *vt* substitute (**à** for). □ **se** ~ **à** *vpr* (remplacer) substitute for. **substitut** *nm* substitute; (Jur) deputy public prosecutor.

subtil, ~e /syptil/ *a* subtle.

subtiliser /syptilize/ [1] *vt* ~ **qch** (**à qn**) steal sth.

subvenir /sybvənir/ [59] *vi* ~ **à** provide for.

subvention /sybvãsjõ/ *nf* subsidy. **subventionner** [1] *vt* subsidize.

subversif, **-ive** /sybvɛrsif, -v/ *a* subversive.

suc /syk/ *nm* juice.

succédané /syksedane/ *nm* substitute (**de** for).

succéder /syksede/ [14] *vi* ~ **à** succeed. □ **se** ~ *vpr* succeed one another.

succès /syksɛ/ *nm* success; **à** ~ (film, livre,) successful; **avoir du** ~ be a success.

successeur /syksesœr/ *nm* successor. **successif**, **-ive** *a* successive. **succession** *nf* succession; (Jur) inheritance.

succinct, ~e /syksɛ̃, -t/ *a* succinct.

succomber /sykõbe/ [1] *vi* die; ~ **à** succumb to.

succulent, ~e /sykylã, -t/ *a* delicious.

succursale /sykyrsal/ *nf* (Comm) branch.

sucer /syse/ [10] *vt* suck.

sucette /sysɛt/ *nf* (bonbon) lollipop; (tétine) dummy; (US) pacifier.

sucre /sykr/ *nm* sugar; ~ **d'orge** barley sugar; ~ **en poudre** caster sugar; ~ **glace** icing sugar; ~ **roux** brown sugar.

sucré /sykre/ *a* sweet; (additionné de sucre) sweetened. **sucrer** [1] *vt* sugar, sweeten. **sucreries** *nfpl* sweets.

sucrier, **-ière** /sykrije, -jɛr/ *a* sugar. ● *nm* (récipient) sugar-bowl.

sud /syd/ *nm* south. ● *a inv* south; (partie) southern.

sud-est /sydɛst/ *nm* south-east.

sud-ouest /sydwɛst/ *nm* south-west.

Suède /sɥɛd/ *nf* Sweden.

suédois, ~e /sɥedwa, -z/ *a* Swedish. ● *nm* (Ling) Swedish. **S**~, ~e *nm, f* Swede.

suer /sɥe/ [1] *vt/i* sweat; **faire** ~ **qn** 🔢 get on sb's nerves.

sueur /sɥœr/ *nf* sweat; **en** ~ covered in sweat.

suffire /syfir/ [57] *vi* be enough (**à qn** for sb); **il suffit de compter** all you have to do is count; **une goutte suffit** a drop is enough; ~ **à** (besoin) satisfy. □ **se** ~ *vpr* **se** ~ **à soi-même** be self-sufficient.

suffisamment /syfizamã/ *adv* sufficiently; ~ **de qch** enough of sth. **suffisance** *nf* (vanité) conceit. **suffisant**, ~e *a* sufficient; (vaniteux) conceited.

suffixe /syfiks/ *nm* suffix.

suffoquer /syfɔke/ [1] *vt/i* choke, suffocate.

suffrage /syfraʒ/ *nm* (voix: Pol) vote; (système) suffrage.

suggérer /sygʒere/ [14] *vt*

S

suggest. **suggestion** *nf*
suggestion.
suicidaire /sɥisidɛʀ/ *a* suicidal.
suicide *nm* suicide. **suicider
(se)** [1] *vpr* commit suicide.
suinter /sɥɛ̃te/ [1] *vi* ooze.
suis /sɥi/ ⇒ÊTRE [4], SUIVRE [57].
Suisse /sɥis/ *nf* Switzerland.
● *nmf* Swiss. **suisse** *a* Swiss.
suite /sɥit/ *nf* continuation, rest;
(d'un film) sequel; (série) series;
(appartement, escorte) suite; (résultat)
consequence; **à la ~, de ~**
(successivement) in a row; **à la ~ de**
(derrière) behind; **à la ~ de, par ~
de** (en conséquence) as a result of;
faire ~ (à) follow; **par la ~**
afterwards; **~ à votre lettre du**
further to your letter of the; **des
~s de** as a result of.
suivant[1], **~e** /sɥivɑ̃, -t/ *a*
following, next. ● *nm, f* following
ou next person.
suivant[2] /sɥivɑ̃/ *prép* (selon)
according to.
suivi, ~e /sɥivi/ *a* (effort) steady,
sustained; (cohérent) consistent;
peu/très ~ (cours) poorly/well
attended.
suivre /sɥivʀ/ [57] *vt/i* follow;
(comprendre) follow; **faire ~** (courrier)
forward. □ **se ~** *vpr* follow each
other.
sujet, ~te /syʒɛ, -t/ *a* **~ à** liable
ou subject to. ● *nm* (d'un royaume)
subject; (question) subject; (motif)
cause; (Gram) subject; **au ~ de**
about.
super /sypɛʀ/ *nm* (essence) four-
star. ● *a inv* 🆃 (très) great. ● *adv*
🆃 ultra, really.
superbe /sypɛʀb/ *a* superb.
supérette /sypeʀɛt/ *nf*
minimarket.
superficie /sypɛʀfisi/ *nf* area.
superficiel, ~le /sypɛʀfisjɛl/ *a*
superficial.
superflu /sypɛʀfly/ *a*

superfluous. ● *nm* (excédent)
surplus.
supérieur, ~e /sypeʀjœʀ/ *a* (plus
haut) upper; (quantité, nombre)
greater (à than); (études,
principe) higher (à than); (meilleur,
hautain) superior (à to). ● *nm, f*
superior. **supériorité** *nf*
superiority.
superlatif, -ive /sypɛʀlatif, -v/ *a*
& *nm* superlative.
supermarché /sypɛʀmaʀʃe/ *nm*
supermarket.
superposer /sypɛʀpoze/ [1] *vt*
superimpose; **lits superposés**
bunk beds.
superproduction
/sypɛʀpʀɔdyksjɔ̃/ *nf* (film)
blockbuster.
superpuissance /sypɛʀpɥisɑ̃s/
nf superpower.
superstitieux, -ieuse /sypɛʀs-
tisjø, -z/ *a* superstitious.
superviser /sypɛʀvize/ [1] *vt*
supervise.
suppléant, ~e /sypleɑ̃, -t/ *nmf* &
a (professeur) **~** supply teacher;
(juge) **~** deputy (judge).
suppléer /syplee/ [15] *vt*
(remplacer) fill in for. ● *vi* **~ à**
(compenser) make up for.
supplément /syplemɑ̃/ *nm*
(argent) extra charge; (de frites,
légumes) extra portion; **en ~** extra;
un ~ de (travail) additional; **payer
un ~** pay a supplement.
supplémentaire *a* extra,
additional.
supplice /syplis/ *nm* torture.
supplier /syplije/ [45] *vt* beg,
beseech (**de** to).
support /sypɔʀ/ *nm* support;
(Ordinat) medium.
supportable /sypɔʀtabl/ *a*
bearable.
supporter[1] /sypɔʀte/ [1] *vt*
(privations) bear; (personne) put
up with; (structure: Ordinat)

support; **il ne supporte pas les enfants/de perdre** he can't stand children/losing.

supporter² /sypɔʀtɛʀ/ *nm* (Sport) supporter.

supposer /sypoze/ [1] *vt* suppose; (*impliquer*) imply; **à ~ que** supposing that.

suppression /sypʀesjɔ̃/ *nf* (de taxe) abolition; (de sanction) lifting; (de mot) deletion. **supprimer** [1] *vt* (*allocation*) withdraw; (*contrôle*) lift; (*train*) cancel; (*preuve*) suppress.

suprématie /sypʀemasi/ *nf* supremacy.

suprême /sypʀɛm/ *a* supreme.

sur /syʀ/ *prép* on, upon; (par-dessus) over; (au sujet de) about, on; (proportion) out of; (mesure) by; **~ la photo** in the photograph; **mettre/jeter ~** put/throw on to; **~ mesure** made to measure; **~ place** on the spot; **~ ce, je pars** with that, I must go; **~ le moment** at the time.

sûr /syʀ/ *a* certain, sure; (sans danger) safe; (digne de confiance) reliable; (*main*) steady; (*jugement*) sound; **être ~ de soi** be self-confident; **j'en étais ~!** I knew it!

surabondance /syʀabɔ̃dɑ̃s/ *nf* overabundance.

surcharge /syʀʃaʀʒ/ *nf* overloading; (poids) excess load. **surcharger** [1] *vt* overload; (*texte*) alter.

surchauffer /syʀʃofe/ [1] *vt* overheat.

surcroît /syʀkʀwa/ *nm* increase (**de** in); **de ~** in addition.

surdité /syʀdite/ *nf* deafness.

surélever /syʀelve/ [6] *vt* raise.

sûrement /syʀmɑ̃/ *adv* certainly; (sans danger) safely; **il a ~ oublié** he must have forgotten.

surenchère /syʀɑ̃ʃɛʀ/ *nf* higher

bid. **surenchérir** [2] *vi* bid higher (**sur** than).

surestimer /syʀɛstime/ [1] *vt* overestimate.

sûreté /syʀte/ *nf* safety; (de pays) security; (d'un geste) steadiness; **être en ~** be safe; **S~ (nationale)** police (+ *pl*).

surexcité, **~e** /syʀɛksite/ *a* very excited.

surf /sœʀf/ *nm* surfing.

surface /syʀfas/ *nf* surface; **faire ~** (sous-marin, fig) surface; **en ~** on the surface.

surfait, **~e** /syʀfɛ, -t/ *a* overrated.

surfer /sœʀfe/ [1] *vi* go surfing; **~ sur l'Internet** surf the Internet.

surgelé, **~e** /syʀʒəle/ *a* (deep-) frozen; **aliments ~s** frozen food (+ *sg*).

surgir /syʀʒiʀ/ [2] *vi* appear (suddenly); (difficulté) crop up.

sur-le-champ /syʀləʃɑ̃/ *adv* right away.

surlendemain /syʀlɑ̃dmɛ̃/ *nm* **le ~** two days later; **le ~ de** two days after.

surligneur /syʀliɲœʀ/ *nm* highlighter (pen).

surmenage /syʀmənaʒ/ *nm* overwork.

surmonter /syʀmɔ̃te/ [1] *vt* (vaincre) overcome, surmount; (être au-dessus de) surmount, top.

surnaturel, **~le** /syʀnatyʀɛl/ *a* supernatural.

surnom /syʀnɔ̃/ *nm* nickname. **surnommer** [1] *vt* nickname.

surpeuplé, **~e** /syʀpœple/ *a* overpopulated.

surplomber /syʀplɔ̃be/ [1] *vt/i* overhang.

surplus /syʀply/ *nm* surplus.

suprenant, **~e** /syʀpʀənɑ̃, -t/ *a* surprising. **surprendre** [50] *vt* (étonner) surprise; (prendre au dépourvu) catch, surprise; (entendre)

S

overhear. **surpris**, ~e *a* surprised (**de** at).

surprise /syʀpʀiz/ *nf* surprise.

surréaliste /syʀʀealist/ *a & nmf* surrealist.

sursaut /syʀso/ *nm* start, jump; **en** ~ with a start; ~ **de** (*regain*) burst of. **sursauter** [1] *vi* start, jump.

sursis /syʀsi/ *nm* reprieve; (Mil) deferment; **deux ans** (**de prison**) **avec** ~ a two-year suspended sentence.

surtaxe /syʀtaks/ *nf* surcharge.

surtout /syʀtu/ *adv* especially; (*avant tout*) above all; ~ **pas** certainly not.

surveillance /syʀvɛjɑ̃s/ *nf* watch; (*d'examen*) supervision; (*de la police*) surveillance. **surveillant**, ~e *nm, f* (*de prison*) warder; (*au lycée*) supervisor (in charge of discipline). **surveiller** [1] *vt* watch; (*travaux, élèves*) supervise.

survenir /syʀvəniʀ/ [58] *vi* occur, take place; (*personne*) turn up.

survêtement /syʀvɛtmɑ̃/ *nm* (Sport) tracksuit.

survie /syʀvi/ *nf* survival.

survivant, ~e /syʀvivɑ̃, -t/ *a* surviving. ● *nm, f* survivor.

survivre /syʀvivʀ/ [63] *vi* survive; ~ **à** (*conflit*) survive; (*personne*) outlive.

survoler /syʀvɔle/ [1] *vt* fly over; (*livre*) skim through.

sus: **en** ~ /ɑ̃sys/ *loc* in addition.

susceptible /sysɛptibl/ *a* touchy; ~ **de faire** likely to do.

susciter /sysite/ [1] *vt* (*éveiller*) arouse; (*occasionner*) create.

suspect, ~e /syspɛ, -ɛkt/ *a* (*individu, faits*) suspicious; (*témoignage*) suspect; ~ **de** suspected of. ● *nm, f* suspect. **suspecter** [1] *vt* suspect.

suspendre /syspɑ̃dʀ/ [3] *vt* (accrocher) hang (up); (interrompre, destituer) suspend; **suspendu à** hanging from. □ **se** ~ **à** *vpr* hang from.

suspens: **en** ~ /ɑ̃syspɑ̃/ *loc* (*affaire*) outstanding; (*dans l'indécision*) in suspense.

suspense /syspɛns/ *nm* suspense.

suture /sytyʀ/ *nf* **point de** ~ stitch.

svelte /svɛlt/ *a* slender.

S.V.P. *abrév* (**s'il vous plaît**) please.

syllabe /silab/ *nf* syllable.

symbole /sɛ̃bɔl/ *nm* symbol. **symboliser** [1] *vt* symbolize.

symétrie /simetʀi/ *nf* symmetry.

sympa /sɛ̃pa/ *a inv* Ⅱ nice; **sois** ~ be a pal.

sympathie /sɛ̃pati/ *nf* (*goût*) liking; (*compassion*) sympathy; **avoir de la** ~ **pour** like. **sympathique** *a* nice, pleasant. **sympathisant**, ~e *nm, f* sympathizer. **sympathiser** [1] *vi* get on well (**avec** with).

symphonie /sɛ̃fɔni/ *nf* symphony.

symptôme /sɛ̃ptom/ *nm* symptom.

synagogue /sinagɔg/ *nf* synagogue.

synchroniser /sɛ̃kʀɔnize/ [1] *vt* synchronize.

syncope /sɛ̃kɔp/ *nf* (Méd) blackout.

syndic /sɛ̃dik/ *nm* ~ (**d'immeuble**) property manager.

syndicaliste /sɛ̃dikalist/ *nmf* (trade-)unionist. ● *a* (trade-) union.

syndicat /sɛ̃dika/ *nm* (trade) union; ~ **d'initiative** tourist office.

syndiqué, ~e /sɛ̃dike/ *a* **être** ~ be a (trade-)union member.

synonyme /sinɔnim/ *a* synonymous. ● *nm* synonym.

syntaxe /sɛ̃taks/ *nf* syntax.

synthèse /sɛ̃tɛz/ *nf* synthesis.
synthétique *a* synthetic.

synthé(tiseur) /sɛ̃te(tizœʀ)/ *nm* synthesizer.

systématique /sistematik/ *a* systematic.

système /sistɛm/ *nm* system; **le ~ D** 🔲 resourcefulness.

t' /t/ ⇒TE.

ta /ta/ ⇒TON¹.

tabac /taba/ *nm* tobacco; (magasin) tobacconist's shop.

table /tabl/ *nf* table; **à ~!** dinner is ready!; **~ de nuit** bedside table; **~ des matières** table of contents; **~ à repasser** ironing board; **~ roulante** (tea-)trolley; (US) (serving) cart.

tableau (*pl* ~**x**) /tablo/ *nm* picture; (peinture) painting; (panneau) board; (graphique) chart; (Scol) blackboard; **~ d'affichage** notice-board; **~ de bord** dashboard.

tablette /tablɛt/ *nf* shelf; **~ de chocolat** bar of chocolate.

tableur /tablœʀ/ *nm* spreadsheet.

tablier /tablije/ *nm* apron; (de pont) platform; (de magasin) shutter.

tabou /tabu/ *nm & a* taboo.

tabouret /tabuʀɛ/ *nm* stool.

tache /taʃ/ *nf* mark, spot; (salissure) stain; **faire ~ d'huile** spread; **~ de rousseur** freckle.

tâche /taʃ/ *nf* task, job.

tacher /taʃe/ [1] *vt* stain. □ **se ~** *vpr* (personne) get oneself dirty.

tâcher /taʃe/ [1] *vi* **~ de faire** try to do.

tacheté, **~e** /taʃte/ *a* spotted.

tact /takt/ *nm* tact.

tactique /taktik/ *a* tactical. ● *nf* (Mil) tactics; **une ~** a tactic.

taie /tɛ/ *nf* **~ (d'oreiller)** pillowcase.

taille /taj/ *nf* (milieu du corps) waist; (hauteur) height; (grandeur) size; **de ~** sizeable; **être de ~ à faire** be up to doing.

taille-crayons /tajkʀejɔ̃/ *nm inv* pencil-sharpener.

tailler /taje/ [1] *vt* cut, (arbre) prune; (crayon) sharpen; (vêtement) cut out. □ **se ~** *vpr* 🔲 clear off.

tailleur /tajœʀ/ *nm* (costume) woman's suit; (couturier) tailor; **en ~** cross-legged; **~ de pierre** stone-cutter.

taire /tɛʀ/ [47] *vt* not to reveal; **faire ~** silence. □ **se ~** *vpr* be silent *ou* quiet; (devenir silencieux) fall silent.

talc /talk/ *nm* talcum powder.

talent /talɑ̃/ *nm* talent.
talentueux, **-euse** *a* talented, gifted.

talon /talɔ̃/ *nm* heel; (de chèque) stub.

tambour /tɑ̃buʀ/ *nm* drum; (d'église) vestibule.

Tamise /tamiz/ *nf* Thames.

tampon /tɑ̃pɔ̃/ *nm* (de bureau) stamp; (ouate) wad, pad; **~ (hygiénique)** tampon.

tamponner /tɑ̃pɔne/ [1] *vt* (document) stamp; (véhicule) crash into; (plaie) swab.

tandem /tɑ̃dɛm/ *nm* (vélo) tandem; (personnes: fig) duo.

tandis que /tɑ̃di(s)/ *conj* while.

tanière /tanjɛʀ/ *nf* den.

tant /tɑ̃/ *adv* (travailler, manger) so much; **~ de** (quantité) so much; (nombre) so many; **~ que** as long

T

as; **en ~ que** as; **~ mieux!** all the better!; **~ pis!** too bad!

tante /tɑ̃t/ *nf* aunt.

tantôt /tɑ̃to/ *adv* sometimes.

tapage /tapaʒ/ *nm* din.

tape /tap/ *nf* slap. **tape-à-l'œil** *a inv* flashy, tawdry.

taper /tape/ [1] *vt* hit; (prendre Ⅱ) scrounge; **~ (à la machine)** type. ● *vi* (cogner) bang; (soleil) beat down; **~ dans** (puiser dans) dig into; **~ sur** hit; **~ sur l'épaule de qn** tap sb on the shoulder. □ *se ~ vpr* (corvée Ⅱ) get stuck with Ⅱ.

tapis /tapi/ *nm* carpet; (petit) rug; **~ de bain** bathmat; **~ roulant** (pour objets) conveyor belt; (pour piétons) moving walkway.

tapisser /tapise/ [1] *vt* (wall) paper; (fig) cover (**de** with).

tapisserie *nf* tapestry; (papier peint) wallpaper.

taquin, ~e /takɛ̃, -in/ *a* fond of teasing. ● *nm, f* tease(r).

tard /taʀ/ *adv* late; **au plus ~** at the latest; **plus ~** later; **sur le ~** late in life.

tarder /taʀde/ [1] *vi* (être lent à venir) be a long time coming; **~ (à faire)** take a long time (doing), delay (doing); **sans (plus) ~** without (further) delay; **il me tarde de** I'm longing to.

tardif, -ive /taʀdif, -v/ *a* late.

tare /taʀ/ *nf* (défaut) defect.

tarif /taʀif/ *nm* rate; (de train, taxi) fare; **plein ~** full price.

tarir /taʀiʀ/ [2] *vt/i* dry up. □ *se ~ vpr* dry up.

tarte /taʀt/ *nf* tart. ● *a inv* (ridicule Ⅱ) ridiculous.

tartine /taʀtin/ *nf* slice of bread; **~ de beurre** slice of bread and butter. **tartiner** [1] *vt* spread.

tartre /taʀtʀ/ *nm* (de bouilloire) fur, scale; (sur les dents) tartar.

tas /tɑ/ *nm* pile, heap; **un** *ou* **des ~ de** Ⅱ lots of.

tasse /tɑs/ *nf* cup; **~ à thé** teacup.

tasser /tase/ [1] *vt* pack, squeeze; (terre) pack (down). □ *se ~ vpr* (terrain) sink; (se serrer) squeeze up.

tâter /tate/ [1] *vt* feel; (opinion: fig) sound out. ● *vi* **~ de** try out.

tatillon, ~ne /tatijɔ̃, -jɔn/ *a* finicky.

tâtonnements /tatɔnmɑ̃/ *nmpl* (essais) trial and error (+ *sg*).

tâtons: **à ~** /atatɔ̃/ *loc* **avancer à ~** grope one's way along.

tatouage /tatwaʒ/ *nm* (dessin) tattoo.

taupe /top/ *nf* mole.

taureau (*pl* **~x**) /tɔʀo/ *nm* bull; **le T~** Taurus.

taux /to/ *nm* rate.

taxe /taks/ *nf* tax.

taxi /taksi/ *nm* taxi(-cab); (personne Ⅱ) taxi driver.

taxiphone® /taksifɔn/ *nm* pay phone.

Tchécoslovaquie /tʃekɔslɔvaki/ *nf* Czechoslovakia.

tchèque /tʃɛk/ *a* Czech; **République ~** Czech Republic. **T~** *nmf* Czech.

te, t' /tə, t/ *pron* you; (indirect) (to) you; (réfléchi) yourself.

technicien, ~ne /tɛknisjɛ̃, -ɛn/ *nm, f* technician.

technique /tɛknik/ *a* technical. ● *nf* technique.

techno /tɛkno/ *nf* (Mus) techno.

technologie /tɛknɔlɔʒi/ *nf* technology.

teindre /tɛ̃dʀ/ [22] *vt* dye. □ *se ~ vpr* **se ~ les cheveux** dye one's hair.

teint /tɛ̃/ *nm* complexion.

teinte /tɛ̃t/ *nf* shade. **teinter** [1] *vt* (verre) tint; (bois) stain.

teinture /tɛ̃tyʀ/ *nf* (produit) dye.

teinturier, -ière /tɛ̃tyʀje, -jɛʀ/ *nm, f* dry-cleaner.

tel, ∼**le** /tɛl/ a such; un ∼ livre such a book; ∼ **que** such as, like; (ainsi que) (just) as; ∼ **ou** ∼ such-and-such; ∼ **quel** (just) as it is.

télé /tele/ nf ▢ TV.

télécharger /teleʃaʀʒe/ [40] vt (Ordinat) download.

télécommande /telekɔmɑ̃d/ nf remote control.

télécommunications /telekɔmynikasjɔ̃/ nfpl telecommunications.

téléconférence /telekɔ̃feʀɑ̃s/ nf teleconferencing.

télécopie /telekɔpi/ nf fax. **télécopieur** nm fax machine.

téléfilm /telefilm/ nm TV film.

télégramme /telegʀam/ nm telegram.

télégraphier /telegʀafje/ [45] vt/i ∼ (à) cable.

téléguidé, ∼**e** /telegide/ a radio-controlled.

télématique /telematik/ nf telematics (+ sg).

téléphérique /teleferik/ nm cable car.

téléphone /telefɔn/ nm (tele-) phone; ∼ **à carte** cardphone. **téléphoner** [1] vt/i ∼ (à) (tele) phone.

téléphonie /telefɔni/ nf telephony; ∼**mobile** mobile telephony. **téléphonique** a (tele)phone.

télé-réalité /teleʀealite/ nf reality TV.

téléserveur /teleseʀvœʀ/ nm (Internet) remote server.

télésiège /telesjɛʒ/ nm chairlift.

téléski /teleski/ nm ski tow.

téléspectateur, **-trice** /telespɛktatœʀ, -tʀis/ nm, f (television) viewer.

télévente /televɑ̃t/ nf telesales (+ pl).

télévisé, ∼**e** /televize/ a (débat) televised; **émission** ∼**e** television programme. **télévision** nf television.

télex /telɛks/ nm telex.

tellement /tɛlmɑ̃/ adv (tant) so much; (si) so; ∼ **de** (quantité) so much; (nombre) so many.

téméraire /temeʀɛʀ/ a (personne) reckless.

témoignage /temwaɲaʒ/ nm testimony, evidence; (récit) account; ∼ **de** (marque) token of.

témoigner /temwaɲe/ [1] vi testify (de to). ● vt (montrer) show; ∼ **que** testify that.

témoin /temwɛ̃/ nm witness; (Sport) baton; **être** ∼ **de** witness; ∼ **oculaire** eyewitness.

tempe /tɑ̃p/ nf (Anat) temple.

tempérament /tɑ̃peʀamɑ̃/ nm temperament, disposition.

température /tɑ̃peʀatyʀ/ nf temperature.

tempête /tɑ̃pɛt/ nf storm; ∼ **de neige** snowstorm.

temple /tɑ̃pl/ nm temple; (protes-tant) church.

temporaire /tɑ̃pɔʀɛʀ/ a temporary.

temps /tɑ̃/ nm (notion) time; (Gram) tense; (étape) stage; **à** ∼ **partiel/plein** part-/full-time; **ces derniers** ∼ lately; **dans le** ∼ at one time; **dans quelque** ∼ in a while; **de** ∼ **en** ∼ from time to time; ∼ **d'arrêt** pause; **avoir tout son** ∼ have plenty of time; (météo) weather; ∼ **de chien** filthy weather; **quel** ∼ **fait-il?** what's the weather like?

tenace /tənas/ a stubborn.

tenaille /tənɑj/ nf pincers (+ pl).

tendance /tɑ̃dɑ̃s/ nf tendency; (évolution) trend; **avoir** ∼ **à** tend to.

tendon /tɑ̃dɔ̃/ nm tendon.

tendre[1] /tɑ̃dʀ/ [3] vt stretch; (piège) set; (bras) stretch out; (main) hold out; (cou) crane; ∼ **qch à qn** hold sth out to sb; ∼ **l'oreille** prick up one's ears. ● vi ∼ **à** tend to.

tendre[2] /tɑ̃dʀ/ a tender; (couleur, bois) soft. **tendresse** nf tenderness.

T

tendu, ~e /tɑ̃dy/ a (corde) tight; (personne, situation) tense.

ténèbres /tenɛbʀ/ nfpl darkness (+ sg).

teneur /tənœʀ/ nf content.

tenir /təniʀ/ [59] vt hold; (pari, promesse, hôtel) keep; (place) take up; (propos) utter; (rôle) play; ~ de (avoir reçu de) have got from; ~ pour regard as; ~ chaud keep warm; ~ compte de take into account; ~ le coup hold out; ~ tête à stand up to. ● vi hold; ~ à be attached to; ~ à faire be anxious to do; ~ bon stand firm; ~ dans fit into; ~ de qn take after sb; tiens! (surprise) hey! □ se ~ vpr (debout) stand; (avoir lieu) be held; se ~ à hold on to; s'en ~ à (se limiter à) confine oneself to.

tennis /tenis/ nm tennis; ~ de table table tennis. ● nmpl (chaussures) sneakers.

ténor /tenɔʀ/ nm tenor.

tension /tɑ̃sjɔ̃/ nf tension; avoir de la ~ have high blood-pressure.

tentation /tɑ̃tasjɔ̃/ nf temptation.

tentative /tɑ̃tativ/ nf attempt.

tente /tɑ̃t/ nf tent.

tenter /tɑ̃te/ [1] vt (allécher) tempt; (essayer) try (de faire to do).

tenture /tɑ̃tyʀ/ nf curtain; ~s draperies.

tenu, ~e /təny/ a bien ~ well kept; ~ de required. ● ⇒TENIR [58].

tenue /təny/ nf (habillement) dress; (de maison) upkeep; (conduite) (good) behaviour; (maintien) posture; ~ de soirée evening dress.

Tergal® /tɛʀgal/ nm Terylene®.

terme /tɛʀm/ nm (mot) term; (date limite) time-limit; (fin) end; né avant ~ premature; à long/court ~ long-/short-term; en bons ~s on good terms (avec with).

terminaison /tɛʀminɛzɔ̃/ nf (Gram) ending.

terminal, ~e (mpl -aux) /tɛʀminal, -o/ a terminal. ● nm terminal. **terminale** nf (Scol) ≈ sixth form; (US) twelfth grade.

terminer /tɛʀmine/ [1] vt/i finish; (discours) end, finish. □ se ~ vpr end (par with).

terne /tɛʀn/ a dull, drab.

ternir /tɛʀniʀ/ [2] vt/i tarnish. □ se ~ vpr tarnish.

terrain /tɛʀɛ̃/ nm ground; (parcelle) piece of land; (à bâtir) plot; ~ d'aviation airfield; ~ de camping campsite; ~ de golf golf course; ~ de jeu playground; ~ vague waste ground.

terrasse /tɛʀas/ nf terrace; à la ~ (d'un café) outside (a café).

terrasser /tɛʀase/ [1] vt (adversaire) knock down; (maladie) strike down.

terre /tɛʀ/ nf (planète, matière) earth; (étendue, pays) land; (sol) ground; à ~ (Naut) ashore; par ~ (dehors) on the ground; (dedans) on the floor; ~ (cuite) terracotta; la ~ ferme dry land; ~ glaise clay.

terreau (pl ~x) nm compost.

terre-plein (pl terres-pleins) nm platform; (de route) central reservation.

terrestre /tɛʀɛstʀ/ a (animaux) land; (de notre planète) of the Earth.

terreur /tɛʀœʀ/ nf terror.

terrible /tɛʀibl/ a terrible; (formidable Ⅱ) terrific.

terrier /tɛʀje/ nm (trou) burrow; (chien) terrier.

terrifier /tɛʀifje/ [45] vt terrify.

territoire /tɛʀitwaʀ/ nm territory.

terroir /tɛʀwaʀ/ nm land; du ~ local.

terroriser /tɛʀɔʀize/ [1] vt terrorize.

terrorisme /tɛʀɔʀism/ nm

terrorism. **terroriste** *nmf* terrorist.

tertiaire /tɛRsjɛR/ *a* (*secteur*) service.

tes /te/ ⇒TON¹.

test /tɛst/ *nm* test.

testament /tɛstamɑ̃/ *nm* (Jur) will; (politique, artistique) testament; **Ancien/Nouveau T~** Old/New Testament.

tétanos /tetanos/ *nm* tetanus.

têtard /tɛtaR/ *nm* tadpole.

tête /tɛt/ *nf* head; (visage) face; (cheveux) hair; **à ~ de** at the head of; **à ~ reposée** at one's leisure; **de ~** (calculer) in one's head; **faire la ~** sulk; **tenir ~ à qn** stand up to sb; **il n'en fait qu'à sa ~** he does just as he pleases; **en ~** (Sport) in the lead; **faire une ~** (au football) head the ball; **une forte ~** a rebel; **la ~ la première** head first; **de la ~ aux pieds** from head to toe.

tête-à-tête /tɛtatɛt/ *nm inv* tête-à-tête; **en ~** in private.

tétée /tete/ *nf* feed.

tétine /tetin/ *nf* (de biberon) teat; (sucette) dummy; (US) pacifier.

têtu, ~e /tety/ *a* stubborn.

texte /tɛkst/ *nm* text; (de leçon) subject; (morceau choisi) passage.

texteur /tɛkstœR/ *nm* (Ordinat) word-processor.

textile /tɛkstil/ *nm & a* textile.

texto /tɛksto/ *nm* 🄼 text message.

TGV *abrév m* (**train à grande vitesse**) TGV, high-speed train.

thé /te/ *nm* tea.

théâtre /teatR/ *nm* theatre; (d'un crime) scene; **faire du ~** act.

théière /tejɛR/ *nf* teapot.

thème /tɛm/ *nm* theme; (traduction: Scol) prose.

théorie /teoRi/ *nf* theory. **théorique** *a* theoretical.

thérapie /teRapi/ *nf* therapy.

thermique /tɛRmik/ *a* thermal.

thermomètre /tɛRmɔmetR/ *nm* thermometer.

thermos® /tɛRmos/ *nm ou f* Thermos® (flask).

thermostat /tɛRmɔsta/ *nm* thermostat.

thèse /tɛz/ *nf* thesis.

thon /tɔ̃/ *nm* tuna.

thym /tɛ̃/ *nm* thyme.

tibia /tibja/ *nm* shinbone.

tic /tik/ *nm* (contraction) tic, twitch; (manie) habit.

ticket /tikɛ/ *nm* ticket.

tiède /tjɛd/ *a* lukewarm; (nuit) warm.

tiédir /tjediR/ [2] *vt/i* (faire) ~ warm up.

tien, ~ne /tjɛ̃, -ɛn/ *pron* **le ~, la ~ne, les ~(ne)s** yours; **à la ~ne!** cheers!

tiens, tient /tjɛ̃/ ⇒TENIR [59].

tiercé /tjɛRse/ *nm* place-betting.

tiers, tierce /tjɛR, tjɛRs/ *a* third. ● *nm* (fraction) third; (personne) third party. **tiers-monde** *nm* Third World.

tige /tiʒ/ *nf* (Bot) stem, stalk; (en métal) shaft, rod.

tigre /tigR/ *nm* tiger.

tigresse /tigRɛs/ *nf* tigress.

tilleul /tijœl/ *nm* lime tree.

timbre /tɛ̃bR/ *nm* stamp; (sonnette) bell; (de voix) tone. **~ poste** (pl **~s poste**) *nm* postage stamp. **timbrer** [1] *vt* stamp.

timide /timid/ *a* shy, timid. **timidité** *nf* shyness.

timoré, ~e /timoRe/ *a* timorous.

tintement /tɛ̃tmɑ̃/ *nm* (de sonnette) ringing; (de clés) jingling.

tique /tik/ *nf* tick.

tir /tiR/ *nm* (Sport) shooting; (action de tirer) firing; (feu, rafale) fire; **~ à l'arc** archery; **~ au pigeon** clay pigeon shooting.

tirage /tiRaʒ/ *nm* (de photo)

T

printing; (de journal) circulation; (de livre) edition; (Ordinat) hard copy; (de cheminée) draught; ~ **au sort** draw.

tire-bouchon (pl ~s) /tiʀbuʃɔ̃/ nm corkscrew.

tirelire /tiʀliʀ/ nf piggy bank.

tirer /tiʀe/ [1] vt pull; (langue) stick out; (conclusion, trait, rideaux) draw; (coup de feu) fire; (gibier) shoot; (photo) print; ~ **de** (sortir) take ou get out of; (extraire) extract from; (plaisir, nom) derive from; ~ **parti de** take advantage of; ~ **profit de** profit from; **se faire ~ l'oreille** get told off. ● vi shoot, fire (**sur** at); ~ **sur** (corde) pull at; (couleur) verge on; ~ **à sa fin** be drawing to a close; ~ **au clair** clarify; ~ **au sort** draw lots (for). □ **se ~** vpr ▣ clear off; **se ~ de** get out of; **s'en ~** (en réchapper) pull through; (réussir ▣) cope.

tiret /tiʀɛ/ nm dash.

tireur /tiʀœʀ/ nm gunman; ~ **d'élite** marksman; ~ **isolé** sniper.

tiroir /tiʀwaʀ/ nm drawer. **tiroir-caisse** (pl **tiroirs-caisses**) nm till, cash register.

tisane /tizan/ nf herbal tea.

tissage /tisaʒ/ nm weaving. **tisser** [1] vt weave. **tisserand** nm weaver.

tissu /tisy/ nm fabric, material; (biologique) tissue; **un ~ de mensonges** (fig) a pack of lies. **tissu-éponge** (pl **tissus-éponge**) nm towelling.

titre /titʀ/ nm title; (diplôme) qualification; (Comm) bond; ~**s** (droits) claims; (gros) ~**s** headlines; **à ~ d'exemple** as an example; **à juste ~** rightly; **à ~ privé** in a private capacity; **à double ~** on two accounts; ~ **de propriété** title deed.

tituber /titybe/ [1] vi stagger.

titulaire /titylɛʀ/ a **être ~** be a permanent staff member; **être ~ de** hold. ● nmf (de permis) holder.

titulariser [1] vt give permanent status to.

toast /tost/ nm (pain) piece of toast; (canapé, allocution) toast.

toboggan /tɔbɔgɑ̃/ nm (de jeu) slide; (Auto) flyover.

toi /twa/ pron you; (réfléchi) yourself; **dépêche-~** hurry up.

toile /twal/ nf cloth; (tableau) canvas; ~ **d'araignée** cobweb; ~ **de fond** (fig) backdrop; **la ~** (Internet) the Web.

toilette /twalɛt/ nf (habillement) outfit; ~**s** (cabinets) toilet(s); **de ~** (articles, savon) toilet; **faire sa ~** have a wash.

toi-même /twamɛm/ pron yourself.

toit /twa/ nm roof; ~ **ouvrant** (Auto) sunroof.

toiture /twatyʀ/ nf roof.

tôle /tol/ nf (plaque) iron sheet; ~ **ondulée** corrugated iron.

tolérant, ~**e** /tɔleʀɑ̃, -t/ a tolerant. **tolérer** [14] vt tolerate.

tomate /tɔmat/ nf tomato.

tombe /tɔ̃b/ nf grave; (pierre) gravestone.

tombeau (pl ~**x**) /tɔ̃bo/ nm tomb.

tomber /tɔ̃be/ [1] vi (aux être) fall; (fièvre, vent) drop; **faire ~** knock over; (gouvernement) bring down; **laisser ~** (objet, amoureux) drop; (collègue) let down; (activité) give up; **laisse ~!** ▣ forget it!; ~ **à l'eau** (projet) fall through; ~ **bien** ou **à point** come at the right time; ~ **en panne** break down; ~ **en syncope** faint; ~ **sur** (trouver) run across.

tombola /tɔ̃bɔla/ nf tombola; (US) lottery.

tome /tɔm/ nm volume.

ton¹, ta (**ton** before vowel or mute h) (pl **tes**) /tɔ̃, ta, tɔ̃n, te/ a your.

ton² /tɔ̃/ nm (hauteur de voix) pitch; **d'un ~ sec** drily; **de bon ~** in good taste.

tonalité /tɔnalite/ nf (Mus) key; (de téléphone) dialling tone; (US) dial tone.

tondeuse /tɔ̃døz/ nf (à moutons) shears (+ pl); (à cheveux) clippers (+ pl); **~ à gazon** lawn-mower.
tondre [3] vt (herbe) mow; (mouton) shear; (cheveux) clip.

tonne /tɔn/ nf tonne.

tonneau (pl **~x**) /tɔno/ nm barrel; (en voiture) somersault.

tonnerre /tɔnɛʀ/ nm thunder.

tonton /tɔ̃tɔ̃/ nm 🄙 uncle.

tonus /tɔnys/ nm energy.

torche /tɔʀʃ/ nf torch.

torchon /tɔʀʃɔ̃/ nm (pour la vaisselle) tea towel.

tordre /tɔʀdʀ/ [3] vt twist. □ **se ~** vpr **se ~ la cheville** twist one's ankle; **se ~ de douleur** writhe in pain; **se ~ (de rire)** split one's sides.

tordu, ~e /tɔʀdy/ a twisted, bent; (esprit) warped, twisted.

torpille /tɔʀpij/ nf torpedo.

torrent /tɔʀɑ̃/ nm torrent.

torride /tɔʀid/ a torrid; (chaleur) scorching.

torse /tɔʀs/ nm chest; (Anat) torso.

tort /tɔʀ/ nm wrong; **avoir ~** be wrong (**de faire** to do); **donner ~ à** prove wrong; **être dans son ~** be in the wrong; **faire (du) ~ à** harm; **à ~** wrongly; **à ~ et à travers** without thinking.

torticolis /tɔʀtikɔli/ nm stiff neck.

tortiller /tɔʀtije/ [1] vt twist, twirl. □ **se ~** vpr wriggle.

tortionnaire /tɔʀsjɔnɛʀ/ nm torturer.

tortue /tɔʀty/ nf tortoise; (d'eau) turtle.

tortueux, -euse /tɔʀtɥø, -z/ a (chemin) twisting; (explication) tortuous.

torture /tɔʀtyʀ/ nf torture.
torturer [1] vt torture.

tôt /to/ adv early; **au plus ~** at the earliest; **le plus ~ possible** as soon as possible; **~ ou tard** sooner or later; **ce n'est pas trop ~!** it's about time!

total, ~e (mpl **-aux**) /tɔtal, -o/ a total. ● nm (pl **-aux**) total; **au ~** all in all. **totalement** adv totally. **totaliser** [1] vt total. **totalitaire** a totalitarian.

totalité /tɔtalite/ nf **la ~ de** all of.

touche /tuʃ/ nf (de piano) key; (de peinture) touch; (**ligne de**) **~** (Sport) touchline.

toucher /tuʃe/ [1] vt touch; (émouvoir) move, touch; (contacter) get in touch with; (cible) hit; (argent) draw; (chèque) cash; (concerner) affect. ● vi **~ à** touch; (question) touch on; (fin, but) approach; **je vais lui en ~ deux mots** I'll talk to him about it. □ **se ~** vpr (lignes) touch. ● nm (sens) touch.

touffe /tuf/ nf (de poils, d'herbe) tuft, (de plantes) clump.

toujours /tuʒuʀ/ adv always; (encore) still; (de toute façon) anyway; **pour ~** for ever; **~ est-il que** the fact remains that.

toupet /tupɛ/ nm (culot 🄙) cheek, nerve.

tour /tuʀ/ nf tower; (immeuble) tower block; (échecs) rook; **~ de contrôle** control tower. ● nm (mouvement, succession, tournure) turn; (excursion) trip; (à pied) walk; (en auto) drive; (artifice) trick; (circonférence) circumference; (Tech) lathe; **~ (de piste)** lap; **à ~ de rôle** in turn; **à mon ~** when it is my turn; **c'est mon ~ de** it is my turn to; **faire le ~ de** go round; (question) survey; **~ d'horizon**

T

survey; **~ de potier** potter's wheel; **~ de taille** waist measurement; (ligne) waistline.

tourbillon /tuʀbijɔ̃/ *nm* whirlwind; (d'eau) whirlpool; (fig) swirl.

tourisme /tuʀism/ *nm* tourism; **faire du ~** do some sightseeing.

touriste /tuʀist/ *nmf* tourist. **touristique** *a* tourist; (*route*) scenic.

tourmenter /tuʀmɑ̃te/ *vt* torment. □ se ~ *vpr* worry.

tournant, **~e** /tuʀnɑ̃, -t/ *a* (qui pivote) revolving. ● *nm* bend; (fig) turning-point.

tourne-disque (*pl* ~s) /tuʀnədisk/ *nm* record-player.

tournée /tuʀne/ *nf* (de facteur, au café) round; **c'est ma ~** I'll buy this round; (d'artiste) tour.

tourner /tuʀne/ [1] *vt* turn; (*film*) shoot, make; **~ le dos à** turn one's back on; **~ en dérision** mock. ● *vi* turn; (*toupie, tête*) spin; (*moteur, usine*) run; **~ autour de** go round; (*personne, maison*) hang around; (*terre*) revolve round; (*question*) centre on; **~ de l'œil** 🖸 faint; **mal ~** (*affaire*) turn out badly. □ se ~ *vpr* turn.

tournesol /tuʀnəsɔl/ *nm* sunflower.

tournevis /tuʀnəvis/ *nm* screwdriver.

tournoi /tuʀnwa/ *nm* tournament.

tourte /tuʀt/ *nf* pie.

tourterelle /tuʀtəʀɛl/ *nf* turtle dove.

Toussaint /tusɛ̃/ *nf* **la ~** All Saints' Day.

tousser /tuse/ [1] *vi* cough.

tout, **~e** (*pl* **tous, toutes**) /tu, tut/ *nm* (ensemble) whole; **en ~** in all; **pas du ~!** not at all! ● *a* all; (n'importe quel) any; **~ le pays** the whole country, all the country;

~e la nuit/journée the whole night/day; **~ un paquet** a whole pack; **tous les jours** every day; **tous les deux ans** every two years; **~ le monde** everyone; **tous les deux, toutes les deux** both of them; **tous les trois** all three (of them). ● *pron* everything; all; anything; **tous** /tus/, **toutes** all; **tous ensemble** all together; **prends ~** take everything; **~ ce que tu veux** everything you want. ● *adv* (très) very; (entièrement) all; **~ au bout/début** right at the end/ beginning; **~ en marchant** while walking; **~ à coup** all of a sudden; **~ à fait** quite, completely; **~ à l'heure** in a moment; (passé) a moment ago; **~ au** *ou* **le long de** throughout; **~ au plus/moins** at most/least; **~ de même** all the same; **~ de suite** straight away; **~ entier** whole; **~ neuf** brand new; **~ nu** stark naked. **tout-à-l'égout** *nm inv* main drainage.

toutefois /tutfwa/ *adv* however.

tout(-)terrain /tuteʀɛ̃/ *a inv* all terrain.

toux /tu/ *nf* cough.

toxicomane /tɔksikɔman/ *nmf* drug addict.

toxique /tɔksik/ *a* toxic.

trac /tʀak/ *nm* **le ~** nerves; (Théât) stage fright.

traçabilité /tʀasabilite/ *nf* traceability.

tracas /tʀaka/ *nm* worry.

trace /tʀas/ *nf* (traînée, piste) trail; (d'animal, de pneu) tracks; **~s de pas** footprints.

tracer /tʀase/ [10] *vt* draw; (écrire) write; (route) open up.

trachée-artère /tʀaʃeaʀtɛʀ/ *nf* windpipe.

tracteur /tʀaktœʀ/ *nm* tractor.

tradition /tʀadisjɔ̃/ *nf* tradition. **traditionnel**, **~le** *a* traditional.

traducteur, **-trice** /tʀadyktœʀ,

-tRis/ *nm, f* translator. **traduction** *nf* translation.

traduire /tRadʉiR/ [17] *vt* translate; ∼ **en justice** take to court.

trafic /tRafik/ *nm* (commerce, circulation) traffic.

trafiquant, ∼**e** /tRafikɑ̃, -t/ *nm, f* trafficker; (d'armes, de drogues) dealer.

trafiquer /tRafike/ [1] *vi* traffic. ● *vt* ▣ (moteur) fiddle with.

tragédie /tRaʒedi/ *nf* tragedy. **tragique** *a* tragic.

trahir /tRaiR/ [2] *vt* betray. **trahison** *nf* betrayal; (Mil) treason.

train /tRɛ̃/ *nm* (Rail) train; (allure) pace; **aller bon** ∼ walk briskly; **en** ∼ **de faire** (busy) doing; ∼ **d'atterrissage** undercarriage; ∼ **électrique** (jouet) electric train set; ∼ **de vie** lifestyle.

traîne /tRɛn/ *nf* (de robe) train; **à la** ∼ lagging behind.

traîneau (*pl* ∼**x**) /tRɛno/ *nm* sleigh.

traînée /tRɛne/ *nf* (trace) trail; (longue) streak; (femme: péj) slut.

traîner /tRɛne/ [1] *vt* drag (along); ∼ **les pieds** drag one's feet. ● *vi* (pendre) trail; (rester en arrière) trail behind; (flâner) hang about; (*papiers, affaires*) lie around; ∼ (**en longueur**) drag on. ▫ **se** ∼ *vpr* (par terre) crawl.

traire /tRɛR/ [29] *vt* milk.

trait /tRɛ/ *nm* line; (en dessinant) stroke; (caractéristique) feature, trait; ∼**s** (du visage) features; **avoir** ∼ **à** relate to; **d'un** ∼ (boire) in one gulp; ∼ **d'union** hyphen; (fig) link.

traite /tRɛt/ *nf* (de vache) milking; (Comm) draft; **d'une** (**seule**) ∼ in one go, at a stretch.

traité /tRɛte/ *nm* (pacte) treaty; (ouvrage) treatise.

traitement /tRɛtmɑ̃/ *nm* treatment; (salaire) salary; ∼ **de données** data processing; ∼ **de texte** word processing.

traiter /tRɛte/ [1] *vt* treat; (*affaire*) deal with; (*données, produit*) process; ∼ **qn de lâche** call sb a coward. ● *vi* deal (**avec** with); ∼ **de** (*sujet*) deal with.

traiteur /tRɛtœR/ *nm* caterer; (boutique) delicatessen.

traître, -esse /tRɛtR, -ɛs/ *a* treacherous. ● *nm, f* traitor.

trajectoire /tRaʒɛktwaR/ *nf* path.

trajet /tRaʒɛ/ *nm* (voyage) journey; (itinéraire) route.

trame /tRam/ *nf* (de tissu) weft.

tramway /tRamwɛ/ *nm* tram; (US) streetcar.

tranchant, ∼**e** /tRɑ̃ʃɑ̃, -t/ *a* sharp; (fig) cutting. ● *nm* cutting edge; **à double** ∼ two-edged.

tranche /tRɑ̃ʃ/ *nf* (rondelle) slice; (bord) edge; (d'âge, de revenu) bracket.

tranchée /tRɑ̃ʃe/ *nf* trench.

trancher /tRɑ̃ʃe/ [1] *vt* cut; (*question*) decide; (contraster) contrast (**sur** with).

tranquille /tRɑ̃kil/ *a* quiet; (*esprit*) at rest; (*conscience*) clear; **être/laisser** ∼ be/leave in peace; **tiens-toi** ∼! be quiet!

tranquillisant *nm* tranquillizer.

tranquilliser [1] *vt* reassure.

tranquillité *nf* (peace and) quiet; (d'esprit) peace of mind.

transcription /tRɑ̃skɾipsjɔ̃/ *nf* transcription; (copie) transcript.

transcrire [30] *vt* transcribe.

transe /tRɑ̃s/ *nf* **en** ∼ in a trance.

transférer /tRɑ̃sfeRe/ [14] *vt* transfer.

transfert /tRɑ̃sfɛR/ *nm* transfer; ∼ **d'appel** (au téléphone) call diversion.

T

transformation /tʀɑ̃sfɔʀmasjɔ̃/ nf change; transformation.

transformer /tʀɑ̃sfɔʀme/ [1] vt change; (radicalement) transform; (vêtement) alter. □ se ~ vpr change; (radicalement) be transformed; (se) ~ en turn into.

transgénique /tʀɑ̃sʒenik/ a genetically modified.

transiger /tʀɑ̃siʒe/ [40] vi compromise.

transiter /tʀɑ̃zite/ [1] vt/i ~ par pass through.

transitif, -ive /tʀɑ̃zitif, -v/ a transitive.

translucide /tʀɑ̃slysid/ a translucent.

transmettre /tʀɑ̃smɛtʀ/ [42] vt (savoir, maladie) pass on; (ondes) transmit; (à la radio) broadcast. **transmission** nf transmission; (radio) broadcasting.

transparence /tʀɑ̃spaʀɑ̃s/ nf transparency. **transparent**, ~e a transparent.

transpercer /tʀɑ̃spɛʀse/ [10] vt pierce.

transpiration /tʀɑ̃spiʀasjɔ̃/ nf perspiration. **transpirer** [1] vi perspire.

transplanter /tʀɑ̃splɑ̃te/ [1] vt (Bot, Méd) transplant.

transport /tʀɑ̃spɔʀ/ nm transport (ation); **durant le** ~ in transit; **les** ~s transport (+ sg); **les** ~s **en commun** public transport (+ sg).

transporter /tʀɑ̃spɔʀte/ [1] vt transport; (à la main) carry. **transporteur** nm haulier; (US) trucker.

transversal, ~e (mpl -aux) /tʀɑ̃svɛʀsal, -o/ a cross, transverse.

trapu, ~e /tʀapy/ a stocky.

traumatisant, ~e /tʀomatizɑ̃, -t/ a traumatic. **traumatiser** vt [1] traumatize. **traumatisme** nm trauma.

travail (pl -aux) /tʀavaj, -o/ nm work; (emploi, tâche) job; (façonnage) working; **travaux** work (+ sg); (routiers) roadworks; ~ **à la chaîne** production line work; **travaux dirigés** (Scol) practical; **travaux forcés** hard labour; **travaux manuels** handicrafts; **travaux ménagers** housework.

travailler /tʀavaje/ [1] vi work; (se déformer) warp. ● vt (façonner) work; (étudier) work at ou on.

travailleur, -euse /tʀavajœʀ, -øz/ nm, f worker. ● a hardworking.

travailliste /tʀavajist/ a Labour. ● nmf Labour party member.

travers /tʀavɛʀ/ nm (défaut) failing; **à** ~ through; **au** ~ (**de**) through; **de** ~ (chapeau, nez) crooked; (regarder) askance; **j'ai avalé de** ~ it went the wrong way; **en** ~ (**de**) across.

traversée /tʀavɛʀse/ nf crossing.

traverser /tʀavɛʀse/ [1] vt cross; (transpercer) go (right) through; (période, forêt) go ou pass through.

traversin /tʀavɛʀsɛ̃/ nm bolster.

travesti /tʀavɛsti/ nm transvestite.

trébucher /tʀebyʃe/ [1] vi stumble, trip (over); **faire** ~ trip (up).

trèfle /tʀɛfl/ nm (plante) clover; (cartes) clubs.

treillis /tʀeji/ nm trellis; (en métal) wire mesh; (tenue militaire) combat uniform.

treize /tʀɛz/ a & nm thirteen.

tréma /tʀema/ nm diaeresis.

tremblement /tʀɑ̃bləmɑ̃/ nm shaking; ~ **de terre** earthquake.

trembler [1] vi shake, tremble; (lumière, voix) quiver.

tremper /tʀɑ̃pe/ [1] vt/i soak; (plonger) dip; (acier) temper; **faire**

~ soak; ~ **dans** (fig) be mixed up.
□ **se ~** *vpr* (se baigner) have a dip.
tremplin /tʀɑ̃plɛ̃/ *nm*
springboard.

trente /tʀɑ̃t/ *a & nm* thirty; **se
mettre sur son ~ et un** dress up;
tous les ~-six du mois once in a
blue moon.

trépied /tʀepje/ *nm* tripod.

très /tʀɛ/ *adv* very; ~ **aimé/estimé**
much liked/esteemed.

trésor /tʀezɔʀ/ *nm* treasure; **le
T~ public** the revenue
department.

trésorerie /tʀezɔʀʀi/ *nf* (bureaux)
accounts department; (du Trésor
public) revenue office; (argent)
funds (+ *pl*); (gestion) accounts (+
pl). **trésorier, -ière** *nm, f*
treasurer.

tressaillement /tʀesajmɑ̃/ *nm*
quiver; start.

tresse /tʀɛs/ *nf* braid, plait.

trêve /tʀɛv/ *nf* truce; (fig) respite;
~ **de plaisanteries** that's enough
joking.

tri /tʀi/ *nm* (classement) sorting;
(sélection) selection; **faire le ~ de**
(classer) sort; (choisir) select; **centre
de ~** sorting office.

triangle /tʀijɑ̃gl/ *nm* triangle.

tribal, ~e (*mpl* **-aux**) /tʀibal, -o/
a tribal.

tribord /tʀibɔʀ/ *nm* starboard.

tribu /tʀiby/ *nf* tribe.

tribunal (*mpl* **-aux**) /tʀibynal, -o/
nm court.

tribune /tʀibyn/ *nf* (de stade)
grandstand; (d'orateur) rostrum;
(débat) forum; (d'église) gallery.

tribut /tʀiby/ *nm* tribute.

tributaire /tʀibytɛʀ/ *a* ~ **de**
dependent on.

tricher /tʀiʃe/ [1] *vi* cheat.
tricheur, -euse *nm, f* cheat.

tricolore /tʀikɔlɔʀ/ *a* three-
coloured; (écharpe) red, white
and blue; (équipe) French.

tricot /tʀiko/ *nm* (activité) knitting;
(pull) sweater; **en ~** knitted; ~ **de
corps** vest; (US) undershirt.

tricoter [1] *vt/i* knit.

trier /tʀije/ [45] *vt* (classer) sort;
(choisir) select.

trimestre /tʀimɛstʀ/ *nm* quarter;
(Scol) term. **trimestriel, ~le** *a*
quarterly; (bulletin) end-of-term.

tringle /tʀɛ̃gl/ *nf* rail.

trinquer /tʀɛ̃ke/ [1] *vi* clink
glasses.

triomphant, ~e /tʀijɔ̃fɑ̃, -t/ *a*
triumphant. **triomphe** *nm*
triumph. **triompher** [1] *vi*
triumph (**de** over); (jubiler) be
triumphant.

tripes /tʀip/ *nfpl* (mets) tripe (+
sg); (entrailles 田) guts.

triple /tʀipl/ *a* triple, treble. ● *nm*
le ~ three times as much (**de** as).
triplés, -es *nm, fpl* triplets.

tripot /tʀipo/ *nm* gambling den.

tripoter /tʀipɔte/ [1] *vt* 田
(personne) grope; (objet) fiddle
with.

trisomique /tʀizɔmik/ *a* **être ~**
have Down's syndrome.

triste /tʀist/ *a* sad; (rue, temps,
couleur) dreary; (lamentable)
dreadful. **tristesse** *nf* sadness;
dreariness.

trivial, ~e (*mpl* **-iaux**) /tʀivjal,
-jo/ *a* coarse.

troc /tʀɔk/ *nm* exchange; (Comm)
barter.

trognon /tʀɔɲɔ̃/ *nm* (de fruit) core.

trois /tʀwa/ *a & nm* three; **hôtel
~ étoiles** three-star hotel.
troisième *a & nmf* third.

trombone /tʀɔ̃bɔn/ *nm* (Mus)
trombone; (agrafe) paperclip.

trompe /tʀɔ̃p/ *nf* (d'éléphant) trunk;
(Mus) horn.

tromper /tʀɔ̃pe/ [1] *vt* deceive,
mislead; (déjouer) elude. □ **se ~**
vpr be mistaken; **se ~ de route/**

T

d'heure take the wrong road/get the time wrong.

trompette /tʀɔ̃pɛt/ *nf* trumpet.

trompeur, -euse /tʀɔ̃pœʀ, -øz/ *a* (*apparence*) deceptive.

tronc /tʀɔ̃/ *nm* trunk; (*boîte*) collection box.

tronçon /tʀɔ̃sɔ̃/ *nm* section.

tronçonneuse /tʀɔ̃sɔnøz/ *nf* chain saw.

trône /tʀon/ *nm* throne. **trôner** [1] *vi* (*vase*) have pride of place (**sur** on).

trop /tʀo/ *adv* (*grand, loin*) too; (*boire, marcher*) too much; ~ (**de**) (*quantité*) too much; (*nombre*) too many; **ce serait** ~ **beau** one should be so lucky; **de** ~, **en** ~ too much; too many; **il a bu un verre de** ~ he's had one too many; **se sentir de** ~ feel one is in the way.

trophée /tʀɔfe/ *nm* trophy.

tropical, ~e (*mpl* **-aux**) /tʀɔpikal, -o/ *a* tropical. **tropique** *nm* tropic.

trop-plein (*pl* ~**s**) /tʀoplɛ̃/ *nm* excess; (*dispositif*) overflow.

troquer /tʀɔke/ [1] *vt* exchange; (*Comm*) barter (**contre** for).

trot /tʀo/ *nm* trot; **aller au** ~ trot. **trotter** [1] *vi* trot.

trotteuse /tʀɔtøz/ *nf* (*de montre*) second hand.

trottoir /tʀɔtwaʀ/ *nm* pavement; (*US*) sidewalk; ~ **roulant** moving walkway.

trou /tʀu/ *nm* hole; (*moment*) gap; (*lieu: péj*) dump; ~ (**de mémoire**) memory lapse; ~ **de serrure** keyhole; **faire son** ~ carve one's niche.

trouble /tʀubl/ *a* (*eau, image*) unclear; (*louche*) shady. ● *nm* (*émoi*) emotion; ~**s** (*Pol*) disturbances; (*Méd*) disorder (+ *sg*).

troubler /tʀuble/ [1] *vt* disturb;

(*eau*) make cloudy; (*inquiéter*) trouble. □ **se** ~ *vpr* (*personne*) become flustered.

trouer /tʀue/ [1] *vt* make a hole *ou* holes in; **mes chaussures sont trouées** my shoes have got holes in them.

troupe /tʀup/ *nf* troop; (*d'acteurs*) company.

troupeau (*pl* ~**x**) /tʀupo/ *nm* herd; (*de moutons*) flock.

trousse /tʀus/ *nf* case, bag; **aux** ~**s de** hot on sb's heels; ~ **de toilette** toilet bag.

trousseau (*pl* ~**x**) /tʀuso/ *nm* (*de clefs*) bunch; (*de mariée*) trousseau.

trouver /tʀuve/ [1] *vt* find; (*penser*) think; **il est venu me** ~ he came to see me. □ **se** ~ *vpr* be; (*se sentir*) feel; **il se trouve que** it happens that; **si ça se trouve** maybe; **se** ~ **mal** faint.

truand /tʀyɑ̃/ *nm* gangster.

truc /tʀyk/ *nm* (*moyen*) way; (*artifice*) trick; (*chose* ▣) thing.

trucage *nm* (*cinéma*) special effect.

truffe /tʀyf/ *nf* (*champignon, chocolat*) truffle; (*de chien*) nose.

truffer /tʀyfe/ [1] *vt* (*fig*) fill, pack (**de** with).

truie /tʀɥi/ *nf* (*animal*) sow.

truite /tʀɥit/ *nf* trout.

truquer /tʀyke/ [1] *vt* fix, rig; (*photo*) fake; (*résultats*) fiddle.

tsar /tsaʀ/ *nm* tsar, czar.

tu /ty/ *pron* (*parent, ami, enfant*) you. ● ⇒TAIRE [47].

tuba /tyba/ *nm* (*Mus*) tuba; (*Sport*) snorkel.

tube /tyb/ *nm* tube.

tuberculose /tybɛʀkyloz/ *nf* tuberculosis.

tuer /tɥe/ [1] *vt* kill; (*d'une balle*) shoot, kill; (*épuiser*) exhaust; ~ **par balles** shoot dead. □ **se** ~ *vpr* kill oneself; (*accident*) be killed.

tuerie /tyʀi/ *nf* killing.

tue-tête: à ~ /atytɛt/ *loc* at the top of one's voice.

tuile /tɥil/ *nf* tile; (malchance ⊞) (stroke of) bad luck.

tulipe /tylip/ *nf* tulip.

tumeur /tymœʀ/ *nf* tumour.

tumulte /tymylt/ *nm* commotion; (désordre) turmoil.

tunique /tynik/ *nf* tunic.

Tunisie /tynizi/ *nf* Tunisia.

tunnel /tynɛl/ *nm* tunnel.

turbo /tyʀbo/ *a* turbo. ● *nf* (voiture) turbo.

turbulent, ~e /tyʀbylɑ̃, -t/ *a* boisterous, turbulent.

turc, -que /tyʀk/ *a* Turkish. ● *nm* (Ling) Turkish. **T~, -que** Turk.

turfiste /tyʀfist/ *nmf* racegoer.

Turquie /tyʀki/ *nf* Turkey.

tutelle /tytɛl/ *nf* (Jur) guardianship; (fig) protection.

tuteur, -trice /tytœʀ, -tʀis/ *nm, f* (Jur) guardian. ● *nm* (bâton) stake.

tutoiement /tytwamɑ̃/ *nm* use of the 'tu' form. **tutoyer** [31] *vt* address using the 'tu' form.

tuyau (*pl* ~**x**) /tɥijo/ *nm* pipe; (conseil ⊞) tip; **~ d'arrosage** hosepipe.

TVA *abrév f* (**taxe à la valeur ajoutée**) VAT.

tympan /tɛ̃pɑ̃/ *nm* ear-drum.

type /tip/ *nm* (genre, traits) type; (individu ⊞) bloke, guy; **le ~ même de** a classic example of. ● *a inv* typical.

typique /tipik/ *a* typical.

tyran /tiʀɑ̃/ *nm* tyrant. **tyrannie** *nf* tyranny. **tyranniser** [1] *vt* oppress, tyrannize.

UE *abrév f* (**Union européenne**) European Union.

Ukraine /ykʀɛn/ *nf* Ukraine.

ulcère /ylsɛʀ/ *nm* (Méd) ulcer.

ULM *abrév m* (**ultraléger motorisé**) microlight.

ultérieur, ~e /ylteʀjœʀ/ *a* later. **ultérieurement** *adv* later.

ultime /yltim/ *a* final.

---

un, une /œ̃, yn/

●*déterminant*

····▶ a; (devant voyelle) an; **~ animal** an animal; **~ jour** one day; **pas ~ arbre** not a single tree; **il fait ~ froid!** it's so cold!

●*pronom*

····▶ one; **l'~ d'entre nous** one of us; **les ~s croient que...** some believe...

····▶ **la une** the front page.

····▶ **j'en veux une** I want one.

●*adjectif*

····▶ one, a, an; **j'ai ~ garçon et deux filles** I have a *ou* one boy and two girls; **il est une heure** it is one o'clock.

●*nom masculin & féminin*

····▶ **~ par ~** one by one.

---

unanime /ynanim/ *a* unanimous.

unanimité /ynanimite/ *nf* unanimity; **à l'~** unanimously.

uni, ~e /yni/ *a* united; (*couple*) close; (*surface*) smooth; (*tissu*) plain.

unième /ynjɛm/ a -first; **vingt et ~** twenty-first; **cent ~** one hundred and first.

unifier /ynifje/ [45] vt unify.

uniforme /ynifɔʀm/ nm uniform. ● a uniform. **uniformiser** [1] vt standardize. **uniformité** nf uniformity.

unilatéral, **~e** (mpl **-aux**) /ynilateʀal, -o/ a unilateral.

union /ynjɔ̃/ nf union; **l'U~** européenne the European Union.

unique /ynik/ a (seul) only; (prix, voie) one; (incomparable) unique; **enfant ~** only child; **sens ~** one-way street. **uniquement** adv only, solely.

unir /yniʀ/ [2] vt unite. □ **s'~** vpr unite, join.

unité /ynite/ nf unit; (harmonie) unity.

univers /ynivɛʀ/ nm universe.

universel, **~le** /ynivɛʀsɛl/ a universal.

universitaire /ynivɛʀsitɛʀ/ a (résidence) university; (niveau) academic. ● nmf academic.

université /ynivɛʀsite/ nf university.

uranium /yʀanjɔm/ nm uranium.

urbain, **~e** /yʀbɛ̃, -ɛn/ a urban. **urbanisme** nm town planning.

urgence /yʀʒɑ̃s/ nf (cas) emergency; (de situation, tâche) urgency; **d'~** (mesure) emergency; (transporter) urgently; **les ~s** casualty (+ sg). **urgent**, **~e** a urgent.

urine /yʀin/ nf urine. **urinoir** nm urinal.

urne /yʀn/ nf (électorale) ballot box; (vase) urn; **aller aux ~s** go to the polls.

urticaire /yʀtikɛʀ/ nf hives (+ pl), urticar.

us /ys/ nmpl **les ~ et coutumes** habits and customs.

usage /yzaʒ/ nm use; (coutume) custom; (de langage) usage; **à l'~ de** for; **d'~** (habituel) customary; **faire ~ de** make use of.

usagé, **~e** /yzaʒe/ a worn.

usager /yzaʒe/ nm user.

usé, **~e** /yze/ a worn (out); (banal) trite.

user /yze/ [1] vt wear (out). ● vi **~ de** use. □ **s'~** vpr (tissu) wear (out).

usine /yzin/ nf factory, plant; **~ sidérurgique** ironworks (+ pl).

usité, **~e** /yzite/ a common.

ustensile /ystɑ̃sil/ nm utensil.

usuel, **~le** /yzɥɛl/ a ordinary, everyday.

usure /yzyʀ/ nf (détérioration) wear (and tear).

utérus /yteʀys/ nm womb, uterus.

utile /ytil/ a useful.

utilisable /ytilizabl/ a usable. **utilisation** nf use. **utiliser** [1] vt use.

utopie /ytɔpi/ nf Utopia; (idée) Utopian idea. **utopique** a Utopian.

UV[1] abrév f (**unité de valeur**) course unit.

UV[2] abrév mpl (**ultraviolets**) ultraviolet rays; **faire des ~** use a sunbed.

va /va/ ⇨ALLER [8].

vacance /vakɑ̃s/ nf (poste) vacancy.

vacances /vakɑ̃s/ nfpl holiday (s); (US) vacation; **en ~** on holiday; **~ d'été, grandes ~**

summer holidays. **vacancier,
-ière** *nm, f* holidaymaker; (US)
vacationer.

vacant, ~e /vakã, -t/ *a* vacant.

vacarme /vakaʀm/ *nm* din.

vaccin /vaksẽ/ *nm* vaccine.
vacciner [1] *vt* vaccinate.

vache /vaʃ/ *nf* cow. ● *a* (méchant
) nasty.

vaciller /vasije/ [1] *vi* sway,
wobble; (*lumière*) flicker; (*hésiter*)
falter; (*santé, mémoire*) fail.

vadrouiller /vadʀuje/ [1] *vi*
wander about.

va-et-vient /vaevjẽ/ *nm inv* toing
and froing; (*de personnes*) comings
and goings; **faire le ~** go to and
fro; (*interrupteur*) two-way switch.

vagabond, ~e /vagabõ, -d/ *nm, f*
vagrant.

vagin /vaʒẽ/ *nm* vagina.

vague /vag/ *a* vague. ● *nm*
regarder dans le ~ stare into
space; **il est resté dans le ~** he
was vague about it. ● *nf* wave; **~
de fond** ground swell; **~ de froid**
cold spell; **~ de chaleur** heatwave.

vaillant, ~e /vajã, -t/ *a* brave;
(*vigoureux*) strong.

vaille /vaj/ ⇒VALOIR [60].

vain, ~e /vẽ, vɛn/ *a* vain, futile;
en ~ in vain.

vaincre /vẽkʀ/ [59] *vt* defeat;
(*surmonter*) overcome. **vaincu, ~e**
nm, f (Sport) loser. **vainqueur** *nm*
victor; (Sport) winner.

vais /vɛ/ ⇒ALLER [8].

vaisseau (*pl ~x*) /vɛso/ *nm* ship;
(veine) vessel; **~ spatial** spaceship.

vaisselle /vɛsɛl/ *nf* crockery; (à
laver) dishes; **faire la ~** do the
washing-up, wash the dishes;
liquide ~ washing-up liquid.

valable /valabl/ *a* valid; (de
qualité) worthwhile.

valet /valɛ/ *nm* (aux cartes) jack; **~
(de chambre)** manservant.

valeur /valœʀ/ *nf* value; (mérite)

worth, value; **~s** (Comm) stocks
and shares; **avoir de la ~** be
valuable; **prendre/perdre de la ~**
go up/down in value; **objets de ~**
valuables; **sans ~** worthless.

valide /valid/ *a* (*personne*) fit;
(*billet*) valid. **valider** [1] *vt*
validate.

valise /valiz/ *nf* (suit)case; **faire
ses ~s** pack (one's bags).

vallée /vale/ *nf* valley.

valoir /valwaʀ/ [60] *vi* (mériter) be
worth; (égaler) be as good as; (être
valable) (*règle*) apply; **faire ~**
(*mérite, qualité*) emphasize;
(*terrain*) cultivate; (*droit*) assert;
se faire ~ put oneself forward; **~
cher/100 francs** be worth a lot/100
francs; **que vaut ce vin?** what's
this wine like?; **ne rien ~** be
useless *ou* no good; **ça ne me dit
rien qui vaille** I don't like the
sound of that; **~ la peine** *or* **le
coup** be worth it; **il vaut/vaudrait
mieux faire** it is/would be better to
do. ● *vt* **~ qch à qn** (*éloges,
critiques*) earn sb sth.;
(*admiration*) win sb sth. □ **se ~**
vpr (être équivalents) be as good as
each other; **ça se vaut** it's all the
same.

valoriser /valɔʀize/ [1] *vt* add
value to; (*produit*) promote;
(*profession*) make attractive;
(*région, ressources*) develop.

valse /vals/ *nf* waltz.

vandale /vãdal/ *nmf* vandal.

vanille /vanij/ *nf* vanilla.

vanité /vanite/ *nf* vanity.
vaniteux, -euse *a* vain,
conceited.

vanne /van/ *nf* (d'écluse) sluice-
gate; (propos) dig .

vantard, ~e /vãtaʀ, -d/ *a*
boastful. ● *nm, f* boaster.

vanter /vãte/ [1] *vt* praise. □ **se
~** *vpr* boast (de about); **se ~ de
faire** pride oneself on doing.

vapeur /vapœR/ *nf* (eau) steam; (brume, émanation) vapour; ~s fumes; à ~ (*bateau, locomotive*) steam; faire cuire à la ~ steam.

vaporisateur /vapoRizatœR/ *nm* spray, atomizer. **vaporiser** [1] *vt* spray.

varappe /vaRap/ *nf* rock-climbing.

variable /vaRjabl/ *a* variable; (*temps*) changeable.

varicelle /vaRisɛl/ *nf* chickenpox.

varié, ~e /vaRje/ *a* (non monotone, étendu) varied; (divers) various; sandwichs ~s a selection of sandwiches.

varier /vaRje/ [45] *vt/i* vary.

variété /vaRjete/ *nf* variety; spectacle de ~s variety show.

vase /vɑz/ *nm* vase. ● *nf* silt, mud.

vaseux, -euse /vɑzø, -z/ *a* (confus 🔟) woolly, hazy.

vaste /vast/ *a* vast, huge.

vaurien, ~ne /voRjɛ̃, -ɛn/ *nm, f* good-for-nothing.

vautour /votuR/ *nm* vulture.

vautrer (se) /(sə)votRe/ [1] *vpr* sprawl; se ~ dans (*vice, boue*) wallow in.

veau (*pl* ~x) /vo/ *nm* calf; (viande) veal; (cuir) calfskin.

vécu, ~e /veky/ *a* (réel) true, real. ● ⇒VIVRE [62].

vedette /vədɛt/ *nf* (artiste) star; en ~ (*objet*) in a prominent position; (*personne*) in the limelight; joueur ~ star player; (bateau) launch.

végétal (*mpl* -aux) /veʒetal, -o/ *a* plant. ● *nm* (*pl* -aux) plant.

végétalien, ~ne /veʒetaljɛ̃, -ɛn/ *a* & *nm, f* vegan.

végétarien, ~ne /veʒetaRjɛ̃, -ɛn/ *a* & *nm, f* vegetarian.

végétation /veʒetasjɔ̃/ *nf* vegetation; ~s (Méd) adenoids.

véhicule /veikyl/ *nm* vehicle.

veille /vɛj/ *nf* (état) wakefulness; (jour précédent) la ~ (de) the day before; la ~ de Noël Christmas Eve; à la ~ de on the eve of; la ~ au soir the previous evening.

veillée /veje/ *nf* evening (gathering).

veiller /veje/ [1] *vi* stay up; (monter la garde) be on watch. ● *vt* (*malade*) watch over; ~ à attend to; ~ sur watch over.

veilleur /vejœR/ *nm* ~ de nuit night-watchman.

veilleuse /vejøz/ *nf* night light; (de véhicule) sidelight; (de réchaud) pilot light; mettre qch en ~ put sth on the back burner.

veine /vɛn/ *nf* (Anat) vein; (nervure, filon) vein; (chance 🔟) luck; avoir de la ~ 🔟 be lucky.

véliplanchiste /veliplɑ̃ʃist/ *nmf* windsurfer.

vélo /velo/ *nm* bike; (activité) cycling; faire du ~ go cycling; ~ tout terrain mountain bike.

vélomoteur /velomotœR/ *nm* moped.

velours /v(ə)luR/ *nm* velvet; ~ côtelé corduroy.

velouté, ~e /vəlute/ *a* smooth. ● *nm* (Culin) ~ d'asperges cream of asparagus soup.

vendanges /vɑ̃dɑ̃ʒ/ *nfpl* grape harvest.

vendeur, -euse /vɑ̃dœR, -øz/ *nm, f* shop assistant; (marchand) salesman, saleswoman; (Jur) vendor, seller.

vendre /vɑ̃dR/ [3] *vt* sell; à ~ for sale. □ se ~ *vpr* (être vendu) be sold; (trouver acquéreur) sell; se ~ bien sell well.

vendredi /vɑ̃dRədi/ *nm* Friday; V~ saint Good Friday.

vénéneux, -euse /venenø, -z/ *a* poisonous.

vénérer /veneRe/ [14] *vt* revere.

vénérien, ~**ne** /veneʀjɛ̃, -ɛn/ a
maladie ~**ne** venereal disease.

vengeance /vãʒãs/ nf revenge,
vengeance.

venger /vãʒe/ [40] vt avenge.
□ se ~ vpr take ou get one's
revenge (**de qch** for sth; **de qn** on
sb).

vengeur, -**eresse** /vãʒœʀ, -əʀɛs/
a vengeful. ● nm, f avenger.

venimeux, -**euse** /vənimø, -z/ a
poisonous, venomous.

venin /vənɛ̃/ nm venom.

venir /vəniʀ/ [58] vi (aux être)
come (**de** from); **faire ~ qn** send
for sb, call sb; **en ~ à** come to; **en
~ aux mains** come to blows; **où
veut-elle en ~?** what is she
driving at?; **il m'est venu à l'esprit**
or **à l'idée que** it occurred to me
that; **s'il venait à pleuvoir** if it
should rain; **dans les jours à ~** in
the next few days. ● v aux ~ **de
faire** have just done; **il vient/venait
d'arriver** he has/had just arrived;
~ **faire** come to do; **viens voir**
come and see.

vent /vã/ nm wind; **il fait du ~** it
is windy; **être dans le ~** be
trendy.

vente /vãt/ nf sale; ~ (**aux
enchères**) auction; **en ~** on ou for
sale; **mettre qch en ~** put sth up
for sale; ~ **de charité** (charity)
bazaar; ~ **au détail/en gros**
retailing/wholesaling; **équipe de
~** sales team.

ventilateur /vãtilatœʀ/ nm fan,
ventilator. **ventiler** [1] vt
ventilate.

ventouse /vãtuz/ nf suction pad;
(pour déboucher) plunger.

ventre /vãtʀ/ nm stomach;
(d'animal) belly; (utérus) womb; **avoir
du ~** have a paunch.

venu, ~**e** /vəny/ a **bien ~** (à
propos) apt, timely; **mal ~** badly
timed; **il serait mal ~ de faire** it

wouldn't be a good idea to do.
● ⇒VENIR [59].

venue /vəny/ nf coming.

ver /vɛʀ/ nm worm; (dans la
nourriture) maggot; (du bois)
woodworm; ~ **luisant** glow-worm;
~ **à soie** silkworm; ~ **solitaire**
tapeworm; ~ **de terre** earthworm.

verbal, ~**e** (mpl -**aux**) /vɛʀbal,
-o/ a verbal.

verbe /vɛʀb/ nm verb.

verdir /vɛʀdiʀ/ [2] vi turn green.

véreux, -**euse** /veʀø, -z/ a
wormy; (malhonnête) shady.

verger /vɛʀʒe/ nm orchard.

verglas /vɛʀgla/ nm black ice.

véridique /veʀidik/ a true.

vérification /veʀifikasjɔ̃/ nf
check(ing), verification.

vérifier /veʀifje/ [45] vt check,
verify; (confirmer) confirm.

véritable /veʀitabl/ a true, real;
(authentique) real.

vérité /veʀite/ nf truth; (de tableau,
roman) realism; **en ~** in fact,
actually.

vermine /vɛʀmin/ nf vermin.

verni, ~**e** /vɛʀni/ a (chaussures)
patent (leather); (chanceux Ⅱ)
lucky.

vernir /vɛʀniʀ/ [2] vt varnish.
□ se ~ vpr se ~ **les ongles** apply
nail polish.

vernis /vɛʀni/ nm varnish; (de
poterie) glaze; ~ **à ongles** nail
polish.

verra, **verrait** /vɛʀa, vɛʀɛ/ ⇒VOIR
[64].

verre /vɛʀ/ nm glass; (de lunettes)
lens; ~ **à vin** wine glass; **prendre**
ou **boire un ~** have a drink; ~ **de
contact** contact lens; ~ **dépoli**
frosted glass.

verrière /vɛʀjɛʀ/ nf (toit) glass
roof; (paroi) glass wall.

verrou /vɛʀu/ nm bolt; **sous les
~s** behind bars.

verrouillage /vɛʀujaz/ nm ~

central or **centralisé (des portes)** central locking.

verrue /vɛʀy/ nf wart; ~ **plantaire** verruca.

vers¹ /vɛʀ/ prép towards; (aux environs de) (temps) about; (lieu) near, around; (période) towards; ~ **le soir** towards evening.

vers² /vɛʀ/ nm (poésie) line of verse.

versatile /vɛʀsatil/ a unpredictable, volatile.

verse: **à ~** /avɛʀs/ loc in torrents.

Verseau /vɛʀso/ nm **le ~** Aquarius.

versement /vɛʀsəmɑ̃/ nm payment; (échelonné) instalment.

verser /vɛʀse/ [1] vt/i pour; (larmes, sang) shed; (payer) pay. ● vi pour; (voiture) overturn; ~ **dans** (fig) lapse into.

version /vɛʀsjɔ̃/ nf version; (traduction) translation.

verso /vɛʀso/ nm back (of the page); **voir au ~** see overleaf.

vert, ~e /vɛʀ, -t/ a green; (vieillard) sprightly. ● nm green; **les ~s** the Greens.

vertèbre /vɛʀtɛbʀ/ nf vertebra; **se déplacer une ~** slip a disc.

vertical, ~e (mpl **-aux**) /vɛʀtikal, -o/ a vertical.

vertige /vɛʀtiʒ/ nm dizziness; ~**s** dizzy spells; **avoir le ~** feel dizzy.

vertigineux, -euse a dizzy; (très grand) staggering.

vertu /vɛʀty/ nf virtue; **en ~ de** in accordance with. **vertueux, -euse** a virtuous.

verveine /vɛʀvɛn/ nf verbena.

vessie /vesi/ nf bladder.

veste /vɛst/ nf jacket.

vestiaire /vɛstjɛʀ/ nm cloakroom; (Sport) changing-room; (US) locker-room.

vestibule /vɛstibyl/ nm hall; (Théât, d'hôtel) foyer.

vestige /vɛstiʒ/ nm (objet) relic; (trace) vestige.

veston /vɛstɔ̃/ nm jacket.

vêtement /vɛtmɑ̃/ nm article of clothing; ~**s** clothes, clothing.

vétéran /veterɑ̃/ nm veteran.

vétérinaire /veteʀinɛʀ/ nmf vet, veterinary surgeon, (US) veterinarian.

vêtir /vetiʀ/ [61] vt dress. □ **se ~** vpr dress.

veto /veto/ nm inv veto.

vêtu, ~e /vety/ a dressed (**de** in).

veuf, veuve /vœf, -v/ a widowed. ● nm, f widower, widow.

veuille /vœj/ ⇒VOULOIR [64].

veut, veux /vø/ ⇒VOULOIR [64].

vexation /vɛksasjɔ̃/ nf humiliation.

vexer /vɛkse/ [1] vt upset, hurt. □ **se ~** vpr be upset, be hurt.

viable /vjabl/ a viable; (projet) feasible.

viande /vjɑ̃d/ nf meat.

vibrer /vibʀe/ [1] vi vibrate; **faire ~** (âme, foules) stir.

vicaire /vikɛʀ/ nm curate.

vice /vis/ nm (moral) vice; (physique) defect.

vicier /visje/ [45] vt contaminate; (air) pollute.

vicieux, -ieuse /visjø, -z/ a depraved. ● nm, f pervert.

victime /viktim/ nf victim; (d'un accident) casualty.

victoire /viktwaʀ/ nf victory; (Sport) win. **victorieux, -ieuse** a victorious; (équipe) winning.

vidange /vidɑ̃ʒ/ nf emptying; (Auto) oil change; (tuyau) waste pipe ou outlet.

vide /vid/ a empty. ● nm (absence, manque) vacuum, void; (espace) space; (trou) gap; (sans air) vacuum; **à ~** empty; **emballé sous ~** vacuum packed; **suspendu dans le ~** dangling in space.

vidéo /video/ a inv video; **jeu ~**

video game. ● *nf* video.
vidéocassette *nf* video(tape).
vidéoclip *nm* music video.
vidéoconférence *nf*
videoconferencing; (séance)
videoconference. **vidéodisque**
nm videodisc. **vidéophone** *nm*
videophone.
vide-ordures /vidɔRdyR/ *nm inv*
rubbish chute.
vidéothèque /videotɛk/ *nf* video
library.
vider /vide/ [1] *vt* empty;
(*poisson*) gut; (expulser 🔢) throw
out. □ **se** ∼ *vpr* empty.
vie /vi/ *nf* life; (durée) lifetime; **à**
∼, **pour la** ∼ for life; **donner la** ∼
à give birth to; **en** ∼ alive; **la** ∼
est chère the cost of living is
high.
vicil /vjɛj/ ⇒VIEUX.
vieillard /vjɛjaR/ *nm* old man.
vieille /vjɛj/ ⇒VIEUX.
vieillesse /vjɛjɛs/ *nf* old age.
vieillir /vjɛjiR/ [2] *vi* grow old,
age; (*mot, idée*) become old-
fashioned. ● *vt* age.
vieillissement *nm* ageing.
viens, vient /vjɛ̃/ ⇒VENIR [59].
vierge /vjɛRʒ/ *nf* virgin; **la V**∼
Virgo. ● *a* virgin; (*feuille,
cassette*) blank; (*cahier, pellicule*)
unused, new.
vieux (**vieil** *before vowel or mute
h*), **vieille** (*mpl* **vieux**) /vjø, vjɛj/
a old. ● *nm, f* old man, old
woman; **petit** ∼ little old man; **les**
∼ old people; **vieille fille** (péj)
spinster; ∼ **garçon** old bachelor.
vieux jeu *a inv* old-fashioned.
vif, vive /vif, viv/ *a* (animé) lively;
(*émotion, vent*) keen; (*froid*)
biting; (*lumière*) bright; (*douleur,
contraste, parole*) sharp; (*souvenir, style, teint*) vivid; (*succès,
impatience*) great; **brûler/enterrer**
∼ burn/bury alive; **de vive voix**
personally. ● *nm* **à** ∼ (*plaie*)

open; **avoir les nerfs à** ∼ be on
edge; **blessé au** ∼ cut to the
quick.
vigie /viʒi/ *nf* lookout.
vigilant, ∼e /viʒilɑ̃, -t/ *a* vigilant.
vigne /viɲ/ *nf* (plante) vine;
(vignoble) vineyard. **vigneron, ∼ne**
nm, f wine-grower.
vignette /viɲɛt/ *nf* (étiquette) label;
(Auto) road tax disc.
vignoble /viɲɔbl/ *nm* vineyard.
vigoureux, -euse /viguRø, -z/ *a*
vigorous, sturdy.
vigueur /vigœR/ *nf* vigour; **être/
entrer en** ∼ (*loi*) be/come into
force; **en** ∼ current.
VIH *abrév m* (**virus immunodé-
ficitaire humain**) HIV.
vilain, ∼e /vilɛ̃, -ɛn/ *a* (mauvais)
nasty; (laid) ugly. ● *nm, f* naughty
boy, naughty girl.
villa /villa/ *nf* detached house.
village /vilaʒ/ *nm* village.
villageois, ∼e /vilaʒwa, -z/ *a*
village. ● *nm, f* villager.
ville /vil/ *nf* town; (importante) city;
∼ **d'eaux** spa.
vin /vɛ̃/ *nm* wine; ∼ **d'honneur**
reception.
vinaigre /vinɛgR/ *nm* vinegar.
vinaigrette *nf* oil and vinegar
dressing, vinaigrette.
vingt /vɛ̃/ (/vɛ̃t/ *before vowel and
in numbers 22-29*) *a & nm* twenty.
vingtaine /vɛtɛn/ *nf* **une** ∼ (de)
about twenty.
vingtième /vɛ̃tjɛm/ *a & nmf*
twentieth.
vinicole /vinikɔl/ *a* wine(-
producing).
viol /vjɔl/ *nm* (de femme) rape; (de
lieu, loi) violation.
violemment /vjɔlamɑ̃/ *adv*
violently.
violence /vjɔlɑ̃s/ *nf* violence;
(acte) act of violence. **violent, ∼e**
a violent.

violer /vjɔle/ [1] *vt* rape; (*lieu, loi*) violate.

violet, ∼te /vjɔlɛ, -t/ *a* purple. ●*nm* purple. **violette** *nf* violet.

violon /vjɔlɔ̃/ *nm* violin; ∼ **d'Ingres** hobby.

violoncelle /vjɔlɔ̃sɛl/ *nm* cello.

vipère /vipɛR/ *nf* viper, adder.

virage /viRaʒ/ *nm* bend; (en ski) turn; (changement d'attitude: fig) change of course.

virée /viRe/ *nf* ⊞ trip, tour; (en voiture) drive; (à vélo) ride.

virement /viRmɑ̃/ *nm* (Comm) (credit) transfer; ∼ **automatique** standing order.

virer /viRe/ [1] *vi* turn; ∼ **de bord** tack; (fig) do a U-turn; ∼ **au rouge** turn red. ●*vt* (*argent*) transfer; (expulser ⊞) throw out; (*élève*) expel; (licencier ⊞) fire.

virgule /viRgyl/ *nf* comma; (dans un nombre) (decimal) point.

viril, ∼e /viRil/ *a* virile.

virtuel, ∼le /viRtɥɛl/ *a* (potentiel) potential; (*mémoire, réalité*) virtual.

virulent, ∼e /viRylɑ̃, -t/ *a* virulent.

virus /viRys/ *nm* virus.

vis¹ /vi/ ⇒VIVRE [62], VOIR [63].

vis² /vis/ *nf* screw.

visa /viza/ *nm* visa.

visage /vizaʒ/ *nm* face.

vis-à-vis /vizavi/ *prép* ∼ **de** (en face de) opposite; (à l'égard de) in relation to; (comparé à) compared to, beside. ●*nm inv* (personne) person opposite; **en ∼** opposite each other.

visée /vize/ *nf* aim; **avoir des ∼s sur** have designs on.

viser /vize/ [1] *vt* (*cible, centre*) aim at; (*poste, résultats*) aim for; (concerner) be aimed at; (*document*) stamp; ∼ **à** aim at; (*mesure, propos*) be aimed at; ∼ **à faire** aim to do. ●*vi* aim.

viseur /vizœR/ *nm* (d'arme) sights (+ *pl*); (Photo) viewfinder.

visière /vizjɛR/ *nf* (de casquette) peak; (de casque) visor.

vision /vizjɔ̃/ *nf* vision.

visite /vizit/ *nf* visit; (pour inspecter) inspection; (personne) visitor; **heures de ∼** visiting hours; ∼ **guidée** guided tour; ∼ **médicale** medical; **rendre ∼ à, faire une ∼ à** pay a visit; **être en ∼ (chez qn)** be visiting (sb); **avoir de la ∼** have visitors.

visiter /vizite/ [1] *vt* visit; (*appartement*) view. **visiteur, -euse** *nm, f* visitor.

visser /vise/ *vt* screw (on).

visuel, ∼le /vizɥɛl/ *a* visual. ●*nm* (Ordinat) visual display unit, VDU.

vit /vi/ ⇒VIVRE [62], VOIR [63].

vital, ∼e (*mpl* -**aux**) /vital, -o/ *a* vital.

vitamine /vitamin/ *nf* vitamin.

vite /vit/ *adv* fast, quickly; (tôt) soon; ∼! quick!; **faire ∼** be quick; **au plus ∼, le plus ∼ possible** as quickly as possible.

vitesse /vitɛs/ *nf* speed; (régime: Auto) gear; **à toute ∼** at top speed; **en ∼** in a hurry, quickly; **boîte à cinq ∼s** five-speed gearbox.

viticole /vitikɔl/ *a* (*industrie*) wine; (*région*) wine-producing. **viticulteur** *nm* wine-grower.

vitrage /vitraʒ/ *nm* (vitres) windows; **double ∼** double glazing.

vitrail (*pl* -**aux**) /vitraj, -o/ *nm* stained-glass window.

vitre /vitR/ *nf* (window) pane; (de véhicule) window.

vitrine /vitrin/ *nf* (shop) window; (meuble) display cabinet.

vivace /vivas/ *a* (*plante*) perennial; (durable) enduring.

vivacité /vivasite/ *nf* liveliness; (agilité) quickness; (d'émotion, d'intelligence) keenness; (de souvenir, style, teint) vividness.

vivant, ~e /vivã, -t/ *a* (*example, symbole*) living; (en vie) alive, living; (actif, vif) lively. ●*nm* un bon ~ a bon viveur; de son ~ in his lifetime; les ~s the living.

vive[1] /viv/ ⇒VIF.

vive[2] /viv/ *interj* ~ le roi! long live the king!

vivement /vivmã/ *adv* (fortement) strongly; (vite, sèchement) sharply; (avec éclat) vividly; (beaucoup) greatly; ~ la fin! I'll be glad when it's the end!

vivier /vivje/ *nm* fish pond; (artificiel) fish tank.

vivifier /vivifje/ [45] *vt* invigorate.

vivre /vivʀ/ [62] *vi* live; ~ de (nourriture) live on; ~ encore be still alive; faire ~ (famille) support. ●*vt* (vie) live; (période, aventure) live through.

vivres /vivʀ/ *nmpl* supplies.

VO *abrév f* (**vorcion originale**) en ~ in the original language.

vocabulaire /vɔkabylɛʀ/ *nm* vocabulary.

vocal, ~e (*mpl* **-aux**) /vɔkal, -o/ *a* vocal.

vœu (*pl* ~**x**) /vø/ *nm* (souhait) wish; (promesse) vow; meilleurs ~x best wishes.

vogue /vɔg/ *nf* fashion, vogue; en ~ in fashion *ou* vogue.

voguer /vɔge/ [1] *vi* sail.

voici /vwasi/ *prép* here is, this is; (au pluriel) here are, these are; me ~ here I am; ~ un an (temps passé) a year ago; ~ un an que it is a year since.

voie /vwa/ *nf* (route) road; (partie de route) lane; (chemin) way; (moyen) means, way; (rails) track; (quai) platform; en ~ de in the process of; en ~ de développement (*pays*)

developing; espèce en ~ de disparition endangered species; par la ~ des airs by air; par ~ orale orally; sur la bonne/mauvaise ~ (fig) on the right/wrong track; montrer la ~ lead the way; ~ de dégagement slip-road; ~ ferrée railway; (US) railroad; V~ lactée Milky Way; ~ navigable waterway; ~ publique public highway; ~ sans issue (sur panneau) no through road; (fig) dead end.

voilà /vwala/ *prép* there is, that is; (au pluriel) there are, those are; (voici) here is, here are; le ~ there he is; ~! right!; (en offrant qch) there you are!; ~ un an (temps passé) a year ago; tu en veux? en ~ do you want some? here you are; en ~ des histoires! what a fuss!; et ~ que and then.

voilage /vwalaʒ/ *nm* net curtain.

voile /vwal/ *nf* (de bateau) sail; (Sport) sailing. ●*nm* veil; (tissu léger) net.

voilé, ~e /vwale/ *a* (allusion, femme) veiled; (flou) hazy.

voiler /vwale/ [1] *vt* (dissimuler) veil; (déformer) buckle. □ se ~ *vpr* (devenir flou) become hazy; (se déformer) (roue) buckle.

voilier /vwalje/ *nm* sailing ship.

voir /vwaʀ/ [63] *vt* see; faire ~ qch à qn show sth to sb; laisser ~ show; avoir quelque chose à ~ avec have something to do with; ça n'a rien à ~ that's got nothing to do with it; je ne peux pas le ~ 🔲 I can't stand him. ●*vi* y ~ be able to see; je n'y vois rien I cannot see; ~ trouble have blurred vision; voyons let's see now; voyons, soyez sages! come on now, behave yourselves! □ se ~ *vpr* (dans la glace) see oneself; (être visible) show; (se produire) be seen; (se trouver) find oneself; (se fréquenter, se rencontrer) see each other; (être vu) be seen.

voire /vwaʀ/ adv or even, not to say.

voirie /vwaʀi/ nf (service) highway maintenance.

voisin, ~e /vwazɛ̃, -in/ a (de voisinage) neighbouring; (proche) nearby; (adjacent) next (de to); (semblable) similar (de to). ● nm, f neighbour; le ~ the man next door, the neighbour. **voisinage** nm neighbourhood; (proximité) proximity.

voiture /vwatyʀ/ nf (motor) car; (wagon) coach, carriage; en ~! all aboard!; ~ bélier ramraiding car; ~ à cheval horse-drawn carriage; ~ de course racing car; ~ école driving school car; ~ d'enfant pram; (US) baby carriage; ~ de tourisme saloon car.

voix /vwa/ nf voice; (suffrage) vote; à ~ basse in a whisper.

vol /vɔl/ nm (d'avion, d'oiseau) flight; (groupe d'oiseaux) flock, flight; (délit) theft; (hold-up) robbery; ~ à l'étalage shoplifting; ~ à la tire pickpocketing; à ~ d'oiseau as the crow flies; de haut ~ high-ranking; ~ libre hang-gliding; ~ à voile gliding.

volaille /vɔlaj/ nf la ~ (poules) poultry; une ~ a fowl.

volant /vɔlɑ̃/ nm (steering-) wheel; (de jupe) flounce; (de badminton) shuttlecock; **donner un coup de ~** turn the wheel sharply.

volcan /vɔlkɑ̃/ nm volcano.

volée /vɔle/ nf flight; (oiseaux) flight, flock; (de coups, d'obus, au tennis) volley; **à toute ~** hard; **à la ~** in flight, in mid-air.

voler /vɔle/ [1] vi (oiseau) fly; (dérober) steal (à from). ● vt steal; ~ qn rob sb; il ne l'a pas volé he deserved it.

volet /vɔlɛ/ nm (de fenêtre) shutter; (de document) (folded ou tear-off) section; **trié sur le ~** hand-picked.

voleur, -euse /vɔlœʀ, -øz/ nm, f thief; **au ~!** stop thief! ● a thieving.

volley-ball /vɔlɛbol/ nm volleyball.

volontaire /vɔlɔ̃tɛʀ/ a (délibéré) voluntary; (opiniâtre) determined. ● nmf volunteer. **volontairement** adv voluntarily; (exprès) intentionally.

volonté /vɔlɔ̃te/ nf (faculté, intention) will; (souhait) wish; (énergie) will-power; **à ~** (comme on veut) as required; **du vin à ~** unlimited wine; **bonne ~** goodwill; **mauvaise ~** ill will.

volontiers /vɔlɔ̃tje/ adv (de bon gré) with pleasure, willingly, gladly; (admettre) readily.

volt /vɔlt/ nm volt.

volte-face /vɔltəfas/ nf inv (fig) U-turn; **faire ~** do a U-turn.

voltige /vɔltiʒ/ nf acrobatics (+ pl).

volume /vɔlym/ nm volume.

volumineux, -euse /vɔlyminø, -z/ a bulky; (livre, dossier) thick.

volupté /vɔlypte/ nf voluptuousness.

vomi /vɔmi/ nm vomit.

vomir /vɔmiʀ/ [2] vt vomit; (fig) belch out. ● vi be sick, vomit.

vomissement /vɔmismɑ̃/ nm vomiting; ~s du matin morning sickness.

vont /vɔ̃/ ⇒ALLER [8].

vorace /vɔʀas/ a voracious.

vos /vo/ ⇒VOTRE.

votant, ~e /vɔtɑ̃, -t/ nm, f voter.

vote /vɔt/ nm (action) voting; (suffrage) vote; ~ d'une loi passing of a bill; ~ par correspondance/ procuration postal/proxy vote.

voter /vɔte/ [1] vi vote. ● vt vote for; (adopter) pass; (crédits) vote.

votre (*pl* **vos**) /vɔtʀ, vo/ *a* your.

vôtre /votʀ/ *pron* le *ou* la ~, les ~s yours.

vouer /vwe/ [1] *vt* (*vie, temps*) dedicate (à to); **voué à l'échec** doomed to failure.

vouloir /vulwaʀ/ [64] *vt* (exiger) want (**faire** to do); (souhaiter) want; **que veux-tu boire?** what would you like to drink?; **je voudrais bien y aller** I'd really like to go; **je veux bien venir** I'm happy to come; **comme tu voudras** as you wish; (accepter) **veuillez vous asseoir** please sit down; **veuillez patienter** (au téléphone) please hold the line; (signifier) ~ **dire** mean; **qu'est-ce que cela veut dire?** what does that mean?; **en** ~ **à qn** bear a grudge against sb. □ **s'en** ~ *vpr* regret; **je m'en veux de lui avoir dit** I really regret having told her.

voulu, ~**e** /vuly/ *a* (délibéré) intentional; (requis) required.

vous /vu/ *pron* (sujet, complément) you; (indirect) (to) you, (réfléchi) yourself; (pluriel) yourselves; (l'un l'autre) each other. **vous-même** *pron* yourself. **vous-mêmes** *pron* yourselves.

voûte /vut/ *nf* (plafond) vault; (porche) archway.

vouvoiement /vuvwamã/ *nm* use of the 'vous' form. **vouvoyer** [31] *vt* address using the 'vous' form.

voyage /vwajaʒ/ *nm* trip; (déplacement) journey; (par mer) voyage; ~(**s**) (action) travelling; ~ **d'affaires** business trip; ~ **d'études** study trip; ~ **de noces** honeymoon; ~ **organisé** (package) tour.

voyager /vwajaʒe/ [40] *vi* travel.

voyageur, **-euse** /vwajaʒœʀ, -øz/ *nm, f* traveller; (passager) passenger; ~ **de commerce** travelling salesman.

voyant, ~**e** /vwajã, -t/ *a* gaudy. ● *nm* (signal) (warning) light.

voyelle /vwajɛl/ *nf* vowel.

voyou /vwaju/ *nm* hooligan.

vrac: **en** ~ /ãvʀak/ *loc* (pêle-mêle) haphazardly; (sans emballage) loose; (en gros) in bulk.

vrai, ~**e** /vʀɛ/ *a* true; (authentique) real. ● *nm* truth; **à** ~ **dire** to tell the truth; **pour de** ~ for real.

vraiment *adv* really.

vraisemblable /vʀɛsãblabl/ *a* (probable) likely; (*excuse, histoire*) plausible. **vraisemblablement** *adv* probably. **vraisemblance** *nf* likelihood, plausibility.

vrombir /vʀɔ̃biʀ/ [2] *vi* roar.

VRP *abrév m* (**voyageur représentant placier**) rep, representative.

VTT *abrév m* (**vélo tout terrain**) mountain bike.

vu, ~**e** /vy/ *a* **bien** ~ well thought of; **ce serait plutôt mal** ~ it wouldn't go down well; **bien** ~! good point! ● *prép* in view of; ~ **que** seeing that. ● ⇒VOIR [63].

vue /vy/ *nf* (spectacle) sight; (vision) (eye)sight; (panorama, idée, image, photo) view; **avoir en** ~ have in mind; **à** ~ (*tirer*) on sight; (*payable*) at sight; **de** ~ by sight; **perdre de** ~ lose sight of; **en** ~ (proche) in sight; (célèbre) in the public eye; **en** ~ **de faire** with a view to doing; **à** ~ **d'œil** visibly; **avoir des** ~**s sur** have designs on.

vulgaire /vylgɛʀ/ *a* (grossier) vulgar; (ordinaire) common.

vulnérable /vylneʀabl/ *a* vulnerable.

wagon /vagɔ̃/ *nm* (de voyageurs)
carriage; (de marchandises) wagon.
wagon-lit (*pl* **wagons-lits**) *nm*
sleeper. **wagon-restaurant** (*pl*
wagons-restaurants) *nm*
restaurant car.
walkman® /wokman/ *nm*
personal stereo, walkman®.
waters /watɛR/ *nmpl* toilets.
watt /wat/ *nm* watt.
wc /(dublə)vese/ *nmpl* toilet (+
sg).
Web /wɛb/ *nm* Web; **un site ~** a
website; **une page ~** web page.
webcam /wɛbkam/ *nf* webcam.
webmestre /wɛbmɛstR/ *nm*
webmaster.
week-end /wikɛnd/ *nm*
weekend.
whisky (*pl* **-ies**) /wiski/ *nm*
whisky.

xénophobe /gzenɔfɔb/ *a*
xenophobic. ● *nmf* xenophobe.
xérès /gzeRɛs/ *nm* sherry.
xylophone /ksilɔfɔn/ *nm*
xylophone.

y /i/

● *adverbe*

····▸ there; (dessus) on it; (pluriel) on
them; (dedans) in it; (pluriel) in
them; **j'~ vais** I'm on my way;
n'~ va pas don't go; **du lait? il
n'~ en a pas** milk? there's none;
tu n'~ arriveras jamais you'll
never manage it.

● *pronom*

····▸ **s'~ habituer** get used to it.

····▸ **s'~ attendre** expect it.

····▸ **~ penser** think about it.

····▸ **~ être pour qch** have sth to do
with it.

yaourt /'jauR(t)/ *nm* yoghurt.
yaourtière *nf* yoghurt-maker.
yard /'jaRd/ *nm* yard (= *91,44 cm*).
yen /'jɛn/ *nm* yen.
yeux /jø/ ⇒ŒIL.
yoga /'jɔga/ *nm* yoga.
yougoslave /'jugoslav/ *a*
Yugoslav. **Y~** *nmf* Yugoslav.
Yougoslavie /'jugoslavi/ *nf*
Yugoslavia.
yo-yo® /'jojo/ *nm inv* yo-yo®.

zapper /zape/ [1] *vi* (à la télévision) channel-hop.

zèbre /zɛbʀ/ *nm* zebra.

zèle /zɛl/ *nm* zeal.

zéro /zeʀo/ *nm* nought, zero; (température) zero; (Sport) nil; (tennis) love; (personne) nonentity; **partir de ∼** start from scratch; **repartir à ∼** start all over again.

zeste /zɛst/ *nm* peel; **un ∼ de** (fig) a touch of.

zézayer /zezeje/ [31] *vi* lisp.

zigzag /zigzag/ *nm* zigzag; **en ∼** winding.

zinc /zɛ̃g/ *nm* (métal) zinc; (comptoir 🄻) bar.

zizanie /zizani/ *nf* discord; **semer la ∼** put the cat among the pigeons.

zizi /zizi/ *nm* 🄻 willy.

zodiaque /zɔdjak/ *nm* zodiac.

zona /zona/ *nm* (Méd) shingles (+ *sg*).

zone /zon/ *nf* zone, area; (banlieue pauvre) slums; **∼ bleue** restricted parking zone; **∼ euro** euro zone.

zoo /zo(o)/ *nm* zoo.

zoom /zum/ *nm* zoom lens.

zut /zyt/ *interj* 🄻 damn 🄻.

Z

Test yourself with word games

This section contains a number of word games which will help you to use your dictionary more effectively and to build up your knowledge of French vocabulary and usage in an entertaining way. You will find answers to all puzzles and games at the end of the section.

1 Madame Irma

Madame Irma is very good at predicting the future, but she is not very good at conjugating French verbs in the future tense. Help her to replace all the verbs in brackets with the correct future form.

Lion 23 juillet–22 août

Cette semaine, les Lions (être) à la fête. **Travail**: Il ne (falloir) pas vous laisser démoraliser par les problèmes et les discussions qui (pouvoir) surgir en début de semaine. Les 19 et 20 avril vous (offrir) la possibilité d'un changement radical dans votre carrière. Pourquoi ne pas saisir votre chance? **Santé**: Le stress ne vous (épargner) pas, surtout le 18. Attention! Pour décompresser, faites un peu de sport et tout (aller) bien. **Amitié**: Vous êtes très sociable et cette semaine, vous vous (faire) encore de nouveaux amis. **Côté cœur**: Vénus (veiller) sur vous. Une nouvelle rencontre (survenir) peut-être. Si vous avez un partenaire, votre relation (être) au beau fixe.

2 Power cut

Unfortunately, there was a power cut while Jean was writing a computer manual for his office staff. He had just begun to label his diagram of a computer. Can you help Jean unscramble the letters and get on with his labelling?

TURANIDORE

VARICLE

ROUSSI

QUITTEDES

NARCE

RUCRUSE

MOCR-D

3 The odd meaning out

Watch out: one word can have different meanings. In the following exercise, only two of the suggested translations are correct. Use the dictionary to spot the odd one out, then find the correct French translation for it.

example:

blindé
- ❑ armoured
- ☑ blind
- ❑ immune

blind = aveugle

gauche
- ❑ left
- ❑ gauge
- ❑ awkward

lentille
- ❑ lentil
- ❑ lens
- ❑ lent

porte
- ❑ door
- ❑ carry
- ❑ port (wine)

duvet
- ❑ duvet
- ❑ down
- ❑ sleeping-bag

4 Word magnets

Antoine's brother took all his magnets off the fridge door to wipe it clean. He put them back the wrong way round. Can you help Antoine rewrite the correct sentences?

| heure | hier | suis | me | levé | bonne | de | je |

| dit | pourtant | je | fois | lui | plusieurs | ai | le |

| sur | sortant | table | les | prends | clés | en | la |

| ira | Portugal | elle | prochaine | au | vacances | l'année | en |

| film | voir | un | allés | cinéma | sommes | nous | au |

| voisine | de | là | frère | pas | le | la | n'est |

5 What are they like?

Here are two lists of adjectives you can use to describe people's characteristics. Each word in the second column is the opposite of one of the adjectives in the first column. Can you link them?

1. grand	A. intelligent
2. blond	B. méchant
3. bête	C. gros
4. énervé	D. petit
5. gentil	E. sympathique
6. timide	F. brun
7. patient	G. calme
8. désagréable	H. extraverti
9. poli	I. impatient
10. maigre	J. malpoli

example: 1.D. *grand* est le contraire de *petit*.

6 The odd one out

In each of the following series, all the words but one are related.
Find the odd one out and explain why. If there are words you
don't know, use your dictionary to find out what they mean.

example: stylo, agenda, livre, carnet scolaire, brosse à dents

The odd one out is 'brosse à dents', because you wouldn't find it in a
schoolbag.

1. voiture, avion, moteur, train, autocar

2. casserole, poêle, cafetière, cendrier, saladier

3. télévision, cassette, chaîne-hifi, magnétoscope, baladeur

4. ski nautique, natation, plongée, varappe, planche à voile

5. redoubler, courir, sauter, glisser, descendre, monter

6. chou, sou, caillou, genou, hibou, bijou

7 The shopping list

Paul has prepared a shopping list. When his friend sees the list, he realises that he needs exactly the same things. He asks Paul whether he would mind buying two of everything. Help Paul rewrite his list.

Watch out: the plurals of compound nouns are irregular. If in doubt, look them up in your dictionary.

Acheter:	Acheter:
- un taille-crayons	deux taille-crayons
- un bloc-notes	....
- un timbre-poste	....
- un abat-jour	....
- un couvre-lit	....
- un cache-nez	....
- un tire-bouchon	....
- un ouvre-boîtes	....
- un réveille-matin	....
- un chou-fleur	....

8 The mystery word

To fill in the grid, find the French words for all the musical instruments illustrated below. Once you have completed the grid, you'll discover the name of a famous classical composer.

The composer is _____ .

9 Body parts

Can you put the right number in the boxes next to the French words in the list?

☐ la bouche
☐ le bras
☐ la cheville
☐ le cou
☐ le coude
☐ la cuisse
☐ le doigt
☐ l'épaule
☐ le front
☐ le genou
☐ la hanche
☐ la jambe
☐ la joue
☐ la main
☐ le menton
☐ le mollet
☐ le nez
☐ le nombril
☐ l'œil
☐ l'oreille
☐ l'orteil
☐ le pied
☐ le poignet
☐ la tête

10 Liar liar!

Today, Sabine had a day off. She tells her mother what she has been up to:

> *Ce matin, je me suis levée juste après ton départ. J'ai bu du café au lait et j'ai mangé des tartines. Après avoir fait ma toilette et m'être habillée, je suis allée au parc. Il faisait très beau et j'avais envie de me promener. Je suis revenue à la maison pour chercher mon maillot de bain et je suis allée à la piscine découverte. J'y suis restée pendant deux heures. En sortant, j'avais très faim, alors je me suis installée dans un café. J'ai commandé un sandwich. Après ça, je suis allée au cinéma. Le film était super! Je suis rentrée à la maison un peu avant que tu arrives.*

What she doesn't say is that her little brother, Adrien, skipped school to spend the day with her. Rewrite her statement.

> *Ce matin, nous nous sommes levés juste après ton départ...*

Answers

1

seront	ira
faudra	ferez
pourront	veillera
offriront	surviendra
épargnera	sera

2

ordinateur	écran
clavier	curseur
souris	cd-rom
disquette	

3

lent = prêté
port = porto
gauge = jauge
duvet = couette

4

Hier, je me suis levé de bonne heure.
Pourtant, je le lui ai dit plusieurs fois.
Prends les clés sur la table en sortant.
L'année prochaine, elle ira en vacances au Portugal.
Nous sommes allés voir un film au cinéma.
Le frère de la voisine n'est pas là.

5

1.D. *grand* est le contraire de *petit*.
2.F. *blond* est le contraire de *brun*.
3.A. *bête* est le contraire d'*intelligent*.
4.G. *énervé* est le contraire de *calme*.
5.B. *gentil* est le contraire de *méchant*.
6.H. *timide* est le contraire d'*extraverti*.
7.I. *patient* est le contraire d'*impatient*.
8.E. *désagréable* est le contraire de *sympathique*.
9.J. *poli* est le contraire de *malpoli*.
10.C. *maigre* est le contraire de *gros*.

6

1. moteur—because it isn't a vehicle
2. cendrier—because it is not used for cooking
3. cassette—because it isn't an electrical device
4. varappe—because it is the only sport in the list which isn't a water-sport
5. redoubler—because it is the only verb in the list which doesn't describe a movement
6. sou—because it ends in "-s" in the plural, not in "-x" like the other five

7

deux taille-crayons
deux blocs-notes
deux timbres-poste
deux abat-jour
deux couvre-lits

deux cache-nez
deux tire-bouchons
deux ouvre-boîtes
deux réveille-matin
deux choux-fleurs

8

```
C O N T R E B A S S E
        F L U T E
    T R O M P E T T E
        G U I T A R E
            H A R P E
        S A X O P H O N E
            V I O L O N
V I O L O N C E L L E
        P I A N O
```

9

6. la bouche	15. le doigt	4. la joue	3. l'œil
11. le bras	10. l'épaule	14. la main	8. l'oreille
22. la cheville	2. le front	7. le menton	24. l'orteil
9. le cou	20. le genou	21. le mollet	23. le pied
12. le coude	17. la hanche	5. le nez	13. le poignet
18. la cuisse	19. la jambe	16. le nombril	1. la tête

10

*"Ce matin, nous nous sommes levés, juste après ton départ.
Nous avons bu du café au lait et nous avons mangé des tartines.
Après avoir fait notre toilette et nous être habillés, nous sommes
allés au parc. Il faisait très beau et nous avions envie de nous
promener. Nous sommes revenus à la maison pour chercher nos
maillots de bain et nous sommes allés à la piscine découverte.
Nous y sommes restés pendant deux heures. En sortant, nous
avions très faim, alors nous nous sommes installés dans un café.
Nous avons commandé des sandwichs. Après ça, nous sommes
allés au cinéma. Le film était super! Nous sommes rentrés à la
maison un peu avant que tu arrives."*

Calendar of French traditions, festivals, and holidays

January
1 8 15 22 29
2 9 16 23 30
3 10 17 24 31
4 11 18 25
5 12 19 26
6 13 20 27
7 14 21 28

February
1 8 15 22
2 9 16 23
3 10 17 24
4 11 18 25
5 12 19 26
6 13 20 27
7 **14** 21 28

March
1 8 15 22 29
2 9 16 23 30
3 10 17 24 31
4 11 18 25
5 12 19 26
6 13 20 27
7 14 21 28

April
1 8 15 22 29
2 9 16 23 30
3 10 17 24 31
4 11 18 25
5 12 19 26
6 13 20 27
7 14 21 28

May
1 **8** 15 22 29
2 9 16 23 30
3 10 17 24 31
4 11 18 25
5 12 19 26
6 13 20 27
7 14 21 28

June
1 8 15 22 29
2 9 16 23 30
3 10 17 **24**
4 11 18 25
5 12 19 26
6 13 20 27
7 14 21 28

July
1 8 15 22 29
2 9 16 23 30
3 10 17 24 31
4 11 18 25
5 12 19 26
6 13 20 27
7 **14** 21 28

August
1 8 **15** 22 29
2 9 16 23 30
3 10 17 24 31
4 11 18 25
5 12 19 26
6 13 20 27
7 14 21 28

September
1 8 15 22 29
2 9 16 23 30
3 10 17 24
4 11 18 25
5 12 19 26
6 13 20 27
7 14 21 28

October
1 8 15 22 29
2 9 16 23 30
3 10 17 24 31
4 11 18 25
5 12 19 26
6 13 20 27
7 14 21 28

November
1 8 15 22 29
2 9 16 23 30
3 10 17 24
4 **11** 18 25
5 12 19 26
6 13 20 27
7 14 21 28

December
1 **8** 15 22 29
2 9 16 23 30
3 10 17 **24** **31**
4 11 18 **25**
5 12 19 **26**
6 13 20 27
7 14 21 28

1 January

le jour de l'an (New Year's Day) is a public holiday and a day of family celebration, with a large lunch, traditionally featuring seafood of various kinds.

6 January

la Fête des Rois (Epiphany or Twelfth Night). Around this time, most families have a *galette des Rois*, a rich pastry cake filled with *frangipane* (almond paste). The cake contains a *fève*, literally a bean, as this is what was originally used. Nowadays the *fève* takes the form of a tiny plastic or ceramic figure. The person who gets the *fève* in their portion puts on the cardboard crown which comes with the cake.

2 February

la Chandeleur (Candlemas) is celebrated in the church but is not a public holiday. However, it is traditional to eat *crêpes* (pancakes) on this day.

14 February

la Saint Valentin (St Valentine's Day). As in many other countries, people celebrate a romantic relationship with gifts of flowers or chocolates.

1 April

le premier avril (April Fool's Day). The French also take advantage of this occasion to play tricks on one another, calling out *poisson d'avril!* (literally 'April fish').

1 May

La Fête du Travail (International Labour Day) is a public holiday.

8 May

le 8 mai or la Fête de la Victoire is a public holiday commemorating Victory in Europe on 8 May 1945.

24 June

la Saint-Jean (Midsummer's Day). In many areas, bonfires (*les feux de la Saint-Jean*) are lit on Midsummer's Night. People are supposed to jump over these, re-enacting a pagan custom intended to ward off the cold of winter.

14 July

la Fête Nationale or le 14 juillet is usually called Bastille Day in English and is a public holiday in France. It commemorates the taking of the Bastille prison in Paris and the liberation of its prisoners by the people of Paris in 1789, one of the first events of the Revolution. All over France there are parades on the day of the 14th and firework displays and *bals* (local dances) either on the night of the 13th or of the 14th.

15 August

l'Assomption (Feast of the
Assumption) is a public holiday. Many people in France are
either setting off on holiday
around the 15th or else return-
ing home, so this is traditionally a very busy time on the
roads.

1 November

la Toussaint (All Saints' Day)
is a public holiday and the day
when people remember their
dead relatives and friends,
although properly speaking it
is All Souls' Day the following
day that is set aside for this in
the church. People take flowers
to the cemetery, particularly
chrysanthemums, as these are
in bloom at this time. Because
of this association, it is best to
avoid taking chrysanthemums
as a gift for someone. School-
children have a two-week holiday around this time.

11 November

le 11 novembre is a public holiday to commemorate the
Armistice of 1918 and a day of
remembrance for those who
died in the two world wars and
in subsequent conflicts. All
towns and villages hold
parades in which war veterans
accompany local officials and a
brass band to lay wreaths on
the war memorial. In Paris, the
President lays a wreath on the
tomb of the unknown soldier

beneath the *Arc de Triomphe*
on the *Champs-Élysées*.

8 December

la fête de l'Immaculée Conception (Feast of the Immaculate Conception).
In the city of Lyons, this is celebrated as la Fête de la
Lumière (Festival of Light)
said to commemorate the Virgin's intervention to prevent
the plague reaching Lyons in
the Middle Ages. People put
rows of candles in coloured
glass jars on the outsides of
their windowsills, so that all
the buildings in the centre of
the city are illuminated.

24 December

la veille de Noël (Christmas
Eve) is the time when most
people exchange presents.
Many people go to *la messe de
minuit* (midnight mass).

25 December

Noël (Christmas) is a public
holiday and a day of eating and
drinking. Lunch will often
start with a variety of seafood,
oysters being particularly popular. Turkey is often eaten as a
main course, sometimes with
chestnut stuffing. A variety of
cheeses will be followed by *la
bûche de Noël*, a rich chocolate
cake in the form of a snow-covered log. French people do not
usually send Christmas cards,
the custom being to send wish-

es for the coming year to more distant friends and relatives during the month of January.

26 December

There is no particular name for the day after Christmas Day and it is not a public holiday.

31 December

la Saint-Sylvestre (New Year's Eve). Many people have parties to celebrate *le réveillon du Nouvel An* (New Year's Eve Party). Once again, food plays a major part and, as at Christmas, this is a time to splash out on luxury foods such as *foie gras*. There will often be dancing and the New Year will be welcomed in with champagne.

Movable feasts

Mardi gras
Shrove Tuesday, the last day of carnival before the beginning of Lent on Ash Wednesday. Traditionally, *crepes* (pancakes) are eaten for supper. In many areas of France, sugared fritters called *bugnes* in and around Lyons and *oreillettes* farther south, are eaten between *la fête des Rois* and *mardi gras*.

le Vendredi saint
Good Friday is celebrated in the church, but is not a public holiday.

Pâques
Easter Sunday, *le dimanche de Pâques*, is for many people the occasion for a big family lunch. Easter hunts are organised for children, with chocolate eggs, rabbits, hens, or fish traditionally hidden in the family garden. *Le lundi de Pâques* (Easter Monday) is a public holiday.

l'Ascension the Thursday forty days after Easter is a public holiday in France.

la Pentecôte (Whitsun) on the seventh Sunday after Easter represents for many people the first long weekend of the summer, as *le lundi de la Pentecôte* (Whit Monday) is a public holiday. Many families go to stay with friends or relatives in the country.

la Fête des mères (Mother's Day) is the Sunday after *Pentecôte*. This is another occasion for a big family meal, with presents for the mother. La fête des pères (Father's Day) is celebrated in similar fashion two weeks later.

A–Z of French life and culture

Académie française
A learned body whose main role nowadays is to monitor new developments in the French language and to make decisions as to what is acceptable and what is not, although these decisions are not always taken entirely seriously by the public at large. Its 40 members are elected for life on the basis of their contribution to scholarship or literature.

Alliance Française
A private organization which aims to spread awareness of French language and culture. It has centres in cities throughout the world, providing classes and a variety of cultural activities.

année scolaire
The French school year starts with the RENTRÉE des classes in early September and ends in early July. There is a week's holiday in late October/early November around *la Toussaint* (All Saints' Day, 1 November), two weeks around Christmas and New Year, two weeks in February, and two weeks in April.

Antenne 2 ▸ FRANCE 2

arrondissement
The three largest cities in France – Paris, Lyons, and Marseilles – are divided into numbered administrative areas called *arrondissements*. Each has its own mayor and council, and the number of the *arrondissement* is usually part of the postcode. The system makes for a convenient way for people to talk about which part of the city they live in e.g. '*le neuvième arrondissement*' or simply '*le neuvième*'. An *arrondissement* is also a sub-division of a DÉPARTEMENT.

ARTE
A television channel, run jointly by France and Germany, which provides a high standard of cultural programmes.

Assemblée Nationale
The lower house of the French parliament, also called the *Chambre des députés*. There are 577 DÉPUTÉS, elected for a five-year term, often after two rounds of voting as at least 50% of the vote must be obtained.

Astérix

A hugely popular comic-book character invented by cartoonists Goscinny and Uderzo. *Astérix* is a tiny but invincible village leader in the ancient province of Gaul, whose fictional adventures with his fellow-villagers often involve fighting and outwitting the occupying Romans and make for gentle mockery of cultures outside Gaul. The *Astérix* books have been translated into 40 languages.

autoroute

France has an extensive motorway system, which is largely financed by tolls calculated according to the distance travelled and the vehicle type. Tickets are obtained and tolls paid at *péages* (tollgates). There is a speed limit for standard vehicles of 130 km/h (approx. 80 mph) and 110 km/h (approx. 70 mph) in wet weather.

baccalauréat

The *baccalauréat*, generally known informally as the *Bac*, is the examination sat in the final year of the LYCÉE (la *terminale*), so usually at age 17 or 18. Students sit exams in a fairly broad range of subjects in a particular category: the *Bac S* places emphasis on the sciences, for example, whilst the *Bac L* has a literary bias. Some categories cater for students specializing in more directly job-based subjects such as agriculture. The final result is given as a single overall mark or grade out of 20, although the scores for individual subjects are also given. It is common to use the *Bac* as a point of reference in job advertisements, so that *Bac + 4* would mean a person who had completed 4 years of full-time study after the *Bac*, with appropriate diplomas to show for it.

bachelier

The holder of the BACCALAURÉAT, entitled to enrol for university courses.

bande dessinée (BD)

Comic books of all sorts and for a wide variety of age and interest groups are immensely popular in France and form an important part of French culture. Cartoon characters such as *Astérix*, *Lucky Luke*, and *Tintin* are household names and older comic books are often collectors' items.

Basque

The Basque country extends on both sides of the Pyrenees with about one quarter of a million Basques living in France and ten times that number in Spain. The French Basque region (*le Pays basque français*) does not have any autonomous status nor is

Basque recognized as an official language. It is, however, taught in some schools, and there are an estimated 40,000 Basque speakers in France.

boules

A type of bowls, also called PÉTANQUE, played all over France, using metal boules and a jack known as a *cochonnet*. Special areas (*terrains de boules*) are set aside for the game in towns and villages, although one of the obvious attractions of the game is that it can be played virtually anywhere. There are some regional variations, notably in the size and form of the playing area and the size of the bowls.

brasserie

The original meaning of *brasserie* is 'brewery', and although the word is still used in this sense, it has come also to mean a type of bar-restaurant, usually serving simple, traditional French food at reasonable prices. Most *brasseries* offer a fixed-price menu, especially at lunchtime.

Breton

The ancient Celtic language of Brittany (*Bretagne*). It is related to Welsh, Irish, Scottish Gaelic, and Cornish. Recent decades have seen a revival of interest in the language going hand in hand with the assertion of a regional cultural identity and a movement for independence from France. Breton is fairly widely spoken and is taught in secondary schools in the region, although it is not recognized as an official language in France.

Brevet d'études professionnelles (BEP)

A vocational qualification awarded at the end of a two-year, practically-based course in a LYCÉE specializing in providing teaching directly related to the workplace.

Brevet de technicien (BT)

A vocational qualification awarded at the end of a three-year course in a special section of a LYCÉE. There is considerable competition for entry to courses, and the standards required result in a high dropout rate.

Brevet de technicien supérieur (BTS)

A vocational qualification awarded at the end of a two-year course after the BACCALAURÉAT in a specific professional field.

Brevet des collèges

A general educational qualification taken in a range of subjects by students aged around 15 in the final year of COLLÈGE.

bureau de tabac

Tobacconists are either individual shops or else are to be found in a *bar-tabac* or *café-tabac*. They are also often combined with a newsagents (*marchand de journaux*). As well as being licensed to sell tobacco and cigarettes, they have a state licence to sell stamps, LOTO tickets, the *vignette* (road tax disc for motor vehicles), and certain other official documents.

Canal Plus (Canal+)

A privately-owned French television channel broadcasting mainly feature films. Viewers pay a subscription and access the channel using a decoder.

CAPES - certificat d'aptitude au professorat de l'enseignement du second degré

The qualification normally required in order to teach in a secondary school. Qualification is by means of a competitive examination (CONCOURS) usually at the end of a two-year course in a specialist teacher-training institute (*IUFM: Institut universitaire pour la formation des maîtres*).

Carte bleue

A credit card issued by French banks as part of the international Visa network.

Carte grise

The registration document for a motor vehicle. It is an offence not to carry it when driving the vehicle, and police checks are frequent. Vehicle registration numbers depend on the DÉPARTEMENT in which the owner lives and have to be changed if the owner moves to a different one.

Carte nationale d'identité

Although not obligatory, most French citizens possess a *carte nationale d'identité* (national identity card), obtained from their local MAIRIE, PREFECTUR, or *commissariat de police* (police station), as proof of identity is often required, for example when paying by cheque. It is also accepted as a travel document by all EC countries.

Catalan

The language spoken by 25 per cent of people in Spain and by some people in the Perpignan area of southwest France. It is taught in schools in the area but is not recognized as an official language in France.

CDI - Centre de documentation et d'information

A resource and information centre providing library and IT facilities in a school or college. The term has largely replaced *bibliothèque* (library) in this context.

CE - cycle élémentaire
Also called *cours élémentaire*, this is the programme for the two years of primary school for children aged 7 to 9 (*CE1* and *CE2*).

Césars
Prizes awarded annually for achievements in the film industry, so the French equivalent of the Oscars.

Chambre des députés ▸
ASSEMBLÉE NATIONALE

champignons
The French use the word *champignons* (mushrooms) to refer to any of the types of mushroom-like fungi that are to be found in the countryside, whether edible or not. Cultivated button mushrooms are called *champignons de Paris*. Hunting for edible *champignons* is almost a national leisure activity, and many varieties are highly prized. Advice on whether a *champignon* is edible or not can usually be obtained in a PHARMACIE.

Champs-Élysées
The world-famous avenue in central Paris, known for its luxury shops, hotels, and clubs. At one end is the *Arc de Triomphe*, the scene of the remembrance ceremony each year for the Armistice of 1918 and under which is the tomb of an unknown soldier, killed in World War I.

charcuterie
A shop or supermarket counter selling a wide variety of pork products. As well as cuts of pork, *charcutiers* usually sell chicken, both raw and ready-cooked, and there will be various types of raw and cooked ham, a variety of pâtés, often homemade in small shops, and a selection of *saucissons*. Most *charcuteries* also offer a variey of salads, various types of savoury pastries, and a number of dishes, different every day, which can be reheated at home or on the premises. Some also offer a catering service, in which case the shop will probably call itself a *charcutier-traiteur*. The word *charcuterie* is also used to mean pork products such as ham and *saucisson*.

chasse
La chasse (hunting) is a widely practised sport in France. Legislation as to the rights of hunters to hunt over privately-owned land varies according to the region and the amount of land concerned. During the hunting season, hunting is permitted on Thursdays, Saturdays, and Sundays. It is advisable not to stray from public footpaths when walking in the country-

side on these days. The hunters (*les chasseurs*) are a powerful political lobby and are represented in the **ASSEMBLÉE NATIONALE**.

Cinquième

La Cinquième is an educational television channel which broadcasts on the **ARTE** channel during the day.

Cinquième république

This is the present régime in France. The constitution was established in 1958 according to principles put forward by Charles de Gaulle.

classe de neige

A period, generally a week, which a school class, usually of under-twelves, spends in a mountain area. Ski tuition is integrated with normal school work.

classe préparatoire

An intensive two-year course, provided by some prestigious **LYCÉES**, which prepares students for the competitive examinations (**CONCOURS**) by means of which students are selected for the **GRANDES ÉCOLES**.

classes

In French schools, after CM, classes go in reverse order, starting at age 11-12 in *sixième* and progressing through *cinquième, quatrième, troisième, seconde, première,*

and ending in *terminale* at age 17 or 18, the year in which the **BACCALAURÉAT** is taken. Education in France is compulsory up to the end of *seconde*.

CM - Cycle moyen

Also called *Cours moyen* this is the programme for the two years of primary school for children aged 9 to 11 (*CM1* and *CM2*).

collège

A state school for pupils between the ages of 11 and 15, between the **ÉCOLE PRIMAIRE** and the **LYCÉE**. The organisation of the school and the curriculum followed are laid down at national level.

colonie de vacances

A holiday village or summer camp for children. Originally set up as a means of giving poorer city children a means of getting out into the countryside, these are still largely state-subsidized. The informal word for them is *colo*.

commune

The *commune* is the smallest administrative unit of French local government. Each has its own **MAIRE** (mayor).

concours

Entry into many areas of the public services, including the teaching profession, as well as the most prestigious institutes of higher education, depends on succeeding in a competitive examination or *concours*.

The number of candidates admitted depends on the number of posts or places available in a given year.

conduite accompagnée (CA)

A learner driver who has passed the theory part of the driving test (*code de la route*) in a state-approved driving school is allowed to practise driving a vehicle accompanied by a qualified driver over the age of 28. Such drivers are not allowed to drive on AUTOROUTES and are required to have a white sticker with a red 'A' displayed on the rear of their vehicle.

conseil de classe

A committee representing each class in a COLLÈGE or LYCÉE consisting of the class teachers, two elected parent members, and two elected class members. It is chaired by the head teacher. The *conseil de classe* meets regularly to discuss the progress of the class and any problems that have arisen.

CP - Cycle préparatoire

Also called *Cours préparatoire*, this is the first year of primary school, starting a child's formal education off at the statutory age of 6.

Most children will have already attended an ÉCOLE MATERNELLE.

CRS – compagnies républicaines de sécurité

Special police units trained in public order techniques and riot control. They also police the AUTOROUTES and support mountain rescue and lifeguard work.

département

An administrative unit of government in France. Each *département* has a number and this appears as the first two digits in postcodes for addresses within the département and as the two-digit number at the end of registration numbers on motor vehicles.

député

An elected member of the ASSEMBLÉE NATIONALE.

droguerie

As a shop or supermarket section, there seems little connection between the name, which might be literally translated as 'drugstore', and the merchandise displayed. However, *drogue* can also mean the raw ingredients of dyes, and *droguistes* were originally dye merchants. Nowadays you will find not only dyes but household products and cleaning utensils, can-

dles, and a variey of other useful household items.

école libre
Private sector school education, provided predominantly
by the Catholic Church.

école maternelle
A school providing free nursery education from age 2 to 6.
Many children start at 2 and
virtually all children attend
between the ages of 4 and 6,
which is the statutory school
starting age and the time at
which children move into the
ÉCOLE PRIMAIRE.

école primaire
A primary school for children
between the ages of 6, the
statutory minimum age for
starting school, and 11.

école secondaire
Secondary education in
France consists of two phases:
COLLÈGE (11–15 years) and
LYCÈE (15/16 –17/18 years).

Élysée ▸ PALAIS DE
L' ÉLYSÉE

Europe 1
A popular commercial
French-language radio station, which broadcasts news,
popular music, sport, and
light entertainment from the
Saarland in Germany.

Événement du jeudi -
l'Événement du jeudi
A popular weekly news maga-

zine.

Express - l'Express
A weekly news magazine
offering in-depth coverage of
political and cultural matters.

faculté
La faculté – and more usually
and informally *la fac* – is the
way that students refer to
their university, particularly
the location itself, so that *aller
à la fac* would be the equivalent of 'to go into college'.

Figaro - le Figaro
A right-wing national daily
newspaper with a wide circulation.

France 2
This is the main publicly-
owned television channel and
aims to provide a wide range
of quality programmes.

France 3
A state-owned television
channel which is regionally
based and is required to promote regional diversity and to
cover a wide range of beliefs
and opinions.

France Culture
A 24-hour RADIO FRANCE radio
station featuring serious talk
programmes on a wide variety of cultural and social topics.

France Info
A 24-hour radio news station
run by RADIO FRANCE.

France Inter

A **RADIO FRANCE** radio station broadcasting mainly light entertainment, including a considerable proportion of studio comedy shows, but also offering good news coverage.

France Musiques

A 24-hour **RADIO FRANCE** radio station. Its main focus is classical music but it also provides considerable coverage of jazz and world music.

Gendarmerie nationale

A section of the military which provides police services outside the major towns.

gîte rural

A farmhouse or other building in the country which has been turned into a holiday cottage. Houses displaying the official *gîte de France* sign must conform to certain standards.

grande école

A prestigious higher education establishment admitting students on the results of a **CONCOURS**. They have different areas of specialization and competition for entry is fierce, as they are widely believed to offer the highest level of education available and thus a guarantee of subsequent career success.

hôtel de ville ▸ **MAIRIE**

Humanité - l'Humanité

The communist national daily newspaper.

Internet

A wealth of useful information on French culture, society, and current affairs can be obtained on the Internet. All the main French newspapers have websites (e.g. http://www.lemonde.fr), as do the television channels (e.g. http://www.france3.fr and http://www.tf1.fr). The *Louvre* museum has an interesting site at http://web.culture.fr/louvre.

immatriculation ▸ **PLAQUE D'IMMATRICULATION**

Libération

A left-wing national daily newspaper published in Paris. A separate edition is published for Lyons.

licence

A university degree awarded after a year's study following the **DEUG**.

Loto

The French national lottery. People play the *Loto* using special machines which can be found in **BUREAUX DE TABAC** throughout France.

Luxembourg ▸ **PALAIS DU LUXEMBOURG**

lycée

A school providing the last

three years of secondary education after **COLLÈGE**. The first year is *seconde* at the age of 15/16, going through *première*, and ending with *terminale* at age 17/18. As well as those which provide a conventional academic education, there are a number of different types of *lycée* offering a more vocationally-based education.

M6

A popular, privately-owned, commercial television channel.

magasins

Opening and closing times of shops (*les magasins*) vary according to the type of shop and the location. Department stores (*les grands magasins*) are generally open all day from 9 a.m. to 7 p.m. In larger towns, most other shops, with the exception of small food shops, are also open all day. Privately-owned food shops such as butchers and fishmongers generally open at 8 a.m. and do not close in the evening until 7 or 7.30. Most, however, are closed between midday and 2 or 3 p.m. In small towns, all the shops, with the exception of bakers, generally close for 2 or 3 hours in the middle of the day. In both small and large towns, it is always possible to find all types of food shops open on Sunday mornings until midday. In smaller towns, however, many of the shops are closed on Mondays.

maire

The chief officer of a **COMMUNE**, he or she represents state authority locally, officiates at marriages, and supervises local elections.

mairie

The *mairie* (town hall) is the administrative headquarters of the **CONSEIL MUNICIPAL**. In larger towns the *mairie* is often called the **HÔTEL DE VILLE**.

marchés

All towns in France have a weekly market with stalls selling a variety of produce, and some areas in big cities have a market every day. Many stalls are held by local people selling their own produce. Despite supermarkets, many people do much of their food shopping *au marché*.

Marianne

The symbolic female figure often used to represent the French Republic. There are statues of her in public places all over France, and she also appears on the standard French stamp. She is always depicted wearing the Phrygian bonnet, a pointed cap which became one of the symbols of liberty as represented by the 1789 Revolution.

Marseillaise
The French national anthem, so called because it was the marching song of a group of republican volunteers from Marseilles a few years after the 1789 revolution.

Médecins du monde
A charitable organization which provides medical and humanitarian aid in areas stricken by war, famine, or natural disaster.

Médecins sans frontières
A charitable organisation which sends medical teams anywhere in the world where they are needed to cope with the effects on people of war and disaster.

Minitel
A computer terminal available in a variety of models to the subscribers of FRANCE TÉLÉCOM. It gives users access to the *Télétel* network, which has a huge variety of services, payable at different rates, including the telephone directory. It can now be accessed via the Internet.

MJC - Maison des jeunes et de la culture
A community youth centre offering a wide variety of services and activities.

Monde - le Monde
A national daily newspaper. Its political stance is left of centre, and it is entirely owned by its staff. It provides full coverage of national and international news and is known for its in-depth analysis of current issues. It is unusual in publishing virtually no photographs of current events.

Nouvel Observateur - le Nouvel Observateur
A left-wing weekly magazine providing in-depth articles on current political issues and good coverage of culture and the arts.

Palais Bourbon
A large eighteenth-century residence on the left bank of the Seine which is now the seat of the ASSEMBLÉE NATIONALE.

Palais de l'Élysée
The official residence and office of the French President, situated just off the CHAMPS-ÉLYSÉES in Paris.

Palais du Luxembourg
A seventeenth century palace in the jardin du Luxembourg in Paris. It is now the seat of the SÉNAT.

paysan
Since *paysan* can be used in French to mean both 'small farmer' and, more offensively, 'peasant', small farmers are

generally referred to as *agriculteurs*. However, many small farmers take pride in their identity as *paysans*, particularly in the more remote areas of the country, where small farms are still the usual form of cultivation. The difficulty of making a living with a limited amount of land has, however, led to many such farms being abandoned or amalgamated into larger units and a general movement of the traditional rural population towards the towns.

permis de conduire
A driving licence can be issued to a person over the age of 18 who has passed both parts of the driving test. The first part is the theory test (*code de la route*) and consists of forty questions based on the highway code. This can be sat from the age of 16 onwards and gives the right to CONDUITE ACCOMPAGNÉE. The practical driving test has to be taken within two years of the theory test. It is compulsory to carry your driving licence with you when you are driving a vehicle.

pétanque ▸ BOULES

pharmacie
Pharmacies in France generally sell only medicines and closely related products such as toiletries and some brands of make-up and perfume. The products of the major perfume houses are to be found in *parfumeries*. Pharmacists traditionally play an active paramedical role, and people will often consult them rather than a doctor in the case of minor ailments and accidents. Pharmacies are easily spotted by the green cross, which is lit up when the pharmacy is open. A *pharmacie de garde* (duty chemist) can dispense medicines outside normal opening hours as part of a local rota.

plaque d'immatriculation
A vehicle's registration plate. The last two figures indicate the number of the DÉPARTEMENT in which the owner lives. If you move into another *département*, you are obliged by law to change your registration plate accordingly.

Point – le Point
A centre-right weekly news magazine offering in-depth coverage of politics and economics.

police
There are three principal police forces: the *police municipale* who are responsible for routine local policing such as traffic offences, who are locally organized and are not armed, the *police nationale* who are nationally organized

and generally armed, and the *gendarmerie nationale* which is a branch of the military.

Poste – La Poste

The state monopoly postal service. Postboxes in France are yellow.

préfet

The most senior offical responsible for representing the state within the **DÉPARTEMENT**.

préfecture

The administrative headquarters of a DÉPARTEMENT.

Premier ministre

The chief minister of the government, appointed by the **PRÉSIDENT DE LA RÉPUBLIQUE** and responsible for the overall management of government affairs.

Président de la République

The president is the head of state and is elected for a term of 7 years. Under the constitution of the **CINQUIÈME RÉPUBLIQUE** the president plays a strong executive role in the governing of the country.

Quai d'Orsay

The *ministère des Affaires étrangères* (ministry of Foreign Affairs) is situated here, so *Quai d'Orsay* is often used by journalists to mean the ministry.

Radio France

The state-owned radio broadcasting company.

région

The largest administrative unit in France, consisting of a number of **DÉPARTEMENTS**. Each has its own *conseil régional* (regional council) which has responsibilities in education and economic planning.

rentrée

The week at the beginning of September when the new school year starts and around which much of French administrative life revolves. The preceding weeks see intensive advertising of associated merchandise, from books and stationery to clothes and sports equipment. *La rentrée littéraire* marks the start of the literary year and *la rentrée parlementaire* signals the reassembly of parliament after the recess.

repas

Traditionally the midday meal was the big meal of the day, and for people who live in country areas this is still largely the case. Even in big cities many people continue to eat a big meal in the middle of the day, though they are tending more and more to have a snack lunch and to eat their main meal in the evening. In either case, the main meal virtually always consists of a number of courses, typically a starter such as pâté, *saucisson*, or salad, then meat or fish with a vegetable dish, followed by cheese and dessert. Cheese is virtually always eaten and is served before the dessert. In town and country alike, Sunday is the day for a big family meal in the middle of the day, and the **PÂTISSERIES** are usually crowded on Sunday mornings as people queue up to buy a large tart or cake for their hosts or guests.

restaurants

France is rightly famed for the quality of its restaurants. It is always possible to find restaurants and **BRASSERIES** offering fixed-price menus which are generally good value for money. A basket of bread is usually included in the price of the meal, and most restaurants will have several inexpensive house wines, available in *pichets* (jugs) of 1/4, 1/2, and 1 litre. Service is included in the bill, although many people do leave a tip if the meal and the service have been good.

route départementale

These are signalled on French road maps as 'D' followed by a number and are marked in yellow. They are roads maintained by the **DÉPARTEMENT** and are secondary roads, not intended to be used for fast travel from place to place. Many of them have stretches marked in green on maps to highlight areas or views of particular beauty.

route nationale

A *route nationale* forms part of the state-maintained road network, outside the **AUTOROUTES** but providing fast roads for travel between towns and cities. They are signalled by 'N' followed by the road number and are marked in red on French road maps.

SAMU – service d'aide médicale d'urgence

A 24 hour service coordinated by each **DÉPARTEMENT** to provide mobile medical services and staff, ambulances, and helicopters to accident scenes and emergencies.

Sénat

The upper house of parliament which meets in the **PALAIS DU LUXEMBOURG**. It consists of 321 elected *sénateurs*. It votes laws and the state budget.

SNCF – Société nationale des chemins de fer français

The state-owned railway company, which also has access to private finance.

tabac ▶ **BUREAU DE TABAC**

télécarte
A phone card for use in telephone kiosks, widely available from *France Télécom* (the state owned telephone company), *bureaux de poste*, *tabacs* and *marchands de journaux*.

TF1 - Télévision française 1
Originally a state-controlled television channel, now privately-owned, *TF1* has an obligation to ensure that 50% of its programmes are of French origin.

TGV - train à grande vitesse
The new-generation high-speed electric train. It runs on special tracks and can reach speeds of up to 300 km/h.

Tintin
A comic-book character invented by the Belgian cartoonist Hergé in 1929. Tintin's adventures with the irrepressible Capitaine Haddock are still bestsellers and have been translated into more than 40 languages.

Tour de France
Probably the most famous cycle race in the world, the *Tour de France* takes place over a different route each year but always ends around July 14 on the **CHAMPS ÉLYSÉES**. The overall winner after each section of the race is entitled to wear *le maillot jaune* (yellow jersey).

Letter-writing in French

Holiday postcard

- Beginnings (informal): *Cher* is used for a man, *Chère* for a woman. A letter to two males or to a male and female begins with *Chers*. For two female correspondents *Chères Madeleine et Hélène*. For friends and relatives: *Chers amis*, *Chers cousins*, etc. For a family: *Chère tous*.

- Address: On an envelope Mr, Mrs, and Miss can be abbreviated to *M.*, *Mme*, *Mlle*, although the full forms are considered preferable in more formal letters. There is no direct equivalent for Ms. If you do not know a woman's marital status use *Madame* (*Mme*).

  Road names such as *rue*, *avenue*, *place* are not generally given capital letters.

  The name of the town comes after the postcode and on the same line.

14.7.2000

Cher Alexandre,

Grosses bises d'Edimbourg! Cela fait trois jours que nous sommes ici et nous n'avons pas encore vu la pluie! Espérons que ça va durer. La vieille ville est très belle et du château on a une vue splendide jusqu'à l'estuaire. Et en Normandie, comment ça va?

A bientôt pour des retrouvailles parisiennes,

Marie et Dominique

M. A. Pilnard

38 rue Glacière

75013 Paris

- Endings (informal): *Bien amicalement*, *Amitiés*; *A bientôt* = see you soon.

Christmas and New Year wishes (informal)

■ On most personal letters French speakers do not put their address at the top of the letter. The date is given preceded by *le*. For the first day of the month le *1er* is used. Generally, the name of the town in which the letter is written is placed before the date.

   1 The tradition of Christmas cards is much less widespread in France than in Great Britain. While Christmas greetings may be sent, it is more customary to send best wishes for the New Year in January.

   2 In the year 2000/2001 etc. = *en l'an 2000/2001* etc., but *bonne année 2000/2001* etc.

---

le 18 décembre 2000 **1**

Chers Steve et Michelle,

Nous vous souhaitons un Joyeux Noël **1** et une très bonne année 2001 **2**! En espérant que ce nouveau millénaire vous apportera tout ce que vous désirez et que nous trouverons une occasion pour nous revoir!

Bises à vous deux,

Gérard

New Year wishes (formal)

---

le 5 janvier 2001

Je vous **1** présente mes meilleurs vœux pour l'année 2001. Que cette année vous apporte, à vous et à votre famille, bonheur et prospérité.

Pierre Carlier

---

1 Note the use of the formal form *vous*.

Invitation (informal)

Invitations to parties are usually by word of mouth, but for more formal events such as weddings, invitations are sent out.

1 Note the use of the informal form *tu* betweeen good friends.

Paris, le 28/04/01

Cher Denis,

Que fais-tu 1 cet été? Pascal et moi avons décidé d'inviter tous les copains d'Orléans à nous rejoindre dans notre maison de Dordogne pour le weekend du 14 juillet. Il y aura fête au village avec bal populaire et feu d'artifice. Le petit vin du pays n'est pas mal non plus!

Nous comptons sur toi pour venir trinquer avec nous,

Bises,

Martine

■ Endings (informal): *Bises* (= lots of love) is very informal and is appropriate for very good friends and family. Alternatives for close friends and family include *Bien à toi, Bons baisers* or affectionately *Je t'embrasse*. If the letter is addressed to more than one person use *Bien à vous* or *Je vous embrasse*.

Invitation (formal)

Christine et Félix Prévost
81 rue Esque moise
59000 Lille

Lille, le 28 avril 2001

Chers amis,

Nous avons l'immense plaisir de vous
annoncer le mariage de notre fils Victor
et de mademoiselle Stéphanie Heusdens.

La cérémonie aura lieu à l'Hôtel de
Ville à 15 heures le samedi 5 juin. Vous
recevrez bientôt un faire-part et une
invitation à dîner mais nous tenions à
vous prévenir suffisamment tôt pour que
vous puissiez arranger votre voyage.
Nous espérons qu'il vous sera possible
de vous joindre à nous.

Amicalement,1

Christine et Félix

- In a more formal letter, especially where a reply is generally required, the sender's address is written on the left-hand side of the page. An alternative is in the centre of the page, particularly on printed stationery.

1 Endings: Alternatives could be *Amitiés*, *Bien amicalement*.

Accepting an Invitation

Emilie Joly
2 rue de la Pompe
75016 Paris

le 16 mars 2001

Chère Madame Dubois,

Je vous 1 remercie de bien vouloir me recevoir pour les deux premières semaines de juillet. Je serai très heureuse de vous revoir ainsi que Natalie, bien entendu. Nous avons passé un si bon séjour linguistique à Manchester l'été dernier que nous avions très envie de nous retrouver. Mes parents ne pouvant m'envoyer en Angleterre cette année, c'est avec un immense plaisir que j'accepte votre invitation.

Je vous prie de bien vouloir accepter, Madame, l'expression de mes sentiments les meilleurs,

Emilie

■ In a more formal social letter where the correspondent is known personally by name it can be used in the opening greeting.

■ The title of the person receiving the letter must be repeated in the closing formula. These formulas are more elaborate than in English, with a number of possible variations. Some of these are shown in the following letters in this section.

1 Since the letter is from a young person to the mother of a friend, she uses the formal *vous* form and writes to her as Madame Dubois. Madame Dubois would address Emilie using *tu*.

Seeking a job as an au pair

Sally Paledra
5 Avon Crescent
Kenilworth
Warwickshire
CV8 2PQ

le 3 mars 2001

Madame,

Vos coordonnées m'ont été communiquées par l'agence 'Au Pair International', qui m'a demandé de vous écrire directement. Je suis en effet à la recherche d'un emploi au pair pour une période de neuf à dix mois à partir de septembre prochain.

J'aime beaucoup les enfants et ils apprécient également ma compagnie. J'ai une grande expérience du baby-sitting. J'ai aussi fait un stage d'un mois dans une crèche privée **1**.

Je suis enthousiaste, discrète et je sais prendre des initiatives. J'ai étudié le français au lycée pendant cinq ans et je connais un peu la France pour y avoir passé des vacances à plusieurs reprises. J'ai aussi mon permis de conduire.

Dans l'espoir d'une réponse positive de votre part, je vous prie d'agréer, Madame, l'expression de mes salutations respectueuses.

S. Paledra

P.J. : un CV avec photo

---

1 Or be more specific, e.g. *pour des enfants de 3 mois à 3 ans.*

■ To supply references: *Vous trouverez également ci-joint les adresses de personnes pouvant fournir une lettre de recommandation* or *pouvant me recommander.*

Enquiry to a tourist office

M. et Mme Baude
13 La Faverolle
45000 Orléans

> Syndicat d'initiative
> de St Gervais
> 74170 Saint-Gervais-les-Bains

> Orléans, le 24 mars 2001

Monsieur,

Nous vous serions reconnaissants de bien vouloir nous
faire parvenir toute la documentation dont vous disposez
sur les villas de location à proximité de la station thermale.
Nous désirons également recevoir des informations sur les
activités de loisirs durant l'été.
Vous trouverez ci-joint une enveloppe timbrée **1** pour la
réponse.

Dans l'attente de votre réponse, je vous prie d'agréer,
Monsieur, l'expression de nos salutations distinguées.

J. Baude

---

1 *enveloppe timbrée* = stamped addressed envelope.

■ Note that, unlike in English, a reference or the purpose of a
business letter is placed, where required, above the opening
greeting. e.g. *Objet: commande 99/08/21* or *Réf: 000/23*.

Booking a hotel room

Miss Sylvia Daley
The Willows
49 North Terrace
Kings Barton
Nottinghamshire
NG8 4LQ
England

Hôtel Beauséjour
Chemin des Mimosas
06100 Grasse

le 8 avril 2001

Madame,

J'ai bien reçu le dépliant de votre hôtel et je vous en remercie.

Je souhaite réserver une chambre calme avec salle de bains, en pension complète **1** pour la période du 7 au 18 juin. Pour les arrhes, je vous prie de m'informer de leur montant et des modalités de paiement possibles depuis la Grande-Bretagne.

En vous remerciant d'avance, je vous prie de croire, Madame, en mes sentiments les meilleurs.

S. Daley

---

1 Or *une chambre avec douche en demi-pension* or *avec petit déjeuner*. The term en suite does not exist for bathroom facilities in French.

Booking a campsite

Frances Good
22 Daniel Avenue
Caldwood
Leeds LS8 7RR
tel. 0113 2998767

Camping 'Les Embruns'
18 allée des Capucins
22116 Moëlan-sur-Mer

le 25 avril 2001

Monsieur,

Nous souhaitons réserver dans votre camping, pour la période du 2 au 15 juillet, deux emplacements de tente côte à côte **1** et, si possible, pas trop loin de la plage **2**. Il s'agit de deux tentes de deux personnes. Nous aurons également deux motos de 1000cc chacune.

Dès que nous aurons confirmation de votre part, nous vous adresserons le montant de la réservation.

Pouvez-vous nous indiquer à cet effet, les possibilités de paiement depuis l'étranger.

Veuillez croire, Monsieur, en l'expression de nos sentiments les meilleurs.

F. Good

1 Or if you have a caravan *un emplacement de caravane*.
2 Other requirements might be *ombragé* (shady), or *abrité* (sheltered).

Cancelling a reservation

Mrs J. Warrington
Downlands
Steyning
West Sussex

> Hôtel des Voyageurs
> BN44 6LZ
> 9 cours Gambetta
> 91949 Les Ulis
>
> le 15 février 2001

Monsieur,

Je suis au regret de devoir annuler la réservation de chambre pour deux personnes pour la nuit du 24 au 25 mars, que j'avais effectuée par téléphone le 18 janvier dernier. **1**

Je vous remercie de votre compréhension et vous prie d'agréer, Monsieur, l'expression de mes sentiments distingués.

J. Warrington

---

1 If reasons for the cancellation are specified these could include: *pour raisons de santé/de famille, en raison d'un décès dans la famille*, etc.

sending an email

1 Note that *mél* is an abbreviated form of *message électronique*. To send an attachment = *joindre un fichier*.
2 Endings (informal): An alternative could be *A bientôt* or simply *Bises* to a close friend in an informal context.

a *determiner*

an avant voyelle ou h muet.

➡️ For expressions such as make a noise, make a fortune ⇒ noise, fortune.

····➤ un/une; ~ **tree** un arbre; ~ **chair** une chaise.

····➤ (per) **two euros** ~ **kilo** deux euros le kilo; **three times** ~ **day** trois fois par jour.

❗ When talking about what people do or are, a is not translated into French: she's a teacher elle est professeur; he's a widower il est veuf.

aback *adv* taken ~ déconcerté.
abandon *vt* abandonner. ● *n* abandon *m*.
abate *vi* (*flood, fever*) baisser; (*storm*) se calmer. ● *vt* diminuer.
abbey *n* abbaye *f*.
abbot *n* abbé *m*.
abbreviate *vt* abréger.
abbreviation *n* abréviation *f*.
abdicate *vt/i* abdiquer.
abdomen *n* abdomen *m*.
abduct *vt* enlever. **abductor** *n* ravisseur/-euse *m/f*.
abhor *vt* (*pt* **abhorred**) exécrer.
abide *vt* supporter; ~ **by** respecter.
ability *n* capacité *f* (**to do** à faire); (*talent*) talent *m*.
abject *a* (*state*) misérable; (*coward*) abject.
ablaze *a* en feu.
able *a* (skilled) compétent; **be** ~ **to do** pouvoir faire; (know how to) savoir faire. **ably** *adv* avec compétence.
abnormal *a* anormal.
abnormality *n* anomalie *f*.
aboard *adv* à bord. ● *prep* à bord de.
abode *n* demeure *f*; **of no fixed** ~ sans domicile fixe.
abolish *vt* abolir.
Aborigine *n* aborigène *mf* (d'Australie).
abort *vt* faire avorter; (Comput) abandonner. ● *vi* avorter.
abortion *n* avortement *m*; **have an** ~ se faire avorter.
abortive *a* (*attempt*) avorté; (*coup*) manqué.
about *adv* (approximately) environ; ~ **the same** à peu près pareil; **there was no-one** ~ il n'y avait personne. ● *prep* **it's** ~ ... il s'agit de ...; **what I like** ~ **her is** ce que j'aime chez elle c'est; **to wander** ~ **the streets** errer dans les rues; **how/what** ~ **some tea?** et si on prenait un thé?; **what** ~ **you?** et toi? ● *adj* **be** ~ **to do** être sur le point de faire; **be up and** ~ être debout. ~-**face**, ~-**turn** *n* (fig) volte-face *f inv*.
above *prep* au-dessus de; **he is not** ~ **lying** il n'est pas incapable de mentir; ~ **all** surtout. ● *adv* **the apartment** ~ l'appartement du dessus; **see** ~ voir ci-dessus. ~-**board** *a* honnête.
~-**mentioned** *a* susmentionné.
abrasive *a* abrasif; (*manner*) mordant. ● *n* abrasif *m*.
abreast *adv* de front; **keep** ~ **of** se tenir au courant de.
abroad *adv* à l'étranger.

abrupt *a* (sudden, curt) brusque;
(steep) abrupt. **abruptly** *adv*
(suddenly) brusquement; (curtly)
avec brusquerie.

abscess *n* abcès *m*.

abseil *vi* descendre en rappel.

absence *n* absence *f*; (lack)
manque *m*; **in the ~ of** faute de.

absent *a* absent.

absentee *n* absent/-e *m/f*.

absent-minded *a* distrait.

absolute *a* (monarch, majority)
absolu; (chaos, idiot) véritable.
absolutely *adv* absolument.

absolve *vt* **~ sb of sth** décharger
qn de qch.

absorb *vt* absorber.

abstain *vi* s'abstenir (from de).

abstract¹ *a* abstrait. ● *n* (summary)
résumé *m*; **in the ~** dans
l'abstrait.

abstract² *vt* tirer.

absurd *a* absurde.

abundance *n* abondance *f*.
abundant *a* abondant.
abundantly *adv* (entirely) tout à
fait.

abuse¹ *vt* (position) abuser de;
(person) maltraiter; (insult)
injurier.

abuse² *n* (misuse) abus *m* (of de);
(cruelty) mauvais traitement *m*;
(insults) injures *fpl*.

abusive *a* (person) grossier;
(language) injurieux.

abysmal *a* épouvantable.

abyss *n* abîme *m*.

academic *a* (career)
universitaire; (year) académique;
(scholarly) intellectuel; (theoretical)
théorique. ● *n* universitaire *mf*.

academy *n* (school) école *f*;
(society) académie *f*.

accelerate *vi* (speed up)
s'accélérer; (Auto) accélérer.
accelerator *n* accélérateur *m*.

accent¹ *n* accent *m*.

accent² *vt* accentuer.

accept *vt* accepter. **acceptable**
a acceptable. **acceptance** *n* (of
offer) acceptation *f*; (of proposal)
approbation *f*.

access *n* accès *m*. **accessible** *a*
accessible.

accessory *a* accessoire. ● *n* (Jur)
complice *mf* (to de).

accident *n* accident *m*; (chance)
hasard *m*; **by ~** par hasard.
accidental *a* (death) accidentel;
(meeting) fortuit. **accidentally**
adv accidentellement; (by chance)
par hasard.

acclaim *vt* applaudir. ● *n*
louanges *fpl*.

acclimatize *vt/i* (s')acclimater
(to à).

accommodate *vt* loger; (adapt to)
s'adapter à; (satisfy) satisfaire.
accommodating *a*
accommodant. **accommodation**
n logement *m*.

accompaniment *n*
accompagnement *m*. **accompany**
vt accompagner.

accomplice *n* complice *mf* (in, to
de).

accomplish *vt* accomplir;
(objective) réaliser.
accomplished *a* très compétent.
accomplishment *n* (feat) réussite
f; (talent) talent *m*.

accord *vi* concorder (with avec).
● *vt* accorder (sb sth qch à qn).
● *n* accord *m*; **of my own ~** de
moi-même.

accordance *n* **in ~ with**
conformément à.

according *adv* **~ to** (principle,
law) selon; (person, book)
d'après. **accordingly** *adv* en
conséquence.

accordion *n* accordéon *m*.

accost *vt* aborder.

account *n* (Comm) compte *m*;
(description) compte-rendu *m*; **on ~**

of à cause de; **on no ~** en aucun cas; **it's of no ~** peu importe. □ **~ for** (explain) expliquer; (represent) représenter. **accountability** n responsabilité f. **accountable** a responsable (**for** de; **to** envers).

accountancy n comptabilité f. **accountant** n comptable mf. **accounts** npl comptabilité f, comptes mpl.

accumulate vt/i (s')accumuler.

accuracy n (of figures) justesse f; (of aim) précision f; (of forecast) exactitude f. **accurate** a juste, précis. **accurately** adv exactement, précisément.

accusation n accusation f.

accuse vt accuser; **the ~d** l'accusé/-e m/f.

accustomed a accoutumé; **become ~ to** s'accoutumer à.

ace n (card, person) as m.

ache n douleur f. ● vi (person) avoir mal; **my leg ~s** ma jambe me fait mal.

achieve vt (aim) atteindre; (result) obtenir; (ambition) réaliser. **achievement** n (feat) réussite f; (fulfilment) réalisation f (**of** de).

acid a & n acide (m). **acidity** n acidité f. **~ rain** n pluies fpl acides.

acknowledge vt (error, authority) reconnaître; (letter) accuser réception de. **acknowledgement** n reconnaissance f.

acne n acné f.

acorn n (Bot) gland m.

acoustic a acoustique. **acoustics** npl acoustique f.

acquaint vt **~ sb with sth** mettre qn au courant de qch; **be ~ed with** (person) connaître; (fact) savoir. **acquaintance** n connaissance f.

acquire vt acquérir; (habit) prendre.

acquit vt (pt **acquitted**) (Jur) acquitter. **acquittal** n acquittement m.

acre n acre f, ≈ demi-hectare m.

acrid a âcre.

acrimonious a acrimonieux.

acrobat n acrobate mf. **acrobatics** npl acrobaties fpl.

acronym n acronyme m.

across adv & prep (side to side) d'un côté à l'autre (de); (on other side) de l'autre côté (**from** de); **go** or **walk ~** traverser; **lie ~ the bed** se coucher en travers du lit; **~ the world** partout dans le monde.

act n acte m; (Jur, Pol) loi f; **put on an ~** jouer la comédie. ● vi agir; (Theat) jouer; **~ as** servir de. ● vt (part, role) jouer.

acting n (Theat) jeu m ● a (temporary) intérimaire.

action n action f; (Mil) combat m; **out of ~** hors service; **take ~** agir.

activate vt (machine) faire démarrer; (alarm) déclencher.

active a actif; (volcano) en activité; **take an ~ interest** in s'intéresser activement à.

activist n activiste mf. **activity** n activité f.

actor n acteur m. **actress** n actrice f.

actual a réel; **the ~ words** les mots exacts; **in the ~ house** (the house itself) dans la maison elle-même. **actuality** n réalité f. **actually** adv (in fact) en fait; (really) vraiment.

acute a (anxiety) vif; (illness) aigu; (shortage) grave; (mind) pénétrant.

ad n (TV) pub f 🔢; **small ~** petite annonce f.

AD abbr (**Anno Domini**) ap. J.-C.

adamant a catégorique.

adapt vt/i (s')adapter (**to** à).
adaptability n adaptabilité f.
adaptable a souple. **adaptation**
n adaptation f. **adaptor** n (Electr)
adaptateur m.

add vt/i ajouter (**to** à); (in maths)
additionner. □ ~ **up** (facts,
figures) s'accorder; ~ **sth up**
additionner qch; ~ **up to** s'élever
à.

adder n vipère f.

addict n toxicomane mf; (fig)
accro mf ▣.

addicted a **be** ~ avoir une
dépendance (**to** à); (fig) être accro
▣ (**to** à). **addiction** n (Med)
dépendance f (**to** à); passion f (**to**
pour). **addictive** a qui crée une
dépendance.

addition n (item) ajout m; (in maths)
addition f; **in** ~ en plus.
additional a supplémentaire.

additive n additif m.

address n adresse f; (speech)
discours m. ●vt (letter) mettre
l'adresse sur; (crowd) s'adresser
à; ~ **sth to** adresser qch à.
addressee n destinataire mf.

adequate a suffisant; (satisfactory)
satisfaisant.

adhere vi (lit, fig) adhérer (**to** à); ~
to (policy) observer.

adjacent a contigu; ~ **to** attenant
à.

adjective n adjectif m.

adjoin vt être contigu à.
adjoining a (room) voisin.

adjourn vt (trial) ajourner; **the
session was ~ed** la séance a été
levée. ●vi s'arrêter; (Parliament)
lever la séance; ~ **to** passer à.

adjust vt (level, speed) régler;
(price) ajuster; (clothes) rajuster.
●vt/i ~ (**oneself**) **to** s'adapter à.
adjustable a réglable.
adjustment n (of rates)
rajustement m; (of control) réglage
m; (of person) adaptation f.

ad lib vt/i (pt **ad libbed**)
improviser.

administer vt administrer.

administration n administration
f. **administrative** a administratif.
administrator n administrateur/
-trice m/f.

admiral n amiral m.

admiration n admiration f.
admire vt admirer. **admirer** n
admirateur/-trice m/f.

admission n (to a place) entrée f;
(confession) aveu m.

admit vt (pt **admitted**)
(acknowledge) reconnaître,
admettre; (crime) avouer; (new
member) admettre; ~ **to**
reconnaître. **admittance** n
entrée f. **admittedly** adv il est
vrai.

ado n **without more** ~ sans plus de
cérémonie.

adolescence n adolescence f.
adolescent n & a adolescent/-e
(m/f).

adopt vt adopter. **adopted** a
(child) adoptif. **adoption** n
adoption f. **adoptive** a adoptif.

adorable a adorable. **adoration**
n adoration f. **adore** vt adorer.

adorn vt orner.

adrift a & adv à la dérive.

adult a & n adulte (mf).

adultery n adultère m.

adulthood n âge m adulte.

advance vt (sum) avancer; (tape,
career) faire avancer; (interests)
servir. ●vi (lit) avancer; (progress)
progresser. ●n avance f; (progress)
progrès m; **in** ~ à l'avance.
advanced a avancé; (studies)
supérieur.

advantage n avantage m; **take** ~
of profiter de; (person) exploiter.
advantageous a avantageux.

adventure n aventure f.
adventurer n aventurier/-ière m/
f. **adventurous** a aventureux.

adverb *n* adverbe *m*.

adverse *a* défavorable.

advert *n* annonce *f*; (TV) pub *f* 🔲.

advertise *vt* faire de la publicité pour; (*car, house, job*) mettre une annonce pour. ● *vi* faire de la publicité; (for staff) passer une annonce. **advertisement** *n* publicité *f*; (in newspaper) annonce *f*. **advertiser** *n* annonceur *m*. **advertising** *n* publicité *f*.

advice *n* conseils *mpl*; **some ~, a piece of ~** un conseil.

advise *vt* conseiller; (inform) aviser; **~ against** déconseiller. **adviser** *n* conseiller/-ère *m/f*. **advisory** *a* consultatif.

advocate[1] *n* (Jur) avocat *m*; (supporter) partisan *m*.

advocate[2] *vt* recommander.

aerial *a* aérien. ● *n* antenne *f*.

aerobics *n* aérobic *m*.

aeroplane *n* avion *m*.

aerosol *n* bombe *f* aérosol.

aesthetic *a* esthétique.

afar *adv* **from ~** de loin.

affair *n* (matter) affaire *f*; (romance) liaison *f*.

affect *vt* affecter.

affection *n* affection *f*. **affectionate** *a* affectueux.

affinity *n* affinité *f*.

afflict *vt* affliger.

affluence *n* richesse *f*.

afford *vt* avoir les moyens d'acheter; (provide) fournir; **can you ~ the time?** avez-vous le temps?

afloat *adj & adv* (boat) à flot.

afoot *adv* **sth is ~** il se prépare qch.

afraid *a* **be ~** (frightened) avoir peur (**of, to** de; **that** que); (worried) craindre (**that** que); **I'm ~ I can't come** je suis désolé mais je ne peux pas venir.

Africa *n* Afrique *f*.

African *n* Africain/-e *m/f*. ● *a* africain.

after *adv & prep* après; **soon ~** peu après; **be ~ sth** rechercher qch; **~ all** après tout. ● *conj* après que; **~ doing** après avoir fait.

aftermath *n* conséquences *fpl* (**of** de).

afternoon *n* après-midi *m or f inv*; **in the ~** (dans) l'après-midi.

after: ~shave *n* après-rasage *m*. **~thought** *n* pensée *f* après coup.

afterwards *adv* après, par la suite.

again *adv* encore; **~ and ~** à plusieurs reprises; **start ~** recommencer; **she never saw him ~** elle ne l'a jamais revu.

against *prep* contre; **~ the law** illégal.

age *n* âge *m*; (era) ère *f*, époque *f*; **I've been waiting for ~s** j'attends depuis des heures. ● *vt/i* (*pres p* **ageing**) vieillir.

aged[1] *a* **~ six** âgé de six ans.

aged[2] *a* âgé.

ageism *n* discrimination *f* en raison de l'âge.

agency *n* agence *f*.

agenda *n* ordre *m* du jour; (fig) programme *m*.

agent *n* agent *m*.

aggravate *vt* (make worse) aggraver; (annoy) exaspérer. **aggravation** *n* (worsening) aggravation *f*; (annoyance) ennuis *mpl*.

aggression *n* agression *f*.

aggressive *a* agressif. **aggressiveness** *n* agressivité *f*. **aggressor** *n* agresseur *m*.

ago *adv* il y a; **a month ~** il y a un mois; **long ~** il y a longtemps; **how long ~?** il y a combien de temps?

agonize *vi* se tourmenter (**over** à

propos de). **agonized** *a* angoissé.

agonizing *a* déchirant. **agony** *n* douleur *f* atroce; (mental) angoisse *f*.

agree *vi* être d'accord (**on** sur; **with** avec); ~ **to** consentir à; ~ **with** (approve of) approuver. ● *vt* être d'accord (**that** sur le fait que); (admit) convenir (**that** que); (date, solution) se mettre d'accord sur.

agreeable *a* agréable; **be** ~ (willing) être d'accord.

agreed *a* (time, place) convenu; **we're** ~ nous sommes d'accord.

agreement *n* accord *m*; **in** ~ d'accord.

agricultural *a* agricole.

agriculture *n* agriculture *f*.

aground *adv* **run** ~ (ship) s'échouer.

ahead *adv* (in front) en avant, devant; (in advance) à l'avance; **be 10 points** ~ avoir 10 points d'avance; ~ **of time** en avance; **go** ~! allez-y!

aid *vt* aider. ● *n* aide *f*; **in** ~ **of** au profit de.

aide *n* aide *mf*.

Aids *n* (Med) sida *m*.

aim *vt* (gun) braquer (**at** sur); **be** ~**ed at sb** (campaign, remark) viser qn. ● *vi* ~ **for/at sth** viser qch; ~ **to do** avoir l'intention de faire. ● *n* but *m*; **take** ~ viser. **aimless** *a* sans but.

air *n* air *m*; **by** ~ par avion; **on the** ~ à l'antenne. ● *vt* aérer; (views) exprimer. ● *a* (base, disaster) aérien; (pollution, pressure) atmosphérique. ~**-bed** *n* matelas *m* pneumatique. ~**-conditioning** *n* climatisation *f*. ~**craft** *n inv* avion *m*. ~**craft carrier** *n* porte-avions *m inv*. ~**field** *n* terrain *m* d'aviation. ~ **force** *n* armée *f* de l'air. ~ **freshener** *n* désodorisant *m* d'atmosphère. ~ **hostess** *n*

hôtesse *f* de l'air. ~**lift** *vt* transporter par pont aérien. ~**line** *n* compagnie *f* aérienne. ~**liner** *n* avion *m* de ligne. ~**lock** *n* (in pipe) bulle *f* d'air; (chamber) sas *m*. ~**mail** *n* (by) ~**mail** par avion. ~**plane** *n* (US) avion *m*. ~**port** *n* aéroport *m*. ~ **raid** *n* attaque *f* aérienne. ~**tight** *a* hermétique. ~ **traffic controller** *n* contrôleur/-euse *m/f* aérien/-ne. ~**waves** *npl* ondes *fpl*.

airy *a* (**-ier, -iest**) (room) clair et spacieux.

aisle *n* (of church) allée *f* centrale; (in train) couloir *m*.

ajar *adv & a* entrouvert.

akin *a* ~ **to** semblable à.

alarm *n* alarme *f*; (clock) réveil *m*; (feeling) frayeur *f*. ● *vt* inquiéter. ~**-clock** *n* réveil *m*.

alas *interj* hélas.

Albania *n* Albanie *f*.

album *n* album *m*.

alcohol *n* alcool *m*.

alcoholic *a* alcoolique; (drink) alcoolisé. ● *n* alcoolique *mf*.

ale *n* bière *f*.

alert *a* alerte; (watchful) vigilant. ● *n* alerte *f*; **on the** ~ sur le qui-vive. ● *vt* alerter; ~ **sb to** prévenir qn de. **alertness** *n* vivacité *f*; vigilance *f*.

A-level *n* ≈ baccalauréat *m*.

algebra *n* algèbre *f*.

Algeria *n* Algérie *f*.

alias *n* (pl ~**es**) faux nom *m*. ● *prep* alias.

alibi *n* alibi *m*.

alien *n & a* étranger/-ère (m/f) (**to** à).

alienate *vt* éloigner.

alight *a* en feu, allumé.

alike *a* semblable. ● *adv* de la même façon; **look** ~ se ressembler.

alive *a* vivant; ~ **to** conscient de; ~ **with** grouillant de.

....

all

● *pronoun*

····▸ (everything) tout; **is that ~?** c'est tout?; **that was ~ (that) he said** c'est tout ce qu'il a dit; **I ate it ~** j'ai tout mangé.

> **!** Use the translation **tous** for a group of masculine or mixed gender people or objects and **toutes** for a group of feminine gender: **we were all delighted** *nous étions tous ravis*; **'where are the cups?'—'they're all in the kitchen'** *'où sont les tasses?'—'elles sont toutes dans la cuisine'*.

● *determiner*

····▸ tout/toute/tous/toutes; ~ **the time** tout le temps; ~ **his life** toute sa vie; ~ **of us** nous tous; ~ **(the) women** toutes les femmes.

● *adverb*

····▸ (completely) tout; **they were ~ alone** ils étaient tout seuls, **tell me ~ about it** raconte-moi tout; ~ **for** tout à fait pour; **not ~ that well** pas si bien que ça; ~ **too** bien trop.

> **!** When the adjective that follows is in the feminine and begins with a consonant, the translation is *toute/toutes*: **she was all alone** *elle était toute seule*.

....

allege *vt* prétendre. **allegedly** *adv* prétendument.

allergic *a* allergique (**to** à). **allergy** *n* allergie *f*.

alleviate *vt* alléger.

alley *n* (street) ruelle *f*.

alliance *n* alliance *f*.

allied *a* allié.

alligator *n* alligator *m*.

allocate *vt* (*funds*) affecter; (*time*) accorder; (*task*) assigner.

allot *vt* (*pt* allotted) (*money*) attribuer; (*task*) assigner.

allotment *n* attribution *f*; (land) parcelle *f* de terre.

all-out *a* (*effort*) acharné; (*strike*) total.

allow *vt* (authorize) autoriser à; (let) laisser; (enable) permettre; (concede) accorder; ~ **for** tenir compte de.

allowance *n* allocation *f*; **make ~s for sth** tenir compte de qch; **make ~s for sb** essayer de comprendre qn.

alloy *n* alliage *m*.

all right *a* (not bad) pas mal; **are you ~?** ça va?; **is it ~ if ...?** est-ce que ça va si ...? ● *adv* (see) bien; (*function*) comme il faut. ● *interj* d'accord.

ally[1] *n* allié/-e *m/f*.

ally[2] *vt* allier; ~ **oneself with** s'allier avec.

almighty *a* tout-puissant; (very great) formidable.

almond *n* amande *f*. ~ **tree** *n* amandier *m*.

almost *adv* presque; **he ~ died** il a failli mourir.

alone *a & adv* seul.

along *prep* le long de; **walk ~ the beach** marcher sur la plage. ● *adv* **come ~** venir; **walk ~** marcher; **push/pull sth ~** pousser/tirer qch; **all ~** (time) depuis le début; ~ **with** avec.

alongside *adv* à côté; **come ~** (Naut) accoster. ● *prep* (next to) à côté de; (all along) le long de.

aloof *a* distant.

aloud *adv* à haute voix.

alphabet n alphabet m.
 alphabetical a alphabétique.

alpine a (*landscape*) alpestre;
 (*climate*) alpin.

already adv déjà.

alright a & adv = ALL RIGHT.

Alsatian n (dog) berger m
 allemand.

also adv aussi.

altar n autel m.

alter vt/i changer; (*building*)
 transformer; (*garment*)
 retoucher. **alteration** n
 changement m; (to building)
 transformation f; (to garment)
 retouche f.

alternate[1] vt/i alterner.

alternate[2] a en alternance; **on ~
 days** un jour sur deux.
 alternately adv alternativement.

alternative a autre; (*solution*) de
 rechange. ● n (specified option)
 alternative f; (possible option) choix
 m. **alternatively** adv sinon.

alternator n alternateur m.

although conj bien que.

altitude n altitude f.

altogether adv (completely) tout à
 fait; (on the whole) tout compte fait.

aluminium n aluminium m.

always adv toujours.

am ⇒BE.

a.m. adv du matin.

amalgamate vt/i (merge)
 fusionner; (*metals*)
 (s')amalgamer.

amateur n & a amateur (m).

amaze vt stupéfaire. **amazed** a
 stupéfait. **amazement** n
 stupéfaction f. **amazing** a
 stupéfiant; (great) exceptionnel.

ambassador n ambassadeur m.

amber n ambre m; (Auto) orange
 m.

ambiguity n ambiguïté f.
 ambiguous a ambigu.

ambition n ambition f.
 ambitious a ambitieux.

ambulance n ambulance f.

ambush n embuscade f. ● vt
 tendre une embuscade à.

amenable a obligeant; **~ to**
 (responsive) sensible à.

amend vt modifier. **amendment**
 n (to rule) amendement m.

amends npl **make ~** réparer son
 erreur.

amenities npl équipements mpl.

America n Amérique f.

American n Américain/-e m/f.
 ● a américain.

amiable a aimable.

amicable a amical.

amid(st) prep au milieu de.

amiss a **there is something ~** il y
 a quelque chose qui ne va pas.

ammonia n (gas) ammoniac m;
 (solution) ammoniaque f.

ammunition n munitions fpl.

amnesty n amnistie f.

among(st) prep parmi; (affecting a
 group) chez; **be ~ the poorest** être
 un des plus pauvres; **be ~ the
 first** être dans les premiers.

amorous a amoureux.

amount n quantité f; (total)
 montant m; (sum of money) somme
 f. ● vi **~ to** (add up to) s'élever à;
 (be equivalent to) revenir à.

amp n ampère m.

amphibian n amphibie m.

ample a (*resources*) largement
 suffisant; (*proportions*) généreux.

amplifier n amplificateur m.

amputate vt amputer.

amuse vt amuser.

amusement n (mirth) amusement
 m; (diversion) distraction f. **~
 arcade** n salle f de jeux.

an ⇒A.

anaemia n anémie f.

anaesthetic n anesthésique m.

analyse *vt* analyser. **analysis** *n* (*pl* **-yses**) analyse *f*. **analyst** *n* analyste *mf*.

anarchist *n* anarchiste *mf*.

anatomical *a* anatomique. **anatomy** *n* anatomie *f*.

ancestor *n* ancêtre *m*.

anchor *n* ancre *f*. ● *vt* mettre à l'ancre. ● *vi* jeter l'ancre.

anchovy *n* anchois *m*.

ancient *a* ancien.

ancillary *a* auxiliaire.

and *conj* et; **two hundred ~ sixty** deux cent soixante; **go ~ see him** allez le voir; **richer ~ richer** de plus en plus riche.

anew *adv* (once more) encore, de nouveau; (in a new way) à nouveau.

angel *n* ange *m*.

anger *n* colère *f*. ● *vt* mettre en colère, fâcher.

angle *n* angle *m*. ● *vi* pêcher (à la ligne); **~ for** (fig) quêter de. **angler** *n* pêcheur/-euse *m/f*.

Anglo-Saxon *a* anglo-saxon. ● *n* Anglo-Saxon/-ne *m/f*.

angry *a* (**-ier**, **-iest**) fâché, en colère; **get ~** se fâcher, se mettre en colère (with contre); **make sb ~** mettre qn en colère.

anguish *n* angoisse *f*.

animal *n* & *a* animal (*m*).

animate[1] *a* (*person*) vivant; (*object*) animé.

animate[2] *vt* animer.

aniseed *n* anis *m*.

ankle *n* cheville *f*. **~ sock** *n* socquette *f*.

annex *vt* annexer.

anniversary *n* anniversaire *m*.

announce *vt* annoncer (**that** que). **announcement** *n* (spoken) annonce *f*; (written) avis *m*. **announcer** *n* (radio, TV) speaker/ -ine *m/f*.

annoy *vt* agacer, ennuyer. **annoyance** *n* contrariété *f*.

annoyed *a* fâché (**with** contre); **get ~ed** se fâcher. **annoying** *a* ennuyeux.

annual *a* annuel. ● *n* publication *f* annuelle. **annually** *adv* (*earn*, *produce*) par an; (*do*, *inspect*) tous les ans.

annul *vt* (*pt* **annulled**) annuler.

anonymity *n* anonymat *m*. **anonymous** *a* anonyme.

anorak *n* anorak *m*.

another *det* & *pron* un/-e autre; **~ coffee** (one more) encore un café; **~ ten minutes** encore dix minutes, dix minutes de plus; **can I have ~?** est-ce que je peux en avoir un autre?

answer *n* réponse *f*; (solution) solution *f*; (phone) **there's no ~** ça ne répond pas. ● *vt* répondre à; (*prayer*) exaucer; **~ the door** ouvrir la porte. ● *vi* répondre. □ **~ back** répondre; **~ for** répondre de; **~ to** (*superior*) dépendre de; (*description*) répondre à. **answerable** *a* responsable (**for** de; **to** devant).

answering machine *n* répondeur *m*.

ant *n* fourmi *f*.

antagonism *n* antagonisme *m*. **antagonize** *vt* provoquer l'hostilité de.

Antarctic *n* **the ~** l'Antarctique *m*. ● *a* antarctique.

antenatal *a* prénatal.

antenna *n* (*pl* **-ae**) (of insect) antenne *f*; (*pl* **-as**; aerial: US) antenne *f*.

anthem *n* (Relig) motet *m*; (of country) hymne *m* national.

anthrax *n* charbon *m*.

antibiotic *n* & *a* antibiotique (*m*).

antibody *n* anticorps *m*.

anticipate *vt* (foresee, expect) prévoir, s'attendre à.

anticipation *n* attente *f*; **in ~ of** en prévision *or* attente de.

anticlimax n (let-down) déception f.

anticlockwise adv & a dans le sens inverse des aiguilles d'une montre.

antics npl pitreries fpl.

antifreeze n antigel m.

antiquated a (idea) archaïque; (building) vétuste.

antique a (old) ancien; (old-style) à l'ancienne. ●n objet m ancien, antiquité f. ~ **dealer** n antiquaire mf. ~ **shop** n magasin m d'antiquités.

anti-Semitic a antisémite.

antiseptic a & n antiseptique (m).

antisocial a asocial, antisocial; (reclusive) sauvage.

antlers npl bois mpl.

anxiety n (worry) anxiété f; (eagerness) impatience f.

anxious a (troubled) anxieux; (eager) impatient (to de).

any det (some) du, de l', de la, des; (after negative) de, d'; (every) tout; (no matter which) n'importe quel; **at ~ moment** à tout moment; **have you ~ water?** avez-vous de l'eau? ●pron (no matter which one) n'importe lequel; (any amount of it or them) en; **I do not have ~** je n'en ai pas; **did you see ~ of them?** en avez-vous vu? ●adv (a little) un peu; **do you have ~ more?** en avez-vous encore?; **do you have ~ more tea?** avez-vous encore du thé?; **I don't do it ~ more** je ne le fais plus.

anybody pron (no matter who) n'importe qui; (somebody) quelqu'un; (after negative) personne; **he did not see ~** il n'a vu personne.

anyhow adv (anyway) de toute façon; (carelessly) n'importe comment.

anyone pron = ANYBODY.

anything pron (no matter what) n'importe quoi; (something) quelque chose; (after negative) rien; **he did not see ~** il n'a rien vu; **~ but** nullement; **~ you do** tout ce que tu fais.

anyway adv de toute façon.

anywhere adv (no matter where) n'importe où; (somewhere) quelque part; (after negative) nulle part; **he does not go ~** il ne va nulle part; **~ you go** partout où tu vas, où que tu ailles; **~ else** partout ailleurs.

apart adv (on or to one side) à part; (separated) séparé; (into pieces) en pièces; **~ from** à part, excepté; **ten metres ~** à dix mètres l'un de l'autre; **come ~** (break) tomber en morceaux; (machine) se démonter; **legs ~** les jambes écartées; **keep ~** séparer; **take ~** démonter.

apartment n (US) appartement m.

ape n singe m. ●vt singer.

aperitif n apéritif m.

apex n sommet m.

apologetic a (tone) d'excuse; **be ~** s'excuser. **apologetically** adv en s'excusant.

apologize vi s'excuser (**for** de; **to** auprès de).

apology n excuses fpl.

apostrophe n apostrophe f.

appal vt (pt **appalled**) horrifier. **appalling** a épouvantable.

apparatus n appareil m.

apparent a apparent. **apparently** adv apparemment.

appeal n appel m; (attractiveness) attrait m, charme m. ●vi (Jur) faire appel; **~ to sb** (beg) faire appel à qn; (attract) plaire à qn; **~ to sb for sth** demander qch à qn. **appealing** a (attractive) attirant.

appear vi apparaître; (arrive) se présenter; (seem, be published) paraître; (Theat) jouer; ~ **on TV** passer à la télé. **appearance** n apparition f; (aspect) apparence f.

appease vt apaiser.

appendix n (pl **-ices**) appendice m.

appetite n appétit m.

appetizer n (snack) amuse-gueule m inv; (drink) apéritif m.

appetizing a appétissant.

applaud vt/i applaudir; (decision) applaudir à. **applause** n applaudissements mpl.

apple n pomme f. ~**-tree** n pommier m.

appliance n appareil m.

applicable a valable; if ~ le cas échéant.

applicant n candidat/-e m/f (**for** à).

application n application f; (request, form) demande f; (for job) candidature f.

apply vt appliquer. ● vi ~ **to** (refer) s'appliquer à; (ask) s'adresser à; ~ **for** (job) postuler pour; (grant) demander; ~ **oneself to** s'appliquer à.

appoint vt (to post) nommer; (fix) désigner; **well-~ed** bien équipé.

appointment n nomination f; (meeting) rendez-vous m inv; (job) poste m; **make an** ~ prendre rendez-vous (**with** avec).

appraisal n évaluation f. **appraise** vt évaluer.

appreciate vt (like) apprécier; (understand) comprendre; (be grateful for) être reconnaissant de. ● vi prendre de la valeur.

appreciation n appréciation f; (gratitude) reconnaissance f; (rise) augmentation f. **appreciative** a reconnaissant; (audience) enthousiaste.

apprehend vt (arrest) appréhender; (understand) comprendre. **apprehension** n

(arrest) appréhension f; (fear) crainte f.

apprehensive a inquiet; **be** ~ **of** craindre.

apprentice n apprenti m. ● vt mettre en apprentissage.

approach vt (s')approcher de; (accost) aborder; (with request) s'adresser à. ● vi (s')approcher. ● n approche f; **an** ~ **to** (problem) une façon d'aborder; (person) une démarche auprès de.

approachable a abordable.

appropriate[1] vt s'approprier.

appropriate[2] a approprié, propre. **appropriately** adv à propos.

approval n approbation f; **on** ~ à or sous condition.

approve vt approuver. ● vi ~ **of** approuver. **approving** a approbateur.

approximate[1] vi ~ **to** se rapprocher de.

approximate[2] a approximatif. **approximately** adv environ. **approximation** n approximation f.

apricot n abricot m.

April n avril m. ~ **Fools Day** n le premier avril.

apron n tablier m.

apt a (suitable) approprié; **be** ~ **to** avoir tendance à.

aptitude n aptitude f.

aptly adv à propos.

Aquarius n Verseau m.

aquatic a aquatique; (Sport) nautique.

Arab n Arabe mf. ● a arabe.

Arabian a d'Arabie.

Arabic a & n (Ling) arabe (m).

arbitrary a arbitraire.

arbitrate vi arbitrer. **arbitration** n arbitrage m. **arbitrator** n médiateur/-trice m/f.

arcade n (shops) galerie f; (arches) arcades fpl.

arch n arche f; (of foot) voûte f plantaire. ● vt/i (s')arquer. ● a (playful) malicieux.

archaeological a archéologique. **archaeologist** n archéologue mf. **archaeology** n archéologie f.

archbishop n archevêque m.

archery n tir m à l'arc.

architect n architecte mf; (of plan) artisan m. **architectural** a architectural. **architecture** n architecture f.

archives npl archives fpl.

archway n voûte f.

Arctic n the ~ l'Arctique m. ● a (climate) arctique; (expedition) polaire; (conditions) glacial.

ardent a ardent.

are ⇒BE.

area n (region) région f; (district) quartier m; (fig) domaine m; (in geometry) aire f; **parking/picnic** ~ aire f de parking/de pique-nique.

arena n arène f.

aren't = ARE NOT.

Argentina n Argentine f.

arguable a discutable. **arguably** adv selon certains.

argue vi (quarrel) se disputer; (reason) argumenter. ● vt (debate) discuter; ~ **that** alléguer que.

argument n dispute f; (reasoning) argument m; (discussion) débat m. **argumentative** a ergoteur.

Aries n Bélier m.

arise vi (pt arose; pp arisen) (problem) survenir; (question) se poser; ~ **from** résulter de.

aristocrat n aristocrate mf.

arithmetic n arithmétique f.

ark n (Relig) arche f.

arm n bras m; ~ **in arm** bras dessus bras dessous. ● vt armer; ~**ed robbery** vol m à main armée.

armament n armement m.

arm: ~**-band** n brassard m. ~**chair** n fauteuil m.

armour n armure f. **armoured** a blindé. **armoury** n arsenal m.

armpit n aisselle f.

arms npl (weapons) armes fpl. ~ **dealer** n trafiquant m d'armes.

army n armée f.

aroma n arôme m. **aromatic** a aromatique.

arose ⇒ARISE.

around adv (tout) autour; (here and there) çà et là. ● prep autour de; ~ **here** par ici.

arouse vt (awaken, cause) éveiller; (excite) exciter.

arrange vt arranger; (time, date) fixer; ~ **to** s'arranger pour.

arrangement n arrangement m; (agreement) entente f; **make** ~**s** prendre des dispositions.

array n an ~ of (display) un étalage impressionnant de.

arrears npl arriéré m; **in** ~ (rent) arriéré; **he is in** ~ il a des retards dans ses paiements.

arrest vt arrêter; (attention) retenir. ● n arrestation f; **under** ~ en état d'arrestation.

arrival n arrivée f; **new** ~ nouveau venu m, nouvelle venue f.

arrive vi arriver; ~ **at** (destination) arriver à; (decision) parvenir à.

arrogance n arrogance f.

arrow n flèche f.

arse n ▨ cul m ▨.

arson n incendie m criminel. **arsonist** n incendiaire mf.

art n art m; (fine arts) beaux-arts mpl.

artery n artère f.

art gallery n (public) musée m (d'art); (private) galerie f (d'art).

arthritis n arthrite f.

artichoke n artichaut m.

article n article m; ~ **of clothing** vêtement m.

articulate a (person) capable de s'exprimer clairement; (speech) distinct.

articulated lorry n semi-remorque m.

artificial a artificiel.

artist n artiste mf.

arts npl the ~ les arts mpl; (Univ) lettres fpl.

artwork n (of book) illustrations fpl.

as conj comme; (while) pendant que; (over gradual period of time) au fur et à mesure que; ~ **she grew older** au fur et à mesure qu'elle vieillissait; **do ~ I say** fais ce que je dis; ~ **usual** comme d'habitude. ●prep ~ **a mother** en tant que mère; ~ **a gift** un cadeau; ~ **from Monday** à partir de lundi; ~ **for**, ~ **to** quant à; ~ **if** comme si; **you look ~ if you're tired** vous avez l'air (d'être) fatigué. ●adv ~ **tall ~** aussi grand que; ~ **much ~**, ~ **many ~** autant que; ~ **soon ~** aussitôt que; ~ **well ~** aussi bien que; ~ **wide ~ possible** aussi large que possible.

asbestos n amiante f.

ascend vt gravir. ●vi monter.

ascertain vt établir (**that** que).

ash n cendre f; ~(-**tree**) frêne m

ashamed a **be ~** avoir honte (**of** de).

ashore adv à terre.

ashtray n cendrier m.

Asia n Asie f.

Asian n Asiatique mf. ●a asiatique.

aside adv de côté; ~ **from** à part. ●n aparté m.

ask vt/i demander; (a question) poser; (invite) inviter; ~ **sb sth** demander qch à qn; ~ **sb to do** demander à qn de faire; ~ **about**

(thing) se renseigner sur; (person) demander des nouvelles de; ~ **for** demander.

asleep a endormi; (numb) engourdi. ●adv **fall ~** s'endormir.

asparagus n (plant) asperge f; (Culin) asperges fpl.

aspect n aspect m; (direction) orientation f.

asphyxiate vt/i (s')asphyxier.

aspire vi aspirer (**to** à; **to do** à faire).

aspirin n aspirine® f.

ass n âne m; (person 🔲) idiot/-e mf.

assail vt attaquer. **assailant** n agresseur m

assassin n assassin m.
assassinate vt assassiner.
assassination n assassinat m.

assault n (Mil) assaut m; (Jur) agression f. ●vt (person: Jur) agresser

assemble vt (construct) assembler; (gather) rassembler. ●vi se rassembler.

assembly n assemblée f. ~ **line** n chaîne f de montage.

assent n assentiment m. ●vi consentir.

assert vt affirmer; (rights) revendiquer. **assertion** n affirmation f. **assertive** a assuré.

assess vt évaluer; (payment) déterminer le montant de. **assessment** n évaluation f. **assessor** n (valuer) expert m.

asset n (advantage) atout m; (financial) bien m; ~**s** (Comm) actif m.

assign vt (allot) assigner; ~ **sb to** (appoint) affecter qn à.

assignment n (task) mission f; (diplomatic) poste m; (academic) devoir m.

assist vt/i aider. **assistance** n aide f.

assistant n aide mf; (in shop) vendeur/-euse m/f. ● a (manager) adjoint.

associate¹ n & a associé/-e (m/f).

associate² vt associer. ● vi ~ with fréquenter. **association** n association f.

assorted a divers; (foods) assorti.

assortment n assortiment m; (of people) mélange m.

assume vt supposer; (power, attitude) prendre; (role, burden) assumer.

assurance n assurance f.

assure vt assurer.

asterisk n astérisque m.

asthma n asthme m.

astonish vt étonner.

astound vt stupéfier.

astray adv go ~ s'égarer; lead ~ égarer.

astride adv & prep à califourchon (sur).

astrologer n astrologue mf. **astrology** n astrologie f.

astronaut n astronaute mf.

astronomer n astronome mf.

asylum n asile m.

....

at preposition

⇒ For expressions such as laugh at, look at ⇒laugh, look.

⋯▶ (in position or place) à; he's ~ his desk il est à son bureau; she's ~ work/school elle est au travail/à l'école.

⋯▶ (at someone's house or business) chez; ~ Mary's/the dentist's chez Mary/le dentiste.

⋯▶ (in times, ages) à; ~ four o'clock à quatre heures; ~ two years of age à l'âge de deux ans.

....

ate ⇒EAT.

atheist n athée mf.

athlete n athlète mf. **athletic** a athlétique. **athletics** npl athlétisme m; (US) sports mpl.

Atlantic a atlantique. ● n the ~ (Ocean) l'Atlantique m.

atlas n atlas m.

atmosphere n (air) atmosphère f; (mood) ambiance f. **atmospheric** a atmosphérique; d'ambiance.

atom n atome m.

atrocious a atroce.

atrocity n atrocité f.

attach vt/i (s')attacher; (letter) joindre (to à).

attaché n (Pol) attaché/-e m/f. ~ **case** n attaché-case m.

attached a be ~ to (like) être attaché à; the ~ letter la lettre ci-jointe.

attachment n (accessory) accessoire m; (affection) attachement m; (e-mail) pièces fpl jointes.

attack n attaque f; (Med) crise f. ● vt attaquer.

attain vt atteindre (à); (gain) acquérir.

attempt vt tenter. ● n tentative f; an ~ on sb's life un attentat contre qn.

attend vt assister à; (class) suivre; (school, church) aller à. ● vi assister; ~ (to) (look after) s'occuper de. **attendance** n présence f; (people) assistance f.

attendant n employé/-e m/f. ● a associé.

attention n attention f; ~! (Mil) garde-à-vous!; pay ~ faire or prêter attention (to à).

attentive a attentif; (considerate)

attentionné. **attentively** adv attentivement. **attentiveness** n attention f.

attest vt/i ~ (to) attester.

attic n grenier m.

attitude n attitude f.

attorney n (US) avocat/-e m/f.

attract vt attirer. **attraction** n attraction f; (charm) attrait m.

attractive a attrayant, séduisant. **attractively** adv agréablement. **attractiveness** n attrait m, beauté f.

attribute[1] vt ~ to attribuer à.

attribute[2] n attribut m.

aubergine n aubergine f.

auction n vente f aux enchères. ● vt vendre aux enchères. **auctioneer** n commissaire-priseur m.

audacious a audacieux.

audience n (theatre, radio) public m; (interview) audience f.

audiovisual a audiovisuel.

audit n vérification f des comptes. ● vt vérifier.

audition n audition f. ● vt/i auditionner (**for** pour).

auditor n commissaire m aux comptes.

August n août m.

aunt n tante f.

auspicious a favorable.

Australia n Australie f.

Australian n Australien/-ne m/f. ● a australien.

Austria n Autriche f.

Austrian n Autrichien/-ne m/f. ● a autrichien.

authentic a authentique.

author n auteur m.

authoritarian a autoritaire.

authoritative a (credible) qui fait autorité; (manner) autoritaire.

authority n autorité f; (permission) autorisation f.

authorization n autorisation f. **authorize** vt autoriser.

autistic a (person) autiste; (response) autistique.

autograph n autographe m. ● vt signer, dédicacer.

automate vt automatiser.

automatic a automatique. ● n (Auto) voiture f automatique.

automobile n (US) auto(mobile) f.

autonomous a autonome.

autumn n automne m.

auxiliary a & n auxiliaire (mf); ~ (verb) auxiliaire m.

avail vt ~ oneself of profiter de. ● n of no ~ inutile; to no ~ sans résultat.

availability n disponibilité f. **available** a disponible.

avenge vt venger; ~ oneself se venger (**on** de).

avenue n avenue f; (line of approach: fig) voie f.

average n moyenne f; on ~ en moyenne. ● a moyen. ● vt faire la moyenne de; (produce, do) faire en moyenne.

aviary n volière f.

avocado n avocat m.

avoid vt éviter. **avoidance** n (of injuries) prévention f; (of responsibility) refus m.

await vt attendre.

awake vt/i (pt awoke; pp awoken) (s')éveiller. ● a be ~ ne pas dormir, être (r)éveillé.

award vt (grant) attribuer; (prize) décerner; (points) accorder. ● n récompense f, prix m; (scholarship) bourse f; pay ~ augmentation f (de salaire).

aware a (well-informed) averti; **be** ~ **of** (danger) être conscient de; (fact) savoir; **become** ~ **of** prendre conscience de. **awareness** n conscience f.

away *adv* (far) (au) loin; (absent) absent, parti; **~ from** loin de; **move ~** s'écarter; (to new home) déménager; **six kilometres ~** à six kilomètres (de distance); **take ~** emporter; **he was snoring ~** il ronflait. ● *a & n* **~** (**match**) match *m* à l'extérieur.

awe *n* crainte *f* (révérencielle).

awe-inspiring *a* impressionnant.

awesome *a* redoutable.

awful *a* affreux. **awfully** *adv* (badly) affreusement; (very 🔟) rudement.

awkward *a* difficile; (inconvenient) inopportun; (clumsy) maladroit; (embarrassing) gênant; (embarrassed) gêné. **awkwardly** *adv* maladroitement; avec gêne. **awkwardness** *n* maladresse *f*; (discomfort) gêne *f*.

awning *n* auvent *m*; (of shop) store *m*.

awoke, awoken ⇒AWAKE.

axe *n* hache *f*. ● *vt* (*pres p* **axing**) réduire; (eliminate) supprimer; (employee) renvoyer.

axis *n* (*pl* **axes**) axe *m*.

axle *n* essieu *m*.

BA *abbr* ⇒BACHELOR OF ARTS.

babble *vi* babiller; (stream) gazouiller. ● *n* babillage *m*.

baby *n* bébé *m*. **~ carriage** *n* (US) voiture *f* d'enfant. **~-sit** *vi* faire du babysitting, garder des enfants. **~-sitter** *n* baby-sitter *mf*.

bachelor *n* célibataire *m*. **B~ of Arts** licencié/-e *m/f* ès lettres.

back *n* (of person, hand, page, etc.) dos *m*; (of house) derrière *m*; (of vehicle) arrière *m*; (of room) fond *m*; (of chair) dossier *m*; (in football) arrière *m*; **at the ~ of the book** à la fin du livre; **in ~ of** (US) derrière. ● *a* (leg, wheel) arrière *inv*; (door, gate) de derrière; (taxes) arriéré. ● *adv* en arrière; (returned) de retour, rentré; **come ~** revenir; **give ~** rendre; **take ~** reprendre; **I want it ~** je veux le récupérer. ● *vt* (support) appuyer; (bet on) miser sur; (vehicle) faire reculer. ● *vi* (of person, vehicle) reculer. □ **~ down** céder; **~ out** se désister; (Auto) sortir en marche arrière; **~ up** (support) appuyer. **~ache** *n* mal *m* de dos. **~-bencher** *n* (Pol) député *m*. **~bone** *n* colonne *f* vertébrale. **~date** *vt* antidater. **~fire** *vi* (Auto) pétarader; (fig) mal tourner. **~gammon** *n* trictrac *m*.

background *n* fond *m*, arrière-plan *m*; (context) contexte *m*; (environment) milieu *m*; (experience) formation *f*. ● *a* (music, noise) de fond.

backhand *n* revers *m*.

backhander *n* (bribe) pot-de-vin *m*.

backing *n* soutien *m*.

back: ~lash *n* retour *m* de bâton; réaction *f* violente (**against** contre). **~log** *n* retard *m*. **~ number** *n* vieux numéro *m*. **~pack** *n* sac *m* à dos. **~side** *n* (buttocks 🔟) derrière *m*. **~stage** *a & adv* dans les coulisses. **~stroke** *n* dos *m* crawlé. **~track** *vi* rebrousser chemin; (change one's opinion) faire marche arrière.

back-up *n* soutien *m*; (Comput) sauvegarde *f*. ● *a* de secours; (Comput) de sauvegarde.

backward *a* (step etc.) en arrière; (retarded) arriéré.

backwards *adv* en arrière; (*walk*) à reculons; (*read*) à l'envers; **go ~ and forwards** aller et venir.

bacon *n* lard *m*; (in rashers) bacon *m*.

bacteria *npl* bactéries *fpl*.

bad *a* (**worse, worst**) mauvais; (*wicked*) méchant; (*ill*) malade; (*accident*) grave; (*food*) gâté; **feel ~** se sentir mal; **go ~** se gâter; **~ language** gros mots *mpl*; **too ~!** tant pis!; (I'm sorry) dommage!

badge *n* badge *m*; (coat of arms) insigne *m*.

badger *n* blaireau *m*. ● *vt* harceler.

badly *adv* mal; (*hurt*) gravement; **want ~** avoir grande envie de.

badminton *n* badminton *m*.

bad-tempered *a* irritable.

baffle *vt* déconcerter.

bag *n* sac *m*; **~s** (luggage) bagages *mpl*; (under eyes 🔲) valises *fpl*, **~s of** plein de.

baggage *n* bagages *mpl*, **~ reclaim** réception *f* des bagages.

baggy *a* large.

bagpipes *npl* cornemuse *f*.

bail *n* caution *f*; **on ~** sous caution; (cricket) bâtonnet *m*. ● *vt* mettre en liberté provisoire.

bailiff *n* huissier *m*.

bait *n* appât *m*. ● *vt* appâter; (fig) tourmenter.

bake *vt* faire cuire au four; **~ a cake** faire un gâteau. ● *vi* cuire; (*person*) faire du pain. **baked beans** *npl* haricots *mpl* blancs à la tomate. **baked potato** *n* pomme *f* de terre en robe des champs. **baker** *n* boulanger/-ère *m*/*f*. **bakery** *n* boulangerie *f*.

balance *n* équilibre *m*; (scales) balance *f*; (outstanding sum: Comm) solde *m*; (of payments, of trade) balance *f*; (remainder) restant *m*. ● *vt* mettre en équilibre; (weigh up also Comm) balancer; (*budget*) équilibrer; (to compensate) contrebalancer. ● *vi* être en équilibre.

balcony *n* balcon *m*.

bald *a* chauve; (*tyre*) lisse; (fig) simple.

balk *vt* contrecarrer. ● *vi* **~ at** reculer devant.

ball *n* (golf, tennis, etc.) balle *f*; (football) ballon *m*; (billiards) bille *f*; (of wool) pelote *f*; (sphere) boule *f*; (dance) bal *m*.

ballet *n* ballet *m*.

balloon *n* ballon *m*.

ballot *n* scrutin *m*. ● *vt* consulter par vote (**on** sur). **~ box** *n* urne *f*. **~-paper** *n* bulletin *m* de vote.

ballpoint pen *n* stylo *m* (à) bille.

ban *vt* (*pt* **banned**) interdire; **~ sb from** exclure qn de; **~ sb from doing** interdire à qn de faire. ● *n* interdiction *f* (**on** de).

banal *a* banal.

banana *n* banane *f*.

band *n* (strip, group of people) bande *f*; (pop group) groupe *m*; (brass band) fanfare *f*. ● *vi* **~ together** se réunir.

bandage *n* bandage *m*. ● *vt* bander.

B and B *abbr* ⇒BED AND BREAKFAST.

bandit *n* bandit *m*.

bandstand *n* kiosque *m* à musique.

bang *n* (blow, noise) coup *m*; (explosion) détonation *f*; (of door) claquement *m*. ● *vt*/*i* taper; (*door*) claquer; **~ one's head** se cogner la tête. ● *interj* vlan. ● *adv* 🔲 **~ in the middle** en plein milieu; **~ on time** à l'heure pile.

banger *n* (*firework*) pétard *m*; (Culin) saucisse *f*; (**old**) **~** (*car* 🔲) guimbarde *f*.

banish *vt* bannir.

banister n rampe f d'escalier.

bank n (Comm) banque f; (of river) rive f; (of sand) banc m. ● vt mettre en banque. ● vi (Aviat) virer; ~ **with** avoir un compte à; ~ **on** compter sur. ~ **account** n compte m en banque. ~ **card** n carte f bancaire. ~ **holiday** n jour m férié.

banking n opérations fpl bancaires; (as career) la banque.

banknote n billet m de banque.

bankrupt a be ~ être en faillite; **go** ~ faire faillite. ● n failli/-e m/f. ● vt mettre en faillite. **bankruptcy** n faillite f.

bank statement n relevé m de compte.

banner n bannière f.

baptism n baptême m. **baptize** vt baptiser.

bar n (of metal) barre f; (on window, cage) barreau m; (of chocolate) tablette f; (pub) bar m; (counter) comptoir m; (Mus) mesure f; (fig) obstacle m; ~ **of soap** savonnette f; **the** ~ (Jur) le barreau. ● vt (pt **barred**) (obstruct) barrer; (prohibit) interdire; (exclude) exclure. ● prep sauf.

barbecue n barbecue m. ● vt faire au barbecue.

barbed wire n fil m de fer barbelé.

barber n coiffeur m (pour hommes).

bar code n code m (à) barres.

bare a nu; (cupboard) vide. ● vt mettre à nu. ~**foot** a nu-pieds inv, pieds nus. **barely** adv à peine.

bargain n (deal) marché m; (cheap thing) occasion f. ● vi négocier; (haggle) marchander; **not** ~ **for** ne pas s'attendre à.

barge n péniche f. ● vi ~ **in** interrompre; (into room) faire irruption.

bark n (of tree) écorce f; (of dog) aboiement m. ● vi aboyer.

barley n orge f.

bar: ~**maid** n serveuse f. ~**man** n (pl -**men**) barman m.

barn n grange f.

barracks npl caserne f.

barrel n tonneau m; (of oil) baril m; (of gun) canon m.

barren a stérile.

barricade n barricade f. ● vt barricader.

barrier n barrière f; **ticket** ~ guichet m.

barrister n avocat m.

bartender n (US) barman m.

barter n troc m. ● vt troquer (**for** contre).

base n base f. ● vt baser (**on** sur; **in** à). ● a ignoble. **baseball** n base-ball m.

basement n sous-sol m.

bash ⚇ vt cogner; ~**ed in** enfoncé. ● n coup m violent; **have a** ~ **at** s'essayer à.

basic a fondamental, élémentaire; **the** ~**s** l'essentiel m. **basically** adv au fond.

basil n basilic m.

basin n (for liquids) cuvette f; (for food) bol m; (for washing) lavabo m; (of river) bassin m.

basis n (pl **bases**) base f.

bask vi se prélasser (**in** à).

basket n corbeille f; (with handle) panier m. **basketball** n basket(-ball) m.

Basque n (person) Basque mf; (Ling) basque m. ● a basque.

bass[1] a (voice, part) de basse; (sound, note) grave. ● n (pl **basses**) basse f.

bass[2] n inv (freshwater fish) perche f; (sea) bar m.

bassoon n basson m.

bastard n (illegitimate) bâtard/-e m/f; (insult ⚇) salaud m ⚇.

bat n (cricket etc.) batte f; (table tennis) raquette f; (animal) chauve-souris f. ● vt (pt **batted**) (ball) frapper; **not ~ an eyelid** ne pas sourciller.

batch n (of cakes, people) fournée f; (of goods, text also Comput) lot m.

bath n (pl **-s**) bain m; (tub) baignoire f; **have a ~** prendre un bain; (swimming) **~s** piscine f. ● vt donner un bain à.

bathe vt baigner. ● vi se baigner; (US) prendre un bain.

bathing n baignade f. **~-costume** n maillot m de bain.

bath: **~robe** n (US) robe f de chambre. **~room** n salle f de bains.

baton n (policeman's) matraque f; (Mus) baguette f.

batter vt battre. ● n (Culin) pâte f (à frire).

battery n (Mil, Auto) batterie f; (of torch, radio) pile f.

battle n bataille f; (fig) lutte f. ● vi se battre. **~field** n champ m de bataille.

baulk vt/i = BALK.

bay n (Bot) laurier m; (Geog, Archit) baie f; (area) aire f; (bark) aboiement m; **keep** or **hold at ~** tenir à distance. ● vi aboyer. **~-leaf** n feuille f de laurier. **~ window** n fenêtre f en saillie.

bazaar n (shop, market) bazar m; (sale) vente f.

BC abbr (**before Christ**) avant J.-C.

BBS abbr (**Bulletin Board System**) (Internet) babillard m électronique, BBS m.

....

be

present **am, is, are**; past **was, were**; past participle **been**.

●*intransitive verb*

····➤ être; **I am tired** je suis fatigué; **it's me** c'est moi.

····➤ (feelings) avoir; **I am hot** j'ai chaud; **he is hungry/thirsty** il a faim/soif; **her hands are cold** elle a froid aux mains.

····➤ (age) avoir; **I am 15** j'ai 15 ans.

····➤ (weather) faire; **it's warm** il fait chaud; **it's 25** il fait 25.

····➤ (health) aller; **how are you?** comment allez-vous or comment vas-tu?

····➤ (visit) aller; **I've never been to Italy** je ne suis jamais allé en Italie.

●*auxiliary verb*

····➤ (in tenses) **I am working** je travaille; **he was writing to his mother** il écrivait à sa mère; **she is to do it at once** (obligation) elle doit le faire tout de suite.

····➤ (in passives) **he was killed** il a été tué; **the window has been fixed** on a réparé la fenêtre.

····➤ (in tag questions) **their house is lovely, isn't it?** leur maison est très jolie, n'est-ce pas?

····➤ (in short answers) '**I am a painter**'—'**are you?**' 'je suis peintre'—'ah oui?'; '**are you a doctor?**'—'**yes, I am**' 'êtes-vous médecin?'—'oui'; '**you're not going out**'—'**yes I am**' 'tu ne sors pas'—'si'

....

beach n plage f.

beacon n (lighthouse) phare m; (marker) balise f.

bead n perle f.

beak n bec m.

beaker n gobelet m.

beam n (timber) poutre f; (of light) rayon m; (of torch) faisceau m. ● vi rayonner. ● vt (broadcast) transmettre.

bean n haricot m.

bear n ours m. ● vt (pt **bore**; pp

borne) (carry, show, feel) porter; (endure, sustain) supporter; (child) mettre au monde. ●vi ~ **left** (go) prendre à gauche; ~ **in mind** tenir compte de. □ ~ **out** confirmer; ~ **up** tenir le coup. **bearable** a supportable.

beard n barbe f.

bearer n porteur/-euse m/f.

bearing n (behaviour) maintien m; (relevance) rapport m; **get one's ~s** s'orienter.

beast n bête f; (person) brute f.

beat vt/i (pt **beat**; pp **beaten**) battre; ~ **a retreat** battre en retraite; ~ **it!** dégage! 🄴; **it ~s me** 🄴 ça me dépasse. ●n (of drum, heart) battement m; (Mus) mesure f; (of policeman) ronde f. □ ~ **off** repousser; ~ **up** tabasser. **beating** n raclée f.

beautiful a beau.

beauty n beauté f. ~ **parlour** n institut m de beauté. ~ **spot** n grain m de beauté; (place) site m pittoresque.

beaver n castor m.

became ⇒BECOME.

because conj parce que; ~ **of** à cause de.

become vt/i (pt **became**; pp **become**) devenir; (befit) convenir à; **what has ~ of her?** qu'est-ce qu'elle est devenue?

bed n lit m; (layer) couche f; (of sea) fond m; (of flowers) parterre m; **go to ~** (aller) se coucher. ●vi (pt **bedded**) ~ **down** se coucher. **bed and breakfast** n chambre f avec petit déjeuner, chambre f d'hôte. ~**bug** n punaise f. ~**clothes** npl couvertures fpl.

bedding n literie f.

bed: ~**ridden** a cloué au lit. ~**room** n chambre f (à coucher). ~**side** n chevet m. ~**sit**, ~**sitter** n chambre f meublée, studio m.

~**spread** n dessus m de lit. ~**time** n heure f du coucher.

bee n abeille f; **make a ~-line for** aller tout droit vers.

beech n hêtre m.

beef n bœuf m. ~**burger** n hamburger m.

beehive n ruche f.

been ⇒BE.

beer n bière f.

beetle n scarabée m.

beetroot n inv betterave f.

before prep (time) avant; (place) devant; **the day ~ yesterday** avant-hier. ●adv avant; (already) déjà; **the day ~** la veille. ●conj ~ **leaving** avant de partir; ~ **I forget** avant que j'oublie. **beforehand** adv à l'avance.

beg vt (pt **begged**) (food, money, favour) demander (from à); ~ **sb to do** supplier qn de faire. ●vi mendier; **it is going ~ging** personne n'en veut.

began ⇒BEGIN.

beggar n mendiant/-e m/f.

begin vt/i (pt **began**, pp **begun**, pres p **beginning**) commencer (**to do** à faire). **beginner** n débutant/-e m/f. **beginning** n commencement m, début m.

begun ⇒BEGIN.

behalf n **on ~ of** (act, speak, campaign) pour; (phone, write) de la part de.

behave vi se conduire; ~ (**oneself**) se conduire bien.

behaviour, (US) **behavior** n comportement m (**towards** envers).

behead vt décapiter.

behind prep derrière; (in time) en retard sur. ●adv derrière; (late) en retard; **leave ~** oublier. ●n (buttocks 🄴) derrière m 🄴.

beige a & n beige (m).

being n (person) être m.

belch vi avoir un renvoi. ● vt ~
out (smoke) s'échapper. ● n
renvoi m.
Belgian n Belge mf. ● a belge
Belgium n Belgique f.
belief n conviction f; (trust)
confiance f; (faith: Relig) foi f.
believe vt/i croire; ~ **in** croire à;
(deity) croire en. **believer** n
croyant/-e m/f.
bell n cloche f; (small) clochette f;
(on door) sonnette f.
belly n ventre m. ~ **button** n
nombril m.
belong vi ~ **to** appartenir à;
(club) être membre de.
belongings npl affaires fpl.
beloved a & n bien-aimé/-e (m/
f)
below prep sous, au-dessous de;
(fig) indigne de. ● adv en dessous;
(on page) ci-dessous.
belt n ceinture f; (Tech) courroie f;
(fig) zone f. ● vt (hit 🅸) rosser. ● vi
(rush 🅸) ~ **in/out** entrer/sortir à
toute vitesse.
beltway n (US) périphérique m.
bemused a perplexe.
bench n banc m; the ~ (Jur) la
magistrature (assise).
bend vt (pt bent) (knee, arm,
wire) plier; (head, back) courber.
● vi (road) tourner; (person) ~
down/over se pencher. ● n courbe
f; (in road) virage m; (of arm, knee)
pli m.
beneath prep sous, au-dessous
de; (fig) indigne de. ● adv en
dessous.
benefactor n bienfaiteur/-trice
m/f.
beneficial a bénéfique.
benefit n avantage m; (allowance)
allocation f. ● vt (be useful to)
profiter à; (do good to) faire du
bien à. ● vi profiter; ~ **from** tirer
profit de.

benign a (kindly) bienveillant;
(Med) bénin.
bent ⇒BEND. ● n (talent) aptitude f;
(inclination) penchant m ● a tordu;
🅱 corrompu; ~ **on doing** décidé à
faire.
bequest n legs m.
bereaved a endeuillé; the ~ la
famille endeuillée. **bereavement**
n deuil m.
berry n baie f.
berserk a fou furieux.
berth n (in train, ship) couchette f;
(anchorage) mouillage m; **give a
wide** ~ **to** éviter. ● vi mouiller.
beside prep à côté de; ~ **oneself**
hors de soi; ~ **the point** sans
rapport.
besides prep en plus de. ● adv
en plus.
besiege vt assiéger.
best a meilleur; the ~ **book** le
meilleur livre; the ~ **part of** la
plus grande partie de; the ~ **thing
is to** le mieux est de. ● adv (the)
~ (behave, play) le mieux. ● n the
~ le meilleur, la meilleure; **do
one's** ~ faire de son mieux; **make
the** ~ **of** s'accommoder de. ~
man n témoin. ~-**seller** n
bestseller m, livre m à succès.
bet n pari m. ● vt/i (pt bet or
betted, pres p **betting**) parier
(on sur).
betray vt trahir.
better a meilleur; the ~ **part of** la
plus grande partie de; **get** ~
s'améliorer; (recover) se remettre.
● adv mieux; **I had** ~ **go** je ferais
mieux de partir. ● vt (improve)
améliorer; (do better than)
surpasser. ● n **get the** ~ **of**
l'emporter sur; **so much the** ~
tant mieux. ~ **off** a (richer) plus
riche; **he is/would be** ~ **off at home**
il est/serait mieux chez lui.
betting-shop n bureau m du
PMU.

between *prep* entre. ● *adv* in ∼ au milieu.

beverage *n* boisson *f*.

beware *vi* prendre garde (**of** à).

bewilder *vt* déconcerter.

beyond *prep* au-delà de; (*control, reach*) hors de; (*besides*) excepté. ● *adv* au-delà; **it is** ∼ **me** ça me dépasse.

bias *n* (*inclination*) tendance *f*; (*prejudice*) parti *m* pris. ● *vt* (*pt* **biased**) influer sur. **biased** *a* partial.

bib *n* bavoir *m*.

Bible *n* Bible *f*.

biceps *n* biceps *m*.

bicycle *n* vélo *m*, bicyclette *f*. ● *a* (*bell, chain*) de vélo; (*pump, clip*) à vélo.

bid *n* (*at auction*) enchère *f*; (*attempt*) tentative *f*. ● *vt/i* (*pt* **bade**, *pp* **bidden** or **bid**, *pres p* **bidding**) (*offer*) offrir, mettre une enchère (de) (**for** pour); ∼ **sb good morning** dire bonjour à qn; ∼ **sb farewell** faire ses adieux à qn.

bidding *n* (*at auction*) enchères *fpl*; **he did my** ∼ il a fait ce que je lui ai dit.

bifocals *npl* verres *mpl* à double foyer.

big *a* (**bigger**, **biggest**) grand; (*in bulk*) gros.

bike *n* vélo *m*.

bikini *n* bikini *m*.

bilberry *n* myrtille *f*.

bilingual *a* bilingue.

bill *n* (*invoice*) facture *f*; (*in hotel, for gas*) note *f*; (*in restaurant*) addition *f*; (*of sale*) acte *m*; (*Pol*) projet *m* de loi; (*banknote: US*) billet *m* de banque; (*Theat*) **on the** ∼ à l'affiche; (*of bird*) bec *m*. ● *vt* (*person: Comm*) envoyer la facture à. ∼**board** *n* panneau *m* d'affichage.

billet *n* cantonnement *m*. ● *vt* (*pt* **billeted**) cantonner (**on** chez).

billiards *n* billard *m*.

billion *n* billion *m*; (*US*) milliard *m*.

bin *n* (*for rubbish*) poubelle *f*; (*for storage*) casier *m*.

bind *vt* (*pt* **bound**) attacher; (*book*) relier; **be bound by** être tenu par. ● *n* (*bore*) corvée *f*.

binding *n* reliure *f*. ● *a* (*agreement, contract*) qui lie.

binge *n* (*drinking*) beuverie *f*; (*eating*) gueuleton *m*.

binoculars *npl* jumelles *fpl*.

biochemistry *n* biochimie *f*.

biodegradable *a* biodégradable.

biographer *n* biographe *mf*.

biography *n* biographie *f*.

biological *a* biologique.

biologist *n* biologiste *mf*.

biology *n* biologie *f*.

bioterrorism *n* bioterrorisme *m*.

birch *n* (*tree*) bouleau *m*; (*whip*) fouet *m*.

bird *n* oiseau *m*; (*girl* 🔲) nana *f*.

Biro® *n* stylo *m* à bille, bic® *m*.

birth *n* naissance *f*; **give** ∼ accoucher. ∼ **certificate** *n* acte *m* de naissance. ∼**-control** *n* contraception *f*. ∼**day** *n* anniversaire *m*. ∼**mark** *n* tache *f* de naissance. ∼**-rate** *n* taux *m* de natalité.

biscuit *n* biscuit *m*; (*US*) petit pain *m* (au lait).

bishop *n* évêque *m*.

bit ⇒BITE. ● *n* morceau *m*; (*of horse*) mors *m*; (*of tool*) mèche *f*; **a** ∼ (*a little*) un peu; (*Comput*) bit *m*.

bitch *n* chienne *f*; (*woman* 🔲) garce *f* 🔲. ● *vi* dire du mal (**about** de).

bite *vt/i* (*pt* **bit**; *pp* **bitten**) mordre; ∼ **one's nails** se ronger les ongles. ● *n* morsure *f*; (*by insect*) piqûre *f*; (*mouthful*) bouchée *f*; **have a** ∼ manger un morceau.

bitter a amer; (weather) glacial. ● n
bière f. **bitterly** adv amèrement;
it is ~ly cold il fait un temps
glacial.

bizarre a bizarre.

black a noir; **~ and blue** couvert
de bleus. ● n (colour) noir m; **B~**
(person) Noir/-e m/f. ● vt noircir;
(goods) boycotter. **~berry** n mûre
f. **~bird** n merle m. **~board** n
tableau m noir. **~currant** n
cassis m.

blacken vt/i noircir.

black: ~ eye n œil m poché.
~head n point m noir. **~ ice** n
verglas m. **~leg** n jaune m.

blacklist n liste f noire. ● vt
mettre à l'index.

blackmail n chantage m. ● vt
faire chanter. **blackmailer** n
maître-chanteur m.

black: ~ market n marché m
noir. **~out** n panne f de courant,
(Med) syncope f. **~ pudding** n
boudin m. **~ sheep** n brebis f
galeuse. **~smith** n forgeron m. **~
spot** n point m noir.

bladder n vessie f.

blade n (of knife) lame f; (of propeller,
oar) pale f; **~ of grass** brin m
d'herbe.

blame vt accuser; **~ sb for sth**
reprocher qch à qn; **he is to ~** il
est responsable (**for** de). ● n
responsabilité f (**for** de).

bland a (insipid) fade.

blank a (page) blanc; (screen)
vide; (cheque) en blanc; **to look ~**
avoir l'air ébahi. ● n blanc m; **~
(cartridge)** cartouche f à blanc.

blanket n couverture f; (layer)
couche f.

blasphemous a blasphématoire;
(person) blasphémateur.

blast n explosion f; (wave of air)
souffle m; (of wind) rafale f; (noise
from siren etc.) coup m. ● vt (blow up)
faire sauter. □ **~ off** décoller. **~-**

furnace n haut-fourneau m. **~-
off** n lancement m.

blatant a (obvious) flagrant;
(shameless) éhonté.

blaze n feu m; (accident) incendie
m. ● vt **~ a trail** faire œuvre de
pionnier. ● vi (fire) brûler; (sky,
eyes) flamboyer.

bleach n (for cleaning) eau f de
Javel; (for hair, fabric) décolorant m.
● vt/i blanchir; (hair) décolorer.

bleak a (landscape) désolé;
(outlook, future) sombre.

bleed vt/i (pt bled) saigner.

bleep n bip m.

blemish n imperfection f; (on fruit,
reputation) tache f. ● vt entacher.

blend vt mélanger. ● vi se fondre
ensemble; **to ~ with** se marier à.
● n mélange m. **blender** n
mixeur n, mixer n.

bless vt bénir; **be ~ed with** jouir
de; **~ you!** à vos souhaits!
blessed a (holy) saint; (damned 🗆)
sacré. **blessing** n bénédiction f;
(benefit) avantage m; (stroke of luck)
chance f.

blew ⇒BLOW.

blight n (disease: Bot) rouille f; (fig)
plaie f.

blind a aveugle (**to** à); (corner,
bend) sans visibilité. ● vt
aveugler. ● n (on window) store m;
the ~ les aveugles mpl.

blindfold a be **~** avoir les yeux
bandés. ● adv les yeux bandés.
● n bandeau m. ● vt bander les
yeux à.

blindness n (Med) cécité f; (fig)
aveuglement m.

blind spot n (Auto) angle m mort.

blink vi cligner des yeux; (light)
clignoter.

bliss n délice m. **blissful** a
délicieux.

blister n ampoule f; (on paint)
cloque f. ● vi cloquer.

blitz n (Aviat) raid m éclair. ● vt bombarder.

blob n (drop) (grosse) goutte f; (stain) tache f.

block n bloc m; (buildings) pâté m de maisons; (in pipe) obstruction f; ~ (of flats) immeuble m; ~ letters majuscules fpl. ● vt bloquer.

blockade n blocus m. ● vt bloquer.

blockage n obstruction f.

block-buster n gros succès m.

bloke n ▣ type m.

blond a & n blond (m).

blonde a & n blonde (f).

blood n sang m. ● a (donor, bath) de sang; (bank, poisoning) du sang; (group, vessel) sanguin. ~-**pressure** n tension f artérielle. ~**shed** n effusion f de sang. ~**shot** a injecté de sang. ~**stream** n sang m. ~ **test** n prise f de sang.

bloody a (-ier, -iest) sanglant; ▣ sacré. ● adv ▣ vachement ▣. ~-**minded** a ▣ hargneux, obstiné.

bloom n fleur f. ● vi fleurir; (person) s'épanouir.

blossom n fleur(s) f(pl). ● vi fleurir; (person) s'épanouir.

blot n tache f. ● vt (pt blotted) tacher; (dry) sécher; ~ out effacer.

blotch n tache f.

blouse n chemisier m.

blow vt/i (pt blew; pp blown) souffler; (fuse) (faire) sauter; (squander ▣) claquer; (opportunity) rater; ~ one's nose se moucher; ~ a whistle siffler. ● n coup m. □ ~ **away** or **off** emporter; ~ **out** souffler; ~ **over** passer; ~ **up** (faire) sauter; (tyre) gonfler; (Photo) agrandir.

blow-dry n brushing m. ● vt faire un brushing à.

blown ⇒BLOW.

bludgeon n matraque f. ● vt matraquer.

blue a bleu; (movie) porno. ● n bleu m; **come out of the** ~ être inattendu; **have the** ~s avoir le cafard. ~**bell** n jacinthe f des bois. ~**print** n projet m.

bluff vt/i bluffer. ● n bluff m; **call sb's** ~ dire chiche à qn. ● a (person) carré.

blunder vi faire une bourde; (move) avancer à tâtons. ● n gaffe f.

blunt a (knife) émoussé; (person) brusque. ● vt émousser. **bluntly** adv carrément.

blur n image f floue. ● vt (pt blurred) brouiller.

blurb n résumé m publicitaire.

blush vi rougir. ● n rougeur f.

blusher n fard m à joues.

blustery a ~ **wind** bourrasque f.

boar n sanglier m.

board n planche f; (for notices) tableau m; (food) pension f; **full** ~ pension f complète; **half** ~ demi-pension f; (committee) conseil m; ~ **of directors** conseil m d'administration; **go by the** ~ tomber à l'eau; **on** ~ à bord. ● vt/i (bus, train) monter dans; (Naut) monter à bord (de); ~ **with** être en pension chez.

boarding-school n école f privée avec internat.

boast vi se vanter (about). ● vt s'enorgueillir de. ● n vantardise f.

boat n bateau m; (small) canot m; **in the same** ~ logé à la même enseigne.

bode vi ~ **well/ill** être de bon/mauvais augure.

bodily a (need, well-being) physique; (injury) corporel. ● adv physiquement; (in person) en personne.

body n corps m; (mass) masse f;

(organization) organisme m; ∼**(work)**
(Auto) carrosserie f; **the main** ∼ **of**
le gros de. ∼**-building** n
culturisme m. ∼**guard** n garde m
du corps.

bog n marais m. ● vt (pt **bogged**)
get ∼**ged down** s'enliser dans.

bogus a faux.

boil n furoncle m; **bring to the** ∼
porter à ébullition. ● vt/i bouillir.
□ ∼ **down to** se ramener à; ∼
over déborder. **boiled** a (egg) à
la coque; (potatoes) à l'eau.

boiler n chaudière f; ∼ **suit** bleu
m (de travail).

boisterous a tapageur; (child)
turbulent.

bold a hardi; (cheeky) effronté;
(type) gras.

Bolivia n Bolivie f.

bollard n (on road) balise f.

bolt n (on door) verrou m; (for nut)
boulon m; (lightning) éclair m. ● vt
(door) verrouiller; (food)
engouffrer. ● vi s'emballer.

bomb n bombe f; ∼ **scare** alerte f
à la bombe. ● vt bombarder.

bomber n (aircraft) bombardier m;
(person) plastiqueur m.

bombshell n **be a** ∼ tomber
comme une bombe.

bond n (agreement) engagement m;
(link) lien m; (Comm) obligation f,
bon m; **in** ∼ (entrepasé en
douane.

bone n os m; (of fish) arête f. ● vt
désosser. ∼**-dry** a tout à fait sec.

bonfire n feu m; (for celebration) feu
m de joie.

bonnet n (hat) bonnet m; (of
vehicle) capot m.

bonus n prime f.

bony a (**-ier**, **-iest**) (thin) osseux;
(fish) plein d'arêtes.

boo interj hou. ● vt/i huer. ● n
huée f.

booby-trap n mécanisme m
piégé. ● vt (pt **-trapped**) piéger.

book n livre m; (exercise) cahier
m; (of tickets etc.) carnet m; ∼**s**
(Comm) comptes mpl. ● vt (reserve)
réserver; (driver) dresser un PV
à; (player) prendre le nom de;
(write down) inscrire. ● vi retenir
des places; (fully) ∼**ed** complet.
∼**case** n bibliothèque f.

booking-office n guichet m.
∼**keeping** n comptabilité f.

booklet n brochure f. ∼**maker** n
bookmaker m. ∼**mark** n (for book,
Internet) signet m. ∼**seller** n
libraire mf. ∼**shop** n librairie f.
∼**stall** n kiosque m (à journaux).

boom vi (gun, wind, etc.) gronder;
(trade) prospérer. ● n
grondement m; (Comm) boom m,
prospérité f.

boost vt stimuler; (morale)
remonter; (price) augmenter;
(publicize) faire de la réclame pour.

boot n (knee-length) botte f; (ankle-
length) chaussure f (montante); (for
walking) chaussure f de marche;
(Sport) chaussure f de sport; (of
vehicle) coffre m; **get the** ∼ 🄳 se
faire virer. ● vt/i ∼ **up** (Comput)
amorcer.

booth n (for telephone) cabine f; (at
fair) baraque f.

booze vi 🄸 boire (beaucoup). ● n
🄸 alcool m.

border n (edge) bord m; (frontier)
frontière f; (in garden) bordure f.
● vi ∼ **on** être voisin de,
avoisiner.

bore vt ennuyer; **be** ∼**d**
s'ennuyer; ⇒BEAR. ● vi (Tech)
forer. ● n raseur/-euse m/f; (thing)
ennui m. **boredom** n ennui m.
boring a ennuyeux.

born a né; **be** ∼ naître.

borne ⇒BEAR.

borough n municipalité f.

borrow vt emprunter (**from** à).

Bosnia n Bosnie f.

Bosnian a bosniaque. ● n Bosniaque.

bosom n poitrine f; ~ **friend** ami/-e m/f intime.

boss n ⊞ patron/-ne m/f. ● vt ~ **(about)** ⊞ mener par le bout du nez.

bossy a autoritaire.

botch vt bâcler, saboter.

both det les deux; ~ **the books** les deux livres. ● pron tous/toutes (les) deux, l'un/-e et l'autre; **we** ~ **agree** nous sommes tous les deux d'accord; **I bought** ~ **(of them)** j'ai acheté les deux; **I saw** ~ **of you** je vous ai vus tous les deux; ~ **Paul and Anne** (et) Paul et Anne. ● adv à la fois.

bother vt (annoy, worry) ennuyer; (disturb) déranger. ● vi se déranger; **don't** ~ **(calling)** ce n'est pas la peine (d'appeler); **don't** ~ **about us** ne t'inquiète pas pour nous; **I can't be** ~**ed** j'ai la flemme ⊞. ● n ennui m; (effort) peine f; **it's no** ~ ce n'est rien.

bottle n bouteille f; (for baby) biberon m. ● vt mettre en bouteille. □ ~ **up** contenir. ~ **bank** n collecteur m (de verre usagé). ~**neck** n (traffic jam) embouteillage m. ~**-opener** n ouvre-bouteilles m inv.

bottom n fond m; (of hill, page, etc.) bas m; (buttocks) derrière m ⊞. ● a inférieur, du bas.

bought ⇒BUY.

bounce vi rebondir; (person) faire des bonds, bondir; (cheques ⊞) être refusé. ● vt faire rebondir. ● n rebond m.

bound vi (leap) bondir; ~**ed by** limité par; ⇒BIND. ● n bond m. ● a **be** ~ **for** être en route pour, aller vers; ~ **to** (obliged) obligé de; (certain) sûr de.

boundary n limite f.

bounds npl limites fpl; **out of** ~ être interdit d'accès.

bout n période f; (Med) accès m; (boxing) combat m.

bow¹ n (weapon) arc m; (of violin) archet m; (knot) nœud m.

bow² n salut m; (of ship) proue f. ● vt/i (s')incliner.

bowels npl intestins mpl; (fig) profondeurs fpl.

bowl n (for washing) cuvette f; (for food) bol m; (for soup) assiette f creuse. ● vt/i (cricket) lancer; ~ **over** bouleverser.

bowler n (cricket) lanceur m; ~ **(hat)** (chapeau) melon m.

bowling n (ten-pin) bowling m; (on grass) jeu m de boules. ~**-alley** n bowling m.

bow-tie n nœud m papillon.

box n boîte f; (cardboard) carton m; (Theat) loge f; **the** ~ ⊞ la télé. ● vt mettre en boîte; (Sport) boxer; ~ **sb's ears** gifler qn; ~ **in** enfermer.

boxing n boxe f. ● a de boxe. **B**~ **Day** n le lendemain de Noël.

box office n guichet m.

boy n garçon m.

boycott vt boycotter. ● n boycottage m.

boyfriend n (petit) ami m.

bra n soutien-gorge m.

brace n (fastener) attache f; (dental) appareil m; (tool) vilbrequin m; ~**s** (for trousers) bretelles fpl. ● vt soutenir; ~ **oneself** rassembler ses forces.

bracket n (for shelf etc.) tasseau m, support m; (group) tranche f; **in** ~**s** entre parenthèses. ● vt mettre entre parenthèses or crochets.

braid n (trimming) galon m; (of hair) tresse f.

brain n cerveau m; ~**s** (fig) intelligence f. ● vt assommer.

brainless a stupide. ~**wash** vt

B

faire subir un lavage de cerveau à. ~**wave** n idée f géniale, trouvaille f. **brainy** a (-ier, -iest) doué.

brake n (Auto also fig) frein m. ● vt/i freiner. ~ **light** n feu m stop.

bran n son m.

branch n (of tree) branche f; (of road) embranchement m; (Comm) succursale f; (of bank) agence f. ● vi ~ (**off**) bifurquer.

brand n marque f. ● vt ~ **sb as** désigner qn comme qch.

brand-new a tout neuf.

brandy n cognac m.

brass n cuivre m; **get down to** ~ **tacks** en venir aux choses sérieuses; **the** ~ (Mus) les cuivres mpl; **top** ~ 🗓 galonnés mpl.

brat n 🗓 môme mf 🗓.

brave a courageux; (smile) brave. ● n (American Indian) brave m. ● vt braver. **bravery** n courage m.

brawl n bagarre f. ● vi se bagarrer.

Brazil n Brésil m.

breach n (of copyright, privilege) violation f; (in relationship) rupture f; (gap) brèche f. ● vt ouvrir une brèche dans.

bread n pain m; ~ **and butter** tartine f. ~-**bin**, (US) ~-**box** n boîte f à pain. ~**crumbs** npl chapelure f.

breadth n largeur f.

bread-winner n soutien m de famille.

break vt (pt **broke**, pp **broken**) casser; (smash into pieces) briser; (vow, silence, rank, etc.) rompre; (law) violer; (a record) battre; (news) révéler; (journey) interrompre; (heart, strike, ice) briser; ~ **one's arm** se casser le bras. ● vi (se) casser; se briser. ● n cassure f, rupture f; (in relationship, continuity) rupture f;

(interval) interruption f; (at school) récréation f, récré f; (for coffee) pause f; (luck 🗓) chance f. □ ~ **away from** se détacher; ~ **down** vi (collapse) s'effondrer; (negotiations) échouer; (machine) tomber en panne; vt (door) enfoncer; (analyse) analyser; ~ **even** rentrer dans ses frais; ~ **into** cambrioler; ~ **off** (se) détacher; (suspend) rompre; (stop talking) s'interrompre; ~ **out** (fire, war, etc.) éclater; ~ **up** (end) (faire) cesser; (couple) rompre; (marriage) (se) briser; (crowd) (se) disperser; (schools) être en vacances. **breakable** a fragile.

breakage n casse f.

breakdown n (Tech) panne f; (Med) dépression f; (of figures) analyse f. ● a (Auto) de dépannage.

breakfast n petit déjeuner m.

break. ~-**in** n cambriolage m. ~**through** n percée f.

breast n sein m; (chest) poitrine f. ~-**feed** vt (pt -**fed**) allaiter. ~-**stroke** n brasse f.

breath n souffle m, haleine f; **out of** ~ à bout de souffle; **under one's** ~ tout bas.

breathalyser® n alcootest m.

breathe vt/i respirer. □ ~ **in** inspirer; ~ **out** expirer.

breathless a à bout de souffle.

breathtaking a à vous couper le souffle.

bred ⇒BREED.

breed vt (pt **bred**) élever; (give rise to) engendrer. ● vi se reproduire. ● n race f.

breeze n brise f.

brew vt (beer) brasser; (tea) faire infuser. ● vi (beer) fermenter; (tea) infuser; (fig) se préparer. ● n décoction f. **brewer** n brasseur m. **brewery** n brasserie f.

bribe n pot-de-vin m. ● vt soudoyer. **bribery** n corruption f.

brick n brique f. **~layer** n maçon m.

bridal a (dress) de mariée; (car, chamber) des mariés.

bride n mariée f. **~groom** n marié m. **~smaid** n demoiselle f d'honneur.

bridge n pont m; (Naut) passerelle f; (of nose) arête f; (card game) bridge m. ● vt ~ **a gap** combler une lacune.

bridle n bride f. ● vt brider. **~-path** n piste f cavalière.

brief a bref. ● n instructions fpl; (Jur) dossier m. ● vt donner des instructions à.

briefcase n serviette f.

briefs npl slip m.

bright a brillant, vif; (day, room) clair; (cheerful) gai; (clever) intelligent.

brighten vt égayer. ● vi (weather) s'éclaircir; (face) s'éclairer.

brilliant a (student, career) brillant; (light) éclatant; (very good 🔲) super.

brim n bord m. ● vi (pt **brimmed**); ~ **over** déborder (**with** de).

bring vt (pt **brought**) (thing) apporter; (person, vehicle) amener; ~ **to bear** (pressure etc.) exercer. □ ~ **about** provoquer; ~ **back** rapporter; (colour, shine) redonner; ~ **down** faire tomber; (shoot down, knock down) abattre; ~ **forward** avancer; ~ **off** réussir; ~ **out** (take out) sortir; (show) faire ressortir; (book) publier; ~ **round** faire revenir à soi; ~ **up** (child) élever; (Med) vomir; (question) aborder.

brink n bord m.

brisk a vif.

bristle n poil m. ● vi se hérisser; **bristling with** hérissé de.

Britain n Grande-Bretagne f.

British a britannique; **the ~** les Britanniques mpl.

Briton n Britannique mf.

Brittany n Bretagne f.

brittle a fragile.

broad a large; (choice, range) grand. ~ **bean** n fève.

broadcast vt/i (pt **broadcast**) diffuser; (person) parler à la télévision or à la radio. ● n émission f.

broadly adv en gros.

broad-minded a large d'esprit.

broccoli n inv brocoli m.

brochure n brochure f.

broke ⇒BREAK. ● a (penniless 🔲) fauché.

broken ⇒BREAK. ● a ~ **English** mauvais anglais m.

bronchitis n bronchite f.

bronze n bronze m.

brooch n broche f.

brood n nichée f, couvée f. ● vi méditer tristement.

broom n balai m.

broth n bouillon m.

brothel n maison f close.

brother n frère m. **~hood** n fraternité f. **~-in-law** n (pl **~s-in-law**) beau-frère m.

brought ⇒BRING.

brow n front m; (of hill) sommet m.

brown a (object) marron; (hair) brun; ~ **bread** pain m complet; ~ **sugar** sucre m roux. ● n marron m; brun m. ● vt/i brunir; (Culin) (faire) dorer.

Brownie n jeannette f.

browse vi flâner; (animal) brouter. ● vt (Comput) naviguer. **browser** n (Comput) navigateur m.

bruise n bleu m. ● vt (knee, arm

etc.) faire un bleu à; (*fruit*) abîmer.

brush n brosse f; (skirmish) accrochage m; (bushes) broussailles fpl. ●vt brosser. □ ~ **against** frôler; ~ **aside** (dismiss) repousser; (move) écarter; ~ **up** (**on**) se remettre à.

Brussels n Bruxelles. ~ **sprouts** npl choux mpl de Bruxelles.

brutal a brutal.

brute n brute f; **by** ~ **force** par la force.

BSE abbr (**bovine spongiform encephalopathy**) encéphalopathie f spongiforme bovine, ESB f.

bubble n bulle f; **blow** ~**s** faire des bulles. ●vi bouillonner; ~ **over** déborder. ~ **bath** n bain m moussant.

buck n mâle m; (US, ▣) dollar m; **pass the** ~ rejeter la responsabilité (**to** sur). ●vi (horse) ruer; ~ **up** ▣ prendre courage; (hurry ▣) se grouiller ▣.

bucket n seau m (of de).

buckle n boucle f. ●vt/i (fasten) (se) boucler; (bend) voiler.

bud n bourgeon m. ●vi (pt **budded**) bourgeonner.

Buddhism n bouddhisme m.

budding a (talent) naissant; (athlete) en herbe.

budge vt/i (faire) bouger.

budgerigar n perruche f.

budget n budget m. ●vi ~ **for** prévoir (dans son budget).

buff n (colour) chamois m; ▣ fanatique mf.

buffalo n (pl **-oes** or **-o**) buffle m; (US) bison m.

buffer n tampon m; ~ **zone** zone f tampon.

buffet[1] n (meal, counter) buffet m; ~ **car** buffet m.

buffet[2] n (blow) soufflet m. ●vt (pt **buffeted**) souffleter.

bug n (bedbug) punaise f; (any small insect) bestiole f; (germ) microbe m; (stomachache ▣) ennuis mpl gastriques; (device) micro m; (defect) défaut m; (Comput) bogue f, bug m. ●vt (pt **bugged**) mettre des micros dans; ▣ embêter.

buggy n poussette f.

build vt/i (pt **built**) bâtir, construire. ●n carrure f. □ ~ **up** (increase) augmenter, monter; (accumulate) (s')accumuler. **builder** n entrepreneur m en bâtiment; (workman) ouvrier m du bâtiment.

building n (structure) bâtiment m; (dwelling) immeuble m. ~ **society** n caisse f d'épargne.

build-up n accumulation f; (fig) publicité f.

built ⇒BUILD.

built-in a encastré.

built-up area a agglomération f, zone f urbanisée.

bulb n (Bot) bulbe m; (Electr) ampoule f.

Bulgaria n Bulgarie f.

Bulgarian n (person) Bulgare mf; (Ling) bulgare m. ●a bulgare.

bulge n renflement m. ●vi se renfler, être renflé; **be bulging with** être gonflé or bourré de.

bulimia n boulimie f.

bulk n volume f; **in** ~ (buy, sell) en gros; (transport) en vrac; **the** ~ **of** la majeure partie de.

bull n taureau m. ~**dog** n bouledogue m. ~**doze** vt raser au bulldozer.

bullet n balle f.

bulletin n bulletin m.

bullet-proof a (vest) pare-balles inv; (vehicle) blindé.

bullfight n corrida f.

bullion n or m or argent m en lingots.

bullring n arène f.

bull's-eye n mille m.

bully n (child) petite brute f; (adult) tyran m. ●vt maltraiter.

bum n ⊠ derrière m ⊡; (US, ⊠) vagabond/-e m/f.

bumble-bee n bourdon m.

bump n (swelling) bosse f; (on road) bosse f. ● vt/i cogner, heurter. □ ~ **along** cahoter; ~ **into** (hit) rentrer dans; (meet) tomber sur.

bumper n pare-chocs m inv. ● a exceptionnel.

bumpy a (road) accidenté.

bun n (cake) petit pain m; (hair) chignon m.

bunch n (of flowers) bouquet m; (of keys) trousseau m; (of people) groupe m; (of bananas) régime m; ~ **of grapes** grappe f de raisin.

bundle n paquet m. ● vt mettre en paquet; (push) fourrer.

bung n bouchon m. ● vt (stop up) boucher; (throw ⊠) flanquer ⊡.

bunion n (Med) oignon m.

bunk n (on ship, train) couchette f. ~-**beds** npl lits mpl superposés.

buoy n bouée f. ● vt ~ **up** (hearten) soutenir, encourager.

buoyancy n (of floating object) flottabilité f; (cheerfulness) gaieté f.

burden n fardeau m. ● vt ennuyer (**with** de).

bureau n (pl -**eaux**) bureau m.

bureaucracy n bureaucratie f.

burglar n cambrioleur m; ~ **alarm** alarme f. **burglarize** vt (US) cambrioler. **burglary** n cambriolage m. **burgle** vt cambrioler.

Burgundy n (wine) bourgogne m.

burial n enterrement m.

burn vt/i (pt **burned** or **burnt**) brûler. ● n brûlure f. □ ~ **down** être réduit en cendres. **burning** a en flammes; (fig) brûlant.

burnt ⇒BURN.

burp n ⊡ rot m. ● vi ⊡ roter.

burrow n terrier m. ● vt creuser.

bursar n intendant/-e m/f.

bursary n bourse f.

burst vt/i (pt **burst**) (balloon, bubble) crever; (pipe) (faire) éclater. ● n explosion f; (of laughter) éclat m; (surge) élan m. □ ~ **into** (room) faire interruption dans; ~ **into tears** fondre en larmes; ~ **out** ~ **out laughing** éclater de rire; ~ **with** be ~**ing with** déborder de.

bury vt (person etc.) enterrer; (hide, cover) enfouir; (engross, thrust) plonger.

bus n (pl **buses**) (auto)bus m. ● vt transporter en bus. ● vi (pt **bussed**) prendre l'autobus.

bush n (shrub) buisson m; (land) brousse f.

business n (task, concern) affaire f; (commerce) affaires fpl; (line of work) métier m; (shop) commerce m; he has no ~ **to** il n'a pas le droit de; mean ~ être sérieux; that's none of your ~! ça ne vous regarde pas! ~**like** a sérieux. ~**man** n homme m d'affaires.

busker n musicien/-ne m/f des rues.

bus-stop n arrêt m d'autobus.

bust n (statue) buste m; (bosom) poitrine f. ● vt/i (pt **busted** or **bust**) (burst ⊠) crever; (break ⊠) (se) casser. ● a (broken, finished ⊠) fichu; go ~ ⊠ faire faillite.

bustle vi s'affairer. ● n affairement m, remue-ménage m.

busy a (-**ier**, -**iest**) (person) occupé; (street) animé; (day) chargé. ● vt ~ **oneself with** s'occuper à.

but conj mais. ● prep sauf; ~ **for** sans; **nobody** ~ personne d'autre que; **nothing** ~ rien que. ● adv (only) seulement.

butcher n boucher m. ● vt massacrer.

butler n maître m d'hôtel.

butt n (of gun) crosse f; (of cigarette) mégot m; (of joke) cible f; (barrel) tonneau m; (US, 🛑) derrière m 🛑. ● vi ~ in interrompre.

butter n beurre m. ● vt beurrer. **~-bean** n haricot m blanc. **~cup** n bouton-d'or m.

butterfly n papillon m.

buttock n fesse f.

button n bouton m. ● vt/i ~ (up) (se) boutonner.

buttonhole n boutonnière f. ● vt accrocher.

buy vt (pt **bought**) acheter (from à); ~ sth for sb acheter qch à qn, prendre qch pour qn; (believe 🛑) croire, avaler.

buzz n bourdonnement m. ● vi bourdonner. **buzzer** n sonnerie f.

by prep par, de; (near) à côté de; (before) avant; (means) en, à, par; ~ bike à vélo; ~ car en auto; ~ day de jour; ~ the kilo au kilo; ~ running en courant; ~ sea par mer; ~ that time à ce moment-là; ~ the way à propos; ~ oneself tout seul. ● adv close ~ tout près; ~ and large dans l'ensemble.

bye(-bye) interj 🛑 au revoir, salut 🛑.

by-election n élection f partielle

Byelorussia n Biélorussie f.

by-law n arrêté m municipal.

bypass n (Auto) rocade f; (Med) pontage m. ● vt contourner.

by-product n dérivé m; (fig) conséquence f.

byte n octet m.

cab n taxi m; (of lorry, train) cabine f.

cabbage n chou m.

cabin n (hut) cabane f; (in ship, aircraft) cabine f.

cabinet n petit placard m; (glass-fronted) vitrine f; (Pol) cabinet m.

cable n câble m. ● vt câbler. **~-car** n téléphérique m. ~ **television** n télévision f par câble.

cache n (hoard) cache f; (place) cachette f.

cackle n (of hen) caquet m; (laugh) ricanement m. ● vi caqueter; (laugh) ricaner.

cactus n (pl -ti or ~es) cactus m.

cadet n élève m officier.

Caesarean a ~ (**section**) césarienne f.

café n café m, snack-bar m.

caffeine n caféine f.

cage n cage f. ● vt mettre en cage.

cagey a réticent.

cagoule n K-way® m.

cajole vt ~ sb into doing sth amener qn à faire qch par la cajolerie.

cake n gâteau m; (of soap) pain m. ● vi former une croûte (**on** sur).

calculate vt calculer; (estimate) évaluer. **calculated** a délibéré; (risk) calculé. **calculating** a calculateur. **calculation** n calcul m. **calculator** n calculatrice f.

calculus n (pl **-li** or **~es**) calcul m.

calendar n calendrier m.

calf n (pl **calves**) (young cow or bull) veau m; (of leg) mollet m.

calibre n calibre m.

call vt/i appeler; (loudly) crier; **he's ~ed John** il s'appelle John; **~ sb stupid** traiter qn d'imbécile. ● n appel m; (of bird) cri m; (visit) visite f; **make/pay a ~ on** rendre visite à; **be on ~** être de garde; **~ box** cabine f téléphonique. □ **~ back** rappeler; (visit) repasser; **~ for** (help) appeler à; (demand) demander; (require) exiger; (collect) passer prendre; **~ in** passer; **~ off** annuler; **~ on** (visit) rendre visite à; (urge) demander à (**to do** de faire); **~ out** (**to**) appeler; **~ round** venir; **~ up** appeler.

calling n vocation f.

callous a inhumain.

calm a calme. ● n calme m. ● vt/i **~ (down)** (se) calmer.

calorie n calorie f.

camcorder n caméscope® m.

came ⇒COME.

camel n chameau m.

camera n appareil(-photo) m; (TV, cinema) caméra f; **in ~** à huis clos. **~man** n (pl **-men**) cadreur m, cameraman m.

camouflage n camouflage m. ● vt camoufler.

camp n camp m. ● vi camper.

campaign n campagne f. ● vi faire campagne.

camper n campeur/-euse m/f. **~(-van)** n camping-car m.

camping n camping m; **go ~** faire du camping.

campsite n camping m.

campus n (pl **~es**) campus m.

can¹

infinitive **be able to**; present **can**; present negative **can't**, **cannot** (formal); past **could**; past participle **been able to**

● auxiliary verb

····▶ pouvoir; **where ~ I buy stamps?** où est-ce que je peux acheter des timbres?; **she can't come** elle ne peut pas venir.

····▶ (be allowed to) pouvoir; **~ I smoke?** est-ce que je peux fumer?

····▶ (know how to) savoir; **she ~ swim** elle sait nager; **he can't drive** il ne sait pas conduire.

····▶ (with verbs of perception) **I ~ hear you** je t'entends; **~ they see us?** est-ce qu'ils nous voient?

can² n (for food) boîte f; (of petrol) bidon m. ● vt (pt **canned**) mettre en conserve.

Canada n Canada m.

Canadian n Canadien/-ne m/f. ● a canadien.

canal n canal m.

canary n canari m.

cancel vt/i (pt **cancelled**) (call off, revoke) annuler; (cross out) barrer; (a stamp) oblitérer; **~ out** (se) neutraliser. **cancellation** n annulation f.

cancer n cancer m; **have ~** avoir un cancer.

Cancer n Cancer m.

cancerous a cancéreux.

candid a franc.

candidate n candidat/-e m/f.

candle n bougie f; (in church) cierge m. **~stick** n bougeoir m.

candy n (US) bonbon(s) m(pl). **~-floss** n barbe f à papa.

cane n canne f; (for baskets) rotin

m; (for punishment) badine *f*. ● *vt*
donner des coups de badine à.

canister *n* boîte *f*.

cannabis *n* cannabis *m*.

cannibal *n* cannibale *mf*.

cannon *n* (*pl* ~ *or* ~**s**) canon *m*.
~**-ball** *n* boulet *m* de canon.

cannot = CAN NOT.

canoe *n* canoë *m*. ● *vi* faire du
canoë. **canoeist** *n* canoéiste *mf*.

canon *n* (clergyman) chanoine *m*;
(rule) canon *m*.

can-opener *n* ouvre-boîtes *m*
inv.

canopy *n* dais *m*; (for bed)
baldaquin *m*.

can't = CAN NOT.

canteen *n* (restaurant) cantine *f*;
(flask) bidon *m*.

canter *n* petit galop *m*. ● *vi* aller
au petit galop.

canvas *n* toile *f*.

canvass *vt/i* (Comm, Pol) faire du
démarchage (auprès de); ~
opinion sonder l'opinion.

canyon *n* cañon *m*.

cap *n* (hat) casquette *f*; (of bottle,
tube) bouchon *m*; (of beer or milk
bottle) capsule *f*; (of pen) capuchon
m; (for toy gun) amorce *f*. ● *vt* (*pt*
capped) couronner.

capability *n* capacité *f*.

capable *a* (person) compétent; ~
of doing capable de faire.

capacity *n* capacité *f*; **in my ~ as
a doctor** en ma qualité de
médecin.

cape *n* (cloak) cape *f*; (Geog) cap *m*.

caper *vi* gambader. ● *n* (leap)
cabriole *f*; (funny film) comédie *f*;
(Culin) câpre *f*.

capital *a* (letter) majuscule;
(offence) capital. ● *n* (town)
capitale *f*; (money) capital *m*; ~
(**letter**) majuscule *f*.

capitalism *n* capitalisme *m*.

capitalize *vi* ~ **on** tirer parti de.

capitulate *vi* capituler.

Capricorn *n* Capricorne *m*.

capsize *vt/i* (faire) chavirer.

capsule *n* capsule *f*.

captain *n* capitaine *m*.

caption *n* (under photo) légende *f*;
(subtitle) sous-titre *m*.

captivate *vt* captiver.

captive *a & n* captif/-ive (*m/f*).
captivity *n* captivité *f*.

capture *vt* (person, animal)
capturer; (moment, likeness)
saisir. ● *n* capture *f*.

car *n* voiture *f*. ● *a* (industry,
insurance) automobile; (accident,
phone) de voiture; (journey,
chase) en voiture.

caravan *n* caravane *f*.

carbohydrate *n* hydrate *m* de
carbone.

carbon *n* carbone *m*.

carburettor *n* carburateur *m*.

card *n* carte *f*.

cardboard *n* carton *m*.

cardiac *a* cardiaque; ~ **arrest**
arrêt *m* du cœur.

cardigan *n* cardigan *m*.

cardinal *a* (sin) capital; (rule)
fondamental; (number) cardinal.
● *n* cardinal *m*.

card-index *n* fichier *m*.

care *n* (attention) soin *m*, attention
f; (worry) souci *m*; (looking after)
soins *mpl*; **take ~ of** (deal with)
s'occuper de; (be careful with)
prendre soin de; **take ~ to do sth**
faire bien attention à faire qch.
● *vi* ~ **about** s'intéresser à; ~ **for**
s'occuper de; (invalid) soigner; ~
to do vouloir faire; **I don't ~** ça
m'est égal.

career *n* carrière *f*. ● *vi* ~ **in/out**
entrer/sortir à toute vitesse.

carefree *a* insouciant.

careful *a* prudent; (research,
study) méticuleux; (**be**) ~**!** (fais)

attention! **carefully** *adv* avec soin; (*cautiously*) prudemment.

careless *a* négligent; (*work*) bâclé.

caress *n* caresse *f*. ● *vt* caresser.

caretaker *n* concierge *mf*. ● *a* (*president*) par intérim.

car ferry *n* ferry *m*.

cargo *n* (*pl* ∼**es**) chargement *m*; (Naut) cargaison *f*.

Caribbean *a* des Caraïbes, des Antilles. ● *n* **the** ∼ (*sea*) la mer des Antilles; (*islands*) les Antilles *fpl*.

caring *a* affectueux.

carnation *n* œillet *m*.

carnival *n* carnaval *m*.

carol *n* chant *m* de Noël.

carp *n inv* carpe *f*. ● *vi* maugréer.

car-park *n* parc *m* de stationnement, parking *m*.

carpenter *n* (*joiner*) menuisier *m*; (*builder*) charpentier *m*. **carpentry** *n* menuiserie *f*; (*structural*) charpenterie *f*.

carpet *n* (*fitted*) moquette *f*; (*loose*) tapis *m*. ● *vt* (*pt* **carpeted**) mettre de la moquette dans.

carriage *n* (*rail*) wagon *m*; (*ceremonial*) carrosse *m*; (*of goods*) transport *m*; (*cost*) port *m*.

carriageway *n* chaussée *f*.

carrier *n* transporteur *m*; (Med) porteur/-euse *m/f*; ∼ (**bag**) sac *m* en plastique.

carrot *n* carotte *f*.

carry *vt/i* porter; (*goods*) transporter; (*involve*) comporter; (*motion*) voter; **be carried away** s'emballer. □ ∼ **off** emporter; (*prize*) remporter; ∼ **on** (*continue*) continuer; (*business*) conduire; (*conversation*) mener; ∼ **out** (*order, plan*) exécuter; (*duty*) remplir; (*experiment, operation*,

repair) effectuer. ∼**-cot** *n* porte-bébé *m*.

car sharing *n* covoiturage *m*.

cart *n* charrette *f*. ● *vt* (*heavy bag* 🔢) trimballer 🔢.

carton *n* (*box*) boîte *f*; (*of yoghurt, cream*) pot *m*; (*of cigarettes*) cartouche *f*.

cartoon *n* dessin *m* humoristique; (*cinema*) dessin *m* animé; (*strip cartoon*) bande *f* dessinée.

cartridge *n* cartouche *f*.

carve *vt* tailler; (*meat*) découper.

car-wash *n* lavage *m* automatique.

cascade *n* cascade *f*. ● *vi* tomber en cascade.

case *n* cas *m*; (Jur) affaire *f*; (*suitcase*) valise *f*; (*crate*) caisse *f*; (*for spectacles*) étui *m*; (**just**) **in** ∼ au cas où; **in** ∼ **he comes** au cas où il viendrait; **in** ∼ **of fire** en cas d'incendie; **in any** ∼ de toute façon; **the** ∼ **for sth** les arguments *mpl* en faveur de qch; **the** ∼ **for the defence** la défense.

cash *n* espèces *fpl*, argent *m*; **in** ∼ en espèces. ● *a* (*price*) comptant. ● *vt* encaisser; ∼ **in** (**on**) profiter (de). ∼**-back** *n* retrait *m* d'argent à la caisse. ∼ **desk** *n* caisse *f*. ∼ **dispenser** *n* distributeur *m* de billets.

cashew *n* cajou *m*.

cash-flow *n* marge *f* brute d'auto-financement.

cashier *n* caissier/-ière *m/f*.

cashmere *n* cachemire *m*.

cash: ∼ **point** *n* distributeur *m* de billets. ∼ **point card** *n* carte *f* de retrait. ∼ **register** *n* caisse *f* enregistreuse.

casino *n* casino *m*.

casket *n* (*box*) coffret *m*; (*coffin*) cercueil *m*.

casserole *n* (*pan*) daubière *f*; (*food*) ragoût *m*.

cassette n cassette f.

cast vt (pt cast) (object, glance) jeter; (shadow) projeter; (metal) couler; ~ (off) (shed) se dépouiller de; ~ one's vote voter; ~ iron fonte f. ● n (cinema, Theat, TV) distribution f; (Med) plâtre m.

castaway n naufragé/-e m/f.

cast-iron a de fonte; (fig) en béton.

castle n château m; (chess) tour f.

cast-offs npl vieux vêtements mpl.

castor n (wheel) roulette f.

castrate vt châtrer.

casual a (informal) décontracté; (remark) désinvolte; (acquaintance) de passage; (work) temporaire. **casually** adv (remark) d'un air détaché; (dress) simplement.

casualty n victime f; (part of hospital) urgences fpl.

cat n chat m; (feline) félin m.

catalogue n catalogue m. ● vt dresser un catalogue de.

catalyst n catalyseur m.

catalytic a ~ converter pot m catalytique.

catapult n lance-pierres m inv. ● vt projeter.

cataract n (Med, Geog) cataracte f.

catarrh n catarrhe m.

catastrophe n catastrophe f.

catch vt (pt caught) attraper; (bus, plane) prendre; (understand) saisir; ~ sb doing surprendre qn en train de faire; ~ fire prendre feu; ~ sight of apercevoir; ~ sb's attention/eye attirer l'attention de qn. ● vi (get stuck) se prendre (in dans); (start to burn) prendre. ● n (fastening) fermeture f; (drawback) piège m; (in sport) prise f. □ ~ on devenir populaire; ~ out prendre de court; ~ up rattraper

son retard; ~ up with sb rattraper qn.

catching a contagieux.

catchment n ~ area (School) secteur m.

catch-phrase n formule f favorite.

catchy a entraînant.

category n catégorie f.

cater vi organiser des réceptions; ~ for/to (guests) accueillir; (needs) pourvoir à; (reader) s'adresser à. **caterer** n traiteur m.

caterpillar n chenille f.

cathedral n cathédrale f.

catholic a éclectique. **Catholic** a & n catholique (mf).

Catholicism n catholicisme m.

Catseye® n plot m rétroréfléchissant.

cattle npl bétail m.

caught ⇒CATCH.

cauliflower n chou-fleur m.

cause n cause f; (reason) raison f, motif m. ● vt causer; ~ sth to grow/move faire pousser/bouger qch.

causeway n chaussée f.

caution n prudence f; (warning) avertissement m. ● vt avertir.

cautious a prudent. **cautiously** adv prudemment.

cave n grotte f. ● vi ~ in s'effondrer; (agree) céder. ~**man** n (pl -**men**) homme m des cavernes.

cavern n caverne f.

caviare n caviar m.

caving n spéléologie f.

CCTV abbr (**closed circuit television**) télévision f en circuit fermé.

CD abbr (**compact disc**) disque m compact, CD m.

CD-ROM n disque m optique compact, CD-ROM m.

cease vt/i cesser. ~**-fire** n cessez-le-feu m inv.

cedar n cèdre m.
cedilla n cédille f.
ceiling n plafond m.
celebrate vt (occasion) fêter; (Easter, mass) célébrer. ●vi faire la fête. **celebrated** a célèbre. **celebration** n fête f.
celebrity n célébrité f.
celery n céleri m.
cell n cellule f; (Electr) élément m.
cellar n cave f.
cellist n violoncelliste mf. **cello** n violoncelle m.
Celt n Celte mf.
cement n ciment m. ●vt cimenter. **~-mixer** n bétonnière f.
cemetery n cimetière m.
censor n censeur m. ●vt censurer.
censure n censure f. ●vt critiquer.
census n recensement m.
cent n cent m.
centenary n centenaire m.
centigrade a centigrade.
centilitre, (US) **centiliter** n centilitre m.
centimetre, (US) **centimeter** n centimètre m.
centipede n millepattes m inv.
central a central; **~ heating** chauffage m central; **~ locking** fermeture f centralisée des portes. **centralize** vt centraliser. **centrally** adv (situated) au centre.
centre, (US) **center** n centre m. ●vt (pt **centred**) centrer. ●vi **~ on** tourner autour de.
century n siècle m.
ceramic a (art) céramique; (object) en céramique.
cereal n céréale f.
ceremonial a (dress) de cérémonie. ●n cérémonial m. **ceremony** n cérémonie f.
certain a certain; **for ~** avec

certitude; **make ~ of** s'assurer de.
certainly adv certainement.
certainty n certitude f.
certificate n certificat m.
certify vt certifier.
cesspit, **cesspool** n fosse f d'aisances.
chafe vt/i frotter (contre).
chagrin n dépit m.
chain n chaîne f; **~ reaction** réaction f en chaîne; **~ store** magasin m à succursales multiples. ●vt enchaîner. **~-smoke** vi fumer sans arrêt.
chair n chaise f; (armchair) fauteuil m; (Univ) chaire f; (chairperson) président/-e m/f. ●vt (preside over) présider. **~man** n (pl **-men**) président/-e m/f. **~woman** n (pl **-women**) présidente f.
chalk n craie f.
challenge n défi m; (opportunity) challenge m. ●vt (summon) défier (to do de faire); (question truth of) contester. **challenger** n (Sport) challenger m. **challenging** a stimulant.
chamber n (old use) chambre f. **~maid** n femme f de chambre. **~ music** n musique f de chambre. **~-pot** n pot m de chambre.
champagne n champagne m.
champion n champion/-ne m/f. ●vt défendre. **championship** n championnat m.
chance n (luck) hasard m; (opportunity) occasion f; (likelihood) chances fpl; (risk) risque m; **by ~** par hasard; **by any ~** par hasard; **~s are that** il est probable que. ●a fortuit. ●vt **~ doing** prendre le risque de faire; **~ it** tenter sa chance.
chancellor n chancelier m; **C~ of the Exchequer** Chancelier de l'Échiquier.
chandelier n lustre m.

change vt (alter) changer; (exchange) échanger (for contre); (money) changer; ~ **trains/one's dress** changer de train/de robe; ~ **one's mind** changer d'avis. ● vi changer; (change clothes) se changer; ~ **into** se transformer en; ~ **over** passer (to à). ● n changement m; (money) monnaie f; **a** ~ **for the better** une amélioration; **a** ~ **for the worse** un changement en pire; **a** ~ **of clothes** des vêtements de rechange; **for a** ~ pour changer. **changeable** a changeant. **changing room** n (in shop) cabine f d'essayage; (Sport) vestiaire m.

channel n (for liquid, information) canal m; (TV) chaîne f; (groove) rainure f. ● vt (pt **channelled**) canaliser. **C**~ n **the (English) C**~ la Manche; **the C**~ **tunnel** le tunnel sous la Manche; **the C**~ **Islands** les îles fpl Anglo-Normandes.

chant n (Relig) mélopée f; (of demonstrators) chant m scandé. ● vt/i scander; (Relig) psalmodier.

chaos n chaos m.

chap n (man 🔲) type m 🔲.

chapel n chapelle f.

chaplain n aumônier m.

chapped a gercé.

chapter n chapitre m.

char vt (pt **charred**) carboniser.

character n caractère m; (in novel, play) personnage m; **of good** ~ de bonne réputation.

characteristic a & n caractéristique (f).

charcoal n charbon m de bois; (art) fusain m.

charge n (fee) frais mpl; (Mil) charge f; (Jur) inculpation f; (task, custody) charge f; **in** ~ **of** responsable de; **take** ~ **of** prendre en charge, se charger de. ● vt (customer) faire payer; (enemy, gun) charger; (Jur)

inculper (with de); ~ **£20 an hour** prendre 20 livres de l'heure; ~ **card** carte f d'achat. ● vi faire payer; (bull) foncer; (person) se précipiter.

charisma n charisme m.

charismatic a charismatique.

charitable a charitable. **charity** n charité f; (organization) organisation f caritative.

charm n charme m; (trinket) amulette f. ● vt charmer. **charming** a charmant.

chart n (graph) graphique m; (table) tableau m; (map) carte f. ● vt (route) porter sur la carte.

charter n charte f; ~ **(flight)** charter m. ● vt affréter; ~**ed accountant** expert-comptable m.

chase vt poursuivre; ~ **away** or **off** chasser. ● vi courir (after après). ● n chasse f.

chassis n châssis m.

chastise vt châtier.

chat n conversation f; (on Internet) causette f, bavardage m, chat m; **have a** ~ bavarder; ~ **show** n talk-show m; ~**room** n salle f de causette, salle f de bavardage. ● vi (pt **chatted**) bavarder. □ ~ **up** 🔲 draguer 🔲.

chatter n bavardage m. ● vi bavarder; **his teeth are** ~**ing** il claque des dents. ~**box** n bavard/-e m/f.

chatty a bavard.

chauffeur n chauffeur m.

chauvinist n chauvin/-e m/f; macho m.

cheap a bon marché inv; (fare, rate) réduit; (joke, gimmick) facile; ~**er** meilleur marché inv. **cheapen** vt déprécier. **cheaply** adv à bas prix.

cheat vi tricher. ● vt tromper. ● n tricheur/-euse m/f.

check vt/i vérifier; (tickets, rises, inflation) contrôler; (stop) arrêter;

(tick off: US) cocher. ● *n* contrôle *m*; (curb) frein *m*; (chess) échec *m*; (pattern) carreaux *mpl*; (bill: US) addition *f*; (cheque: US) chèque *m*. □ ~ **in** remplir la fiche; (at airport) enregistrer; ~ **out** partir; ~ **sth out** vérifier qch; ~ **up** vérifier; ~ **up on** (*story*) vérifier; (*person*) faire une enquête sur.

check: ~**-in** *n* enregistrement *m*. **checking account** *n* (US) compte *m* courant. ~**-list** *n* liste *f* de contrôle. ~**mate** *n* échec *m* et mat. ~**-out** *n* caisse *f*. ~**-point** *n* contrôle *m*. ~**-up** *n* examen *m* médical.

cheek *n* joue *f*; (impudence) culot *m* ▣. **cheeky** *a* effronté.

cheer *n* gaieté *f*; ~**s** acclamations *fpl*; (when drinking) à la vôtre. ● *vt/i* applaudir; ~ **sb** (**up**) (gladden) remonter le moral à qn; ~ **up** prendre courage. **cheerful** *a* joyeux. **cheerfulness** *n* gaieté *f*.

cheerio *interj* ▣ salut ▣.

cheese *n* fromage *m*.

cheetah *n* guépard *m*.

chef *n* chef *m*.

chemical *a* chimique. ● *n* produit *m* chimique.

chemist *n* pharmacien/-ne *m/f*; (scientist) chimiste *mf*; ~**'s** (shop) pharmacie *f*. **chemistry** *n* chimie *f*.

cheque *n* chèque *m*. ~**-book** *n* chéquier *m*. ~ **card** *n* carte *f* bancaire.

chequered *a* (pattern) à damiers; (fig) en dents de scie.

cherish *vt* chérir; (hope) caresser.

cherry *n* cerise *f*; (tree, wood) cerisier *m*.

chess *n* échecs *mpl*. ~**-board** *n* échiquier *m*.

chest *n* (Anat) poitrine *f*; (box) coffre *m*; ~ **of drawers** commode *f*.

chestnut *n* (nut) marron *m*,

châtaigne *f*; (tree) marronnier *m*; (sweet) châtaignier *m*.

chew *vt* mâcher.

chic *a* chic *inv*.

chick *n* poussin *m*.

chicken *n* poulet *m*. ● *a* ▣ froussard. ● *vi* ~ **out** ▣ se dégonfler. ~**-pox** *n* varicelle *f*.

chick-pea *n* pois *m* chiche.

chicory *n* (for salad) endive *f*; (in coffee) chicorée *f*.

chief *n* chef *m*. ● *a* principal. **chiefly** *adv* principalement.

chilblain *n* engelure *f*.

child *n* (*pl* **children**) enfant *mf*. ~**birth** *n* accouchement *m*. **childhood** *n* enfance *f*. **childish** *a* puéril. **childless** *a* sans enfants. **childlike** *a* enfantin. ~**-minder** *n* nourrice *f*.

Chile *n* Chili *m*.

chill *n* froid *m*; (Med) refroidissement *m*. ● *a* froid. ● *vt* (*person*) faire frissonner; (*wine*) rafraîchir; (*food*) mettre à refroidir.

chilli *n* (*pl* ~**es**) piment *m*.

chilly *a* froid; **it's** ~ il fait froid.

chime *n* carillon *m*. ● *vt/i* carillonner.

chimney *n* cheminée *f*. ~**-sweep** *n* ramoneur *m*.

chimpanzee *n* chimpanzé *m*.

chin *n* menton *m*.

china *n* porcelaine *f*.

China *n* Chine *f*.

Chinese *n* (person) Chinois/-e *m/f*; (Ling) chinois *m*. ● *a* chinois.

chip *n* (on plate) ébréchure *f*; (piece) éclat *m*; (of wood) copeau *m*; (Culin) frite *f*; (Comput) puce *f*; (**potato**) ~**s** (US) chips *fpl*. ● *vt/i* (*pt* **chipped**) (s')ébrécher; ~ **in** ▣ dire son mot; (with money) contribuer.

chiropodist *n* pédicure *mf*.

chirp *n* pépiement *m*. ● *vi* pépier. **chirpy** *a* gai.

chisel n ciseau m. ● vt (pt **chiselled**) ciseler.

chit n note f; (voucher) bon m.

chitchat n ▯ bavardage m.

chivalrous a galant.

chives npl ciboulette f.

chlorine n chlore m.

choc-ice n esquimau m.

chock-a-block a plein à craquer.

chocolate n chocolat m.

choice n choix m. ● a de choix.

choir n chœur m. ~**boy** n jeune choriste m.

choke vt/i (s')étrangler; ~ (**up**) boucher. ● n starter m.

cholesterol n cholestérol m.

choose vt/i (pt **chose**; pp **chosen**) choisir; ~ **to do** décider de faire. **choosy** a difficile.

chop vt/i (pt **chopped**) (wood) couper; (food) hacher; **chopping board** planche f à découper; ~ **down** abattre. ● n (meat) côtelette f. **chopper** n hachoir m; ▯ hélico m ▯.

choppy a (sea) agité.

chopstick n baguette f (chinoise).

chord n (Mus) accord m.

chore n (routine) tâche f; (unpleasant) corvée f.

chortle n gloussement m. ● vi glousser.

chorus n chœur m; (of song) refrain m.

chose, chosen ⇒CHOOSE.

Christ n le Christ.

christen vt baptiser. **christening** n baptême m.

Christian a & n chrétien/-ne (m/f); ~ **name** nom m de baptême. **Christianity** n christianisme m.

Christmas n Noël m; ~ **Day/Eve** le jour/la veille de Noël. ● a (card, tree) de Noël.

chronic a (situation, disease) chronique; (bad ▯) nul.

chronicle n chronique f.

chronological a chronologique.

chrysanthemum n chrysanthème m.

chubby a (-ier, -iest) potelé.

chuck vt ▯ lancer; ~ **away** or **out** ▯ balancer.

chuckle n gloussement m. ● vi glousser.

chuffed a ▯ vachement content ▯.

chunk n morceau m. **chunky** a (sweater, jewellery) gros; (person) costaud.

church n église f. ~**goer** n pratiquant/-e m/f. ~**yard** n cimetière m.

churn n baratte f; (milk-can) bidon m. ● vt baratter; ~ **out** produire en série.

chute n toboggan m; (for rubbish) vide-ordures m inv.

chutney n condiment m aigre-doux.

cider n cidre m.

cigar n cigare m.

cigarette n cigarette f; ~ **end** mégot m.

cinder n cendre f.

cinema n cinéma m.

cinnamon n cannelle f.

circle n cercle m; (Theat) balcon m. ● vt (go round) tourner autour de; (word, error) encercler. ● vi tourner en rond.

circuit n circuit m. ~ **board** carte f de circuit imprimé. ~**breaker** n disjoncteur m.

circuitous a indirect.

circular a & n circulaire (f).

circulate vt/i (faire) circuler. **circulation** n circulation f; (of newspaper) tirage m.

circumcise vt circoncire.

circumference *n* circonférence *f*.

circumflex *n* circonflexe *m*.

circumstance *n* circonstance *f*; ~**s** (financial) situation *f*; **under no** ~**s** en aucun cas.

circus *n* cirque *m*.

cistern *n* réservoir *m*.

citizen *n* citoyen/-ne *m/f*; (of town) habitant/-e *m/f*. **citizenship** *n* nationalité *f*.

citrus *a* ~ **fruit(s)** agrumes *mpl*; ~ **tree** citrus *m*.

city *n* (grande) ville *f*.

civic *a* (official) municipal; (pride, duty) civique.

civil *a* civil. ~ **disobedience** *n* résistance *f* passive. ~ **engineer** *n* ingénieur *m* des travaux publics.

civilian *a* & *n* civil/-e (*m/f*).

civilization *n* civilisation *f*. **civilize** *vt* civiliser.

civil: ~ **law** *n* droit *m* civil. ~ **liberties** *npl* libertés *fpl* individuelles. ~ **rights** *npl* droits *mpl* civils. ~ **servant** *n* fonctionnaire *mf*. ~ **service** *n* fonction *f* publique. ~ **war** *n* guerre *f* civile.

claim *vt* (demand) revendiquer; (assert) prétendre. ● *n* revendication *f*; (assertion) affirmation *f*; (for insurance) réclamation *f*; (right) droit *m*. **claimant** *n* (of benefits) demandeur/-euse *m/f*.

clairvoyant *n* voyant/-e *m/f*.

clam *n* palourde *f*.

clamber *vi* grimper.

clammy *a* (-ier, -iest) moite.

clamour *n* clameur *f*. ● *vi* ~ **for** réclamer.

clamp *n* valet *m*; (Med) pince *f*; (wheel) ~ sabot *m* de Denver. ● *vt*

cramponner; (jaw) serrer; (car) mettre un sabot de Denver à; ~ **down on** faire de la répression contre.

clan *n* clan *m*.

clang *n* son *m* métallique.

clap *vt/i* (*pt* **clapped**) applaudir; (put forcibly) mettre; ~ **one's hands** frapper dans ses mains. ● *n* applaudissement *m*; (of thunder) coup *m*.

claret *n* bordeaux *m* rouge.

clarification *n* clarification *f*. **clarify** *vt/i* (se) clarifier.

clarinet *n* clarinette *f*.

clarity *n* clarté *f*.

clash *n* choc *m*; (fig) conflit *m*. ● *vi* (metal objects) s'entrechoquer; (armies) s'affronter; (meetings) avoir lieu en même temps; (colours) jurer.

clasp *n* (fastener) fermoir *m*. ● *vt* serrer.

class *n* classe *f*. ● *vt* classer; ~ **sb/sth as** assimiler qn/qch à.

classic *a* & *n* classique (*m*); ~**s** (Univ) lettres *fpl* classiques. **classical** *a* classique.

classified *a* (information) secret; ~ (**ad**) petite annonce *f*.

classroom *n* salle *f* de classe.

clatter *n* cliquetis *m*. ● *vi* cliqueter.

clause *n* clause *f*; (Gram) proposition *f*.

claw *n* (of animal, small bird) griffe *f*; (of bird of prey) serre *f*; (of lobster) pince *f*. ● *vt* griffer.

clay *n* argile *f*.

clean *a* propre; (shape, stroke) net. ● *adv* complètement. ● *vt* nettoyer; ~ **one's teeth** se brosser les dents. ● *vi* ~ **up** faire le nettoyage. **cleaner** *n* (at home) femme *f* de ménage; (industrial) agent *m* de nettoyage; (of clothes)

teinturier/-ière *m/f*. **cleanliness**
n propreté *f*. **cleanly** *adv*
proprement; (*sharply*) nettement.
cleanse *vt* nettoyer; (*fig*) purifier.
clean-shaven *a* glabre.
clear *a* (*explanation*) clair; (*need,
sign*) évident; (*glass*) transparent;
(*profit*) net; (*road*) dégagé; **make
sth** ~ être très clair sur qch; ~ **of**
(*away from*) à l'écart de. ● *adv*
complètement; **stand** ~ **of**
s'éloigner de. ● *vt* (*free*) dégager
(*of* de); (*table*) débarrasser;
(*building*) évacuer; (*cheque*)
compenser; (*jump over*) franchir;
(*debt*) liquider; (Jur) disculper.
● *vi* (*fog*) se dissiper; (*cheque*)
être compensé. □ ~ **away** *or* **off**
(*remove*) enlever; ~ **off** *or* **out**
Ⓘ décamper; ~ **out** (*clean*)
nettoyer; ~ **up** (*tidy*) ranger;
(*weather*) s'éclaircir.
clearance *n* (*permission*)
autorisation *f*; (*space*) espace *m*;
~ **sale** liquidation *f*.
clear-cut *a* net.
clearing *n* clairière *f*.
clearly *adv* clairement.
clef *n* (Mus) clé *f*.
cleft *n* fissure *f*.
clench *vt* serrer.
clergy *n* clergé *m*. ~**man** *n* (*pl*
-men) ecclésiastique *m*.
cleric *n* clerc *m*. **clerical** *a* (Relig)
clérical; (*staff, work*) de bureau.
clerk *n* employé/-e *m/f* de
bureau; (US) (**sales**) ~ vendeur/
-euse *m/f*.
clever *a* intelligent; (*skilful*) habile.
click *n* déclic *m*; (Comput) clic *m*.
● *vi* faire un déclic; (*people* Ⓘ)
sympathiser; (Comput) cliquer (**on**
sur). ● *vt* (*heels, tongue*) faire
claquer.
client *n* client/-e *m/f*.
clientele *n* clientèle *f*.
cliff *n* falaise *f*.
climate *n* climat *m*.

climax *n* (*of story, contest*) point *m*
culminant; (*sexual*) orgasme *m*.
climb *vt* grimper; (*steps*) monter;
(*tree, ladder*) grimper à;
(*mountain*) faire l'ascension de.
● *vi* grimper; ~ **into** (*car*) monter
dans; ~ **into bed** se mettre au lit.
● *n* (*of mountain*) escalade *f*; (*steep
hill, rise*) montée *f*. □ ~ **down** (fig)
reculer. **climber** *n* (Sport)
alpiniste *mf*.
clinch *vt* (*deal*) conclure; (*victory,
order*) décrocher.
cling *vi* (*pt* **clung**) se
cramponner (**to** à); (*stick*) coller.
~**-film** *n* scellofrais® *m*.
clinic *n* centre *m* médical; (*private*)
clinique *f*. **clinical** *a* clinique.
clink *n* tintement *m*. ● *vt/i* (faire)
tinter.
clip *n* (*for paper*) trombone *m*; (*for
hair*) barrette *f*; (*for tube*) collier *m*;
(*of film*) extrait *m*. ● *vt* (*pt*
clipped) (*fasten*) attacher (**to** à);
(*cut*) couper.
clippers *npl* tondeuse *f*; (*for nails*)
coupe-ongles *m inv*.
clipping *n* (*from press*) coupure *f*
de presse.
cloak *n* cape *f*; (*man's*)
houppelande *f*. ~**room** *n*
vestiaire *m*; (*toilet*) toilettes *fpl*.
clobber *n* Ⓘ attirail *m*. ● *vt* (hlt Ⓘ)
tabasser Ⓘ.
clock *n* pendule *f*; (*large*) horloge
f. ● *vi* ~ **on/in** *or* **off/out** pointer;
~ **up** (*miles*) faire. ~**-tower** *n*
beffroi *m*. ~**wise** *a & adv* dans le
sens des aiguilles d'une montre.
clockwork *n* mécanisme *m*. ● *a*
mécanique.
clog *n* sabot *m*. ● *vt/i* (*pt*
clogged) (se) boucher.
cloister *n* cloître *m*.
clone *n* clone *m*. ● *vt* cloner.
close[1] *a* (*friend, relative*) proche
(**to** de); (*link, collaboration*) étroit;
(*examination*) minutieux; (*result,
match*) serré; (*weather*) lourd; ~

together (crowded) serrés; ~ **by**, ~
at hand tout près; **have a ~ shave**
l'échapper belle; **keep a ~ watch**
on surveiller de près. ● *adv* près.
● *n* (street) impasse *f*.

close² *vt* fermer; (*meeting, case*)
mettre fin à. ● *vi* se fermer;
(*shop*) fermer; (*meeting, play*)
prendre fin. ● *n* fin *f*.

closely *adv* (follow) de près.
closeness *n* proximité *f*.

closet *n* (US) placard *m*.

close-up *n* gros plan *m*.

closure *n* fermeture *f*.

clot *n* (of blood) caillot *m*; (in sauce)
grumeau *m*. ● *vt/i* (*pt* **clotted**)
(se) coaguler.

cloth *n* (fabric) tissu *m*; (duster)
chiffon *m*; (table-cloth) nappe *f*.

clothe *vt* vêtir.

clothes *npl* vêtements *mpl*.
~-**hanger** *n* cintre *m*. ~-**line** *n*
corde *f* à linge.

clothing *n* vêtements *mpl*.

cloud *n* nuage *m*. ● *vi* ~ (**over**) se
couvrir (de nuages); (*face*)
s'assombrir. **cloudy** *a* (*sky*)
couvert; (*liquid*) trouble.

clout *n* (blow) coup *m* de poing;
(power) influence *f*. ● *vt* frapper.

clove *n* clou *m* de girofle; ~ **of**
garlic gousse *f* d'ail.

clover *n* trèfle *m*.

clown *n* clown *m*. ● *vi* faire le
clown.

club *n* (group) club *m*; (weapon)
massue *f*; (**golf**) ~ **club** *m* (de
golf); ~**s** (cards) trèfle *m*. ● *vt/i*
(*pt* **clubbed**) matraquer. □ ~
together cotiser.

cluck *vi* glousser.

clue *n* indice *m*; (in crossword)
définition *f*; **I haven't a ~** 🖾 je
n'en ai pas la moindre idée.

clump *n* massif *m*.

clumsy *a* (**-ier**, **-iest**) maladroit;
(*tool*) peu commode.

clung ⇒CLING.

cluster *n* (of people, islands) groupe
m; (of flowers, berries) grappe *f*. ● *vi*
se grouper.

clutch *vt* (hold) serrer fort; (grasp)
saisir. ● *vi* ~ **at** (try to grasp)
essayer de saisir. ● *n* (Auto)
embrayage *m*; (of eggs) couveé *f*;
(of people) groupe *m*.

clutter *n* désordre *m*. ● *vt* ~ (**up**)
encombrer.

coach *n* autocar *m*; (of train)
wagon *m*; (horse-drawn) carrosse *m*;
(Sport) entraîneur/-euse *m/f*. ● *vt*
(*team*) entraîner; (*pupil*) donner
des leçons particulières à.

coal *n* charbon *m*. ~-**field** *n*
bassin *m* houiller. ~-**mine** *n*
mine *f* de charbon.

coarse *a* grossier.

coast *n* côte *f*. ● *vi* (car, bicycle)
descendre en roue libre. **coastal**
a côtier.

coast: ~-**guard** *n* (person)
gardecôte *m*; (organization)
gendarmerie *f* maritime. ~-**line** *n*
littoral *m*.

coat *n* manteau *m*; (of animal)
pelage *m*; (of paint) couche *f*; ~ **of**
arms armoiries *fpl*. ● *vt* enduire,
couvrir; (with chocolate) enrober
(with de). **coating** *n* couche *f*.

coax *vt* cajoler.

cob *n* (of corn) épi *m*.

cobbler *n* cordonnier *m*.

cobblestones *npl* pavés *mpl*.

cobweb *n* toile *f* d'araignée.

cocaine *n* cocaïne *f*.

cock *n* (rooster) coq *m*; (oiseau)
mâle *m*. ● *vt* (*gun*) armer; (*ears*)
dresser.

cockerel *n* jeune coq *m*.

cockle *n* (Culin) coque *f*.

cock: ~-**pit** *n* poste *m* de pilotage.
~-**roach** *n* cafard *m*. ~-**tail** *n*
cocktail *m*.

cocky a (**-ier, -iest**) trop sûr de soi.

cocoa n cacao m.

coconut n noix f de coco.

COD abbr (**cash on delivery**) envoi m contre remboursement.

cod n inv morue f; ~**-liver oil** huile f de foie de morue.

code n code m. ● vt coder.

coerce vt contraindre.

coexist vi coexister.

coffee n café m. ~ **bar** n café m. ~ **bean** n grain m de café. ~**-pot** n cafetière f. ~**-table** n table f basse.

coffin n cercueil m.

cog n pignon m; (fig) rouage m.

cognac n cognac m.

coil vt/i (s')enrouler. ● n (of rope) rouleau m; (of snake) anneau m; (contraceptive) stérilet m.

coin n pièce f (de monnaie). ● vt (word) inventer.

coincide vi coïncider. **coincidence** n coïncidence f. **coincidental** a dû à une coïncidence.

colander n passoire f.

cold a froid; (person) be or feel ~ avoir froid; **it is** ~ il fait froid; **get** ~ **feet** avoir les jetons 🄸; ~**-blooded** (lit) à sang froid; (fig) sans pitié. ● n froid m; (Med) rhume m; ~ **sore** bouton m de fièvre. **coldness** n froideur f.

coleslaw n salade f de chou cru.

colic n coliques fpl.

collaborate vi collaborer.

collapse vi s'effondrer; (person) s'écrouler; (fold) se plier. ● n effondrement m.

collar n col m; (of dog) collier m. ~**-bone** n clavicule f.

collateral n nantissement m.

colleague n collègue mf.

collect vt rassembler; (pick up) ramasser; (call for) passer prendre; (money, fare) encaisser; (taxes, rent) percevoir; (as hobby) collectionner. ● vi se rassembler; (dust) s'amasser. ● adv **call** ~ (US) appeler en PCV. **collection** n collection f; (of money) collecte f; (in church) quête f; (of mail) levée f.

collective a collectif.

collector n (as hobby) collectionneur/-euse m/f; (of taxes) percepteur m; (of rent, debt) encaisseur m.

college n (for higher education) établissement m d'enseignement supérieur; (within university) collège m; **be at** ~ faire des études supérieures.

collide vi entrer en collision (with avec).

colliery n houillère f.

collision n collision f.

colloquial a familier. **colloquialism** n expression f familière.

Colombia n Colombie f.

colon n (Gram) deux-points m inv; (Anat) côlon m.

colonel n colonel m.

colonial a & n colonial/-e (m/f).

colour, (US) **color** n couleur f; ~**-blind** daltonien. ● a (photo) en couleur; (TV set) couleur inv. ● vt colorer; (with crayon) colorier. **coloured** a de couleur. **colourful** a aux couleurs vives; (fig) haut en couleur. **colouring** n (of skin) teint m; (in food) colorant m.

colt n poulain m.

column n colonne f.

coma n coma m.

comb n peigne m. ● vt peigner; ~ **one's hair** se peigner; ~ **a place** passer un lieu au peigne fin.

combat n combat m. ● vt (pt **combated**) combattre.

combination n combinaison f.

combine[1] *vt/i* (se) combiner, (s')unir.

combine[2] *n* (Comm) groupe *m*; ∼ (**harvester**) moissonneuse-batteuse *f*.

come *vi* (*pt* **came**; *pp* **come**) venir; (*bus, letter*) arriver; (*postman*) passer; ∼ **and look!** viens voir!; ∼ **in** (*size, colour*) exister en; **when it** ∼**s to** lorsqu'il s'agit de. □ ∼ **about** survenir; ∼ **across** (*meaning*) passer; ∼ **across sth** tomber sur qch; ∼ **away** (*leave*) partir; (*come off*) se détacher; ∼ **back** revenir; ∼ **by** obtenir; ∼ **down** descendre; (*price*) baisser; ∼ **forward** se présenter; ∼ **in** entrer; ∼ **in useful** être utile; ∼ **in for** recevoir; ∼ **into** (*money*) hériter de; ∼ **off** (*succeed*) réussir; (*fare*) s'en tirer; (*detach*) se détacher; ∼ **on** (*actor*) entrer en scène; (*light*) s'allumer; (*improve*) faire des progrès; ∼ **on!** allez!; ∼ **out** sortir; ∼ **round** reprendre connaissance; (*change mind*) changer d'avis; ∼ **through** s'en tirer; ∼ **to** reprendre connaissance; ∼ **to sth** (*amount*) revenir à qch; (*decision, conclusion*) arriver à qch; ∼ **up** (*problem*) être soulevé; (*opportunity*) se présenter; (*sun*) se lever; ∼ **up against** se heurter à; ∼ **up with** trouver.

comedian *n* comique *m*.

comedy *n* comédie *f*.

comfort *n* confort *m*; (*consolation*) réconfort *m*. ●*vt* consoler. **comfortable** *a* (*chair, car*) confortable; (*person*) à l'aise; (*wealthy*) aisé.

comfortably *adv* confortablement; ∼ **off** aisé.

comfy *a* ⊞ = COMFORTABLE.

comic *a* comique. ●*n* (*person*)

comique *m*; ∼ (**book**), ∼ **strip** bande *f* dessinée.

coming *n* arrivée *f*; ∼**s and goings** allées et venues *fpl*. ●*a* à venir.

comma *n* virgule *f*.

command *n* (*authority*) commandement *m*; (*order*) ordre *m*; (*mastery*) maîtrise *f*. ●*vt* ordonner à (**to do** de faire); (*be able to use*) disposer de; (*respect*) inspirer. **commandeer** *vt* réquisitionner. **commander** *n* commandant *m*. **commanding** *a* imposant. **commandment** *n* commandement *m*.

commando *n* commando *m*.

commemorate *vt* commémorer.

commence *vt/i* commencer.

commend *vt* (*praise*) louer; (*entrust*) confier.

commensurate *a* proportionné.

comment *n* commentaire *m*. ●*vi* faire des commentaires; ∼ **on** commenter. **commentary** *n* commentaire *m*; (*radio, TV*) reportage *m*. **commentate** *vi* faire un reportage. **commentator** *n* commentateur/-trice *m/f*.

commerce *n* commerce *m*.

commercial *a* commercial; (*traveller*) de commerce. ●*n* publicité *f*.

commiserate *vi* compatir (**with** avec).

commission *n* commission *f*; (*order for work*) commande *f*; **out of** ∼ hors service. ●*vt* (*order*) commander; (Mil) nommer officier; ∼ **to do** charger de faire. **commissioner** *n* préfet *m* (de police); (*in EC*) membre *m* de la Commission européenne.

commit *vt* (*pt* **committed**) commettre; (*entrust*) confier; ∼ **oneself** s'engager; ∼ **perjury** se parjurer; ∼ **suicide** se suicider; ∼

to memory apprendre par cœur.
commitment n engagement m.
committee n comité m.
commodity n article m.
common a (shared by all) commun
(to à); (usual) courant; (vulgar)
vulgaire, commun; **in ~** en
commun; **~ people** le peuple; **~
sense** bon sens m. ●n terrain m
communal; **the C~s** Chambre f
des Communes.
commoner n roturier/-ière m/f.
common law n droit m
coutumier.
commonly adv communément.
commonplace a banal. ●n
banalité f.
common-room n salle f de
détente.
Commonwealth n **the ~** le
Commonwealth m.
commotion n (noise) vacarme m;
(disturbance) agitation f.
communal a (shared) commun;
(life) collectif.
commune n (group) communauté
f.
communicate vt/i
communiquer. **communication** n
communication f.
communicative a communicatif.
communion n communion f.
Communism n communisme m.
Communist a & n communiste
(mf).
community n communauté f.
commute vi faire la navette. ●vt
(Jur) commuer. **commuter** n
navetteur/-euse m/f.
compact a compact; (lady's case)
poudrier m.
compact disc n disque m
compact. **~ player** n platine f
laser.
companion n compagnon/-agne
m/f. **companionship** n
camaraderie f.

company n (companionship, firm)
compagnie f; (guests) invités/-es
m/fpl.
comparative a (study, form)
comparatif; (comfort) relatif.
compare vt comparer (with, to à);
~d with par rapport à. ●vi être
comparable. **comparison** n
comparaison f.
compartment n compartiment
m.
compass n (for direction) boussole
f; (scope) portée f; **a pair of ~es**
compas m.
compassionate a compatissant.
compatible a compatible.
compel vt (pt **compelled**)
contraindre. **compelling** a
irrésistible.
compensate vt/i (financially)
dédommager (for de); **~ for sth**
compenser qch. **compensation** n
compensation f; (financial)
dédommagement m
compete vi concourir; **~ with**
rivaliser avec.
competent a compétent.
competition n (contest) concours
m; (Sport) compétition f; (Comm)
concurrence f.
competitive a (prices)
compétitif; (person) qui a l'esprit
de compétition.
competitor n concurrent/-e m/f.
compile vt (list) dresser; (book)
rédiger.
complacency n suffisance f.
complain vi se plaindre (about, of
de). **complaint** n plainte f; (official)
réclamation f; (illness) maladie f.
complement n complément m.
●vt compléter. **complementary**
a complémentaire.
complete a complet; (finished)
achevé; (downright) parfait. ●vt
achever; (a form) remplir.
completely adv complètement.
completion n achèvement m.

complex *a* complexe. ●*n* (Psych) complexe *m*.

complexion *n* (of face) teint *m*; (fig) caractère *m*.

compliance *n* (agreement) conformité *f*.

complicate *vt* compliquer. **complicated** *a* compliqué. **complication** *n* complication *f*.

compliment *n* compliment *m*. ●*vt* complimenter. **complimentary** *a* (offert) à titre gracieux; (praising) flatteur.

comply *vi* ~ **with** se conformer à, obéir à.

component *n* (of machine) pièce *f*; (chemical substance) composant *m*; (element: fig) composante *f*. ●*a* constituant.

compose *vt* composer; ~ **oneself** se calmer. **composed** *a* calme. **composer** *n* (Mus) compositeur *m*. **composition** *n* composition *f*.

composure *n* calme *m*.

compound *n* (substance, word) composé *m*; (enclosure) enclos *m*. ●*a* composé.

comprehend *vt* comprendre. **comprehension** *n* compréhension *f*.

comprehensive *a* étendu, complet; (*insurance*) tous risques *inv*. ~ **school** *n* collège *m* d'enseignement secondaire.

compress *vt* comprimer.

comprise *vt* comprendre, inclure.

compromise *n* compromis *m*. ●*vt* compromettre. ●*vi* transiger, arriver à un compromis.

compulsive *a* (Psych) compulsif; (*liar, smoker*) invétéré.

compulsory *a* obligatoire.

computer *n* ordinateur *m*; ~ **science** informatique *f*. **computerize** *vt* informatiser.

comrade *n* camarade *mf*.

con¹ *vt* (*pt* **conned**) 🅺 rouler 🅳, escroquer (**out of** de). ●*n* 🅺 escroquerie *f*.

con² ⇒PRO.

conceal *vt* dissimuler (**from** à).

concede *vt* concéder. ●*vi* céder.

conceited *a* vaniteux.

conceive *vt/i* concevoir; ~ **of** concevoir.

concentrate *vt/i* (se) concentrer. **concentration** *n* concentration *f*.

concept *n* concept *m*.

conception *n* conception *f*.

concern *n* (interest, business) affaire *f*; (worry) inquiétude *f*; (firm: Comm) entreprise *f*, affaire *f*. ●*vt* concerner; ~ **oneself with**, **be** ~**ed with** s'occuper de. **concerned** *a* inquiet. **concerning** *prep* en ce qui concerne.

concert *n* concert *m*.

concession *n* concession *f*.

conciliation *n* conciliation *f*.

concise *a* concis.

conclude *vt* conclure. ●*vi* se terminer. **conclusion** *n* conclusion *f*. **conclusive** *a* concluant.

concoct *vt* confectionner; (invent: fig) fabriquer. **concoction** *n* mélange *m*.

concourse *n* (Rail) hall *m*.

concrete *n* béton *m*. ●*a* de béton; (fig) concret. ●*vt* bétonner.

concur *vi* (*pt* **concurred**) être d'accord.

concurrently *adv* simultanément.

concussion *n* commotion *f* (cérébrale).

condemn *vt* condamner.

condensation *n* (on walls) condensation *f*; (on windows) buée *f*. **condense** *vt/i* (se) condenser.

condition *n* condition *f*; **on** ~ **that** à condition que. ●*vt* conditionner. **conditional** a conditionnel.

conditioner n après-shampooing m.

condolences npl condoléances fpl.

condom n préservatif m.

condone vt pardonner, fermer les yeux sur.

conducive a ~ to favorable à.

conduct[1] n conduite f.

conduct[2] vt conduire; (orchestra) diriger. **conductor** n chef m d'orchestre; (of bus) receveur m; (on train: US) chef m de train; (Electr) conducteur m. **conductress** n receveuse f.

cone n cône m; (of ice-cream) cornet m.

confectioner n confiseur/-euse m/f. **confectionery** n confiserie f.

confer vt/i (pt **conferred**) conférer.

conference n conférence f.

confess vt/i avouer; (Relig) (se) confesser. **confession** n confession f; (of crime) aveu m.

confide vt confier. ● vi ~ in se confier à.

confidence n (trust) confiance f; (boldness) confiance f en soi; (secret) confidence f; in ~ en confidence. **confident** a sûr.

confidential a confidentiel.

confine vt enfermer; (limit) limiter; ~d space espace m réduit; ~d to limité à.

confirm vt confirmer. **confirmed** a (bachelor) endurci; (smoker) invétéré.

confiscate vt confisquer.

conflict[1] n conflit m.

conflict[2] vi (statements, views) être en contradiction (with avec); (appointments) tomber en même temps (with que). **conflicting** a contradictoire.

conform vt/i (se) conformer.

confound vt confondre.

confront vt affronter; ~ with confronter avec.

confuse vt (bewilder) troubler; (mistake, confound) confondre; **become** ~d s'embrouiller; **I am** ~d je m'y perds. **confusing** a déroutant. **confusion** n confusion f.

congeal vt/i (se) figer.

congested a (road) embouteillé; (passage) encombré; (Med) congestionné. **congestion** n (traffic) encombrement(s) m(pl); (Med) congestion f.

congratulate vt féliciter (on de). **congratulations** npl félicitations fpl.

congregate vi se rassembler. **congregation** n assemblée f.

congress n congrès m; C~ (US) le Congrès.

conjugate vt conjuguer. **conjugation** n conjugaison f.

conjunction n (Ling) conjonction f; in ~ with conjointement avec.

conjunctivitis n conjonctivite f.

conjure vi faire des tours de passe-passe. ● vt ~ up faire apparaître. **conjuror** n prestidigitateur/-trice m/f.

con man n ▣ escroc m.

connect vt/i (se) relier; (in mind) faire le rapport entre; (install, wire up to mains) brancher; ~ with (of train) assurer la correspondance avec; ~ed (idea, event) lié; **be** ~ed with avoir rapport à.

connection n rapport m; (Rail) correspondance f; (phone call) communication f; (Electr) contact m; (joining piece) raccord m; ~s (Comm) relations fpl.

connive vi ~ at se faire le complice de.

conquer vt vaincre; (country) conquérir. **conqueror** n conquérant m.

conquest n conquête f.

conscience n conscience f. **conscientious** a consciencieux.

conscious a conscient; (deliberate) voulu. **consciously** adv consciemment. **consciousness** n conscience f; (Med) connaissance f.

conscript n appelé m.

consecutive a consécutif.

consensus n consensus m.

consent vi consentir (**to** à). ● n consentement m.

consequence n conséquence f. **consequently** adv par conséquent.

conservation n préservation f; ~ **area** zone f protégée. **conservationist** n défenseur m de l'environnement.

conservative a conservateur; (estimate) minimal.

Conservative Party n parti m conservateur.

conservatory n (greenhouse) serre f; (room) véranda f.

conserve vt conserver; (energy) économiser.

consider vt considérer; (allow for) tenir compte de; (possibility) envisager (**doing** de faire).

considerable a considérable; (much) beaucoup de.

considerate a prévenant, attentionné. **consideration** n considération f; (respect) égard(s) m(pl).

considering prep compte tenu de.

consignment n envoi m.

consist vi consister (**of** en; **in doing** à faire).

consistency n (of liquids) consistance f; (of argument) cohérence f.

consistent a cohérent; ~ **with** conforme à.

consolation n consolation f.

consolidate vt/i (se) consolider.

consonant n consonne f.

conspicuous a (easily seen) en évidence; (showy) voyant; (noteworthy) remarquable.

conspiracy n conspiration f.

constable n agent m de police, gendarme m.

constant a (questions) incessant; (unchanging) constant; (friend) fidèle. ● n constante f. **constantly** adv constamment.

constellation n constellation f.

constipation n constipation f.

constituency n circonscription f électorale.

constituent a constitutif. ● n élément m constitutif; (Pol) électeur/-trice m/f.

constitution n constitution f.

constrain vt contraindre. **constraint** n contrainte f.

constrict vt (flow) comprimer; (movement) gêner.

construct vt construire. **construction** n construction f. **constructive** a constructif.

consulate n consulat m.

consult vt consulter. ● vi ~ **with** conférer avec. **consultant** n conseiller/-ère m/f; (Med) spécialiste mf. **consultation** n consultation f.

consume vt consommer; (destroy) consumer. **consumer** n consommateur/-trice m/f.

consummate vt consommer.

consumption n consommation f; (Med) phtisie f.

contact n contact m; (person) relation f. ● vt contacter. ~

lenses *npl* lentilles *fpl* (de contact).

contagious *a* contagieux.

contain *vt* contenir; ~ **oneself** se contenir. **container** *n* récipient *m*; (for transport) container *m*.

contaminate *vt* contaminer.

contemplate *vt* (gaze at) contempler; (think about) envisager.

contemporary *a* & *n* contemporain/-e (*m/f*).

contempt *n* mépris *m*. **contemptible** *a* méprisable. **contemptuous** *a* méprisant.

contend *vt* soutenir. ● *vi* ~ **with** (compete) rivaliser avec; (face) faire face à. **contender** *n* adversaire *mf*.

content[1] *n* (of letter) contenu *m*; (amount) teneur *f*. ~**s** contenu *m*.

content[2] *a* satisfait. ● *vt* contenter. **contented** *a* satisfait. **contentment** *n* contentement *m*.

contest[1] *n* (competition) concours *m*; (struggle) lutte *f*.

contest[2] *vt* contester; (compete for or in) disputer. **contestant** *n* concurrent/-e *m/f*.

context *n* contexte *m*.

continent *n* continent *m*; **the C~** l'Europe *f* (continentale). **continental** *a* continental, européen. **continental quilt** *n* couette *f*.

contingency *n* éventualité *f*; ~ **plan** plan *m* d'urgence.

continual *a* continuel.

continuation *n* continuation *f*; (after interruption) reprise *f*; (new episode) suite *f*.

continue *vt/i* continuer; (resume) reprendre. **continued** *a* continu.

continuous *a* continu. **continuously** *adv* (without a break) sans interruption; (repeatedly) continuellement.

contort *vt* tordre; ~ **oneself** se contorsionner.

contour *n* contour *m*.

contraband *n* contrebande *f*.

contraception *n* contraception *f*. **contraceptive** *a* & *n* contraceptif (*m*).

contract[1] *n* contrat *m*.

contract[2] *vt/i* (se) contracter. **contraction** *n* contraction *f*.

contractor *n* entrepreneur/-euse *m/f*.

contradict *vt* contredire. **contradictory** *a* contradictoire.

contrary[1] *a* contraire (**to** à). ● *n* contraire *m*; **on the ~** au contraire. ● *adv* ~ **to** contrairement à.

contrary[2] *a* entêté.

contrast[1] *n* contraste *m*.

contrast[2] *vt/i* contraster.

contravention *n* infraction *f*.

contribute *vt* donner. ● *vi* ~ **to** contribuer à; (take part) participer à; (newspaper) collaborer à. **contribution** *n* contribution *f*. **contributor** *n* collaborateur/ -trice *m/f*.

contrive *vt* imaginer; ~ **to do** trouver moyen de faire.

control *vt* (*pt* **controlled**) (firm) diriger; (check) contrôler; (restrain) maîtriser. ● *n* contrôle *m*; (mastery) maîtrise *f*; ~**s** commandes *fpl*; (knobs) boutons *mpl*; **have under ~** (event) avoir en main; **in ~ of** maître de. ~ **tower** *n* tour *f* de contrôle.

controversial *a* discutable, discuté. **controversy** *n* controverse *f*.

conurbation *n* agglomération *f*, conurbation *f*.

convalesce *vi* être en convalescence.

convene *vt* convoquer. ● *vi* se réunir.

convenience *n* commodité *f;* ~s toilettes *fpl;* all modern ~s tout le confort moderne; at your ~ quand cela vous conviendra, à votre convenance. ~ foods *npl* plats *mpl* tout préparés.

convenient *a* commode, pratique; *(time)* bien choisi; be ~ for convenir à.

convent *n* couvent *m.*

convention *n* (assembly, agreement) convention *f;* (custom) usage *m.* **conventional** *a* conventionnel.

conversation *n* conversation *f.* **conversational** *a* (tone) de la conversation; *(French)* de tous les jours.

converse¹ *vi* s'entretenir, converser (with avec).

converse² *a* & *n* inverse (*m*). **conversely** *adv* inversement.

conversion *n* conversion *f.*

convert¹ *vt* convertir; *(house)* aménager. ● *vi* ~ into se transformer en.

convert² *n* converti/-e *m/f.*

convertible *a* convertible. ● *n* (car) décapotable *f.*

convey *vt* (wishes, order) transmettre; *(goods, people)* transporter; *(idea, feeling)* communiquer. **conveyor belt** *n* tapis *m* roulant.

convict¹ *vt* déclarer coupable.

convict² *n* prisonnier/-ière *m/f.*

conviction *n* (Jur) condamnation *f;* (opinion) conviction *f.*

convince *vt* convaincre.

convoke *vt* convoquer.

convoy *n* convoi *m.*

convulse *vt* convulser; (fig) bouleverser; be ~d with laughter se tordre de rire.

cook *vt/i* (faire) cuire; (of person) faire la cuisine; ~ up 🔲 fabriquer. ● *n* cuisinier/-ière

m/f. **cooker** *n* (stove) cuisinière *f.* **cookery** *n* cuisine *f.*

cookie *n* (US) biscuit *m.*

cooking *n* cuisine *f.* ● *a* de cuisine.

cool *a* frais; (calm) calme; (unfriendly) froid. ● *n* fraîcheur *f;* (calmness 🔲) sang-froid *m;* in the ~ au frais. ● *vt/i* rafraîchir. ~ box *n* glacière *f.*

coolly *adv* calmement; froidement.

coop *n* poulailler *m.* ● *vt* ~ up enfermer.

co-operate *vi* coopérer.

co-operation *n* coopération *f.*

co-operative *a* coopératif. ● *n* coopérative *f.*

co-ordinate *vt* coordonner.

cop *vt* (*pt* copped) 🔲 piquer. ● *n* (policeman 🔲) flic *m.* □ ~ out 🔲 se dérober.

cope *vi* s'en sortir 🔲, se débrouiller; ~ with (problem) faire face à.

copper *n* cuivre *m;* (coin) sou *m;* 🔲 flic *m.* ● *a* de cuivre.

copulate *vi* s'accoupler.

copy *n* copie *f;* (of book, newspaper) exemplaire *m;* (print: Photo) épreuve *f.* ● *vt/i* copier.

copyright *n* droit *m* d'auteur, copyright *m.*

copy-writer *n* rédacteur-concepteur *m,* rédactrice-conceptrice *f.*

cord *n* (petite) corde *f;* (of curtain, pyjamas) cordon *m;* (Electr) cordon *m* électrique; (fabric) velours *m* côtelé.

cordial *a* cordial. ● *n* (drink) sirop *m.*

corduroy *n* velours *m* côtelé.

core *n* (of apple) trognon *m;* (of problem) cœur *m;* (Tech) noyau *m.* ● *vt* (apple) évider.

cork *n* liège *m;* (for bottle) bouchon

m. ● *vt* boucher. **corkscrew** *n* tire-bouchon *m.*

corn *n* blé *m;* (maize: US) maïs *m;* (seed) grain *m;* (hard skin) cor *m.*

cornea *n* cornée *f.*

corner *n* coin *m;* (bend in road) virage *m;* (football) corner *m.* ● *vt* coincer, acculer; (market) accaparer. ● *vi* prendre un virage.

cornflour *n* farine *f* de maïs.

cornice *n* corniche *f.*

corny *a* (-**ier**, -**iest**) (joke) éculé.

corollary *n* corollaire *m.*

coronary *n* infarctus *m.*

coronation *n* couronnement *m.*

corporal *n* caporal *m.* ~ **punishment** *n* châtiment *m* corporel.

corporate *a* (ownership) en commun; (body) constitué.

corporation *n* (Comm) société *f.*

corpse *n* cadavre *m.*

corpuscle *n* globule *m.*

correct *a* (right) exact, juste, correct; (proper) correct; **you are** ~ vous avez raison. ● *vt* corriger.

correction *n* correction *f.*

correlate *vt/i* (faire) correspondre.

correspond *vi* correspondre. **correspondence** *n* correspondance *f.*

corridor *n* couloir *m.*

corrode *vt/i* (se) corroder.

corrugated *a* ondulé; ~ **iron** tôle *f* ondulée.

corrupt *a* corrompu. ● *vt* corrompre. **corruption** *n* corruption *f.*

Corsica *n* Corse *f.*

cosh *n* matraque *f.* ● *vt* matraquer.

cosmetic *n* produit *m* de beauté. ● *a* cosmétique; (fig, pej) superficiel. ~ **surgery** *n* chirurgie *f* esthétique

cosmopolitan *a* & *n* cosmopolite (*mf*).

cosmos *n* cosmos *m.*

cost *vt* (*pt* **cost**) coûter; (*pt* **costed**) établir le prix de. ● *n* coût *m;* ~**s** (Jur) dépens *mpl;* **at all** ~**s** à tout prix; **to one's** ~ à ses dépens; ~ **price** prix *m* de revient; ~ **of living** coût *m* de la vie. ~-**effective** *a* rentable.

costly *a* (-**ier**, -**iest**) coûteux; (valuable) précieux.

costume *n* costume *m;* (for swimming) maillot *m.* ~ **jewellery** *npl* bijoux *mpl* de fantaisie.

cosy *a* (-**ier**, -**iest**) confortable, intime.

cot *n* lit *m* d'enfant; (camp-bed: US) lit *m* de camp.

cottage *n* petite maison *f* de campagne; (thatched) chaumière *f.* ~ **pie** *n* hachis *m* Parmentier.

cotton *n* coton *m;* (for sewing) fil *m* (à coudre). ● *vi* ~ **on** ▣ piger. ~ **wool** *n* coton *m* hydrophile.

couch *n* canapé *m.* ● *vt* (express) formuler.

cough *vi* tousser. ● *n* toux *f.* □ ~ **up** ▣ cracher, payer.

could ⇒CAN¹.

couldn't = COULD NOT.

council *n* conseil *m.* ~ **house** *n* maison *f* louée par la municipalité, ≈ H.L.M. *m or f.*

councillor *n* conseiller/-ère *m/f* municipal/-e.

counsel *n* conseil *m.* ● *n inv* (Jur) avocat/-e *m/f.* **counsellor** *n* conseiller/-ère *m/f.*

count *vt/i* compter. ● *n* (numerical record) décompte *m;* (nobleman) comte *m.* □ ~ **on** compter sur.

counter *n* comptoir *m;* (in bank) guichet *m;* (token) jeton *m.* ● *adv* ~ **to** à l'encontre de. ● *a* opposé. ● *vt* opposer; (blow) parer. ● *vi* riposter.

counteract *vt* neutraliser.

counterbalance n contrepoids m. ●vt contrebalancer.

counterfeit a & n faux (m). ●vt contrefaire.

counterfoil n souche f.

counter-productive a qui produit l'effet contraire.

countess n comtesse f.

countless a innombrable.

country n (land, region) pays m; (homeland) patrie f; (countryside) campagne f.

countryman n (pl **-men**) campagnard m; (fellow citizen) compatriote m.

countryside n campagne f.

county n comté m.

coup n (achievement) joli coup m; (Pol) coup m d'état.

couple n (people, animals) couple m; **a ~ (of)** (two or three) deux ou trois. ●vt/i (s')accoupler.

coupon n coupon m; (for shopping) bon m or coupon m de réduction.

courage n courage m.

courgette n courgette f.

courier n messager/-ère m/f; (for tourists) guide m.

course n cours m; (for training) stage m; (series) série f; (Culin) plat m; (for golf) terrain m; (at sea) itinéraire m; **change ~** changer de cap; **~ (of action)** façon f de faire; **during the ~ of** pendant; **in due ~** en temps utile; **of ~** bien sûr.

court n cour f; (tennis) court m; **go to ~** aller devant les tribunaux. ●vt faire la cour à; (danger) rechercher.

courteous a courtois.

courtesy n courtoisie f; **by ~ of** avec la permission de.

court-house n (US) palais m de justice.

court-martial vt (pt **-martialled**) faire passer en conseil de guerre. ●n cour f martiale.

court: **~room** n salle f de tribunal. **~shoe** n escarpin m. **~yard** n cour f.

cousin n cousin/-e m/f; **first ~** cousin/-e m/f germain/-e.

cove n anse f, crique f.

covenant n convention f.

cover vt couvrir. ●n (for bed, book) couverture f; (lid) couvercle m; (for furniture) housse f; (shelter) abri m; **take ~** se mettre à l'abri. □ **~ up** cacher; (crime) couvrir; **~ up for** couvrir.

coverage n reportage m.

covering n enveloppe f; **~ letter** lettre f d'accompagnement.

covert a (activity) secret; (threat) voilé; (look) dérobé.

cover-up n opération f de camouflage.

cow n vache f.

coward n lâche mf.

cowboy n cow-boy m.

cowshed n étable f.

coy a (faussement) timide, qui fait le or la timide.

cozy US = **cosy**.

crab n crabe m. **~-apple** n pomme f sauvage.

crack n fente f; (in glass) fêlure f; (noise) craquement m; (joke) plaisanterie f. ●a 🅸 d'élite. ●vt/i (break partially) (se) fêler; (split) (se) fendre; (nut) casser; (joke) raconter; (problem) résoudre; **get ~ing** 🅸 s'y mettre. □ **~ down on** 🅸 sévir contre; **~ up** 🅸 craquer.

cracker n (Culin) biscuit m (salé); (for Christmas) diablotin m.

crackle vi crépiter. ●n crépitement m.

cradle n berceau m. ●vt bercer.

craft n métier m artisanal; (technique) art m; (boat) bateau m.

craftsman n (pl **-men**) artisan m. **craftsmanship** n art m.

crafty a (**-ier, -iest**) rusé.

crag n rocher m à pic.

cram vt/i (pt **crammed**); (for an exam) bachoter (**for** pour); ~ **into** (pack) (s')entasser dans; ~ **with** (fill) bourrer de.

cramp n crampe f.

cramped a à l'étroit.

cranberry n canneberge f.

crane n grue f. ● vt (neck) tendre.

crank n excentrique mf; (Tech) manivelle f.

crap n (nonsense ⊠) conneries fpl ⊠; (faeces ⊠) merde f ⊠.

crash n accident m; (noise) fracas m; (of thunder) coup m; (of firm) faillite f. ● vt/i avoir un accident (avec), (of plane) s'écraser; (two vehicles) se percuter; ~ **into** rentrer dans. ~ **course** n cours m intensif. ~**helmet** n casque m (anti-choc). ~**land** vi atterrir en catastrophe.

crate n cageot m.

cravat n foulard m.

crave vt/i ~ (**for**) désirer ardemment. **craving** n envie f irrésistible.

crawl vi (insect) ramper; (vehicle) se traîner; **be** ~**ing with** grouiller de. ● n (pace) pas m; (swimming) crawl m.

crayfish n inv écrevisse f.

crayon n craie f grasse.

craze n engouement m.

crazy a (**-ier, -iest**) fou; ~ **about** (person) fou de; (thing) fana or fou de.

creak n grincement m. ● vi grincer.

cream n crème f. ● a crème inv. ● vt écrémer.

crease n pli m. ● vt/i (se) froisser.

create vt créer. **creation** n

création f. **creative** a (person) créatif; (process) créateur.

creator n créateur/-trice m/f.

creature n créature f.

crèche n garderie f.

credentials npl (identity) pièces fpl d'identité; (competence) références fpl.

credibility n crédibilité f.

credit n (credence) crédit m; (honour) honneur m; **in** ~ créditeur; ~**s** (cinema) générique m. ● a (balance) créditeur. ● vt croire; (Comm) créditer; ~ **sb with** attribuer à qn. ~ **card** n carte f de crédit. ~ **note** n avoir m.

creditor n créancier/-ière m/f.

credit-worthy a solvable.

creed n credo m.

creek n (US) ruisseau m; **up the** ~ ⊠ dans le pétrin ⊠.

creep vi (pt **crept**) (insect, cat) ramper; (fig) se glisser. ● n (person ⊠) pauvre type m ⊠; **give sb the** ~**s** faire frissonner qn. **creeper** n liane f.

cremate vt incinérer. **cremation** n incinération f. **crematorium** n (pl **-ia**) crématorium m.

crêpe n crêpe m. ~ **paper** n papier m crêpon.

crept ⇒CREEP.

crescent n croissant m; (of houses) rue f en demi-lune.

cress n cresson m.

crest n crête f; (coat of arms) armoiries fpl.

cretin n crétin/-e m/f.

crevice n fente f.

crew n (of plane, ship) équipage m; (gang) équipe f. ~ **cut** n coupe f en brosse. ~ **neck** n (col) ras du cou m.

crib n lit m d'enfant. ● vt/i (pt **cribbed**) copier.

cricket n (Sport) cricket m; (insect) grillon m.

crime n crime m; (minor) délit m; (acts) criminalité f.

criminal a & n criminel/-le (m/f).

crimson a & n cramoisi (m).

cringe vi reculer; (fig) s'humilier.

crinkle vt/i (se) froisser. ● n pli m.

cripple n infirme mf. ● vt estropier; (fig) paralyser.

crisis n (pl **crises**) crise f.

crisp a (Culin) croquant; (air, reply) vif. **crisps** npl chips fpl.

criss-cross a entrecroisé. ● vt/i (s')entrecroiser.

criterion n (pl **-ia**) critère m.

critic n critique m. **critical** a critique. **critically** adv d'une manière critique; (ill) gravement.

criticism n critique f.

criticize vt/i critiquer.

croak n (bird) croassement m; (frog) coassement m. ● vi croasser; coasser.

Croatia n Croatie f.

Croatian n Croate mf. ● a Croate.

crochet n crochet m. ● vt faire du crochet.

crockery n vaisselle f.

crocodile n crocodile m.

crook n (criminal 🔲) escroc m; (stick) houlette f.

crooked a tordu; (winding) tortueux; (askew) de travers; (dishonest: fig) malhonnête.

crop n récolte f; (fig) quantité f. ● vt (pt **cropped**) couper. ● vi ~ up se présenter.

cross n croix f; (hybrid) hybride m. ● vt/i traverser; (legs, animals) croiser; (cheque) barrer; (paths) se croiser; ~ sb's mind venir à l'esprit de qn. ● a en colère, fâché (with contre). talk at ~ purposes parler sans se comprendre. □ ~ off or out rayer. ~-check vt vérifier (pour confirmer). ~-country (running)

n cross m. ~-examine vt faire subir un contre-interrogatoire à. ~-eyed a be ~-eyed loucher. ~fire n feux mpl croisés.

crossing n (by boat) traversée f; (on road) passage m clouté.

crossly adv avec colère.

cross: ~-reference n renvoi m. ~roads n carrefour m. ~word n mots mpl croisés.

crotch n (of garment) entrejambes m inv.

crouch vi s'accroupir.

crow n corbeau m; as the ~ flies à vol d'oiseau. ● vi (of cock) chanter; (fig) jubiler. ~bar n pied-de-biche m.

crowd n foule f. **crowded** a plein.

crown n couronne f; (top part) sommet m. ● vt couronner.

Crown Court n Cour f d'assises.

crucial a crucial.

crucifix n crucifix m.

crucify vt crucifier.

crude a (raw) brut; (rough, vulgar) grossier.

cruel a (**crueller**, **cruellest**) cruel.

cruise n croisière f. ● vi (ship) croiser; (tourists) faire une croisière; (vehicle) rouler; **cruising speed** vitesse f de croisière.

crumb n miette f.

crumble vt/i (s')effriter; (bread) (s')émietter; (collapse) s'écrouler.

crumple vt/i (se) froisser.

crunch vt croquer. ● n (event) moment m critique; **when it comes to the** ~ quand ça devient sérieux.

crusade n croisade f. **crusader** n (knight) croisé m; (fig) militant/-e m/f.

crush vt écraser; (clothes) froisser. ● n (crowd) presse f; **a** ~ **on** 🔲 le béguin pour.

crust n croûte f. **crusty** a croustillant.

crutch n béquille f; (crotch) entrejambes m inv.

crux n the ~ of (problem) le point crucial de.

cry n cri m. ● vi (weep) pleurer; (call out) crier. □ ~ off se décommander.

crying a (need) urgent; a ~ shame une vraie honte. ● n pleurs mpl.

cryptic a énigmatique.

crystal n cristal m. ~-clear a parfaitement clair.

cub n petit m; **Cub** (Scout) louveteau m.

Cuba n Cuba f.

cube n cube m. **cubic** a cubique; (metre) cube.

cubicle n (in room, hospital) box m; (at swimming-pool) cabine f.

cuckoo n coucou m.

cucumber n concombre m.

cuddle vt câliner. ● vi (kiss and) ~ s'embrasser. ● n caresse f. **cuddly** a câlin; **cuddly toy** peluche f.

cue n signal m; (Theat) réplique f; (billiards) queue f.

cuff n manchette f; (US: on trousers) revers m; **off the** ~ impromptu. ● vt gifler. ~-link n bouton m de manchette.

cul-de-sac n (pl culs-de-sac) impasse f.

cull vt (select) choisir; (kill) massacrer.

culminate vi ~ in se terminer par. **culmination** n point m culminant.

culprit n coupable mf.

cult n culte m.

cultivate vt cultiver. **cultivation** n culture f.

cultural a culturel.

culture n culture f. **cultured** a cultivé.

cumbersome a encombrant.

cunning a rusé. ● n astuce f, ruse f.

cup n tasse f; (prize) coupe f; **Cup final** finale f de la coupe.

cupboard n placard m.

cup-tie n match m de coupe.

curate n vicaire m.

curator n (of museum) conservateur m.

curb n (restraint) frein m; (of path) (US) bord m du trottoir. ● vt (desires) refréner; (price increase) freiner.

cure vt guérir; (fig) éliminer; (Culin) fumer; (in brine) saler. ● n (recovery) guérison f; (remedy) remède m.

curfew n couvre-feu m.

curiosity n curiosité f. **curious** a curieux.

curl vt/i (hair) boucler. ● n boucle f. □ ~ up se pelotonner; (shrivel) se racornir.

curler n bigoudi m.

curly a (-ier, -iest) bouclé.

currant n raisin m de Corinthe.

currency n (money) monnaie f; (of word) fréquence f; **foreign** ~ devises fpl étrangères.

current a (term, word) usité; (topical) actuel; (year) en cours. ● n courant m. ~ **account** n compte m courant. ~ **events** npl l'actualité f.

currently adv actuellement.

curriculum n (pl -la) programme m scolaire. ~ **vitae** n curriculum vitae m.

curry n curry m. ● vt ~ **favour with** chercher les bonnes grâces de.

curse n (spell) malédiction f; (swearword) juron m. ● vt maudire. ● vi (swear) jurer.

cursor n curseur m.

curt a brusque.

curtain n rideau m.

curve n courbe f. ● vi (line) s'incurver; (edge) se recourber; (road) faire une courbe. ● vt courber.

cushion n coussin m. ● vt (a blow) amortir; (fig) protéger.

custard n crème f anglaise; (set) flan m.

custody n (of child) garde f; (Jur) détention f préventive.

custom n coutume f; (patronage: Comm) clientèle f. **customary** a habituel.

customer n client/-e m/f; (person ▣) type m.

customize vt personnaliser.

custom-made a fait sur mesure.

customs npl douane f. ● a douanier. ~ **officer** n douanier m.

cut vt/i (pt cut; pres p cutting) vt couper; (hedge) tailler; (prices) réduire. ● vi couper. ● n (wound) coupure f; (of clothes) coupe f; (in surgery) incision f; (share) part f; (in prices) réduction f. □ ~ **back** vi faire des économies. vt réduire. ~ **down** (**on**) réduire; ~ **in** (in conversation) intervenir; ~ **off** couper; (tide, army) isoler; ~ **out** vt découper; (leave out) supprimer; vi (engine) s'arrêter. ~ **short** (visit) écourter; ~ **up** couper; (carve) découper.

cut-back n réduction f.

cute a ▣ mignon.

cutlery n couverts mpl.

cutlet n côtelette f.

cut-price a à prix réduit.

cutting a cinglant. ● n (from newspaper) coupure f; (plant) bouture f.

CV abbr ⇒CURRICULUM VITAE.

cyanide n cyanure m.

cyberspace n cyberespace m.

cycle n cycle m; (bicycle) vélo m. ● vi aller à vélo.

cycling n cyclisme m. ~ **shorts** npl cycliste m.

cyclist n cycliste mf.

cylinder n cylindre m.

cymbal n cymbale f.

cynic n cynique mf. **cynical** a cynique. **cynicism** n cynisme m.

cypress n cyprès m.

Cypriot n Cypriote mf. ● a cypriote.

Cyprus n Chypre f.

cyst n kyste m.

czar n tsar m.

Czech n (person) Tchèque mf; (Ling) tchèque m. ~ **Republic** n République f tchèque.

dab vt (pt dabbed) tamponner; ~ **sth on** appliquer qch par petites touches. ● n touche f.

dabble vi ~ **in sth** faire qch en amateur.

dad n ▣ papa m. **daddy** n ▣ papa m.

daffodil n jonquille f.

daft a bête.

dagger n poignard m.

daily a quotidien. ● adv tous les jours. ● n (newspaper) quotidien m.

dainty a (-ier, -iest) (lace, food) délicat; (shoe, hand) mignon.

dairy n (on farm) laiterie f; (shop) crémerie f. ● a (farm, cow, product) laitier; (butter) fermier.

daisy n pâquerette f.

dam n barrage m.

damage n (to property) dégâts mpl; (Med) lésions fpl; **to do sth ~** (cause, trade) porter atteinte à; **~s** (Jur) dommages-intérêts mpl. ● vt (property) endommager; (health) nuire à; (reputation) porter atteinte à. **damaging** a (to health) nuisible; (to reputation) préjudiciable.

damn vt (Relig) damner; (condemn: fig) condamner. ● interj 🅸 zut 🅸, merde 🅷. ● n **not give/care a ~ about** se ficher de 🅸. ● a fichu 🅸. ● adv franchement.

damp n humidité f. ● a humide. **dampen** vt (lit) humecter; (fig) refroidir. **dampness** n humidité f.

dance vt/i danser. ● n danse f; (gathering) bal m; **~ hall** dancing m. **dancer** n danseur/-euse m/f.

dandelion n pissenlit m.

dandruff n pellicules fpl.

Dane n Danois/-e m/f.

danger n danger m; (risk) risque m; **be in ~ of** risquer de. **dangerous** a dangereux

dangle vt (object) balancer; (legs) laisser pendre. ● vi (object) se balancer (**from** à).

Danish n (Ling) danois m. ● a danois.

dare vt/i oser ((**to**) **do** faire); **~ sb to do** défier qn de faire. ● n défi m. **daring** a audacieux.

dark a (day, colour, suit, mood, warning) sombre; (hair, eyes, skin) brun; (secret, thought) noir. ● n noir m; (nightfall) tombée f de la nuit; **in the ~** (fig) dans le noir. **darken** vt/i (sky) (s')obscurcir; (mood) (s')assombrir. **darkness** n obscurité f. **~-room** n chambre f noire.

darling a & n chéri/-e (m/f).

dart n fléchette f; **~s** (game)

fléchettes fpl. ● vi **~ in/away** entrer/filer comme une flèche.

dash vi se précipiter; **~ off** se sauver. ● vt (hope) anéantir; **~ sth against** projeter qch contre. ● n course f folle; (of liquid) goutte f; (of colour) touche f; (in punctuation) tiret m.

dashboard n tableau m de bord.

data npl données fpl. **~base** n base f de données. **~ capture** n saisie f de données. **~ processing** n traitement m des données. **~ protection** n protection f de l'information.

date n date f; (meeting) rendez-vous m; (fruit) datte f; **out of ~** (old-fashioned) démodé; (passport) périmé; **to ~** à ce jour; **up to ~** (modern) moderne; (list) à jour. ● vt/i dater; (go out with) sortir avec; **~ from** dater de. **dated** a démodé.

daughter n fille f. **~-in-law** n (pl **~s-in-law**) belle-fille f.

daunt vt décourager.

dawdle vi flâner, traînasser 🅸.

dawn n aube f. ● vi (day) se lever; **it ~ed on me that** je me suis rendu compte que.

day n jour m; (whole day) journée f; (period) époque f; **the ~ before** la veille; **the following** or **next ~** le lendemain. **~break** n aube f.

daydream n rêves mpl. ● vi rêvasser (**about** de).

day: **~light** n jour m. **~time** n journée f. **~ trader** n spéculateur m à la journée, scalper m.

daze n **in a ~** (from blow) étourdi; (from drug) hébété. **dazed** a (by blow) abasourdi; (by news) ahuri.

dazzle vt éblouir.

dead a mort; (numb) engourdi. ● adv complètement; **in ~ centre** au beau milieu; **stop ~** s'arrêter net. ● n **in the ~ of** au cœur de; **the ~** les morts m. **deaden** vt (sound, blow) amortir; (pain)

calmer. ~ **end** n impasse f.
~**line** n date f limite. ~**lock** n
impasse f.

deadly a (-ier, -iest) mortel;
(weapon) meurtrier.

deaf a sourd. **deafen** vt
assourdir. **deafness** n surdité f.

deal vt (pt **dealt**) donner; (blow)
porter. ● vi (trade) être en activité;
~ **in** être dans le commerce de.
● n affaire f; (cards) donne f; **a
great** or **good** ~ beaucoup (**of** de).
□ ~ **with** (handle, manage)
s'occuper de; (be about) traiter de.
dealer n marchand/-e m/f; (agent)
concessionnaire m/f. **dealings** npl
relations fpl.

dear a cher; ~ **Sir/Madam**
Monsieur/Madame. ● n (**my**) ~
mon chéri/ma chérie m/f. ● adv
cher. ● interj oh ~! oh mon Dieu!

death n mort f; ~ **penalty** peine f
de mort.

debatable a discutable.

debate n (formal) débat m; (informal)
discussion f. ● vt (formally)
débattre de; (informally) discuter.

debit n débit m. ● a (balance)
débiteur. ● vt (pt **debited**)
débiter.

debris n débris mpl; (rubbish)
déchets mpl.

debt n dette f; **be in** ~ avoir des
dettes.

debug vt (Comput) déboguer.

decade n décennie f.

decadent a décadent.

decaffeinated a décaféiné.

decay vi (vegetation) pourrir;
(tooth) se carier; (fig) décliner. ● n
pourriture f; (of tooth) carie f; (fig)
déclin m.

deceased a décédé. ● n défunt/
-e m/f.

deceit n tromperie f. **deceitful** a
trompeur.

deceive vt tromper.

December n décembre m.

decent a (respectable) comme il
faut; (adequate) convenable; (good)
bon; (kind) gentil; (not indecent)
décent. **decently** adv
convenablement.

deception n tromperie f.
deceptive a trompeur.

decide vt/i décider (**to do** de
faire); (question) régler; ~ **on** se
décider pour. **decided** a (firm)
résolu; (clear) net. **decidedly** adv
nettement.

decimal a décimal. ● n décimale
f; ~ **point** virgule f.

decipher vt déchiffrer.

decision n décision f.

decisive a (conclusive) décisif; (firm)
décidé.

deck n pont m; (of cards: US) jeu
m; (of bus) étage m. ~**-chair** n
chaise f longue.

declaration n déclaration f.
declare vt déclarer.

decline vt/i refuser; (fall) baisser.
● n (waning) déclin m; (drop) baisse
f; **in** ~ sur le déclin.

decode vt décoder.

decommission vt (arms) mettre
hors service; (reactor)
démanteler.

decompose vt/i (se)
décomposer.

decor n décor m.

decorate vt décorer; (room)
refaire, peindre. **decoration** n
décoration f. **decorative** a
décoratif.

decorator n peintre m; (interior)
~ décorateur/-trice m/f.

decoy n (person, vehicle) leurre m;
(for hunting) appeau m.

decrease¹ vt/i diminuer.

decrease² n diminution f.

decree n (Pol, Relig) décret m; (Jur)
jugement m. ● vt (pt **decreed**)
décréter.

decrepit a (building) délabré; (person) décrépit.

dedicate vt dédier; ~ oneself to se consacrer à.

dedicated a dévoué; ~ line (Internet) ligne f spécialisée.

dedication n dévouement m; (in book) dédicace f.

deduce vt déduire.

deduct vt déduire; (from wages) retenir.

deed n acte m.

deem vt considérer.

deep a profond; (mud, carpet) épais. ● adv profondément; ~ in thought absorbé dans ses pensées. **deepen** vt/i (admiration, concern) augmenter.

deep-freeze n congélateur m. ● vt congeler.

deep vein thrombosis n thrombose f veineuse profonde.

deer n inv cerf m; (doe) biche f.

deface vt dégrader.

default vi (Jur) ~ (on payments) ne pas régler ses échéances. ● n (on payments) non-remboursement m; **by** ~ par défaut; **win by** ~ gagner par forfait. ● a (Comput) par défaut.

defeat vt vaincre; (thwart) faire échouer. ● n défaite f.

defect[1] n défaut m.

defect[2] vi faire défection; ~ **to** passer à.

defective a défectueux.

defector n transfuge mf.

defence n défense f.

defend vt défendre. **defendant** n (Jur) accusé/-e m/f. **defender** défenseur m.

defensive a défensif. ● n défensive f.

defer vt (pt **deferred**) (postpone) reporter; (judgement) suspendre; (payment) différer.

deference n déférence f. **deferential** a déférent.

defiance n défi m; **in** ~ **of** contre. **defiant** a rebelle. **defiantly** adv avec défi.

deficiency n insuffisance f; (fault) défaut m.

deficient a insuffisant; **be** ~ **in** manquer de.

deficit n déficit m.

define vt définir.

definite a (exact) précis; (obvious) net; (firm) ferme; (certain) certain. **definitely** adv certainement; (clearly) nettement.

definition n définition f.

deflate vt dégonfler.

deflect vt (missile) dévier; (criticism) détourner.

deforestation n déforestation f.

deform vt déformer.

defraud vt (client, employer) escroquer; (state, customs) frauder; ~ **sb of sth** escroquer qch à qn.

defrost vt dégivrer.

deft a adroit.

defunct a défunt.

defuse vt désamorcer.

defy vt défier; (attempts) résister à.

degenerate[1] vi dégénérer (into en).

degenerate[2] a & n dégénéré/-e (m/f).

degrade vt (humiliate) humilier; (damage) dégrader.

degree n degré m; (Univ) diplôme m universitaire; (Bachelor's degree) licence f; **to such a** ~ **that** à tel point que.

dehydrate vt/i (se) déshydrater.

deign vt ~ **to do** daigner faire.

dejected a découragé.

delay vt (flight) retarder; (decision) différer; ~ **doing**

attendre pour faire. ●*n* (of plane, post) retard *m*; (time lapse) délai *m*.

delegate[1] *n* délégué/-e *m/f*.

delegate[2] *vt* déléguer.
delegation *n* délégation *f*.

delete *vt* supprimer; (Comput) effacer; (with pen) barrer. **deletion** *n* suppression *f*; (with line) rature *f*.

deliberate[1] *vi* délibérer.

deliberate[2] *a* délibéré; (*steps, manner*) mesuré. **deliberately** *adv* (*do, say*) exprès; (*sarcastically, provocatively*) délibérément.

delicacy *n* délicatesse *f*; (food) mets *m* raffiné.

delicate *a* délicat.

delicatessen *n* épicerie *f* fine.

delicious *a* délicieux.

delight *n* joie *f*, plaisir *m*. ●*vt* ravir. ●*vi* ~ in prendre plaisir à. **delighted** *a* ravi. **delightful** *a* charmant/-e.

delinquent *a* & *n* délinquant/-e (*m/f*).

delirious *a* délirant.

deliver *vt* (*message*) remettre; (*goods*) livrer; (*speech*) faire; (*baby*) mettre au monde; (rescue) délivrer. **delivery** *n* (of goods) livraison *f*; (of mail) distribution *f*; (of baby) accouchement *m*.

delude *vt* tromper; ~ oneself se faire des illusions.

deluge *n* déluge *m*. ●*vt* submerger (**with** de).

delusion *n* illusion *f*.

delve *vi* fouiller.

demand *vt* (request, require) demander; (forcefully) exiger. ●*n* (request) demande *f*; (pressure) exigence *f*; **in** ~ très demandé; **on** ~ à la demande. **demanding** *a* exigeant.

demean *vt* ~ oneself s'abaisser.

demeanour, (US) **demeanor** *n* comportement *m*.

demented *a* fou.

demise *n* disparition *f*.

demo *n* (demonstration 🔲) manif *f* 🔲.

democracy *n* démocratie *f*.

democrat *n* démocrate *mf*.
democratic *a* démocratique.

demolish *vt* démolir.

demon *n* démon *m*.

demonstrate *vt* démontrer; (*concern, skill*) manifester. ●*vi* (Pol) manifester. **demonstration** *n* démonstration *f*; (Pol) manifestation *f*. **demonstrative** *a* démonstratif. **demonstrator** *n* manifestant/-e *m/f*.

demoralize *vt* démoraliser.

demote *vt* rétrograder.

den *n* (of lion) antre *m*; (room) tanière *f*.

denial *n* (of rumour) démenti *m*; (of rights) négation *f*; (of request) rejet *m*.

denim *n* jean *m*; ~s (jeans) jean *m*.

Denmark *n* Danemark *m*.

denomination *n* (Relig) confession *f*; (money) valeur *f*.

denounce *vt* dénoncer.

dense *a* dense. **densely** *adv* (*packed*) très. **density** *n* densité *f*.

dent *n* bosse *f*. ●*vt* cabosser.

dental *a* dentaire; ~ **floss** fil *m* dentaire; ~ **surgeon** chirurgien-dentiste *m*.

dentist *n* dentiste *mf*. **dentistry** *n* médecine *f* dentaire.

dentures *npl* dentier *m*.

deny *vt* nier (**that** que); (*rumour*) démentir; ~ **sb sth** refuser qch à qn.

deodorant *n* déodorant *m*.

depart *vi* partir; ~ **from** (deviate) s'éloigner de.

department *n* (in shop) rayon *m*; (in hospital, office) service *m*; (Univ) département *m*; **D**~ **of Health**

ministère *m* de la santé; ~ **store** grand magasin *m*.

departure *n* départ *m*; **a ~ from** (*custom, truth*) une entorse à.

depend *vi* dépendre (**on** de); ~ **on** (rely on) compter sur; **it** (all) ~**s** ça dépend; ~**ing on the season** suivant la saison. **dependable** *a* (*person*) digne de confiance. **dependant** *n* personne *f* à charge. **dependence** *n* dépendance *f*.

dependent *a* dépendant; **be ~ on** dépendre de.

depict *vt* (describe) dépeindre; (in picture) représenter.

deplete *vt* réduire.

deport *vt* expulser.

depose *vt* déposer.

deposit *vt* (*pt* **deposited**) déposer. ● *n* (in bank) dépôt *m*; (on house) versement *m* initial; (on holiday) acompte *m*; (against damage) caution *f*; (on bottle) consigne *f*; (of mineral) gisement *m*; ~ **account** compte *m* de dépôt. **depositor** *n* (Comm) déposant/-e *m/f*.

depot *n* dépôt *m*; (US) gare *f*.

depreciate *vt/i* (se) déprécier.

depress *vt* déprimer. **depressing** *a* déprimant. **depression** *n* dépression *f*; (Econ) récession *f*.

deprivation *n* privation *f*.

deprive *vt* ~ **of** priver de. **deprived** *a* démuni.

depth *n* profondeur *f*; (of knowledge, ignorance) étendue *f*; (of colour, emotion) intensité *f*.

deputize *vi* ~ **for** remplacer.

deputy *n* adjoint/-e *m/f*. ● *a* adjoint; ~ **chairman** vice-président *m*.

derail *vt* faire dérailler. **derailment** *n* déraillement *m*.

deranged *a* dérangé.

derelict *a* abandonné.

deride *vt* ridiculiser. **derision** *n*

moqueries *fpl*. **derisory** *a* dérisoire.

derivative *a & n* dérivé (*m*).

derive *vt* ~ **sth from** tirer qch de. ● *vi* ~ **from** découler de.

derogatory *a* (*word*) péjoratif; (*remark*) désobligeant.

descend *vt/i* descendre; **be ~ed from** descendre de. **descendant** *n* descendant/-e *m/f*. **descent** *n* descente *f*; (lineage) origine *f*.

describe *vt* décrire; ~ **sb as sth** qualifier qn de qch. **description** *n* description *f*. **descriptive** *a* descriptif.

desert[1] *n* désert *m*.

desert[2] *vt/i* abandonner; (*cause*) déserter. **deserted** *a* désert. **deserter** *n* déserteur *m*.

deserts *npl* **got one's ~** avoir ce qu'on mérite.

deserve *vt* mériter (**to** de). **deservedly** *adv* à juste titre. **deserving** *a* (*person*) méritant; (*action*) louable.

design *n* (sketch) plan *m*; (idea) conception *f*; (pattern) motif *m*; (art of designing) design *m*; (aim) dessein *m*. ● *vt* (sketch) dessiner; (devise, intend) concevoir.

designate *vt* désigner.

designer *n* concepteur/-trice *m/f*; (of fashion, furniture) créateur/-trice *m/f*. ● *a* (clothes) de haute couture; (sunglasses, drink) de dernière mode.

desirable *a* (outcome) souhaitable; (person) désirable.

desire *n* désir *m*. ● *vt* désirer.

desk *n* bureau *m*; (of pupil) pupitre *m*; (in hotel) réception *f*; (in bank) caisse *f*.

desolate *a* (place) désolé; (person) affligé.

despair *n* désespoir *m*. ● *vi* désespérer (**of** de).

desperate *a* désespéré; (criminal) prêt à tout; **be ~ for** avoir

désespérément besoin de.
desperately adv désespérément;
(worried) terriblement; (ill)
gravement.

desperation n désespoir m; in ~
en désespoir de cause.

despicable a méprisable.

despise vt mépriser.

despite prep malgré.

despondent a découragé.

dessert n dessert m. ~**spoon** n
cuillère f à dessert.

destination n destination f.

destiny n destin m.

destitute a sans ressources.

destroy vt détruire; (animal)
abattre. **destroyer** n (warship)
contre-torpilleur m.

destruction n destruction f.
destructive a destructeur.

detach vt détacher; ~ed house
maison f (individuelle).

detail n détail m; go into ~ entrer
dans les détails. ●vt (plans)
exposer en détail.

detain vt retenir; (in prison) placer
en détention. **detainee** n détenu/
-e m/f.

detect vt (error, trace) déceler;
(crime, mine, sound) détecter.
detection n détection f.
detective n inspecteur/-trice m/
f; (private) détective m.

detention n détention f; (School)
retenue f.

deter vt (pt **deterred**) dissuader
(**from** de).

detergent a & n détergent (m).

deteriorate vi se détériorer.

determine vt déterminer; ~ **to do**
résoudre de faire. **determined** a
(person) décidé; (air) résolu.

deterrent n moyen m de
dissuasion. ●a (effect) dissuasif.

detest vt détester.

detonate vt/i (faire) détoner.

detonation n détonation f.
detonator n détonateur m.

detour n détour m.

detract vi ~ **from** (success, value)
porter atteinte à; (pleasure)
diminuer.

detriment n to the ~ of au
détriment de. **detrimental** a
nuisible (**to** à).

devalue vt dévaluer.

devastate vt (place) ravager;
(person) accabler.

develop vt (plan) élaborer;
(mind, body) développer; (land)
mettre en valeur; (illness)
attraper; (habit) prendre. ●vi
(child, country, plot, business) se
développer; (hole, crack) se
former.

development n développement
m; (housing) ~ lotissement m;
(new) ~ fait m nouveau.

deviate vi dévier; ~ **from** (norm)
s'écarter de.

device n appareil m; (means)
moyen m; (bomb) engin m
explosif.

devil n diable m.

devious a (person) retors.

devise vt (scheme) concevoir;
(product) inventer.

devoid a ~ **of** dépourvu de.

devolution n (Pol) régionalisation
f.

devote vt consacrer (**to** à).
devoted a dévoué. **devotion** n
dévouement m; (Relig) dévotion f.

devour vt dévorer.

devout a fervent.

dew n rosée f.

diabetes n diabète m.

diabolical a diabolique; (bad 🔲)
atroce.

diagnose vt diagnostiquer.
diagnosis n (pl **-oses**) diagnostic
m.

diagonal *a* diagonal. ● *n* diagonale *f*.

diagram *n* schéma *m*.

dial *n* cadran *m*. ● *vt* (*pt* **dialled**) (*number*) faire; (*person*) appeler; **dialling code** indicatif *m*; **dialling tone** tonalité *f*.

dialect *n* dialecte *m*.

dialogue *n* dialogue *m*.

diameter *n* diamètre *m*

diamond *n* diamant *m*; (*shape*) losange *m*; (*baseball*) terrain *m*; **~s** (*cards*) carreau *m*.

diaper *n* (US) couche *f*.

diaphragm *n* diaphragme *m*.

diarrhoea, (US) **diarrhea** *n* diarrhée *f*.

diary *n* (for appointments) agenda *m*; (journal) journal *m* intime.

dice *n inv* dé *m*. ● *vt* (*food*) couper en dés.

dictate *vt/i* dicter.

dictation *n* dictée *f*.

dictator *n* dictateur *m*. **dictatorship** *n* dictature *f*.

dictionary *n* dictionnaire *m*.

did ⇒DO.

didn't = DID NOT.

die *vi* (*pres p* **dying**) mourir; (*plant*) crever; **be dying to do** mourir d'envie de faire. □ **~ down** diminuer; **~ out** disparaître.

diesel *n* gazole *m*; **~ engine** moteur *m* diesel.

diet *n* (usual food) alimentation *f*; (restricted) régime *m*. ● *vi* être au régime. **dietary** *a* alimentaire. **dietician** *n* diététicien/-ne *m/f*.

differ *vi* différer (**from** de).

difference *n* différence *f*; (disagreement) différend *m*.

different *a* différent (**from, to** de).

differentiate *vt* différencier. ● *vi* faire la différence (**between** entre).

differently *adv* différemment (**from** de).

difficult *a* difficile. **difficulty** *n* difficulté *f*.

diffuse[1] *a* diffus.

diffuse[2] *vt* diffuser.

dig *vt/i* (*pt* **dug**; *pres p* **digging**) (excavate) creuser; (in garden) bêcher. ● *n* (poke) coup *m* de coude; (remark) pique *f* 🗆; (Archeol) fouilles *fpl*. □ **~ up** déterrer.

digest *vt/i* digérer. **digestible** *a* digestible. **digestion** *n* digestion *f*.

digger *n* excavateur *m*.

digit *n* chiffre *m*.

digital *a* (clock) à affichage numérique; (display, recording) numérique. **~ audio tape** *n* cassette *f* audionumérique. **~ camera** *n* appareil *m* photo numérique.

dignified *a* digne.

dignitary *n* dignitaire *m*.

dignity *n* dignité *f*.

digress *vi* faire une digression.

dilapidated *a* délabré.

dilate *vt/i* (se) dilater.

dilemma *n* dilemme *m*.

diligent *a* appliqué.

dilute *vt* diluer.

dim *a* (**dimmer**, **dimmest**) (weak) faible; (dark) sombre; (indistinct) vague; 🗆 stupide. ● *vt/i* (*pt* **dimmed**) (light) baisser.

dime *n* (US) (pièce *f* de) dix cents.

dimension *n* dimension *f*.

diminish *vt/i* diminuer.

dimple *n* fossette *f*.

din *n* vacarme *m*.

dine *vi* dîner. **diner** *n* dîneur/-euse *m/f*; (US) restaurant *m* à service rapide.

dinghy *n* dériveur *m*.

dingy *a* (-ier, -iest) minable.

dining room *n* salle *f* à manger.

dinner *n* (evening meal) dîner *m*;

(lunch) déjeuner m; **have ~** dîner.
~-jacket n smoking m. **~ party**
n dîner m.

dinosaur n dinosaure m.

dip vt/i (pt **dipped**) plonger; **~
into** (book) feuilleter; (savings)
puiser dans; **~ one's headlights** se
mettre en code. ● n (slope)
déclivité f; (in sea) bain m rapide.

diploma n diplôme m (**in** en).

diplomacy n diplomatie f.

diplomat n diplomate mf.

diplomatic a (Pol) diplomatique;
(tactful) diplomate.

dire a affreux; (need, poverty)
extrême.

direct a direct. ● adv
directement. ● vt diriger; (letter,
remark) adresser; (a play) mettre
en scène; **~ sb to** indiquer à qn
le chemin de; (order) signifier à qn
de.

direction n direction f; (Theat)
mise f en scène; **~s** indications
fpl; **ask ~s** demander le chemin;
~s for use mode m d'emploi.

directly adv directement; (at once)
tout de suite. ● conj dès que.

director n directeur/-trice m/f;
(Theat) metteur m en scène.

directory n (phone book) annuaire
m. **~ enquiries** npl
renseignements mpl
téléphoniques.

dirt n saleté f; (earth) terre f; **~
cheap** ⊠ très bon marché inv.
~-track n (Sport) cendrée f.

dirty a (-ier, -iest) sale; (word)
grossier; **get ~** se salir. ● vt/i (se)
salir.

disability n handicap m.

disable vt rendre infirme.
disabled a handicapé.

disadvantage n désavantage m.
disadvantaged a défavorisé.

disagree vi ne pas être d'accord
(**with** avec); **~ with sb** (food,
climate) ne pas convenir à qn.

disagreement n désaccord m;
(quarrel) différend m.

disappear vi disparaître.
disappearance n disparition f
(**of** de).

disappoint vt décevoir.
disappointment n déception f.

disapproval n désapprobation f
(**of** de).

disapprove vi **~ (of)**
désapprouver.

disarm vt/i désarmer.
disarmament n désarmement m.

disarray n désordre m.

disaster n désastre m.
disastrous a désastreux.

disband vi disperser. ● vt
dissoudre.

disbelief n incrédulité f.

disc n disque m; (Comput) = DISK.

discard vt se débarrasser de;
(beliefs) abandonner.

discharge vt (unload) décharger;
(liquid) déverser; (duty) remplir;
(dismiss) renvoyer; (prisoner)
libérer. ● vi (of pus) s'écouler.

disciple n disciple m.

disciplinary a disciplinaire.

discipline n discipline f. ● vt
discipliner; (punish) punir.

disc jockey n disc-jockey m,
animateur m.

disclaimer n démenti m.

disclose vt révéler. **disclosure** n
révélation f (**of** de).

disco n (club ▣) discothèque f;
(event) soirée f disco.

discolour vt/i (se) décolorer.

discomfort n gêne f.

disconcert vt déconcerter.

disconnect vt détacher; (unplug)
débrancher; (cut off) couper.

discontent n mécontentement
m.

discontinue vt (service)
supprimer; (production) arrêter.

discord n discorde f; (Mus) discordance f.

discount[1] n remise f; (on minor purchase) rabais m.

discount[2] vt (advice) ne pas tenir compte de; (possibility) écarter.

discourage vt décourager.

discourse n discours m.

discourteous a peu courtois.

discover vt découvrir. **discovery** n découverte f.

discreet a discret.

discrepancy n divergence f.

discretion n discrétion f.

discriminate vt/i distinguer; ~ **against** faire de la discrimination contre. **discriminating** a qui a du discernement. **discrimination** n discernement m; (bias) discrimination f.

discus n disque m.

discuss vt (talk about) discuter de; (in writing) examiner. **discussion** n discussion f.

disdain n dédain m.

disease n maladie f.

disembark vt/i débarquer.

disenchanted a désabusé.

disentangle vt démêler.

disfigure vt défigurer.

disgrace n (shame) honte f; (disfavour) disgrâce f. ● vt déshonorer. **disgraced** a (in disfavour) disgracié. **disgraceful** a honteux.

disgruntled a mécontent.

disguise vt déguiser. ● n déguisement m; in ~ déguisé.

disgust n dégoût m. ● vt dégoûter.

dish n plat m; the ~es (crockery) la vaisselle. ● vt ~ **out** 🔟 distribuer; ~ **up** servir.

dishcloth n lavette f; (for drying) torchon m.

dishearten vt décourager.

dishevelled a échevelé.

dishonest a malhonnête.

dishonour, (US) **dishonor** n déshonneur m.

dishwasher n lave-vaisselle m inv.

disillusion vt désabuser. **disillusionment** n désillusion f.

disincentive n be a ~ to décourager.

disinclined a ~ to peu disposé à.

disinfect vt désinfecter. **disinfectant** n désinfectant m.

disintegrate vt/i (se) désintégrer.

disinterested a désintéressé.

disjointed a (talk) décousu.

disk n (US) = disc; (Comput) disque m. ~ **drive** n drive m, lecteur m de disquettes.

diskette n disquette f.

dislike n aversion f. ● vt ne pas aimer.

dislocate vt (limb) disloquer.

dislodge vt (move) déplacer; (drive out) déloger.

disloyal a déloyal (to envers).

dismal a morne, triste.

dismantle vt démonter, défaire.

dismay n consternation f (at devant). ● vt consterner.

dismiss vt renvoyer; (appeal) rejeter; (from mind) écarter. **dismissal** n renvoi m.

dismount vi descendre, mettre pied à terre.

disobedient a désobéissant.

disobey vt désobéir à. ● vi désobéir.

disorder n désordre m; (ailment) trouble(s) m(pl). **disorderly** a désordonné.

disorganized a désorganisé.

disown vt renier.

disparaging a désobligeant.

dispassionate a impartial; (unemotional) calme.

dispatch vt (send, complete)

expédier; (troops) envoyer. ● *n*
expédition *f*; envoi *m*; (report)
dépêche *f*.

dispel *vt* (*pt* **dispelled**) dissiper.

dispensary *n* (in hospital)
pharmacie *f*, (in chemist's) officine
f.

dispense *vt* distribuer; (*medicine*)
préparer. ● *vi* ∼ **with** se passer
de. **dispenser** *n* (container)
distributeur *m*.

disperse *vt/i* (se) disperser.

display *vt* montrer, exposer;
(*feelings*) manifester. ● *n*
exposition *f*; manifestation *f*;
(Comm) étalage *m*; (of computer)
visuel *m*.

displeased *a* mécontent (**with**
de).

disposable *a* jetable.

disposal *n* (of waste) évacuation *f*;
at sb's ∼ à la disposition de qn.

dispose *vt* disposer. ● *vi* ∼ **of** se
débarrasser de; **well** ∼**d to** bien
disposé envers.

disposition *n* disposition *f*;
(character) naturel *m*.

disprove *vt* réfuter.

dispute *vt* contester. ● *n*
discussion *f*; (Pol) conflit *m*; **in** ∼
contesté.

disqualify *vt* rendre inapte;
(Sport) disqualifier; ∼ **from driving**
retirer le permis à.

disquiet *n* inquiétude *f*.
disquieting *a* inquiétant.

disregard *vt* ne pas tenir compte
de. ● *n* indifférence *f* (**for** à).

disrepair *n* délabrement *m*.

disreputable *a* peu
recommandable.

disrepute *n* discrédit *m*.

disrespect *n* manque *m* de
respect. **disrespectful** *a*
irrespectueux.

disrupt *vt* (disturb, break up)
perturber; (*plans*) déranger.

disruption *n* perturbation *f*.
disruptive *a* perturbateur.

dissatisfied *a* mécontent.

dissect *vt* disséquer.

disseminate *vt* diffuser.

dissent *vi* différer (**from** de). ● *n*
dissentiment *m*.

dissertation *n* mémoire *m*.

disservice *n* **do a** ∼ **to sb** rendre
un mauvais service à qn.

dissident *a & n* dissident/-e (*m/
f*).

dissimilar *a* dissemblable,
différent.

dissipate *vt/i* (se) dissiper.
dissipated *a* (person) dissolu.

dissolve *vt/i* (se) dissoudre.

dissuade *vt* dissuader.

distance *n* distance *f*; **from a** ∼
de loin; **in the** ∼ au loin. **distant**
a éloigné, lointain; (*relative*)
éloigné; (aloof) distant.

distaste *n* dégoût *m*. **distasteful**
a désagréable.

distil *vt* (*pt* **distilled**) distiller.

distinct *a* distinct; (definite) net; **as**
∼ **from** par opposition à.
distinction *n* distinction *f*; (in
exam) mention *f* très bien.
distinctive *a* distinctif.

distinguish *vt/i* distinguer.

distort *vt* déformer. **distortion** *n*
distorsion *f*; (of facts) déformation
f.

distract *vt* distraire. **distracted**
a (distraught) éperdu. **distracting** *a*
gênant. **distraction** *n* (lack of
attention, entertainment) distraction *f*.

distraught *a* éperdu.

distress *n* douleur *f*; (poverty,
danger) détresse *f*. ● *vt* peiner.
distressing *a* pénible.

distribute *vt* distribuer.

district *n* région *f*; (of town)
quartier *m*.

distrust *n* méfiance *f*. ● *vt* se
méfier de.

disturb *vt* déranger; (alarm, worry) troubler. **disturbance** *n* dérangement *m* (of de); (noise) tapage *m*. **disturbances** *npl* (Pol) troubles *mpl*. **disturbed** *a* troublé; (psychologically) perturbé. **disturbing** *a* troublant.

disused *a* désaffecté.

ditch *n* fossé *m*. ● *vt* ▣ abandonner.

ditto *adv* idem.

dive *vi* plonger; (rush) se précipiter. ● *n* plongeon *m*; (of plane) piqué *m*; (place ▣) bouge *m*. **diver** *n* plongeur/-euse *m/f*.

diverge *vi* diverger. **divergent** *a* divergent.

diverse *a* divers.

diversion *n* détournement *m*; (distraction) diversion *f*; (of traffic) déviation *f*. **divert** *vt* détourner; (traffic) dévier.

divide *vt/i* (se) diviser.

dividend *n* dividende *m*.

divine *a* divin.

diving *n*. **~-board** *n* plongeoir *m*. **~-suit** *n* scaphandre *m*.

division *n* division *f*.

divorce *n* divorce *m* (from avec). ● *vt/i* divorcer (d'avec).

divulge *vt* divulguer.

DIY *abbr* ⇒DO-IT-YOURSELF.

dizziness *n* vertige *m*.

dizzy *a* (**-ier**, **-iest**) vertigineux; be *or* feel ~ avoir le vertige.

....

do

present do, does; *present negative* don't, do not; *past* did; *past participle* done

● *transitive and intransitive verb*
····▸ faire; **she is doing her homework** elle fait ses devoirs.
····▸ (progress, be suitable) aller; **how are you doing?** comment ça va?

····▸ (be enough) suffire; **will five dollars ~?** cinq dollars, ça suffira?

● *auxiliary verb*
····▸ (in questions) **~ you like Mozart?** aimes-tu Mozart?, est-ce que tu aimes Mozart?; **did your sister phone?** est-ce que ta sœur a téléphoné?, ta sœur a-t-elle téléphoné?
····▸ (in negatives) **I don't like Mozart** je n'aime pas Mozart.
····▸ (emphatic uses) **I ~ like your dress** j'aime beaucoup ta robe; **I ~ think you should go** je pense vraiment que tu devrais y aller.
····▸ (referring back to another verb) **I live in Oxford and so does Lily** j'habite à Oxford et Lily aussi; **she gets paid more than I ~** elle est payée plus que moi; **'I don't like carrots'—'neither ~ I'** 'je n'aime pas les carottes'—'moi non plus'.
····▸ (imperatives) **don't shut the door** ne ferme pas la porte, **~ be quiet** tais-toi!
····▸ (short questions and answers) **you like fish, don't you?** tu aimes le poisson, n'est-ce pas?; **Lola didn't phone, did she?** Lola n'a pas téléphoné par hasard?; **'does he play tennis?'—'no he doesn't/yes he does'** 'est-ce qu'il joue au tennis?'—'non/oui'; **'Marion didn't say that'—'yes she did'** 'Marion n'a pas dit ça'—'si'.

□ **do away with** supprimer; **do up** (fasten) fermer; (house) refaire;
do with it's to ~ with c'est à propos de; **it's nothing to ~ with** ça n'a rien à voir avec;
do without se passer de.

....

docile *a* docile.

dock *n* (Jur) banc *m* des accusés; dock *m*. ● *vi* arriver au port. ● *vt* mettre à quai; (*wages*) faire une retenue sur.

doctor *n* médecin *m*, docteur *m*; (Univ) docteur *m*. ●*vt* (*cat*) châtrer; (*fig*) altérer.

doctorate *n* doctorat *m*.

document *n* document *m*. **documentary** *a* & *n* documentaire (*m*). **documentation** *n* documentation *f*.

dodge *vt* esquiver. ●*vi* faire un saut de côté. ●*n* mouvement *m* de côté.

dodgems *npl* autos *fpl* tamponneuses.

dodgy *a* (-ier, -iest) (🔲: difficult) épineux, délicat; (untrustworthy) louche 🔲.

doe *n* (deer) biche *f*.

does ⇒DO.

doesn't = DOES NOT.

dog *n* chien *m*. ●*vt* (*pt* dogged) poursuivre. ∼-**collar** *n* col *m* romain. ∼-**eared** *a* écorné.

dogged *a* obstiné.

dogma *n* dogme *m*. **dogmatic** *a* dogmatique.

dogsbody *n* bonne *f* à tout faire.

do-it-yourself *n* bricolage *m*.

doldrums *npl* be in the ∼ (person) avoir le cafard.

dole *vt* ∼ out distribuer. ●*n* 🔲 indemnité *f* de chômage; on the ∼ 🔲 au chômage.

doll *n* poupée *f*. ●*vt* ∼ up 🔲 bichonner.

dollar *n* dollar *m*.

dollop *n* (of food 🔲) gros morceau *m*.

dolphin *n* dauphin *m*.

domain *n* domaine *m*.

dome *n* dôme *m*.

domestic *a* familial; (*trade, flights*) intérieur; (*animal*) domestique. **domesticated** *a* (*animal*) domestiqué.

domestic science *n* arts *mpl* ménagers.

dominant *a* dominant.

dominate *vt/i* dominer. **domination** *n* domination *f*.

domineering *a* dominateur.

domino *n* (*pl* ∼es) domino *m*; ∼es (game) dominos *mpl*.

donate *vt* faire don de. **donation** *n* don *m*.

done ⇒DO.

donkey *n* âne *m*. ∼ work *n* travail *m* pénible.

donor *n* donateur/-trice *m/f*; (of blood) donneur/-euse *m/f*.

don't = DO NOT.

doodle *vi* griffonner.

doom *n* (ruin) ruine *f*; (fate) destin *m*. ●*vt* be ∼ed to être destiné *or* condamné à; ∼ed (to failure) voué à l'échec.

door *n* porte *f*; (of vehicle) portière *f*, porte *f*. ∼**bell** *n* sonnette *f*. ∼**man** *n* (*pl* -men) portier *m*. ∼**mat** *n* paillasson *m*. ∼**step** *n* pas *m* de (la) porte, seuil *m*. ∼**way** *n* porte *f*.

dope *n* 🔲 cannabis *m*; (idiot 🔲) imbécile *mf*. ●*vt* doper. **dopey** *a* (foolish 🔲) imbécile.

dormant *a* en sommeil.

dormitory *n* dortoir *m*; (Univ, US) résidence *f*.

dosage *n* dose *f*; (on label) posologie *f*.

dose *n* dose *f*.

dot *n* point *m*; on the ∼ 🔲 à l'heure pile.

dot-com *n* (société) point com *f*; ∼ millionaire millionnaire *mf* de l'Internet. ∼ shares actions *fpl* des sociétés point com.

dote *vi* ∼ on adorer.

dotted *a* (fabric) à pois; ∼ line pointillé *m*; ∼ with parsemé de.

double *a* double; (room, bed) pour deux personnes; ∼ the size deux fois plus grand. ●*adv* deux fois; **pay** ∼ payer le double. ●*n* double *m*; (stuntman) doublure *f*; ∼**s** (tennis) double *m*; **at** or **on the** ∼ au pas de course. ●*vt/i* doubler; (fold) plier en deux. ∼**-bass** *n* (Mus) contrebasse *f*. ∼**-check** *vt* revérifier. ∼ **chin** *n* double menton *m*. ∼**-cross** *vt* tromper. ∼**-decker** *n* autobus *m* à impériale.

doubt *n* doute *m*. ●*vt* douter de; ∼ **if** or **that** douter que. **doubtful** *a* incertain, douteux; (*person*) qui a des doutes. **doubtless** *adv* sans doute.

dough *n* pâte *f*; (money ▣) fric *m* ▣.

doughnut *n* beignet *m*.

douse *vt* arroser; (*light, fire*) éteindre.

dove *n* colombe *f*.

Dover *n* Douvres.

dowdy *a* (**-ier, -iest**) (*clothes*) sans chic, monotone; (*person*) sans élégance.

down *adv* en bas; (of sun) couché; (lower) plus bas; **come** or **go** ∼ descendre; **go** ∼ **to the post office** aller à la poste; ∼ **under** aux antipodes; ∼ **with** à bas. ●*prep* en bas de; (along) le long de. ●*vt* (knock down, shoot down) abattre; (drink) vider. ●*n* (fluff) duvet *m*.

down: ∼**-and-out** *n* clochard/-e *m/f*. ∼**cast** *a* démoralisé. ∼**fall** *n* chute *f*. ∼**grade** *vt* déclasser. ∼**-hearted** *a* découragé.

downhill *adv* **go** ∼ descendre; (pej) baisser.

down: ∼**load** *n* (Comput) télécharger. ∼**-market** *a* bas de gamme. ∼ **payment** *n* acompte *m*. ∼**pour** *n* grosse averse *f*.

downright *a* (utter) véritable; (honest) franc. ●*adv* carrément.

downsize *vt/i* dégraisser.

downstairs *adv* en bas. ●*a* d'en bas.

down: ∼**stream** *adv* en aval. ∼**-to-earth** *a* pratique.

downtown *a* (US) du centre-ville; ∼ **Boston** le centre de Boston.

downward *a* & *adv*, **downwards** *adv* vers le bas.

doze *vi* somnoler; ∼ **off** s'assoupir. ●*n* somme *m*.

dozen *n* douzaine *f*; **a** ∼ **eggs** une douzaine d'œufs; ∼**s of** ▣ des dizaines de.

Dr *abbr* (**Doctor**) Docteur.

drab *a* terne.

draft *n* (outline) brouillon *m*; (Comm) traite *f*; **the** ∼ (Mil, US) la conscription; **a** ∼ **treaty** un projet de traité; (US) = DRAUGHT. ●*vt* faire le brouillon de; (draw up) rédiger.

drag *vt/i* (*pt* **dragged**) traîner; (*river*) draguer; (pull away) arracher; ∼ **on** s'éterniser. ●*n* (task ▣) corvée *f*; (person ▣) raseur/-euse *m/f*; **in** ∼ en travesti.

dragon *n* dragon *m*.

drain *vt* (*land*) drainer; (*vegetables*) égoutter; (*tank, glass*) vider; (use up) épuiser; ∼ **(off)** (*liquid*) faire écouler. ●*vi* ∼ **(off)** (of liquid) s'écouler. ●*n* (sewer) égout *m*; ∼**-pipe** tuyau *m* d'écoulement; **a** ∼ **on** une ponction sur. **draining-board** *n* égouttoir *m*.

drama *n* art *m* dramatique, théâtre *m*; (play, event) drame *m*. **dramatic** *a* (situation) dramatique; (increase) spectaculaire. **dramatist** *n* dramaturge *m*. **dramatize** *vt* adapter pour la scène; (fig) dramatiser.

drank ⇒DRINK.

drape *vt* draper. **drapes** *npl* (US) rideaux *mpl*.

drastic *a* sévère.

draught *n* courant *m* d'air; ∼**s**

(game) dames *fpl*. ~ **beer** *n* bière *f* pression.

draughty *a* plein de courants d'air.

draw *vt* (*pt* **drew**; *pp* **drawn**) (*picture*) dessiner; (*line*) tracer; (*pull*) tirer; (*attract*) attirer. ● *vi* dessiner; (Sport) faire match nul; (*come, move*) venir. ● *n* (Sport) match *m* nul; (in lottery) tirage *m* au sort. □ ~ **back** reculer; ~ **near** (s')approcher (**to** de); ~ **out** (*money*) retirer; ~ **up** *vi* (stop) s'arrêter; *vt* (*document*) dresser; (*chair*) approcher.

drawback *n* inconvénient *m*.

drawbridge *n* pont-levis *m*.

drawer *n* tiroir *m*.

drawing *n* dessin *m*. ~-**board** *n* planche *f* à dessin. ~-**pin** *n* punaise *f*. ~-**room** *n* salon *m*.

drawl *n* voix *f* traînante.

drawn ⇒DRAW. ● *a* (*features*) tiré; (*match*) nul.

dread *n* terreur *f*, crainte *f*. ● *vt* redouter. **dreadful** *a* épouvantable, affreux. **dreadfully** *adv* terriblement.

dream *n* rêve *m*. ● *vt/i* (*pt* **dreamed** *or* **dreamt**) rêver; ~ **up** imaginer. ● *a* (ideal) de ses rêves.

dreary *a* (-**ier**, -**iest**) triste; (boring) monotone.

dredge *vt* (*river*) draguer; ~ **sth up** (fig) exhumer.

dregs *npl* lie *f*.

drench *vt* tremper.

dress *n* robe *f*; (clothing) tenue *f*. ● *vt/i* (s')habiller; (*food*) assaisonner; (*wound*) panser; ~ **up as** se déguiser en; **get** ~**ed** s'habiller. ~ **circle** *n* premier balcon *m*.

dresser *n* (furniture) buffet *m*; **be a stylish** ~ s'habiller avec chic.

dressing *n* (sauce) assaisonnement *m*; (bandage) pansement *m*. ~-**gown** *n* robe *f*

de chambre. ~-**room** *n* (Sport) vestiaire *m*; (Theat) loge *f*. ~-**table** *n* coiffeuse *f*.

dressmaker *n* couturière *f*.

dressmaking *n* couture *f*.

dress rehearsal *n* répétition *f* générale.

dressy *a* (-**ier**, -**iest**) chic *inv*.

drew ⇒DRAW.

dribble *vi* (*liquid*) dégouliner; (*person*) baver; (football) dribbler.

dried *a* (fruit) sec.

drier *n* séchoir *m*.

drift *vi* aller à la dérive; (pile up) s'amonceler; ~ **towards** glisser vers. ● *n* dérive *f*; amoncellement *m*; (of events) tournure *f*; (meaning) sens *m*; **snow** ~ congère *f*.

driftwood *n* bois *m* flotté.

drill *n* (tool) perceuse *f*; (for teeth) roulette *f*; (training) exercice *m*; (procedure 🅔) marche *f* à suivre; (**pneumatic**) ~ marteau *m* piqueur. ● *vt* percer; (train) entraîner. ● *vi* être à l'exercice.

drink *vt/i* (*pt* **drank**; *pp* **drunk**) boire. ● *n* (liquid) boisson *f*; (glass of alcohol) verre *m*; **a** ~ **of water** un verre d'eau. **drinking water** *n* eau *f* potable.

drip *vi* (*pt* **dripped**) (é)goutter; (washing) s'égoutter. ● *n* goutte *f*; (person 🅔) lavette *f*.

drip-dry *vt* laisser égoutter. ● *a* sans essorage.

drive *vt* (*pt* **drove**; *pp* **driven**) (*vehicle*) conduire; (sb somewhere) chasser, pousser; (*machine*) actionner; ~ **mad** rendre fou. ● *vi* conduire. ● *n* promenade *f* en voiture; (private road) allée *f*; (fig) énergie *f*; (Psych) instinct *m*; (Pol) campagne *f*; (Auto) traction *f*; (golf, Comput) drive *m*; **it's a two-hour** ~ il y a deux heures de route; **left-hand** ~ conduite *f* à gauche. □ ~ **at** en venir à.

drivel *n* bêtises *fpl*.

driver n conducteur/-trice m/f,
chauffeur m. ~'**s license** n (US)
permis m de conduire.
driving n conduite f; **take one's** ~
test passer son permis. ● a (rain)
battant; (wind) cinglant. ~
licence n permis m de conduire.
~ **school** n auto-école f.
drizzle n bruine f. ● vi bruiner.
drone n (of engine) ronronnement
m; (of insects) bourdonnement m.
● vi ronronner; bourdonner.
drool vi baver (over sur).
droop vi pencher, tomber.
drop n goutte f; (fall, lowering) chute
f. ● vt/i (pt **dropped**) (laisser)
tomber; (decrease, lower) baisser; ~
(off) (person from car) déposer; ~
a line écrire un mot (to à). □ ~ **in**
passer (on chez); ~ **off** (doze)
s'assoupir; ~ **out** se retirer (of
de); (of student) abandonner.
drop-out n marginal/-e m/f, raté/
-e m/f.
droppings npl crottes fpl.
drought n sécheresse f.
drove ⇒DRIVE.
droves npl foules fpl.
drown vt/i (se) noyer.
drowsy a somnolent; **be** or **feel** ~
avoir envie de dormir.
drug n drogue f; (Med)
médicament m. ● vt (pt **drugged**)
droguer. ~ **addict** n drogué/-e
m/f. **drugstore** n (US) drugstore
m.
drum n tambour m; (for oil) bidon
m; ~s batterie f. ● vi (pt
drummed) tambouriner. ● vt ~
into sb répéter sans cesse à qn; ~
up (support) susciter; (business)
créer. **drummer** n tambour m; (in
pop group) batteur m.
drumstick n baguette f de
tambour; (of chicken) pilon m.
drunk ⇒DRINK. ● a ivre; **get** ~
s'enivrer. ● n ivrogne/-esse m/f.
drunkard n ivrogne/-esse m/f.

drunken a ivre. **drunkenness** n
ivresse f.
dry a (**drier, driest**) sec; (day)
sans pluie; **be** or **feel** ~ avoir soif.
● vt/i (faire) sécher; ~ **up** (dry
dishes) essuyer la vaisselle; (of
supplies) (se) tarir; (be silent 🗊) se
taire. ~-**clean** vt nettoyer à sec.
~-**cleaner** n teinturier m. ~ **run**
n galop m d'essai.
dual a double. ~ **carriageway** n
route f à quatre voies.
~-**purpose** a qui fait double
emploi.
dub vt (pt **dubbed**) (film) doubler
(into en); (nickname) surnommer.
dubious a (pej) douteux; **be** ~
about avoir des doutes sur.
duck n canard m. ● vi se baisser
subitement. ● vt (head) baisser;
(person) plonger dans l'eau.
duct n conduit m.
dud a (tool 🗊) mal fichu; (coin 🗊)
faux; (cheque 🗊) sans provision.
● n **be a** ~ (not work 🗊) ne pas
marcher.
due a (owing) dû; (expected) attendu;
(proper) qui convient; ~ **to** à cause
de; (caused by) dû à; **she's** ~ **to**
leave now il est prévu qu'elle
parte maintenant; **in** ~ **course** (at
the right time) en temps voulu; (later)
plus tard. ● adv ~ **east** droit vers
l'est. ● n dû m; ~s droits mpl; (of
club) cotisation f.
duel n duel m.
duet n duo m.
dug ⇒DIG.
duke n duc m.
dull a ennuyeux; (colour) terne;
(weather) maussade; (sound)
sourd. ● vt (pain) atténuer;
(shine) ternir.
duly adv comme il convient; (as
expected) comme prévu.
dumb a muet; (stupid 🗊) bête. □ ~
down (course, TV coverage)
baisser le niveau intellectuel de.

dumbfound vt sidérer, ahurir.

dummy n (of tailor) mannequin m; (of baby) sucette f. ● a factice. ~ **run** n galop m d'essai.

dump vt déposer; (get rid of 🔟) se débarrasser de. ● n tas m d'ordures; (refuse tip) décharge f; (Mil) dépôt m; (dull place 🔟) trou m 🔟; **be in the ~s** 🔟 avoir le cafard.

dune n dune f.

dung n (excrement) bouse f, crotte f; (manure) fumier m.

dungarees npl salopette f.

dungeon n cachot m.

duplicate[1] n double m. ● a identique.

duplicate[2] vt faire un double de; (on machine) polycopier.

durable a (tough) résistant; (enduring) durable.

duration n durée f.

during prep pendant.

dusk n crépuscule m.

dusky a (-ier, -iest) foncé.

dust n poussière f. ● vt/i épousseter; (sprinkle) saupoudrer (with de). ~**bin** n poubelle f.

duster n chiffon m.

dust: ~**man** n (pl -men) éboueur m. ~**pan** n pelle f (à poussière).

dusty a (-ier, -iest) poussiéreux.

Dutch a néerlandais; **go ~** partager les frais. ● n (Ling) néerlandais m. ~**man** n Néerlandais m. ~**woman** n Néerlandaise f.

dutiful a obéissant.

duty n devoir m; (tax) droit m; (of official) fonction f; **on ~** de service. ~**-free** a hors-taxe.

duvet n couette f.

dwarf n nain/-e m/f. ● vt rapetisser.

dwell vi (pt dwelt) demeurer; ~ **on** s'étendre sur. **dweller** n habitant/-e m/f. **dwelling** n habitation f.

dwindle vi diminuer.

dye vt teindre. ● n teinture f.

dying a mourant; (art) qui se perd.

dynamic a dynamique.

dynamite n dynamite f.

dysentery n dysenterie f.

dyslexia n dyslexie f. **dyslexic** a & n dyslexique (mf).

each det chaque inv; ~ **one** chacun/-e m/f. ● pron chacun/-e m/f; **oranges at 30p ~** des oranges à 30 pence pièce.

each other pron l'un/l'une l'autre, les uns/les unes les autres; **know ~** se connaître; **love ~** s'aimer.

eager a impatient (**to** de); (person, acceptance) enthousiaste; ~ **for** avide de.

eagle n aigle m.

ear n oreille f; (of corn) épi m. ~**ache** n mal m à l'oreille. ~**drum** n tympan m.

earl n comte m.

early (-ier, -iest) adv tôt, de bonne heure; (ahead of time) en avance; **as I said earlier** comme je l'ai déjà dit. ● a (attempt, years) premier; (hour) matinal; (fruit) précoce; (retirement) anticipé; **have an ~ dinner** dîner tôt; **in ~ summer** au début de l'été; **at the earliest** au plus tôt.

earmark vt désigner (**for** pour).

earn vt gagner; (interest: Comm) rapporter.

earnest a sérieux; **in ~** sérieusement.

earnings npl salaire m; (profits) gains mpl.

ear: **~phones** npl casque m. **~-ring** n boucle f d'oreille. **~shot** n **within/in ~shot** à portée de voix.

earth n terre f; **why/how/where on ~...?** pourquoi/comment/où diable...? ● vt (Electr) mettre à la terre. **earthenware** n faïence f. **~quake** n tremblement m de terre.

ease n facilité f; (comfort) bien-être m; **at ~** à l'aise; (Mil) au repos; **with ~** facilement. ● vt (pain, pressure) atténuer; (congestion) réduire; (transition) faciliter. ● vi (pain, pressure) s'atténuer; (congestion, rain) diminuer.

easel n chevalet m.

east n est m; **the E~** (Orient) l'Orient m. ● a (side, coast) est; (wind) d'est. ● adv à l'est.

Easter n Pâques m; **~ egg** œuf m de Pâques.

easterly a (wind) d'est; (direction) de l'est.

eastern de l'est; **~ France** l'est de la France.

eastward a (side) est inv; (journey) vers l'est.

easy a (-ier, -iest) facile; **go ~ with** 𝄚 y aller doucement avec; **take it ~** ne te fatigue pas. **~going** a accommodant.

eat vt/i (pt ate; pp eaten) manger; **~ into** ronger.

eavesdrop vi (pt -dropped) écouter aux portes.

ebb n reflux m. ● vi descendre; (fig) décliner.

EC abbr (**European Community**) CE f.

eccentric a & n excentrique (mf).

echo n (pl -oes) écho m. ● vt répercuter; (idea, opinion) reprendre. ● vi retentir, résonner (**to, with** de).

eclipse n éclipse f. ● vt éclipser.

ecological a écologique.

ecology n écologie f.

e-commerce n commerce m électronique, commerce m en ligne.

economic a économique; (profitable) rentable. **economical** a économique; (person) économe.

economics n économie f, sciences fpl économiques.

economist n économiste mf.

economize vi **~ (on)** économiser.

economy n économie f. **~-class syndrome** n syndrome m de la classe économique.

ecosystem n écosystème m.

ecstasy n extase f; (drug) ecstasy m.

edge n bord m; (of town) abords mpl; (of knife) tranchant m; **have the ~ on** 𝄚 l'emporter sur; **on ~** énervé. ● vt (trim) border. ● vi **~ forward** avancer doucement.

edgeways adv **I can't get a word in ~** je n'arrive pas à placer un mot.

edgy a énervé.

edible a comestible.

edit vt (pt edited) (newspaper, page) être le rédacteur/la rédactrice de; (check) réviser; (cut) couper; (TV, cinema) monter.

edition n édition f.

editor n (writer) rédacteur/-trice m/f; (of works, anthology) éditeur/-trice m/f; (TV, cinema) monteur/-teuse m/f; **the ~ (in chief)** le rédacteur en chef.

editorial a de la rédaction. ● n éditorial m.

educate vt instruire; (mind, public) éduquer. **educated** a instruit. **education** n éducation f; (schooling) études fpl. **educational**

a éducatif; (*establishment, method*) d'enseignement.

eel *n* anguille *f*.

eerie *a* (**-ier, -iest**) sinistre.

effect *n* effet *m*; **come into ~** entrer en vigueur; **in ~** effectivement; **take ~** agir. ● *vt* effectuer.

effective *a* efficace; (*actual*) effectif. **effectively** *adv* efficacement; (*in effect*) en réalité. **effectiveness** *n* efficacité *f*.

effeminate *a* efféminé.

effervescent *a* effervescent.

efficiency *n* efficacité *f*; (*of machine*) rendement *m*. **efficient** *a* efficace. **efficiently** *adv* efficacement.

effort *n* efforts *mpl*; **make an ~** faire un effort; **be worth the ~** en valoir la peine. **effortless** *a* facile.

effusive *a* expansif.

e.g. *abbr* par ex.

egg *n* œuf *m*. ● *vt* **~ on** pousser. **~-cup** *n* coquetier *m*. **~-plant** *n* (*US*) aubergine *f*. **~shell** *n* coquille *f* d'œuf.

ego *n* amour-propre *m*; (*Psych*) moi *m*. **egotism** *n* égotisme *m*. **egotist** *n* égotiste *mf*.

Egypt *n* Égypte *f*.

eiderdown *n* édredon *m*.

eight *a & n* huit (*m*). **eighteen** *a & n* dix-huit (*m*). **eighth** *a & n* huitième (*mf*). **eighty** *a & n* quatre-vingts (*m*).

either *det & pron* l'un/une ou l'autre; (*with negative*) ni l'un/une ni l'autre; **you can take ~** tu peux prendre n'importe lequel/ laquelle. ● *adv* non plus. ● *conj* **~...or** ou (bien)...ou (bien); (*with negative*) ni...ni.

eject *vt* (*troublemaker*) expulser; (*waste*) rejeter.

elaborate[1] *a* compliqué.

elaborate[2] *vt* élaborer. ● *vi* préciser; **~ on** s'étendre sur.

elastic *a & n* élastique (*m*); **~ band** élastique *m*. **elasticity** *n* élasticité *f*.

elated *a* transporté de joie.

elbow *n* coude *m*; **~ room** espace *m* vital.

elder *a & n* aîné/-e (*m/f*); (*tree*) sureau *m*.

elderly *a* âgé; **the ~** les personnes *fpl* âgées.

eldest *a & n* aîné/-e (*m/f*).

elect *vt* élire; **~ to do** choisir de faire. ● *a* (*president etc.*) futur. **election** *n* élection *f*. **elector** *n* électeur/-trice *m/f*. **electoral** *a* électoral. **electorate** *n* électorat *m*.

electric *a* électrique; **~ blanket** couverture *f* chauffante. **electrical** *a* électrique. **electrician** *n* électricien/-ne *m/f*. **electricity** *n* électricité *f*. **electrify** *vt* électrifier; (*excite*) électriser. **electrocute** *vt* électrocuter.

electronic *a* électronique. **~ publishing** *n* éditique *f*. **electronics** *n* électronique *f*.

elegance *n* élégance *f*.

element *n* élément *m*; (*of heater etc.*) résistance *f*. **elementary** *a* élémentaire.

elephant *n* éléphant *m*.

elevate *vt* élever. **elevation** *n* élévation *f*. **elevator** *n* (*US*) ascenseur *m*.

eleven *a & n* onze (*m*). **eleventh** *a & n* onzième (*mf*).

elicit *vt* obtenir (**from** de).

eligible *a* admissible (**for** à); **be ~ for** (*entitled to*) avoir droit à.

eliminate *vt* éliminer.

elm *n* orme *m*.

elongate *vt* allonger.

elope *vi* s'enfuir (**with** avec).

elopement n fugue f
(amoureuse).

eloquence n éloquence f.

else adv d'autre; **somebody/
nothing** ∼ quelqu'un/rien d'autre;
everybody ∼ tous les autres;
somewhere/something ∼ autre
part/chose; **or** ∼ ou bien.
elsewhere adv ailleurs.

elude vt échapper à.

elusive a insaisissable.

e-mail n (medium) courrier m
électronique; (item) e-mail m, mél
m. ● vt ∼ **sb** envoyer un e-mail
à qn; ∼ **sth** envoyer qch par
courrier électronique.

emancipate vt émanciper.

embankment n (of river) quai m;
(of railway) remblai m.

embark vt embarquer. ● vi (Naut)
embarquer; ∼ **on** (journey)
entreprendre; (campaign, career)
se lancer dans.

embarrass vt plonger dans
l'embarras; **be/feel** ∼**ed** être/se
sentir gêné. **embarrassment** n
confusion f, gêne f.

embassy n ambassade f.

embed vt (pt **embedded**)
enfoncer (**in** dans).

embellish vt embellir.

embers npl braises fpl.

embezzle vt détourner (**from** de).
embezzlement n détournement
m de fonds.

emblem n emblème m.

embodiment n incarnation f.
embody vt incarner; (legally)
incorporer.

emboss vt (metal) repousser;
(paper) gaufrer.

embrace vt (person) étreindre;
(religion) embrasser; (include)
comprendre. ● n étreinte f.

embroider vt broder.
embroidery n broderie f.

embryo n embryon m.

emerald n émeraude f.

emerge vi (person) sortir (**from**
de); **it** ∼**d that** il est apparu que.

emergence n apparition f.

emergency n (crisis) crise f; (urgent
case: Med) urgence f; **in an** ∼ en
cas d'urgence. ● a d'urgence; ∼
exit n sortie f de secours. ∼
landing n atterrissage m forcé. ∼
room n (US) salle f des urgences.

emigrant n émigrant/-e m/f.

emigrate vi émigrer.

eminence n éminence f.
eminent a éminent.

emission n émission f.

emit vt (pt **emitted**) émettre.

emotion n émotion f. **emotional**
a (development) émotif; (reaction)
émotionel; (film, scene)
émouvant.

emotive a qui soulève les
passions.

emperor n empereur m.

emphasis n accent m; **lay** ∼ **on**
mettre l'accent sur. **emphasize**
vt mettre l'accent sur. **emphatic**
a catégorique; (manner) énergique.

empire n empire m.

employ vt employer. **employee** n
employé/-e m/f. **employer** n
employeur/-euse m/f.

employment n emploi m; **find** ∼
trouver du travail.

empower vt autoriser (**to do** à
faire).

empty a (-ier, -iest) vide; (street)
désert; (promise) vain; **on an** ∼
stomach à jeun. ● vt/i (se) vider.
∼-**handed** a les mains vides.

emulate vt imiter.

enable vt ∼ **sb to** permettre à qn
de.

enamel n émail m. ● vt (pt
enamelled) émailler.

encase vt revêtir, recouvrir (**in**
de).

enchant vt enchanter.

enclose vt entourer; (land) clôturer; (with letter) joindre. **enclosed** a (space) clos; (with letter) ci-joint. **enclosure** n enceinte f; (with letter) pièce f jointe.

encompass vt inclure.

encore interj & n bis (m).

encounter vt rencontrer. ● n rencontre f.

encourage vt encourager.

encroach vi ~ **upon** empiéter sur.

encyclopaedia n encyclopédie f. **encyclopaedic** a encyclopédique.

end n fin f; (farthest part) bout m; **come to an ~** prendre fin; **~-product** produit m fini; **in the ~** finalement; **no ~** ⓣ énormément de; **on ~** (upright) debout; (in a row) de suite; **put an ~ to** mettre fin à. ● vt (marriage) mettre fin à; **~ one's days** finir ses jours. ● vi se terminer; **~ up doing** finir par faire.

endanger vt mettre en danger.

endearing a attachant.

endeavour, (US) **endeavor** n (attempt) tentative f; (hard work) effort m. ● vi faire tout son possible (**to do** pour faire).

ending n fin f.

endive n chicorée f.

endless a interminable; (supply) inépuisable; (patience) infini.

endorse vt (candidate, decision) appuyer; (product, claim) approuver; (cheque) endosser.

endurance n endurance f.

endure vt supporter. ● vi durer. **enduring** a durable.

enemy n & a ennemi/-e (m/f).

energetic a énergique. **energy** n énergie f.

enforce vt (rule, law) appliquer, faire respecter; (silence,

discipline) imposer (**on** à); **~d** forcé.

engage vt (staff) engager; (attention) retenir; **be ~d in** se livrer à. ● vi ~ **in** se livrer à. **engaged** a fiancé; (busy) occupé; **get ~d** se fiancer. **engagement** n fiançailles fpl; (meeting) rendez-vous m; (undertaking) engagement m.

engaging a attachant, engageant.

engine n moteur m; (of train) locomotive f; (of ship) machines fpl. **~-driver** n mécanicien m.

engineer n ingénieur m; (repairman) technicien m; (on ship) mécanicien m. ● vt (contrive) manigancer.

engineering n ingénierie f; (industry) mécanique f; **civil ~** génie m civil.

England n Angleterre f.

English a anglais. ● n (Ling) anglais m; **the ~** les Anglais mpl. **~man** n Anglais m. **~-speaking** a anglophone. **~woman** n Anglaise f.

engrave vt graver.

engrossed a absorbé (**in** dans).

engulf vt engouffrer.

enhance vt (prospects, status) améliorer; (price, value) augmenter.

enjoy vt aimer (**doing** faire); (benefit from) jouir de; **~ oneself** s'amuser; **~ your meal!** bon appétit! **enjoyable** a agréable. **enjoyment** n plaisir m.

enlarge vt agrandir. ● vi s'agrandir; (pupil) se dilater; **~ on** s'étendre sur. **enlargement** n agrandissement m.

enlighten vt éclairer (**on** sur). **enlightenment** n instruction f; (information) éclaircissement m.

enlist vt (person) recruter; (fig) obtenir. ● vi s'engager.

enmity n inimitié f.

enormous a énorme.
enormously adv énormément.
enough adv & n assez; **have ~ of** en avoir assez de. ●det assez de; **~ glasses/time** assez de verres/de temps.
enquire ⇒INQUIRE. **enquiry** ⇒INQUIRY.
enrage vt mettre en rage, rendre furieux.
enrol vt/i (pt **enrolled**) (s')inscrire. **enrolment** n inscription f.
ensure vt garantir; **~ that** (ascertain) s'assurer que.
entail vt entraîner.
entangle vt emmêler.
enter vt (room, club, phase) entrer dans; (note down, register) inscrire; (data) entrer, saisir. ●vi entrer (**into** dans); **~ for** s'inscrire à.
enterprise n entreprise f; (boldness) initiative f. **enterprising** a entreprenant.
entertain vt amuser, divertir; (guests) recevoir; (ideas) considérer. **entertainer** n artiste mf. **entertaining** a divertissant. **entertainment** n divertissement m; (performance) spectacle m.
enthral vt (pt **enthralled**) captiver.
enthusiasm n enthousiasme m (**for** pour).
enthusiast n passionné/-e m/f (**for** de). **enthusiastic** a (supporter) enthousiaste; **be ~ic about** être enthousiasmé par.
enthusiastically adv avec enthousiasme.
entice vt attirer; **~ to do** entraîner à faire.
entire a entier. **entirely** adv entièrement. **entirety** n **in its ~ty** en entier.
entitle vt donner droit à (**to sth** à qch; **to do** de faire); **~d** (book)

intitulé; **be ~d to sth** avoir droit à qch.
entrance[1] n (entering, way in) entrée f (**to** de); (right to enter) admission f. ●a (charge, exam) d'entrée.
entrance[2] vt transporter.
entrant n (Sport) concurrent/-e m/f; (in exam) candidat/-e m/f.
entrenched a (opinion) inébranlable; (Mil) retranché.
entrepreneur n entrepreneur/-euse m/f.
entrust vt confier; **~ sb with sth** confier qch à qn.
entry n entrée f; **~ form** fiche f d'inscription.
envelop vt (pt **enveloped**) envelopper.
envelope n enveloppe f.
envious a envieux (**of** de).
environment n (ecological) environnement m; (social) milieu m. **environmental** a du milieu; de l'environnement.
environmentalist n écologiste mf.
envisage vt prévoir (**doing** de faire).
envoy n envoyé/-e m/f.
envy n envie f. ●vt envier; **~ sb sth** envier qch à qn.
epic n épopée f. ●a épique.
epidemic n épidémie f.
epilepsy n épilepsie f.
episode n épisode m.
epitome n modèle m. **epitomize** vt incarner.
equal a & n égal/-e (m/f); **~ opportunities/rights** égalité f des chances/droits; **~ to** (task) à la hauteur de. ●vt (pt **equalled**) égaler. **equality** n égalité f.
equalize vt/i égaliser. **equalizer** n (goal) but m égalisateur. **equally** adv (divide) en parts égales; (just as) tout aussi.

E

equanimity n sérénité f.

equate vt assimiler (**with** à).
equation n équation f.

equator n équateur m.

equilibrium n équilibre m.

equip vt (pt **equipped**) équiper
(**with** de). **equipment** n
équipement m.

equity n équité f.

equivalence n équivalence f.

era n ère f, époque f.

eradicate vt éliminer; (disease)
éradiquer.

erase vt effacer. **eraser** n (rubber)
gomme f.

erect a droit. ● vt ériger.
erection n érection f.

erode vt éroder; (fig) saper.
erosion n érosion f.

erotic a érotique.

errand n commission f, course f.

erratic a (behaviour, person)
imprévisible; (performance)
inégal.

error n erreur f.

erupt vi (volcano) entrer en
éruption; (fig) éclater.

escalate vt intensifier. ● vi
(conflict) s'intensifier. **escalation**
n intensification f. **escalator** n
escalier m mécanique, escalator®
m.

escapade n frasque f.

escape vt échapper à. ● vi
s'enfuir, s'évader; (gas) fuir. ● n
fuite f, évasion f; (of gas etc.) fuite
f; **have a lucky** or **narrow** ~
l'échapper belle.

escapism n évasion f (du réel).

escort[1] n (guard) escorte f;
(companion) compagnon/compagne
m/f.

escort[2] vt escorter.

Eskimo n Esquimau/-de m/f.

especially adv en particulier.

espionage n espionnage m.

espresso n (café) express m.

essay n (in literature) essai m;
(School) rédaction f; (Univ)
dissertation f.

essence n essence f.

essential a essentiel; **the** ~**s**
l'essentiel m. **essentially** adv
essentiellement.

establish vt établir; (business)
fonder.

establishment n (process)
instauration f; (institution)
établissement m; **the E**~ l'ordre
m établi.

estate n (house and land) domaine
m; (possessions) biens mpl; (housing
estate) cité f. ~ **agent** n agent m
immobilier. ~ **car** n break m.

esteem n estime f.

esthetic a (US) = AESTHETIC.

estimate[1] n (calculation) estimation
f; (Comm) devis m.

estimate[2] vt évaluer; ~ **that**
estimer que. **estimation** n
(esteem) estime f; (judgment)
opinion f.

Estonia n Estonie f.

estuary n estuaire m.

eternal a éternel.

eternity n éternité f.

ethic n éthique f; ~**s** moralité f.
ethical a éthique.

ethnic a ethnique. ~ **cleansing**
n nettoyage m ethnique.

EU abbr (**European Union**) UE f,
Union f européenne.

euphoria n euphorie f.

euro n euro m. ~ **zone** n zone f
euro.

euroland euroland m.

Europe n Europe f.

European a & n européen/-ne
(m/f); ~ **Community** Communauté
f Européenne.

eurosceptic n eurosceptique mf.

euthanasia n euthanasie f.

evacuate vt évacuer.

evade vt (*blow*) esquiver;
(*question*) éluder.

evaporate vi s'évaporer; ∼d **milk**
lait m condensé.

evasion n fuite f (of devant);
(excuse) faux-fuyant m; **tax** ∼
évasion f fiscale. **evasive** a
évasif.

eve n veille f (of de).

even a (*surface, voice, contest*)
égal; (*teeth, hem*) régulier;
(*number*) pair; **get** ∼ **with** se venger
de. ● adv même; ∼ **better**/*etc.*
(still) encore mieux/*etc.*; ∼ **so**
quand même. □ ∼ **out**
(*differences*) s'atténuer; ∼ **sth out**
(*inequalities*) réduire qch; ∼ **up**
équilibrer.

evening n soir m; (*whole evening,
event*) soirée f.

evenly adv (*spread, apply*)
uniformément; (*breathe*)
régulièrement; (*equally*) en parts
égales.

event n événement m; (Sport)
épreuve f; **in the** ∼ **of** en cas de.
eventful a mouvementé.

eventual a (*outcome, decision*)
final; (*aim*) à long terme.
eventuality n éventualité f.
eventually adv finalement; (in
future) un jour ou l'autre.

ever adv jamais; (at all times)
toujours.

evergreen n arbre m à feuilles
persistantes.

everlasting a éternel.

ever since prep & adv depuis.

every a ∼ **house**/**window** toutes
les maisons/les fenêtres; ∼ **time**/
minute chaque fois/minute; ∼ **day**
tous les jours; ∼ **other day** tous
les deux jours. **everybody** pron
tout le monde. **everyday** a
quotidien. **everyone** pron tout le
monde. **everything** pron tout.
everywhere adv partout; ∼**where**
he goes partout où il va.

evict vt expulser (from de).

evidence n (proof) preuves fpl
(that que; of, for de); (testimony)
témoignage m; (traces) trace f (of
de); **give** ∼ témoigner; **be in** ∼
être visible. **evident** a manifeste.
evidently adv (apparently)
apparemment; (obviously)
manifestement.

evil a malfaisant. ● n mal m.

evoke vt évoquer.

evolution n évolution f.

evolve vi évoluer. ● vt élaborer.

ewe n brebis f.

ex- pref ex-, ancien.

exact a exact; **the** ∼ **opposite**
exactement le contraire. ● vt
exiger (from de). **exactly** adv
exactement.

exaggerate vt/i exagérer.

exalted a élevé.

exam n 🄸 examen m.

examination n examen m.

examine vt examiner; (witness)
interroger. **examiner** n
examinateur/-trice m/f.

example n exemple m; **for** ∼ par
exemple; **make an** ∼ **of** punir
pour l'exemple.

exasperate vt exaspérer.

excavate vt fouiller.
excavations npl fouilles fpl.

exceed vt dépasser.
exceedingly adv extrêmement.

excel vi (pt **excelled**) exceller
(at, in en; at doing à faire). ● vt
surpasser.

excellence n excellence f.

excellent a excellent.

except prep sauf, excepté; ∼ **for**
à part. ● vt excepter. **excepting**
prep sauf, excepté.

exception n exception f; **take** ∼
to s'offusquer. **exceptional** a
exceptionnel.

excerpt n extrait m.

excess[1] n excès m.

excess² *a* ~ **weight** excès *m* de poids; ~ **baggage** excédent *m* de bagages.

excessive *a* excessif.

exchange *vt* échanger (**for** contre). ● *n* échange *m*; (between currencies) change *m*; ~ **rate** taux *m* de change; **telephone** ~ central *m* téléphonique.

Exchequer *n* (Pol) ministère *m* britannique des finances.

excise *n* excise *f*, taxe *f*.

excite *vt* exciter; (enthuse) enthousiasmer. **excited** *a* excité; **get** ~**d** s'exciter. **excitement** *n* excitation *f*. **exciting** *a* passionnant.

exclaim *vt* s'exclamer.

exclamation *n* exclamation *f*; ~ **mark** or **point** (US) point *m* d'exclamation.

exclude *vt* exclure.

exclusive *a* (club) fermé; (rights) exclusif; (news item) en exclusivité; ~ **of meals** repas non compris. **exclusively** *adv* exclusivement.

excruciating *a* atroce.

excursion *n* excursion *f*.

excuse¹ *vt* excuser; ~ **from** (exempt) dispenser de; ~ **me!** excusez-moi!, pardon!

excuse² *n* (reason) excuse *f*; (pretext) prétexte *m* (**for sth** à qch; **for doing** pour faire).

ex-directory *a* sur liste rouge.

execute *vt* exécuter. **executioner** *n* bourreau *m*.

executive *n* (person) cadre *m*; (committee) exécutif *m*. ● *a* exécutif.

exemplary *a* exemplaire.

exemplify *vt* illustrer.

exempt *a* exempt (**from** de). ● *vt* exempter.

exercise *n* exercice *m*; ~ **book** cahier *m*. ● *vt* exercer; (restraint, patience) faire preuve de. ● *vi* faire de l'exercice.

exert *vt* exercer; ~ **oneself** se fatiguer. **exertion** *n* effort *m*.

exhaust *vt* épuiser. ● *n* (Auto) pot *m* d'échappement.

exhaustive *a* exhaustif.

exhibit *vt* exposer; (fig) manifester. ● *n* objet *m* exposé.

exhibition *n* exposition *f*; (of skill) démonstration *f*. **exhibitionist** *n* exhibitionniste *mf*.

exhibitor *n* exposant/-e *m/f*.

exhilarate *vt* griser.

exile *n* exil *m*; (person) exilé/-e *m/f*. ● *vt* exiler.

exist *vi* exister. **existence** *n* existence *f*; **be in** ~**ence** exister. **existing** *a* actuel.

exit *n* sortie *f*. ● *vt/i* (also Comput) sortir (de).

exodus *n* exode *m*.

exonerate *vt* disculper.

exotic *a* exotique.

expand *vt* développer; (workforce) accroître. ● *vi* se développer; (population) s'accroître; (metal) se dilater.

expanse *n* étendue *f*.

expansion *n* développement *m*; (Pol, Comm) expansion *f*.

expatriate *a & n* expatrié/-e (*m/ f*).

expect *vt* s'attendre à; (suppose) supposer; (demand) exiger; (baby) attendre.

expectancy *n* attente *f*.

expectant *a* ~ **mother** future maman *f*.

expectation *n* (assumption) prévision *f*; (hope) aspiration *f*; (demand) exigence *f*.

expedient *a* opportun. ● *n* expédient *m*.

expedition *n* expédition *f*.

expel *vt* (*pt* **expelled**) expulser; (pupil) renvoyer.

expend vt consacrer.

expenditure n dépenses fpl.

expense n frais mpl; **at sb's ~** aux frais de qn; **~ account** frais mpl de représentation.

expensive a cher; (tastes) de luxe. **expensively** adv luxueusement.

experience n expérience f. ● vt (undergo) connaître; (feel) éprouver; **~d** expérimenté.

experiment n expérience f. ● vi expérimenter, faire des essais.

expert n spécialiste mf. ● a spécialisé, expert. **expertise** n compétence f. **expertly** adv de manière experte.

expire vi expirer; **~d** périmé. **expiry** n expiration f.

explain vt expliquer. **explanation** n explication f. **explanatory** a explicatif.

explicit a explicite.

explode vt/i (faire) exploser.

exploit[1] n exploit m

exploit[2] vt exploiter.

exploration n exploration f. **exploratory** a (talks) exploratoire. **explore** vt explorer; (fig) étudier. **explorer** n explorateur/-trice m/f.

explosion n explosion f. **explosive** a & n explosif (m).

exponent n avocat/-e m/f (of de).

export[1] vt exporter.

export[2] n (process) exportation f; (product) produit m d'exportation.

expose vt exposer; (disclose) révéler.

exposure n révélation f; (Photo) pose f; **die of ~** mourir de froid.

express vt exprimer. ● a exprès. ● adv **send sth ~** envoyer qch en exprès. ● n (train) rapide m. **expression** n expression f. **expressive** a expressif. **expressly** adv expressément.

exquisite a exquis.

extend vt (visit) prolonger; (house) agrandir; (range) élargir; (arm, leg) étendre. ● vi (stretch) s'étendre; (in time) se prolonger.

extension n (of line, road) prolongement m; (of visa, loan) prorogation f; (building) addition f; (phone number) poste m; (cable) rallonge f.

extensive a vaste; (study) approfondi; (damage) considérable. **extensively** adv (much) beaucoup; (very) très.

extent n (size, scope) étendue f; (degree) mesure f; **to some ~** dans une certaine mesure; **to such an ~ that** à tel point que.

extenuating a atténuant.

exterior a & n extérieur (m).

exterminate vt exterminer.

external a extérieur; (cause, medical use) externe.

extinct a (species) disparu; (volcano, passion) éteint.

extinguish vt éteindre. **extinguisher** n extincteur m.

extol vt (pt **extolled**) louer, chanter les louanges de.

extort vt extorquer (from à). **extortion** n (Jur) extorsion f. **extortionate** a exorbitant.

extra a supplémentaire; **~ charge** supplément m; **~ time** (football) prolongation f; **~ strong** extra-fort. ● adv encore; plus. ● n supplément m; (cinema) figurant/-e m/f.

extract[1] vt sortir (from de); (tooth) extraire; (promise) arracher.

extract[2] n extrait m.

extra-curricular a parascolaire.

extradite vt extrader.

extramarital a extraconjugal.

extramural a (Univ) hors faculté.

extraordinary a extraordinaire.

E

extravagance *n* prodigalité *f*.
extravagant *a* (*person*)
dépensier; (*claim*) extravagant.
extreme *a & n* extrême (*m*).
extremely *adv* extrêmement.
extremist *n* extrémiste *mf*.
extremity *n* extrémité *f*.
extricate *vt* dégager.
extrovert *n* extraverti/-e *m/f*.
exuberance *n* exubérance *f*.
exude *vt* (*charm*) respirer; (*smell*)
exhaler.
eye *n* œil *m* (*pl* yeux); **keep an ~**
on surveiller. ● *vt* (*pt* **eyed**; *pres*
p **eyeing**) regarder. **~ball** *n*
globe *m* oculaire. **~brow** *n*
sourcil *m*. **~-catching** *a*
attrayant. **~lash** *n* cil *m*. **~lid** *n*
paupière *f*. **~-opener** *n*
révélation *f*. **~-shadow** *n* ombre
f à paupières. **~sight** *n* vue *f*.
~sore *n* horreur *f*. **~witness** *n*
témoin *m* oculaire.

fable *n* fable *f*.
fabric *n* (*cloth*) tissu *m*.
fabulous *a* fabuleux; (*marvellous* 🄸)
formidable.
face *n* visage *m*, figure *f*;
(*expression*) air *m*; (*appearance, dignity*)
face *f*; (*of clock*) cadran *m*; (*Geol*)
face *f*; (*of rock*) paroi *f*; **in the ~ of**
face à; **make a (funny) ~** faire la
grimace; **~ to ~** face à face. ● *vt*
être en face de; (*risk*) devoir
affronter; (*confront*) faire face à;
(*deal with*) **I can't ~ him** je n'ai pas
le courage de le voir. ● *vi*
(*person*) regarder; (*chair*) être
tourné vers; (*window*) donner

sur; **~ up to** faire face à; **~d with**
face à.
face-lift *n* lifting *m*; **give a ~ to**
donner un coup de neuf à.
face value *n* valeur *f* nominale;
take sth at ~ prendre qch au pied
de la lettre.
facial *a* (*hair*) du visage; (*injury*)
au visage. ● *n* soin *m* du visage.
facility *n* (*building*) complexe *m*;
(*feature*) fonction *f*; **facilities**
(*equipment*) équipements *mpl*.
facsimile *n* fac-similé *m*.
fact *n* fait *m*; **as a matter of ~, in**
~ en fait; **know for a ~ that** savoir
de source sûre que; **owing/due to**
the ~ that étant donné que.
factor *n* facteur *m*.
factory *n* usine *f*.
factual *a* (*account, description*)
basé sur les faits; (*evidence*)
factuel.
faculty *n* faculté *f*.
fade *vi* (*sound*) s'affaiblir;
(*memory*) s'effacer; (*flower*) se
faner; (*material*) se décolorer;
(*colour*) passer.
fail *vi* échouer; (grow weak) (s'af)
faiblir; (run short) manquer;
(*engine*) tomber en panne. ● *vt*
(*exam*) échouer à; **~ to do** (not do)
ne pas faire; (not be able) ne pas
réussir à faire; **without ~** à coup
sûr.
failing *n* défaut *m*; **~ that/this**
sinon.
failure *n* échec *m*; (*person*) raté/-e
m/f; (*breakdown*) panne *f*; **~ to do**
(inability) incapacité *f* de faire.
faint *a* léger, faible; **feel ~** (ill) se
sentir mal; **I haven't the ~est idea**
je n'en ai pas la moindre idée.
● *vi* s'évanouir. ● *n*
évanouissement *m*. **~-hearted** *a*
timide.
fair *n* foire *f*. ● *a* (*hair, person*)
blond; (*skin*) clair; (*weather*)
beau; (*amount, quality*)

raisonnable; (just) juste, équitable.
● *adv* (*play*) loyalement.

fairground *n* champ *m* de foire.

fairly *adv* (*justly*) équitablement;
(rather) assez.

fairness *n* justice *f*.

fairy *n* fée *f*. ~ **story**, ~**-tale** *n*
conte *m* de fées.

faith *n* (belief) foi *f*; (confidence)
confiance *f*.

faithful *a* fidèle.

fake *n* (forgery) faux *m*; (person)
imposteur *m*; **it is a** ~ c'est un
faux. ● *a* faux. ● *vt* (*signature*)
contrefaire; (*results*) falsifier;
(*illness*) feindre.

falcon *n* faucon *m*.

fall *vi* (*pt* **fell**; *pp* **fallen**) tomber;
~ **short** être insuffisant. ● *n*
chute *f*; (autumn: US) automne *m*;
Niagara F~s chutes *fpl* du
Niagara. □ ~ **back on** se
rabattre sur; ~ **behind** prendre
du retard; ~ **down** *or* **off** tomber;
~ **for** (*person* ⊞) tomber
amoureux de; (*a trick* ⊞) se
laisser prendre à; ~ **in** (Mil) se
mettre en rangs; ~ **off** (decrease)
diminuer; ~ **out** se brouiller
(**with** avec); ~ **over** tomber (par
terre), ~ **through** (*plans*) tomber
à l'eau.

fallacy *n* erreur *f*.

false *a* faux. ~ **teeth** *npl* dentier
m.

falter *vi* (*courage*) faiblir; (when
speaking) bafouiller ⊞.

fame *n* renommée *f*. **famed** *a*
célèbre (**for** pour).

familiar *a* familier; **be** ~ **with**
connaître.

family *n* famille *f*.

famine *n* famine *f*.

famished *a* affamé.

famous *a* célèbre (**for** pour).

fan *n* (mechanical) ventilateur *m*;
(hand-held) éventail *m*; (of person)
fan *mf* ⊞, admirateur/-trice *m/f*;
(enthusiast) fervent/-e *m/f*,
passionné/-e *m/f*. ● *vt* (*pt*
fanned) (*face*) éventer; (fig)
attiser. ● *vi* ~ **out** se déployer en
éventail.

fanatic *n* fanatique *mf*.

fan belt *n* courroie *f* de
ventilateur.

fancy *n* (whim, fantasy) fantaisie *f*;
take a ~ **to sb** se prendre
d'affection pour qn; **it took my** ~
ça m'a plu. ● *a* (buttons etc.)
fantaisie *inv*; (prices)
extravagant; (impressive)
impressionnant. ● *vt* s'imaginer;
(want ⊞) avoir envie de; (like ⊞)
aimer. ~ **dress** *n* déguisement
m.

fang *n* (of dog) croc *m*; (of snake)
crochet *m*.

fantasize *vi* fantasmer.

fantastic *a* fantastique.

fantasy *n* (whim) fantaisie *f*; (daydream)
fantasme *m*.

fanzine *n* magazine *m* des fans,
fanzine *m*.

FAQ *abbr* (**Frequently Asked
Questions**) (Internet) FAQ *f*, foire *f*
aux questions.

far *adv* loin; (much) beaucoup;
(very) très; ~ **away**, ~ **off** au loin;
as ~ **as** (up to) jusqu'à; **as** ~ **as I
know** autant que je sache; **by** ~
de loin; ~ **from** loin de. ● *a*
lointain; (end, side) autre. ~**away**
a lointain.

farce *n* farce *f*.

fare *n* (prix du) billet *m*; (food)
nourriture *f*. ● *vi* (progress) aller;
(manage) se débrouiller.

Far East *n* Extrême-Orient *m*.

farewell *interj* & *n* adieu (*m*).

farm *n* ferme *f*. ● *vt* cultiver; ~
out céder en sous-traitance. ● *vi*
être fermier. **farmer** *n* fermier *m*.
~**house** *n* ferme *f*. **farming** *n*

F

agriculture f. ~**yard** n basse-cour f.

fart ▣ vi péter ▣. ●n pet m ▣.

farther adv plus loin. ●a plus éloigné.

farthest adv le plus loin. ●a le plus éloigné.

fascinate vt fasciner.

Fascism n fascisme m.

fashion n (current style) mode f; (manner) façon f; **in** ~ à la mode; **out of** ~ démodé. ●vt façonner. **fashionable** a à la mode.

fast a rapide; (colour) grand teint inv; (firm) fixe, solide; **be** ~ (of a clock) avancer. ●adv vite; (firmly) ferme; **be** ~ **asleep** dormir d'un sommeil profond. ●vi jeûner. ●n jeûne m.

fasten vt/i (s')attacher. **fastener**, **fastening** n attache f, fermeture f.

fast food n fast-food m; restauration f rapide.

fat n graisse f; (on meat) gras m. ●a (**fatter, fattest**) gros, gras; (meat) gras; (profit) gros; **a** ~ **lot** ▣ bien peu (**of** de).

fatal a mortel; (fateful, disastrous) fatal. **fatality** n mort m. **fatally** adv mortellement.

fate n sort m. **fateful** a fatidique.

father n père m. ~**hood** n paternité f. ~**-in-law** n (pl ~**s-in-law**) beau-père m.

fathom n brasse f (=1.8 m). ●vt ~ (**out**) comprendre.

fatigue n épuisement m; (Tech) fatigue f. ●vt fatiguer.

fatten vt/i engraisser. **fattening** a qui fait grossir.

fatty a (food) gras; (tissue) adipeux.

faucet n (US) robinet m.

fault n (defect, failing) défaut m; (blame) faute f; (Geol) faille f; **at** ~ fautif; **find** ~ **with** critiquer. ●vt

~ **sth/sb** prendre en défaut qn/ qch. **faulty** a défectueux.

favour, (US) **favor** n faveur f; **do sb a** ~ rendre service à qn; **in** ~ **of** pour. ●vt favoriser; (support) être en faveur de; (prefer) préférer. **favourable** a favorable.

favourite a & n favori/-te (m/f).

fawn n (animal) faon m; (colour) beige m foncé. ●vi ~ **on** flagorner.

fax n fax m, télécopie f. ●vt faxer, envoyer par télécopie. ~ **machine** n fax m; télécopieur m; (for public use) Publifax® m.

FBI abbr (**Federal Bureau of Investigation**) (US) Police f judiciaire fédérale.

fear n crainte f, peur f; (fig) risque m; **for** ~ **of/that** de peur de/que. ●vt craindre.

feasible a faisable; (likely) plausible.

feast n festin m; (Relig) fête f. ●vi festoyer. ●vt régaler (**on** de).

feat n exploit m.

feather n plume f. ●vt ~ **one's nest** s'enrichir.

feature n caractéristique f; (of person, face) trait m; (film) long métrage m; (article) article m de fond. ●vt (advert) représenter; (give prominence to) mettre en vedette. ●vi figurer (**in** dans).

February n février m.

fed ⇒FEED. ●a **be** ~ **up** ▣ en avoir marre ▣ (**with** de).

federal a fédéral.

fee n (for entrance) prix m; ~**(s)** (of doctor) honoraires mpl; (of actor, artist) cachet m; (for tuition) frais mpl; (for enrolment) droits mpl.

feeble a faible.

feed vt (pt **fed**) nourrir, donner à manger à; (suckle) allaiter; (supply) alimenter. ●vi se nourrir (**on** de); ~ **in information** rentrer des données. ● *n* nourriture *f*; (of baby) tétée *f*.

feedback *n* réaction(s) *f(pl)*; (Med, Tech) feed-back *m*.

feel *vt* (*pt* felt) (touch) tâter; (be conscious of) sentir; (*emotion*) ressentir; (experience) éprouver; (think) estimer. ● *vi* (tired, lonely) se sentir; ~ **hot/thirsty** avoir chaud/soif; ~ **as if** avoir l'impression que; ~ **awful** (ill) se sentir malade; ~ **like** (want 🔲) avoir envie de.

feeler *n* antenne *f*; **put out** ~s tâter le terrain.

feeling *n* (emotion) sentiment *m*; (physical) sensation *f*; (impression) impression *f*.

feet ⇒FOOT.

feign *vt* feindre.

fell ⇒FALL. ● *vt* (cut down) abattre.

fellow *n* compagnon *m*, camarade *m*; (of society) membre *m*; (man 🔲) type *m* 🔲. ~-**countryman** *n* compatriote *m*. ~-**passenger** *n* compagnon *m* de voyage.

fellowship *n* camaraderie *f*; (group) association *f*.

felony *n* crime *m*.

felt ⇒FEEL. ● *n* feutre *m*. ~-**tip** *n* feutre *m*.

female *a* (*animal*) femelle; (voice, sex) féminin. ● *n* femme *f*; (animal) femelle *f*.

feminine *a* & *n* féminin (*m*). **femininity** *n* féminité *f*. **feminist** *n* féministe *mf*.

fence *n* barrière *f*; **sit on the** ~ ne pas prendre position. ● *vt* ~ (in) clôturer. ● *vi* (Sport) faire de l'escrime. **fencing** *n* escrime *f*.

fend *vi* ~ **for oneself** se débrouiller tout seul. ● *vt* ~ **off** (blow, attack) parer.

fender *n* (for fireplace) garde-cendre *m*; (mudguard: US) garde-boue *m inv*.

ferment¹ *n* ferment *m*; (excitement: fig) agitation *f*.

ferment² *vt/i* (faire) fermenter.

fern *n* fougère *f*.

ferocious *a* féroce.

ferret *n* (animal) furet *m*. ● *vi* ~ **about** fureter. ● *vt* ~ **out** dénicher.

ferry *n* (long-distance) ferry *m*; (short-distance) bac *m*. ● *vt* transporter.

fertile *a* fertile; (person, animal) fécond. **fertilizer** *n* engrais *m*.

festival *n* festival *m*; (Relig) fête *f*.

festive *a* de fête, gai; ~ **season** période *f* des fêtes. **festivity** *n* réjouissances *fpl*.

fetch *vt* (go for) aller chercher; (bring person) amener; (bring thing) apporter; (be sold for) rapporter.

fête *n* fête *f*; (church) kermesse *f*. ● *vt* fêter.

fetish *n* (object) fétiche *m*; (Psych) obsession *f*.

feud *n* querelle *f*.

fever *n* fièvre *f*. **feverish** *a* fiévreux.

few *det* peu de; **a** ~ **houses** quelques maisons; **quite a** ~ **people** un bon nombre de personnes. ● *pron* quelques-uns/ quelques-unes.

fewer *det* moins de; **be** ~ être moins nombreux (**than** que). **fewest** *det* le moins de.

fiancé *n* fiancé *m*. **fiancée** *n* fiancée *f*.

fibre, (US) **fiber** *n* fibre *f*. ~**glass** *n* fibre *f* de verre.

fiction *n* fiction *f*; (works of) ~ romans *mpl*. **fictional** *a* fictif.

fiddle *n* 🔲 violon *m*; (swindle 🔲) combine *f*. ● *vi* 🔲 frauder. ● *vt* 🔲 falsifier; ~ **with** 🔲 tripoter 🔲.

fidget *vi* gigoter sans cesse.

field *n* champ *m*; (Sport) terrain *m*; (fig) domaine *m*. ● *vt* (ball: cricket) bloquer.

F

fierce a féroce; (*storm, attack*) violent.

fiery a (**-ier, -iest**) (hot) ardent; (spirited) fougueux.

fifteen a & n quinze (m).

fifth a & n cinquième (mf).

fifty a & n cinquante (m).

fig n figue f.

fight vi (pt **fought**) se battre; (struggle: fig) lutter; (quarrel) se disputer. ● vt se battre avec; (*evil*: fig) lutter contre. ● n (struggle) lutte f; (quarrel) dispute f; (brawl) bagarre f; (Mil) combat m. □ ~ **back** se défendre (**against** contre); ~ **off** surmonter; ~ **over** se disputer qch. **fighter** n (determined person) lutteur/-euse m/f; (plane) avion m de chasse. **fighting** n combats mpl.

figment n a ~ **of the imagination** un produit de l'imagination.

figure n (number) chiffre m; (diagram) figure f; (shape) forme f; (body) ligne f; ~**s** arithmétique f. ● vt s'imaginer. ● vi (appear) figurer; **that**~**s** (US, 🔲) c'est logique; ~ **out** comprendre. ~ **of speech** n façon f de parler.

file n (tool) lime f; dossier m, classeur m; (Comput) fichier m; (row) file f. ● vt limer; (*papers*) classer; (Jur) déposer. □ ~ **in** entrer en file; ~ **past** défiler devant.

filing cabinet n classeur m.

fill vt/i (se) remplir. ● n have had one's ~ en avoir assez. □ ~ **in** (*form*) remplir; ~ **out** prendre du poids; ~ **up** (Auto) faire le plein (de carburant); (*bath, theatre*) (se) remplir.

fillet n filet m. ● vt découper en filets.

filling n (of tooth) plombage m; (of sandwich) garniture f. ~ **station** n station-service f.

film n film m; (Photo) pellicule f.

● vt filmer. ~**-goer** n cinéphile mf. ~ **star** n vedette f de cinéma.

filter n filtre m; (traffic signal) flèche f. ● vt/i filtrer; (of traffic) suivre la flèche. ~ **coffee** n café m filtre.

filth n crasse f. **filthy** a crasseux.

fin n (of fish, seal) nageoire f; (of shark) aileron m.

final a dernier; (conclusive) définitif. ● n (Sport) finale f.

finale n (Mus) finale m.

finalize vt mettre au point, fixer.

finally adv (lastly, at last) enfin, finalement; (once and for all) définitivement.

finance n finance f. ● a financier. ● vt financer. **financial** a financier.

find vt (pt **found**) trouver; (sth lost) retrouver. ● n trouvaille f. ~ **out** vt découvrir; vi se renseigner (**about** sur). **findings** npl conclusions fpl.

fine a fin; (excellent) beau; ~ **arts** beaux-arts mpl. ● n amende f. ● vt condamner à une amende.

finger n doigt m. ● vt palper. ~**-nail** n ongle m. ~**print** n empreinte f digitale. ~**tip** n bout m du doigt.

finish vt/i finir; ~ **doing** finir de faire; ~ **up doing** finir par faire; ~ **up in** se retrouver à. ● n fin f; (of race) arrivée f; (appearance) finition f.

finite a fini.

Finland n Finlande f. **Finn** n Finlandais/-e m/f.

Finnish a finlandais. ● n (Ling) finnois m.

fir n sapin m.

fire n (element) feu m; (blaze) incendie m; (heater) radiateur m; **set** ~ **to** mettre le feu à. ● vt (bullet) tirer; (dismiss) renvoyer; (fig) enflammer. ● vi tirer (**at** sur); ~ **a gun** tirer un coup de revolver/de fusil. ~ **alarm** n alarme f

incendie. ~**arm** n arme f à feu.
~ **brigade** n pompiers mpl. ~
engine n voiture f de pompiers.
~ **escape** n escalier m de
secours. ~ **extinguisher** n
extincteur m. ~**man** n (pl -**men**)
pompier m. ~**place** n cheminée
f. ~ **station** n caserne f de
pompiers. ~**wall** n mur m
coupe-feu; (Internet) pare-feu m
inv. ~**wood** n bois m de
chauffage. ~**work** n feu m
d'artifice.

firing-squad n peloton m
d'exécution.

firm n entreprise f, société f. ● a
ferme; (belief) solide.

first a premier; **at ~ hand** de
première main; **at ~ sight** à
première vue; ~ **of all** tout
d'abord. ● n premier/-ière m/f.
● adv d'abord, premièrement;
(arrive) le premier, la première; **at
~** d'abord. ~ **aid** n premiers
soins mpl. ~**class** a de
première classe. ~ **floor** n
premier étage m; (US) rez-de-
chaussée m inv. ~ **gear** n
première (vitesse) f. **F~ Lady** n
(US) épouse f du Président.

firstly adv premièrement.

first name n prénom m.

fish n poisson m; ~ **shop**
poissonnerie f. ● vi pêcher; ~ **for**
(cod) pêcher; ~ **out** (from water)
repêcher; (take out ⊞) sortir.
fisherman n (pl -**men**) n pêcheur
m.

fishing n pêche f; **go ~** aller à la
pêche. ~ **rod** n canne f à pêche.

fishmonger n poissonnier/-ière
m/f.

fist n poing m.

fit n accès m, crise f; **be a good ~**
(dress) être à la bonne taille. ● a
(**fitter**, **fittest**) en bonne santé;
(proper) convenable; (good enough)
bon; (able) capable; **in no ~ state**

to do pas en état de faire. ● vt/i
(pt **fitted**) (into space) aller; (install)
poser. □ ~ **in** vt caser; vi
(newcomer) s'intégrer; ~ **out**, ~
up équiper.

fitness n forme f; (of remark)
justesse f.

fitted a (wardrobe) encastré. ~
carpet n moquette f.

fitting a approprié. ● n essayage
m. ~ **room** n cabine f d'essayage.

five a & n cinq (m).

fix vt (make firm, attach, decide) fixer;
(mend) réparer; (deal with) arranger;
~ **sb up with sth** trouver qch à qn.

fixture n (Sport) match m; ~**s** (in
house) installations fpl.

fizz vi pétiller. ● n pétillement m.
fizzy a gazeux.

flabbergast vt sidérer.

flabby a flasque.

flag n drapeau m; (Naut) pavillon
m. ● vt (pt **flagged**) ~ (**down**)
faire signe de s'arrêter à. ● vi
(weaken) faiblir; (sick person)
s'affaiblir. ~**pole** n mât m.
~**stone** n dalle f.

flake n flocon m; (of paint, metal)
écaille f. ● vi s'écailler.

flamboyant a (colour) éclatant;
(manner) extravagant.

flame n flamme f; **burst into ~s**
exploser; **go up in ~s** brûler. ● vi
flamber.

flamingo n flamant m (rose).

flammable a inflammable.

flan n tarte f; (custard tart) flan m.

flank n flanc m. ● vt flanquer.

flannel n (material) flannelle f; (for
face) gant m de toilette.

flap vi (pt **flapped**) battre. ● vt ~
its wings battre des ailes. ● n (of
pocket) rabat m; (of table) abattant
m.

flare vi ~ **up** (fighting) éclater. ● n
flamboiement m; (Mil) fusée f

F

éclairante; (in skirt) évasement *m*.
flared *a* évasé.

flash *vi* briller; (on and off) clignoter; **~ past** passer à toute vitesse. ● *vt* faire briller; (aim torch) diriger (**at** sur); (flaunt) étaler; **~ one's headlights** faire un appel de phares. ● *n* (of news, camera) flash *m*; **in a ~** en un éclair. **~back** *n* retour *m* en arrière. **~light** *n* lampe *f* de poche.

flask *n* (for chemicals) flacon *m*; (for drinks) thermos® *m* or *f* *inv*.

flat *a* (**flatter, flattest**) plat; (tyre) à plat; (refusal) catégorique; (fare, rate) fixe. ● *adv* (say) carrément. ● *n* (rooms) appartement *m*; (tyre Ⓜ) crevaison *f*; (Mus) bémol *m*.

flat out *adv* (drive) à toute vitesse; (work) d'arrache-pied.

flatten *vt/i* (s')aplatir.

flatter *vt* flatter.

flaunt *vt* étaler, afficher.

flavour, (US) **flavor** *n* goût *m*; (of ice-cream) parfum *m*. ● *vt* parfumer (**with** à), assaisonner (**with** de). **flavouring** *n* arôme *m* artificiel.

flaw *n* défaut *m*.

flea *n* puce *f*. **~ market** *n* marché *m* aux puces.

fleck *n* petite tache *f*.

fled ⇒FLEE.

flee *vt/i* (*pt* **fled**) fuir.

fleece *n* toison *f*; (garment) polaire *f*. ● *vt* plumer.

fleet *n* (Naut, Aviat) flotte *f*; **a ~ of vehicles** (in reserve) parc *m*; (on road) convoi *m*.

fleeting *a* très bref.

Flemish *a* flamand. ● *n* (Ling) flamand *m*.

flesh *n* chair *f*; **one's (own) ~ and blood** la chair de sa chair.

flew ⇒FLY.

flex *vt* (knee) fléchir; (muscle) faire jouer. ● *n* (Electr) fil *m*.

flexible *a* flexible.

flexitime *n* horaire *m* variable.

flick *n* petit coup *m*. ● *vt* donner un petit coup à; **~ through** feuilleter.

flight *n* (of bird, plane) vol *m*; **~ of stairs** escalier *m*; (fleeing) fuite *f*; **take ~** prendre la fuite. **~-deck** *n* poste *m* de pilotage.

flimsy *a* (**-ier, -iest**) (pej) mince, peu solide.

flinch *vi* (wince) broncher; (draw back) reculer.

fling *vt* (*pt* **flung**) jeter.

flint *n* (rock) silex *m*.

flip *vt* (*pt* **flipped**) donner un petit coup à; **~ through** feuilleter. ● *n* chiquenaude *f*.

flippant *a* désinvolte.

flipper *n* (of seal) nageoire *f*; (of swimmer) palme *f*.

flirt *vi* flirter. ● *n* flirteur/-euse *m*/*f*.

float *vt/i* (faire) flotter. ● *n* flotteur *m*; (cart) char *m*.

flock *n* (of sheep) troupeau *m*; (of people) foule *f*. ● *vi* affluer.

flog *vt* (*pt* **flogged**) (beat) fouetter; (sell Ⓜ) vendre.

flood *n* inondation *f*; (fig) flot *m*. ● *vt* inonder. ● *vi* (building) être inondé; (river) déborder; (people: fig) affluer.

floodlight *n* projecteur *m*. ● *vt* (*pt* **floodlit**) illuminer.

floor *n* sol *m*, plancher *m*; (for dancing) piste *f*; (storey) étage *m*. ● *vt* (knock down) terrasser; (baffle) stupéfier. **~-board** *n* planche *f*.

flop *vi* (*pt* **flopped**) (drop) s'affaler; (fail Ⓜ) échouer; (head) tomber. ● *n* Ⓜ échec *m*, fiasco *m*.

floppy *a* lâche, flasque. **~ (disk)** *n* disquette *f*.

florist *n* fleuriste *mf*.

flounder *vi* (animal, person) se débattre (**in** dans); (economy) stagner. ● *n* flet *m*; (US) poisson *m* plat.

flour *n* farine *f*.

flourish *vi* prospérer. ● *vt* brandir. ● *n* geste *m* élégant.

flout *vt* se moquer de.

flow *vi* couler; (circulate) circuler; (traffic) s'écouler; (hang loosely) flotter; ~ **in** affluer; ~ **into** (of river) se jeter dans. ● *n* (of liquid, traffic) écoulement *m*; (of tide) flux *m*; (of orders, words: fig) flot *m*. ~ **chart** *n* organigramme *m*.

flower *n* fleur *f*. ● *vi* fleurir.

flown ⇒FLY.

flu *n* grippe *f*.

fluctuate *vi* varier.

fluent *a* (style) aisé; **be ~** (**in a language**) parler (une langue) couramment.

fluff *n* peluche(s) *f(pl)*; (down) duvet *m*.

fluid *a* & *n* fluide (*m*).

fluke *n* coup *m* de chance.

flung ⇒FLING.

fluoride *n* fluor *m*.

flush *vi* rougir. ● *vt* nettoyer à grande eau; ~ **the toilet** tirer la chasse d'eau. ● *n* (blush) rougeur *f*. (fig) excitation *f*. ● *a* ~ **with** (level with) au ras de. □ ~ **out** chasser.

fluster *vt* énerver.

flute *n* flûte *f*.

flutter *vi* voleter; (of wings) battre. ● *n* (wings) battement *m*; (fig) agitation *f*; (bet 🇬🇧) pari *m*.

flux *n* changement *m* continuel.

fly *n* mouche *f*; (of trousers) braguette *f*. ● *vi* (*pt* **flew**; *pp* **flown**) voler; (passengers) voyager en avion; (flag) flotter; (rush) filer. ● *vt* (aircraft) piloter; (passengers, goods) transporter par avion; (flag) arborer. □ ~ **off** s'envoler.

flyer *n* (person) aviateur *m*; (circular) prospectus *m*.

flying *a* (saucer) volant; **with ~ colours** haut la main; ~ **start** excellent départ *m*; ~ **visit** visite *f* éclair (*a inv*). ● *n* (activity) aviation *f*.

flyover *n* pont *m* (routier).

foal *n* poulain *m*.

foam *n* écume *f*, mousse *f*; ~ (**rubber**) caoutchouc *m* mousse. ● *vi* écumer, mousser.

focus *n* (*pl* ~**es** or **-ci**) foyer *m*; (fig) centre *m*; **be in/out of ~** être/ne pas être au point. ● *vt/i* (faire) converger; (instrument) mettre au point; (with camera) faire la mise au point (**on** sur); (fig) (se) concentrer. ~ **group** *n* groupe *m* de discussion.

fodder *n* fourrage *m*.

foe *n* ennemi/-e *m/f*.

foetus *n* fœtus *m*.

fog *n* brouillard *m*. ● *vt/i* (*pt* **fogged**) (window) (s')embuer.

foggy *a* brumeux; **it is ~** il fait du brouillard.

foil *n* (tin foil) papier *m* d'aluminium; (deterrent) repoussoir *m*. ● *vt* (thwart) déjouer.

fold *vt/i* (paper, clothes) (se) plier; (arms) croiser; (tail) s'effondrer. ● *n* pli *m*; (for sheep) parc *m* à moutons; (Relig) bercail *m*. **folder** *n* (file) chemise *f*; (leaflet) dépliant *m*. **folding** *a* pliant.

foliage *n* feuillage *m*.

folk *n* gens *mpl*; ~**s** parents *mpl*. ● *a* (dance) folklorique; (music) folk.

folklore *n* folklore *m*.

follow *vt/i* suivre; **it ~s that** il s'ensuit que; ~ **suit** en faire autant; ~ **up** (letter) donner suite à. **follower** *n* partisan *m*.

following *n* partisans *mpl*. ● *a* suivant; ~ **day** lendemain. ● *prep* à la suite de.

F

fond a (loving) affectueux; (hope) cher; be ~ of aimer.

fondle vt caresser.

fondness n affection f; (for things) attachement m.

food n nourriture f; French ~ la cuisine française. ● a alimentaire. ~ **processor** n robot m (ménager).

fool n idiot/-e m/f. ● vt duper. ● vi ~ **around** faire l'idiot. **foolish** a idiot.

foot n (pl feet) pied m; (measure) pied m (=30.48 cm); (of stairs, page) bas m; on ~ à pied; on or to one's feet debout; under sb's feet dans les jambes de qn. ● vt (bill) payer. **foot-and-mouth disease** n fièvre f aphteuse.

football n (ball) ballon m; (game) football m. **footballer** n footballeur m.

foot: ~-**bridge** n passerelle f. ~**hold** n prise f.

footing n on an equal ~ sur un pied d'égalité; be on a friendly ~ with sb avoir des rapports amicaux avec qn; lose one's ~ perdre pied.

foot: ~**note** n note f (en bas de la page). ~**path** n (in countryside) sentier m; (in town) chemin m. ~**print** n empreinte f (de pied). ~**step** n pas m. ~**wear** n chaussures fpl.

for

● preposition

····▸ pour; ~ me pour moi; music ~ dancing de la musique pour danser; what is it ~? ça sert à quoi?

····▸ (with a time period that is still continuing) depuis; I've been waiting ~ two hours j'attends depuis deux hours; I haven't seen him

~ ten years je ne l'ai pas vu depuis dix ans.

····▸ (with a time period that has ended) pendant; I waited ~ two hours j'ai attendu pendant deux heures.

····▸ (with a future time period) pour; I'm going to Paris ~ six weeks je vais à Paris pour six semaines.

····▸ (with distances) pendant; I drove ~ 50 kilometres j'ai roulé pendant 50 kilomètres.

forbid vt (pt forbade; pp forbidden) interdire, défendre (sb to do à qn de faire); ~ sb sth interdire or défendre qch à qn; you are forbidden to leave il vous est interdit de partir. **forbidding** a menaçant.

force n force f; come into ~ entrer en vigueur; the ~s les forces fpl armées. ● vt forcer. □ ~ **into** faire entrer de force; ~ **on** imposer à. **forced** a forcé.

force-feed vt (pt -fed) (person) nourrir de force; (animal) gaver.

forceful a énergique.

ford n gué m. ● vt passer à gué.

forearm n avant-bras m inv.

forecast vt (pt forecast) prévoir. ● n weather ~ météo f.

forecourt n (of garage) devant m; (of station) cour f.

forefinger n index m.

forefront n at/in the ~ of à la pointe de.

foregone a it's a ~ conclusion c'est couru d'avance.

foreground n premier plan m.

forehead n front m.

foreign a étranger; (trade) extérieur; (travel) à l'étranger. **foreigner** n étranger/-ère m/f.

foreman n (pl -men) contremaître m.

foremost *a* le plus éminent.
● *adv* first and ~ tout d'abord.

forensic *a* médico-légal; ~ **medicine** médecine *f* légale.

foresee *vt* (*pt* **-saw**; *pp* **-seen**) prévoir.

forest *n* forêt *f*. **forestry** *n* sylviculture *f*.

foretaste *n* avant-goût *m*.

forever *adv* toujours.

foreword *n* avant-propos *m inv*.

forfeit *n* (penalty) peine *f*; (in game) gage *m*. ● *vt* perdre.

forgave ⇒FORGIVE.

forge *n* forge *f*. ● *vt* (*metal, friendship*) forger; (*copy*) contrefaire, falsifier. ● *vi* ~ **ahead** aller de l'avant, avancer. **forger** *n* faussaire *m*. **forgery** *n* faux *m*, contrefaçon *f*.

forget *vt/i* (*pt* **forgot**; *pp* **forgotten**) oublier; ~ **oneself** s'oublier. **forgetful** *a* distrait. ~**-me-not** *n* myosotis *m*.

forgive *vt* (*pt* **forgave**; *pp* **forgiven**) pardonner (**sb for sth** qch à qn).

fork *n* fourchette *f*; (for digging) fourche *f*; (in road) bifurcation *f*. ● *vi* (*road*) bifurquer; ~ **out** Ⓣ payer. **forked** *a* fourchu. ~**-lift truck** *n* chariot *m* élévateur.

form *n* forme *f*; (document) formulaire *m*; (School) classe *f*; on ~ en forme. ● *vt/i* (se) former.

formal *a* officiel, en bonne et due forme; (*person*) compassé, cérémonieux; (*dress*) de cérémonie; (*denial, grammar*) formel; (*language*) soutenu. **formality** *n* cérémonial *m*; (requirement) formalité *f*.

format *n* format *m*. ● *vt* (*pt* **formatted**) (*disk*) formater.

former *a* ancien; (first of two) premier. ● *n* the ~ celui-là, celle-là. **formerly** *adv* autrefois.

formula *n* (*pl* **-ae** *or* **-as**) formule *f*. **formulate** *vt* formuler.

fort *n* (Mil) fort *m*; **to hold the** ~ s'occuper de tout.

forth *adv* from this day ~ à partir d'aujourd'hui; **and so** ~ et ainsi de suite; **go back and** ~ aller et venir.

forthcoming *a* à venir, prochain; (sociable Ⓣ) communicatif.

forthright *a* direct.

forthwith *adv* sur-le-champ.

fortnight *n* quinze jours *mpl*, quinzaine *f*.

fortnightly *a* bimensuel. ● *adv* tous les quinze jours.

fortunate *a* heureux; **be** ~ avoir de la chance. **fortunately** *adv* heureusement.

fortune *n* fortune *f*; **make a** ~ faire fortune; **have the good** ~ **to** avoir la chance de. ~**-teller** *n* diseur/-euse *m/f* de bonne aventure.

forty *a & n* quarante (*m*); ~ **winks** un petit somme.

forward *a* en avant; (advanced) précoce; (bold) effronté. ● *n* (Sport) avant *m*. ● *adv* en avant; **come** ~ se présenter; **go** ~ avancer. ● *vt* (*letter, e-mail*) faire suivre; (*goods*) expédier; (*fig*) favoriser. **forwardness** *n* précocité *f*. **forwards** *adv* en avant.

fossil *n & a* fossile (*m*).

foster *vt* (promote) encourager; (*child*) élever. ● *a* (*child, parent*) adoptif; (*family, home*) de placement.

fought ⇒FIGHT.

foul *a* (*smell, weather*) infect; (*place, action*) immonde; (*language*) ordurier. ● *n* (*football*) faute *f*. ● *vt* souiller, encrasser; ~ **up** Ⓣ gâcher. ~**-mouthed** *a* grossier.

found ⇒FIND. ● *vt* fonder.

foundation *n* fondation *f*; (basis)

fondement *m*; (make-up) fond *m* de
teint. **founder** *n* fondateur/-trice
m/f.

fountain *n* fontaine *f*. ~**-pen** *n*
stylo *m* à encre.

four *a & n* quatre (*m*).

fourteen *a & n* quatorze (*m*).

fourth *a & n* quatrième (*mf*).

four-wheel drive *n* (car) quatre-
quatre *m*.

fowl *n* (one bird) poulet *m*; (group)
volaille *f*.

fox *n* renard *m*. ● *vt* (baffle)
mystifier; (deceive) tromper.

fraction *n* fraction *f*.

fracture *n* fracture *f*. ● *vt/i* (se)
fracturer.

fragile *a* fragile.

fragment *n* fragment *m*.

fragrance *n* parfum *m*.

frail *a* frêle.

frame *n* (of building, boat) charpente
f; (of picture) cadre *m*; (of window)
châssis *m*; (of spectacles) monture *f*;
~ **of mind** humeur *f*. ● *vt*
encadrer; (fig) formuler; (Jur, ▣)
monter un coup contre. ~**work** *n*
structure *f*; (context) cadre *m*.

France *n* France *f*.

franchise *n* (Pol) droit *m* de vote;
(Comm) franchise *f*.

frank *a* franc. ● *vt* affranchir.
frankly *adv* franchement.

frantic *a* frénétique; ~ **with** fou
de.

fraternity *n* (bond) fraternité *f*;
(group, club) confrérie *f*.

fraud *n* (deception) fraude *f*; (person)
imposteur *m*. **fraudulent** *a*
frauduleux.

fray *n* the ~ la bataille. ● *vt/i*
(s')effilocher.

freckle *n* tache *f* de rousseur.

free *a* libre; (gratis) gratuit; (lavish)
généreux; ~ **(of charge)** gratuit
(ement); **a** ~ **hand** carte *f*

blanche. ● *vt* (*pt* **freed**) libérer;
(clear) dégager.

freedom *n* liberté *f*.

free: ~ **enterprise** *n* la libre
entreprise. ~ **kick** *n* coup *m*
franc. ~**lance** *a & n* free-lance
(*mf*), indépendant/-e (*m/f*).

freely *adv* librement.

Freemason *n* franc-maçon *m*.

Freenet *n* (Comput) Libertel *m*.

free: ~ **phone**, ~ **number** *n*
numéro *m* vert. ~**-range** *a* (eggs)
de ferme.

Freeware *n* (Comput) Gratuiciel *m*.

freeway *n* (US) autoroute *f*.

freeze *vt/i* (*pt* **froze**; *pp* **frozen**)
geler; (Culin) (se) congeler;
(*wages*) bloquer. ● *n* gel *m*;
blocage *m*. ~**-dried** *a* lyophilisé.

freezer *n* congélateur *m*.

freezing *a* glacial; **below** ~
au-dessous de zéro.

freight *n* fret *m*.

French *a* français. ● *n* (Ling)
français *m*; **the** ~ les Français
mpl. ~ **bean** *n* haricot *m* vert. ~
fries *npl* frites *fpl*. ~**man** *n*
Français *m*. ~**-speaking** *a*
francophone. ~ **window** *n* porte-
fenêtre *f*. ~**woman** *n* Française
f.

frenzied *a* frénétique. **frenzy** *n*
frénésie *f*.

frequent[1] *a* fréquent.

frequent[2] *vt* fréquenter.

fresco *n* fresque *f*.

fresh *a* frais; (different, additional)
nouveau; (cheeky ▣) culotté.

freshen *vi* (*weather*) fraîchir; ~
up (*person*) se rafraîchir.

freshly *adv* nouvellement.

freshness *n* fraîcheur *f*.

freshwater *a* d'eau douce.

friction *n* friction *f*.

Friday *n* vendredi *m*.

fridge *n* frigo *m*.

fried ⇒FRY. ●a frit; ~ **eggs** œufs *mpl* sur le plat.

friend n ami/-e m/f. **friendly** a (-ier, -iest) amical, gentil. **friendship** n amitié f.

frieze n frise f.

fright n peur f; (person, thing) horreur f.

frighten vt effrayer; ~ **off** faire fuir; **frightened** a effrayé; be ~ed avoir peur (of de). **frightening** a effrayant.

frill n (trimming) fanfreluche f; with no ~s très simple.

fringe n (edging, hair) frange f; (of area) bordure f; (of society) marge f. ~ **benefits** npl avantages mpl sociaux.

frisk vt (search) fouiller.

fritter n beignet m. ●vt ~ **away** gaspiller.

frivolity n frivolité f.

frizzy a crépu.

fro ⇒TO AND FRO.

frog n grenouille f; a ~ **in one's throat** un chat dans la gorge.

frolic vi (pt **frolicked**) s'ébattre. ●n ébats mpl.

from prep de; (with time, prices) à partir de, de; (habit, conviction) par; (according to) d'après; **take** ~ **sb** prendre à qn; **take** ~ **one's pocket** prendre dans sa poche.

front n (of car, train) avant m; (of garment, building) devant m; (Mil, Pol) front m; (of book, pamphlet) début m; (appearance: fig) façade f. ●a de devant, avant inv; (first) premier; ~ **door** porte f d'entrée; **in** ~ (of) devant. **frontage** n façade f.

frontier n frontière f.

frost n gel m, gelée f; (on glass) givre m. ●vt/i (se) givrer. ~-**bite** n gelure f.

frosty a (weather, welcome) glacial; (window) givré.

froth n (on beer) mousse f; (on water) écume f. ●vi mousser, écumer.

frown vi froncer les sourcils; ~ **on** désapprouver. ●n froncement m de sourcils.

froze ⇒FREEZE.

frozen ⇒FREEZE. ●a congelé.

fruit n fruit m; (collectively) fruits mpl. **fruitful** a (discussions) fructueux. ~ **machine** n machine f à sous.

frustrate vt (plan) faire échouer; (person: Psych) frustrer; (upset ⑤) exaspérer. **frustration** n (Psych) frustration f; (disappointment) déception f.

fry vt/i (pt **fried**) (faire) frire. **frying-pan** n poêle f (à frire).

FTP abbr (**File Transfer Protocol**) (Internet) protocole m FTP.

fudge n caramel m mou. ●vt (issue) esquiver.

fuel n combustible m; (for car engine) carburant m. ●vt (pt **fuelled**) alimenter en combustible.

fugitive n & a fugitif/-ive (m/f).

fulfil vt (pt **fulfilled**) accomplir, réaliser; (condition) remplir; ~ **oneself** s'épanouir. **fulfilling** a satisfaisant. **fulfilment** n réalisation f; épanouissement m.

full a plein (of de); (bus, hotel) complet; (programme) chargé; (skirt) ample; **be** ~ (**up**) n'avoir plus faim; **at** ~ **speed** à toute vitesse. ●n **in** ~ intégralement; **to the** ~ complètement. ~ **back** n (Sport) arrière m. ~ **moon** n pleine lune f. ~ **name** n nom m et prénom m. ~-**scale** a (drawing etc.) grandeur nature inv; (fig) de grande envergure. ~ **stop** n point m. ~-**time** a & adv à plein temps.

fully adv complètement; ~ **fledged** (member, citizen) à part entière.

fume vi rager. **fumes** npl émanations fpl, vapeurs fpl.

fun n amusement m; **be ~** être chouette; **for ~** pour rire; **make ~ of** se moquer de.

function n (purpose, duty) fonction f; (event) réception f. ● vi fonctionner.

fund n fonds m. ● vt fournir les fonds pour.

fundamental a fondamental. **fundamentalist** n intégriste mf.

funeral n enterrement m. ● a funèbre.

fun-fair n fête f foraine.

fungus n (pl -gi) (plant) champignon m; (mould) moisissure f.

funnel n (for pouring) entonnoir m; (of ship) cheminée f.

funny a (-ier, -iest) drôle; (odd) bizarre.

fur n (for garment) fourrure f; (on animal) poils mpl; (in kettle) tartre m.

furious a furieux.

furnace n fourneau m.

furnish vt (room) meubler; (supply) fournir. **furnishings** npl ameublement m.

furniture n meubles mpl, mobilier m.

furry a (animal) à fourrure; (toy) en peluche.

further a plus éloigné; (additional) supplémentaire. ● adv plus loin; (more) davantage. ● vt avancer. **~ education** n formation f continue.

furthermore adv en outre, de plus.

furthest a le plus éloigné. ● adv le plus loin.

fury n fureur f.

fuse vt/i (melt) fondre; (unite: fig) fusionner; **~ the lights** faire sauter les plombs. ● n (of plug) fusible m; (of bomb) amorce f.

fuss n (when upset) histoire(s) f(pl); (when excited) agitation f; **make a ~** faire des histoires; s'agiter; (about food) faire des chichis; **make a ~ of** faire grand cas de. ● vi s'agiter. **fussy** a (finicky) tatillon; (hard to please) difficile.

future a futur. ● n avenir m; (Gram) futur m; **in ~** à l'avenir.

fuzzy a (hair) crépu; (photograph) flou; (person ⊞) à l'esprit confus.

Gaelic n gaélique m.

gag n (on mouth) bâillon m; (joke) blague f. ● vt (pt **gagged**) bâillonner.

gain vt (respect, support) gagner; (speed, weight) prendre. ● vi (of clock) avancer. ● n (increase) augmentation f (**in** de); (profit) gain m.

galaxy n galaxie f.

gale n tempête f.

gallery n galerie f; (art) ~ musée m.

Gallic a français.

gallon n gallon m (imperial = 4.546 litres; Amer. = 3.785 litres).

gallop n galop m. ● vi (pt **galloped**) galoper.

galore adv (prizes, bargains) en abondance; (drinks, sandwiches) à gogo ⊞.

gamble vt/i jouer; **~ on** miser sur. ● n (venture) entreprise f risquée; (bet) pari m; (risk) risque m. **gambling** n jeu m.

game n jeu m; (football) match m; (tennis) partie f; (animals, birds) gibier *m*. ● *a* (brave) courageux; ~ for prêt à. ~**keeper** *n* garde-chasse *m*.

games console *n* console *f* de jeux.

gammon *n* jambon *m*.

gang *n* (of youths) bande *f*; (of workmen) équipe *f*. ● *vi* ~ up se liguer (on, against contre).

gangway *n* passage *m*; (aisle) allée *f*; (of ship) passerelle *f*.

gaol *n & vt* = JAIL.

gap *n* trou *m*, vide *m*; (in time) intervalle *m*; (difference) écart *m*. ~ **year** *n* année *f* de coupure (*avant d'entrer à l'université*).

gape *vi* rester bouche bée. **gaping** *a* béant.

garage *n* garage *m*. ● *vt* mettre au garage.

garbage *n* (US) ordures *fpl*.

garden *n* jardin *m*. ● *vi* jardiner. **gardener** *n* jardinier/-ière *m/f*. **gardening** *n* jardinage *m*.

gargle *vi* se gargariser.

garish *a* (clothes) tape-à-l'œil.

garland *n* guirlande *f*.

garlic *n* ail *m*.

garment *n* vêtement *m*.

garnish *vt* garnir (with de). ● *n* garniture *f*.

garter *n* jarretière *f*.

gas *n* (*pl* ~**es**) gaz *m*; (Med) anesthésie *m*; (petrol: US) essence *f*. ● *a* (*mask, pipe*) à gaz. ● *vt* asphyxier; (Mil) gazer.

gash *n* entaille *f*. ● *vt* entailler.

gasoline *n* (petrol: US) essence *f*.

gasp *vi* haleter; (in surprise: fig) avoir le souffle coupé. ● *n* halètement *m*.

gate *n* (in garden, airport) porte *f*; (of field, level crossing) barrière *f*. ~**way** *n* porte *f*; (Internet) passerelle *f*.

gather *vt* (*people, objects*) rassembler; (pick up) ramasser; (*flowers*) cueillir; (fig) comprendre; ~ **speed** prendre de

la vitesse; (sewing) froncer. ● *vi* (*people*) se rassembler; (pile up) s'accumuler. **gathering**. *n* réunion *m*.

gauge *n* jauge *f*, indicateur *m*. ● *vt* (*speed, distance*) jauger; (*reaction, mood*) évaluer.

gaunt *a* décharné.

gauze *n* gaze *f*.

gave ⇒GIVE.

gay *a* (joyful) gai; (homosexual) gay *inv*. ● *n* gay *mf*.

gaze *vi* ~ (**at**) regarder (fixement). ● *n* regard *m* (fixe).

GB *abbr* ⇒GREAT BRITAIN.

gear *n* (equipment) matériel *m*; (Tech) engrenage *m*; (Auto) vitesse *f*; in ~ en prise; out of ~ au point mort. ● *vt* to be geared to s'adresser à. ~**box** *n* (Auto) boîte *f* de vitesses. ~-**lever**, (US) ~-**shift** *n* levier *m* de vitesse.

geese ⇒GOOSE.

gel *n* (for hair) gel *m*.

gem *n* pierre *f* précieuse.

Gemini *n* Gémeaux *mpl*.

gender *n* (Ling) genre *m*; (of person) sexe *m*.

gene *n* gène *m*. ~ **library** *n* génothèque *f*.

general *a* général. ● *n* général *m*; in ~ en général.

general election *n* élections *fpl* législatives.

generalization *n* généralisation *f*. **generalize** *vt/i* généraliser.

general practitioner *n* (Med) généraliste *m*.

generate *vt* produire.

generation *n* génération *f*.

generator *n* (Electr) groupe *m* électrogène.

generosity *n* générosité *f*. **generous** *a* généreux; (plentiful) copieux.

genetics *n* génétique *f*.

Geneva *n* Genève.

genial *a* affable, sympathique.

genitals *npl* organes *mpl* génitaux.

genius *n* (*pl* ~es) génie *m*.

genome *n* génome *m*.

gentle *a* (mild, kind) doux; (*pressure, breeze*) léger; (*reminder, hint*) discret.

gentleman *n* (*pl* -men) (man) monsieur *m*; (well-bred) gentleman *m*.

gently *adv* doucement.

gents *npl* (toilets) toilettes *fpl*; (on sign) 'Messieurs'.

genuine *a* (*reason, motive*) vrai; (*jewel, substance*) véritable; (*person, belief*) sincère.

geography *n* géographie *f*.

geology *n* géologie *f*.

geometry *n* géométrie *f*.

geriatric *a* gériatrique.

germ *n* (Med) microbe *m*.

German *n* (person) Allemand/-e *m/f*; (Ling) allemand *m*. ● *a* allemand.

German measles *n* rubéole *f*.

Germany *n* Allemagne *f*.

gesture *n* geste *m*.

· ·

get

> *past* **got**; *past participle* **got**, **gotten** (US); *present participle* **getting**

● *transitive verb*

····▸ recevoir; **we got a letter** nous avons reçu une lettre.

····▸ (obtain) **I got a job in Paris** j'ai trouvé un travail à Paris; **I'll ~ sth to eat at the airport** je mangerai qch à l'aéroport.

····▸ (buy) acheter; **~ sb a present** acheter un cadeau à qn.

····▸ (achieve) obtenir; **he got it right** il a obtenu le bon résultat; **~**

good grades avoir de bonnes notes.

····▸ (fetch) chercher; **go and ~ a chair** va chercher une chaise.

····▸ (transport) prendre; **we can ~ the bus** on peut prendre le bus.

····▸ (understand 🔲) comprendre; **now let me ~ this right** alors si je comprends bien...

····▸ (experience) **~ a surprise** être surpris; **~ a shock** avoir un choc.

····▸ (illness) **~ measles** attraper la rougeole; **~ a cold** s'enrhumer.

····▸ (ask or persuade) **~ him to call me** dis-lui de m'appeler; **I'll ~ her to help me** je lui demanderai de m'aider.

····▸ (cause to be done) **~ a TV repaired** faire réparer une télévision; **~ one's hair cut** se faire couper les cheveux.

● *intransitive verb*

····▸ devenir; **he's getting old** il vieillit; **it's getting late** il se fait tard.

····▸ (in passives) **~ married** se marier; **~ hurt** être blessé.

····▸ (arrive) arriver; **~ to the airport** arriver à l'aéroport.

▢ **get about** (*person*) se déplacer.

get along (manage) se débrouiller; (progress) avancer.

get along with s'entendre avec.

get at (reach) atteindre; (imply) vouloir dire.

get away partir; (escape) s'échapper.

get back *vi* revenir. *vt* récupérer.

get by *vi* (manage) se débrouiller. *vt* (pass) passer.

get down *vt/i* descendre. *vt* (depress) déprimer.

get in entrer.

get into (*car*) monter dans; (*dress*) mettre.

get off vt (*bus*) descendre; (remove) enlever. vi (from bus) descendre; (leave) partir; (Jur) être acquitté.

get on vi (to bus) monter; (succeed) réussir. vt (*bus*) monter.

get on with (*person*) s'entendre avec; (*job*) attaquer.

get out sortir.

get out of (fig) se soustraire.

get over (*illness*) se remettre de.

get round (*rule*) contourner; (*person*) entortiller.

get through vi passer; (on phone) ~ **through to sb** avoir qn. vt traverser.

get up se lever.

: **get up to** faire.

getaway n fuite f.

ghastly a (-ier, -iest) affreux.

gherkin n cornichon m.

ghetto n ghetto m.

ghost n fantôme m.

giant n & a géant (m).

gibberish n baragouin m, charabia m.

giblets npl abats mpl.

giddy a (-ier, -iest) vertigineux; **be** or **feel** ~ avoir le vertige.

gift n (present) cadeau m; (ability) don m.

gifted a doué.

gift-wrap n paquet-cadeau m.

gigantic a gigantesque.

giggle vi ricaner (sottement), glousser. ● n ricanement m; **the** ~**s** le fou rire.

gimmick n truc m.

gin n gin m.

ginger n gingembre m. ● a (*hair*) roux. ~ **beer** n boisson f gazeuse au gingembre. ~**bread** n pain m d'épices.

gingerly adv avec précaution.

giraffe n girafe f.

girl n (child) (petite) fille f; (young woman) (jeune) fille f. ~**friend** n amie f; (of boy) petite amie f.

giro n virement m bancaire; (cheque) mandat m.

gist n essentiel m.

give vt (pt **gave**; pp **given**) donner; (gesture) faire; (laugh, sigh) pousser; ~ **sb sth** donner qch à qn. ● vi donner; (yield) céder; (stretch) se détendre. ● n élasticité f. □ ~ **away** donner; (secret) trahir; ~ **back** rendre; ~ **in** (yield) céder (**to** à); ~ **off** (heat, fumes) dégager; (signal, scent) émettre; ~ **out** vt distribuer; ~ **over** (devote) consacrer; (stop 🗓) cesser; ~ **up** vt/i (renounce) renoncer (à); (yield) céder; ~ **oneself up** se rendre; ~ **way** céder; (collapse) s'effondrer.

given →GIVE. ● a donné. ~ **name** n prénom m.

glad a content. **gladly** adv avec plaisir.

glamorous a séduisant, ensorcelant.

glamour, (US) **glamor** n enchantement m, séduction f.

glance n coup m d'œil. ● vi ~ **at** jeter un coup d'œil à.

gland n glande f.

glare vi briller très fort; ~ **at** regarder d'un air furieux. ● n (of lights) éclat m (aveuglant); (stare: fig) regard m furieux. **glaring** a (dazzling) éblouissant; (obvious) flagrant.

glass n verre m. **glasses** npl (spectacles) lunettes fpl.

glaze vt (door) vitrer; (pottery) vernisser. ● n vernis m.

gleam n lueur f. ● vi luire.

glide vi glisser; (of plane) planer. **glider** n planeur m.

glimpse n (insight) aperçu m; **catch a** ~ **of** entrevoir.

G

glitter vi scintiller. ● n scintillement m.

global a (world-wide) mondial; (all-embracing) global. ~ **warming** n réchauffement m de la planète. **globalization** n mondialisation f.

globe n globe m.

gloom n obscurité f; (sadness: fig) tristesse f. **gloomy** a triste; (pessimistic) pessimiste.

glorious a splendide; (deed, hero) glorieux.

glory n gloire f; (beauty) splendeur f. ● vi ~ **in** être très fier de.

gloss n lustre m, brillant m. ● a brillant. ● vi ~ **over** (make light of) glisser sur; (cover up) dissimuler.

glossary n glossaire m.

glossy a brillant.

glove n gant m. ~ **compartment** n (Auto) boîte f à gants.

glow vi (fire) rougeoyer; (person, eyes) rayonner. ● n rougeoiement m, éclat m. **glowing** a (report) enthousiaste.

glucose n glucose m.

glue n colle f. ● vt (pres p **gluing**) coller.

GM abbr (**genetically modified**) transgénique.

gnaw vt/i ronger.

GNP abbr (**Gross National Product**) produit m national brut, PNB m.

....

go

⇒ present **go**, **goes**; past **went**; past participle **gone**

● intransitive verb

····▸ aller; ~ **to school/town/market** aller à l'école/en ville/au marché; ~ **for a swim/walk** aller nager/se promener.

····▸ (leave) s'en aller; **I must be** ~**ing** il faut que je m'en aille.

····▸ (vanish) **the money's gone** il n'y a plus d'argent; **my bike's gone** mon vélo n'est plus là.

····▸ (work, function) marcher; **is the car** ~**ing?** est-ce que la voiture marche?

····▸ (become) devenir; ~ **blind** devenir aveugle; ~ **pale/red** pâlir/rougir.

····▸ (turn out, progress) aller; **how's it going?** comment ça va?; **how did the exam** ~**?** comment s'est passé l'examen?

····▸ (in future tenses) **be** ~**ing to do** aller faire.

● noun

····▸ (turn) tour m; (try) essai m; **have a** ~**!** essaie!; **full of** ~ Ⓘ dynamique.

□ **go across** traverser.

go after poursuivre.

go away partir; ~ **away!** va-t'en!, allez-vous-en!

go back retourner; ~ **back in** rentrer; ~ **back to work** reprendre le travail.

go down (quality, price) baisser; (person) descendre; (sun) se coucher.

go in entrer.

go in for (exam) se présenter à.

go off (leave) partir; (bomb) exploser; (alarm clock) sonner; (milk) tourner; (light) s'éteindre.

go on (continue) continuer; (light) s'allumer; ~ **on doing** continuer à faire; **what's** ~**ing on?** qu'est-ce qui se passe?

go out sortir; (light, fire) s'éteindre.

go over vérifier.

go round (be enough) être assez; ~ **round to see sb** passer voir qn.

go through (check) examiner; (search) fouiller; ~ **through a difficult time** traverser une période difficile.

go together aller ensemble.

go under (sink) couler; (fail) échouer.

go up (*person*) monter; (*price, salary*) augmenter.

go without se passer de.

....

go-ahead *n* feu *m* vert. ● *a* dynamique.

goal *n* but *m*. ∼**keeper** *n* gardien *m* de but. ∼**post** *n* poteau *m* de but.

goat *n* chèvre *f*.

gobble *vt* engouffrer.

go-between *n* intermédiaire *mf*.

god *n* dieu *m*. ∼**child** *n* (*pl* **-children**) filleul/-e *m/f*. ∼**daughter** *n* filleule *f*.

goddess *n* déesse *f*.

god: ∼**father** *n* parrain *m*. ∼**mother** *n* marraine *f*. ∼**send** *n* aubaine *f*. ∼**son** *n* filleul *m*.

goggles *npl* lunettes *fpl* (protectrices).

going *n* **it is slow/hard** ∼ c'est lent/difficile. ● *a* (*price, rate*) actuel.

go-kart *n* kart *m*.

gold *n* or *m*. ● *a* en or, d'or.

golden *a* en or, d'or; (in colour) doré; (opportunity) unique.

gold: ∼**fish** *n* poisson *m* rouge. ∼**plated** *a* plaqué or. ∼**smith** *n* orfèvre *m*.

golf *n* golf *m*. ∼**course** *n* terrain *m* de golf.

gone ⇒GO. ● *a* parti; ∼ **six o'clock** six heures passées; **the butter's all** ∼ il n'y a plus de beurre.

good *a* (**better, best**) bon; (weather) beau; (well-behaved) sage; **as** ∼ **as** (almost) pratiquement; **that's** ∼ **of you** c'est gentil (de ta part); **be** ∼ **with** savoir s'y prendre avec; **feel** ∼ se sentir bien; **it is** ∼ **for you** ça vous fait du bien. ● *n* bien *m*; **do** ∼ faire

du bien; **is it any** ∼? est-ce que c'est bien?; **it's no** ∼ ça ne vaut rien; **it is no** ∼ **shouting** ça ne sert à rien de crier; **for** ∼ pour toujours. ∼ **afternoon** *interj* bonjour. ∼**bye** *interj & n* au revoir (*m inv*). ∼ **evening** *interj* bonsoir. G∼ **Friday** *n* Vendredi *m* saint. ∼**-looking** *a* beau. ∼ **morning** *interj* bonjour. ∼**-natured** *a* gentil.

goodness *n* bonté *f*; **my** ∼! mon Dieu!

good-night *interj* bonsoir, bonne nuit.

goods *npl* marchandises *fpl*.

goodwill *n* bonne volonté *f*.

goose *n* (*pl* **geese**) oie *f*.

gooseberry *n* groseille *f* à maquereau. ∼**-pimples** *npl* chair *f* de poule.

gorge *n* (Geog) gorge *f*. ● *vt* ∼ **oneself** se gaver (**on** de).

gorgeous *a* magnifique, splendide, formidable.

gorilla *n* gorille *m*.

gory *a* (**-ier, -iest**) sanglant; (horrific: fig) horrible.

gospel *n* évangile *m*; **the** G∼ l'Évangile *m*.

gossip *n* bavardages *mpl*, commérages *mpl*. (person) bavard/ -e *m/f*. ● *vi* bavarder.

got ⇒GET. ● **have** ∼ avoir; **have** ∼ **to do** devoir faire.

govern *vt/i* gouverner.

governess *n* gouvernante *f*.

government *n* gouvernement *m*.

governor *n* gouverneur *m*.

gown *n* robe *f*; (of judge, teacher) toge *f*.

GP *abbr* ⇒GENERAL PRACTITIONER.

grab *vt* (*pt* **grabbed**) saisir.

grace *n* grâce *f*. ● *vt* (honour) honorer; (adorn) orner. **graceful** *a* gracieux.

gracious *a* (kind) bienveillant; (elegant) élégant.

grade n catégorie f; (of goods) qualité f; (on scale) grade m; (school mark) note f; (class: US) classe f. ●vt classer; (school work) noter. ~**school** n (US) école f primaire.

gradual a progressif, graduel. **gradually** adv progressivement, peu à peu.

graduate¹ n (Univ) diplômé/-e m/f.

graduate² vi obtenir son diplôme. ●vt graduer. **graduation** n remise f des diplômes.

graffiti npl graffiti mpl.

graft n (Med, Bot) greffe f; (work) boulot m. ●vt greffer (**on to** sur); (work) trimer.

grain n (seed, quantity, texture) grain m; (in wood) fibre f.

gram n gramme m.

grammar n grammaire f.

grand a magnifique; (duke, chorus) grand.

grandad n Ⓘ papy m.

grand: ~**child** n (girl) petite-fille f; (boy) petit-fils m; **her** ~**children** ses petits-enfants mpl. ~**daughter** n petite-fille f. ~**father** n grand-père m. ~**ma** n = GRANNY. ~**mother** n grand-mère f. ~**parents** npl grands-parents mpl. ~ **piano** n piano m à queue. ~**son** n petit-fils m. ~**stand** n tribune f.

granny n Ⓘ mémé f, mamie f.

grant vt (permission) accorder; (request) accéder à; (admit) admettre (**that** que); **take sth for** ~**ed** considérer qch comme une chose acquise. ●n subvention f; (Univ) bourse f.

granule n (of sugar, salt) grain m; (of coffee) granulé m.

grape n grain m de raisin; ~**s** raisin(s) m(pl).

grapefruit n inv pamplemousse m.

graph n graphique m.

graphic a (arts) graphique; (fig) vivant, explicite. **graphics** npl (Comput) graphiques mpl.

grasp vt saisir. ●n (hold) prise f; (strength of hand) poigne f; (reach) portée f; (fig) compréhension f.

grass n herbe f. ~**hopper** n sauterelle f. ~**land** n prairie f.

grass roots npl peuple m. ●a (movement) populaire; (support) de base.

grate n (hearth) âtre m; (fire basket) grille f. ●vt râper. ●vi grincer.

grateful a reconnaissant.

grater n râpe f.

gratified a très heureux. **gratify** vt faire plaisir à.

grating n (bars) grille f; (noise) grincement m.

gratitude n reconnaissance f.

gratuity n (tip) pourboire m; (bounty: Mil) prime f.

grave¹ n tombe f. ●a (serious) grave.

grave² a ~ **accent** accent m grave.

gravel n graviers mpl.

grave: ~**stone** n pierre f tombale. ~**yard** n cimetière m.

gravity n (seriousness) gravité f; (force) pesanteur f.

gravy n jus m (de viande).

gray (US) a & n = GREY.

graze vi (eat) paître. ●vt (touch) frôler; (scrape) écorcher. ●n écorchure f.

grease n graisse f. ●vt graisser. **greasy** a graisseux.

great a grand; (very good Ⓘ) génial Ⓘ, formidable Ⓘ, (grandfather, grandmother) arrière.

Great Britain n Grande-Bretagne f.

greatly adv (very) très; (much) beaucoup.

Greece n Grèce f.

greed n avidité f; (for food)
gourmandise f. **greedy** a avide;
gourmand.

Greek n (person) Grec/-que m/f;
(Ling) grec m. ● a grec.

green a vert; (fig) naïf. ● n vert m;
(grass) pelouse f; (golf) green m;
~s légumes mpl verts. ~**grocer**
n marchand/-e m/f de fruits et
légumes.

green house n serre f; ~ **effect**
effet m de serre.

greet vt (welcome) accueillir;
(address politely) saluer. **greeting** n
accueil m.

greetings interj salutations!
● npl (Christmas) vœux mpl. ~
card n carte f de vœux.

grew →GROW.

grey a gris; (fig) triste; **go** ~ (hair,
person) grisonner. ● n gris m.
~**hound** n lévrier m.

grid n grille f; (network: Electr)
réseau m.

grief n chagrin m; **come to** ~
(person) avoir un malheur; (fall)
tourner mal.

grievance n griefs mpl.

grieve vt/i (s')affliger; ~ **for**
pleurer.

grill n (cooking device) gril m; (food)
grillade f; (Auto) calandre f. ● vt/i
(faire) griller; (interrogate) mettre
sur la sellette.

grim a sinistre.

grimace n grimace f. ● vi
grimacer.

grime n crasse f.

grin vi (pt **grinned**) sourire. ● n
(large) sourire m.

grind vt (pt **ground**) (grain)
écraser; (coffee) moudre; (sharpen)
aiguiser; ~ **one's teeth** grincer
des dents. ● vi ~ **to a halt**
s'immobiliser. ● n corvée f.

grip vt (pt **gripped**) saisir; (interest)
passionner. ● n prise f; (strength of

hand) poigne f; **come to** ~**s with** en
venir aux prises avec.

grisly a (-ier, -iest) (remains)
macabre; (sight) horrible.

gristle n cartilage m.

grit n (for roads) sable m; (fig)
courage m. ● vt (pt **gritted**)
(road) sabler; (teeth) serrer.

groan vi gémir. ● n gémissement
m.

grocer n (person) épicier/-ière m/f;
(shop) épicerie f. **groceries** npl
(shopping) courses fpl; (goods)
épicerie f. **grocery** n (shop)
épicerie f.

groin n aine f.

groom n marié m; (for horses)
palefrenier/-ière m/f. ● vt (horse)
panser; (fig) préparer.

groove n (for door etc.) rainure f; (in
record) sillon m.

grope vi tâtonner; ~ **for** chercher
à tâtons.

gross a (behaviour) vulgaire;
(Comm) brut. ● n inv grosse f.

grotto n (pl -**es**) grotte f.

grouch vi (grumble 🔲) rouspéter,
râler.

ground¹ n terre f, sol m; (area)
terrain m; (reason) raison f; (Electr,
US) masse f; ~**s** terres fpl, parc
m; (of coffee) marc m; **on the** ~ par
terre; **lose** ~ perdre du terrain.
● vt/i (Naut) échouer; (aircraft)
retenir au sol.

ground² →GRIND. ● a ~ **beef** (US)
bifteck m haché.

ground: ~ **floor** n rez-de-
chaussée m inv. ~**work** n travail
m préparatoire.

group n groupe m. ● vt/i (se)
grouper. ~**ware** n (Comput)
logiciel m de groupe.

grovel vi (pt **grovelled**) ramper.

grow vi (pt **grew**; pp **grown**)
(person) grandir; (plant) pousser;
(become) devenir; (crime)
augmenter. ● vt cultiver; ~ **up**

G

devenir adulte, grandir. **grower** n cultivateur/-trice m/f.

growl vi (dog) gronder; (person) grogner. ● n grognement m.

grown ⇒GROW. ● a adulte. **~-up** a & n adulte (mf).

growth n (of person, plant) croissance f; (in numbers) accroissement m; (of hair, tooth) pousse f; (Med) grosseur f, tumeur f.

grudge vt ~ **doing** faire à contrecœur; ~ **sb sth** (success, wealth) en vouloir à qn de qch. ● n rancune f; **have a ~ against** en vouloir à.

grumble vi ronchonner, grogner (at après).

grumpy a (-ier, -iest) grincheux, grognon.

grunt vi grogner. ● n grognement m.

guarantee n garantie f. ● vt garantir.

guard vt protéger; (watch) surveiller. ● vi ~ **against** se protéger contre. ● n (Mil) garde f; (person) garde m; (on train) chef m de train.

guardian n gardien/-ne m/f; (of orphan) tuteur/-trice m/f.

guess vt/i deviner; (suppose) penser. ● n conjecture f.

guest n invité/-e m/f; (in hotel) client/-e m/f. **~-house** n pension f. **~-room** n chambre f d'amis.

guidance n (advice) conseils mpl; (information) information f.

guide n (person, book) guide m; (girl) guide f. ● vt guider. **~book** n guide m. **~-dog** n chien m d'aveugle. **~line** n indication f; (advice) conseils mpl.

guillotine n (for execution) guillotine f; (for paper) massicot m.

guilt n culpabilité f. **guilty** a coupable.

guinea-pig n (animal) cochon m d'Inde; (fig) cobaye m.

guitar n guitare f.

gulf n (part of sea) golfe m; (hollow) gouffre m.

gull n mouette f, (larger) goéland m.

gullible a crédule.

gully n (ravine) ravin m; (drain) rigole f.

gulp vt ~ **(down)** avaler en vitesse. ● vi (from fear etc.) avoir la gorge serrée. ● n gorgée f.

gum n (Anat) gencive f; (glue) colle f; (for chewing) chewing-gum m. ● vt (pt **gummed**) gommer.

gun n (pistol) revolver m; (rifle) fusil m; (large) canon m. ● vt (pt **gunned**) ~ **down** abattre. **~fire** n fusillade f. **~powder** n poudre f à canon. **~shot** n coup m de feu.

gurgle n (of water) gargouillement m; (of baby) gazouillis m. ● vi (water) gargouiller; (baby) gazouiller.

gush vi ~ **(out)** jaillir. ● n jaillissement m.

gust n rafale f; (of smoke) bouffée f.

gut n (belly 🄵) ventre m. ● vt (pt **gutted**) (fish) vider; (of fire) dévaster. **gutted** a 🄵 abattu.

guts npl 🄵 (insides of human) tripes fpl 🄵; (insides of animal, building) entrailles fpl; (courage) cran m 🄵.

gutter n (on roof) gouttière f; (in street) caniveau m.

guy n (man 🄵) type m.

gym n (place) gymnase m; (activity) gym(nastique) f.

gymnasium n gymnase m.

gymnastics npl gymnastique f.

gynaecologist n gynécologue mf.

gypsy n bohémien/-ne m/f.

habit n habitude f; (costume: Relig) habit m; **bo in/got into the ~e of** avoir/prendre l'habitude de.

habitual a (usual) habituel; (smoker, liar) invétéré.

hack n (writer) écrivaillon m. ● vi (Comput) pirater; **~ into** s'introduire dans. ● vt tailler.

haoker n (Comput) pirate m informatique.

hackneyed a rebattu.

had ⇒HAVE.

haddock n inv églefin m.

haemorrhage n hémorragie f.

haggard a (person) exténué; (face, look) défait.

haggle vi marchander; **~ over sth** discuter du prix de qch.

hail n grêle f. ● vt (greet) saluer; (taxi) héler. ● vi grêler; **~ from** venir de. **~stone** n grêlon m.

hair n (on head) cheveux mpl; (on body, of animal) poils mpl; (single strand on head) cheveu m; (on body) poil m. **~brush** n brosse f à cheveux. **~cut** n coupe f de cheveux. **~do** n □ coiffure f. **~dresser** n coiffeur/-euse m/f. **~drier** n séchoir m (à cheveux). **~pin** n épingle f à cheveux. **~remover** n dépilatoire m. **~style** n coiffure f.

hairy a (-ier, -iest) poilu; (terrifying □) horrifiant.

half n (pl halves) (part) moitié f; (fraction) demi m; **~ a dozen** une demi-douzaine; **~ an hour** une demi-heure; **four and a ~** quatre et demi; **an hour and a ~** une

heure et demie; **~ and half** moitié moitié; **in ~** en deux. ● a demi; **~ price** à moitié prix. ● adv à moitié. **~-back** n (Sport) demi m. **~-hearted** a tiède. **~-mast** n at **~-mast** en berne. **~-term** n vacances fpl de demi-trimestre. **~-time** n mi-temps f. **~-way** adv à mi-chemin. **~-wit** n imbécile mf.

hall n (in house) entrée f, (corridor) couloir m; (in airport) hall m; (for events) salle f; **~ of residence** résidence f universitaire.

hallmark n (on gold) poinçon m; (fig) caractéristique f.

hallo = HELLO.

Hallowe'en n la veille de la Toussaint.

halt n arrêt m; (temporary) suspension f; (Mil) halte f. ● vt (proceedings) interrompre; (arms sales, experiments) mettre fin à. ● vi (vehicle) s'arrêter; (army) faire halte.

halve vt (time) réduire de moitié; (fruit) couper en deux.

ham n jambon m.

hamburger n hamburger m.

hammer n marteau m. ● vt/i marteler; **~ sth into sth** enfoncer qch dans qch; **~ sth out** (agreement) parvenir à qch.

hammock n hamac m.

hamper n panier m. ● vt gêner.

hamster n hamster m.

hand n main f; (of clock) aiguille f; (writing) écriture f; (worker) ouvrier/-ière m/f; (cards) jeu m; **give sb a ~** donner un coup de main à qn; **at ~** proche; **on ~** disponible; **on the one ~...on the other ~** d'une part...d'autre part; **to ~** à portée de la main. ● vt **~ sb sth, ~ sth to sb** donner qch à qn. □ **~ in** or **over** remettre; **~ out** distribuer. **~bag** n sac m à main.

~baggage n bagages mpl à

main. ∼**book** n manuel m.
∼**brake** n frein m à main.
∼**cuffs** npl menottes fpl.

handicap n handicap m. ● vt (pt
handicapped) handicaper.

handkerchief n (pl ∼s)
mouchoir m.

handle n (of door, bag) poignée f;
(of implement) manche m; (of cup,
bucket) anse f; (of frying pan) queue
f. ● vt (manage) manier; (deal with)
traiter; (touch) manipuler.

handout n document m; (leaflet)
prospectus m; (money) aumône f.

hands-free kit n kit m mains
libres conducteur.

handshake n poignée f de main.

handsome a (good looking) beau;
(generous) généreux.

handwriting n écriture f.

handy a (-ier, -iest) (book, skill)
utile; (size, shape, tool) pratique;
(person) doué. ∼**man** n (pl
-men) bricoleur m.

hang vt (pt **hung**) (from hook,
hanger) accrocher; (from rope)
suspendre; (pt **hanged**) (person)
pendre. ● vi (from hook) être
accroché; (from rope) être
suspendu; (person) être pendu.
● n get the ∼ of doing 🔲 piger
comment faire 🔲. □ ∼**about**
traîner; ∼ **on** 🔲 (hold out) tenir;
(wait) attendre; ∼ **on to sth**
s'agripper à qch; ∼ **out** vi 🔲 (live)
crécher 🔲; (spend time) passer son
temps; vt (washing) étendre; ∼
up (telephone) raccrocher.

hanger n (for clothes) cintre m.

hang-gliding n vol m libre.

hangover n gueule f de bois 🔲.

hang-up n 🔲 complexe m.

haphazard a peu méthodique.

happen vi arriver, se passer; ∼ **to**
sb arriver à qn; **it so** ∼**s that** il se
trouve que.

happily adv joyeusement;
(fortunately) heureusement.

happiness n bonheur m.

happy a (-ier, -iest) heureux; **I'm**
not ∼ **about it** je ne suis pas
content; ∼ **with sth** satisfait de
qch; ∼ **medium** juste milieu m.

harass vt harceler. **harassment**
n harcèlement m.

harbour, (US) **harbor** n port m.
● vt (shelter) héberger.

hard a dur; (difficult) difficile, dur;
(evidence, fact) solide; **find it** ∼ **to**
do avoir du mal à faire; ∼ **on sb**
dur envers qn. ● adv (work) dur;
(pull, hit, cry) fort; (think, study)
sérieusement. ∼**board** n
aggloméré m. ∼ **copy** n (Comput)
tirage m. ∼ **disk** n disque m dur.

hardly adv à peine; (expect, hope)
difficilement; ∼ **ever** presque
jamais.

hardship n (poverty) privations fpl;
(ordeal) épreuve f.

hard: ∼ **shoulder** n bande f
d'arrêt d'urgence. ∼ **up** a
🔲 fauché 🔲. ∼**ware** n (Comput)
matériel m, hardware m; (goods)
quincaillerie f. ∼**-working** a
travailleur.

hardy a (-ier, -iest) résistant.

hare n lièvre m.

harm n mal m; **there is no** ∼ **in** il
n'y a pas de mal à. ● vt (person)
faire du mal à; (object)
endommager. **harmful** a nuisible.
harmless a inoffensif.

harmony n harmonie f.

harness n harnais m. ● vt (horse)
harnacher; (use) exploiter.

harp n harpe f. ● vi ∼ **on** (about)
rabâcher.

harrowing a (experience) atroce;
(story) déchirant.

harsh a (punishment) sévère;
(person) dur; (light) cru; (voice)

rude; (*chemical*) corrosif.
harshness *n* dureté *f*.
harvest *n* récolte *f*; **the wine** ～ les vendanges *fpl*. ● *vt* (*corn*) moissonner; (*vegetables*) récolter.
has ⇒HAVE.
hassle *n* complications *fpl*. ● *vt* Ⓣ talonner (**about** à propos de); (*worry*) stresser.
haste *n* hâte *f*; **in** ～ à la hâte; **make** ～ se dépêcher.
hasty *a* (**-ier, -iest**) précipité.
hat *n* chapeau *m*.
hatch *n* (Aviat) panneau *m* mobile; (Naut) écoutille *f*; (for food) passe plats *m inv*. ● *vt/i* (*eggs*) (faire) éclore.
hate *n* haine *f*. ● *vt* détester; (*violently*) haïr; (*sport, food*) avoir horreur de.
hatred *n* haine *f*.
haughty *a* (**-ier, -iest**) hautain.
haul *vt* tirer. ● *n* (by thieves) butin *m*; (by customs) saisie *f*; **it will be a long** ～ l'étape sera longue; **long/short** ～ (*transport*) long/court courrier *m*. **haulage** *n* transport *m* routier. **haulier** *n* (firm) société *f* de transports routiers.
haunt *vt* hanter. ● *n* lieu *m* de prédilection.

---

have

  present **have, has**; past **had**;
  past participle **had**

● *transitive verb*

····▸ (possess) avoir; **I** ～ (**got**) **a car** j'ai une voiture; **they** ～ (**got**) **problems** ils ont des problèmes.

····▸ (do sth) ～ **a try** essayer; ～ **a bath** prendre un bain.

····▸ ～ **sth done** faire faire qch; ～ **your hair cut** se faire couper les cheveux.

● *auxiliary verb*

····▸ (in perfect tenses) avoir; être; **I** ～ **seen him** je l'ai vu; **she had fallen** elle était tombée.

····▸ (in tag questions) **you've seen her, haven't you?** tu l'as vue, n'est-ce pas?; **you haven't seen her,** ～ **you?** tu ne l'as pas vue, par hasard?

····▸ (in short answers) '**you've never met him**'—'**yes I** ～' 'tu ne l'as jamais rencontré' 'mais si!'

····▸ (must) ～ **to do sth; I** ～ **to go** je dois partir; **you don't** ～ **to do it** tu n'es pas obligé de le faire.

⮞ For expressions such as **have a walk, have dinner** ⇒**walk, dinner**.

---

haven *n* refuge *m*; (fig) havre *m*.
havoc *n* dévastation *f*.
hawk *n* faucon *m*.
hay *n* foin *m*; ～ **fever** rhume *m* des foins.
haywire *a* **go** ～ (*plans*) dérailler; (*machine*) se détraquer.
hazard *n* risque *m*; ～ (**warning**) **lights** feux *mpl* de détresse. ● *vt* hasarder.
haze *n* brume *f*.
hazel *n* (bush) noisetier *m*. ～**nut** *n* noisette *f*.
hazy *a* (**-ier, -iest**) (misty) brumeux; (fig) vague.
he *pron* il; (emphatic) lui; **here** ～ **is** le voici.
head *n* tête *f*; (leader) chef *m*; (of beer) mousse *f*; ～**s or tails?** pile ou face? ● *vt* (list) être en tête de; (team) être à la tête de; (chapter) intituler; ～ **the ball** faire une tête. ● *vi* ～ **for** se diriger vers.
headache *n* mal *m* de tête; **have a** ～ avoir mal à la tête.
heading *n* titre *m*; (subject category) rubrique *f*.
head: ～**lamp**, ～**light** *n* phare *m*. ～**line** *n* gros titre *m*. ～**master** *n*

directeur m. **~mistress** n
directrice f. **~ office** n siège m
social. **~-on** a & adv de front.
~phones npl casque m.
~quarters npl siège m social;
(Mil) quartier m général. **~ rest** n
(Auto) repose-tête m inv. **~strong**
a têtu.

heal vt/i guérir.

health n santé f. **~ centre** n
centre m médico-social. **~ food** n
produits mpl diététiques. **~
insurance** n assurance f maladie.

healthy a (person, plant, skin,
diet) sain; (air) salutaire.

heap n tas m; **~s of** 🔲 un tas de.
● vt **~** (up) entasser.

hear vt (pt heard) entendre;
(news, rumour) apprendre;
(lecture, broadcast) écouter. ● vi
entendre; **~ from** recevoir des
nouvelles de; **~ of** or **about**
entendre parler de.

hearing n ouïe f; (of case)
audience f; **give sb a ~** écouter
qn. **~-aid** n prothèse f auditive.

hearse n corbillard m.

heart n cœur m; **~s** (cards) cœur
m; **at ~** au fond; **by ~** par cœur;
be ~-broken avoir le cœur brisé;
lose ~ perdre courage. **~ attack**
n crise f cardiaque. **~burn** n
brûlures fpl d'estomac. **~felt** a
sincère.

hearth n foyer m.

heartily adv (greet)
chaleureusement; (laugh, eat) de
bon cœur.

hearty a (-ier, -iest) (sincere)
chaleureux; (meal) solide.

heat n chaleur f; (contest) épreuve
f éliminatoire. ● vt (house)
chauffer; **~ (up)** (food) faire
chauffer; (reheat) réchauffer.
heated a (fig) passionné; (lit)
(pool) chauffé. **heater** n appareil
m de chauffage.

heather n bruyère f.

heating n chauffage m.

heave vt (lift) hisser; (pull) traîner
péniblement; **~ a sigh** pousser
un soupir. ● vi (pull) tirer de
toutes ses forces; (retch) avoir un
haut-le-cœur.

heaven n ciel m.

heavily adv lourdement; (smoke,
drink) beaucoup.

heavy a (-ier, -iest) lourd; (cold,
work) gros; (traffic) dense. **~
goods vehicle** n poids m lourd.
~-handed a maladroit. **~weight**
n poids m lourd.

Hebrew n (person) Hébreu m;
(Ling) hébreu m. ● a hébreu; (Ling)
hébraïque.

hectic a (activity) intense;
(period, day) mouvementé.

hedge n haie f. ● vi (in answering)
se dérober.

hedgehog n hérisson m.

heel n talon m.

hefty a (-ier, -iest) (person)
costaud 🔲; (object) pesant.

height n hauteur f; (of person)
taille f; (of plane, mountain) altitude f;
(of fame, glory) apogée m; (of joy, folly,
pain) comble m.

heir n héritier/-ière m/f. **heiress**
n héritière f. **heirloom** n objet m
de famille.

held ⇒HOLD.

helicopter n hélicoptère m.

hell n enfer m.

hello interj bonjour!; (on phone)
allô!

helmet n casque m.

help vt/i aider (**to do** à faire); **~
(sb) with a bag/the housework** aider
qn à porter un sac/à faire le
ménage; **~ oneself** se servir; **he
can't ~ it** ce n'est pas de sa faute.
● n aide f. ● interj au secours!
helper n aide mf. **helpful** a utile;
(person) serviable. **helping** n
portion f. **helpless** a impuissant.

hem *n* ourlet *m*. ● *vt* (*pt* **hemmed**) faire un ourlet à; ~ **in** cerner.

hen *n* poule *f*.

hence *adv* (for this reason) d'où; (from now) d'ici. **henceforth** *adv* désormais.

hepatitis *n* hépatite *f*.

her *pron* la, l'; (indirect object) lui; it's ~ c'est elle; for ~ pour elle. ● *a* son, sa; *pl* ses.

herb *n* herbe *f*; ~**s** (Culin) fines herbes *fpl*.

herd *n* troupeau *m*.

here *adv* ici; ~! (take this) tiens!; tenez!; ~ **is**, ~ **are** voici; **I'm** ~ je suis là. **hereabouts** *adv* par ici. **hereafter** *adv* après; (in book) ci-après. **hereby** *adv* par le présent acte; (in letter) par la présente.

herewith *adv* ci-joint.

heritage *n* patrimoine *m*.

hernia *n* hernie *f*.

hero *n* (*pl* ~**es**) héros *m*.

heroic *a* héroïque.

heroin *n* héroïne *f*.

heroine *n* héroïne *f*.

heron *n* héron *m*.

herring *n* hareng *m*.

hers *pron* le sien, la sienne, les sien(ne)s; **it is** ~ c'est à elle *or* le sien *or* la sienne.

herself *pron* (emphatic) elle-même; (reflexive) se; **proud of** ~ fière d'elle; **by** ~ toute seule.

hesitate *vi* hésiter. **hesitation** *n* hésitation *f*.

heterosexual *a* & *n* hétérosexuel/-le (*m/f*).

hexagon *n* hexagone *m*.

heyday *n* apogée *m*.

HGV *abbr* ⇒HEAVY GOODS VEHICLE.

hi *interj* 🔲 salut! 🔲.

hiccup *n* hoquet *m*; (the) ~**s** le hoquet. ● *vi* hoqueter.

hide *vt* (*pt* **hid**; *pp* **hidden**) cacher (from à). ● *vi* se cacher (from de); **go into hiding** se cacher. ● *n* (skin) peau *f*.

hideous *a* (monster, object) hideux; (noise) affreux.

hiding *n* **go into** ~ se cacher; **give sb a** ~ administrer une correction à qn.

hierarchy *n* hiérarchie *f*.

hi-fi *n* (chaîne *f*) hi-fi *f inv*.

high *a* haut; (price, number) élevé; (priest, speed) grand; (voice) aigu; **in the** ~ **season** en pleine saison. ● *n* **a (new)** ~ un niveau record. ● *adv* haut. ~**brow** *a* & *n* intellectuel/-le (*m/ f*). ~ **chair** *n* chaise *f* haute. ~ **court** *n* cour *f* suprême. **higher education** *n* enseignement *m* supérieur. ~**-jump** *n* saut *m* en hauteur. ~**-level** *a* à haut niveau.

highlight *n* (best moment) point *m* fort; ~**s** (in hair) reflet *m*; (artificial) mèches *fpl*; (Sport) résumé *m*. ● *vt* (emphasize) souligner.

highly *adv* extrêmement; (paid) très bien; **speak/think** ~ **of** dire/ penser beaucoup de bien de.

Highness *n* Altesse *f*.

high: ~**-rise** (building) *n* tour *f*. ~ **school** *n* lycée *m*. ~**-speed** *a* (train) à grande vitesse; (film) ultrarapide. ~ **street** *n* rue *f* principale. ~**-tech** *a* de pointe.

highway *n* route *f* nationale; (US) autoroute *f*; ~ **code** code *m* de la route.

hijack *vt* détourner. ● *n* détournement *m*. **hijacker** *n* pirate *m* (de l'air).

hike *n* randonnée *f*; **price** ~ hausse *f* de prix. ● *vi* faire de la randonnée.

hilarious *a* désopilant.

hill *n* colline *f*; (slope) côte *f*. **hilly** *a* vallonné.

him *pron* le, l'; (indirect object) lui;
it's ~ c'est lui; for ~ pour lui.

himself *pron* (emphatic) lui-même;
(reflexive) se; **proud of** ~ fier de lui;
by ~ tout seul.

hind *a* de derrière.

hinder *vt* (hamper) gêner; (prevent)
empêcher. **hindrance** *n* obstacle
m, gêne *f*.

hindsight *n* **with** ~
rétrospectivement.

Hindu *n* Hindou/-e *m/f*. ●*a*
hindou.

hinge *n* charnière *f*. ●*vi* ~ **on**
dépendre de.

hint *n* allusion *f*; (of spice, accent)
pointe *f*; (of colour) touche *f*; (advice)
conseil *m*. ●*vt* laisser entendre.
●*vi* ~ **at** faire allusion à.

hip *n* hanche *f*.

hippopotamus *n* (*pl* ~**es**)
hippopotame *m*.

hire *vt* (thing) louer; (person)
engager. ●*n* location *f*. ~**-car** *n*
voiture *f* de location.
~**-purchase** *n* achat *m* à crédit.

his *a* son, sa, *pl* ses. ●*pron* le
sien, la sienne, les sien(ne)s; **it is**
~ c'est à lui *or* le sien *or* la
sienne.

hiss *n* sifflement *m*. ●*vt/i* siffler.

history *n* histoire *f*; **make** ~
entrer dans l'histoire.

hit *vt* (*pt* **hit**; *pres p* **hitting**)
frapper; (collide with) heurter; (find)
trouver; (affect, reach) toucher. ●*vi*
~ **on** (find) tomber sur; ~ **it off**
s'entendre bien (**with** avec). ●*n*
(blow) coup *m*; (fig) succès *m*; (song)
tube *m* Ⅲ; (on Internet) (visit) visite *f*,
accès *m*; (result) page *f* trouvée,
résultat *m*.

hitch *vt* (fasten) accrocher; ~ **up**
remonter. ●*n* (snag) anicroche *f*.
~**-hike** *vi* faire du stop Ⅲ.
~**-hiker** *n* auto-stoppeur/-euse
m/f.

hi-tech *a* & *n* = HIGH-TECH.

HIV *abbr* (**human
immunodeficiency virus**) VIH
m.

hive *n* ruche *f*. ●*vt* ~ **off** séparer;
(industry) céder.

HIV-positive *a* séropositif.

hoard *vt* amasser; (supplies)
stocker. ●*n* trésor *m*; (of provisions)
provisions *fpl*.

hoarse *a* enroué.

hoax *n* canular *m*.

hobby *n* passe-temps *m inv*.

hockey *n* hockey *m*.

hog *n* cochon *m*. ●*vt* (*pt* **hogged**)
Ⅲ monopoliser.

hold *vt* (*pt* **held**) tenir; (contain)
contenir; (conversation, opinion)
avoir; (shares, record, person)
détenir; ~ (**the line**), **please** ne
quittez pas. ●*vi* (rope, weather)
tenir. ●*n* prise *f*; **get** ~ **of**
attraper; (ticket) se procurer;
(person) (by phone) joindre; **on** ~
en attente. □ ~ **back** (contain)
retenir; (hide) cacher; ~ **down**
(job) garder; (person) tenir;
(costs) limiter; ~ **on** (stand firm)
tenir bon; (wait) attendre; ~ **on to**
(keep) garder; (cling to) se
cramponner à; ~ **out** *vt* (offer)
offrir; *vi* (resist) tenir le coup; ~
up (support) soutenir; (delay)
retarder; (rob) attaquer.

holder *n* détenteur/-trice *m/f*; (of
passport, post) titulaire *mf*; (for object)
support *m*.

hold-up *n* retard *m*; (of traffic)
embouteillage *m*; (robbery) hold-up
m inv.

hole *n* trou *m*.

holiday *n* vacances *fpl*; (public)
jour *m* férié; (time off) congé *m*.
●*vi* passer ses vacances. ●*a* de
vacances. ~**-maker** *n* vacancier/
-ière *m/f*.

Holland *n* Hollande *f*.

hollow *a* creux; (fig) faux. ●*n*
creux *m*. ●*vt* creuser.

holly *n* houx *m*.

holy *a* (**-ier, -iest**) saint; (water) bénit; **H~ Ghost, H~ Spirit** Saint-Esprit *m*.

homage *n* hommage *m*.

home *n* (place to live) logement *m*; maison *f*; (institution) maison *f*; (family base) foyer *m*; (country) pays *m*. ●*a* de la maison, du foyer; (of family) de famille; (Pol) intérieur; (*match, visit*) à domicile. ●*adv* (at) ~ à la maison, chez soi; **come** *or* **go** ~ rentrer; (from abroad) rentrer dans son pays; **feel at** ~ **with** être à l'aise avec. ~ **computer** *n* ordinateur *m*, PC *m*.

homeless *a* sans abri. ●*n* the ~ les sans-abri *mpl*.

homely *a* (**-ier, -iest**) (cosy) accueillant; (simple) sans prétention; (person: US) sans attraits.

home: ~**-made** *a* (fait) maison. **H~ Office** *n* ministère *m* de l'Intérieur. ~ **page** *n* (Internet) page *f* d'accueil. **H~ Secretary** *n* Ministre *m* de l'Intérieur. ~**sick** *a* **be** ~**sick** avoir le mal du pays. ~**work** *n* devoirs *mpl*.

homosexual *a & n* homosexuel/-le (*m/f*).

honest *a* (truthful) intègre; (trustworthy) honnête; (sincere) franc. **honestly** *adv* honnêtement; franchement. **honesty** *n* honnêteté *f*.

honey *n* miel *m*; (person ⯅) chéri/-e *m/f*. ~**moon** *n* voyage *m* de noces; (fig) lune *f* de miel.

honk *vi* klaxonner.

honorary *a* (*person*) honoraire; (*degree*) honorifique.

honour, (US) **honor** *n* honneur *m*. ●*vt* honorer.

hood *n* capuchon *m*; (on car, pram) capote *f*; (car engine cover: US) capot *m*.

hoof *n* (*pl* ~**s**) sabot *m*.

hook *n* crochet *m*; (on garment) agrafe *f*; (for fishing) hameçon *m*; **off the** ~ tiré d'affaire; (phone) décroché. ●*vt* accrocher.

hoot *n* (of owl) (h)ululement *m*; (of car) coup *m* de klaxon. ●*vi* (owl) (h)ululer; (car) klaxonner; (jeer) huer.

hoover *vt* ~ **a room** passer l'aspirateur dans une pièce. **Hoover®** *n* aspirateur *m*.

hop *vi* (*pt* **hopped**) sauter (à cloche-pied); ~ **in!** ⯅ vas-y, monte! ●*n* bond *m*; ~**s** houblon *m*.

hope *n* espoir *m*. ●*vt/i* espérer; ~ **for** espérer avoir; **I** ~ **so** je l'espère.

hopeful *a* (*news, sign*) encourageant; (*person*) plein d'espoir; (*mood*) optimiste. **hopefully** *adv* (with luck) avec un peu de chance; (with hope) avec optimisme.

hopeless *a* désespéré; (useless: fig) nul ⯅.

horizon *n* horizon *m*.

horizontal *a* horizontal.

hormone *n* hormone *f*.

horn *n* corne *f*; (of car) klaxon® *m*; (Mus) cor *m*.

horoscope *n* horoscope *m*.

horrible *a* horrible.

horrid *a* horrible.

horrific *a* horrifiant.

horrify *vt* horrifier.

horror *n* horreur *f*. ●*a* (*film, story*) d'épouvante.

horse *n* cheval *m*. ~**back** *n* **on** ~**back** à cheval. ~**chestnut** *n* marron *m* (d'Inde). ~**man** *n* (*pl* -**men**) cavalier *m*. ~**power** *n* puissance *f* (en chevaux). ~**race** *n* course *f* de chevaux. ~**radish** *n* raifort *m*. ~**shoe** *n* fer *m* à cheval. ~**show** *n* concours *m* hippique.

H

hose n tuyau m. ●vt arroser.
~-**pipe** n tuyau m.

hospitable a hospitalier.

hospital n hôpital m.

host n (to guests) hôte m; (on TV)
animateur m; (Internet) ordinateur
m hôte; **a ~ of** une foule de;
(Relig) hostie f.

hostage n otage m; **hold sb ~**
garder qn en otage.

hostel n foyer m; (youth) ~
auberge f (de jeunesse).

hostess n hôtesse f.

hostile a hostile.

hot a (**hotter, hottest**) chaud;
(Culin) épicé; **be** or **feel ~** avoir
chaud; **it is ~** il fait chaud; **in ~
water** 🔟 dans le pétrin. ●vt/i (pt
hotted) ~ **up** 🔟 chauffer. ~ **air
balloon** n montgolfière f. ~ **dog**
n hot-dog m.

hotel n hôtel m.

hot: ~-**headed** a impétueux. ~
list n (Internet) signets mpl favoris.
~-**plate** n plaque f chauffante. ~
water bottle n bouillotte f.

hound n chien m de chasse. ●vt
poursuivre.

hour n heure f.

hourly a horaire; **on an ~ basis** à
l'heure. ●adv toutes les heures.

house[1] n maison f; (Pol) Chambre
f; **on the ~** aux frais de la
maison.

house[2] vt loger; (of building)
abriter.

household n (house, family)
ménage m. ●a ménager.

house: ~**keeper** n gouvernante
f. ~-**proud** a méticuleux.
~-**warming** n pendaison f de
crémaillère. ~**wife** n (pl -**wives**)
ménagère f. ~**work** n travaux
mpl ménagers.

housing n logement m; ~
association service m de
logement; ~ **development** cité f;
(smaller) lotissement m.

hover vi (bird) voleter; (vacillate)
vaciller. **hovercraft** n
aéroglisseur m.

how adv comment; ~ **are you?**
comment allez-vous?; ~ **long/tall
is...?** quelle est la longueur/
hauteur de...?; ~ **many?**, ~
much? combien?; ~ **pretty!**
comme or que c'est joli!; ~ **about
a walk?** si on faisait une
promenade?; ~ **do you do?**
(greeting) enchanté.

however adv (nevertheless)
cependant; ~ **hard I try** j'ai beau
essayer; ~ **much it costs** quel que
soit le prix; ~ **young/poor he is** si
jeune/pauvre soit-il; ~ **you like**
comme tu veux.

howl n hurlement m. ●vi hurler.

HP abbr ⇒HIRE-PURCHASE.

hp abbr ⇒HORSEPOWER.

HQ abbr ⇒HEADQUARTERS.

hub n moyeu m; (fig) centre m.

hug vt (pt **hugged**) serrer dans
ses bras. ●n étreinte f; **give sb a
~** serrer qn dans ses bras.

huge a énorme.

hull n (of ship) coque f.

hum vt/i (pt **hummed**) (person)
fredonner; (insect) bourdonner;
(engine) ronronner. ●n
bourdonnement m;
ronronnement m.

human a humain. ●n humain m.
~ **being** n être m humain.

humane a (person) humain; (act)
d'humanité; (killing) sans
cruauté.

humanitarian a humanitaire.

humanity n humanité f.

humble a humble.

humid a humide.

humiliate vt humilier.

humorous a humoristique;
(person) plein d'humour.

humour, (US) **humor** n humour

m; (mood) humeur *f.* ● *vt*
amadouer.

hump *n* bosse *f.* ● *vt* 🔲 porter.

hunchback *n* bossu/-e *m/f.*

hundred *a* & *n* cent (*m*); **two ~
and one** deux cent un; **~s of** des
centaines de. **hundredth** *a* & *n*
centième (*mf*).

hung →HANG.

Hungarian *n* (person) Hongrois/-e
m/f; (Ling) hongrois *m.* ● *a*
hongrois. **Hungary** *n* Hongrie *f.*

hunger *n* faim *f.* ● *vi* **~ for** avoir
faim de.

hungry *a* (-ier, -iest) affamé; **be
~** avoir faim.

hunt *vt/i* chasser; **~ for** chercher.
● *n* chasse *f.* **hunter** *n* chasseur
m. **hunting** *n* chasse *f.*

hurdle *n* (Sport) haie *f*; (fig)
obstacle *m.*

hurricane *n* ouragan *m.*

hurry *vi* se dépêcher; **~ out** sortir
précipitamment. ● *vt* (*work*)
terminer à la hâte; (*person*)
bousculer. ● *n* hâte *f*; **in a ~**
pressé.

hurt *vt/i* (*pt* hurt) faire mal (à);
(*injure, offend*) blesser. ● *a* blessé.
● *n* blessure *f.*

hurtle *vi* **~ down** dévaler; **~ along
a road** foncer sur une route.

husband *n* mari *m.*

hush *vt* faire taire; **~ up** (*news*)
étouffer. ● *n* silence *m.* ● *interj*
chut!

husky *a* (-ier, -iest) enroué. ● *n*
husky *m.*

hustle *vt* (push, rush) bousculer.
● *vi* (hurry) se dépêcher; (work: US)
se démener. ● *n* **~ and bustle**
agitation *f.*

hut *n* cabane *f.*

hyacinth *n* jacinthe *f.*

hydrant *n* (fire) **~** bouche *f*
d'incendie.

hydraulic *a* hydraulique.

hydroelectric *a* hydroélectrique.

hydrogen *n* hydrogène *m*; **~
bomb** bombe *f* à hydrogène.

hyena *n* hyène *f.*

hygiene *n* hygiène *f.* **hygienic** *a*
hygiénique.

hymn *n* cantique *m*; (fig) hymne
m.

hype 🔲 battage *m* publicitaire.
● *vt* **~ (up)** (*film, book*) faire du
battage pour.

hyperactive *a* hyperactif.

hyperlink *n* hyperlien *m.*

hypermarket *n* hypermarché *m.*

hypertext *n* hypertexte *m.*

hyphen *n* trait *m* d'union.

hypnosis *n* hypnose *f.*

hypocrisy *n* hypocrisie *f.*
hypocrite *n* hypocrite *mf.*
hypocritical *a* hypocrite.

hypothesis *n* (*pl* -ses)
hypothèse *f.*

hysteria *n* hystérie *f.* **hysterical**
a hystérique.

hysterics *npl* crise *f* de nerfs; **be
in ~** rire aux larmes.

I *pron* je, j'; (stressed) moi.

ice *n* glace *f*; (on road) verglas *m.*
● *vt* (*cake*) glacer. ● *vi* **~ (up)**
(*window*) se givrer; (*river*) geler.
~box *n* (US) réfrigérateur *m.*
~-cream *n* glace *f.* **~-cube** *n*
glaçon *m.* **~ hockey** *n* hockey *m*
sur glace.

Iceland *n* Islande *f.* **Icelander** *n*
Islandais/-e *m/f.* **Icelandic** *a* & *n*
islandais (*m*).

ice: **~ lolly** *n* glace *f* (sur

bâtonnet). ~ **rink** *n* patinoire *f*. ~
skate *n* patin *m* à glace.

icicle *n* stalactite *f* (de glace).

icing *n* (sugar) glaçage *m*.

icy *a* (**-ier, -iest**) (*hands, wind*)
glacé; (*road*) verglacé; (*manner,
welcome*) glacial.

ID *n* pièce *f* d'identité; ~ **card**
carte *f* d'identité.

idea *n* idée *f*.

ideal *a* idéal. ● *n* idéal *m*.

identical *a* identique.

identification *n* identification *f*;
(*papers*) pièce *f* d'identité.

identify *vt* identifier. ● *vi* ~ **with**
s'identifier à.

identikit *n* ~ **picture** portrait-
robot *m*.

identity *n* identité *f*.

ideological *a* idéologique.

idiom *n* (*phrase*) idiome *m*;
(*language*) parler *m*, langue *f*.
idiomatic *a* idiomatique.

idiosyncrasy *n* particularité *f*.

idiot *n* idiot/-e *m/f*. **idiotic** *a*
idiot.

idle *a* (lazy) paresseux; (*doing
nothing*) oisif; (*boast, threat*) vain.
● *vi* (*engine*) tourner au ralenti.
● *vt* ~ **away** gaspiller.

idol *n* idole *f*. **idolize** *vt* idolâtrer.

idyllic *a* idyllique.

i.e. *abbr* c-à-d, c'est-à-dire.

if *conj* si.

ignite *vt/i* (s')enflammer.

ignition *n* (Auto) allumage *m*; ~
(**switch**) contact *m*; ~ **key** clé *f* de
contact.

ignorance *n* ignorance *f*.

ignorant *a* ignorant (**of** de).

ignorantly *adv* par ignorance.

ignore *vt* (*person*) ignorer;
(*mistake, remark*) ne pas relever;
(*feeling, fact*) ne pas tenir
compte de.

ill *a* malade. ● *adv* mal. ● *n* mal
m. ~**-advised** *a* malavisé. ~ **at**

ease *a* mal à l'aise. ~**-bred** *a*
mal élevé.

illegal *a* illégal.

illegible *a* illisible.

illegitimate *a* illégitime.

ill: ~**-fated** *a* malheureux. ~
feeling *n* ressentiment *m*.

illiterate *a* & *n* analphabète (*mf*).

illness *n* maladie *f*.

ill-treat *vt* maltraiter.

illuminate *vt* éclairer; (decorate with
lights) illuminer. **illumination** *n*
éclairage *m*; illumination *f*.

illusion *n* illusion *f*.

illustrate *vt* illustrer. **illustration**
n illustration *f*. **illustrative** *a* qui
illustre.

image *n* image *f*; (of firm, person)
image *f* de marque. **imagery** *n*
images *fpl*.

imaginable *a* imaginable.
imaginary *a* imaginaire.
imagination *n* imagination *f*.
imaginative *a* plein
d'imagination.

imagine *vt* (s')imaginer (**that**
que); ~ **being rich** s'imaginer
riche.

imbalance *n* déséquilibre *m*.

imitate *vt* imiter.

immaculate *a* impeccable.

immaterial *a* sans importance
(**to** pour; **that** que).

immature *a* (*person*) immature;
(*plant*) qui n'est pas arrivé à
maturité.

immediate *a* immédiat.

immediately *adv*
immédiatement. ● *conj* dès que.

immense *a* immense.

immensely *adv* extrêmement,
immensément. **immensity** *n*
immensité *f*.

immerse *vt* plonger (**in** dans).
immersion *n* immersion *f*;
immersion heater chauffe-eau *m*
inv électrique.

immigrant n & a immigré/-e (m/f); (newly-arrived) immigrant/-e (m/f). **immigrate** vi immigrer. **immigration** n immigration f.

imminent a imminent.

immobilizer n système m antidémarrage.

immoral a immoral.

immortal a immortel.

immune a immunisé (from, to contre); (reaction, system) immunitaire. **immunity** n immunité f. **immunization** n immunisation f. **immunize** vt immuniser.

impact n impact m.

impair vt (performance) affecter; (ability) affaiblir.

impart vt communiquer, transmettre.

impartial a impartial.

impassable a (barrier) infranchissable, (road) impraticable.

impassive a impassible.

impatience n impatience f. **impatient** a impatient; **get impatient** s'impatienter. **impatiently** adv impatiemment.

impeccable a impeccable.

impede vt entraver.

impediment n entrave f; **speech** ~ défaut m d'élocution.

impending a imminent.

imperative a urgent. ● n impératif m.

imperfect a incomplet; (faulty) défectueux. ● n (Gram) imparfait m. **imperfection** n imperfection f.

imperial a impérial; (measure) conforme aux normes britanniques. **imperialism** n impérialisme m.

impersonal a impersonnel.

impersonate vt se faire passer pour; (mimic) imiter.

impertinent a impertinent.

impervious a imperméable (to à).

impetuous a impétueux.

impetus n impulsion f.

impinge vi ~ on affecter; (encroach) empiéter sur.

implement n instrument m; (tool) outil m. ● vt exécuter, mettre en application; (software) implanter.

implicit a (implied) implicite (in dans); (unquestioning) absolu.

imply vt (assume, mean) impliquer; (insinuate) laisser entendre.

impolite a impoli.

import[1] vt importer.

import[2] n (article) importation f; (meaning) signification f.

importance n importance f. **important** a important.

impose vt imposer (on sb à qn; on sth sur qch). ● vi s'imposer; ~ on sb abuser de la bienveillance de qn. **imposing** a imposant.

impossible a impossible. ● n the ~ l'impossible m.

impotent a impuissant.

impound vt confisquer, saisir.

impoverish vt appauvrir.

impractical a peu réaliste.

impregnable a imprenable.

impress vt impressionner; ~ sth on sb faire bien comprendre qch à qn. **impression** n impression f. **impressionable** a impressionnable. **impressive** a impressionnant.

imprint[1] n empreinte f.

imprint[2] vt (fix) graver (on dans); (print) imprimer.

imprison vt emprisonner.

improbable a (not likely) improbable; (incredible) invraisemblable.

improper a (unseemly) malséant; (dishonest) irrégulier.

improve vt/i (s')améliorer.
 improvement n amélioration f.

improvise vt/i improviser.

impudent a impudent.

impulse n impulsion f; on ~ sur un coup de tête. **impulsive** a impulsif. **impulsively** adv par impulsion.

impurity n impureté f.

in prep (inside, within) dans; (expressing place, position) à, en; (expressing time) en, dans; ~ **the box/garden** dans la boîte/le jardin; ~ **Paris/school** à Paris/l'école; ~ **town** en ville; ~ **the country** à la campagne; ~ **English** en anglais; ~ **India** en Inde; ~ **Japan** au Japon; ~ **winter** en hiver; ~ **spring** au printemps; ~ **an hour** (at end of) au bout d'une heure; ~ **an hour('s time)** dans une heure; ~ **(the space of) an hour** en une heure; ~ **doing** en faisant; ~ **the evening** le soir; **one** ~ **ten** un sur dix; ~ **between** entre les deux; (time) entretemps; ~ **a firm voice** d'une voix ferme; ~ **blue** en bleu; ~ **ink** à l'encre; ~ **uniform** en uniforme; ~ **a skirt** en jupe; ~ **a whisper** en chuchotant; ~ **a loud voice** d'une voix forte; **the best** ~ le meilleur de; **we are** ~ **for** on va avoir; **have it** ~ **for sb** 🅸 avoir qn dans le collimateur. ● adv (inside) dedans; (at home) là, à la maison; (in fashion) à la mode; **come** ~ entrer; **run** ~ entrer en courant.

inability n incapacité f (**to do** of faire).

inaccessible a inaccessible.

inaccurate a inexact.

inactive a inactif. **inactivity** n inaction f.

inadequate a insuffisant.

inadvertently adv par mégarde.

inadvisable a inopportun, à déconseiller.

inane a idiot, débile.

inanimate a inanimé.

inappropriate a inopportun; (term) inapproprié.

inarticulate a qui a du mal à s'exprimer.

inasmuch as adv dans la mesure où; (because) vu que.

inaugurate vt (open, begin) inaugurer; (person) investir.

inborn a inné.

inbred a (inborn) inné.

Inc. abbr (incorporated) S.A.

incapable a incapable (**of doing** de faire).

incapacitate vt immobiliser.

incense[1] n encens m.

incense[2] vt mettre en fureur.

incentive n motivation f; (payment) prime f.

incessant a incessant. **incessantly** adv sans cesse.

incest n inceste m. **incestuous** a incestueux.

inch n pouce m (=2.54 cm.). ● vi ~ **towards** se diriger petit à petit vers.

incidence n fréquence f.

incident n incident m. **incidental** a secondaire. **incidentally** adv à propos; (by chance) par la même occasion.

incinerate vt incinérer. **incinerator** n incinérateur m.

incite vt inciter, pousser.

inclination n (tendency) tendance f; (desire) envie f.

incline[1] vt/i (s')incliner; **be** ~**d to** avoir tendance à.

incline[2] n pente f.

include vt comprendre, inclure. **including** prep (y) compris. **inclusion** n inclusion f.

inclusive a & adv inclus; ~ **of delivery** livraison comprise.

income n revenus mpl; ~ **tax** impôt m sur le revenu.

incoming a (*tide*) montant; (*tenant, government*) nouveau; (*call*) qui vient de l'extérieur.

incompatible a incompatible.

incompetent a incompétent.

incomplete a incomplet.

incomprehensible a incompréhensible.

inconceivable a inconcevable.

inconclusive a peu concluant.

incongruous a déconcertant, surprenant.

inconsiderate a (*person*) peu attentif à autrui; (*act*) maladroit.

inconsistent a (*argument*) incohérent; (*performance*) inégal; (*behaviour*) changeant; ~ **with** en contradiction avec.

inconspicuous a qui passe inaperçu.

incontinent a incontinent.

inconvenience n dérangement m; (*drawback*) inconvénient m. ● vt déranger. **inconvenient** a incommode; **if it's not inconvenient for you** si cela ne vous dérange pas.

incorporate vt incorporer (**into** dans); (*contain*) comporter.

incorrect a incorrect.

increase¹ n augmentation f (**in**, **of** de); **be on the** ~ être en progression.

increase² vt/i augmenter. **increasing** a croissant. **increasingly** adv de plus en plus.

incredible a incroyable.

incriminate vt incriminer. **incriminating** a compromettant.

incubate vt (*eggs*) couver. **incubation** n incubation f. **incubator** n couveuse f.

incur vt (*pt* **incurred**) (*penalty, anger*) encourir; (*debts*) contracter.

indebted a ~ **to sb** redevable à

qn (**for** de); (*grateful*) reconnaissant à qn.

indecent a indécent.

indecisive a indécis; (*ending*) peu concluant.

indeed adv en effet; (*emphatic*) vraiment.

indefinite a vague; (*period, delay*) illimité. **indefinitely** adv indéfiniment.

indelible a indélébile.

indemnity n (*protection*) assurance f; (*payment*) indemnité f.

indent vt (*text*) renfoncer. **indentation** n (*dent*) marque f.

independence n indépendance f. **independent** a indépendant. **independently** adv de façon indépendante; **independently of** indépendamment de.

index n (*pl* ~**es**) (*in book*) index m; (*in library*) catalogue m; (*in economy*) indice m; ~ **card** fiche f; ~ (**finger**) index m. ● vt classer. ~**-linked** a indexé.

India n Inde f.

Indian n Indien/-ne m/f. ● a indien.

indicate vt indiquer. **indication** n indication f.

indicative a & n indicatif (m).

indicator n (*pointer*) aiguille f; (*on vehicle*) clignotant m; (*board*) tableau m.

indict vt inculper. **indictment** n accusation f.

indifferent a indifférent; (*not good*) médiocre.

indigenous a indigène.

indigestible a indigeste. **indigestion** n indigestion f.

indignant a indigné.

indirect a indirect. **indirectly** adv indirectement.

indiscreet a indiscret. **indiscretion** n indiscrétion f.

indiscriminate a sans

distinction. **indiscriminately** *adv*
sans distinction.
indisputable *a* indiscutable.
individual *a* individuel; (*tuition*)
particulier. ●*n* individu *m*.
individualist *n* individualiste *mf*.
individuality *n* individualité *f*.
individually *adv*
individuellement.
indoctrinate *vt* endoctriner.
indoctrination *n* endoctrinement
m.
indolent *a* indolent.
Indonesia *n* Indonésie *f*.
indoor *a* (*clothes*) d'intérieur;
(pool, court) couvert. **indoors** *adv* à
l'intérieur.
induce *vt* (influence) persuader;
(stronger) inciter (**to do** à faire).
inducement *n* (financial)
récompense *f*; (incentive)
motivation *f*.
induction *n* (Electr) induction *f*;
(inauguration) installation *f*.
indulge *vt* (*person, whim*) céder
à; (*child*) gâter. ●*vi* ~ **in** se livrer
à. **indulgence** *n* indulgence *f*;
(treat) plaisir *m*. **indulgent** *a*
indulgent.
industrial *a* industriel; (accident)
du travail; ~ **action** grève *f*; ~
dispute conflit *m* social.
industrialist *n* industriel/-le *m/f*.
industrialized *a* industrialisé.
industrious *a* diligent.
industry *n* industrie *f*; (zeal) zèle
m.
inebriated *a* ivre.
inedible *a* immangeable.
ineffective *a* inefficace.
inefficient *a* inefficace; (person)
incompétent.
ineligible *a* inéligible; **be** ~ **for**
ne pas avoir droit à.
inept *a* incompétent; (tactless)
maladroit.
inequality *n* inégalité *f*.

inescapable *a* indéniable.
inevitable *a* inévitable.
inexcusable *a* inexcusable.
inexhaustible *a* inépuisable.
inexpensive *a* pas cher.
inexperience *n* inexpérience *f*.
inexperienced *a* inexpérimenté.
infallible *a* infaillible.
infamous *a* (*person*) tristement
célèbre; (*deed*) infâme.
infancy *n* petite enfance *f*; **in its**
~ (fig) à ses débuts *mpl*. **infant** *n*
(baby) bébé *m*; (at school) enfant *m*.
infantile *a* infantile.
infatuated *a* ~ **with** entiché de.
infatuation *n* engouement *m*.
infect *vt* contaminer; ~ **sb with**
sth transmettre qch à qn.
infection *n* infection *f*.
infectious *a* contagieux.
infer *vt* (*pt* **inferred**) (deduce)
déduire.
inferior *a* inférieur (**to** à); (*work,*
product) de qualité inférieure.
●*n* inférieur/-e *m/f*. **inferiority** *n*
infériorité *f*.
inferno *n* (hell) enfer *m*; (blaze)
brasier *m*.
infertile *a* infertile.
infest *vt* infester (**with** de).
infidelity *n* infidélité *f*.
infighting *n* conflits *mpl* internes.
infinite *a* infini. **infinitely** *adv*
infiniment. **infinitive** *n* infinitif
m. **infinity** *n* infinité *f*.
infirm *a* infirme. **infirmary** *n*
hôpital *m*; (sick-bay) infirmerie *f*.
infirmity *n* infirmité *f*.
inflame *vt* enflammer.
inflammable *a* inflammable.
inflammation *n* inflammation *f*.
inflammatory *a* incendiaire.
inflatable *a* gonflable. **inflate** *vt*
(lit, fig) gonfler.
inflation *n* inflation *f*.
inflection *n* (of word root) flexion *f*;
(of vowel, voice) inflexion *f*.

inflict *vt* infliger (**on** à).

influence *n* influence *f*; **under the ~** (drunk 🔲) éméché. ● *vt* (*person*) influencer; (*choice*) influer sur. **influential** *a* (powerful) influent; (*theory, artist*) très suivi.

influenza *n* grippe *f*.

influx *n* afflux *m*.

inform *vt* informer (**of** de); **keep ~ed** tenir au courant.

informal *a* (simple) simple, sans façons; (unofficial) officieux; (colloquial) familier. **informality** *n* simplicité *f*. **informally** *adv* (*dress*) en tenue décontractée; (*speak*) en toute simplicité.

informant *n* indicateur/-trice *m/f*.

information *n* renseignements *mpl*, informations *fpl*; **some ~** un renseignement. **~ superhighway** *n* autoroute *f* de l'information. **~ technology** *n* informatique *f*.

informative *a* (*book*) riche en renseignements; (*visit*) instructif.

informer *n* indicateur/-trice *m/f*.

infrequent *a* rare.

infringe *vt* (*rule*) enfreindre; (*rights*) ne pas respecter. **infringement** *n* infraction *f*

infuriate *vt* exaspérer.

ingenuity *n* ingéniosité *f*.

ingot *n* lingot *m*.

ingrained *a* (hatred) enraciné; (dirt) bien incrusté.

ingratiate *vt* **~ oneself with** se faire bien voir de.

ingredient *n* ingrédient *m*.

inhabit *vt* habiter. **inhabitable** *a* habitable. **inhabitant** *n* habitant/ -e *m/f*.

inhale *vt* inhaler; (smoke) avaler. **inhaler** *n* inhalateur *m*.

inherent *a* inhérent (**in** à). **inherently** *adv* en soi, par sa nature.

inherit *vt* hériter de; **~ sth from sb** hériter qch de qn. **inheritance** *n* héritage *m*.

inhibit *vt* (restrain) inhiber; (prevent) entraver.

inhospitable *a* inhospitalier.

inhuman *a* inhumain.

initial *n* initiale *f*. ● *vt* (*pt* **initialled**) parapher. ● *a* initial.

initiate *vt* (*project*) mettre en œuvre; (*talks*) amorcer; (*person*) initier (**into** à). **initiation** *n* initiation *f*; (start) amorce *f*.

initiative *n* initiative *f*.

inject *vt* injecter (**into** dans); (*new element*: fig) insuffler (**into** à). **injection** *n* injection *f*, piqûre *f*.

injure *vt* blesser; (damage) nuire à. **injury** *n* blessure *f*.

injustice *n* injustice *f*.

ink *n* encre *f*.

inkling *n* petite idée *f*.

inland *a* intérieur; **I~ Revenue** service *m* des impôts britannique.

in-laws *npl* (parents) beaux-parents *mpl*; (family) belle-famille *f*.

inlay[1] *vt* (*pt* **inlaid**) incruster (**with** de); (on wood) marqueter.

inlay[2] *n* incrustation *f*; (on wood) marqueterie *f*.

inlet *n* bras *m* de mer; (Tech) arrivée *f*.

inmate *n* (of asylum) interné/-e *m/f*; (of prison) détenu/-e *m/f*.

inn *n* auberge *f*.

innate *a* inné.

inner *a* intérieur; **~ city** quartiers *mpl* déshérités; **~ tube** chambre *f* à air.

innocent *a & n* innocent/-e (*m/f*).

innocuous *a* inoffensif.

innovate *vi* innover.

innuendo *n* (*pl* **~es**)

insinuations *fpl*; (sexual) allusions *fpl* grivoises.

innumerable *a* innombrable.

inoculate *vt* vacciner (**against** contre).

inopportune *a* inopportun.

in-patient *n* malade *mf* hospitalisé/-e.

input *n* (of energy) alimentation *f* (**of** en); (contribution) contribution *f*; (data) données *fpl*; (computer process) saisie *f* des données. ● *vt* (data) saisir.

inquest *n* enquête *f*.

inquire *vi* se renseigner (**about, into** sur). ● *vt* demander.

inquiry *n* demande *f* de renseignements; (inquest) enquête *f*.

inquisitive *a* curieux.

inroad *n* make ∼s **into** faire une avancée sur.

insane *a* fou; (Jur) aliéné. **insanity** *n* folie *f*; (Jur) aliénation *f* mentale.

inscribe *vt* inscrire. **inscription** *n* inscription *f*.

inscrutable *a* énigmatique.

insect *n* insecte *m*. **insecticide** *n* insecticide *m*.

insecure *a* (person) qui manque d'assurance; (job) précaire; (lock, property) peu sûr. **insecurity** *n* (of person) manque *m* d'assurance; (of situation) insécurité *f*.

insensitive *a* insensible; (remark) indélicat.

inseparable *a* inséparable (**from** de).

insert *vt* insérer (**in** dans).

in-service *a* (training) continu.

inshore *a* côtier.

inside *n* intérieur *m*; ∼s
Ⅱ entrailles *fpl*. ● *a* intérieur.
● *adv* à l'intérieur; **go** ∼ entrer.
● *prep* à l'intérieur de; (of time) en

moins de; ∼ **out** à l'envers; (thoroughly) à fond.

insight *n* (perception) perspicacité *f*; (idea) aperçu *m*.

insignia *npl* insigne *m*.

insignificant *a* (cost, difference) négligeable; (person) insignifiant.

insincere *a* peu sincère.

insinuate *vt* insinuer.

insist *vt/i* insister (**that** pour que); ∼ **on** exiger; ∼ **on doing** vouloir à tout prix faire. **insistence** *n* insistance *f*. **insistent** *a* insistant. **insistently** *adv* avec insistance.

insofar as *adv* dans la mesure où.

insolent *a* insolent.

insolvent *a* insolvable.

insomnia *n* insomnie *f*. **insomniac** *n* insomniaque *mf*.

inspect *vt* (school, machinery) inspecter; (tickets) contrôler. **inspection** *n* inspection *f*; (of passport, ticket) contrôle *m*. **inspector** *n* inspecteur/-trice *m*/ *f*; (on bus) contrôleur/-euse *m*/*f*.

inspiration *n* inspiration *f*. **inspire** *vt* inspirer.

install *vt* installer.

instalment *n* (payment) versement *m*; (of serial) épisode *m*.

instance *n* exemple *m*; (case) cas *m*; **for** ∼ par exemple; **in the first** ∼ en premier lieu.

instant *a* immédiat; (food) instantané. ● *n* instant *m*. **instantaneous** *a* instantané. **instantly** *adv* immédiatement.

instead *adv* plutôt; ∼ **of doing** au lieu de faire; ∼ **of sb** à la place de qn.

instep *n* cou-de-pied *m*.

instigate *vt* (attack) lancer; (proceedings) engager.

instil *vt* (*pt* **instilled**) inculquer; (fear) insuffler.

instinct n instinct m. **instinctive** a instinctif.

institute n institut m. ● vt instituer; (*proceedings*) engager. **institution** n institution f; (school, hospital) établissement m.

instruct vt (teach) instruire; (order) ordonner; ~ **sb in sth** enseigner qch à qn; ~ **sb to do** donner l'ordre à qn de faire. **instruction** n instruction f. **instructions** npl (for use) mode m d'emploi. **instructive** a instructif. **instructor** n (skiing, driving) moniteur/-trice m/f.

instrument n instrument m. **instrumental** a instrumental; **be** ~ **in** contribuer à. **instrumentalist** n instrumentaliste mf.

insubordinate a insubordonné.

insufficient a insuffisant.

insular a (Geog) insulaire; (mind, person; fig) borné.

insulate vt (room, wire) isoler.

insulin n insuline f.

insult[1] vt insulter.

insult[2] n insulte f.

insurance n assurance f (against contre).

insure vt assurer; ~ **that** (US) s'assurer que.

intact a intact.

intake n (of food) consommation f; (School, Univ) admissions fpl.

integral a intégral (**to** à).

integrate vt/i (s')intégrer (**with** à; **into** dans).

integrity n intégrité f.

intellect n intelligence f. **intellectual** a & n intellectuel/-le (m/f).

intelligence n intelligence f; (Mil) renseignements mpl. **intelligent** a intelligent. **intelligently** adv intelligemment.

intend vt (*outcome*) vouloir; ~ **to** do avoir l'intention de faire. **intended** a (*result*) voulu; (*visit*) projeté.

intense a intense; (person) sérieux. **intensely** adv (very) extrêmement.

intensify vt/i (s')intensifier.

intensive a intensif; **in** ~ **care** en réanimation.

intent n intention f. ● a absorbé; ~ **on doing** résolu à faire.

intention n intention f

intentional a intentionnel.

intently adv attentivement.

interact vi (*factors*) agir l'un sur l'autre; (*people*) communiquer. **interactive** a (TV, video) interactif.

intercept vt intercepter.

interchange n (road junction) échangeur m; (exchange) échange m.

interchangeable a interchangeable.

intercom n interphone® m.

interconnected a (*parts*) raccordé; (*problems*) lié.

intercourse n rapports mpl.

interest n intérêt m; ~ **rate** taux m d'intérêt. ● vt intéresser (**in** à). **interested** a intéressé, **be** ~**ed in** s'intéresser à. **interesting** a intéressant.

interfere vi se mêler des affaires des autres; ~ **in** se mêler de; ~ **with** (*freedom*) empiéter sur; (tamper with) toucher. **interference** n ingérence f; (sound, light waves) brouillage m; (radio) parasites mpl.

interim n **in the** ~ entre-temps. ● a (*government*) provisoire; (*payment*) intermédiaire.

interior n intérieur m. ● a intérieur.

interjection n interjection f.

interlock vt/i (Tech) (s')emboîter, (s')enclencher.

interlude n intervalle m; (Theat, Mus) intermède m.

intermediary a & n intermédiaire (mf).

intermediate a intermédiaire; (exam, level) moyen.

intermission n (Theat) entracte m.

intermittent a intermittent.

intern[1] vt interner.

intern[2] n (US) stagiaire mf; (Med) interne mf.

internal a interne; (domestic: Pol) intérieur; **I~ Revenue** (US) service m des impôts américain.

international a international.

Internet n Internet m; **on the ~** sur Internet; **~ access** accès à Internet; **~ service provider** fournisseur m d'accès Internet.

interpret vt interpréter (as comme). ● vi faire l'interprète.

interpretation n interprétation f.

interpreter n interprète mf.

interrelated a interdépendant, lié.

interrogate vt interroger.

interrogative a & n (Ling) interrogatif (m).

interrupt vt/i interrompre.

interruption n interruption f.

intersect vt/i (lines, roads) (se) croiser. **intersection** n intersection f.

interspersed a parsemé (with de).

intertwine vt/i (s')entrelacer.

interval n intervalle m; (Theat) entracte m.

intervene vi intervenir; (of time) s'écouler (**between** entre); (happen) arriver.

interview n (for job) entretien m; (by a journalist) interview f. ● vt (candidate) faire passer un entretien à; (celebrity) interviewer.

intestine n intestin m.

intimacy n intimité f.

intimate[1] vt (state) annoncer; (hint) laisser entendre.

intimate[2] a intime. **intimately** adv intimement.

intimidate vt intimider.

into prep (put, go, fall) dans; (divide, translate, change) en; be **~ jazz** être fana du jazz ▣; **8 ~ 24 is 3** 24 divisé par 8 égale 3.

intolerant a intolérant.

intonation n intonation f.

intoxicate vt enivrer. **intoxicated** a ivre. **intoxication** n ivresse f.

intractable a (person) intraitable; (problem) rebelle.

Intranet n (Comput) Intranet m.

intransitive a intransitif.

intravenous a (Med) intraveineux.

intricate a complexe.

intrigue vt intriguer. ● n intrigue f. **intriguing** a fascinant; (curious) curieux.

intrinsic a intrinsèque (**to** à).

introduce vt (person, idea, programme) présenter; (object, law) introduire (**into** dans). **introduction** n introduction f; (of person) présentation f. **introductory** a (words) préliminaire.

introvert n introverti/-e m/f.

intrude vi (person) s'imposer (**on sb** à qn), déranger. **intruder** n intrus/-e m/f. **intrusion** n intrusion f.

intuition n intuition f. **intuitive** a intuitif.

inundate vt inonder (with de).

invade vt envahir.

invalid[1] n malade mf; (disabled) infirme mf.

invalid[2] a (passport) pas valable; (claim) sans fondement.

invalidate vt (*argument*) infirmer; (*claim*) annuler.

invaluable a inestimable.

invariable a invariable. **invariably** adv invariablement.

invasion n invasion f.

invent vt inventer. **invention** n invention f. **inventive** a inventif. **inventor** n inventeur/-trice m/f.

inventory n inventaire m.

invert vt (*order*) intervertir; (*image, values*) renverser; **~ed commas** guillemets mpl.

invest vt investir; (*time, effort*) consacrer. ● vi faire un investissement; **~ in** (buy) s'acheter.

investigate vt examiner; (*crime*) enquêter sur. **investigation** n investigation f. **investigator** n (police) enquêteur/-euse m/f.

investment n investissement m; **emotional ~** engagement m personnel. **investor** n investisseur/-euse m/f; (in shares) actionnaire mf.

invigilate vi (*exam*) surveiller. **invigilator** n surveillant/-e m/f.

invigorate vt revigorer.

invisible a invisible.

invitation n invitation f. **invite** vt inviter; (ask for) demander. **inviting** a engageant.

invoice n facture f. ● vt facturer.

involuntary a involontaire.

involve vt impliquer; (*person*) faire participer (in à). **involved** a (complex) compliqué; (at stake) en jeu; **be ~d in** (work) participer à; (*crime*) être mêlé à. **involvement** n participation f (in à).

inward a (*feeling*) intérieur. **inwardly** adv intérieurement. **inwards** adv vers l'intérieur.

iodine n iode m; (antiseptic) teinture f d'iode.

iota n iota m; **not one ~ of** pas un grain de.

IOU abbr (**I owe you**) reconnaissance f de dette.

IQ abbr (**intelligence quotient**) QI m.

Iran n Iran m.

Iraq n Irak m.

irate a furieux.

IRC abbrev (**Internet Relay Chat**) (Internet) conversation f IRC.

Ireland n Irlande f.

Irish n & a irlandais (m). **~man** n Irlandais m. **~woman** n Irlandaise f.

iron n fer m; (appliance) fer m (à repasser). ● a (will) de fer; (bar) en fer. ● vt repasser.

ironic(al) a ironique.

iron: ironing-board n planche f à repasser. **~monger** n quincaillier m.

irony n ironie f.

irrational a irrationnel; (person) pas raisonnable.

irregular a irrégulier.

irrelevant a hors de propos.

irreplaceable a irremplaçable.

irresistible a irrésistible.

irrespective a **~ of** sans tenir compte de.

irresponsible a irresponsable.

irreverent a irrévérencieux.

irrigate vt irriguer.

irritable a irritable.

irritate vt irriter. **irritating** a irritant.

is ⇒BE.

ISDN abbr (**integrated services digital network**) RNIS m, réseau m numérique à intégration de services.

Islam n (faith) islam m; (Muslims) Islam m. **Islamic** a islamique.

island n île f.

isle n île f.

isolate vt isoler. **isolation** n isolement m.

Israel *n* Israël *m*.

Israeli *n* Israélien/-ne *m/f*. ● *a* israélien.

issue *n* question *f*; (outcome) résultat *m*; (of magazine) numéro *m*; (of stamps) émission *f*; (offspring) descendance *f*; **at ~** en cause. ● *vt* distribuer; (stamps) émettre; (book) publier; (order) délivrer. ● *vi* **~ from** provenir de.

it

● *pronoun*

····➤ (subject) il, elle; **'where's the book/chair?'—'~'s in the kitchen'** 'où est le livre/la chaise?'—'il/ elle est dans la cuisine'.

····➤ (object) le, la, l'; **~'s my book and I want ~** c'est mon livre et je le veux; **I liked his shirt, did you notice ~?** sa chemise m'a plu, l'as-tu remarquée?; **give ~ to me** donne-le-moi.

····➤ (with preposition) **we talked a lot about ~** on en a beaucoup parlé; **Elliott went to ~** Elliott y est allé.

····➤ (impersonal) il; **~'s raining** il pleut; **~ will snow** il va neiger.

IT *abbr* ⇒INFORMATION TECHNOLOGY.

Italian *n* (person) Italien/-ne *m/f*; (Ling) italien *m*. ● *a* italien.

italics *npl* italique *m*.

Italy *n* Italie *f*.

itch *n* démangeaison *f*. ● *vi* démanger; **my arm ~es** j'ai le bras qui me démange; **be ~ing to do** mourir d'envie de faire.

item *n* article *m*; (on agenda) point *m*.

itemize *vt* détailler; **~d bill** facture *f* détaillée.

itinerary *n* itinéraire *m*.

its *det* son, sa; *pl* ses.

it's = IT IS, IT HAS.

itself *pron* lui-même, elle-même; (reflexive) se.

ivory *n* ivoire *m*; **~ tower** tour *f* d'ivoire.

ivy *n* lierre *m*.

jab *vt* (*pt* **jabbed**) **~ sth into sth** planter qch dans qch. ● *n* coup *m*; (injection) piqûre *f*.

jack *n* (Auto) cric *m*; (cards) valet *m*; (Electr) jack *m*. ● *vt* **~ up** soulever avec un cric.

jackal *n* chacal *m*.

jacket *n* veste *f*, veston *m*; (of book) jaquette *f*.

jack-knife *n* couteau *m* pliant. ● *vi* (lorry) se mettre en portefeuille.

jackpot *n* gros lot *m*; **hit the ~** gagner le gros lot.

jade *n* (stone) jade *m*.

jaded *a* (tired) fatigué; (bored) blasé.

jagged *a* (rock) déchiqueté; (knife) dentelé.

jail *n* prison *f*. ● *vt* mettre en prison.

jam *n* confiture *f*; (traffic) **~** embouteillage *m*. ● *vt/i* (*pt* **jammed**) (wedge) (se) coincer; (cram) (s')entasser; (street) encombrer; (radio) brouiller.

Jamaica *n* Jamaïque *f*.

jam-packed *a* ▣ bondé; **~ with** bourré de.

jangle *n* tintement *m*. ● *vt/i* (faire) tinter.

janitor *n* (US) gardien *m*.

January *n* janvier *m*.

Japan n Japon m.
Japanese n (person) Japonais/-e m/f; (Ling) japonais m. ● a japonais.
jar n pot m, bocal m. ● vi (pt **jarred**) rendre un son discordant; (colours) détonner. ● vt ébranler.
jargon n jargon m.
jaundice n jaunisse f.
javelin n javelot m.
jaw n mâchoire f.
jay n geai m.
jazz n jazz m. ● vt ~ **up** (dress) rajeunir; (event) ranimer.
jealous a jaloux. **jealousy** n jalousie f.
jeans npl jean m.
jeer vt/i ~ (at) huer. ● n huée f.
jelly n gelée f. ~**fish** n méduse f.
jeopardize vt (career, chance) compromettre; (lives) mettre en péril.
jerk n secousse f; (fool ⊞) crétin m ⊞. ● vt tirer brusquement. ● vi tressaillir. **jerky** a saccadé.
jersey n (garment) pull-over m; (fabric) jersey m.
jet n (plane, stream) jet m; (mineral) jais m; ~ **lag** décalage m horaire.
jettison vt jeter par-dessus bord; (Aviat) larguer; (fig) rejeter.
jetty n jetée f.
Jew n juif/juive m/f.
jewel n bijou m. **jeweller** n bijoutier/-ière m/f. **jeweller('s)** n (shop) bijouterie f. **jewellery** n bijoux mpl.
Jewish a juif.
jibe n moquerie f.
jigsaw n puzzle m.
jingle vt/i (faire) tinter. ● n tintement m; (advertising) refrain m publicitaire, sonal m.
jinx n (person) porte-malheur m inv; (curse) sort m.
jitters npl have the ~ ⊞ être nerveux. **jittery** a nerveux.

job n emploi m; (post) poste m; out of a ~ sans emploi; it is a good ~ that heureusement que; just the ~ tout à fait ce qu'il faut. ~ **centre** n bureau m des services nationaux de l'emploi. **jobless** a sans emploi.
jockey n jockey m.
jog n go for a ~ aller faire un jogging. ● vt (pt **jogged**) heurter; (memory) rafraîchir. ● vi faire du jogging. **jogging** n jogging m.
join vt (attach) réunir, joindre; (club) devenir membre de; (company) entrer dans; (army) s'engager dans; (queue) se mettre dans; ~ **sb** (in activity) se joindre à qn; (meet) rejoindre qn. ● vi (become member) adhérer; (pieces) se joindre; (roads) se rejoindre. ● n raccord m. □ ~ **in** participer; ~ **in sth** participer à qch; ~ **up** (Mil) s'engager; ~ **sth up** relier qch. **joiner** n menuisier/-ière m/f.
joint a (action) collectif; (measures, venture) commun; (winner) ex aequo inv; (account) joint; ~ **author** coauteur m. ● n (join) joint m; (Anat) articulation f; (Culin) rôti m; out of ~ déboîté.
joke n plaisanterie f; (trick) farce f; it's no ~ ce n'est pas drôle. ● vi plaisanter. **joker** n blagueur/-euse m/f; (cards) joker m.
jolly a (-ier, -iest) (person) enjoué; (tune) joyeux. ● adv ⊞ drôlement.
jolt vt secouer. ● vi cahoter. ● n secousse f; (shock) choc m.
jostle vt/i (se) bousculer.
jot vt (pt **jotted**) ~ (down) noter.
journal n journal m. **journalism** n journalisme m. **journalist** n journaliste mf.
journey n (trip) voyage m; (short or habitual) trajet m. ● vi voyager.
joy n joie f. **joyful** a joyeux.

J

joy: ~**riding** n rodéo m à la
voiture volée. ~**stick** n (Comput)
manette f; (Aviat) manche m à
balai.

jubilant a (person) exultant;
(mood) réjoui.

Judaism n judaïsme m.

judge n juge m. ●vt juger;
(distance) estimer; **judging by/from**
à en juger par. **judg(e)ment** n
jugement m.

judicial a judiciaire. **judiciary** n
magistrature f.

judo n judo m.

jug n (glass) carafe f; (pottery)
pichet m.

juggernaut n (lorry) poids m
lourd.

juggle vt/i jongler (avec). **juggler**
n jongleur/-euse m/f.

juice n jus m. **juicy** a juteux;
(details ▣) croustillant.

jukebox n juke-box m.

July n juillet m.

jumble vt mélanger. ●n (of objects)
tas m; (of ideas) fouillis m; ~ **sale**
vente f de charité.

jumbo n (also ~ **jet**) gros-porteur
m.

jump vt sauter; ~ **the lights** passer
au feu rouge; ~ **the queue** passer
devant tout le monde. ●vi sauter;
(in surprise) sursauter; (price)
monter en flèche; ~ **at**
(opportunity) sauter sur. ●n saut
m, bond m; (increase) bond m.

jumper n pull(-over) m; (dress: US)
robe f chasuble.

jump-leads npl câbles mpl de
démarrage.

jumpy a nerveux.

junction n (of roads) carrefour m;
(on motorway) échangeur m.

June n juin m.

jungle n jungle f.

junior a (young) jeune; (in rank)
subalterne; (school) primaire. ●n
cadet/-te m/f; (School) élève mf du
primaire.

junk n bric-à-brac m inv; (poor
quality) camelote f; ~ **food**
nourriture f industrielle.

junkie n ▣ drogué/-e m/f.

junk: ~ **mail** n prospectus mpl.
~-**shop** n boutique f de bric-à-
brac.

jurisdiction n compétence f; (Jur)
juridiction f.

juror n juré m.

jury n jury m.

just a (fair) juste. ●adv (immediately,
slightly) juste; (simply) tout
simplement; (exactly) exactement;
he has/had ~ **left** il vient/venait
de partir; **have** ~ **missed** avoir
manqué de peu; **I'm** ~ **leaving** je
suis sur le point de partir; **it's** ~
a cold ce n'est qu'un rhume; ~ **as
tall/well as** tout aussi grand/bien
que; ~ **listen!** écoutez donc!; **it's**
~ **ridiculous** c'est vraiment
ridicule.

justice n justice f; **J**~ **of the
Peace** juge m de paix.

justification n justification f.
justify vt justifier.

jut vi (pt **jutted**) ~ (**out**) s'avancer
en saillie.

juvenile a (childish) puéril;
(offender) mineur; (delinquent)
jeune. ●n jeune mf; (Jur) mineur/
-e m/f.

juxtapose vt juxtaposer.

kangaroo n kangourou m.

karate n karaté m.

kebab n brochette f.

keel n (of ship) quille f. ●vi ~ **over** (bateau) chavirer; (person) s'écrouler.

keen a (interest, wind, feeling) vif; (mind, analysis) pénétrant; (edge, appetite) aiguisé; (eager) enthousiaste; **be ~ on** être passionné de; **be ~ to do** or **on doing** tenir beaucoup à faire. **keenly** adv vivement. **keenness** n enthousiasme m.

keep vt (pt **kept**) garder; (promise, shop, diary) tenir; (family) faire vivre; (animals) élever; (rule) respecter; (celebrate) célébrer; (delay) retenir; ~ **sth clean/warm** garder qch propre/au chaud; ~ **sb in/out** empêcher qn de sortir/d'entrer; ~ **sb from doing** empêcher qn de faire. ●vi (food) se conserver; ~ (**on**) continuer (**doing** à faire). ●n pension f; (of castle) donjon m. □ ~ **down** rester allongé; ~ **sth down** limiter qch; ~ **your voice down!** baisse la voix!; ~ **to** (road) ne pas s'écarter de; (rules) respecter; ~ **up** (car, runner) suivre; (rain) continuer; ~ **up with sb** (in speed) aller aussi vite que; (class, inflation, fashion, news) suivre.

keeper n gardien/-ne m/f.

keepsake n souvenir m.

kennel n niche f.

kept ⇒KEEP.

kerb n bord m du trottoir.

kernel n amande f; ~ **of truth** fond m de vérité.

kettle n bouilloire f.

key n clé f; (of computer, piano) touche f. ●a (industry, figure) clé (inv). ●vt ~ (**in**) saisir. ~**board** n clavier m. ~**hole** n trou m de serrure. ~**pad** n clavier m numérique. ~**ring** n porte-clés m inv. ~**stroke** n (Comput) frappe f.

khaki a kaki inv.

kick vt/i donner un coup de pied (à); (horse) botter. ●n coup m de pied; (of gun) recul m; **get a ~ out of doing** prendre plaisir à faire. □ ~ **out** 🔟 virer 🔟.

kick-off n coup m d'envoi

kid n (goat, leather) chevreau m; (child 🔟) gosse mf 🔟. ●vt/i (pt **kidded**) blaguer.

kidnap vt (pt **kidnapped**) enlever. **kidnapping** n enlèvement m

kidney n rein m; (Culin) rognon m.

kill vt tuer; (rumour: fig) arrêter. ●n mise f à mort. **killer** n tueur/-euse m/f. **killing** n meurtre m.

kiln n four m.

kilo n kilo m.

kilobyte n kilo-octet m.

kilogram n kilogramme m.

kilometre, (US) **kilometer** n kilomètre m.

kilowatt n kilowatt m.

kin n parents mpl.

kind n genre m, sorte f; **in ~** en nature; ~ **of** (somewhat 🔟) assez. ●a gentil, bon.

kindergarten n jardin m d'enfants.

kindle vt/i (s')allumer.

kindly a (-ier, -iest) (person) gentil; (interest) bienveillant. ●adv avec gentillesse; **would you**

~ **do** auriez-vous l'amabilité de faire.

kindness n bonté f.

king n roi m. **kingdom** n royaume m; (Bot) règne m. **~fisher** n martin-pêcheur m. **~-size(d)** a géant.

kiosk n kiosque m; telephone ~ cabine f téléphonique; (Internet) borne f interactive, kiosque m.

kiss n baiser m. ●vt/i (s')embrasser.

kit n (clothing) affaires fpl; (set of tools) trousse f; (for assembly) kit m. ●vt (pt **kitted**) ~ **out** équiper.

kitchen n cuisine f.

kite n (toy) cerf-volant m; (bird) milan m.

kitten n chaton m.

kitty n (fund) cagnotte f.

knack n tour m de main (**of doing** pour faire).

knead vt pétrir.

knee n genou m. **~cap** n rotule f.

kneel vi (pt **knelt**) ~ (**down**) se mettre à genoux; (in prayer) s'agenouiller.

knew ⇒KNOW.

knickers npl petite culotte f, slip m.

knife n (pl **knives**) couteau m. ●vt poignarder.

knight n chevalier m; (chess) cavalier m. ●vt anoblir. **~hood** n titre m de chevalier.

knit vt/i (pt **knitted** or **knit**) tricoter; (bones) (se) souder. **knitting** n tricot m. **knitwear** n tricots mpl.

knob n bouton m.

knock vt/i cogner; (criticize 🄛) critiquer; ~ **sth off/out** faire tomber qch. ●n coup m. □ ~ **down** (chair, pedestrian) renverser; (demolish) abattre; (reduce) baisser; ~ **off** (stop work 🄛) arrêter de travailler; ~ **£10 off** faire une réduction de 10 livres; ~ **it off!** 🄛 ça suffit!; ~ **out** assommer; ~ **over** renverser; ~ **up** (meal) préparer en vitesse.

knock-out n (boxing) knock-out m.

knot n nœud m. ●vt (pt **knotted**) nouer.

know vt/i (pt **knew**; pp **known**) (answer, reason, language) savoir (that que); (person, place, name, rule, situation) connaître; (recognize) reconnaître; ~ **how to do** savoir faire; ~ **about** (event) être au courant de; (subject) s'y connaître en; ~ **of** (from experience) connaître; (from information) avoir entendu parler de. **~-how** n savoir-faire m inv.

knowingly adv (intentionally) délibérément; (meaningfully) d'un air entendu.

knowledge n connaissance f; (learning) connaissances fpl. **knowledgeable** a savant.

knuckle n jointure f, articulation f.

Koran n Coran m.

Korea n Corée f.

kosher a casher inv.

lab n 🄛 labo m.

label n étiquette f. ●vt (pt **labelled**) étiqueter.

laboratory n laboratoire m.

laborious a laborieux.

labour, (US) **labor** n travail m; (workers) main-d'œuvre f; in ~ en train d'accoucher. ●vi peiner (**to do** à faire). ●vt trop insister sur.

Labour n le parti travailliste. ● a travailliste.

laboured a laborieux.

labourer n ouvrier/-ière m/f; (on farm) ouvrier/-ière m/f agricole.

lace n dentelle f; (of shoe) lacet m. ● vt (shoe) lacer; (drink) arroser.

lacerate vt lacérer.

lack n manque m; **for ~ of** faute de. ● vt manquer de; **be ~ing** manquer (in de).

lad n garçon m, gars m.

ladder n échelle f; (in stocking) maille f filée. ● vt/i (stocking) filer.

laden a chargé (with de).

ladle n louche f.

lady n (pl **ladies**) dame f; **ladies and gentlemen** mesdames et messieurs; **young ~** jeune femme or fille f. **~bird** n coccinelle f.

ladylike a distingué.

lag vi (pt **lagged**) traîner. ● vt (pipes) calorifuger. ● n (interval) décalage m.

lager n bière f blonde.

lagoon n lagune f.

laid ⇒LAY¹. **~ back** a décontracté.

lain ⇒LIE².

lake n lac m.

lamb n agneau m; **leg of ~** gigot m d'agneau.

lame a boiteux.

lament n lamentation f. ● vt/i se lamenter (sur).

laminated a laminé.

lamp n lampe f. **~post** n réverbère m. **~shade** n abat-jour m inv.

lance vt (Med) inciser.

land n terre f; (plot) terrain m; (country) pays m. ● a terrestre; (policy, reform) agraire. ● vt/i débarquer; (aircraft) (se) poser, (faire) atterrir; (fall) tomber;

(obtain) décrocher; (a blow) porter; **~ up** se retrouver.

landing n débarquement m; (Aviat) atterrissage m; (top of stairs) palier m. **~-stage** n débarcadère m.

land: **~lady** n propriétaire f; (of pub) patronne f. **~lord** n propriétaire m; (of pub) patron m. **~mark** n (point de) repère m. **~mine** n mine f terrestre.

landscape n paysage m. ● vt aménager.

landslide n glissement m de terrain; (Pol) raz-de-marée m inv (électoral).

lane n (path, road) chemin m; (strip of road) voie f; (of traffic) file f; (Aviat) couloir m.

language n langue f; (speech, style) langage m. **~ engineering** n ingénierie f des langues. **~ laboratory** n laboratoire m de langue.

lank a (hair) plat.

lanky a (-ier, -iest) grand et maigre.

lantern n lanterne f.

lap n genoux mpl; (Sport) tour m (de piste). ● vi (pt **lapped**) (waves) clapoter. □ **~ up** laper.

lapel n revers m.

lapse vi (decline) se dégrader; (expire) se périmer; **~ into** retomber dans. ● n défaillance f, erreur f; (of time) intervalle m.

laptop n (Comput) portable m.

lard n saindoux m.

larder n garde-manger m inv.

large a grand, gros; **at ~** en liberté; **by and ~** en général.

largely adv en grande mesure.

lark n (bird) alouette f; (bit of fun 🄓) rigolade f. ● vi 🄓 rigoler.

larva n (pl **-vae**) larve f.

laryngitis n laryngite f.

laser n laser m. **~ printer** n

imprimante *f* laser. ~ **treatment** *n* (Med) laserothérapie *f*.

lash *vt* fouetter. ● *n* coup *m* de fouet; (eyelash) cil *m*. □ ~ **out** (spend) dépenser follement; ~ **out against** attaquer.

lass *n* jeune fille *f*.

lasso *n* lasso *m*.

last *a* dernier; **the ~ straw** le comble; **the ~ word** le mot de la fin; **on its ~ legs** sur le point de rendre l'âme; ~ **night** hier soir. ● *adv* en dernier; (most recently) la dernière fois. ● *n* dernier/-ière *m/f*; (remainder) reste *m*; **at (long) ~** enfin. ● *vi* durer. ~**-ditch** *a* ultime. **lasting** *a* durable. **lastly** *adv* en dernier lieu. ~**-minute** *a* de dernière minute.

latch *n* loquet *m*.

late *a* (not on time) en retard; (former) ancien; (hour, fruit) tardif; **the ~ Mrs X** feu Mme X. ● *adv* (not early) tard; (not on time) en retard; **in ~ July** fin juillet; **of ~** dernièrement. **lately** *adv* dernièrement. **latest** *a* ⇒LATE; (last) dernier.

lathe *n* tour *m*.

lather *n* mousse *f*. ● *vt* savonner. ● *vi* mousser.

Latin *n* (Ling) latin *m*. ● *a* latin. ~ **America** *n* Amérique *f* latine.

latitude *n* latitude *f*.

latter *a* dernier. ● *n* **the ~** celui-ci, celle-ci.

Latvia *n* Lettonie *f*.

laudable *a* louable.

laugh *vi* rire (**at** de). ● *n* rire *m*. **laughable** *a* ridicule.

laughing stock *n* risée *f*.

laughter *n* (act) rire *m*; (sound of laughs) rires *mpl*.

launch *vt* (rocket) lancer; (boat) mettre à l'eau; ~ (**out**) **into** se lancer dans. ● *n* lancement *m*; (boat) vedette *f*. **launching pad** *n* aire *f* de lancement.

launderette *n* laverie *f* automatique.

laundry *n* (place) blanchisserie *f*; (clothes) linge *m*.

laurel *n* laurier *m*.

lava *n* lave *f*.

lavatory *n* toilettes *fpl*.

lavender *n* lavande *f*.

lavish *a* (person) généreux; (lush) somptueux. ● *vt* prodiguer (**on** à). **lavishly** *adv* luxueusement.

law *n* loi *f*; (profession, subject of study) droit *m*; ~ **and order** ordre public. ~**-abiding** *a* respectueux des lois. ~**court** *n* tribunal *m*.

lawful *a* légal.

lawn *n* pelouse *f*, gazon *m*. ~**-mower** *n* tondeuse *f* à gazon.

lawsuit *n* procès *m*.

lawyer *n* avocat *m*.

lax *a* (government) laxiste; (security) relâché.

laxative *n* laxatif *m*.

lay[1] *a* (non-clerical) laïque; (worker) non-initié. ● *vt* (*pt* **laid**) poser, mettre; (trap) tendre; (table) mettre; (plan) former; (eggs) pondre. ● *vi* pondre; ~ **waste** ravager. □ ~ **aside** mettre de côté; ~ **down** (dé)poser; (condition) (im-)poser; ~ **off** *vt* (worker) licencier; *vi* 🔲 arrêter; ~ **on** (provide) fournir; ~ **out** (design) dessiner; (display) disposer; (money) dépenser.

lay[2] ⇒LIE[2].

lay-by *n* (*pl* ~**s**) aire *f* de repos.

layer *n* couche *f*.

layman *n* (*pl* **-men**) profane *m*.

layout *n* disposition *f*.

laze *vi* paresser. **laziness** *n* paresse *f*. **lazy** *a* (**-ier, -iest**) paresseux.

lead[1] *vt/i* (*pt* **led**) mener; (team) diriger; (life) mener; (induce) amener; ~ **to** conduire à, mener à. ● *n* avance *f*; (clue) indice *m*;

(leash) laisse *f*; (Theat) premier rôle *m*; (wire) fil *m*; **in the ~** en tête. □ **~ away** emmener; **~ up to** (come to) en venir à; (precede) précéder.

lead² *n* plomb *m*; (of pencil) mine *f*.

leader *n* chef *m*; (of country, club) dirigeant/-e *m/f*; (leading article) éditorial *m*. **leadership** *n* direction *f*.

lead-free *a* (petrol) sans plomb.

leading *a* principal.

leaf *n* (pl leaves) feuille *f*; (of table) rallonge *f*. ● *vi* **~ through** feuilleter.

leaflet *n* prospectus *m*.

leafy *a* feuillu.

league *n* ligue *f*; (Sport) championnat *m*; **in ~ with** de mèche avec.

leak *n* fuite *f*. ● *vi* fuir; (news: fig) s'ébruiter. ● *vt* répandre; (fig) divulguer.

lean¹ *a* maigre. ● *n* (of meat) maigre *m*.

lean² *vt/i* (pt leaned or leant) (rest) (s')appuyer; (slope) pencher. □ **~ out** se pencher à l'extérieur; **~ over** (of person) se pencher.

leaning *a* penché. ● *n* tendance *f*.

leap *vi* (pt leaped or leapt) bondir. ● *n* bond *m*. **~ year** *n* année *f* bissextile.

learn *vt/i* (pt learned or learnt) apprendre (**to do** à faire). **learned** *a* érudit. **learner** *n* débutant/-e *m/f*.

lease *n* bail *m*. ● *vt* louer à bail.

leash *n* laisse *f*.

least *a* **the ~** (smallest amount of) le moins de; (slightest) le *or* la moindre. ● *n* le moins. ● *adv* le moins; (with adjective) le *or* la moins; **at ~** au moins.

leather *n* cuir *m*.

leave *vt* (pt left) laisser; (depart from) quitter; (person) laisser

tranquille; **be left (over)** rester. ● *n* (holiday) congé *m*; (consent) permission *f*; **take one's ~** prendre congé (**of** de); **on ~** (Mil) en permission. □ **~ alone** (thing) ne pas toucher; (person) laisser tranquille; **~ behind** laisser; **~ out** omettre.

Lebanon *n* Liban *m*.

lecture *n* cours *m*, conférence *f*; (rebuke) réprimande *f*. ● *vt/i* faire un cours *or* une conférence (à); (rebuke) réprimander. **lecturer** *n* conférencier/-ière *m/f*; (Univ) enseignant/-e *m/f*

led ⇒LEAD¹.

ledge *n* (window) rebord *m*; (rock) saillie *f*.

ledger *n* grand livre *m*.

leech *n* sangsue *f*.

leek *n* poireau *m*.

leer *vi* **~ (at)** lorgner. ● *n* regard *m* sournois.

leeway *n* (fig) liberté *f* d'action; (Naut) dérive *f*.

left ⇒LEAVE. ● *a* gauche. ● *adv* à gauche. ● *n* gauche *f*. **~-hand** *a* à *or* de gauche. **~-handed** *a* gaucher.

left luggage (**office**) *n* consigne *f*.

left-overs *npl* restes *mpl*.

left-wing *a* de gauche.

leg *n* jambe *f*; (of animal) patte *f*; (of table) pied *m*; (of chicken) cuisse *f*; (of lamb) gigot *m*; (of journey) étape *f*.

legacy *n* legs *m*.

legal *a* légal; (affairs) juridique.

legend *n* légende *f*.

leggings *npl* (for woman) caleçon *m*.

legible *a* lisible.

legionnaire *n* légionnaire *m*.

legislation *n* (body of laws) législation *f*; (law) loi *f*.

legislature *n* corps *m* législatif.

L

legitimate *a* légitime.

leisure *n* loisirs *mpl*; **at one's** ~ à tête reposée. ● *a* (*centre*) de loisirs.

leisurely *a* lent. ● *adv* sans se presser.

lemon *n* citron *m*.

lemonade *n* (fizzy) limonade *f*; (still) citronnade *f*.

lend *vt* (*pt* **lent**) prêter; (*credibility*) conférer; ~ **itself to** se prêter à.

length *n* longueur *f*; (in time) durée *f*; (section) morceau *m*; **at** ~ (at last) enfin; **at (great)** ~ longuement.

lengthen *vt/i* (s')allonger.

lengthways *adv* dans le sens de la longueur.

lengthy *a* long.

lenient *a* indulgent.

lens *n* lentille *f*; (of spectacles) verre *m*; (Photo) objectif *m*.

lent ⇒LEND.

Lent *n* Carême *m*.

lentil *n* lentille *f*.

Leo *n* Lion *m*.

leopard *n* léopard *m*.

leotard *n* body *m*.

leprosy *n* lèpre *f*.

lesbian *n* lesbienne *f*. ● *a* lesbien.

less *a* (in quantity) moins de (than que). ● *adv, n & prep* moins; ~ **than** (with numbers) moins de; **work** ~ **than** travailler moins que; **ten pounds** ~ dix livres de moins; ~ **and** ~ de moins en moins.

lessen *vt/i* diminuer. **lesser** *a* moindre.

lesson *n* leçon *f*.

let *vt* (*pt* **let**; *pres p* **letting**) laisser; (lease) louer. ● *v aux* ~ **us do**, ~**'s do** faisons; ~ **him do** qu'il fasse; ~ **me know the results** informe-moi des résultats. ● *n* location *f*. □ ~ **down** baisser;

(deflate) dégonfler; (fig) décevoir; ~ **go** *vt* lâcher; *vi* lâcher prise; ~ **sb in/out** laisser *or* faire entrer/ sortir qn; ~ **a dress out** élargir une robe; ~ **oneself in for** (*task*) s'engager à; (*trouble*) s'attirer; ~ **off** (explode, fire) faire éclater *or* partir; (excuse) dispenser; (not punish) ne pas punir; ~ **up** □ s'arrêter.

let-down *n* déception *f*.

lethal *a* mortel; (weapon) meurtrier.

letter *n* lettre *f*. ~**-bomb** *n* lettre *f* piégée. ~**-box** *n* boîte *f* à *or* aux lettres.

lettering *n* (letters) caractères *mpl*.

lettuce *n* laitue *f*, salade *f*.

let-up *n* répit *m*.

leukaemia *n* leucémie *f*.

level *a* plat, uni; (on surface) horizontal; (in height) au même niveau (with que); (in score) à égalité. ● *n* niveau *m*; (spirit) ~ niveau *m* à bulle; **be on the** ~ □ être franc. ● *vt* (*pt* **levelled**) niveler; (aim) diriger. ~ **crossing** *n* passage *m* à niveau. ~**-headed** *a* équilibré.

lever *n* levier *m*. ● *vt* soulever au moyen d'un levier.

leverage *n* influence *f*.

levy *vt* (*tax*) prélever. ● *n* impôt *m*.

lexicon *n* lexique *m*.

liability *n* responsabilité *f*; □ handicap *m*; **liabilities** (debts) dettes *fpl*.

liable *a* **be** ~ **to do** avoir tendance à faire, pouvoir faire; ~ **to** (illness) sujet à; (fine) passible de; ~ **for** responsable de.

liaise *vi* □ faire la liaison. **liaison** *n* liaison *f*.

liar *n* menteur/-euse *m/f*.

libel *n* diffamation *f*. ● *vt* (*pt* **libelled**) diffamer.

liberal *a* libéral; (generous) généreux, libéral.

Liberal *a & n* (Pol) libéral/-e (*m/f*).

liberate *vt* libérer.

liberty *n* liberté *f*; **at ~ to** libre de; **take liberties** prendre des libertés.

Libra *n* Balance *f*.

librarian *n* bibliothécaire *mf*.

library *n* bibliothèque *f*.

libretto *n* livret *m*.

lice ⇒LOUSE.

licence, (US) **license** *n* permis *m*, (for television) redevance *f*; (Comm) licence *f*; (liberty: fig) licence *f*. **~ plate** *n* plaque *f* minéralogique.

license *vt* accorder un permis à, autoriser.

lick *vt* lécher; (defeat 🔲) rosser; (fig) **a ~ of paint** un petit coup de peinture. ● *n* coup *m* de langue.

lid *n* couvercle *m*.

lie¹ *n* mensonge *m*. ● *vi* (*pt* **lied**; *pres p* **lying**) (tell lies) mentir.

lie² *vi* (*pt* **lay**; *pp* **lain**; *pres p* **lying**) s'allonger; (remain) rester; (be) se trouver, être; (in grave) reposer; **be lying** être allongé. □ **~ down** s'allonger; **~ in** faire la grasse matinée; **~ low** se cacher.

lieutenant *n* lieutenant *m*.

life *n* (*pl* **lives**) vie *f*. **~belt** *n* bouée *f* de sauvetage. **~boat** *n* canot *m* de sauvetage. **~buoy** *n* bouée *f* de sauvetage. **~ cycle** *n* cycle *m* de vie. **~guard** *n* sauveteur *m*. **~ insurance** *n* assurance-vie *f*. **~jacket** *n* gilet *m* de sauvetage.

lifeless *a* inanimé.

lifelike *a* très ressemblant.

life: **~long** *a* de toute la vie. **~ sentence** *n* condamnation *f* à perpétuité. **~size(d)** *a* grandeur

nature *inv*. **~ story** *n* vie *f*. **~-style** *n* style *m* de vie. **~ support machine** *n* appareil *m* de respiration artificielle.

lifetime *n* vie *f*; **in one's ~** de son vivant.

lift *vt* lever; (steal 🔲) voler. ● *vi* (of fog) se lever. ● *n* (in building) ascenseur *m*; **give a ~ to** emmener (en voiture). **~-off** *n* (Aviat) décollage *m*.

light *n* lumière *f*; (lamp) lampe *f*; (for fire, on vehicle) feu *m*; (headlight) phare *m*; **bring to ~** révéler; **come to ~** être révélé; **have you got a ~?** vous avez du feu? ● *a* (not dark) clair; (not heavy) léger. ● *vt* (*pt* **lit** *or* **lighted**) allumer; (room) éclairer; (match) frotter. □ **~ up** *vi* s'allumer; *vt* (room) éclairer. **~ bulb** *n* ampoule *f*.

lighten *vt* (give light to) éclairer; (make brighter) éclaircir; (make less heavy) alléger.

lighter *n* briquet *m*; (for stove) allume-gaz *m inv*.

light: **~-headed** *a* (dizzy) qui a un vertige; (frivolous) étourdi. **~-hearted** *a* gai. **~house** *n* phare *m*

lighting *n* éclairage *m*.

lightly *adv* légèrement.

lightning *n* éclair *m*, foudre *f*. ● *a* (visit) éclair *inv*.

lightweight *a* léger. ● *n* (boxing) poids *m* léger.

light-year *n* année *f* lumière.

like¹ *a* semblable, pareil; **be ~-minded** avoir les mêmes sentiments. ● *prep* comme. ● *conj* 🔲 comme. ● *n* pareil *m*; **the ~s of you** les gens comme vous.

like² *vt* aimer (bien); **I should ~** je voudrais, j'aimerais; **would you ~?** voudriez-vous?, voudrais-tu?; **~s** goûts *mpl*. **likeable** *a* sympathique.

likelihood *n* probabilité *f*.

L

likely a (-ier, -iest) probable.
●adv probablement; **he is ~ to do** il fera probablement; **not ~!** ⊡ pas question!

likeness n ressemblance f.

likewise adv également.

liking n (for thing) penchant m; (for person) affection f.

lilac n lilas m. ●a lilas inv.

Lilo® n matelas m pneumatique.

lily n lis m, lys m.

limb n membre m.

limber vi ~ **up** faire des exercices d'assouplissement.

limbo n **be in ~** (forgotten) être tombé dans l'oubli.

lime n (fruit) citron m vert; ~(-tree) tilleul m.

limelight n **in the ~** en vedette.

limestone n calcaire m.

limit n limite f. ●vt limiter.

limited company n société f anonyme.

limp vi boiter. ●n **have a ~** boiter. ●a mou.

line n ligne f; (track) voie f; (wrinkle) ride f; (row) rangée f, file f; (of poem) vers m; (rope) corde f; (of goods) gamme f; (queue: US) queue f; **be in ~ for** avoir de bonnes chances de; **hold the ~** ne quittez pas; **in ~ with** en accord avec; **stand in ~** faire la queue. ●vt (paper) régler; (streets) border; (garment) doubler; (fill) remplir, garnir. □ ~ **up** (s')aligner; (in queue) faire la queue; ~ **sth up** prévoir qch. ~ **dancing** n danse f en ligne

linen n (sheets) linge m; (material) lin m.

liner n paquebot m.

linesman n (football) juge m de touche; (tennis) juge m de ligne.

linger vi s'attarder; (smells) persister.

linguist n linguiste mf.

linguistics n linguistique f.

lining n doublure f.

link n lien m; (of chain) maillon m. ●vt relier; (relate) (re)lier; ~ **up** (of roads) se rejoindre. **linkage** n lien m. **links** n inv terrain m de golf. ~**-up** n liaison f.

lino n lino m.

lion n lion m. **lioness** n lionne f.

lip n lèvre f; (edge) rebord m; **pay ~-service to** n'approuver que pour la forme. ~**-read** vt/i lire sur les lèvres. ~**salve** n baume m pour les lèvres. ~**stick** n rouge m (à lèvres).

liquid n & a liquide (m).

liquidation n liquidation f; **go into ~** déposer son bilan.

liquidize vt passer au mixeur. **liquidizer** n mixeur m.

liquor n alcool m.

liquorice n réglisse f.

lisp n zézaiement m; **with a ~** en zézayant. ●vi zézayer.

list n liste f. ●vt dresser la liste de. ●vi (ship) gîter.

listen vi écouter; ~ **to**, ~ **in** (to) écouter. **listener** n auditeur/-trice m/f.

listless a apathique.

lit ⇒LIGHT.

liter ⇒LITRE.

literal a (meaning) littéral; (translation) mot à mot. **literally** adv littéralement; mot à mot.

literary a littéraire.

literate a qui sait lire et écrire.

literature n littérature f; (brochures) documentation f.

Lithuania n Lituanie f.

litigation n litiges mpl.

litre, (US) **liter** n litre m.

litter n (rubbish) détritus mpl, papiers mpl; (animals) portée f. ●vt éparpiller; (make untidy) laisser

des détritus dans; ~ed with
jonché de. ~-bin n poubelle f.

little a petit; (not much) peu de. ● n
peu m; a ~ un peu (de). ● adv
peu.

live¹ a vivant; (wire) sous tension;
(broadcast) en direct; be a ~ wire
être très dynamique.

live² vt/i vivre; (reside) habiter,
vivre; ~ it up mener la belle vie.
□ ~ down faire oublier; ~ on
(feed oneself on) vivre de; (continue)
survivre; ~ up to se montrer à la
hauteur de.

livelihood n moyens mpl
d'existence.

lively a (-ier, -iest) vif, vivant.

liven vt/i ~ up (s')animer; (cheer
up) (s')égayer.

liver n foie m.

livestock n bétail m.

livid a livide; (angry) furieux.

living a vivant. ● n vie f; make a
~ gagner sa vie; ~ conditions
conditions fpl de vie. ~-room n
salle f de séjour.

lizard n lézard m.

load n charge f; (loaded goods)
chargement m, charge f; (weight,
strain) poids m; ~s of ▯ des tas de
▯. ● vt charger.

loaf n (pl loaves) pain m. ● vi ~
(about) fainéanter.

loan n prêt m; (money borrowed)
emprunt m. ● vt prêter.

loathe vt détester (doing faire).
loathing n dégoût m.

lobby n entrée f, vestibule m; (Pol)
lobby m, groupe m de pression.
● vt faire pression sur.

lobster n homard m.

local a local; (shops) du quartier;
~ government administration f
locale. ● n personne f du coin;
(pub ▯) pub m du coin.

locally adv localement; (nearby)
dans les environs.

locate vt (situate) situer; (find)
repérer.

location n emplacement m; on ~
(cinema) en extérieur.

lock n (of door) serrure f; (on canal)
écluse f; (of hair) mèche f. ● vt/i
fermer à clef; (wheels: Auto) (se)
bloquer. □ ~ in or up (person)
enfermer; ~ out (by mistake)
enfermer dehors.

locker n casier m.

locket n médaillon m.

locksmith n serrurier m.

locum n (doctor) remplaçant/-e
m/f.

lodge n (house) pavillon m (de
gardien or de chasse); (of porter)
loge f. ● vt (accommodate) loger;
(money, complaint) déposer. ● vi
être logé (with chez); (become fixed)
se loger. **lodger** n locataire mf,
pensionnaire mf. **lodgings** n
logement m.

loft n grenier m.

lofty a (-ier, -iest) (tall, noble)
élevé; (haughty) hautain.

log n (of wood) bûche f; ~(-book)
(Naut) journal m de bord; (Auto) ≈
carte f grise. ● vt (pt logged)
noter; (distance) parcourir. □ ~ on
(Comput) se connecter; ~ off
(Comput) se déconnecter.

logic a logique. **logical** a logique.

logistics n logistique f.

loin n (Culin) filet m; ~s reins mpl.

loiter vi traîner.

loll vi se prélasser.

lollipop n sucette f.

London n Londres. **Londoner** n
Londonien/-ne m/f.

lone a solitaire.

lonely (-ier, -iest) solitaire;
(person) seul, solitaire.

long a long; how ~ is? quelle est
la longueur de?; (in time) quelle
est la durée de?; how ~?
combien de temps?; a ~ time

longtemps. ● *adv* longtemps; **he will not be ~** il n'en a pas pour longtemps; **as** *or* **so ~ as** pourvu que; **before ~** avant peu; **I no ~er do** je ne fais plus. ● *vi* avoir bien *or* très envie (**for, to** de); **~ for sb** (pine for) se languir de qn. **~-distance** *a* (*flight*) sur long parcours; (*phone call*) interurbain; (*runner*) de fond. **~ face** *n* grimace *f*. **~hand** *n* écriture *f* courante.

longing *n* envie *f* (**for** de); (nostalgia) nostalgie *f* (**for** de).

longitude *n* longitude *f*.

long: ~ jump *n* saut *m* en longueur. **~-range** *a* (*missile*) à longue portée; (*forecast*) à long terme. **~-sighted** *a* presbyte. **~-standing** *a* de longue date. **~-term** *a* à long terme. **~ wave** *n* grandes ondes *fpl*. **~-winded** *a* verbeux.

loo *n* 🄸 toilettes *fpl*.

look *vi* regarder; (seem) avoir l'air; **~ like** ressembler à, avoir l'air de. ● *n* regard *m*; (appearance) air *m*, aspect *m*; (good) **~s** beauté *f*. □ **~ after** s'occuper de, soigner; **~ at** regarder; **~ back on** repenser à; **~ down on** mépriser; **~ for** chercher; **~ forward to** attendre avec impatience; **~ in on** passer voir; **~ into** examiner; **~ out** faire attention; **~ out for** (*person*) guetter; (*symptoms*) guetter l'apparition de; **~ round** se retourner; **~ up** (*word*) chercher; (visit) passer voir; **~ up to** respecter.

look-out *n* (Mil) poste *m* de guet; (person) guetteur *m*; **be on the ~ for** rechercher.

loom *vi* surgir; (*war*) menacer; (*interview*) être imminent. ● *n* métier *m* à tisser.

loony *n & a* 🄸 fou, folle (*mf*).

loop *n* boucle *f*. ● *vt* boucler. **~hole** *n* lacune *f*.

loose *a* (*knot*) desserré; (*page*) détaché; (*clothes*) ample, lâche; (*tooth*) qui bouge; (lax) relâché; (not packed) en vrac; (inexact) vague; (pej) immoral; **at a ~ end** désœuvré; **come ~** *vt* bouger. **loosely** *adv* sans serrer; (roughly) vaguement. **loosen** *vt* (slacken) desserrer; (untie) défaire.

loot *n* butin *m*. ● *vt* piller.

lord *n* seigneur *m*; (British title) lord *m*; **the L~** le Seigneur; (good) **L~!** mon Dieu!

lorry *n* camion *m*.

lose *vt/i* (*pt* **lost**) perdre; **get lost** se perdre. **loser** *n* perdant/-e *m/f*.

loss *n* perte *f*; **be at a ~** être perplexe; **be at a ~ to** être incapable de; **heat ~** déperdition *f* de chaleur.

lost ⇒LOSE. ● *a* perdu. **~ property** *n* objets *mpl* trouvés.

lot *n* **the ~** (le) tout *m*; (people) tous *mpl*, toutes *fpl*; **a ~ (of)**, **~s (of)** 🄸 beaucoup (de); **quite a ~ (of)** 🄸 pas mal (de); (fate) sort *m*; (at auction) lot *m*; (land) lotissement *m*.

lotion *n* lotion *f*.

lottery *n* loterie *f*.

loud *a* bruyant, fort. ● *adv* fort; **out ~** tout haut. **loudly** *adv* fort. **~speaker** *n* haut-parleur *m*.

lounge *vi* paresser. ● *n* salon *m*.

louse *n* (*pl* **lice**) pou *m*.

lousy *a* (**-ier, -iest**) 🄸 infect.

lout *n* rustre *m*.

lovable *a* adorable.

love *n* amour *m*; (tennis) zéro *m*; **in ~** amoureux (**with** de); **make ~** faire l'amour. ● *vt* (*person*) aimer; (like greatly) aimer (beaucoup) (**to do** faire). **~ affair** *n* liaison *f* amoureuse. **~ life** *n* vie *f* amoureuse.

lovely *a* (**-ier, -iest**) joli; (delightful 🇬🇧) très agréable.

lover *n* (male) amant *m*; (female) maîtresse *f*; (devotee) amateur *m* (of de).

loving *a* affectueux.

low *a & adv* bas; ~ **in sth** à faible teneur en qch. ● *n* (low pressure) dépression *f*; **reach a (new)** ~ atteindre son niveau le plus bas. ● *vi* meugler. ~**-calorie** *a* basses-calories. ~**-cut** *a* décolleté.

lower *a & adv* ⇒LOW. ● *vt* baisser; ~ **oneself** s'abaisser.

low: ~**-fat** *a* (*diet*) sans matières grasses; (*cheese*) allégé. ~**-key** *a* modéré; (discreet) discret. ~**lands** *npl* plaine(s) *f(pl)*. ~**-lying** *a* à faible altitude.

loyal *a* loyal (to envers).

loyalty *n* fidélité *f*. ~ **card** *n* carte *f* de fidélité.

lozenge *n* (shape) losange *m*; (tablet) pastille *f*.

LP *n* (disque *m*) 33 tours *m*.

Ltd. *abbr* (**Limited**) SA.

lubricant *n* lubrifiant *m*.
lubricate *vt* lubrifier.

luck *n* chance *f*; **bad** ~ malchance *f*; **good** ~! bonne chance!

luckily *adv* heureusement.

lucky *a* (**-ier, -iest**) qui a de la chance, heureux; (event) heureux; (number) qui porte bonheur; **it's** ~ **that** heureusement que.

ludicrous *a* ridicule.

lug *vt* (*pt* **lugged**) traîner.

luggage *n* bagages *mpl*. ~**-rack** *n* porte-bagages *m inv*.

lukewarm *a* tiède.

lull *vt* **he** ~**ed them into thinking that** il leur a fait croire que. ● *n* accalmie *f*.

lullaby *n* berceuse *f*.

lumber *n* bois *m* de charpente. ● *vt* 🇬🇧 ~ **sb with** (*chore*) coller à qn 🇬🇧. ~**jack** *n* bûcheron *m*.

luminous *a* lumineux.

lump *n* morceau *m*; (swelling on body) grosseur *f*; (in liquid) grumeau *m*. ● *vt* ~ **together** réunir. ~ **sum** *n* somme *f* globale.

lunacy *n* folie *f*.

lunar *a* lunaire.

lunatic *n* fou/ folle *m/f*.

lunch *n* déjeuner *m*. ● *vi* déjeuner.

luncheon *n* déjeuner *m*. ~ **voucher** *n* chèque-repas *m*.

lung *n* poumon *m*.

lunge *vi* bondir (at sur; forward en avant).

lurch *n* **leave in the** ~ planter là, laisser en plan. ● *vi* (*person*) tituber.

lure *vt* appâter, attirer. ● *n* (attraction) attrait *m*, appât *m*.

lurid *a* choquant, affreux; (gaudy) voyant.

lurk *vi* se cacher; (in ambush) s'embusquer; (prowl) rôder; (*suspicion, danger*) menacer.

luscious *a* appétissant.

lush *a* luxuriant.

lust *n* luxure *f*.

Luxemburg *n* Luxembourg *m*.

luxurious *a* luxueux.

luxury *n* luxe *m*. ● *a* de luxe.

lying ⇒LIE¹, LIE². ● *n* mensonges *mpl*.

lyric *a* lyrique. **lyrical** *a* lyrique. **lyrics** *npl* paroles *fpl*.

MA *abbr* ⇒MASTER OF ARTS.
mac *n* Ⓑ imper *m*.
machine *n* machine *f*. ● *vt* (sew) coudre à la machine; (Tech) usiner. **~-gun** *n* mitrailleuse *f*.
mackerel *n inv* maquereau *m*.
mackintosh *n* imperméable *m*.
mad *a* (**madder, maddest**) fou; (foolish) insensé; (dog) enragé; (angry Ⓑ) furieux; **be ~ about** se passionner pour; (person) être fou de; **drive sb ~** exaspérer qn; **like ~** comme un fou. **~ cow disease** *n* maladie *f* de la vache folle.
madam *n* madame *f*; (unmarried) mademoiselle *f*.
made ⇒MAKE.
madly *adv* (interested, in love) follement; (frantically) comme un fou.
madman *n* (*pl* **-men**) fou *m*.
madness *n* folie *f*.
magazine *n* revue *f*, magazine *m*; (of gun) magasin *m*.
maggot *n* (in fruit) ver *m*, (for fishing) asticot *m*.
magic *n* magie *f*. ● *a* magique.
magician *n* magicien/-ne *m/f*.
magistrate *n* magistrat *m*.
magnet *n* aimant *m*. **magnetic** *a* magnétique.
magnificent *a* magnifique.
magnify *vt* grossir; (sound) amplifier; (fig) exagérer.
magnifying glass *n* loupe *f*.
magpie *n* pie *f*.
mahogany *n* acajou *m*.

maid *n* (servant) bonne *f*; (in hotel) femme *f* de chambre.
maiden *n* (old use) jeune fille *f*. ● *a* (aunt) célibataire; (voyage) premier. **~ name** *n* nom *m* de jeune fille.
mail *n* (postal service) poste *f*; (letters) courrier *m*; (armour) cotte *f* de mailles. ● *a* (bag, van) postal. ● *vt* envoyer par la poste. **~ box** *n* boîte *f* aux lettres; (Comput) boîte *f* aux lettres électronique.
mailing list *n* liste *f* d'adresses. **~man** *n* (*pl* **-men**) (US) facteur *m*. **~ order** *n* vente *f* par correspondance. **~ shot** *n* publipostage *m*.
main *a* principal; **a ~ road** une grande route. ● *n* (water/gas) **~** conduite *f* d'eau/de gaz; **the ~s** (Electr) le secteur; **in the ~** en général. **~frame** *n* unité *f* centrale. **~land** *n* continent *m*. **~stream** *n* tendance *f* principale, ligne *f*.
maintain *vt* (continue, keep, assert) maintenir; (house, machine, family) entretenir; (rights) soutenir.
maintenance *n* (care) entretien *m*; (continuation) maintien *m*; (allowance) pension *f* alimentaire.
maisonette *n* duplex *m*.
maize *n* maïs *m*.
majestic *a* majestueux.
majesty *n* majesté *f*.
major *a* majeur. ● *n* commandant *m*. ● *vi* **~ in** (Univ, US) se spécialiser en.
majority *n* majorité *f*; **the ~ of people** la plupart des gens. ● *a* majoritaire.
make *vt/i* (*pt* **made**) faire; (manufacture) fabriquer; (friends) se faire; (money) gagner; (decision) prendre; (place, position) arriver à; (cause to be) rendre; **~ sb do sth** faire faire qch à qn; (force) obliger

qn à faire qch; **be made of** être fait de; **~ oneself at home** se mettre à l'aise; **~ sb happy** rendre qn heureux; **~ it** arriver; (succeed) réussir; **I ~ it two o'clock** j'ai deux heures; **I ~ it 150** d'après moi, ça fait 150; **I cannot ~ anything of it** je n'y comprends rien; **can you ~ Friday?** vendredi, c'est possible?; **~ as if to** faire mine de. ● *n* (brand) marque *f*. □ **~ do** (manage) se débrouiller (with avec); **~ for** se diriger vers; (cause) tendre à créer; **~ good** *vi* réussir; *vt* compenser; (repair) réparer; **~ off** filer (with avec); **~ out** distinguer, (understand) comprendre; (draw up) faire; (assert) prétendre; **~ up** *vt* faire, former; (story) inventer; (deficit) combler; *vi* se réconcilier; **~ up for** compenser; (time) rattraper; **~ up one's mind** se décider.

make-believe *a* feint, illusoire. ● *n* fantaisie *f*.

maker *n* fabricant *m*.

makeshift *a* improvisé.

make-up *n* maquillage *m*; (of object) constitution *f*; (Psych) caractère *m*.

malaria *n* paludisme *m*.

Malaysia *n* Malaisie *f*.

male *a* (voice, sex) masculin; (Bot, Tech) mâle. ● *n* mâle *m*.

malfunction *n* mauvais fonctionnement *m*. ● *vi* mal fonctionner.

malice *n* méchanceté *f*. **malicious** *a* méchant.

malignant *a* malveillant; (tumour) malin.

mall *n* (shopping) **~** (in suburbs) centre *m* commercial; (in town) galerie *f* marchande.

malnutrition *n* sous-alimentation *f*.

Malta *n* Malte *f*.

mammal *n* mammifère *m*.

mammoth *n* mammouth *m*. ● *a* (task) gigantesque; (organization) géant.

man *n* (pl **men**) homme *m*; (in sports team) joueur *m*; (chess) pièce *f*; **~ to man** d'homme à homme. ● *vt* (pt **manned**) (desk) tenir; (ship) armer; (guns) servir; (be on duty at) être de service à.

manage *vt* (project, organization) diriger; (shop, affairs) gérer; (handle) manier; **I could ~ another drink** □ je prendrais bien encore un verre; **can you ~ Friday?** vendredi, c'est possible? ● *vi* se débrouiller, **~ to do** réussir à faire. **manageable** *a* (tool, size, person) maniable; (job) faisable.

management *n* (managers) direction *f*; (of shop) gestion *f*.

manager *n* directeur/-trice *m/f*; (of shop) gérant/-e *m/f*; (of actor) impresario *m*.

mandate *n* mandat *m*.

mandatory *a* obligatoire.

mane *n* crinière *f*.

mango *n* (pl **~es**) mangue *f*.

manhandle *vt* maltraiter, malmener.

man: ~hole *n* regard *m*. **~hood** *n* âge *m* d'homme; (quality) virilité *f*.

maniac *n* maniaque *mf*, fou *m*, folle *f*.

manicure *n* manucure *f*. ● *vt* soigner, manucurer.

manifest *a* manifeste. ● *vt* manifester.

manipulate *vt* (tool, person) manipuler.

mankind *n* genre *m* humain.

manly *a* viril.

man-made *a* (fibre) synthétique; (pond) artificiel; (disaster) d'origine humaine.

manned *a* (spacecraft) habité.

manner *n* manière *f*; (attitude)

M

attitude f; (kind) sorte f; ~s (social behaviour) manières fpl.

mannerism n particularité f; (quirk) manie f.

manoeuvre n manœuvre f. ● vt/i manœuvrer.

manor n manoir m.

manpower n main-d'œuvre f.

mansion n (in countryside) demeure f; (in town) hôtel m particulier.

manslaughter n homicide m involontaire.

mantelpiece n (manteau m de) cheminée.

manual a (labour) manuel; (typewriter) mécanique. ● n (handbook) manuel m.

manufacture vt fabriquer. ● n fabrication f.

manure n fumier m.

many a & n beaucoup (de); **a great** or **good** ~ un grand nombre (de); ~ **a** bien des.

map n carte f; (of streets) plan m. ● vt (pt **mapped**) faire la carte de; ~ **out** (route) tracer; (arrange) organiser.

mar vt (pt **marred**) gâcher.

marble n marbre m; (for game) bille f.

March n mars m.

march vi (Mil) marcher (au pas). ● vt ~ **off** (lead away) emmener. ● n marche f.

margin n marge f.

marginal a marginal; (increase) léger, faible; (seat: Pol) disputé.

marinate vt faire mariner (**in** dans).

marine a marin. ● n (shipping) marine f; (sailor) fusilier m marin.

marital a conjugal. ~ **status** n situation f de famille.

mark n (currency) mark m; (stain) tache f; (trace) marque f; (School) note f; (target) but m. ● vt marquer; (exam) corriger; ~ **out**

délimiter; (person) désigner; ~ **time** marquer le pas.

marker n (pen) marqueur m; (tag) repère m; (School, Univ) examinateur/-trice m/f.

market n marché m; **on the** ~ en vente. ● vt (sell) vendre; (launch) commercialiser. ~ **research** n étude f de marché.

marmalade n confiture f d'oranges.

maroon n bordeaux m inv. ● a bordeaux inv.

marooned a abandonné; (snowbound) bloqué.

marquee n grande tente f; (of circus) chapiteau m; (awning: US) auvent m.

marriage n mariage m (**to** avec).

married a marié (**to** à); (life) conjugal; **get** ~ se marier (**to** avec).

marrow n (of bone) moelle f; (vegetable) courge f.

marry vt épouser; (give or unite in marriage) marier. ● vi se marier.

marsh n marais m.

marshal n maréchal m; (at event) membre m du service d'ordre. ● vt (pt **marshalled**) rassembler.

martyr n martyr/-e m/f. ● vt martyriser.

marvel n merveille f. ● vi (pt **marvelled**) s'émerveiller (**at** de).

marvellous a merveilleux.

marzipan n pâte f d'amandes.

masculine a & n masculin (m).

mash n (potatoes 🇬🇧) purée f. ● vt écraser. **mashed potatoes** npl purée f (de pommes de terre).

mask n masque m. ● vt masquer.

Mason n franc-maçon m.

masonry n maçonnerie f.

mass n (Relig) messe f; masse f; **the** ~**es** les masses fpl. ● vt/i (se) masser.

massacre n massacre m. ● vt massacrer.

massage n massage m. ● vt masser.

massive a (large) énorme; (heavy) massif.

mass media n médias mpl.

mass-produce vt fabriquer en série.

mast n (on ship) mât m; (for radio, TV) pylône m.

master n maître m; (in secondary school) professeur m; **M~ of Arts** titulaire mf d'une maîtrise ès lettres. ● vt maîtriser.

masterpiece n chef-d'œuvre m.

mastery n maîtrise f.

mat n (petit) tapis m; (at door) paillasson m.

match n (for lighting fire) allumette f; (Sport) match m; (equal) égal/-e m/f; (marriage) mariage m; (sb to marry) parti m; **be a ~ for** pouvoir tenir tête à. ● vt opposer; (go with) aller avec; (cups) assortir; (equal) égaler. ● vi (be alike) être assorti.

matchbox n boîte f à allumettes.

matching a assorti.

mate n camarade mf; (of animal) compagnon m, compagne f; (assistant) aide mf; (chess) mat m. ● vt/i (s')accoupler (**with** avec).

material n matière f; (fabric) tissu m; (documents, for building) matériau (x) m(pl); ~**s** (equipment) matériel m. ● a matériel; (fig) important.

materialistic a matérialiste.

materialize vi se matérialiser, se réaliser.

maternal a maternel.

maternity n maternité f. ● a (clothes) de grossesse. ~ **hospital** n maternité f. ~ **leave** n congé m maternité.

mathematics n & npl mathématiques fpl.

maths, (US) **math** n maths fpl.

mating n accouplement m.

matrimony n mariage m.

matron n (married, elderly) dame f âgée; (in hospital) infirmière f en chef.

matt a mat.

matter n (substance) matière f; (affair) affaire f; **as a ~ of fact** en fait; **what is the ~?** qu'est-ce qu'il y a? ● vi importer; **it does not ~** ça ne fait rien; **no ~ what happens** quoi qu'il arrive.

mattress n matelas m.

mature a (psychologically) mûr; (plant) adulte. ● vt/i (se) mûrir.

maturity n maturité f.

mauve a & n mauve (m).

maverick n non-conformiste mf.

maximize vt porter au maximum.

maximum a & n (pl -ima) maximum (m).

may

past **might**

●*auxiliary verb*

····▸ (possibility) **they ~ be able to come** ils pourront peut-être venir; **she ~ not have seen him** elle ne l'a peut-être pas vu; **it ~ rain** il risque de pleuvoir; **'will you come?'—'I might'** 'tu viendras?'—'peut-être'.

····▸ (permission) **you ~ leave** vous pouvez partir; **~ I smoke?** puis-je fumer?

····▸ (wish) **~ he be happy** qu'il soit heureux.

May n mai m.

maybe adv peut-être.

mayhem n (havoc) ravages mpl.

mayonnaise n mayonnaise f.

mayor n maire m.

maze n labyrinthe m.

Mb *abbr* (**megabyte**) (Comput) Mo.

me *pron* me, m'; (after prep.) moi; (indirect object) me, m'; **he knows ~** il me connaît.

meadow *n* pré *m*.

meagre *a* maigre.

meal *n* repas *m*; (grain) farine *f*.

mean *a* (poor) misérable; (miserly) avare; (unkind) méchant; (average) moyen. ● *n* milieu *m*; (average) moyenne *f*; **in the ~ time** en attendant. ● *vt* (*pt* **meant**) vouloir dire, signifier; (involve) entraîner; **I ~ that!** je suis sérieux; **be meant for** être destiné à; **~ to do** avoir l'intention de faire.

meaning *n* sens *m*, signification *f*. **meaningful** *a* significatif. **meaningless** *a* dénué de sens.

means *n* moyen(s) *m*(*pl*); **by ~ of sth** au moyen de qch. ● *npl* (wealth) moyens *mpl* financiers; **by all ~** certainement; **by no ~** nullement.

meant ⇒MEAN.

meantime, **meanwhile** *adv* en attendant.

measles *n* rougeole *f*.

measure *n* mesure *f*; (ruler) règle *f*. ● *vt/i* mesurer; **~ up to** être à la hauteur de.

meat *n* viande *f*. **meaty** *a* de viande; (fig) substantiel.

mechanic *n* mécanicien/-ne *m/f*.

mechanical *a* mécanique.

mechanism *n* mécanisme *m*.

medal *n* médaille *f*.

meddle *vi* (interfere) se mêler (**in** de); (tinker) toucher (**with** à).

media *n* ⇒MEDIUM. ● *npl* **the ~** les média *mpl*; **talk to the ~** parler à la presse.

median *a* médian. ● *n* médiane *f*.

mediate *vi* servir d'intermédiaire.

medical *a* médical; (student) en médecine. ● *n* visite *f* médicale.

medication *n* médicaments *mpl*.

medicine *n* (science) médecine *f*; (substance) médicament *m*.

medieval *a* médiéval.

mediocre *a* médiocre.

meditate *vt/i* méditer.

Mediterranean *a* méditerranéen. ● *n* **the ~** la Méditerranée *f*.

medium *n* (*pl* **media**) (mid-point) milieu *m*; (for transmitting data) support *m*; (*pl* **mediums**) (person) médium *m*. ● *a* moyen.

medley *n* mélange *m*; (Mus) pot-pourri *m*.

meet *vt* (*pt* **met**) rencontrer; (see again) retrouver; (be introduced to) faire la connaissance de; (face) faire face à; (requirement) satisfaire. ● *vi* se rencontrer; (see each other again) se retrouver; (in session) se réunir.

meeting *n* réunion *f*; (between two people) rencontre *f*.

megabyte *n* (Comput) mégaoctet *m*.

melancholy *n* mélancolie *f*. ● *a* mélancolique.

mellow *a* (fruit) mûr; (sound, colour) moelleux, doux; (person) mûri. ● *vt/i* (mature) mûrir; (soften) (s')adoucir.

melody *n* mélodie *f*.

melon *n* melon *m*.

melt *vt/i* (faire) fondre.

member *n* membre *m*. **M~ of Parliament** *n* député *m*. **membership** *n* adhésion *f*; (members) membres *mpl*; (fee) cotisation *f*.

memento *n* (*pl* **~es**) (object) souvenir *m*.

memo *n* note *f*.

memoir *n* (record, essay) mémoire *m*.

memorandum n note f.

memorial n monument m. ●a commémoratif.

memorize vt apprendre par cœur.

memory n (mind, in computer) mémoire f; (thing remembered) souvenir m; **from ∼** de mémoire; **in ∼ of** à la mémoire de.

men ⇒MAN.

menace n menace f; (nuisance) peste f. ●vt menacer.

mend vt réparer; (darn) raccommoder; **∼ one's ways** s'amender. ●n raccommodage m; **on the ∼** en voie de guérison.

meningitis n méningite f.

menopause n ménopause f.

mental a mental; (hospital) psychiatrique.

mentality n mentalité f.

mention vt mentionner; **don't ∼ it!** il n'y a pas de quoi!, je vous en prie! ●n mention f.

menu n (food, on computer) menu m; (list) carte f.

MEP abbr (**Member of the European Parliament**) député m au Parlement européen.

mercenary a & n mercenaire (m).

merchandise n marchandises fpl.

merchant n marchand m. ●a (ship, navy) marchand. **∼ bank** n banque f de commerce.

merciful a miséricordieux.

mercury n mercure m.

mercy n pitié f; **at the ∼ of** à la merci de.

mere a simple. **merest** a moindre.

merge vt/i (se) mêler (with à); (companies: Comm) fusionner. **merger** n fusion f.

mermaid n sirène f.

merrily adv (happily) joyeusement; (unconcernedly) avec insouciance.

merry a (-ier, -iest) gai; **make ∼** faire la fête. **∼-go-round** n manège m.

mesh n maille f; (fabric) tissu m à mailles; (network) réseau m.

mesmerize vt hypnotiser.

mess n désordre m, gâchis m; (dirt) saleté f; (Mil) mess m; **make a ∼ of** gâcher. ●vt **∼ up** gâcher. ●vi **∼ about** s'amuser; (dawdle) traîner; **∼ with** (tinker with) tripoter.

message n message m.

messenger n messager/-ère m/f.

messy a (-ier, -iest) en désordre; (dirty) sale.

met ⇒MEET.

metal n métal m. ●a de métal. **metallic** a métallique; (paint, colour) métallisé.

metallurgy n métallurgie f.

metaphor n métaphore f.

meteor n météore m.

meteorite n météorite f.

meteorology n météorologie f.

meter n compteur m; (US) = METRE.

method n méthode f.

methylated spirit(s) n alcool m à brûler.

meticulous a méticuleux.

metre, (US) **meter** n mètre m.

metric a métrique.

metropolis n métropole f. **metropolitan** a métropolitain.

mew n miaulement m. ●vi miauler.

mews npl appartements mpl chic aménagés dans d'anciennes écuries.

Mexico n Mexique m.

miaow n & vi = MEW.

mice ⇒MOUSE.

mickey n take the **∼ out of** ⊞ se moquer de.

microchip n puce f; circuit m
intégré.

microlight n ULM m.

microprocessor n
microprocesseur m.

microscope n microscope m.

microwave n micro-onde f; ~
(oven) four m à micro-ondes. ● vt
passer au four à micro-ondes.

mid a in ~ air en plein ciel; in ~
March à la mi-mars; ~ afternoon
milieu m de l'après-midi; he's in
his ~ twenties il a environ vingt-
cinq ans.

midday n midi m.

middle a (door, shelf) du milieu;
(size) moyen. ● n milieu m; in the
~ of au milieu de. ~-aged a
d'âge mûr. M~ Ages n Moyen
Âge m. ~ class n classe f
moyenne. M~ East n Moyen-
Orient m.

midge n moucheron m.

midget n nain/-e m/f. ● a
minuscule.

midnight n minuit f; it's ~ il est
minuit.

midst n in the ~ of au beau
milieu de; in our ~ parmi nous.

midsummer n milieu m de l'été;
(solstice) solstice m d'été.

midway adv ~ between/along à
mi-chemin entre/le long de.

midwife n (pl -wives) sage-
femme f.

might[1] v aux I ~ have been killed!
j'aurais pu être tué; you ~ try
doing sth vous pourriez faire qch;
⇒MAY.

might[2] n puissance f.

mighty a puissant; (huge ⓣ)
énorme. ● adv ⓣ vachement ⓣ.

migrant a & n (bird) migrateur
(m); (worker) migrant/-e (m/f).

migrate vi émigrer. **migration** n
migration f.

mild a (surprise, taste, tobacco,

attack) léger; (weather, cheese,
soap, person) doux; (case,
infection) bénin.

mile n mile m (= 1.6 km); walk for
~s marcher pendant des
kilomètres; ~s better ⓣ bien
meilleur. **mileage** n nombre m
de miles, kilométrage m.

milestone n (lit) borne f; (fig)
étape f importante.

military a militaire.

militia n milice f.

milk n lait m. ● vt (cow) traire;
(fig) pomper.

milkman n (pl -men) laitier m.

milky a (skin, colour) laiteux;
(tea) au lait; M~ Way Voie f
lactée.

mill n moulin m; (factory) usine f.
● vt moudre. ● vi ~ around
grouiller.

millennium n (pl ~s) millénaire
m.

millimetre, (US) **millimeter** n
millimètre m.

million n million m; a ~ pounds
un million de livres. **millionaire**
n millionnaire m.

millstone n meule f; (fig) boulet
m.

mime n (actor) mime mf; (art)
mime m. ● vt/i mimer.

mimic vt (pt mimicked) imiter.
● n imitateur/-trice m/f.

mince vt hacher; not to ~ matters
ne pas mâcher ses mots. ● n
viande f hachée.

mind n esprit m; (sanity) raison f;
(opinion) avis m; be on sb's ~
préoccuper qn; bear that in ~ ne
l'oubliez pas; change one's ~
changer d'avis; make up one's ~
se décider (to à). ● vt (have charge
of) s'occuper de; (heed) faire
attention à; I do not ~ the noise le
bruit ne me dérange pas; I don't
~ ça m'est égal; would you ~

checking? je peux vous demander de vérifier?

minder n (bodyguard) garde m de corps; (**child**) ~ nourrice f.

mindless a (programme) bête; (work) abrutissant; (vandalism) gratuit.

mine n mine f. ● vt extraire; (Mil) miner. ● pron le mien, la mienne, les mien(ne)s; **the blue car is** ~ la voiture bleue est la mienne or à moi.

minefield n (lit) champ m de mines; (fig) terrain m miné.

miner n mineur m.

mineral n & a minéral (m); ~ **water** eau f minérale.

minesweeper n (ship) dragueur m de mines.

mingle vt/i (se) mêler (with à).

minibus n minibus m.

minicab n taxi m (non agréé).

minimal a minimal.

minimize vt minimiser; (Comput) réduire.

minimum a & n (pl **-ima**) minimum (m).

minister n ministre m.
ministerial a ministériel.
ministry n ministère m.

mink n vison m.

minor a (change, surgery) mineur; (injury, burn) léger; (road) secondaire. ● n (Jur) mineur/-e m/f.

minority n minorité f; **in the** ~ en minorité. ● a minoritaire.

mint n (Bot, Culin) menthe f; (sweet) bonbon m à la menthe; (fortune 🔢) fortune f. ● vt frapper; **in** ~ **condition** à l'état neuf.

minus prep moins; (without 🔢) sans. ● n moins m; (drawback) inconvénient m.

minute[1] n minute f; ~**s** (of meeting) compte-rendu m.

minute[2] a (object) minuscule; (risk, variation) minime.

miracle n miracle m.

mirror n miroir m, glace f; (Auto) rétroviseur. ● vt refléter.

misbehave vi se conduire mal.

miscalculation n (lit) erreur f de calcul; (fig) mauvais calcul m.

miscarriage n fausse couche f; ~ **of justice** erreur f judiciaire.

miscellaneous a divers.

mischief n (playfulness) espièglerie f; (by children) bêtises fpl.
mischievous a espiègle; (malicious) méchant.

misconduct n mauvaise conduite f.

misconstrue vt mal interpréter.

misdemeanour, (US) **misdemeanor** n (Jur) délit m.

miser n avare mf.

miserable a (sad) malheureux; (wretched) misérable; (performance, result) lamentable.

misery n (unhappiness) souffrance f; (misfortune) misère f; (person 🔢) rabat-joie mf inv.

misfit n inadapté/-e m/f.

misfortune n malheur m.

misgiving n (doubt) doute m; (apprehension) crainte f.

misguided a (foolish) imprudent; (mistaken) erroné; **be** ~ (person) se tromper.

mishap n incident m.

misjudge vt (distance, speed) mal évaluer; (person) mal juger.

mislay vt (pt **mislaid**) égarer.

mislead vt (pt **misled**) tromper.
misleading a trompeur.

misplace vt mal ranger; (lose) égarer. **misplaced** a (fear, criticism) déplacé.

misprint n coquille f, faute f typographique.

misread vt (pt **misread**) mal lire; (intentions) mal interpréter.

M

miss *vt/i* manquer; (*bus*) rater; **he ~es her/Paris** elle/Paris lui manque; **you're ~ing the point** tu n'as rien compris; **~ sth out** omettre qch; **~ out on sth** laisser passer qch. ● *n* coup *m* manqué; **it was a near ~** on l'a échappé belle.

Miss *n* Mademoiselle *f*; **~ Smith** (written) Mlle Smith.

misshapen *a* difforme.

missile *n* (Mil) missile *m*; (thrown) projectile *m*.

mission *n* mission *f*. **missionary** *n* missionnaire *mf*.

misspell *vt* (*pt* **misspelt** or **misspelled**) mal écrire.

mist *n* brume *f*; (on window) buée *f*. ● *vt/i* (s')embuer.

mistake *n* erreur *f*; **by ~** par erreur; **make a ~** faire une erreur. ● *vt* (*pt* **mistook**; *pp* **mistaken**) (*meaning*) mal interpréter; **~ for** prendre pour.

mistaken *a* (*enthusiasm*) mal placé; **be ~** avoir tort.

mistletoe *n* gui *m*.

mistreat *vt* maltraiter.

mistress *n* maîtresse *f*.

misty *a* (-ier, -iest) brumeux; (*window*) embué.

misunderstanding *n* malentendu *m*.

misuse *vt* (*word*) mal employer; (*power*) abuser de; (*equipment*) faire mauvais usage de.

mitten *n* moufle *f*.

mix *n* mélange *m*. ● *vt* mélanger; (*drink*) préparer; (*cement*) malaxer. ● *vi* se mélanger (with avec, à); (socially) être sociable; **~ with sb** fréquenter qn. □ **~ up** (confuse) confondre; (jumble up) mélanger; **get ~ed up in** se trouver mêlé à.

mixed *a* (*school*) mixte; (*collection, diet*) varié; (*nuts, sweets*) assorti.

mixer *n* (Culin) batteur *m* électrique; **be a good ~** être sociable; **~ tap** mélangeur *m*.

mixture *n* mélange *m*.

mix-up *n* confusion *f* (over sur).

moan *n* gémissement *m*. ● *vi* gémir; (complain 🔲) râler 🔲.

mob *n* (crowd) foule *f*; (gang) gang *m*; **the M~** la Mafia. ● *vt* (*pt* **mobbed**) assaillir.

mobile *a* mobile; **~ phone** téléphone *m* portable. ● *n* mobile *m*.

mobilize *vt/i* mobiliser.

mock *vt/i* se moquer (de). ● *a* faux.

mockery *n* moquerie *f*; **a ~ of** une parodie de.

mock-up *n* maquette *f*.

mode *n* mode *m*.

model *n* (Comput, Auto) modèle *m*; (scale representation) maquette *f*; (person showing clothes) mannequin *m*. ● *a* modèle; (*car*) modèle réduit *inv*; (*railway*) miniature. ● *vt* (*pt* **modelled**) modeler; (*clothes*) présenter. ● *vi* être mannequin; (pose) poser.

modelling *n* métier *m* de mannequin.

modem *n* modem *m*.

moderate *a & n* modéré/-e (*m/f*).

moderation *n* modération *f*; **in ~** avec modération.

modern *a* moderne; **~ languages** langues *fpl* vivantes. **modernize** *vt* moderniser.

modest *a* modeste. **modesty** *n* modestie *f*.

modification *n* modification *f*. **modify** *vt* modifier.

module *n* module *m*.

moist *a* (*soil*) humide; (*skin, palms*) moite; (*cake*) moelleux. **moisten** *vt* humecter. **moisture** *n* humidité *f*. **moisturizer** *n* crème *f* hydratante.

molar n molaire f.

mold (US) = MOULD.

mole n grain m de beauté; (animal) taupe f.

molecule n molécule f.

molest vt (pester) importuner; (sexually) agresser sexuellement.

moment n (short time) instant m; (point in time) moment m.
momentarily adv momentanément; (soon: US) très bientôt. **momentary** a momentané.

momentum n élan m.

monarch n monarque m.
monarchy n monarchie f.

Monday n lundi m.

monetary a monétaire.

money n argent m; **make ~** (person) gagner de l'argent; (business) rapporter de l'argent. **~-box** n tirelire f. **~ order** n mandat m postal.

monitor n dispositif m de surveillance; (Comput) moniteur m. ● vt surveiller; (broadcast) être à l'écoute de.

monk n moine m.

monkey n singe m.

monopolize vt monopoliser.
monopoly n monopole m.

monotonous a monotone.
monotony n monotonie f.

monsoon n mousson f.

monster n monstre m.
monstrous a monstrueux.

month n mois m.

monthly a mensuel. ● adv (pay) au mois; (publish) tous les mois. ● n (periodical) mensuel m.

monument n monument m.

moo vi meugler.

mood n humeur f; **in a good/bad ~** de bonne/mauvaise humeur.
moody a d'humeur changeante.

moon n lune f.

moonlight n clair m de lune.

moonlighting n [①] travail m au noir.

moor n lande f. ● vt amarrer.

mop n balai m à franges; **~ of hair** crinière f [①]. ● vt (pt **mopped**) **~ (up)** éponger.

moped n vélomoteur m.

moral a moral. ● n morale f; **~s** moralité f.

morale n moral m.

morbid a morbide.

more adv plus; **~ serious** plus sérieux; **work ~** travailler plus; **sleep ~ and ~** dormir de plus en plus; **once ~** une fois de plus; **I don't go there any ~** je n'y vais plus; **~ or less** plus ou moins ● det plus de; **a little ~ wine** un peu plus de vin; **~ bread** encore un peu de pain; **there's no ~ bread** il n'y a plus de pain; **nothing ~** rien de plus. ● pron plus; **cost ~ than** coûter plus cher que; **I need ~ of it** il m'en faut davantage.

moreover adv de plus.

morning n matin m; (whole morning) matinée f.

Morocco n Maroc m.

morsel n morceau m.

mortal a & n mortel/-le (m/f).

mortgage n emprunt-logement m. ● vt hypothéquer.

mortuary n morgue f.

mosaic n mosaïque f.

mosque n mosquée f.

mosquito n (pl **~es**) moustique m.

moss n mousse f.

most det (nearly all) la plupart de; **~ people** la plupart des gens; **the ~ votes/money** le plus de voix/ d'argent. ● n le plus. ● pron la plupart; **~ of us** la plupart d'entre nous; **~ of the money** la plus grande partie de l'argent; **the ~ I can do is ...** tout ce que je

M

peux faire c'est … ● adv the ~
beautiful house/hotel in Oxford la
maison la plus belle/l'hôtel le
plus beau d'Oxford; ~ interesting
très intéressant; what I like ~ (of
all) is ce que j'aime le plus c'est.
mostly adv surtout.
moth n papillon m de nuit; (in
cloth) mite f.
mother n mère f. ● vt (lit)
materner; (fig) dorloter.
motherhood n maternité f. ~-in-
law n (pl ~s-in-law) belle-mère
f. ~-of-pearl n nacre f. M~'s
Day n la fête des mères. ~-to-be
n future maman f. ~ tongue n
langue f maternelle.
motion n mouvement m; (proposal)
motion f; ~ picture (US) film m.
● vt/i ~ (to) sb to faire signe à qn
de. **motionless** a immobile.
motivate vt motiver.
motive n motif m; (Jur) mobile m.
motor n moteur m; (car) auto f.
● a (industry, insurance, vehicle)
automobile; (activity, disorder:
Med) moteur. ~bike n moto f. ~
car n auto f. ~-cyclist n
motocycliste mf. ~ home n auto-
caravane f.
motorist n automobiliste mf.
motorway n autoroute f.
mottled a tacheté.
motto n (pl ~es) devise f.
mould n (shape) moule m; (fungus)
moisissure f. ● vt mouler;
(influence) former. **moulding** n
moulure f. **mouldy** a moisi.
mount n (hill) mont m; (horse)
monture f. ● vt (stairs) gravir;
(platform, horse, bike) monter
sur; (jewel, picture, campaign,
exhibit) monter. ● vi monter;
(number, toll) augmenter;
(concern) grandir.
mountain n montagne f; ~ bike
(vélo) tout terrain m, VTT m.
mountaineer n alpiniste mf.

mourn vt/i ~ (for) pleurer.
mournful a mélancolique.
mourning n deuil m.
mouse n (pl mice) souris f.
~trap n souricière f.
mouth n bouche f; (of dog, cat)
gueule f; (of cave, tunnel) entrée f.
mouthful n bouchée f. ~wash n
eau f dentifrice. ~watering a
appétissant.
move vt (object) déplacer; (limb,
head) bouger; (emotionally)
émouvoir; ~ house déménager.
● vi bouger; (vehicle) rouler;
(change address) déménager; (act)
agir. ● n mouvement m; (in game)
coup m; (player's turn) tour m; (step,
act) manœuvre f; (house change)
déménagement m; on the ~ en
mouvement. □ ~ back reculer;
~ in emménager; ~ in with
s'installer avec; ~ on (person) se
mettre en route; (vehicle)
repartir; (time) passer; ~ sth on
faire avancer qch; ~ sb on faire
circuler qn; ~ over or up se
pousser.
movement n mouvement m.
movie n (US) film m; the ~s le
cinéma.
moving a (vehicle) en marche;
(part, target) mobile; (staircase)
roulant; (touching) émouvant.
mow vt (pp mowed or mown)
(lawn) tondre; (hay) couper; ~
down faucher. **mower** n tondeuse
f.
MP abbr ⇒MEMBER OF
PARLIAMENT.
Mr n (pl Messrs) ~ Smith
Monsieur or M. Smith; ~
President Monsieur le Président.
Mrs n (pl Mrs) ~ Smith Madame
or Mme Smith.
Ms n Mme.
much adv beaucoup; too ~ trop;
very ~ beaucoup; I like them as ~
as you (do) je les aime autant que

toi. ● *pron* beaucoup; **not ~** pas grand-chose; **he didn't say ~** il n'a pas dit grand-chose; **I ate so ~ that** j'ai tellement mangé que. ● *det* beaucoup de; **too ~ money** trop d'argent; **how ~ time is left?** combien de temps reste-t-il?

muck *n* saletés *fpl*; (manure) fumier *m*. □ **~ about** Ⅱ faire l'imbécile. **mucky** *a* sale.

mud *n* boue *f*.

muddle *n* (mix-up) malentendu *m*; (mess) pagaille *f* Ⅱ; **get into a ~** s'embrouiller. □ **~ through** se débrouiller; **~ up** embrouiller.

muddy *a* couvert de boue.

muffle *vt* emmitoufler; (bell) assourdir; (voice) étouffer.

mug *n* grande tasse *f*; (for beer) chope *f*; (face Ⅱ) gueule *f* Ⅱ; (fool Ⅱ) poire *f* Ⅱ. ● *vt* (*pt* **mugged**) agresser. **mugger** *n* agresseur *m*.

muggy *a* lourd.

mule *n* mulet *m*.

multicoloured *a* multicolore.

multiple *a & n* multiple (*m*); **~ sclerosis** sclérose *f* en plaques.

multiplication *n* multiplication *f*

multiply *vt/i* (se) multiplier.

multistorey *a* (car park) à niveaux multiples.

mum *n* Ⅱ maman *f*.

mumble *vt/i* marmonner.

mummy *n* (mother Ⅱ) maman *f*; (embalmed body) momie *f*.

mumps *n* oreillons *mpl*.

munch *vt* mâcher.

mundane *a* terre-à-terre.

municipal *a* municipal.

mural *a* mural. ● *n* peinture *f* murale.

murder *n* meurtre *m*. ● *vt* assassiner. **murderer** *n* meurtrier *m*, assassin *m*.

murky *a* (-ier, -iest) (water) glauque; (past) trouble.

murmur *n* murmure *m*. ● *vt/i* murmurer.

muscle *n* muscle *m*. ● *vi* **~ in** Ⅱ s'imposer (on dans).

muscular *a* (tissue, disease) musculaire; (body, person) musclé.

museum *n* musée *m*.

mushroom *n* champignon *m*. ● *vi* (town) proliférer; (demand) s'accroître rapidement.

music *n* musique *f*.

musical *a* (person) musicien; (voice) mélodieux; (accompaniment) musical; (instrument) de musique. ● *n* comédie *f* musicale.

musician *n* musicien/-ne *m/f*.

Muslim *n* Musulman/-e *m/f*. ● *a* musulman.

mussel *n* moule *f*.

must *v aux* devoir; **you ~ go** vous devez partir, il faut que vous partiez; **she ~ be consulted** il faut la consulter; **he ~ be old** il doit être vieux; **I ~ have done it** j'ai dû le faire. ● *n* **be a ~** Ⅱ être indispensable.

mustard *n* moutarde *f*.

musty *a* (-ier, -iest) (room) qui sent le renfermé; (smell) de moisi.

mute *a & n* muet/-te (*m/f*). **muted** *a* (colour) sourd; (response) tiède; (celebration) mitigé.

mutilate *vt* mutiler.

mutter *vt/i* marmonner.

mutton *n* mouton *m*.

mutual *a* (reciprocal) réciproque; (common) commun; (consent) mutuel. **mutually** *adv* mutuellement.

muzzle *n* (snout) museau *m*; (device) muselière *f*; (of gun) canon *m*. ● *vt* museler.

my *a* mon, ma, *pl* mes.

myself pron (reflexive) me, m'; **I've hurt ~** je me suis fait mal; (emphatic) moi-même; **I did it ~** je l'ai fait moi-même; (after preposition) moi, moi-même; **I am proud of ~** je suis fier de moi.

mysterious a mystérieux.

mystery n mystère m.

mystic a & n mystique (mf).
mystical a mystique.

myth n mythe m. **mythical** a mythique. **mythology** n mythologie f.

nag vt/i (pt **nagged**) critiquer; (pester) harceler. **nagging** a persistant.

nail n clou m; (of finger, toe) ongle m; **on the ~** sans tarder, tout de suite. ●vt clouer. **~ polish** n vernis m à ongles.

naïve a naïf.

naked a nu; **to the ~ eye** à l'œil nu.

name n nom m; (fig) réputation f. ●vt nommer; (terms) fixer; **be ~d after** porter le nom de.

namely adv à savoir.

nanny n nurse f.

nap n somme m.

nape n nuque f.

napkin n serviette f.

nappy n couche f.

narcotic a & n narcotique (m).

narrative n récit m. **narrator** n narrateur/-trice m/f.

narrow a étroit. ●vt/i (se) rétrécir; (limit) (se) limiter; **~ down the choices** limiter les choix.

~-minded a à l'esprit étroit; (ideas) étroit.

nasal a nasal.

nasty a (-ier, -iest) mauvais, désagréable; (malicious) méchant.

nation n nation f.

national a national. ●n ressortissant/-e m/f.

nationality n nationalité f.

nationalize vt nationaliser.

nationally adv à l'échelle nationale.

native n (local inhabitant) autochtone mf; (non-European) indigène mf; **be a ~ of** être originaire de. ●a indigène; (country) natal; (inborn) inné; **~ language** langue f maternelle; **~ speaker of French** personne f de langue maternelle française.

natural a naturel.

naturally adv (normally, of course) naturellement; (by nature) de nature.

nature n nature f.

naughty a (-ier, -iest) vilain, méchant; (indecent) grivois.

nausea n nausée f. **nauseous** a (smell) écœurant.

nautical a nautique.

naval a (battle) naval; (officer) de marine.

navel n nombril m.

navigate vt (sea) naviguer sur; (ship) piloter. ●vi naviguer. **navigation** n navigation f.

navy n marine f. ●a **~ (blue)** bleu inv marine.

near adv près; **draw ~** (s')approcher (to de). ●prep près de. ●a proche; **~ to** près de. ●vt approcher de.

nearby a proche. ●adv à proximité.

nearly adv presque; **I ~ forgot** j'ai failli oublier; **not ~ as pretty as** loin d'être aussi joli que.

nearness n proximité f.

nearside a (Auto) du côté du passager.

neat a soigné, net; (room) bien rangé; (clever) habile; (drink) sec. **neatly** adv avec soin; habilement.

necessarily adv nécessairement.

necessary a nécessaire.

necessitate vt nécessiter.

necessity n nécessité f; (thing) chose f indispensable.

neck n cou m; (of dress) encolure f. ~ **and neck** a à égalité. ~**lace** n collier m. ~**line** n encolure f. ~**tie** n cravate f.

nectarine n brugnon m, nectarine f.

need n besoin m. ● vt avoir besoin de; (demand) demander; **you** ~ **not come** vous n'êtes pas obligé de venir.

needle n aiguille f.

needless a inutile.

needlework n couture f; (object) ouvrage m (à l'aiguille).

needy a (-ier, -iest) nécessiteux. ● n the ~ les indigents.

negative a négatif. ● n (of photograph) négatif m; (word: Gram) négation f; **in the** ~ (answer) par la négative, (Gram) à la forme négative.

neglect vt négliger, laisser à l'abandon; ~ **to do** négliger de faire. ● n manque m de soins; (state of) ~ abandon m.

negligent a négligent.

negotiate vt/i négocier.

negotiation n négociation f.

neigh n hennissement m. ● vi hennir.

neighbour, (US) **neighbor** n voisin/-e m/f. **neighbourhood** n voisinage m, quartier m; **in the** ~**hood of** aux alentours de. **neighbouring** a voisin. **neighbourly** a amical.

neither a & pron aucun/-e des deux, ni l'un/-e ni l'autre. ● adv ni; ~ **big nor small** ni grand ni petit. ● conj (ne) non plus; ~ **am I coming** je ne viendrai pas non plus.

nephew n neveu m.

nerve n nerf m; (courage) courage m; (calm) sang-froid m; (impudence 🔲) culot m; ~**s** (before exams) trac m. ~**-racking** a éprouvant.

nervous a nerveux; **be** or **feel** ~ (afraid) avoir peur; ~ **breakdown** dépression f nerveuse. **nervousness** n nervosité f; (fear) crainte f.

nest n nid m. ● vi nicher. ~**-egg** n pécule m.

nestle vi se blottir.

net n filet m; (Comput) net m, Internet m. ● vt (pt **netted**) prendre au filet. ● a (weight) net. ~**ball** n netball m.

Netherlands n the ~ les Pays-Bas mpl.

netiquette n nétiquette f.

Netsurfer n Internaute mf.

nettle n ortie f.

network n réseau m.

neurotic a & n névrosé/-e (m/f).

neuter a & n neutre (m). ● vt (castrate) castrer.

neutral a neutre; ~ (**gear**) (Auto) point m mort.

never adv (ne) jamais; **he** ~ **refuses** il ne refuse jamais; **I** ~ **saw him** 🔲 je ne l'ai pas vu; ~ **again** plus jamais; ~ **mind** (don't worry) ne vous en faites pas; (it doesn't matter) peu importe.

nevertheless adv néanmoins, toutefois.

new a nouveau; (brand-new) neuf. ~**-born** a nouveau-né. ~**comer** n nouveau venu m, nouvelle venue f.

N

newly *adv* nouvellement. **~-weds** *npl* jeunes mariés *mpl*.

news *n* nouvelle(s) *f(pl)*; (radio, press) informations *fpl*; (TV) actualités *fpl*, informations *fpl*. **~ agency** *n* agence *f* de presse. **~agent** *n* marchand/-e *m/f* de journaux. **~caster** *n* présentateur/-trice *m/f*. **~group** *n* (Internet) forum *m* de discussion. **~letter** *n* bulletin *m*. **~paper** *n* journal *m*.

new year *n* nouvel an *m*. **New Year's Day** *n* le jour de l'an. **New Year's Eve** *n* la Saint-Sylvestre.

New Zealand *n* Nouvelle-Zélande *f*.

next *a* prochain; (adjoining) voisin; (following) suivant; **~ to** à côté de; **~ door** à côté (**to** de). ● *adv* la prochaine fois; (afterwards) ensuite. ● *n* suivant/-e *m/f*; (e-mail) message *m* suivant. **~-door** *a* d'à côté. **~ of kin** *n* parent *m* le plus proche.

nib *n* plume *f*.

nibble *vt/i* grignoter.

nice *a* agréable, bon; (kind) gentil; (pretty) joli; (respectable) bien *inv*; (subtle) délicat. **nicely** *adv* agréablement; gentiment; (well) bien.

nicety *n* subtilité *f*.

niche *n* (recess) niche *f*; (fig) place *f*, situation *f*.

nick *n* petite entaille *f*; **be in good/bad ~** être en bon/mauvais état. ● *vt* (steal, arrest 🔲) piquer.

nickel *n* (metal) nickel *m*; (US) pièce *f* de cinq cents.

nickname *n* surnom *m*. ● *vt* surnommer.

nicotine *n* nicotine *f*.

niece *n* nièce *f*.

niggling *a* (person) tatillon; (detail) insignifiant.

night *n* nuit *f*; (evening) soir *m*. ● *a* de nuit. **~-cap** *n* boisson *f* (avant d'aller se coucher). **~-club** *n* boîte *f* de nuit. **~-dress** *n* chemise *f* de nuit. **~fall** *n* tombée *f* de la nuit. **nightie** *n* chemise *f* de nuit.

nightingale *n* rossignol *m*.

nightly *a & adv* (de) chaque nuit *or* soir.

night: **~mare** *n* cauchemar *m*. **~-time** *n* nuit *f*.

nil *n* (Sport) zéro *m*. ● *a* (chances, risk) nul.

nimble *a* agile.

nine *a & n* neuf (*m*).

nineteen *a & n* dix-neuf (*m*).

ninety *a & n* quatre-vingt-dix (*m*).

ninth *a & n* neuvième (*mf*).

nip *vt/i* (*pt* **nipped**) (pinch) pincer; (rush 🔲) courir; **~ out/back** sortir/rentrer rapidement. ● *n* pincement *m*.

nipple *n* mamelon *m*; (of baby's bottle) tétine *f*.

nippy *a* (**-ier**, **-iest**) (air) piquant; (car) rapide.

nitrogen *n* azote *m*.

no *det* aucun/-e; pas de; **~ man** aucun homme; **~ money/time** pas d'argent/de temps; **~ one** = NOBODY; **~ smoking/entry** défense de fumer/d'entrer; **~ way!** 🔲 pas question! ● *adv* non. ● *n*(*pl* **noes**) non *m inv*.

nobility *n* noblesse *f*.

noble *a* noble. **~ man** *n* (*pl* **-men**) noble *m*.

nobody *pron* (ne) personne; **he knows ~** il ne connaît personne. ● *n* nullité *f*.

nocturnal *a* nocturne.

nod *vt/i* (*pt* **nodded**); **~ (one's head)** faire un signe de tête; **~ off** s'endormir. ● *n* signe *m* de tête.

noise *n* bruit *m*; **make a ~** faire du bruit. **noisily** *adv*.

bruyamment. **noisy** a (**-ier, -iest**) bruyant.

no man's land n no man's land m.

nominal a symbolique, nominal; (*value*) nominal.

nominate vt nommer; (put forward) proposer.

none pron aucun/-e; ~ **of us** aucun/-e de nous; **I have** ~ je n'en ai pas.

non-existent a inexistant.

nonplussed a perplexe.

nonsense n absurdités fpl.

non-smoker n non-fumeur m.

non-stick a antiadhésif.

non-stop a (*train, flight*) direct. ● adv sans arrêt.

noodles npl nouilles fpl.

noon n midi m.

nor adv ni. ● conj (ne) non plus; ~ **shall I come** je ne viendrai pas non plus.

norm n norme f.

normal a normal.

Norman n Normand/-e m/f. ● a (*village*) normand; (*arch*) roman.

north n nord m. ● a nord inv, du nord. ● adv vers le nord.

North America n Amérique f du Nord.

north-east n nord-est m.

northerly a (*wind, area*) du nord; (*point*) au nord.

northern a (*accent*) du nord; (*coast*) nord. **northerner** n habitant/-e m/f du nord.

northward a (*side*) nord inv; (*journey*) vers le nord.

north-west n nord-ouest m.

Norway n Norvège f.

Norwegian n (*person*) Norvégien/-ne m/f; (*language*) norvégien m. ● a norvégien.

nose n nez m. ● vi ~ **about** fouiner.

nosedive n piqué m. ● vi descendre en piqué.

nostalgia n nostalgie f.

nostril n narine f; (of horse) naseau m.

nosy a (**-ier, -iest**) ⊡ curieux, indiscret.

not adv (ne) pas; **I do** ~ **know** je ne sais pas; ~ **at all** du tout; ~ **yet** pas encore; **I suppose** ~ je suppose que non.

notably adv notamment.

notch n entaille f. ● vt ~ **up** (score) marquer.

note n note f; (banknote) billet m; (short letter) mot m. ● vt noter; (notice) remarquer. ~**book** n carnet m.

nothing pron (ne) rien; **he eats** ~ il ne mange rien; ~ **else** rien d'autre; ~ **much** pas grand-chose; **for** ~ pour rien, gratis. ● n rien m; (person) nullité f. ● adv nullement.

notice n avis m, annonce f; (poster) affiche f; (advance) ~ préavis m; **at short** ~ dans des délais très brefs; **give in one's** ~ donner sa démission; **take** ~ faire attention (**of à**). ● vt remarquer, observer. **noticeable** a visible. ~**-board** n tableau m d'affichage.

notify vt (inform) aviser; (make known) notifier.

notion n idée f, notion f.

notorious a (criminal) notoire; (district) mal famé; (case) tristement célèbre.

notwithstanding prep malgré. ● adv néanmoins.

nought n zéro m.

noun n nom m.

nourish vt nourrir. **nourishing** a nourrissant. **nourishment** n nourriture f.

novel n roman m. ● a nouveau. **novelist** n romancier/-ière m/f. **novelty** n nouveauté f.

N

November *n* novembre *m*.

now *adv* maintenant. ● *conj* maintenant que; **just ~** maintenant; (a moment ago) tout à l'heure; **~ and again, ~ and then** de temps à autre.

nowadays *adv* de nos jours.

nowhere *adv* nulle part.

nozzle *n* (tip) embout *m*; (of hose) jet *m*.

nuclear *a* nucléaire.

nude *a* nu. ● *n* nu/-e *m/f*; **in the ~** tout nu.

nudge *vt* pousser du coude. ● *n* coup *m* de coude.

nudism *n* nudisme *m*. **nudity** *n* nudité *f*.

nuisance *n* (thing, event) ennui *m*; (person) peste *f*; **be a ~** être embêtant.

null *a* nul.

numb *a* engourdi (**with** par). ● *vt* engourdir.

number *n* nombre *m*; (of ticket, house, page) numéro *m*; (written figure) chiffre *m*; **a ~ of people** plusieurs personnes. ● *vt* numéroter; (count; include) compter. **~-plate** *n* plaque *f* d'immatriculation.

numeral *n* chiffre *m*.

numerate *a* qui sait compter.

numerical *a* numérique.

numerous *a* nombreux.

nun *n* religieuse *f*.

nurse *n* infirmier/-ière *m/f*; (nanny) nurse *f*. ● *vt* soigner; (hope) nourrir.

nursery *n* (room) chambre *f* d'enfants; (for plants) pépinière *f*; (day) crèche *f*. **~ rhyme** *n* comptine *f*. **~ school** *n* (école) maternelle *f*.

nursing home *n* maison *f* de retraite.

nut *n* (walnut, Brazil nut) noix *f*; (hazelnut) noisette *f*; (peanut) cacahuète *f*; (Tech) écrou *m*. **~crackers** *npl* casse-noix *m inv*.

nutmeg *n* muscade *f*.

nutrient *n* substance *f* nutritive.

nutritious *a* nutritif.

nuts *a* (crazy 🔲) cinglé.

nutshell *n* coquille *f* de noix; **in a ~** en un mot.

nylon *n* nylon *m*.

oak *n* chêne *m*.

OAP *abbr* (**old-age pensioner**) retraité/-e *m/f*.

oar *n* rame *f*.

oath *n* (promise) serment *m*; (swear-word) juron *m*.

oats *npl* avoine *f*.

obedience *n* obéissance *f*.

obedient *a* obéissant.

obediently *adv* docilement.

obese *a* obèse.

obey *vt/i* obéir (à).

object[1] *n* (thing) objet *m*; (aim) but *m*; (Gram) complément *m* d'objet; **money is no ~** l'argent n'est pas un problème.

object[2] *vi* protester. ● *vt* **~ that** objecter que; **~ to** (behaviour) désapprouver; (plan) protester contre. **objection** *n* objection *f*; (drawback) inconvénient *m*.

objective *a & n* objectif (*m*).

obligation *n* devoir *m*.

obligatory *a* obligatoire.

oblige *vt* obliger (**to do** à faire).

oblivion *n* oubli *m*. **oblivious** *a* inconscient (**to, of** de).

oblong *a* oblong. ● *n* rectangle *m*.

obnoxious a odieux.

oboe n hautbois m.

obscene a obscène.

obscure a obscur. ● vt obscurcir; (conceal) cacher.

observance n (of law) respect m; (of sabbath) observance f.
  observant a observateur.

observation n observation f.

observe vt observer; (remark) remarquer.

obsess vt obséder. **obsession** n obsession f. **obsessive** a (person) maniaque; (thought) obsédant; (illness) obsessionnel.

obsolete a dépassé.

obstacle n obstacle m.

obstinate a obstiné.

obstruct vt (road) bloquer; (view) cacher; (progress) gêner.
  obstruction n (act) obstruction f; (thing) obstacle m; (in traffic) encombrement m.

obtain vt obtenir. ● vi avoir cours. **obtainable** a disponible.

obvious a évident. **obviously** adv manifestement.

occasion n occasion f; (big event) événement m; **on** ~ à l'occasion.

occasional a (event) qui a lieu de temps en temps; **the** ~ **letter** une lettre de temps en temps.
  occasionally adv de temps à autre.

occupation n (activity) occupation f; (job) métier m, profession f.
  occupational therapy n ergothérapie f.

occupier n occupant/-e m/f.

occupy vi occuper.

occur vi (pt **occurred**) se produire; (arise) se présenter; ~ **to sb** venir à l'esprit de qn.

occurrence n (event) fait m; (instance) occurrence f.

ocean n océan m.

Oceania n Océanie f.

o'clock adv **it is six** ~ il est six heures; **at one** ~ à une heure.

October n octobre m.

octopus n (pl ~**es**) pieuvre f.

odd a bizarre; (number) impair; (left over) qui reste; (sock) dépareillé; **write the** ~ **article** écrire un article de temps en temps; ~ **jobs** menus travaux mpl; **twenty** ~ vingt et quelques.
  oddity n bizarrerie f.

odds npl chances fpl; (in betting) cote f (**on** de); **at** ~ en désaccord; **it makes no** ~ ça ne fait rien; ~ **and ends** des petites choses.

odour, (US) **odor** n odeur f.
  odourless a inodore.

of

➡ For expressions such as **of course**, **consist of** ➡**course**, **consist**.

● preposition

⋯▸ de; **a photo** ~ **the dog** une photo du chien; **the king** ~ **the beasts** le roi des animaux; (made) ~ **gold** en or; **it's kind** ~ **you** c'est très gentil de votre part; **some** ~ **us** quelques-uns d'entre nous; ~ **it/them** en; **have you heard** ~ **it?** est-ce que tu en as entendu parler?

off adv **be** ~ partir, s'en aller, **I'm** ~ je m'en vais; **30 metres** ~ à 30 mètres; **a month** ~ dans un mois.
  ● a (gas, water) coupé; (tap) fermé; (light, TV) éteint; (party, match) annulé; (bad) (food) avarié; (milk) tourné; **Friday is my day** ~ je ne travaille pas le vendredi; **25%** ~ 25% de remise.
  ● prep **3 metres** ~ **the ground** 3 mètres (au-dessus) du sol; **just** ~ **the kitchen** juste à côté de la cuisine; **that is** ~ **the point** là n'est pas la question.

offal n abats mpl.

offence n (Jur) infraction f; give ~ to offenser; take ~ s'offenser (at de).

offend vt offenser; be ~ed s'offenser (at de). ● vi (Jur) commettre une infraction.

offender n délinquant/-e m/f.

offensive a (remark) injurieux; (language) grossier; (smell) repoussant; (weapon) offensif. ● n offensive f.

offer vt (pt offered) offrir. ● n offre f; on ~ en promotion.

offhand a désinvolte. ● adv à l'improviste.

office n bureau m; (duty) fonction f; in ~ au pouvoir. ● a de bureau.

officer n (army) officier m; (police) ~ policier m; (government) ~ fonctionnaire mf.

official a officiel. ● n (civil servant) fonctionnaire mf; (of party, union) officiel/-le m/f; (of police, customs) agent m.

off: ~-**licence** n magasin m de vins et spiritueux. ~-**line** a autonome; (switched off) déconnecté; (Comput) hors connexion. ~-**load** vt (stock) écouler; (Comput) décharger. ~-**peak** a (call) au tarif réduit; (travel) en période creuse. ~-**putting** a rebutant. ~**set** vt (pt -**set**; pres p -**setting**) compenser. ~**shore** a (waters) du large; (funds) hors-lieu inv. ~**side** a (Sport) hors jeu inv; (Auto) du côté du conducteur. ~**spring** n inv progéniture f.

often adv souvent; how ~ do you meet? vous vous voyez tous les combien?; every so ~ de temps en temps.

oil n (for lubrication, cooking) huile f; (for fuel) pétrole m; (for heating) mazout m. ● vt huiler. ~**field** n gisement m pétrolifère.

~-**painting** n peinture f à l'huile. ~**skins** npl ciré m. ~-**tanker** n pétrolier m.

oily a graisseux.

ointment n pommade f.

OK, okay a d'accord; is it ~ if...? ça va si...?; feel ~ aller bien.

old a vieux; (person) vieux, âgé; (former) ancien; how ~ is he? quel âge a-t-il?; he is eight years ~ il a huit ans; ~er, ~est aîné. ~ age n vieillesse f. ~-**age** pensioner n retraité/-e m/f. ~-**fashioned** a démodé; (person) vieux jeu inv. ~ man n vieillard m, vieux m. ~ woman n vieille f.

olive n olive f; ~ oil huile f d'olive. ● a olive inv.

Olympic a olympique. ~ **Games** npl Jeux mpl olympiques.

omelette n omelette f.

omen n augure m.

ominous a (presence, cloud) menaçant; (sign) de mauvais augure.

omission n omission f. **omit** vt (pt omitted) omettre.

on prep sur; ~ the table sur la table; put the key ~ it mets la clé dessus; ~ 22 March le 22 mars; ~ Monday lundi; ~ TV à la télé; ~ video en vidéo; be ~ steroids prendre des stéroïdes; ~ arriving en arrivant. ● a (TV, oven, light) allumé; (dishwasher, radio) en marche; (tap) ouvert; (lid) mis; the match is still ~ le match aura lieu quand même; the news is ~ in 10 minutes les informations sont dans 10 minutes. ● adv have sth ~ porter qch; 20 years ~ 20 ans plus tard; from that day ~ à partir de ce jour-là; further ~ plus loin; ~ and off (occasionally) de temps en temps; go ~ and ~ (person) parler pendant des heures.

once adv une fois; (formerly)

autrefois. ● *conj* une fois que; **all at ~** tout d'un coup.

oncoming *a* (*vehicle*) qui approche.

one *det & n* un/-e (*m/f*). ● *pron* un/-e *m/f*; (impersonal) on; **~ (and only)** seul (et unique); **a big ~** un grand/une grande; **this/that ~** celui-ci/-là, celle-ci/-là; **~ another** l'un/-e l'autre. **~-off** *a* 🇬🇧 unique, exceptionnel. **~self** *pron* soi-même; (reflexive) se. **~-way** *a* (*street*) à sens unique; (*ticket*) simple.

ongoing *a* (*process*) continu; **be ~** être en cours.

onion *n* oignon *m*.

on-line *a & adv* en ligne.

onlooker *n* spectateur/-trice *m/f*.

only *a* seul; **~ son** fils unique. ● *adv & conj* seulement; **he is ~ six** il n'a que six ans.

onset *n* début *m*.

onward(s) *adv* en avant.

open *a* ouvert; (*view*) dégagé; (free to all) public; (undisguised) manifeste; (*question*) en attente; **in the ~ air** en plein air. ● *vt/i* (*door*) (s')ouvrir, (*shop, play*) ouvrir; **~ out** *or* **up** (s')ouvrir. **~-ended** *a* (*stay*) de durée indéterminée; (*debate, question*) ouvert. **~-heart** *a* (*surgery*) à cœur ouvert.

opening *n* (of book) début *m*; (of exhibition, shop) ouverture *f*; (of film) première *f*; (in market) débouché *m*; (job) poste *m* (disponible).

open: **~-minded** *a* **be ~-minded** avoir l'esprit ouvert. **~-plan** *a* paysagé.

opera *n* opéra *m*.

operate *vt/i* opérer; (Tech) (faire) fonctionner; **~ on** (Med) opérer; **operating theatre** salle *f* d'opération.

operation *n* opération *f*; **have an ~** se faire opérer; **in ~** (*plan*) en vigueur; (*mine*) en service.

operative *n* employé/-e *m/f*. ● *a* (*law*) en vigueur.

operator *n* opérateur/-trice *m/f*; (telephonist) standardiste *mf*.

opinion *n* opinion *f*, avis *m*.

opinionated *a* qui a des avis sur tout.

opponent *n* adversaire *mf*.

opportunity *n* occasion *f* (**to do** de faire).

oppose *vt* s'opposer à; **as ~d to** par opposition à. **opposing** *a* opposé.

opposite *a* (*direction, side*) opposé; (*building*) d'en face. ● *n* contraire *m*. ● *adv* en face. ● *prep* **~ (to)** en face de.

opposition *n* opposition *f*.

oppress *vt* opprimer. **oppressive** *a* (cruel) oppressif; (heat) oppressant.

opt *vi* **~ for** opter pour; **~ out** refuser de participer (**of** à); **~ to do** choisir de faire.

optical *a* optique. **~ illusion** *n* illusion *f* d'optique. **~ scanner** *n* lecteur *m* optique.

optician *n* opticien/-ne *m/f*.

optimism *n* optimisme *m*.

optimist *n* optimiste *mf*.

optimistic *a* optimiste.

option *n* option *f*; (choice) choix *m*.

optional *a* facultatif; **~ extras** accessoires *mpl* en option.

or *conj* ou; (with negative) ni.

oral *n & a* oral (*m*).

orange *n* (fruit) orange *f*; (*colour*) orange *m*. ● *a* (colour) orange *inv*.

orbit *n* orbite *f*. ● *vt* décrire une orbite autour de.

orchard *n* verger *m*.

orchestra *n* orchestre *m*.

orchid *n* orchidée *f*.

ordeal *n* épreuve *f*.

order *n* ordre *m*; (Comm)

commande *f*; **in ~** (tidy) en ordre; (*document*) en règle; **in ~ that** pour que; **in ~ to** pour. ● *vt* ordonner; (*goods*) commander; **~ sb to** ordonner à qn de.

orderly *a* (tidy) ordonné; (not unruly) discipliné. ● *n* (Mil) planton *m*; (Med) aide-soignant/-e *m/f*.

ordinary *a* (usual) ordinaire; (average) moyen.

ore *n* minerai *m*.

organ *n* organe *m*; (Mus) orgue *m*.

organic *a* organique; (*produce*) biologique.

organization *n* organisation *f*.

organize *vt* organiser.

organizer *n* organisateur/-trice *m/f*; **electronic ~** agenda *m* électronique.

orgasm *n* orgasme *m*.

Orient *n* **the ~** l'Orient *m*. **oriental** *a* oriental.

origin *n* origine *f*.

original *a* original; (*inhabitant*) premier; (*member*) originaire. **originality** *n* originalité *f*. **originally** *adv* (at the outset) à l'origine.

originate *vi* (plan) prendre naissance; **~ from** provenir de; (person) venir de. ● *vt* être l'auteur de. **originator** *n* (of idea) auteur *m*; (of invention) créateur/-trice *m/f*.

ornament *n* (decoration) ornement *m*; (object) objet *m* décoratif.

orphan *n* orphelin/-e *m/f*. ● *vt* rendre orphelin. **orphanage** *n* orphelinat *m*.

orthopaedic *a* orthopédique.

ostentatious *a* tape-à-l'œil *inv*.

osteopath *n* ostéopathe *mf*.

ostrich *n* autruche *f*.

other *a* autre; **the ~ one** l'autre *mf*. ● *n* & *pron* autre *mf*; (some) **~s** d'autres. ● *adv* **~ than** (apart from) à part; (otherwise than)

autrement que. **otherwise** *adv* autrement.

otter *n* loutre *f*.

ouch *interj* aïe!

ought *v aux* devoir; **you ~ to stay** vous devriez rester; **he ~ to succeed** il devrait réussir; **I ~ to have done it** j'aurais dû le faire.

ounce *n* once *f* (= 28.35 g).

our *a* notre, *pl* nos.

ours *poss* le *or* la nôtre, les nôtres.

ourselves *pron* (reflexive) nous; (emphatic) nous-mêmes; (after preposition) **for ~** pour nous, pour nous-mêmes.

out *adv* dehors; **he's ~** il est sorti; **further ~** plus loin; **be ~** (*book*) être publié; (*light*) être éteint; (*sun*) briller; (*flower*) être épanoui; (*tide*) être bas; (*player*) être éliminé; **~ of** hors de; **go/ walk/get ~ of** sortir de; **~ of pity** par pitié; **made ~ of** fait de; **5 ~ of 6** 5 sur 6. **~break** *n* (of war) déclenchement *m*; (of violence, boils) éruption *f*. **~burst** *n* explosion *f*. **~cast** *n* paria *m*. **~class** *vt* surclasser. **~come** *n* résultat *m*. **~cry** *n* tollé *m*. **~dated** *a* démodé. **~door** *a* (activity) de plein air; (*pool*) en plein air. **~doors** *adv* dehors.

outer *a* extérieur; **~ space** espace *m* extra-atmosphérique.

outfit *n* (clothes) tenue *f*.

outgoing *a* (minister, tenant) sortant; (sociable) ouvert. **outgoings** *npl* dépenses *fpl*.

outgrow *vt* (*pt* **-grew**; *pp* **-grown**) (*clothes*) devenir trop grand pour; (*habit*) dépasser.

outing *n* sortie *f*.

outlaw *n* hors-la-loi *m inv*. ● *vt* déclarer illégal.

outlet *n* (for water, gas) tuyau *m* de sortie; (for goods) débouché *m*; (for feelings) exutoire *m*.

outline n contour m; (of plan) grandes lignes fpl; (of essay) plan m. ●vt tracer le contour de; (summarize) exposer brièvement.

out: ~**live** vt survivre à. ~**look** n perspective f. ~**number** vt surpasser en nombre. ~ **of date** a démodé; (expired) périmé. ~ **of hand** a incontrôlable. ~ **of order** a en panne. ~ **of work** a sans travail. ~**patient** n malade mf externe.

output n rendement m; (Comput) sortie f. ●vt/i (Comput) sortir.

outrage n (anger) indignation f, (atrocity) attentat m; (scandal) outrage m. ●vt (morals) outrager; (person) scandaliser. **outrageous** a scandaleux.

outright adv (completely) catégoriquement; (killed) sur le coup. ●a (majority) absolu; (ban) catégorique; (hostility) pur et simple.

outset n début m.

outside n extérieur m. ●adv dehors. ●prep en dehors de; (in front of) devant. ●a extérieur. **outsider** n étranger/-ère m/f; (Sport) outsider m.

out: ~**skirts** npl périphérie f. ~**spoken** a franc. ~**standing** a exceptionnel; (not settled) en suspens.

outward a & adv vers l'extérieur; (sign) extérieur; (journey) d'aller. **outwards** adv vers l'extérieur.

oval n & a ovale (m).

ovary n ovaire m.

oven n four m.

over prep (across) par-dessus; (above) au-dessus de; (covering) sur; (more than) plus de; **it's ~ the road** c'est de l'autre côté de la rue; ~ **here/there** par ici/là; **children ~ six** les enfants de plus de six ans; ~ **the weekend** pendant le week-end; **all ~ the house** partout dans

la maison. ●a, adv (term) terminé; (war) fini; **get sth ~ with** en finir avec qch; **ask sb ~** inviter qn; ~ **and** ~ (again) à plusieurs reprises; **five times ~** cinq fois de suite.

overall a global, d'ensemble; (length) total. ●adv globalement.

overalls npl combinaison f.

over: ~**board** adv par-dessus bord. ~**cast** a couvert. ~**charge** vt faire payer trop cher à. ~**coat** n pardessus m.

overcome vt (pt -**came**; pp -**come**) (enemy) vaincre; (difficulty, fear) surmonter; ~ **by** accablé de.

overcrowded a bondé; (country) surpeuplé.

overdo vt (pt -**did**; pp -**done**) (Culin) trop cuire; ~ **it** (overwork) en faire trop.

over: ~**dose** n surdose f, overdose f. ~**draft** n découvert m. ~**draw** vt (pt -**drew**; pp -**drawn**) faire un découvert sur. ~**due** a en retard; (bill) impayé.

overflow¹ vi déborder.

overflow² n (outlet) trop-plein m.

overhaul vt réviser.

overhead¹ adv au-dessus; (in sky) dans le ciel.

overhead² a aérien; ~ **projector** rétroprojecteur m. **overheads** npl frais mpl généraux.

over: ~**hear** vt (pt -**heard**) entendre par hasard. ~**lap** vt/i (pt -**lapped**) (se) chevaucher. ~**leaf** adv au verso. ~**load** vt surcharger. ~**look** vt (window) donner sur; (miss) ne pas voir.

overnight¹ adv dans la nuit; (instantly) du jour au lendemain.

overnight² a (train) de nuit; (stay) d'une nuit; (fig) soudain.

over: ~**power** vt (thief) maîtriser; (army) vaincre; (fig) accabler. ~**priced** a trop cher.

~**rate** *vt* surestimer. ~**react** *vi* réagir de façon excessive. ~**riding** *a* (*consideration*) numéro un; (*importance*) primordial. ~**rule** *vt* (*decision*) annuler.

overrun *vt* (*pt* -**ran**; *pp* -**run**; *pres p* -**running**) (*country*) envahir; (*budget*) dépasser. ● *vi* (*meeting*) durer plus longtemps que prévu.

overseas *a* étranger. ● *adv* outre-mer, à l'étranger.

over: ~**see** *vt* (*pt* -**saw**; *pp* -**seen**) surveiller. ~**sight** *n* omission *f*. ~**sleep** *vi* (*pt* -**slept**) se réveiller trop tard. ~**take** *vt/i* (*pt* -**took**; *pp* -**taken**) dépasser; (*fig*) frapper. ~**time** *n* heures *fpl* supplémentaires. ~**turn** *vt/i* (se) renverser. ~**weight** *a* trop gros.

overwhelm *vt* (*enemy*) écraser; (*shame*) accabler. **overwhelmed** *a* (with offers, calls) submergé (**with**, **by** de); (with shame, work) accablé; (by sight) ébloui. **overwhelming** *a* (*heat, grief*) accablant; (*defeat, victory*) écrasant; (*urge*) irrésistible.

overwork *vt/i* (se) surmener. ● *n* surmenage *m*.

owe *vt* devoir. **owing** *a* dû; **owing to** en raison de.

owl *n* hibou *m*.

own *a* propre. ● *pron* **my** ~ le mien, la mienne; **a house of one's** ~ sa propre maison; **on one's** ~ tout seul. ● *vt* posséder; ~ **up (to)** 🔟 avouer. **owner** *n* propriétaire *mf*. **ownership** *n* propriété *f*; (of land) possession *f*.

oxygen *n* oxygène *m*.

oyster *n* huître *f*.

ozone *n* ozone *m*; ~ **layer** couche *f* d'ozone.

PA *abbr* ⇒PERSONAL ASSISTANT.

pace *n* pas *m*; (speed) allure *f*; **keep** ~ **with** suivre. ● *vt* (*room*) arpenter. ● *vi* ~ (**up and down**) faire les cent pas.

Pacific *n* ~ (**Ocean**) océan *m* Pacifique.

pack *n* paquet *m*; (Mil) sac *m*; (of hounds) meute *f*; (of thieves) bande *f*; (of lies) tissu *m*. ● *vt* (into case) mettre dans une valise; (into box, crate) emballer; (for sale) conditionner; (*crowd*) remplir complètement; ~ **one's suitcase** faire sa valise. ● *vi* faire ses valises; ~ **into** (cram) s'entasser dans; ~ **off** expédier; **send** ~**ing** envoyer promener.

package *n* paquet *m*; (Comput) progiciel *m*; ~ **deal** offre *f* globale; ~ **holiday** voyage *m* organisé. ● *vt* empaqueter.

packed *a* (crowded) bondé; ~ **lunch** repas *m* froid.

packet *n* paquet *m*.

packing *n* (action, material) emballage *m*.

pad *n* (of paper) bloc *m*; (to protect) protection *f*; (for ink) tampon *m*; (launch) ~ **rampe** *f* de lancement. ● *vt* (*pt* **padded**) rembourrer; (text: fig) délayer. ● *vi* (*pt* **padded**) (walk) marcher à pas feutrés. **padding** *n* rembourrage *m*.

paddle *n* pagaie *f*. ● *vt* ~ **a canoe** pagayer. ● *vi* patauger.

padlock *n* cadenas *m*. ● *vt* cadenasser.

paediatrician *n* pédiatre *mf*.

pagan a & n païen/-ne (m/f).

page n (of book) page f. ● vt (on pager) rechercher; (over speaker) faire appeler. **pager** n radiomessageur m.

pain n douleur f; ~s efforts mpl; be in ~ souffrir; take ~s to se donner du mal pour. ● vt (grieve) peiner. **painful** a douloureux; (laborious) pénible. ~-**killer** n analgésique m. **painless** a (operation) indolore; (death) sans souffrance; (trouble-free) sans peine. **painstaking** a minutieux.

paint n peinture f; ~s (in tube, box) couleurs fpl. ● vt/i peindre. ~**brush** n pinceau m. **painter** n peintre m. **painting** n peinture f. ~**work** n peintures fpl.

pair n paire f; (of people) couple m; a ~ of trousers un pantalon. ● vi ~ off former un couple.

pajamas npl (US) = PYJAMAS.

Pakistan n Pakistan m

palace n palais m.

palatable a (food) savoureux; (solution) acceptable. **palate** n palais m.

pale a pâle. ● vi pâlir.

Palestine n Palestine f.

pallid a pâle.

palm n (of hand) paume f; (tree) palmier m; (symbol) palme f. □ ~ off ⊡ ~ sth off as faire passer qch pour; ~ sth off on sb refiler qch à qn ⊡.

palpitate vi palpiter.

paltry a (-ier, -iest) dérisoire, piètre.

pamper vt choyer.

pamphlet n brochure f.

pan n casserole f; (for frying) poêle f.

pancake n crêpe f.

pandemonium n tohu-bohu m.

pander vi ~ to (person, taste) flatter bassement.

pane n carreau m, vitre f.

panel n (of door) panneau m; (of experts, judges) commission f; (on discussion programme) invités mpl; (instrument) ~ tableau m de bord.

pang n serrement m au cœur; ~s of conscience remords mpl.

panic n panique f. ● vt/i (pt panicked) (s')affoler. ~-**stricken** a pris de panique, affolé.

pansy n (Bot) pensée f.

pant vi haleter.

panther n panthère f.

pantomime n (show) spectacle m de Noël; (mime) mime m.

pantry n garde-manger m inv.

pants npl (underwear) slip m; (trousers: US) pantalon m.

paper n papier m; (newspaper) journal m; (exam) épreuve f; (essay) exposé m; (wallpaper) papier m peint; (identity) ~s papiers mpl (d'identité); on ~ par écrit. ● vt (room) tapisser. ~-**back** n livre m de poche. ~-**clip** n trombone m. ~ **feed tray** n (Comput) bac m d'alimentation en papier. ~**work** n (work) travail m administratif; (documentation) documents mpl.

par n be below ~ ne pas être en forme; on a ~ with (performance) comparable à; (person) l'égal de; (golf) par m.

parachute n parachute m. ● vi descendre en parachute.

parade n (procession) parade f; (Mil) défilé m. ● vi défiler. ● vt faire étalage de.

paradise n paradis m.

paradox n paradoxe m.

paraffin n pétrole m (lampant); (wax) paraffine f.

paragliding n parapente m.

paragon n modèle m.

paragraph n paragraphe m.

P

parallel *a* parallèle. ● *n* parallèle *m*; (maths) parallèle *f*.

paralyse *vt* paralyser. **paralysis** *n* paralysie *f*.

paramedic *n* auxiliaire *mf* médical/-e.

paramount *a* suprême.

paranoia *n* paranoïa *f*. **paranoid** *a* paranoïaque; (Psych) paranoïde *a*.

paraphernalia *n* attirail *m*.

parasol *n* ombrelle *f*; (on table, at beach) parasol *m*.

paratrooper *n* (Mil) parachutiste *mf*.

parcel *n* paquet *m*.

parchment *n* parchemin *m*.

pardon *n* pardon *m*; (Jur) grâce *f*; **I beg your ~** je vous demande pardon. ● *vt* (*pt* **pardoned**) pardonner (*sb for sth* qch à qn); (Jur) gracier.

parent *n* parent *m*.

parenthesis *n* (*pl* **-theses**) parenthèse *f*.

parenthood *n* (fatherhood) paternité *f*; (motherhood) maternité *f*.

Paris *n* Paris.

parish *n* (Relig) paroisse *f*; (municipal) commune *f*.

park *n* parc *m*. ● *vt/i* (se) garer; (remain parked) stationner. **~ and ride** *n* parc *m* relais.

parking *n* stationnement *m*; **no ~** stationnement interdit. **~-lot** *n* (US) parking *m*. **~-meter** *n* parcmètre *m*. **~ ticket** *n* (fine) contravention *f*, PV *m* ⊡.

parliament *n* parlement *m*. **parliamentary** *a* parlementaire.

parlour, (US) **parlor** *n* salon *m*.

parody *n* parodie *f*. ● *vt* parodier.

parole *n* **on ~** en liberté conditionnelle.

parrot *n* perroquet *m*.

parry *vt* (Sport) parer; (*question*) éluder. ● *n* parade *f*.

parsley *n* persil *m*.

parsnip *n* panais *m*.

part *n* partie *f*; (of serial) épisode *m*; (of machine) pièce *f*; (Theat) rôle *m*; (side in dispute) parti *m*; **in ~** en partie; **on the ~ of** de la part de; **take ~ in** participer à. ● *a* partiel. ● *adv* en partie. ● *vt/i* (separate) (se) séparer; **~ with** se séparer de.

part-exchange *n* reprise *f*; **take sth in ~** reprendre qch.

partial *a* partiel; (biased) partial; **be ~ to** avoir un faible pour.

participant *n* participant/-e *m/f*. **participate** *vi* participer (*in* à). **participation** *n* participation *f*.

participle *n* participe *m*.

particular *n* détail *m*; **~s** détails *mpl*; **in ~** en particulier. ● *a* particulier; (fussy) difficile; (careful) méticuleux; **that ~ man** cet homme-là. **particularly** *adv* particulièrement.

parting *n* séparation *f*; (in hair) raie *f*. ● *a* d'adieu.

partition *n* (of room) cloison *f*; (Pol) partition *f*. ● *vt* (*room*) cloisonner; (*country*) partager.

partly *adv* en partie.

partner *n* (professional) associé/-e *m/f*; (economic, sporting) partenaire *mf*; (spouse) époux/-se *m/f*; (unmarried) partenaire *mf*.

partnership *n* association *f*.

partridge *n* perdrix *f*.

part-time *a & adv* à temps partiel.

party *n* fête *f*; (formal) réception *f*; (group) groupe *m*; (Pol) parti *m*; (Jur) partie *f*.

pass *vt/i* (*pt* **passed**) passer; (overtake) dépasser; (in exam) réussir; (approve) (*candidate*) admettre; (*invoice*) approuver; (*remark*) faire; (*judgement*) prononcer; (*law, bill*) adopter; **~ (by)** (*building*) passer devant;

(*person*) croiser. ● *n* (permit)
laisser-passer *m inv*; (ticket) carte
f d'abonnement; (Geog) col *m*;
(Sport) passe *f*; ∼ (**mark**) (in exam)
moyenne *f*. □ ∼ **away** mourir; ∼
out (faint) s'évanouir; ∼ **sth out**
distribuer qch; ∼ **over** (overlook)
délaisser; ∼ **up** (forego) laisser
passer.

passage *n* (way through, text)
passage *m*; (voyage) traversée *f*;
(corridor) couloir *m*.

passenger *n* (in car, plane, ship)
passager/-ère *m/f*; (in train, bus,
tube) voyageur/-euse *m/f*.

passer-by *n* (*pl* **passers-by**)
passant/-e *m/f*.

passing *a* (*motorist*) qui passe;
(*whim*) passager; (*reference*) en
passant.

passion *n* passion *f*. **passionate**
a passionné.

passive *a* passif.

passport *n* passeport *m*.

password *n* mot *m* de passe.

past *a* (*times, problems*) passé;
(*president*) ancien; **the** ∼ **months**
ces derniers mois. ● *n* passé *m*.
● *prep* (beyond) après; **walk/go** ∼
sth passer devant qch; **10** ∼ **6** six
heures dix; **it's** ∼ **11** il est 11
heures passées. ● *adv* **go/walk** ∼
passer.

pasta *n* pâtes *fpl* (alimentaires).

paste *n* (glue) colle *f*; (dough) pâte
f; (of fish, meat) pâté *m*; (jewellery)
strass *m*. ● *vt* coller.

pasteurize *vt* pasteuriser.

pastime *n* passe-temps *m inv*.

pastry *n* (dough) pâte *f*; (tart)
pâtisserie *f*.

pat *vt* (*pt* **patted**) tapoter. ● *n*
petite tape *f*.

patch *n* pièce *f*; (over eye) bandeau
m; (spot) tache *f*; (of snow, ice)
plaque *f*; (of vegetables) carré *m*;
bad ∼ période *f* difficile. □ ∼ **up**

(*trousers*) rapiécer; (*quarrel*)
résoudre.

patent *a* (obvious) manifeste;
(patented) breveté; ∼ **leather** cuir *m*
verni. ● *n* brevet *m*. ● *vt* faire
breveter.

path *n* (*pl* **-s**) sentier *m*, chemin
m; (in park) allée *f*; (of rocket)
trajectoire *f*.

pathetic *a* misérable; (bad ⬚)
lamentable.

patience *n* patience *f*.

patient *a* patient. ● *n* patient/-e
m/f. **patiently** *adv* patiemment.

patriotic *a* patriotique; (*person*)
patriote.

patrol *n* patrouille *f*; ∼ **car**
voiture *f* de police. ● *vi/t*
patrouiller (dans).

patron *n* (of the arts) mécène *m*;
(customer) client/-e *m/f*.
patronage *n* clientèle *f*; (support)
patronage *m*. **patronize** *vt*
(*person*) traiter avec
condescendance; (*establishment*)
fréquenter.

patter *n* (of steps) bruit *m*; (of rain)
crépitement *m*.

pattern *n* motif *m*, dessin *m*; (for
sewing) patron *m*; (for knitting)
modèle *m*.

paunch *n* ventre *m*.

pause *n* pause *f*. ● *vi* faire une
pause; (hesitate) hésiter.

pave *vt* paver; ∼ **the way** ouvrir la
voie (**for** à).

pavement *n* trottoir *m*; (US)
chaussée *f*.

paving stone *n* pavé *m*.

paw *n* patte *f*. ● *vt* (*animal*)
donner des coups de patte à;
(touch ⬚) peloter ⬚.

pawn *n* pion *m*. ● *vt* mettre en
gage. ∼**broker** *n* prêteur/-euse
m/f sur gages. ∼**-shop** *n* mont-
de-piété *m*.

pay *vt* (*pt* **paid**) payer; (*interest*)
rapporter; (*compliment, attention*)

P

faire; (*visit, homage*) rendre. ● *vi* payer; (*business*) rapporter; ~ **for sth** payer qch. ● *n* salaire *m*; ~ **rise** augmentation *f* (*de salaire*). □ ~ **back** rembourser; ~ **in** déposer; ~ **off** (*loan*) rembourser; (*worker*) congédier; (succeed) être payant; ~ **out** payer, débourser.

payable *a* payable; ~ **to** (*cheque*) à l'ordre de.

payment *n* paiement *m*; (regular) versement *m*; (reward) récompense *f*.

payroll *n* fichier *m* des salaires; **be on the** ~ **of** être employé par.

PC *abbr* ⇒PERSONAL COMPUTER.

PDA *abbr* (**personal digital assistant**) assistant *m* personnel numérique.

PE *abbr* (**physical education**) éducation *f* physique, EPS *f*.

pea *n* (petit) pois *m*.

peace *n* paix *f*; ~ **of mind** tranquillité *f* d'esprit. **peaceful** *a* (tranquil) paisible; (peaceable) pacifique.

peach *n* pêche *f*.

peacock *n* paon *m*.

peak *n* (of mountain) pic *m*; (of cap) visière *f*; (maximum) maximum *m*; (on graph) sommet *m*; (of career) apogée *m*; (of fitness) meilleur *m*; ~ **hours** heures *fpl* de pointe.

peal *n* (of bells) carillon *m*; (of laughter) éclat *m*.

peanut *n* cacahuète *f*; ~**s** (money 🔊) clopinettes *fpl* 🔊.

pear *n* poire *f*.

pearl *n* perle *f*.

peasant *n* paysan/-ne *m/f*.

peat *n* tourbe *f*.

pebble *n* caillou *m*; (on beach) galet *m*.

peck *vt/i* (*food*) picorer; (attack) donner des coups de bec (à). ● *n* coup *m* de bec; **a** ~ **on the cheek** une bise.

peckish *a* **be** ~ 🔊 avoir faim.

peculiar *a* (odd) bizarre; (special) particulier (**to** à). **peculiarity** *n* bizarrerie *f*.

pedal *n* pédale *f*. ● *vi* pédaler.

pedantic *a* pédant.

peddle *vt* colporter; (*drugs*) faire du trafic de.

pedestrian *n* piéton *m*. ● *a* (*precinct, street*) piétonnier; (fig) prosaïque; ~ **crossing** passage *m* pour piétons.

pedigree *n* (of animal) pedigree *m*; (of person) ascendance *f*. ● *a* (*dog*) de pure race.

pee *vi* 🔊 faire pipi 🔊.

peek *vi & n* = PEEP.

peel *n* (on fruit) peau *m*; (removed) épluchures *fpl*. ● *vt* (*fruit, vegetables*) éplucher; (*prawn*) décortiquer. ● *vi* (of skin) peler; (of paint) s'écailler.

peep *vi* jeter un coup d'œil (furtif) (**at** à). ● *n* coup *m* d'œil (furtif). ~**hole** *n* judas *m*.

peer *vi* ~ (**at**) regarder fixement. ● *n* (equal, noble) pair *m*. **peerage** *n* pairie *f*.

peg *n* (for clothes) pince *f* à linge; (to hang coats) patère *f*; (for tent) piquet *m*. ● *vt* (*pt* **pegged**) (*clothes*) accrocher avec des pinces; (*prices*) indexer.

pejorative *a* péjoratif.

pelican *n* pélican *m*; ~ **crossing** passage *m* pour piétons.

pellet *n* (round mass) boulette *f*; (for gun) plomb *m*.

pelt *vt* bombarder (**with** de). ● *n* (skin) peau *f*.

pelvis *n* (Anat) bassin *m*.

pen *n* stylo *m*; (for sheep) enclos *m*; (for baby, cattle) parc *m*.

penal *a* pénal. **penalize** *vt* pénaliser.

penalty *n* peine *f*; (fine) amende *f*; (in football) penalty *m*.

penance n pénitence f.

pence ⇒PENNY.

pencil n crayon m. ● vt (pt **pencilled**) crayonner; ~ **in** noter provisoirement. ~**-sharpener** n taille-crayons m inv.

pending a (matter) en souffrance; (Jur) en instance. ● prep (until) en attendant.

penetrate vt pénétrer; (silence, defences) percer; (organization) infiltrer. ● vi pénétrer.

penetrating a pénétrant.

pen-friend n correspondant/-e m/f.

penguin n manchot m, pingouin m.

pen: ~**knife** n (pl **-knives**) canif m. ~**-name** n pseudonyme m.

penniless a sans le sou.

penny n (pl **pennies** or **pence**) (unit of currency) penny m; (small amount) centime m.

pension n (from state) pension f; (from employer) retraite f; ~ **scheme** plan m de retraite. ● vt ~ **off** mettre à la retraite. **pensioner** n retraité/-e m/f.

pensive a songeur.

penthouse n appartement m de luxe (au dernier étage).

penultimate a avant-dernier.

people npl gens mpl, personnes fpl; **English** ~ les Anglais mpl; ~ **say** on dit. ● n peuple m. ● vt peupler. ~ **carrier** n monospace m.

pepper n poivre m; (vegetable) poivron m. ● vt (Culin) poivrer.

peppermint n (plant) menthe f poivrée; (sweet) bonbon m à la menthe.

per prep par; ~ **annum** par an; ~ **cent** pour cent; ~ **kilo** le kilo; **ten km** ~ **hour** dix km à l'heure.

percentage n pourcentage m.

perception n perception f.

perceptive a perspicace.

perch n (of bird) perchoir m. ● vi (se) percher.

perennial a perpétuel; (plant) vivace.

perfect¹ vt perfectionner.

perfect² a parfait. ● n (Ling) parfait m. **perfectly** adv parfaitement.

perfection n perfection f; **to** ~ à la perfection.

perforate vt perforer.

perform vt (task) exécuter; (function) remplir; (operation) procéder à; (play) jouer; (song) chanter. ● vi (actor, musician, team) jouer; ~ **well/badly** (candidate, business) avoir de bons/de mauvais résultats.

performance n interprétation f; (of car, team) performance f; (show) représentation f; (fuss) histoire f.

performer n artiste mf.

perfume n parfum m.

perhaps adv peut être.

peril n péril m. **perilous** a périlleux.

perimeter n périmètre m.

period n période f; (era) époque f; (lesson) cours m; (Gram) point m; (Med) règles fpl. ● a d'époque.

periodical n périodique m.

peripheral a (vision, suburb) périphérique; (issue) annexe. ● n (Comput) périphérique m.

perish vi périr; (rubber) se détériorer.

perjury n faux témoignage m.

perk n ⊞ avantage m. ● vt/i ~ **up** ⊞ (se) remonter. **perky** a ⊞ gai.

perm n permanente f. ● vt **have one's hair** ~**ed** se faire faire une permanente.

permanent a permanent.

permanently adv (happy) en permanence; (employed) de façon permanente.

P

permissible *a* permis.

permission *n* permission *f*.

permissive *a* libéral; (pej) permissif.

permit¹ *vt* (*pt* **permitted**) permettre (**sb to** à qn de), autoriser (**sb to** qn à).

permit² *n* permis *m*.

perpendicular *a* perpendiculaire.

perpetrator *n* auteur *m*.

perpetuate *vt* perpétuer.

perplexed *a* perplexe.

persecute *vt* persécuter.

perseverance *n* persévérance *f*. **persevere** *vi* persévérer.

persist *vi* persister (**in doing** à faire). **persistence** *n* persistance *f*. **persistent** *a* (*cough, snow*) persistant; (*obstinate*) obstiné; (*noise, pressure*) continuel.

person *n* personne *f*; **in** ~ en personne.

personal *a* (*life, problem, opinion*) personnel; (*safety, freedom, insurance*) individuel. ~ **ad** *n* petite annonce *f*. ~ **assistant** *n* secrétaire *mf* de direction. ~ **computer** *n* ordinateur *m* (personnel), micro-ordinateur *m*.

personality *n* personnalité *f*; (star) vedette *f*.

personal: ~ **organizer** *n* agenda *m*. ~ **stereo** *n* baladeur *m*.

personnel *n* personnel *m*.

perspiration *n* (*sweat*) sueur *f*; (*sweating*) transpiration *f*. **perspire** *vi* transpirer.

persuade *vt* persuader (**to** de). **persuasion** *n* persuasion *f*. **persuasive** *a* persuasif.

pertinent *a* pertinent.

perturb *vt* troubler.

Peru *n* Pérou *m*.

pervasive *a* (*smell*) pénétrant; (*feeling*) envahissant.

perverse *a* (*desire*) pervers; (*refusal, attitude*) illogique. **perversion** *n* perversion *f*.

pervert¹ *vt* (*truth*) travestir; (*values*) fausser; (*justice*) entraver.

pervert² *n* pervers/-e *m/f*.

pessimist *n* pessimiste *mf*. **pessimistic** *a* pessimiste.

pest *n* (insect) insecte *m* nuisible; (animal) animal *m* nuisible; (person 🔲) enquiquineur/-euse *m/f* 🔲.

pester *vt* harceler.

pet *n* animal *m* de compagnie; (favourite) chouchou/-te *m/f*. ●*a* (*theory, charity*) favori; ~ **hate** bête *f* noire; ~ **name** petit nom *m*. ●*vt* (*pt* **petted**) caresser; (spoil) chouchouter 🔲.

petal *n* pétale *m*.

peter *vi* ~ **out** (*conversation*) tarir; (*supplies*) s'épuiser.

petite *a* (*woman*) menue.

petition *n* pétition *f*. ●*vt* adresser une pétition à.

petrol *n* essence *f*. ~ **bomb** *n* cocktail *m* molotov. ~ **station** *n* station-service *f*. ~ **tank** *n* réservoir *m* d'essence.

petticoat *n* jupon *m*.

petty *a* (**-ier**, **-iest**) (minor) petit; (mean) mesquin; ~ **cash** petite caisse *f*.

pew *n* banc *m* (d'église).

pharmacist *n* pharmacien/-ne *m/f*. **pharmacy** *n* pharmacie *f*.

phase *n* phase *f*. ●*vt* ~ **in/out** introduire/supprimer peu à peu.

PhD *abbr* (**Doctor of Philosophy**) doctorat *m*.

pheasant *n* faisan/-e *m/f*.

phenomenon *n* (*pl* **-ena**) phénomène *m*.

phew *interj* ouf.

philosopher *n* philosophe *mf*. **philosophical** *a* philosophique;

(resigned) philosophe. **philosophy** n philosophie f.

phlegm n (Med) mucosité f.

phobia n phobie f.

phone n téléphone m; **on the ~** au téléphone. ● vt (person) téléphoner à; **~ England** téléphoner en Angleterre. ● vi téléphoner; **~ back** rappeler. **~ book** n annuaire m. **~ booth**, **~ box** n cabine f téléphonique. **~ call** n coup m de fil 🔲. **~card** n télécarte f. **~-in** n émission f à ligne ouverte. **~ number** n numéro m de téléphone.

phonetic a phonétique.

phoney a (-ier, -iest) 🔲 faux. ● n 🔲 (person) charlatan m; **it's a ~** c'est un faux.

photocopier n photocopieuse f.

photocopy n photocopie f. ● vt photocopier.

photograph n photographie f. ● vt photographier.

photographer n photographe mf.

phrase n expression f; (idiom) locution f. ● vt exprimer, formuler. **~-book** n guide m de conversation.

physical a physique.

physicist n physicien/-ne m/f.

physics n physique f.

physiotherapist n kinésithérapeute mf.

physiotherapy n kinésithérapie f.

physique n physique m.

piano n piano m.

pick n choix m; (best) meilleur/-e m/f; (tool) pioche f. ● vt choisir; (flower) cueillir; (lock) crocheter; **~ a quarrel with** chercher querelle à; **~ one's nose** se curer le nez. 🔲 **~ on** harceler; **~ out** choisir; (identify) distinguer; **~ up** vt ramasser; (sth fallen) relever; (weight) soulever; (habit,

passenger, speed) prendre; (learn) apprendre; vi s'améliorer.

pickaxe n pioche f.

picket n (striker) gréviste mf; (stake) piquet m; **~ (line)** piquet m de grève. ● vt (pt **picketed**) installer un piquet de grève devant.

pickle n conserves fpl au vinaigre; (gherkin) cornichon m. ● vt conserver dans du vinaigre.

pick-up n (stylus-holder) lecteur m; (on guitar) capteur m; (collection) ramassage m; (improvement) reprise f.

picnic n pique-nique m. ● vi (pt **picnicked**) pique-niquer.

pictorial a (magazine) illustré; (record) graphique.

picture n image f; (painting) tableau m; (photograph) photo f; (drawing) dessin m; (film) film m; (fig) description f; **the ~s** le cinéma. ● vt s'imaginer; **be ~d** (shown) être représenté.

picturesque a pittoresque.

pie n (sweet) tarte f; (savoury) tourte f.

piece n morceau m; (of string, ribbon) bout m; (of currency, machine) pièce f; **a ~ of advice/furniture** un conseil/meuble; **go to ~s** (fig) s'effondrer; **take to ~s** démonter.

pier n jetée f.

pierce vt percer.

pig n porc m, cochon m.

pigeon n pigeon m. **~-hole** n casier m.

pig-headed a entêté.

pigsty n porcherie f.

pigtail n natte f.

pike n inv (fish) brochet m.

pile n (heap) tas m; (stack) pile f; (of carpet) poil m; **~s of** 🔲 un tas de 🔲. ● vt **~ (up)** entasser. ● vi **~ into** s'engouffrer dans; **~ up** (snow, leaves) s'entasser; (debts,

P

work) s'accumuler. **~-up** n (Auto) carambolage m.

pilgrim n pèlerin m. **pilgrimage** n pèlerinage m.

pill n pilule f.

pillar n pilier m. **~-box** n boîte f aux lettres.

pillion n siège m de passager; **ride ~** monter en croupe.

pillow n oreiller m. **~case** n taie f d'oreiller.

pilot n pilote m. ● a pilote. ● vt (*pt* **piloted**) piloter. **~-light** n veilleuse f.

pimple n bouton m.

pin n épingle f; (*of plug*) fiche f; (*for wood, metal*) goujon m; (*in surgery*) broche f; **have ~s and needles** avoir des fourmis. ● vt (*pt* **pinned**) épingler, attacher; (*trap*) coincer; **~ sb down** (fig) forcer qn à se décider; **~ up** accrocher.

pinafore n tablier m.

pincers npl tenailles fpl.

pinch vt pincer; (*steal* ⊞) piquer. ● vi (*be too tight*) serrer. ● n (*mark*) pinçon m; (*of salt*) pincée f; **at a ~** à la rigueur.

pine n (*tree*) pin m. ● vi **~** (*away*) dépérir; **~ for** languir après.

pineapple n ananas m.

pinecone n pomme f de pin.

pink a & n rose (m).

pinpoint vt (*problem, cause, location*) indiquer; (*time*) déterminer.

pint n pinte f (GB = *0.57 litre*; US = *0.47 litre*).

pin-up n ⊞ pin-up f inv ⊞.

pioneer n pionnier m. ● vt **~ the use of** être le premier à utiliser.

pious a pieux.

pip n (*seed*) pépin m; (*sound*) top m.

pipe n tuyau m; (*to smoke*) pipe f; (*Mus*) chalumeau m; **~s** cornemuse f. ● vt transporter par tuyau. □ **~ down** se taire.

pipeline n oléoduc m; **in the ~** en cours.

piping n tuyauterie f; **~ hot** fumant.

pirate n pirate m. ● vt pirater.

Pisces n Poissons mpl.

pistol n pistolet m.

pit n fosse f; (*mine*) puits m; (*quarry*) carrière f; (*for orchestra*) fosse f; (*of stomach*) creux m; (*of cherry*: US) noyau m. ● vt (*pt* **pitted**) marquer; (fig) opposer; **~ oneself against** se mesurer à.

pitch n (*Sport*) terrain m; (*of voice, note*) hauteur f; (*degree*) degré m; (*Mus*) ton m; (*tar*) brai m. ● vt jeter; (*tent*) planter. ● vi (*ship*) tanguer. □ **~ in** ⊞ contribuer.

pitfall n écueil m.

pitiful a pitoyable. **pitiless** a impitoyable.

pit stop n arrêt m mécanique.

pittance n **earn a ~** gagner trois fois rien.

pity n pitié f; (*regrettable fact*) dommage m; **take ~ on** avoir pitié de; **what a ~!** quel dommage! ● vt avoir pitié de.

pivot n pivot m. ● vi (*pt* **pivoted**) pivoter.

placard n affiche f.

place n endroit m, lieu m; (*house*) maison f; (*seat, rank*) place f; **at** or **to my ~** chez moi; **change ~s** changer de place; **in the first ~** d'abord; **out of ~** déplacé; **take ~** avoir lieu. ● vt placer; (*order*) passer; (*remember*) situer; **be ~d** (*in race*) se placer. **~-mat** n set m.

placid a placide.

plagiarism n plagiat m. **plagiarize** vt/i plagier.

plague n (*bubonic*) peste f; (*epidemic*) épidémie f; (*of ants, locusts*) invasion f. ● vt harceler.

plaice n inv carrelet m.

plain a (*obvious*) clair; (*candid*)

franc; (simple) simple; (not pretty) sans beauté; (not patterned) uni; ~ **chocolate** chocolat *m* noir; **in** ~ **clothes** en civil. ● *adv* franchement. ● *n* plaine *f*.
plainly *adv* clairement; franchement; simplement.

plaintiff *n* plaignant/-e *m/f*.

plaintive *a* plaintif.

plait *vt* tresser. ● *n* natte *f*.

plan *n* projet *m*, plan *m*; (diagram) plan *m*. ● *vt* (*pt* **planned**) projeter (**to do** de faire); (timetable, day) organiser; (economy, work) planifier. ● *vi* prévoir; ~ **on** s'attendre à.

plane *n* (level) plan *m*; (aeroplane) avion *m*; (tool) rabot *m*. ● *a* plan. ● *vt* raboter.

planet *n* planète *f*.

plank *n* planche *f*.

planning *n* (of economy, work) planification *f*; (of holiday, party) organisation *f*; (of town) urbanisme *m*; **family** ~ **planning** *m* familial; ~ **permission** permis *m* de construire.

plant *n* plante *f*; (Tech) matériel *m*; (factory) usine *f*. ● *vt* planter; (bomb) placer.

plaster *n* plâtre *m*; (adhesive) sparadrap *m*. ● *vt* plâtrer; (cover) couvrir (**with** de).

plastic *a* en plastique; (art, substance) plastique; ~ **surgery** chirurgie *f* esthétique. ● *n* plastique *m*.

plate *n* assiette *f*; (of metal) plaque *f*; (silverware) argenterie *f*; (in book) gravure *f*. ● *vt* (metal) plaquer.

plateau *n* (*pl* ~**x**) plateau *m*; (fig) palier *m*.

platform *n* (stage) estrade *f*; (for speaking) tribune *f*; (Rail) quai *m*; (Pol) plate-forme *f*.

platoon *n* (Mil) section *f*.

play *vt/i* jouer; (instrument) jouer de; (record) mettre; (game) jouer

à; (opponent) jouer contre; (match) disputer; ~ **safe** ne pas prendre de risques. ● *n* jeu *m*; (Theat) pièce *f*. □ ~ **down** minimiser; ~ **on** (fears) exploiter; ~ **up** 🔢 commencer à faire des siennes 🔢; ~ **up sth** mettre l'accent sur qch.

playful *a* (remark) taquin; (child) joueur.

play: ~**ground** *n* cour *f* de récréation. ~**-group**, ~**-school** *n* garderie *f*.

playing *n* (Sport) jeu *m*; (Theat) interprétation *f*. ~**-card** *n* carte *f* à jouer. ~**-field** *n* terrain *m* de sport.

play: ~**-pen** *n* parc *m* (pour bébé). ~**wright** *n* auteur *m* dramatique.

plc *abbr* (**public limited company**) SA.

plea *n* (for mercy, tolerance) appel *m*; (for food, money) demande *f*; (reason) excuse *f*; **make a** ~ **of guilty** plaider coupable.

plead *vt/i* supplier; (Jur) plaider.

pleasant *a* agréable.

please *vt/i* plaire (à), faire plaisir (à); ~ **oneself, do as one** ~**s** faire ce qu'on veut. ● *adv* s'il vous or te plaît. **pleased** *a* content (**with** de). **pleasing** *a* agréable.

pleasure *n* plaisir *m*; **with** ~ avec plaisir; **my** ~ je vous en prie.

pleat *n* pli *m*. ● *vt* plisser.

pledge *n* (token) gage *m*; (promise) promesse *f*. ● *vt* promettre; (pawn) mettre en gage.

plentiful *a* abondant.

plenty *n* abondance *f*; ~ (**of**) (a great deal) beaucoup (de); (enough) assez (de).

pliers *npl* pinces *fpl*.

plight *n* détresse *f*.

plinth *n* socle *m*.

plod *vi* (*pt* **plodded**) avancer péniblement.

plonk *n* Ⓘ pinard *m* Ⓘ.

plot *n* (*conspiracy*) complot *m*; (of novel) intrigue *f*; ~ (**of land**) terrain *m*. ● *vt/i* (*pt plotted*) (plan) comploter; (mark out) tracer.

plough *n* charrue *f*. ● *vt/i* labourer. □ ~ **back** réinvestir; ~ **through** avancer péniblement dans.

plow *n* & *vt/i* (US) = PLOUGH.

ploy *n* stratagème *m*.

pluck *vt* (*flower, fruit*) cueillir; (*bird*) plumer; (*eyebrows*) épiler; (*strings*: Mus) pincer; ~ **up courage** prendre son courage à deux mains. **plucky** *a* courageux.

plug *n* (for sink) bonde *f*; (Electr) fiche *f*, prise *f*. ● *vt* (*pt plugged*) (*hole*) boucher; (publicize Ⓘ) faire du battage autour de. □ ~ **in** brancher. ~**-hole** *n* bonde *f*.

plum *n* prune *f*; ~ **pudding** (plum-)pudding *m*.

plumber *n* plombier *m*.

plume *n* (of feathers) panache *m*.

plummet *vi* tomber, plonger.

plump *a* potelé, dodu.

plunge *vt/i* (dive, thrust) plonger; (fall) tomber. ● *n* plongeon *m*; (fall) chute *f*; **take the** ~ se jeter à l'eau. **plunger** *n* (for sink) ventouse *f*.

plural *a* pluriel; (*noun*) au pluriel; (*ending*) du pluriel. ● *n* pluriel *m*.

plus *prep* plus; **ten** ~ plus de dix. ● *a* (Electr & fig) positif. ● *n* signe *m* plus; (fig) atout *m*.

ply *vt* (*tool*) manier; (*trade*) exercer. ● *vi* faire la navette; ~ **sb with drink** offrir continuellement à boire à qn.

plywood *n* contreplaqué *m*.

p.m. *adv* de l'après-midi *or* du soir.

pneumatic drill *n* marteau-piqueur *m*.

pneumonia *n* pneumonie *f*.

PO *abbr* ⇨POST OFFICE.

poach *vt/i* (*game*) braconner; (*staff*) débaucher; (Culin) pocher.

PO Box *n* boîte *f* postale.

pocket *n* poche *f*; **be out of** ~ avoir perdu de l'argent. ● *a* de poche. ● *vt* empocher. ~**-book** *n* (notebook) carnet *m*; (wallet: US) portefeuille *m*; (handbag: US) sac *m* à main. ~**-money** *n* argent *m* de poche.

pod *n* (peas) cosse *f*; (vanilla) gousse *f*.

podgy *a* (**-ier, -iest**) dodu.

poem *n* poème *m*. **poet** *n* poète *m*. **poetic** *a* poétique. **poetry** *n* poésie *f*.

point *n* (position) point *m*; (tip) pointe *f*; (decimal point) virgule *f*; (remark) remarque *f*; ~ **good** ~**s** qualités *fpl*; **on the** ~ **of** sur le point de; ~ **in time** moment *m*; ~ **of view** point *m* de vue; **to the** ~ pertinent; **what is the** ~? à quoi bon? ● *vt* (aim) braquer; (show) indiquer; ~ **out** signaler. ● *vi* indiquer du doigt; ~ **out that, make the** ~ **that** faire remarquer que. ~**-blank** *a* & *adv* à bout portant.

pointed *a* (sharp) pointu; (window) en pointe; (*remark*) lourd de sens.

pointless *a* inutile.

poise *n* (confidence) assurance *f*; (physical elegance) aisance *f*.

poison *n* poison *m*. ● *vt* empoisonner. **poisonous** *a* (*substance*) toxique; (*plant*) vénéneux; (*snake*) venimeux.

poke *vt/i* (push) pousser; (*fire*) tisonner; (thrust) fourrer; ~ **fun at** se moquer de. ● *n* (petit) coup *m*. □ ~ **out** (*head*) sortir.

poker *n* (for fire) tisonnier *m*; (cards) poker *m*.

Poland *n* Pologne *f*.

polar *a* polaire.

pole n (stick) perche f; (for flag) mât m; (Geog) pôle m.

Pole n Polonais/-e m/f.

pole-vault n saut m à la perche.

police n police f. ● vt faire la police dans. ~ **constable** n agent m de police. ~**man** n (pl -men) agent m de police. ~ **station** n commissariat m de police. ~**woman** n (pl -women) femme-agent f.

policy n politique f; (insurance) police f (d'assurance).

polish vt polir; (shoes, floor) cirer. ● n (for shoes) cirage m; (for floor) encaustique f; (for nails) vernis m; (shine) poli m; (fig) raffinement m. □ ~ **off** finir en vitesse. ~ **up** (language) perfectionner.

Polish a polonais. ● n (Ling) polonais m.

polished a raffiné.

polite a poli.

political a politique.

politician n homme m politique, femme f politique.

politics n politique f.

poll n (vote casting) scrutin m; (survey) sondage m; go to the ~s aller aux urnes. ● vt (votes) obtenir.

pollen n pollen m.

polling booth n isoloir m.

polling station n bureau m de vote.

pollution n pollution f.

polo n polo m. ~ **neck** n col m roulé.

pomegranate n grenade f.

pomp n pompe f.

pompous a pompeux.

pond n étang m; (artificial) bassin m; (stagnant) mare f.

ponder vt/i réfléchir (à), méditer (sur).

pong n (stink 🔲) puanteur f. ● vi 🔲 puer.

pony n poney m. ~**tail** n queue f de cheval.

poodle n caniche m.

pool n (puddle) flaque f; (pond) étang m; (of blood) mare f; (for swimming) piscine f; (fund) fonds m commun; (of ideas) réservoir m; (snooker) billard m américain; ~s pari m mutuel sur le football. ● vt mettre en commun.

poor a (not wealthy) pauvre; (not good) médiocre, mauvais.

poorly a malade. ● adv mal.

pop n (noise) pan m; (music) pop m. ● a pop inv. ● vt/i (pt popped) (burst) crever; (put) mettre; ~ in/ out/off entrer/sortir/partir. □ ~ up surgir.

pope n pape m.

poppy n pavot m; (wild) coquelicot m.

popular a populaire; (in fashion) en vogue; be ~ with plaire à.

population n population f.

porcelain n porcelaine f.

porcupine n porc-épic m.

pork n porc m

pornography n pornographie f.

port n (harbour) port m; (left: Naut) bâbord m; ~ **of call** escale f; (wine) porto m.

portable a portable.

porter n (carrier) porteur m; (door-keeper) portier m.

portfolio n (Pol, Comm) portefeuille m.

portion n (at meal) portion f; (part) partie f.

portrait n portrait m.

portray vt représenter.

Portugal n Portugal m.

Portuguese n (Ling) portugais m; (person) Portugais/-e m/f. ● a portugais.

P

pose vt/i poser; ~ **as** (expert) se poser en. ● n pose f.

poser n (person) frimeur/-euse m/f; (puzzle) colle f.

posh a ▣ chic inv.

position n position f; (job, state) situation f. ● vt placer.

positive a positif; (sure) sûr, certain; (real) réel, vrai.

possess vt posséder.

possession n possession f; take ~ **of** prendre possession de.

possessive a possessif.

possible a possible.

possibly adv peut-être; if I ~ **can** si cela m'est possible; I cannot ~ **leave** il m'est impossible de partir.

post n (pole) poteau m; (station, job) poste m; (mail service) poste f; (letters) courrier m. ● a postal. ● vt (letter) poster; **keep** ~ed tenir au courant; ~ **(up)** (a notice) afficher; (appoint) affecter.

postage n affranchissement m; tarif m postal.

postal a postal. ~ **order** n mandat m.

post: ~ **box** n boîte f aux lettres. ~ **card** n carte f postale. ~ **code** n code m postal.

poster n (for information) affiche f; (for decoration) poster m.

postgraduate n étudiant/-e m/f de troisième cycle.

posthumous a posthume.

post: ~ **man** n (pl -**men**) facteur m. ~ **mark** n cachet m de la poste.

post-mortem n autopsie f.

post office n poste f.

postpone vt remettre.

postscript n (to letter) post-scriptum m inv.

posture n posture f. ● vi prendre des poses.

pot n pot m; (drug ▣) hasch m; **go**

to ~ ▣ aller à la ruine; **take** ~ **luck** tenter sa chance. ● vt (plants) mettre en pot.

potato n (pl ~**es**) pomme f de terre.

pot-belly n bedaine f.

potential a & n potentiel (m).

pot-hole n (in rock) caverne f; (in road) nid m de poule. **pot-holing** n spéléologie f.

potter n potier m. ● vi bricoler.

pottery n (art) poterie f; (objects) poteries fpl.

potty a (-**ier**, -**iest**) (crazy ▣) toqué. ● n pot m.

pouch n poche f; (for tobacco) blague f.

poultry n volailles fpl.

pounce vi bondir (**on** sur). ● n bond m.

pound n (weight) livre f (= 454 g); (money) livre f; (for dogs, cars) fourrière f. ● vt (crush) piler; (bombard) pilonner. ● vi frapper fort; (of heart) battre fort; (walk) marcher à pas lourds.

pour vt verser. ● vi couler, ruisseler (**from** de); (rain) pleuvoir à torrents. □ ~ **in/out** (people) arriver/sortir en masse; ~ **off** or **out** vider. **pouring rain** n pluie f torrentielle.

pout vi faire la moue.

poverty n misère f, pauvreté f.

powder n poudre f. ● vt poudrer.

power n (strength) puissance f; (control) pouvoir m; (energy) énergie f; (Electr) courant m. ● vt (engine) faire marcher; (plane) propulser; ~ed by (engine) propulsé par; (generator) alimenté par. ~ **cut** n coupure f de courant.

powerful a puissant.

powerless a impuissant.

power: ~ **point** n prise f de courant. ~**-station** n centrale f électrique.

practical *a* pratique. ~ **joke** *n* farce *f*.

practice *n* (procedure) pratique *f*; (of profession) exercice *m*; (Sport) entraînement *m*; **in ~** (in fact) en pratique; (well-trained) en forme; **out of ~** rouillé; **put into ~** mettre en pratique.

practise *vt/i* (*musician, typist*) s'exercer (à); (Sport) s'entraîner (à); (put into practice) pratiquer; (*profession*) exercer.

praise *vt* faire l'éloge de; (*God*) louer. ● *n* éloges *mpl*, louanges *fpl*.

pram *n* landau *m*.

prance *vi* caracoler.

prawn *n* crevette *f* rose.

pray *vi* prier. **prayer** *n* prière *f*.

preach *vt/i* prêcher; ~ **at** *or* **to** prêcher.

precarious *a* précaire.

precaution *n* précaution *f*.

precede *vt* précéder.

precedence *n* (in importance) priorité *f*; (in rank) préséance *f*.

precedent *n* précédent *m*.

precinct *n* quartier *m* commerçant; (pedestrian area) zone *f* piétonne; (district: US) circonscription *f*.

precious *a* précieux.

precipitate *vt* (*person, event, chemical*) précipiter.

précis *n* résumé *m*.

precise *a* précis; (careful) méticuleux. **precision** *n* précision *f*.

precocious *a* précoce.

preconceived *a* préconçu.

predator *n* prédateur *m*.

predicament *n* situation *f* difficile.

predict *vt* prédire. **predictable** *a* prévisible. **prediction** *n* prédiction *f*.

predispose *vt* prédisposer (**to do** à faire).

predominant *a* prédominant.

pre-empt *vt* (anticipate) anticiper; (*person*) devancer.

preface *n* (to book) préface *f*; (to speech) préambule *m*.

prefect *n* (pupil) élève *m/f* chargé/-e de la discipline; (official) préfet *m*.

prefer *vt* (*pt* **preferred**) préférer (**to do** faire). **preferably** *adv* de préférence. **preference** *n* préférence *f*. **preferential** *a* préférentiel.

prefix *n* préfixe *m*.

pregnancy *n* grossesse *f*.

pregnant *a* (*woman*) enceinte; (*animal*) pleine; (*pause*) éloquent.

prehistoric *a* préhistorique.

prejudge *vt* (*issue*) préjuger de; (*person*) juger d'avance.

prejudice *n* préjugé(s) *m(pl)*; (harm) préjudice *m*. ● *vt* (*claim*) porter préjudice à; (*person*) léser. **prejudiced** *a* partial; (person) qui a des préjugés.

premature *a* prématuré.

premeditated *a* prémédité.

premises *npl* locaux *mpl*; **on the ~** sur les lieux.

premium *n* (*insurance*) prime *f*; **be at a ~** être précieux.

preoccupied *a* préoccupé.

preparation *n* préparation *f*; ~**s** préparatifs *mpl*.

preparatory *a* préparatoire. ~ **school** *n* école *f* primaire privée; (US) école *f* secondaire privée.

prepare *vt/i* (se) préparer (**for** à); **be ~d for** (expect) s'attendre à; ~**d to** prêt à.

preposition *n* préposition *f*.

preposterous *a* absurde, ridicule.

prep school n = PREPARATORY SCHOOL.

prerequisite n condition f préalable.

prescribe vt prescrire.

prescription n (Med) ordonnance f.

presence n présence f; ~ **of mind** présence f d'esprit.

present[1] a présent. ●n présent m; (gift) cadeau m; **at ~** à présent; **for the ~** pour le moment.

present[2] vt présenter; (film, concert) donner; ~ **sb with** offrir à qn. **presentation** n présentation f. **presenter** n présentateur/-trice m/f.

preservation n (of food) conservation f; (of wildlife) préservation f.

preservative n (Culin) agent m de conservation.

preserve vt préserver; (Culin) conserver. ●n réserve f; (fig) domaine m; (jam) confiture f.

presidency n présidence f.

president n président/-e m/f.

press vt/i (button) appuyer (sur); (squeeze) presser; (iron) repasser; (pursue) poursuivre; **be ~ed for** (time) manquer de; ~ **for sth** faire pression pour avoir qch; ~ **sb to do sth** pousser qn à faire qch; ~ **on** continuer (**with sth** qch). ●n (newspapers, machine) presse f; (for wine) pressoir m. ~ **cutting** n coupure f de presse.

pressing a pressant.

press: ~ **release** n communiqué m de presse. ~-**stud** n bouton-pression m. ~-**up** n pompe f.

pressure n pression f. ●vt faire pression sur. ~-**cooker** n cocotte-minute f. ~ **group** n groupe m de pression.

pressurize vt (cabin) pressuriser; (person) faire pression sur.

prestige n prestige m.

presumably adv vraisemblablement.

presume vt (suppose) présumer.

pretence, (US) **pretense** n feinte f, simulation f; (claim) prétention f; (pretext) prétexte m.

pretend vt/i faire semblant (**to do** de faire); ~ **to** (lay claim to) prétendre à.

pretentious a prétentieux.

pretext n prétexte m.

pretty a (-ier, -iest) joli. ●adv assez; ~ **much** presque.

prevail vi (be usual) prédominer; (win) prévaloir; ~ **on** persuader (**to do** de faire). **prevailing** a actuel; (wind) dominant.

prevalent a répandu.

prevent vt empêcher (**from doing** de faire). **prevention** n prévention f. **preventive** a préventif.

preview n avant-première f; (fig) aperçu m.

previous a précédent, antérieur; ~ **to** avant. **previously** adv auparavant.

prey n proie f; **bird of ~** rapace m. ●vi ~ **on** faire sa proie de; (worry) préoccuper.

price n prix m. ●vt fixer le prix de. **priceless** a inestimable; (amusing 🗵) impayable 🗵.

prick vt (with pin) piquer; ~ **up one's ears** dresser l'oreille. ●n piqûre f.

prickle n piquant m.

pride n orgueil m; (satisfaction) fierté f; ~ **of place** place f d'honneur. ●vpr ~ **oneself on** s'enorgueillir de.

priest n prêtre m.

prim a (primmer, primmest) guindé, méticuleux.

primarily adv essentiellement.

primary a (school, elections) primaire; (chief, basic) premier,

fondamental. ●*n* (Pol: US)
primaire *f*.

prime *a* principal, premier; (first-rate) excellent. ●*vt* (*pump, gun*)
amorcer; (*surface*) apprêter. **P~
Minister** *n* Premier Ministre *m*.

primitive *a* primitif.

primrose *n* primevère *f* (*jaune*).

prince *n* prince *m*. **princess** *n*
princesse *f*.

principal *a* principal. ●*n* (of
school) directeur/-trice *m/f*.

principle *n* principe *m*; **in/on ~**
en/par principe.

print *vt* imprimer; (write in capitals)
écrire en majuscules; **~ed matter**
imprimés *mpl*. ●*n* (of foot)
empreinte *f*; (letters) caractères
mpl; (photograph) épreuve *f*;
(engraving) gravure *f*; **in ~**
disponible; **out of ~** épuisé.
printer *n* (person) imprimeur *m*;
(Comput) imprimante *f*.

prion *n* prion *m*.

prior *a* précédent. ●*n* (Relig)
prieur *m*. **~ to** *prep* avant (de).

priority *n* priorité *f*; **take ~** avoir
la priorité (**over** sur).

prise *vt* forcer; **~ open** ouvrir en
forçant.

prison *n* prison *f*. **prisoner** *n*
prisonnier/-ière *m/f*. **~ officer** *n*
gardien/-ne *m/f* de prison.

pristine *a* **be in ~ condition** être
comme neuf.

privacy *n* intimité *f*, solitude *f*.

private *a* privé; (confidential)
personnel; (*lessons, house*)
particulier; (*ceremony*) intime; **in
~** en privé; (of ceremony) dans
l'intimité. ●*n* (soldier) simple
soldat *m*. **privately** *adv* en privé;
dans l'intimité; (inwardly)
intérieurement.

privilege *n* privilège *m*.
privileged *a* privilégié; **be ~d to**
avoir le privilège de.

prize *n* prix *m*. ●*vt* (value) priser.

pro *n* **the ~s and cons** le pour et
le contre.

probable *a* probable. **probably**
adv probablement.

probation *n* (testing) essai *m*; (Jur)
liberté *f* surveillée.

probe *n* (device) sonde *f*; (fig)
enquête *f*. ●*vt* sonder. ●*vi* **~
into** sonder.

problem *n* problème *m*. ●*a*
difficile. **problematic** *a*
problématique.

procedure *n* procédure *f*; (way of
doing sth) démarche *f* à suivre.

proceed *vi* (go) aller, avancer;
(pass) passer (**to** à); (act) procéder;
~ (with) continuer; **~ to do** se
mettre à faire.

proceedings *npl* (discussions)
débats *mpl*; (meeting) réunion *f*;
(report) actes *mpl*; (Jur) poursuites
fpl.

proceeds *npl* (profits) produit *m*,
bénéfices *mpl*.

process *n* processus *m*; (method)
procédé *m*; **in ~** en cours; **in the
~ of doing** en train de faire. ●*vt*
(*material, data*) traiter.

procession *n* défilé *m*.

procrastinate *vi* différer,
tergiverser.

procure *vt* obtenir.

prod *vt/i* (*pt* **prodded**) pousser
doucement. ●*n* petit coup *m*.

prodigy *n* prodige *m*.

produce[1] *n* produits *mpl*.

produce[2] *vt/i* produire; (bring out)
sortir; (show) présenter; (cause)
provoquer; (Theat, TV) mettre en
scène; (radio) réaliser; (cinema)
produire. **producer** *n* metteur *m*
en scène; réalisateur *m*;
producteur *m*.

product *n* produit *m*.

production *n* production *f*; (Theat,
TV) mise *f* en scène; (radio)
réalisation *f*.

P

productive *a* productif.
 productivity *n* productivité *f*.
profession *n* profession *f*.
professional *a* professionnel; (of
 high quality) de professionnel;
 (*person*) qui exerce une
 profession libérale. ● *n*
 professionnel/-le *m/f*.
professor *n* professeur *m*
 (*titulaire d'une chaire*).
proficient *a* compétent.
profile *n* (of face) profil *m*; (of body,
 mountain) silhouette *f*; (by journalist)
 portrait *m*.
profit *n* profit *m*, bénéfice *m*. ● *vi*
 ∼ **by** tirer profit de. **profitable** *a*
 rentable.
profound *a* profond.
profusely *adv* (*bleed*)
 abondamment; (*apologize*) avec
 effusion. **profusion** *n* profusion *f*.
program *n* (US) = PROGRAMME;
 (**computer**) ∼ programme *m*. ● *vt*
 (*pt* **programmed**) programmer.
programme *n* programme *m*;
 (broadcast) émission *f*.
programmer *n* programmeur/
 -euse *m/f*.
programming *n* (Comput)
 programmation *f*.
progress[1] *n* progrès *m*(*pl*); **in** ∼
 en cours; **make** ∼ faire des
 progrès; ∼ **report** compte-rendu
 m.
progress[2] *vi* (advance, improve)
 progresser.
progressive *a* progressif;
 (reforming) progressiste.
prohibit *vt* interdire (**sb from
 doing** à qn de faire).
project[1] *vt* projeter. ● *vi* (jut out)
 être en saillie.
project[2] *n* (plan) projet *m*;
 (undertaking) entreprise *f*; (School)
 dossier *m*.
projection *n* projection *f*; saillie
 f; (estimate) prévision *f*.

projector *n* projecteur *m*.
proliferate *vi* proliférer.
prolong *vt* prolonger.
prominent *a* (projecting)
 proéminent; (conspicuous) bien en
 vue; (fig) important.
promiscuous *a* de mœurs
 faciles.
promise *n* promesse *f*. ● *vt/i*
 promettre. **promising** *a*
 prometteur; (*person*) qui promet.
promote *vt* promouvoir; (advertise)
 faire la promotion de. **promotion**
 n promotion *f*.
prompt *a* rapide; (punctual) à
 l'heure, ponctuel. ● *adv* (on the
 dot) pile. ● *vt* inciter; (cause)
 provoquer; (Theat) souffler à. ● *n*
 (Comput) message *m* guide-
 opérateur. **prompter** *n* souffleur/
 -euse *m/f*. **promptly** *adv*
 rapidement; ponctuellement.
prone *a* ∼ **to** sujet à.
pronoun *n* pronom *m*.
pronounce *vt* prononcer.
 pronunciation *n* prononciation *f*.
proof *n* (evidence) preuve *f*; (test, trial
 copy) épreuve *f*; (of alcohol) teneur *f*
 en alcool. ● *a* ∼ **against** à
 l'épreuve de.
prop *n* support *m*; (Theat)
 accessoire *m*. ● *vt* (*pt* **propped**)
 ∼ (**up**) (support) étayer; (lean)
 appuyer.
propaganda *n* propagande *f*.
propel *vt* (*pt* **propelled**) (*vehicle,
 ship*) propulser; (*person*)
 pousser.
propeller *n* hélice *f*.
proper *a* correct, bon; (adequate)
 convenable; (real) vrai; (thorough ⊞)
 parfait. **properly** *adv*
 correctement, comme il faut;
 (adequately) convenablement.
proper noun *n* nom *m* propre.
property *n* (house) propriété *f*;
 (things owned) biens *mpl*, propriété
 f. ● *a* immobilier, foncier.

prophecy n prophétie f.

prophet n prophète m.

proportion n (ratio, dimension) proportion f; (amount) partie f.

proposal n proposition f; (of marriage) demande f en mariage.

propose vt proposer. ● vi faire une demande en mariage; ~ to do se proposer de faire.

proposition n proposition f; (matter ▣) affaire f. ● vt ▣ faire des propositions malhonnêtes à.

proprietor n propriétaire mf.

propriety n (correct behaviour) bienséance f.

prose n prose f; (translation) thème m.

prosecute vt poursuivre en justice. **prosecution** n poursuites fpl. **prosecutor** n procureur m.

prospect[1] n (outlook) perspective f; (chance) espoir m.

prospect[2] vt/i prospecter.

prospective a (future) futur; (possible) éventuel.

prospectus n brochure f; (Univ) livret m de l'étudiant.

prosperity n prospérité f. **prosperous** a prospère.

prostitute n prostituée f.

prostrate a (prone) à plat ventre; (exhausted) prostré.

protect vt protéger. **protection** n protection f. **protective** a protecteur; (clothes) de protection.

protein n protéine f.

protest[1] n protestation f; under ~ en protestant.

protest[2] vt/i protester.

Protestant a & n protestant/-e (m/f).

protester n manifestant/-e m/f.

protocol n protocole m.

protrude vi dépasser.

proud a fier, orgueilleux.

prove vt prouver. ● vi ~ (to be)

easy se révéler facile; ~ oneself faire ses preuves. **proven** a éprouvé.

proverb n proverbe m.

provide vt fournir (sb with sth qch à qn). ● vi ~ for (allow for) prévoir; (guard against) parer à; (person) pourvoir aux besoins de.

provided conj ~ that à condition que.

providing conj = PROVIDED.

province n province f; (fig) compétence f.

provision n (stock) provision f; (supplying) fourniture f; (stipulation) dispositions fpl; ~s (food) provisions fpl.

provisional a provisoire.

provocative a provocant.

provoke vt provoquer.

prow n proue f.

prowess n prouesses fpl.

prowl vi rôder.

proxy n by ~ par procuration.

prudish a pudibond, prude.

prune n pruneau m. ● vt (cut) tailler.

pry vi ~ into mettre son nez dans.

psalm n psaume m.

pseudonym n pseudonyme m.

psychiatric a psychiatrique. **psychiatrist** n psychiatre mf. **psychiatry** n psychiatrie f.

psychic a (phenomenon) métapsychique; (person) doué de télépathie.

psychoanalyse vt psychanalyser.

psychological a psychologique. **psychologist** n psychologue mf. **psychology** n psychologie f.

PTO abbr (please turn over) TSVP.

pub n pub m.

puberty n puberté f.

public a public; (*library*) municipal; **in ~** en public.

publican n patron/-ne m/f de pub.

publication n publication f.

public house n pub m.

publicity n publicité f.

publicize vt faire connaître au public.

public: **~ relations** n relations fpl publiques. **~ school** n école f privée; (US) école f publique. **~ transport** n transports mpl en commun.

publish vt publier. **publisher** n éditeur m. **publishing** n édition f.

pudding n dessert m; (steamed) pudding m.

puddle n flaque f d'eau.

puff n (of smoke) bouffée f; (of breath) souffle m. ● vt/i souffler. □ **~ at** (*cigar*) tirer sur. **~ out** (swell) (se) gonfler.

pull vt/i tirer; (*muscle*) se froisser; **~ a face** faire une grimace; **~ one's weight** faire sa part du travail; **~ sb's leg** faire marcher qn. ● n traction f; (fig) attraction f; (influence) influence f; **give a ~** tirer. □ **~ away** (Auto) démarrer; **~ back** or **out** (withdraw) (se) retirer; **~ down** (*building*) démolir; **~ in** (enter) entrer; (stop) s'arrêter; **~ off** enlever; (fig) réussir; **~ out** (from bag) sortir; (extract) arracher; (Auto) déboîter; **~ over** (Auto) se ranger (sur le côté); **~ through** s'en tirer; **~ oneself together** se ressaisir.

pull-down menu n (Comput) menu m déroulant.

pulley n poulie f.

pullover n pull(-over) m.

pulp n (of fruit) pulpe f; (for paper) pâte f à papier.

pulpit n chaire f.

pulsate vi battre.

pulse n (Med) pouls m.

pump n pompe f; (plimsoll) chaussure f de sport. ● vt/i pomper; (*person*) soutirer des renseignements à; **~ up** gonfler.

pumpkin n citrouille f.

pun n jeu m de mots.

punch vt donner un coup de poing à; (*ticket*) poinçonner. ● n coup m de poing; (vigour 🄸) punch m; (device) poinçonneuse f; (drink) punch m. **~-line** n chute f.

punctual a à l'heure; (habitually) ponctuel.

punctuation n ponctuation f.

puncture n crevaison f. ● vt/i crever.

pungent a âcre.

punish vt punir (**for sth** de qch). **punishment** n punition f.

punk n (music, fan) punk m; (US: 🄸) voyou m.

punt n (boat) barque f; (Irish pound) livre f irlandaise.

puny a (-ier, -iest) chétif.

pupil n (person) élève mf; (of eye) pupille f.

puppet n marionnette f.

puppy n chiot m.

purchase vt acheter (**from sb** à qn). ● n achat m.

pure a pur.

purgatory n purgatoire m.

purge vt purger (**of** de). ● n purge f.

purification n (of water, air) épuration f; (Relig) purification f.

purify vt épurer; purifier.

puritan n puritain/-e m/f.

purity n pureté f.

purple a & n violet (m).

purpose n but m; (determination) résolution f; **on ~** exprès; **to no ~** sans résultat.

purr n ronronnement m. ● vi ronronner.

purse n porte-monnaie m inv;

(handbag: US) sac *m* à main. ● *vt*
(*lips*) pincer.

pursue *vt* poursuivre.

pursuit *n* poursuite *f*; (hobby)
activité *f*, occupation *f*.

pus *n* pus *m*.

push *vt/i* pousser; (*button*)
appuyer sur; (thrust) enfoncer;
(recommend Ⓣ) proposer avec
insistance; **be ~ed for** (*time*)
manquer de; **be ~ing thirty**
Ⓣ friser la trentaine; **~ sb around**
bousculer qn. ● *n* poussée *f*;
(effort) gros effort *m*; (drive)
dynamisme *m*; **give the ~ to**
Ⓣ flanquer à la porte Ⓣ. □ **~ in**
resquiller; **~ on** continuer; **~ up**
(lift) relever; (*prices*) faire monter.

pushchair *n* poussette *f*.

pusher *n* revendeur/-euse *m/f*
(de drogue)

push-up *n* pompe *f*.

put *vt/i* (*pt* put; *pres p* putting)
mettre, placer, poser; (*question*)
poser; **~ the damage at a million**
estimer les dégâts à un million;
~ sth tactfully dire qch avec tact.
□ **~ across** communiquer; **~
away** ranger; (in hospital, prison)
enfermer; **~ back** (postpone)
remettre; (delay) retarder; **~
down** (dé)poser; (write) inscrire;
(pay) verser; (suppress) réprimer; **~
forward** (*plan*) soumettre; **~ in**
(insert) introduire; (fix) installer;
(submit) soumettre; **~ in for** faire
une demande de; **~ off** (postpone)
renvoyer à plus tard; (disconcert)
déconcerter; (displease) rebuter; **~
sb off sth** dégoûter
qn de qch; **~ on** (*clothes, radio*)
mettre; (*light*) allumer; (*accent,
weight*) prendre; **~ out** sortir;
(stretch) (é)tendre; (extinguish)
éteindre; (disconcert) déconcerter;
(inconvenience) déranger; **~ up**
lever, remonter; (*building*)
construire; (*notice*) mettre;

(*price*) augmenter; (*guest*)
héberger; (*offer*) offrir; **~ up with**
supporter.

putty *n* mastic *m*.

puzzle *n* énigme *f*; (game) casse-
tête *m inv*; (jigsaw) puzzle *m*. ● *vt*
rendre perplexe. ● *vi* se creuser
la tête.

pyjamas *npl* pyjama *m*.

pylon *n* pylône *m*.

quack *n* (of duck) coin-coin *m inv*;
(doctor) charlatan *m*.

quadrangle (of college) *n* cour *f*.

quadruple *a & n* quadruple (*m*).
● *vt/i* quadrupler.

quail *n* (bird) caille *f*.

quaint *a* pittoresque; (old) vieillot;
(odd) bizarre.

qualification *n* diplôme *m*;
(ability) compétence *f*; (fig) réserve
f, restriction *f*.

qualified *a* diplômé; (able)
qualifié (**to do** pour faire); (fig)
conditionnel.

qualify *vt* qualifier; (modify) mettre
des réserves à; (*statement*)
nuancer. ● *vi* obtenir son
diplôme (**as** de); (Sport) se
qualifier; **~ for** remplir les
conditions requises pour.

quality *n* qualité *f*.

qualm *n* scrupule *m*.

quantity *n* quantité *f*.

quarantine *n* quarantaine *f*.

quarrel *n* dispute *f*, querelle *f*.
● *vi* (*pt* quarrelled) se disputer.

quarry *n* (excavation) carrière *f*;
(prey) proie *f*. ● *vt* extraire.

quart $n \approx$ litre m.

quarter n quart m; (of year) trimestre m; (25 cents: US) quart m de dollar; (district) quartier m; $\sim$s logement m; **from all** $\sim$s de toutes parts. ● vt diviser en quatre; (*troops*) cantonner.

quarterly a trimestriel. ● adv tous les trois mois.

quartet n quatuor m.

quartz n quartz m. ● a (*watch*) à quartz.

quash vt (suppress) étouffer; (Jur) annuler.

quaver vi trembler, chevroter. ● n (Mus) croche f.

quay n (Naut) quai m.

queasy a **feel** $\sim$ avoir mal au cœur.

queen n reine f; (cards) dame f.

queer a étrange; (dubious) louche; ▣ homosexuel.

quench vt éteindre; (*thirst*) étancher; (*desire*) étouffer.

query n question f. ● vt mettre en question.

quest n recherche f.

question n question f; **in** $\sim$ en question; **out of the** $\sim$ hors de question. ● vt interroger; (doubt) mettre en question, douter de. $\sim$ **mark** n point m d'interrogation.

questionnaire n questionnaire m.

queue n queue f. ● vi (*pres p* **queuing**) faire la queue.

quibble vi ergoter.

quick a rapide; (clever) vif/vive; **be** $\sim$ (hurry) se dépêcher. ● adv vite. ● n **cut to the** $\sim$ piquer au vif.

quicken vt/i (s')accélérer.

quickly adv rapidement, vite. $\sim$**sand** n sables mpl mouvants.

quid n inv ▣ livre f sterling.

quiet a (calm, still) tranquille; (silent) silencieux; (gentle) doux; (discreet)

discret; **keep** $\sim$ se taire. ● n tranquillité f; **on the** $\sim$ en cachette. **quieten** vt/i (se) calmer. **quietly** adv (speak) doucement; (*sit*) en silence.

quilt n édredon m; (**continental**) $\sim$ couette f.

quirk n bizarrerie f.

quit vt (*pt* **quitted**) quitter; (*smoking*) arrêter de. ● vi abandonner; (resign) démissionner; $\sim$ **doing** (US) cesser de faire.

quite adv tout à fait, vraiment; (rather) assez; $\sim$ **a few** un bon nombre (de).

quits a quitte (**with** envers); **call it** $\sim$ en rester là.

quiver vi trembler.

quiz n (*pl* **quizzes**) test m; (game) jeu-concours m. ● vt (*pt* **quizzed**) questionner.

quotation n citation f; (price) devis m; (stock exchange) cotation f; $\sim$ **marks** guillemets mpl.

quote vt citer; (*reference, number*) rappeler; (*price*) indiquer; (*share price*) coter. ● vi $\sim$ **for** faire un devis pour; $\sim$ **from** citer. ● n (quotation) citation f; (estimate) devis m; **in** $\sim$**s** ▣ entre guillemets.

rabbi n rabbin m.

rabbit n lapin m.

rabies n (disease) rage f.

race n (contest) course f; (group) race f. ● a racial; $\sim$ **relations**

relations *fpl* inter-raciales. ● *vt* (compete with) faire la course avec; (*horse*) faire courir. ● *vi* courir; (*pulse*) battre précipitamment; (*engine*) s'emballer. ~**course** *n* champ *m* de courses. ~**horse** *n* cheval *m* de course. ~**track** *n* piste *f*; (for horses) champ *m* de courses.

racing *n* courses *fpl*; ~ **car** voiture *f* de course.

racism *n* racisme *m*. **racist** *a & n* raciste (*mf*).

rack *n* (shelf) étagère *f*; (for clothes) portant *m*; (for luggage) compartiment *m* à bagages; (for dishes) égouttoir *m*. ● *vt* ~ **one's brains** se creuser la cervelle.

racket *n* (Sport) raquette *f*; (noise) vacarme *m*; (swindle) escroquerie *f*; (crime) trafic *m*.

radar *n & a* radar (*m*).

radial *n* ~ (**tyre**) pneu *m* radial.

radiate *vt* (*happiness*) rayonner de; (*heat*) émettre. ● *vi* rayonner (from de). **radiation** *n* (radioactivity) radiation *f*. **radiator** *n* radiateur *m*.

radical *n & a* radical/-e (*m/f*).

radio *n* radio *f*; on the ~ à la radio. ● *vt* (*message*) envoyer par radio; (*person*) appeler par radio.

radioactive *a* radioactif.

radiographer *n* manipulateur/ -trice *m/f* radiographe.

radish *n* radis *m*.

radius *n* (*pl* -**dii**) rayon *m*.

raffle *n* tombola *f*.

rag *n* chiffon *m*; ~**s** loques *fpl*.

rage *n* rage *f*, colère *f*; **be all the** ~ faire fureur. ● *vi* (*person*) tempêter; (*storm, battle*) faire rage.

ragged *a* (*clothes*) en loques; (*person*) dépenaillé.

raid *n* (Mil, on stock market) raid *m*; (by police) rafle *f*; (by criminals) hold-up *m inv*. ● *vt* faire un raid

or une rafle or un hold-up dans. **raider** *n* (thief) pillard *m*; (Mil) commando *m*; (corporate) raider *m*.

rail *n* (on balcony) balustrade *f*; (stairs) rampe *f*; (for train) rail *m*; (for curtain) tringle *f*; **by** ~ par chemin de fer.

railing *n* (also ~**s**) grille *f*.

railway, (US) **railroad** *n* chemin *m* de fer. ~ **line** *n* voie *f* ferrée. ~ **station** *n* gare *f*.

rain *n* pluie *f*. ● *vi* pleuvoir. ~**bow** *n* arc-en-ciel *m*. ~**coat** *n* imperméable *m*. ~**fall** *n* précipitation *f*. ~ **forest** *n* forêt *f* tropicale.

rainy *a* (-**ier**, -**iest**) pluvieux; (*season*) des pluies.

raise *vt* (*barrier, curtain*) lever; (*child, cattle*) élever; (*question*) soulever; (*price, salary*) augmenter. ● *n* (US) augmentation *f*.

raisin *n* raisin *m* sec.

rake *n* râteau *m*. ● *vt* (*garden*) ratisser; (search) fouiller dans. □ ~ **in** (*money*) amasser; ~ **up** (*past*) remuer.

rally *vt/i* (se) rallier; (*strength*) reprendre; (after illness) aller mieux; ~ **round** venir en aide. ● *n* rassemblement *m*; (Auto) rallye *m*; (tennis) échange *m*.

ram *n* bélier *m*. ● *vt* (*pt* **rammed**) (thrust) enfoncer; (crash into) rentrer dans.

RAM *abbr* (**random access memory**) RAM *f*.

ramble *n* randonnée *f*. ● *vi* faire une randonnée. □ ~ **on** discourir.

ramp *n* (slope) rampe *f*; (in garage) pont *m* de graissage.

rampage[1] *vi* se déchaîner (**through** dans).

rampage[2] *n* **go on the** ~ tout saccager.

ran ⇒RUN.

R

rancid *a* rance.

random *a* (fait) au hasard. ●*n* at ∼ au hasard.

rang ⇒RING².

range *n* (of prices, products) gamme *f*; (of people, beliefs) variété *f*; (of radar, weapon) portée *f*; (of aircraft) autonomie *f*; (of mountains) chaîne *f*. ●*vi* aller; (vary) varier.

rank *n* rang *m*; (Mil) grade *m*. ●*vt/i* ∼ **among** (se) classer parmi.

ransack *vt* (search) fouiller; (pillage) mettre à sac.

ransom *n* rançon *f*.

rap *n* coup *m* sec; (Mus) rap *m*. ●*vi* (*pt* **rapped**) donner des coups secs (**on** sur).

rape *vt* violer. ●*n* viol *m*.

rapid *a* rapide.

rapist *n* violeur *m*.

rapturous *a* (*delight*) extasié; (*welcome*) enthousiaste.

rare *a* rare; (Culin) saignant.

rarely *adv* rarement.

rascal *n* coquin/-e *m/f*.

rash *n* (Med) rougeurs *fpl*. ●*a* irréfléchi.

raspberry *n* framboise *f*.

rat *n* rat *m*. ●*vi* (*pt* **ratted**) ∼ **on** (desert) lâcher; (inform on) dénoncer.

rate *n* (ratio, level) taux *m*; (speed) rythme *m*; (price) tarif *m*; (of exchange) taux *m*; **at any** ∼ en tout cas. ●*vt* (value) estimer; (deserve) mériter; ∼ **sth highly** admirer beaucoup qch. ●*vi* ∼ **as** être considéré comme.

rather *adv* (by preference) plutôt; (fairly) assez, plutôt; (a little) un peu; **I would** ∼ **go** j'aimerais mieux partir; ∼ **than go** plutôt que de partir.

rating *n* (score, value) cote *f*; **the** ∼**s** (TV) l'indice *m* d'écoute, l'audimat® *m*.

ratio *n* proportion *f*.

ration *n* ration *f*. ●*vt* rationner.

rational *a* rationnel; (*person*) sensé.

rationalize *vt* justifier; (organize) rationaliser.

rattle *vi* (*bottles, chains*) s'entrechoquer; (*window*) vibrer. ●*vt* (*bottles, chains*) faire s'entrechoquer; (fig, 🔲) énerver. ●*n* cliquetis *m*; (toy) hochet *m*. ∼**snake** *n* serpent *m* à sonnette, crotale *m*.

rave *vi* (enthuse) s'emballer; (in fever) délirer; (in anger) tempêter.

raven *n* corbeau *m*.

ravenous *a* **be** ∼ avoir une faim de loup.

ravine *n* ravin *m*.

raving *a* ∼ **lunatic** fou *m* furieux, folle *f* furieuse.

ravishing *a* ravissant.

raw *a* cru; (not processed) brut; (*wound*) à vif; (immature) inexpérimenté; **get a** ∼ **deal** être mal traité; ∼ **material** matière *f* première.

ray *n* (of light) rayon *m*; ∼ **of hope** lueur *f* d'espoir.

razor *n* rasoir *m*. ∼**-blade** *n* lame *f* de rasoir.

re *prep* au sujet de; (at top of letter) objet.

reach *vt* (*place, level*) atteindre; (*decision*) arriver à; (contact) joindre; (*audience, market*) toucher. ●*vi* ∼ **up/down** lever/ baisser le bras; ∼ **across** étendre le bras. ●*n* portée *f*; **within** ∼ **of** à portée de; (close to) à proximité de.

react *vi* réagir. **reaction** *n* réaction *f*. **reactor** *n* réacteur *m*.

read *vt/i* (*pt* **read**) lire; (study) étudier; (*instrument*) indiquer; ∼ **about sb** lire quelque chose sur qn; ∼ **out** lire à haute voix. **reader** *n* lecteur/-trice *m/f*.

reading *n* lecture *f*; (measurement)

indication *f*; (interpretation) interprétation *f*.

readjust *vt* rajuster. ●*vi* se réadapter (**to** à).

read-only memory, ROM *n* mémoire *f* morte.

ready *a* (**-ier, -iest**) prêt; (quick) prompt. ~**-made** *a* tout fait. ~**-to-wear** *a* prêt-à-porter.

real *a* (not imaginary) véritable, réel; (not artificial) vrai; **it's a ~ shame** c'est vraiment dommage. ~ **estate** *n* biens *mpl* immobiliers.

realism *n* réalisme *m*. **realistic** *a* réaliste.

reality *n* réalité *f* ~ **TV** *n* télé-réalité *f*.

realize *vt* se rendre compte de, comprendre; (fulfil, turn into cash) réaliser; (price) atteindre.

really *adv* vraiment.

reap *vt* (crop) recueillir; (benefits) récolter.

reappear *vi* reparaître.

rear *n* arrière *m*; (of person) derrière *m* ⟨Ⅱ⟩. ●*a* (seat) arrière *inv*; (entrance) de derrière. ●*vt* élever. ●*vi* (horse) se cabrer. ~**-view mirror** *n* rétroviseur *m*.

reason *n* raison *f* (**to do, for doing** de faire); **within ~** dans la limite du raisonnable.

reasonable *a* raisonnable.

reassurance *n* réconfort *m*.

reassure *vt* rassurer.

rebate *n* (refund) remboursement *m*; (discount) remise *f*.

rebel[1] *n & a* rebelle (*mf*).

rebel[2] *vi* (*pt* **rebelled**) se rebeller. **rebellion** *n* rébellion *f*.

rebound[1] *vi* rebondir; ~ **on** (backfire) se retourner contre.

rebound[2] *n* *n* rebond *m*.

rebuke *vt* réprimander. ●*n* réprimande *f*.

recall *vt* (remember) se souvenir de; (call back) rappeler. ●*n*

(memory) mémoire *f*; (Comput, Mil) rappel *m*.

recap *vt/i* (*pt* **recapped**) récapituler. ●*n* récapitulation *f*.

recede *vi* s'éloigner; **his hair is receding** son front se dégarnit.

receipt *n* (written) reçu *m*; (of letter) réception *f*; ~**s** (Comm) recettes *fpl*.

receive *vt* recevoir; (stolen goods) receler. **receiver** *n* (telephone) combiné *m*; (TV) récepteur *m*.

recent *a* récent. **recently** *adv* récemment.

receptacle *n* récipient *m*.

reception *n* réception *f*; **give sb a warm ~** donner un accueil chaleureux à qn.

recess *n* (alcove) alcôve *m*; (for door) embrasure *f*; (Jur, Pol) vacances *fpl*; (School, US) récréation *f*.

recession *n* récession *f*.

recharge *vt* recharger.

recipe *n* recette *f*.

recipient *n* (of honour) récipiendaire *mf*; (of letter) destinataire *mf*.

reciprocate *vt* (compliment) retourner; (kindness) payer de retour. ●*vi* en faire autant.

recite *vt* réciter.

reckless *a* imprudent.

reckon *vt/i* calculer; (judge) considérer; (think) penser; ~ **on/with** compter sur/avec.

reckoning *n* (guess) estimation *f*; (calculation) calculs *mpl*.

reclaim *vt* récupérer; (flooded land) assécher.

recline *vi* s'allonger; (seat) s'incliner.

recluse *n* reclus/-e *m/f*.

recognition *n* reconnaissance *f*; **beyond ~** méconnaissable; **gain ~** être reconnu.

recognize *vt* reconnaître.

R

recollect *vt* se souvenir de, se rappeler. **recollection** *n* souvenir *m*.

recommend *vt* recommander. **recommendation** *n* recommandation *f*.

reconcile *vt* (*people*) réconcilier; (*facts*) concilier; ~ **oneself to** se résigner à.

recondition *vt* remettre à neuf.

reconsider *vt* réexaminer. ● *vi* réfléchir.

reconstruct *vt* reconstruire; (*crime*) faire une reconstitution de.

record¹ *vt/i* (in register, on tape) enregistrer; (in diary) noter; ~ **that** rapporter que.

record² *n* (of events) compte-rendu *m*; (official) procès-verbal *m*; (personal, administrative) dossier *m*; (historical) archives *fpl*; (past history) réputation *f*; (Mus) disque *m*; (Sport) record *m*; (criminal) ~ casier *m* judiciaire; **off the** ~ officieusement. ● *a* record *inv*.

recorder *n* (Mus) flûte *f* à bec.

recording *n* enregistrement *m*.

record-player *n* tourne-disque *m*.

recover *vt* récupérer. ● *vi* se remettre; (*economy*) se redresser. **recovery** *n* (Med) rétablissement *m*; (of economy) relance *f*.

recreation *n* récréation *f*.

recruit *n* recrue *f*. ● *vt* recruter. **recruitment** *n* recrutement *m*.

rectangle *n* rectangle *m*.

rectify *vt* rectifier.

recuperate *vt* récupérer. ● *vi* se rétablir.

recur *vi* (*pt* **recurred**) se reproduire.

recycle *vt* recycler.

red *a* (**redder, reddest**) rouge; (*hair*) roux. ● *n* rouge *m*; **in the** ~

en déficit. **R~ Cross** *n* Croix-Rouge *f*. ~**currant** *n* groseille *f*.

redecorate *vt* repeindre, refaire.

redeploy *vt* réorganiser; (*troops*) répartir.

red: ~**-handed** *a* en flagrant délit. ~**-hot** *a* brûlant.

redirect *vt* (*traffic*) dévier; (*letter*) faire suivre.

redness *n* rougeur *f*.

redo *vt* (*pt* **-did**; *pp* **-done**) refaire.

redress *vt* (*wrong*) redresser; (*balance*) rétablir. ● *n* réparation *f*.

reduce *vt* réduire; (*temperature*) faire baisser. **reduction** *n* réduction *f*.

redundancy *n* licenciement *m*.

redundant *a* superflu; (*worker*) licencié; **make** ~ licencier.

reed *n* (plant) roseau *m*.

reef *n* récif *m*, écueil *m*.

reel *n* (of thread) bobine *f*; (of film) bande *f*; (winding device) dévidoir *m*. ● *vi* chanceler. ● *vt* ~ **off** réciter.

refectory *n* réfectoire *m*.

refer *vt/i* (*pt* **referred**) ~ **to** (allude to) faire allusion à; (concern) s'appliquer à; (consult) consulter; (direct) renvoyer à.

referee *n* (Sport) arbitre *m*. ● *vt* (*pt* **refereed**) arbitrer.

reference *n* référence *f*; (mention) allusion *f*; (person) personne *f* pouvant fournir des références; **in** *or* **with** ~ **to** en ce qui concerne; (Comm) suite à.

referendum *n* (*pl* ~**s**) référendum *m*.

refill¹ *vt* (*glass*) remplir à nouveau; (*pen*) recharger.

refill² *n* recharge *f*.

refine *vt* raffiner.

reflect *vt* refléter; (*heat, light*) renvoyer. ● *vi* réfléchir (on à); ~

well/badly on sb faire honneur/du tort à qn.

reflection n réflexion f; (image) reflet m; **on** ∼ à la réflexion.

reflective a (surface) réfléchissant; (person) réfléchi.

reflector n (on car) catadioptre m.

reflex a & n réflexe (m).

reflexive a (Gram) réfléchi.

reform vt réformer. ● vi (person) s'amender. ● n réforme f.

refrain n refrain m. ● vi s'abstenir (**from** de).

refresh vt (drink) rafraîchir; (rest) reposer. **refreshments** npl rafraîchissements mpl.

refrigerate vt réfrigérer. **refrigerator** n réfrigérateur m.

refuel vt/i (pt refuelled) (se) ravitailler.

refuge n refuge m; **take** ∼ se réfugier. **refugee** n réfugié/-e m/f.

refund¹ vt rembourser.

refund² n remboursement m

refurbish vt remettre à neuf.

refuse¹ vt/i refuser.

refuse² n ordures fpl.

regain vt retrouver; (lost ground) regagner.

regard vt considérer; **as** ∼s en ce qui concerne. ● n égard m, estime f; **in this** ∼ à cet égard; ∼s amitiés fpl. **regarding** prep en ce qui concerne.

regardless adv malgré tout; ∼ **of** sans tenir compte de.

regime n régime m.

regiment n régiment m.

region n région f; **in the** ∼ **of** environ.

register n registre m. ● vt (record) enregistrer; (vehicle) faire immatriculer; (birth) déclarer; (letter) recommander; (indicate) indiquer; (express) exprimer. ● vi

(enrol) s'inscrire; (at hotel) se présenter; (fig) être compris.

registrar n officier m de l'état civil; (Univ) responsable m du bureau de la scolarité.

registration n (of voter, student) inscription f; (of birth) déclaration f; ∼ (**number**) (Auto) numéro m d'immatriculation.

registry office n bureau m de l'état civil.

regret n regret m. ● vt (pt **regretted**) regretter (**to do** de faire). **regretfully** adv à regret.

regular a régulier; (usual) habituel. ● n habitué/-e m/f. **regularity** n régularité f. **regularly** adv régulièrement.

regulate vt régler. **regulation** n (rule) règlement m; (process) réglementation f.

rehabilitate vt (in public esteem) réhabiliter; (prisoner) réinsérer.

rehearsal n répétition f. **rehearse** vt/i répéter.

reign n règne m. ● vi régner (**over** sur).

reimburse vt rembourser.

reindeer n inv renne m.

reinforce vt renforcer. **reinforcement** n renforcement m; ∼s renforts mpl.

reinstate vt (person) réintégrer; (law) rétablir.

reject¹ n marchandise f de deuxième choix.

reject² vt (offer, plea) rejeter; (goods) refuser. **rejection** n (personal) rejet m; (of candidate, work) refus m.

rejoice vi se réjouir.

relapse n rechute f. ● vi rechuter; ∼ **into** retomber dans.

relate vt raconter; (associate) associer. ● vi ∼ **to** se rapporter à; (get on with) s'entendre avec. **related** a (ideas) lié; **we are** ∼**d** nous sommes parents.

R

relation n rapport m; (person) parent/-e m/f. **relationship** n relations fpl; (link) rapport m.

relative n parent/-e m/f. ● a relatif; (respective) respectif.

relax vt (grip) relâcher; (muscle) décontracter; (discipline) assouplir. ● vi (person) se détendre; (grip) se relâcher. **relaxation** n détente f. **relaxing** a délassant.

relay[1] n (also ~ race) course f de relais.

relay[2] vt relayer.

release vt (prisoner) libérer; (fastening) faire jouer; (object, hand) lâcher; (film) faire sortir; (news) publier. ● n libération f; (of film) sortie f; (new record, film) nouveauté f.

relevance n pertinence f, intérêt m.

relevant a pertinent; **be ~ to** avoir rapport à.

reliability n (of firm) sérieux m; (of car) fiabilité f; (of person) honnêteté f. **reliable** a (firm) sérieux; (person, machine) fiable.

reliance n dépendance f.

relic n vestige m; (object) relique f.

relief n soulagement m (from à); (assistance) secours m; (outline) relief m; ~ **road** route f de délestage.

relieve vt soulager; (help) secourir; (take over from) relayer.

religion n religion f. **religious** a religieux.

relish n plaisir m; (Culin) condiment m. ● vt (food) savourer; (idea) se réjouir de.

relocate vt muter. ● vi (company) déménager; (worker) être muté.

reluctance n répugnance f.

reluctant a (person) peu enthousiaste; (consent) accordé à contrecœur; ~ **to** peu disposé à.

reluctantly adv à contrecœur.

rely vi ~ **on** (count) compter sur; (be dependent) dépendre de.

remain vi rester. **remainder** n reste m.

remand vt mettre en détention provisoire. ● n **on** ~ en détention provisoire.

remark n remarque f. ● vt remarquer. ● vi ~ **on** faire des remarques sur. **remarkable** a remarquable.

remedy n remède m. ● vt remédier à.

remember vt se souvenir de, se rappeler; ~ **to do** ne pas oublier de faire. **remembrance** n souvenir m.

remind vt rappeler (sb of sth qch à qn); ~ **sb to do** rappeler à qn de faire. **reminder** n rappel m.

reminisce vi évoquer ses souvenirs.

remission n (Med) rémission f; (Jur) remise f.

remnant n reste m; (trace) vestige m; (of cloth) coupon m.

remodel vt (pt **remodelled**) remodeler.

remorse n remords m.

remote a (place, time) lointain; (person) distant; (slight) vague; ~ **control** télécommande f.

removable a amovible.

removal n (of employee) renvoi m; (of threat) suppression f; (of troops) retrait m; (of stain) détachage m; (from house) déménagement m; ~ **men** déménageurs mpl.

remove vt enlever; (dismiss) renvoyer; (do away with) supprimer; (Comput) effacer.

remunerate vt rémunérer. **remuneration** n rémunération f.

render vt rendre.

renegade n renégat/-e m/f.

renew vt renouveler; (resume) reprendre. **renewable** a renouvelable.

renounce vt renoncer à; (disown) renier.

renovate vt rénover.

renown n renommée f.

rent n loyer m. ● vt louer; **for ~** à louer. **rental** n prix m de location.

reopen vt/i rouvrir.

reorganize vt réorganiser.

rep n (Comm) représentant/-e m/f.

repair vt réparer. ● n réparation f; **in good/bad ~** en bon/mauvais état.

repatriate vt rapatrier. **repatriation** n rapatriement m.

repay vt (pt **repaid**) rembourser; (reward) récompenser. **repayment** n remboursement m.

repeal vt abroger. ● n abrogation f.

repeat vt/i répéter; (renew) renouveler; **~ itself, ~ oneself** se répéter. ● n répétition f; (broadcast) reprise f.

repel vt (pt **repelled**) repousser.

repent vi se repentir (**of** de).

repercussion n répercussion f.

repetition n répétition f.

replace vt (put back) remettre; (take the place of) remplacer.

replacement n remplacement m (**of** de); (person) remplaçant/-e m/f; (new part) pièce f de rechange.

replay n (Sport) match m rejoué; (recording) répétition f immédiate.

replenish vt (refill) remplir; (renew) renouveler.

replica n copie f exacte.

reply vt/i répondre. ● n réponse f.

report vt rapporter, annoncer (**that** que); (notify) signaler; (denounce) dénoncer. ● vi faire un rapport; **~ (on)** (news item) faire un reportage sur; **~ to** (go) se présenter chez. ● n rapport m; (in press) reportage m; (School) bulletin m. **reporter** n reporter m.

repossess vt reprendre.

represent vt représenter.

representation n représentation f; **make ~s to** protester auprès de.

representative a représentatif, typique (**of** de). ● n représentant/ -e m/f.

repress vt réprimer.

reprieve n (delay) sursis m; (pardon) grâce f. ● vt accorder un sursis à; gracier.

reprimand vt réprimander. ● n réprimande f.

reprisals npl représailles fpl.

reproach vt reprocher (**sb for sth** qch à qn). ● n reproche m.

reproduce vt/i (se) reproduire. **reproduction** n reproduction f. **reproductive** a reproducteur.

reptile n reptile m.

republic n république f. **republican** a & n républicain/-e (m/f).

repudiate vt répudier; (contract) refuser d'honorer.

reputable a honorable, de bonne réputation.

reputation n réputation f.

repute n réputation f.

request n demande f. ● vt demander (**of, from** à).

require vt (of thing) demander; (of person) avoir besoin de; (demand, order) exiger. **required** a requis. **requirement** n exigence f; (condition) condition f (requise).

rescue vt sauver. ● n sauvetage m (**of** de); (help) secours m.

research n recherche(s) f(pl). ● vt/i faire des recherches (sur). **researcher** n chercheur/-euse m/f.

R

resemblance n ressemblance f.
resemble vt ressembler à.

resent vt être indigné de, s'offenser de. **resentment** n ressentiment m.

reservation n (doubt) réserve f; (booking) réservation f; (US) réserve f (indienne); **make a ~** réserver.

reserve vt réserver. ● n (stock, land) réserve f; (Sport) remplaçant/-e m/f; **in ~** en réserve; **the ~s** (Mil) les réserves fpl. **reserved** a (person, room) réservé.

reshuffle vt (Pol) remanier. ● n (Pol) remaniement m (ministériel).

residence n résidence f; (of students) foyer m; **in ~** (doctor) résidant.

resident a résidant; **be ~** résider. ● n habitant/-e m/f; (foreigner) résident/-e m/f; (in hotel) pensionnaire mf. **residential** a résidentiel.

resign vt abandonner; (job) démissionner de. ● vi démissionner; **~ oneself to** se résigner à. **resignation** n résignation f; (from job) démission f. **resigned** a résigné.

resilience n élasticité f; ressort m.

resin n résine f.

resist vt/i résister (à). **resistance** n résistance f. **resistant** a (Med) rebelle; (metal) résistant.

resolution n résolution f.

resolve vt résoudre (**to do** de faire). ● n résolution f.

resort vi **~ to** avoir recours à. ● n (recourse) recours m; (place) station f; **in the last ~** en dernier ressort.

resource n ressource f; **~s** (wealth) ressources fpl.
resourceful a ingénieux.

respect n respect m; (aspect) égard m; **with ~ to** à l'égard de, relativement à. ● vt respecter.

respectability n respectabilité f.
respectable a respectable.

respectful a respectueux.

respective a respectif.

respite n répit m.

respond vi répondre (**to** à); **~ to** (react to) réagir à. **response** n réponse f.

responsibility n responsabilité f.
responsible a responsable; (job) qui comporte des responsabilités.

responsive a réceptif.

rest vt/i (se) reposer; (lean) (s')appuyer (**on** sur); (be buried, lie) reposer; (remain) demeurer. ● n repos m; (support) support m; **have a ~** se reposer; **the ~** (remainder) le reste (**of** de); (other people) les autres.

restaurant n restaurant m.

restless a agité.

restoration n rétablissement m; restauration f.

restore vt rétablir; (building) restaurer; **~ sth to sb** restituer qch à qn.

restrain vt contenir; **~ sb from** retenir qn de. **restrained** a (moderate) mesuré; (in control of self) maître de soi.

restrict vt restreindre.

rest room n (US) toilettes fpl.

result n résultat m. ● vi résulter; **~ in** aboutir à.

resume vt/i reprendre.

résumé n résumé m; (of career: US) CV m, curriculum vitae m.

resurrect vt ressusciter.

resuscitate vt réanimer.

retail n détail m. ● a & adv au détail. ● vt/i (se) vendre (au détail). **retailer** n détaillant/-e m/f.

retain vt (hold back, remember) retenir; (keep) conserver.

retaliate vi riposter. **retaliation** n représailles fpl.

retch vi avoir un haut-le-cœur.

retire vi (from work) prendre sa retraite; (withdraw) se retirer; (go to bed) se coucher. **retired** a retraité. **retirement** n retraite f.

retort vt/i répliquer. ● n réplique f.

retrace vt ~ one's steps revenir sur ses pas.

retract vt/i (se) rétracter.

retrain vt/i (se) recycler.

retreat vi (Mil) battre en retraite. ● n retraite f.

retrieval n (Comput) extraction f.

retrieve vt (object) récupérer; (situation) redresser; (data) extraire.

retrospect n in ~ rétrospectivement.

return vi (come back) revenir; (go back) retourner; (go home) rentrer. ● vt (give back) rendre; (bring back) rapporter; (send back) renvoyer; (put back) remettre. ● n retour m; (yield) rapport m; ~s (Comm) bénéfices mpl; in ~ for en échange de. ~ **ticket** n aller-retour m.

reunion n réunion f.

reunite vt réunir.

rev n (Auto 🔟) tour m. ● vt/i (pt **revved**) ~ (**up**) (engine 🔟) (s')emballer.

reveal vt révéler; (allow to appear) laisser voir.

revelation n révélation f.

revenge n vengeance f. ● vt venger.

revenue n revenu m.

reverberate vi (sound, light) se répercuter.

reverend a révérend.

reversal n renversement m; (of view) revirement m.

reverse a contraire, inverse. ● n contraire m; (back) revers m, envers m; (gear) marche f arrière. ● vt (situation, bracket) renverser; (order) inverser; (decision) annuler; ~ **the charges** appeler en PCV. ● vi (Auto) faire marche arrière.

review n (inspection, magazine) revue f; (of book) critique f. ● vt passer en revue; (situation) réexaminer; faire la critique de. **reviewer** n critique m.

revise vt réviser; (text) revoir. **revision** n révision f.

revival n (of economy) reprise f; (of interest) regain m.

revive vt (person, hopes) ranimer; (custom) rétablir. ● vi se ranimer.

revoke vt révoquer.

revolt vt/i (se) révolter. ● n révolte f. **revolting** a dégoûtant.

revolution n révolution f.

revolve vi tourner.

revolver n revolver m.

revolving door n porte f à tambour.

reward n récompense f. ● vt récompenser (**for** de). **rewarding** a rémunérateur; (worthwhile) qui (en) vaut la peine.

rewind vt (pt **rewound**) rembobiner.

rewire vt refaire l'installation électrique de.

rhetorical a (de) rhétorique; (question) de pure forme.

rheumatism n rhumatisme m.

rhinoceros n (pl ~es) rhinocéros m.

rhubarb n rhubarbe f.

rhyme n rime f; (poem) vers mpl. ● vt/i (faire) rimer.

rhythm n rythme m. **rhythmic-(al)** a rythmique.

R

rib n côte f.

ribbon n ruban m; **in ~s** en lambeaux.

rice n riz m. **~ pudding** n riz m au lait.

rich a riche.

rid vt (pt **rid**; pres p **ridding**) débarrasser (**of** de); **get ~ of** se débarrasser de.

ridden ⇒RIDE.

riddle n énigme f. ● vt **~ with** (bullets) cribler de; (mistakes) bourrer de.

ride vi (pt **rode**; pp **ridden**) aller (à bicyclette, à cheval); (in car) rouler; (on a horse as sport) monter à cheval. ● vt (a particular horse) monter; (distance) parcourir. ● n promenade f, tour m; (distance) trajet m; **give sb a ~** (US) prendre qn en voiture; **go for a ~** aller faire un tour (à bicyclette, à cheval). **rider** n cavalier/-ière m/ f; (in horse race) jockey m; (cyclist) cycliste mf; (motorcyclist) motocycliste mf.

ridge n arête f, crête f.

ridiculous a ridicule.

riding n équitation f.

rifle n fusil m. ● vt (rob) dévaliser.

rift n (crack) fissure f; (between people) désaccord m.

rig vt (pt **rigged**) (equip) équiper; (election, match) truquer. ● n (for oil) derrick m. □ **~ out** habiller; **~ up** (arrange) arranger.

right a (morally) bon; (fair) juste; (best) bon, qu'il faut; (not left) droit; **be ~** (person) avoir raison (**to** de); (calculation, watch) être exact; **put ~** arranger, rectifier. ● n (entitlement) droit m; (not left) droite f; (not evil) le bien; **be in the ~** avoir raison; **on the ~** à droite. ● vt (a wrong, sth fallen) redresser. ● adv (not left) à droite; (directly) tout droit; (exactly) bien, juste; (completely) tout (à fait); **~ away** tout de suite; **~ now**

(at once) tout de suite; (at present) en ce moment.

righteous a vertueux.

rightful a légitime.

right-handed a droitier.

rightly adv correctement; (with reason) à juste titre.

right of way n (Auto) priorité f.

right wing a de droite.

rigid a rigide.

rigorous a rigoureux.

rim n bord m.

rind n (on cheese) croûte f; (on bacon) couenne f; (on fruit) écorce f.

ring[1] n (hoop) anneau m; (jewellery) bague f; (circle) cercle m; (boxing) ring m; (wedding) ~ alliance f. ● vt entourer; (word in text) entourer d'un cercle.

ring[2] vt/i (pt **rang**; pp **rung**) sonner; (of words) retentir; **~ the bell** sonner. ● n sonnerie f; **give sb a ~** donner un coup de fil à qn. □ **~ back** rappeler; **~ off** raccrocher; **~ up** téléphoner (à).

ring road n périphérique m.

rink n patinoire f.

rinse vt rincer; **~ out** rincer. ● n rinçage m.

riot n émeute f; (of colours) profusion f; **run ~** se déchaîner. ● vi faire une émeute.

rip vt/i (pt **ripped**) (se) déchirer; **let ~** (not check) laisser courir; **~ off** ⊠ rouler. ● n déchirure f.

ripe a mûr. **ripen** vt/i mûrir.

rip-off n ⊡ vol m; arnaque f ⊡.

ripple n ride f, ondulation f. ● vt/i (water) (se) rider.

rise vi (pt **rose**; pp **risen**) (go upwards, increase) monter, s'élever; (stand up, get up from bed) se lever; (rebel) se soulever; (sun) se lever; (water) monter; **~ up** se soulever. ● n (slope) pente f; (increase) hausse f; (in pay) augmentation f;

(progress, boom) essor m; **give ~ to** donner lieu à.

risk n risque m; **at ~** menacé. ●vt risquer; **~ doing** (venture) se risquer à faire. **risky** a risqué.

rite n rite m; **last ~s** derniers sacrements mpl.

rival n rival/-e m/f. ●a rival; (claim) opposé. ●vt (pt **rivalled**) rivaliser avec.

river n rivière f; (flowing into sea) fleuve m. ●a (fishing, traffic) fluvial.

rivet n (bolt) rivet m. ●vt (pt **riveted**) river, riveter.

Riviera n the (French) ~ la Côte d'Azur.

road n route f; (in town) rue f; (small) chemin m; **the ~ to** (glory; fig) le chemin de. ●a (sign, safety) routier. **~-map** n carte f routière. ~ **rage** n violence f au volant. **~worthy** a en état de marche.

roam vi errer. ●vt (streets, seas) parcourir.

roar n hurlement m; (of lion, wind) rugissement m; (of lorry, thunder) grondement m. ●vt/i hurler; (lion, wind) rugir; (lorry, thunder) gronder; **~ with laughter** rire aux éclats.

roast vt/i rôtir. ●n (meat) rôti m. ●a rôti. ~ **beef** n rôti m de bœuf.

rob vt (pt **robbed**) voler (**sb of sth** qch à qn); (bank, house) dévaliser; (deprive) priver (**of** de). **robber** n voleur/-euse m/f. **robbery** n vol m.

robe n (of judge) robe f; (dressing-gown) peignoir m.

robin n rouge-gorge m.

robot n robot m.

robust a robuste.

rock n roche f; (rock face, boulder) rocher m; (hurled stone) pierre f; (sweet) sucre m d'orge; (Mus) rock

m; **on the ~s** (drink) avec des glaçons; (marriage) en crise. ●vt/i (se) balancer; (shake) (faire) trembler; (child) bercer. **~-climbing** n varappe f.

rocket n fusée f.

rocking-chair n fauteuil m à bascule.

rocky a (-ier, -iest) (ground) rocailleux; (hill) rocheux; (shaky: fig) branlant.

rod n (metal) tige f; (wooden) baguette f; (for fishing) canne f à pêche.

rode ⇒RIDE.

roe n œufs mpl de poisson.

rogue n (dishonest) bandit m; (mischievous) coquin/-e m/f.

role n rôle m.

roll vt/i rouler; **~ (about)** (child, dog) se rouler; **be ~ing (in money)** 🄸 rouler sur l'or. ●n rouleau m; (list) liste f; (bread) petit pain m; (of drum, thunder) roulement m; (of ship) roulis m. □ **~ out** étendre, **~over** se retourner; **~ up** (sleeves) retrousser.

roll-call n appel m.

roller n rouleau m. **R~blade**® n patin m en ligne, roller m. **~-coaster** n montagnes fpl russes. **~-skate** n patin m à roulettes.

ROM (abbr) (**read-only memory**) mémoire f morte.

Roman a & n romain/-e (m/f). ~ **Catholic** a & n catholique (mf).

romance n (novel) roman m d'amour; (love) amour m; (affair) idylle f; (fig) poésie f.

Romania n Roumanie f.

Romanian a roumain. ●n (person) Roumain/-e m/f; (language) roumain m.

romantic a (love) romantique; (of the imagination) romanesque.

roof n toit m; (of mouth) palais m. ●vt recouvrir. **~-rack** n galerie f. **~-top** n toit m.

R

room n pièce f; (bedroom) chambre f; (large hall) salle f; (space) place f; ~ **for manoeuvre** marge f de manœuvre. ~**-mate** n camarade mf de chambre.

roomy a spacieux; (clothes) ample.

root n racine f; (source) origine f; take ~ prendre racine. ● vt/i (s')enraciner. □ ~ **about** fouiller; ~ **for** (US 🔟) encourager; ~ **out** extirper.

rope n corde f; know the ~s être au courant. ● vt attacher; ~ **in** (person) enrôler.

rose¹ n rose f. ● ⇒RISE.

rosé n rosé m.

rosy a (-ier, -iest) rose; (hopeful) plein d'espoir.

rot vt/i (pt rotted) pourrir.

rota n liste f (de service).

rotary a rotatif.

rotate vt/i (faire) tourner; (change round) alterner.

rotten a pourri; (tooth) gâté; (bad 🔟) mauvais, sale.

rough a (manners) rude; (to touch) rugueux; (ground) accidenté; (violent) brutal; (bad) mauvais; (estimate) approximatif. ● adv (live) à la dure.

roughage n fibres fpl.

roughly adv rudement; (approximately) à peu près.

round a rond. ● n (circle) rond m; (slice) tranche f; (of visits, drinks) tournée f; (competition) partie f, manche f; (boxing) round m; (of talks) série f; ~ **of applause** applaudissements mpl; go the ~s circuler. ● prep autour de; she lives ~ here elle habite par ici; ~ the clock vingt-quatre heures sur vingt-quatre. ● adv autour; ~ about (nearby) par ici; (fig) à peu près; go or come ~ to (a friend) passer chez; enough to go ~ assez pour tout le monde. ● vt (object) arrondir; (corner) tourner. □ ~ off terminer; ~ up rassembler

roundabout n (in fairground) manège m; (for traffic) rond-point m (à sens giratoire). ● a indirect.

round trip n voyage m aller-retour.

round-up n rassemblement m; (of suspects) rafle f.

route n itinéraire m, parcours m; (Naut, Aviat) route f.

routine n routine f. ● a de routine.

row¹ n rangée f, rang m; in a ~ (consecutive) consécutif. ● vi ramer; (Sport) faire de l'aviron. ● vt ~ **a boat up the river** remonter la rivière à la rame.

row² n (noise 🔟) tapage m; (quarrel 🔟) dispute f. ● vi 🔟 se disputer.

rowdy a (-ier, -iest) tapageur.

rowing n aviron m. ~**-boat** n bateau m à rames.

royal a royal. **royalty** n famille f royale; **royalties** droits mpl d'auteur.

RSI abbr (**repetitive strain injury**) TMS m, trouble m musculo-squelettique.

rub vt/i (pt rubbed) frotter; ~ **it in** insister, en rajouter. ● n friction f. □ ~ **out** (s')effacer.

rubber n caoutchouc m; (eraser) gomme f. ~ **band** n élastique m. ~ **stamp** n tampon m.

rubbish n (refuse) ordures fpl; (junk) saletés fpl; (fig) bêtises fpl.

rubble n décombres mpl.

ruby n rubis m.

rucksack n sac m à dos.

rude a impoli, grossier; (improper) indécent; (blow) brutal.

ruffle vt (hair) ébouriffer; (clothes) froisser; (person) contrarier. ● n (frill) ruche f.

rug n petit tapis m.

rugby n rugby m.

rugged a (*surface*) rude, rugueux; (*ground*) accidenté; (*character, features*) rude.

ruin n ruine f. ● vt (destroy) ruiner; (damage) abîmer; (spoil) gâter.

rule n règle f; (regulation) règlement m; (Pol) gouvernement m; **as a ∼** en règle générale. ● vt gouverner; (master) dominer; (decide) décider; **∼ out** exclure. ● vi régner. **ruler** n dirigeant/-e m/f, gouvernant m; (measure) règle f.

ruling a (*class*) dirigeant; (*party*) au pouvoir. ● n décision f.

rum n rhum m.

rumble vi gronder; (*stomach*) gargouiller. ● n grondement m; gargouillement m

rumour, (US) **rumor** n bruit m, rumeur f; **there's a ∼ that** le bruit court que.

rump n (of animal) croupe f; (of bird) croupion m; (steak) romsteck m.

run vi (pt **ran**; pp **run**; pres p **running**) courir; (flow) couler; (pass) passer; (function) marcher; (melt) fondre; (extend) s'étendre; (of bus) circuler; (of play) se jouer; (last) durer; (of colour in washing) déteindre; (in election) être candidat. ● vt (manage) diriger; (event) organiser; (risk, race) courir; (house) tenir; (temperature, errand) faire; (Comput) exécuter. ● n course f; (journey) parcours m; (outing) promenade f; (rush) ruée f; (series) série f; (for chickens) enclos m; (in cricket) point m; **in the long ∼** avec le temps; **on the ∼** en fuite. □ **∼ across** rencontrer par hasard; **∼ away** s'enfuir; **∼ down**

descendre en courant; (of vehicle) renverser; (*production*) réduire progressivement; (belittle) dénigrer; **∼ into** (hit) heurter; **∼ off** (*copies*) tirer; **∼ out** (be used up) s'épuiser; (of lease) expirer; **∼ out of** manquer de; **∼ over** (of vehicle) écraser; (*details*) revoir; **∼ through** regarder qch rapidement; **∼ sth through sth** passer qch à travers qch; **∼ up** (*bill*) accumuler.

runaway n fugitif/-ive m/f. ● a fugitif; (*horse, vehicle*) fou; (*inflation*) galopant.

rung ⇒RING². ● n (of ladder) barreau m.

runner n coureur/-euse m/f. **∼ bean** n haricot m d'Espagne. **∼-up** n second/-e m/f

running n course f à pied; (of business) gestion f; (of machine) marche f; **be in the ∼ for** être sur les rangs pour. ● a (*commentary*) suivi; (*water*) courant; **four days ∼** quatre jours de suite.

runway n piste f.

rural a rural.

rush vi (move) se précipiter; (be in a hurry) se dépêcher. ● vt (*person*) bousculer; (Mil) prendre d'assaut; **∼ to** envoyer d'urgence à. ● n ruée f; (haste) bousculade f; (plant) jonc m; **in a ∼** pressé. **∼-hour** n heure f de pointe.

Russia n Russie f.

Russian a russe. ● n (person) Russe mf; (language) russe.

rust n rouille f. ● vt/i rouiller.

rustle vt/i (*papers*) froisser.

rusty a rouillé.

ruthless a impitoyable.

rye n seigle m.

R

sabbath n (Jewish) sabbat m; (Christian) jour m du seigneur.

sabbatical a (Univ) sabbatique.

sabotage n sabotage m. ● vt saboter.

saccharin n saccharine f.

sack n (bag) sac m; **get the ~** 🅣 être renvoyé. ● vt 🅣 renvoyer; (plunder) saccager. **sacking** n (cloth) toile f à sac; (dismissal 🅣) renvoi m.

sacrament n sacrement m.

sacred a sacré.

sacrifice n sacrifice m. ● vt sacrifier.

sad a (**sadder**, **saddest**) triste.

saddle n selle f. ● vt (horse) seller.

sadist n sadique mf. **sadistic** a sadique.

sadly adv tristement; (unfortunately) malheureusement.

sadness n tristesse f.

safe a (not dangerous) sans danger; (reliable) sûr; (out of danger) en sécurité; (after accident) sain et sauf; **~ from** à l'abri de. ● n coffre-fort m.

safeguard n sauvegarde f. ● vt sauvegarder.

safely adv sans danger; (in safe place) en sûreté.

safety n sécurité f. **~-belt** n ceinture f de sécurité. **~-pin** n épingle f de sûreté. **~-valve** n soupape f de sûreté.

saffron n safran m.

sag vi (pt **sagged**) (beam, mattress) s'affaisser; (flesh) être flasque.

sage n (herb) sauge f.

Sagittarius n Sagittaire m.

said ⇒SAY.

sail n voile f; (journey) tour m en bateau. ● vi (person) voyager en bateau; (as sport) faire de la voile; (set off) prendre la mer; **~ across** traverser. ● vt (boat) piloter; (sea) traverser. **sailing-boat**, **sailing-ship** n voilier m.

sailor n marin m.

saint n saint/-e m/f.

sake n **for the ~ of** pour.

salad n salade f.

salaried a salarié.

salary n salaire m.

sale n vente f; **for ~** à vendre; **on ~** en vente; (reduced) en solde; **~s** (reductions) soldes mpl; **~s assistant**, (US) **~s clerk** vendeur/ -euse m/f.

salesman n (pl -men) (in shop) vendeur m; (traveller) représentant m.

saline a salin. ● n sérum m physiologique.

saliva n salive f.

salmon n inv saumon m.

salon n salon m.

saloon n (on ship) salon m; **~ (car)** berline f.

salt n sel m. ● vt saler. **salty** a salé.

salutary a salutaire.

salute n salut m. ● vt saluer. ● vi faire un salut.

salvage n sauvetage m; (of waste) récupération f. ● vt sauver; (for re-use) récupérer.

same a même (as que). ● pron **the ~** le même, la même, les mêmes; **at the ~ time** en même temps; **the ~ (thing)** la même chose.

sample n échantillon m; (of blood)

prélèvement *m*. ● *vt* essayer; (*food*) goûter.

sanctimonious *a* (pej) supérieur.

sanction *n* sanction *f*. ● *vt* sanctionner.

sanctity *n* sainteté *f*.

sanctuary *n* (safe place) refuge *m*; (Relig) sanctuaire *m*; (for animals) réserve *f*.

sand *n* sable *m*; ~s (beach) plage *f*.

sandal *n* sandale *f*.

sandpaper *n* papier *m* de verre. ● *vt* poncer.

sandpit *n* bac *m* à sable.

sandwich *n* sandwich *m*: ~ **course** cours *m* avec stage pratique.

sandy *a* (beach) de sable; (soil) sablonneux; (hair) blond roux *inv*.

sane *a* (view) sensé; (person) sain d'esprit.

sang ⇒SING.

sanitary *a* (clean) hygiénique, (system) sanitaire; ~ **towel** serviette *f* hygiénique.

sanitation *n* installations *fpl* sanitaires.

sanity *n* équilibre *m* mental; (sense) bon sens *m*.

sank ⇒SINK.

Santa (**Claus**) *n* le père Noël.

sapphire *n* saphir *m*.

sarcasm *n* sarcasme *m*. **sarcastic** *a* sarcastique.

sash *n* (on uniform) écharpe *f*; (on dress) ceinture *f*.

sat ⇒SIT.

satchel *n* cartable *m*.

satellite *n* & *a* satellite (*m*); ~ **dish** antenne *f* parabolique.

satire *n* satire *f*. **satirical** *a* satirique.

satisfaction *n* satisfaction *f*.

satisfactory *a* satisfaisant.

satisfy *vt* satisfaire; (convince) convaincre.

saturate *vt* saturer. **saturated** *a* (wet) trempé.

Saturday *n* samedi *m*.

sauce *n* sauce *f*.

saucepan *n* casserole *f*.

saucer *n* soucoupe *f*.

Saudi Arabia *n* Arabie *f* saoudite.

sausage *n* (for cooking) saucisse *f*; (ready to eat) saucisson *m*.

savage *a* (blow, temper) violent; (attack) sauvage. ● *n* sauvage *mf*. ● *vt* attaquer sauvagement.

save *vt* sauver; (money) économiser; (time) gagner; (keep) garder; ~ (sb) **doing** sth éviter (à qn) de faire qch. ● *n* (football) arrêt *m*. **saver** *n* épargnant/-e *m/f*. **saving** *n* économie *f*.

savings *npl* économies *fpl*.

saviour, (US) **savior** *n* sauveur *m*.

savour, (US) **savor** *n* saveur *f*. ● *vt* savourer. **savoury** *a* (tasty) savoureux; (Culin) salé.

saw ⇒SEE. ● *n* scie *f*. ● *vt* (*pt* **sawed**; *pp* **sawn** or **sawed**) scier.

sawdust *n* sciure *f*.

saxophone *n* saxophone *m*.

say *vt/i* (*pt* **said**) dire; (prayer) faire. ● **n** have a ~ dire son mot; (in decision) avoir voix au chapitre. **saying** *n* proverbe *m*.

scab *n* croûte *f*.

scaffolding *n* échafaudage *m*.

scald *vt* (injure, cleanse) ébouillanter. ● *n* brûlure *f*.

scale *n* (for measuring) échelle *f*; (extent) étendue *f*; (Mus) gamme *f*; (on fish) écaille *f*; **on a small** ~ sur une petite échelle; ~ **model** maquette *f*. ● *vt* (climb) escalader; ~ **down** réduire. **scales** *npl* (for weighing) balance *f*.

scallop *n* coquille *f* Saint-Jacques.

scalp *n* cuir *m* chevelu.

S

scampi *npl* (fresh) langoustines *fpl*; (breaded) scampi *mpl*.

scan *vt* (*pt* **scanned**) scruter; (quickly) parcourir. ● *n* (ultrasound) échographie *f*; (CAT) scanner *m*.

scandal *n* scandale *m*; (gossip) potins *mpl* 🖾.

Scandinavia *n* Scandinavie *f*.

scanty *a* (**-ier, -iest**) maigre; (clothing) minuscule.

scapegoat *n* bouc *m* émissaire.

scar *n* cicatrice *f*. ● *vt* (*pt* **scarred**) marquer.

scarce *a* rare. **scarcely** *adv* à peine.

scare *vt* faire peur à; be ~d avoir peur. ● *n* peur *f*; bomb ~ alerte *f* à la bombe. **scarecrow** *n* épouvantail *m*.

scarf *n* (*pl* **scarves**) écharpe *f*; (over head) foulard *m*.

scarlet *a* écarlate; ~ fever scarlatine *f*.

scary *a* (**-ier, -iest**) 🖾 qui fait peur.

scathing *a* cinglant.

scatter *vt* (throw) éparpiller, répandre; (disperse) disperser. ● *vi* se disperser.

scavenge *vi* fouiller (dans les ordures). **scavenger** *n* (animal) charognard *m*.

scene *n* scène *f*; (of accident, crime) lieu *m*; (sight) spectacle *m*; behind the ~s en coulisse. **scenery** *n* paysage *m*; (Theat) décors *mpl*. **scenic** *a* panoramique.

scent *n* (perfume) parfum *m*; (trail) piste *f*. ● *vt* flairer; (make fragrant) parfumer.

sceptic *n* sceptique *mf*. **sceptical** *a* sceptique. **scepticism** *n* scepticisme *m*.

schedule *n* horaire *m*; (for job) planning *m*; behind ~ en retard; on ~ dans les temps. ● *vt* prévoir; ~d flight vol *m* régulier.

scheme *n* projet *m*; (dishonest) combine *f*; **pension** ~ plan *m* de retraite. ● *vi* comploter.

schizophrenic *a & n* schizophrène (*mf*).

scholar *n* érudit/-e *m/f*.

school *n* école *f*; go to ~ aller à l'école. ● *a* (age, year, holidays) scolaire. ~**boy** *n* élève *m*. ~**girl** élève *f*. **schooling** *n* scolarité *f*. ~**teacher** *n* (primary) instituteur/ -trice *m/f*; (secondary) professeur *m*.

science *n* science *f*; teach ~ enseigner les sciences. **scientific** *a* scientifique. **scientist** *n* scientifique *mf*.

scissors *npl* ciseaux *mpl*.

scold *vt* gronder.

scoop *n* (shovel) pelle *f*; (measure) mesure *f*; (for ice cream) cuillère *f* à glace; (news) exclusivité *f*.

scooter *n* (child's) trottinette *f*; (motor cycle) scooter *m*.

scope *n* étendue *f*; (competence) compétence *f*; (opportunity) possibilité *f*.

scorch *vt* brûler; (iron) roussir.

score *n* score *m*; (Mus) partition *f*; on that ~ à cet égard. ● *vt* marquer; (success) remporter. ● *vi* marquer un point; (football) marquer un but; (keep score) marquer les points. **scorer** *n* (Sport) marqueur *m*.

scorn *n* mépris *m*. ● *vt* mépriser.

Scorpio *n* Scorpion *m*.

Scot *n* Écossais/-e *m/f*.

Scotland *n* Écosse *f*.

Scottish *a* écossais.

scoundrel *n* gredin *m*.

scour *vt* (pan) récurer; (search) parcourir. **scourer** *n* tampon *m* à récurer.

scourge *n* fléau *m*.

scout *n* éclaireur *m*. ● *vi* ~ **around for** rechercher.

scowl n air m renfrogné. ● vi prendre un air renfrogné.

scramble vi (clamber) grimper. ● vt (eggs) brouiller. ● n (rush) course f.

scrap n petit morceau m; ~s (of metal, fabric) déchets mpl; (of food) restes mpl; (fight 🔲) bagarre f. ● vt (pt scrapped) abandonner; (car) détruire.

scrape vt gratter; (damage) érafler. ● vi ~ against érafler. □ ~ through réussir de justesse.

scrap: ~-paper n papier m brouillon. ~ yard n casse f.

scratch vt/i (se) gratter; (with claw, nail) griffer; (graze) érafler; (mark) rayer. ● n (on body) égratignure f; (on surface) éraflure f; start from ~ partir de zéro; up to ~ à la hauteur. ~ card n jeu m de grattage.

scrawl n gribouillage m. ● vt/i gribouiller.

scrawny a (-ier, -iest) décharné.

scream vt/i crier. ● n cri m (perçant).

screech vi (scream) hurler; (tyres) crisser. ● n cri m strident; (of tyres) crissement f.

screen n écran m; (folding) paravent m. ● vt masquer; (protect) protéger; (film) projeter; (candidates) filtrer; (Med) faire subir un test de dépistage. **screening** n (cinema) projection f; (Med) dépistage m.

screen: ~play n scénario m. ~ saver n protecteur m d'écran.

screw n vis f. ● vt visser; (eyes) plisser; (ruin 🔲) cafouiller 🔲. ~driver n tournevis m.

scribble vt/i griffonner. ● n griffonnage m.

script n script m; (of play) texte m.

scroll n rouleau m. ● vt/i (Comput) (faire) défiler. ~bar n barre f de défilement.

scrounge 🔲 vt (favour) quémander; (cigarette) piquer 🔲; ~ money from sb taper de l'argent à qn. ● vi ~ off sb vivre sur le dos de qn.

scrub n (land) broussailles fpl. ● vt/i (pt scrubbed) nettoyer (à la brosse), frotter.

scruffy a (-ier, -iest) 🔲 dépenaillé.

scrum n (rugby) mêlée f.

scruple n scrupule m.

scrutinize vt scruter. **scrutiny** n examen m minutieux.

scuba-diving n plongée f sous-marine.

scuffle n bagarre f.

sculpt vt/i sculpter. **sculptor** n sculpteur m.

sculpture n sculpture f.

scum n (on liquid) mousse f; (people: pej) racaille f.

scurry vi se précipiter, courir (for pour chercher), ~ off se sauver.

sea n mer f; at ~ en mer; by ~ par mer. ● a (air) marin; (bird) de mer; (voyage) par mer. ~food n fruits mpl de mer. ~gull n mouette f.

seal n (animal) phoque m; (insignia) sceau m; (with wax) cachet m. ● vt sceller; cacheter; (stick down) coller. □ ~ off (area) boucler.

seam n (in cloth) couture f; (of coal) veine f.

search vt/i (examine) fouiller; (seek) chercher; (study) examiner; (Comput) rechercher. ● n fouille f; (quest) recherches fpl; (Comput) recherche f; in ~ of à la recherche de. ~ engine n (Internet) moteur m de recherche. ~light n projecteur m. ~-warrant n mandat m de perquisition.

sea: ~shell n coquillage m. ~shore n (coast) littoral m; (beach) plage f.

S

seasick a be ~ avoir le mal de mer.

seaside n bord m de la mer.

season n saison f; ~ **ticket** carte f d'abonnement. ● vt assaisonner. **seasonal** a saisonnier. **seasoning** n assaisonnement m.

seat n siège m; (place) place f; (of trousers) fond m; **take a** ~ asseyez-vous. ● vt (put) placer; **the room ~s 30** la salle peut accueillir 30 personnes. ~-**belt** n ceinture f (de sécurité).

seaweed n algue f marine.

secluded a retiré.

seclusion n isolement m.

second¹ a deuxième, second; **a ~ chance** une nouvelle chance; **have ~ thoughts** avoir des doutes. ● n deuxième mf, second/-e m/f; (unit of time) seconde f; ~**s** (food) rab m ▣. ● adv (in race) deuxième; (secondly) deuxièmement. ● vt (proposal) appuyer.

second² vt (transfer) détacher (**to** à).

secondary a secondaire; ~ **school** lycée m, école f secondaire.

second-best n pis-aller m.

second-class a (Rail) de deuxième classe; (post) au tarif lent.

second hand n (on clock) trotteuse f.

second-hand a & adv (article) d'occasion; (information) de seconde main.

secondly adv deuxièmement.

second-rate a médiocre.

secrecy n secret m.

secret a secret. ● n secret m; **in ~** en secret.

secretarial a (work) de secrétaire.

secretary n secrétaire mf; **S~ of**

State ministre m; (US) ministre m des Affaires étrangères.

secrete vt (Med) sécréter; (hide) cacher.

secretive a secret. **secretly** adv secrètement.

sect n secte f. **sectarian** a sectaire.

section n partie f; (in store) rayon m; (of newspaper) rubrique f; (of book) passage m.

sector n secteur m.

secular a (school) laïque; (art, music) profane.

secure a (safe) sûr; (job, marriage) stable; (knot, lock) solide; (window) bien fermé; (feeling) de sécurité; (person) sécurisé. ● vt attacher; (obtain) s'assurer; (ensure) assurer.

security n (safety) sécurité f; (for loan) caution f; ~ **guard** vigile m.

sedate a calme. ● vt donner un sédatif à. **sedative** n sédatif m.

seduce vt séduire. **seducer** n séducteur/-trice m/f. **seduction** n séduction f. **seductive** a séduisant.

see vt/i (pt **saw**; pp **seen**) voir; **see you (soon)**! à bientôt!; ~**ing that** vu que. □ ~ **out** (person) raccompagner à la porte; ~ **through** (deception) déceler; (person) percer à jour; ~ **sth through** mener qch à bonne fin; ~ **to** s'occuper de; ~ **to it that** veiller à ce que.

seed n graine f; (collectively) graines fpl; (origin: fig) germe m; (tennis) tête f de série. **seedling** n plant m.

seek vt (pt **sought**) chercher.

seem vi sembler; **he ~s to think** il a l'air de croire.

seen ⇒SEE.

seep vi suinter; ~ **into** s'infiltrer dans.

see-saw n tapecul m. ● vt osciller.

seethe vi ~ with (anger) bouillir de; (people) grouiller de.

segment n segment m; (of orange) quartier m.

segregate vt séparer.

seize vt saisir; (territory, prisoner) s'emparer de. ● vi ~ on (chance) saisir; ~ up (engine) se gripper.

seizure n (Med) crise f.

seldom adv rarement.

select vt sélectionner. ● a privilégié. **selection** n sélection f. **selective** a sélectif.

self n (pl selves) moi m; (on cheque) moi-même. ~-**assured** a plein d'assurance. ~-**catering** a (holiday) en location. ~-**centred**, (US) ~-**centered** a égocentrique. ~-**confident** a sûr de soi. ~-**conscious** a timide. ~-**contained** a (flat) indépendant. ~-**control** n sang-froid m. ~-**defence** n autodéfense f; (Jur) légitime défense f. ~-**employed** a qui travaille à son compte. ~-**esteem** n amour-propre m. ~-**governing** a autonome. ~-**indulgent** a complaisant. ~-**interest** n intérêt m personnel.

selfish a égoïste.

selfless a désintéressé.

self: ~-**portrait** n autoportrait m. ~-**reliant** a autosuffisant. ~-**respect** n respect m de soi. ~-**righteous** a satisfait de soi. ~-**sacrifice** n abnégation f. ~-**satisfied** a satisfait de soi. ~-**seeking** a égoïste. ~-**service** n & a libre-service (m).

sell vt/i (pt sold) vendre; ~ well se vendre bien. □ ~ off liquider; ~ out (items) se vendre; have sold out avoir tout vendu.

Sellotape® n scotch® m.

sell-out n (betrayal) ⊡ revirement m; be a ~ (show) afficher complet.

semester n (Univ) semestre m.

semicircle n demi-cercle m.

semicolon n point-virgule m.

semi-detached a ~ house maison f jumelée.

semifinal n demi-finale f.

seminar n séminaire m.

semolina n semoule f.

senate n sénat m. **senator** n sénateur m.

send vt/i (pt sent) envoyer. □ ~ away (dismiss) renvoyer; ~ (away or off) for commander (par la poste); ~ back renvoyer; ~ for (person, help) envoyer chercher; ~ up ⊡ parodier.

senile a sénile.

senior a plus âgé (to que); (in rank) haut placé; be ~ to sb être le supérieur de qn. ● n aîné/-e m/f. ~ **citizen** n personne f âgée. ~ **school** n lycée m.

sensation n sensation f. **sensational** a sensationnel.

sense n sens m; (mental impression) sentiment m; (common sense) bon sens m, ~s (mind) raison f; there's no ~ in doing cela ne sert à rien de faire; make ~ avoir un sens; make ~ of comprendre. ● vt (pres)sentir. **senseless** a insensé; (Med) sans connaissance.

sensible a raisonnable; (clothing) pratique.

sensitive a sensible (to à); (issue) difficile.

sensory a sensoriel.

sensual a sensuel. **sensuality** n sensualité f.

sensuous a sensuel.

sent ⇒SEND.

sentence n phrase f; (punishment:

S

Jur) peine f. ● vt ~ **to** condamner à.

sentiment n sentiment m.
sentimental a sentimental.

sentry n sentinelle f.

separate[1] a (piece) à part; (issue) autre; (sections) différent; (organizations) distinct.

separate[2] vt/i (se) séparer.

separately adv séparément.

separation n séparation f.

September n septembre m.

septic a (wound) infecté; ~ **tank** fosse f septique.

sequel n suite f.

sequence n (order) ordre m; (series) suite f; (in film) séquence f.

Serb a serbe. ● n (person) Serbe mf; (Ling) serbe m.

Serbia n Serbie f.

sergeant n (Mil) sergent m; (policeman) brigadier m.

serial n feuilleton m. ● a (Comput) série inv.

series n inv série f.

serious a sérieux; (accident, crime) grave.

seriously adv sérieusement; (ill) gravement; **take** ~ prendre au sérieux.

sermon n sermon m.

serpent n serpent m.

serrated a dentelé.

serum n sérum m.

servant n domestique mf.

serve vt/i servir; faire; (transport, hospital) desservir; ~ **as/to** servir de/à; ~ **a purpose** être utile; ~ **a sentence** (Jur) purger une peine.
● n (tennis) service m.

server n serveur m; **remote** ~ téléserveur m.

service n service m; (maintenance) révision f; (Relig) office m; ~**s** (Mil) forces fpl armées. ● vt (car) réviser. ~ **area** n (Auto) aire f de

services. ~ **charge** n service m.
~ **station** n station-service f.

session n séance f; **be in** ~ (Jur) tenir séance.

set vt (pt **set**; pres p **setting**) placer; (table) mettre; (limit) fixer; (clock) mettre à l'heure; (example, task) donner; (TV, cinema) situer; ~ **fire to** mettre le feu à; ~ **free** libérer; ~ **to music** mettre en musique. ● vi (sun) se coucher; (jelly) prendre; ~ **sail** partir. ● n (of chairs, stamps) série f; (of knives, keys) jeu m; (of people) groupe m; (TV, radio) poste m; (Theat) décor m; (tennis) set m; (mathematics) ensemble m. ● a (time, price) fixe; (procedure) bien determiné; (meal) à prix fixe; (book) au programme; ~ **against sth** opposé à; **be** ~ **on doing** tenir absolument à faire. □ ~ **about** se mettre à; ~ **back** (delay) retarder; (cost ▥) coûter; ~ **in** (take hold) s'installer, commencer; ~ **off** or **out** partir; ~ **off** (panic, riot) déclencher; (bomb) faire exploser; ~ **out** (state) présenter; (arrange) disposer; ~ **out to do sth** chercher à faire qch; ~ **up** (stall) monter; (equipment) assembler; (experiment) préparer; (company) créer; (meeting) organiser.
~-**back** n revers m.

settee n canapé m.

setting n cadre m; (on dial) position f.

settle vt (arrange, pay) régler; (date) fixer; (nerves) calmer. ● vi (come to rest) (bird) se poser; (dust) se déposer; (live) s'installer. □ ~ **down** se calmer; (marry etc.) se ranger; ~ **for** accepter; ~ **in** s'installer; ~ **up** (with) régler.

settlement n règlement m (of de); (agreement) accord m; (place) colonie f.

settler n colon m.

seven *a & n* sept (*m*).

seventeen *a & n* dix-sept (*m*).

seventh *a & n* septième (*mf*).

seventy *a & n* soixante-dix (*m*).

sever *vt* (cut) couper; (*relations*) rompre.

several *a & pron* plusieurs; ~ **of us** plusieurs d'entre nous.

severe *a* (harsh) sévère; (serious) grave.

sew *vt/i* (*pt* **sewed**; *pp* **sewn** or **sewed**) coudre.

sewage *n* eaux *fpl* usées.

sewer *n* égout *m*.

sewing *n* couture *f*. ~**-machine** *n* machine *f* à coudre.

sewn ⇒SEW.

sex *n* sexe *m*; **have** ~ avoir des rapports (sexuels). ● *a* sexuel. **sexist** *a & n* sexiste (*mf*). **sexual** *a* sexuel.

shabby *a* (**-ier, -iest**) (*place, object*) miteux; (*person*) habillé de façon miteuse; (*treatment*) mesquin.

shack *n* cabane *f*.

shade *n* ombre *f*; (of colour, opinion) nuance *f*; (for lamp) abat-jour *m inv*; **a** ~ **bigger** légèrement plus grand. ● *vt* (*tree*) ombrager; (*hat*) projeter une ombre sur.

shadow *n* ombre *f*. ● *vt* (follow) filer. **S**~ **Cabinet** *n* cabinet *m* fantôme.

shady *a* (**-ier, -iest**) ombragé; (dubious) véreux.

shaft *n* (of tool) manche *m*; (of arrow) tige *f*; (in machine) axe *m*; (of mine) puits *m*; (of light) rayon *m*.

shake *vt* (*pt* **shook**; *pp* **shaken**) secouer; (*bottle*) agiter; (*belief*) ébranler; ~ **hands with** serrer la main à; ~ **one's head** dire non de la tête. ● *vi* trembler. ● *n* secousse *f*; **give sth a** ~ secouer qch. □ ~ **off** se débarrasser de. ~**-up** *n* (Pol) remaniement *m*.

shaky *a* (**-ier, -iest**) (*hand, voice*) tremblant; (*ladder*) branlant; (weak: fig) instable.

shall *v aux* **I** ~ **do** je ferai; **we** ~ **see** nous verrons; ~ **we go…**? si on allait…?

shallow *a* peu profond; (fig) superficiel.

shame *n* honte *f*; **it's a** ~ c'est dommage. ● *vt* faire honte à.

shampoo *n* shampooing *m*. ● *vt* faire un shampooing à.

shandy *n* panaché *m*.

shan't = SHALL NOT.

shanty *n* (shack) baraque *f*; ~ **town** bidonville *m*.

shape *n* forme *f*. ● *vt* (*clay*) modeler; (*rock*) façonner; (*future, fig*) déterminer; ~ **sth into balls** faire des boules avec qch. ● *vi* ~ **up** (*plan*) prendre tournure; (*person*) faire des progrès.

share *n* part *f*; (Comm) action *f*. ● *vt/i* partager; (*feature*) avoir en commun. ~**holder** *n* actionnaire *mf*. ~**ware** *n* (Comput) logiciel *m* contributif.

shark *n* requin *m*.

sharp *a* (*knife*) tranchant; (*pin*) pointu; (*point, angle, cry*) aigu; (*person, mind*) vif; (*tone*) acerbe. ● *adv* (*stop*) net; (*sing, play*) trop haut; **six o'clock** ~ six heures pile. ● *n* (Mus) dièse *m*.

sharpen *vt* aiguiser; (*pencil*) tailler.

shatter *vt* (*glass*) fracasser; (*hope*) briser. ● *vi* (*glass*) voler en éclats.

shave *vt/i* (se) raser. ● *n* **have a** ~ se raser. **shaver** *n* rasoir *m* électrique.

shaving *n* (of wood) copeau *m*. ● *a* (*cream, foam, gel*) à raser.

shawl *n* châle *m*.

she *pron* elle. ● *n* (animal) femelle *f*.

shear vt (pp **shorn** or **sheared**) (sheep) tondre; ~ **off** se détacher.

shears npl cisaille f.

shed n remise f. ● vt (pt **shed**; pres p **shedding**) perdre; (light, tears) répandre.

sheen n lustre m.

sheep n inv mouton m. ~-**dog** n chien m de berger.

sheepish a penaud.

sheepskin n peau f de mouton.

sheer a pur; (steep) à pic; (fabric) très fin. ● adv à pic.

sheet n drap m; (of paper) feuille f; (of glass, ice) plaque f.

shelf n (pl **shelves**) étagère f; (in shop, fridge) rayon m; (in oven) plaque f.

shell n coquille f; (on beach) coquillage m; (of building) carcasse f; (explosive) obus m. ● vt (nut) décortiquer; (peas) écosser; (Mil) bombarder.

shellfish npl (lobster etc.) crustacés mpl; (mollusc) coquillages mpl.

shelter n abri m. ● vt/i (s')abriter; (give lodging to) donner asile à.

shelve vt (plan) mettre en suspens.

shepherd n berger m; ~'s **pie** hachis m Parmentier. ● vt (people) guider.

sherry n xérès m.

shield n bouclier m; (screen) écran m. ● vt protéger.

shift vt/i (se) déplacer, bouger; (exchange, alter) changer de. ● n changement m; (workers) équipe f; (work) poste m; ~ **work** travail m posté, travail m par roulement.

shifty a (-**ier**, -**iest**) louche.

shimmer vi chatoyer. ● n chatoiement m.

shin n tibia m.

shine vt (pt **shone**) (torch) braquer (**on** sur). ● vi (light, sun,

hair) briller; (brass) reluire. ● n lustre m.

shingle n (pebbles) galets mpl; (on roof) bardeau m.

shingles npl (Med) zona m.

shiny a (-**ier**, -**iest**) brillant.

ship n bateau m, navire m. ● vt (pt **shipped**) transporter.

shipment n (by sea) cargaison f; (by air, land) chargement m.

shipping n (ships) navigation f. ~**wreck** n épave f; (event) naufrage m.

shirt n chemise f; (woman's) chemisier m.

shiver vi frissonner. ● n frisson m.

shock n choc m; (Electr) décharge f; in ~ en état de choc; ~ **absorber** amortisseur m. ● a (result) choc inv; (tactics) de choc. ● vt choquer.

shoddy a (-**ier**, -**iest**) mal fait; (behaviour) mesquin.

shoe n chaussure f; (of horse) fer m; (brake) ~ sabot m (de frein). ● vt (pt **shod** ; pres p **shoeing**) (horse) ferrer. ~**lace** n lacet m. ~ **size** n pointure f.

shone ⇒SHINE.

shook ⇒SHAKE.

shoot vt (pt **shot**) (gun) tirer un coup de; (bullet) tirer; (missile, glance) lancer; (person) tirer sur; (kill) abattre; (execute) fusiller; (film) tourner. ● vi tirer (**at** sur). ● n (Bot) pousse f. □ ~ **down** abattre; ~ **out** (rush) sortir en vitesse; ~ **up** (spurt) jaillir; (grow) pousser vite.

shooting n (killing) meurtre m (par arme à feu); hear ~ entendre des coups de feu.

shop n magasin m; (small) boutique f; (workshop) atelier m. ● vi (pt **shopped**) faire ses courses; ~ **around** comparer les prix. ~ **assistant** n vendeur/

-euse *m/f.* ~**floor** *n* (workers) ouvriers *mpl.* ~**keeper** *n* commerçant/-e *m/f.* ~**lifter** *n* voleur/-euse *m/f* à l'étalage.

shopper *n* acheteur/-euse *m/f.*

shopping *n* (goods) achats *mpl;* go ~ (for food) faire les courses; (for clothes etc.) faire les magasins. ~ **bag** *n* sac *m* à provisions. ~ **centre**, (US) ~ **center** *n* centre *m* commercial.

shop window *n* vitrine *f.*

shore *n* côte *f,* rivage *m;* on ~ à terre.

short *a* court; (*person*) petit; (brief) court, bref; (curt) brusque; be ~ (of) manquer (de); everything ~ of tout sauf; nothing ~ of rien de moins que; cut ~ écourter; cut sb ~ interrompre qn; fall ~ of ne pas arriver à; he is called Tom for ~ son diminutif est Tom; in ~ en bref. ● *adv* (stop) net. ● *n* (Electr) court-circuit *m;* (film) court-métrage *m;* ~s (trousers) short *m.*

shortage *n* manque *m.*

short: ~**bread** *n* sablé *m.* ~**change** *vt* (cheat) rouler 🔲. ~ **circuit** *n* court-circuit *m.* ~**coming** *n* défaut *m.* ~ **cut** *n* raccourci *m.*

shorten *vt* raccourcir.

shortfall *n* déficit *m.*

shorthand *n* sténographie *f;* ~ **typist** sténodactylo *f.*

short: ~ **list** *n* liste *f* des candidats choisis. ~**lived** *a* de courte durée.

shortly *adv* bientôt.

short: ~**sighted** *a* myope. ~**staffed** *a* à court de personnel; ~ **story** *n* nouvelle *f.* ~**term** *a* à court terme.

shot ⇒SHOOT. ● *n* (firing, attempt) coup *m* de feu; (person) tireur *m;* (bullet) balle *f;* (photograph) photo *f;* (injection) piqûre *f;* like a ~ sans

hésiter. ~**gun** *n* fusil *m* de chasse.

should *v aux* devoir; you ~ help me vous devriez m'aider; I ~ have stayed j'aurais dû rester; I ~ like to j'aimerais bien; if he ~ come s'il venait.

shoulder *n* épaule *f.* ● *vt* (*responsibility*) endosser; (*burden*) se charger de. ~**bag** *n* sac *m* à bandoulière. ~**blade** *n* omoplate *f.*

shout *n* cri *m.* ● *vt/i* crier (at après); ~ **sth out** lancer qch à haute voix.

shove *n* give sth a ~ pousser qch. ● *vt/i* pousser; ~ off! 🔲 tire-toi! 🔲.

shovel *n* pelle *f.* ● *vt* (*pt* **shovelled**) pelleter.

show *vt* (*pt* showed; *pp* shown) montrer; (*dial, needle*) indiquer; (put on display) exposer; (*film*) donner; (conduct) conduire; ~ **sb in/out** faire entrer/sortir qn. ● *vi* (be visible) se voir. ● *n* (exhibition) exposition *f,* salon *m;* (Theat) spectacle *m;* (cinema) séance *f;* (of strength) démonstration *f;* for ~ pour l'effet; on ~ exposé. □ ~ **off** faire le fier/la fière; ~ **sth/sb off** exhiber qch/qn; ~ **up** se voir; (appear) se montrer; ~ **sb up** 🔲 faire honte à qn.

shower *n* douche *f;* (of rain) averse *f.* ● *vt* ~ **with** couvrir de. ● *vi* se doucher.

showing *n* performance *f;* (cinema) séance *f.*

show-jumping *n* concours *m* hippique.

shown ⇒SHOW.

show: ~**off** *n* m'as-tu-vu *mf inv* 🔲. ~**room** *n* salle *f* d'exposition.

shrank ⇒SHRINK.

shrapnel *n* éclats *mpl* d'obus.

shred *n* lambeau *m;* (least amount:

fig) parcelle *f*. ● *vt* (*pt* **shredded**) déchiqueter; (Culin) râper.

shrewd *a* (*person*) habile; (*move*) astucieux.

shriek *n* hurlement *m*. ● *vt/i* hurler.

shrill *a* (*voice*) perçant; (*tone*) strident.

shrimp *n* crevette *f*.

shrine *n* (place) lieu *m* de pèlerinage.

shrink *vt/i* (*pt* **shrank**; *pp* **shrunk**) rétrécir; (lessen) diminuer; ~ **from** (se) reculer devant.

shrivel *vt/i* (*pt* **shrivelled**) (se) ratatiner.

shroud *n* linceul *m*. ● *vt* (veil) envelopper.

Shrove Tuesday *n* mardi *m* gras.

shrub *n* arbuste *m*.

shrug *vt* (*pt* **shrugged**) ~ **one's shoulders** hausser les épaules; ~ **sth off** ignorer qch.

shrunk ⇒SHRINK.

shudder *vi* frémir. ● *n* frémissement *m*.

shuffle *vt* (*feet*) traîner; (*cards*) battre. ● *vi* traîner les pieds.

shun *vt* (*pt* **shunned**) fuir.

shut *vt* (*pt* **shut**; *pres p* **shutting**) fermer. ● *vi* (*door*) se fermer; (*shop*) fermer. □ ~ **in** or **up** enfermer; ~ **up** 🔲 se taire; ~ **sb up** faire taire qn.

shutter *n* volet *m*; (Photo) obturateur *m*.

shuttle *n* (bus) navette *f*; ~ **service** navette *f*. ● *vi* faire la navette. ● *vt* transporter.

shuttlecock *n* (badminton) volant *m*.

shy *a* timide. ● *vi* ~ **away from** se tenir à l'écart de.

sibling *n* frère/sœur *m/f*.

sick *a* malade; (*humour*) macabre; (*mind*) malsain; **be** ~

(vomit) vomir; **be** ~ **of** 🔲 en avoir assez *or* marre de 🔲; **feel** ~ avoir mal au cœur. ~**-leave** *n* congé *m* de maladie.

sickly *a* (**-ier, -iest**) (*person*) maladif; (*taste, smell*) écœurant.

sickness *n* maladie *f*.

sick-pay *n* indemnité *f* de maladie.

side *n* côté *m*; (of road, river) bord *m*; (of hill, body) flanc *m*; (Sport) équipe *f*; (TV 🔲) chaîne *f*; ~ **by** ~ côte à côte. ● *a* latéral. ● *vi* ~ **with** se ranger du côté de. ~**board** *n* buffet *m*. ~**-effect** *n* effet *m* secondaire. ~**light** *n* (Auto) feu *m* de position. ~**line** *n* activité *f* secondaire. ~**-show** *n* attraction *f*. ~**-step** *vt* (*pt* **-stepped**) éviter. ~**-street** *n* rue *f* latérale. ~**-track** *vt* fourvoyer. ~**walk** *n* (US) trottoir *m*.

sideways *a* (*look*) de travers. ● *adv* (*move*) latéralement; (*look at*) de travers.

siding *n* voie *f* de garage.

sidle *vi* s'avancer furtivement (**up** to vers).

siege *n* siège *m*.

siesta *n* sieste *f*.

sieve *n* tamis *m*; (for liquids) passoire *f*. ● *vt* tamiser.

sift *vt* tamiser. ● *vi* ~ **through** examiner.

sigh *n* soupir *m*. ● *vt/i* soupirer.

sight *n* vue *f*; (scene) spectacle *m*; (on gun) mire *f*; **at** or **on** ~ à vue; **catch** ~ **of** apercevoir; **in** ~ visible; **lose** ~ **of** perdre de vue. ● *vt* apercevoir.

sightseeing *n* tourisme *m*.

sign *n* signe *m*; (notice) panneau *m*. ● *vt/i* signer. □ ~ **on** (as unemployed) pointer au chômage; ~ **up** (s')engager.

signal *n* signal *m*. ● *vt* (*pt* **signalled**) (gesture) faire signe (**that** que); (indicate) indiquer.

signatory n signataire mf.

signature n signature f; ~ **tune** indicatif m.

significance n importance f; (meaning) signification f.

significant a important; (meaningful) significatif.

significantly adv (much) sensiblement.

signify vt signifier.

signpost n panneau m indicateur.

silence n silence m. ● vt faire taire.

silent a silencieux; (film) muet.
silently adv silencieusement.

silhouette n silhouette f. ● vt be ~d **against** se profiler contre.

silicon n silicium m; ~ **chip** puce f électronique.

silk n soie f.

silly a (-ier, -iest) bête, idiot.

silver n argent m; (silverware) argenterie f. ● a en argent.

similar a semblable (**to** à).
similarity n ressemblance f.
similarly adv de même.

simile n comparaison f.

simmer vt/i (soup) mijoter; (water) (laisser) frémir.

simple a simple.

simplicity n simplicité f.

simplify vt simplifier.

simplistic a simpliste.

simply adv simplement; (absolutely) absolument.

simulate vt simuler.

simultaneous a simultané.

sin n péché m. ● vi (pt **sinned**) pécher.

....

since

●*preposition*

····▸ depuis; **I haven't seen him** ~ **Monday** je ne l'ai pas vu depuis

lundi; **I've been waiting** ~ **yesterday** j'attends depuis hier; **she had been living in Paris** ~ **1985** elle habitait Paris depuis 1985.

●*conjunction*

····▸ (in time expressions) depuis que; ~ **she's been working here** depuis qu'elle travaille ici; ~ **she left** depuis qu'elle est partie or depuis son départ.

····▸ (because) comme; ~ **he was ill, he couldn't go** comme il était malade, il ne pouvait pas y aller.

●*adverb*

····▸ depuis; **he hasn't been seen** ~ on ne l'a pas vu depuis.

....

sincere a sincère. **sincerely** adv sincèrement. **sincerity** n sincérité f.

sinful a immoral; ~ **man** pécheur m.

sing vt/i (pt **sang**; pp **sung**) chanter.

singe vt (pres p **singeing**) brûler légèrement; (with iron) roussir.

singer n chanteur/-euse m/f.

single a seul; (not double) simple; (unmarried) célibataire; (room, bed) pour une personne; (ticket) simple; **in** ~ **file** en file indienne. ● n (ticket) aller simple m; (record) 45 tours m inv; ~**s** (tennis) simple m. ● vt ~ **out** choisir. ~**-handed** a tout seul. ~**-minded** a tenace. ~ **parent** n parent m isolé.

singular n singulier m. ● a (strange) singulier; (noun) au singulier.

sinister a sinistre.

sink vt (pt **sank**; pp **sunk**) (boat) couler; (well) forer; (post) enfoncer. ● vi (boat) couler; (sun, level) baisser; (wall) s'effondrer. ● n (in kitchen) évier m; (wash-basin)

S

lavabo *m*. □ ∼ **in** (*news*) faire son chemin.

sinner *n* pécheur/-eresse *m/f*.

sip *n* petite gorgée *f*. ● *vt* (*pt* **sipped**) boire à petites gorgées.

siphon *n* siphon *m*. ● *vt* ∼ **off** siphonner.

sir *n* Monsieur *m*; **Sir** (*title*) Sir *m*.

siren *n* sirène *f*.

sirloin *n* aloyau *m*.

sister *n* sœur *f*; (*nurse*) infirmière *f* en chef. ∼**-in-law** *n* (*pl* ∼**s-in-law**) belle-sœur *f*.

sit *vt/i* (*pt* **sat**; *pres p* **sitting**) (s')asseoir; (*committee*) siéger; ∼ (**for**) (*exam*) se présenter à; be ∼**ting** être assis. □ ∼ **around** ne rien faire; ∼ **down** s'asseoir.

site *n* emplacement *m*; (**building**) ∼ chantier *m*. ● *vt* construire.

sitting *n* séance *f*; (*in restaurant*) service *m*. ∼**-room** *n* salon *m*.

situate *vt* situer; be ∼d être situé. **situation** *n* situation *f*.

six *a & n* six (*m*).

sixteen *a & n* seize (*m*).

sixth *a & n* sixième (*mf*).

sixty *a & n* soixante (*m*).

size *n* dimension *f*; (*of person, garment*) taille *f*; (*of shoes*) pointure *f*; (*of sum, salary*) montant *m*; (*extent*) ampleur *f*. □ ∼ **up** (*person*) se faire une opinion de; (*situation*) évaluer. **sizeable** *a* assez grand.

skate *n* patin *m*; (fish) raie *f*. ● *vi* patiner.

skateboard *n* skateboard *m*, planche *f* à roulettes. ● *vi* faire du skateboard.

skating *n* patinage *m*.

skeleton *n* squelette *m*; ∼ **staff** effectifs *mpl* minimums.

sketch *n* esquisse *f*; (*hasty*) croquis *m*; (Theat) sketch *m*. ● *vt* faire une esquisse *or* un croquis de. ● *vi* faire des esquisses.

sketchy *a* (**-ier, -iest**) (*details*) insuffisant; (*memory*) vague.

skewer *n* brochette *f*.

ski *n* ski *m*. ● *a* de ski. ● *vi* (*pt* **ski'd** *or* **skied**; *pres p* **skiing**) skier; (go skiing) faire du ski.

skid *vi* (*pt* **skidded**) déraper. ● *n* dérapage *m*.

skier *n* skieur/-euse *m/f*.

skiing *n* ski *m*.

ski jump *n* saut *m* à ski.

skilful *a* habile.

ski lift *n* remontée *f* mécanique.

skill *n* habileté *f*; (*craft*) compétence *f*; ∼**s** connaissances *fpl*. **skilled** *a* (*worker*) qualifié; (*talented*) consommé.

skim *vt* (*pt* **skimmed**) écumer; (*milk*) écrémer; (*pass over*) effleurer. ● *vi* ∼ **through** parcourir.

skimpy *a* (*clothes*) étriqué.

skin *n* peau *f*. ● *vt* (*pt* **skinned**) (*animal*) écorcher; (*fruit*) éplucher.

skinny *a* (**-ier, -iest**) 🄳 maigre.

skip *vi* (*pt* **skipped**) sautiller; (with rope) sauter à la corde. ● *vt* (*page, class*) sauter. ● *n* petit saut *m*; (container) benne *f*.

skipper *n* capitaine *m*.

skirmish *n* escarmouche.

skirt *n* jupe *f*. ● *vt* contourner. **skirting-board** *n* plinthe *f*.

skittle *n* quille *f*.

skull *n* crâne *m*.

sky *n* ciel *m*. ∼**-blue** *a & n* bleu ciel *m inv*. ∼**scraper** *n* gratte-ciel *m inv*.

slab *n* (of stone) dalle *f*.

slack *a* (not tight) détendu; (*person*) négligent; (*period*) creux. ● *n* (in rope) mou *m*. ● *vi* se relâcher.

slacken *vt* (*rope*) donner du mou à; (*grip*) relâcher; (*pace*) réduire. ● *vi* (*grip, rope*) se relâcher;

(*activity*) ralentir; (*rain*) se calmer.

slam *vt/i* (*pt* **slammed**) (*door*) claquer; (*throw*) flanquer; (*criticize* 🗉) critiquer. ●*n* (*noise*) claquement *m*.

slander *n* (*offence*) diffamation *f*; (*statement*) calomnie *f*. ●*vt* calomnier; (*Jur*) diffamer. **slanderous** *a* diffamatoire.

slang *n* argot *m*.

slant *vt/i* (faire) pencher; (*news*) présenter sous un certain jour. ●*n* inclinaison *f*; (*bias*) angle *m*. **slanted** *a* (biased) orienté; (sloping) en pente.

slap *vt* (*pt* **slapped**) (strike) donner une tape à; (*face*) gifler; (put) flanquer 🗉. ●*n* claque *f*; (on face) gifle *f*. ●*adv* tout droit

slapdash *a* (*person*) brouillon 🗉; (*work*) bâclé 🗉.

slash *vt* (*picture, tyre*) taillader; (*face*) balafrer; (*throat*) couper; (fig) réduire (radicalement). ●*n* lacération *f*.

slat *n* (in blind) lamelle *f*; (on bed) latte *f*.

slate *n* ardoise *f*. ●*vt* 🗉 taper sur 🗉.

slaughter *vt* massacrer; (*animal*) abattre. ●*n* massacre *m*; abattage *m*.

slave *n* esclave *mf*. ●*vi* trimer 🗉. **slavery** *n* esclavage *m*.

sleazy *a* (**-ier, -iest**) 🗉 (*story*) scabreux; (*club*) louche.

sledge *n* luge *f*; (horse-drawn) traîneau *m*.

sleek *a* (*hair*) lisse, brillant; (*shape*) élégant.

sleep *n* sommeil *m*; **go to** ~ s'endormir. ●*vi* (*pt* **slept**) dormir; (spend the night) coucher; ~ **in** faire la grasse matinée. ●*vt* loger.

sleeper *n* (Rail) (berth) couchette *f*; (on track) traverse *f*.

sleeping-bag *n* sac *m* de couchage.

sleeping-pill *n* somnifère *m*.

sleep-walker *n* somnambule *mf*.

sleepy *a* (**-ier, -iest**) somnolent; **be** ~ avoir sommeil.

sleet *n* neige *f* fondue.

sleeve *n* manche *f*; (of record) pochette *f*; **up one's** ~ en réserve.

sleigh *n* traîneau *m*.

slender *a* (*person*) mince; (*majority*) faible.

slept ⇒SLEEP.

slice *n* tranche *f*. ●*vt* couper (en tranches).

slick *a* (adept) habile; (insincere) roublard 🗉. ●*n* (oil) ~ marée *f* noire.

slide *vt/i* (*pt* **slid**) glisser; ~ **into** (go silently) se glisser dans. ●*n* glissade *f*; (fall: fig) baisse *f*; (in playground) toboggan *m*; (for hair) barrette *f*; (Photo) diapositive *f*.

sliding *a* (*door*) coulissant, ~ **scale** échelle *f* mobile.

slight *a* petit, léger; (slender) mince; (frail) frêle. ●*vt* (insult) offenser. ●*n* affront *m*. **slightest** *a* moindre. **slightly** *adv* légèrement, un peu.

slim *a* (**slimmer, slimmest**) mince. ●*vi* (*pt* **slimmed**) maigrir.

slime *n* dépôt *m* gluant; (on river-bed) vase *f*. **slimy** *a* visqueux, (fig) servile.

sling *n* (weapon, toy) fronde *f*; (bandage) écharpe *f*. ●*vt* (*pt* **slung**) jeter, lancer.

slip *vt/i* (*pt* **slipped**) glisser; ~**ped disc** hernie *f* discale; ~ **sb's mind** échapper à qn. ●*n* (mistake) erreur *f*; (petticoat) combinaison *f*; (paper) bout *m* de papier; ~ **of the tongue** lapsus *m*. □ ~ **away** s'esquiver; ~ **into** (go) se glisser dans; (*clothes*) mettre; ~ **up** 🗉 faire une gaffe 🗉.

slipper *n* pantoufle *f*.

slippery *a* glissant.

slip road *n* bretelle *f*.

slit *n* fente *f*. ● *vt* (*pt* **slit**; *pres p* **slitting**) déchirer; ~ **sth open** ouvrir qch; ~ **sb's throat** égorger qn.

slither *vi* glisser.

sliver *n* (of glass) éclat *m*; (of soap) reste *m*.

slobber *vi* 🔲 baver.

slog 🔲 *vt* (*pt* **slogged**) (hit) frapper dur. ● *vi* (work) bosser 🔲. ● *n* (work) travail *m* dur.

slogan *n* slogan *m*.

slope *vi* être en pente; (*handwriting*) pencher. ● *n* pente *f*; (of mountain) flanc *m*.

sloppy *a* (**-ier**, **-iest**) (*food*) liquide; (*work*) négligé; (*person*) négligent.

slosh *vt* 🔲 répandre; (hit 🔲) frapper. ● *vi* clapoter.

slot *n* fente *f*. ● *vt/i* (*pt* **slotted**) (s')insérer.

sloth *n* paresse *f*.

slot-machine *n* distributeur *m* automatique; (for gambling) machine *f* à sous.

slouch *vi* être avachi.

Slovakia *n* Slovaquie *f*.

Slovenia *n* Slovénie *f*.

slovenly *a* débraillé.

slow *a* lent; **be** ~ (*clock*) retarder; **in** ~ **motion** au ralenti. ● *adv* lentement. ● *vt/i* ralentir. **slowly** *adv* lentement. **slowness** *n* lenteur *f*.

sludge *n* vase *f*.

slug *n* (mollusc) limace *f*; (bullet 🔲) balle *f*; (blow 🔲) coup *m*.

sluggish *a* (*person*) léthargique; (*circulation*) lent.

slum *n* taudis *m*.

slump *n* (Econ) effondrement *m*; (in support) baisse *f*. ● *vi* (*demand, trade*) chuter; (*economy*) s'effondrer; (*person*) s'affaler.

slung ⇒SLING.

slur *vt/i* (*pt* **slurred**) (*words*) mal articuler. ● *n* calomnie *f* (**on** sur).

slush *n* (snow) neige *f* fondue. ~ **fund** *n* caisse *f* noire.

sly *a* (crafty) rusé; (secretive) sournois. ● *n* **on the** ~ en cachette.

smack *n* tape *f*; (on face) gifle *f*. ● *vt* donner une tape à; gifler. ● *vi* ~ **of sth** sentir qch. ● *adv* 🔲 tout droit.

small *a* petit. ● *n* ~ **of the back** creux *m* des reins. ● *adv* (cut) menu. ~ **ad** *n* petite annonce *f*. ~ **business** *n* petite entreprise *f*. ~ **change** *n* petite monnaie *f*. ~ **pox** *n* variole *f*. ~ **print** *n* petits caractères *mpl*. ~ **talk** *n* banalités *fpl*.

smart *a* élégant; (clever 🔲) malin, habile; (*restaurant*) chic *inv*; (Comput) intelligent. ● *vi* (*wound*) brûler.

smarten *vt/i* ~ (**up**) embellir; ~ (oneself) **up** s'arranger.

smash *vt/i* (se) briser, (se) fracasser; (*opponent, record*) pulvériser. ● *n* (noise) fracas *m*; (blow) coup *m*; (car crash) collision *f*; (hit record 🔲) tube *m* 🔲.

smashing *a* 🔲 épatant.

SME *abbr* (**small and medium enterprises**) PME.

smear *vt* (stain) tacher; (coat) enduire; (discredit: fig) diffamer. ● *n* tache *f*; (effort to discredit) propos *m* diffamatoire; ~ (**test**) frottis *m*.

smell *n* odeur *f*; (sense) odorat *m*. ● *vt/i* (*pt* **smelt** or **smelled**) sentir; ~ **of** sentir. **smelly** *a* qui sent mauvais.

smelt ⇒SMELL.

smile *n* sourire *m*. ● *vi* sourire.

smiley *n* (Internet) binette *f*.

smirk *n* petit sourire *m* satisfait.

smitten a (in love) fou d'amour.

smog n smog m.

smoke n fumée f; **have a ∼** fumer. ● vt/i fumer. **smoked** a fumé. **smokeless** a (fuel) non polluant. **smoker** n fumeur/-euse m/f. **smoky** a (air) enfumé.

smooth a lisse; (movement) aisé; (manners) onctueux; (flight) sans heurts. ● vt lisser; (process) faciliter.

smoothly adv (move, flow) doucement; (brake, start) en douceur; **go ∼** marcher bien.

smother vt (stifle) étouffer; (cover) couvrir.

smoulder vi (lit) se consumer; (fig) couver.

smudge n trace f. ● vt/i (ink) (s')étaler.

smug a (**smugger, smuggest**) suffisant.

smuggle vt passer (en contrebande). **smuggler** n contrebandier/-ière m/f. **smuggling** n contrebande f.

smutty a grivois.

snack n casse-croûte m inv.

snag n inconvénient m; (in cloth) accroc m.

snail n escargot m.

snake n serpent m.

snap vt/i (pt **snapped**) (whip, fingers) (faire) claquer, (break) (se) casser net; (say) dire sèchement. ● n claquement m; (Photo) photo f. ● a soudain. □ **∼ up** (buy) sauter sur.

snapshot n photo f.

snare n piège m.

snarl vi gronder (en montrant les dents). ● n grondement m. **∼-up** n embouteillage m.

snatch vt (grab) attraper; (steal) voler; (opportunity) saisir; **∼ sth from sb** arracher qch à qn. ● n

(theft) vol m; (short part) fragment m.

sneak vi aller furtivement. ● n 🔲 rapporteur/-euse m/f.

sneer n sourire m méprisant. ● vi sourire avec mépris.

sneeze n éternuement m. ● vi éternuer.

snide a narquois.

sniff vt/i renifler. ● n reniflement m.

snigger n ricanement m. ● vi ricaner.

snip vt (pt **snipped**) couper.

sniper n tireur m embusqué.

snippet n bribe f.

snivel vi (pt **snivelled**) pleurnicher.

snob n snob mf.

snooker n snooker m.

snoop vi 🔲 fourrer son nez partout.

snooty a (-ier, -iest) 🔲 snob inv, hautain.

snooze n petit somme m. ● vi sommeiller.

snore n ronflement m. ● vi ronfler.

snorkel n tuba m.

snort n grognement m. ● vi (person) grogner; (horse) s'ébrouer.

snout n museau m.

snow n neige f. ● vi neiger; **be ∼ed under with** être submergé de.

snowball n boule f de neige. ● vi faire boule de neige.

snow: **∼boarding** n surf m des neiges. **∼-bound** a bloqué par la neige. **∼-drift** n congère f. **∼drop** n perce-neige m or f inv. **∼flake** n flocon m de neige. **∼man** n (pl -men) bonhomme m de neige. **∼-plough** n chasse-neige m inv.

snub vt (pt **snubbed**) rembarrer. ● n rebuffade f.

snuffle vi renifler.

snug *a* (**snugger, snuggest**) (cosy) confortable; (tight) bien ajusté.

snuggle *vi* se pelotonner.

so *adv* si, tellement; (thus) ainsi; ~ **am** I moi aussi; ~ **good as** aussi bon que; **that is** ~ c'est ça; I **think** ~ je pense que oui; **five or** ~ environ cinq; ~ **as to** de manière à; ~ **far** jusqu'ici; ~ **long!** ▣ à bientôt!; ~ **many**, ~ **much** tant (de); ~ **that** pour que. ● *conj* donc, alors.

soak *vt/i* (faire) tremper (**in** dans). □ ~ **in** pénétrer; ~ **up** absorber. **soaking** *a* trempé.

soap *n* savon *m*. ● *vt* savonner. ~ **opera** *n* feuilleton *m*. ~ **powder** *n* lessive *f*.

soar *vi* monter (en flèche).

sob *n* sanglot *m*. ● *vi* (*pt* **sobbed**) sangloter.

sober *a* qui n'a pas bu d'alcool; (serious) sérieux. ● *vi* ~ **up** dessoûler.

soccer *n* football *m*.

sociable *a* sociable.

social *a* social. ● *n* réunion *f* (amicale), fête *f*.

socialism *n* socialisme *m*. **socialist** *a & n* socialiste (*mf*).

socialize *vi* se mêler aux autres; ~ **with** fréquenter.

socially *adv* socialement; (meet) en société.

social: ~ **security** *n* aide *f* sociale. ~ **worker** *n* travailleur/ -euse *m/f* social/-e.

society *n* société *f*.

sociological *a* sociologique. **sociologist** *n* sociologue *mf*. **sociology** *n* sociologie *f*.

sock *n* chaussette *f*. ● *vt* (hit ▣) flanquer un coup (de poing) à.

socket *n* (for lamp) douille *f*; (Electr) prise *f* (de courant); (of eye) orbite *f*.

soda *n* soude *f*; ~**(-water)** eau *f* de Seltz.

sodden *a* détrempé.

sofa *n* canapé *m*. ~ **bed** *n* canapé-lit *m*.

soft *a* (gentle, lenient) doux; (not hard) doux, mou; (heart, wood) tendre; (silly) ramolli. ~ **drink** *n* boisson *f* non alcoolisée.

soften *vt/i* (se) ramollir; (tone down, lessen) (s')adoucir.

soft spot *n* to have a ~ for sb avoir un faible pour qn.

software *n* logiciel *m*.

soggy *a* (**-ier, -iest**) (ground) détrempé; (food) ramolli.

soil *n* sol *m*, terre *f*. ● *vt/i* (se) salir.

sold ⇒SELL. ● *a* ~ **out** épuisé.

solder *n* soudure *f*. ● *vt* souder.

soldier *n* soldat *m*. ● *vi* ~ **on** ▣ persévérer.

sole *n* (of foot) plante *f*; (of shoe) semelle *f*; (fish) sole *f*. ● *a* unique, seul. **solely** *adv* uniquement.

solemn *a* solennel.

solicitor *n* notaire *m*; (for court and police work) ≈ avocat/-e *m/f*.

solid *a* solide; (not hollow) plein; (gold) massif; (mass) compact; (meal) substantiel. ● *n* solide *m*; ~**s** (food) aliments *mpl* solides.

solidarity *n* solidarité *f*.

solidify *vt/i* (se) solidifier.

solitary *a* (alone) solitaire; (only) seul.

solo *n* solo *m*. ● *a* (Mus) solo *inv*; (flight) en solitaire.

soluble *a* soluble.

solution *n* solution *f*.

solve *vt* résoudre.

solvent *a* (Comm) solvable. ● *n* (dis)solvant *m*.

....

some

● *determiner*

····▶ (unspecified amount) du/de l'/de la/des; **I have to buy ∼ bread** je dois acheter du pain; **have ∼ water** prenez de l'eau; **∼ sweets** des bonbons.

····▶ (certain) certains/certaines; **∼ people say that** certains disent que.

····▶ (unknown) un/une; **∼ man came to the house** un homme est venu à la maison.

····▶ (considerable amount) **we stayed there for ∼ time** nous sommes restés là assez longtemps; **it will take ∼ doing** ça ne va pas être facile à faire.

> ! In front of a plural adjective *des* changes to *de*: **some pretty dresses** *de jolies robes.*

● *pronoun*

····▶ en; **he wants ∼** il en veut; **have ∼ more** reprenez-en.

····▶ (certain) certains/certaines; **∼ are expensive** certains sont chers.

● *adverb*

····▶ environ; **∼ 20 people** environ 20 personnes.

somebody *pron* quelqu'un. ● *n* **be a ∼** être quelqu'un.

somehow *adv* d'une manière ou d'une autre; (for some reason) je ne sais pas pourquoi.

someone *pron & n* = SOMEBODY.

someplace *adv* (US) = SOMEWHERE.

somersault *n* roulade *f*. ● *vi* faire une roulade.

something *pron & n* quelque chose (*m*); **∼ good** quelque chose de bon; **∼ like** un peu comme.

sometime *adv* un jour; **∼ in June** en juin. ● *a* (former) ancien.

sometimes *adv* quelquefois, parfois.

somewhat *adv* quelque peu, un peu.

somewhere *adv* quelque part.

son *n* fils *m*.

song *n* chanson *f*; (of bird) chant *m*.

son-in-law *n* (*pl* **sons-in-law**) gendre *m*.

soon *adv* bientôt; (early) tôt; **I would ∼er stay** j'aimerais mieux rester; **∼ after** peu après; **∼er or later** tôt ou tard.

soot *n* suie *f*.

soothe *vt* calmer.

sophisticated *a* raffiné; (*machine*) sophistiqué.

sopping *a* trempé.

soppy *a* (**-ier, -iest**) 🔲 sentimental.

sorcerer *n* sorcier *m*.

sordid *a* sordide.

sore *a* douloureux; (vexed) en rogne (**at, with** contre). ● *n* plaie *f*.

sorely *adv* fortement.

sorrow *n* chagrin *m*.

sorry *a* (**-ier, -iest**) (regretful) désolé (**to** de; **that** que); (wretched) triste; **feel ∼ for** plaindre; **∼!** pardon!

sort *n* genre *m*, sorte *f*, espèce *f*; (person 🔲) type *m*; **what ∼ of?** quel genre de?; **be out of ∼s** ne pas être dans son assiette. ● *vt* **∼ (out)** (classify) trier; **∼ out** (tidy) ranger; (arrange) arranger; (*problem*) régler.

so-so *a & adv* comme ci comme ça.

sought ⇒SEEK.

soul *n* âme *f*.

sound *n* son *m*, bruit *m*. ● *a* solide; (healthy) sain; (sensible) sensé. ● *vt/i* sonner; (seem) sembler (**as if** que); (test) sonder; **∼ out** sonder; **∼ a horn** klaxonner; **∼ like** sembler être. ∼

S

asleep a profondément endormi.
~ **barrier** n mur m du son.

soundly adv (sleep) à poings
fermés; (built) solidement.

sound-proof a insonorisé. ● vt
insonoriser.

sound-track n bande f sonore.

soup n soupe f, potage m.

sour a aigre. ● vt/i (s')aigrir.

source n source f.

south n sud m. ● a sud inv, du
sud. ● adv vers le sud.

South Africa n Afrique f du Sud.

South America n Amérique f du
Sud.

south-east n sud-est m.

southern a du sud. **southerner** n
habitant/-e m/f du sud.

southward a (side) sud inv;
(journey) vers le sud.

south-west n sud-ouest m.

souvenir n souvenir m.

sovereign n & a souverain/-e
(m/f).

sow[1] vt (pt **sowed**; pp **sowed** or
sown) (seed) semer; (land)
ensemencer.

sow[2] n (pig) truie f.

soya n soja m. ~ **sauce** n sauce f
soja.

spa n station f thermale.

space n espace m; (room) place f;
(period) période f. ● a (research)
spatial. ● vt ~ (out) espacer.
~**craft** n inv, ~**ship** n engin m
spatial. ~**suit** n combinaison f
spatiale.

spacious a spacieux.

spade n (for garden) bêche f; (child's)
pelle f; (cards) pique m. ~**work** n
(fig) travail m préparatoire.

spaghetti n spaghetti mpl.

Spain n Espagne f.

spam n (Comput) multipostage m
abusif.

span n (of arch) portée f; (of wings)
envergure f; (of time) durée f. ● vt

(pt **spanned**) enjamber; (in time)
embrasser.

Spaniard n Espagnol/-e m/f.

spaniel n épagneul m.

Spanish a espagnol. ● n
espagnol m.

spank vt donner une fessée à.

spanner n (tool) clé f (plate);
(adjustable) clé f à molette.

spare vt (treat leniently) épargner;
(do without) se passer de; (afford to
give) donner, accorder. ● a en
réserve; (surplus) de trop; (tyre,
shoes) de rechange; (room, bed)
d'ami; **are there any** ~ **tickets?** y
a-t-il encore des places? ● n ~
(part) pièce f de rechange. ~
time n loisirs mpl.

sparing a frugal. **sparingly** adv
en petite quantité.

spark n étincelle f. ● vt ~ **off**
(initiate) provoquer.

sparkle vi étinceler. ● n
étincellement m. **sparkling** a
(wine) mousseux; (eyes) brillant.

spark-plug n bougie f.

sparrow n moineau m.

sparse a clairsemé. **sparsely** adv
(furnished) peu.

spasm n (of muscle) spasme m; (of
coughing, anger) accès m.

spat ⇒SPIT.

spate n a ~ **of** (letters) une
avalanche de.

spatter vt éclabousser (with de).

spawn n frai m, œufs mpl. ● vt
pondre. ● vi frayer.

speak vi (pt **spoke**; pp **spoken**)
parler. ● vt (say) dire; (language)
parler. □ ~ **up** parler plus fort.

speaker n (in public) orateur m;
(Pol) président m; (loudspeaker)
baffle m; **be a French/a good** ~
parler français/bien.

spear n lance f.

spearmint n menthe f verte.

special *a* spécial; (exceptional) exceptionnel.

specialist *n* spécialiste *mf*.

speciality, (US) **specialty** *n* spécialité *f*.

specialize *vi* se spécialiser (**in** en).

specially *adv* spécialement.

species *n inv* espèce *f*.

specific *a* précis, explicite.

specification *n* (of design) spécification *f*; (of car equipment) caractéristiques *fpl*. **specify** *vt* spécifier.

specimen *n* spécimen *m*, échantillon *m*.

speck *n* (stain) (petite) tache *f*; (particle) grain *m*.

specs *npl* ⊞ lunettes *fpl*.

spectacle *n* spectacle *m*. **spectacles** *n* lunettes *fpl*. **spectacular** *a* spectaculaire.

spectator *n* spectateur/-trice *m/f*.

spectrum *n* (*pl* **-tra**) spectre *m*; (of ideas) gamme *f*.

speculate *vi* s'interroger (**about** sur); (Comm) spéculer. **speculation** *n* conjectures *fpl*; (Comm) spéculation *f*. **speculator** *n* spéculateur/-trice *m/f*.

speech *n* (faculty) parole *f*; (diction) élocution *f*; (dialect) langage *m*; (address) discours *m*. **speechless** *a* muet (**with** de).

speed *n* (of movement) vitesse *f*; (swiftness) rapidité *f*. ● *vi* (*pt* **sped**) aller vite; (*pt* **speeded**) (drive too fast) aller trop vite. □ ∼ **up** accélérer; (of pace) s'accélérer.

speedboat *n* vedette *f*.

speeding *n* excès *m* de vitesse.

speed limit *n* limitation *f* de vitesse.

speedometer *n* compteur *m* (de vitesse).

spell *n* (magic) charme *m*, sortilège *m*; (curse) sort *m*; (of time) (courte) période *f*. ● *vt/i* (*pt* **spelled** or **spelt**) écrire; (mean) signifier; ∼ **out** épeler; (explain) expliquer. ∼**checker** *n* correcteur *m* orthographique.

spelling *n* orthographe *f*. ● *a* (mistake) d'orthographe.

spend *vt* (*pt* **spent**) (money) dépenser (**on** pour); (time, holiday) passer; (energy) consacrer (**on** à). ● *vi* dépenser.

spent ⇒SPEND. ● *a* (used) utilisé; (person) épuisé.

sperm *n* (*pl* **sperms** or **sperm**) sperme *m*.

sphere *n* sphère *f*.

spice *n* épice *f*; (fig) piquant *m*.

spick-and-span *a* impeccable.

spicy *a* épicé; piquant.

spider *n* araignée *f*.

spike *n* pointe *f*.

spill *vt* (*pt* **spilled** or **spilt**) renverser, répandre. ● *vi* se répandre; ∼ **over** déborder.

spin *vt/i* (*pt* **spun**; *pres p* **spinning**) (wool, web) filer; (turn) (faire) tourner; (story) débiter; ∼ **out** faire durer. ● *n* (movement, excursion) tour *m*.

spinach *n* épinards *mpl*.

spinal *a* vertébral. ∼ **cord** *n* moelle *f* épinière.

spin-drier *n* essoreuse *f*.

spine *n* colonne *f* vertébrale; (prickle) piquant *m*.

spin-off *n* avantage *m* accessoire; (by-product) dérivé *m*.

spinster *n* célibataire *f*; (pej) vieille fille *f*.

spiral *a* en spirale; (staircase) en colimaçon. ● *n* spirale *f*. ● *vi* (*pt* **spiralled**) (prices) monter (en flèche).

spire *n* flèche *f*.

spirit *n* esprit *m*; (boldness) courage *m*; ∼**s** (morale) moral *m*;

S

(drink) spiritueux *mpl*. ●*vt* ~ **away** faire disparaître. **spirited** *a* fougueux. ~-**level** *n* niveau *m* à bulle.

spiritual *a* spirituel.

spit *vt/i* (*pt* **spat** *or* **spit**; *pres p* **spitting**) cracher; (of rain) crachiner; ~ **out** cracher; **the** ~**ting image of** le portrait craché *or* vivant de. ●*n* crachat(s) *m*(*pl*); (for meat) broche *f*.

spite *n* rancune *f*; **in** ~ **of** malgré. ●*vt* contrarier.

splash *vt* éclabousser. ●*vi* faire des éclaboussures; ~ (**about**) patauger. ●*n* (act, mark) éclaboussure *f*; (sound) plouf *m*; (of colour) tache *f*.

spleen *n* (Anat) rate *f*.

splendid *a* magnifique, splendide.

splint *n* (Med) attelle *f*.

splinter *n* éclat *m*; (in finger) écharde *f*. ~ **group** *n* groupe *m* dissident.

split *vt/i* (*pt* **split**; *pres p* **splitting**) (se) fendre; (tear) (se) déchirer; (divide) (se) diviser; (share) partager; ~ **one's sides** se tordre (de rire). ●*n* fente *f*; déchirure *f*; (share 🔲) part *f*, partage *m*; (quarrel) rupture *f*; (Pol) scission *f*. □ ~ **up** (*couple*) rompre. ~ **second** *n* fraction *f* de seconde.

splutter *vi* crachoter; (stammer) bafouiller; (*engine*) tousser.

spoil *vt* (*pt* **spoilt** *or* **spoiled**) (pamper) gâter; (ruin) abîmer; (mar) gâcher, gâter. ●*n* ~(**s**) butin *m*. ~-**sport** *n* trouble-fête *mf inv*.

spoke[1] *n* rayon *m*.

spoke[2], **spoken** ⇒SPEAK.

spokesman *n* (*pl* -**men**) porte-parole *m inv*.

sponge *n* éponge *f*. ●*vt* éponger. ●*vi* ~ **on** vivre aux crochets de.

~-**bag** *n* trousse *f* de toilette. ~-**cake** *n* génoise *f*.

sponsor *n* (of concert) parrain *m*, sponsor *m*; (surety) garant *m*; (for membership) parrain *m*, marraine *f*. ●*vt* parrainer, sponsoriser; (*member*) parrainer.

sponsorship *n* patronage *m*; parrainage *m*.

spontaneous *a* spontané.

spoof *n* 🔲 parodie *f*.

spoon *n* cuiller *f*, cuillère *f*.

spoonful *n* (*pl* ~**s**) cuillerée *f*.

sport *n* sport *m*; (good) ~ (person 🔲) chic type *m*; ~**s car**/**coat** voiture/veste *f* de sport. ●*vt* (display) exhiber, arborer.

sporting *a* sportif; **a** ~ **chance** une assez bonne chance.

sportsman *n* (*pl* -**men**) sportif *m*.

sporty *a* 🔲 sportif.

spot *n* (mark, stain) tache *f*; (dot) point *m*; (in pattern) pois *m*; (drop) goutte *f*; (place) endroit *m*; (pimple) bouton *m*; **a** ~ **of** 🔲 un peu de; **on the** ~ sur place; (without delay) sur le coup. ●*vt* (*pt* **spotted**) 🔲 apercevoir. ~-**check** *n* contrôle *m* surprise.

spotless *a* impeccable.

spotlight *n* (lamp) projecteur *m*, spot *m*.

spotty *a* (skin) boutonneux.

spouse *n* époux *m*, épouse *f*.

spout *n* (of teapot) bec *m*; (of liquid) jet *m*; **up the** ~ (ruined 🔲) fichu. ●*vi* jaillir.

sprain *n* entorse *f*, foulure *f*. ●*vt* ~ **one's wrist** se fouler le poignet.

sprang ⇒SPRING.

sprawl *vi* (*town, person*) s'étaler. ●*n* étalement *m*.

spray *n* (of flowers) gerbe *f*; (water) gerbe *f* d'eau; (from sea) embruns *mpl*; (device) bombe *f*, atomiseur *m*. ●*vt* (*surface, insecticide, plant*)

vaporiser; (*person*) asperger; (*crops*) traiter.
spread vt/i (*pt* **spread**) (stretch, extend) (s')étendre; (*news, fear*) (se) répandre; (*illness*) (se) propager; (*butter*) (s')étaler. ● *n* propagation *f*; (of population) distribution *f*; (paste) pâte *f* à tartiner; (food) belle table *f*. ~**-eagled** *a* bras et jambes écartés. ~**sheet** *n* tableur *m*.
spree *n* go on a ~ (have fun 🆃) faire la noce.
sprig *n* petite branche *f*.
sprightly *a* (-**ier**, -**iest**) alcrtc, vif.
spring vi (*pt* **sprang**; *pp* **sprung**) bondir. ● vt ~ **sth on sb** annoncer qch de but en blanc à qn. ● *n* bond *m*; (device) ressort *m*; (season) printemps *m*; (of water) source *f*. ▫ ~ **from** provenir de; ~ **up** surgir. ~**board** *n* tremplin *m*. ~**onion** *n* oignon *m* blanc.
springy *a* (-**ier**, -**iest**) élastique.
sprinkle vt (with liquid) arroser (**with** de); (with salt, flour) saupoudrer (**with** de); (sand) répandre. **sprinkler** *n* (in garden) arroseur *m*; (for fires) extincteur *m* (à déclenchement) automatique.
sprint vi (Sport) sprinter. ● *n* sprint *m*.
sprout vt/i pousser. ● *n* (on plant) pousse *f*; (**Brussels**) ~**s** choux *mpl* de Bruxelles.
spruce *a* pimpant. ● vt ~ **oneself up** se faire beau. ● *n* (tree) épicéa *m*.
sprung ⇒SPRING.
spud *n* 🆃 patate *f*.
spun ⇒SPIN.
spur *n* (of rider) éperon *m*; (stimulus) aiguillon *m*; **on the** ~ **of the moment** sous l'impulsion du moment. ● vt (*pt* **spurred**) éperonner.
spurious *a* faux.
spurn vt repousser.

spurt vi jaillir; (fig) accélérer. ● *n* jet *m*; (of energy) sursaut *m*.
spy *n* espion/-ne *m/f*. ● vi espionner. ● vt apercevoir.
squabble vi se chamailler. ● *n* chamaillerie *f*.
squad *n* (of soldiers) escouade *f*; (Sport) équipe *f*.
squadron *n* (Mil) escadron *m*; (Aviat) escadrille *f*.
squalid *a* sordide.
squander vt (*money, time*) gaspiller.
square *n* carré *m*; (open space in town) place *f*. ● *a* carré; (honest) honnête; (*meal*) solide; (boring 🆃) ringard; (all) ~ (quits) quitte; ~ **metre** mètre *m* carré. ● vt (settle) régler; ~ **up to** faire face à.
squash vt écraser; (crowd) serrer. ● *n* (game) squash *m*; (marrow: US) courge *f*; **lemon** ~ citronnade *f*; **orange** ~ orangeade *f*.
squat vi (*pt* **squatted**) s'accroupir; ~ **in a house** squattériser une maison. ● *a* (dumpy) trapu. **squatter** *n* squatter *m*.
squawk *n* cri *m* rauque. ● vi pousser un cri rauque.
squeak *n* petit cri *m*; (of door) grincement *m*. ● vi crier, grincer.
squeal *n* cri *m* aigu. ● vi pousser un cri aigu; ~ **on** (inform on 🆃) dénoncer.
squeamish *a* (trop) délicat.
squeeze vt presser; (*hand, arm*) serrer; (extract) exprimer (**from** de); (extort) soutirer (**from** à). ● vi (force one's way) se glisser. ● *n* pression *f*; (Comm) restrictions *fpl* de crédit.
squid *n* calmar *m*.
squint vi loucher; (with half-shut eyes) plisser les yeux. ● *n* (Med) strabisme *m*.
squirm vi se tortiller.
squirrel *n* écureuil *m*.

S

squirt *vt/i* (faire) jaillir. ● *n* jet *m*.

stab *vt* (*pt* **stabbed**) (with knife) poignarder. ● *n* coup *m* (de couteau); **have a ~ at sth** essayer de faire qch.

stability *n* stabilité *f*. **stabilize** *vt* stabiliser.

stable *a* stable. ● *n* écurie *f*. **~-boy** *n* lad *m*.

stack *n* tas *m*. ● *vt* **~ (up)** entasser, empiler.

stadium *n* stade *m*.

staff *n* personnel *m*; (in school) professeurs *mpl*; (Mil) état-major *m*; (stick) bâton *m*. ● *vt* pourvoir en personnel.

stag *n* cerf *m*.

stage *n* (Theat) scène *f*; (phase) stade *m*, étape *f*; (platform in hall) estrade *f*; **go on the ~** faire du théâtre. ● *vt* mettre en scène; (fig) organiser. **~ door** *n* entrée *f* des artistes. **~ fright** *n* trac *m*.

stagger *vi* chanceler. ● *vt* (shock) stupéfier; (*payments*) échelonner. **staggering** *a* stupéfiant.

stagnate *vi* stagner.

stag night *n* soirée *f* pour enterrer une vie de garçon.

staid *a* sérieux.

stain *vt* tacher; (*wood*) colorer. ● *n* tache *f*; (colouring) colorant *m*. **stained glass window** *n* vitrail *m*.

stainless steel *n* acier *m* inoxydable.

stain remover *n* détachant *m*.

stair *n* marche *f*; **the ~s** l'escalier *m*. **~case**, **~way** *n* escalier *m*.

stake *n* (post) pieu *m*; (wager) enjeu *m*; **at ~** en jeu. ● *vt* (*area*) jalonner; (*wager*) jouer; **~ a claim to** revendiquer.

stale *a* pas frais; (*bread*) rassis; (*smell*) de renfermé.

stalk *n* (of plant) tige *f*. ● *vi* marcher de façon guindée. ● *vt*

(*hunter*) chasser; (*murderer*) suivre.

stall *n* (in stable) stalle *f*; (in market) éventaire *m*; **~s** (Theat) orchestre *m*. ● *vt/i* (Auto) caler; **~ (for time)** temporiser.

stallion *n* étalon *m*.

stamina *n* résistance *f*.

stammer *vt/i* bégayer. ● *n* bégaiement *m*.

stamp *vt/i* **~ (one's foot)** taper du pied. ● *vt* (*letter*) timbrer. ● *n* (for postage, marking) timbre *m*; (mark: fig) sceau *m*. □ **~ out** supprimer. **~-collecting** *n* philatélie *f*.

stampede *n* fuite *f* désordonnée; (rush: fig) ruée *f*. ● *vi* s'enfuir en désordre; se ruer.

stand *vi* (*pt* **stood**) être *or* se tenir (debout); (rise) se lever; (be situated) se trouver; (Pol) être candidat (for à); **~ in line** (US) faire la queue; **~ to reason** être logique. ● *vt* mettre (debout); (tolerate) supporter; **~ a chance** avoir une chance. ● *n* (stance) position *f*; (Mil) résistance *f*; (for lamp) support *m*; (at fair) stand *m*; (in street) kiosque *m*; (for spectators) tribune *f*; (Jur, US) barre *f*; **make a ~** prendre position. □ **~ back** reculer; **~ by** *or* **around** ne rien faire; **~ by** (be ready) se tenir prêt; (*promise, person*) rester fidèle à; **~ down** se désister; **~ for** représenter; Ⅱ supporter; **~ in for** remplacer; **~ out** ressortir; **~ up** se lever; **~ up for** défendre; **~ up to** résister à.

standard *n* norme *f*; (level) niveau *m* (voulu); (flag) étendard *m*; **~ of living** niveau *m* de vie; **~s** (morals) principes *mpl*. ● *a* ordinaire.

standard of living *n* niveau *m* de vie.

stand-by *a* de réserve. ● *n* **be a ~** être de réserve.

stand-in *n* remplaçant/-e *m/f*.

standing a debout *inv.* ● n réputation f; (duration) durée f. ~ **order** n prélèvement m bancaire.

standpoint n point m de vue.

standstill n **at a** ~ immobile; **bring/come to a** ~ (s')immobiliser.

stank ⇒STINK.

staple n agrafe. ● vt agrafer. ● a principal, de base. **stapler** n agrafeuse f.

star n étoile f; (person) vedette f. ● vt (pt **starred**) (film) avoir pour vedette. ● vi ~ **in** être la vedette de.

starch n amidon m; (in food) fécule f. ● vt amidonner.

stardom n célébrité f.

stare vi ~ **at** regarder fixement. ● n regard m fixe.

starfish n étoile f de mer.

stark a (desolate) désolé; (severe) austère; (utter) complet; (fact) brutal. ● adv complètement.

starling n étourneau m.

start vt/i commencer; (machine) (se) mettre en marche; (fashion) lancer; (cause) provoquer; (jump) sursauter; (of vehicle) démarrer; ~ **to do** commencer or se mettre à faire; ~**ing tomorrow** à partir de demain. ● n commencement m, début m; (of race) départ m, (lead) avance f; (jump) sursaut m. □ ~ **off** commencer (**doing** par faire); ~ **out** partir; ~ **up** (business) lancer. **starter** n (Auto) démarreur m; (runner) partant m; (Culin) entrée f.

starting point n point m de départ.

startle vt (make jump) faire tressaillir; (shock) alarmer.

starvation n faim f.

starve vi mourir de faim. ● vt affamer; (deprive) priver.

stash vt cacher.

state n état m; (pomp) apparat m; S~ État m; **the** S~**s** les États-Unis; **get into a** ~ s'affoler. ● a d'État, de l'État; (school) public. ● vt affirmer (**that** que); (views) exprimer; (fix) fixer.

stately a (-ier, -iest) majestueux. ~ **home** n château m.

statement n déclaration f; (of account) relevé m.

statesman n (pl -men) homme m d'État.

static a statique. ● n (radio, TV) parasites mpl.

station n (Rail) gare f; (TV) chaîne f; (Mil) poste m; (rank) condition f. ● vt poster, placer; ~**ed at** or **in** (Mil) en garnison à.

stationary a immobile, stationnaire; (vehicle) à l'arrêt.

stationery n papeterie f.

station wagon n (US) break m.

statistic n statistique f; ~**s** statistique f.

statue n statue f.

status n (pl ~**es**) situation f, statut m; (prestige) standing m.

statute n loi f; ~**s** (rules) statuts mpl. **statutory** a statutaire; (holiday) légal.

staunch a (friend) loyal, fidèle.

stave n (Mus) portée f. ● vt ~ **off** éviter, conjurer.

stay vi rester; (spend time) séjourner; (reside) loger. ● vt (hunger) tromper. ● n séjour m. □ ~ **away from** (school) ne pas aller à; ~ **behind** or ~ **on** rester; ~ **in** rester à la maison; ~ **up** veiller, se coucher tard.

stead n **stand sb in good** ~ être utile à qn.

steadfast a ferme.

steady a (-ier, -iest) stable; (hand, voice) ferme; (regular) régulier; (staid) sérieux. ● vt maintenir, assurer; (calm) calmer.

steak n steak m, bifteck m; (of fish) darne f.

steal vt/i (pt **stole**; pp **stolen**)
voler (**from sb** à qn).

steam n vapeur f; (on glass) buée
f. ● vt (cook) cuire à la vapeur.
● vi fumer. ~**-engine** n
locomotive f à vapeur

steamer n (Culin) cuit-vapeur m;
(boat) (bateau à) vapeur m.

steel n acier m; ~ **industry**
sidérurgie f. ● vpr ~ **oneself**
s'endurcir, se cuirasser.

steep a raide, rapide; (price: ▣)
excessif. ● vt (soak) tremper; ~**ed**
in (fig) imprégné de.

steeple n clocher m.

steer vt diriger; (ship) gouverner;
(fig) guider. ● vi (in ship)
gouverner; ~ **clear of** éviter.

steering-wheel n volant m.

stem n tige f; (of glass) pied m.
● vi (pt **stemmed**) ~ **from**
provenir de. ● vt (pt **stemmed**)
(check, stop) endiguer, contenir. ~
cell n cellule f souche.

stench n puanteur f.

stencil n pochoir m. ● vt (pt
stencilled) décorer au pochoir.

step vi (pt **stepped**) marcher,
aller. ● n pas m; (stair) marche f;
(of train) marchepied m; (action)
mesure f; ~**s** (ladder) escabeau m;
in ~ au pas; (fig) conforme (**with**
à). □ ~ **down** (resign)
démissionner; (from ladder)
descendre; ~ **forward** faire un
pas en avant; ~ **in** (intervene)
intervenir; ~ **up** (pressure)
augmenter. ~**brother** n demi-
frère m. ~**daughter** n belle-fille
f. ~**father** n beau-père m.
~**-ladder** n escabeau m.
~**mother** n belle-mère f.

stepping-stone n (fig) tremplin
m. ~**sister** n demi-sœur f. ~**son**
n beau-fils m.

stereo n stéréo f; (record-player)
chaîne f stéréo. ● a stéréo inv.

stereotype n stéréotype m.

sterile a stérile. **sterility** n
stérilité f.

sterilize vt stériliser.

sterling n livre(s) f(pl) sterling.
● a sterling inv; (silver) fin; (fig)
excellent.

stern a sévère. ● n (of ship) arrière
m.

steroid n stéroïde m.

stew vt/i cuire à la casserole;
~**ed fruit** compote f; ~**ed tea** thé
m trop infusé. ● n ragoût m.

steward n (of club) intendant m;
(on ship) steward m. **stewardess**
n hôtesse f.

stick vt (pt **stuck**) (glue) coller;
(put ▣) mettre; (endure ▣)
supporter. ● vi (adhere) coller,
adhérer; (to pan) attacher; (remain
▣) rester; (be jammed) être coincé;
be stuck with sb ▣ se farcir qn.
● n bâton m; (for walking) canne f.
□ ~ **at** persévérer dans; ~ **out** vt
(head) sortir; (tongue) tirer; vi
(protrude) dépasser; ~ **to**
(promise) rester fidèle à; ~ **up**
for ▣ défendre.

sticker n autocollant m.

sticky a (-**ier**, -**iest**) poisseux;
(label, tape) adhésif.

stiff a raide (limb, joint)
ankylosé; (tough) dur; (drink) fort;
(price) élevé; (manner) guindé; ~
neck torticolis m.

stifle vt/i étouffer.

stiletto a & n ~**s**, ~ **heels** talons
mpl aiguille.

still a immobile; (quiet) calme,
tranquille; **keep** ~! arrête de
bouger! ● n silence m. ● adv
encore, toujours; (even) encore;
(nevertheless) tout de même.

stillborn a mort-né.

still life n nature f morte.

stimulate vt stimuler.
stimulation n stimulation f.

stimulus n (pl -**li**) (spur) stimulant
m.

sting n piqûre f; (of insect)
aiguillon m. ● vt/i (pt **stung**)
piquer.

stingy a (**-ier, -iest**) avare (**with**
de).

stink n puanteur f. ● vi (pt **stank**
or **stunk**; pp **stunk**) ~ (**of**) puer.

stipulate vt stipuler.

stir vt/i (pt **stirred**) (move)
remuer; (excite) exciter; ~ **up**
(trouble) provoquer. ● n agitation
f.

stirrup n étrier m.

stitch n point m; (in knitting) maille
f; (Med) point m de suture; (muscle
pain) point m de côté; **be in ~es**
Ⓘ avoir le fou rire. ● vt coudre.

stock n réserve f; (Comm) stock m;
(financial) valeurs fpl; (family)
souche f; (soup) bouillon m; **we're
out of ~** il n'y en a plus; **take ~**
(fig) faire le point; **in ~** en stock.
● a (goods) courant. ● vt (shop)
approvisionner; (sell) vendre. ● vi
~ **up** s'approvisionner (**with** de).
~ **broker** n agent m de change.
~ **cube** n bouillon-cube m. **S~
Exchange** n Bourse f.

stocking n bas m.

stock market n Bourse f.

stockpile n stock m. ● vt stocker;
(arms) amasser.

stock-taking n (Comm) inventaire
m.

stocky a (**-ier, -iest**) trapu.

stodgy a lourd.

stole, stolen ⇒STEAL.

stomach n estomac m; (abdomen)
ventre m. ● vt (put up with)
supporter. ~**ache** n mal m à
l'estomac or au ventre.

stone n pierre f; (pebble) caillou
m; (in fruit) noyau m; (weight) 6,350
kg. ● a de pierre; ~**cold/-deaf**
complètement froid/sourd. ● vt
(throw stones) lapider; (fruit)
dénoyauter.

stony a pierreux.

stood ⇒STAND.

stool n tabouret m.

stoop vi (bend) se baisser;
(condescend) s'abaisser. ● n **have a
~** être voûté.

stop vt/i (pt **stopped**) arrêter
(**doing** de faire); (moving, talking)
s'arrêter; (prevent) empêcher (**from**
de); (hole, leak) boucher; (pain,
noise) cesser; (stay Ⓘ) rester. ● n
arrêt m; (full stop) point m; ~(**-over**)
halte f; (port of call) escale f. □ ~
off s'arrêter; ~ **up** boucher,

stopgap n bouche-trou m. ● a
intérimaire.

stoppage n arrêt m; (of work) arrêt
m de travail, (of pay) retenue f.

stopper n bouchon m.

stop-watch n chronomètre m.

storage n (of goods, food)
emmagasinage m. ● **heater** n
radiateur m électrique à
accumulation.

store n réserve f; (warehouse)
entrepôt m; (shop) grand magasin
m; (US) magasin m; **have in ~ for**
réserver à; **set ~ by** attacher du
prix à. ● vt (for future) mettre en
réserve; (in warehouse, mind)
emmagasiner. ~**room** n réserve
f.

storey n étage m.

stork n cigogne f.

storm n tempête f, orage m. ● vt
prendre d'assaut. ● vi (rage)
tempêter.

story n histoire f; (in press) article
m; (storey: US) étage m. ~**teller** n
conteur/-euse m/f.

stout a corpulent; (strong) solide.
● n bière f brune.

stove n cuisinière f.

stow vt ~ **away** (put away) ranger;
(hide) cacher. ● vi voyager
clandestinement.

straddle vt être à cheval sur,
enjamber.

straggler n traînard/-e m/f.

S

straight *a* droit; (tidy) en ordre; (frank) franc; ~ **face** visage *m* sérieux; **get sth** ~ mettre qch au clair. ● *adv* (in straight line) droit; (direct) tout droit; ~ **ahead** *or* **on** tout droit; ~ **away** tout de suite; ~ **off** Ⓕ sans hésiter. ● *n* (Sport) ligne *f* droite.

straighten *vt* (*nail, situation*) redresser; (tidy) arranger.

straightforward *a* honnête; (easy) simple.

straight off *a* Ⓕ sans hésiter.

strain *vt* (*rope, ears*) tendre; (*limb*) fouler; (*eyes*) fatiguer; (*muscle*) froisser; (filter) passer; (*vegetables*) égoutter; (fig) mettre à l'épreuve. ● *vi* fournir des efforts. ● *n* tension *f*; (fig) effort *m*; (breed) race *f*; (of virus) variété *f*; ~**s** (tune: Mus) accents *mpl*.

strained *a* forcé; (*relations*) tendu. **strainer** *n* passoire *f*.

strait *n* détroit *m*; ~**s** détroit *m*; **be in dire** ~**s** être aux abois. ~**-jacket** *n* camisole *f* de force.

strand *n* (thread) fil *m*, brin *m*; (of hair) mèche *f*.

stranded *a* (*person*) en rade; (*ship*) échoué.

strange *a* étrange; (unknown) inconnu. **stranger** *n* inconnu/-e *m/f*.

strangle *vt* étrangler.

stranglehold *n* **have a** ~ **on** tenir à la gorge.

strap *n* (of leather) courroie *f*; (of dress) bretelle *f*; (of watch) bracelet *m*. ● *vt* (*pt* **strapped**) attacher.

strategic *a* stratégique. **strategy** *n* stratégie *f*.

straw *n* paille *f*; **the last** ~ le comble.

strawberry *n* fraise *f*.

stray *vi* s'égarer; (deviate) s'écarter. ● *a* perdu; (isolated) isolé. ● *n* animal *m* perdu.

streak *n* raie *f*, bande *f*; (trace)

trace *f*; (period) période *f*; (tendency) tendance *f*. ● *vt* (mark) strier. ● *vi* filer à toute allure.

stream *n* ruisseau *m*; (current) courant *m*; (flow) flot *m*; (in school) classe *f* (de niveau). ● *vi* ruisseler (with de); (*eyes, nose*) couler.

streamline *vt* rationaliser. **streamlined** *a* (shape) aérodynamique.

street *n* rue *f*. ~**car** *n* (US) tramway *m*. ~ **lamp** *n* réverbère *m*. ~ **map** *n* indicateur *m* des rues.

strength *n* force *f*; (of wall, fabric) solidité *f*; **on the** ~ **of** en vertu de. **strengthen** *vt* renforcer, fortifier.

strenuous *a* (exercise) énergique; (work) ardu.

stress *n* (emphasis) accent *m*; (pressure) pression *f*; (Med) stress *m*. ● *vt* souligner, insister sur.

stretch *vt* (pull taut) tendre; (*arm, leg*) étendre; (*neck*) tendre; (*clothes*) étirer; (*truth*) forcer; ~ **one's legs** se dégourdir les jambes. ● *vi* s'étendre; (*person*) s'étirer; (*clothes*) se déformer. ● *n* étendue *f*; (period) période *f*; (of road) tronçon *m*; **at a** ~ d'affilée. ● *a* (fabric) extensible.

stretcher *n* brancard *m*.

strew *vt* (*pt* **strewed**; *pp* **strewed** *or* **strewn**) (scatter) répandre; (cover) joncher.

strict *a* strict.

stride *vi* (*pt* **strode**; *pp* **stridden**) faire de grands pas. ● *n* grand pas *m*.

strife *n* conflit(s) *m(pl)*.

strike *vt* (*pt* **struck**) frapper; (*blow*) donner; (*match*) frotter; (*gold*) trouver. ● *vi* faire grève; (attack) attaquer; (*clock*) sonner. ● *n* (of workers) grève *f*; (Mil) attaque *f*; (find) découverte *f*; **on** ~ en grève. □ ~ **off** *or* **out** rayer; ~ **up** (a friendship) lier amitié (**with**

avec). **striker** n gréviste mf;
(football) attaquant/-e m/f. **striking**
a frappant.

string n ficelle f; (of violin, racket)
corde f; (of pearls) collier m; (of lies)
chapelet m; **the ~s** (Mus) les
cordes; **pull ~s** faire jouer ses
relations. ● vt (pt **strung**) (thread)
enfiler. **stringed** a (instrument) à
cordes.

stringent a rigoureux, strict.

stringy a filandreux.

strip vt/i (pt **stripped**) (undress)
(se) déshabiller; (deprive)
dépouiller. ● n bande f.

stripe n rayure f, raie f. **striped** a
rayé.

strip light n néon m.

stripper n strip-teaseur/-euse
m/f; (solvent) décapant.

strip-tease n strip-tease m.

strive vi (pt **strove**; pp **striven**)
s'efforcer (**to** de).

strode ⇒STRIDE.

stroke vt (with hand) caresser. ● n
coup m; (of pen) trait m; (swimming)
nage f; (Med) attaque f, congestion
f; **at a ~** d'un seul coup.

stroll vi flâner; **~ in** entrer
tranquillement. ● n petit tour m.
stroller n (US) poussette f.

strong a fort; (shoes, fabric)
solide; **be fifty ~** être fort de
cinquante personnes. **~hold** n
bastion m.

strongly adv (greatly) fortement;
(with energy) avec force; (deeply)
profondément.

strove ⇒STRIVE.

struck ⇒STRIKE.

structure n (of cell, poem) structure
f; (building) construction f.

struggle vi lutter, se battre. ● n
lutte f; (effort) effort m; **have a ~ to**
avoir du mal à.

strum vt (pt **strummed**) gratter
de.

strung ⇒STRING. ● a **~ up** (tense)
nerveux.

strut n (support) étai m. ● vi (pt
strutted) se pavaner.

stub n bout m; (counterfoil) talon m.
● vt (pt **stubbed**) **~ one's toe** se
cogner le doigt de pied. □ **~ out**
écraser.

stubble n (on chin) barbe f de
plusieurs jours; (remains of wheat)
chaume m.

stubborn a obstiné.

stuck ⇒STICK. ● a (jammed)
coincé; **I'm ~** (for answer) je sèche.
~-up a 🄸 prétentieux.

stud n (on jacket) clou m; (for collar)
bouton m; (stallion) étalon m; (horse
farm) haras m. ● vt (pt **studded**)
clouter.

student n (Univ) étudiant/-e m/f;
(School) élève mf. ● a (restaurant,
life) universitaire.

studio n studio m.

studious a (person) studieux;
(deliberate) étudié.

study n étude f; (office) bureau m.
● vt/i étudier.

stuff n substance f; 🄸 chose(s)
f(pl). ● vt rembourrer; (animal)
empailler; (cram) bourrer; (Culin)
farcir; (block up) boucher; (put)
fourrer. **stuffing** n bourre f;
(Culin) farce f.

stuffy a (-ier, -iest) mal aéré; (dull
🄸) vieux jeu inv.

stumble vi trébucher; **~ across**
or **on** tomber sur. **stumbling-
block** n obstacle m.

stump n (of tree) souche f; (of limb)
moignon m; (of pencil) bout m.

stumped a embarrassé.

stun vt (pt **stunned**) étourdir;
(bewilder) stupéfier.

stung ⇒STING.

stunk ⇒STINK.

stunning a (delightful 🄸)
sensationnel.

S

stunt vt (*growth*) retarder. ● n (feat 🔢) tour m de force; (trick 🔢) truc m; (dangerous) cascade f.

stupid a stupide, bête. **stupidity** n stupidité f.

sturdy a (-ier, -iest) robuste.

stutter vi bégayer. ● n bégaiement m.

sty n (pigsty) porcherie f; (on eye) orgelet m.

style n style m; (fashion) mode f; (sort) genre m; (pattern) modèle m; **do sth in** ~ faire qch avec classe. ● vt (design) créer; ~ **sb's hair** coiffer qn.

stylish a élégant.

stylist n (of hair) coiffeur/-euse m/f.

suave a (urbane) courtois; (smooth: pej) doucereux.

subconscious a & n inconscient (m), subconscient (m).

subcontract vt sous-traiter.

subdue vt (*feeling*) maîtriser; (country) subjuguer. **subdued** a (person, mood) morose; (light) tamisé; (criticism) contenu.

subject[1] a (state) soumis; ~ **to** soumis à; (liable to, dependent on) sujet à. ● n sujet m; (focus) objet m; (School, Univ) matière f; (citizen) ressortissant/-e m/f, sujet/-te m/f.

subject[2] vt soumettre.

subjective a subjectif.

subject-matter n contenu m.

subjunctive a & n subjonctif (m).

sublet vt sous-louer.

submarine n sousmarin m.

submerge vt submerger. ● vi plonger.

submissive a soumis.

submit vt/i (pt **submitted**) (se) soumettre (**to** à).

subordinate a subalterne; (Gram) subordonné. ● n subordonné/-e m/f.

subpoena n (Jur) citation f, assignation f.

subscribe vt/i verser (de l'argent) (**to** à); ~ **to** (loan, theory) souscrire à; (newspaper) s'abonner à, être abonné à. **subscriber** n abonné/-e m/f. **subscription** n abonnement m; (membership dues) cotisation f.

subsequent a (later) ultérieur; (next) suivant. **subsequently** adv par la suite.

subside vi (land) s'affaisser; (flood, wind) baisser.

subsidiary a accessoire. ● n (Comm) filiale f.

subsidize vt subventionner. **subsidy** n subvention f.

substance n substance f.

substandard a de qualité inférieure.

substantial a considérable; (meal) substantiel.

substitute n succédané m; (person) remplaçant/-e m/f. ● vt substituer (**for** à).

subtitle n sous-titre m.

subtle a subtil.

subtract vt soustraire.

suburb n faubourg m, banlieue f; ~s banlieue f. **suburban** a de banlieue. **suburbia** n la banlieue.

subway n passage m souterrain; (US) métro m.

succeed vi réussir (**in doing** à faire). ● vt (follow) succéder à.

success n succès m, réussite f.

successful a réussi, couronné de succès; (favourable) heureux; (in exam) reçu; **be** ~ **in doing** réussir à faire.

succession n succession f; **in** ~ de suite.

successive a successif; **six** ~ **days** six jours consécutifs.

successor n successeur m.

such det & pron tel(le), tel(le)s;

(so much) tant (de). ● *adv* si; ~ **a book** un tel livre; ~ **books** de tels livres; ~ **courage** tant de courage; ~ **a big house** une si grande maison; ~ **as** comme, tel que; **as** ~ en tant que tel; **there's no** ~ **thing** ça n'existe pas. ~-**and**-~ *a* tel ou tel.

suck *vt* sucer. □ ~ **in** *or* **up** aspirer. **sucker** *n* (rubber pad) ventouse *f*; (person 🎩) dupe *f*.

suction *n* succion *f*.

sudden *a* soudain, subit; **all of a** ~ tout à coup. **suddenly** *adv* subitement, brusquement.

sue *vt* (*pres p* **suing**) poursuivre (en justice).

suede *n* daim *m*.

suffer *vt/i* souffrir; (*loss, attack*) subir. **sufferer** *n* victime *f*, malade *mf*. **suffering** *n* souffrance(s) *f(pl)*.

sufficient *a* (enough) suffisamment de; (big enough) suffisant.

suffix *n* suffixe *m*.

suffocate *vt/i* suffoquer.

sugar *n* sucre *m*. ● *vt* sucrer.

suggest *vt* suggérer. **suggestion** *n* suggestion *f*.

suicidal *a* suicidaire.

suicide *n* suicide *m*; **commit** ~ se suicider.

suit *n* (man's) costume *m*; (woman's) tailleur *m*; (cards) couleur *f*. ● *vt* convenir à; (*garment, style*) aller à; (adapt) adapter.

suitable *a* qui convient (**for** à), convenable. **suitably** *adv* convenablement.

suitcase *n* valise *f*.

suite *n* (rooms) suite *f*; (furniture) mobilier *m*.

suited *a* (well) ~ (matched) bien assorti; ~ **to** fait pour, apte à.

sulk *vi* bouder.

sullen *a* maussade.

sultana *n* raisin *m* de Smyrne, raisin *m* sec.

sultry *a* (-ier, -iest) étouffant, lourd; (fig) sensuel.

sum *n* somme *f*; (in arithmetic) calcul *m*. ● *vt/i* (*pt* **summed**) ~ **up** résumer, récapituler; (assess) évaluer.

summarize *vt* résumer.

summary *n* résumé *m*. ● *a* sommaire.

summer *n* été *m*. ● *a* d'été. ~**time** *n* (season) été *m*.

summery *a* estival.

summit *n* sommet *m*; ~ (**conference**) (Pol) (conférence *f* au) sommet *m*.

summon *vt* appeler; ~ **sb to a meeting** convoquer qn à une réunion; ~ **up** (*strength, courage*) rassembler.

summons *n* (Jur) assignation *f*. ● *vt* assigner.

sun *n* soleil *m*. ● *vt* (*pt* **sunned**) ~ **oneself** se chauffer au soleil. ~**burn** *n* coup *m* de soleil.

Sunday *n* dimanche *m*. ~ **school** *n* catéchisme *m*.

sundry *a* divers; **sundries** articles *mpl* divers; **all and** ~ tout le monde.

sunflower *n* tournesol *m*.

sung ⇒SING.

sun-glasses *npl* lunettes *fpl* de soleil.

sunk ⇒SINK.

sunken *a* (ship) submergé; (eyes) creux.

sunlight *n* soleil *m*.

sunny *a* (-ier, -iest) ensoleillé.

sun: ~**rise** *n* lever *m* du soleil. ~**roof** *n* toit *m* ouvrant. ~ **screen** *n* filtre *m* solaire. ~**set** *n* coucher *m* du soleil. ~**shine** *n* soleil *m*. ~**stroke** *n* insolation *f*.

sun-tan *n* bronzage *m*. ~ **lotion**

S

n lotion *f* solaire. ~ **oil** *n* huile *f* solaire.

super *a* 🔲 formidable.

superb *a* superbe.

superficial *a* superficiel.

superfluous *a* superflu.

superimpose *vt* superposer (**on** à).

superintendent *n* directeur/-trice *m/f*; (of police) commissaire *m*.

superior *a & n* supérieur/-e (*m/f*).

superlative *a* suprême. ●*n* (Gram) superlatif *m*.

supermarket *n* supermarché *m*.

supersede *vt* remplacer, supplanter.

superstition *n* superstition *f*. **superstitious** *a* superstitieux.

superstore *n* hypermarché *m*.

supervise *vt* surveiller, diriger. **supervision** *n* surveillance *f*. **supervisor** *n* surveillant/-e *m/f*; (shop) chef *m* de rayon; (firm) chef *m* de service.

supper *n* dîner *m*; (late at night) souper *m*.

supple *a* souple.

supplement[1] *n* supplément *m*. **supplementary** *a* supplémentaire.

supplement[2] *vt* compléter.

supplier *n* fournisseur *m*.

supply *vt* fournir; (equip) pourvoir; (feed) alimenter (**with** en). ●*n* provision *f*; (of gas) alimentation *f*; **supplies** (food) vivres *mpl*; (material) fournitures *fpl*.

support *vt* soutenir; (family) assurer la subsistance de. ●*n* soutien *m*, appui *m*; (Tech) support *m*. **supporter** *n* partisan/-e *m/f*; (Sport) supporter *m*. **supportive** *a* qui soutient et encourage.

suppose *vt/i* supposer; **be ~d to**

do être censé faire, devoir faire; **supposing he comes** supposons qu'il vienne. **supposedly** *adv* soi-disant, prétendument.

suppress *vt* (put an end to) supprimer; (restrain) réprimer; (stifle) étouffer.

supreme *a* suprême.

surcharge *n* supplément *m*; (tax) surtaxe *f*.

sure *a* sûr; **make ~ of** s'assurer de; **make ~ that** vérifier que. ●*adv* (US 🔲) pour sûr. **surely** *adv* sûrement.

surf *n* ressac *m*. ●*vi* faire du surf; (Internet) surfer.

surface *n* surface *f*. ●*a* superficiel. ●*vt* revêtir. ●*vi* faire surface; (fig) réapparaître.

surfer *n* surfeur/-euse *m/f*; (Internet) internaute *mf*.

surge *vi* (waves, crowd) déferler; (increase) monter. ●*n* (wave) vague *f*; (rise) montée *f*.

surgeon *n* chirurgien *m*.

surgery *n* chirurgie *f*; (office) cabinet *m*; (session) consultation *f*; **need ~** devoir être opéré.

surgical *a* chirurgical. ~ **spirit** *n* alcool *m* à 90 degrés.

surly *a* (-ier, -iest) bourru.

surname *n* nom *m* de famille.

surplus *n* surplus *m*. ●*a* en surplus.

surprise *n* surprise *f*. ●*vt* surprendre. **surprised** *a* surpris (**at** de). **surprising** *a* surprenant.

surrender *vi* se rendre. ●*vt* (hand over) remettre; (Mil) rendre. ●*n* (Mil) reddition *f*; (of passport) remise *f*.

surround *vt* entourer; (Mil) encercler. **surrounding** *a* environnant. **surroundings** *npl* environs *mpl*; (setting) cadre *m*.

surveillance *n* surveillance *f*.

survey[1] *vt* (review) passer en

revue; (inquire into) enquêter sur; (building) inspecter.

survey² n (inquiry) enquête f; inspection f; (general view) vue f d'ensemble.

surveyor n expert m (géomètre).

survival n survie f.

survive vt/i survivre (à). **survivor** n survivant/-e m/f.

susceptible a sensible (to à); ~ **to** (prone to) prédisposé à.

suspect¹ vt soupçonner; (doubt) douter de.

suspect² n & a suspect/-e (m/f).

suspend vt (hang, stop) suspendre; (licence) retirer provisoirement. **suspended sentence** n condamnation f avec sursis. **suspender** n jarretelle f; ~**s** (braces: US) bretelles fpl. ~ **belt** n porte-jarretelles m.

suspension n suspension f; retrait m provisoire.

suspicion n soupçon m; (distrust) méfiance f.

suspicious a soupçonneux; (causing suspicion) suspect; **be** ~ **of** se méfier de. **suspiciously** adv de façon suspecte.

sustain vt supporter; (effort) soutenir; (suffer) subir.

sustenance n (food) nourriture f; (nourishment) valeur f nutritive.

swallow vt/i avaler; ~ **up** (absorb, engulf) engloutir. ● n hirondelle f.

swam ⇒SWIM.

swamp n marais m. ● vt (flood, overwhelm) submerger.

swan n cygne m.

swap vt/i (pt swapped) Ⓣ échanger. ● n Ⓣ échange m.

swarm n essaim m. ● vi fourmiller; ~ **into** or **round** (crowd) envahir.

swat vt (pt swatted) (fly) écraser.

sway vt/i (se) balancer; (influence)

influencer. ● n balancement m; (rule) empire m.

swear vt/i (pt swore; pp sworn) jurer (**to sth** de qch); ~ **at** injurier; ~ **by sth** Ⓣ ne jurer que par qch. ~**-word** n juron m.

sweat n sueur f. ● vi suer.

sweater n pull-over m.

sweat-shirt n sweat-shirt m.

swede n rutabaga m.

Swede n Suédois/-e m/f. **Sweden** n Suède f.

Swedish a suédois. ● n (Ling) suédois m.

sweep vt/i (pt swept) (floor) balayer; (carry away) emporter, entraîner; (chimney) ramoner ● n coup m de balai; (curve) courbe f, (mouvement) geste m, mouvement m; (for chimneys) ramoneur m. □ ~ **by** passer rapidement or majestueusement. **sweeper** n (for carpet) balai m mécanique, (football) libero m.

sweet a (not sour, pleasant) doux; (not savoury) sucré, (charming Ⓣ) gentil; **have a** ~ **tooth** aimer les sucreries. ● n bonbon m; (dish) dessert m. ~**corn** n maïs m.

sweeten vt sucrer; (fig) adoucir. **sweetener** n édulcorant m.

sweetheart n petit/-e ami/-e m/f; (term of endearment) chéri/-e m/f.

sweetly adv gentiment.

sweetness n douceur f; goût m sucré.

sweet pea n pois m de senteur.

swell vt/i (pt swelled; pp swollen or swelled) (increase) grossir; (expand) (se) gonfler; (hand, face) enfler. ● n (of sea) houle f. **swelling** n (Med) enflure f.

sweltering a étouffant.

swept ⇒SWEEP.

swerve vi faire un écart.

S

swift *a* rapide. ● *n* (bird) martinet *m*.

swim *vi* (*pt* swam; *pp* swum; *pres p* swimming) nager; (be dizzy) tourner. ● *vt* traverser à la nage; (*distance*) nager. ● *n* baignade *f*; **go for a ~** aller se baigner. **swimmer** *n* nageur/ -euse *m/f*. **swimming** *n* natation *f*.

swimming-pool *n* piscine *f*.

swim-suit *n* maillot *m* (de bain).

swindle *vt* escroquer. ● *n* escroquerie *f*.

swine *npl* (pigs) pourceaux *mpl*. ● *n inv* (person ℗) salaud *m*.

swing *vt/i* (*pt* swung) (se) balancer; (turn round) tourner; (*pendulum*) osciller. ● *n* balancement *m*; (seat) balançoire *f*; (of opinion) revirement *m* (**towards** en faveur de); (Mus) rythme *m*; **be in full ~** battre son plein. □ **~ round** (*person*) se retourner.

swipe *vt* (hit ℗) frapper; (steal ℗) piquer.

swirl *vi* tourbillonner. ● *n* tourbillon *m*.

Swiss *a* suisse. ● *n inv* Suisse *mf*.

switch *n* bouton *m* (électrique), interrupteur *m*; (shift) changement *m*, revirement *m*. ● *vt* (transfer) transférer; (exchange) échanger (**for** contre); (reverse positions of) changer de place; **~ trains** (change) changer de train. ● *vi* changer. □ **~ off** éteindre; **~ on** mettre, allumer.

switchboard *n* standard *m*.

Switzerland *n* Suisse *f*.

swivel *vt/i* (*pt* swivelled) (faire) pivoter.

swollen ⇒SWELL.

swoop *vi* (bird) fondre; (*police*) faire une descente, foncer. ● *n* (police raid) descente *f*.

sword *n* épée *f*.

swore ⇒SWEAR.

sworn ⇒SWEAR. ● *a* (enemy) juré; (ally) dévoué.

swot *vt/i* (*pt* swotted) (study ℗) bûcher ℗. ● *n* ℗ bûcheur/-euse *m/f* ℗.

swum ⇒SWIM.

swung ⇒SWING.

syllabus *n* (*pl* ~es) (School, Univ) programme *m*.

symbol *n* symbole *m*.

symbolic(al) *a* symbolique.

symbolize *vt* symboliser.

symmetrical *a* symétrique.

sympathetic *a* compatissant; (fig) compréhensif.

sympathize *vi* ~ **with** (pity) plaindre; (fig) comprendre les sentiments de. **sympathizer** *n* sympathisant/-e *m/f*.

sympathy *n* (pity) compassion *f*; (fig) compréhension *f*; (solidarity) solidarité *f*; (condolences) condoléances *fpl*; (affinity) affinité *f*; **be in ~ with** comprendre, être en accord avec.

symptom *n* symptôme *m*.

synagogue *n* synagogue *f*.

synonym *n* synonyme *m*.

synopsis *n* (*pl* -opses) résumé *m*.

syntax *n* syntaxe *f*.

synthesis *n* (*pl* -theses) synthèse *f*.

synthetic *a* synthétique.

syringe *n* seringue *f*.

syrup *n* (liquid) sirop *m*; (treacle) mélasse *f* raffinée.

system *n* système *m*; (body) organisme *m*; (order) méthode *f*. **systematic** *a* systématique.

systems analyst *n* analyste- programmeur/-euse *m/f*.

tab *n* (on can) languette *f*; (on garment) patte *f*; (label) étiquette *f*; (US ⊡) addition *f*; (Comput) tabulatrice *f*; (setting) tabulation *f*.

table *n* table *f*; **at (the) ~** à table; **lay** *or* **set the ~** mettre la table. ● *vt* (*motion*) présenter. **~-cloth** *n* nappe *f*. **~-mat** *n* set *m* de table. **~spoon** *n* cuillère *f* de service.

tablet *n* (of stone) plaque *f*; (drug) comprimé *m*.

table tennis *n* tennis *m* de table; ping-pong® *m*.

taboo *n & a* tabou (*m*).

tacit *a* tacite.

tack *n* (nail) clou *m*; (stitch) point *m* de bâti; (course of action) voie *f*. ● *vt* (nail) clouer; (stitch) bâtir; (add) ajouter. ● *vi* (Naut) louvoyer.

tackle *n* équipement *m*; (in soccer) tacle *m*; (in rugby) plaquage *m*. ● *vt* (*problem*) s'attaquer à; (*player*) tacler, plaquer.

tact *n* tact *m*. **tactful** *a* plein de tact.

tactics *npl* tactique *f*.

tadpole *n* têtard *m*.

tag *n* (label) étiquette *f*. ● *vt* (*pt* **tagged**) (label) étiqueter; ● *vi* **~ along** ⊡ suivre.

tail *n* queue *f*; **~s** (coat) habit *m*; **~s!** (on coin) pile! ● *vt* (follow) filer. ● *vi* **~ away** *or* **off** diminuer. **~-back** *n* bouchon *m*. **~-gate** *n* hayon *m*.

tailor *n* tailleur *m*. ● *vt* (*garment*) façonner; (fig) adapter. **~-made** *a* fait sur mesure.

take *vt/i* (*pt* **took**; *pp* **taken**) prendre (**from sb** à qn); (carry) emporter, porter (**to** à); (escort) emmener; (contain) contenir; (tolerate) supporter; (accept) accepter; (*prize*) remporter; (*exam*) passer; (*precedence*) avoir; (view) adopter; **~ sb home** ramener qn chez lui; **be taken by** *or* **with** être impressionné par; **be taken ill** tomber malade; **it ~s time** il faut du temps pour. □ **~ after** tenir de; **~ apart** démonter; (fig) descendre en flammes ⊡; **~ away** (object) enlever; (person) emmener; (pain) supprimer; **~ back** reprendre; (return) rendre; (accompany) raccompagner; (statement) retirer; **~ down** (object) descendre; (notes) prendre; **~ in** (object) rentrer; (include) inclure; (cheat) tromper; **~ off** (Aviat) décoller; **~ sth off** enlever qch; **~ sb off** imiter qn; **~ on** (task, staff, passenger) prendre; (challenger) relever le défi de; **~ out** sortir; (stain) enlever; **~ over** *vt* (country, firm) prendre le contrôle de; *vi* prendre le pouvoir; **~ over from** remplacer; **~ part** participer (**in** à); **~ place** avoir lieu; **~ to** se prendre d'amitié pour; (activity) prendre goût à; **~ to doing** se mettre à faire; **~ up** (object) monter; (hobby) se mettre à; (occupy) prendre; (resume) reprendre; **~ up with** se lier avec. **~-away** *n* (meal) repas *m* à emporter. **~-off** *n* (Aviat) décollage *m*. **~-over** *n* (Pol) prise *f* de pouvoir; (Comm) rachat *m*.

tale *n* conte *m*; (report) récit *m*; (lie) histoire *f*.

talent *n* talent *m*. **talented** *a* doué.

talk *vt/i* parler; (chat) bavarder; **~ sb into doing** persuader qn de faire; **~ sth over** discuter de qch.

● *n* (talking) propos *mpl*; (conversation) conversation *f*; (lecture) exposé *m*.

talkative *a* bavard.

tall *a* (high) haut; (*person*) grand.

tame *a* apprivoisé; (dull) insipide. ● *vt* apprivoiser; (*lion*) dompter.

tamper *vi* ~ **with** (*lock, machine*) tripoter; (*accounts, evidence*) trafiquer.

tan *vt/i* (*pt* **tanned**) bronzer; (*hide*) tanner. ● *n* bronzage *m*.

tangerine *n* mandarine *f*.

tangle *vt/i* ~ (**up**) s'emmêler. ● *n* enchevêtrement *m*.

tank *n* réservoir *m*; (vat) cuve *f*; (for fish) aquarium *m*; (Mil) char *m* (de combat).

tanker *n* (lorry) camion-citerne *m*; (ship) navire-citerne *m*; **oil/petrol** ~ pétrolier *m*.

tantrum *n* crise *f* (de colère).

tap *n* (for water) robinet *m*; (knock) petit coup *m*; **on** ~ disponible. ● *vt* (*pt* **tapped**) (knock) taper (doucement); (*resources*) exploiter; (*phone*) mettre sur écoute.

tape *n* bande *f* (magnétique); (cassette) cassette *f*; (video) cassette *f* vidéo; (fabric) ruban *m*; (sticky) scotch® *m*. ● *vt* (record) enregistrer; ~ **sth to sth** coller qch à qch. ~**-measure** *n* mètre *m* ruban. ~ **recorder** *n* magnétophone *m*.

tapestry *n* tapisserie *f*.

tar *n* goudron *m*. ● *vt* (*pt* **tarred**) goudronner.

target *n* cible *f*; (objective) objectif *m*. ● *vt* (city) prendre pour cible; (*weapon*) diriger; (in marketing) viser.

tariff *n* (price list) tarif *m*; (on imports) droit *m* de douane.

tarmac, Tarmac® *n* macadam *m*; (runway) piste *f*.

tarpaulin *n* bâche *f*.

tarragon *n* estragon *m*.

tart *n* tarte *f*. ● *a* aigrelet.

task *n* tâche *f*.

taste *n* goût *m*; (experience) aperçu *m*. ● *vt* (eat, enjoy) goûter à; (try) goûter; (perceive taste of) sentir (le goût de). ● *vi* ~ **of** *or* **like** avoir un goût de. **tasteful** *a* de bon goût.

tasty *a* (-ier, -iest) 🆃 miteux.

tattoo *vt* tatouer. ● *n* tatouage *m*.

tatty *a* (-ier, -iest) 🆃 miteux.

taught ⇒TEACH.

taunt *vt* railler. ● *n* raillerie *f*.

Taurus *n* Taureau *m*.

tax *n* (on goods, services) taxe *f*; (on income) impôt *m*. ● *vt* imposer; (put to test: fig) mettre à l'épreuve. **taxable** *a* imposable. **taxation** *n* imposition *f*; (taxes) impôts *mpl*.

tax: ~**collector** *n* percepteur *m*. ~**deductible** *a* déductible des impôts. ~ **disc** *n* vignette *f*. ~**-free** *a* exempt d'impôts. ~ **haven** *n* paradis *m* fiscal.

taxi *n* taxi *m*. ~ **rank** *n* station *f* de taxi.

tax: ~**payer** *n* contribuable *mf*. ~ **relief** *n* dégrèvement *m* fiscal. ~ **return** *n* déclaration *f* d'impôts.

tea *n* (drink, meal) thé *m*; (children's snack) goûter *m*; ~ **bag** sachet *m* de thé.

teach *vt* (*pt* **taught**) apprendre (**sb sth** qch à qn); (in school) enseigner (**sb sth** qch à qn). ● *vi* enseigner. **teacher** *n* enseignant/ -e *m/f*; (secondary) professeur *m*; (primary) instituteur/-trice *m/f*.

team *n* équipe *f*; (of animals) attelage *m*. ● *vi* ~ **up** faire équipe (with avec).

teapot *n* théière *f*.

tear[1] *vt/i* (*pt* **tore**; *pp* **torn**) (se) déchirer; (snatch) arracher (**from** à); (rush) aller à toute vitesse. ● *n* déchirure *f*.

tear[2] *n* larme *f*; **in** ~**s** en larmes. ~**-gas** *n* gaz *m* lacrymogène.

tease *vt* taquiner. ● *n* taquin/-e *m/f*.

tea: **~-shop** *n* salon *m* de thé. **~spoon** *n* petite cuillère *f*.

teat *n* tétine *f*.

tea-towel *n* torchon *m*.

technical *a* technique.

technician *n* technicien/-ne *m/f*.

technique *n* technique *f*.

techno *n* (Mus) techno *f*.

technology *n* technologie *f*.

teddy *a* **~ bear** ours *m* en peluche.

tedious *a* ennuyeux.

tee *n* (golf) tee *m*.

teenage *a* (*girl, boy*) adolescent; (*fashion*) des adolescents.

teenager *n* jeune *mf*, adolescent/ -e *m/f*.

teens *npl* in one's **~** adolescent.

teeth ⇒TOOTH.

teethe *vi* faire ses dents.

teetotaller *n* personne *f* qui ne boit pas d'alcool.

telecommunications *npl* télécommunications *fpl*.

telecommuting *n* télétravail *m*.

teleconferencing *n* téléconférence *f*.

telegram *n* télégramme *m*.

telegraph *n* télégraphe *m*. ● *a* télégraphique.

telephone *n* téléphone *m*. ● *vt* (*person*) téléphoner à; (*message*) téléphoner. ● *vi* téléphoner. **~ book** annuaire *m*. **~ booth**, **~-box** *n* cabine *f* téléphonique. **~ call** *n* coup *m* de téléphone. **~ number** *n* numéro *m* de téléphone.

telephoto *a* **~ lens** téléobjectif *m*.

telescope *n* télescope *m*. ● *vt/i* (se) télescoper.

teletext *n* télétexte *m*.

televise *vt* téléviser.

television *n* télévision *f*; **~ set** poste *m* de télévision, téléviseur *m*.

teleworking *n* télétravail *m*.

telex *n* télex *m*. ● *vt* envoyer par télex.

tell *vt* (*pt* told) dire (**sb sth** qch à qn); (*story*) raconter; (distinguish) distinguer; **~ sb to do sth** dire à qn de faire qch; **~ sth from sth** voir la différence entre qch et qch. ● *vi* (show) avoir un effet; (know) savoir. □ **~ off** 🔤 gronder.

temp *n* intérimaire *mf*. ● *vi* faire de l'intérim.

temper *n* humeur *f*; (anger) colère *f*; **lose one's ~** se mettre en colère.

temperament *n* tempérament *m*. **temperamental** *a* capricieux.

temperature *n* température *f*, **have a ~** avoir de la fièvre *or* de la température.

temple *n* temple *m*; (of head) tempe *f*.

temporary *a* temporaire, provisoire.

tempt *vt* tenter; **~ sb to do** donner envie à qn de faire.

ten *a* & *n* dix (*m*).

tenacious *a* tenace.

tenancy *n* location *f*. **tenant** *n* locataire *mf*.

tend *vt* s'occuper de. ● *vi* **~ to** (be apt to) avoir tendance à; (look after) s'occuper de. **tendency** *n* tendance *f*.

tender *a* tendre; (sore, painful) sensible. ● *vt* offrir, donner. ● *vi* faire une soumission. ● *n* (Comm) soumission *f*; **be legal ~** (money) avoir cours.

tendon *n* tendon *m*.

tennis *n* tennis *m*. ● *a* (*court, match*) de tennis.

tenor *n* (meaning) sens *m* général; (Mus) ténor *m*.

tense *n* (Gram) temps *m*. ● *a*

tendu. ●vt (muscles) tendre,
raidir. ●vi (face) se crisper.
tension n tension f.
tent n tente f.
tentative a provisoire; (hesitant)
timide.
tenth a & n dixième (mf).
tepid a tiède.
term n (word, limit) terme m; (of
imprisonment) temps m; (School)
trimestre m; ~s conditions fpl; on
good/bad ~s en bons/mauvais
termes; in the short/long ~ à
court/long terme; come to ~s with
sth accepter qch; ~ of office (Pol)
mandat m. ●vt appeler.
terminal a (point) terminal;
(illness) incurable. ●n (oil,
computer) terminal m; (Rail)
terminus m; (Electr) borne f; (air)
~ aérogare f.
terminate vt mettre fin à. ●vi
prendre fin.
terminus n (pl -ni) (station)
terminus m.
terrace n terrasse f; (houses)
rangée f de maisons contiguës;
the ~s (Sport) les gradins mpl.
terracotta n terre f cuite.
terrible a affreux, atroce.
terrific a (huge) énorme; (great 🄸)
formidable.
terrify vt terrifier; be terrified of
avoir très peur de.
territory n territoire m.
terror n terreur f.
terrorism n terrorisme m.
terrorist n terroriste mf.
test n épreuve f; (written exam)
contrôle m; (of machine, product)
essai m; (of sample) analyse f;
driving ~ examen m du permis
de conduire. ●vt évaluer; (School)
contrôler; (machine, product)
essayer; (sample) analyser;
(patience, strength) mettre à
l'épreuve. ●vi ~ for faire une
recherche de.

testament n testament m; Old/
New T~ Ancien/Nouveau
Testament m.
testicle n testicule m.
testify vt/i témoigner (to de; that
que).
testimony n témoignage m.
test tube n éprouvette f.
tetanus n tétanos m.
text n texte m. ●vt ~ sb envoyer
un message texte à qn. ~book n
manuel m ~ message n
message m texte.
texture n (of paper) grain m; (of
fabric) texture f.
than conj que, qu'; (with numbers)
de; more/less ~ ten plus/moins de
dix.
thank vt remercier; ~ you!, ~s!
merci! **thankful** a reconnaissant
(for de). **thanks** npl
remerciements mpl; ~s to grâce
à. **Thanksgiving** (**Day**) n (US)
jour m d'Action de Grâces

···

that pl those

●determiner

····▸ce, cet, cette, ces; ~ dog ce
chien; ~ man cet homme; ~
woman cette femme; those books
ces livres; at ~ moment à ce
moment-là.

❗ To distinguish from this and
these, you need to add -là
after the noun: I prefer that
car je préfère cette
voiture-là.

●pronoun

····▸cela, ça, ce; what's ~?, what
are those? qu'est-ce que c'est
(que ça)?; who's ~? qui est-ce?;
~ is my brother c'est or voilà
mon frère; those are my parents
ce sont mes parents.
····▸ (emphatic) celui-là, celle-là,
ceux-là, celles-là; all the dresses

are nice but I like ∼/those best toutes les robes sont jolies mais je préfère celle-là/celles-là.

●*relative pronoun*

····▸ (for subject) qui; **the man ∼ stole the car** l'homme qui a volé la voiture.

····▸ (for object) que; **the girl ∼ I met** la fille que j'ai rencontrée.

! With a preposition, use *lequel/laquelle/lesquels/ lesquelles*: **the chair ∼ I was sitting on** *la chaise sur laquelle j'étais assis.*

! With a preposition that translates as *à*, use *auquel/ à laquelle/auxquels/ auxquelles*: **the girls ∼ I was talking to** *les filles auxquelles je parlais.*

! With a preposition that translates as *de*, use *dont*: **the people ∼ I've talked about** *les personnes dont j'ai parlé.*

●*conjunction* que; **she said ∼ she would do it** elle a dit qu'elle le ferait.

thatched *a* de chaume: ∼ **cottage** chaumière *f*.

thaw *vt/i* (faire) dégeler; (*snow*) (faire) fondre. ●*n* dégel *m*.

the *determiner*

····▸ le, l', la, les; ∼ **dog** le chien; ∼ **tree** l'arbre; ∼ **chair** la chaise; **to** ∼ **shops** aux magasins.

! With a preposition that translates as *à*: *à + le = au* and *à + les = aux.*

theatre *n* théâtre *m*.

theft *n* vol *m*.

their *a* leur, *pl* leurs.

theirs *pron* le *or* la leur, les leurs.

them *pron* les; (after preposition) eux, elles; (**to**) ∼ leur; **phone** ∼! téléphone-leur!; **I know** ∼ je les connais; **both of** ∼ tous/toutes les deux.

themselves *pron* eux-mêmes, elles-mêmes; (reflexive) se; (after preposition) eux, elles.

then *adv* alors; (next) ensuite, puis; (therefore) alors, donc. ●*a* d'alors; **from** ∼ **on** dès lors.

theology *n* théologie *f*.

theory *n* théorie *f*.

therapy *n* thérapie *f*.

there *adv* là; (with verb) y; (over there) là-bas; **he goes** ∼ il y va; **on** ∼ là-dessus; ∼ **is**, ∼ **are** il y a; (pointing) voilà. ●*interj*; ∼, ∼! allons, allons!

therefore *adv* donc.

thermal *a* thermal.

thermometer *n* thermomètre *m*.

Thermos® *n* thermos® *m or f inv*.

thermostat *n* thermostat *m*.

thesaurus *n* (*pl* **-ri**) dictionnaire *m* de synonymes.

these ⇒THIS.

thesis *n* (*pl* **theses**) thèse *f*.

they *pron* ils, elles; (emphatic) eux, elles; (people in general) on.

thick *a* épais; (stupid) bête; **be 6 cm** ∼ avoir 6 cm d'épaisseur.

thief *n* (*pl* **thieves**) voleur/-euse *m/f*.

thigh *n* cuisse *f*.

thin *a* (**thinner, thinnest**) mince; (*person*) maigre, mince; (sparse) clairsemé; (fine) fin. ●*vt/i* (*pt* **thinned**) ∼ (**down**) (*paint*) diluer; (*soup*) allonger.

thing *n* chose *f*; ∼**s** (belongings) affaires *fpl*; **the best** ∼ **is to** le mieux est de; **the (right)** ∼ ce qu'il faut (**for sb** à qn).

think *vt/i* (*pt* **thought**) penser

T

(about, of à); (carefully) réfléchir
(about, of à); (believe) croire; I ~ so
je crois que oui; ~ of doing
envisager de faire. □ ~ over bien
réfléchir à; ~ up inventer.

third a troisième. ● n troisième
mf; (fraction) tiers m. **T~ World** n
tiers-monde m.

thirst n soif f.

thirsty a be ~ avoir soif; make ~
donner soif à.

thirteen a & n treize (m).

thirty a & n trente (m).

....
this pl **these**

● determiner

····▸ ce/cet/cette/ces; ~ dog ce
chien; ~ man cet homme; ~
woman cette femme; these books
ces livres.

! To distinguish from that and
those, you need to add -ci
after the noun: I prefer this
car je préfère cette
voiture.

● pronoun

····▸ ce; what's ~?, what are these?
qu'est-ce que c'est?; who is ~?
qui est-ce?; ~ is the kitchen voici
la cuisine; ~ is Sophie je te or
vous présente Sophie; these are
your things voici tes affaires.

····▸ (emphatic) celui-ci/
celle-ci/ceux-ci/celles-ci; all the
dresses are nice but I like ~/these
best toutes les robes sont jolies
mais je préfère celle-ci/celles-ci.
....

thistle n chardon m.

thorn n épine f.

thorough a (detailed) approfondi;
(meticulous) minutieux. **thoroughly**
adv (clean, study) à fond; (very)
tout à fait.

those ⇒THAT.

though conj bien que. ● adv
quand même.

thought ⇒THINK. ● n pensée f,
idée f. **thoughtful** a pensif; (kind)
prévenant.

thousand a & n mille (m inv); ~s
of des milliers de. **thousandth** a
& n millième (mf).

thread n (yarn & fig) fil m; (of screw)
pas m. ● vt enfiler; ~ one's way
se faufiler.

threat n menace f. **threaten** vt/i
menacer (with de).

three a & n trois (m).

threw ⇒THROW.

thrill n frisson m; (pleasure) plaisir
m. ● vt transporter (de joie); be
~ed être ravi. ● vi frissonner (de
joie).

thrive vi (pt thrived or throve;
pp thrived or thriven) prospérer;
he ~s on it cela lui réussit.

throat n gorge f; have a sore ~
avoir mal à la gorge.

throb vi (pt throbbed) (heart)
battre; (engine) vibrer. ● n (pain)
élancement m; (of engine) vibration
f. **throbbing** a (pain) lancinant.

throne n trône m.

through prep à travers; (during)
pendant; (by means or way of, out of)
par; (by reason of) grâce à, à cause
de. ● adv à travers; (entirely)
jusqu'au bout. ● a (train) direct;
be ~ (finished) avoir fini; come or
go ~ (cross, pierce) traverser; I'm
putting you ~ je vous passe votre
correspondant.

throughout prep ~ the country
dans tout le pays; ~ the day
pendant toute la journée. ● adv
(place) partout; (time) tout le
temps.

throw vt (pt threw; pp thrown)
jeter, lancer; (baffle) déconcerter;
~ a party faire une fête. ● n jet
m; (of dice) coup m. □ ~ away
jeter; ~ off (get rid of) se

débarrasser de; ~ **out** jeter; (*person*) expulser; (*reject*) rejeter; ~ **up** (*arms*) lever; (*vomit* 🔲) vomir.

thrust *vt* (*pt* **thrust**) pousser. ● *n* poussée *f*.

thud *n* bruit *m* sourd.

thug *n* voyou *m*.

thumb *n* pouce *m*. ● *vt* (*book*) feuilleter; ~ **a lift** faire de l'auto-stop. ~-**index** *n* répertoire *m* à onglets.

thump *vt/i* cogner (sur); (*heart*) battre fort. ● *n* coup *m*.

thunder *n* tonnerre *m*. ● *vi* (*weather, person*) tonner. ~-**storm** *n* orage *m*.

Thursday *n* jeudi *m*.

thus *adv* ainsi.

thwart *vt* contrecarrer.

thyme *n* thym *m*.

tick *n* (*sound*) tic-tac *m*; (*mark*) coche *f*; (*moment* 🔲) instant *m*; (*insect*) tique *f*. ● *vi* faire tic-tac. ● *vt* ~ (**off**) cocher. □ ~ **over** tourner au ralenti.

ticket *n* billet *m*; (*for bus, cloakroom*) ticket *m*; (*label*) étiquette *f*. ~-**collector** *n* contrôleur/-euse *m/f*. ~-**office** *n* guichet *m*.

tickle *vt* chatouiller; (*amuse: fig*) amuser. ● *n* chatouillement *m*.

tidal *a* (*river*) à marées; ~ **wave** raz-de-marée *m inv*.

tide *n* marée *f*; (*of events*) cours *m*.

tidy *a* (-**ier**, -**iest**) (*room*) bien rangé; (*appearance, work*) soigné; (*methodical*) ordonné; (*amount* 🔲) joli. ● *vt/i* ~ (**up**) faire du rangement; ~ **sth** (**up**) ranger qch; ~ **oneself up** s'arranger.

tie *vt* (*pres p* **tying**) attacher; (*knot*) faire; (*scarf*) nouer; (*link*) lier. ● *vi* (*in football*) faire match nul; (*in race*) être ex aequo. ● *n* (*necktie*) cravate *f*; (*fastener*) attache *f*; (*link*) lien *m*; (*draw*) match *m* nul. □ ~ **down** attacher; ~ **in with**

être lié à; ~ **up** attacher; (*money*) immobiliser; (*occupy*) occuper.

tier *n* étage *m*, niveau *m*; (*in stadium*) gradin *m*.

tiger *n* tigre *m*.

tight *a* (*clothes, budget*) serré; (*grip*) ferme; (*rope*) tendu; (*security*) strict; (*angle*) aigu. ● *adv* (*hold, sleep*) bien; (*squeeze*) fort.

tighten *vt/i* (se) tendre; (*bolt*) (se) resserrer; (*control*) renforcer.

tights *npl* collant *m*.

tile *n* (*on wall, floor*) carreau *m*; (*on roof*) tuile *f*. ● *vt* carreler; couvrir de tuiles.

till *n* caisse *f* (enregistreuse). ● *vt* (*land*) cultiver. ● *prep & conj* = UNTIL.

timber *n* bois *m* (de construction); (*trees*) arbres *mpl*.

time *n* temps *m*; (*moment*) moment *m*; (*epoch*) époque *f*; (*by clock*) heure *f*; (*occasion*) fois *f*; (*rhythm*) mesure *f*; ~**s** (*multiplying*) fois *fpl*; **any** ~ n'importe quand; **for the** ~ **being** pour le moment; **from** ~ **to** ~ de temps en temps; **have a good** ~ s'amuser; **in no** ~ en un rien de temps; **in** ~ à temps; (*eventually*) avec le temps; **a long** ~ longtemps; **on** ~ à l'heure; **what's the** ~? quelle heure est-il?; ~ **off** du temps libre. ● *vt* choisir le moment de; (*measure*) minuter; (Sport) chronométrer. ~-**limit** *n* délai *m*.

timer *n* minuterie *f*; (*for cooker*) minuteur *m*.

time: ~-**scale** *n* délais *mpl*. ~**table** *n* horaire *m*. ~ **zone** *n* fuseau *m* horaire.

timid *a* timide; (*fearful*) peureux.

tin *n* étain *m*; (*container*) boîte *f*; ~(**plate**) fer-blanc *m*. ● *vt* (*pt* **tinned**) mettre en boîte. ~ **foil** *n* papier *m* d'aluminium.

T

tingle vi picoter. ● n picotement m.

tin-opener n ouvre-boîtes m inv.

tint n teinte f; (for hair) shampooing m colorant. ● vt teinter.

tiny a (-ier, -iest) tout petit.

tip n (of stick, pen, shoe, ski) pointe f; (of nose, finger, wing) bout m; (gratuity) pourboire m; (advice) tuyau m; (for rubbish) décharge f. ● vt/i (pt **tipped**) (tilt) pencher; (overturn) (faire) basculer; (pour) verser; (empty) déverser; (give money) donner un pourboire à. □ ~ **off** prévenir.

tiptoe n on ~ sur la pointe des pieds.

tire vt/i (se) fatiguer; ~ **of** se lasser de. ● n (US) pneu m.

tired a fatigué; **be** ~ **of** en avoir assez de.

tiring a fatigant.

tissue n tissu m; (handkerchief) mouchoir m en papier; ~ (**paper**) papier m de soie.

tit n (bird) mésange f; **give** ~ **for tat** rendre coup pour coup.

title n titre m. ~ **deed** n titre m de propriété.

to

● preposition

····▸ à; ~ **Paris** à Paris; **give the book** ~ **Jane** donne le livre à Jane; ~ **the office** au bureau; ~ **the shops** aux magasins.

····▸ (with feminine countries) en; ~ **France** en France.

····▸ (to + personal pronoun) me/te/lui/ nous/vous/leur; **she gave it** ~ **them** elle le leur a donné; **I'll say it** ~ **her** je vais le lui dire.

! à + le = au
à + les = aux.

● in infinitive

to is not normally translated (**to go** aller; **to sing** chanter)

····▸ (in order to) pour; **he's gone into town** ~ **buy a shirt** il est parti en ville pour acheter une chemise.

····▸ (after adjectives) à; de; **be easy/ difficult** ~ **read** être facile/ difficile à lire; **it's easy/difficult to read her writing** c'est facile/ difficile de lire son écriture.

⟹ For verbal expressions using the infinitive 'to' such as **tell sb to do sth, help sb to do sth** ⇒**tell, help**.

toad n crapaud m.

toast n pain m grillé, toast m; (drink) toast m. ● vt (bread) faire griller; (drink to) porter un toast à. **toaster** n grille-pain m inv.

tobacco n tabac m.

tobacconist n marchand/-e m/f de tabac; ~'s (**shop**) tabac m.

toboggan n toboggan m, luge f.

today n & adv aujourd'hui (m).

toddler n bébé m (qui fait ses premiers pas).

toe n orteil m; (of shoe) bout m; **on one's** ~s vigilant. ● vt ~ **the line** se conformer.

together adv ensemble; (at same time) à la fois; ~ **with** avec.

toilet n toilettes fpl.

toiletries npl articles mpl de toilette.

token n (symbol) témoignage m; (voucher) bon m; (coin) jeton m. ● a symbolique.

told ⇒**TELL**.

tolerance n tolérance f.

tolerate vt tolérer.

toll n péage m; **death** ~ nombre m de morts; **take its** ~ faire des ravages. ● vi (bell) sonner.

tomato n (pl ~**es**) tomate f.

tomb n tombeau m.

tomorrow n & adv demain (m);
~ **morning/night** demain matin/
soir; **the day after** ~ après-
demain.

ton n tonne f (= 1016 kg); (**metric**)
~ tonne f (= 1000 kg); ~**s of**
⊡ des masses de.

tone n ton m; (of radio, telephone)
tonalité f. ● vt ~ **down** atténuer.
● vi ~ (**in**) s'harmoniser (**with**
avec).

tongs npl (for coal) pincettes fpl;
(for sugar) pince f; (for hair) fer m.

tongue n langue f.

tonic n (Med) tonique m. ● a
(effect, accent) tonique; ~ (**water**)
tonic m, Schweppes® m.

tonight n & adv (evening) ce soir;
(night) cette nuit.

tonsil n amygdale f.

too adv trop; (also) aussi; ~ **many
people** trop de gens; **I've got** ~
much/many j'en ai trop; **me** ~ moi
aussi.

took ⇒TAKE.

tool n outil m. ~**bar** n barre f
d'outils. ~**box** n boîte f à outils.

toot n coup m de klaxon®. ● vt/i
~ (**the horn**) klaxonner.

tooth n (pl **teeth**) dent f. ~**ache**
n mal m de dents. ~**brush** n
brosse f à dents. ~**paste** n
dentifrice m. ~**pick** n cure-dents
m inv.

top n (highest point) sommet m;
(upper part) haut m; (upper surface)
dessus m; (lid) couvercle m; (of
bottle, tube) bouchon m; (of beer
bottle) capsule f; (of list) tête f; **on** ~
of sur; (fig) en plus de. ● a (shelf)
du haut; (step, floor) dernier; (in
rank) premier; (best) meilleur;
(distinguished) éminent; (maximum)
maximum. ● vt (pt **topped**)
(exceed) dépasser; (list) venir en
tête de; ~ **up** remplir; ~**ped with**

(dome) surmonté de; (cream)
recouvert de.

topic n sujet m.

topless a aux seins nus.

torch n (electric) lampe f de poche;
(flaming) torche f.

tore ⇒TEAR¹.

torment vt tourmenter.

torn ⇒TEAR¹.

torrent n torrent m.

tortoise n tortue f. ~**shell** n
écaille f.

torture n torture f; (fig) supplice
m. ● vt torturer.

Tory n & a tory (mf),
conservateur/-trice (m/f).

toss vt lancer; (salad) tourner,
(pancake) faire sauter. ● vi se
retourner; ~ **a coin**, ~ **up** tirer à
pile ou face (**for** pour).

tot n petit/-e enfant m/f; (drink)
petit verre m.

total n & a total (m). ● vt (pt
totalled) (add up) additionner;
(amount to) se monter à.

touch vt toucher; (tamper with)
toucher à. ● vi se toucher. ● n
(sense) toucher m; (contact) contact
m; (of artist, writer) touche f; **a** ~ **of**
(small amount) un petit peu de; **get
in** ~ **with** se mettre en contact
avec; **out of** ~ **with** déconnecté
de. ☐ ~ **down** (Aviat) atterrir; ~
up retoucher. ~**down** n
atterrissage m; (Sport) essai m.
~**line** n ligne f de touche.
~**tone** a (phone) à touches.

tough a (negotiator) coriace; (law)
sévère; (time) difficile; (robust)
robuste.

tour n voyage m; (visit) visite f; (by
team) tournée f; **on** ~ en tournée.
● vt visiter.

tourist n touriste mf. ● a
touristique. ~ **office** n syndicat
m d'initiative.

tournament n tournoi m.

tout vi ~ (**for**) racoler ⊡. ● vt (sell)

revendre. ● *n* racoleur/-euse *m/f*; revendeur/-euse *m/f*.

tow *vt* remorquer. ● *n* remorque *f*; **on** ~ en remorque.

toward(s) *prep* vers; (of attitude) envers.

towel *n* serviette *f*.

tower *n* tour *f*. ● *vi* ~ **above** dominer.

town *n* ville *f*; **in** ~ en ville. ~ **council** *n* conseil *m* municipal. ~ **hall** *n* mairie *f*.

tow: ~**-path** *n* chemin *m* de halage. ~ **truck** *n* dépanneuse *f*.

toxic *a* toxique.

toy *n* jouet *m*. ● *vi* ~ **with** (object) jouer avec; (idea) caresser.

trace *n* trace *f*. ● *vt* (*person*) retrouver; (*cause*) déterminer; (*life*) retracer; (draw) tracer; (with tracing paper) décalquer.

track *n* (of person, car) traces *fpl*; (of missile) trajectoire *f*; (path) sentier *m*; (Sport) piste *f*; (Rail) voie *f*; (on disc) morceau *m*; **keep** ~ **of** suivre. ● *vt* suivre la trace *or* la trajectoire de. □ ~ **down** retrouver. ~ **suit** *n* survêtement *m*.

tractor *n* tracteur *m*.

trade *n* commerce *m*; (job) métier *m*; (swap) échange *m*. ● *vi* faire du commerce; ~ **on** exploiter. ● *vt* échanger. ● *a* (*route, deficit*) commercial. ~**-in** *n* reprise *f*. ~ **mark** *n* marque *f* (de fabrique); (registered) marque *f* déposée.

trader *n* commerçant/-e *m/f*; (on stockmarket) opérateur/-trice *m/f*.

trade union *n* syndicat *m*.

trading *n* commerce *m*; (on stockmarket) transactions *fpl* (boursières).

tradition *n* tradition *f*.

traffic *n* trafic *m*; (on road) circulation *f*. ● *vi* (*pt* **trafficked**) faire du trafic (**in** de). ~ **jam** *n* embouteillage *m*. ~**-lights** *npl*

feux *mpl* (de circulation). ~ **warden** contractuel/-le *m/f*.

trail *vt/i* traîner; (*plant*) ramper; (track) suivre; ~ **behind** traîner. ● *n* (of powder) traînée *f*; (track) piste *f*; (path) sentier *m*.

trailer *n* remorque *f*; (caravan) caravane *f*; (film) bande-annonce *f*.

train *n* (Rail) train *m*; (underground) rame *f*; (procession) file *f*; (of dress) traîne *f*. ● *vt* (instruct, develop) former; (*sportsman*) entraîner; (*animal*) dresser; (*ear*) exercer; (*aim*) braquer. ● *vi* être formé, étudier; (Sport) s'entraîner.

trained *a* (skilled) qualifié; (*doctor*) diplômé. **trainee** *n* stagiaire *mf*.

trainer *n* (Sport) entraîneur/-euse *m/f*. **trainers** *npl* (shoes) chaussures *fpl* de sport. **training** *n* formation *f*; (Sport) entraînement *m*.

tram *n* tram(way) *m*.

tramp *vi* marcher (d'un pas lourd). ● *vt* parcourir. ● *n* (vagrant) clochard/-e *m/f*; (sound) bruit *m*.

trample *vt/i* ~ (**on**) piétiner; (fig) fouler aux pieds.

tranquil *a* tranquille.

tranquillizer *n* tranquillisant *m*.

transact *vt* négocier.

transaction *n* transaction *f*.

transcript *n* transcription *f*.

transfer[1] *vt* (*pt* **transferred**) transférer; (*power*) céder; (*employee*) muter. ● *vi* être transféré; (*employee*) être muté.

transfer[2] *n* transfert *m*; (of employee) mutation *f*; (image) décalcomanie *f*.

transform *vt* transformer.

transitive *a* transitif.

translate *vt* traduire. **translation** *n* traduction *f*. **translator** *n* traducteur/-trice *m/f*.

transmit *vt* (*pt* **transmitted**)

transmettre. **transmitter** n émetteur m.

transparency n transparence f; (Photo) diapositive f.

transplant n transplantation f; (Med) greffe f.

transport¹ vt transporter.

transport² n transport m.

trap n piège m. ● vt (pt trapped) (jam, pin down) coincer; (cut off) bloquer; (snare) prendre au piège.

trash n (refuse) ordures fpl; (nonsense) idioties fpl. **~-can** n (US) poubelle f.

trauma n traumatisme m. **traumatic** a traumatisant.

travel vi (pt travelled, US traveled) voyager; (vehicle, bullet) aller. ● vt parcourir. ● n voyages mpl. **~ agency** n agence f de voyages.

traveller, (US) **traveler** n voyageur/-euse m/f; **~'s cheque** chèque m de voyage.

trawler n chalutier m.

tray n plateau m; (on office desk) corbeille f.

treacle n mélasse f.

tread vi (pt trod; pp trodden) marcher (on sur). ● vt fouler. ● n (sound) pas m; (of tyre) chape f.

treasure n trésor m. ● vt (gift, memory) chérir, (friendship, possession) tenir beaucoup à.

treasury n trésorerie f; **the T~** le ministère des Finances.

treat vt traiter; **~ sb to sth** offrir qch à qn. ● n (pleasure) plaisir m; (food) gâterie f. **treatment** n traitement m.

treaty n traité m.

treble a triple; **~ clef** clé f de sol. ● vt/i tripler. ● n (voice) soprano m.

tree n arbre m.

trek n randonnée f. ● vi (pt trekked) **~ across/through**

traverser péniblement; **go ~king** faire de la randonnée.

tremble vi trembler.

tremendous a énorme; (excellent) formidable.

tremor n tremblement m; (earth) **~ secousse** f.

trench n tranchée f.

trend n tendance f; (fashion) mode f. **trendy** a ▣ branché ▣.

trespass vi s'introduire illégalement (on dans). **trespasser** n intrus/-e m/f.

trial n (Jur) procès m; (test) essai m; (ordeal) épreuve f; **go on ~** passer en jugement; **by ~ and error** par expérience.

triangle n triangle m.

tribe n tribu f.

tribunal n tribunal m.

tributary n affluent m.

tribute n tribut m; **pay ~ to** rendre hommage à.

trick n tour m; (dishonest) combine f; (knack) astuce f; **do the ~** ▣ faire l'affaire. ● vt tromper. **trickery** n ruse f.

trickle vi dégouliner; **~ in/out** arriver or partir en petit nombre. ● n filet m; (fig) petit nombre m.

tricky a (task) difficile; (question) épineux; (person) malin.

trifle n bagatelle f; (cake) diplomate m; **a ~** (small amount) un peu. ● vi **~ with** jouer avec.

trigger n (of gun) gâchette f; (of machine) manette f. ● vt **~ (off)** (initiate) déclencher.

trim a (trimmer, trimmest) soigné; (figure) svelte. ● vt (pt trimmed) (hair, grass) couper; (budget) réduire; (decorate) décorer. ● n (cut) coupe f d'entretien; (decoration) garniture f; **in ~** en forme.

trinket n babiole f.

trip vt/i (pt tripped) (faire)

trébucher. ●*n* (journey) voyage *m*; (outing) excursion *f*.

triple *a* triple. ●*vt/i* tripler. **triplets** *npl* triplés/-es *m/fpl*.

tripod *n* trépied *m*.

trite *a* banal.

triumph *n* triomphe *m*. ●*vi* triompher (**over** de).

trivial *a* insignifiant.

trod, trodden ⇒TREAD.

trolley *n* chariot *m*.

trombone *n* (Mus) trombone *m*.

troop *n* bande *f*; ∼s (Mil) troupes *fpl*. ●*vi* ∼ **in/out** entrer/sortir en bande.

trophy *n* trophée *m*.

tropic *n* tropique *m*; ∼s tropiques *mpl*.

trot *n* trot *m*; **on the** ∼ 🄸 coup sur coup. ●*vi* (*pt* **trotted**) trotter.

trouble *n* problèmes *mpl*; ennuis *mpl*; (pains, effort) peine *f*; **be in** ∼ avoir des ennuis; **go to a lot of** ∼ se donner du mal; **what's the** ∼? quel est le problème? ●*vt* (bother) déranger; (worry) tracasser. ●*vi* ∼ (oneself) **to do** se donner la peine de faire. ∼**maker** *n* provocateur/ -trice *m/f*. ∼**shooter** *n* conciliateur/-trice *m/f*; (Tech) expert *m*.

troublesome *a* ennuyeux.

trousers *npl* pantalon *m*; **short** ∼ short *m*.

trout *n inv* truite *f*.

trowel *n* (garden) déplantoir *m*; (for mortar) truelle *f*.

truant *n* (School) élève *mf* qui fait l'école buissonnière; **play** ∼ sécher les cours.

truce *n* trève *f*.

truck *n* (lorry) camion *m*; (cart) chariot *m*; (Rail) wagon *m* de marchandises. ∼**-driver** *n* routier *m*.

true *a* vrai; (accurate) exact; (faithful) fidèle.

truffle *n* truffe *f*.

truly *adv* vraiment; (faithfully) fidèlement; (truthfully) sincèrement.

trumpet *n* trompette *f*.

trunk *n* (of tree, body) tronc *m*; (of elephant) trompe *f*; (box) malle *f*; (Auto, US) coffre *m*; ∼s (for swimming) slip *m* de bain.

trust *n* confiance *f*; (association) trust *m*; **in** ∼ en dépôt. ●*vt* avoir confiance en; ∼ **sb with** confier à qn. ●*vi* ∼ **in** *or* **to** s'en remettre à. **trustee** *n* administrateur/-trice *m/f*. **trustworthy** *a* digne de confiance.

truth *n* (*pl* -s) vérité *f*. **truthful** *a* (account) véridique; (person) qui dit la vérité.

try *vt/i* (*pt* **tried**) essayer; (be a strain on) éprouver; (Jur) juger; ∼ **on** *or* **out** essayer; ∼ **to do** essayer de faire. ●*n* (attempt) essai *m*; (rugby) essai *m*.

T-shirt *n* tee-shirt *m*.

tub *n* (for flowers) bac *m*; (of ice cream) pot *m*; (bath) baignoire *f*.

tube *n* tube *m*; **the** ∼ 🄸 le métro.

tuberculosis *n* tuberculose *f*.

tuck *n* pli *m*. ●*vt* (put away, place) ranger; (hide) cacher. ●*vi* ∼ **in** *or* **into** 🄸 attaquer; ∼ **in** (shirt) rentrer; (blanket, person) border.

Tuesday *n* mardi *m*.

tug *vt* (*pt* **tugged**) tirer. ●*vi* ∼ **at/ on** tirer sur. ●*n* (boat) remorqueur *m*.

tuition *n* cours *mpl*; (fee) frais *mpl* pédagogiques.

tulip *n* tulipe *f*.

tumble *vi* (fall) dégringoler. ●*n* chute *f*. ∼**-drier** *n* sèche-linge *m inv*.

tumbler *n* verre *m* droit.

tummy *n* 🄸 ventre *m*.

tumour *n* tumeur *f*.

tuna *n inv* thon *m*.

tune *n* air *m*; **be in** ∼/**out of** ∼

(instrument) être/ne pas être en accord; (singer) chanter juste/faux. ●vt (engine) régler; (Mus) accorder. ●vi ~ **in** (to) (radio, TV) écouter. □ ~ **up** s'accorder.

Tunisia n Tunisie f.

tunnel n tunnel m; (in mine) galerie f. ●vi (pt **tunnelled**) creuser un tunnel (**into** dans).

turf n (pl **turf** or **turves**) gazon m; **the** ~ (racing) le turf. ●vt ~ **out** 🎟 jeter dehors.

Turk n Turc m, Turque f. **Turkey** n Turquie f.

turkey n dinde f.

Turkish a turc. ●n (Ling) turc m.

turn vt/i tourner; (person) se tourner; (to other side) retourner; (change) (se) transformer (**into** en); (become) devenir; (deflect) détourner; (milk) tourner. ●n tour m; (in road) tournant m; (of mind, events) tournure f; **do a good** ~ rendre service; **in** ~ à tour de rôle; **take** ~**s** se relayer. □ ~ **against** se retourner contre; ~ **away** vi se détourner; vt (avert) détourner; (refuse) refuser; (send back) renvoyer; ~ **back** vi (return) retourner; (vehicle) faire demi-tour; vt (fold) rabattre; ~ **down** refuser; (fold) rabattre; (reduce) baisser; ~ **off** (light) éteindre; (engine) arrêter; (tap) fermer; (of driver) tourner; ~ **on** (light) allumer; (engine) allumer; (tap) ouvrir; ~ **out** vt (light) éteindre; (empty) vider; (produce) produire; vi **it** ~**s out that** il se trouve que; ~ **out well/badly** bien/mal se terminer; ~ **over** (se) retourner; ~ **round** (person) se retourner; ~ **up** vi arriver; (be found) se retrouver; vt (find) déterrer; (collar) remonter.

turning n rue f; (bend) virage m.

turnip n navet m.

turn: ~**-out** n assistance f. ~**over**

n (pie) chausson m; (money) chiffre m d'affaires. ~**table** n (for record) platine f.

turquoise a turquoise inv.

turtle n tortue f (de mer). ~**-neck** n col m montant.

tutor n (private) professeur m particulier; (Univ) (GB) chargé/-e m/f de travaux dirigés.

tutorial n (Univ) classe f de travaux dirigés.

tuxedo n (US) smoking m.

TV n télé f.

tweezers npl pince f (à épiler).

twelfth a & n douzième (mf).

twelve a & n douze (m); ~ (o'clock) midi m or minuit m.

twentieth a & n vingtième (mf).

twenty a & n vingt (m).

twice adv deux fois.

twig n brindille f.

twilight n crépuscule m. ●a crépusculaire.

twin n & a jumeau/-elle (m/f). ●vt (pt **twinned**) jumeler.

twinge n (of pain) élancement m; (of conscience, doubt) accès m.

twinkle vi (star) scintiller; (eye) pétiller. ●n scintillement m; pétillement m.

twinning n jumelage m.

twist vt tordre; (weave together) entortiller; (roll) enrouler; (distort) déformer. ●vi (rope) s'entortiller; (road) zigzaguer. ●n torsion f; (in rope) tortillon m; (in road) tournant m; (in play, story) coup m de théâtre.

twitch vi (person) trembloter; (mouth) trembler; (string) vibrer. ●n (tic) tic m; (jerk) secousse f.

two a & n deux (m); **in** ~**s** par deux; **break in** ~ casser en deux.

tycoon n magnat m.

type n type m, genre m; (print) caractères mpl. ●vt/i (write) taper (à la machine). ~**face** n police f

(de caractères). **~writer** n
machine f à écrire.
typical a typique.
typist n dactylo mf.
tyrant n tyran m.
tyre n pneu m.

udder n pis m, mamelle f.
UFO n OVNI m inv.
UHT abbr (**ultra heat treated**) ~
milk lait m longue conservation.
ugly a (**-ier, -iest**) laid.
UK abbr ⇒UNITED KINGDOM.
Ukraine n Ukraine f.
ulcer n ulcère m.
ulterior a ultérieur; ~ **motive**
arrière-pensée f.
ultimate a dernier, ultime;
(definitive) définitif; (basic)
fondamental.
ultrasound n ultrason m.
umbilical cord n cordon m
ombilical.
umbrella n parapluie m.
umpire n arbitre m. ●vt arbitrer.
umpteenth a 🄳 énième.
UN abbr (**United Nations**) ONU
f.
unable a incapable; (through
circumstances) dans l'impossibilité
(**to do** de faire).
unacceptable a (suggestion)
inacceptable; (behaviour)
inadmissible.
unanimous a unanime.
unanimously adv à l'unanimité.
unattended a sans surveillance.

unattractive a (idea) peu
attrayant; (person) peu attirant.
unauthorized a non autorisé.
unavoidable a inévitable.
unbearable a insupportable.
unbelievable a incroyable.
unbiased a impartial.
unblock vt déboucher.
unborn a (child) à naître;
(generation) à venir.
uncalled-for a injustifié, déplacé.
uncanny a (**-ier, -iest**) étrange,
troublant.
uncivilized a barbare.
uncle n oncle m.
uncomfortable a (chair)
inconfortable; (feeling) pénible;
feel or **be** ~ (person) être mal à
l'aise.
uncommon a rare.
unconscious a sans
connaissance, inanimé; (not aware)
inconscient (**of** de). ●n
inconscient m.
unconventional a peu
conventionnel.
uncouth a grossier.
uncover vt découvrir.
undecided a indécis.
under prep sous; (less than) moins
de; (according to) selon. ●adv
au-dessous; ~ **it/there** là-dessous.
~ **age** a mineur. **~cover** a
secret. **~cut** vt (pt **-cut**; pres p
-cutting) (Comm) vendre moins
cher que. **~dog** n (Pol) opprimé/
-e m/f; (socially) déshérité/-e m/f.
~done a pas assez cuit.
~estimate vt sous-estimer.
~fed a sous-alimenté. **~go** vt
(pt **-went**; pp **-gone**) subir.
~graduate n étudiant/-e m/f
(qui prépare la licence).
underground a souterrain;
(secret) clandestin. ●adv sous
terre. ●n (rail) métro m.

under: ~**line** vt souligner. ~**mine** vt saper.

underneath prep sous. ● adv (en) dessous.

under: ~**pants** npl slip m. ~**rate** vt sous-estimer.

understand vt/i (pt -**stood**) comprendre.

understanding a compréhensif. ● n compréhension f; (agreement) entente f.

undertake vt (pt -**took**; pp -**taken**) entreprendre. ~**taker** n entrepreneur m de pompes funèbres. ~**taking** n (task) entreprise f; (promise) promesse f.

underwater a sous-marin. ● adv sous l'eau.

under: ~**wear** n sous-vêtements mpl. ~**world** n (of crime) milieu m, pègre f.

undo vt (pt -**did**; pp -**done**) défaire, détacher; (wrong) réparer; (Comput) annuler.

undress vt/i (se) déshabiller; **get** ~**ed** se déshabiller.

undue a excessif.

unearth vt déterrer.

uneasy a (ill at ease) mal à l'aise; (worried) inquiet; (situation) difficile.

uneducated a (person) inculte; (speech) populaire.

unemployed a en chômage. ● npl **the** ~ les chômeurs mpl.

unemployment n chômage m; ~ **benefit** allocations fpl de chômage.

uneven a inégal.

unexpected a inattendu, imprévu. **unexpectedly** adv (arrive) à l'improviste; (small, fast) étonnamment.

unfair a injuste.

unfaithful a infidèle.

unfit a (Med) pas en forme; (ill) malade; (unsuitable) impropre (**for** à); ~ **to** (unable) pas en état de.

unfold vt déplier; (expose) exposer. ● vi se dérouler.

unforeseen a imprévu.

unforgettable a inoubliable.

unfortunate a malheureux; (event) fâcheux.

ungrateful a ingrat.

unhappy a (-**ier**, -**iest**) (person) malheureux; (face) triste; (not pleased) mécontent (**with** de).

unharmed a indemne, sain et sauf.

unhealthy a (-**ier**, -**iest**) (climate) malsain; (person) en mauvaise santé.

unheard-of a inouï.

unhurt a indemne.

uniform n uniforme m. ● a uniforme.

unify vt unifier.

unintentional a involontaire.

uninterested a indifférent (**in** à).

union n union f; (trade union) syndicat m; **U**~ **Jack** drapeau m du Royaume-Uni.

unique a unique.

unit n unité f; (of furniture) élément m; ~ **trust** ≈ SICAV f.

unite vt/i (s')unir.

United Kingdom n Royaume-Uni m.

United Nations npl Nations fpl Unies.

United States (of America) npl États-Unis mpl (d'Amérique).

unity n unité f.

universal a universel.

universe n univers m.

university n université f. ● a universitaire; (student, teacher) d'université.

unkind a pas gentil, méchant.

unknown a inconnu. ● n **the** ~ l'inconnu m.

unleaded a sans plomb.

unless *conj* à moins que.

unlike *a* différent. ● *prep* contrairement à; (*different from*) différent de.

unlikely *a* improbable.

unload *vt* décharger.

unlock *vt* ouvrir.

unlucky *a* (**-ier, -iest**) malheureux; (*number*) qui porte malheur.

unmarried *a* célibataire.

unnatural *a* pas naturel, anormal.

unnecessary *a* inutile.

unnoticed *a* inaperçu.

unofficial *a* officieux.

unpack *vt* (*suitcase*) défaire; (*contents*) déballer. ● *vi* défaire sa valise.

unpleasant *a* désagréable (**to** avec).

unplug *vt* débrancher.

unpopular *a* impopulaire; ~ **with** mal vu de.

unprofessional *a* peu professionnel.

unqualified *a* non diplômé; (*success*) total; **be** ~ **to** ne pas être qualifié pour.

unravel *vt* (*pt* **unravelled**) démêler.

unreasonable *a* irréaliste.

unrelated *a* sans rapport (**to** avec).

unreliable *a* peu sérieux; (*machine*) peu fiable.

unrest *n* troubles *mpl*.

unroll *vt* dérouler.

unruly *a* indiscipliné.

unsafe *a* (*dangerous*) dangereux; (*person*) en danger.

unscheduled *a* pas prévu.

unscrupulous *a* sans scrupules, malhonnête.

unsettled *a* instable.

unsightly *a* laid.

unskilled *a* (*worker*) non qualifié.

unsound *a* (*roof*) en mauvais état; (*investment*) douteux.

unsteady *a* (*step*) chancelant; (*ladder*) instable; (*hand*) mal assuré.

unsuccessful *a* (*result, candidate*) malheureux; (*attempt*) infructueux; **be** ~ ne pas réussir (**in doing** à faire).

unsuitable *a* inapproprié; **be** ~ ne pas convenir.

unsure *a* incertain.

untidy *a* (**-ier, -iest**) (*person*) désordonné; (*room*) en désordre; (*work*) mal soigné.

untie *vt* (*knot, parcel*) défaire; (*person*) détacher.

until *prep* jusqu'à; **not** ~ pas avant. ● *conj* jusqu'à ce que; **not** ~ pas avant que.

untrue *a* faux.

unused *a* (*new*) neuf; (*not in use*) inutilisé.

unusual *a* exceptionnel; (*strange*) insolite, étrange.

unwanted *a* (*useless*) superflu; (*child*) non désiré.

unwelcome *a* fâcheux; (*guest*) importun.

unwell *a* souffrant.

unwilling *a* peu disposé (**to** à); (*accomplice*) malgré soi.

unwind *vt/i* (*pt* **unwound**) (se) dérouler; (*relax* ▣) se détendre.

unwise *a* imprudent.

unwrap *vt* déballer.

up *adv* en haut, en l'air; (*sun, curtain*) levé; (*out of bed*) levé, debout; (*finished*) fini; **be** ~ (*level, price*) avoir monté. ● *prep* (a hill) en haut de; (a tree) dans; (a ladder) sur; **come** *or* **go** ~ monter; ~ **in the bedroom** là-haut dans la chambre; ~ **there** là-haut; ~ **to** jusqu'à; (*task*) à la hauteur de; **it is** ~ **to you** ça dépend de vous (**to**

de); **be ~ to sth** (able) être capable de qch; (plot) préparer qch; **be ~ to** (in book) en être à; **be ~ against** faire face à; **~ to date** moderne; (news) récent. ● n **~s and downs** les hauts et les bas mpl.

up-and-coming a prometteur.

upbringing n éducation f.

update vt mettre à jour.

upgrade vt améliorer; (person) promouvoir.

upheaval n bouleversement m.

uphill a qui monte; (fig) difficile. ● adv **go ~** monter.

upholstery n rembourrage m; (in vehicle) garniture f.

upkeep n entretien m.

up-market a haut-de-gamme.

upon prep sur.

upper a supérieur; **have the ~ hand** avoir le dessus. ● n (of shoe) empeigne f. **~ class** n aristocratie f. **~most** a (highest) le plus haut.

upright a droit. ● n (post) montant m.

uprising n soulèvement m.

uproar n tumulte m.

uproot vt déraciner.

upset¹ vt (pt upset; pres p upsetting) (overturn) renverser; (plan, stomach) déranger; (person) contrarier, affliger. ● a peiné.

upset² n dérangement m; (distress) chagrin m.

upside-down adv (lit) à l'envers; (fig) sens dessus dessous.

upstairs adv en haut. ● a (flat) du haut.

uptight a ▣ tendu, coincé ▣.

up-to-date a à la mode; (records) à jour.

upward a & adv, **upwards** adv vers le haut.

urban a urbain.

urge vt conseiller vivement (to do de faire); **~ on** encourager. ● n forte envie f.

urgency n urgence f; (of request, tone) insistance f. **urgent** a urgent; (request) pressant.

urinal n urinoir m.

urine n urine f.

us pron nous; (to) **~** nous; **both of ~** tous/toutes les deux.

US abbr ⇒UNITED STATES.

USA abbr ⇒UNITED STATES OF AMERICA.

use¹ vt se servir de, utiliser; (consume) consommer; **~ up** épuiser.

use² n usage m, emploi m; **in ~** en usage; **it is no ~ doing** ça ne sert à rien de faire; **make ~ of** se servir de; **of ~** utile.

used¹ a (car) d'occasion.

used² v aux **he ~ to smoke** il fumait (autrefois). ● a **~ to** habitué à.

useful a utile.

useless a inutile; (person) incompétent.

user n (of road, service) usager m; (of product) utilisateur/-trice m/f. **~-friendly** a facile d'emploi; (Comput) convivial.

usual a habituel, normal; **as ~** comme d'habitude. **usually** adv d'habitude.

utility n utilité f; (public) **~** service m public.

utmost a (furthest, most intense) extrême; **the ~ care** le plus grand soin. ● n **do one's ~** faire tout son possible.

utter a complet, absolu. ● vt prononcer.

U-turn n demi-tour m; (fig) volte-face f inv.

vacancy n (post) poste m vacant; (room) chambre f disponible.

vacant a (post) vacant; (seat) libre; (look) vague.

vacate vt quitter.

vacation n vacances fpl.

vaccinate vt vacciner.

vacuum n vide m. ~ **cleaner** n aspirateur m. ~**-packed** a emballé sous vide.

vagina n vagin m.

vagrant n vagabond/-e m/f.

vague a vague; (outline) flou; **be** ~ **about** ne pas préciser.

vain a (conceited) vaniteux; (useless) vain; **in** ~ en vain.

valentine n ~ (card) carte f de la Saint-Valentin.

valid a (argument, ticket) valable; (passport) valide.

valley n vallée f.

valuable a (object) de valeur; (help) précieux. **valuables** npl objets mpl de valeur.

valuation n (of painting) expertise f; (of house) évaluation f.

value n valeur f; ~ **added tax** taxe f à la valeur ajoutée, TVA f. ● vt (appraise) évaluer; (cherish) attacher de la valeur à.

valve n (Tech) soupape f; (of tyre) valve f; (Med) valvule f.

van n camionnette f.

vandal n vandale mf.

vanguard n **in the** ~ **of** à l'avant-garde f de.

vanilla n vanille f.

vanish vi disparaître.

vapour n vapeur f.

variable a variable.

varicose a ~ **veins** varices fpl.

varied a varié.

variety n variété f; (entertainment) variétés fpl.

various a divers.

varnish n vernis m. ● vt vernir.

vary vt/i varier.

vase n vase m.

vast a (space) vaste; (in quantity) énorme.

vat n cuve f.

VAT abbr (value added tax) TVA f.

vault n (roof) voûte f; (in bank) chambre f forte; (tomb) caveau m; (jump) saut m. ● vt/i sauter.

VCR abbr ⇒VIDEO CASSETTE RECORDER.

VDU abbr ⇒VISUAL DISPLAY UNIT.

veal n veau m.

vegan a & n végétalien/-ne (m/f).

vegetable n légume m. ● a végétal.

vegetarian a & n végétarien/-ne (m/f).

vehicle n véhicule m.

veil n voile m.

vein n (in body, rock) veine f; (on leaf) nervure f.

velvet n velours m.

vending-machine n distributeur m automatique.

veneer n (on wood) placage m; (fig) vernis m.

venereal a vénérien.

venetian a ~ **blind** jalousie f.

vengeance n vengeance f; **with a** ~ de plus belle.

venison n venaison f.

venom n venin m.

vent n bouche f, conduit m; (in coat) fente f. ● vt (anger) décharger (on sur).

ventilate vt ventiler. **ventilator** n ventilateur m.

venture n entreprise f. ●vt/i (se) risquer.

venue n lieu m.

verb n verbe m.

verbal a verbal.

verdict n verdict m.

verge n bord m; **on the ~ of doing** sur le point de faire. ●vi ~ **on** friser, frôler.

verify vt vérifier.

vermin n vermine f.

versatile a (person) aux talents variés; (mind) souple.

verse n strophe f; (of Bible) verset m; (poetry) vers mpl.

version n version f.

versus prep contre.

vertebra n (pl -brae) vertèbre f.

vertical a vertical.

vertigo n vertige m.

very adv très. ●a (actual) même; **the ~ day** le jour même; **at the ~ end** tout à la fin, **the ~ first** le tout premier; ~ **much** beaucoup.

vessel n vaisseau m.

vest n maillot m de corps; (waistcoat: US) gilet m.

vet n vétérinaire mf. ●vt (pt **vetted**) (candidate) examiner (de près).

veteran n vétéran m; (war) ~ ancien combattant m.

veterinary a vétérinaire; ~ **surgeon** vétérinaire mf.

veto n (pl ~es) veto m; (right) droit m de veto. ●vt mettre son veto à.

vibrate vt/i (faire) vibrer.

vicar n pasteur m.

vice n (depravity) vice m; (Tech) étau m.

vicinity n environs mpl; **in the ~ of** à proximité de.

vicious a (spiteful) méchant; (violent) brutal; ~ **circle** cercle m vicieux.

victim n victime f.

victor n vainqueur m. **victory** n victoire f.

video a (game, camera) vidéo inv. ●n (recorder) magnétoscope m; (film) vidéo f; ~ **(cassette)** cassette f vidéo. ●vt enregistrer. ~ **game** n jeu m vidéo. ~**phone** n vidéophone m.

videotape n bande f vidéo. ●vt (programme) enregistrer; (wedding) filmer avec une caméra vidéo.

view n vue f; **in my ~** à mon avis; **in ~ of** compte tenu de; **on ~** exposé; **with a ~ to** dans le but de. ●vt (watch) regarder; (consider) considérer (as comme); (house) visiter. **viewer** n (TV) téléspectateur/-trice m/f.

view: ~**finder** n viseur m. ~**point** n point m de vue.

vigilant a vigilant.

vigour, (US) **vigor** n vigueur f.

vile a (base) vil; (bad) abominable.

villa n pavillon m; (for holiday) villa f.

village n village m.

villain n scélérat m, bandit m; (in story) méchant m.

vindictive a vindicatif.

vine n vigne f.

vinegar n vinaigre m.

vineyard n vignoble m.

vintage n (year) année f, millésime m. ●a (wine) de grand cru; (car) d'époque.

viola n (Mus) alto m.

violate vt violer.

violence n violence f. **violent** a violent.

violet n (Bot) violette f; (colour) violet m.

violin n violon m.

VIP abbr (**very important person**) personnalité f, VIP m.

V

virgin n (woman) vierge f.

Virgo n Vierge f.

virtual a quasi-total; (Comput) virtuel. **virtually** adv pratiquement.

virtue n vertu f; (advantage) mérite m; **by ~ of** en raison de.

virus n virus m.

visa n visa m.

visibility n visibilité f. **visible** a visible.

vision n vision f.

visit vt (pt **visited**) (person) rendre visite à; (place) visiter. ●vi être en visite. ●n (tour, call) visite f; (stay) séjour m. **visitor** n visiteur/-euse m/f; (guest) invité/-e m/f.

visual a visuel. **~ display unit** n visuel m, console f de visualisation.

visualize vt se représenter; (foresee) envisager.

vital a vital.

vitamin n vitamine f.

vivacious a plein de vivacité.

vivid a (colour, imagination) vif; (description, dream) frappant.

vivisection n vivisection f.

vocabulary n vocabulaire m.

vocal a vocal; (person) qui s'exprime franchement. **~ cords** npl cordes fpl vocales.

vocation n vocation f. **vocational** a professionnel.

voice n voix f. ●vt (express) formuler. **~ mail** n messagerie f vocale.

void a vide (of de); (not valid) nul. ●n vide m.

volatile a (person) versatile; (situation) explosif.

volcano n (pl ~es) volcan m.

volley n (of blows, in tennis) volée f; (of gunfire) salve f.

volt n (Electr) volt m. **voltage** n tension f.

volume n volume m.

voluntary a volontaire; (unpaid) bénévole.

volunteer n volontaire mf. ●vi s'offrir (**to do** pour faire); (Mil) s'engager comme volontaire. ●vt offrir.

vomit vt/i (pt **vomited**) vomir. ●n vomi m.

vote n vote m; (right) droit m de vote. ●vt/i voter; **~ sb in** élire qn. **voter** n électeur/-trice m/f.

voting n vote m (of de); (poll) scrutin m.

vouch vi **~ for** se porter garant de.

voucher n bon m.

vowel n voyelle f.

voyage n voyage m (en mer).

vulgar a vulgaire.

vulnerable a vulnérable.

wad n (pad) tampon m; (bundle) liasse f.

wade vi **~ through** (mud) patauger dans; (book: fig) avancer péniblement dans.

wafer n (biscuit) gaufrette f.

waffle n (talk 🔲) verbiage m; (cake) gaufre f. ●vi 🔲 divaguer.

wag vt/i (pt **wagged**) (tail) remuer.

wage vt (campaign) mener; **~ war** faire la guerre. ●n (weekly, daily) salaire m; **~s** salaire m. **~-earner** n salarié/-e m/f.

wagon n (horse-drawn) chariot m; (Rail) wagon m (de marchandises).

wail vi gémir. ●n gémissement m.

waist n taille f. **~coat** n gilet m.

wait vt/i attendre; **I can't ~ to start** j'ai hâte de commencer; **let's ~ and see** attendons voir; **~ for** attendre; **~ on** servir. ●n attente f.

waiter n garçon m, serveur m.

waiting-list n liste f d'attente.

waiting-room n salle f d'attente.

waitress n serveuse f.

waive vt renoncer à.

wake vt/i (pt woke; pp woken) **~ (up)** (se) réveiller. ●n (track) sillage m; **in the ~ of** (after) à la suite de. **~ up call** n réveil m téléphoné.

Wales n pays m de Galles.

walk vi marcher; (not ride) aller à pied; (stroll) se promener. ●vt (streets) parcourir; (distance) faire à pied; (dog) promener. ●n promenade f, tour m; (gait) démarche f; (pace) marche f, pas m; (path) allée f; **have a ~** faire une promenade. □ **~ out** (go away) partir; (worker) faire grève; **~ out on** abandonner.

walkie-talkie n talkie-walkie m.

walking n marche f (à pied). ●a (corpse, dictionary: fig) ambulant.

walkman® n walkman® m, baladeur m.

walk: ~-out n grève f surprise. **~-over** n victoire f facile.

wall n mur m; (of tunnel, stomach) paroi f. ●a mural. **walled** a (city) fortifié.

wallet n portefeuille m.

wallpaper n papier m peint. ●vt tapisser.

walnut n (nut) noix f; (tree) noyer m.

waltz n valse f. ●vi valser.

wander vi errer; (stroll) flâner; (digress) s'écarter du sujet; (in mind) divaguer.

wane vi décroître.

want vt vouloir (**to do** faire); (need) avoir besoin de (**doing** d'être fait); (ask for) demander; **I ~ you to do it** je veux que vous le fassiez. ●vi **~ for** manquer de. ●n (need, poverty) besoin m; (desire) désir m; (lack) manque m; **for ~ of** faute de. **wanted** a (criminal) recherché par la police.

war n guerre f; **at ~** en guerre; **on the ~path** sur le sentier de la guerre.

ward n (in hospital) salle f; (minor: Jur) pupille mf; (Pol) division f électorale. ●vt **~ off** (danger) prévenir.

warden n directeur/-trice m/f; (of park) gardien/-ne m/f; (traffic) ~ contractuel/-le m/f

wardrobe n (furniture) armoire f; (clothes) garde-robe f.

warehouse n entrepôt m.

wares npl marchandises fpl.

warfare n guerre f.

warm a chaud; (hearty) chaleureux; **be or feel ~** avoir chaud; **it is ~** il fait chaud. ●vt/i **~ (up)** (se) réchauffer; (food) chauffer; (liven up) (s')animer; (exercise) s'échauffer.

warmth n chaleur f.

warn vt avertir, prévenir; **~ sb off sth** (advise against) mettre qn en garde contre qch; (forbid) interdire qch à qn.

warning n avertissement m; (notice) avis m; **without ~** sans prévenir. **~ light** n voyant m. **~ triangle** n triangle m de sécurité.

warp vt/i (wood) (se) voiler; (pervert) pervertir; (judgment) fausser.

warrant n (for arrest) mandat m (d'arrêt); (Comm) autorisation f. ●vt justifier.

warranty *n* garantie *f*.

wart *n* verrue *f*.

wartime *n* in ~ en temps de guerre.

wary *a* (-ier, -iest) prudent.

was ⇒BE.

wash *vt/i* (se) laver; (flow over) baigner; ~ one's hands of se laver les mains de. ● *n* lavage *m*; (clothes) lessive *f*; **have a** ~ se laver. □ ~ **up** faire la vaisselle; (US) se laver. ~**-basin** *n* lavabo *m*.

washer *n* rondelle *f*.

washing *n* lessive *f*. ~**-machine** *n* machine *f* à laver. ~**-powder** *n* lessive *f*.

washing-up *n* vaisselle *f*. ~ **liquid** *n* liquide *m* vaisselle.

wash: ~**-out** *n* ▣ fiasco *m*. ~**-room** *n* (US) toilettes *fpl*.

wasp *n* guêpe *f*.

wastage *n* gaspillage *m*.

waste *vt* gaspiller; (time) perdre. ● *vi* ~ **away** dépérir. ● *a* superflu; ~ **products** *or* **matter** déchets *mpl*. ● *n* gaspillage *m*; (of time) perte *f*; (rubbish) déchets *mpl*; **lay** ~ dévaster. **wasteful** *a* peu économique; (person) gaspilleur.

waste: ~ **land** *n* (desolate) terre *f* désolée; (unused) terre *f* inculte; (in town) terrain *m* vague. ~ **paper** *n* vieux papiers *mpl*. ~**-paper basket** *n* corbeille *f* (à papier).

watch *vt/i* (television) regarder; (observe) observer; (guard, spy on) surveiller; (be careful about) faire attention à. ● *n* (for telling time) montre *f*; (Naut) quart *m*; **be on the** ~ guetter; **keep a** ~ **on** surveiller. □ ~ **out** (take care) faire attention (for à); ~ **out for** (keep watch) guetter.

water *n* eau *f*; **by** ~ en bateau. ● *vt* arroser. ● *vi* (eyes) larmoyer; **my/his mouth** ~**s** l'eau me/lui vient à la bouche. □ ~ **down** couper (d'eau); (tone down) édulcorer. ~**-colour** *n* (painting) aquarelle *f*. ~**cress** *n* cresson *m* (de fontaine). ~**fall** *n* chute *f* d'eau, cascade *f*. ~ **heater** *n* chauffe-eau *m*. **watering-can** *n* arrosoir *m*. ~**-lily** *n* nénuphar *m*. ~**-melon** *n* pastèque *f*. ~**proof** *a* (material) imperméable. ~**shed** *n* (in affairs) tournant *m* décisif. ~**-skiing** *n* ski *m* nautique. ~**tight** *a* étanche. ~**way** *n* voie *f* navigable.

watery *a* (colour) délavé; (eyes) humide; (soup) trop liquide.

wave *n* vague *f*; (in hair) ondulation *f*; (radio) onde *f*; (sign) signe *m*. ● *vt* agiter. ● *vi* faire signe (de la main); (move in wind) flotter.

waver *vi* vaciller.

wavy *a* (line) onduleux; (hair) ondulé.

wax *n* cire *f*; (for skis) fart *m*. ● *vt* cirer; farter; (car) lustrer.

way *n* (road, path) chemin *m* (**to** de); (distance) distance *f*; (direction) direction *f*; (manner) façon *f*; (means) moyen *m*; ~**s** (habits) habitudes *fpl*; **be in the** ~ bloquer le passage; (hindrance: fig) gêner (qn); **be on one's** *or* **the** ~ être sur son *or* le chemin; **by the** ~ à propos; **by the** ~**side** au bord de la route; **by** ~ **of** comme; (via) par; **go out of one's** ~ se donner du mal; **in a** ~ dans un sens; **make one's** ~ **somewhere** se rendre quelque part; **push one's** ~ **through** se frayer un passage; **that** ~ par là; **this** ~ par ici; ~ **in** entrée *f*; ~ **out** sortie *f*. ● *adv* ▣ loin.

we *pron* nous.

weak *a* faible; (delicate) fragile.

weakness *n* faiblesse *f*; (fault) point *m* faible; **a** ~ **for** (liking) un faible pour.

wealth n richesse f; (riches, resources) richesses fpl; (quantity) profusion f.

wealthy a (-ier, -iest) riche. ● n the ~ les riches mpl.

weapon n arme f.

wear vt (pt **wore**; pp **worn**) porter; (put on) mettre; (expression) avoir. ● vi (last) durer; ~ (out) (s')user. ● n (use) usage m; (damage) usure f. □ ~ **down** user; ~ **off** (colour, pain) passer; ~ **out** (exhaust) épuiser.

weary a (-ier, -iest) fatigué, las. ● vi ~ **of** se lasser de.

weather n temps m; under the ~ patraque. ● a météorologique. ● vt (survive) réchapper de or à. ~ **forecast** n météo f.

weave vt/i (pt **wove**; pp **woven**) tisser; (basket) tresser; (move) se faufiler. ● n (style) tissage m.

web n (of spider) toile f; (on foot) palmure f. ~**cam** n webcam f. ~**master** n administrateur m de site Internet. ~ **page** n page f Web. ~ **search** n recherche f sur le Web. ~**site** n site m Internet.

Web n (Comput) Web m.

wedding n mariage m. ~**-ring** n alliance f.

wedge n (of wood) coin m; (under wheel) cale f. ● vt caler; (push) enfoncer; (crowd) coincer.

Wednesday n mercredi m.

weed n mauvaise herbe f. ● vt/i désherber; ~ **out** extirper.

week n semaine f; a ~ **today/tomorrow** aujourd'hui/demain en huit. ~**day** n jour m de semaine. ~**end** n week-end m, fin f de semaine.

weekly adv toutes les semaines. ● a & n (periodical) hebdomadaire (m).

weep vt/i (pt **wept**) pleurer (for sb qn).

weigh vt/i peser; ~ **anchor** lever l'ancre. □ ~ **down** lester (avec un poids); (bend) faire plier; (fig) accabler; ~ **up** calculer.

weight n poids m; lose/put on ~ perdre/prendre du poids. ~**-lifting** n haltérophilie f. ~ **training** n musculation f en salle.

weird a bizarre.

welcome a agréable; (timely) opportun; be ~ être le or la bienvenu(e), être les bienvenu (e)s; you're ~! il n'y a pas de quoi!; ~ **to do** libre de faire. ● interj soyez le or la bienvenu (e), soyez les bienvenu(e)s. ● n accueil m. ● vt accueillir; (as greeting) souhaiter la bienvenue à; (fig) se réjouir de.

weld vt souder. ● n soudure f.

welfare n bien-être m; (aid) aide f sociale. **W~ State** n État-providence m.

well[1] n puits m.

well[2] adv (**better**, **best**) bien; do ~ (succeed) réussir; ~ **done!** bravo! ● a bien inv; as ~ aussi; be ~ (healthy) aller bien. ● interj eh bien; (surprise) tiens.

well: ~**-behaved** a sage. ~**-being** n bien-être m inv.

wellington n (boot) botte f de caoutchouc.

well: ~**-known** a (bien) connu. ~**-meaning** a bien intentionné. ~ **off** aisé, riche. ~**-read** a instruit. ~**-to-do** a riche. ~**-wisher** n admirateur/-trice m/f.

Welsh a gallois. ● n (Ling) gallois m.

went ⇒GO.

wept ⇒WEEP.

were ⇒BE.

west n ouest m; the **W~** (Pol) l'Occident m. ● a d'ouest. ● adv vers l'ouest.

western *a* de l'ouest; (Pol)
occidental. ● *n* (film) western *m*.
westerner *n* occidental/-e *m/f*.
West Indies *n* Antilles *fpl*.
westward *a* (side) ouest *inv*;
(journey) vers l'ouest.
wet *a* (**wetter, wettest**) mouillé;
(damp, rainy) humide; (paint) frais;
get ~ se mouiller. ● *vt* (*pt*
wetted) mouiller. ● *n* the ~
l'humidité *f*; (rain) la pluie *f*. ~
suit *n* combinaison *f* de plongée.
whale *n* baleine *f*.
wharf *n* quai *m*.

● *pronoun*
····➤ (in questions as object pronoun)
qu'est-ce que?; ~ **are we going to
do?** qu'est-ce que nous allons
faire?
····➤ (in questions as subject pronoun)
qu'est-ce qui?; ~ **happened?**
qu'est-ce qui s'est passé?
····➤ (introducing clause as object) ce
que; **I don't know ~ he wants** je
ne sais pas ce qu'il veut.
····➤ (introducing clause as subject) ce
qui; **tell me ~ happened** raconte-
moi ce qui s'est passé.
····➤ (with prepositions) quoi; ~ **are
you thinking about?** à quoi
penses-tu?

● *determiner*
····➤ quel/quelle/quels/quelles; ~
train did you catch? quel train
as-tu pris?; ~ **time is it?** quelle
heure est-il?

whatever *a* ~ **book** quel que soit
le livre. ● *pron* (no matter what) quoi
que, quoi qu'; (anything that) tout ce
qui; (object) tout ce que *or* qu'; ~
happens quoi qu'il arrive; ~
happened? qu'est-ce qui est
arrivé?; ~ **the problems** quels que

soient les problèmes; ~ **you want**
tout ce que vous voulez, **nothing
~** rien du tout.
whatsoever *a & pron* =
WHATEVER.
wheat *n* blé *m*, froment *m*.
wheel *n* roue *f*; **at the ~** (of vehicle)
au volant; (helm) au gouvernail.
● *vt* pousser. ● *vi* tourner; ~ **and
deal** faire des combines.
~**barrow** *n* brouette *f*. ~**chair** *n*
fauteuil *m* roulant.
when *adv & pron* quand. ● *conj*
quand, lorsque; **the day/moment
~** le jour/moment où.
whenever *conj & adv* (at whatever
time) quand; (every time that) chaque
fois que.
where *adv, conj & pron* où;
(whereas) alors que; (the place that) là
où.
whereabouts *adv* (à peu près)
où. ● *n* sb's ~ l'endroit où se
trouve qn.
whereas *conj* alors que.
wherever *conj & adv* où que;
(everywhere) partout où; (anywhere)
(là) où; (emphatic where) où donc.
whether *conj* si; **not know ~** ne
pas savoir si; ~ **I go or not** que
j'aille ou non.

● *pronoun*
····➤ (in questions) lequel/laquelle/
lesquels/lesquelles; **there are
three peaches, ~ do you want?** il
y a trois pêches, laquelle
veux-tu?
····➤ (in questions with superlative
adjective) quel/quelle/quels/
quelles; ~ (**apple**) **is the biggest?**
quelle est la plus grosse?
····➤ (in relative clauses as subject) qui;
the book ~ is on the table le livre
qui est sur la table.

····▸ (in relative clauses as object) que; **the book ∼ Tina is reading** le livre que lit Tina.

● *determiner*

····▸ quel/quelle/quels/quelles; **∼ car did you choose?** quelle voiture as-tu choisie?

whichever *a* ∼ **book** quel que soit le livre que *or* qui; **take ∼ book you wish** prenez le livre que vous voulez. ● *pron* celui/celle/ceux/celles qui *or* que.

while *n* moment *m*. ● *conj* (when) pendant que; (although) bien que; (as long as) tant que. ● *vt* ∼ **away** (time) passer.

whilst *conj* = WHILE.

whim *n* caprice *m*.

whine *vi* gémir, se plaindre. ● *n* gémissement *m*.

whip *n* fouet *m*. ● *vt* (*pt* **whipped**) fouetter; (Culin) fouetter, battre; (seize) enlever brusquement. ● *vi* (move) aller en vitesse. □ ∼ **up** exciter; (cause) provoquer; (meal 🅐) préparer.

whirl *vt/i* (faire) tourbillonner. ● *n* tourbillon *m*. ∼**pool** *n* tourbillon *m*. ∼**wind** *n* tourbillon *m* (de vent).

whisk *vt* (snatch) enlever *or* emmener brusquement; (Culin) fouetter. ● *n* (Culin) fouet *m*.

whiskers *npl* (of animal) moustaches *fpl*; (of man) favoris *mpl*.

whisper *vt/i* chuchoter. ● *n* chuchotement *m*; (rumour: fig) rumeur *f*, bruit *m*.

whistle *n* sifflement *m*; (instrument) sifflet *m*. ● *vt/i* siffler; ∼ **at** *or* **for** siffler.

white *a* blanc. ● *n* blanc *m*; (person) blanc/-che *m/f*. ∼ **coffee** *n* café *m* au lait. ∼**-collar worker** *n* employé/-e *m/f* de bureau. ∼ **elephant** *n* projet *m* coûteux et

peu rentable. ∼ **lie** *n* pieux mensonge *m*. **W∼ Paper** *n* livre *m* blanc.

whitewash *n* blanc *m* de chaux. ● *vt* blanchir à la chaux; (*person*: fig) blanchir.

Whitsun *n* la Pentecôte.

whiz *vi* (*pt* **whizzed**) (through air) fendre l'air; (hiss) siffler; (rush) aller à toute vitesse. ∼**-kid** *n* jeune prodige *m*.

who *pron* qui.

whoever *pron* (no matter who) qui que ce soit qui *or* que; (the one who) quiconque; **tell ∼ you want** dites-le à qui vous voulez.

whole *a* entier; (intact) intact; **the ∼ house** toute la maison. ● *n* totalité *f*; (unit) tout *m*; **on the ∼** dans l'ensemble. ∼**-foods** *npl* aliments *mpl* naturels et diététiques. ∼**-hearted** *a* sans réserve. ∼**meal** *a* complet.

wholesale *a* (*firm*) de gros; (fig) systématique. ● *adv* (in large quantities) en gros; (fig) en masse.

wholesome *a* sain.

wholly *adv* entièrement.

whom *pron* (that) que, qu'; (after prepositions & in questions) qui; **of ∼** dont; **with ∼** avec qui.

whooping cough *n* coqueluche *f*.

whose *pron & a* à qui, de qui. ∼ **hat is this?**, ∼ **is this hat?** à qui est ce chapeau?; ∼ **son are you?** de qui êtes-vous le fils?; **the man ∼ hat I see** l'homme dont je vois le chapeau.

why *adv* pourquoi; **the reason ∼** la raison pour laquelle.

wicked *a* méchant, mauvais, vilain.

wide *a* large; (*ocean*) vaste. ● *adv* (*fall*) loin du but; **open ∼** ouvrir tout grand; ∼ **open** grand ouvert; ∼ **awake** éveillé. **widely** *adv* (*spread, space*) largement;

(*travel*) beaucoup; (*generally*) généralement; (*extremely*) extrêmement.

widespread *a* très répandu.

widow *n* veuve *f*. **widowed** *a* (*man*) veuf; (*woman*) veuve. **widower** *n* veuf *m*.

width *n* largeur *f*.

wield *vt* (*axe*) manier; (*power*: fig) exercer.

wife *n* (*pl* **wives**) femme *f*, épouse *f*.

wig *n* perruque *f*.

wiggle *vt/i* remuer; (*hips*) tortiller; (*worm*) se tortiller.

wild *a* sauvage; (*sea, enthusiasm*) déchaîné; (*mad*) fou; (*angry*) furieux. ● *adv* (*grow*) à l'état sauvage.

wildlife *n* faune *f*.

will[1]

present **will**; present negative **won't**, **will not**; past **would**

● *auxiliary verb*

····▸ (in future tense) **he'll come** il viendra; **it ∼ be sunny tomorrow** il va faire du soleil demain.

····▸ (inviting and requesting) **∼ you have some coffee?** est-ce que vous voulez du café?

····▸ (making assumptions) **they won't know what's happened** ils ne doivent pas savoir ce qui s'est passé.

····▸ (in short questions and answers) **you'll come again, won't you?** tu reviendras, n'est-ce pas?; **'they won't forget'—'yes they ∼'** 'ils n'oublieront pas'—'si'.

····▸ (capacity) **the lift ∼ hold 12** l'ascenseur peut transporter 12 personnes.

····▸ (ability) **the car won't start** la voiture ne veut pas démarrer.

● *transitive verb*

····▸ **∼ sb's death** souhaiter ardemment la mort de qn.

will[2] *n* volonté *f*; (*document*) testament *m*; **at ∼** quand *or* comme on veut.

willing *a* (*help, offer*) spontané; (*helper*) bien disposé; **∼ to** disposé à. **willingly** *adv* (with pleasure) volontiers; (not forced) volontairement. **willingness** *n* empressement *m* (**to do** à faire).

willow *n* saule *m*.

will-power *n* volonté *f*.

win *vt/i* (*pt* **won**; *pres p* **winning**) gagner; (*victory, prize*) remporter; (*fame, fortune*) acquérir, trouver; **∼ round** convaincre. ● *n* victoire *f*.

winch *n* treuil *m*. ● *vt* hisser au treuil.

wind[1] *n* vent *m*; (*breath*) souffle *m*; **get ∼ of** avoir vent de; **in the ∼** dans l'air. ● *vt* essouffler. **∼ farm** *n* ferme *f* d'éoliennes.

wind[2] *vt/i* (*pt* **wound**) (s')enrouler; (of path, river) serpenter; **∼ (up)** (*clock*) remonter; **∼ up** (end) (se) terminer; **∼ up in hospital** finir à l'hôpital.

windmill *n* moulin *m* à vent.

window *n* fenêtre *f*; (glass pane) vitre *f*; (in vehicle, train) vitre *f*; (in shop) vitrine *f*; (counter) guichet *m*; (Comput) fenêtre *f*. **∼-box** *n* jardinière *f*. **∼-cleaner** *n* laveur *m* de carreaux. **∼-dresser** *n* étalagiste *mf*. **∼-ledge** *n* rebord *m* de (la) fenêtre. **∼-shopping** *n* lèche-vitrines *m*. **∼-sill** *n* (inside) appui *m* de (la) fenêtre; (outside) rebord *m* de (la) fenêtre.

windscreen *n* pare-brise *m inv*. **∼ wiper** *n* essuie-glace *m*.

windshield *n* (US) = WINDSCREEN.

windsurfing *n* planche *f* à voile.

windy a (**-ier, -iest**) venteux; it is ~ il y a du vent.

wine n vin m. **~-cellar** n cave f (à vin). **~glass** n verre m à vin. **~-grower** n viticulteur m. **~ list** n carte f des vins. **~-tasting** n dégustation f de vins.

wing n aile f; **~s** (Theat) coulisses fpl; **under one's ~** sous son aile. **~ mirror** n rétroviseur m extérieur.

wink vi faire un clin d'œil; (light, star) clignoter. ● n clin m d'œil; clignotement m.

winner n (of game) gagnant/-e m/f; (of fight) vainqueur m.

winning ⇒WIN. ● a (number, horse) gagnant; (team) victorieux; (smile) engageant. **winnings** npl gains mpl.

winter n hiver m.

wipe vt essuyer. ● vi **~ up** essuyer la vaisselle. ● n coup m de torchon or d'éponge. □ **~ out** (destroy) anéantir; (remove) effacer.

wire n fil m; (US) télégramme m.

wiring n (Electr) installation f électrique.

wisdom n sagesse f.

wise a prudent, sage; (look) averti.

wish n (specific) souhait m, vœu m; (general) désir m; **best ~es** (in letter) amitiés fpl; (on greeting card) meilleurs vœux mpl. ● vt souhaiter, vouloir, désirer (**to do** faire); (bid) souhaiter. ● vi **~ for** souhaiter; I **~ he'd leave** je voudrais bien qu'il parte.

wishful a it's **~ thinking** c'est prendre ses désirs pour des réalités.

wistful a mélancolique.

wit n intelligence f; (humour) esprit m; (person) homme m d'esprit, femme f d'esprit.

witch n sorcière f.

with prep avec; (having) à; (because of) de; (at house of) chez; **the man ~** the beard l'homme à la barbe; **fill ~** remplir de; **pleased/shaking ~** content/frémissant de.

withdraw vt/i (pt **withdrew**; pp **withdrawn**) (se) retirer.

withdrawal n retrait m.

wither vt/i (se) flétrir.

withhold vt (pt **withheld**) refuser (de donner); (retain) retenir; (conceal) cacher (**from** à).

within prep & adv à l'intérieur (de); (in distances) à moins de; **~ a month** (before) avant un mois; **~ sight** en vue.

without prep sans; **~ my knowing** sans que je sache.

withstand vt (pt **withstood**) résister à.

witness n témoin m; (evidence) témoignage m; **bear ~ to** témoigner de. ● vt être le témoin de, voir. **~ box, ~ stand** n barre f des témoins.

witty a (**-ier, -iest**) spirituel.

wives ⇒WIFE.

wizard n magicien m; (genius: fig) génie m.

woke, woken ⇒WAKE.

wolf n (pl **wolves**) loup m. ● vt (food) engloutir.

woman n (pl **women**) femme f, **~ doctor** femme f médecin; **~ driver** femme f au volant.

women ⇒WOMAN.

won ⇒WIN.

wonder n émerveillement m; (thing) merveille f; **it is no ~** ce or il n'est pas étonnant (**that** que). ● vt se demander (**if** si). ● vi s'étonner (**at** de); (reflect) songer (**about** à).

wonderful a merveilleux.

won't = WILL NOT.

wood n bois m.

wooden a en or de bois; (stiff: fig) raide, comme du bois.

wood: **~wind** n (Mus) bois mpl.

W

~**work** n (craft, objects) menuiserie f.

wool n laine f. **woollen** a de laine. **woollens** npl lainages mpl.

woolly a laineux; (vague) nébuleux. ●n (garment 🇬🇧) lainage m.

word n mot m; (spoken) parole f, mot m; (promise) parole f; (news) nouvelles fpl; **by ~ of mouth** de vive voix; **give/keep one's ~** donner/tenir sa parole; **have a ~ with** parler à; **in other ~s** autrement dit. ●vt rédiger. **wording** n termes mpl.

word processing n traitement m de texte. **word processor** n machine f à traitement de texte.

wore ⇒WEAR.

work n travail m; (product, book) œuvre f, ouvrage m; (building work) travaux mpl; ~**s** (Tech) mécanisme m; (factory) usine f. ●vi (person) travailler; (drug) agir; (Tech) fonctionner, marcher. ●vt (Tech) faire fonctionner, faire marcher; (land, mine) exploiter; (shape, hammer) travailler; ~ **sb** (make work) faire travailler qn. □ ~ **out** vt (solve) résoudre; (calculate) calculer; (elaborate) élaborer; vi (succeed) marcher; (Sport) s'entraîner; ~ **up** vt développer; vi (to climax) monter vers; ~**ed up** (person) énervé.

workaholic n 🇬🇧 bourreau m de travail.

worker n travailleur/-euse m/f; (manual) ouvrier/-ière m/f.

work-force n main-d'œuvre f.

working a (day, lunch) de travail; ~**s** mécanisme m; **in ~ order** en état de marche.

working class n classe f ouvrière. ●a ouvrier.

workman n (pl -men) ouvrier m.

work: ~ **out** n séance f de mise

en forme. ~**shop** n atelier m. ~**-station** n poste m de travail.

world n monde m; **best in the ~** meilleur au monde. ●a (power) mondial; (record) du monde.

world-wide a universel.

World Wide Web, WWW n World Wide Web m, réseau m des réseaux.

worm n ver m. ●vt ~ **one's way into** s'insinuer dans.

worn ⇒WEAR. ●a usé. ~**-out** a (thing) complètement usé; (person) épuisé.

worried a inquiet.

worry vt/i (s')inquiéter. ●n souci m.

worse a pire, plus mauvais; **be ~ off** perdre. ●adv plus mal. ●n pire m. **worsen** vt/i empirer.

worship n (adoration) culte m. ●vt (pt worshipped) adorer. ●vi faire ses dévotions.

worst a pire, plus mauvais. ●adv (the) ~ (sing) le plus mal. ●n the ~ (one) (person, object) le or la pire; the ~ (thing) le pire.

worth a be ~ valoir; **it is ~ waiting** ça vaut la peine d'attendre; **it is ~ (one's) while** ça (en) vaut la peine. ●n valeur f; **ten pence ~ of** (pour) dix pence de. **worthless** a qui ne vaut rien. **worthwhile** a qui (en) vaut la peine.

worthy a (-ier, -iest) digne (of de); (laudable) louable.

would v aux he ~ do/you ~ sing (conditional tense) il ferait/tu chanterais; **he ~ have done** il aurait fait; **I ~ come every day** (used to) je venais chaque jour; **I ~ like some tea** je voudrais du thé; ~ **you come here?** voulez-vous venir ici?; **he wouldn't come** il a refusé de venir. ~**-be** a soi-disant.

wound¹ n blessure f. ●vt blesser; **the ~ed** les blessés mpl.

wound² ⇒WIND².

wove, woven ⇒WEAVE.

wrap vt (pt **wrapped**) ~ **(up)** envelopper. ●vi ~ **up** (dress warmly) se couvrir; **~ped up in** (engrossed) absorbé dans.

wrapping n emballage m.

wreak vt ~ **havoc** faire des ravages.

wreath n (of flowers, leaves) couronne f.

wreck n (sinking) naufrage m; (ship, remains, person) épave f; (vehicle) voiture f accidentée or délabrée. ●vt détruire; (ship) provoquer le naufrage de. **wreckage** n (pieces) débris mpl; (wrecked building) décombres mpl.

wrestle vi lutter, se débattre (**with** contre).

wrestling n lutte f; (**all-in**) ~ catch m.

wriggle vt/i (se) tortiller.

wring vt (pt **wrung**) (twist) tordre; (clothes) essorer; ~ **out of** (obtain from) arracher à.

wrinkle n (crease) pli m; (on skin) ride f. ●vt/i (se) rider.

wrist n poignet m.

write vt/i (pt **wrote**; pp **written**) écrire. □ ~ **back** répondre; ~ **down** noter; ~ **off** (debt) passer aux profits et pertes; (vehicle) considérer bon pour la casse; ~ **up** (from notes) rédiger.

write-off n perte f totale.

writer n auteur m, écrivain m; ~ **of** auteur de.

write-up n compte-rendu m.

writing n écriture f; ~**(s)** (works) écrits mpl; **in** ~ par écrit. ~**-paper** n papier m à lettres.

written ⇒WRITE.

wrong a (incorrect, mistaken) faux, mauvais; (unfair) injuste; (amiss) qui ne va pas; (clock) pas à l'heure; **be** ~ (person) avoir tort (**to** de); (be mistaken) se tromper; **go** ~ (err) se tromper; (turn out badly) mal tourner; **it is** ~ **to** (morally) c'est mal de; **what's** ~**?** qu'est-ce qui ne va pas?; **what is** ~ **with you?** qu'est-ce que vous avez? ●adv mal. ●n injustice f; (evil) mal m; **be in the** ~ avoir tort. ●vt faire (du) tort à. **wrongful** a injustifié, injuste. **wrongfully** adv à tort. **wrongly** adv mal; (blame) à tort.

wrote ⇒WRITE.

wrought iron n fer m forgé.

wrung ⇒WRING.

Xmas n Noël m.

X-ray n rayon m X; (photograph) radio(graphie) f. ●vt radiographier.

yank vt tirer brusquement. ●n coup m brusque.

yard n (measure) yard m (= 0.9144 metre); (of house) cour f; (garden: US) jardin m; (for storage) chantier m, dépôt m. ~**stick** n mesure f.

yawn vi bâiller. ●n bâillement m.

year n an m, année f; **school/tax**

~ année scolaire/fiscale; **be ten**
~**s old** avoir dix ans.
yearly *a* annuel. ●*adv*
annuellement.
yearn *vi* avoir bien *or* très envie
(**for, to** de).
yeast *n* levure *f*.
yell *vt/i* hurler. ●*n* hurlement *m*.
yellow *a* jaune; (cowardly 🆃)
froussard. ●*n* jaune *m*.
yes *adv* oui; (as answer to negative
question) si. ●*n* oui *m inv*.
yesterday *n & adv* hier (*m*).
yet *adv* encore; (already) déjà.
●*conj* pourtant, néanmoins.
yew *n* if *m*.
yield *vt* (produce) produire, rendre;
(*profit*) rapporter;
(surrender) céder. ●*n* rendement
m.
yoga *n* yoga *m*.
yoghurt *n* yaourt *m*.
yolk *n* jaune *m* (d'œuf).
you *pron* (familiar form) tu, *pl* vous;
(polite form) vous; (object) te, t', *pl*
vous; (polite) vous; (after prep.) toi,
pl vous; (polite) vous; (indefinite) on;
(object) vous; (**to**) ~ te, t', *pl* vous;
(polite) vous; **I gave** ~ **a pen** je vous
ai donné un stylo; **I know** ~ je te
connais *or* je vous connais.
young *a* jeune. ●*n* (people) jeunes
mpl; (of animals) petits *mpl*.
your *a* (familiar form) ton, ta, *pl* tes;
(polite form, & familiar form pl.) votre,
pl vos.
yours *pron* (familiar form) le tien, la
tienne, les tien(ne)s; (polite form, &
familiar form pl.) le *or* la vôtre, les
vôtres; ~ **faithfully/sincerely** je
vous prie d'agréer mes
salutations les meilleures.
yourself *pron* (familiar form) toi-

même; (polite form) vous-même;
(reflexive & after prepositions) te, t';
vous; **proud of** ~ fier de toi.
yourselves *pron* vous-mêmes;
(reflexive) vous.
youth *n* jeunesse *f*; (young man)
jeune *m*. ~ **hostel** *n* auberge *f* de
jeunesse.
Yugoslav *a* yougoslave. ●*n*
Yougoslave *mf*.
Yugoslavia *n* Yougoslavie *f*.

zap *vt* 🆃 (kill) descendre; (Comput)
enlever.
zeal *n* zèle *m*.
zebra *n* zèbre *m*. ~ **crossing** *n*
passage *m* pour piétons.
zero *n* zéro *m*.
zest *n* (gusto) entrain *m*; (spice: fig)
piment *m*; (of orange or lemon peel)
zeste *m*.
zip *n* (vigour) allant *m*; ~(**-fastener**)
fermeture *f* éclair®. ●*vt* (*pt*
zipped) fermer avec une
fermeture éclair®; (Comput)
compresser. **Zip code** (US) *n*
code *m* postal.
zodiac *n* zodiaque *m*.
zone *n* zone *f*.
zoo *n* zoo *m*.
zoom *vi* (rush) se précipiter. □ ~
off *or* **past** filer (comme une
flèche). ~ **lens** *n* zoom *m*.
zucchini *n inv* (US) courgette *f*.

Summary of French grammar

Grammar provides a useful description of the patterns which make up a language. The following pages offer a summary for reference.

1 NOUNS and GENDER

- All nouns are either *masculine* or *feminine* in French
- The gender is an important feature of each noun
- The gender is shown by the article (*definite* or *indefinite*)

1.1 The definite article (= THE)

	Singular	Plural
Masculine	*le*	*les*
Feminine	*la*	*les*

- *le* and *la* are reduced to *l'* before:
  a singular noun starting with a vowel (*école* → *l'école*)
  a singular noun starting with a silent h (*hôtel* → *l'hôtel*)
- *les* is the plural in all cases

1.2 The indefinite article (= A or AN; plural = SOME)

	Singular	Plural
Masculine	*un*	*des*
Feminine	*une*	*des*

- *un* and *une* also indicate the number 1 in counting:
  e.g. *une pomme* = one apple [*see* NUMBERS *section 9.1*]
- *des* is the plural in all cases

⚠ *Note:* Articles are rarely omitted:
e.g. *les enfants aiment les bonbons* = children like sweets
BUT when specifying someone's occupation, the article is dropped:
e.g. *il est boucher* = he is a butcher,
ma soeur est avocat = my sister is a lawyer

2 NOUNS and NUMBER

■ number means *singular* or *plural*

■ nouns in most cases add an ending in the plural

2.1 Typical nouns:

Most nouns add *-s* in the plural:
e.g. *chaise → chaises* (= chairs) *chien → chiens* (= dogs)

2.2 Nouns ending in -eu or -eau:

These nouns usually add *-x* in the plural:
e.g. *jeu → jeux* (= games) *bureau → bureaux* (= desks)

2.3 Nouns ending in -ou:

These nouns usually add *-s* in the plural.
BUT there are 6 common exceptions which add *-x*:
bijou → bijoux (= jewels) *genou → genoux* (= knees)
caillou → cailloux (= pebbles) *hibou→ hiboux* (= owls)
chou → choux (= cabbages) *joujou → joujoux* (= toys)

2.4 Nouns ending in -al:

These nouns usually change from *-al* to *-aux*:
e.g. *rival → rivaux* (= rivals); *cheval → chevaux* (= horses)
BUT there are exceptions: e.g. *bal → bals* (= dances)

2.5 Nouns ending in -ail:

These nouns usually add *-s*:
  e.g. *détail → détails* (= details)
BUT there are exceptions:
  e.g. *travail → travaux* (= works)

2.6 Some nouns have unusual plurals:

These plurals need to be learnt individually:
e.g. *ciel → cieux* (= skies) *oeil → yeux* (= eyes)

⚠ *Note*: the group: monsieur ‡ messieurs; madame ‡ mesdames;
mademoiselle ‡ mesdemoiselles; mon-, ma- in these words meant 'my'
originally (as in 'my lord', 'my lady')
[*See* POSSESSIVE ADJECTIVES *section 6*]

2.7 Hyphenated nouns

- The plurals of this group of nouns vary and depend on how the word is formed (*adjective* + *noun*, *verb* + *noun*, etc.)

- In cases where there is an ADJECTIVE + NOUN, it is normal for both words in the compound to change: e.g. ***beau-père*** → ***beaux-pères*** (= fathers-in-law)

- It is often helpful to translate the compound and find which word will logically become plural: e.g. ***arc-en-ciel*** (= rainbow) → ***arcs-en-ciel*** (= rainbows) (literally 'arc in the sky' → 'arcs in the sky')

⚠ *Note:* sometimes it is logical to leave the word unchanged in the plural because no noun is present in the make-up of the compound: e.g. ***un passe-partout*** = skeleton key ‡ ***des passe-partout*** = skeleton keys (literally 'a go-everywhere' : VERB + ADVERB)

2.8 Nouns showing no change between singular and plural

Nouns already ending in -*s*: e.g. ***bois*** → ***bois*** (= woods)
Nouns already ending in -*x*: e.g. ***voix*** → ***voix*** (= voices)
Nouns already ending in -*z*: e.g. ***nez*** → ***nez*** (= noses)

3 NOUNS and QUANTITY

- There are many nouns which indicate quantity e.g. ***un kilo de*** = a kilo of...; ***une livre de*** = a pound of...; ***une bouteille de*** = a bottle of...

- The word ***de*** is important in quantity expressions

- Sometimes ***de*** combines with ***le / la / l' / les*** to mean 'some'

3.1 The partitive article (= SOME)

```
de + NOUNS
de + le → du    e.g. le pain → du pain = some bread
de + la → de la e.g. la crème → de la crème = some cream
de + l' → de l' e.g. l'huile → de l'huile = some oil
de + les → des  e.g. les oranges → des oranges = some
                                                 oranges
```

⚠ *Note:* After a negative (*not, no more,* etc.: *see* NEGATIVES *section 12*), only use *de* or *d'*: e.g. *je n'ai plus de pain* = I haven't got any more bread; *il ne prend pas d'huile* = he's not buying any oil
After a quantity expression such as *un kilo de*, do not change *de* to *des*: e.g. *un kilo de pommes* = a kilo of apples

4 NOUNS replaced by PRONOUNS

4.1 Subject pronouns

- Subject pronouns (*I, we, they,* etc.) replace nouns
- They refer to people or things
- They govern verbs (e.g. *je chante* = I sing)
  [*see* VERBS *section 10.1*]

Singular	Plural
je = I	*nous* = we
tu = you	*vous* = you
il = he /it	*ils* = they [*masculine*]
elle = she / it	*elles* = they [*feminine*]
on = one*	

- *on* is used as a less specific subject pronoun to mean 'one', 'you', 'people', 'we', 'they':
  e.g. *on mange ici?* = shall we eat here?
  on n'aime pas refuser = one doesn't like to refuse
  on parle français là? = do they speak French there?

4.2 Object pronouns

4.2.a Direct object pronouns

- Direct object pronouns (*it, him, us,* etc.) replace nouns
- They refer to people or things
- They are the object (= affected by the action) of verbs:
  e.g. hit the ball; go on, hit it! = *frappe la balle; allez, frappe-la!*

French	English
me / m'	me
te / t'	you [*singular*]
le / l'	him /it
la / l'	her / it
se / s'	himself/ herself/ itself
nous	us
vous	you [*plural*]
les	them
se / s'	themselves

- *m' / t' / l' / s'* are used if the word that follows starts
  with a vowel or a silent h:
  e.g. *ils l'aiment* = they love her
  elles l'ont humidifié = they sprayed it with water
- object pronouns affect the ending of a past participle
  [*see* VERBS *section 10.1.f*] if the object is feminine or
  plural:
  e.g. *elle a poli la table* → *elle l'a polie* (she polished it)

4.2.b Indirect object pronouns

- Indirect object pronouns (*to it, to him, to us*, etc.)
  replace nouns
- They refer to people or things
- They are the indirect object (= *indirectly* affected
  by the action) of verbs:
  e.g. *donnez-lui la balle!* = give the ball to him
  (or to her)!
  il m'a montré la photo = he showed me the photo

French	English
me / m'	(to) me
te / t'	(to) you [*singular*]
lui	(to) him or it
lui	(to) her or it
nous	(to) us
vous	(to) you [*plural*]
leur	(to) them

- (to) shows that the word 'to' is understood in the sentence even though it may not actually be said:
  e.g. give them that! = give that to them! = *donne-le*-leur!

4.2.c Indirect object pronouns: places and quantities
- The indirect object pronoun referring to a place is:
  y (= there) e.g. *j'y vais* = I'm going there
- The indirect object pronoun referring to a quantity is:
  en (= of it, of them, some) e.g. *j'en voudrais 3* = I'd like 3 (of them); *offrez-leur-en* = offer them some

4.3 Order of object pronouns in the sentence
- Object pronouns come before most verb parts:
  e.g. *elle leur rend les livres* = she returns the books to them
- Object pronouns come before an infinitive:
  e.g. *elle va leur rendre les livres* = she is going to return the books to them
- Object pronouns come before the first part of a compound tense (= conjugated with *avoir* or *être*: see VERBS *section 10.1.f*)
  e.g. *elle leur a rendu les livres* = she returned the books to them
- Object pronouns follow the imperative form of the verb and are linked to it by a hyphen:
  e.g. *rends-leur les livres!* = return the books to them!
- Object pronouns return to normal order even with an imperative if it is negative:
  e.g. *ne les rendez pas!* = don't return them!
- When they occur in multiples in a sentence, object pronouns have a fixed order

OBJECT PRONOUN ORDER (see above tables for meanings):

me				
te	*le*	*lui*	*y*	*en*
se*	*la*	*leur*		
nous	*les*			
vous				
se*				

- the first column (me, te, se) is also used with reflexive verbs [*see* VERBS *section 10.1*]
- *se* means: (to) himself, (to) herself, (to) oneself, (to) themselves

⚠ *Note:* any combination of object pronouns will fall in this order:
e.g. *ils y en ont mis 6* = they put 6 of them there
il le lui a payé = he bought it for her
ils le leur y ont expliqué = they explained it to them there

4.4 Disjunctive or emphatic pronouns

■ Pronouns are sometimes used for emphasis:

Disjunctive Pronouns	
moi	*nous*
toi	*vous*
lui	*eux*
elle	*elles*

■ They take on these spellings:
  * after prepositions:
  e.g. *avec moi* = with me
  * after *que* or *qu'* in comparative sentences [*see* COMPARISON *section 8.1*]:
  e.g. *plus petit que lui* = smaller than him
  * to emphasize the subject:
  e.g. *lui, il n'aime pas le vin rouge mais elle, elle l'adore*
  = he doesn't like red wine but she loves it
  * with *même* meaning 'self' (*myself, yourself*, etc.):
  e.g. *toi-même* = yourself
  vous-mêmes = yourselves

⚠️ *Note:* that -*s* is added to *même* in the plural

⚠️ *Note: moi* and *toi* are also used as 'emphatics' in imperatives when pronouns follow the verb: e.g. ***donnez-le-moi****!* = give it to me! ***mettez-toi là****!* = sit yourself there!

5 ADJECTIVES

- Adjectives qualify nouns
- They usually follow the noun in French
- They reflect the noun in both gender and number
- Many determiners (*this, my, all, three*, etc.) are adjectival
- Some adjectives are used alone as nouns
  e.g. ***il est intelligent, le petit*** = the little one (= boy) is bright

5.1 Common adjectival endings:
- The masculine form is that given in the dictionary
- Add -*e* to form the feminine:
  e.g. ***une jupe courte*** = a short skirt
- Add -*s* to the masculine to form the masculine plural:
  e.g. ***des voyages intéressants*** = interesting journeys
- Add -*s* to the feminine to form the feminine plural
  e.g. ***des histoires amusantes*** = funny stories

5. 2 Adjectives ending in -e
These stay the same in the feminine:
e.g. ***aimable*** → feminine ***aimable***

⚠️ *Note:* unless the -*e* has an acute accent:
e.g. ***aimé*** → feminine ***aimée***

-*s* is added in the normal way in the plural:
e.g. ***aimable*** → plural ***aimables***

⚠️ *Note:* this is true of all adjectives:
unless the ending is -*x* (e.g. ***curieux*** → masculine plural ***curieux***)
unless there is already a final -*s* (***bas*** → masculine plural ***bas***)

5.3 Table of adjectives showing typical endings and their feminines:

Typical ending	Adjective	Feminine	English
The following double the last letter and add an -e			
-as	*bas*	*basse*	low
-eil	*pareil*	*pareille*	similar
-el	*mortel*	*mortelle*	fatal
-en	*ancien*	*ancienne*	ancient
-et	*muet*	*muette*	mute
! sometimes !	*inquiet*	*inquiète*	anxious
-on	*bon*	*bonne*	good
-ul	*nul*	*nulle*	no good
The following add a final -e and lengthen the syllable by adding an accent or changing a consonant or consonant group			
-er	*premier*	*première*	first
-ef	*bref*	*brève*	brief
-if	*actif*	*active*	active
-eux	*fameux*	*fameuse*	infamous
-eur	*menteur*	*menteuse*	untruthful
-nc	*blanc*	*blanche*	white
-ic	*public*	*publique*	public
-gu	*aigu*	*aiguë*	acute

The following are examples of irregular adjectives which show additional variations

doux → douce (= sweet); *faux → fausse* (= false)
favori → favorite (= favourite); *frais → fraîche* (= fresh)
gentil → gentille (= kind); *jaloux → jalouse* (= jealous)
malin → maligne (= cunning); *roux → rousse* (= red)
sot → sotte (=silly)

5.4 Position of adjectives

■ Most adjectives follow the noun; this is because an adjective distinguishes the noun in some way (colour, shape, etc.) and this position gives more emphasis in French: e.g. *un chocolat chaud* (= a hot chocolate)

■ Some adjectives go before the noun: these are usually common adjectives where a distinguishing feature is less pronounced:
e.g. *un vieil ami de la famille* (= an old family friend)

These may almost become part of the noun as
a compound:

e.g. *un jeune homme* (= a young man)
les petits enfants (= the little children;
the grandchildren)

- Some adjectives change meaning if they go before
  the noun: e.g. *la pauvre fille* (= the poor girl!)
  la fille pauvre (= the girl with little money)
  la mauvaise clé (= the wrong key)
  un animal mauvais (= a vicious animal)
  un seul président (= only one president)
  elle, seule, le sait (= she alone knows that)

5.4.a beau, nouveau, vieux

- These 3 adjectives go before the noun
- They form a group because they have an extra spelling:

Masculine	Masculine with vowel*	Masculine Plural	Feminine	Feminine Plural	English
beau	*bel*	*beaux*	*belle*	*belles*	beautiful
nouveau	*nouvel*	*nouveaux*	*nouvelle*	*nouvelles*	new
vieux	*vieil*	*vieux*	*vieille*	*vieilles*	old

• The extra spelling is used if the noun is masculine and
starts with a vowel:

e.g. *arbre* → *un bel arbre* (= a lovely tree)

Examples: *une belle femme* (= a beautiful woman)
de nouveaux livres (= new books)
de vieilles histoires (= old stories)

 Note: des changes to *de* in front of a plural adjective

6 POSSESSION

- Possession is commonly expressed by using *de*
- The style used is:
  'the dog of Paul' = *le chien de Paul* = Paul's dog
  'the clothes of Sophie' = *les vêtements de Sophie*
  = Sophie's clothes

■ Possession is also shown by possessive adjectives
(*my*, *your*, etc.):

POSSESSIVE ADJECTIVES

Masculine	Feminine	Plural	English
mon	*ma*	*mes*	my
ton	*ta*	*tes*	your
son	*sa*	*ses*	his/her/its/one's
notre	*notre*	*nos*	our
votre	*votre*	*vos*	your
leur	*leur*	*leurs*	their

• The word matches the gender and number of the 'thing'
possessed NOT the speaker:
e.g. *ma soeur* = my sister (the speaker may be male)
• *ma*, *ta*, and *sa* end in vowels; therefore they are not used
before a vowel:
e.g. NOT *sa amie* BUT *son amie* = his girlfriend

6.1 mine, yours, etc.

■ These are expressed by possessive pronouns
■ They reflect the gender and number of the 'thing'
possessed:

POSSESSIVE PRONOUNS

| | | Masculine | Feminine | |
Masculine	Feminine	Plural	Plural	English
le mien	*la mienne*	*les miens*	*les miennes*	mine
le tien	*la tienne*	*les tiens*	*les tiennes*	yours
le sien	*la sienne*	*les siens*	*les siennes*	his/hers/its
le nôtre	*la nôtre*	*les nôtres*	*les nôtres*	ours
le vôtre	*la vôtre*	*les vôtres*	*les vôtres*	yours
le leur	*la leur*	*les leurs*	*les leurs*	theirs

• The word matches the gender and number of the 'thing'
possessed NOT the speaker:
e.g. *cette chaise est la mienne* = this chair is mine (*the
speaker may be male*)

7 ADVERBS

- Adverbs usually give additional information about a verb's action: i.e. they say 'how' (= in what way or manner), 'when', 'where' something happens
- Most adverbs are formed from the feminine adjective by adding -*ment*
  e.g. *heureux* → *heureuse* → *heureusement* (= happily, fortunately)

Exceptions include:

7.1 masculine adjectives ending in a vowel

The feminine -*e* is dropped:
e.g. *hardi* → *hardiment* (= robustly)
résolu → *résolument* (= resolutely)

7.2 adjectives ending in -ant or -ent

The -*nt* is dropped and the -*m*- is doubled:
e.g. *constant* → *constamment* (= constantly)
intelligent → *intelligemment* (= intelligently)
Note however *lent* → *lentement* (= slowly)

8 COMPARISON

8.1 Comparative of adjectives and adverbs

- The comparative in English is usually expressed by:
  'more...' (e.g. *more interesting*)
  'as...' (e.g. *as big*)
  'less...' (e.g. *less intelligent*)
  or the suffix '-er' (e.g. *bigger*)
- The comparative in French is expressed in most cases by: 'plus...' (e.g. *plus intéressant*)
  'aussi...' (e.g. *aussi grand*)
  'moins...' (e.g. *moins intelligent*)
- The word for 'than' in French is *que* (or *qu'*)
- The adjective reflects the gender and number of the noun described. Examples:
  il est plus grand que toi = he is taller than you
  cette rue est moins longue que celui-là = this road is shorter than that one

SOME IRREGULAR COMPARATIVES		
Adjective	Comparative	English
bon = good	***meilleur***	better
mauvais = bad	***pire***	worse
petit = small	***moindre***	lesser, less great,
! *sometimes* !	***plus petit***	smaller
bien = well	***mieux***	better
mal = badly	***pis***	worse
! *sometimes* !	***plus mal***	
peu = little	***moins***	less

8.2 Superlative of adjectives and adverbs

- The superlative in English is usually expressed by 'most...' (e.g. *most interesting*)
  or the suffix '-est' (e.g. *biggest*)
- The superlative in French is expressed in most cases by: '*le/la/les plus* ' (e.g. *le plus intéressant*)
- The article is repeated reflecting the gender and number of the noun described:
  e.g. *la ville la plus belle* = the most beautiful city
- The superlative is often followed by 'in' which is translated by *de*...:
  e.g. *la ville la plus belle du monde* = the most beautiful city in the world

9 TIMES

- Time phrases begin with *il est*... (= it is...)
- The French equivalent of 'o' clock' is *heures*
  BUT 1 o' clock = *une heure* (i.e. no -*s* required in the singular)
- The 24 hour clock is often used to make a.m. and p.m. clear
- The number of hours is stated first before any minutes are detailed:
    minutes 'past' the hour are simply added to the end of the phrase: e.g. *il est sept heures dix*

'quarter past' is expressed by *et quart*:
e.g. *il est sept heures et quart*
minutes 'to' the hour follow the word *moins* (= minus):
e.g. *il est quatre heures moins cinq* (= five to four)
'quarter to' is expressed by *moins le quart*:
e.g. *il est quatre heures moins le quart*
'half past' is expressed by *et demie*:
e.g. *il est trois heures et demie*

⚠ *Note: midi* (= midday) and *minuit* (= midnight) are masculine;
therefore *et demie* changes to *et demi*: e.g. *il est midi et demi*

9.1 The cardinal numbers 1-24
[*see* ORDINAL NUMBERS *section 9.5*]

1 un/e	7 sept	13 treize	19 dix-neuf
2 deux	8 huit	14 quatorze	20 vingt
3 trois	9 neuf	15 quinze	21 vingt et un/e
4 quatre	10 dix	16 seize	22 vingt-deux
5 cinq	11 onze	17 dix-sept	23 vingt-trois
6 six	12 douze	18 dix-huit	24 vingt-quatre

Examples:
1.00 = *il est une heure*
2.00 = *il est deux heures*
2.10 = *il est deux heures dix*
2.15 = *il est deux heures et quart*
      [also *il est deux heures quinze*]
2.30 = *il est deux heures et demie*
      [also *il est deux heures trente*]
2.35 = *il est trois heures moins vingt-cinq*
      [also *il est deux heures trente-cinq*]

9.2 The numbers 30-100 (in 10s)

30 trente		70 soixante-dix	
40 quarante		80 quatre-vingts	
50 cinquante		90 quatre-vingt-dix	
60 soixante		100 cent	

9.3 Numbers: norms and exceptions

■ Numbers normally count up by linking each digit to 20,
30, etc. by a hyphen: e.g. *vingt-deux, vingt-trois*...

Exceptions worthy of note include:

- Numbers ending in 1 (*31, 41*, etc.) add *et un* (= and one)
  to the main number: e.g. 61 = *soixante et un*
  EXCEPT for:
  81 (*quatre-vingt-un*); 91 (*quatre-vingt-onze*); 101
  (*cent un*):
- Numbers 70-79 are unusual in that they count literally
  as:
  sixty-ten (*soixante-dix*) = 70
  sixty-eleven (*soixante et onze*) = 71
  sixty-twelve (*soixante-douze*) = 72 etc.
- Numbers 80-100 are unusual in that they count literally
  as:
  four-twenties (*quatre vingts*) = 80
  four-twenties-one (*quatre-vingt-un*) = 81
  four-twenties-two (*quatre-vingt-deux*) = 82 etc.
  and over 90...
  four-twenties-seventeen (*quatre-vingt-dix-sept*) = 97 etc.

 Note: the final *-s* of *vingts* is dropped if any digit follows

- Over 100, there is no hyphen linking the 100, 200, etc.
  with following digits: e.g. *trois cent dix-huit* = 318

 Note: the final *s* of *cents* is dropped if any digit follows

9.4 1000 and year dates

The number 1000 = *mille* However, in written dates, *mille*
changes to *mil*:
e.g. 1914 = *mil neuf cent quatorze*

 Note: the word *cent* is not omitted

9.4.a Other dates

- The article *le* is used to specify the day of the month:
  e.g. *c'est aujourd'hui le six septembre* = today is the 6th
  of September
- The cardinal numbers (*un, deux,* ...) are used
  (NOT the ordinal numbers as in English style: *1st, 2nd,*
  etc.)

- sometimes the article *le* goes before the day :
  e.g. *c'est le mardi deux juillet* = it's Tuesday 2 July

9.5 Ordinal numbers

- The ordinal numbers count focusing on sequence or
  priority (*first, second, third,* etc.)
- Ordinal numbers in French are usually formed by
  adding *-ième* to the cardinal number:
  e.g. *deuxième* (= 2nd), *troisième* (= 3rd), etc.
  BUT there are exceptions:
  e.g. *premier* = 1st

⚠ *Note:* numbers like 21st do not follow this change:
e.g. 31st = *trente-et-unième*

- There is sometimes a spelling change:
  e.g. *neuvième* = 9th (*-f-* changes to *-v-*)
  onzième = 11th (*onze* drops the final *-e*)

10 VERBS

- Verbs add action to a phrase (*he kicks the ball*) or they
  describe a state (*she is lazy*)
- A sentence needs a verb for it to make sense
  (*he... the dog* → *he strokes the dog*)
- An infinitive is a verb preceded by 'to' (*I want to go*)
- A finite verb indicates tense (*will go; went*)
- Tense is the time at which something happens, exists,
  etc.

10.1 Regular verbs

- Some verbs belong to 'regular' groups where they follow
  the same pattern
- Regular patterns are identified by the endings *-er, -ir*,
  and *-re*
- Some regular verbs are REFLEXIVE which means the
  action involves *oneself*:
  e.g. *je me lave* = I wash myself [*see* PRONOUNS
  section 4.3]

10.1.a Regular verbs in the present tense

The present tense describes what is happening now (*it is raining*) or what regularly happens (*he plays football on Tuesdays*) or a current truth (*she does love chips*)

---

parler 'to speak' AN EXAMPLE OF AN -ER VERB

je parle = I speak	*nous parlons* = we speak
tu parles = you speak	*vous parlez* = you speak
il parle = he speaks	*ils (masc) parlent* = they speak
elle parle = she speaks	*elles (fem) parlent* = they speak

- *tu* is used to speak to a child or someone known well
- *vous* is used in polite speech or to more than one person
- *ils* also means 'they' referring to a mixed male and female group
- the translation *I speak*, etc., may also be *I am speaking* and *I do speak*

---

finir 'to finish' AN EXAMPLE OF AN -IR VERB

je finis = I finish	*nous finissons* = we finish
tu finis = you finish	*vous finissez* = you finish
il finit = he finishes	*ils (masc) finissent* = they finish
elle finit = she finishes	*elles (fem) finissent* = they finish

- note the lengthened stem *-iss-* in the plural

---

vendre 'to sell' AN EXAMPLE OF AN -RE VERB

je vends – I sell	*nous vendons* = we sell
tu vends = you sell	*vous vendez* = you sell
il vend = he sells	*ils (masc) vendent* = they sell
elle vend = she sells	*elles (fem) vendent* = they sell

- note the dropped verb ending with *il* and *elle*

Other present tense patterns are individual to each verb or to a small number of verbs; these are known as 'irregular' verbs. [*see* VERB TABLES]

10.1.b Regular verbs in the imperative

- The imperative is a way of ordering, suggesting strongly
- 3 parts of the present tense are used: *tu, nous, vous*

- The *-s* is dropped from the *tu* part of the verb:
  e.g. *parle!* (= talk!); *parlons!* (= let's talk!); *parlez!*
  (= talk!)
- BUT there are exceptions [*see* VERB TABLES]:
  e.g. *aie!* (= have!); *ayons!* (= let's have!); *ayez!* (= have!)
  sois! (= be!); *soyons!* (= let's be!); *soyez!* (= be!)
  sache! (= know!); *sachons!* (= let's know!); *sachez!*
  (= know!)

10.1.c Regular verbs in the imperfect tense

The imperfect tense describes what was happening in the past (*it was raining*) or what used to be a fact or occurrence (*he used to like chocolate; he used to go to classes*); in French it also expresses what happened regularly (*il jouait au football tous les jeudis* = he played football every Tuesday)

Imperfect tense endings	
-ais	*-ions*
-ais	*-iez*
-ait	*-aient*
-ait	*-aient*

- these endings apply to all verbs
- they are added to a stem
- the stem is taken from the *nous* part of the present tense
  e.g. *nous finissons* → *finiss-* → *je finissais*
- the only irregular stem is *ét-* from *être*:
  e.g. *j'étais* (= I was), *tu étais* (= you were)...etc.

10.1.d Regular verbs in the future tense

The future tense describes what will happen (*it will rain*) or what is expected to be a fact (*it will be easy*)

Future tense endings	
-ai	*-ons*
-as	*-ez*
-a	*-ont*
-a	*-ont*

- these endings apply to all verbs
- they are added to a stem: the stem is the infinitive
  e.g. *finir* → *je finirai* (= I shall finish)
  BUT *-re* verbs drop the final *-e*:
  e.g. *vendre* → *je vendrai* (= I shall sell)
- some irregular stems have to be learnt
- the future may also be expressed by:
  the verb ALLER + INFINITIVE = *je vais finir...*
  (I am going to finish...)

TABLE of irregular future stems: [*see* VERB TABLES]

Infinitive	Future Stem	Infinitive	Future Stem
avoir	*j'aurai* = I shall have	tenir	*je tiendrai* = I shall hold
être	*je serai* = I shall be	vouloir	*je voudrai* = I shall want
faire	*je ferai* = I shall make	pouvoir	*je pourrai* = I shall be able
savoir	*je saurai* = I shall know	recevoir	*je recevrai* = I shall get
voir	*je verrai* = I shall see	devoir	*je devrai* = I shall have to
envoyer	*j'enverrai* = I shall send	courir	*je courrai* = I shall run
venir	*je viendrai* = I shall come	mourir	*je mourrai* = I shall die

- compounds of the above have the same stem:
  e.g. *retenir* (= to hold back) → *je retiendrai*

10.1.e Regular verbs in the conditional tense
The conditional tense describes what would happen (*it would make him angry*) or what would be a fact (*it would be easy*)

Formation: = FUTURE STEM + CONDITIONAL ENDINGS

Conditional tense endings	
-ais	*-ions*
-ais	*-iez*
-ait	*-aient*
-ait	*-aient*

- these endings apply to all verbs
  e.g. *il commencerait* (= he would begin)
  tu devrais (= you ought to)
- the word *si* (= if) is often present or understood in the
  meaning: e.g. *il le ferait si tu le lui demandais*
  (= he'd do it if you asked him)

10.1.f Regular verbs in the perfect tense
The perfect tense describes what has happened (*it has
snowed*; *they have written*). In French it is also used for
what happened and remained the case until a specific point
in time (*ils y sont restés jusqu'à mardi* = they stayed
there until Tuesday) or to state an action as part of a
series, each action being complete in itself (*je me suis
approché de la maison, j'ai sonné à la porte*... = I went
up to the house, rang the doorbell...)

Formation of the perfect tense:
- Two common verbs are important in the formation
  of this tense: AVOIR and ÊTRE

avoir = to have		être = to be	
j'ai	*nous avons*	*je suis*	*nous sommes*
tu as	*vous avez*	*tu es*	*vous êtes*
il a	*ils ont*	*il est*	*ils sont*
elle a	*elles ont*	*elle est*	*elles sont*

- 3 parts are needed to make the perfect tense:
  SUBJECT + AVOIR/ÊTRE + PAST PARTICIPLE
- The past participle of regular verbs is made by removing
  the last syllable of the infinitive (*regarder, choisir,*

rendre) and by replacing it with *é, -i, -u* respectively:
e.g. *regarder* → *regardé* → *j'ai regardé* (= I have watched)
choisir → *choisi* → *tu as choisi* (= you have chosen)
rendre → *rendu* → *il a rendu* (= he has given back)
BUT some past participles have to be learnt [*see* VERB TABLES].

TABLE giving common irregular past participles following the auxiliary (= 'helper') verb *avoir*:

Infinitive	Past Participle	Infinitive	Past Participle
avoir	*j'ai eu* = I have had	croire	*j'ai cru* = I have believed
être	*j'ai été* = I have been	savoir	*j'ai su* = I have known
faire	*j'ai fait* = I have made	voir	*j'ai vu* = I have seen
boire	*j'ai bu* = I have drunk	pleuvoir	*il a plu* = it has rained
pouvoir	*j'ai pu* = I have been able	dire	*j'ai dit* = I have said
devoir	*j'ai dû* = I have had to	écrire	*j'ai écrit* = I have written
lire	*j'ai lu* = I have read	mettre	*j'ai mis* = I have put
vouloir	*j'ai voulu* = I have wanted	prendre	*j'ai pris* = I have taken

• the past participle does not change its spelling after *avoir* unless there is a direct object preceding it: e.g. *j'ai vendu la table* (= I sold the table)
BUT *où est la table que tu as vendue*? (= where is the table you've sold?)

■ Most verbs make their perfect tense with *avoir* but
the exceptions are: 1 reflexive verbs and 2 a small group
of verbs of 'motion'. These take *être* and the past
participle behaves like an adjective.

---

1 *se laver* = to get washed / to wash oneself

je me suis lavé(e) = I got washed
tu t'es lavé(e) = you got washed
il s'est lavé = he got washed
elle s'est lavée = she got washed
nous nous sommes lavé(e)s = we got washed
vous vous êtes lavé(e)(s) = you got washed
ils se sont lavés = they got washed
elles se sont lavées = they got washed

• The alternatives in brackets depend on gender (masculine
or feminine) and number (singular or plural)

---

2 VERBS OF MOTION WHICH TAKE ÊTRE

arriver	*je suis arrivé(e)* = I arrived
partir	*je suis parti(e)* = I left
retourner	*je suis retourné(e)* = I returned
rester	*je suis resté(e)* = I stayed
tomber	*je suis tombé(e)* = I fell
mourir	*je suis mort(e)* = I died
naître	*je suis né(e)* = I was born
monter	*je suis monté(e)* = I went up
descendre	*je suis descendu(e)* = I went down
entrer	*je suis entré(e)* = I entered
aller	*je suis allé(e)* = I went
sortir	*je suis sorti(e)* = I went out
venir	*je suis venu(e)* = I came
revenir	*je suis revenu(e)* = I came back

• compounds of the above also take *être* e.g. *devenir*
(= to become) → *je suis devenu(e)*

10.1.g Regular verbs in the pluperfect tense

The pluperfect tense describes what had happened
(*it had snowed; they had written*) or what had been the case
(*it had been easy*).

Formation: = IMPERFECT TENSE OF AVOIR OR ÊTRE +
PAST PARTICIPLE [*see* VERB TABLES]

Examples:
j'avais fini = I had finished
nous avions vendu l'appartement = we had sold the flat
elle s'était réveillée = she had woken up
nous étions partis = we had left

⚠ *Note:* past participles after *être* behave in the same way as
they do for the perfect tense: i.e. they look like adjectives reflecting
the gender and number of the subject

10.1.h Regular verbs in the future perfect tense

The future perfect tense describes what will have happened
(*he will have arrived*) or what will have been the case
(*it will not have been easy*)

Formation: = FUTURE TENSE OF AVOIR OR ÊTRE +
PAST PARTICIPLE [*see* VERB TABLES]

Examples:
j'aurai fini = I shall have finished
nous aurons vendu la voiture = we shall have sold the car
nous serons descendus = we shall have gone down

⚠ *Note:* past participles after *être* behave in the same way as
they do for the perfect tense: i.e. they look like adjectives reflecting
the gender and number of the subject

10.2 Irregular verbs [*see* VERB TABLES]

11 NEGATIVES

- The negative expresses *not, never, no-one*, etc.
- In French the negative usually has 2 parts:
  e.g. *ne... pas* (= not), *ne... jamais* (= never),
  ne...personne (= nobody), etc.
- If the negative is the SUBJECT (*nobody knows*), then
  the negative reverses:
  i.e. *ne...personne* → *personne ne...*
  e.g. *personne ne sait*!
- Usually however with verbs, the 2 parts 'sandwich'
  the finite verb: e.g. *il ne mange pas* = he is not eating
BUT if an infinitive is present, they exclude the infinitive
from the 'sandwich':
  e.g. *il ne veut pas manger* = he doesn't want to eat
AND in a compound tense (e.g. *perfect, pluperfect*), they
only sandwich the first verb:
  e.g. *il n'est pas allé* = he didn't go
ALSO if object pronouns are present, these 'cling' to the
verb within the 'sandwich':
  e.g. *elle l'a acheté* → *elle ne l'a pas acheté*
  (= she didn't buy it)
- If no verb is present, as in a short response, then
  the *ne*... is omitted:
  e.g. '*Qui a frappé*?' - '*Personne!*' (= 'Who knocked ?'
  'Nobody!')

French verbs

1 chanter

Present indicative

je	chante
tu	chantes
il	chante
nous	chantons
vous	chantez
ils	chantent

Present subjunctive

(que)	je	chante
(que)	tu	chantes
(qu')	il	chante
(que)	nous	chantions
(que)	vous	chantiez
(qu')	ils	chantent

Future indicative

je	chanterai
tu	chanteras
il	chantera
nous	chanterons
vous	chanterez
ils	chanteront

Present conditional

je	chanterais
tu	chanterais
il	chanterait
nous	chanterions
vous	chanteriez
ils	chanteraient

Imperfect indicative

je	chantais
tu	chantais
il	chantait
nous	chantions
vous	chantiez
ils	chantaient

Past participle

chanté/chantée

Pluperfect indicative

j'	avais	chanté
tu	avais	chanté
il	avait	chanté
elle	avait	chanté
nous	avions	chanté
vous	aviez	chanté
ils	avaient	chanté
elles	avaient	chanté

Perfect indicative

j'	ai	chanté
tu	as	chanté
il	a	chanté
elle	a	chanté
nous	avons	chanté
vous	avez	chanté
ils	ont	chanté
elles	ont	chanté

2 finir

Present indicative

je	finis
tu	finis
il	finit
nous	finissons
vous	finissez
ils	finissent

Present subjunctive

(que)	je	finisse
(que)	tu	finisses
(qu')	il	finisse
(que)	nous	finissions
(que)	vous	finissiez
(qu')	ils	finissent

Future indicative

je	finirai
tu	finiras
il	finira
nous	finirons
vous	finirez
ils	finiront

Present conditional

je	finirais
tu	finirais
il	finirait
nous	finirions
vous	finiriez
ils	finiraient

Imperfect indicative

je	finissais
tu	finissais
il	finissait
nous	finissions
vous	finissiez
ils	finissaient

Past participle

fini/finie

Perfect indicative

j'	ai	fini
tu	as	fini
il	a	fini
elle	a	fini
nous	avons	fini
vous	avez	fini
ils	ont	fini
elles	ont	fini

Pluperfect indicative

j'	avais	fini
tu	avais	fini
il	avait	fini
elle	avait	fini
nous	avions	fini
vous	aviez	fini
ils	avaient	fini
elles	avaient	fini

3 attendre

Present indicative

j'	attends
tu	attends
il	attend
nous	attendons
vous	attendez
ils	attendent

Present subjunctive

(que)	j'	attende
(que)	tu	attendes
(qu')	il	attende
(que)	nous	attendions
(que)	vous	attendiez
(qu')	ils	attendent

Future indicative

j'	attendrai
tu	attendras
il	attendra
nous	attendrons
vous	attendrez
ils	attendront

Present conditional

j'	attendrais
tu	attendrais
il	attendrait
nous	attendrions
vous	attendriez
ils	attendraient

Imperfect indicative

j'	attendais
tu	attendais
il	attendait
nous	attendions
vous	attendiez
ils	attendaient

Past participle

attendu/attendue

Perfect indicative

j'	ai	attendu
tu	as	attendu
il	a	attendu
elle	a	attendu
nous	avons	attendu
vous	avez	attendu
ils	ont	attendu
elles	ont	attendu

Pluperfect indicative

j'	avais	attendu
tu	avais	attendu
il	avait	attendu
elle	avait	attendu
nous	avions	attendu
vous	aviez	attendu
ils	avaient	attendu
elles	avaient	attendu

4 être

Present indicative

je	suis
tu	es
il	est
nous	sommes
vous	êtes
ils	sont

Present subjunctive

(que)	je	sois
(que)	tu	sois
(qu')	il	soit
(que)	nous	soyons
(que)	vous	soyez
(qu')	ils	soient

Future indicative

je	serai
tu	seras
il	sera
nous	serons
vous	serez
ils	seront

Present conditional

je	serais
tu	serais
il	serait
nous	serions
vous	seriez
ils	seraient

Imperfect indicative

j'	étais
tu	étais
il	était
nous	étions
vous	étiez
ils	étaient

Past participle

été (*invariable*)

Perfect indicative

j'	ai	été
tu	as	été
il	a	été
elle	a	été
nous	avons	été
vous	avez	été
ils	ont	été
elles	ont	été

Pluperfect indicative

j'	avais	été
tu	avais	été
il	avait	été
elle	avait	été
nous	avions	été
vous	aviez	été
ils	avaient	été
elles	avaient	été

5 avoir

Present indicative

j'	ai
tu	as
il	a
nous	avons
vous	avez
ils	ont

Present subjunctive

(que)	j'	aie
(que)	tu	aies
(qu')	il	ait
(que)	nous	ayons
(que)	vous	ayez
(qu')	ils	aient

Future indicative

j'	aurai
tu	auras
il	aura
nous	aurons
vous	aurez
ils	auront

Present conditional

j'	aurais
tu	aurais
il	aurait
nous	aurions
vous	auriez
Ils	auraient

Imperfect indicative

j'	avais
tu	avais
il	avait
nous	avions
vous	aviez
ils	avaient

Past participle

eu/eue

Perfect indicative

j'	ai	eu
tu	as	eu
il	a	eu
elle	a	eu
nous	avons	eu
vous	avez	eu
ils	ont	eu
elles	ont	eu

Pluperfect indicative

j'	avais	eu
tu	avais	eu
il	avait	eu
elle	avait	eu
nous	avions	eu
vous	avlez	eu
ils	avaient	eu
elles	avaient	eu

[6] acheter
1 j'achète 2 j'achèterai
3 j'achetais 4 que j'achète
5 acheté

[7] acquérir
1 j'acquiers, nous acquérons,
ils acquièrent 2 j'acquerrai
3 j'acquérais 4 que
j'acquière 5 acquis

[8] aller
1 je vais, tu vas, il va, nous
allons, vous allez, ils vont
2 j'irai 3 j'allais 4 que
j'aille, que nous allions,
qu'ils aillent 5 allé

[9] asseoir
1 j'assois, tu assois, il assoit,
nous assoyons, vous assoyez,
ils assoient 2 j'assoirai
3 j'assoyais 4 que j'assoie,
que nous assoyions, qu'ils
assoient 5 assis

[10] avancer
1 nous avançons 3 j'avançais

[11] battre
1 je bats, il bat, nous battons
2 je battrai 3 je battais
4 que je batte 5 battu

[12] boire
1 je bois, il boit, nous
buvons, ils boivent 2 je
boirai 3 je buvais 4 que je
boive 5 bu

[13] bouillir
1 je bous, il bout, nous
bouillons, ils bouillent
2 je bouillirai 3 je bouillais
4 que je bouille 5 bouilli

[14] céder
1 je cède, nous cédons,
ils cèdent 2 je céderai 3 je
cédais 4 que je cède 5 cédé

[15] créer
1 je crée, nous créons 2 je
créerai 3 je créais 4 que je
crée 5 créé

[16] conclure
1 je conclus, il conclut, nous
concluons, ils concluent
2 je conclurai 3 je concluais
4 que je conclue 5 conclu
(*but* inclus)

[17] conduire
1 je conduis, nous
conduisons 2 je conduirai
3 je conduisais 4 que je
conduise 5 conduit (*but* lui,
nui)

[18] connaître
1 je connais, il connaît, nous
connaissons 2 je connaîtrai
3 je connaissais 4 que je
connaisse 5 connu

[19] coudre
1 je couds, il coud, nous
cousons, ils cousent 2 je
coudrai 3 je cousais 4 que
je couse 5 cousu

[20] courir
1 je cours, il court, nous
courons, ils courent 2 je
courrai 3 je courais 4 que
je coure 5 couru

[21] couvrir
1 je couvre 2 je couvrirai

---

1 Present Indicative 2 Future Indicative 3 Imperfect Indicative 4 Present Subjunctive 5 Past Participle

3 je couvrais 4 que je couvre
5 couvert

[22] **craindre**
1 je crains, il craint, nous
craignons, ils craignent
2 je craindrai 3 je craignais
4 que je craigne 5 craint

[23] **croire**
1 je crois, il croit, nous
croyons, ils croient 2 je
croirai 3 je croyais, nous
croyions 4 que je croie, que
nous croyions 5 cru

[24] **croître**
1 je croîs, il croît, nous
croissons 2 je croîtrai 3 je
croissais 4 que je croisse
5 crû/crue (*but* accru, décru)

[25] **cueillir**
1 je cueille 2 je cueillerai
3 je cueillais 4 que je cueille
5 cueilli

[26] **devoir**
1 je dois, il doit, nous devons,
ils doivent 2 je devrai 3 je
devais 4 que je doive, que
nous devions 5 dû/due

[27] **dire**
1 je dis, il dit, nous disons,
vous dites, ils disent 2 je
dirai 3 je disais 4 que je
dise 5 dit

[28] **dissoudre**
1 je dissous, il dissout, nous
dissolvons, ils dissolvent
2 je dissoudrai 3 je dissolvais
4 que je dissolve 5 dissous/
dissoute

[29] **distraire**
1 je distrais, il distrait, nous
distrayons 2 je distrairai
3 je distrayais 4 que je
distraie 5 distrait

[30] **écrire**
1 j'écris, il écrit, nous
écrivons 2 j'écrirai
3 j'écrivais 4 que j'écrive
5 écrit

[31] **employer**
1 j'emploie, nous employons,
ils emploient 2 j'emploierai
3 j'employais 4 que j'emploie,
que nous employions
5 employé

[32] **envoyer**
1 j'envoie, nous envoyons,
ils envoient 2 j'enverrai
3 j'envoyais, nous envoyions
4 que j'envoie, que nous
envoyions 5 envoyé

[33] **faire**
1 je fais, nous faisons (*say*
/fəzɔ̃/), vous faites, ils font
2 je ferai 3 je faisais (*say*
/fəzɛ/) 4 que je fasse, que
nous fassions 5 fait

[34] **falloir** (*impersonal*)
1 il faut 2 il faudra 3 il
fallait 4 qu'il faille 5 fallu

[35] **fuir**
1 je fuis, nous fuyons
2 je fuirai 3 je fuyais, nous
fuyions 4 que je fuie, que
nous fuyions 5 fui

---

1 Present Indicative 2 Future Indicative 3 Imperfect Indicative 4 Present Subjunctive 5 Past Participle

[36] haïr
1 je hais, il hait, nous haïssons, ils haïssent 2 je haïrai 3 je haïssais 4 que je haïsse 5 haï

[37] interdire
1 j'interdis, vous interdisez 2 j'interdirai 3 j'interdisais 4 que j'interdise 5 interdit

[38] jeter
1 je jette, nous jetons, ils jettent 2 je jetterai 3 je jetais 4 que je jette 5 jeté

[39] lire
1 je lis, il lit, nous lisons 2 je lirai 3 je lisais 4 que je lise 5 lu

[40] manger
1 je mange, nous mangeons 2 je mangerai 3 je mangeais 4 que je mange, que nous mangions 5 mangé

[41] maudire
1 je maudis, il maudit, nous maudissons 2 je maudirai 3 je maudissais 4 que je maudisse 5 maudit

[42] mettre
1 je mets, tu mets, nous mettons 2 je mettrai 3 je mettais 4 que je mette 5 mis

[43] mourir
1 je meurs, il meurt, nous mourons 2 je mourrai 3 je mourais 4 que je meure 5 mort

[44] naître
1 je nais, il naît, nous naissons 2 je naîtrai 3 je naissais 4 que je naisse 5 né

[45] oublier
1 j'oublie, nous oublions, ils oublient 2 j'oublierai 3 j'oubliais, nous oubliions, vous oubliiez 4 que nous oubliions, que vous oubliiez 5 oublié

[46] partir
1 je pars, nous partons 2 je partirai 3 je partais 4 que je parte 5 parti

[47] plaire
1 je plais, il plaît (*but* il tait), nous plaisons 2 je plairai 3 je plaisais 4 que je plaise 5 plu

[48] pleuvoir (*impersonal*)
1 il pleut 2 il pleuvra 3 il pleuvait 4 qu'il pleuve 5 plu

[49] pouvoir
1 je peux, il peut, nous pouvons, ils peuvent 2 je pourrai 3 je pouvais 4 que je puisse, que nous puissions 5 pu

[50] prendre
1 je prends, il prend, nous prenons 2 je prendrai 3 je prenais 4 que je prenne 5 pris

[51] prévoir
1 je prévois, il prévoit, nous prévoyons, ils prévoient 2 je prévoirai 3 je prévoyais,

---

1 Present Indicative 2 Future Indicative 3 Imperfect Indicative 4 Present Subjunctive 5 Past Participle

nous prévoyions 4 que je
prévoie, que nous prévoyions
5 prévu

[52] recevoir
1 je reçois, il reçoit, nous
recevons, ils reçoivent 2 je
recevrai 3 je recevais 4 que
je reçoive, que nous recevions
5 reçu

[53] résoudre
1 je résous, il résout, nous
résolvons, ils résolvent
2 je résoudrai 3 je résolvais
4 que je résolve 5 résolu

[54] rire
1 je ris, nous rions, ils rient
2 je rirai 3 je riais, nous
riions 4 que je rie, que nous
riions 5 ri

[55] savoir
1 je sais, il sait, nous savons,
ils savent 2 je saurai 3 je
savais 4 que je sache, que
nous sachions 5 su

[56] suffire
1 il suffit, ils suffisent 2 il
suffira 3 il suffisait 4 qu'il
suffise 5 suffi (*but* frit)

[57] suivre
1 je suis, il suit, nous suivons
2 je suivrai 3 je suivais
4 que je suive 5 suivi

[58] tenir
1 je tiens, il tient, nous

tenons, ils tiennent 2 je
tiendrai 3 je tenais 4 que je
tienne, que nous tenions
5 tenu

[59] vaincre
1 je vaincs, il vainc, nous
vainquons, ils vainquent
2 je vaincrai 3 je vainquais
4 que je vainque 5 vaincu

[60] valoir
1 je vaux, il vaut, nous
valons 2 je vaudrai 3 je
valais 4 que je vaille, que
nous valions 5 valu

[61] vêtir
1 je vêts, il vêt, nous vêtons
2 je vêtirai 3 je vêtais 4 que
je vête 5 vêtu

[62] vivre
1 je vis, il vit, nous vivons,
ils vivent 2 je vivrai 3 je
vivais 4 que je vive 5 vécu

[63] voir
1 je vois, nous voyons, ils
voient 2 je verrai
3 je voyais, nous voyions
4 que je voie, que nous
voyions 5 vu

[64] vouloir
1 je veux, il veut, nous
voulons, ils veulent 2 je
voudrai 3 je voulais 4 que
je veuille, que nous voulions
5 voulu

---

1 Present Indicative 2 Future Indicative 3 Imperfect Indicative 4 Present Subjunctive 5 Past Participle

What are the equivalent tenses in English

Present indicative
  je chante = *I sing, I'm singing*

Future indicative
  je chanterai = *I will sing*

Imperfect indicative
  je chantais = *I was singing*

Perfect indicative
  j'ai chanté
  = *I sang, I have sung*

Pluperfect indicative
  j'avais chanté = *I had sung*

Present subjunctive
  bien que je chante
  = *although I sing*

Present conditional
  si je pouvais, je chanterais
  = *if I could, I would sing*

Past participle
  chanté/chantée = *sung*

How to conjugate a reflexive verb

Present indicative and other simple tenses
  je me lave
  tu te laves
  il se lave
  elle se lave
  nous nous lavons
  vous vous lavez
  ils se lavent
  elles se lavent

in the negative form
  je ne me lave pas
  tu ne te laves pas
  il ne se lave pas
  elle ne se lave pas
  nous ne nous lavons pas
  vous ne vous lavez pas
  ils ne se lavent pas
  elles ne se lavent pas

Perfect indicative and other compound tenses
*(always with auxiliary **être**)*
  je me suis lavé
  tu t'es lavé
  il s'est lavé
  elle s'est lavée
  nous nous sommes lavés
  vous vous êtes lavés
  ils se sont lavés
  elles se sont lavées

in the negative form
  je ne me suis pas lavé
  tu ne t'es pas lavé
  il ne s'est pas lavé
  elle ne s'est pas lavée
  nous ne nous sommes pas lavés
  vous ne vous êtes pas lavés
  ils ne se sont pas lavés
  elles ne se sont pas lavées